VISUAL C++ .NET
A MANAGED CODE APPROACH
FOR EXPERIENCED PROGRAMMERS
DEITEL™ DEVELOPER SERIES

DEITEL™ Books, Cyber Classrooms, Complete Tra
published by

DEITEL™ Developer Series

C#: A Programmer's Introduction
C# for Experienced Programmers
Java™ Web Services for Experienced Programmers
Visual Basic® .NET for Experienced Programmers
Visual C++® .NET: A Managed Code Approach
*   For Experienced Programmers*
Web Services: A Technical Introduction
ASP .NET and Web Services with Visual Basic® .NET for Experienced Programmers (2003)
ASP .NET and Web Services with C# for Experienced Programmers (2003)
.NET: A Technical Introduction (2003)
Java 2 Micro Edition for Experienced Programmers (2003)
Java 2 Enterprise Edition for Experienced Programmers (2003)

How to Program Series

Advanced Java™ 2 Platform How to Program
C How to Program, 3/E
C++ How to Program, 4/E
C# How to Program
e-Business and e-Commerce How to Program
Internet and World Wide Web How to Program, 2/E
Java™ How to Program, 4/E
Perl How to Program
Python How to Program
Visual C++® .NET How to Program (2003)
Visual Basic® 6 How to Program
Visual Basic® .NET How to Program, 2/E
Wireless Internet & Mobile Business How to Program
XML How to Program

.NET How to Program Series

C# How to Program
Visual C++® .NET How to Program (2003)
Visual Basic® .NET How to Program, 2/E

Visual Studio® Series

C# How to Program
Visual C++® .NET How to Program (2003)
Visual Basic® .NET How to Program, 2/E
Getting Started with Microsoft® Visual C++™ 6 with an Introduction to MFC
Visual Basic® 6 How to Program

For Managers Series

e-Business and e-Commerce for Managers

Coming Soon

e-books and e-whitepapers
Premium CourseCompass, WebCT and Blackboard Multimedia Cyber Classroom versions

ining Courses and Web-Based Training Courses
Prentice Hall

Multimedia Cyber Classroom and *Web-Based Training* Series

(For information regarding DEITEL™ Web-based training visit **www.ptgtraining.com**)

C++ Multimedia Cyber Classroom, 4/E

C# Multimedia Cyber Classroom

e-Business and e-Commerce Multimedia Cyber Classroom

Internet and World Wide Web Multimedia Cyber Classroom, 2/E

Java™ 2 Multimedia Cyber Classroom, 4/E

Perl Multimedia Cyber Classroom

Python Multimedia Cyber Classroom

Visual Basic® 6 Multimedia Cyber Classroom

Visual Basic® .NET Multimedia Cyber Classroom, 2/E

Wireless Internet & Mobile Business Programming Multimedia Cyber Classroom

XML Multimedia Cyber Classroom

The Complete Training Course Series

The Complete C++ Training Course, 4/E

The Complete C# Training Course

The Complete e-Business and e-Commerce Programming Training Course

The Complete Internet and World Wide Web Programming Training Course, 2/E

The Complete Java™ 2 Training Course, 4/E

The Complete Perl Training Course

The Complete Python Training Course

The Complete Visual Basic® 6 Training Course

The Complete Visual Basic® .NET Training Course, 2/E

The Complete Wireless Internet & Mobile Business Programming Training Course

The Complete XML Programming Training Course

To follow the Deitel publishing program, please register at

> **www.deitel.com/newsletter/subscribe.html**

for the *DEITEL™ BUZZ ONLINE* e-mail newsletter.

To communicate with the authors, send e-mail to:

> **deitel@deitel.com**

For information on corporate on-site seminars and public seminars offered by Deitel & Associates, Inc. worldwide, visit:

> **www.deitel.com**

For continuing updates on Prentice Hall and Deitel publications visit:

> **www.deitel.com,**
> **www.prenhall.com/deitel** or
> **www.InformIT.com/deitel**

Library of Congress Cataloging-in-Publication Data

On file

Acquisitions Editor: *Karen McLean*
Project Manager: *Mike Ruel*
Executive Managing Editor: *Vince O'Brien*
Managing Editor: *Tom Manshreck*
Production Editor: *Chirag Thakkar*
Director of Creative Services: *Paul Belfanti*
Art Editor: *Xiaohong Zhu*
Creative Director: *Carole Anson*
Design Technical Support: *John Christiana*
Chapter Opener and Cover Designers: *Laura Treibick, Dr. Harvey M. Deitel and Tamara L. Newnam*
Manufacturing Manager: *Trudy Pisciotti*
Manufacturing Buyer: *Lisa McDowell*
Marketing Manager: *Kate Hargett*
Marketing Assistant: *Corrine Mitchell*

© 2003 Pearson Education, Inc.
Upper Saddle River, New Jersey 07458

Cover photo: *Yann Arthus-Bertrand/CORBIS*

10 9 8 7 6 5 4 3 2 1

ISBN 0-13-045821-X

Pearson Education Ltd., *London*
Pearson Education Australia Pty. Ltd., *Sydney*
Pearson Education Singapore, Pte. Ltd.
Pearson Education North Asia Ltd., *Hong Kong*
Pearson Education Canada, Inc., *Toronto*
Pearson Educacion de Mexico, S.A. de C.V.
Pearson Education–Japan, *Tokyo*
Pearson Education Malaysia, Pte. Ltd.
Pearson Education, Inc., *Upper Saddle River, New Jersey*

VISUAL C++ .NET
A MANAGED CODE APPROACH
FOR EXPERIENCED PROGRAMMERS
DEITEL™ DEVELOPER SERIES

H. M. Deitel
Deitel & Associates, Inc.

P. J. Deitel
Deitel & Associates, Inc.

C. J. Courtemarche
Deitel & Associates, Inc.

J. C. Hamm

J. P. Liperi

T. R. Nieto
Deitel & Associates, Inc.

C. H. Yaeger
Deitel & Associates, Inc.

PRENTICE HALL, Upper Saddle River, New Jersey 07458

Trademarks

In memory of Edsger W. Dijkstra:

It is a privilege to keep learning from your work in the fields of program-ming languages, software engineering and operating systems.

Harvey and Paul Deitel

To my mother and my husband, the two most important people in my life, for their patience, love and support. Thank you.

Christina J. Courtemarche

To my parents and Adele:

I could not succeed without your support. It is you, those that I love most, who guide me when I am lost, and right me when I stumble.

Jeffrey C. Hamm

To the Wolfroms:

For always filling me with food and laughter. Thank you for every-thing—I will never forget your generosity.

Jonathan P. Liperi

To Craig M. Smith:

For all the memories, stories, jokes and laughs. I am truly blessed to have you as a friend.

Tem R. Nieto

To my parents, for always helping me get back up when I am down.

Cheryl H. Yaeger

Contents

3 Control Structures   52

4 Functions and Arrays   80

5 Object-Based Programming   118

13   Graphics and Multimedia   546

14   Files and Streams   637

Illustrations

6   Object-Oriented Programming: Inheritance   179

7   Object-Oriented Programming: Polymorphism   221

10   Graphical User Interface Concepts: Part 2   361

13 Graphics and Multimedia   546

15   Extensible Markup Language (XML)   **742**

18   Networking: Streams-Based Sockets and Datagrams   949

19   Data Structures and Collections   996

20   Accessibility   1072

Preface

Live in fragments no longer. Only connect.
Edward Morgan Forster

We wove a web in childhood,
A web of sunny air.
Charlotte Brontë

Welcome to Visual C++ .NET and the world of Windows, Internet and World-Wide-Web programming with Visual Studio® .NET and the .NET platform! This book is part of the new *Deitel™ Developer Series*, which presents leading-edge computing technologies to software developers and IT professionals.

Visual C++ was enhanced with *Managed Extensions for C++ (MC++)* by Microsoft expressly for its .NET platform. MC++ provides support for managed programming. Using MC++, programmers can access powerful classes provided by the .NET Framework as well as benefit from automatic garbage collection. Visual C++ .NET provides the features that are most important to programmers, such as object-oriented programming, graphics, graphical-user-interface (GUI) components, exception handling, multithreading, multimedia (audio, images, animation and video), file processing, prepackaged data structures, database processing, networking, Web services and distributed computing. [*Note*: The different implementations of C++ and Visual C++ have yielded several industry terms. For the remainder of this book, we use the term "C++" when referring to standard C++. We use the term "Managed Extensions for C++ (MC++)" when referring to features of managed C++ or code that uses these features. Finally, we use the term "Visual C++ .NET" when referring to the Microsoft product/compiler, which can be used to write both managed and unmanaged code.]

The .NET platform offers powerful capabilities for software development and deployment, including language and platform independence. For example, developers writing code in any (or several) of the .NET languages (such as MC++, C# and Visual Basic .NET) can contribute components to the same software product. In addition to providing language interoperability, .NET extends program portability by enabling .NET applications to reside on, and communicate across, multiple platforms. This facilitates the creation and use of *Web services*, which are applications that expose functionality to clients via the Internet. The capabilities that Microsoft has incorporated into the .NET platform increase programmer productivity and decrease development time.

Visual C++ .NET does not currently include a *Windows Form designer* that is included in other Visual Studio products (such as Visual C# .NET). This form designer simplifies the creation of GUIs for the programmer by autogenerating code. For this reason, all GUIs in this book were created using C#. The auto-generated code then was converted to MC++. Microsoft is currently working on a Windows Form designer for Visual C++ .NET that is available in beta format. Further editions of this book will use the GUI tools as they become available to the public.

Who Should Read This Book

Deitel & Associates, Inc. has two Visual C++ .NET publications, intended for different audiences. We provide information on **www.deitel.com**, here and inside this book's back cover to help you determine which publication is best for you.

This book, *Visual C++ .NET: A Managed Code Approach for Experienced Programmers*, is part of the *Deitel™ Developer Series*. This publication is a part of the *For Experienced Programmers* subseries, designed for the experienced software developer who wants a deep treatment of a new technology with minimal, if any, introductory material. *Visual C++ .NET: A Managed Code Approach for Experienced Programmers* delves deeply into the more sophisticated topics.

Our *Visual C++ .NET How to Program*, available Fall 2003, is part of our *How to Program Series*, for college and university students. It provides a comprehensive treatment of Visual C++ .NET and includes learning aids and extensive ancillary support. *Visual C++ .NET How to Program* assumes that the reader has little or no programming experience. Early chapters focus on fundamental programming principles. The book builds on this to create increasingly complex and sophisticated programs that demonstrate how to use Visual C++ .NET to create graphical user interfaces, networking applications, multi-threaded applications, Web-based applications and more.

Each of these Visual C++ .NET books presents many complete, working programs and depicts their inputs and outputs in actual screen shots of running programs. This is our signature *LIVE-CODE™ approach*—we present all concepts in the context of complete working programs. Each book's source code is available free for download at **www.deitel.com**.

Please examine both the *Deitel™ Developer Series* professional book and the *How to Program Series* textbook to determine which best suits your needs. For a detailed listing of Deitel™ products and services, please see the "advertorial" pages at the back of this book and visit **www.deitel.com**. Readers also may want to register for our new *Deitel™ Buzz Online* e-mail newsletter (**www.deitel.net/newsletter/subscribe.html**), which provides information about our publications, company announcements, links to informative technical articles, programming tips, teaching tips, challenges and anecdotes.

As you proceed, if you would like to communicate with us, please send an e-mail to **deitel@deitel.com**—we always respond promptly. Please check our Web sites, **www.deitel.com**, **www.prenhall.com/deitel** and **www.InformIT.com/ deitel** for frequent updates, errata, FAQs, etc. When sending an e-mail, please include the book's title and edition number. We sincerely hope that you enjoy learning Visual C++ .NET with our publications.

Features of Visual C++ .NET: A Managed Code Approach for Experienced Programmers

This book contains many features, including:

- *Syntax Highlighting.* This book uses five-way syntax highlighting to emphasize Visual C++ programming elements in a manner similar to that of Visual Studio .NET. Our syntax-highlighting conventions are as follows:

  ```
  comments
  keywords
  literal values
  errors and ASP .NET directives
  text, class, method and variable names
  ```

- *"Code Washing."* This is our term for the process we use to format the book's programs so that they have a carefully commented, open layout. The code is grouped into small, well-documented pieces. This greatly improves code readability—an especially important goal for us, considering that this book contains approximately 34,131 lines of code in 228 complete LIVE-CODE™ programs.

- *Web Services.* Microsoft's .NET strategy embraces the Internet and Web as integral to software development and deployment. Web-services technology enables information sharing, e-commerce and other interactions using standard Internet protocols and technologies, such as Hypertext Transfer Protocol (HTTP), Extensible Markup Language (XML) and Simple Object Access Protocol (SOAP). Web services enable programmers to package application functionality in a manner that turns the Web into a library of reusable software components. Chapter 17, Web Services, presents a Web service that allows users to manipulate "huge integers"—integers too large to be contained in .NET's built-in data types. In this example, a user enters two huge integers and presses buttons to invoke a Web service that adds, subtracts and compares the two huge integers.

- *Object-Oriented Programming.* Object-oriented programming is the most widely employed technique for developing robust, reusable software. This text offers a rich treatment of MC++'s object-oriented programming features. Chapter 5, Object-Based Programming, introduces how to create classes and objects. These concepts are extended in Chapter 6, Object-Oriented Programming: Inheritance, which discusses how programmers can create powerful new classes quickly by "absorbing" the capabilities of existing classes. [*Note*: This book assumes that the reader has some prior knowledge of C++ pointers.]

- *XML.* Use of Extensible Markup Language (XML) is exploding in the software-development industry, in the e-business and e-commerce communities, and is pervasive throughout the .NET platform. Because XML is a platform-independent technology for describing data and for creating markup languages, XML's data portability integrates well with MC++-based applications and services. Chapter 15, Extensible Markup Language (XML), introduces XML. In this chapter, we present XML markup and discuss the Document Object Model (DOM™), which is used to manipulate XML documents programmatically.

- *Multithreading.* Computers enable programmers to perform many tasks in parallel (i.e., concurrently), such as printing documents, downloading files from a network and surfing the Web. Multithreading is the technology through which programmers can develop applications that perform concurrent tasks. Historically, a computer has contained a single, expensive processor, which its operating system would share among all applications. Today, processors are becoming increasingly inexpensive, making it possible to build affordable computers with many processors working in parallel—such computers are called multiprocessors. Multithreading is effective on both single-processor and multiprocessor systems. .NET's multithreading capabilities make the platform and its related technologies better prepared to handle today's sophisticated multimedia-intensive, database-intensive, network-based, multiprocessor-based, distributed applications. Chapter 11, Multithreading, introduces this powerful capability.

- *ADO .NET.* Databases store vast amounts of information that individuals and organizations must access to conduct business. As an evolution of Microsoft's ActiveX Data Objects (ADO) technology, ADO .NET represents a new approach for building applications that interact with databases. ADO .NET uses XML and an enhanced object model to provide developers with the tools they need to access and manipulate databases for large-scale, extensible, mission-critical multi-tier applications. Chapter 16, Database, SQL and ADO .NET, introduces the capabilities of ADO .NET and the Structured Query Language (SQL) to manipulate databases.

- *Unmanaged Code*. Unmanaged code is any code that cannot use the services provided by the Common Language Runtime (CLR). The CLR is the .NET environment that provides basic services such as garbage collection and array-bounds checking to .NET applications. Although most of this book focuses on managed code, Chapters 21–25 provide an in-depth discussion on unmanaged code in .NET. These chapters cover changes and additions to unmanaged code in Visual C++ .NET, including attributed programming, which enables the programmer to easily insert additional functionality into a program, and ATL Server, which enables the creation of Web applications in Visual C++ .NET. The last two chapters introduce the reader to .NET's interoperability features between managed and unmanaged code. Microsoft has put tremendous effort into ensuring that legacy Visual C++ code can be used with managed code, without having to be rewritten.

- *Graphical User Interfaces*. This book presents several GUI (Graphical User Interface) applications to demonstrate different topics in Visual C++ .NET. GUI applications are programs that display graphical elements, such as buttons and labels, with which the user interacts. Visual Studio .NET contains built-in GUI development tools for both C# and Visual Basic .NET, but not Visual C++ .NET as of yet. To create the graphical user interfaces for this book, we converted C# code (created by the Visual Studio .NET IDE) into Visual C++ .NET code. We walk the reader through the code so that they can create their own graphical user interfaces in Visual C++ .NET. As a result, the reader will gain an understanding of creating programs that are easy to understand and use.

- *XHTML*™. The World Wide Web Consortium (W3C) has declared HTML to be a legacy technology that will undergo no further development. HTML is being replaced by the Extensible Hypertext Markup Language (XHTML)—an XML-based technology that is rapidly becoming the standard for describing Web content. We use XHTML in Chapter 15, Extensible Markup Language (XML), and offer an introduction to the technology in Appendix E, Introduction to XHTML: Part 1, and Appendix F, Introduction to XHTML: Part 2. These appendices overview headers, images, lists, image maps and other features of this emerging markup language.

- *Accessibility.* Although the World Wide Web has become an important part of many people's lives, the medium currently presents many challenges to people with disabilities. Individuals with hearing and visual impairments, in particular, have difficulty accessing multimedia-rich Web sites. In an attempt to improve this situation, the World Wide Web Consortium (W3C) launched the Web Accessibility Initiative (WAI), which provides guidelines for making Web sites accessible to people with disabilities. Chapter 20, Accessibility, describes these guidelines and highlights various products and services designed to improve the Web-browsing experiences of individuals with disabilities. For example, the chapter introduces VoiceXML™ and CallXML™—two XML-based technologies for increasing the accessibility of Web-based content for people with visual impairments.

- *Unicode®.* As computer systems evolved worldwide, computer vendors developed numeric representations of character sets and special symbols for the local languages spoken in different countries. In some cases, different representations were developed for the same languages. Such disparate character sets hindered communication among computer systems. Visual C++ .NET supports the *Unicode® Standard* (maintained by a non-profit organization called the *Unicode® Consortium*), which maintains a single character set that specifies unique numeric values for characters and special symbols in most of the world's languages. Appendix D, Unicode®, discusses the standard, overviews the Unicode® Consortium Web site, **www.unicode.org** and presents an MC++ application that displays "Welcome to Unicode!" in several languages.

- *Bit Manipulation*. Computers work with data in the form of binary digits, or bits, which can assume the values 1 or 0. Computer circuitry performs various simple bit manipulations, such as examining the value of a bit, setting the value of a bit and reversing a bit (from 1 to 0 or from 0 to 1). Operating systems, test-equipment, networking software and many other kinds of software require that programs communicate "directly with the hardware" by using bit manipulation. Appendix I, Bit Manipulation, overviews the bit manipulation capabilities that the .NET Framework provides.

Pedagogic Approach

Visual C++ .NET: A Managed Code Approach for Experienced Programmers contains a rich collection of examples that have been tested on Windows 2000 and Windows XP. The book concentrates on the principles of good software engineering and stresses program clarity. We are educators who teach edge-of-the-practice topics in industry classrooms worldwide. We avoid arcane terminology and syntax specifications in favor of teaching by example. The text emphasizes good pedagogy.

We use fonts to distinguish between Visual Studio .NET's Integrated Development Environment (IDE) features (such as menu names and menu items) and other elements that appear in the IDE. Our convention is to emphasize IDE features in a sans-serif bold Helvetica font (e.g., **Project** menu) and to emphasize program text in a serif bold Courier font (e.g., `bool x = true;`).

LIVE-CODE™ Teaching Approach

Visual C++ .NET: A Managed Code Approach for Experienced Programmers is loaded with numerous LIVE-CODE™ examples. This style exemplifies the way we teach and write about programming and is the focus of our multimedia *Cyber Classrooms* and Web-based training courses as well. Each new concept is presented in the context of a complete, working example that is followed by one or more windows showing the program's input/output. We call this method of teaching and writing the ***LIVE-CODE™ Approach***. *We use programming languages to teach programming languages.* Reading the examples in the text is much like entering and running them on a computer. Readers have the option of downloading all of the book's code examples from `www.deitel.com`, under the **Downloads/Resources** link. Other links provide errata and answers to frequently asked questions.

World Wide Web Access

All of the source code for the examples in *Visual C++ .NET: A Managed Code Approach for Experienced Programmers* (and our other publications) is available on the Internet as downloads from the following Web sites:

> `www.deitel.com`
> `www.prenhall.com/deitel`

Registration is quick and easy and these downloads are free. We suggest downloading all the examples, then running each program as you read the corresponding portion of the book. Make changes to the examples and immediately see the effects of those changes—this is a great way to improve your programming skills. Any instructions for running the examples assumes that the user is running Windows 2000 or Windows XP and is using Microsoft's Internet Information Services (IIS). Additional setup instructions for IIS and other software can be found at our Web sites along with the examples. [*Note*: This is copyrighted material. Feel free to use it as you study, but you may not republish any portion of it in any form without explicit permission from Prentice Hall and the authors.]

Visual Studio .NET belongs to a family of products that are available for purchase and download from Microsoft. Visual Studio .NET, which includes Visual C++ .NET, comes in four different editions—Academic, Professional, Enterprise Developer and Enterprise Architect. Visual Studio .NET Academic contains Visual Studio .NET Professional's features in addition to features designed for students and professors (e.g., an Assignment Manager that documents assignment submission, Application Publishing Tools that aid in the notification of assignments, code samples and more).

Visual Studio .NET provides a powerful debugger that combines aspects of previous Visual Studio debuggers and that allows the programmer to debug applications that include both managed code and unmanaged code. More information about the Visual Studio .NET debugger, including instructions on using the debugger, can be found at

```
msdn.microsoft.com/library/default.asp?url=/library/en-us/
vsdebug/html/vc_debugging_your_application_home_page.asp
```

Microsoft also offers stand-alone products (Visual C++ .NET Standard, Visual C# .NET Standard and Visual Basic .NET Standard) for various .NET-languages. Each product provides an integrated development environment (similar to Visual Studio .NET) and a compiler. Visit **msdn.microsoft.com/vstudio/howtobuy** for descriptions and ordering information.

Objectives
Each chapter begins with objectives that inform readers of what to expect and gives them an opportunity, after reading the chapter, to determine whether they have met the intended goals. The objectives serve as confidence builders and as a source of positive reinforcement.

Quotations
The chapter objectives are followed by sets of quotations. Some are humorous, some are philosophical and some offer interesting insights. We have found that readers enjoy relating the quotations to the chapter material. Many of the quotations are worth a "second look" *after* you read each chapter.

Outline
The chapter outline enables readers to approach the material in top-down fashion. Along with the chapter objectives, the outline helps readers anticipate topics and set a comfortable and effective learning pace.

Approximately 34,131 Lines of Code in 228 Example Programs (with Program Outputs)
We present Visual C++ .NET features in the context of complete, working programs. The programs range in size from just a few lines of code to substantial examples containing hundreds of lines of code. All examples are available as downloads from our Web site, **www.deitel.com**.

884 Illustrations/Figures
An abundance of charts, line drawings and program outputs is included.

388 Programming Tips
We have included programming tips to help readers focus on important aspects of program development. We highlight hundreds of these tips in the form of *Good Programming Practices*, *Common Programming Errors*, *Testing and Debugging Tips*, *Performance Tips*, *Portability Tips*, *Software Engineering Observations* and *Look-and-*

Feel Observations. These tips and practices represent the best the authors have gleaned from many decades of programming and teaching experience. One of our customers—a mathematics major—told us that she feels this approach is like the highlighting of axioms, theorems and corollaries in mathematics books; it provides a foundation on which to build good software.

58 Good Programming Practices

Good Programming Practices *are tips that call attention to techniques that will help developers produce programs that are clearer, more understandable and more maintainable.*

132 Common Programming Errors

Developers learning a language tend to make certain kinds of errors frequently. Pointing out these Common Programming Errors *reduces the likelihood that readers will make the same mistakes.*

26 Testing and Debugging Tips

When we first designed this "tip type," we thought the tips would contain suggestions strictly for exposing bugs and removing them from programs. In fact, many of the tips prevent "bugs" from getting into programs in the first place, thus simplifying the testing and debugging processes.

46 Performance Tips

Developers like to "turbo charge" their programs. We have included 44 Performance Tips *that highlight opportunities for improving program performance—making programs run faster or minimizing the amount of memory that they occupy.*

12 Portability Tips

We include Portability Tips *to help developers write portable code and to provide insights on how Visual C++ .NET achieves its high degree of portability.*

93 Software Engineering Observations

The object-oriented programming paradigm necessitates a complete rethinking of the way we build software systems. Visual C++ .NET is effective for achieving good software engineering. The Software Engineering Observations *highlight architectural and design issues that affect the construction of software systems, especially large-scale systems.*

21 Look-and-Feel Observations

We provide Look-and-Feel Observations *to highlight graphical-user-interface conventions. These observations help developers design attractive, user-friendly graphical user interfaces that conform to industry norms.*

Summary
Each chapter ends with a summary that helps readers review and reinforce key concepts.

Approximately 5,838 Index Entries (with approximately 7,261 Page References)
We have included an extensive index. This resource enables readers to search for any term or concept by keyword. The index is especially useful for practicing programmers who use the book as a reference.

"Double Indexing" of All Visual C++ LIVE-CODE™ Examples

Visual C++ .NET: A Managed Code Approach for Experienced Programmers has 228 LIVE-CODE™ examples, which we have "double indexed." For every source-code program in the book, we took the file names with the **.h** and **.cpp** extensions, such as **ShowColors.cpp**, and indexed each both alphabetically (in this case, under "S") and as a subindex item under "Examples." We have double-indexed the figure captions using this same method. This makes it easier to find examples using particular features.

Deitel e-Learning Initiatives

e-Books and Support for Wireless Devices

Wireless devices will have an enormous role in the future of the Internet. Given recent bandwidth enhancements and the emergence of 2.5 and 3G technologies, it is projected that, within a few years, more people will access the Internet through wireless devices than through desktop computers. Deitel & Associates is committed to wireless accessibility and recently published *Wireless Internet & Mobile Business How to Program*. To fulfill the needs of a wide range of customers, we currently are developing our content both in traditional print formats and in newly developed electronic formats, such as wireless e-books so that students and professors can access content virtually anytime, anywhere. For periodic updates on these initiatives subscribe to the *Deitel™ Buzz Online* e-mail newsletter, **www.deitel.com/newsletter/subscribe.html** or visit **www.deitel.com**.

e-Matter

Deitel & Associates is partnering with Prentice Hall's parent company, Pearson PLC, and its information technology Web site, **www.InformIT.com**, to launch the DEITEL™ e-Matter series at **www.InformIT.com/deitel** in Spring 2003. This series will provide professors, students and professionals with an additional source of information on programming and software topics. e-Matter consists of stand-alone sections taken from published texts, forthcoming texts or pieces written during the Deitel research-and-development process. Developing e-Matter based on pre-publication books allows us to offer significant amounts of the material to early adopters for use in academic and corporate courses.

Course Management Systems: WebCT, Blackboard, CourseCompass and Premium CourseCompass

We are working with Prentice Hall to integrate our *How to Program Series* courseware into four series of Course Management Systems-based products: WebCT, Blackboard™, CourseCompass and Premium CourseCompass. These enable instructors to create, manage and use sophisticated Web-based educational programs. Course Management Systems feature course customization (such as posting contact information, policies, syllabi, announcements, assignments, grades, performance evaluations and progress tracking), class and student management tools, a grade book, reporting tools, communication tools (such as chat rooms), a whiteboard, document sharing, bulletin boards and more. Instructors can use these products to communicate with their students, create online quizzes and exams from questions directly linked to the text and efficiently grade and track test results. Visit **www.prenhall.com/cms** for more information about these upcoming products. For demonstrations of existing WebCT, Blackboard and CourseCompass course materials, visit **cms.prenhall.com/webct**, **cms.prenhall.com/blackboard** and **cms.prenhall.com/coursecompass**, respectively.

Deitel and InformIT Newsletters

Deitel Newsletter

Our own free newsletter, the DEITEL™ BUZZ ONLINE, includes commentary on industry trends and developments, links to free articles and resources from our published books and upcoming publications, product-release schedules, challenges, anecdotes, information on our corporate instructor-led training courses and more. To subscribe, visit

```
www.deitel.com/newsletter/subscribe.html
```

Deitel Column in the InformIT Newsletters

Deitel & Associates, Inc., contributes articles to two free *InformIT* weekly e-mail newsletters, currently subscribed to by more than 1,000,000 IT professionals worldwide.

- *Editorial Newsletter*—Contains dozens of new articles per week on various IT topics, including programming, advanced computing, networking, business, Web development, software engineering, operating systems and more. Deitel & Associates contributes 2–3 articles per week taken from our extensive content base or from material being created during our research and development process.

- *Promotional Newsletter*—Features weekly specials and discounts on most Pearson publications. Each week a new DEITEL™ product is featured along with information about our corporate instructor-led training courses.

To subscribe, visit **www.InformIT.com**.

The New DEITEL™ Developer Series

Deitel & Associates, Inc., is making a major commitment to .NET programming through the launch of our *Deitel™ Developer Series*. *Visual C++ .NET: A Managed Code Approach for Experienced Programmers, C#: A Programmer's Introduction, C# for Experienced Programmers* and *Visual Basic .NET for Experienced Programmers* are the first .NET books in this new series. These will be followed by several additional books, beginning with *ASP .NET with Visual Basic .NET for Experienced Programmers, ASP .NET with C# for Experienced Programmers*, and *.NET: A Technical Introduction*. Please visit **www.deitel.com** for continuous updates on all published and forthcoming *DEITEL™ Developer Series* titles.

The *DEITEL™ Developer Series* is divided into three subseries. The *A Technical Introduction* subseries provides IT managers and developers with detailed overviews of emerging technologies. The *A Programmer's Introduction* subseries is designed to teach the fundamentals of new languages and software technologies to programmers and novices from the ground up; these books discuss programming fundamentals, followed by brief introductions to more sophisticated topics. The *For Experienced Programmers* subseries is designed for seasoned developers seeking a deeper treatment of new programming languages and technologies, without the encumbrance of introductory material; the books in this subseries move quickly to in-depth coverage of the features of the programming languages and software technologies being covered.

Acknowledgments

One of the great pleasures of writing a book is acknowledging the efforts of many people whose names may not appear on the cover, but whose hard work, cooperation, friendship and understanding were crucial to the production of the book.

Many other people at Deitel & Associates, Inc., devoted long hours to this project. Below is a list of our full-time employees who contributed to this publication:

Rashmi Jayaprakash
Laura Treibick
Betsy DuWaldt

We would also like to thank the participants in the Deitel & Associates, Inc., College Internship Program who contributed to this publication.[1]

Jimmy Nguyen (Northeastern)
Nicholas Cassie (Northeastern)
Thiago da Silva (Northeastern)
Mike Dos'Santos (Northeastern)
Emanuel Achildiev (Northeastern)
Christina Carney (Framingham State)

We are fortunate to have been able to work with the talented and dedicated team of publishing professionals at Prentice Hall. We especially appreciate the extraordinary efforts of our editors, Petra Recter and Karen McLean of Prentice Hall and PH/PTR, respectively and Michael Ruel, who managed the extraordinary review processes for our *Deitel™ Developer Series* Visual C++ .NET publication. We would also like to thank Mark L. Taub, Editor-in-Chief for computer publications at PH/PTR, for conceptualizing the *Deitel™ Developer Series*. He provided the necessary environment and resources to help us generate the many books in this series. A special note of appreciation goes to Marcia Horton, Editor-in-Chief of Engineering and Computer Science at Prentice Hall. Marcia has been our mentor and our friend for 18 years at Prentice Hall. She is responsible for all aspects of Deitel publications at all Pearson divisions including Prentice Hall, PH/PTR and Pearson International.

Laura Treibick, the Director of Multimedia at Deitel & Associates, Inc., designed the cover. Tamara Newnam (`smart_art@earthlink.net`) carried the cover through to completion, and produced the art work for our programming-tip icons.

We wish to acknowledge the efforts of our reviewers. Adhering to a tight time schedule, these reviewers scrutinized the text and the programs, providing countless sug-

---

1. The *Deitel & Associates, Inc. College Internship Program* offers a limited number of salaried positions to Boston-area college students majoring in Computer Science, Information Technology, Marketing, Management and English. Students work at our corporate headquarters in Maynard, Massachusetts full-time in the summers and (for those attending college in the Boston area) part-time during the academic year. We also offer full-time internship positions for students interested in taking a semester off from school to gain industry experience. Regular full-time positions are available to college graduates. For more information about this competitive program, please contact Abbey Deitel at `deitel@deitel.com` and visit `www.deitel.com`.

gestions for improving the accuracy and completeness of the presentation. We sincerely appreciate the time these people took from their busy professional schedules to help us ensure the quality, accuracy and timeliness of this book.

Reviewers:
Neal Patel (Microsoft)
Paul Randal (Microsoft)
Scott Woodgate (Microsoft)
David Weller (Microsoft)
Dr. Rekha Bhowmik (St. Cloud State University)
Carl Burnham (Hosting Resolve)
Kyle Gabhart (StarMaker Technologies)
Doug Harrison (Eluent Software)
Christian Hessler (Sun Microsystems)
Michael Hudson (Blue Print Tech)
John Paul Mueller (DataCon Services)
Nicholas Paldino (Exis Consulting)
Chris Platt (RealAge Inc./ UC San Diego Extension)
Teri Radichel (Radical Software)
Ivan Rancati
Tomas Restrepo (Intergrupo S.A)

Under tight deadlines, these reviewers scrutinized every aspect of the text and made countless suggestions for improving the accuracy and completeness of the presentation.

Contacting Deitel & Associates

We would sincerely appreciate your comments, criticisms, corrections and suggestions for improving the text. Please address all correspondence to:

`deitel@deitel.com`

We will respond promptly.

Errata

We will post all errata for this publication at **www.deitel.com**.

Well, that's it for now. Welcome to the exciting world of Visual C++ .NET programming. We hope you enjoy this look at Microsoft Visual C++ .NET. Good luck!

Dr. Harvey M. Deitel
Paul J. Deitel
Christina J. Courtemarche
Jeffrey C. Hamm
Jonathan P. Liperi
Tem R. Nieto
Cheryl H. Yaeger

About the Authors

Dr. Harvey M. Deitel, Chairman and Chief Strategy Officer of Deitel & Associates, Inc., has 41 years experience in the computing field, including extensive industry and academic experience. Dr. Deitel earned B.S. and M.S. degrees from the Massachusetts Institute of Technology and a Ph.D. from Boston University. He worked on the pioneering virtual-memory operating-systems projects at IBM and MIT that developed techniques now widely implemented in systems such as Unix, Linux™ and Windows. He has 20 years of college teaching experience, including earning tenure and serving as the Chairman of the Computer Science Department at Boston College before founding Deitel & Associates, Inc., with his son, Paul J. Deitel. He is the author or co-author of several dozen books and multimedia packages and continues to write more. With translations published in Japanese, Russian, Spanish, Traditional Chinese, Simplified Chinese, Korean, French, Polish, Italian, Portuguese and Greek, Dr. Deitel's texts have earned international recognition. Dr. Deitel has delivered professional seminars to major corporations, and to government organizations and various branches of the military.

Paul J. Deitel, CEO and Chief Technical Officer of Deitel & Associates, Inc., is a graduate of the Massachusetts Institute of Technology's Sloan School of Management, where he studied Information Technology. Through Deitel & Associates, Inc., he has delivered C++, C, Java and Internet and World Wide Web programming courses to industry clients including Compaq, Sun Microsystems, White Sands Missile Range, Rogue Wave Software, Boeing, Dell, Stratus, Fidelity, Cambridge Technology Partners, Open Environment Corporation, One Wave, Hyperion Software, Lucent Technologies, Adra Systems, Entergy, CableData Systems, NASA at the Kennedy Space Center, the National Severe Storms Laboratory, IBM and many other organizations. He has lectured on C++ and Java for the Boston Chapter of the Association for Computing Machinery and has taught satellite-based Java courses through a cooperative venture of Deitel & Associates, Inc., Prentice Hall and the Technology Education Network. He and his father, Dr. Harvey M. Deitel, are the world's best-selling programming language textbook authors.

Tem R. Nieto, Director of Product Development at Deitel & Associates, Inc., is a graduate of Massachusetts Institute of Technology, where he studied engineering and computing. Through Deitel & Associates, Inc., he has delivered courses for industry clients including Sun Microsystems, Compaq, EMC, Stratus, Fidelity, NASDAQ, Art Technology, Progress Software, Toys "R" Us, Operational Support Facility of the National Oceanographic and Atmospheric Administration, Jet Propulsion Laboratory, Nynex, Motorola, Federal Reserve Bank of Chicago, Banyan, Schlumberger, University of Notre Dame, NASA, various military installations and many others. He has co-authored numerous books and multimedia packages with the Deitels and has contributed to virtually every Deitel & Associates, Inc. publication.

Christina J. Courtemarche graduated from Boston University *magna cum laude* with a Bachelor's degree in Computer Science. Deitel publications she has contributed to include *Python How to Program* and *Wireless Internet & Mobile Business How to Program*.

Jeffrey C. Hamm is a third-year Computer Science and Mathematics student at Northeastern University. He has programming experience in C++, Java, C# and Visual Basic .NET and has a special interest in Windows technologies such as DirectX, MFC and

ATL. Jeff has contributed to other Deitel publications including *Advanced Java 2 Platform How to Program, C# How to Program* and *Visual Basic .NET How to Program, Second Edition*.

Jonathan P. Liperi is a graduate student at Boston University. He will earn his Master's degree in Computer Science in May 2003. His coursework has included advanced algorithms, queueing theory, computer architecture, computer networks, artificial intelligence, computer graphics, database systems, software engineering and various programming courses (C++, C, Python and Java). Jon also co-authored the Deitel & Associates, Inc. publication, *Python How to Program*.

Cheryl H. Yaeger, Director of Microsoft Software Publications with Deitel & Associates, Inc., graduated from Boston University in three years with a bachelor's degree in Computer Science. Cheryl has co-authored various Deitel & Associates publications, including *C# How to Program, C#: A Programmer's Introduction, C# for Experienced Programmers* and *Visual Basic .NET for Experienced Programmers* as well as contributed to other Deitel publications including *Perl How to Program, Wireless Internet & Mobile Business How to Program, Internet and World Wide Web How to Program, Second Edition* and *Visual Basic .NET How to Program, Second Edition*.

About Deitel & Associates, Inc.

Deitel & Associates, Inc., is an internationally recognized corporate instructor-led training and content-creation organization specializing in Internet/World Wide Web software technology, e-business/e-commerce software technology, object technology and computer programming languages education. The company provides courses in Internet and World Wide Web programming, wireless Internet programming, Web services (in both .NET and Java languages), object technology, and major programming languages and platforms, such as Visual C++ .NET, Visual Basic .NET, C#, ASP .NET, ADO .NET, C++, C, Java, Advanced Java, C, C++, XML, Perl, Python and more. Deitel & Associates, Inc., was founded by Dr. Harvey M. Deitel and Paul J. Deitel, the world's leading programming-language textbook authors. The company's clients include many of the largest computer companies, government agencies, branches of the military and business organizations. Through its 25-year publishing partnership with Prentice Hall, Deitel & Associates, Inc., publishes leading-edge programming textbooks, professional books, interactive CD-ROM-based multimedia *Cyber Classrooms, Complete Training Courses*, e-books, e-matter, Web-based training courses and course management systems e-content. Deitel & Associates, Inc., and the authors can be reached via e-mail at:

   deitel@deitel.com

To learn more about Deitel & Associates, Inc., its publications and its worldwide corporate on-site curriculum, see the last few pages of this book or visit:

   www.deitel.com

Individuals wishing to purchase Deitel books and Web-based training courses can do so through bookstores, online booksellers and:

   www.deitel.com

```
www.prenhall.com/deitel
www.InformIT.com/deitel
www.InformIT.com/cyberclassrooms
```

Bulk orders by corporations and academic institutions should be placed directly with Prentice Hall. See the last few pages of this book for worldwide ordering details. To follow the Deitel publishing program, please register at

```
www.deitel.com/newsletter/subscribe.html
```

1

Introduction to .NET and Visual C++® .NET

Objectives

- To learn the history of the Internet and the World Wide Web.
- To become familiar with the World Wide Web Consortium (W3C).
- To learn what the Extensible Markup Language (XML) is and why it is an important technology.
- To understand the impact of object technology on software development.
- To understand the Microsoft® .NET initiative.
- To introduce Managed Extensions for C++.
- To preview the remaining chapters of the book.

Things are always at their best in their beginning.
Blaise Pascal

High thoughts must have high language.
Aristophanes

Our life is frittered away by detail…Simplify, simplify.
Henry David Thoreau

Before beginning, plan carefully….
Marcus Tullius Cicero

Look with favor upon a bold beginning.
Virgil

I think I'm beginning to learn something about it.
Auguste Renoir

Outline

1.1 Introduction

Welcome to Visual C++ .NET! We have worked hard to provide programmers with the most accurate and complete information regarding Visual C++ .NET and the .NET platform. We hope that this book will provide an informative, entertaining and challenging learning experience for you. In this chapter, we present the history of the Internet and World Wide Web and introduce Microsoft's .NET initiative. The chapter concludes by touring the remainder of the book.

1.2 History of the Internet and World Wide Web

In the late 1960s, at a conference at the University of Illinois Urbana-Champaign, ARPA—the Advanced Research Projects Agency of the Department of Defense—rolled out the blueprints for networking the main computer systems of approximately a dozen ARPA-funded universities and research institutions. The computers were to be connected with communications lines operating at a then-stunning 56 Kbps (1 Kbps is equal to 1,024 bits per second), at a time when most people (of the few who had access to networking technologies) were connecting over telephone lines to computers at a rate of 110 bits per second. Researchers at Harvard talked about communicating with the Univac 1108 "supercomputer," which was located across the country at the University of Utah, to handle calculations related to their computer graphics research. Many other intriguing possibilities were discussed. Academic research was about to take a giant leap forward. Shortly after this conference, ARPA proceeded to implement what quickly became called the *ARPAnet*, the grandparent of today's *Internet*.

Things worked out differently from the original plan. Although the ARPAnet did enable researchers to network their computers, its chief benefit proved to be its capability for quick and easy communication via what came to be known as *electronic mail (e-mail)*. This is true even on today's Internet, with e-mail, instant messaging and file transfer facilitating communications among hundreds of millions of people worldwide.

The network was designed to operate without centralized control. This meant that if a portion of the network should fail, the remaining working portions would still be able to route data packets from senders to receivers over alternative paths.

The protocol (i.e., set of rules) for communicating over the ARPAnet became known as the *Transmission Control Protocol (TCP)*. TCP ensured that messages were routed properly from sender to receiver and that those messages arrived intact.

In parallel with the early evolution of the Internet, organizations worldwide were implementing their own networks to facilitate both intra-organization (i.e., within the organization) and inter-organization (i.e., between organizations) communication. A huge variety of networking hardware and software appeared. One challenge was to enable these diverse products to communicate with each other. ARPA accomplished this by developing the *Internet Protocol (IP),* which created a true "network of networks," the current architecture of the Internet. The combined set of protocols is now commonly called *TCP/IP*.

Initially, the use of the Internet was limited to universities and research institutions; later, the military adopted the technology. Eventually, the government decided to allow access to the Internet for commercial purposes. When this decision was made, there was resentment among the research and military communities—it was felt that response times would become poor as "the Net" became saturated with so many users.

In fact, the opposite has occurred. Businesses rapidly realized that, by making effective use of the Internet, they could refine their operations and offer new and better services to their clients. Companies started spending vast amounts of money to develop and enhance their Internet presence. This generated fierce competition among communications carriers and hardware and software suppliers to meet the increased infrastructure demand. The result is that *bandwidth* (i.e., the information-carrying capacity of communications lines) on the Internet has increased tremendously, while hardware costs have plummeted. The Internet has played a significant role in the economic growth that many industrialized nations experienced over the last decade.

The *World Wide Web* allows computer users to locate and view multimedia-based documents (i.e., documents with text, graphics, animations, audios or videos) on almost any subject. Even though the Internet was developed more than three decades ago, the introduction of the World Wide Web (WWW) was a relatively recent event. In 1989, Tim Berners-Lee of CERN (the European Organization for Nuclear Research) began to develop a technology for sharing information via hyperlinked text documents. Basing the new language on the well-established *Standard Generalized Markup Language (SGML)*—a standard for business data interchange—Berners-Lee called his invention the *HyperText Markup Language (HTML)*. He also wrote communication protocols to form the backbone of his new hypertext information system, which he referred to as the World Wide Web.

Surely, historians will list the Internet and the World Wide Web among the most important and profound creations of humankind. In the past, most computer applications ran on "stand-alone" computers (computers that were not connected to one another). Today's applications can be written to communicate among the world's hundreds of millions of computers. The Internet and World Wide Web merge computing and communications technologies, expediting and simplifying our work. They make information instantly and conveniently accessible to large numbers of people. They enable individuals and small businesses to achieve worldwide exposure. They are changing the way we do business and conduct our personal lives.

1.3 World Wide Web Consortium (W3C)

In October 1994, Tim Berners-Lee founded an organization, called the *World Wide Web Consortium (W3C)*, that is devoted to developing nonproprietary, interoperable technologies for the World Wide Web. One of the W3C's primary goals is to make the Web universally accessible—regardless of its users' disabilities, languages or cultures.

The W3C is also a standardization organization and is composed of three *hosts*—the Massachusetts Institute of Technology (MIT), France's INRIA (Institut National de Recherche en Informatique et Automatique) and Keio University of Japan—and over 400 members, including Deitel & Associates, Inc. Members provide the primary financing for the W3C and help set the strategic direction of the Consortium. To learn more about the W3C, visit **www.w3.org**.

Web technologies standardized by the W3C are called *Recommendations*. Current W3C Recommendations include Extensible HyperText Markup Language (XHTML™) for marking up content for the Web (discussed in Section 1.4), *Cascading Style Sheets (CSS™)* for describing how content is formatted and the *Extensible Markup Language (XML)* for creating markup languages. Recommendations are not actual software products, but documents that specify the role, syntax and rules of a technology. Before becoming a W3C Recommendation, a document passes through three major phases: *Working Draft*, which, as its name implies, specifies an evolving draft; *Candidate Recommendation,* a stable version of the document that industry can begin to implement; and *Proposed Recommendation*, a Candidate Recommendation that is considered mature (i.e., has been implemented and tested over a period of time) and is ready to be considered for W3C Recommendation status. For detailed information about the W3C Recommendation track, see "6.2 The W3C Recommendation track" at

```
www.w3.org/Consortium/Process/Process-19991111/
process.html#RecsCR
```

1.4 Extensible Markup Language (XML)

As the popularity of the Web exploded in the 1990s, HTML's limitations became apparent. Although HTML was created as a common format for the Web, HTML's lack of *extensibility* (the ability to change or add features) frustrated developers, and the lack of correctly structured documents allowed erroneous HTML to proliferate. Browser vendors attempting to gain market share created platform-specific tags. This forced Web developers to support multiple browsers, which significantly complicated Web development. To address these and other problems, the W3C developed XML.

XML combines the power and extensibility of its parent language, SGML, with simplicity. XML is a *meta-language*—a language used as a basis for other languages—that offers a high level of extensibility. Using XML, the W3C created the *Extensible HyperText Markup Language (XHTML)*, an XML *vocabulary* (i.e., an XML-based markup language that is developed for a specific industry or purpose) that provides a common, extensible format for the Web. XHTML is expected to replace HTML. The W3C also developed the *Extensible Stylesheet Language (XSL)*, which is composed of several technologies, to manipulate data in XML documents for presentation purposes. XSL provides developers the flexibility to transform data from an XML document into other types of documents—for example, Web pages or reports. In addition to serving as the basis for other markup languages, developers use XML for data interchange and e-commerce systems. At the time of this writing, there were more than 450 XML standards.

Unlike many technologies, which begin as proprietary solutions and become standards, XML was defined as an open, standard technology. XML's development has been supervised by the W3C's *XML Working Group*, which prepared the XML specification and approved it for publication. In 1998, the XML version 1.0 specification (**www.w3.org/TR/REC-xml**) was accepted as a *W3C Recommendation*. This means that the technology is stable for wide deployment in industry.

The W3C continues to oversee the development of XML, as well as Simple Object Access Protocol (SOAP), a technology for the distribution of data (marked up as XML) over the Internet. Developed initially by Microsoft and DevelopMentor, SOAP is a W3C Working Draft that provides a framework for expressing application semantics and encoding and packaging data. Microsoft .NET (discussed in Sections 1.6 and 1.7) uses XML and SOAP to mark up and transfer data over the Internet. XML and SOAP are at the core of .NET—they allow software components to interoperate (i.e., communicate easily with one another). SOAP is supported by many platforms, because of its foundations in XML and HTTP. We discuss XML in Chapter 15, Extensible Markup Language (XML), and SOAP in Chapter 17, Web Services.

1.5 Key Software Trend: Object Technology

What are objects, and why are they special? Object technology is a packaging scheme that facilitates the creation of meaningful software units. These units are large and focused on particular application areas. There are date objects, time objects, paycheck objects, invoice objects, audio objects, video objects, file objects, record objects and so on. In fact, almost any noun can be represented as a software object. Objects have *properties* (i.e., *attributes*, such as color, size and weight) and perform *actions* (i.e., *behaviors*, such as moving, sleeping and drawing). Classes represent groups of related objects. For example, all cars belong to the "car" class, even though individual cars vary in make, model, color and options packages. A class specifies the general format of its objects; the properties and actions available to an object depend on its class.

We live in a world of objects. Just look around you—there are cars, planes, people, animals, buildings, traffic lights, elevators and so on. Before object-oriented languages appeared, *procedural programming languages* (such as Fortran, Pascal, BASIC and C) focused on actions (verbs) rather than things or objects (nouns). We live in a world of objects, but earlier programming languages forced individuals to program primarily with verbs. This paradigm shift made writing programs a bit awkward. However, with the advent of popular object-oriented languages, such as C++, Java™ and C#, programmers can program in an object-oriented manner that reflects the way in which they perceive the world. This process, which seems more natural than procedural programming, has resulted in significant productivity gains.

One of the key problems with procedural programming is that the program units created do not mirror real-world entities effectively and therefore are difficult to reuse. Programmers often write and rewrite similar software for various projects. This wastes precious time and money as programmers repeatedly "reinvent the wheel." With object technology, properly designed software entities (called objects) can be reused on future projects. Using libraries of reusable componentry can reduce the amount of effort required to implement certain kinds of systems (compared with the effort that would be required to reinvent these capabilities in new projects). Visual C++ .NET programmers use the .NET Framework Class Library (known commonly as the FCL), which is introduced in Section 1.8.

Some organizations report that software reusability is not, in fact, the key benefit of object-oriented programming. Rather, they indicate that object-oriented programming tends to produce software that is more understandable because it is better organized and has fewer maintenance requirements. As much as 80 percent of software costs are not associated with the original efforts to develop the software, but instead are related to the continued evolution and maintenance of that software throughout its lifetime. Object orientation allows programmers to abstract the details of software and focus on the "big picture." Rather than worrying about minute details, the programmer can focus on the behaviors and interactions of objects. A roadmap that showed every tree, house and driveway would be difficult, if not impossible, to read. When such details are removed and only the essential information (roads) remains, the map becomes easier to understand. In the same way, a program that is divided into objects is easy to understand, modify and update because it hides much of the detail. It is clear that object-oriented programming will be the key programming methodology for at least the next decade.

 Software Engineering Observation 1.1

Use a building-block approach to create programs. By using existing pieces in new projects, programmers avoid reinventing the wheel. This is called software reuse, *and it is central to object-oriented programming.*

[*Note*: We will include many of these *Software Engineering Observations* throughout the book to explain concepts that affect and improve the overall architecture and quality of a software system and, particularly, of large software systems. We also will highlight *Good Programming Practices* (practices that can help programmers write programs that are clearer, more understandable, more maintainable and easier to test and debug), *Common Programming Errors* (problems we highlight to ensure that programmers avoid the most common errors), *Performance Tips* (techniques that will help programmers write programs that run faster and use less memory), *Portability Tips* (techniques that will help programmers write programs that can run, with little or no modification, on a variety of computers), *Testing and Debugging Tips* (techniques that will help programmers remove bugs from their programs and, more importantly, write bug-free programs in the first place) and *Look-and-Feel Observations* (techniques that will help programmers design the "look and feel" of their graphical user interfaces for appearance and ease of use). Many of these techniques and practices are only guidelines; you will, no doubt, develop your own preferred programming style.]

The advantage of writing your own code is that you will know exactly how it works. The code will be yours to examine, modify and improve. The disadvantage is the time and effort that goes into designing, developing and testing new code.

 Performance Tip 1.1

Reusing proven code components instead of writing your own versions can improve program performance, because these components normally are written to perform efficiently.

Software Engineering Observation 1.2

Extensive class libraries of reusable software components are available over the Internet and the World Wide Web; many are offered free of charge.

1.6 Introduction to Microsoft .NET

In June 2000, Microsoft announced its *.NET* (pronounced "dot-net") *initiative*. The *.NET platform* is one that provides significant enhancements to earlier developer platforms. .NET offers a new software-development model that allows applications created in disparate programming languages to communicate with each other. The platform also allows developers to create Web-based applications that can be distributed to a great variety of devices (even wireless phones) and to desktop computers.

Microsoft's .NET initiative is a broad new vision for embracing the Internet and the Web in the development, engineering and use of software. One key aspect of the .NET strategy is its independence from a specific language or platform. Rather than requiring programmers to use a single programming language, developers can create a .NET application by using any combination of .NET-compatible languages (Fig. 1.1). Programmers can contribute to the same software project, writing code in the .NET languages (such as Visual C++ .NET, C#, Visual Basic® .NET and many others) in which they are most proficient.

A key component of the .NET architecture is *Web services*, which are applications that expose (i.e., make available) functionality to clients via the Internet. Clients and other applications can use these Web services as reusable building blocks. One example of a Web service is Dollar Rent a Car's reservation system, known as Quick Keys.[1] Dollar wanted to expose the functionality of its mainframe-based system, so that other companies could provide customers with the ability to make rental-car reservations. Dollar could have created

Programming Languages	
APL	Oberon
C#	Oz
COBOL	Pascal
Component Pascal	Perl
Curriculum	Python
Eiffel	RPG
Fortran	Scheme
Haskell	Smalltalk
J#	Standard ML

Fig. 1.1   .NET Languages (tabular information from Microsoft Web site, `www.microsoft.com`). (Part 1 of 2.)

1. Microsoft Corporation, "Dollar Rent A Car Breathes New Life Into Legacy Systems Using .NET Connected Software," 15 March 2002 **<www.microsoft.com/business/ casestudies/b2c/dollarrentacar.asp>**.

Programming Languages	
JScript .NET	Visual Basic .NET
Mercury	Visual C++ .NET

Fig. 1.1   .NET Languages (tabular information from Microsoft Web site, **www.microsoft.com**.). (Part 2 of 2.)

individual, proprietary solutions for its business partners. To expose its functionality in a reusable way, Dollar implemented its solution using Web services. Through the newly created Web service, airlines and hotels can use Dollar's reservation system to reserve cars for their clients. Dollar's business partners do not need to use the same platform as Dollar uses, nor do they need to understand how the reservation system is implemented. Reimplementing its application as a Web service has provided Dollar with millions of dollars of additional revenue, as well as thousands of new customers.

Web services extend the concept of software reuse by allowing programmers to concentrate on their specialties without having to implement every component of every application. Instead, companies can buy Web services and devote their time and energy to developing their products. Object-oriented programming has become popular, because it enables programmers to create applications easily, using prepackaged components. Similarly, programmers may create an application using Web services for databases, security, authentication, data storage and language translation without having to know the internal details of those components.

When companies link their products via Web services, a new user experience emerges. For example, a single application could manage bill payments, tax refunds, loans and investments, using Web services from various companies. An online merchant could buy Web services for online credit-card payments, user authentication, network security and inventory databases to create an e-commerce Web site.

The keys to this interaction are XML and SOAP, which enable Web services to communicate. XML gives meaning to data, and SOAP is the protocol that allows Web services to communicate easily with one another. XML and SOAP act as the "glue" that combines various Web services to form applications.

Universal data access is another essential .NET concept. If two copies of a file exist (e.g., on a personal and a company computer), the oldest version must be updated constantly—this is called file *synchronization*. If the files are different, they are *unsynchronized*, a situation that could lead to errors. With .NET, data can reside in one central location rather than on separate systems. Any Internet-connected device can access the data (under tight control, of course), which would then be formatted appropriately for use or display on the accessing device. Thus, the same document could be seen and edited on a desktop PC, a PDA, a wireless phone or some other device. Users would not need to synchronize the information, because it would be fully up-to-date in a central location.

.NET is an immense undertaking. We discuss various aspects of .NET throughout this book. Additional information is available at **www.microsoft.com/net**.

1.7 Visual C++ .NET

Standard C++ evolved from C, which was developed from two previous programming languages, BCPL and B. BCPL was created in 1967 by Martin Richards as a language for writing operating-systems software and compilers. Ken Thompson modeled many features in his language B after their counterparts in BCPL and used B to create early versions of the UNIX operating system at Bell Laboratories in 1970 on a DEC PDP-7 computer. Both BCPL and B were "typeless" languages—every data item occupied one "word" in memory and the burden of treating a data item as a whole number or a real number, for example, was the responsibility of the programmer.

The C language was developed by Dennis Ritchie at Bell Laboratories and was originally implemented on a DEC PDP-11 computer in 1972. C uses many important concepts of BCPL and B while adding data typing and other features. By the late 1970s, C had evolved into what now is referred to as "traditional C," "classic C," or "Kernighan and Ritchie C." The publication by Prentice-Hall in 1978 of Kernighan and Ritchie's book, *The C Programming Language,* brought attention to the language.

C initially became widely known as the development language of the UNIX operating system. The widespread use of C with various types of computers (sometimes called *hardware platforms*) led to many variations of the language that were similar, but often incompatible. This was a serious problem for program developers who needed to write portable programs to run on disparate platforms. It became clear that a standard version of C was needed. In 1983, the X3J11 technical committee was created under the American National Standards Committee on Computers and Information Processing (X3) to "provide an unambiguous and machine-independent definition of the language." In 1989, the standard was approved. ANSI cooperated with the International Organization for Standardization (ISO) to standardize C; the joint standard document was published in 1990 and is referred to as *ANSI/ISO 9899: 1990.* Copies of this document can be ordered from ANSI. The second edition of Kernighan and Ritchie, published in 1988, reflects this version called ANSI C, a version of the language now used worldwide.

 Portability Tip 1.1

Because C is a standardized, hardware-independent, widely available language, applications written in C often can be run with little or no modifications on a wide range of different computer systems.

C++, an extension of C, was developed by Bjarne Stroustrup in the early 1980s at Bell Laboratories. C++ provides a number of features that "spruce up" the C language, but more importantly, it provides capabilities for *object-oriented programming.*

Building software quickly, correctly and economically remains an elusive goal, and this at a time when the demand for new and more powerful software is soaring. *Objects* are essentially reusable software *components* that model items in the real world. Software developers are discovering that using a modular, object-oriented design and implementation approach can make software development groups much more productive than is possible with previous popular programming techniques, such as structured programming. Object-oriented programs are easier to understand, correct and modify.

Developed in the early 1990s, Visual C++ is a Microsoft implementation of C++ that includes Microsoft's proprietary extensions to the language. Over the past decade, Microsoft has released several versions of Visual C++—most recently, Visual C++ .NET.

Visual C++ .NET is known as a *visual programming language*—the developer uses graphical tools (via Visual Studio .NET) to create applications. We discuss Visual Studio .NET later in this section.

Early graphics and *graphical user interface* (*GUI*) programming (i.e., the programming of an application's visual interface) with Visual C++ was implemented using the *Microsoft Foundation Classes* (*MFC*). The *Microsoft Foundation Classes library* is a collection of classes that help Visual C++ programmers create powerful Windows-based applications. Now, with the introduction of .NET, Microsoft provides an additional library (.NET's FCL, discussed in Section 1.8) for implementing GUI, graphics, networking, multithreading and other capabilities. This library is available to .NET-compliant languages such as Visual C++ .NET, Visual Basic .NET and Microsoft's new language, C#. However, developers still can use MFC—Microsoft has, in fact, upgraded MFC to MFC 7, which includes new classes and documentation that can be accessed using Visual Studio .NET. MFC often is used to develop *unmanaged code*, or code that does not make use of the .NET Framework.[2] We discuss unmanaged code in more detail shortly.

The .NET platform enables Web-based applications to be distributed to a variety of devices, including desktop computers and cell phones. The platform offers a new software-development model that allows applications created in disparate programming languages to communicate with each other. Visual C++ .NET was designed specifically for the .NET platform so Visual C++ programmers could migrate easily to .NET. However, Microsoft also designed Visual C++ .NET to be backward compatible with its previous version, 6.0, and has continued to emphasize compliance with the ANSI/ISO standard for C++.

Visual C++ .NET introduces *Managed Extensions for C++* (*MC++*) that enable a programmer to access the .NET Framework. Programmers can use the .NET Framework to create objects that provide automatic garbage collection, memory management and language interoperability (with other .NET languages). Such objects are known as *managed objects*; the code that defines these objects is known as *managed code*. With managed objects, memory leaks are extremely rare. [*Note*: The different implementations of C++ and Visual C++ have yielded several industry terms. For the remainder of this book, we use the term "C++" when referring to standard C++. We use the term "Managed Extensions for C++ (MC++)" when referring to features of managed C++ or code that uses these features. Finally, we use the term "Visual C++ .NET" when referring to the Microsoft product/compiler, which can be used to write both managed and unmanaged code.]

MC++ provides the programmer access to new data types provided by the .NET Framework. These new data types aid in standardization across different platforms and .NET programming languages. In MC++, standard C++ data types are mapped to these new types. [*Note*: We discuss .NET data types in more detail in Chapter 2, Visual Studio® .NET IDE and Visual C++ .NET Programming.]

The true power of Visual C++ .NET lies in its interoperability between managed and unmanaged code. All legacy Visual C++ code is unmanaged. Rather than forcing developers to discard large amounts of legacy code, Visual C++ .NET enables programmers to mix managed (MC++) and unmanaged (standard C++) code. We discuss mixing managed and unmanaged code in detail in Chapter 24, Managed and Unmanaged Interoperability.

---

2. Readers can learn more about what is new in MFC 7 at **msdn.microsoft.com/library/ default.asp?url=/library/en-us/vcedit/html/ vcrefwhatsnewlibrariesvisualc70.asp**.

In addition to providing interoperability between managed and unmanaged code, Microsoft has upgraded several of the technologies used in unmanaged code. One example of this is the *Active Template Library (ATL)*, a set of template classes that simplify the creation of COM components.[3] The newest version of ATL, *ATL 7*, contains several enhancements. An example of one enhancement is the *ATL Server*, which is a set of classes designed to simplify Web development while providing the ability to call unmanaged C++ from within a Web page. *Attributes* are a new feature that allow a programmer to inject precompiled code into an application. An attribute can be used to modify different portions of an application. We discuss attributed programming in Chapter 22 and ATL Server in Chapter 23.

Although Visual C++ .NET is powerful, it lacks some tools, such as a Windows Form designer, a visual programming tool that simplifies GUI and database programming. With the Windows Form Designer, Visual Studio .NET generates program code from various programmer *actions* (such as using the mouse for pointing, clicking, dragging and dropping). Because Visual C++ .NET does not yet provide the programmer with a Form designer, programmers must manually generate code for their graphical user interfaces.[4]

In Visual C++ .NET, programs are created using Visual Studio .NET, an *Integrated Development Environment (IDE)*. With the IDE, a programmer can create, run, test and debug programs conveniently, thereby reducing the time it takes to produce a working program to a fraction of the time it would have taken without using the IDE. The process of rapidly creating an application using an IDE typically is referred to as *Rapid Application Development (RAD)*.

Visual C++ .NET enables a new degree of language interoperability: Software components from different languages can interact as never before. Developers can package even old software to work with new Visual C++ .NET programs. In addition, Visual C++ .NET applications can interact via the Internet, using industry standards such as the Simple Object Access Protocol (SOAP) and XML, which we discuss in Chapter 15, Extensible Markup Language (XML) and Chapter 17, Web Services. The programming advances embodied in .NET and Visual C++ .NET will lead to a new style of programming, in which applications are created from building blocks available over the Internet.

1.8 .NET Framework and the Common Language Runtime

The *.NET Framework* is at the heart of .NET. This framework manages and executes applications, contains a class library (called the *Framework Class Library*, or *FCL*), enforces security and provides many other programming capabilities. The details of the .NET Framework are found in the *Common Language Specification (CLS)*, which contains information about the storage of objects and other information. The CLS has been submitted for standardization to ECMA (the European Computer Manufacturers Association). This allows independent software vendors to create the .NET Framework for other platforms. The .NET Framework exists only for the Windows platform, but is being developed for other

---

3. *COM* (the *Component Object Model*) is a specification that provides a platform-, language- and location-independent environment to develop reusable, binary object-oriented software components.
4. For convenience, we used C# to generate all of the GUI code for this book. We then converted the autogenerated C# code to MC++. Normally, however, programmers should not modify autogenerated code.

platforms, as well, such as Microsoft's *Shared Source CLI* (*Common Language Infrastructure*). The Shared Source CLI is an archive of source code that provides a subset of the Microsoft .NET Framework for both Windows XP and the FreeBSD[5] operating systems.[6] For more information in the Shared Source CLI, visit **msdn.microsoft.com/ library/default.asp?url=/library/en-us/dndotnet/html/ mssharsourcecli.asp**.

The *Common Language Runtime (CLR)* is another central part of the .NET Framework—it executes managed code. Programs are compiled into machine-specific instructions in two steps. First, the program is compiled into *Microsoft Intermediate Language (MSIL)*, which defines instructions for the CLR. Code converted into MSIL from other languages and sources is woven together by the CLR. Then, another compiler in the CLR compiles the MSIL into machine code (for a particular platform), creating a single application.

Why bother having the extra step of converting from Visual C++ .NET to MSIL, instead of compiling directly into machine language? The key reasons are portability between operating systems, interoperability between languages and execution-management features such as memory management and security.

If the .NET Framework exists (and is installed) for a platform, that platform can run any .NET program. The ability of a program to run (without modification) across multiple platforms is known as *platform independence*. Code written once can be used on another machine without modification, saving both time and money. In addition, software can target a wider audience—previously, companies had to decide whether converting (sometimes called *porting*) their programs to different platforms was worth the cost. With .NET, porting is simplified.

The .NET Framework also provides a high level of *language interoperability*. Programs written in different languages are all compiled into MSIL—the different parts can be combined to create a single, unified program. MSIL allows the .NET Framework to be *language independent*, because MSIL is not tied to a particular programming language. Any language that can be compiled into MSIL is called a *.NET-compliant language*.

Language interoperability offers many benefits to software companies. Visual C++ .NET, Visual Basic .NET and C# developers, for example, can work side-by-side on the same project without having to learn another programming language—all their code is compiled into MSIL and linked together to form one program. In addition, the .NET Framework can package preexisting components (i.e., components created using tools that predate .NET) and .NET components to work together. This allows companies to reuse the code that they have spent years developing and integrate it with the .NET code that they write. Integration is crucial, because companies cannot migrate easily to .NET unless they can stay productive, using their existing developers and software.

Another benefit of the .NET Framework is the CLR's execution-management features. The CLR manages memory, security and other features, relieving the programmer of these responsibilities. With languages like C++, programmers must manage their own memory. This leads to problems if programmers request memory and never release it—programs

---

5. The FreeBSD project provides a freely available and open-source UNIX-like operating system that is based on UC Berkeley's *Berkeley System Distribution* (*BSD*). For more information on BSD, visit **www.freebsd.org**.
6. Microsoft Corporation, "The Microsoft Shared Source CLI Implementation," March 2002, **<msdn.microsoft.com/library/en-us/Dndotnet/html/ mssharsourcecli.asp>**.

could consume all available memory, which would prevent applications from running. By managing the program's memory, the .NET Framework allows programmers to concentrate on program logic.

The .NET Framework also provides programmers with a huge library of reusable classes. This library, called the Framework Class Library (FCL), can be used by any .NET language.

This book explains how to develop .NET software with Visual C++ .NET and the FCL. Steve Ballmer, Microsoft's CEO, stated in May 2001 that Microsoft was "betting the company" on .NET. Such a dramatic commitment surely indicates a bright future for Visual C++ .NET and its community of developers.

1.9 Tour of the Book

In this section, we tour the chapters and appendices of *Visual C++ .NET for Experienced Programmers: A Managed Code Approach*. In addition to the topics presented in each chapter, several of the chapters contain an Internet and Web Resources section that lists additional sources from which readers can enhance their knowledge of Visual C++ programming.

Chapter 1—Introduction to .NET and Visual C++® .NET
The first chapter presents the history of the Internet, World Wide Web and various technologies (such as XML and SOAP) that have led to advances in computing. We introduce the Microsoft .NET initiative and Visual C++ .NET, including Web services. We explore the impact of .NET on software development and software reusability. The chapter concludes with a tour of the book.

Chapter 2—Visual Studio® .NET IDE and Visual C++ .NET Programming
Chapter 2 introduces Visual Studio .NET, an integrated development environment (IDE) that allows programmers to create applications using standard C++ and Managed Extensions for C++ (MC++). Visual Studio .NET contains tools for debugging and writing code. The chapter presents features of Visual Studio .NET, including its key windows, and shows how to compile and run programs. The chapter also introduces readers to console-application programming in MC++. Every concept is presented in the context of a complete working MC++ program and is followed by one or more screen shots showing actual inputs and outputs as the program executes. This is our LIVE-CODE™ approach. We discuss fundamental tasks, such as how a program inputs data from its users and how to write arithmetic expressions.

Chapter 3—Control Structures
This chapter introduces the principles of structured programming, a set of techniques that will help the reader develop clear, understandable and maintainable programs. The chapter then introduces the use of control structures that affect the sequence in which statements are executed. Control structures produce programs that are easily understood, debugged and maintained. We discuss the three forms of program control—sequence, selection and repetition—focusing on the **if/else**, **while**, **for**, **do/while** and **switch** structures. We explain the break and continue statements and the logical operators. We build on information presented in the previous chapter to create programs that are interactive (i.e., they change their behavior to suit user-supplied inputs).

Chapter 4—Functions and Arrays

A function allows the programmer to create a block of code that can be called upon from various points in a program. Larger programs can be divided into interacting classes, each consisting of functions—this is sometimes called the "divide and conquer" strategy. Programs are divided into simple components that interact in straightforward ways. We discuss how to create our own functions that can take inputs, perform calculations and return outputs. Recursive functions (functions that call themselves) and function overloading, which allows multiple functions to have the same name, are introduced. We demonstrate overloading by creating two square functions that each take an integer (i.e., a whole number) and a floating-point number (i.e., a number with a decimal point), respectively. This chapter also introduces arrays, our first data structure. Data structures are crucial to storing, sorting, searching and manipulating large amounts of information. Arrays are groups of related data items that allow the programmer to access any element directly. Rather than creating 100 separate variables that are all related in some way, the programmer can create an array of 100 elements and access these elements by their location in the array. We discuss how to declare and allocate managed arrays, and we build on the techniques of the previous chapter by passing arrays to functions. Chapter 3 provides essential background for the discussion of arrays, because repetition structures are used to iterate through elements in the array. The combination of these concepts helps the reader create highly structured and well-organized programs. We discuss multidimensional arrays (both rectangular and jagged), which can be used to store tables of data.

Chapter 5—Object-Based Programming

Chapter 5 introduces objects and classes. Object technology has led to considerable improvements in software development, allowing programmers to create reusable software components. Objects allow programs to be organized in natural and intuitive ways. This chapter presents the fundamentals of object-based programming, such as encapsulation, data abstraction and abstract data types (ADTs). These techniques hide the details of components so that the programmer can concentrate on the "big picture." We create a **Time** class, which displays the time in standard and universal formats. We show how to create reusable software components with assemblies, namespaces and dynamic-link-library (DLL) files. We create classes and namespaces, and discuss properties and the **const** keyword. This chapter lays the groundwork for the next two chapters, which introduce object-oriented programming.

Chapter 6—Object-Oriented Programming: Inheritance

In this chapter, we discuss inheritance—a form of software reusability in which classes (called *derived classes*) are created by absorbing attributes and methods of existing classes (called *base classes*). The inherited class (i.e., the derived class) can contain additional attributes and methods. We show how finding the commonality between classes of objects can reduce the amount of work it takes to build large software systems. A detailed case study demonstrates software reuse and good programming techniques by finding the commonality among a three-level inheritance hierarchy: The **Point**, **Circle** and **Cylinder** classes. We discuss the software engineering benefits of object-oriented programming. Crucial object-oriented programming concepts, such as creating and extending classes, are presented in this chapter.

Chapter 7—Object-Oriented Programming: Polymorphism

Chapter 7 continues our presentation of object-oriented programming. We discuss polymorphic programming and its advantages. *Polymorphism* permits classes to be treated in a general manner, allowing the same method call to act differently depending on context (e.g., "move" messages sent to a bird and a fish result in dramatically different types of action—a bird flies and a fish swims). In addition to treating existing classes in a general manner, polymorphism allows new classes to be added to a system easily. We identify situations in which polymorphism is useful. A payroll system case study demonstrates polymorphism—the system determines the wages for each employee differently to suit the type of employee (bosses, paid fixed salaries; hourly workers, paid by the hour; commission workers, who receive a base salary plus commission; and piece workers, who are paid per item produced). These programming techniques and those of the previous chapter allow the programmer to create extensible and reusable software components.

Chapter 8—Exception Handling

Exception handling is one of the most important topics in Visual C++ .NET from the standpoint of building mission-critical and business-critical applications. Users can enter incorrect data, data can be corrupted and clients can try to access records that do not exist or are restricted. A simple division-by-zero error may cause a calculator program to crash, but what if such an error occurs in the navigation system of an airplane while it is in flight? In some cases, the results of program failure could be disastrous. Programmers need to know how to recognize the errors (*exceptions*) that could occur in software components and handle those exceptions effectively, allowing programs to deal with problems and continue executing instead of "crashing." Programmers who construct software systems from reusable components built by other programmers must deal with the exceptions that those components may "throw." This chapter covers the details of MC++ exception handling, the termination model of exception handling, throwing and catching exceptions and FCL class **Exception**.

Chapter 9—Graphical User Interface Concepts: Part 1

Chapter 9 introduces techniques for designing graphical user interfaces. We discuss how to construct user interfaces with Windows Forms controls such as labels, buttons, text boxes and picture boxes. We also introduce events, which are messages sent by a program to signal to an object or a set of objects that an action has occurred. Events most commonly are used to signal user interactions with GUI controls, but also can signal internal actions in a program. We overview event handling and discuss how to handle events specific to controls, the keyboard and the mouse. Tips are included throughout the chapter to help the programmer create visually appealing, well-organized and consistent GUIs.

Chapter 10—Graphical User Interface Concepts: Part 2

Chapter 10 introduces more complex GUI components, including menus, link labels, panels, list boxes, combo boxes and tab controls. The chapter presents *Multiple Document Interface* (*MDI*) programming, which allows multiple documents (i.e., forms) to be open simultaneously in a single GUI. We introduce visual inheritance, which enables programmers to combine the GUI concepts presented in this chapter with the object-oriented concepts presented in Chapter 6 to create user interfaces that can be used and extended by other programmers. The chapter concludes with a discussion of creating user-defined controls.

Chapter 11—Multithreading

We have come to expect much from our applications. We want to download files from the Internet, listen to music, print documents and browse the Web—all at the same time! To do this, we need a technique called multithreading, which allows applications to perform multiple activities concurrently. MC++ gives programmers access to the multithreading classes provided by the FCL, while shielding programmers from complex details. MC++ is better equipped to deal with more sophisticated multimedia, network-based and multiprocessor-based applications than other languages that do not have multithreading features. This chapter overviews the threading classes in the FCL and covers threads, thread life-cycles, time-slicing, scheduling and priorities. We analyze the producer-consumer relationship, thread synchronization and circular buffers. This chapter lays the foundation for creating the impressive multithreaded programs that clients demand.

Chapter 12—Strings, Characters and Regular Expressions

In this chapter, we discuss the processing of words, sentences, characters and groups of characters. In MC++, *strings* (groups of characters) are objects of type **String ***. This is yet another benefit of MC++'s emphasis on object-oriented programming. Objects of type **String *** contain methods that can copy, search, extract substrings and concatenate strings with one another. We introduce class ***StringBuilder***, which defines string-like objects that can be modified after initialization. As an interesting example of strings, we create a card shuffling-and-dealing simulation. We discuss regular expressions, a powerful tool for searching and manipulating text.

Chapter 13—Graphics and Multimedia

In this chapter, we discuss *GDI+* (an extension of the *Graphics Device Interface—GDI*), the Windows service that provides the graphical features used by .NET applications. The extensive graphical capabilities of GDI+ can make programs more visual and fun to create and use. We discuss Visual C++ .NET's treatment of graphics objects and color control. We also discuss how to draw arcs, polygons and other shapes. This chapter also demonstrates how to use various pens and brushes to create color effects and includes an example that demonstrates gradient fills and textures. We also introduce techniques for turning text-only applications into aesthetically pleasing programs that even novice programmers can write with ease. The second half of the chapter focuses on audio, video and speech technology. We discuss adding sound, video and animated characters to programs (primarily via existing audio and video clips). You will see how easy it is to incorporate multimedia into Visual C++ .NET applications. This chapter introduces a technology called *Microsoft Agent* for adding *interactive animated characters* to a program. Each character allows users to interact with the application, using more natural human communication techniques, such as speech. The agent characters respond to mouse and keyboard events, speak and hear (i.e., they support speech synthesis and speech recognition). With these capabilities, your applications can speak to users and actually respond to their voice commands!

Chapter 14—Files and Streams

Imagine a program that could not save data to a file. Once the program is closed, all the work performed by the program is lost forever. For this reason, this chapter is one of the most important for programmers who will be developing commercial applications. We introduce FCL classes for inputting and outputting data. A detailed example demonstrates these concepts by allowing users to read and write bank account information to and from files. We introduce the FCL classes and methods that help perform input and output conveniently—they demonstrate the power of object-oriented programming and reusable classes. We discuss benefits of sequential files, random-access files and buffering. This chapter lays the groundwork for the material presented in Chapter 18, Networking: Streams-Based Sockets and Datagrams.

Chapter 15—Extensible Markup Language (XML)

The Extensible Markup Language (XML) derives from SGML (Standard Generalized Markup Language), which became an industry standard in 1986. Although SGML is employed in publishing applications worldwide, it has not been incorporated into the mainstream programming community because of its sheer size and complexity. XML is an effort to make SGML-like technology available to a much broader community. XML, created by the World Wide Web Consortium (W3C), describes data in a portable format. XML differs in concept from markup languages such as HTML, which only describes how information is rendered in a browser. XML is a technology for creating markup languages for virtually any type of information. Document authors use XML to create entirely new markup languages to describe specific types of data, including mathematical formulas, chemical molecular structures, music, recipes and much more. Markup languages created with XML include XHTML (Extensible HyperText Markup Language, for Web content), MathML (for mathematics), VoiceXML™ (for speech), SMIL™ (Synchronized Multimedia Integration Language, for multimedia presentations), CML (Chemical Markup Language, for chemistry) and XBRL (Extensible Business Reporting Language, for financial data exchange). The extensibility of XML has made it one of the most important technologies in industry today and is being integrated into almost every field. Companies and individuals constantly are finding new and innovative uses for XML. In this chapter, we present examples that illustrate the basics of marking up data with XML. We demonstrate several XML-derived markup languages, such as *XML Schema* (for checking an XML document's grammar), and *XSLT (Extensible Stylesheet Language Transformations*, for transforming an XML document's data into another text-based format such as XHTML). (For readers who are unfamiliar with XHTML, we provide Appendices E and F, which provide a detailed introduction to XHTML.)

Chapter 16—Database, SQL and ADO .NET

Data storage and access are integral to creating powerful software applications. This chapter discusses .NET support for database manipulation. Today's most popular database systems are relational databases. In this chapter, we introduce the *Structured Query Language (SQL)* for performing queries on relational databases. We also introduce *ActiveX Data Objects (ADO .NET)*—an extension of ADO that enables .NET applications to access and manipulate databases. ADO .NET allows data to be exported as XML, which enables applications that use ADO .NET to communicate with a variety of programs that understand XML. We show the reader how to create database connections and how to use ADO .NET classes to query a database.

Chapter 17—Web Services

Previous chapters demonstrated how to create applications that execute locally on the user's computer. In this chapter, we introduce Web services, which are programs that "expose" services (i.e., methods) to clients over the Internet, intranets and extranets. Web services offer increased software reusability by allowing services on disparate platforms to interact with each other seamlessly. We discuss .NET Web services basics and related technologies, including *Simple Object Access Protocol* (*SOAP*) and *Active Server Pages* (*ASP*) .NET. This chapter presents an interesting example of a Web service that manipulates huge integers (up to 100 digits). We present a Black Jack application that demonstrates session tracking, a form of personalization that enables the application to "recognize" a user. We conclude with a discussion of Microsoft's Global XML Web Services Architecture (GXA), a series of specifications that provide additional capabilities to Web services developers.

Chapter 18—Networking: Streams-Based Sockets and Datagrams

Chapter 18 introduces the fundamental techniques of streams-based networking. We demonstrate how streams-based *sockets* allow programmers to hide many networking details. With sockets, networking is as simple as if the programmer were reading from and writing to a file. We also introduce *datagrams,* in which packets of information are sent between programs. Each packet is addressed to its recipient and sent out to the network, which routes the packet to its destination. The examples in this chapter focus on communication between applications. One example demonstrates using streams-based sockets to communicate between two MC++ programs. Another, similar example sends datagrams between applications. We also show how to create a multithreaded-server application that can communicate with multiple clients in parallel. In this client/server tic-tac-toe game, the server maintains the status of the game, and two clients communicate with the server to play the game.

Chapter 19—Data Structures and Collections

This chapter discusses arranging data into aggregations such as linked lists, stacks, queues and trees. Each data structure has properties that are useful in a wide variety of applications, from sorting elements to keeping track of method calls. We discuss how to build each of these data structures. This is also a valuable experience in crafting useful classes. In addition, we cover pre-built collection classes in the FCL. These classes store sets, or collections, of data and provide functionality that allow the developer to sort, insert, delete and retrieve data items. Different collection classes store data in different ways. This chapter focuses on classes **Array**, **ArrayList**, **Stack** and **Hashtable**, discussing the details of each. When possible, MC++ programmers should use the FCL to find appropriate data structures, rather than implementing these data structures themselves. This chapter reinforces much of the object technology discussed in Chapters 5–7, including classes, inheritance and composition.

Chapter 20—Accessibility

The World Wide Web presents challenges to individuals with disabilities. Multimedia-rich Web sites are difficult for text readers and other programs to interpret; thus, users with hearing and visual impairments may have difficulty browsing such sites. To help rectify this situation, the World Wide Web Consortium (W3C) launched the *Web Accessibility Initiative* (*WAI*), which provides guidelines for making Web sites accessible to people with disabilities. This chapter provides a description of these guidelines, such as the use of the **headers** element to make tables more accessible to page readers, the **alt** attribute of the **img** element to describe images and the combination of XHTML and Cascading Style

Sheets (CSS) to ensure that a page can be viewed on almost any type of display or reader. We illustrate key accessibility features of Visual Studio .NET, Internet Explorer 6 and Windows XP. We also introduce *VoiceXML™* and *CallXML™*, two technologies for increasing the accessibility of Web-based content. VoiceXML helps people with visual impairments to access Web content via speech synthesis and speech recognition. CallXML allows users with visual impairments to access Web-based content through a telephone.

Chapter 21—Introduction to Unmanaged Code in Visual C++ .NET
This chapter introduces the unmanaged aspect of Visual C++ .NET. We highlight the differences between managed and unmanaged code, discuss how unmanaged code fits into Microsoft's .NET strategy and suggest a possible future for unmanaged code. In addition, we discuss the new Unified Event Model, designed to provide a simplified syntax for Visual C++ .NET event handling. The chapter includes a presentation of the changes to unmanaged code designed to increase ANSI/ISO compliance and increase native code Wide-Character and 64-bit processing support. The chapter's examples include a demonstration of the new compiler features designed to provide program run-time checking into the debugging mode of native code. This chapter (as well as Chapters 22–25) assumes knowledge of standard C++, including pointers.

Chapter 22—Attributed Programming in ATL/COM
Attributed programming is a new feature in Visual C++ .NET designed to simplify common programming tasks, most notably in the area of COM development. In this chapter, we discuss how attributes simplify COM and ATL. This chapter is targeted towards developers with previous COM and ATL knowledge and is designed to demonstrate the power of attributed programming in COM. While attributes simplify COM development, a solid understanding of COM basics is essential to use attributes correctly. The chapter's examples demonstrate basic COM component creation, the Unified Event Model in COM and include a case study demonstrating an attributed ATL ActiveX control.

Chapter 23—ATL Server Web Applications
In this chapter, we discuss how to create Web-based applications using ATL Server. This technology provides rapid Web-application development coupled with native code performance. ATL Server is an integral technology for creating dynamic Web content in a native context. Server Response Files (SRFs) provide dynamic content using replacement tags (or stencils) coupled with HTML markup. An ATL Server Web application dynamically replaces SRF stencils with native C++ generated HTML. This chapter presents many interesting examples, which include an online guest book application and a multi-tier, database intensive application that allows users to query a database for a list of publications by a specific author.

Chapter 24—Managed and Unmanaged Interoperability
This chapter focuses on the differences between managed and unmanaged code, and the technologies used to surmount the differences to allow interoperability between code contexts. Unlike other .NET languages, Visual C++ .NET allows side-by-side execution of managed and unmanaged code within the same application. This is possible due to the separation of execution into a managed and unmanaged context and managing all communication between the contexts. The interoperability features of Visual C++ .NET may be split into three technologies, the It Just Works (IJW) compiler design goal, the Platform Invoke

Services and COM Interop Services. This chapter discusses IJW and the Platform Invoke Services, while Chapter 25 discusses the COM interoperability features. This chapter contains a set of examples designed to demonstrate common interoperability uses, such as using Win32 API functions and templated classes.

Chapter 25—COM Interoperability Services
This chapter overviews the services provided by Visual C++ .NET that allow interoperability between the COM and .NET architectures. The COM and .NET component architectures are fundamentally different technologies, from data type representation and object construction to the descriptions and layout of their respective component libraries. The COM interoperability services enable the .NET programmer to bypass these difficulties and provide seamless interaction between both component architectures. The chapter demonstrates type-library and assembly conversions, discusses the Runtime Callable Wrapper and the COM Callable Wrapper and provides examples that show COM objects in .NET and .NET objects in COM.

Appendix A—Operator Precedence Chart
This appendix lists MC++ operators and their precedence.

Appendix B—Number Systems
This appendix explains the binary, octal, decimal and hexadecimal number systems. It also reviews the conversion of numbers among these bases and illustrates mathematical operations in each base.

Appendix C—ASCII Character Set
This appendix contains a table of the 128 ASCII (American Standard Code for Information Interchange) alphanumeric symbols and their corresponding integer values.

Appendix D—Unicode®
This appendix introduces the Unicode Standard, an encoding scheme that assigns unique numeric values to the characters of most of the world's languages. We include a Windows application that uses Unicode encoding to print welcome messages in several languages.

Appendices E and F—Introduction to XHTML: Parts 1 & 2
In these appendices, we introduce the Extensible HyperText Markup Language (XHTML), an emerging W3C technology designed to replace HTML as the primary means of describing Web content. As an XML-based language, XHTML is more robust and extensible than HTML. XHTML incorporates most of HTML's elements and attributes—the focus of these appendices. Appendices E and F are included for our readers who do not know XHTML or who would like a review of XHTML before studying Chapter 15, Extensible Markup Language (XML), and Chapter 20, Accessibility.

Appendix G—XHTML Special Characters
This appendix provides many commonly used XHTML special characters, called *character entity references*.

Appendix H—XHTML Colors
This appendix lists commonly used XHTML color names and their corresponding hexadecimal values.

Appendix I—Bit Manipulation
This appendix discusses Visual C++ .NET's powerful bit-manipulation capabilities. This helps programs process bit strings, set individual bits on or off and store information more compactly. Such capabilities are characteristic of low-level assembly languages and are valued by programmers writing systems software, such as operating system and networking software.

1.10 Summary

In the late 1960s, at a conference at the University of Illinois Urbana-Champaign, ARPA—the Advanced Research Projects Agency of the Department of Defense—rolled out the blueprints for networking the main computer systems of approximately a dozen ARPA-funded universities and research institutions. Shortly after this conference, ARPA proceeded to implement the ARPAnet, the grandparent of today's Internet.

Although the ARPAnet did enable researchers to network their computers, its chief benefit proved to be its capability for quick and easy communication via what came to be known as electronic mail (e-mail). This is true even on today's Internet, with e-mail, instant messaging and file transfer facilitating communications among hundreds of millions of people worldwide.

The protocol (i.e., set of rules) for communicating over the ARPAnet became known as the Transmission Control Protocol (TCP). TCP ensured that messages were routed properly from sender to receiver and that those messages arrived intact. ARPA developed the Internet Protocol (IP), which created a true "network of networks," the current architecture of the Internet. The combined set of protocols is now commonly called TCP/IP.

The World Wide Web allows computer users to locate and view multimedia-based documents (i.e., documents with text, graphics, animations, audios or videos) on almost any subject. In 1989, Tim Berners-Lee of CERN (the European Organization for Nuclear Research) began to develop a technology for sharing information via hyperlinked text documents. Berners-Lee called his invention the HyperText Markup Language (HTML). He also wrote communication protocols to form the backbone of his new hypertext information system, which he referred to as the World Wide Web.

In October 1994, Berners-Lee founded the World Wide Web Consortium (W3C), an organization that is devoted to developing nonproprietary, interoperable technologies for the World Wide Web. One of the W3C's primary goals is to make the Web universally accessible—regardless of an individual's disabilities, language or culture.

XML combines the power and extensibility of its parent language, SGML, with simplicity. XML is a meta-language that offers a high level of extensibility. Using XML, the W3C created the Extensible HyperText Markup Language (XHTML), an XML vocabulary that provides a common, extensible format for the Web. In addition to serving as the basis for other markup languages, developers use XML for data interchange and e-commerce systems. At the time of this writing, there were more than 450 XML standards.

Unlike many technologies, which begin as proprietary solutions and become standards, XML was defined as an open, standard technology. XML's development has been supervised by the W3C's XML Working Group, which prepared the XML specification and approved it for publication. In 1998, the XML version 1.0 specification was accepted as a W3C Recommendation.

Object technology is a packaging scheme that facilitates the creation of meaningful software units. Objects have properties (i.e., attributes, such as color, size and weight) and perform actions (i.e., behaviors, such as moving, sleeping or drawing). Classes represent groups of related objects.

With the advent of popular object-oriented languages, such as C++, Java and C#, programmers can program in an object-oriented manner that reflects the way in which they perceive the world. This process, which seems more natural than procedural programming, has resulted in significant productivity gains.

With object technology, properly designed software entities (called objects) can be reused on future projects. Using libraries of reusable componentry can reduce the amount of effort required to implement certain kinds of systems (as compared to the effort that would be required to reinvent these capabilities in new projects). Visual C++ .NET programmers use the .NET Framework Class Library (FCL).

In June 2000, Microsoft announced its .NET initiative. The .NET platform is one that provides significant enhancements to earlier developer platforms. .NET offers a new software-development model that allows applications created in disparate programming languages to communicate with each other. The platform also allows developers to create Web-based applications that can be distributed to a great variety of devices (even wireless phones) and to desktop computers.

One key aspect of the .NET strategy is its independence from a specific language or platform. Rather than requiring programmers to use a single programming language, developers can create a .NET application by using any combination of .NET-compatible languages. Programmers can contribute to the same software project, writing code in the .NET languages in which they are most proficient.

A key component of the .NET architecture is Web services, which are applications that expose functionality to clients via the Internet. Clients and other applications can use these Web services as reusable building blocks.

Universal data access is another essential .NET concept. With .NET, data can reside in one central location rather than on separate systems. Any Internet-connected device can access the data (under tight control, of course), which would then be formatted appropriately for use or display on the accessing device.

Developed in the early 1990s, Visual C++ is a Microsoft implementation of C++ that includes Microsoft's proprietary extensions to the language. Over the past decade, Microsoft has released several versions of Visual C++—most recently, Visual C++ .NET. Visual C++ .NET is known as a visual programming language—the developer uses graphical tools (via Visual Studio .NET) to create applications.

Early graphics and graphical user interface (GUI) programming (i.e., the programming of an application's visual interface) with Visual C++ was implemented using the Microsoft Foundation Classes (MFC). The Microsoft Foundation Classes library is a collection of classes that help Visual C++ programmers create powerful Windows-based applications. Now, with the introduction of .NET, Microsoft provides an additional library (.NET's FCL) for implementing GUI, graphics, networking, multithreading and other capabilities.

This library is available to .NET-compliant languages such as Visual C++ .NET, Visual Basic .NET and Microsoft's new language, C#. However, developers still can use MFC—Microsoft has, in fact, upgraded MFC to MFC 7, which includes new classes and documentation that can be accessed using Visual Studio .NET. MFC often is used to develop unmanaged code, or code that does not make use of the .NET Framework.

Visual C++ .NET introduces Managed Extensions for C++ (MC++) that enable a programmer to access the .NET Framework. Programmers can use the .NET Framework to create objects that provide automatic garbage collection, memory management and language interoperability (with other .NET languages). Such objects are known as managed objects; the code that defines these objects is known as managed code. With managed objects, memory leaks are extremely rare.

The true power of Visual C++ .NET lies in its interoperability between managed and unmanaged code. All legacy Visual C++ code is unmanaged. Rather than forcing developers to discard large amounts of legacy code, Visual C++ .NET enables programmers to mix managed (MC++) and unmanaged (standard C++) code.

Microsoft has upgraded several of the technologies used in unmanaged code. One example of this is the Active Template Library (ATL), a set of template classes that simplify the creation of COM components. The newest version of ATL, ATL 7, contains several enhancements. An example of one enhancement is the ATL Server, which is a set of classes designed to simplify Web development while providing the ability to call unmanaged C++ from within a Web page.

In Visual C++ .NET, programs are created using Visual Studio .NET, an Integrated Development Environment (IDE). With the IDE, a programmer can create, run, test and debug programs conveniently, thereby reducing the time it takes to produce a working program to a fraction of the time it would have taken without using the IDE. The process of rapidly creating an application using an IDE typically is referred to as Rapid Application Development (RAD).

The .NET Framework is at the heart of .NET. This framework manages and executes applications, contains the FCL, enforces security and provides many other programming capabilities. The details of the .NET Framework are found in the Common Language Specification (CLS), which contains information about the storage of data types, objects and so on.

The Common Language Runtime (CLR) is another central part of the .NET Framework—it executes Visual C++ .NET programs. Programs are compiled into machine-specific instructions in two steps. First, the program is compiled into Microsoft Intermediate Language (MSIL), which defines instructions for the CLR. Code converted into MSIL from other languages and sources is woven together by the CLR. Then, another compiler in the CLR compiles the MSIL into machine code (for a particular platform), creating a single application.

1.11 Internet and World Wide Web Resources

www.deitel.com
This is the official Deitel & Associates, Inc. Web site. Here you will find updates, corrections, downloads and additional resources for all Deitel publications. In addition, this site provides information about Deitel & Associates, Inc., information on international translations and much more.

www.deitel.com/newsletter/subscribe.html
You can register here to receive the *DEITEL™ BUZZ ONLINE* e-mail newsletter. This free monthly newsletter updates readers on our publishing program, instructor-led corporate training courses, hottest industry trends and topics and much more. The newsletter is available in full-color HTML and plain-text formats.

www.prenhall.com/deitel
This is Prentice Hall's Web site for Deitel publications, which contains information about our products and publications, downloads, Deitel curriculum and author information.

www.InformIT.com/deitel
This is the Deitel & Associates, Inc. page on Pearson's InformIT Web site. (Pearson owns our publisher Prentice Hall.) InformIT is a comprehensive resource for IT professionals providing articles, electronic publications and other resources for today's hottest information technologies. The Deitel kiosk at **InformIT.com** provides two or three free articles per week and for-purchase electronic publications. All Deitel publications can be purchased at this site.

www.w3.org
The World Wide Web Consortium (W3C) is an organization that develops and recommends technologies for the Internet and World Wide Web. This site includes links to W3C technologies, news, mission statements and frequently asked questions (FAQs). Deitel and Associates, Inc. is a member of the W3C.

www.microsoft.com
The Microsoft Corporation Web site provides information and technical resources for all Microsoft products, including .NET, enterprise software and the Windows operating system.

www.microsoft.com/net
The .NET home page provides downloads, news and events, certification information and subscription information.

Visual Studio® .NET IDE and Visual C++ .NET Programming

Objectives

- To become familiar with the Visual Studio .NET integrated development environment (IDE).
- To use the commands contained in the IDE's menus and toolbars.
- To become familiar with the windows in Visual Studio .NET.
- To understand Visual Studio .NET's help features.
- To create, compile and execute a simple Managed Extensions for C++ (MC++) program.
- To become familiar with primitive data types.
- To use input and output statements.
- To use arithmetic operators.
- To write decision-making statements.
- To use relational and equality operators.

Seeing is believing.
Proverb

Form ever follows function.
Louis Henri Sullivan

Intelligence… is the faculty of making artificial objects, especially tools to make tools.
Henri-Louis Bergson

2.1 Introduction

Visual Studio .NET is Microsoft's integrated development environment (IDE) for creating, running and debugging programs written in a variety of .NET programming languages. Visual Studio .NET also offers editing tools for manipulating several types of files (HTML, XML, etc.). Visual Studio .NET is a powerful and sophisticated tool for creating business-critical and mission-critical applications. In this chapter, we provide an overview of the Visual Studio .NET features needed to create a simple program. We introduce additional IDE features throughout the book.

This chapter also introduces the *Managed Extensions for C++ (MC++)* programming language. MC++ is an extension of traditional C++ that allows programmers to access the .NET Framework. With MC++, programmers can rely on the *common language runtime (CLR)* to handle memory management.

In Chapters 2–20, we present examples that illustrate important features of MC++; in Chapters 21–25, we present examples that illustrate how to combine the features of MC++ with the features of traditional C++ (or, *unmanaged C++*).

In this chapter, we create *console applications*—applications that contain output consisting predominantly of text. There are several types of projects that we can create in Visual C++ .NET; the console application is one of the basic types. Text output in a console application is displayed in a *console window* (also called a *command window*). On Microsoft Windows 95/98, the console window is the **MS-DOS Prompt**. On Microsoft Windows NT/2000/XP, the console window is called the **Command Prompt**. In this chapter, we provide a detailed treatment of *program development* and *program control* in MC++.

2.2 Visual Studio .NET Integrated Development Environment (IDE) Overview

When Visual Studio .NET is executed for the first time, the **Start Page** is displayed (Fig. 2.1). This page contains helpful links, which appear on the left side. Users can click the name of a section (such as **Get Started**) to browse its contents. We refer to single-clicking with the left mouse button as *selecting* or *clicking*. We refer to clicking twice with the left mouse button as *double-clicking*. [*Note*: Readers should be aware that there are slight differences in the way Visual Studio .NET appears, depending on the version being used.]

Figure 2.1 displays the way the **Start Page** looks when the ***Get Started*** link is selected. The **Get Started** section contains links to recently opened projects (such as **ASimpleProject** in Fig. 2.1), along with the modification dates of the projects. Alternatively, the user can select **Recent Projects** from the **File** menu. The first time Visual Studio .NET is loaded, this section will be empty. Notice the two buttons on the page: ***Open Project*** and ***New Project***.

We now provide a brief overview of the other **Start Page** links,[1] shown in Fig. 2.1. When clicked, the ***What's New*** link displays new features and updates for Visual Studio .NET, including downloads for code samples and new programming tools. The ***Online Community*** provides ways to contact other software developers, using newsgroups, Web pages and other online resources. The ***Headlines*** link provides a way to browse

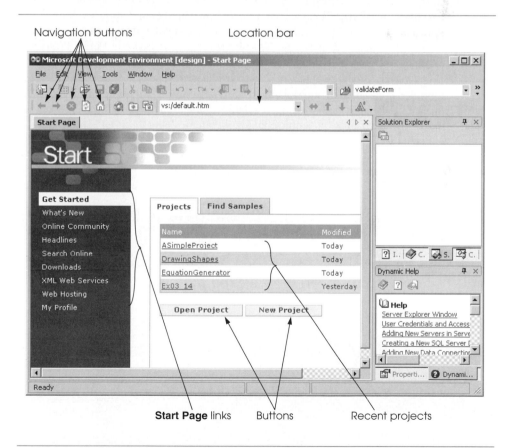

Fig. 2.1   **Start Page** in Visual Studio .NET.

---

1. Note that, for many of the links provided by the **Start Page**, an Internet connection is required.

news, articles and how-to guides. The **Search Online** link allows users to browse through the *MSDN* (*Microsoft Developer Network*) online library. The MSDN site includes numerous articles, downloads and tutorials for a variety of technologies. The **Downloads** link allows users to obtain updates and code samples. The **XML Web Services** page provides programmers with information about *Web services*, which are reusable pieces of software accessible via the Internet. **Web Hosting** provides information for developers who wish to post their software (such as Web services) online for public use. The **My Profile** page allows users to customize Visual Studio .NET, such as by setting keyboard and window layout preferences. Users also can customize Visual Studio .NET by selecting **Options...** or **Customize...** from the **Tools** menu. [*Note*: From this point forward, we use the **>** character to indicate the selection of a menu command. For example, we use the notation **Tools > Options...** and **Tools > Customize...** to indicate the selection of the **Options...** and **Customize...** commands, respectively, from the **Tools** menu.]

Users can browse the Web through Visual Studio .NET—the Internet Explorer Web browser is accessible from within the IDE. To access a Web page, type its address into the location bar (see Fig. 2.1) and press the *Enter* key. Several other windows appear in the IDE in addition to the **Start Page**. We discuss these windows in the upcoming sections.

To create a new Visual C++ .NET program, click the **New Project** button in the **Get Started** section. This action displays the **New Project** *dialog* shown in Fig. 2.2 (alternatively, the **New Project** dialog can be opened via **File > New > Project...**. Visual Studio .NET organizes programs into *projects* and *solutions*. A project is a group of related files, such as C++ code, images and documentation. A solution is a group of projects that represents a complete application or a set of related applications. Each project in the solution may perform a different task. In this chapter, we create a single-project solution.

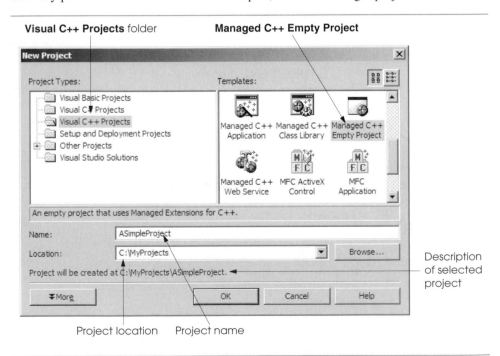

Fig. 2.2   **New Project** dialog.

Visual Studio .NET allows programmers to create projects in a variety of programming languages. This book focuses on MC++, so select the **Visual C++ Projects** folder (Fig. 2.2). There are a variety of project types from which to choose, several of which are used throughout this book. In this case, a ***Managed C++ Empty Project*** is selected.[2] Windows applications are programs that execute inside the Windows operating system (OS), like Microsoft Word, Internet Explorer and Visual Studio .NET. Typically, they contain *controls*—graphical elements, such as buttons and labels—with which the user interacts.

The default location for new projects or files is the folder where the last project or file was created. The first time Visual Studio .NET executes, the default folder is the **Visual Studio Projects** folder in the **My Documents** folder. The user can change both the name and the location of the folder in which to save the project. Name the project **ASimpleProject** and select a directory in which to save the project. To do this, click the **Browse...** button, which opens a **Project Location** dialog (Fig. 2.3). Navigate through the directories to the location where you want to store the project and select **OK**. This selection returns the user to the **New Project** dialog; the selected folder appears in the **Location** text field. When you are satisfied with the project's name, location and type, click **OK**. Visual Studio .NET will create and load the new solution. The IDE will then change its appearance, as shown in Fig. 2.4.

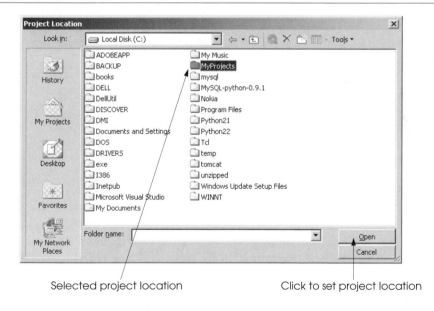

Selected project location   Click to set project location

Fig. 2.3   Setting the project location.

---

2. We use **Managed C++ Empty Project** to create most of the applications in this book. This is because the other MC++ project types create extra files that usually are unnecessary. As we develop our applications, we will create the files we need and add them to our projects. For more information about the various MC++ project types, visit **msdn.microsoft.com/library/default.asp?url=/library/en-us/vcmex/html/vcgrfManagedCProjectTypes.asp**.

Menu   Toolbar   Title bar   Menu bar   **Solution Explorer**

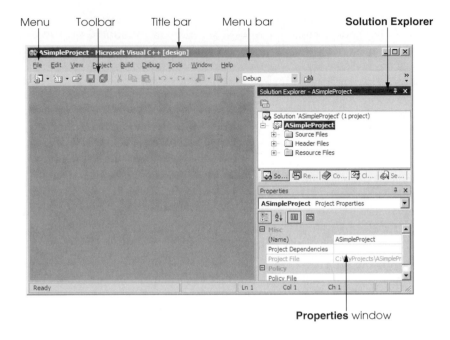

Properties window

Fig. 2.4   Visual Studio .NET environment after a new project has been created.

The top of the IDE window (the *title bar* in Fig. 2.4) displays **ASimpleProject - Microsoft Visual C++ [design]**. This title provides the name of the project (**ASimpleProject**), the project type (**Microsoft Visual C++**) and the mode of the file being viewed (**Design** mode). We discuss the various modes in Section 2.6.

2.3 Menu Bar and Toolbar

Commands for managing the IDE and for developing, maintaining and executing programs are contained in the menus. Figure 2.5 shows the menus displayed on the Visual Studio .NET menu bar. Menus contain groups of related commands that, when selected, cause the IDE to perform various actions (e.g., opening a window). For example, new projects also can be created by selecting **File > New > Project...**. The contents of the menus shown in Fig. 2.5 are summarized in Fig. 2.6. Visual Studio .NET provides different modes in which the user can work. One of these modes is the design mode, which will be discussed in Section 2.6. Certain menu items appear only in specific IDE modes.

Rather than having to navigate the menus for certain commonly used commands, the programmer can access the commands from the *toolbar* (Fig. 2.7). The toolbar contains pictures called *icons* that represent commands. To execute a command, click its icon. Some icons represent multiple actions that are related. Click the *down arrows* beside such icons to display a list of commands. Figure 2.7 shows the standard (default) toolbar and an icon that provides access to two commands.

Placing the mouse pointer over an icon on the toolbar highlights that icon and displays a description called a *tooltip* (Fig. 2.8). Tooltips help users understand the purposes of unfamiliar icons.

File   Edit   View   Project   Build   Debug   Tools   Window   Help

Fig. 2.5   Visual Studio .NET menu bar.

Menu	Description
File	Contains commands for opening projects, closing projects, printing files, etc.
Edit	Contains commands such as cut, paste, find, undo, etc.
View	Contains commands for displaying IDE windows and toolbars.
Project	Contains commands for adding features, such as forms, to the project.
Build	Contains commands for compiling a program.
Debug	Contains commands for debugging and executing a program.
Tools	Contains commands for additional IDE tools and options for customizing the environment.
Window	Contains commands for arranging and displaying windows.
Help	Contains commands for getting help.

Fig. 2.6   Visual Studio .NET menus summary.

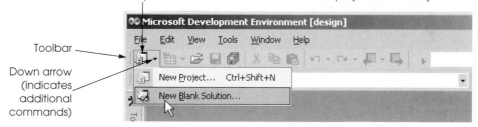

Fig. 2.7   Visual Studio .NET toolbar.

Fig. 2.8   Tooltip demonstration.

Toolbars can be further customized via the **Toolbars** tab on the **Customize** dialog that is displayed when **Tools > Customize...** is selected. Here users can delete icons, rename icons and change icon images (among other options).

2.4 Visual Studio .NET Windows

Visual Studio .NET provides users with windows for exploring files and customizing controls. In this section, we discuss the windows that are essential for developing MC++ applications. These windows can be accessed using the toolbar icons below the menu bar and on the right edge of the toolbar (Fig. 2.9), or by selecting the name of the desired window from the **View** menu.

2.4.1 Solution Explorer

The ***Solution Explorer*** window (Fig. 2.10) lists all the files in the solution. When Visual Studio .NET is first loaded, the **Solution Explorer** is empty—there are no files to display. After a new project has been created or an existing project has been loaded, the **Solution Explorer** displays that project's contents.

The *startup project* of the solution is the project that runs when the solution is executed. It appears in bold text in the **Solution Explorer**. For our single-project solution, the startup project (**ASimpleProject**) is the only project.

The plus and minus boxes to the left of the project and solution names expand and collapse the tree, respectively (similar to those in Windows Explorer). Click a plus box to display more options; click a minus box to collapse a tree that already is expanded. Users also can expand or collapse a tree by double-clicking the name of the folder. Many other Visual Studio .NET windows use the plus/minus boxes as well.

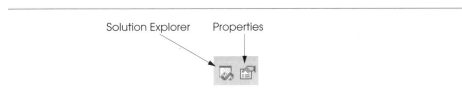

Fig. 2.9   Toolbar icons for two Visual Studio .NET windows.

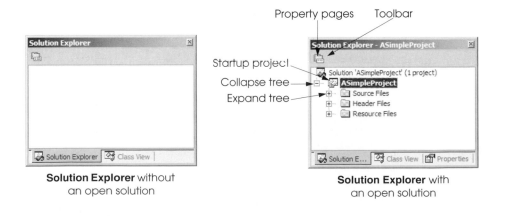

Fig. 2.10   **Solution Explorer** window.

The **Solution Explorer** contains a toolbar (Fig. 2.10). The icon displays the **Property Pages** dialog for the selected (highlighted) item. The **Property Pages** dialog allows users to configure compilation options. If there are no open projects, selecting this icon opens the **Properties** window (Section 2.4.2).

2.4.2 Properties Window

The *Properties* window (Fig. 2.11) allows manipulation of the *properties* for a project or a class. Properties specify information about a project, such as its full path name and its dependences (if any). Each project has its own set of properties. The bottom of the **Properties** window contains a description of the selected property.

The left column of the **Properties** window lists the properties (Fig. 2.11). The right column displays their current values. As with the **Solution Explorer**, the **Properties** window has a toolbar. Icons on this toolbar sort properties either alphabetically (by clicking the *alphabetic icon*) or categorically (by clicking the *categorized icon*). If there are too many properties to list in the window, a vertical scrollbar is provided by the IDE. Users can scroll through the list of properties by *dragging* the scrollbar *thumb*—the rectangle that represents the current position in the scrollbar—up or down (i.e., holding down the left mouse button while the mouse cursor is over the thumb, moving the mouse up or down and releasing the mouse button).

2.5 Using Help

Visual Studio .NET has an extensive help mechanism. The *Help* menu contains a variety of options. The *Contents* menu item displays a categorized table of contents that lists available help topics. *Menu item* **Index** displays an alphabetical index that users can browse. The *Search* feature allows users to find particular help articles, based on a few search words. Each of these features includes a subset of available topics, or filter, that can narrow the search to articles related only to Visual C++ .NET.

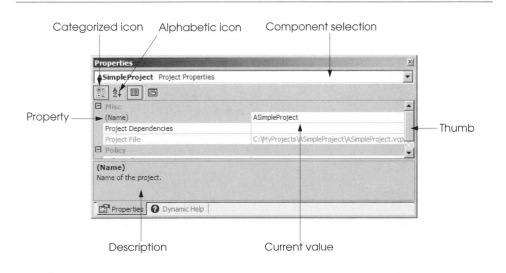

Fig. 2.11   Properties window.

Dynamic help (Fig. 2.12) provides a list of articles, based on the content in the text-editor window. To open dynamic help (if it is not already open), select **Help > Dynamic Help**. The window lists relevant help entries, samples and "Getting Started" information, in addition to providing a toolbar for the regular help features. Dynamic help is an excellent way to get information about the features of Visual Studio .NET. Note, however, that **Dynamic Help** may slow down Visual Studio .NET.

Performance Tip 2.1

If you experience slow response times from Visual Studio .NET, you can close **Dynamic Help** *by clicking the* **X** *in the upper right corner of the* **Dynamic Help** *window.*

In addition to dynamic help, Visual Studio .NET provides *context-sensitive help*. Context-sensitive help is similar to dynamic help, except that context-sensitive help immediately brings up a relevant help article rather than presenting a list. To use context-sensitive help, select an item and press the *F1* key. Help can appear either *internally* or *externally*. With external help, a relevant article immediately pops up in a separate window, outside the IDE. With internal help, a help article appears as a tabbed window inside Visual Studio .NET. The help options can be set from the **My Profile** section of the **Start Page** as well as from the **Tools > Options > Help** menu item.

Selected item   **Dynamic Help** window

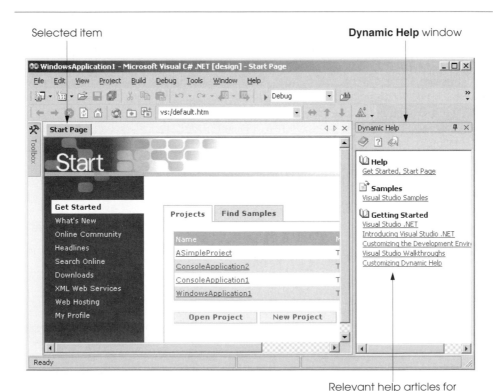

Relevant help articles for
selected item (**Start Page**)

Fig. 2.12   Dynamic Help window.

2.6 Creating a Simple Console Application

In this section, we create a program that prints the text "**Welcome to Visual C++ .NET!**" to the screen. The program consists of a single **.cpp** (the file extension for an MC++ program) file that displays a message. Figure 2.13 shows the program's output.

To create, run and terminate this first program, perform the following steps:

1. *Create the new project.* If you have not yet created the project (**ASimpleProject** from Fig. 2.4), refer to Section 2.2 to create it. However, if another project is already open, first close it by selecting **File > Close Solution** from the menu. A dialog asking whether to save the current solution may appear. Save the solution to keep any unsaved changes. Then create **ASimpleProject**.

2. *Create a new code file.* Select **File > New > File...** to open a new code file. In the **New File** dialog (Fig. 2.14), select the type of file needed and click **Open**. In the dialog that appears, browse to the project folder and save the file in this location. For this example, we select **C++ File (.cpp)** from the **Visual C++** folder. Visual Studio .NET names the file **Source1** by default. To rename the file, select **File > Save Source1 As...** and specify the filename (**Welcome.cpp**) in the **Save File As** dialog (Fig. 2.15). Note that the **File > Save Source1 As...** option appears only if the **Source1** text-editor window is the active window.

```
Welcome to Visual C++ .NET!
```

Fig. 2.13   Simple program as it executes.

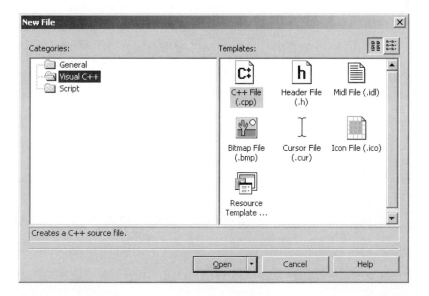

Fig. 2.14   Creating a new code file.

Fig. 2.15   Renaming a source file.

3. *Add the file to the project.* Select **File > Move Welcome.cpp into Project**, or right click inside the editor and select **Move Welcome.cpp into Project** from the popup menu. The submenu that appears lists any open projects. Select **ASimpleProject** from this list. [*Note*: Some users prefer to combine steps 2 and 3 by right-clicking **Source Files** in the **Solution Explorer** and selecting **Add > Add New Item...** from the context menu.]

4. *Write the program.* Add the code in Fig. 2.16 to **Welcome.cpp**. The program displays a message. We introduce the reader to program syntax in Section 2.7.

5. *Save the project.* Select **File > Save All** to save the entire solution. To save an individual file, select it in the **Solution Explorer**, and select **File > Save Welcome.cpp**. The IDE stores the source code in file **Welcome.cpp**. The project file **ASimpleProject.vcproj** contains the names and locations of all the files in the project. Choosing **Save All** saves the project, the solution and the code file.

```
1   // Fig. 2.16: Welcome.cpp
2   // Simple welcome program.
3
4   #using <mscorlib.dll>
5
6   using namespace System;
7
8   int main()
9   {
10     Console::WriteLine( S"Welcome to Visual C++ .NET!" );
11
12     return 0;
13  }
```

Fig. 2.16   Code for IDE demonstration.

6. *Run the project*. Prior to this step, we have been working in the IDE *design mode* (i.e., the program being created is not executing). This mode is indicated by the text **Microsoft Visual C++ [design]** in the title bar. While in design mode, programmers have access to all the environment windows (e.g., **Toolbox** and **Properties**), menus, toolbars and so on. While in *run mode*, however, the program is executing, and users can interact with only a few IDE features. Features that are not available are disabled or grayed out. To execute or run the program, we first need to compile it, which is accomplished by clicking on the **Build Solution** command in the **Build** *menu* (or typing *Ctrl + Shift + B*). The program can then be executed by clicking the start button (the blue triangle), selecting the **Debug** menu's **Start** command or pressing the *F5* key. Figure 2.17 shows the IDE in run mode. Note that the IDE title bar displays **[run]** and that many toolbar icons are disabled.

The console window closes as soon as the program finishes executing. To keep the console window open, users can select **Debug > Start Without Debugging** or press *Ctrl + F5*. This causes the console window to prompt the user to press a key after the program terminates, allowing the user to observe the program's output. Throughout this book, we execute programs using the **Start Without Debugging** command so that the reader can see the output.

7. *Terminating execution*. To terminate the program, click the running application's close button (the **x** in the top-right corner). Alternatively, click the **End** button (the blue square) in the toolbar or type *Shift + F5*. All of these actions terminate program execution and return the IDE to design mode.

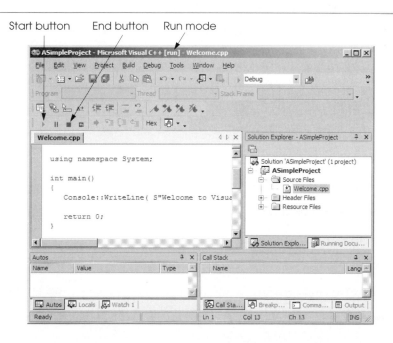

Fig. 2.17   IDE in run mode.

2.7 Simple Program: Printing a Line of Text

We begin by considering the **Welcome.cpp** program that displays a line of text. The program and its output are shown in Fig. 2.18. The program is followed by an output window that displays the program's results. When you execute this program, the output will appear in a console window.

This program illustrates several important features of MC++. All programs we present in this book will include line numbers for the reader's convenience; these line numbers are not part of the programs. Line 10 in Fig. 2.18 does the "real work" of the program (i.e., displaying the phrase **Welcome to Visual C++ .NET!** on the screen).

Line 1 begins with **//**, indicating that the remainder of the line is a *comment*. Programmers insert comments to *document* and improve the readability of their code. Comments also help other programmers read and understand your programs. A comment that begins with **//** is called a *single-line comment*, because the comment terminates at the end of the line. Single-line comments can be placed almost anywhere in the program.

There is also a syntax for writing *multiple-line comments*. A multiple-line comment, such as

```
/* This is a multiple-line
   comment. It can be
   split over many lines. */
```

begins with *delimiter* **/*** and ends with *delimiter* ***/**. By default, all comment text in the Visual Studio .NET IDE appears in green. Comments of the form **//** and **/*** ... ***/** are ignored by the compiler—they do not cause the computer to perform any action when the program executes. Throughout this book, we use mostly single-line comments.

Common Programming Error 2.1

Forgetting one of the delimiters of a multiple-line comment is a syntax error. A syntax error is caused when the compiler cannot recognize a statement. The compiler normally issues an error message to help the programmer locate and fix the incorrect statement. Syntax errors are violations of the language rules. Syntax errors are also called compile errors, compile-time errors *or* compilation errors *because they are detected during the compilation phase. A program cannot compile or execute until all the syntax errors are corrected.*

```
1   // Fig. 2.18: Welcome.cpp
2   // Simple welcome program.
3
4   #using <mscorlib.dll>
5
6   using namespace System;
7
8   int main()
9   {
10      Console::WriteLine( S"Welcome to Visual C++ .NET!" );
11
12      return 0;
13  }
```

Fig. 2.18 Sample code for IDE demonstration. (Part 1 of 2.)

```
Welcome to Visual C++ .NET!
```

Fig. 2.18   Sample code for IDE demonstration. (Part 2 of 2.)

Programmers often use blank lines and space characters throughout a program to make the code easier to read. Blank lines, space characters, newline characters and tab characters are collectively known as *whitespace*. (Space characters and tabs are known specifically as *whitespace characters*.) *Newline characters* are "special characters" that indicate when to position the output cursor at the beginning of the next line in the console window. The compiler ignores blank lines, tabs and extra spaces that separate language elements. Several conventions for using whitespace characters are discussed in this and subsequent chapters.

Good Programming Practice 2.1

Use blank lines, space characters and tab characters in a program to enhance program readability.

Line 4 (known as a *using* directive) references **mscorlib.dll**, a prepackaged unit of code. We will discuss **.dll** *(dynamic link library)* files in further detail in Chapter 5, Object-Based Programming. The **using** statement (line 6) declares that the program uses features in the **System** *namespace* (part of **mscorlib.dll**). A *namespace* groups various MC++ features into related categories. One of the great strengths of MC++ is that programmers can use the rich set of namespaces provided by the .NET Framework. These namespaces contain code that programmers can reuse, rather than "reinventing the wheel." This makes programming easier and faster. The namespaces that are defined in the .NET Framework contain preexisting code known as the *.NET Framework Class Library*. An example of one of the features in namespace **System** is class **Console**, which we discuss momentarily. The various features are organized into namespaces that enable programmers to locate them easily. We discuss many namespaces and their features throughout the book.

Line 8 begins *main*, which is known as the *entry point* of the program. The parentheses after **main** indicate that **main** is a program building block, called a *function*. Functions can perform tasks and return information when these tasks complete. Information also can be passed (as *arguments*) to a function. This information may be necessary for the function to complete its task. Functions are explained in detail in Chapter 4, Functions and Arrays. [*Note*: In Visual Studio .NET, functions are sometimes also referred to as *methods* and *subroutines*.]

For an MC++ application, exactly one function must define the entry point of the program; otherwise, the program is not executable. Throughout this book, we use function **main** as the entry point of console applications and function *WinMain*[3] as the entry point of *GUI* *(graphical user interface)* applications. GUI applications are programs that display

---

3. Another possible entry point, **_tmain**, ensures that, if the support is available, a program uses Unicode® strings; if Unicode® is unavailable, the program still compiles and runs normally. However, we use **main** in console applications because it is the widely recognized standard C++ entry point. We use **WinMain** as the entry point in all GUI applications because it is a standard entry point in Windows programming and ensures that the console window does not appear when the application runs. For more information about entry points **main**, **_tmain** and **WinMain**, visit **sunlightd.virtualave.net/Windows/GUI/Intro.html**.

graphical elements, such as buttons and labels, with which the user interacts. We discuss GUI applications and function **WinMain** in more detail in Chapter 9, Graphical User Interface Concepts: Part 1.

The left brace (**{**) on line 9 begins the *body of the function definition* (the code that will be executed as a part of our program). A corresponding right brace (**}**) terminates the function definition's body (line 13). Notice that the line in the body of the function is indented between these braces.

Good Programming Practice 2.2

*Indent the entire body of each function definition one "level" of indentation between the left brace (**{**) and the right brace (**}**) that define the function body. This makes the structure of the function stand out, improving the function definition's readability.*

Line 10 instructs the computer to perform an *action*, namely, to print a series of characters contained between the double quotation marks. Characters delimited in this manner are called *strings*, *character strings* or *string literals*. We refer to characters between double quotation marks generically as strings. Whitespace characters in strings are significant—the compiler does not ignore these characters.

The **Console** class enables programs to output information to the computer's *standard output*. *Classes* are logical groupings of members (e.g., methods)[4] that simplify program organization. Class **Console** provides methods that allow MC++ programs to display strings and other types of information in the Windows console window.

Method **Console::WriteLine** *displays* (or *prints*) a line of text in the console window. When **Console::WriteLine** completes its task, it positions the *output cursor* (the location where the next character will be displayed) at the beginning of the next line in the console window. (This is similar to pressing the *Enter* key when typing in a text editor—the cursor is repositioned at the beginning of the next line in the file.)

The entire line, including **Console::WriteLine**, its *argument* in the parentheses (**S"Welcome to Visual C++ .NET Programming!"**) and the *semicolon* (**;**), is called a *statement*. Every statement must end with a semicolon (known as the *statement terminator*). When this statement executes, it displays the message **Welcome to Visual C++ .NET Programming!** in the console window (Fig. 2.18).

The **S** *prefix* in line 10 indicates that the string that follows is of type **String ***, a string-literal type in MC++. We will discuss type **String *** in more detail in Chapter 12, Strings, Characters and Regular Expressions.

Performance Tip 2.2

*Preceding managed strings with the **S** prefix offers better performance than a standard C++ string literal.*

In MC++ statements, we normally precede each class name with its namespace name and the *scope resolution operator (**::**)*. For example, line 10 normally would be

```
System::Console::WriteLine( S"Welcome to Visual C++ .NET "
    S"Programming!" );
```

for the program to compile successfully. The **using** statement on line 6 eliminates the need to precede every use of **Console** with **System::**.

---

4. Functions that are members of a class are called methods.

Common Programming Error 2.2

Omitting the semicolon at the end of a statement is a syntax error.

Testing and Debugging Tip 2.1

When the compiler reports a syntax error, the error might not be on the line indicated by the error message. First, check the line where the error was reported. If that line does not contain a syntax error, check the lines that precede the one reported.

Program execution begins with function **main**, which is the entry point to the program. Next, the statement at line 10 of **main** displays **Welcome to Visual C++ .NET Programming!**

Line 12 introduces the **return** statement. MC++ keyword **return** is one of several means we will use to *exit a function* (or method). When the **return** statement is used at the end of **main** as shown here, the value **0** indicates that the program has terminated successfully. In Chapter 4, Functions and Arrays, we discuss the reasons for including this statement. For now, simply include this statement in each program, or the compiler might produce a warning on some systems. Figure 2.19 shows the result of executing the program.

The message **Welcome to Visual C++ .NET Programming!** can be displayed via multiple method calls. File **Welcome1.cpp** of Fig. 2.20 uses two statements to produce the output shown in Fig. 2.19.

Fig. 2.19 Execution of the **Welcome1** program.

```
1   // Fig. 2.20: Welcome1.cpp
2   // Printing a line with multiple statements.
3
4   #using <mscorlib.dll>
5
6   using namespace System;
7
8   int main()
9   {
10     Console::Write( S"Welcome to " );
11     Console::WriteLine( S"Visual C++ .NET Programming!" );
12
13     return 0;
14  }
```

```
Welcome to Visual C++ .NET Programming!
```

Fig. 2.20 Printing on one line with separate statements.

Lines 10–11 of Fig. 2.20 display one line in the console window. The first statement calls **Console** method *Write* to display a string. Unlike **WriteLine**, method **Write** does not position the output cursor at the beginning of the next line in the console window after displaying its string. Rather, the cursor remains immediately after the last character displayed. This way, the next character displayed in the console window appears immediately after the last character displayed with **Write**. Thus, when line 11 executes, the first character displayed (**V**) appears immediately after the last character displayed with **Write** (i.e., the space character after the word **"to"** in line 10).

A single statement can display multiple lines by using newline characters. Recall that these characters indicate when to position the output cursor at the beginning of the next line in the console window to continue output. Figure 2.21 demonstrates using newline characters.

Lines 10–11 produce four separate lines of text in the console window. Programmers can continue a string on the next line and the pieces will be concatenated (combined). *Concatenation* is the process that enables a **String *** and a value of another data type (including another **String ***) to be combined to form a new **String ***. Normally, the characters in a string are displayed exactly as they appear between the double quotes. However, notice that the two characters "****" and "**n**" do not appear on the screen. The *backslash* (****) is called an *escape character*. It indicates that a "special" character is to be output. When a backslash is encountered in a string of characters, the next character is combined with the backslash to form an *escape sequence*. This escape sequence **\n** is the *newline character*. It causes the *cursor* (i.e., the current screen position indicator) to move to the beginning of the next line in the console window. Some common escape sequences are listed in Fig. 2.22. Notice that Fig. 2.22 also contains escape sequences for the backslash character (****) and the double quote character (**"**). Because these are special characters, programmers must use their respective escape sequences when adding them to a string.

```
1   // Fig. 2.21: Welcome2.cpp
2   // Printing multiple lines with a single statement.
3
4   #using <mscorlib.dll>
5
6   using namespace System;
7
8   int main()
9   {
10      Console::WriteLine( S"Welcome\nto\nVisual C++ .NET\n"
11          S"Programming!" );
12
13      return 0;
14  }
```

```
Welcome
to
Visual C++ .NET
Programming!
```

Fig. 2.21   Printing on multiple lines with a single statement.

Escape sequence	Description
\n	Newline. Position the screen cursor to the beginning of the next line.
\t	Horizontal tab. Move the screen cursor to the next tab stop.
\r	Carriage return. Position the screen cursor to the beginning of the current line; do not advance to the next line. Any characters output after the carriage return overwrite the previous characters output on that line.
\\	Backslash. Used to print a backslash character.
\"	Double quote. Used to print a double quote (") character.

Fig. 2.22 Some common escape sequences.

2.8 Arithmetic

Most programs perform arithmetic calculations. Figure 2.23 summarizes the *arithmetic operators* used in programs. Note the use of various special symbols not used in algebra. The *asterisk* (*****) indicates multiplication, and the *percent sign* (**%**) represents the *modulus operator*. The modulus operator, **%**, yields the remainder after division. The expression **x % y** yields the remainder after **x** is divided by **y**. Thus, **7 % 4** yields **3** and **17 % 5** yields **2**. This operator is used most commonly with integer operands, but also can be used with other arithmetic types.

The arithmetic operators in Fig. 2.23 are binary operators, because they each require two operands. For example, the expression **sum + value** contains the binary operator **+** and the two operands **sum** and **value**.

MC++ applies the operators in arithmetic expressions in a precise sequence, determined by the following *rules of operator precedence*, which are generally the same as those followed in algebra:

1. Operators in expressions contained within pairs of parentheses are evaluated first. Thus, *parentheses may be used to force the order of evaluation to occur in any sequence desired by the programmer*. Parentheses are at the highest level of precedence. With *nested* (or *embedded*) parentheses, the operators in the innermost pair of parentheses are applied first.

2. Multiplication, division and modulus operations are applied next. If an expression contains several multiplication, division and modulus operations, operators are applied from left to right. Multiplication, division and modulus are said to have the same level of precedence.

MC++ Operation	Arithmetic operator	Algebraic expression	MC++ expression
Addition	+	$f + 7$	**f + 7**

Fig. 2.23 Arithmetic operators. (Part 1 of 2.)

MC++ Operation	Arithmetic operator	Algebraic expression	MC++ expression
Subtraction	–	$p - c$	p - c
Multiplication	*	bm	b * m
Division	/	x / y or $\dfrac{x}{y}$ or $x \div y$	x / y
Modulus	%	$r \bmod s$	r % s

Fig. 2.23 Arithmetic operators. (Part 2 of 2.)

3. Addition and subtraction operations are applied last. If an expression contains several addition and subtraction operations, operators are applied from left to right. Addition and subtraction have the same level of precedence.

The rules of operator precedence enable MC++ to apply operators in the correct order. When we say that operators are applied from left to right, we are referring to the *associativity* of the operators. If there are multiple operators, each with the same precedence, the associativity determines the order in which the operators are applied. Later, we will see that some operators associate from right to left. Figure 2.24 summarizes the rules of operator precedence. This table will expand as we introduce additional MC++ operators in subsequent chapters. See Appendix A for a complete operator-precedence chart.

2.9 Decision Making: Equality and Relational Operators

This section introduces the **if** structure, which allows a program to make a decision based on the truth or falsity of some *condition*. If the condition is met (i.e., the condition is *true*), the statement in the body of the **if** structure executes. If the condition is not met (i.e., the condition is *false*), the body statement does not execute. Conditions in **if** structures can be formed by using the *equality operators* and *relational operators*, summarized in Fig. 2.25. The relational operators all have the same level of precedence and associate from left to right. The equality operators both have the same level of precedence, which is lower than the precedence of the relational operators. The equality operators also associate from left to right.

Operator(s)	Operation	Order of evaluation (precedence)
( )	Parentheses	Evaluated first. If the parentheses are nested, the expression in the innermost pair is evaluated first. If there are several pairs of parentheses on the same level (i.e., not nested), they are evaluated from left to right.

Fig. 2.24 Precedence of arithmetic operators. (Part 1 of 2.)

Operator(s)	Operation	Order of evaluation (precedence)
*, / or %	Multiplication Division Modulus	Evaluated second. If there are several such operators, they are evaluated from left to right.
+ or –	Addition Subtraction	Evaluated last. If there are several such operators, they are evaluated from left to right.

Fig. 2.24   Precedence of arithmetic operators. (Part 2 of 2.)

Standard algebraic equality operator or relational operator	MC++ equality or relational operator	Example of MC++ condition	Meaning of MC++ condition
Equality operators			
=	==	x == y	**x** is equal to **y**.
≠	!=	x != y	**x** is not equal to **y**.
Relational operators			
>	>	x > y	**x** is greater than **y**.
<	<	x < y	**x** is less than **y**.
≥	>=	x >= y	**x** is greater than or equal to **y**.
≤	<=	x <= y	**x** is less than or equal to **y**.

Fig. 2.25   Equality and relational operators.

Common Programming Error 2.3

It is a syntax error if the operators ==, !=, >= and <= contain spaces between their symbols (as in = =, ! =, > =, < =).

Common Programming Error 2.4

Reversing the operators != , >= and <= (as in =! , => and =<) is a syntax error.

Common Programming Error 2.5

Confusing the equality operator == with the assignment operator = is a logic error. The equality operator should be read "is equal to," and the assignment operator should be read "gets" or "gets the value of." Some people prefer to read the equality operator as "double equals" or "equals equals."

The next example uses six **if** statements to compare two numbers input into a program by the user. If the condition in any of these **if** statements is true, the assignment statement associated with that **if** executes. The user inputs values—**input1** and **input2**—that the program converts to integers and stores in variables **number1** and **number2**. The program compares the numbers and displays the results of the comparison in the command prompt. The program and sample outputs are shown in Fig. 2.26.

Function **main** begins on line 9. Lines 11–15 declare the variables used in function **main**. Note that there are two variables of type integer (**int**). Variables of the same type may be declared in one declaration (lines 11–12) or in multiple declarations (lines 14–15). Also recall that, if more than one variable is placed in one declaration (lines 11–12), those variables are separated by commas (**,**).

```cpp
1   // Fig. 2.26: Comparison.cpp
2   // Using if statements, relational operators and equality
3   // operators.
4
5   #using <mscorlib.dll>
6
7   using namespace System;
8
9   int main()
10  {
11     int number1,        // first number to compare
12         number2;        // second number to compare
13
14     String *input1;     // first user input
15     String *input2;     // second user input
16
17     Console::Write( S"Please enter first integer: " );
18     input1 = Console::ReadLine();
19     number1 = Int32::Parse( input1 );
20
21     Console::Write( S"\nPlease enter second integer: " );
22     input2 = Console::ReadLine();
23     number2 = Int32::Parse( input2 );
24
25     if ( number1 == number2 )
26        Console::WriteLine( S"{0} == {1}", input1, input2 );
27
28     if ( number1 != number2 )
29        Console::WriteLine( S"{0} != {1}", input1, input2 );
30
31     if ( number1 < number2 )
32        Console::WriteLine( S"{0} < {1}", input1, input2 );
33
34     if ( number1 > number2 )
35        Console::WriteLine( S"{0} > {1}", input1, input2 );
36
37     if ( number1 <= number2 )
38        Console::WriteLine( S"{0} <= {1}", input1, input2 );
39
40     if ( number1 >= number2 )
41        Console::WriteLine( S"{0} >= {1}", input1, input2 );
42
43     return 0;
44  }
```

Fig. 2.26 Using equality and relational operators. (Part 1 of 2.)

```
Please enter first integer: 2000

Please enter second integer: 1000
2000 != 1000
2000 > 1000
2000 >= 1000
```

```
Please enter first integer: 1000

Please enter second integer: 2000
1000 != 2000
1000 < 2000
1000 <= 2000
```

```
Please enter first integer: 1000

Please enter second integer: 1000
1000 == 1000
1000 <= 1000
1000 >= 1000
```

Fig. 2.26   Using equality and relational operators. (Part 2 of 2.)

Lines 17–18 prompt the user to input an integer and read from the user a **String ***
representing the first of the two integers that the program will add. The message on line 17
is called a *prompt*, because it prompts the user to take a specific action. Method ***ReadLine***
(line 18) causes the program to pause and wait for user input. The user inputs characters
from the keyboard, then presses the *Enter* key to return the string to the program. Line 18
reads in the first number from the user and stores it in **input1**, a variable of type
String *. Recall from Section 2.7 that **String *** is a string literal in MC++. Arithmetic
operators, relational and equality operators cannot be used with strings. Therefore, the two
input strings must be converted to integers. Line 19 converts the **String *** to an **int**
using method ***Parse*** of class ***System::Int32*** and stores the result in variable
number1. [*Note*: In these earlier chapters, we receive user input through the command
prompt. In Chapters 9–10 (Graphical User Interface Concepts: Part 1 and Part 2), we introduce an alternative means of receiving user input.]

In MC++, type **int** is an alias (i.e., **int** is an alternative name for **Int32** and the two
are interchangeable) for structure **Int32**, a fundamental data type supplied by the .NET
Framework.[5] Throughout this book, we use **int** rather than **Int32** for the convenience of
standard C++ programmers. However, we use **Int32** explicitly when using methods or

---

5. *Structures*, which are defined with keyword **struct**, are aggregate data types built using ele-
    ments of other types. Only **String** in Fig. 2.27 is a class rather than a **struct**.

properties of **Int32**. Figure 2.27 lists some data types[6] supplied by the .NET Framework and their MC++ aliases.[7]

Line 22 reads in the second number from the user. This value is stored in variable **input2**. Line 23 then parses the **String ***[8] and stores the result in variable **number2**.

Lines 18–19 and 22–23 both get an input **String ***, convert the input to type **int** and assign the values to the appropriate variable. Notice that these steps can be combined with the variable declarations and placed on two lines with the statements

```
String *input1 = Console::ReadLine();
int number1 = Int32::Parse( input1 );
```

which declare the variables, read a string from the user, store it in one variable, convert the string to an integer and store the integer in another variable.

The **if** structure in lines 25–26 compares the values of the variables **number1** and **number2** for equality. If the values are equal, the program outputs the value of **"{0} == {1}"**, where **0** corresponds to **input1** and **1** corresponds to **input2**. The **{0}** and **{1}** *formats* indicate that we are printing out the contents of two variables, namely **input1** and **input2**.

FCL Structure/ Class Name	Description	MC++ Data Type
Int16	16-bit signed (i.e., could be positive or negative) integer	*short*
Int32	32-bit signed integer	*int* or *long*
Int64	64-bit signed integer	*__int64*
Single	single-precision (32-bit) floating-point number	*float*
Double	double-precision (64-bit) floating-point number	*double*
Boolean	boolean value (*true* or *false*)	*bool*
Char	Unicode® (16-bit) character	*wchar_t* or *__wchar_t*
String	immutable, fixed-length string of Unicode® characters	*String **

Fig. 2.27   Some data types supplied by the .NET Framework and their aliases.

6. The **__wchar_t** data type is a Microsoft-specific data type, and **wchar_t** is an standard C++ data type. For the Visual C++ .NET compiler to recognize the **wchar_t** data type, programmers must specify compiler option **/Zc:wchar_t** by setting **Project > Properties > Configuration Properties > C/C++ > Language > Treat wchar_t as Built-in Type** to **Yes**. For simplicity, we use the **__wchar_t** data type throughout this book.

7. For more information about the .NET data types, visit **msdn.microsoft.com/library/ en-us/cpguide/html/cpconthenetframeworkclasslibrary.asp**.

8. Because **String *** is an MC++ alias for .NET's **String** class, some sources tend to use these terms interchangeably, or to use one term and not the other. In this book, we will use **String *** to represent objects of type **String *** and **String** when referring to class **String**.

As the program proceeds through the **if** structures, more strings will be output by these **Console::WriteLine** statements. For example, given the value **1000** for **number1** and **number2**, the **if** conditions at lines 37 (**<=**) and 40 (**>=**) also will be true. Thus, the output displayed will be

```
1000 == 1000
1000 <= 1000
1000 >= 1000
```

The third output window of Fig. 2.26 demonstrates this case. Notice the indentation in the **if** statements throughout the program. Such indentation enhances program readability.

Good Programming Practice 2.3

Indent the statement in the body of an **if** *structure to make the body of the structure stand out and to enhance program readability.*

Common Programming Error 2.6

Forgetting the left and right parentheses for the condition in an **if** *structure is a syntax error. The parentheses are required.*

There is no semicolon (**;**) at the end of the first line of each **if** structure. Such a semicolon would result in a logic error at execution time. For example,

```
if ( number1 == number2 );
    Console::WriteLine( S"{0} == {1}", input1, input2 );
```

actually would be interpreted by the compiler as

```
if ( number1 == number2 )
    ;

Console::WriteLine( S"{0} == {1}", input1, input2 );
```

where the semicolon on the line by itself—called the *empty statement*—is the statement to execute if the condition is true. When the empty statement executes, no task is performed. The program continues with the **Console::WriteLine** statement, which executes regardless of whether the condition is true or false.

Notice the use of spacing in Fig. 2.26. Remember that the compiler normally ignores whitespace characters, such as tabs, newlines and spaces. Statements may be split over several lines and may be spaced according to the programmer's preferences without affecting the meaning of a program. For example, line 23 (of Fig. 2.26) could be changed to

```
number2 = Int32::Parse(
    input2 );
```

without affecting the program. It is, however, incorrect to split identifiers and string literals. Ideally, statements should be kept small, but it is not always possible to do so.

Good Programming Practice 2.4

A lengthy statement may be spread over several lines. If a single statement must be split across lines, choose breaking points that make sense, such as after a comma in a comma-separated list or after an operator in a lengthy expression. If a statement is split across two or more lines, indent all subsequent lines with one level of indentation.

The chart in Fig. 2.28 shows the precedence of the operators introduced in this chapter. The operators are displayed from top to bottom in decreasing order of precedence. Notice that all these operators, with the exception of the assignment operator **=**, associate from left to right. Addition is left associative, so an expression such as **x + y + z** is evaluated as if it were written **(x + y) + z**. The assignment operator **=** associates from right to left, so an expression such as **x = y = 0** is evaluated as if it were written **x = (y = 0)**. The latter expression, **x = (y = 0)**, first assigns the value **0** to variable **y** and then assigns the result of that assignment, **0**, to **x**.

Good Programming Practice 2.5

Refer to the operator-precedence chart when writing expressions containing many operators. Confirm that the operators in the expression are performed in the expected order. If you are uncertain about the order of evaluation in a complex expression, use parentheses to force the order, as you would do in an algebraic expression. Remember that some operators, such as assignment (=), associate from right to left rather than from left to right.

In this chapter, we have introduced important features of Visual Studio .NET and the various tools provided by this IDE. Important MC++ features of C++ also have been introduced, including those for displaying data on the screen, inputting data from the keyboard, performing calculations and making decisions. The next chapter introduces control structures and how they can be used to specify the order in which statements execute.

2.10 Summary

The Visual Studio .NET integrated development environment (IDE) is the environment used for creating, running and debugging programs. There are various windows used in Visual Studio .NET. These windows include the **Solution Explorer**, which lists all the files in a solution, and the **Properties** window, which displays a control's characteristics (e.g., colors and fonts). Visual Studio .NET provides several help features, including context-sensitive and dynamic help.

For an MC++ application, exactly one function must define the entry point of the program; otherwise, the program is not executable. Functions can perform tasks and return information when these tasks complete. Information also can be passed (as arguments) to a function. This information may be necessary for the function to complete its task.

Operators	Associativity	Type
( )	left to right	parentheses
* / %	left to right	multiplicative
+ -	left to right	additive
< <= > >=	left to right	relational
== !=	left to right	equality
=	right to left	assignment

Fig. 2.28 Precedence and associativity of operators discussed in this chapter.

     C++ provides arithmetic, equality and relational operators for manipulating values in a program. Often times, values will need to be input by the user. Data can be read from the user via method **ReadLine** and (if necessary) converted into values of various types, such as type **int**.

Control Structures

Objectives

- To use the **if** and **if/else** selection structures to choose among alternative actions.
- To use the **while** repetition structure to execute statements in a program repeatedly.
- To use the increment, decrement and assignment operators.
- To use the **for** and **do/while** repetition structures to execute statements in a program repeatedly.
- To understand multiple selection as facilitated by the **switch** selection structure.
- To use the **break** and **continue** program-control statements.
- To use the logical operators.

Let's all move one place on.
Lewis Carroll

The wheel is come full circle.
William Shakespeare

How many apples fell on Newton's head before he took the hint?
Robert Frost

Who can control his fate?
William Shakespeare

Outline

3.1 Introduction

In this chapter, we present control structures that enable programmers to control the order of execution in their programs. MC++'s sequence, selection and repetition structures are used to select and repeat various statements, thereby enabling the execution of complex algorithms. In the process of presenting these structures, we introduce commonly used shorthand operators, which allow the programmer to calculate and assign new values to variables conveniently. When we study object-based programming in more depth in Chapter 5, we will see that control structures are helpful in building and manipulating objects.

3.2 Control Structures

Normally, statements in a program execute one after the other in the order in which they appear in the program. This process is called *sequential execution*. Various MC++ statements, however, enable the programmer to specify that the next statement to execute may not be the next one in sequence. A *transfer of control* occurs when a statement other than the next one in the program executes.

MC++ has only seven control structures—one *sequence structure* (sequential execution), three types of *selection structures* and three types of *repetition structures*. Each program is formed by combining as many of each type of control structure as is necessary.

MC++ provides three types of selection structures. The **if** selection structure performs (selects) an action if a condition is true or skips the action if the condition is false. The **if/else** selection structure performs an action if a condition is true and performs a different action if the condition is false. The **switch** selection structure selects among many actions, depending on the value of an expression.

The **if** structure is called a *single-selection structure*, because it selects or ignores a single action (or a single group of actions). The **if/else** structure is called a *double-selection structure*, because it selects between two different actions (or groups of actions). The **switch** structure is called a *multiple-selection structure*, because it selects among many different actions (or groups of actions).

MC++ provides three repetition structures: **while**, **do/while** and **for**. The words **if**, **else**, **switch**, **while**, **do** and **for** are examples of standard C++ keywords. Figure 3.1 lists the keywords available to Visual C++ .NET developers.[1] The first section displays the standard C++ keywords. The second section displays keywords added by Microsoft to the core C++ language. The third and final section lists the MC++ keywords. The keywords in the first two sections can be used for both managed and unmanaged code, whereas the keywords in the last section can be used only with managed code. MC++ applications can use all keywords listed in Fig. 3.1. Notice that many of the Microsoft-specific keywords are preceded by double underscores.

Visual C++ .NET Keywords

Standard C++ keywords

auto	bool	break	case	catch
char	class	const	const_cast	continue
default	delete	do	double	dynamic_cast
else	enum	explicit	extern	false
float	for	friend	goto	if
inline	int	long	mutable	namespace
new	operator	private	property	protected
public	register	reinterpret_cast	return	short
signed	sizeof	static	static_cast	struct
switch	template	this	throw	true
try	typedef	typeid	typename	union
unsigned	using	virtual	void	volatile
wchar_t	while			

Microsoft-specific keywords for C++

__alignof	__asm	__assume	__based	__cdecl
__declspec	__event	__except	__fastcall	__finally

Fig. 3.1   Visual C++ .NET keywords. (Part 1 of 2.)

1. For more information on C++ and MC++ keywords, visit **msdn.microsoft.com/library/default.asp?url=/library/en-us/vclang/html/_pluslang_C.2b2b_.Keywords.asp**.

Visual C++ .NET Keywords				
__force inline	__hook	__identifier	__if_exists	__if_not_ exists
__inline	__int8	__int16	__int32	__int64
__interface	__leave	__m64	__m128	__m128d
__m128i	__multiple_ inheritance	__noop	__raise	__single_ inheritance
__stdcall	__super	__try/ __except	__try/ __finally	__unhook
__uuidof	__virtual_ inheritance	__w64	__wchar_t	deprecated
dllexport	dllimport	naked	noinline	noreturn
nothrow	novtable	selectany	thread	uuid

MC++ keywords (also Microsoft-specific)

__abstract	__box	__delegate	__gc	__nogc
__pin	__property	__sealed	__try_cast	__value

Fig. 3.1   Visual C++ .NET keywords. (Part 2 of 2.)

Single-entry/single-exit control structures make it easy to build programs; the control structures are attached to one another by connecting the exit point of one control structure to the entry point of the next. This construction is similar to the stacking of building blocks; thus, we call it *control-structure stacking*. There is only one other way in which control structures may be connected, and that is through *control-structure nesting*, where one control structure can be placed inside another. Thus, algorithms in MC++ programs are constructed from only seven different types of control structures, combined in only two ways.

3.3 if Selection Structure

In a program, a selection structure chooses among alternative courses of action. For example, suppose that the passing grade on an examination is 60 (out of 100). Then the **if** statement

```
if ( studentGrade >= 60 )
    Console::WriteLine( S"Passed" );
```

determines whether the condition **studentGrade >= 60** is true or false. If the condition is true, then **"Passed"** is printed, and the next statement in order is performed. If the condition is false, then the print statement is ignored, and the next statement in order is performed. The decision is made based on the condition. A decision can be based on any expression that evaluates to a value of type *bool*, i.e., any expression that evaluates to *true* (any nonzero value) or *false* (zero).

3.4 `if/else` Selection Structure

The **if** selection structure performs an indicated action only when the condition evaluates to true; otherwise, the action is skipped. The **if/else** selection structure allows the programmer to specify different actions to perform when the condition is true and when the condition is false. For example, the statement

```
if ( studentGrade >= 60 )
    Console::WriteLine( S"Passed" );
else
    Console::WriteLine( S"Failed" );
```

prints **"Passed"** if the student's grade is greater than or equal to **60** and prints **"Failed"** if the student's grade is less than **60**. In either case, after printing occurs, the next statement in sequence is performed.

The *conditional operator* (**?:**) is related closely to the **if/else** structure. The **?:** is MC++'s only *ternary operator*—it takes three operands. The operands and the **?:** form a *conditional expression*. The first operand is a *condition* (i.e., an expression that evaluates to a **bool** value); the second is the value for the conditional expression if the condition evaluates to true; and the third is the value for the conditional expression if the condition evaluates to false. For example, the output statement

```
Console::WriteLine( studentGrade >= 60 ? S"Passed" :
    S"Failed" );
```

contains a conditional expression that evaluates to the string **"Passed"** if the condition **studentGrade >= 60** is true and evaluates to the string **"Failed"** if the condition is false.

The statement with the conditional operator performs in the same manner as the preceding **if/else** statement. The precedence of the conditional operator is low, so the entire conditional expression normally is placed in parentheses. Conditional operators can be used in some situations where **if/else** statements cannot, such as in the argument to the **WriteLine** method.

Good Programming Practice 3.1

*Although the conditional operator provides a convenient alternative to the **if/else** structure, it can sometimes make code less readable. Only use the conditional operator when performing simple, straight-forward tasks.*

The **if** selection structure can have more than one statement in its body. To include several statements in the body of an **if** structure, enclose the statements in braces (**{** and **}**). A set of statements contained in a pair of braces is called a *block*. A block may contain declarations. The declarations in a block commonly are placed first in the block, before any action statements, but declarations may be intermixed with action statements as well.

Good Programming Practice 3.2

Declarations placed at the beginning of a block are easier to find than declarations intermixed with other statements. Place declarations at the beginning of a block to make the code easier to read, debug and maintain.

3.5 `while` Repetition Structure

A *repetition structure* allows the programmer to specify that an action is to be repeated while a condition remains true. As an example of a **while** structure, consider a program segment designed to find the first power of 2 larger than 1000. Suppose that **int** variable **product** contains the value **2**. When the following **while** structure finishes executing, **product** contains the result (i.e., the first power of 2 larger than 1000).

```
int product = 2;

while ( product <= 1000 )
    product = 2 * product;
```

When the **while** structure begins executing, **product** is 2. Variable **product** is repeatedly multiplied by 2, successively taking on the values 4, 8, 16, 32, 64, 128, 256, 512 and 1024. When **product** becomes 1024, the condition **product <= 1000** in the **while** structure becomes false. The repetition then terminates, with 1024 as **product**'s final value. Execution continues with the next statement after the **while** structure. [*Note*: If a **while** structure's condition is initially false, the body statement(s) will never be executed.]

We provide a program that demonstrates the **while** structure in Fig. 3.2. This program was created to solve the following problem:

> *A college offers a course that prepares students for the state licensing examination for real-estate brokers. Last year, several of the students who completed this course took the licensing examination. The college wants to know how well its students did on the exam. You have been asked to write a program to summarize the results, which consists of a list of the 10 students. Next to each name is written a 1 if the student passed the exam and a 2 if the student failed the exam. If more than eight students passed the exam, print the message "Raise tuition."*

```
1   // Fig. 3.2: Analysis.cpp
2   // Analysis of examination results.
3
4   #using <mscorlib.dll>
5
6   using namespace System;
7
8   int main()
9   {
10      int passes = 0,      // number of passes
11          failures = 0,    // number of failures
12          student = 1,     // student counter
13          result;          // one exam result
14
15      // process 10 students; counter-controlled loop
16      while ( student <= 10 ) {
17          Console::Write( S"Enter result (1=pass, 2=fail): " );
18          result = Int32::Parse( Console::ReadLine() );
19
20          if ( result == 1 )
21              passes = passes + 1;
22          else
23              failures = failures + 1;
```

Fig. 3.2   Examination-results problem. (Part 1 of 2.)

```
24
25          student = student + 1;
26      }
27
28      // termination phase
29      Console::WriteLine( S"\nPassed: {0}\nFailed: {1}",
30          passes.ToString(), failures.ToString() );
31
32      if ( passes > 8 )
33          Console::WriteLine( S"Raise Tuition\n" );
34
35      return 0;
36  }
```

```
Enter result (1=pass, 2=fail): 1
Enter result (1=pass, 2=fail): 2
Enter result (1=pass, 2=fail): 2
Enter result (1=pass, 2=fail): 2
Enter result (1=pass, 2=fail): 2
Enter result (1=pass, 2=fail): 2
Enter result (1=pass, 2=fail): 1
Enter result (1=pass, 2=fail): 1
Enter result (1=pass, 2=fail): 1
Enter result (1=pass, 2=fail): 1

Passed: 5
Failed: 5
```

Fig. 3.2   Examination-results problem. (Part 2 of 2.)

Lines 10–13 declare the variables used in **main** to process the examination results. We have taken advantage of an MC++ feature that incorporates variable initialization into declarations (**passes** is assigned **0**, **failures** is assigned **0** and **student** is assigned **1**). Line 18 reads the information entered by the user, converts the input to type **int** and assigns the value to **result**, successfully combining several actions into one statement. Notice the use of the nested **if/else** structure (lines 20–23) in the **while** structure's body.

Lines 29–30 display the final values of **passes** and **failures**. The syntax

```
passes.ToString()
```

obtains the string representation of variable **passes** by calling method *ToString*. Method **ToString** of variable **passes** is invoked using the *dot operator (.)*. The dot operator accesses an object via the variable name for the object or via a reference to the object. We discuss objects in more detail in Chapter 5, Object-Based Programming.

3.6 Assignment Operators

MC++ provides several assignment operators for abbreviating assignment expressions. For example, the statement

```
c = c + 3;
```

can be abbreviated with the *addition assignment operator* (+=) as

```
c += 3;
```

The += operator adds the value of the expression on the right of the operator to the value of the variable on the left of the operator and stores the result in the variable on the left of the operator. Any statement of the form

    variable = *variable operator expression*;

where *operator* is one of the binary operators +, -, *, / or % (or others we will discuss later in the book), can be written in the form

    variable operator= expression;

    Figure 3.3 lists the arithmetic assignment operators, provides sample expressions that use these operators and gives an explanation of the meaning of each sample expression.

Common Programming Error 3.1

Placing a space character between the two characters that compose an arithmetic assignment operator is a syntax error.

3.7 Increment and Decrement Operators

MC++ provides the unary *increment operator*, ++, and the unary *decrement operator*, --, the definitions of which are summarized in Fig. 3.4. A program can use the increment operator to increment the value of a variable called c by 1, rather than using the expression c = c + 1 or c += 1. If an increment or decrement operator is placed before a variable, it is referred to as the *preincrement* or *predecrement operator*, respectively. If an increment or decrement operator is placed after a variable, it is referred to as the *postincrement* or *postdecrement operator*, respectively.

    Preincrementing (or predecrementing) a variable causes the variable to be incremented (or decremented) by 1, and then the new value of the variable is used in the expression in which it appears. Postincrementing (or postdecrementing) the variable causes the value of the variable to be used in the expression in which it appears, and then the variable value is incremented (or decremented) by 1.

Assignment operator	Sample expression	Explanation	Assigns
Assume: int c = 3, d = 5, e = 4, f = 6, g = 12;			
+=	c += 7	c = c + 7	10 to c
-=	d -= 4	d = d - 4	1 to d
*=	e *= 5	e = e * 5	20 to e
/=	f /= 3	f = f / 3	2 to f
%=	g %= 9	g = g % 9	3 to g

Fig. 3.3   Arithmetic assignment operators.

Operator	Called	Sample expression	Explanation
++	preincrement	++a	Increment **a** by 1; then use the new value of **a** in the expression in which **a** resides.
++	postincrement	a++	Use the value of **a** in the expression in which **a** resides; then increment **a** by 1.
--	predecrement	--b	Decrement **b** by 1; then use the new value of **b** in the expression in which **b** resides.
--	postdecrement	b--	Use the value of **b** in the expression in which **b** resides; then decrement **b** by 1.

Fig. 3.4   Increment and decrement operators.

Common Programming Error 3.2

Attempting to use an increment or decrement operator on an expression other than a lvalue *("left value") is a syntax error. An* lvalue *is a variable or expression that can appear on the left side of an assignment operation. For example, writing* **++(x + 1)** *is a syntax error, because* **(x + 1)** *is not an* lvalue.

Figure 3.5 shows the precedence and associativity of the operators that have been introduced thus far. The operators are shown from top to bottom in decreasing order of precedence. The second column describes the associativity of the operators at each level of precedence. Notice that the conditional operator (**? :**), the unary preincrement (**++**) and predecrement (**--**) operators, the plus (**+**) operator, the minus (**-**) operator and the assignment operators (**=, +=, -=, *=, /=** and **%=**) associate from right to left. All other operators in the operator precedence chart in Fig. 3.5 associate from left to right. The third column names the groups of operators. Note that the parentheses and the unary postfix operators have the same level of precedence.

Operators	Associativity	Type
( )	left to right	parentheses
++ --	left to right	unary postfix
++ -- + -	right to left	unary prefix
* / %	left to right	multiplicative
+ -	left to right	additive
< <= > >=	left to right	relational
== !=	left to right	equality
? :	right to left	conditional
= += -= *= /= %=	right to left	assignment

Fig. 3.5   Precedence and associativity of the operators discussed thus far in this book.

3.8 `for` Repetition Structure

The `for` repetition structure handles the details of *counter-controlled repetition*, where a counter is used to control the number of times a set of statements will execute. We illustrate the power of the `for` structure in Fig. 3.6. Function `main` (lines 8–16) operates as follows: When the `for` structure (line 12) begins executing, the program initializes the control variable `counter` to **1** (the first two elements of counter-controlled repetition—control variable *name* and *initial value*). Next, the program tests the loop-continuation condition, `counter <= 5`. The initial value of `counter` is **1**; thus, the condition is true, so line 13 outputs the `counter`'s value. Then, the program increments variable `counter` in the expression `counter++`, and the loop begins again with the loop-continuation test. The control variable is now equal to **2**. This value does not exceed the final value, so the program performs the body statement again (i.e., performs the next iteration of the loop). This process continues until the control variable `counter` becomes **6**, causing the loop-continuation test to fail and repetition to terminate. The program continues by performing the first statement after the `for` structure. (In this case, function `main` terminates because the program reaches the `return` statement on line 15.)

The first line of the `for` structure (including the keyword `for` and everything in parentheses after `for`) sometimes is called the *`for` structure header*. Notice that the `for` structure specifies each of the items needed for counter-controlled repetition with a control variable. If there is more than one statement in the body of the `for` structure, braces (`{` and `}`) are required to define the loop's body.

Figure 3.6 uses the loop-continuation condition `counter <= 5`. If the programmer incorrectly writes `counter < 5` instead, the loop executes only four times. This common logic error is called an *off-by-one error*.

The general format of the `for` structure is

> *for* (*expression1*; *expression2*; *expression3*)
>   *statement*;

where *expression1* names the loop's control variable and provides its initial value, *expression2* is the loop-continuation condition and *expression3* usually increments or decrements the control variable.

Programmers can declare the control variable in *expression1* of the `for` structure header (i.e., the control variable's type is specified before the variable name), rather than earlier in the code. In Visual C++ .NET, this approach is equivalent to declaring the control variable immediately before the `for` structure. Therefore, the `for` structure

```
for ( int counter = 1; counter <= 5; counter++ )
    Console::WriteLine( counter );
```

```
1   // Fig. 3.6: forCounter.cpp
2   // Counter-controlled repetition with the for structure.
3
4   #using <mscorlib.dll>
5
6   using namespace System;
7
```

Fig. 3.6   Counter-controlled repetition with the `for` structure. (Part 1 of 2.)

```
 8   int main()
 9   {
10      // initialization, repetition condition and incrementing
11      // are all included in the for structure
12      for ( int counter = 1; counter <= 5; counter++ )
13         Console::WriteLine( counter );
14
15      return 0;
16   }
```

```
1
2
3
4
5
```

Fig. 3.6   Counter-controlled repetition with the **for** structure. (Part 2 of 2.)

is equivalent to

```
int counter;

for ( counter = 1; counter <= 5; counter++ )
   Console::WriteLine( counter );
```

Both code segments create variables with the same *scope*. The scope of a variable specifies where it can be used in a program. Scope is discussed in detail in Chapter 4, Functions and Arrays. [*Note*: Unlike standard C++, the variable can be used outside of the **for** structure. If this behavior is undesirable, the programmer can simulate the behavior of standard C++ using the **/Zc:forScope** compiler option. This option can be set in the IDE by selecting **Project > Properties > Configuration Properties > C/C++ > Language**, and changing option **Force Conformance In For Loop Scope** to **Yes (/Zc:forScope)**.]

Good Programming Practice 3.3

*When a control variable is declared in the initialization section (e.g., expression1) of a **for** structure header, avoid declaring the control variable again after the **for** structure's body.*

Expression1 and *expression3* in a **for** structure also can be comma-separated lists of expressions, which enables the programmer to use multiple initialization expressions, multiple increment or decrement expressions. For example, there may be several control variables in a single **for** structure that must be initialized and incremented or decremented.

Good Programming Practice 3.4

*Place only expressions involving control variables in the initialization and increment or decrement sections of a **for** structure. Manipulations of other variables should appear either before the loop (if they execute only once, like initialization statements) or in the body of the loop (if they execute once per iteration of the loop, like incrementing or decrementing statements).*

The three expressions in the **for** structure are optional. If *expression2* is omitted, Visual C++ .NET assumes that the loop-continuation condition is always true, thus creating an *infinite loop*. Infinite loops occur when loop-continuation conditions never become false. A programmer might omit *expression1* if the program initializes the control variable before the loop. *Expression3* might be omitted if statements in the body of the **for** structure perform the incrementation or decrementation themselves, or if no incrementation or decrementation is necessary. The increment (or decrement) expression in the **for** structure acts as if it were a stand-alone statement at the end of the body of the **for** structure. Therefore, the expressions

```
counter = counter + 1
counter += 1
++counter
counter++
```

are equivalent when used in *expression3*. Some programmers prefer the form **counter++**, because the **++** is at the end of the expression. For this reason, the postincrementing (or postdecrementing) form, in which the variable is incremented after it is used, seems more natural. However, because the variable being either incremented or decremented does not appear in a larger expression, preincrementing (or predecrementing) and postincrementing (or postdecrementing) the variable have the same effect. The two semicolons in the **for** structure are required.

Common Programming Error 3.3

*Using commas in a **for** structure header instead of the two required semicolons is a syntax error.*

Common Programming Error 3.4

*Placing a semicolon immediately to the right of a **for** structure header's right parenthesis makes the body of that **for** structure an empty statement. This is normally a logic error.*

The initialization, loop-continuation condition, and increment or decrement portions of a **for** structure can contain arithmetic expressions. For example, assume that $x = 2$ and $y = 10$. If x and y are not modified in the body of the loops, then the statement

```
for ( int j = x; j <= 4 * x * y; j += y / x )
```

is equivalent to the statement

```
for ( int j = 2; j <= 80; j += 5 )
```

The increment of a **for** structure may be negative, in which case it is really a decrement, and the loop actually counts downward.

Testing and Debugging Tip 3.1

*Avoid changing the value of the control variable in the body of a **for** loop, to avoid subtle errors.*

3.9 Example: Using the for Structure to Compute Compound Interest

Our next example demonstrates a simple application of the **for** repetition structure. The program in Fig. 3.7 uses the **for** structure to solve the following problem:

A person invests $1000.00 in a savings account that yields 5% interest annually. Assuming that all interest is left on deposit, calculate and print the amount of money in the account at the end of each year for 10 years. To determine these amounts, use the formula

$$a = p(1 + r)^n,$$

where

p is the original amount invested (i.e., the principal)
r is the annual interest rate
n is the number of years
a is the amount on deposit at the end of the *n*th year.

This problem involves a loop that performs the indicated calculation for each of the 10 years that the money remains on deposit.

```
1   // Fig. 3.7: interest.cpp
2   // Calculating compound interest.
3
4   #using <mscorlib.dll>
5
6   using namespace System;
7
8   int main()
9   {
10     Decimal amount, principal = 1000.00;
11     double rate = .05;
12
13     Console::WriteLine( S"Year\tAmount on deposit" );
14
15     for ( int year = 1; year <= 10; year++ ) {
16        amount = principal * Math::Pow( 1.0 + rate, year );
17
18        Console::WriteLine( String::Concat( year.ToString(), S"\t",
19           amount.ToString( "C" ) ) );
20     }
21
22     return 0;
23  }
```

```
Year      Amount on deposit
1         $1,050.00
2         $1,102.50
3         $1,157.63
4         $1,215.51
5         $1,276.28
6         $1,340.10
7         $1,407.10
8         $1,477.46
9         $1,551.33
10        $1,628.89
```

Fig. 3.7   Calculating compound interest with **for**.

Line 10 in function **main** declares two *Decimal* variables—**amount** and **prin-cipal**—and initializes **principal** to **1000.00**. The type **Decimal** is a data type used for monetary calculations. Line 11 declares **double** variable **rate**, which we initialize to **.05**.

The **for** structure executes its body 10 times, varying control variable **year** from **1** to **10** in increments of **1**. Note that **year** represents n in the problem statement. MC++ does not have an exponentiation operator, so we use **static** method **Pow** in class **Math** for this purpose. **Math::Pow(x, y)** calculates the value of **x** raised to the **y**th power. Method **Math::Pow** takes two arguments of type **double** and returns a **double** value. Lines 16 performs the calculation from the problem statement

$$a = p\,(1 + r)^{\,n},$$

where a is **amount**, p is **principal**, r is **rate** and n is **year**.

Lines 18–19 use method **Concat** of class **Sytem::String** to build an output **String**. Method *Concat* concatenates multiple **String**s and returns a new **String** containing the combined characters from the original **String**s. We discuss method **Concat** in more detail in Chapter 12, Strings, Characters and Regular Expressions.

Common Programming Error 3.5

Attempting to use **+** *to concatenate* **String**s *is a syntax error.*

The concatenated text (lines 18–19) includes the current value of year (**year.ToString()**), a tab character (**\t**) to position to the second column, the amount on deposit (**amount.ToString("C")**) and a newline character to position the output cursor to the next line. The call to method **ToString** converts **amount** to a **String *** and formats this **String *** as a monetary amount. The argument to method **ToString** specifies the formatting of the string and is referred to as the *formatting code*. In this case, we use formatting code *C* (for "currency"), which indicates that the string should be displayed as a monetary amount. There are several other formatting codes, which can be found in the MSDN documentation.[2] [*Note*: Method **ToString** uses .NET's string formatting codes to represent numeric and monetary values in a form that is appropriate to the execution environment. For example, U.S. dollars are represented as **$634,307.08**, whereas Malaysian ringgits are represented as **R636.307,08**.] Figure 3.8 shows several formatting codes. If no formatting code is specified (e.g., **year.ToString()**), the formatting code **G** is used.

The variables **amount** and **principal** were declared to be of type **Decimal** because the program deals with fractional parts of dollars. In such cases, programs need a type that allows decimal points in its values. Variable **rate** is of type **double** because it is used in the calculation **1.0 + rate**, which appears as a **double** argument to method **Pow** of class **Math**. Note that the calculation **1.0 + rate** appears in the body of the **for** statement. The calculation produces the same result each time through the loop, so repeating the calculation is unnecessary.

---

2. For more information on formatting types, visit **msdn.microsoft.com/library/ default.asp?url=/library/en-us/cpguide/html/ cpconformattingtypes.asp**.

Format Code	Description
C or c	Formats the string as currency. Precedes the number with an appropriate currency symbol ($ for U.S. settings). Separates digits with an appropriate separator character (comma for U.S. settings) and sets the number of decimal places to two by default.
D or d	Formats the string as a decimal.
N or n	Formats the string with comma-separator characters and two decimal places.
E or e	Formats the string in scientific notation with a default of six decimal places (e.g., the value **27,900,000** becomes **2.790000E+007**).
F or f	Formats the string with a fixed number of decimal places (two by default).
G or g	Formats the string as decimal, using the **E** or **F** format code, whichever provides the most compact result.
P or p	Formats the string as a percentage. By default, the value is multiplied by 100, and a percent sign is appended to it.
R or r	Ensures that a value converted to string can be converted back without loss of precision or data.
X or x	Formats the string as hexadecimal.

Fig. 3.8   Numeric formatting codes.

Performance Tip 3.1

Avoid placing expressions containing values that do not change inside a loop. Such expressions should be evaluated only once before the loop. Most compilers will prevent redundant evaluations with a process that compilers perform called optimization.

3.10 `switch` Multiple-Selection Structure

Occasionally, an algorithm contains a series of decisions in which the algorithm tests a variable or expression separately for each *constant integral expression* the variable or expression may assume. A constant integral expression is any expression involving character and integer constants that evaluates to an integer value (e.g., values of type **int** or **__wchar_t**). The algorithm then takes different actions, based on those values. MC++ provides the ***switch** multiple-selection structure* to handle such decision making.

In the next example (Fig. 3.9), let us assume that a class of 10 students took an exam and that each student received a letter grade of A, B, C, D or F. The program will input the letter grades and summarize the results by using **switch** to count the number of each different letter grade that students earned on an exam. Line 10 declares variable **grade** as type **__wchar_t**. Lines 11–15 define counter variables that the program uses to count each letter grade. This variable stores the user's input for each grade. Line 17 begins a **for** structure that loops 10 times. At each iteration, line 18 prompts the user for the next grade, and line 19 invokes **Char** method **Parse** to read the user input as a **__wchar_t**. The **Char** structure represents Unicode® characters. Nested in the body of the **for** structure is a **switch** structure (lines 21–52) that processes the letter grades. The **switch** structure consists of a series of *case* labels and an optional ***default*** case.

```
1    // Fig. 3.9: switchtest.cpp
2    // Counting letter grades.
3
4    #using <mscorlib.dll>
5
6    using namespace System;
7
8    int main()
9    {
10       __wchar_t grade;     // one grade
11       int aCount = 0,      // number of As
12           bCount = 0,      // number of Bs
13           cCount = 0,      // number of Cs
14           dCount = 0,      // number of Ds
15           fCount = 0;      // number of Fs
16
17       for ( int i = 1; i <= 10; i++ ) {
18          Console::Write( S"Enter a letter grade: " );
19          grade = Char::Parse( Console::ReadLine() );
20
21          switch ( grade ) {
22             case 'A':        // grade is uppercase A
23             case 'a':        // or lowercase a
24                ++aCount;
25                break;
26
27             case 'B':        // grade is uppercase B
28             case 'b':        // or lowercase b
29                ++bCount;
30                break;
31
32             case 'C':        // grade is uppercase C
33             case 'c':        // or lowercase c
34                ++cCount;
35                break;
36
37             case 'D':        // grade is uppercase D
38             case 'd':        // or lowercase d
39                ++dCount;
40                break;
41
42             case 'F':        // grade is upppercase F
43             case 'f':        // or lowercase f
44                ++fCount;
45                break;
46
47             default:         // processes all other characters
48                Console::WriteLine(
49                   S"Incorrect letter grade entered."
50                   S"\nGrade not added to totals." );
51                break;
52          } // end switch
53       } // end for
```

Fig. 3.9   **switch** multiple-selection structure. (Part 1 of 2.)

```
54
55      Console::WriteLine(
56        S"\nTotals for each letter grade are: \nA: {0} "
57        S"\nB: {1}\nC: {2}\nD: {3}\nF: {4}", aCount.ToString(),
58        bCount.ToString(), cCount.ToString(), dCount.ToString(),
59        fCount.ToString() );
60
61      return 0;
62  } // end function main
```

```
Enter a letter grade: a
Enter a letter grade: A
Enter a letter grade: c
Enter a letter grade: F
Enter a letter grade: z
Incorrect letter grade entered.
Grade not added to totals.
Enter a letter grade: D
Enter a letter grade: d
Enter a letter grade: B
Enter a letter grade: a
Enter a letter grade: C

Totals for each letter grade are:
A: 3
B: 1
C: 2
D: 2
F: 1
```

Fig. 3.9   **switch** multiple-selection structure. (Part 2 of 2.)

When the flow of control reaches the **switch** structure, the program evaluates the *controlling expression* (**grade** in this example) in the parentheses following keyword **switch**. The value of this expression is compared with each **case** label until a match occurs. Assume that the user entered the letter **B** as the grade. **B** is compared to each **case** in the **switch**, until a match occurs at line 27 (**case 'B':**). When this happens, the statements for that **case** execute. For the letter **B**, lines 29–30 increment the number of **B** grades stored in variable **bCount**, and the **switch** structure exits immediately with the **break** *statement*. The **break** statement causes program control to proceed with the first statement after the **switch** structure. In this case, we reach the end of the **for** structure's body, so control flows to the control-variable increment expression in the **for** structure header. Then the counter variable in the **for** structure is incremented, and the loop-continuation condition is evaluated to determine whether another iteration of the loop is necessary.

Good Programming Practice 3.5

*Indent the body statements of each **case** in a **switch** structure.*

If no match occurs between the controlling expression's value and a **case** label, the **default** case (line 47) executes. Lines 48–50 display an error message. Note that the

default case is optional in the **switch** structure. If the controlling expression does not match a **case** and there is no **default** case, program control proceeds to the next statement after the **switch** structure.

Each **case** can contain multiple actions or no actions at all. A **case** with no statements is considered an *empty* **case**. The last **case** in a **switch** structure must not be an empty **case**.

If a **case** label matches our controlling expression, and the case contains no **break** statement, *fall through* occurs. This means that the **switch** structure executes the statements in the current case as well as those in the next case. If that **case** also contains no **break** statement, this process will continue until a **break** statement is found, or the statements for the last case are executed. This provides the programmer with a way to specify that statements are to be executed for several **case**s. Figure 3.9 demonstrates this. Lines 24–25 execute for both cases on lines 22–23 (if the grade entered was either **A** or **a**), lines 29–30 execute for both cases on lines 27–28 (if the grade entered was either **B** or **b**) and so on. Furthermore, if all the **break** statements were removed from Fig. 3.9, and the user entered the letter **A**, the statements for every **case** would be executed (including the **default** case).

Common Programming Error 3.6

*Not including a **break** statement at the end of each **case** in a **switch** structure can lead to logic errors. Only omit **break** statements from **case**s that should result in fall through.*

Common Programming Error 3.7

*Be sure to check all possible values when creating **case**s to confirm that no two **case**s in a **switch** statement are for the same integral value. If any values are the same, a compile-time error will occur.*

Finally, it is important to notice that the **switch** structure is different than other structures in that braces are not required around multiple actions in a **case**. [*Note*: One exception occurs when a **case** contains a combined variable declaration and initialization statement (e.g., **int x = 2;**). In this scenario, the **case** statements must be enclosed in braces.]

Good Programming Practice 3.6

*Provide a **default** case in every **switch** structure. Cases not explicitly tested in a **switch** structure that lacks a **default** case are ignored. Including a **default** case focuses the programmer on processing exceptional conditions. There are situations, however, in which no **default** processing is required.*

Good Programming Practice 3.7

*Although the **case**s in a **switch** structure can occur in any order, it is considered good programming practice to order the **case**s in some logical order and to place the **default** case last.*

When using the **switch** structure, remember that the expression after each **case** in a particular **switch** structure must be a constant integral expression, i.e., any combination of character constants and integer constants that evaluates to a constant integer value. A *character constant* is represented as a specific character in single quotes (such as **'A'**). An integer constant is simply an integer value. The expression after each **case** also can be a *constant*—a variable that contains a value that does not change throughout the entire program. Such a variable is declared with keyword **const** (discussed in Chapter 4, Functions and Arrays).

Chapter 7, Object-Oriented Programming: Polymorphism, presents a more elegant way of implementing **switch** logic. In that chapter, we use a technique called *polymorphism* to create programs that are clearer and easier to maintain and extend than programs that use **switch** logic.

3.11 do/while Repetition Structure

The *do/while* repetition structure is similar to the **while** structure. The main difference is that, in the **while** structure, the test of the loop-continuation condition occurs at the beginning of the loop, before the body of the loop executes, while the **do/while** structure tests the loop-continuation condition *after* the body of the loop executes: Therefore, the loop body always executes at least once with the **do/while** structure. When a **do/while** structure terminates, execution continues with the statement after the **while** clause. Figure 3.10 uses a **do/while** structure to output the values 1–5.

Lines 12–15 demonstrate the **do/while** structure. When program execution reaches the **do/while** structure, the program executes lines 13–14, which display the value of **counter** (at this point, **1**) and increment **counter** by **1**. Then the program evaluates the condition on line 15. At this point, variable **counter** is **2**, which is less than or equal to **5**, so the **do/while** structure's body executes again. The fifth time the structure executes, line 13 outputs the value **5** and line 14 increments **counter** to **6**. Then the condition on line 15 evaluates to false, and the **do/while** structure exits.

Note that it is not necessary to use braces in the **do/while** structure if there is only one statement in the body. However, the braces normally are included to avoid confusion between the **while** and **do/while** structures. For example,

> **while** (*condition*)

```
1   // Fig. 3.10: doWhileLoop.cpp
2   // The do/while repetition structure.
3
4   #using <mscorlib.dll>
5
6   using namespace System;
7
8   int main()
9   {
10      int counter = 1;
11
12      do {
13         Console::WriteLine( counter );
14         counter++;
15      } while ( counter <= 5 );
16
17      return 0;
18  }
```

Fig. 3.10 do/while repetition structure. (Part 1 of 2.)

```
1
2
3
4
5
```

Fig. 3.10 do/while repetition structure. (Part 2 of 2.)

typically is the header for a **while** structure. A **do/while** structure with no braces around a single-statement body appears as

> *do*
> >   *statement;*
> *while* (*condition*)*;*

which can be confusing. The last line—**while(** *condition* **);**—might be misinterpreted by the reader as a **while** structure containing an empty statement (the semicolon by itself). Thus, the **do/while** structure with a single-statement body often is written as follows, to avoid confusion:

> *do* {
> >   *statement;*
> } *while* (*condition*)*;*

Good Programming Practice 3.8

*Some programmers always include braces in a **do/while** structure, even when the braces are unnecessary. This practice helps eliminate ambiguity between a **while** structure and a **do/while** structure that contains only one statement.*

Common Programming Error 3.8

*Infinite loops occur when the loop-continuation condition in a **while**, **for** or **do/while** structure never becomes false. To prevent this, make sure there is no semicolon immediately after the header of a **while** or **for** structure. In a counter-controlled loop, make sure the control variable is incremented (or decremented) in the body of the loop. In a sentinel-controlled loop, make sure the* sentinel value *(i.e., the value indicating "end of data entry") eventually is input.*

Common Programming Error 3.9

*Placing a semicolon immediately after the word **do** in a **do/while** statement is a syntax error.*

3.12 Statements break and continue

The **break** and **continue** statements alter the flow of control. The **break** statement, when executed in a **while**, **for**, **do/while** or **switch** structure, causes immediate exit from the structure. Execution continues with the first statement that follows the structure. Common uses of the **break** statement are to exit prematurely from a loop or to exit a **switch** structure (as in Fig. 3.9). Figure 3.11 demonstrates use of the **break** statement in a **for** repetition structure.

```
1   // Fig. 3.11: BreakTest.cpp
2   // Using the break statement in a for structure.
3
4   #using <mscorlib.dll>
5
6   using namespace System;
7
8   int main()
9   {
10     int count;
11
12     for ( count = 1; count <= 10; count++ ) {
13
14        if ( count == 5 )
15           break;     // skip remaining code in loop if count == 5
16
17        Console::Write( String::Concat( count.ToString(), S" " ) );
18     }
19
20     Console::WriteLine( String::Concat(
21        S"\nBroke out of loop at count = ", count.ToString() ) );
22
23     return 0;
24  }
```

```
1 2 3 4
Broke out of loop at count = 5
```

Fig. 3.11   **break** statement in a **for** structure.

When the **if** structure in line 14 detects that **count** is **5**, **break** is executed. This terminates the **for** structure and the program proceeds to line 20 (immediately after the **for**). The output statement produces the string that is displayed in lines 20–21. The loop executes its body only four times.

The **continue** statement, when executed in a **while**, **for** or **do/while** structure, skips the remaining statements in the body of that structure and proceeds with the next iteration of the loop. In **while** and **do/while** structures, the loop-continuation condition evaluates immediately after the **continue** statement executes. In a **for** structure, the increment or decrement expression executes; then the loop-continuation test evaluates.

The **while** structure can replace the **for** structure in most cases. One exception occurs when the increment or decrement expression in the **while** structure follows the **continue** statement. In this case, the increment or decrement expression does not execute before the repetition-continuation condition is tested, and the **while** structure thus does not execute in the same manner as the **for** structure.

Figure 3.12 uses the **continue** statement in a **for** structure to skip the output statement on line 16 when the **if** structure (line 12) determines that the value of **count** is **5**. When the **continue** statement executes, program control continues with the increment of the control variable in the **for** structure.

```
1    // Fig. 3.12: continueTest.cpp
2    // Using the continue statement in a for structure.
3
4    #using <mscorlib.dll>
5
6    using namespace System;
7
8    int main()
9    {
10      for ( int count = 1; count <= 10; count++ ) {
11
12        if ( count == 5 )
13           continue;   // skip remaining code in loop
14                       // only if count == 5
15
16        Console::Write( String::Concat( count.ToString(), S" " ) );
17      }
18
19      Console::WriteLine( S"\nUsed continue to skip printing 5" );
20
21      return 0;
22   }
```

```
1 2 3 4 6 7 8 9 10
Used continue to skip printing 5
```

Fig. 3.12 `continue` statement in a `for` structure.

Good Programming Practice 3.9

*Some programmers believe that the **break** and **continue** statements violate the concept of structured programming. As the effects of these statements can be achieved by structured-programming techniques, these programmers simply avoid using **break** and **continue**.*

Performance Tip 3.2

*When used properly, the **break** and **continue** statements perform faster than their corresponding structured-programming techniques.*

Software Engineering Observation 3.1

There is a debate between achieving quality software engineering and achieving the best-performing software. Often, one of these goals is achieved at the expense of the other. For all but the most performance-intensive situations, apply the following rule of thumb: First, make your code simple and correct; then make it fast and small, but only if necessary.

3.13 Logical and Conditional Operators

MC++ provides several *logical and conditional operators* that may be used to form complex conditions by combining simple conditions. The operators are **&&** (*conditional AND*), **&** (*logical AND*), **| |** (*conditional OR*), **|** (*logical OR*), **^** (*logical exclusive OR, or logical XOR*) and **!** (*logical NOT, or logical negation*). In this section, we consider examples that use each of these operators.

Common Programming Error 3.10

Placing a space between the characters of the && and || operators is a syntax error.

Suppose that we wish to ensure that two conditions are *both* true in a program before we choose a certain path of execution. In this case, we can use the conditional **&&** operator as follows:

```
if ( gender == 1 && age >= 65 )
   ++seniorFemales;
```

This **if** statement contains two simple conditions. The condition **gender == 1** might be evaluated to determine whether a person is female. The condition **age >= 65** is evaluated to determine whether a person is a senior citizen. The two simple conditions are evaluated first, because the precedences of **==** and **>=** are both higher than the precedence of **&&**. The **if** statement then considers the combined condition

```
gender == 1 && age >= 65
```

This condition is true *if and only if* both of the simple conditions are true. Finally, if this combined condition is true, the body statement increments the count of **seniorFemales** by **1**. If either or both of the simple conditions are false, the program skips the incrementation step and proceeds to the statement that follows the **if** structure.

Now let us consider the || (conditional OR) operator. Suppose that we wish to ensure that either *or* both of two conditions are true before we choose a certain path of execution. In this case, we use the || operator as follows:

```
if ( semesterAverage >= 90 || finalExam >= 90 )
   Console::WriteLine( S"Student grade is A" );
```

This **if** statement also contains two simple conditions. The condition **semesterAverage >= 90** determines whether the student deserves an "A" in the course because of a solid performance throughout the semester. The condition **finalExam >= 90** determines whether the student deserves an "A" in the course because of an outstanding performance on the final exam. The **if** statement then considers the combined condition

```
semesterAverage >= 90 || finalExam >= 90
```

and awards the student an "A" if either or both of the simple conditions are true. Note that the message "**Student grade is A**" prints unless *both* of the simple conditions are false.

The **&&** operator has a higher precedence than the || operator. Both operators associate from left to right. An expression containing **&&** or || operators is evaluated only until truth or falsity is known. Thus, evaluation of the expression

```
gender == 1 && age >= 65
```

stops immediately if **gender** is not equal to **1** (i.e., if one condition is **false**, then the entire expression is **false**) and continues if **gender** is equal to **1** (i.e., the entire expression could still be **true** if the condition **age >= 65** is **true**). This performance feature for the evaluation of conditional AND and conditional OR expressions is called *short-cir-cuit evaluation.*

Performance Tip 3.3

*In expressions using operator **&&**, if the separate conditions are independent of one another, then make the condition most likely to be false the leftmost condition. In expressions using operator **||**, make the condition most likely to be true the leftmost condition. This use of short-circuit evaluation can reduce a program's execution time.*

Short-circuit evaluation is useful in cases where one condition could cause an error in the program. For example, the expression

```
grades > 0 && ( total / grades > 60 )
```

stops immediately if **grades** is not greater than **0**; otherwise the expression evaluates the second condition. Notice that if we omit the first condition (**grades > 0**), and **grades** is **0**, the second condition (**total/grades > 60**) will attempt to divide **total** by **0**. This will result in a program error called an *exception*, which could cause the program to terminate. We discuss exceptions in detail in Chapter 8, Exception Handling.

The *logical AND* (**&**) and *logical OR* (**|**) operators are similar to the conditional AND and conditional OR operators, respectively. However, the logical operators always evaluate both of their operands (i.e., there is no short-circuit evaluation). Therefore, the expression

```
gender == 1 & age >= 65
```

evaluates **age >= 65**, regardless of whether **gender** is equal to **1**. This feature is useful if the right operand of the logical AND or logical OR operator includes a needed *side effect*, such as a modification of a variable's value. For example, the expression

```
birthday == true & Console::WriteLine( age )
```

guarantees that variable **age** is printed in the preceding expression, regardless of whether the overall expression is true or false. Likewise, if we want the condition in the right operand to be the result of a mathematical operation, and we want the operation to execute in any case, then we can use the **|** operator.

Testing and Debugging Tip 3.2

Avoid using expressions with side effects in conditions. The side effects might look clever, but they often cause subtle errors and can be confusing to other people who read or maintain your code.

The logical operators (**&** and **|**) also differ from the conditional operators (**&&** and **||**) in their return values. While the conditional operators return boolean values (**true** or **false**), the logical operators are *bitwise* operators and return integer values (**0** or **1**). We discuss bitwise operators in Appendix I, Bit Manipulation.

A condition containing the *logical exclusive OR* (^) operator (sometimes known as the logical XOR operator) is true *if and only if one of its operands results in a true value and one results in a false value*. If both operands are true or both are false, the result of the entire condition is false. This operator evaluates both of its operands (i.e., there is no short-circuit evaluation).

MC++ provides the **!** (logical negation) operator to enable a programmer to "reverse" the meaning of a condition. Unlike the operators **&&**, **&**, **||**, **|** and **^**, which combine two conditions (and thus are binary operators), the logical negation operator has only a single condition as an operand (and thus is a unary operator). The logical negation operator is placed before a condition to choose a path of execution if the original condition (without the logical negation operator) is false. For example, the following **if** structure

```
if ( !finished )
    Console::WriteLine( "Not finished." );
```

will execute its body only if **finished** is false.

The console application in Fig. 3.13 demonstrates all the conditional and logical operators by displaying their truth tables in the console window.

```
1   // Fig. 3.13: LogicalOperators.cpp
2   // Demonstrating the logical operators.
3
4   #using <mscorlib.dll>
5
6   using namespace System;
7
8   int main()
9   {
10
11      // testing conditional AND operator (&&)
12      Console::WriteLine( String::Concat(
13         S"Conditional AND (&&)",
14         S"\nfalse && false: ", ( false && false ).ToString(),
15         S"\nfalse && true:  ", ( false && true ).ToString(),
16         S"\ntrue && false:  ", ( true && false ).ToString(),
17         S"\ntrue && true:   ", ( true && true ).ToString() ) );
18
19      // testing conditional OR operator (||)
20      Console::WriteLine( String::Concat(
21         S"\n\nConditional OR (||)",
22         S"\nfalse || false: ", ( false || false ).ToString(),
23         S"\nfalse || true:  ", ( false || true ).ToString(),
24         S"\ntrue || false:  ", ( true || false ).ToString(),
25         S"\ntrue || true:   ", ( true || true ).ToString() ) );
26
27      // testing logical AND operator (&)
28      Console::WriteLine( String::Concat(
29         S"\n\nLogical AND (&)",
30         S"\nfalse & false: ",
31         ( false & false ) ? S"True" : S"False",
32         S"\nfalse & true:  ",
33         ( false & true ) ? S"True" : S"False",
34         S"\ntrue & false:  ",
35         ( true & false ) ? S"True" : S"False",
36         S"\ntrue & true:   ",
37         ( true & true ) ? S"True" : S"False" ) );
```

Fig. 3.13   Conditional and logical operators. (Part 1 of 3.)

```
38
39        // testing logical OR operator (|)
40        Console::WriteLine( String::Concat(
41           S"\n\nLogical OR (|)",
42           S"\nfalse | false: ",
43           ( false | false ) ? S"True" : S"False",
44           S"\nfalse | true:  ",
45           ( false | true ) ? S"True" : S"False",
46           S"\ntrue | false:  ",
47           ( true | false ) ? S"True" : S"False",
48           S"\ntrue | true:   ",
49           ( true | true ) ? S"True" : S"False" ) );
50
51        // testing logical exclusive OR operator (^)
52        Console::WriteLine( String::Concat(
53           S"\n\nLogical exclusive OR (^)",
54           S"\nfalse ^ false: ",
55           ( false ^ false ) ? S"True" : S"False",
56           S"\nfalse ^ true:  ",
57           ( false ^ true ) ? S"True" : S"False",
58           S"\ntrue ^ false:  ",
59           ( true ^ false ) ? S"True" : S"False",
60           S"\ntrue ^ true:   ",
61           ( true ^ true ) ? S"True" : S"False" ) );
62
63        // testing logical NOT operator (!)
64        Console::WriteLine( String::Concat(
65           S"\n\nLogical NOT (!)",
66           S"\n!false: ", ( !false ).ToString(),
67           S"\n!true: ", ( !true ).ToString() ) );
68
69        return 0;
70     } // end main
```

```
Conditional AND (&&)
false && false: False
false && true:  False
true && false:  False
true && true:   True


Conditional OR (||)
false || false: False
false || true:  True
true || false:  True
true || true:   True

Logical AND (&)
false & false: False
false & true:  False
true & false:  False
true & true:   True
```

continued at the top of the next page

Fig. 3.13   Conditional and logical operators. (Part 2 of 3.)

continued from the previous page

```
Logical OR (|)
false | false: False
false | true:  True
true  | false: True
true  | true:  True


Logical exclusive OR (^)
false ^ false: False
false ^ true:  True
true  ^ false: True
true  ^ true:  False


Logical NOT (!)
!false: True
!true:  False
```

Fig. 3.13   Conditional and logical operators. (Part 3 of 3.)

Lines 12–17 demonstrate the **&&** operator; lines 28–37 demonstrate the **&** operator. The remainder of the program demonstrates the **||**, **|**, **^** and **!** operators. Lines 12–25 output the string representations of the expressions using method **ToString**. In the case of **&&**, **||** and **!**, the string representation of the expression is **"False"** or **"True"**. For **&**, **|** and **^**, however, the expressions evaluate to **0** or **1**. We use the ternary conditional operator **?:** (lines 28–61) to output **"False"** instead of **0** and **"True"** instead of **1**. This is simply to create consistent output.

Figure 3.14 shows the precedence and associativity of the MC++ operators that have been introduced thus far. The operators are shown from top to bottom in decreasing order of precedence.

Operators	Associativity	Type
( )	left to right	parentheses
++ --	right to left	unary postfix
++ -- + - ! (*type*)	right to left	unary prefix
* / %	left to right	multiplicative
+ -	left to right	additive
< <= > >=	left to right	relational
== !=	left to right	equality
&	left to right	logical AND
^	left to right	logical exclusive OR (XOR)
		left to right	logical inclusive OR
&&	left to right	conditional AND

Fig. 3.14   Precedence and associativity of the operators discussed thus far. (Part 1 of 2.)

Operators	Associativity	Type
||	left to right	conditional OR
?:	right to left	conditional
= += -= *= /= %=	right to left	assignment

Fig. 3.14 Precedence and associativity of the operators discussed thus far. (Part 2 of 2.)

3.14 Summary

Program control is important in any programming language, as it specifies the order in which statements execute in a computer program. Normally, statements in a program execute one after the other in the order in which they appear. This process is called sequential execution. There are several control structures that enable the programmer to specify that the next statement to execute may be other than the next one in sequence. This technique is called transfer of control.

The **if** and **if/else** selection structures are used to select actions to perform, based on the truth or falsity of a condition. These structures are known as the single-selection and double-selection structures, respectively. The **switch** structure, known as a multiple-selection structure, selects among several actions.

Repetition structures repeat actions, based on the truth or falsity of a condition. MC++'s repetition structures include the **while**, **for** and **do/while** repetition structures.

The **break** statement is used to perform an immediate exit from a structure, while the **continue** statement is used to perform the next iteration in a repetition structure.

The unary increment and decrement operators add or subtract **1** from a variable. The conditional and logical operators are used to form complex conditions by combining simple conditions.

Functions and Arrays

Objectives

- To construct programs modularly from functions and methods.
- To become familiar with common math methods available in the Framework Class Library.
- To understand the mechanisms for passing data between functions.
- To understand how the visibility of identifiers is limited to specific regions of programs.
- To become familiar with the array data structure.
- To understand how to declare a managed array, initialize a managed array and refer to individual elements of a managed array.
- To declare and manipulate multiple-subscripted managed arrays.

Form ever follows function.
Louis Henri Sullivan

E pluribus unum.
(One composed of many.)
Virgil

Now go, write it before them in a table,
and note it in a book.
Isaiah 30:8

When you call me that, smile.
Owen Wister

Outline

4.1 Introduction

Most computer programs that solve real problems are much larger than the programs presented in the first few chapters of this text. Experience has shown that the best way to develop and maintain a large program is to construct it from small, simple pieces. This technique is known as *divide and conquer.* In the previous chapters, we called various methods and functions to perform specific tasks. We also defined our own **main** functions, specifying the actions to occur in our program. This chapter investigates functions in depth, describing many key features of Managed Extensions for C++ that facilitate the design, implementation, operation and maintenance of large programs.

The chapter also introduces data structures. *Arrays* are data structures consisting of data items of the same type. Arrays are "static" entities, which means that they remain the same size once they are created. In this chapter, we show how to create and access arrays; We then demonstrate how to create more sophisticated arrays that have multiple dimensions. Chapter 19, Data Structures and Collections, introduces dynamic data structures, such as lists, queues, stacks and trees, which can grow and shrink as programs execute. In that chapter, we also introduce the .NET Framework's predefined data structures that enable the programmer to use existing data structures for lists, queues, stacks and tree rather than having to "reinvent the wheel."

4.2 Functions and Methods in Managed Extensions for C++

MC++ programs are written by combining new functions, methods and classes that the programmer writes with "prepackaged" methods and classes available in the *.NET Framework*

Class Library (*FCL*). In this chapter, we concentrate on functions and methods. We discuss classes in detail in Chapter 5, Object-Based Programming.

A *method* is a function that is a member of a class. The FCL provides a rich collection of classes and methods for performing common mathematical calculations, string manipulations, character manipulations, input/output operations, error checking and many other useful operations. This set of preexisting code makes the programmer's job easier by providing many capabilities that programmers need. The FCL methods are part of the .NET Framework, which includes the FCL classes **Console** and **String** used in earlier examples.

Software Engineering Observation 4.1

*Familiarize yourself with the rich collection of classes and methods in the FCL (**msdn.mi-crosoft.com/library/en-us/cpref/html/cpref_start.asp**).*

Software Engineering Observation 4.2

When possible, use .NET Framework classes and methods instead of writing new classes and methods. This practice reduces both program development time and errors.

Programmers can write functions to define specific tasks that may be used at many points in a program. Such functions are known as *programmer-defined* (or *user-defined*) *functions*. The actual statements defining the function are written only once and are hidden from other functions.

A function is *invoked* (i.e., made to perform its designated task) by a *function call*. The function call specifies the name of the function and may provide information (as *arguments*) that the called function requires to perform its task. When the function call completes, the function either returns a result to the *calling function* (or *caller*) or simply returns control to the calling function. The calling function does not "know" *how* the called function performs its designated tasks; in particular, the called function may call other functions, and the calling function will be "unaware" of these calls. We will see how this "hiding" of implementation details promotes good software engineering.

Functions are called by writing the name of the function, followed by a left parenthesis, the *argument* (or a comma-separated list of arguments) of the function and a right parenthesis. The parentheses may be empty if the called function needs no arguments.

Variables declared in function definitions are *local variables*—only the function that defines them "knows" they exist. Most functions have a list of *parameters* that enable function calls to communicate information between functions. A function's parameters are also variables local to that function and are not visible in any other functions. Local variables are discussed in more detail in Section 4.8.

4.3 Function Definitions

The programs that have been presented thus far have each contained a function **main** that called existing FCL methods to accomplish the program's tasks. We now consider how to write programmer-defined functions.

Consider a program that calculates the square of the integers from 1–10 (Fig. 4.1). The program invokes programmer-defined function **Square** on line 15. The parentheses, **()**, after **Square** represent the *function-call operator*. At this point, the program makes a copy of the value of **counter** (the argument to the function call), and program control transfers to function **Square** (defined at lines 21–24). Function **Square** receives the copy of the value of **counter** in the *parameter* **y**. Then **Square** calculates **y * y** in a ***return*** statement (line 23) to return (i.e., give back) the result of the calculation to the statement that invoked **Square** (located in line 15). Lines 13–15 concatenate **"The square of"**, the value of **counter**, **" is "**, the value of the function call and a newline character to the console output.

Line 8 is the *function prototype* for function **Square**. A function prototype provides the compiler with the name of the function, the type of data returned by the function, the number of parameters the function expects to receive, the types of the parameters and the order in which these parameters are expected. The compiler uses function prototypes to validate function calls. The data type **int** in parentheses informs the compiler that function **Square** expects an integer parameter. The data type **int** to the left of the function name informs the caller that **Square** returns an integer result. Parameter **y** (line 21) is the name that holds the value passed to **Square** as an argument. The parameter name provides access to the argument value, so that code in the function body can use the value. The **return** statement in **Square** (line 23) passes the result of the calculation **y * y** back to the calling statement.

Good Programming Practice 4.1

Place a blank line between adjacent function definitions to separate the functions and enhance program readability.

The format of a function definition is

> *return-value-type function-name* **(** *parameter-list* **)**
> **{**
>   *declarations and statements*
> **}**

The first line is sometimes called the *function header*. The *function name* is any valid identifier. The *return-value-type* is the data type of the result that the function returns to its caller. The *return-value-type* ***void*** indicates that a function does not return a value. Functions can return at most one value.

```
1   // Fig. 4.1: SquareInt.cpp
2   // Demonstrates a programmer-defined square function.
3
4   #using <mscorlib.dll>
5
6   using namespace System;
7
8   int Square( int );    // function prototype
9
10  int main()
11  {
12     for ( int counter = 1; counter <= 10; counter++ )
13        Console::WriteLine( String::Concat( S"The square of ",
14           counter.ToString(), S" is ",
15           Square( counter ).ToString() ) );
16
17     return 0;
18  }
```

Fig. 4.1   Programmer-defined function **Square**. (Part 1 of 2.)

```
19
20   // function definition
21   int Square( int y )
22   {
23       return y * y;  // return square of y
24   } // end function square
```

```
The square of 1 is 1
The square of 2 is 4
The square of 3 is 9
The square of 4 is 16
The square of 5 is 25
The square of 6 is 36
The square of 7 is 49
The square of 8 is 64
The square of 9 is 81
The square of 10 is 100
```

Fig. 4.1   Programmer-defined function **Square**. (Part 2 of 2.)

Common Programming Error 4.1

Omitting the return-value-type *in a function definition is a syntax error. If a function does not return a value, the function's* return-value-type *must be **void**.*

Common Programming Error 4.2

Forgetting to return a value from a function that is supposed to return a value may cause a syntax error. If a return-value-type *other than **void** is specified, the function should contain a **return** statement that returns a value.*

Common Programming Error 4.3

*Returning a value from a function whose return type has been declared **void** causes a syntax error.*

Common Programming Error 4.4

Omitting the opening or closing brace of a function is a syntax error.

The *parameter-list* is a comma-separated list in which the function declares each parameter's type and name. The function call normally must specify one argument for each parameter in the function definition, and the arguments must appear in the same order as the parameters in the function definition. The arguments also must be compatible with the parameter's type. For example, a parameter of type **double** could receive the values 7.35, 22 or –.03546, but not **"hello"**, because a **double** variable cannot contain a **String *** value. If a function does not receive any values, the parameter list is empty (i.e., the function name is followed by an empty set of parentheses). Each parameter in a function's parameter list must have a data type; otherwise, a syntax error occurs.

Common Programming Error 4.5

*Declaring function parameters of the same type as **float x, y** instead of **float x, float y** is a syntax error, because a type is required for each parameter in the parameter list.*

Common Programming Error 4.6

Placing a semicolon after the right parenthesis enclosing the parameter list of a function definition is a syntax error.

Common Programming Error 4.7

Redefining a function parameter in the function's body is a syntax error.

Common Programming Error 4.8

Passing to a function an argument that is not compatible with the corresponding parameter's type is a syntax error.

The declarations and statements within braces form the *function body*. The function body also is referred to as a block. Variables can be declared in any block, and blocks can be nested.

Common Programming Error 4.9

Defining a function inside another function is a syntax error (i.e., functions cannot be nested).

Good Programming Practice 4.2

Choosing meaningful function names and parameter names makes programs more readable and helps avoid excessive use of comments.

Software Engineering Observation 4.3

As a rule of thumb, a function should fit in an editor window. Regardless of how long a function is, it should perform one task well. Small functions promote software reusability.

Testing and Debugging Tip 4.1

Small functions are easier to test, debug and understand than large functions.

Software Engineering Observation 4.4

A function requiring a large number of parameters might be performing too many tasks. If possible, consider dividing the function into smaller functions that perform separate tasks. As a rule of thumb, the function header should be able to fit on one line.

Software Engineering Observation 4.5

The number, type and order of arguments in a function call usually must exactly match those of the parameters in the corresponding function header.

There are three ways to return control to the point at which a function was invoked. If the function does not return a result (i.e., the function has a **void** return type), control returns when the program reaches the function-ending right brace or when the statement

```
return;
```

executes. If the function does return a result, the statement

```
return expression;
```

returns the value of *expression* to the caller. When a **return** statement executes, control returns immediately to the point at which the function was invoked.

Function calls commonly pass values for each function argument. Programmers can specify that such an argument be a *default argument*, and the programmer can provide a default value for that argument. When a default argument is omitted in a function call, the default value of that argument is inserted by the compiler and passed in the call. Default arguments must be the rightmost (trailing) arguments in a function's parameter list. When one is calling a function with two or more default arguments, if an omitted argument is not the rightmost argument in the argument list, all arguments to the right of that argument also must be omitted. Default arguments are specified with the first occurrence of the function name—typically, in the prototype. For example, to specify a default value of **2** for argument **y** in function **Square**, we would change the function prototype to:

```
int Square( int y = 2 );
```

while leaving the function definition exactly the same. We could then call function **Square** without any arguments (as **Square()**), and the compiler would insert the value **2** for argument **y**. However, we would not lose the ability to specify a different value for **y** (e.g., **Square(5)**).

Good Programming Practice 4.3

Using default arguments can simplify writing function calls. However, some programmers feel that explicitly specifying all arguments is clearer.

Common Programming Error 4.10

Default arguments must be the rightmost (trailing) arguments. Specifying a default argument that is not a rightmost argument is a syntax error.

Notice the syntax that invokes function **Square** in Fig. 4.1—we use the function name, followed by the arguments to the function in parentheses. There are four ways to call a function or a method with arguments—by using a function name by itself (such as **Square(x)**), by using a pointer to an object followed by the arrow operator (**->**) and the function name (such as **string1->CompareTo(string2)**), by using the variable name for the object or a reference to the object followed by the dot operator (**.**) and the function name (such as **x.ToString()**) and by using a class name followed by the scope resolution operator and the method name (such as **Math::Sqrt(9.0)**, where we want to call method **Sqrt** of class **Math**, located in namespace **System**). Pointers and references are used to access reference types, such as **String**s (Section 4.6). We discuss the arrow operator (**->**) and the dot operator (**.**) in Chapter 5, Object-Based Programming.

4.4 Argument Promotion

Another important feature of function definitions is the *coercion of arguments* (i.e., the forcing of arguments to the type appropriate to pass to a function). This process commonly is referred to as *implicit conversion*, in that a copy of the variable's value is converted to a different type without an explicit cast. *Explicit conversion* occurs when an explicit cast specifies that conversion is to occur. Such conversions also can be done with class **Convert** in namespace **System**. Visual C++ .NET supports both widening and narrowing conversions—*widening conversion* occurs when a type is converted to a type that holds at least the same amount of data, and *narrowing conversion* occurs when a type is converted to a type that holds a smaller amount of data. Figure 4.2 provides size information for the various built-in types of .NET, and Fig. 4.3 shows safe widening conversions—widening conversions that do not result in the loss of data. Note that the data types shown in Fig. 4.3 are those provided by the .NET Framework.[1]

Type	Bits	Values	Standard
Boolean (*bool*)	8	**true** or **false**	
Char (*__wchar_t*)	8	**'\u0000'** to **'\uFFFF'**	(Unicode® character set)
Byte (*char*)	8	0 to 255	(unsigned)
SByte (*signed char*)	8	−128 to +127	
Int16 (*short*)	16	−32,768 to +32,767	
UInt16 (*unsigned short*)	16	0 to 65,535	(unsigned)
Int32 (*int* or *long*)	32	−2,147,483,648 to +2,147,483,647	
UInt32 (*unsigned int/long*)	32	0 to 4,294,967,295	(unsigned)
Int64 (*__int64*)	64	−9,223,372,036,854,775,808 to +9,223,372,036,854,775,807	
UInt64 (*unsigned __int64*)	64	0 to 18,446,744,073,709,551,615	(unsigned)
Decimal (*Decimal*)	96	$-7.9 \infty 10^{28}$ to $+7.9 \infty 10^{28}$	
Single (*float*)	32	$-3.4 \infty 10^{38}$ to $+3.4 \infty 10^{38}$	(IEEE 754 floating point)
Double (*double*)	64	$-1.7 \infty 10^{308}$ to $+1.7 \infty 10^{308}$	(IEEE 754 floating point)
Object (Object *)			
String (String *)			(Unicode® character set)

Fig. 4.2   Built-in data types in the .NET Framework.

Type	Can be Safely Converted to Type(s)
Byte	UInt16, Int16, UInt32, Int32, UInt64, Int64, Single, Double or Decimal
SByte	Int16, Int32, Int64, Single, Double or Decimal
Int16	Int32, Int64, Single, Double or Decimal
UInt16	UInt32, Int32, UInt64, Int64, Single, Double or Decimal

Fig. 4.3   Safe widening conversions. (Part 1 of 2.)

1. For more information about type conversions in the .NET Framework, visit **msdn.microsoft.com/library/en-us/cpguide/html/cpcontypeconversiontables.asp**.

Type	Can be Safely Converted to Type(s)
Char	UInt16, UInt32, Int32, UInt64, Int64, Single, Double or Decimal
Int32	Int64, Double or Decimal
UInt32	Int64, Double or Decimal
Int64	Decimal
UInt64	Decimal
Single	Double

Fig. 4.3   Safe widening conversions. (Part 2 of 2.)

For example, method **Sqrt** of class **Math** can be called with an integer argument, even though the method is defined in class **Math** to receive a **double** argument. The statement

```
Console::WriteLine( Math::Sqrt( 4 ) );
```

correctly evaluates **Math::Sqrt(4)** and displays the value **2**. Visual C++ .NET implicitly converts the **int** value **4** to the **double** value **4.0** before passing the value to **Math::Sqrt**. In many cases, Visual C++ .NET applies implicit conversions to argument values that do not correspond precisely to the parameter types in the function definition. In some cases, attempting these conversions leads to compiler warnings because Visual C++ .NET uses conversion rules to judge when a widening conversion can occur. In our previous **Math::Sqrt** example, Visual C++ .NET converts an **int** to a **double** without changing its value. However, converting a **double** to an **int** truncates the fractional part of the **double** value. Converting large integer types to small integer types (e.g., **int** to **short**) also can result in changed values. Such narrowing conversions, as well as some widening conversions, can result in a loss of information; therefore, the programmer could be forced to perform the conversion with a cast operation to avoid compiler warnings. The conversion rules apply to expressions containing values of two or more data types (also referred to as *mixed-type expressions*) and to primitive data-type values passed as arguments to functions. Primitive data types (e.g., **int**) also are referred to as built-in data types because they are provided by the language and consequently do not need to be defined by the programmer. Visual C++ .NET converts the type of each value in a mixed-type expression to the "highest" type in the expression. Visual C++ .NET creates a temporary copy of each value and uses it in the expression—the original values remain unchanged. A function argument's type can be promoted to any "higher" type. The table of Fig. 4.3 can be used to determine the highest type in an expression. For each type in the left column, the corresponding types in the right column are considered to be of higher type. For instance, types **Int64**, **Double** and **Decimal** are higher than type **Int32**.

Converting values to lower types can result in data loss. In cases where information could be lost through conversion, the compiler might issue a warning (although the program might still be executable). To avoid such compiler warnings, programmers can use a cast to force the conversion to occur. To invoke our **Square** function, which takes an **int** parameter (Fig. 4.1) with the **double** variable **y**, the function call would be written as

```
int result = Square( static_cast< int >( y ) );
```

This statement explicitly casts (converts) a copy of the value of **y** to an integer for use in function **Square**. Thus, if **y**'s value is **4.5**, function **Square** returns **16**, not **20.25**. In the previous function call, we use *cast operator* **static_cast** to perform the cast operation. The **static_cast** operator performs an unchecked conversion (i.e., the compiler does not determine whether the conversion can be performed at run time) between data types at compile time. For operator **static_cast**, the value to cast is contained in parentheses (e.g., **(y)**), and the desired data type is contained in angle brackets (e.g., **< int >**). There are four other cast operators available in MC++. We discuss these in Chapter 7, Object-Oriented Programming: Polymorphism.

Performance Tip 4.1

*It is preferable to use operator **static_cast** when converting numeric data types because it does not incur the overhead of a run time check.*

Common Programming Error 4.11

*When performing a narrowing conversion (e.g., **double** to **int**), converting a primitive-data-type value to another primitive data type might result in a loss of data.*

4.5 Managed Extensions for C++ Namespaces

As we have seen, MC++ contains many predefined classes that are grouped into namespaces. Collectively, we refer to this preexisting code as the .NET Framework Class Library (FCL). The actual code for the classes is located in **.dll** files called *assemblies*. Assemblies are the packaging units for code. [*Note*: Assemblies can be composed of many different types of files.]

Throughout the text, **using** statements specify the namespaces we use in each program. For example, a program includes the statement

```
using namespace System;
```

to tell the compiler that we are using the **System** namespace. This **using** statement allows us to write **Console::WriteLine** rather than **System::Console::Write-Line** throughout the program.

We exercise a large number of the FCL classes in this book. Figure 4.4 lists a subset of the many namespaces in the FCL and provides a brief description of each. We use classes from these namespaces and others throughout the book. This table introduces readers to the variety of reusable components in the FCL. When learning MC++, spend time reading the descriptions of the classes in the documentation.

Namespace	Description
System	Contains essential classes and data types (**Int32**, **Char**, **String**, etc.).
System::Data	Contains classes that form ADO .NET, used for database access and manipulation.

Fig. 4.4   Some namespaces in the Framework Class Library. (Part 1 of 2.)

Namespace	Description
`System::Drawing`	Contains classes used for drawing and graphics.
`System::IO`	Contains classes for the input and output of data, such as with files.
`System::Threading`	Contains classes for multithreading, used to run multiple parts of a program simultaneously.
`System::Windows::Forms`	Contains classes used to create graphical user interfaces.
`System::Xml`	Contains classes used to process XML data.

Fig. 4.4 Some namespaces in the Framework Class Library. (Part 2 of 2.)

The set of namespaces available in the FCL is quite large. In addition to the namespaces summarized in Fig. 4.4, the FCL includes namespaces for complex graphics, advanced graphical user interfaces, printing, advanced networking, security, multimedia, accessibility (for people with disabilities) and many more. For an overview of the namespaces in the FCL, look up "Class Library" in the **Help** index or visit:

```
msdn.microsoft.com/library/default.asp?url=/library/en-us/
cpref/html/cpref_start.asp
```

4.6 Value Types and Reference Types

In the next section, we will discuss passing arguments to functions by value and by reference. To understand this, we first need to make a distinction between types in MC++. Data types are either *value types* or *reference types*. A variable of a value type contains data of that type. A variable of a reference type, in contrast, contains the address of the location in memory where the data is stored. Value types are accessed directly and are passed by value; reference types is accessed through pointers or references[2] and are passed by reference.

Value types normally contain small pieces of data, such as **int** or **bool** values. Reference types, on the other hand, usually refer to large objects. We discuss objects in detail in Chapters 5–7 (Object-Based Programming, Object-Oriented Programming: Inheritance and Object-Oriented Programming: Polymorphism).

MC++ includes built-in value types and reference types. The built-in value types are the *integral types* (**signed char**, **char**, **__wchar_t**, **short**, **unsigned short**, **int**, **unsigned int**, **long**, **unsigned long**, **__int64** and **unsigned __int64**), the *floating-point types* (**float** and **double**) and the types **Decimal** and **bool**. In MC++, these data types map to data types provided by the .NET Framework (**Int32**, **Char**, **Double**, etc.). The built-in reference types are **String *** and **Object ***. Programmers can create new value types and reference types; the reference types and value

---

2. References provide functionality similar to that of pointers. Developers can use references to access and modify objects (just as with pointers), using a slightly different syntax. However, pointers are more common in MC++ than are references. For simplicity, we exclusively use pointers to refer to reference type objects. More information about references can be found at **msdn.microsoft.com/library/en-us/vcmxspec/html/ vcManagedExtensionsSpec_8.asp**.

types that programmers can create include classes (Chapter 5), interfaces (Chapter 5) and delegates (Chapter 6).

The table in Fig. 4.2 lists the .NET primitive data types, which are building blocks for more complicated types.[3] Their MC++ aliases are shown in parentheses. Like C and C++, MC++ requires all variables to have a type before they can be used in a program. For this reason, MC++ is referred to as a *strongly typed language*.

In C and C++ programs, programmers frequently must write separate program versions to support different computer platforms, because the primitive data types are not guaranteed to be identical from computer to computer. For example, an **int** value on one computer might occupy 16 bits (2 bytes) of memory, whereas an **int** value on another computer might occupy 32 bits (4 bytes) of memory. In MC++, **int** (**Int32**) values are always 32 bits (4 bytes).

Each data type in Fig. 4.2 is listed with its size in bits (there are 8 bits to a byte) and its range of values. The architects of .NET wanted code to be portable; therefore, they chose to use internationally recognized standards for both character formats (Unicode®) and floating-point numbers (IEEE 754). Unicode® is discussed in Appendix D.

4.7 Passing Arguments: Pass-by-Value vs. Pass-by-Reference

Two ways to pass arguments to functions in many programming languages are *pass-by-value* and *pass-by-reference*. When an argument is passed by value, the called function receives a *copy* of the argument's value.

Testing and Debugging Tip 4.2

With pass-by-value, changes to the called function's copy do not affect the original variable's value. This prevents some possible side effects that hinder the development of correct and reliable software systems.

When an argument is passed via pass-by-reference, the caller gives the function the ability to access and modify the caller's original data directly. Pass-by-reference can improve performance because it eliminates the overhead of copying large data items (i.e., reference types); however, pass-by-reference can weaken security, because the called function can modify the caller's data.

Software Engineering Observation 4.6

*When returning information from a function via a **return** statement, value-type variables always are returned by value (i.e., a copy is returned), and reference-type variables are always returned by reference (i.e., a pointer to the object is returned).*

To pass a pointer to a function, specify the pointer name in the function call. Then, in the function body, refer to the object, using the parameter name. This refers to the original object in memory, to allow the called function to access the original object directly.

In Section 4.6, we discussed value types and reference types. One of the major differences between the two data types is that value-type variables are passed to methods by value and reference-type variables are passed to methods by reference. What if the programmer would like to pass a value type by reference? In this section, we introduce *refer-*

---

3. For more information about data types provided by the .NET Framework (and their MC++ aliases), visit **msdn.microsoft.com/library/en-us/cpguide/html/ cpconthenetframeworkclasslibrary.asp**.

ence parameters, a means by which MC++ performs call-by-reference. A reference parameter is an alias for its corresponding argument. To indicate that a function parameter is passed by reference, follow the parameter's type in the function prototype by an ampersand (**&**); use the same convention when listing the parameter's type in the function header. In the function call, pass the variable name, and it will be passed by reference. The original variable in the calling function can be modified directly by the called function.

Figure 4.5 compares pass-by-value and pass-by-reference with reference parameters. The "styles" of the arguments in the calls to **squareByValue** and **squareByReference** are identical, i.e., both variables are mentioned by name. Without checking the function prototypes or function definitions, it is not possible to tell from the calls alone whether either function can modify its arguments.

```
1   // Fig. 4.5: PassByReference.cpp
2   // Comparing pass-by-value and pass-by-reference.
3
4   #using <mscorlib.dll>
5
6   using namespace System;
7
8   int squareByValue( int );
9   void squareByReference( int & );
10
11  int main()
12  {
13     int y = 2, z = 4;
14
15     Console::Write( S"Original value of y: " );
16     Console::WriteLine( y.ToString() );
17     Console::Write( S"Original value of z: " );
18     Console::WriteLine( z.ToString() );
19
20     Console::Write( S"Value of y after squareByValue: " );
21     squareByValue( y );
22     Console::WriteLine( y.ToString() );
23
24     Console::Write( S"Value of z after squareByReference: " );
25     squareByReference( z );
26     Console::WriteLine( z.ToString() );
27
28     return 0;
29  }
30
31  int squareByValue( int a )
32  {
33     return a * a;   // caller's argument not modified
34  }
35
36  void squareByReference( int &cRef )
37  {
38     cRef *= cRef;   // caller's argument modified
39  }
```

Fig. 4.5   Call-by-reference demonstration. (Part 1 of 2.)

```
Original value of y: 2
Original value of z: 4
Value of y after squareByValue: 2
Value of z after squareByReference: 16
```

Fig. 4.5   Call-by-reference demonstration. (Part 2 of 2.)

Common Programming Error 4.12

Because reference parameters are mentioned only by name in the body of the called function, the programmer might inadvertently treat reference parameters as pass-by-value parameters. This can cause unexpected side effects if the original copies of the variables are changed by the calling function.

4.8 Scope Rules

The *scope* (sometimes called *declaration space*) of an identifier for a variable, pointer or function is the portion of the program in which the identifier can be accessed. A local variable or pointer declared in a block can be used only in that block or in blocks nested within that block. Four scopes for an identifier are *file scope*, *function scope*, *block scope* and *function-prototype scope*. Later we will see two other scopes—*class scope* (Chapter 5) and *namespace scope*.

An identifier declared outside any function has *file scope*. Such an identifier is "known" in all functions from the point at which the identifier is declared until the end of the file. *Global variables* (i.e., variables that can be referenced anywhere in an application), function prototypes placed outside a function and function definitions have file scope.

Labels, identifiers followed by a colon (such as **start:**), are implementation details that functions hide from one another. Labels are the only identifiers with *function scope*. Labels can be used anywhere in the function in which they appear, but cannot be referenced outside the function body. Labels are used in **switch** structures (as **case** labels). Hiding—more formally called *information hiding*—implementation details is one of the fundamental principles of good software engineering.

Identifiers declared inside a block have *block scope* (*local-variable declaration space*). Block scope begins at the identifier's declaration and ends at the block's terminating right brace (**}**). Local variables of a function have block scope, as do function parameters, which are local variables of the function. Any block may contain variable declarations. When blocks are nested in a function's body and an identifier declared in an outer block has the same name as an identifier declared in an inner block, the identifier in the outer block is "hidden" until the inner block terminates. While executing, the inner block sees the value of its own local identifier and not the value of the identically named identifier in the enclosing block. In Chapter 5, Object-Based Programming, we discuss how to access such "hidden" instance variables. The reader should note that block scope also applies to functions and **for** structures. However, any variable declared in the initialization portion of the **for** header will still be in scope after that **for** structure terminates.[4] Refer to Chapter 3, Control Structures, for a discussion of the scope of **for** structures.

---

4. Recall from Chapter 3, Control Structures, that this behavior can be avoided using compiler option **/Zc:forScope**.

The only identifiers with *function-prototype scope* are those used in the parameter list of a function prototype. Function prototypes do not require names in the parameter list—only types are required. If a name is used in the parameter list of a function prototype, the compiler ignores the name. Identifiers used in a function prototype can be redeclared and reused elsewhere in the program without ambiguity.

Common Programming Error 4.13

Accidentally using the same name for the identifiers of both an inner block and an outer block, when in fact that programmer wants the identifier in the outer block to be active for the duration of the inner block, is normally a logic error.

Good Programming Practice 4.4

Avoid variable names that hide names in outer scopes.

The program in Fig. 4.6 demonstrates scoping issues with global variables, *automatic local variables* and **static** local variables. Automatic local variables are created when the block in which they are declared is entered, and they are destroyed when the block is exited. Local variables declared as **static** retain their values even when they are out of scope.

A global variable **x** is declared and initialized to **1** (line 12). This global variable is hidden in any block (or function) in which another variable **x** is declared. In **main**, a local variable **x** is declared and initialized to **5** (line 16). This variable is printed to show that the global **x** is hidden in **main**.

```
1   // Fig. 4.6: Scoping.cpp
2   // Demonstrating variable scope.
3
4   #using <mscorlib.dll>
5
6   using namespace System;
7
8   void FunctionA();
9   void FunctionB();
10  void FunctionC();
11
12  int x = 1;    // global variable
13
14  int main()
15  {
16     int x = 5;    // local variable to main
17
18     Console::WriteLine( S"local x in outer scope of main is {0}",
19        x.ToString() );
20
21     {  // start new scope
22        int x = 7;
23        Console::Write( S"local x in inner scope of main is {0}",
24           x.ToString() );
25     }
```

Fig. 4.6   Scoping. (Part 1 of 3.)

```
26
27      Console::WriteLine( S"local x in outer scope of main is {0}",
28         x.ToString() );
29
30      FunctionA();    // functionA has automatic local x
31      FunctionB();    // functionB has static local x
32      FunctionC();    // functionC uses global x
33      FunctionA();    // functionA reinitializes automatic local x
34      FunctionB();    // static local x retains its previous value
35      FunctionC();    // global x also retains its value
36
37      Console::WriteLine( S"local x in main is {0}", x.ToString() );
38
39      return 0;
40   } // end main
41
42   void FunctionA()
43   {
44      int x = 25;     // initialized each time functionA is called
45
46      Console::WriteLine( S"local x in functionA is {0} {1}",
47         x.ToString(), S"after entering functionA" );
48
49      ++x; // increment local variable x
50
51      Console::WriteLine( S"local x in functionA is {0} {1}",
52         x.ToString(), S"before exiting functionA" );
53   } // end functionA
54
55   void FunctionB()
56   {
57      static int x = 50;    // static initialization only
58                            // first time functionB is called
59
60      Console::WriteLine( S"local static x is {0} {1}",
61         x.ToString(), S"on entering functionB" );
62
63      ++x;
64
65      Console::WriteLine( S"local static x is {0} {1}",
66         x.ToString(), S"before exiting functionB" );
67   } // end functionB
68
69   void FunctionC()
70   {
71      Console::WriteLine( S"global x is {0} {1}", x.ToString(),
72         S"on entering functionC" );
73
74      x *= 10;
75
76      Console::WriteLine( S"global x is {0} {1}", x.ToString(),
77         S"on exiting functionC" );
78   } // end functionC
```

Fig. 4.6   Scoping. (Part 2 of 3.)

```
local x in outer scope of main is 5
local x in inner scope of main is 7
local x in outer scope of main is 5
local x in functionA is 25 after entering functionA
local x in functionA is 26 before exiting functionA
local static x is 50 on entering functionB
local static x is 51 before exiting functionB
global x is 1 on entering functionC
global x is 10 on exiting functionC
local x in functionA is 25 after entering functionA
local x in functionA is 26 before exiting functionA
local static x is 51 on entering functionB
local static x is 52 before exiting functionB
global x is 10 on entering functionC
global x is 100 on exiting functionC
local x in main is 5
```

Fig. 4.6   Scoping. (Part 3 of 3.)

Next, a new block is defined in **main**, with another local variable **x** initialized to **7**. This variable is printed to show that it hides **x** in the outer block **main**. The variable **x** with value **7** is destroyed when the block is exited, and the local variable **x** in the outer block is printed to show that it is no longer hidden. The program defines three functions—each takes no arguments and returns nothing.

Function **functionA** (lines 42–53) defines automatic variable **x** and initializes it to **25**. When **functionA** is called, the variable is printed, incremented and printed again before exiting the function. Each time this function is called, an automatic variable is recreated and initialized to **25**.

Function **functionB** (lines 55–67) declares **static** variable **x** and initializes it to **50**. When **functionB** is called, **x** is printed, incremented and printed again before exiting the function. In the next call to this function, **static** local variable **x** will contain the value **51**.

Function **functionC** (lines 69–78) does not declare any variables. Therefore, when it refers to variable **x**, the global **x** is used. When **functionC** is called, the global variable is printed, multiplied by **10** and printed again before exiting the function. The next time function **functionC** is called, the global variable has its modified value, **10**. Finally, the program prints the local variable **x** in **main** again to show that none of the function calls modified the value of **x**, because the functions all referred to variables in other scopes.

4.9 Recursion

The programs we have discussed thus far generally have been structured as functions that call one another in a hierarchical manner. For some problems, it is useful to have a function actually call itself. A *recursive function* is a function that calls itself, either directly or indirectly through another function. In this section, we consider recursion conceptually first; we then examine a program containing a simple recursive function.

Recursive problem-solving approaches have a number of elements in common. A recursive function is called to solve a problem. The function actually "knows" how to solve only the simplest case(s), or *base case(s)*. If the function is called with a base case, the function returns a result. If the function is called with a more complex problem, the function divides the problem into two conceptual pieces—a piece that the function knows how to perform (the base case) and a piece that the function does not know how to perform. To make recursion feasible, the latter piece must resemble the original problem, but be a slightly simpler or smaller version of it. The function invokes (calls) a fresh copy of itself to work on the smaller problem; this call is referred to as a *recursive call*, or a *recursion step*. The recursion step also normally includes the keyword **return**, because its result will be combined with the portion of the problem that the function knew how to solve. Such a combination will form a result that will be passed back to the original caller.

The recursion step executes while the original call to the function is still "open" (i.e., it has not finished executing). The recursion step may result in many more recursive calls, as the function divides each new subproblem into two conceptual pieces. As the function calls itself over and over, each time with a slightly simpler version of the original problem, the sequence of smaller and smaller problems must converge on the base case, so that the recursion can terminate eventually. At that point, the function recognizes the base case and returns a result to the previous copy of the function. A sequence of returns ensues up the line until the original function call returns the final result to the caller. As an example of these concepts, let us write a recursive program to perform a popular mathematical calculation.

The factorial of a nonnegative integer n, written $n!$ (and pronounced "n factorial"), is the product

$$n \cdot (n-1) \cdot (n-2) \cdot \ldots \cdot 1$$

where $1!$ is equal to 1 and $0!$ is defined as 1. For example, $5!$ is the product $5 \cdot 4 \cdot 3 \cdot 2 \cdot 1$, which is equal to 120.

The factorial of an integer **number** greater than or equal to **0** can be calculated *iteratively* (nonrecursively) via a **for** structure, as follows:

```
int factorial = 1;

for ( int counter = number; counter >= 1; counter-- )
    factorial *= counter;
```

We arrive at a recursive definition of the factorial function via the following relationship:

$$n! = n \cdot (n-1)!$$

For example, $5!$ is clearly equal to $5 \cdot 4!$, as is shown by the following calculations:

$$5! = 5 \cdot 4 \cdot 3 \cdot 2 \cdot 1$$
$$5! = 5 \cdot (4 \cdot 3 \cdot 2 \cdot 1)$$
$$5! = 5 \cdot (4!)$$

Figure 4.7 uses recursion to calculate and print the factorials of the integers 0–10. The recursive function **Factorial** (lines 20–26) first determines whether its terminating condition is **true** (i.e., **number** is less than or equal to **1**). If **number** is less than or equal to **1**, **factorial** returns **1**, no further recursion is necessary and the function returns. If **number** is greater than **1**, line 25 expresses the problem as the product of **number** and a recursive call to **Factorial**, evaluating the factorial of **number** - **1**. Note that **Factorial(number - 1)** is a slightly simpler problem than the original calculation **Factorial(number)**.

```
1    // Fig. 4.7: FactorialTest.cpp
2    // Calculating factorials with recursion.
3
4    #using <mscorlib.dll>
5
6    using namespace System;
7
8    long Factorial( long );
9
10   int main()
11   {
12      for ( long i = 0; i <= 10; i++ ) {
13         Console::Write( S"{0}! = {1}", i.ToString(),
14            Factorial( i ).ToString() );
15      }
16
17      return 0;
18   }
19
20   long Factorial( long number )
21   {
22      if ( number <= 1 )         // base case
23         return 1;
24      else
25         return number * Factorial( number - 1 );
26   }
```

```
0! = 1
1! = 1
2! = 2
3! = 6
4! = 24
5! = 120
6! = 720
7! = 5040
8! = 40320
9! = 362880
10! = 3628800
```

Fig. 4.7   Recursively calculating factorials.

Function **Factorial** receives a parameter of type **long** and returns a result of type **long**. As is seen in Fig. 4.7, factorial values become large quickly. Using data type **long** programs can calculate factorials greater than 20!. Unfortunately, the **Factorial** function produces large values so quickly that even **long** does not help us print many more factorial values before the size even of a **long** variable is exceeded.

Calculating factorials of larger numbers requires the program to use **float** and **double** variables. This condition points to a weakness in most programming languages, namely, that the languages are not easily extended to handle the unique requirements of various applications. As we will see in our treatment of object-oriented programming, beginning in Chapter 5, MC++ is an extensible language; programmers with unique requirements can extend the language with new data types (called *classes*). A programmer could create a

HugeInteger class, for example, that would enable a program to calculate the factorials of arbitrarily large numbers.

Common Programming Error 4.14

Forgetting to return a value from a recursive function can result in syntax or logic errors.

Common Programming Error 4.15

Omitting the base case or writing the recursion step so that it does not converge on the base case will cause infinite recursion, eventually exhausting memory. Infinite recursion is analogous to the problem of an infinite loop in an iterative (nonrecursive) solution.

4.10 Function Overloading

MC++ enables several functions of the same name to be defined in the same scope, as long as these functions have different sets of parameters (number of parameters, types of parameters or order of parameters). This is called *function overloading*. When an overloaded function is called, the Visual C++ .NET compiler selects the proper function by examining the number, types and order of the call's arguments. Function overloading commonly is used to create several functions with the same name that perform similar tasks, but on different data types. Figure 4.8 uses overloaded function **Square** to calculate the square of an **int** and that of a **double**.

Good Programming Practice 4.5

Overloading a function to perform closely related tasks can make a program more readable and understandable.

```
1   // Fig. 4.8: FunctionOverload.cpp
2   // Using overloaded functions.
3
4   #using <mscorlib.dll>
5
6   using namespace System;
7
8   int Square( int );
9   double Square( double );
10
11  int main()
12  {
13     Console::Write( S"The square of integer 7 is " );
14     Console::WriteLine( Square( 7 ).ToString() );
15
16     Console::Write( S"The square of double 7.5 is " );
17     Console::WriteLine( Square( 7.5 ).ToString() );
18
19     return 0;
20  }
21
```

Fig. 4.8   Function overloading. (Part 1 of 2.)

```
22   // first version, takes one integer
23   int Square( int x )
24   {
25      return x * x;
26   }
27
28   // second version, takes one double
29   double Square( double y )
30   {
31      return y * y;
32   }
```

```
The square of integer 7 is 49
The square of double 7.5 is 56.25
```

Fig. 4.8   Function overloading. (Part 2 of 2.)

The compiler distinguishes overloaded functions by their *signatures*. A function's signature is a combination of the function's name and its parameter types. If the compiler looked only at function names during compilation, the code in Fig. 4.8 would be ambiguous—the compiler would not know how to distinguish the two **Square** functions. The compiler uses *overload resolution* to determine which function to call. This process first searches for all the functions that *can* be used in the context, based on the number and type of arguments that are present. It might seem that only one function would match, but recall that MC++ can convert variable values to other data types implicitly. Once all matching functions are found, the closest match is chosen. This matching uses a "best-fit" algorithm that analyzes the implicit conversions that will take place.

Let us look at an example. In Fig. 4.8, the compiler might use the logical name "**Square** of **int**" for the **Square** function that specifies an **int** parameter (line 8) and "**Square** of **double**" for the **Square** function that specifies a **double** parameter (line 9). If a function **Foo**'s definition begins as

```
void Foo( int a, float b )
```

the compiler might use the logical name "**Foo** of **int** and **float**." If the parameters are specified as

```
void Foo( float a, int b )
```

the compiler might use the logical name "**Foo** of **float** and **int**." The order of the parameters is important to the compiler; it considers the preceding two **Foo** functions distinct.

So far, the logical names of functions that have been used by the compiler have not mentioned the functions' return types. This is because function calls cannot be distinguished by return type. The program in Fig. 4.9 illustrates the syntax error that is generated when two functions have the same signature and different return types. Overloaded functions with different parameter lists can have different return types. Overloaded functions need not have the same number of parameters.

```
1    // Fig. 4.9: InvalidFunctionOverload.cpp
2    // Demonstrating incorrect function overloading.
3
4    int Square( double x )
5    {
6        return x * x;
7    }
8
9    // ERROR! Second Square function takes same number, order
10   // and type of arguments.
11   double Square( double y )
12   {
13       return y * y;
14   }
```

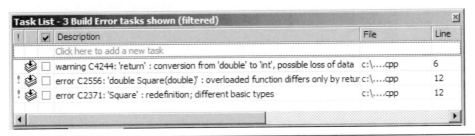

Fig. 4.9   Incorrect function overloading.

 Common Programming Error 4.16

Creating overloaded functions with identical parameter lists and different return types is a syntax error.

4.11 Arrays

An array is a group of memory locations that all have the same name and type. A program can refer to any *element* of an array by giving the name of the array followed by the *position number* (a value that indicates a specific location within the array) of the element in square brackets ([ ]). The first element in every array is called the *zeroth element.* Thus, the first element of array c is referred to as c[0], the second element of array c is referred to as c[1] (one element from the beginning of the array), and, in general, the *i*th element of array c is referred to as c[i-1]. The position number in square brackets is more formally called a *subscript* (or an *index*). A subscript must be an integer or an integer expression. If a program uses an integer expression as a subscript, the program evaluates the expression first to determine the subscript.

The brackets that enclose the subscript of an array are operators. Brackets have the same level of precedence as parentheses. Figure 4.10 shows the precedence and associativity of the operators introduced thus far in the text. They are displayed from top to bottom in decreasing order of precedence, with their associativity and type. The reader should note that the ++ and -- operators in the second row represent the postincrement and postdecrement operators, respectively, and that the ++ and -- operators in the third row represent the preincrement and predecrement operators, respectively.

Operators	Associativity	Type
: :	left to right	scope resolution
( ) [ ] . -> ++ --	left to right	postfix
++ -- + - ! (*type*)	right to left	prefix
* / %	left to right	multiplicative
+ -	left to right	additive
< <= > >=	left to right	relational
== !=	left to right	equality
&	left to right	logical AND
^	left to right	logical exclusive OR (XOR)
|	left to right	logical OR
&&	left to right	conditional AND
||	left to right	conditional OR
? :	right to left	conditional
= += -= *= /= %=	right to left	assignment

Fig. 4.10 Precedence and associativity of the operators discussed so far.

4.12 Declaring and Allocating Arrays

Arrays occupy space in memory. The programmer specifies the type of the elements and uses *operator **new*** to allocate the number of elements required by each array dynamically. Arrays are allocated with **new** because arrays are reference types, and all reference types must be created with **new**. We will see an exception to this shortly, however.

The declaration

```
int c __gc[] = new int __gc[ 12 ];
```

allocates 12 elements for integer array **c**. The preceding statement also can be performed in two steps as follows:

```
// declare managed array
int c __gc[];

// allocate space for array; set pointer to that space
c = new int __gc[ 12 ];
```

When arrays are allocated, the elements are initialized to zero for numeric primitive-data-type variables, to **false** for **bool** variables and to **0** for pointers.

MC++ keyword __***gc*** in the array declarations specifies that arrays are *managed arrays.*[5] In general, keyword __***gc*** declares a *managed type.* Managed types are *garbage*

---

5. For more information about managed arrays, visit **msdn.microsoft.com/library/ default.asp?url=/library/en-us/vcmxspec/html/ vcManagedExtensionsSpec_4_5.asp**.

collected (i.e., memory no longer in use is freed) and managed by the CLR,[6] a runtime environment provided by the .NET Framework. Managed arrays[7] (sometimes called **__gc** arrays) inherit from class **System::Array**. We discuss **__gc** classes and garbage collection in Chapter 5, Object-Based Programming.

Conversely, keyword **__nogc** declares an *unmanaged array*. Unmanaged arrays (sometimes called **__nogc** arrays) are standard C++ arrays and do not receive the benefits of managed arrays, such as garbage collection. Unmanaged arrays are also not considered objects in C++ as managed arrays are in MC++. Throughout this book, we will use managed arrays unless otherwise specified.

A single declaration may be used to reserve memory for several arrays. The following declaration reserves 100 elements for **String *** array **b** and 27 elements for **String *** array **x**:

```
String *b[] = new String *[ 100 ], *x[] = new String *[ 27 ];
```

Similarly, the following declaration reserves 10 elements for **array1** and 20 elements for **array2** (both of type **double**):

```
double array1 __gc[] = new double __gc[ 10 ],
       array2 __gc[] = new double __gc[ 20 ];
```

Notice that, in the **String *** array declaration, we have to prefix **x[]** with ***** to declare it as a **String *** array (in the same way that we prefix **b[]** with *****). Also notice that we do not have to include keyword **__gc**. Because **String *** is a pointer to a managed type (**System::String**), arrays **b** and **x** are managed arrays by default. Keyword **__gc** is optional in the declaring of managed arrays of all managed types (e.g., **Int32**, **Double** and **Boolean**). However, we must use keyword **__gc** when using MC++ aliases (e.g, **int**, **double** and **bool**) to declare managed arrays. For example, we must use keyword **__gc** when declaring **array1** and **array2**, because **double** is only an MC++ alias for .NET type **Double** (located in namespace **System**). If we replace **double** with **Double**, we can declare the arrays as follows:

```
Double array1[] = new Double[ 10 ],
       array2[] = new Double[ 20 ];
```

Refer to Fig. 4.2 to review data types of the .NET Framework and their MC++ aliases.

Managed arrays may be declared to contain any managed data type. In an array of value types, every element of the array contains one value of the declared type. For example, every element of an **int** array is an **int** value.

In an array of pointers, every element of the array points to an object of the data type of the array. For example, every element of a **String *** array is a pointer to an object of class **String**; each of the **String *** pointers points to an object containing the empty string by default.

---

6. For more information about the CLR, visit **msdn.microsoft.com/library/default.asp?url=/library/en-us/cpguide/html/cpconthecommonlanguageruntime.asp**.

7. For more information about managed types, visit **msdn.microsoft.com/library/default.asp?url=/library/en-us/vcmex/html/vclrf__gc.asp**.

The next example demonstrates declaration, allocation, initialization and manipulation of array elements. Figure 4.11 creates three 10-element integer arrays and displays those arrays in tabular format. The program demonstrates several techniques for declaring and initializing arrays.

Line 10 declares **x** as a pointer to an array of integers. Each element in the array is of type **int**. The variable **x** is of type **int[]**, which denotes an array whose elements are of type **int**. Line 11 allocates the 10 elements of the array with **new** and assigns the array to pointer **x**. Each element of this array has the default value **0**.

Line 15 creates another **int** array and initializes each element via an *initializer list*. In this case, the number of elements in the initializer list determines the array's size. For example, line 15 creates a 10-element array with the indices **0–9** and the values **32**, **27**, **64** and so on. Note that this declaration does not require the **new** operator to create the array object—the compiler allocates memory for the object when it encounters an array declaration that includes an initializer list.

```
1   // Fig. 4.11: InitArray.cpp
2   // Different ways of initializing arrays.
3
4   #using <mscorlib.dll>
5
6   using namespace System;
7
8   int main()
9   {
10     int x __gc[];              // declare pointer to an array
11     x = new int __gc[ 10 ];    // dynamically allocate array
12
13     // initializer list specifies number of elements
14     // and value of each element
15     int y __gc[] = { 32, 27, 64, 18, 95, 14, 90, 70, 60, 37 };
16
17     const int ARRAY_SIZE = 10;    // named constant
18     int z __gc[];                 // pointer to int array
19
20     // allocate array of ARRAY_SIZE (i.e., 10) elements
21     z = new int __gc[ ARRAY_SIZE ];
22
23     // set the values in the array
24     for ( int i = 0; i < z->Length; i++ )
25        z[ i ] = 2 + 2 * i;
26
27     Console::WriteLine( S"Subscript\tArray x\tArray y\tArray z" );
28
29     // output values for each array
30     for ( int i = 0; i < ARRAY_SIZE; i++ )
31        Console::WriteLine( S"{0}\t\t{1}\t\t{2}\t\t{3}", i.ToString(),
32           x[ i ].ToString(), y[ i ].ToString(), z[ i ].ToString() );
33
34     return 0;
35  }
```

Fig. 4.11   Initializing element arrays in three different ways. (Part 1 of 2.)

Subscript	Array x	Array y	Array z
0	0	32	2
1	0	27	4
2	0	64	6
3	0	18	8
4	0	95	10
5	0	14	12
6	0	90	14
7	0	70	16
8	0	60	18
9	0	37	20

Fig. 4.11   Initializing element arrays in three different ways. (Part 2 of 2.)

On line 17, we create constant integer **ARRAY_SIZE**, using keyword **const**. *Constants* are values that cannot change during program execution. A constant must be initialized in the same statement where it is declared and cannot be modified thereafter. If an attempt is made to modify a **const** variable after it is declared, the compiler issues a compilation error.

Constants also are called *named constants*. They often are used to make a program more readable and usually are denoted with variable names in all capital letters.

Common Programming Error 4.17

Assigning a value to a constant after the constant has been initialized is a compilation error.

Good Programming Practice 4.6

Using constants instead of literal constants (e.g., values such as 8) makes programs clearer. This technique is used to eliminate so-called magic numbers; *i.e., repeatedly mentioning the number 10, for example, as a counter for a loop gives the number 10 an artificial significance and could unfortunately confuse the reader when the program includes other 10s that have nothing to do with the counter.*

Line 21 creates integer array **z** of length 10, using the **ARRAY_SIZE** named constant. The **for** structure in lines 24–25 initializes each element in array **z**. The **for** loop uses property **Length** to determine the number of elements in array **z**. Array **z** has access to property **Length** because, as a managed array, it is also an object of type **System::Array**. The values are generated by multiplying each successive value of the loop counter by **2** and adding **2** to the product. After this initialization, array **z** contains the even integers **2, 4, 6, …, 20**.

The **for** structure in lines 30–32 displays the values in arrays **x, y** and **z**. Zero-based counting (remember, array subscripts start at 0) allows the loop to access every element of the array. The constant **ARRAY_SIZE** in the **for** structure condition (line 30) specifies the arrays' lengths.

4.13 Arrays and Functions

To pass an array argument to a function, specify the name of the array without using brackets. For example, if array **hourlyTemperatures** is declared as

```
int hourlyTemperatures __gc[] = new int __gc[ 24 ];
```

then the function call

```
ModifyArray( hourlyTemperatures );
```

passes array **hourlyTemperatures** (by reference) to function **ModifyArray**. Every array object "knows" its own size (via the **Length** property), so that, when we pass an array object into a function, we do not pass the size of the array as an additional argument.

Although entire arrays are passed by reference, individual array elements of primitive data types are passed by value. (The objects referred to by individual elements of a non-primitive-type array are passed by reference.) Such simple single pieces of data are sometimes called *scalars* or *scalar quantities*. To pass an array element to a function, use the subscripted name of the array element as an argument in the function call; for example, the zeroth element of array **scores** is passed as **scores[0]**.

For a function to receive an array through a function call, the function's parameter list must specify that an array will be received. For example, the function header for function **ModifyArray** might be written as

```
void ModifyArray( int b __gc[] )
```

indicating that **ModifyArray** expects to receive an integer array in parameter **b**. Arrays are passed by reference; when the called function uses the array parameter name **b**, it refers to the actual array in the caller.

A programmer can return an array from a function by appending **__gc[]** to both the function prototype and function-definition header.[8] For instance, the following is the general syntax for a function that returns an array of integers

```
int FunctionName( parameter-list ) __gc[];
```

The **__gc[]** indicates that function *FunctionName* returns a managed array, and **int** indicates that the array returned is an integer array. The header of the function definition follows the same syntax, except without the semicolon. As with the declaration of managed arrays, the **__gc** is optional when managed types' aliases are not used. For instance,

```
Int32 FunctionName( parameter-list ) [];
```

also would declare a function that returns a managed array of integers.

4.14 Passing Arrays by Value and by Reference

In MC++, a variable that "stores" a reference type, such as a managed array, does not actually store the object itself. Instead, such a variable usually stores a pointer to the object (i.e., the location in the computer's memory where the object itself is stored). The distinction between value-type variables and reference-type variables raises some subtle issues that programmers must understand to create secure, stable programs.

---

8. This is the syntax used to indicate that the function returns a one-dimensional array. We will discuss returning multiple-subscripted arrays from functions in Section 4.15.

When a program passes an argument to a function, the called function receives a copy of that argument's value. Changes to the local copy do not affect the original variable that the program passed to the function. If the argument is of a reference type, the function makes a local copy only of the pointer, not a copy of the actual object to which the pointer refers. The local copy of the pointer also refers to the original object in memory. Thus, reference types always are passed by reference, which means that changes to those objects in called functions affect the original objects in memory.

Performance Tip 4.2

Passing arrays and other objects by reference makes sense for performance reasons. If arrays were passed by value, a copy of each element would be passed. For large, frequently passed arrays, this would waste time and would consume considerable storage for the copies of the arrays—both of these problems cause poor performance.

However, we also can pass the pointers themselves by reference, using two MC++ operators. We discuss them here briefly. The **&**, or *address operator*, is a unary operator that returns the address of its operand. For example, assuming the declarations

```
int y = 5;
int *yPtr;
```

the statement

```
yPtr = &y;
```

assigns the address of variable **y** to pointer variable **yPtr**. Variable **yPtr** is then said to "point to" **y**.

The ***** *operator*, commonly referred to as the *indirection operator* or *dereferencing operator*, returns an alias for the object to which its operand (i.e., a pointer) points. For example, the statement

```
*yPtr = 9;
```

would assign **9** to **y**. The dereferenced pointer is an *lvalue*.

This is a subtle capability, which, if misused, can lead to problems. For instance, when a reference type is passed to a function through these operators, the called function actually gains control over the passed pointer itself, allowing the called function to replace the original object in the caller with a different object or even with **0**. Such behavior can lead to unpredictable results, which can be disastrous in mission-critical applications. The program in Fig. 4.12 demonstrates the difference between passing a managed array pointer by value and passing a managed array pointer by reference (using operators **&** and *****).

Lines 16 and 19 declare two integer array variables, **firstArray** and **firstArray-Copy**. (We make the copy so we can determine whether pointer **firstArray**'s value gets overwritten.) Line 16 initializes **firstArray** with the values **1**, **2** and **3**. The assignment statement on line 19 copies pointer **firstArray** to variable **firstArrayCopy**, causing these variables to point to the same array object in memory. The **for** structure on lines 28–30 prints the contents of **firstArray** before it is passed to function **FirstDouble** (line 33) so we can verify that this array is passed by reference (i.e., the called function indeed changes the array's contents).

```cpp
1   // Fig. 4.12: ArrayReferenceTest.cpp
2   // Testing the effects of passing arrays
3   // by value and by reference.
4
5   #using <mscorlib.dll>
6
7   using namespace System;
8
9   void FirstDouble( int __gc[] );
10  void SecondDouble( int (*) __gc[] );
11  void DisplayArray( int __gc[] );
12
13  int main()
14  {
15
16     // create and initialize firstArray
17     int firstArray __gc[] = { 1, 2, 3 };
18
19     // copy firstArray pointer
20     int firstArrayCopy __gc[] = firstArray;
21
22     Console::WriteLine( S"Test passing firstArray by value\n"
23        S"\nContents of firstArray before calling FirstDouble:" );
24
25     // print contents of firstArray
26     DisplayArray( firstArray );
27
28     // pass firstArray by value to FirstDouble
29     FirstDouble( firstArray );
30
31     Console::WriteLine( S"\n\nContents of firstArray after "
32        S"calling FirstDouble" );
33
34     // print contents of firstArray
35     DisplayArray( firstArray );
36
37     // test whether FirstDouble changed firstArray pointer
38     if ( firstArray == firstArrayCopy )
39        Console::WriteLine(
40           S"\n\nThe pointers point to the same array" );
41     else
42        Console::WriteLine(
43           S"\n\nThe pointers point to different arrays" );
44
45     // create and initialize secondArray
46     int secondArray __gc[] = { 1, 2, 3 };
47
48     // copy secondArray pointer
49     int secondArrayCopy __gc[] = secondArray;
50
51     Console::WriteLine( S"\nTest passing secondArray by reference"
52        S"\n\nContents of secondArray before calling SecondDouble:" );
53
```

Fig. 4.12   Passing an array by value and by reference. (Part 1 of 3.)

```
54      // print contents of secondArray before function call
55      DisplayArray( secondArray );
56
57      SecondDouble( &secondArray );
58
59      Console::WriteLine( S"\n\nContents of secondArray "
60         S"after calling SecondDouble:" );
61
62      // print contents of secondArray after function call
63      DisplayArray( secondArray );
64
65      // test whether SecondDouble changed secondArray pointer
66      if ( secondArray == secondArrayCopy )
67         Console::WriteLine(
68            S"\n\nThe pointers point to the same array" );
69      else
70         Console::WriteLine(
71            S"\n\nThe pointers refer to different arrays" );
72
73      return 0;
74   } // end main
75
76   // modify elements of array and attempt to modify pointer
77   void FirstDouble( int array __gc[] )
78   {
79
80      // double each element's value
81      for ( int i = 0; i < array->Length; i++ )
82         array[ i ] *= 2;
83
84      // create new pointer and assign it to array
85      array = new int __gc[ 3 ];
86
87      for ( int j = 0; j < array->Length; j++ )
88         array[ j ] = j + 11;
89   } // end function FirstDouble
90
91   // modify elements of array and change array pointer
92   // to point to a new array
93   void SecondDouble( int ( *array ) __gc[] )
94   {
95
96      // double each element's value
97      for ( int i = 0; i < ( *array )->Length; i++ )
98         ( *array )[ i ] *= 2;
99
100     // create new pointer and assign it to array
101     *array = new int __gc[ 3 ];
102
103     for ( int j = 0; j < ( *array )->Length; j++ )
104        ( *array )[ j ] = j + 11;
105  } // end function SecondDouble
106
```

Fig. 4.12   Passing an array by value and by reference. (Part 2 of 3.)

```
107    // display array contents
108    void DisplayArray( int array __gc[] )
109    {
110        for ( int i = 0; i < array->Length; i++ )
111            Console::Write( S"{0} ", array[ i ].ToString() );
112    }
```

```
Test passing firstArray by value

Contents of firstArray before calling FirstDouble:
1 2 3

Contents of firstArray after calling FirstDouble
2 4 6

The pointers point to the same array

Test passing secondArray by reference

Contents of secondArray before calling SecondDouble:
1 2 3

Contents of secondArray after calling SecondDouble:
11 12 13

The pointers point to different arrays
```

Fig. 4.12   Passing an array by value and by reference. (Part 3 of 3.)

The **for** structure in function **FirstDouble** (lines 94–95) multiplies the values of all the elements in the array by **2**. Lines 98–101 allocate a new array containing the values **11**, **12** and **13**; the pointer for this array then is assigned to parameter **array** (in an attempt to overwrite pointer **firstArray**—this, of course, will not happen, because the pointer to the array was passed by value). After function **FirstDouble** executes, the **for** structure on lines 40–41 prints the contents of **firstArray**, demonstrating that the values of the elements have been changed by the function (and confirming that, in MC++, arrays are always passed by reference). The **if/else** structure on lines 44–49 uses the **==** operator to compare pointers **firstArray** (which we just attempted to overwrite) and **firstArrayCopy**. The expression on line 44 evaluates to **true** if the operands to binary operator **==** indeed point to the same object. In this case, the object represented is the array allocated on line 16, not the array allocated in function **FirstDouble** (line 98), so the expression evaluates to true.

Lines 52–86 perform similar tests, using array variables **secondArray** and **secondArrayCopy** and function **SecondDouble** (lines 106–118). Line 68 passes **secondArray** to function **SecondDouble**, using the address operator (**&**). This ensures that function **SecondDouble** receives the address of pointer **secondArray**, allowing **SecondDouble** to modify the pointer itself in the same manner that **FirstDouble** is able to modify the array referred to by **firstArray** (i.e., the actual pointer to the array is passed by reference rather than the array object being passed by reference). Function **SecondDouble** performs the same operations as **FirstDouble**, but receives its argument through the dereferencing operator (*), indicating that it is receiving the address of an array pointer.

Lines 110–111 double the value of each element in the array. To access the array pointer itself, we again use the dereferencing operator (as ***array**). Note the parentheses around ***array** when it is used with various operators, such as the arrow member-selection operator (**->**). The parentheses are needed because the arrow operator has higher precedence than the ***** operator. Without the parentheses, the expression

```
*array->Length
```

would be evaluated as if it were parenthesized as follows:

```
*( array->Length )
```

Notice that line 114 does not require the parentheses because it does not use operators of higher precedence with ***array**.

When the function call returns, the pointer stored in **secondArray** points to the array allocated on lines 114–117 of **SecondDouble**, demonstrating that a pointer passed with the address operator (**&**) can be modified by the called function so that the pointer actually points to a different object—an array allocated in function **SecondDouble**. The **if/else** structure in lines 79–84 demonstrates that **secondArray** and **secondArray-Copy** no longer point to the same array.

Software Engineering Observation 4.7

*When a function receives a reference type by value, the object is not passed by value—the object still passes by reference. Rather, the object's pointer is passed by value. This prevents a function from overwriting pointers passed to that function. In the vast majority of cases, protecting the caller's pointer from modification is the desired behavior. If you encounter a situation where you truly want the called function to modify the argument's pointer, pass the reference type with operators **&** and *****—but, again, such cases are rare.*

4.15 Multiple-Subscripted Arrays

So far, we have studied *single-subscripted* (or *one-dimensional*) arrays—i.e., those that contain single lists of values. In this section, we introduce *multiple-subscripted* (often called *multi-dimensional*) arrays. Such arrays require two or more subscripts to identify particular elements. Arrays that require two subscripts to identify a particular element commonly are called *double-subscripted arrays*. We concentrate on *double-subscripted arrays* (often called *two-dimensional arrays*). There are two types of multiple-subscripted arrays—*rectangular* and *jagged*. Rectangular arrays (also called *ranked arrays*) with two subscripts often represent *tables* of values consisting of information arranged in *rows* and *columns*, where each row is the same size and each column is the same size. To identify a particular table element, we must specify the two subscripts—by convention, the first identifies the element's row, the second the element's column. Multiple-subscripted arrays can have two or more subscripts. Figure 4.13 illustrates a double-subscripted array, **a**, containing three rows and four columns (i.e., a 3-by-4 array). An array with m rows and n columns is called an *m-by-n array*.

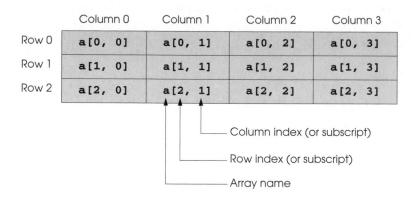

Fig. 4.13   Double-subscripted array with three rows and four columns.

Every element in array **a** is identified in Fig. 4.13 by an element name of the form **a[i, j]**, in which **a** is the name of the array and **i** and **j** are the subscripts that uniquely identify the row and column of each element in **a**. Notice that the names of the elements in the first row all have a first subscript of **0**; the names of the elements in the fourth column all have a second subscript of **3**.

Multiple-subscripted arrays can be initialized in declarations like single-subscripted arrays. A double-subscripted array **b** with two rows and two columns could be declared and initialized with

```
int b __gc[,] = new int __gc[ 2, 2 ];

b[ 0, 0 ] = 1;
b[ 0, 1 ] = 2;
b[ 1, 0 ] = 3;
b[ 1, 1 ] = 4;
```

Method **GetLength** returns the length of a particular array dimension. In the preceding example, **b->GetLength(0)** returns the length of the zeroth dimension of **b**, which is **2**. The number of dimensions in an array is called its *rank*. The rank of an array is one more than the number of commas used in its declaration. For example, array **b** is declared via the notation **[,]**, which contains one comma. Therefore, the rank of array **b** is two. To declare a three-dimensional array, we would use the notation **[,,]**.

In Section 4.13, we discussed returning arrays from functions. Programmers also can specify multiple-subscripted rectangular arrays to be returned, using the notation above. For instance, the programmer indicates that a function returns a double-subscripted array of integers using the following syntax

```
int FunctionName( parameter-list ) __gc[,];
```

Jagged arrays are maintained as arrays of arrays. In MC++, jagged arrays are explicitly declared as **System::Array** objects. Unlike rectangular arrays, arrays that compose jagged arrays can be of different lengths. The following code

```
// allocate array of two arrays with managed type Int32
Array *c = Array::CreateInstance( __typeof( Int32[] ), 2 );

// allocate and initialize elements for row 0
int row0 __gc[] = { 1, 2, 3 };

// allocate and initialize elements for row 1
int row1 __gc[] = { 4, 5 };

// set row0 as first element of c
c->SetValue( row0, 0 );

// set row1 as second element of c
c->SetValue( row1, 1 );
```

instantiates **c** which points to an integer **Array** object with row **0** (which is an array itself) that contains three elements (**1**, **2**, and **3**) and row **1** (another array) that contains two elements (**4** and **5**). **Array** method *CreateInstance* is used to create the jagged array. We use a version of method **CreateInstance** that creates a one-dimensional array. We specify the type of the array using MC++ keyword __*typeof*, which returns the *System::Type* of a specified managed type name. In this case, we want an array of integer arrays (i.e., an array of **Int32[]** objects). The second argument to method **CreateInstance** is the length of the array, **2**.

Each element of array **c** is an array itself, so jagged arrays can use property **Length** to determine the length of each subarray. For the jagged array **c**, the size of the zeroth row is

```
( dynamic_cast< Int32[] >( c->GetValue( 0 ) ) )->Length
```

which is **3**. Function *GetValue* returns a generic **Object** pointer to the subarray (in this case, **row0**), which must be cast to an **Array** pointer to access the **Length** property. We perform the necessary cast, using cast operator *dynamic_cast*. Operator **dynamic_cast** performs a checked conversion between data types. To determine the number of subarrays in a jagged array, we can use the **Length** property on the jagged array itself, as in **c->Length** (which would evaluate to **2** in this example).

Figure 4.14 demonstrates the initialization of double-subscripted arrays in declarations and the use of nested **for** loops to traverse the arrays (i.e., to manipulate each array element).

The declaration of **array1** (line 15) creates a 2-by-3 managed array. Lines 17–19 populate the multidimensional array. The first row of the array has the values **1**, **2** and **3**. The second row of the array contains the values **2**, **4** and **6**.

Method **CreateInstance** (lines 27–28) creates an instance (**array2**) of the **Array** class with three rows. Each row is an integer array. Note that the first argument to **CreateInstance** must be a managed type, such as **Int32[]**. Lines 31–33 initialize each subarray so that the first subarray contains the values **1** and **2**, the second contains the value **3** and the last contains the values **4**, **5** and **6**. Lines 36–38 call **SetValue** to create a jagged array of three arrays.

```
1   // Fig. 4.14: TwoDimensionalArrays.cpp
2   // Initializing two-dimensional arrays.
```

Fig. 4.14   Initializing two-dimensional arrays. (Part 1 of 3.)

```
3
4   #using <mscorlib.dll>
5
6   using namespace System;
7
8   void BuildOutput( int __gc[,] );
9   void BuildOutput( Array * );
10
11  int main()
12  {
13
14     // declaration and initialization of 2D array
15     int array1 __gc[,] = new int __gc[ 2, 3 ];
16
17     for ( int i = 0; i < array1->GetLength( 0 ); i++ )
18        for ( int j = 0; j < array1->GetLength( 1 ); j++ )
19           array1[ i, j ] = ( i + 1 ) * ( j + 1 );
20
21     Console::WriteLine( S"Values in array1 by row are" );
22
23     // display 2D square array
24     BuildOutput( array1 );
25
26     // declaration and initialization of jagged array
27     Array *array2 = Array::CreateInstance( __typeof( Int32[] ),
28        3 );
29
30     // create and initialize three rows
31     int row0 __gc[] = { 1, 2 };
32     int row1 __gc[] = { 3 };
33     int row2 __gc[] = { 4, 5, 6 };
34
35     // set rows as elements of array2
36     array2->SetValue( row0, 0 );
37     array2->SetValue( row1, 1 );
38     array2->SetValue( row2, 2 );
39
40     Console::WriteLine( S"\nValues in array2 by row are" );
41     BuildOutput( array2 );
42
43     return 0;
44  } // end main
45
46  void BuildOutput( int array __gc[,] )
47  {
48     for ( int i = 0; i < array->GetLength( 0 ); i++ ) {
49
50        for ( int j = 0; j < array->GetLength( 1 ); j++ )
51           Console::Write( S"{0} ", array[ i, j ].ToString() );
52
53        Console::WriteLine();
54     }
55  } // end function BuildOutput
```

Fig. 4.14   Initializing two-dimensional arrays. (Part 2 of 3.)

```
56
57    void BuildOutput( Array *array )
58    {
59        Int32 temp[];
60
61        for ( int i = 0; i < array->Length; i++ ) {
62            temp = dynamic_cast< Int32[] >( array->GetValue( i ) );
63
64            for ( int x = 0; x < temp->Length; x++ )
65                Console::Write( S"{0} ", temp[ x ].ToString() );
66
67            Console::WriteLine();
68        }
69    } // end overloaded function BuildOutput
```

```
Values in array1 by row are
1 2 3
2 4 6

Values in array2 by row are
1 2
3
4 5 6
```

Fig. 4.14   Initializing two-dimensional arrays. (Part 3 of 3.)

Function **buildOutput** (lines 46–55) appends the elements of **array1** to **String *output**. Note the use of a nested **for** structure to output the rows of each double-subscripted array. In the nested **for** structures for **array1**, we use function **GetLength** to determine the number of elements in each dimension of the array. Line 48 determines the number of rows in the array by invoking **array1->GetLength(0)**; line 50 determines the number of columns by invoking **array1->GetLength(1)**. Arrays with additional dimensions would require additional **for** loops.

The overloaded version of function **buildOutput** (lines 57–69) accepts a pointer to an **Array** object. Note that the array of arrays must be a .NET data type, such as **Int32[]**. The nested **for** structures (lines 61–68) append the elements of jagged array **array2** to **output**. Line 61 uses the **Length** property of **array2** to determine the number of rows in the jagged array. Recall that a jagged array is essentially an array that contains additional arrays as its elements. Method **GetValue** (line 62) retrieves each subarray as an **Object ***, casts the subarray to an **Int32** array and assigns it to pointer **temp**. Line 64 determines the number of elements in each subarray using the expression **temp->Length**.

Many common array manipulations use **for** repetition structures. Imagine a jagged array **a**, which contains three rows, or arrays of type **Int32[]**. The following **for** structure sets all the elements in the third row of array **a** to zero:

```
Int32 row2[] = dynamic_cast< Int32[] >( a->GetValue( 2 ) );
for ( int col = 0; col < row2->Length; col++ )
    row2[ col ] = 0;
```

We specified the *third* row; therefore, we know that the first subscript is always **2**. (**0** specifies the first row, **1** the second row.) The **for** loop varies only the second subscript (i.e., the column subscript). Notice the use of **row2->Length** in the **for** structure's conditional expression. This statement demonstrates that each row of **a** is an array in itself; therefore, the program can access a typical array's properties, such as **Length**. Assuming the length of the third row of the jagged array is **4**, the preceding **for** structure is equivalent to the assignment statements

```
row2[ 0 ] = 0;
row2[ 1 ] = 0;
row2[ 2 ] = 0;
row2[ 3 ] = 0;
```

The following nested **for** structure sums the elements in array **a**. We use **a->Length** in the conditional expression of the outer **for** structure to determine the number of rows (i.e., the number of subarrays) in **a**, in this case, 3:

```
int total = 0;

for ( int row = 0; row < a->Length; row++ )
    Int32 t[] = dynamic_cast< Int32[] >( a->GetValue( row ) );

    for ( int col = 0; col < t->Length; col++ )
        total += t[ col ];
```

The **for** structure totals the elements of the array one row at a time. The outer **for** structure begins by setting the **row** subscript to **0**, so the elements of the first row may be totaled by the inner **for** structure. Then the outer **for** structure increments **row** to **1**, so the second row can be totaled. Finally, the outer **for** structure increments **row** to **2**, so the third row can be totaled. The result can be displayed when the nested **for** structure terminates.

4.16 Summary

The best way to develop and maintain a large program is to construct it from reusable pieces, such as functions, methods and classes. This technique is called divide and conquer. Programs are written by combining new functions, methods and classes that the programmer writes with prepackaged functions, classes and methods in the .NET Framework Class Library (FCL) and in various other class libraries. The FCL provides a rich collection of classes and methods for performing common mathematical calculations, string manipulations, character manipulations, input/output, error checking and other useful operations. The programmer can write functions to define specific tasks that may be used at many points in a program. These functions are referred to as programmer-defined functions.

Data types are either value types or reference types. A variable of a value type contains data of that type. A variable of a reference type, in contrast, contains the address of the location in memory where the data is stored. Value types are accessed directly and are passed by value; reference types are accessed through pointers or references and are passed by reference. Value types normally contain small pieces of data, such as **int** or **bool** values. Reference types, on the other hand, usually refer to large objects.

When an argument is passed by value, the called function receives a copy of the argument's value. When an argument is passed via pass-by-reference, the caller gives the function the ability to access and modify the caller's original data directly. Pass-by-reference can improve performance, because it eliminates the overhead of copying large data items (i.e., reference types); however, pass-by-reference can weaken security, because the called function can modify the caller's data.

The scope of a variable is the portion of a program where that variable can be referenced. An identifier's duration (its lifetime) is the period during which the identifier exists in memory.

Recursion is a powerful problem-solving technique wherein functions can call themselves to solve a problem. With function overloading, several functions in a class can be defined with the same name, as long as they have different sets of parameters.

Arrays are groups of memory locations that all have the same name and type. Arrays group lists of logically related data together. Each piece of data, or element, can be accessed via a subscript, a numeric value placed within square brackets after the name of the array. The number in square brackets determines which element in the array is accessed. In MC++, managed arrays inherit from class **System::Array**.

MC++ also allows the creation of multiple-subscripted managed arrays—arrays that contain two or more subscripts. There are two types of such multiple-subscripted arrays—rectangular and jagged. Rectangular arrays with two subscripts often represent tables of values consisting of information arranged in rows and columns, where each row is the same size and each column is the same size. Jagged arrays are maintained as arrays of arrays. Unlike rectangular arrays, rows in jagged arrays can be of different lengths.

Object-Based Programming

Objectives

- To understand encapsulation and data hiding.
- To understand the concepts of data abstraction and abstract data types (ADTs).
- To create, use and destroy objects.
- To control access to object instance variables and methods.
- To use properties to keep objects in consistent states.
- To understand the use of the **this** pointer.
- To understand namespaces and assemblies.
- To use the **Class View**.

My object all sublime
I shall achieve in time.
W. S. Gilbert

Is it a world to hide virtues in?
William Shakespeare

Your public servants serve you right.
Adlai Stevenson

This above all: to thine own self be true.
William Shakespeare

Outline

5.1 Introduction

In this chapter, we investigate object orientation in MC++. Some readers might ask, why have we deferred this topic until now? There are several reasons. First, the objects we build in this chapter partially are composed of structured program pieces. To explain the organization of objects, we needed to establish a basis in structured programming with control structures. We also wanted to study functions in detail before introducing object orientation.

Let us briefly overview some key concepts and terminology of object orientation. Object orientation uses classes to *encapsulate* (i.e., wrap together) data (*attributes*) and methods (*behaviors*). Objects have the ability to hide their implementation from other object (this principle is called *information hiding*). Although some objects can communicate with one another across well-defined *interfaces* (just like the driver's interface to a car includes a steering wheel, accelerator pedal, brake pedal and gear shift), objects are unaware of how other objects are implemented (just as the driver is unaware of how the steering, engine, brake and transmission mechanisms are implemented). Normally, implementation details are hidden within the objects themselves. Surely, it is possible to drive a car effectively without knowing the details of how engines, transmissions and exhaust systems work. Later, we will see why information hiding is so crucial to good software engineering.

In *procedural programming languages* (like C), programming tends to be *action oriented*. MC++ programming, however, is *object oriented*. In C, the unit of programming is the *function*. In MC++, the unit of programming is the *class*. Objects eventually are *instantiated* (i.e., created) from these classes, and functions are encapsulated within the "boundaries" of classes as *methods*.

C programmers concentrate on writing functions. They group actions that perform some task into a function and then group functions to form a program. Data are certainly important in C, but they exist primarily to support the actions that functions perform. C programmers use the *verbs* in a system-requirements document to determine the set of functions needed to implement a system.

By contrast, MC++ programmers concentrate on creating their own *user-defined types*, called *classes*. We also refer to classes as *programmer-defined types*. Each class contains both data and a set of methods that manipulate the data. The data components of a class are called *data members*, *member variables* or *instance variables* (many MC++ programmers prefer the term *fields*). Just as we call an instance of a built-in type—such as **int**—a *variable*, we call an instance of a programmer-defined type (i.e., a class) an *object*. In MC++, attention is focused on classes, rather than on methods. Whereas C programmers use the verbs in a system-requirements document, MC++ programmers use the *nouns*. These nouns can be used to determine an initial set of classes with which to begin the design process. Programmers use these classes to instantiate objects that work together to implement a system.

This chapter explains how to create and use classes and objects, a subject known as *object-based programming (OBP)*. Chapters 6 and 7 introduce *inheritance* and *polymorphism*—key technologies that enable *object-oriented programming (OOP)*.

5.2 Implementing a Time Abstract Data Type with a Class

Classes in MC++ facilitate the creation of *abstract data types (ADT)*, which hide their implementation from clients (or users of the class object). A problem in procedural programming languages is that client code often is dependent on implementation details of the data used in the code. This dependency might necessitate rewriting the client code if the data implementation changes. ADTs eliminate this problem by providing implementation-independent *interfaces* to their clients. The creator of a class can change the internal implementation of that class without affecting the clients of that class.

 Software Engineering Observation 5.1

It is important to write programs that are understandable and easy to maintain. Change is the rule, rather than the exception. Programmers should anticipate that their code will be modified. As we will see, classes facilitate program modifiability.

Our first example consists of class **Time1** (Fig. 5.1 and Fig. 5.2) and the driver program **TimeTest1.cpp** (Fig. 5.3), which we use to test the class. Class **Time1** contains the time of day in 24-hour clock format. Program **TimeTest1.cpp** contains function **WinMain**, which creates an instance of class **Time1** and demonstrates the features of that class.

```
1   // Fig. 5.1: Time1.h
2   // Demonstrating class Time1.
3
```

Fig. 5.1   Abstract data type **Time** implementation as a class. (Part 1 of 2.)

```
 4    #pragma once
 5
 6    #using <mscorlib.dll>
 7
 8    using namespace System;
 9
10    public __gc class Time1
11    {
12    public:
13       Time1();    // constructor
14       void SetTime( int, int, int ); // set function
15       String *ToUniversalString();
16       String *ToStandardString();
17
18    private:
19       int hour;      // 0-23
20       int minute;    // 0-59
21       int second;    // 0-59
22    }; // end class Time1
```

Fig. 5.1   Abstract data type **Time** implementation as a class. (Part 2 of 2.)

```
 1    // Fig. 5.2: Time1.cpp
 2    // Implementing class Time1.
 3
 4    #include "Time1.h"
 5
 6    // Time1 constructor initializes instance variables to
 7    // zero to set default time to midnight
 8    Time1::Time1()
 9    {
10       SetTime( 0, 0, 0 );
11    }
12
13    // set new time value in 24-hour format. Perform validity
14    // checks on the data. Set invalid value to zero.
15    void Time1::SetTime( int hourValue, int minuteValue,
16       int secondValue )
17    {
18       hour = ( hourValue >= 0 && hourValue < 24 ) ? hourValue : 0;
19       minute = ( minuteValue >= 0 && minuteValue < 60 ) ?
20          minuteValue : 0;
21       second = ( secondValue >= 0 && secondValue < 60 ) ?
22          secondValue : 0;
23    }
24
25    // convert time to universal-time (24 hour) format string
26    String *Time1::ToUniversalString()
27    {
28       return String::Concat( hour.ToString( S"D2" ), S":"
29          minute.ToString( S"D2" ), S":", second.ToString( S"D2" ) );
30    }
```

Fig. 5.2   Class **Time** method definitions. (Part 1 of 2.)

```
31
32    // convert time to standard-time (12 hour) format string
33    String *Time1::ToStandardString()
34    {
35       return String::Concat(
36          ( ( hour == 12 || hour == 0 ) ? 12 : hour % 12 ).ToString(),
37          S":", minute.ToString( S"D2" ), S":",
38          second.ToString( S"D2" ), S" ",
39          ( hour < 12 ? S"AM" : S"PM" ) );
40    }
```

Fig. 5.2   Class **Time** method definitions. (Part 2 of 2.)

```
1     // Fig. 5.3: TimeTest1.cpp
2     // Demonstrating class Time1.
3
4     #using <system.windows.forms.dll>
5
6     using namespace System::Windows::Forms;
7
8     #include "Time1.h"
9
10    int __stdcall WinMain()
11    {
12       Time1 *time = new Time1(); // calls Time1 constructor
13       String *output;
14
15       // assign string representation of time to output
16       output = String::Concat( S"Initial universal time is: ",
17          time->ToUniversalString(), S"\nInitial standard time is: ",
18          time->ToStandardString() );
19
20       // attempt valid time settings
21       time->SetTime( 13, 27, 6 );
22
23       // append new string representations of time to output
24       output = String::Concat( output,
25          S"\n\nUniversal time after SetTime is: ",
26          time->ToUniversalString(),
27          S"\nStandard time after SetTime is: ",
28          time->ToStandardString() );
29
30       // attempt invalid time settings
31       time->SetTime( 99, 99, 99 );
32
33       output = String::Concat( output,
34          S"\n\nAfter attempting invalid settings: ",
35          S"\nUniversal time: ", time->ToUniversalString(),
36          S"\nStandard time: ", time->ToStandardString() );
37
```

Fig. 5.3   Using an abstract data type. (Part 1 of 2.)

```
38       MessageBox::Show( output, S"Testing Class Time1" );
39
40       return 0;
41   } // end function WinMain
```

Fig. 5.3   Using an abstract data type. (Part 2 of 2.)

When building an MC++ application, each class definition normally is placed in a *header file,* and that class's method definitions are placed in *source-code files* with the same name and the extension **.cpp**. A header file (extension **.h**) contains the names and types of all methods (or *member functions*[1]), member data and other information about the class needed by the compiler. The header files are included (via **#include**) in each file in which the class is used, and the source-code file is compiled and linked with the file containing the main program. The **#include** directive instructs the compiler to treat the header file contents as if they are inserted into the **.cpp** file in place of the **#include**. To add a header file to a project in Visual Studio .NET, right-click **Header Files** in the **Solution Explorer** and selecting **Add > Add New Item...** (or **Add > Add Existing Item...** if the file already exists) from the popup menu.

Figure 5.1 consists of the header file **Time1.h** in which class **Time1** is defined. Line 4 introduces the **#pragma once** compile directive. This directive instructs the compiler to process a header file only once even if it is included in more than one file in a project. The compiler normally generates an error if a class definition is included more than once; the directive ensures that, regardless of how many files in a project include a header file, the compiler processes the definition only once.

Line 10 begins the **Time1** class definition. Class **Time1** implicitly inherits from class **Object** (namespace **System**). MC++ programmers use *inheritance* to create classes from existing classes. Every class in MC++ (except **Object**) inherits from an existing class definition. It is not necessary to understand inheritance to learn the concepts and programs in this chapter. We explore inheritance and class **Object** in detail in Chapter 6.

Line 10 uses keyword **__gc** to specify that **Time1** is a managed class (i.e., the CLR manages its lifetime). The .NET Framework garbage collector destroys unused objects of managed classes in your programs. We discuss garbage collection in Section 5.10.

The opening left brace (**{**) at line 11 and closing right brace (**}**) at line 22 delineate the *body* of class **Time1**. Any information that we place in this body is said to be encapsulated

---

1. In C++, the methods of a class usually are referred to as member functions. However, in the .NET community, the term "methods" is the proper idiom. Therefore, we use "methods" throughout this book.

(i.e., wrapped) in the class. For example, lines 18–20 of class **Time1** declare three **int** variables—**hour, minute** and **second**—that represent the time of day in *universal-time* format (*24-hour clock* format). Variables declared in a class definition, but not inside a method definition, are called *instance variables*—each instance (object) of the class contains its own separate copy of the class's instance variables. The semicolon (**;**) at line 22 ends the class definition. Every class definition must end with a semicolon.

Common Programming Error 5.1

Failure to end a class definition with a semicolon is a syntax error.

The **public:** and **private:** labels are *member access specifiers*. Any data member or method declared after member access specifier **public** (and before the next member access specifier) is accessible wherever the program has a pointer to an object of class **Time1**. Any data member or method declared after member access specifier **private** (and up to the next member access specifier) is accessible only to methods of the class. Member access specifiers are always followed by a colon (**:**) and can appear multiple times and in any order in a class definition. For the remainder of the text, we will refer to the member access specifiers as **public** and **private**, without the colon. In Chapter 6, Object-Oriented Programming: Inheritance, we introduce a third member access specifier, **protected**, as we study inheritance and the part it plays in object-oriented programming.

Good Programming Practice 5.1

*Even though **private** and **public** members can be intermixed, use each member access specifier only once in a class definition for clarity and readability. Place **public** members first so that they are easy to locate.*

The default member access for objects created with keyword **class** is **private**. Thus, if we did not provide any member access specifiers in Fig. 5.1, all of the data members and methods of the class would be considered **private**. *Structures*, another available MC++ construct, have default member access **public**. Structures, which are similar to classes, are created with keyword **struct**.[2]

The three integer members appear after the **private** member access specifier. Lines 19–21 declare each of the three **private int** instance variables—**hour, minute** and **second**—indicating that these instance variables of the class are accessible only to members of the class. (This is known as *data hiding*.) When an object of the class encapsulates such instance variables, only data members of that object's class can access the variables. Normally, instance variables are declared **private**, and methods are declared **public**. However, it is possible to have **private** methods and **public** instance variables, as we will see later. Often, **private** methods are called *utility methods*, or *helper methods*, because they can be called only by other methods of that class. The purpose of utility methods is to support the operation of a class's other methods. Declaring instance variables and utility methods as **public** is a dangerous practice. Providing such access to these data members is unsafe—foreign code (i.e., code in other classes) could set **public** data members to invalid values, producing potentially disastrous results.

---

2. Structures are not discussed in this book. More information about structures can be found at **msdn.microsoft.com/library/default.asp?url=/library/en-us/ vclang/html/vcsmpstruct.asp**.

Software Engineering Observation 5.2

Declare all instance variables of a class as **private***. The architecture of accessing* **private** *data through* **public** *methods that first validate the data allows the developer to ensure that an object's data remains in a consistent state.*

Software Engineering Observation 5.3

Make a class member **private** *if there is no reason for that member to be accessed outside of the class definition.*

Classes often include *accessor methods* that can read or display data. Another common use for access methods is to test the truth of conditions—such methods often are called *predicate methods.* For example, we could design predicate method **IsEmpty** for a *container class*—a class capable of holding many objects, such as a linked list, a stack or a queue. (These data structures are discussed in detail in Chapter 19, Data Structures and Collections.) **IsEmpty** would return **true** if the container is empty and **false** otherwise. A program might test **IsEmpty** before attempting to read another item from the container object. Similarly, a program might call another predicate method (e.g., **IsFull**) before attempting to insert an item into a container object.

Class **Time1** (Fig. 5.1) contains constructor **Time1** (line 13) and methods **SetTime** (line 14), **ToUniversalString** (line 15) and **ToStandardString** (line 16). These are the **public** methods (also called the **public** *services* or the **public** *interface*) of the class. Clients of class **Time1**, such as class **TimeTest1.cpp** (Fig. 5.3), use **Time1**'s **public** interface to manipulate the data stored in **Time1** objects or to cause class **Time1** to perform some service. The class definition contains prototypes for the following four methods after the **public** member access specifier—**Time1**, **SetTime**, **ToStandardString** and **ToUniversalString**. These methods are known as the **public** methods, **public** *services* or **public** *behaviors* of the class. *Clients* (i.e., portions of a program that use the class) will use these class methods to manipulate the class's data. The data members of the class support the delivery of the *services* the class provides to the clients of the class.

Figure 5.2 consists of the source-code file **Time1.cpp** in which the methods of class **Time1** are defined. Lines 8-11 define the *constructor* of class **Time1**. A class's constructor initializes objects of that class. When a program creates an object of class **Time1** with operator **new**, the constructor is called to initialize the object. Class **Time1**'s constructor calls method **SetTime** (lines 15–23) to initialize instance variables **hour**, **minute** and **second** to **0** (representing midnight). Constructors can take arguments, but cannot return values. As we will see, a class can have overloaded constructors. An important difference between constructors and other methods is that constructors cannot specify a return type. Generally, constructors are **public**. Note that the constructor name must be the same as the class name.

Common Programming Error 5.2

Attempting to **return** *a value from a constructor is a syntax error.*

Method **SetTime** (lines 15–23) is a **public** method that receives three **int** parameters and uses them to set the time. A conditional expression tests each argument to determine whether the value is in a specified range. For example, the **hour** value must be greater than or equal to 0 and less than 24, because universal-time format represents hours as integers from 0 to 23. Similarly, both minute and second values must be greater than or equal to 0 and less than 60. Any values outside these ranges are invalid values and default to zero. Setting invalid values to zero ensures that a **Time1** object always contains valid data (because, in this example, zero is a valid value for **hour**, **minute** and **second**). Rather than simply assigning a default value, developers might want to indicate to the client that the time entered was invalid. In Chapter 8, we discuss exception handling, which can be used to indicate invalid initialization values.

Software Engineering Observation 5.4

Always define a class so that each of its instance variables contains valid values.

Method **ToUniversalString** (lines 26–30) takes no arguments and returns a **String *** in universal-time format, consisting of six digits—two for the hour, two for the minute and two for the second. For example, if the time were 1:30:07 PM, method **ToUniversalString** would return **13:30:07**. Lines 28–29 use **String** method **Concat** to configure the universal-time string. Method **ToString** is called on each integer with argument **D2** (a two-digit base 10-decimal number format) for display purposes. The **D2** format specification causes single-digit values to appear as two digits with a leading **0** (e.g., **8** would be represented as **08**). The two colons separate the hour from the minute and the minute from the second in the resulting **String *** object.

Method **ToStandardString** (lines 33–40) takes no arguments and returns a **String *** object in standard-time format, consisting of the **hour**, **minute** and **second** values separated by colons and followed by an AM or a PM indicator (e.g., **1:27:06 PM**). Like method **ToUniversalString**, method **ToStandardString** uses **String** method **Concat** to format the **minute** and **second** as two-digit values with leading zeros if necessary. Line 36 determines the value for **hour** in the **String *** object—if the **hour** is **0** or **12** (AM or PM), the **hour** appears as 12; otherwise, the **hour** appears as a value from 1–11.

After defining the class, we can use it as a type in declarations such as

```
Time1 *sunset; // pointer to a Time1 object
```

The class name (**Time1**) is a type name. A class can yield many objects, just as a primitive data type, such as **int**, can yield many variables. Programmers can create class types as needed; this is one reason why MC++ is known as an *extensible language*.

The main program **TimeTest1** (Fig. 5.3) uses an instance of class **Time1**. Note that line 8 uses **#include** to link to the class header file. This allows the driver to create **Time1** objects and access the class's **public** methods.

Although all of the programs in the previous chapters displayed output in the command prompt, most MC++ applications use windows or *dialogs* to display output. Dialogs are windows that typically display important messages to the user of an application. The .NET Framework Class Library includes class **MessageBox** for creating dialogs. Class **MessageBox** is defined in namespace **System::Windows::Forms**. The program in Fig. 5.3 displays its output in a message dialog using class **MessageBox**.

Note that line 10 uses **WinMain** as the entry point of the application. This is because **WinMain** is the standard entry point for Windows programs; **WinMain** ensures that the console window does not appear when the application is executed. We discuss Windows programming and **WinMain** in more detail in Chapter 9, Graphical User Interface Concepts: Part 1.

Function **WinMain** (lines 10–41) declares and initializes **Time1** instance **time** (line 12). When the object is instantiated, *operator **new*** allocates the memory in which the **Time1** object will be stored, then calls the **Time1** constructor (lines 8–11 of Fig. 5.2) to initialize the instance variables of the **Time1** object. As mentioned before, this constructor invokes method **SetTime** of class **Time1** to initialize each **private** instance variable to **0**. Operator **new** (line 12 of Fig. 5.3) then returns a pointer to the newly created object; this pointer is assigned to **time**.

Software Engineering Observation 5.5

*Note the relationship between operator **new** and the constructor of a class. When operator **new** creates an object of a class, that class's constructor is called to initialize the object's instance variables.*

Line 13 declares **String** pointer **output** to store the **String** containing the results, which later will be displayed in a **MessageBox**. Lines 16–18 assign to **output** the time in universal-time format (by invoking method **ToUniversalString** of the **Time1** object) and standard-time format (by invoking method **ToStandardString** of the **Time1** object). Note the syntax of the method call in each case—the pointer **time** is followed by the member access operator (**->**) followed by the method name. Members of a class are accessed using the *member access operators*—the *dot operator* (**.**) and the *arrow operator* (**->**). The dot operator accesses a class member via the variable name for the object or via a reference to the object; for instance, we often access a variable's **ToString** method with the dot operator. The arrow operator—consisting of a minus sign (**-**) and a greater than sign (**>**) with no intervening spaces—accesses a class member via a pointer to the object.

The expression **time->hour** is equivalent to **(*time).hour**, which dereferences the pointer and accesses the member **hour** using the dot operator. The parentheses are needed here because the dot operator (**.**) has a higher precedence than the pointer dereferencing operator (*****).

Common Programming Error 5.3

*The expression **(*time).hour** refers to the **hour** member of the class pointed to by **time**. Omitting the parentheses as in ***time.hour** would be a syntax error because **.** has a higher precedence than *****, so the expression would execute as if parenthesized as ***(time.hour)**.*

Line 21 sets the time for the **Time1** object to which **time** points by passing valid hour, minute and second arguments to **Time1** method **SetTime**. Lines 24–28 append to **output** the new time in both universal and standard formats to confirm that the time was set correctly.

To illustrate that method **SetTime** validates the values passed to it, line 31 passes invalid time arguments to method **SetTime**. Lines 33–36 append to **output** the new time in both formats. All three values passed to **SetTime** are invalid, so instance variables **hour**, **minute** and **second** are set to **0**. Line 38 displays a **MessageBox** with the results of our program. Notice in the last two lines of the output window that the time was indeed set to midnight when invalid arguments were passed to **SetTime**.

Note that the class declares instance variables **hour**, **minute** and **second** as **private**. Such instance variables are not accessible outside the class in which they are defined. A class's clients should not be concerned with the data representation of that class. Clients of a class should be interested only in the services provided by that class. For example, the class could represent the time internally as the number of seconds that have elapsed since the previous midnight. Suppose the data representation changes. Clients still are able to use the same **public** methods and obtain the same results without being aware of the change in internal representation. In this sense, the implementation of a class is said to be *hidden* from its clients.

Software Engineering Observation 5.6

Information hiding promotes program modifiability and simplifies the client's perception of a class.

Software Engineering Observation 5.7

Clients of a class can (and should) use the class without knowing the internal details of how the class is implemented. If the class implementation changes (to improve performance, for example), but the class interface remains constant, the client's source code need not change. This makes it much easier to modify systems.

In this program, the **Time1** constructor initializes the instance variables to **0** (the universal-time equivalent of 12 midnight) to ensure that the object is created in a *consistent state*—i.e., all instance variables have valid values. The instance variables of a **Time1** object cannot store invalid values, because the constructor, which calls **SetTime**, is called to initialize the instance variables when the **Time1** object is created. Method **SetTime** scrutinizes subsequent attempts by a client to modify the instance variables.

Normally, the instance variables of a class are initialized in that class's constructor, but they also can be initialized when they are declared in the class body. If a programmer does not initialize instance variables explicitly, the compiler implicitly initializes them. When this occurs, the compiler sets primitive numeric variables to **0**, **bool** values to **false** and pointers to **NULL**. [*Note*: Readers should recall that in MC++, **0** represents a null pointer. However, sometimes in this book, we use **NULL** in place of **0**. **NULL** is defined in a number of headers, including ***tchar.h***, and is interchangeable with **0**.]

Methods **ToUniversalString** and **ToStandardString** take no arguments, because, by default, these methods manipulate the instance variables of the particular **Time1** object on which they are invoked. This often makes method calls more concise than conventional function calls in procedural programming languages. It also reduces the likelihood of passing the wrong arguments, the wrong types of arguments or the wrong number of arguments.

Software Engineering Observation 5.8

The use of an object-oriented programming approach often simplifies method calls by reducing the number of parameters that must be passed. This benefit of object-oriented programming derives from the fact that encapsulation of instance variables and methods within an object gives the object's methods the right to access the object's instance variables.

Classes simplify programming, because the client need be concerned only with the **public** operations encapsulated in the object. Usually, such operations are designed to be client oriented, rather than implementation oriented. Clients are neither aware of, nor involved in, a class's implementation. Interfaces change less frequently than do implementations. When an implementation changes, implementation-dependent code must change accordingly. By hiding the implementation, we eliminate the possibility that other program parts will become dependent on the class-implementation details.

Often, programmers do not have to create classes "from scratch." Rather, they can derive classes from other classes that provide behaviors required by the new classes. Classes also can include pointers to objects as members. Such *software reuse* can greatly enhance programmer productivity. Chapter 6 discusses *inheritance*—the process by which new classes are derived from existing classes. Section 5.8 discusses *composition* (or *aggregation*), in which classes include as members pointers to objects of other classes.

Many compiled classes in the .NET Framework Class Library (including **MessageBox**) need to be referenced before they can be used in a program. Depending on the type of application we create, classes may be compiled into files with an **.exe** (*executable*) extension, a **.dll** (or *dynamic link library*) extension or one of several other extensions. Dynamic link libraries, which cannot be run as programs by themselves, contain executable code (e.g., functions and classes). Programs link to DLLs, which can be shared among several executing programs. DLLs are loaded at runtime dynamically. Executable files contain an application entry point (e.g., a **main** function). Such files are called *assemblies* and are the packaging units for code in MC++. [*Note*: Assemblies can be comprised of files of different types.] The assembly is a package containing the Microsoft Intermediate Language (MSIL) code that a project has been compiled into, plus any other information that is needed for these classes. The assembly that we need to reference can be found in the Visual Studio .NET documentation for the class we wish to use. The easiest way to access this information is to go to the **Help** menu in Visual Studio .NET and choose **Index**. The reader then can type in the name of the class to access the documentation. Class **MessageBox** is located in assembly **System.Windows.Forms.dll**. Other classes that create GUI components will be described in Chapters 9 and 10, Graphical User Interface Concepts: Part 1 and Graphical User Interface Concepts: Part 2, respectively.

In **WinMain**, line 38 calls method *Show* of class **MessageBox** (Fig. 5.3). This overloaded version of the method takes two strings as arguments. The first string (**output**) is the message to be displayed. The second string is the title of the message dialog (**"Testing Class Time1"**). If the second argument is omitted, the message dialog will have no title. Method **Show** is called a *static method*. Such methods always are called by using their class name (in this case, **MessageBox**) followed by the scope resolution operator (**::**) and the method name (in this case, **Show**). We discuss static methods in Section 5.11.

Line 38 displays the dialog shown in Fig. 5.4. The dialog includes an **OK** button that allows the user to *dismiss (close)* the dialog. Positioning the mouse cursor (also called the mouse pointer) over the **OK** button and clicking the mouse dismisses the dialog. The user can close the dialog by clicking the **OK** button or the close box. Once this occurs, the program terminates, because the **WinMain** function terminates.

5.3 Class Scope

In Section 4.8, we discussed method scope; now, we discuss *class scope*. A class's instance variables and methods belong to that class's scope. Within a class's scope, class members are immediately accessible to that class's methods and can be referenced by name. Outside

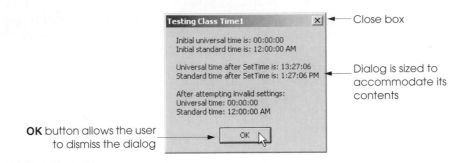

OK button allows the user
to dismiss the dialog

Close box

Dialog is sized to
accommodate its
contents

Fig. 5.4   Dialog displayed by calling **MessageBox::Show**.

a class's scope, class members cannot be referenced directly by name. Those class members that are visible (such as **public** members) can be accessed only through a "handle" (i.e., members can be referenced via the format *pointerName->memberName*).

If a variable is defined in a method, only that method can access the variable (i.e., the variable is a local variable of that method). Such variables are said to have *block scope*. If a method defines a variable that has the same name as a variable with class scope (i.e., an instance variable), the method-scope variable hides the class-scope variable in that method's scope. A hidden instance variable can be accessed in a method by preceding its name with the keyword **this** and the member access operator, as in **this->hour**. We discuss keyword **this** in Section 5.9.

5.4 Controlling Access to Members

The member access modifiers **public** and **private** control access to a class's data and methods. (In Chapter 6, Object-Oriented Programming: Inheritance, we introduce another access modifier—**protected**.)

As previously stated, **public** methods present to the class's clients a view of the *services* that the class provides (i.e., the **public** interface of the class). Previously, we mentioned the merits of writing methods that perform only one task. If a method must execute other tasks to calculate its final result, these tasks should be performed by a helper method. A client does not need to call these helper methods, nor does it need to be concerned with how the class uses its helper methods. For these reasons, helper methods are declared as **private** members of a class.

Common Programming Error 5.4

*Attempting to access a **private** class member from outside that class is a compilation error.*

The application of Fig. 5.5 (which uses the **Time1** class from Fig. 5.1–Fig. 5.2) demonstrates that **private** class members are not accessible outside the class. Lines 12–14 attempt to access the **private** instance variables **hour**, **minute** and **second** of the **Time1** object to which **time** points. When this program is compiled, the compiler generates errors stating that the **private** members **hour**, **minute** and **second** are not accessible.

```
1   // Fig. 5.5: RestrictedAccess.cpp
2   // Demonstrate compilation errors from attempt to access
3   // private class members.
4
5   #include "Time1.h"
6
7   // main entry point for application
8   int main()
9   {
10      Time1 *time = new Time1();
11
12      time->hour = 7;
13      time->minute = 15;
14      time->second = 30;
15
16      return 0;
17  }
```

Fig. 5.5   Accessing **private** class members from client code generates syntax errors.

Access to **private** data should be controlled carefully by a class's methods. To allow clients to read the values of **private** data, the class can define a *property* that enables client code to access this **private** data safely. Properties, which we discuss in detail in Section 5.7, contain *accessor methods* that handle the details of modifying and returning data. A property definition can contain a *get accessor*, a *set accessor* or both. A *get* accessor enables a client to read a **private** data member; a *set* accessor enables the client to modify a **private** data member. Such modification would seem to violate the notion of **private** data. However, a *set* accessor can provide data-validation capabilities (such as range checking) to ensure that the value is set properly. A *set* accessor also can translate between the format of the data used in the interface and the format used in the underlying implementation. Similarly, a *get* accessor need not expose the data in "raw" format; rather, the *get* accessor can alter the data and limit the client's view of that data.

Software Engineering Observation 5.9

Class designers need not provide set *or* get *accessors for each* **private** *data member; these capabilities should be provided only when doing so makes sense.*

Testing and Debugging Tip 5.1

Declaring the instance variables of a class as **private** *and the methods and properties of the class as* **public** *facilitates debugging, because problems with data manipulations are localized to the class methods that manipulate that data.*

5.5 Initializing Class Objects: Constructors

When a program creates an instance of a class, the program invokes the class's constructor to initialize the class's instance variables (data members). A class can contain overloaded constructors to provide multiple ways to initialize objects of that class.

Common Programming Error 5.5

*Only **static** instance variables can be initialized in the body of a managed class. Attempting to initialize a non-**static** instance variable is a syntax error.*

Regardless of whether instance variables receive explicit initialization values, the instance variables always are initialized. In such cases, instance variables receive their default values (**0** for primitive numeric type variables, **false** for **bool** variable and **NULL** for pointers).

Performance Tip 5.1

Because instance variables always are initialized to default values by the runtime, avoid initializing instance variables to their default values in the constructor.

Software Engineering Observation 5.10

When appropriate, provide a constructor to ensure that every object is initialized with meaningful values.

When creating an object of a class, the programmer can provide *initializers* in parentheses to the right of the class name. These initializers are the arguments to the constructor. In general, declarations take the form

ClassName ***objectPointer* = *new** ClassName* (*arguments*) **;**

where *objectPointer* is a pointer of the appropriate data type, **new** indicates that an object is being created, *ClassName* indicates the type of the new object (and the name of the constructor being called) and *arguments* specifies a comma-separated list of the values used by the constructor to initialize the object.

If a class does not define any constructors, the compiler provides a *default (no-argument) constructor*. This compiler-provided default constructor contains no code (i.e., the constructor has an empty body) and takes no parameters. The programmer also can provide a default constructor, as we demonstrated in class **Time1** (Fig. 5.1 and Fig. 5.2). Programmer-provided default constructors can have code in their bodies.

Common Programming Error 5.6

*If a class has constructors, but none of the **public** constructors is a default constructor, and a program attempts to call a no-argument constructor to initialize an object of the class, a compilation error occurs. A constructor can be called with no arguments only if there are no constructors for the class (in which case the compiler-provided default constructor is called) or if the class defines a **public** no-argument constructor.*

5.6 Using Overloaded Constructors

Like methods, constructors of a class can be overloaded. The **Time1** constructor in Fig. 5.2 initialized **hour, minute** and **second** to **0** (i.e., midnight in universal time) via a call to the method **SetTime**. However, class **Time2** (Fig. 5.6 and Fig. 5.7) overloads the constructor to provide a variety of ways to initialize **Time2** objects. Each constructor calls

Time2 method **SetTime**, which ensures that the object begins in a consistent state by setting out-of-range values to zero. MC++ invokes the appropriate constructor by matching the number, types and order of arguments specified in the constructor call with the number, types and order of parameters specified in each constructor definition. Figure 5.6–Fig. 5.7 demonstrate using initializers and overloaded constructors.

```
1   // Fig. 5.6: Time2.h
2   // Class Time2 header file.
3
4   #pragma once
5
6   #using <mscorlib.dll>
7
8   using namespace System;
9
10  // Time2 class definition
11  public __gc class Time2
12  {
13  public:
14      Time2();
15
16      // overloaded constructors
17      Time2( int );
18      Time2( int, int );
19      Time2( int, int, int );
20      Time2( Time2 * );
21
22      void SetTime( int, int, int );
23      String *ToUniversalString();
24      String *ToStandardString();
25
26  private:
27      int hour;      // 0-23
28      int minute;    // 0-59
29      int second;    // 0-59
30  }; // end class Time2
```

Fig. 5.6 Overloaded constructors provide flexible object-initialization options.

```
1   // Fig. 5.7: Time2.cpp
2   // Class Time2 provides overloaded constructors.
3
4   #include "Time2.h"
5
6   // Time2 constructor initializes instance variables to
7   // zero to set default time to midnight
8   Time2::Time2()
9   {
10      SetTime( 0, 0, 0 );
11  }
12
```

Fig. 5.7 **Time2** class method definitions. (Part 1 of 3.)

```
13   // Time2 constructor: hour supplied, minute and second
14   // defaulted to 0
15   Time2::Time2( int hourValue )
16   {
17      SetTime( hourValue, 0, 0 );
18   }
19
20   // Time2 constructor: hour and minute supplied, second
21   // defaulted to 0
22   Time2::Time2( int hourValue, int minuteValue )
23   {
24      SetTime( hourValue, minuteValue, 0 );
25   }
26
27   // Time2 constructor: hour, minute, and second supplied
28   Time2::Time2( int hourValue, int minuteValue, int secondValue )
29   {
30      SetTime( hourValue, minuteValue, secondValue);
31   }
32
33   // Time2 constructor: initialize using another Time2 object
34   Time2::Time2( Time2 *time )
35   {
36      SetTime( time->hour, time->minute, time->second );
37   }
38
39   // set new time value in 24-hour format. Perform validity
40   // check on the data. Set invalid values to zero.
41   void Time2::SetTime( int hourValue, int minuteValue,
42      int secondValue )
43   {
44      hour = ( hourValue >= 0 && hourValue < 24 ) ?
45         hourValue : 0;
46      minute = ( minuteValue >= 0 && minuteValue < 60 ) ?
47         minuteValue : 0;
48      second = ( secondValue >= 0 && secondValue < 60 ) ?
49         secondValue : 0;
50   }
51
52   // convert time to universal-time (24 hour) format string
53   String *Time2::ToUniversalString()
54   {
55      return String::Concat( hour.ToString( S"D2" ), S":"
56         minute.ToString( S"D2" ), S":", second.ToString( S"D2" ) );
57   }
58
59   // convert time to standard-time (12 hour) format string
60   String *Time2::ToStandardString()
61   {
62      return String::Concat(
63         ( ( hour == 12 || hour == 0 ) ? 12 : hour % 12 ).ToString(),
64         S":", minute.ToString( S"D2" ), S":",
65         second.ToString( S"D2" ), S" ",
```

Fig. 5.7   **Time2** class method definitions. (Part 2 of 3.)

```
66          ( hour < 12 ? S"AM" : S"PM" ) );
67      }
```

Fig. 5.7 **Time2** class method definitions. (Part 3 of 3.)

Because most of the code in class **Time2** is identical to that in class **Time1**, this discussion concentrates only on the overloaded constructors. Lines 8–11 (of Fig. 5.7) define the no-argument constructor that sets the time to midnight. Lines 15–18 define a **Time2** constructor that receives a single **int** argument representing the **hour** and sets the time using the specified **hour** value and zero for **minute** and **second**. Lines 22–25 define a **Time2** constructor that receives two **int** arguments representing the **hour** and **minute** and sets the time using those values and zero for the **second**. Lines 28–31 define a **Time2** constructor that receives three **int** arguments representing the **hour**, **minute** and **second** and uses those values to set the time. Lines 34–37 define a **Time2** constructor that receives a pointer to another **Time2** object. When this last constructor is called, the values from the **Time2** argument are used to initialize the **hour**, **minute** and **second** values of the new **Time2** object. Even though class **Time2** declares **hour**, **minute** and **second** as **private** (lines 27–29 of Fig. 5.6), the **Time2** constructor can access these values in its **Time2** argument directly using the expressions **time->hour**, **time->minute** and **time->second**.

Software Engineering Observation 5.11

*When one object of a class has a pointer to another object of the same class, the first object can access all the second object's data and methods (including those that are **private**).*

Notice that the second, third and fourth constructors (beginning on lines 15, 22 and 28 of Fig. 5.7) have some arguments in common and that those arguments are kept in the same order. For instance, the constructor that starts at line 22 has as its two arguments an integer representing the hour and an integer representing the minute. The constructor beginning on line 28 has these same two arguments in the same order, followed by its last argument (an integer representing the second).

Good Programming Practice 5.2

When defining overloaded constructors, keep the order of arguments as similar as possible; this makes client programming easier.

Common Programming Error 5.7

Unlike functions, constructors and methods cannot have default arguments. Attempting to specify a default value for a constructor or method argument generates a compilation error.

Constructors cannot specify return types; doing so results in syntax errors. Also, notice that each constructor receives a different number or different types of arguments. Even though only two of the constructors receive values for the **hour**, **minute** and **second**, each constructor calls **SetTime** with values for **hour**, **minute** and **second** and uses zeros for the missing values to satisfy **SetTime**'s requirement of three arguments.

Driver **TimeTest2** (Fig. 5.8) starts the application that demonstrates the use of overloaded constructors. Line 15 creates six **Time2** objects that invoke various constructors of the class. Line 17 invokes the no-argument constructor by placing an empty set of parentheses after the class name. Lines 18–22 invoke the **Time2** constructors that receive arguments. To invoke the appropriate constructor, pass the proper number, types and order of arguments (specified by the constructor's definition) to that constructor. For example, line 18 invokes the constructor that is defined in lines 19–22 of Fig. 5.7. Lines 24–52 invoke methods **ToUniversalString** and **ToStandardString** for each **Time2** object to demonstrate that the constructors initialize the objects correctly.

```cpp
1   // Fig. 5.8: TimeTest2.cpp
2   // Using overloaded constructors.
3
4   #using <system.dll>
5   #using <system.windows.forms.dll>
6
7   using namespace System;
8   using namespace System::Windows::Forms;
9
10  #include "Time2.h"
11
12  // main entry point for application
13  int __stdcall WinMain()
14  {
15     Time2 *time1, *time2, *time3, *time4, *time5, *time6;
16
17     time1 = new Time2();                  // 00:00:00
18     time2 = new Time2( 2 );               // 02:00:00
19     time3 = new Time2( 21, 34 );          // 21:34:00
20     time4 = new Time2( 12, 25, 42 );      // 12:25:42
21     time5 = new Time2( 27, 74, 99 );      // 00:00:00
22     time6 = new Time2( time4 );           // 12:25:42
23
24     String *output = String::Concat( S"Constructed with: ",
25        S"\ntime1: all arguments defaulted",
26        S"\n\t", time1->ToUniversalString(),
27        S"\n\t", time1->ToStandardString() );
28
29     output = String::Concat( output,
30        S"\ntime2: hour specified; minute and ",
31        S"second defaulted", S"\n\t", time2->ToUniversalString(),
32        S"\n\t", time2->ToStandardString() );
33
34     output = String::Concat( output,
35        S"\ntime3: hour and minute specified; ",
36        S"second defaulted", S"\n\t", time3->ToUniversalString(),
37        S"\n\t", time3->ToStandardString() );
38
39     output = String::Concat( output,
40        S"\ntime4: hour, minute and second specified", S"\n\t",
41        time4->ToUniversalString(), S"\n\t",
42        time4->ToStandardString() );
43
44     output = String::Concat( output,
45        S"\ntime5: all invalid values specified ",
46        S"\n\t", time5->ToUniversalString(), S"\n\t",
47        time5->ToStandardString() );
```

Fig. 5.8   Using overloaded constructors. (Part 1 of 2.)

```
48
49      output = String::Concat( output,
50          S"\ntime6: Time2 object time4 specified", S"\n\t",
51          time6->ToUniversalString(), S"\n\t",
52          time6->ToStandardString() );
53
54      MessageBox::Show( output,
55          S"Demonstrating Overloaded Constructors" );
56
57      return 0;
58  } // end function WinMain
```

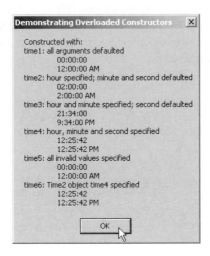

Fig. 5.8   Using overloaded constructors. (Part 2 of 2.)

Each **Time2** constructor can be written to include a copy of the appropriate statements from method **SetTime**. This might be slightly more efficient, because it eliminates the extra call to **SetTime**. However, consider what would happen if the programmer were to change the representation of the time from three **int** values (requiring 12 bytes of memory) to a single **int** value representing the total number of seconds that have elapsed in the day (requiring 4 bytes of memory). Placing identical code in the **Time2** constructors and method **SetTime** makes such a change in the class definition more difficult, because every constructor's body would require modifications to manipulate the data as a single **int** rather than three **int**s. If the **Time2** constructors call **SetTime** directly, any changes to the implementation of **SetTime** must be made only once, in the body of **Set-Time**. This reduces the likelihood of introducing a programming error when altering the implementation, because we make only one change in the class, rather than changing every constructor and method **SetTime**.

Software Engineering Observation 5.12

If a method of a class provides functionality required by a constructor (or other method) of the class, call that method from the constructor (or other method). This simplifies the maintenance of the code and reduces the likelihood of introducing errors into the code.

5.7 Properties

Methods of a class can manipulate that class's **private** instance variables. A typical manipulation might be the adjustment of a customer's bank balance—a **private** instance variable of a class **BankAccount**—by a **ComputeInterest** method.

Classes often provide **public** *properties* to allow clients to *set* (i.e., assign values to) or *get* (i.e., obtain the values of) **private** instance variables. Figure 5.9 enhances our **Time** class, now called **Time3**, to include three properties—**Hour**, **Minute** and **Second**—for the **private** instance variables **hour**, **minute** and **second**. Each property contains a *get accessor* (to retrieve the field value) and a *set accessor* (to modify the field value). The *set* accessors of these properties strictly control the setting of the instance variables to valid values. An attempt to set any instance variable to an incorrect value causes the instance variable to be set to zero (thus leaving the instance variable in a consistent state). Each *get* accessor returns the appropriate instance variable's value. We create which access variables **hour**, **minute** and **second**, respectively. Figure 5.10 contains the method definitions of class **Time3**.

```
1   // Fig. 5.9: Time3.h
2   // Class Time3 introduces properties.
3
4   #pragma once
5
6   #using <mscorlib.dll>
7   #using <system.dll>
8
9   using namespace System;
10
11  // Time3 class definition
12  public __gc class Time3
13  {
14  public:
15     Time3();
16     Time3( int );
17     Time3( int, int );
18     Time3( int, int, int );
19     Time3( Time3 * );
20     void SetTime( int, int, int );
21
22     // get accessor for property Hour
23     __property int get_Hour()
24     {
25        return hour;
26     }
27
28     // set accessor for property Hour
29     __property void set_Hour( int value )
30     {
31        hour = ( ( value >= 0 && value < 24 ) ? value : 0 );
32     }
33
```

Fig. 5.9   Properties provide controlled access to an object's data. (Part 1 of 2.)

```
34        // get accessor for property Minute
35        __property int get_Minute()
36        {
37           return minute;
38        }
39
40        // set accessor for property Minute
41        __property void set_Minute( int value )
42        {
43           minute = ( ( value >= 0 && value < 60 ) ? value : 0 );
44        }
45
46        // get accessor for property Second
47        __property int get_Second()
48        {
49           return second;
50        }
51
52        // set accessor for property Second
53        __property void set_Second( int value )
54        {
55           second = ( ( value >= 0 && value < 60 ) ? value : 0 );
56        }
57
58        String *ToUniversalString();
59        String *ToStandardString();
60
61     private:
62        int hour;    // 0-23
63        int minute;  // 0-59
64        int second;  // 0-59
65     }; // end class Time3
```

Fig. 5.9   Properties provide controlled access to an object's data. (Part 2 of 2.)

```
1     // Fig. 5.10: Time3.cpp
2     // Method definitions for class Time3.
3
4     #include "Time3.h"
5
6     // Time3 constructor initializes instance variables to
7     // zero to set default time to midnight
8     Time3::Time3()
9     {
10        SetTime( 0, 0, 0 );
11    }
12
13    // Time3 constructor: hour supplied, minute and second
14    // defaulted to 0
15    Time3::Time3( int hourValue )
16    {
17        SetTime( hourValue, 0, 0 );
18    }
```

Fig. 5.10   **Time3** class method definitions. (Part 1 of 2.)

```
19
20    // Time3 constructor: hour and minute supplied, second
21    // defaulted to 0
22    Time3::Time3( int hourValue, int minuteValue )
23    {
24       SetTime( hourValue, minuteValue, 0 );
25    }
26
27    // Time3 constructor: hour, minute and second supplied
28    Time3::Time3( int hourValue, int minuteValue, int secondValue )
29    {
30       SetTime( hourValue, minuteValue, secondValue );
31    }
32
33    // Time3 constructor: intialize using another Time3 object
34    Time3::Time3( Time3 *time )
35    {
36       SetTime( time->Hour, time->Minute, time->Second );
37    }
38
39    // set new time value in 24-hour format
40    void Time3::SetTime(
41       int hourValue, int minuteValue, int secondValue )
42    {
43       Hour = hourValue;
44       Minute = minuteValue;
45       Second = secondValue;
46    }
47
48    // convert time to universal-time (24 hour) format string
49    String *Time3::ToUniversalString()
50    {
51       return String::Concat( Hour.ToString( S"D2" ), S":",
52          Minute.ToString( S"D2" ), S":", Second.ToString( S"D2" ) );
53    }
54
55    // convert time to standard-time (12 hour) format string
56    String *Time3::ToStandardString()
57    {
58       return String::Concat(
59          ( ( Hour == 12 || Hour == 0 ) ? 12 : Hour % 12 ).ToString(),
60          S":", Minute.ToString( S"D2" ), S":",
61          Second.ToString( S"D2" ), S" ",
62          ( Hour < 12 ? S"AM" : S"PM" ) );
63    }
```

Fig. 5.10 Time3 class method definitions. (Part 2 of 2.)

Providing *set* and *get* capabilities appears to be the same as making the instance variables **public**. However, this is another one of MC++'s subtleties that makes it so attractive from a software-engineering standpoint. If an instance variable is **public**, the instance variable can be read or written to by any method in the program. If an instance variable is **private**, a **public** *get* accessor seems to allow other methods to read the data at will. However, the *get* accessor can control the formatting and display of the data.

Similarly, a **public** *set* accessor can scrutinize attempts to modify the instance variable's value, thus ensuring that the new value is appropriate for that data member. For example, an attempt to *set* the day of the month to 37 would be rejected, and an attempt to *set* a person's weight to a negative value would be rejected. So, *set* and *get* accessors can provide access to **private** data, but the implementation of these accessors controls what the client code can do to the data.

The declaration of instance variables as **private** does not guarantee their integrity. Programmers must provide validity checking—MC++ provides only the framework with which programmers can design better programs.

Testing and Debugging Tip 5.2

*Methods that set the values of **private** data should verify that the intended new values are valid; if they are not, the methods should take appropriate action. The* set *accessors could display an error message, they could place the **private** instance variables into an appropriate consistent state or they could retain the current values of the variables.*

The *set* accessors of a property cannot return values indicating a failed attempt to assign invalid data to objects of the class. Such return values could be useful to a client of a class when handling errors. The client could take appropriate actions if the objects occupy invalid states. Chapter 8 presents exception handling—a mechanism that can be used to indicate attempts to set an object's members to invalid values.

Lines 22–56 (Fig. 5.9) define **Time3** properties **Hour**, **Minute** and **Second** by defining their *get* and *set* accessor methods. A property does not necessarily need both a *get* and a *set* accessor method. A *set* accessor definition has the general form

      __property void set_PropertyName(*type* **value)**

Its corresponding *get* accessor has the general form

      __property *type* **get_PropertyName()**

Every property method name must have be preceded by either **set_** or **get_**. The **PropertyName** portion of the method declaration sets the name of the property.

The *get* accessor methods are on lines 23–26, 35–38 and 47–50. These accessors return the **hour**, **minute** and **second** instance variable values that objects request. The *set* accessors are defined on lines 29–32, 41–44 and 53–56. The body of each *set* accessor performs the same conditional statement that was performed by method **SetTime** previously to set the **hour**, **minute** and **second**.

Common Programming Error 5.8

The accessor methods of a property are prefixed with get *or* set. *If the* get *or* set *prefixes are omitted, a compilation error will occur.*

Method **SetTime** (lines 40–46 of Fig. 5.10) now uses properties **Hour**, **Minute** and **Second** to ensure that instance variables **hour**, **minute** and **second** have valid values. Properties **Hour**, **Minute** and **Second** are *scalar properties*. Scalar properties are properties that can be accessed like fields or variables. We assign values to scalar properties using the **=** (assignment) operator. When this assignment occurs, the code in the *set* accessor for that property executes. Similarly, methods **ToUniversalString** (lines 49–53) and **ToStandardString** (lines 56–63) now use properties **Hour**, **Minute** and

Second to obtain the values of instance variables **hour**, **minute** and **second**. Referencing the scalar property executes the *get* accessor for that property. We discuss another type of property, *indexed properties*, in Section 5.13.

Using *set* and *get* accessor methods throughout the constructors and other methods of class **Time3**, we minimize the changes that we must make to the class definition in the event that we alter the data representation from **hour**, **minute** and **second** to another representation (such as total elapsed seconds in the day). When such changes are made, we must provide only new *set* and *get* accessor bodies. Using this technique also enables programmers to change the implementation of a class without affecting the clients of that class (as long as all the **public** methods of the class still are called in the same way).

Software Engineering Observation 5.13

*Accessing **private** data through* set *and* get *accessors not only protects the instance variables from receiving invalid values, but also hides the internal representation of the instance variables from that class's clients. Thus, if representation of the data changes (typically, to reduce the amount of required storage or to improve performance), only the method implementations need to change—the client implementations need not change, as long as the interface provided by the methods is preserved.*

Time3Test.cpp (Fig. 5.11) defines a console-based application for manipulating an object of class **Time3**.

Line 8 creates an object of class **Time3** and assigns it to **time**. Line 10 creates boolean variable **finished** and initializes it to **false** to indicate that the user is not finished with the program. The **while** loop (lines 13–71) executes until **finished** becomes **true**. Lines 16–19 use the **Time3** properties to display the **hour**, **minute** and **second** values. Lines 20–22 use **Time3** methods **ToUniversalString** and **ToStandardString** to display the universal- and standard-time representations.

```
1   // Fig. 5.11: Time3Test.cpp
2   // Demonstrating Time3 properties Hour, Minute and Second.
3
4   #include "Time3.h"
5
6   int main()
7   {
8      Time3 *time = new Time3();
9      int choice;
10     bool finished = false;
11
12     // loop until user decides to quit
13     while ( !finished ) {
14
15        // display current time
16        Console::WriteLine( String::Concat( S"\nHour: ",
17           time->Hour.ToString(), S"; Minute: ",
18           time->Minute.ToString(), S"; Second: ",
19           time->Second.ToString() ) );
20        Console::WriteLine( String::Concat( S"Standard time: ",
```

Fig. 5.11   Properties demonstration for class **Time3**. (Part 1 of 4.)

```
21              time->ToStandardString(), S"\nUniversal time: ",
22              time->ToUniversalString() ) );
23
24          // display options
25          Console::WriteLine( S"   1: Set Hour" );
26          Console::WriteLine( S"   2: Set Minute" );
27          Console::WriteLine( S"   3: Set Second" );
28          Console::WriteLine( S"   4: Add 1 to Second" );
29          Console::WriteLine( S"  -1: Quit" );
30          Console::Write( S"=> " );
31          choice = Int32::Parse( Console::ReadLine() );
32
33          switch ( choice ) {
34
35              // set Hour property
36              case 1:
37                 Console::Write( S"New Hour: " );
38                 time->Hour = Int32::Parse( Console::ReadLine() );
39                 break;
40
41              // set Minute property
42              case 2:
43                 Console::Write( S"New Minute: " );
44                 time->Minute = Int32::Parse( Console::ReadLine() );
45                 break;
46
47              // set Second property
48              case 3:
49                 Console::Write( S"New Second: " );
50                 time->Second = Int32::Parse( Console::ReadLine() );
51                 break;
52
53              // add one to Second property
54              case 4:
55                 time->Second = ( time->Second + 1 ) % 60;
56
57                 if ( time->Second == 0 ) {
58                    time->Minute = ( time->Minute + 1 ) % 60;
59
60                    if ( time->Minute == 0 )
61                       time->Hour = ( time->Hour + 1 ) % 24;
62                 }
63                 break;
64
65              // exit loop
66              default:
67                 finished = true;
68                 break;
69          } // end switch
70       } // end while
71
72       return 0;
73    } // end function main
```

Fig. 5.11 Properties demonstration for class **Time3**. (Part 2 of 4.)

```
Hour: 0; Minute: 0; Second: 0
Standard time: 12:00:00 AM
Universal time: 00:00:00
   1: Set Hour
   2: Set Minute
   3: Set Second
   4: Add 1 to Second
  -1: Quit
=> 1
New Hour: 23
```

```
Hour: 23; Minute: 0; Second: 0
Standard time: 11:00:00 PM
Universal time: 23:00:00
   1: Set Hour
   2: Set Minute
   3: Set Second
   4: Add 1 to Second
  -1: Quit
=> 2
New Minute: 59
```

```
Hour: 23; Minute: 59; Second: 0
Standard time: 11:59:00 PM
Universal time: 23:59:00
   1: Set Hour
   2: Set Minute
   3: Set Second
   4: Add 1 to Second
  -1: Quit
=> 3
New Second: 58
```

```
Hour: 23; Minute: 59; Second: 58
Standard time: 11:59:58 PM
Universal time: 23:59:58
   1: Set Hour
   2: Set Minute
   3: Set Second
   4: Add 1 to Second
  -1: Quit
=> 4
```

Fig. 5.11   Properties demonstration for class **Time3**. (Part 3 of 4.)

```
Hour: 23; Minute: 59; Second: 59
Standard time: 11:59:59 PM
Universal time: 23:59:59
   1: Set Hour
   2: Set Minute
   3: Set Second
   4: Add 1 to Second
  -1: Quit
=> 4
```

```
Hour: 0; Minute: 0; Second: 0
Standard time: 12:00:00 AM
Universal time: 00:00:00
   1: Set Hour
   2: Set Minute
   3: Set Second
   4: Add 1 to Second
  -1: Quit
=> -1
```

Fig. 5.11　Properties demonstration for class **Time3**. (Part 4 of 4.)

Lines 25–29 then display the available options to the user. The **switch** structure (lines 33–69) executes statements corresponding to the user's choice. Choices **1–3** (lines 36–51) alter the values of a **Time3** property (**Hour**, **Minute** or **Second**). Choice **4** (lines 54–63) enables the user to increment the **second** value by **1**. Lines 55–61 use the **Time3** object's properties to determine and set the new time. For example, **23:59:59** becomes **00:00:00** when the user selects choice **4**. Any other choice (such as **-1**) sets **finished** to **false**, exiting the program.

Properties are not limited to accessing **private** data—properties also can be used to calculate values associated with an object. One example of this would be a **student** object with a property representing the student's GPA (called **GPA**). Programmers can either provide code that calculates the student's GPA in the *get* accessor for this property, or they can simply return a **private** variable containing the GPA, called **gpa**. (The value in this variable will need to be calculated in some other way, such as using a **CalculateGPA** method.) The programmer can use either technique, but we recommend using a property that calculates the GPA. Remember that client code should not be required to tell the **student** object when to calculate the GPA. The client code simply should use the GPA property. The client should not be aware of the underlying implementation.

5.8 Composition: Objects Pointers as Instance Variables of Other Classes

In many situations, referencing existing objects is more convenient than rewriting the objects' code for new classes in new projects. Suppose that we were to implement an **Alarm-Clock** object that needs to know when to sound its alarm. Referencing an existing **Time** object (like those from earlier examples in this chapter) is easier than writing a new **Time** object. The use of pointers to objects of preexisting classes as members of new objects is called *composition* (or *aggregation*).

Software Engineering Observation 5.14

One form of software reuse is composition, in which a class has as members pointers to objects of other classes.

    The application of Fig. 5.12–Fig. 5.16 demonstrates composition. The program contains two classes. Class **Date** (Fig. 5.12 and Fig. 5.13) encapsulates information relating to a specific date. Class **Employee** (Fig. 5.14 and Fig. 5.15) encapsulates the name of the employee and two **Date** objects representing the **Employee**'s birthday and hire date. The main program **CompositionTest** (Fig. 5.16) creates an object of class **Employee** to demonstrate composition.

```
1   // Fig. 5.12: Date.h
2   // Date class definition encapsulates month, day and year.
3
4   #pragma once
5
6   #using <mscorlib.dll>
7   #using <system.dll>
8
9   using namespace System;
10
11  // Date class definition
12  public __gc class Date
13  {
14  public:
15     Date( int, int, int );
16
17     String *ToDateString();
18
19  private:
20
21     // utility method
22     int CheckDay( int );
23
24     int month;   // 1-12
25     int day;     // 1-31 based on month
26     int year;    // any year
27  }; // end class Date
```

Fig. 5.12 **Date** class encapsulates day, month and year information.

```
1   // Fig. 5.13: Date.cpp
2   // Method definitions for class Date.
3
4   #include "Date.h"
5
6   // constructor confirms proper value for month;
7   // call method CheckDay to confirm proper
```

Fig. 5.13 **Date** class method definitions. (Part 1 of 2.)

```cpp
 8    // value for day
 9    Date::Date( int theMonth, int theDay, int theYear )
10    {
11       // validate month
12       if ( theMonth > 0 && theMonth <= 12 )
13          month = theMonth;
14       else {
15          month = 1;
16          Console::WriteLine( S"Month {0} invalid. Set to month 1.",
17             theMonth.ToString() );
18       }
19
20       year = theYear;              // could validate year
21       day = CheckDay( theDay );    // validate day
22    } // end Date constructor
23
24    // utility method confirms proper day value
25    // based on month and year
26    int Date::CheckDay( int testDay )
27    {
28       int daysPerMonth[] =
29          { 0, 31, 28, 31, 30, 31, 30, 31, 31, 30, 31, 30, 31 };
30
31       // check if day in range for month
32       if ( testDay > 0 && testDay <= daysPerMonth[ month ] )
33          return testDay;
34
35       // check for leap year
36       if ( month == 2 && testDay == 29 &&
37          ( year % 400 == 0 ||
38          ( year % 4 == 0 && year % 100 != 0 ) ) )
39          return testDay;
40
41       Console::WriteLine( S"Day {0} invalid. Set to day 1.",
42          testDay.ToString() );
43
44       return 1; // leave object in consistent state
45    } // end method CheckDay
46
47    // return date string as month/day/year
48    String *Date::ToDateString()
49    {
50       return String::Concat( month.ToString(), S"/",
51          day.ToString(), S"/", year.ToString() );
52    } // end method ToDateString
```

Fig. 5.13   Date class method definitions. (Part 2 of 2.)

```cpp
1    // Fig. 5.14: Employee.h
2    // Employee class definition encapsulates employee's first name,
3    // last name, birth date and hire date.
```

Fig. 5.14   Employee class encapsulates employee name, birthday and hire date.
(Part 1 of 2.)

```
4
5    #pragma once
6
7    #using <mscorlib.dll>
8    #using <system.dll>
9
10   using namespace System;
11
12   #include "date.h"
13
14   // Employee class definition
15   public __gc class Employee
16   {
17   public:
18      Employee( String *, String *, int, int, int, int, int, int );
19      String *ToEmployeeString();
20
21   private:
22      String *firstName;
23      String *lastName;
24      Date *birthDate;      // pointer to a Date object
25      Date *hireDate;       // pointer to a Date object
26   }; // end class Employee
```

Fig. 5.14 **Employee** class encapsulates employee name, birthday and hire date. (Part 2 of 2.)

```
1    // Fig. 5.15: Employee.cpp
2    // Method definitions for class Employee.
3
4    #include "Employee.h"
5
6    // constructor initializes name, birth date and hire date
7    Employee::Employee( String *first, String *last, int birthMonth,
8       int birthDay, int birthYear, int hireMonth, int hireDay,
9       int hireYear )
10   {
11      firstName = first;
12      lastName = last;
13
14      // create and initialize new Date objects
15      birthDate = new Date( birthMonth, birthDay, birthYear );
16      hireDate = new Date( hireMonth, hireDay, hireYear );
17   } // end Employee constructor
18
19   // return Employee as String * object
20   String *Employee::ToEmployeeString()
21   {
22      return String::Concat( lastName, S", ", firstName,
23         S" Hired: ", hireDate->ToDateString(), S" Birthday: ",
24         birthDate->ToDateString() );
25   }
```

Fig. 5.15 **Employee** class method definitions.

```
1   // Fig. 5.16: CompositionTest.cpp
2   // Demonstrates an object with member object pointer.
3
4   #using <system.windows.forms.dll>
5
6   using namespace System::Windows::Forms;
7
8   #include "Employee.h"
9
10  // main entry point for application
11  int __stdcall WinMain()
12  {
13     Employee *e = new Employee( S"Bob", S"Jones", 7, 24, 1949, 3,
14        12, 1988 );
15
16     MessageBox::Show( e->ToEmployeeString(),
17        S"Testing Class Employee" );
18  } // end function WinMain
```

```
Testing Class Employee                        [X]

   Jones, Bob Hired: 3/12/1988 Birthday: 7/24/1949

                  [  OK  ]
```

Fig. 5.16 Composition demonstration.

Class **Date** declares **int** instance variables **month**, **day** and **year** (lines 24–26 of Fig. 5.12). Figure 5.13 (lines 9–22) defines the constructor, which receives values for **month**, **day** and **year** as arguments and assigns these values to the instance variables after ensuring that the values are in a consistent state. Note that lines 16–17 print an error message if the constructor receives an invalid month value. Ordinarily, rather than printing error messages, a constructor would "throw an exception." We discuss exceptions in Chapter 8, Exception Handling. Method **ToDateString** (lines 48–52) returns the **String *** representation of a **Date**.

Class **Employee** encapsulates information relating to an employee's name, birthday and hire date (lines 22–25 of Fig. 5.14) using instance variables **firstName**, **lastName**, **birthDate** and **hireDate**. Members' **birthDate** and **hireDate** are pointers to **Date** objects, each of which contains instance variables **month**, **day** and **year**. In this example, class **Employee** is *composed of* two pointers of type **String** and two pointers of class **Date**. The **Employee** constructor (lines 7–17 of Fig. 5.15) takes eight arguments (**first**, **last**, **birthMonth**, **birthDay**, **birthYear**, **hireMonth**, **hireDay** and **hireYear**). Line 15 passes arguments **birthMonth**, **birthDay** and **birthYear** to the **Date** constructor to create the **birthDate** object. Similarly, line 16 passes arguments **hireMonth**, **hireDay** and **hireYear** to the **Date** constructor to create the **hireDate** object. Method **ToEmployeeString** (lines 20–25) returns a pointer to a string containing the name of the **Employee** and the string representations of the **Employee**'s **birthDate** and **hireDate**.

CompositionTest (Fig. 5.16) runs the application with function **WinMain**. Lines 13–14 instantiate an **Employee** object, and lines 16–17 display the string representation of the **Employee** to the user.

5.9 Using the `this` Pointer

Every object can access a pointer to itself, called the ***this*** *pointer*. The **this** pointer is used to reference implicitly the instance variables, properties and methods of an object; it can be used explicitly as well. Keyword **this** is commonly used within methods, where **this** is a pointer to the object on which the method is performing operations. Chapters 9–10 contain Windows applications that use keyword **this** to reference the window that is being initialized.

We now demonstrate implicit and explicit use of the **this** pointer to display the **private** data of a **Time4** object. Class **Time4** (Fig. 5.17 and Fig. 5.18) defines three **private** instance variables—**hour**, **minute** and **second** (lines 20–22 of Fig. 5.17). The constructor (lines 7–12 of Fig. 5.18) receives three **int** arguments to initialize a **Time4** object. Note that, for this example, we have made the parameter names for the constructor (line 7) identical to the instance variable names for the class (Fig. 5.17, lines 20–22). We did this to illustrate explicit use of the **this** pointer. If a method contains a local variable with the same name as an instance variable of that class, that method will refer to the local variable, rather than to the instance variable (i.e., the local variable hides the instance variable in that method's scope). However, the method can use the **this** pointer to refer to the hidden instance variables explicitly (lines 9–11 of Fig. 5.18).

```
1   // Fig. 5.17: Time4.h
2   // Class Time4 demonstrates the this pointer.
3
4   #pragma once
5
6   #using <mscorlib.dll>
7
8   using namespace System;
9
10  // Time4 class definition
11  public __gc class Time4
12  {
13  public:
14     Time4( int, int, int );
15
16     String *BuildString();
17     String *ToStandardString();
18
19  private:
20     int hour;        // 0-23
21     int minute;      // 0-59
22     int second;      // 0-59
23  }; // end class Time4
```

Fig. 5.17 `this` pointer used implicitly and explicitly to enable an object to manipulate its own data and invoke its own methods.

```
1   // Fig. 5.18: Time4.cpp
2   // Method definitions for class Time4.
```

Fig. 5.18 `Time4` class method definitions. (Part 1 of 2.)

```
3
4    #include "Time4.h"
5
6    // constructor
7    Time4::Time4( int hourValue, int minuteValue, int secondValue )
8    {
9        this->hour = hourValue;
10       this->minute = minuteValue;
11       this->second = secondValue;
12   }
13
14   // create string using this and implicit pointers
15   String *Time4::BuildString()
16   {
17       return String::Concat(
18           S"this->ToStandardString(): ", this->ToStandardString(),
19           S"\n( *this ).ToStandardString(): ",
20           ( *this ).ToStandardString(),
21           S"\nToStandardString(): ", ToStandardString() );
22   }
23
24   // convert time to standard-time (12 hour) format string
25   String *Time4::ToStandardString()
26   {
27       return String::Concat(
28           ( ( this->hour == 12 || this->hour == 0 ) ? S"12"
29           : ( this->hour % 12 ).ToString( S"D2" ) ), S":",
30           this->minute.ToString( S"D2" ), S":",
31           this->second.ToString( S"D2" ), S" ",
32           ( this->hour < 12 ? S"AM" : S"PM" ) );
33   }
```

Fig. 5.18 **Time4** class method definitions. (Part 2 of 2.)

Recall from Chapter 4, Functions and Arrays, that the dereferencing operator (*****) can be used to refer to an object directly. Thus, the notation of line 9 is equivalent to

```
( *this ).hour = hour;
```

Note the parentheses around ***this** when used with the dot member selection operator (**.**). The parentheses are needed because the dot operator has higher precedence than the ***** operator. We demonstrate this alternative notation in method **BuildString**.

Method **BuildString** (lines 15–22) returns a pointer to a **String** created by a statement that uses the **this** pointer explicitly and implicitly. Lines 18 and 20 use the **this** pointer explicitly to call method **ToStandardString**, whereas line 21 uses the **this** pointer implicitly to call the same method. Note that lines 18, 20 and 21 all perform the same task. Therefore, programmers usually do not use the **this** pointer explicitly to reference methods within the current object.

Method **ToStandardString** (lines 25–33) builds and returns a pointer to a **String** that represents the specified time. The correct notation is determined based on the values of the **hour, minute** and **second** instance variables.

Common Programming Error 5.9

*For a method in which a parameter (or local variable) has the same name as an instance variable, use pointer **this** if you wish to access the instance variable; otherwise, the method parameter (or local variable) will be referenced.*

Testing and Debugging Tip 5.3

Avoid method-parameter names (or local variable names) that conflict with instance variable names to prevent subtle, hard-to-trace bugs.

Good Programming Practice 5.3

*The explicit use of the **this** pointer can increase program clarity in some contexts where **this** is optional.*

Driver **ThisTest.cpp** (Fig. 5.19) runs the application that demonstrates explicit use of the **this** pointer. Line 12 instantiates an instance of class **Time4**. Lines 14–15 invoke method **BuildString** of the **Time4** object, then display the results to the user in a **MessageBox**.

The problem of parameters (or local variables) hiding instance variables can be solved by using properties. If we have a property **Hour** that accesses the **hour** instance variable, then we would not need to use **(*this).hour** or **this->hour** to distinguish between a parameter (or local variable) **hour** and the instance variable **hour**—we would simply assign **hour** to **Hour**.

```
1   // Fig. 5.19: ThisTest.cpp
2   // Using the this pointer.
3
4   #using <system.windows.forms.dll>
5
6   using namespace System::Windows::Forms;
7
8   #include "Time4.h"
9
10  int __stdcall WinMain()
11  {
12     Time4 *time = new Time4( 12, 30, 19 );
13
14     MessageBox::Show( time->BuildString(),
15        S"Demonstrating the \"this\" Pointer" );
16
17     return 0;
18  } // end function WinMain
```

Fig. 5.19   **this** pointer demonstration.

5.10 Garbage Collection

In previous examples, we have seen how a constructor initializes data in an object of a class after the object is created. Operator **new** allocates memory for the object, then calls that object's constructor. The constructor might acquire other system resources, such as network connections and databases or files. Objects must have a disciplined way to return memory and release resources when the program no longer uses those objects. Failure to release such resources causes *resource leaks*—potentially exhausting the pool of available resources that programs might need to continue executing.

Unlike C and standard C++, in which programmers must manage memory explicitly, managed C++ performs memory management internally. The .NET Framework performs *garbage collection* of memory to return to the system memory that is no longer needed. When the *garbage collector* executes, it locates objects for which the application has no references or pointers. Such objects can be collected at that time or during a subsequent execution of the garbage collector. Therefore, the *memory leaks* that are common in such languages as C and C++, where memory is not reclaimed by the runtime, are rare in managed C++.

Allocation and deallocation of other resources, such as network connections, database connections and files, must be handled explicitly by the programmer. One technique employed to handle these resources (in conjunction with the garbage collector) is to define a *destructor* that returns resources to the system. The garbage collector calls an object's destructor to perform *termination housekeeping* on that object just before the garbage collector reclaims the object's memory (called *finalization*).

Each class can contain only one destructor. The name of a destructor is formed by preceding the class name with a ~ character. For example, the destructor for class **Time** would be **~Time()**. Destructors do not receive arguments, so destructors cannot be overloaded. When the garbage collector is removing an object from memory, the garbage collector first invokes that object's destructor to clean up resources used by the class. However, we cannot determine exactly when the destructor is called, because we cannot determine exactly when garbage collection occurs. When a program terminates, the destructor is called on any objects that have not yet been garbage collected.

5.11 static Class Members

Each object of a class has its own copy of all the instance variables of the class. However, in certain cases, all class objects should share only one copy of a particular variable. Such variables are called **static** *variables*. A program contains only one copy of each of a class's **static** variables in memory, no matter how many objects of the class have been instantiated. A **static** variable represents *class-wide information*—all class objects share the same **static** data item.

The declaration of a **static** member begins with the keyword **static**. A **static** variable can be initialized in its declaration by following the variable name with an **=** and an initial value. In cases where a **static** variable requires more complex initialization, programmers can define a **static** *constructor* to initialize only the **static** members. Such constructors are optional and must be declared with the **static** keyword, followed by the name of the class. **static** constructors are called before any **static** members are used and before any class objects are instantiated.

We now consider a video-game example to justify the need for **static** class-wide data. Suppose that we have a video game involving **Martian**s and other space creatures. Each **Martian** tends to be brave and willing to attack other space creatures when the **Martian** is aware that there are at least four other **Martian**s present. If there are fewer than five **Martian**s present, each **Martian** becomes cowardly. For this reason, each **Martian** must know the **martianCount**. We could endow class **Martian** with **martianCount** as instance data. However, if we were to do this, then every **Martian** would have a separate copy of the instance data, and every time we create a **Martian**, we would have to update the instance variable **martianCount** in every **Martian**. The redundant copies waste space, and updating those copies is time consuming. Instead, we declare **martianCount** to be **static** so that **martianCount** is class-wide data. Each **Martian** can see the **martianCount** as if it were instance data of that **Martian**, but only one copy of the **static** variable **martianCount** is actually maintained to save space. This technique also saves time; because there is only one copy, we do not have to increment separate copies of **martianCount** for each **Martian** object.

Performance Tip 5.2

When a single copy of the data will suffice, use **static** *variables to save storage.*

Although **static** variables might seem like *global variables* (variables that can be referenced anywhere in a program) in other programming languages, **static** variables need not be globally accessible. Static variables have class scope.

The **public static** data members of a class can be accessed through the class name using the scope resolution operator (**::**) (e.g., **Math::PI**). The **private static** members can be accessed only through methods or properties of the class. Static members are available as soon as the class is loaded into memory at execution time and they exist for the duration of program execution, even when no objects of that class exist. To enable a program to access a **private static** member when no objects of the class exist, the class must provide a **public static** method or property.

A **static** method cannot access instance (non-**static**) members. Unlike instance methods, a **static** method has no **this** pointer, because **static** variables and **static** methods exist independently of any class objects, even when there are no objects of that class.

Common Programming Error 5.10

Using the **this** *pointer in a* **static** *method or* **static** *property is a compilation error.*

Common Programming Error 5.11

A call to an instance method or an attempt to access an instance variable from a **static** *method is a compilation error.*

Class **Employee** (Fig. 5.20 and Fig. 5.21) demonstrates a **public static** property that enables a program to obtain the value of a **private static** variable. The **static** variable **count** (line 43 of Fig. 5.20) is not initialized explicitly, so it receives the value zero by default. Class variable **count** maintains a count of the number of objects of class **Employee** that have been instantiated, including those objects that have already been marked for garbage collection, but have not yet been reclaimed by the garbage collector.

```
1    // Fig. 5.20: Employee.h
2    // Employee class contains static data and a static property.
3
4    #pragma once
5
6    #using <mscorlib.dll>
7    #using <system.dll>
8
9    using namespace System;
10
11   // Employee class definition
12   public __gc class Employee
13   {
14   public:
15
16      // constructor increments static Employee count
17      Employee( String *fName, String *lName );
18
19      // destructor decrements static Employee count
20      ~Employee();
21
22      // FirstName property
23      __property String *get_FirstName()
24      {
25         return firstName;
26      }
27
28      // LastName property
29      __property String *get_LastName()
30      {
31         return lastName;
32      }
33
34      // static Count property
35      __property static int get_Count()
36      {
37         return count;
38      }
39
40   private:
41      String *firstName;
42      String *lastName;
43      static int count;      // Employee objects in memory
44   }; // end class Employee
```

Fig. 5.20 `static` members are accessible to all objects of a class.

```
1    // Fig. 5.21: Employee.cpp
2    // Method definitions for class Employee.
3
4    #include "Employee.h"
5
```

Fig. 5.21 `Employee` class method definitions. (Part 1 of 2.)

```
 6    // constructor increments static Employee count
 7    Employee::Employee( String *fName, String *lName )
 8    {
 9       firstName = fName;
10       lastName = lName;
11
12       ++count;
13
14       Console::WriteLine( String::Concat(
15          S"Employee object constructor: ", firstName, S" ",
16          lastName, S"; count = ", Count.ToString() ) );
17    }
18
19    // destructor decrements static Employee count
20    Employee::~Employee()
21    {
22       --count;
23
24       Console::WriteLine( String::Concat(
25          S"Employee object destructor: ", firstName, S" ",
26          lastName, S"; count = ", Count.ToString() ) );
27    }
```

Fig. 5.21 **Employee** class method definitions. (Part 2 of 2.)

When objects of class **Employee** exist, **static** member **count** can be used in any method of an **Employee** object—in this example, the constructor (lines 7–17 of Fig. 5.21) increments **count**, and the destructor (lines 20–27) decrements **count**. If no objects of class **Employee** exist, the value of member **count** can be obtained through **static** property **Count** (Fig. 5.20, lines 35–38); this also works when there are **Employee** objects in memory.

Driver **StaticTest.cpp** (Fig. 5.22) runs the application that demonstrates the **static** members of class **Employee** (Fig. 5.20 and Fig. 5.21). Lines 9–11 use the **static** property **Count** of class **Employee** to obtain the current **count** value before the program creates **Employee** objects. Notice that the syntax used to access a **static** member is

>   *ClassName***::***StaticMember*

On line 11, *ClassName* is **Employee** and *StaticMember* is **Count**. Recall that we used this syntax in prior examples to call the **static** methods of class **Math** (e.g., **Math::Pow**, **Math::Abs**, etc.) and other methods, such as **Int32::Parse** and **MessageBox::Show**.

```
1    // Fig. 5.22: StaticTest.cpp
2    // Demonstrating static class members.
3
4    #include "Employee.h"
5
```

Fig. 5.22 **static** member demonstration. (Part 1 of 2.)

```
6    // main entry point for application
7    int main()
8    {
9       Console::WriteLine( String::Concat(
10         S"Employees before instantiation: ",
11         ( Employee::Count ).ToString(), S"\n" ) );
12
13      // create two Employees
14      Employee *employee1 = new Employee( S"Susan", S"Baker" );
15      Employee *employee2 = new Employee( S"Bob", S"Jones" );
16
17      Console::WriteLine( String::Concat(
18         S"Employees after instantiation: ",
19         ( Employee::Count ).ToString(), S"\n" ) );
20
21      // display Employees
22      Console::WriteLine( String::Concat( S"Employee1: ",
23         employee1->FirstName, S" ", employee1->LastName,
24         S"\nEmployee2: ", employee2->FirstName, S" ",
25         employee2->LastName, S"\n" ) );
26
27      // remove references to objects to indicate that
28      // objects can be garbage collected
29      employee1 = 0;
30      employee2 = 0;
31
32      // force garbage collection
33      System::GC::Collect();
34
35      // wait until collection completes
36      System::GC::WaitForPendingFinalizers();
37
38      Console::WriteLine(
39         String::Concat( S"\nEmployees after garbage collection: ",
40         ( Employee::Count ).ToString() ) );
41
42      return 0;
43   } // end function main
```

```
Employees before instantiation: 0

Employee object constructor: Susan Baker; count = 1
Employee object constructor: Bob Jones; count = 2
Employees after instantiation: 2

Employee1: Susan Baker
Employee2: Bob Jones

Employee object destructor: Bob Jones; count = 1
Employee object destructor: Susan Baker; count = 0

Employees after garbage collection: 0
```

Fig. 5.22 `static` member demonstration. (Part 2 of 2.)

Next, lines 14–15 instantiate two **Employee** objects and assign them to pointers **employee1** and **employee2**. Each call to the **Employee** constructor increments the **count** value by one. Lines 22–25 display the value of **Count** as well as the names of the two employees. Lines 29–30 set pointers **employee1** and **employee2** to **0**, so they no longer point to the **Employee** objects. Because these were the only pointers in the program to the **Employee** objects, those objects can now be garbage collected.

The garbage collector is not invoked directly by the program. Either the garbage collector reclaims the memory for objects when the runtime determines garbage collection is appropriate, or the operating system recovers the memory when the program terminates. However, it is possible to request that the garbage collector attempt to collect available objects. Line 33 uses **public static** method *Collect* from class *GC* (namespace **System**) to make this request. The garbage collector is not guaranteed to collect all objects that are currently available for collection. If the garbage collector decides to collect objects, the garbage collector first invokes the destructor of each object. It is important to understand that the garbage collector executes as an independent entity called a *thread*. (Threads are discussed in Chapter 11, Multithreading.) It is possible for multiple threads to execute in parallel on a multiprocessor system or to share a processor on a single-processor system. Thus, a program could run in parallel with garbage collection. For this reason, we call **static** method *WaitForPendingFinalizers* of class *GC* (line 36), which forces the program to wait until the garbage collector invokes the destructors for all objects that are ready for collection and reclaims those objects. When the program reaches lines 38, we are assured that both destructor calls completed and that the value of **count** has been decremented accordingly.

Software Engineering Observation 5.15

Programs normally do not call methods **Collect** *and* **WaitForPendingFinalizers** *explicitly because they might decrease performance.*

In this example, the output shows that the destructor was called for each **Employee**, which decrements the **count** value by two (once per **Employee** being collected). Lines 38–40 use property **Count** to obtain the value of **count** after invoking the garbage collector. If the objects had not been collected, the **count** would be greater than zero.

Toward the end of the output, notice that the **Employee** object for **Bob Jones** was finalized before the **Employee** object for **Susan Baker**. However, the output of this program on your system could differ. The garbage collector is not guaranteed to collect objects in a specific order.

5.12 const Keyword and Read-Only Properties

MC++ allows programmers to create *constants* whose values cannot change during program execution.

Testing and Debugging Tip 5.4

If a variable's value should never change, make it a constant. This helps eliminate errors that might occur if the value of the variable were to change.

To create a constant data member of a class, either declare that member using the **const** keyword or create a property for the data member and provide only a *get* accessor method. Data members declared as **const** implicitly are **static** and must be initialized in their declaration. Once they are initialized, **const** values cannot be modified.

Common Programming Error 5.12

*Declaring a class data member as **const**, but failing to initialize it in that class's declaration is a syntax error.*

Common Programming Error 5.13

*Assigning a value to a **const** data member after that data member has been initialized is a compilation error.*

A read-only property provides only a *get* accessor method. Without a *set* accessor method, the property's value cannot be changed. The property usually controls access to a **private** data member. The value of the data member can be changed within its class.

Common Programming Error 5.14

Declaring a property with only a get *accessor method and attempting to use it before it is initialized is a logic error.*

Members that are declared as **const** must be assigned values at compile time. Therefore, **const** members can be initialized only with other constant values, such as integers, string literals, characters and other **const** members. Constant members with values that cannot be determined at compile time must be declared as properties without *set* accessor methods. The constant member then can be assigned a value in the constructor and the programmer can only retrieve the private constant data member's value using the *set* accessor.

The application of Fig. 5.23–Fig. 5.25 demonstrates constants. Class **Constants** defines constant **PI** (line 16 of Fig. 5.23), the source file implements the constructor (lines 6–9 of Fig. 5.24) and driver **UsingConstMain.cpp** (Fig. 5.25) demonstrates the constants in class **Constants**.

```
1   // Fig. 5.23: Const.h
2   // Class Constants contains a const data member.
3
4   #pragma once
5
6   #using <mscorlib.dll>
7
8   using namespace System;
9
10  // Constants class definition
11  public __gc class Constants
12  {
13  public:
14
15      // create constant PI
16      static const double PI = 3.14159;
17
18      Constants( int );
19
```

Fig. 5.23 **const** class member demonstration. (Part 1 of 2.)

```
20      // radius is readonly
21      __property int get_Radius()
22      {
23         return radius;
24      }
25
26   private:
27      int radius;
28   }; // end class Constants
```

Fig. 5.23 **const** class member demonstration. (Part 2 of 2.)

```
1    // Fig. 5.24: Const.cpp
2    // Method definitions for class Constants.
3
4    #include "Const.h"
5
6    Constants::Constants( int radiusValue )
7    {
8       radius = radiusValue;
9    }
```

Fig. 5.24 **Constants** class method definitions.

```
1    // Fig. 5.25: UsingConstMain.cpp
2    // Demonstrating constant values.
3
4    #using <system.windows.forms.dll>
5
6    using namespace System::Windows::Forms;
7
8    #include "Const.h"
9
10   // create Constants object and display its values
11   int __stdcall WinMain()
12   {
13      Random *random = new Random();
14
15      Constants *constantValues = new Constants(
16         random->Next( 1, 20 ) );
17
18      String *output = String::Concat( S"Radius = ",
19         constantValues->Radius.ToString(), S"\nCircumference = ",
20         ( 2 * Constants::PI * constantValues->Radius ).ToString() );
21
22      MessageBox::Show( output, S"Circumference" );
23
24      return 0;
25   } // end function WinMain
```

Fig. 5.25 Using **const** data members demonstration. (Part 1 of 2.)

Fig. 5.25 Using **const** data members demonstration. (Part 2 of 2.)

Line 16 in class **Constants** (Fig. 5.23) creates constant **PI** using keyword **const** and initializes **PI** with the **double** value **3.14159**—an approximation of π that the program uses to calculate the circumferences of circles. Note that we could have used the predefined constant **PI** of class **Math** (**Math::PI**) as the value, but we wanted to demonstrate how to define a **const** member explicitly. The compiler must be able to determine a **const** variable's value at compile time; otherwise, a compilation error will occur. For example, if line 16 initialized **PI** with the expression

```
Double::Parse( S"3.14159" )
```

the compiler would generate an error. Although the expression uses **String *** literal **"3.14159"** (a constant value) as an argument, the compiler cannot evaluate the method call **Double::Parse** at compile time.

Line 27 declares variable **radius**, but does not initialize it. Property **Radius** only has a *get* accessor method (lines 21–24). Clients of the class can only read the value of the **private** data member **radius** after it has been initialized. The **Constants** constructor (lines 6–9 of Fig. 5.24) receives an **int** value and assigns it to **radius** when the program creates a **Constants** object. Note that **radius** also can be initialized with a more complex expression, such as a method call that returns an **int**.

The element of chance can be introduced into computer applications with the *Random* class (located in namespace **System**). Line 13 (Fig. 5.25) creates a **Random** object; lines 15–16 use method *Next* of class **Random** to generate a random **int** between **1** and **20** that corresponds to a circle's **radius**. Then, that value is passed to the **Constants** constructor to initialize the read-only variable **radius**. If **Next** produces values at random, every value in this range has an equal *chance* (or *probability*) of being chosen when **Next** is called. Note that values returned by **Next** are actually *pseudo-random numbers*—a sequence of values produced by a complex mathematical calculation. A *seed* value is required in this mathematical calculation. When we create our **Random** object, we use the current time of day as the seed. A particular seed value always produces the same series of random numbers. Programmers commonly use the current time of day as a seed value, because it changes each second and, therefore produces different random-number sequences each time the program executes.

Line 19 uses **Constant** pointer **constantValues** to access read-only property **Radius**. Line 20 computes the circle's circumference using **const** variable **Constants::PI** and property **Radius**. Note that we use **static** syntax to access **const** variable **PI**, because **const** variables implicitly are **static**. Line 22 outputs the radius and circumference in a **MessageBox**.

5.13 Indexed Properties

Sometimes a class encapsulates data that a program can manipulate as a list of elements. Such a class can define special properties called *indexed properties* that allow array-style indexed access to lists of elements. With "conventional" managed arrays, the subscript number must be an integer value. A benefit of indexed properties is that the programmer can define both integer subscripts and non-integer subscripts. For example, a programmer could allow client code to manipulate data using strings as subscripts that represent the data items' names or descriptions. When manipulating managed array elements, the array subscript operator always returns the same data type—i.e., the type of the array. Index properties are more flexible—they can return any data type, even one that is different from the type of the data in the list of elements. Although an indexed property's subscript operator is used like an array-subscript operator, indexed properties are defined as properties in a class.

Common Programming Error 5.15

*Defining an indexed property as **static** is a syntax error.*

    The application of Fig. 5.26–Fig. 5.28 demonstrates indexed properties. Fig. 5.26–Fig. 5.27 define class **Box**—a box with a length, a width and a height. Fig. 5.28 is the main entry point of the application that demonstrates class **Box**'s indexed properties.

```
1   // Fig. 5.26: Box.h
2   // Class Box represents a box with length,
3   // width and height dimensions.
4
5   #pragma once
6
7   #using <mscorlib.dll>
8
9   using namespace System;
10
11  public __gc class Box
12  {
13  public:
14
15     // constructor
16     Box( double, double, double );
17
18     // access dimensions by index number
19     __property double get_Dimension( int index )
20     {
21        return ( index < 0 || index > dimensions.Length ) ?
22           -1 : dimensions[ index ];
23     }
24
25     __property void set_Dimension( int index, double value )
26     {
27        if ( index >= 0 && index < dimensions.Length )
28           dimensions[ index ] = value;
```

Fig. 5.26   **Box** class represents a box with length, width and height dimensions. (Part 1 of 2.)

```
29
30       } // end numeric indexed property
31
32       // access dimensions by their names
33       __property double get_Dimension( String *name )
34       {
35          // locate element to get
36          int i = 0;
37
38          while ( i < names->Length &&
39             name->ToLower()->CompareTo( names[ i ] ) != 0 )
40             i++;
41
42          return ( i == names->Length ) ? -1 : dimensions[ i ];
43       }
44
45       __property void set_Dimension( String *name, double value )
46       {
47          // locate element to set
48          int i = 0;
49
50          while ( i < names->Length &&
51             name->ToLower()->CompareTo( names[ i ] ) != 0 )
52             i++;
53
54          if ( i != names->Length )
55             dimensions[ i ] = value;
56
57       } // end String indexed property
58
59    private:
60       static String *names[] = { S"length", S"width", S"height" };
61       static double dimensions __gc[] = new double __gc[ 3 ];
62    }; // end class Box
```

Fig. 5.26   **Box** class represents a box with length, width and height dimensions.
(Part 2 of 2.)

```
1    // Fig. 5.27: Box.cpp
2    // Method definitions for class Box.
3
4    #include "Box.h"
5
6    Box::Box( double length, double width, double height )
7    {
8       dimensions[ 0 ] = length;
9       dimensions[ 1 ] = width;
10      dimensions[ 2 ] = height;
11   }
```

Fig. 5.27   **Box** class method definition.

The **private** data members of class **Box** are **String *** array **names** (line 60), which contains the names (i.e., **"length"**, **"width"** and **"height"**) for the dimensions of a **Box**, and **double** array **dimensions** (line 61), which contains the size of each dimension. Each element in array **names** corresponds to an element in array **dimensions** (e.g., **dimensions[2]** contains the height of the **Box**).

Box defines two indexed properties (lines 19–30 and lines 33–57) that each return a **double** value representing the size of the dimension specified by the property's parameter. Indexed properties can be overloaded like methods. The first indexed property uses an **int** subscript to manipulate an element in the **dimensions** array. The second indexed property uses a **String *** subscript representing the name of the dimension to manipulate an element in the **dimensions** array. Unlike scalar properties, the *get* accessors of indexed properties accept arguments (which are specified as subscripts). Each property in Fig. 5.26 returns **-1** if its *get* accessor encounters an invalid subscript. Each indexed property's *set* accessor assigns **value** to the appropriate element of **dimensions** only if the index is valid. Normally, the programmer would have an indexed property throw an exception if it received an invalid index. We discuss how to throw exceptions in Chapter 8, Exception Handling.

```cpp
1   // Fig. 5.28: BoxTest.cpp
2   // Indexed properties provide access to an object's members
3   // via a subscript operator.
4
5   #include "Box.h"
6
7   void ShowValueAtIndex( Box *, String *, int );
8   void ShowValueAtIndex( Box *, String *, String * );
9
10  int main()
11  {
12     Box *box = new Box( 0.0, 0.0, 0.0 );
13     int choice;
14     bool finished = false;
15     int index = 0;
16     String *name = S"";
17
18     // loop until user decides to quit
19     while ( !finished ) {
20
21        // display options
22        Console::Write( S"\n   1: Get Value by Index\n" );
23           S"   2: Set Value by Index\n   3: Get Value by Name\n"
24           S"   4: Set Value by Name\n  -1: Quit\n  -1: Quit\n=> " );
25        choice = Int32::Parse( Console::ReadLine() );
26
27        switch ( choice ) {
28
29           // get value at specified index
30           case 1:
31              Console::Write( S"Index to get: " );
```

Fig. 5.28 Indexed properties provide subscripted access to an object's members. (Part 1 of 3.)

```
32              ShowValueAtIndex( box, S"get: ",
33                 Int32::Parse( Console::ReadLine() ) );
34              break;
35
36           // set value at specified index
37           case 2:
38              Console::Write( S"Index to set: " );
39              index = Int32::Parse( Console::ReadLine() );
40              Console::Write( S"Value to set: " );
41              box->Dimension[ index ] = Double::Parse(
42                 Console::ReadLine() );
43
44              ShowValueAtIndex( box, S"set: ", index );
45              break;
46
47           // get value with specified name
48           case 3:
49              Console::Write( S"Name to get: " );
50              ShowValueAtIndex( box, S"get: ",
51                 Console::ReadLine() );
52              break;
53
54           // set value with specified name
55           case 4:
56              Console::Write( S"Name to set: " );
57              name = Console::ReadLine();
58              Console::Write( S"Value to set: " );
59              box->Dimension[ name ] = Double::Parse(
60                 Console::ReadLine() );
61
62              ShowValueAtIndex( box, S"set: ", name );
63              break;
64
65           // exit loop
66           default:
67              finished = true;
68              break;
69        } // end switch
70     } // end while
71
72     return 0;
73  } // end function main
74
75  // display value at specified index number
76  void ShowValueAtIndex( Box *box, String *prefix, int index )
77  {
78     Console::WriteLine( String::Concat( prefix, S"box[ ",
79        index.ToString(), S" ] = ", box->Dimension[ index ] ) );
80  }
81
```

Fig. 5.28   Indexed properties provide subscripted access to an object's members.
(Part 2 of 3.)

```
82    // display value with specified name
83    void ShowValueAtIndex( Box *box, String *prefix, String *name )
84    {
85        Console::WriteLine( String::Concat( prefix, S"box[ ",
86            name, S" ] = ", box->Dimension[ name ] ) );
87    }
```

```
    1: Get Value by Index
    2: Set Value by Index
    3: Get Value by Name
    4: Set Value by Name
   -1: Quit
=> 2
Index to set: 0
Value to set: 123.45
set: box[ 0 ] = 123.45
```

```
    1: Get Value by Index
    2: Set Value by Index
    3: Get Value by Name
    4: Set Value by Name
   -1: Quit
=> 3
Name to get: length
get: box[ length ] = 123.45
```

```
    1: Get Value by Index
    2: Set Value by Index
    3: Get Value by Name
    4: Set Value by Name
   -1: Quit
=> 4
Name to set: width
Value to set: 33.33
set: box[ width ] = 33.33
```

```
    1: Get Value by Index
    2: Set Value by Index
    3: Get Value by Name
    4: Set Value by Name
   -1: Quit
=> 1
Index to get: 1
get: box[ 1 ] = 33.33
```

Fig. 5.28 Indexed properties provide subscripted access to an object's members.
(Part 3 of 3.)

Notice that the **String** indexed properties use **while** structures to search for a matching **String *** object in the **names** array. If a match is found, the indexed property manipulates the corresponding element in array **dimensions**.

BoxTest.cpp (Fig. 5.28) is a console-based application that manipulates the **private** data members of class **Box** through **Box**'s indexed properties. Figure 5.28 declares variable **box** and initializes its dimensions to **0.0** (line 12). The **while** loop in lines 19–70 executes until boolean variable **finished** becomes **true** (line 67). Lines 22–24 display available options to the user. Choice **1** (lines 30–34) and choice **3** (lines 48–52) retrieve the value at the specified index or name, respectively. Choice **1** invokes method **ShowValueAtIndex** (lines 76–80) to retrieve the value at the specified index number. Similarly, choice **3** invokes method **ShowValueAtIndex** (lines 83–87) to retrieve the value with the specified name. Choice **2** (lines 37–45) and choice **4** (lines 55–63) set a value at the specified index or name, respectively. Any other choice (such as **-1**) sets **finished** to **false**, exiting the program.

5.14 Data Abstraction and Information Hiding

As we pointed out at the beginning of this chapter, classes normally hide the details of their implementation from their clients. This is called information hiding. As an example of information hiding, let us consider a data structure called a *stack*.

Readers can think of a stack as analogous to a pile of dishes. When a dish is placed on the pile, it is always placed at the top (referred to as *pushing* the dish onto the stack). Similarly, when a dish is removed from the pile, it is always removed from the top (referred to as *popping* the dish off the stack). Stacks are known as *last-in, first-out (LIFO) data structures*—the last item pushed (inserted) on the stack is the first item popped (removed) from the stack.

Stacks can be implemented with arrays and with other data structures, such as linked lists. (We discuss stacks and linked lists in Chapter 19, Data Structures and Collections.) A client of a stack class need not be concerned with the stack's implementation. The client knows only that when data items are placed in the stack, these items will be recalled in last-in, first-out order. The client cares about *what* functionality a stack offers, but not about *how* that functionality is implemented. This concept is referred to as *data abstraction*. Although programmers might know the details of a class's implementation, they should not write code that depends on these details. This enables a particular class (such as one that implements a stack and its operations, *push* and *pop*) to be replaced with another version without affecting the rest of the system. As long as the **public** services of the class do not change (i.e., every method still has the same name, return type and parameter list in the new class definition), the rest of the system is not affected.

Most programming languages emphasize actions. In these languages, data exist to support the actions that programs must take. Data are "less interesting" than actions. Data are "crude." Only a few built-in data types exist, and it is difficult for programmers to create their own data types. MC++ and the object-oriented style of programming elevate the importance of data. The primary activities of object-oriented programming in MC++ is the creation of data types (i.e., classes) and the expression of the interactions among objects of those data types. To create languages that emphasize data, the programming-languages community needed to formalize some notions about data. The formalization we consider here is the notion of *abstract data types (ADTs)*. ADTs receive as much attention today as structured programming did decades earlier. ADTs, however, do not replace structured programming. Rather, they provide an additional formalization to improve the program-development process.

Consider built-in type **int**, which most people would associate with an integer in mathematics. Rather, an **int** is an abstract representation of an integer. Unlike mathematical integers, computer **int**s are fixed in size. For example, type **int** in .NET is limited approximately to the range –2 billion to +2 billion. If the result of a calculation falls outside this range, an error occurs, and the computer responds in some machine-dependent manner. It might, for example, "quietly" produce an incorrect result. Mathematical integers do not have this problem. Therefore, the notion of a computer **int** is only an approximation of the notion of a real-world integer. The same is true of **float** and other built-in types.

We have taken the notion of **int** for granted until this point, but we now consider it from a new perspective. Types like **int**, **float**, **__wchar_t** and others are all examples of abstract data types. These types are representations of real-world notions to some satisfactory level of precision within a computer system.

An ADT actually captures two notions: A *data representation* and the *operations* that can be performed on that data. For example, in MC++, an **int** contains an integer value (data) and provides addition, subtraction, multiplication, division and modulus operations; however, division by zero is undefined. MC++ programmers use classes to implement abstract data types.

Software Engineering Observation 5.16

Programmers can create types through the use of the class mechanism. These new types can be designed so that they are as convenient to use as the built-in types. This marks MC++ as an extensible language. *Although the language is easy to extend via new types, the programmer cannot alter the base language itself.*

Another abstract data type we discuss is a *queue*, which is similar to a "waiting line." Computer systems use many queues internally. A queue offers well-understood behavior to its clients: Clients place items in a queue one at a time via an *enqueue* operation, then get those items back one at a time via a *dequeue* operation. A queue returns items in *first-in, first-out (FIFO)* order, which means that the first item inserted in a queue is the first item removed. Conceptually, a queue can become infinitely long, but real queues are finite.

The queue hides an internal data representation that keeps track of the items currently waiting in line, and it offers a set of operations to its clients (*enqueue* and *dequeue*). The clients are not concerned about the implementation of the queue—clients simply depend upon the queue to operate "as advertised." When a client enqueues an item, the queue should accept that item and place it in some kind of internal FIFO data structure. Similarly, when the client wants the next item from the front of the queue, the queue should remove the item from its internal representation and deliver the item in FIFO order (i.e., the item that has been in the queue the longest should be the next one returned by the next dequeue operation).

The queue ADT guarantees the integrity of its internal data structure. Clients cannot manipulate this data structure directly—only the queue ADT has access to its internal data. Clients are able to perform only allowable operations on the data representation; the ADT rejects operations that its public interface does not provide.

5.15 Software Reusability

MC++ programmers concentrate both on crafting new classes and on reusing classes from the Framework Class Library (FCL), which contains thousands of predefined classes. Developers construct software by combining programmer-defined classes with well-defined, carefully tested, well-documented, portable and widely available FCL classes. This kind of software reusability speeds the development of powerful, high-quality software. *Rapid applications development (RAD)* is of great interest today.

The FCL allows MC++ programmers to achieve software reusability across platforms that support .NET and rapid applications development. MC++ programmers focus on the high-level programming issues and leave the low-level implementation details to classes in the FCL. For example, an MC++ programmer who writes a graphics program does not need to know the details of every .NET-platform graphics capability. Instead, MC++ programmers concentrate on learning and using the FCL's graphics classes.

The FCL enables MC++ developers to build applications faster by reusing preexisting, extensively tested classes. In addition to reducing development time, FCL classes also improve programmers' abilities to debug and maintain applications, because proven software components are being used. For programmers to take advantage of the FCL's classes, they must familiarize themselves with the FCL's rich set of capabilities.

Software reuse is not limited to Windows-application development. The FCL also includes classes for creating *Web services*, which are applications packaged as services that clients can access via the Internet. Any MC++ application is a potential Web service, so programmers can reuse existing applications as building blocks to form larger more sophisticated Web-enabled applications. Visual C++ .NET provides all the features necessary for creating scalable, robust Web services. We formally introduce Web services in Chapter 17, Web Services.

5.16 Namespaces and Assemblies

As we have seen in almost every example in the text, classes from preexisting libraries, such as the .NET Framework, must be imported into an MC++ program by adding a reference to the appropriate libraries (a process we demonstrated in Section 2.7). Remember that each class in the Framework Class Library belongs to a specific namespace. The preexisting code in the FCL facilitates software reuse.

Programmers should concentrate on making the software components they create reusable. However, doing so often results in *naming collisions*. For example, two classes defined by different programmers can have the same name. If a program needs both of those classes, the program must have a way to distinguish between the two classes in the code.

 Common Programming Error 5.16

Attempting to compile code that contains naming collisions will generate compilation errors.

Namespaces help minimize this problem by providing a convention for *unique class names*. No two classes in a given namespace can have the same name, but different namespaces can contain classes of the same name. With hundreds of thousands of people writing MC++ programs, there is a good chance the names that one programmer chooses to describe classes will conflict with the names that other programmers choose for their classes.

We begin our discussion of reusing existing class definitions in Fig. 5.29–Fig. 5.30, which provides the code for class **Time3** (originally defined in Fig. 5.9–Fig. 5.10). When reusing class definitions between programs, programmers create class libraries that can be imported for use in a program via a **#using** statement. Only **public** classes can be reused from class libraries. Non-**public** classes can be used only by other classes in the same assembly.

```cpp
1   // Fig. 5.29: TimeLibrary.h
2   // Class Time3 is defined within namespace TimeLibrary.
3
4   #pragma once
5
6   using namespace System;
7
8   namespace TimeLibrary
9   {
10
11      // Time3 class definition
12      public __gc class Time3
13      {
14      public:
15         Time3();
16         Time3( int );
17         Time3( int, int );
18         Time3( int, int, int );
19         Time3( Time3 * );
20         void SetTime( int, int, int );
21
22         __property int get_Hour()
23         {
24            return hour;
25         }
26
27         __property void set_Hour( int value )
28         {
29            hour = ( ( value >= 0 && value < 24 ) ? value : 0 );
30         }
31
32         __property int get_Minute()
33         {
34            return minute;
35         }
36
37         __property void set_Minute( int value )
38         {
39            minute = ( ( value >= 0 && value < 60 ) ? value : 0 );
40         }
41
42         __property int get_Second()
43         {
44            return second;
45         }
```

Fig. 5.29 Assembly **TimeLibrary** contains class **Time3**. (Part 1 of 2.)

```
46
47            __property void set_Second( int value )
48            {
49                second = ( ( value >= 0 && value < 60 ) ? value : 0 );
50            }
51
52            String *ToUniversalString();
53            String *ToStandardString();
54
55        private:
56            int hour;    // 0-23
57            int minute;  // 0-59
58            int second;  // 0-59
59        }; // end class Time3
60    } // end namespace TimeLibrary
```

Fig. 5.29   Assembly **TimeLibrary** contains class **Time3**. (Part 2 of 2.)

```
 1    // Fig. 5.30: TimeLibrary.cpp
 2    // Method definitions for class Time3.
 3
 4    #include "stdafx.h"
 5
 6    #include "TimeLibrary.h"
 7
 8    using namespace TimeLibrary;
 9
10    // Time3 constructor initializes instance variables to
11    // zero to set default time to midnight
12    Time3::Time3()
13    {
14        SetTime( 0, 0, 0 );
15    }
16
17    // Time3 constructor: hour supplied, minute and second
18    // defaulted to 0
19    Time3::Time3( int hourValue )
20    {
21        SetTime( hourValue, 0, 0 );
22    }
23
24    // Time3 constructor: hour and minute supplied, second
25    // defaulted to 0
26    Time3::Time3( int hourValue, int minuteValue )
27    {
28        SetTime( hourValue, minuteValue, 0 );
29    }
30
31    // Time3 constructor: hour, minute and second supplied
32    Time3::Time3( int hourValue, int minuteValue, int secondValue )
33    {
34        SetTime( hourValue, minuteValue, secondValue );
35    }
```

Fig. 5.30   **Time3** class method definitions. (Part 1 of 2.)

```
36
37   // Time3 constructor: intialize using another Time3 object
38   Time3::Time3( Time3 *time )
39   {
40      SetTime( time->Hour, time->Minute, time->Second );
41   }
42
43   // set new time value in 24-hour format
44   void Time3::SetTime(
45      int hourValue, int minuteValue, int secondValue )
46   {
47      Hour = hourValue;
48      Minute = minuteValue;
49      Second = secondValue;
50   }
51
52   // convert time to universal-time (24 hour) format string
53   String *Time3::ToUniversalString()
54   {
55      return String::Concat( Hour.ToString( S"D2" ), S":",
56         Minute.ToString( S"D2" ), S":", Second.ToString( S"D2" ) );
57   }
58
59   // convert time to standard-time (12 hour) format string
60   String *Time3::ToStandardString()
61   {
62      return String::Concat(
63         ( ( Hour == 12 || Hour == 0 ) ? 12 : Hour % 12 ).ToString(),
64         S":", Minute.ToString( S"D2" ), S":",
65         Second.ToString( S"D2" ), S" ",
66         ( Hour < 12 ? S"AM" : S"PM" ) );
67   }
```

Fig. 5.30   **Time3** class method definitions. (Part 2 of 2.)

The only difference between class **Time3** in this example and the version in Fig. 5.9 and Fig. 5.10 is that we define class **Time3** in namespace **TimeLibrary**. Each class library is defined in a namespace that contains all the classes in the library. We will demonstrate momentarily how to package class **Time3** into **TimeLibrary.dll**—the *dynamic link library* that we create for reuse in other programs. Programs can load dynamic link libraries at execution time to access common functionality that can be shared among many programs. A dynamic link library represents an assembly. When a project uses a class library, the project must contain a reference to the assembly that defines the class library.

We now describe, step-by-step, how to create the class library **TimeLibrary** containing class **Time3**:

1. *Create a class library project.* First select **File > New > Project...**. In the **New Project** dialog, ensure that **Visual C++ Projects** is selected in the **Project Types** section and click **Managed C++ Class Library**. Name the project **TimeLibrary** and choose the directory in which you would like to store the project. A simple class library will be created, as shown in Fig. 5.31. There are two important points to note about the generated code. The first is that the class does

not contain a **main** function. This indicates that the class in the class library cannot be used to begin the execution of an application. This class is designed to be used by other programs. Also notice that **Class1** is created as a **public** class. If another project uses this library, only the library's **public** classes are accessible. We created class **Time3** as **public** for this purpose (line 12 of Fig. 5.29) by renaming the class **Class1** (created by Visual Studio .NET as part of the project) to **Time3**.

2. *Add the code for class **Time3***. Delete the code for **Class1**. Then copy the remainder of the **Time3** code (lines 14–58) from Fig. 5.29 and paste the code in the body of the class definition shown in Fig. 5.31. Add line 8 from Fig. 5.30 to **TimeLibrary.cpp**, followed by the method definitions in lines 12–67.

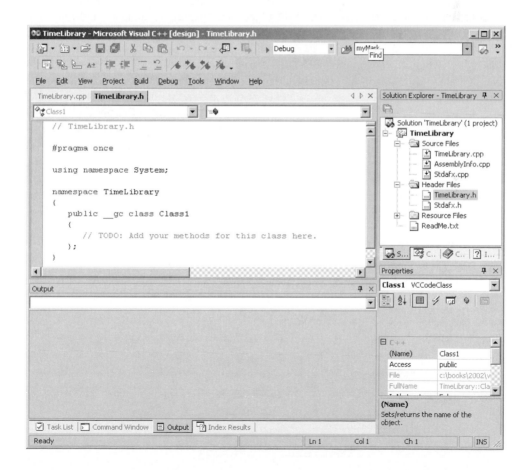

Fig. 5.31 Simple class library.

3. *Compile the code.* From the **Build** menu, choose option **Build Solution**. The code should compile successfully. Remember that this code cannot be executed— there is no entry point into the program. In fact, if you try running the program by selecting **Debug > Start**, Visual Studio .NET prompts the programmer to locate the executable file.

Compiling the project creates an assembly (a dynamic link library) that represents the new class library. This assembly can be found in the **Debug** directory of the project. By default, the assembly name will include the namespace name. (In this case, the name will be **TimeLibrary.dll**.) The assembly file contains class **Time3**, which other projects can use. Assembly files, which have file extensions **.dll** and **.exe** (as well as others), are integral to MC++ applications. The Windows operating system uses executable files (**.exe**) to run applications, whereas it uses library files (**.dll**, or *dynamic link library*) to represent code libraries that can be loaded dynamically by many applications and shared among those applications.

Next, we define a console application (Fig. 5.32) that uses class **Time3** in assembly **TimeLibrary.dll** to create a **Time3** object and display its standard and universal string formats.

Before Fig. 5.32 can use class **Time3**, the project must have access to the **TimeLibrary** assembly. During compilation the current project must be able to find **TimeLibrary.dll** (located in the **Debug** directory of the **TimeLibrary** project). The programmer can copy the DLL into the current project directory or the programmer can specify where the compiler can find the DLL by selecting **Project > Properties > Configuration Properties > C/C++ > General > Resolve #using References**. For execution, the DLL needs to be in the **Debug** directory of the current project.[3] After copying the DLL, use lines 5 and 8 to include the DLL and inform the compiler that we will use classes from namespace **TimeLibrary** (line 8 in Fig. 5.29).

```
1   // Fig. 5.32: AssemblyTest.cpp
2   // Using class Time3 from assembly TimeLibrary.
3
4   #using <mscorlib.dll>
5   #using <TimeLibrary.dll>
6
7   using namespace System;
8   using namespace TimeLibrary;
9
10  int main()
11  {
12     Time3 *time = new Time3( 13, 27, 6 );
13
14     Console::WriteLine(
15        S"Standard time: {0}\nUniversal time: {1}\n",
16        time->ToStandardString(), time->ToUniversalString() );
```

Fig. 5.32 Using assembly **TimeLibrary**. (Part 1 of 2.)

3. The **TimeLibrary** DLL also may be placed in the Global Assembly Cache (GAC) for execution. Please see the Visual Studio .NET documentation for more information about the GAC.

```
17
18      return 0;
19  }
```

```
Standard time: 1:27:06 PM
Universal time: 13:27:06
```

Fig. 5.32   Using assembly **TimeLibrary**. (Part 2 of 2.)

5.17 Class View

Now that we have introduced key concepts of object-based programming, we present a feature of Visual Studio .NET that facilitates the design of object-oriented applications—*Class View*.

The **Class View** displays the variables and methods for all classes in a project. To access this feature, select **View > Class View**. Figure 5.33 shows the **Class View** for the **TimeTest1** project of Fig. 5.1, Fig. 5.2 and Fig. 5.3 (class **Time1**). The view follows a hierarchical structure, positioning the project name (**TimeTest1**) as the root and including a series of nodes (e.g., classes, variables, methods, etc.). If a plus sign (**+**) appears to the left of a node, that node can be expanded to show other nodes. By contrast, if a minus sign (**-**) appears to the left of a node, that node has been expanded (and can be collapsed). According to the **Class View**, project **TimeTest** contains class **Time1** and class **TimeTest1** as a *child*. Class **Time1** contains methods **SetTime**, **Time1**, **ToStandardString** and **ToUniversalString** (indicated by purple boxes) and instance variables **hour**, **minute** and **second** (indicated by blue boxes). The lock icons, placed to the left of the blue-box icons for the instance variables, specify that the variables are **private**. Project **TimeTest1** also includes global functions and variables, including the **main** function. Note that class **Time1** contains the **Bases and Interfaces** node. If you expand this node, you will see class **Object**, because each class inherits from class **System::Object** (discussed in Chapter 6).

Fig. 5.33   **Class View** of class **Time1** (Fig. 5.1).

This chapter is the first in a series of three chapters that cover the fundamentals of object-based and object-oriented programming. In this chapter, we discussed how to create class definitions, how to control access to class members and several features commonly used to craft valuable classes for reuse by other programmers. Chapter 6 focuses on inheritance. In Chapter 6, you will learn how to build classes that inherit data and functionality from existing class definitions. You also will learn other MC++ features that are specific to the inheritance relationship between classes. These features serve as the basis for the object-oriented programming concept called polymorphism that we present in Chapter 7.

5.18 Summary

Object orientation uses classes to encapsulate (i.e., wrap together) data (attributes) and methods (behaviors). Objects have the ability to hide their implementation from other object (this principle is called information hiding). MC++ programmers concentrate on creating their own programmer-defined types, called classes. Each class contains both data and a set of methods that manipulate the data. The data components, or data members, of a class are called member variables, or instance variables.

MC++ and the object-oriented style of programming elevate the importance of data. The primary activities of object-oriented programming in MC++ are the creation of data types (i.e., classes) and the expression of the interactions among objects of those data types. MC++ programmers concentrate on crafting new classes and reusing existing classes. Object orientation uses classes to encapsulate data (attributes) and methods (behaviors). Classes normally hide their implementation details from the clients of the classes. This is called information hiding.

Keywords **public** and **private** are member access modifiers. Instance variables and methods that are declared with member access modifier **public** are accessible wherever the program has a pointer to an object of that class. Instance variables and methods that are declared with member access modifier **private** are accessible only to non-**static** methods of the class in which the **private** members are defined. The **private** methods often are called utility methods, or helper methods, because they can be called only by other methods of that class and are used to support the operation of those methods. Classes simplify programming, because the client code need only be concerned with the **public** operations encapsulated in an object of the class.

Access methods can read or display data. Another common use for access methods is to test the truth of conditions—such methods often are called predicate methods.

When an object is created, its members can be initialized by a constructor of that object's class. If no constructors are defined for a class, a default constructor will be provided by the compiler. This constructor contains no code and takes no parameters. Methods and constructors of a class can be overloaded. To overload a method/constructor of a class, simply provide a separate method/constructor definition with the same name for each version of the method/constructor. Overloaded methods/constructors must have different parameter lists.

Instance variables can be initialized by the class constructor, or they can be assigned values by the *set* accessor of a property. Instance variables that are not initialized explicitly by the programmer are initialized by the compiler. (Primitive numeric variables are set to **0**, **bool** values are set to **false** and pointers are set to **0**.) A class's constructor is called when an object of that class is instantiated. It is common to have overloaded constructors for a class. Normally, constructors are **public**.

Class **MessageBox** allows you to display a dialog containing information. Class **MessageBox** is defined in namespace **System::Windows::Forms**. Method **MessageBox::Show** is a method of class **MessageBox**, called a static method. Such methods are called with their class name followed by a scope resolution operator (**::**) and the method name.

A class's non-**static** instance variables and methods belong to that class's scope. Within a class's scope, class members are immediately accessible to all of that class's non-**static** methods and can be referenced simply by name. Outside a class's scope, class members cannot be referenced directly by name.

In certain cases, all objects of a class should share only one copy of a particular variable. Programmers use **static** variables for this and other reasons. A **static** variable represents class-wide information—all objects of the class share the same piece of data. The declaration of a **static** member begins with the keyword **static**. Such variables have class scope. A class's **public static** members can be accessed via the class name and the scope resolution operator (e.g., **Math::PI**). A class's **private static** members can be accessed only through methods or properties of the class. A method declared **static** cannot access non-**static** members.

Depending on the type of application we create, classes may be compiled into files with a **.exe** (executable) extension, a **.dll** (or dynamic link library) extension or one of several other extensions. This file is called an assembly, which is the packaging unit for code in MC++.

To allow clients to manipulate the value of **private** data, the class can provide a property definition, which will enable the user to access this **private** data in a safe way. A property definition contains accessor methods that handle the details of modifying and returning data. A property definition can contain a *set* accessor, a *get* accessor or both. A *get* accessor enables the client to read the field's value, and the *set* accessor enables the client to modify the value. Although *set* and *get* accessors can provide access to **private** data, the access is restricted by the programmer's implementation of those methods.

Every object can access a pointer to itself, called the **this** pointer. The **this** pointer is used implicitly and explicitly to refer to both the instance variables and the non-**static** methods of an object.

The .NET Framework performs automatic garbage collection. Every class can have a programmer-defined destructor that typically returns resources to the system. The destructor for an object is guaranteed to be called to perform termination housekeeping on the object just before the garbage collector reclaims the memory for the object (called finalization).

MC++ allows programmers to create constants whose values cannot change during program execution. To create a constant member of a class, the programmer must declare that member using keyword **const**. Members declared **const** must be initialized in the declaration. Once they are initialized, **const** values cannot be modified.

A class can define indexed properties to provide subscripted access to the data in an object of that class. Indexed properties can be defined to use any data type as the subscript. Each indexed property can define a *get* and *set* accessor.

Software reusability speeds the development of powerful, high-quality software. Rapid applications development (RAD) is of great interest today. One form of software reuse is composition, in which a class contains as members pointers to objects of other classes.

Every class in MC++, such as the classes from the .NET Framework, belongs to a namespace that contains a group of related classes and interfaces. If the programmer does not specify the namespace for a class, the class is placed in the default namespace, which includes the compiled classes in the current directory. Namespaces provide a mechanism for software reuse.

The Visual Studio .NET **Class View** feature displays the variables and methods for all classes in a project. To access this feature, select **View > Class View**.

6

Object-Oriented Programming: Inheritance

Objectives

- To understand inheritance and software reusability.
- To understand the concepts of base classes and derived classes.
- To understand member access modifier **protected**.
- To understand the use of constructors and destructors in base classes and derived classes.
- To present a case study that demonstrates the mechanics of inheritance.

Say not you know another entirely, till you have divided an inheritance with him.
Johann Kasper Lavater

This method is to define as the number of a class the class of all classes similar to the given class.
Bertrand Russell

Good as it is to inherit a library, it is better to collect one.
Augustine Birrell

6.1 Introduction

In this chapter, we continue our discussion of *object-oriented programming (OOP)* by introducing one of its main features—*inheritance*. Inheritance is a form of software reusability in which classes are created by absorbing an existing class's data and behaviors and embellishing them with new capabilities. Software reusability saves time during program development. It also encourages the reuse of proven and debugged high-quality software, which increases the likelihood that a system will be implemented effectively.

When creating a class, instead of writing completely new instance variables and methods, the programmer can designate that the new class should *inherit* the class variables, properties and methods of another class. The previously defined class is called the *base class*, and the new class is referred to as the *derived class*. (Other programming languages, such as Java, refer to the base class as the *superclass* and the derived class as the *subclass*.) Once created, each derived class can become the base class for future derived classes. A derived class, to which unique class variables, properties and methods normally are added, is often larger than its base class. Therefore, a derived class is more specific than its base class and represents a more specialized group of objects. Typically, the derived class contains the behaviors of its base class and additional behaviors. The *direct base class* is the base class from which the derived class explicitly inherits. An *indirect base class* is inherited from two or more levels up the *class hierarchy*. In the case of *single inheritance,* a class is derived from one base class. Unlike standard C++, MC++ does not support *multiple inheritance,* which occurs when a class is derived from more than one direct base class.

Every object of a derived class is also an object of that derived class's base class. However, base-class objects are not objects of their derived classes. For example, all cars are vehicles, but not all vehicles are cars. As we continue our study of object-oriented programming here and in Chapter 7, we take advantage of this relationship to perform some interesting manipulations.

Experience in building software systems indicates that significant amounts of code deal with closely related special cases. When programmers are preoccupied with special cases, the details can obscure the "big picture." With object-oriented programming, programmers focus on the commonalities among objects in the system, rather than on the special cases. This process is called *abstraction*.

We distinguish between the *"is-a" relationship* and the *"has-a" relationship*. "Is-a" represents inheritance. In an "is-a" relationship, an object of a derived class also can be treated as an object of its base class. For example, a car *is a* vehicle. By contrast, "has-a" stands for composition (composition is discussed in Chapter 5, Object-Oriented Programming). In a "has-a" relationship, a class object contains one or more objects of other classes as members. For example, a car *has a* steering wheel.

Derived-class methods might require access to their base-class instance variables, properties and methods. A derived class can access the non-**private** members of its base class. Base-class members that should be inaccessible to properties or methods of any of its derived classes are declared **private** in the base class. A derived class can effect state changes in **private** base-class members, but only through non-**private** methods and properties provided in the base class and inherited into the derived class.

Software Engineering Observation 6.1

*Properties and methods of a derived class cannot directly access **private** members of their base class.*

Software Engineering Observation 6.2

*Hiding **private** members helps programmers test, debug and correctly modify systems. If a derived class could access its base class's **private** members, classes that inherit from that derived class could access that data as well. This would propagate access to what should be **private** data, and the benefits of information hiding would be lost.*

One problem with inheritance is that a derived class can inherit properties and methods it does not need or should not have. It is the class designer's responsibility to ensure that the capabilities provided by a class are appropriate for future derived classes. Even when a base-class property or method is appropriate for a derived class, that derived class often requires the property or method to perform its task in a manner specific to the derived class. In such cases, the base-class property or method can be *overridden* (redefined) in the derived class with an appropriate implementation.

New classes can inherit from abundant *class libraries*. Organizations develop their own class libraries and can take advantage of other libraries available worldwide. Someday, the vast majority of new software likely will be constructed from *standardized reusable components*, as most hardware is constructed today. This will facilitate the development of more powerful and abundant software.

6.2 Base Classes and Derived Classes

Often, an object of one class "is an" object of another class, as well. For example, a rectangle *is a* quadrilateral (as are squares, parallelograms and trapezoids). Thus, class **Rectangle** can be said to *inherit* from class **Quadrilateral**. In this context, class **Quadrilateral** is a base class, and class **Rectangle** is a derived class. A rectangle *is a* specific type of quadrilateral, but it is incorrect to claim that a quadrilateral *is a* rectangle—the quadrilateral could be a parallelogram or some other type of **Quadrilateral**. Figure 6.1 lists several simple examples of base classes and derived classes.

Every derived-class object "is an" object of its base class, and one base class can have many derived classes; therefore, the set of objects represented by a base class typically is larger than the set of objects represented by any of its derived classes. For example, the base class **Vehicle** represents all vehicles, including cars, trucks, boats, bicycles and so on. By contrast, derived-class **Car** represents only a small subset of all **Vehicle**s.

Base class	Derived classes
Student	GraduateStudent UndergraduateStudent
Shape	Circle Triangle Rectangle
Loan	CarLoan HomeImprovementLoan MortgageLoan
Employee	FacultyMember StaffMember
Account	CheckingAccount SavingsAccount

Fig. 6.1   Inheritance examples.

Inheritance relationships form tree-like hierarchical structures. A class exists in a hierarchical relationship with its derived classes. Although classes can exist independently, once they are employed in inheritance arrangements, they become affiliated with other classes. A class becomes either a base class, supplying data and behaviors to other classes, or a derived class, inheriting its data and behaviors from other classes.

Let us develop a simple inheritance hierarchy. A university community has thousands of members. These members consist of employees, students and alumni. Employees are either faculty members or staff members. Faculty members are either administrators (such as deans and department chairpersons) or teachers. This organizational structure yields the inheritance hierarchy depicted in Fig. 6.2. Note that the inheritance hierarchy could contain many other classes. For example, students can be graduate or undergraduate students. Undergraduate students can be freshmen, sophomores, juniors and seniors. Each arrow in the hierarchy represents an "is-a" relationship. For example, as we follow the arrows in this class hierarchy, we can state, "an **Employee** *is a* **CommunityMember**" and "a **Teacher** *is a* **Faculty** member." **CommunityMember** is the *direct base class* of **Employee**, **Student** and **Alumnus**. In addition, **CommunityMember** is an *indirect base class* of all the other classes in the hierarchy diagram.

Starting from the bottom of the diagram, the reader can follow the arrows and apply the *is-a* relationship to the topmost base class. For example, an **Administrator** *is a* **Faculty** member, *is an* **Employee** and *is a* **CommunityMember**. In MC++, an **Administrator** also *is an* **Object**, because all classes[1] have **System::Object** as either a direct or indirect base class. Thus, all classes are connected via a hierarchical relationship in which they share the eight methods defined by class **Object**. We discuss some of these methods inherited from **Object** throughout the text.

---

1. Throughout this book, when we use the general term *classes*, we refer to __**gc** classes, unless otherwise specified.

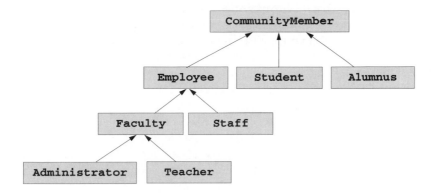

Fig. 6.2   Inheritance hierarchy for university **CommunityMember**s.

Another inheritance hierarchy is the **Shape** hierarchy (Fig. 6.3). To specify that class **TwoDimensionalShape** is derived from (or inherits from) class **Shape**, class **TwoDimensionalShape** could be defined in MC++ as follows:

```
public __gc class TwoDimensionalShape : public Shape
```

 Common Programming Error 6.1

*Using the keyword **private** or omitting the keyword **public** in front of the base class leads to compilation errors because private inheritance is strictly forbidden.[2]*

In Chapter 5, Object-Based Programming, we briefly discussed *has-a* relationships, in which classes have as members objects of other classes. Such relationships create classes by *composition* of existing classes. For example, given the classes **Employee**, **BirthDate** and **TelephoneNumber**, it is improper to say that an **Employee** *is a* **BirthDate** or that an **Employee** *is a* **TelephoneNumber**. However, it is appropriate to say that an **Employee** *has a* **BirthDate** and that an **Employee** *has a* **TelephoneNumber**.

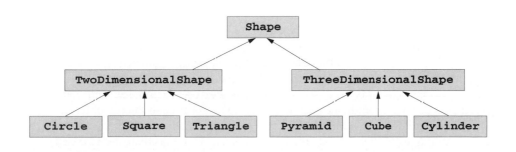

Fig. 6.3   **Shape** class hierarchy.

---

2. Currently, MC++ supports only public inheritance of a base class.

With inheritance, **private** members of a base class are not accessible directly from that class's derived classes, but these **private** base-class members are still inherited. All other base-class members retain their original member access when they become members of the derived class (e.g., **public** members of the base class become **public** members of the derived class, and, as we will soon see, **protected** members of the base class become **protected** members of the derived class). Through these inherited base-class members, the derived class can manipulate **private** members of the base class (if these inherited members provide such functionality in the base class).

It is possible to treat base-class objects and derived-class objects similarly; their commonalities are expressed in the instance variables, properties and methods of the base class. Objects of all classes derived from a common base class can be treated as objects of that base class. In Chapter 7, Object-Oriented Programming: Polymorphism, we consider many examples that take advantage of this relationship.

Software Engineering Observation 6.3

Constructors are never inherited—they are specific to the class in which they are defined.

6.3 **protected** Members

Chapter 5, Object-Based Programming, discussed **public** and **private** member access modifiers. A base class's **public** members are accessible anywhere that the program has a pointer to an object of that base class or one of its derived classes. A base class's **private** members are accessible only within the body of that base class. In this section, we introduce an additional member access modifier, *protected*.

Using **protected** access offers an intermediate level of protection between **public** and **private** access. A base class's **protected** members can be accessed only in that base class or in any classes derived from that base class.

Derived-class methods normally can refer to **public** and **protected** members of the base class simply using the member names. Note that **protected** data "breaks" encapsulation—a change to **protected** members of a base class may require modification of all derived classes.

6.4 Relationship Between Base Classes and Derived Classes

In this section, we use a point-circle hierarchy[3] to discuss the relationship between a base class and a derived class. We divide our discussion of the point-circle relationship into several parts. First, we create class **Point**, which directly inherits from class **System::Object** and contains as **private** data an *x-y* coordinate pair. Then, we create class **Circle**, which also directly inherits from class **System::Object** and contains as **private** data an *x-y* coordinate pair (representing the location of the center of the circle) and a radius. We do not use inheritance to create class **Circle**; rather, we construct the class by writing every line of code the class requires. Next, we create a **Circle2** class, which directly inherits from class **Point** (i.e., class **Circle2** "is a" **Point** but also con-

---

3. The point-circle relationship may seem unnatural when we discuss it in the context of a circle "is a" point. This example teaches what is sometimes called *structural inheritance*; the example focuses on the "mechanics" of inheritance and how a base class and a derived class relate to one another.

tains a radius) and attempts to use the **Point private** members—this results in compilation errors, because the derived class does not have access to the base-class's **private** data. We then show that if **Point**'s data is declared as **protected**, a **Circle3** class that inherits from class **Point** can access that data. Both the inherited and noninherited **Circle** classes contain identical functionality, but we show how the inherited **Circle3** class is easier to create and manage. After discussing the merits of using **protected** data, we set the **Point** data back to **private** (to enforce good software engineering), then show how a separate **Circle4** class (which also inherits from class **Point**) can use **Point** methods and properties to manipulate **Point**'s **private** data.

Let us first examine class **Point** (Fig. 6.4–Fig. 6.5). The **public** services of class **Point** include two **Point** constructors (lines 16–17 of Fig. 6.4), properties **X** and **Y** (lines 19–39) and method **ToString** (line 41). The instance variables **x** and **y** of **Point** are specified as **private** (line 44), so objects of other classes cannot access **x** and **y** directly. Technically, even if **Point**'s variables **x** and **y** were made **public**, **Point** can never maintain an inconsistent state, because the x-y coordinate plane is infinite in both directions, so **x** and **y** can hold any **int** value. In general, however, declaring data as **private**, while providing non-**private** properties to manipulate and perform validation checking on that data, enforces good software engineering.

```
1   // Fig. 6.4: Point.h
2   // Point class represents an x-y coordinate pair.
3
4   #pragma once
5
6   #using <mscorlib.dll>
7   #using <system.windows.forms.dll>
8
9   using namespace System::Windows::Forms;
10  using namespace System;
11
12  // Point class definition implicitly inherits from Object
13  public __gc class Point
14  {
15  public:
16     Point();                    // default constructor
17     Point( int, int );          // constructor
18
19     // property X
20     __property int get_X()
21     {
22        return x;
23     }
24
25     __property void set_X( int value )
26     {
27        x = value;
28     }
29
```

Fig. 6.4   **Point** class represents an x-y-coordinate pair. (Part 1 of 2.)

```
30      // property Y
31      __property int get_Y()
32      {
33         return y;
34      }
35
36      __property void set_Y( int value )
37      {
38         y = value;
39      }
40
41      String *ToString();    // return string representation of Point
42
43   private:
44      int x, y;              // point coordinates
45   }; // end class Point
```

Fig. 6.4   **Point** class represents an *x-y*-coordinate pair. (Part 2 of 2.)

```
1    // Fig. 6.5: Point.cpp
2    // Method definitions for class Point.
3
4    #include "Point.h"
5
6    // default (no-argument) constructor
7    Point::Point()
8    {
9       // implicit call to Object constructor occurs here
10   }
11
12   // constructor
13   Point::Point( int xValue, int yValue )
14   {
15
16      // implicit call to Object constructor occurs here
17      x = xValue;
18      y = yValue;
19   }
20
21   // return string representation of Point
22   String *Point::ToString()
23   {
24      return String::Concat( S"[", x.ToString(), S", ",
25         y.ToString(), S"]" );
26   }
```

Fig. 6.5   **Point** class method definitions.

We mentioned in Section 6.2 that constructors are not inherited. Therefore, header file **Point** does not inherit class **Object**'s constructor. However, class **Point**'s constructors (lines 7–19 of Fig. 6.5) call class **Object**'s constructor implicitly. In fact, the first task of any derived-class constructor is to call its direct base class's constructor, either implicitly or explicitly. (The syntax for calling a base-class constructor is discussed later in this section.) If the code does not include an explicit call to the base-class constructor, an implicit call is made to the base class's default (no-argument) constructor. The comments in lines 9 and 16 indicate where the implicit calls to the base-class **Object**'s default constructor occur. The driver (Fig. 6.6) executes the application.

Every **__gc** class in MC++ (such as class **Point**) inherits either directly or indirectly from class **System::Object**, which is the root of the class hierarchy. As we mentioned previously, this means that every class inherits the eight methods defined by class **Object**. One of these methods is **ToString**, which returns a pointer to a **String** object containing the object's type preceded by its namespace—this method obtains an object's string representation and sometimes is called implicitly (such as when an object is concatenated to a string). Method **ToString** of class **Point** *overrides* the original **ToString** from class **Object**—when invoked, method **ToString** of class **Point** returns a string containing an ordered pair of the values **x** and **y** (lines 24–25 of Fig. 6.5).

```cpp
1    // Fig. 6.6: PointTest.cpp
2    // Testing class Point.
3
4    #include "Point.h"
5
6    // main entry point for application
7    int _stdcall WinMain()
8    {
9
10       // instantiate Point object
11       Point *point = new Point( 72, 115 );
12
13       // display point coordinates via X and Y properties
14       String *output = String::Concat( S"X coordinate is ",
15          point->X.ToString(), S"\nY coordinate is ",
16          point->Y.ToString() );
17
18       point->X = 10;      // set x-coordinate via X property
19       point->Y = 10;      // set y-coordinate via Y property
20
21       // display new point value
22       output = String::Concat( output,
23          S"\n\nThe new location of point is ", point->ToString() );
24
25       MessageBox::Show( output, S"Demonstrating Class Point" );
26
27       return 0;
28    } // end function WinMain
```

Fig. 6.6   **PointTest** demonstrates **Point** functionality.

Software Engineering Observation 6.4

*The Visual C++ .NET compiler sets the base class of a derived class to **Object** when the program does not specify a base class explicitly.*

Method **ToString** of class **Object** is, in fact, declared *virtual*. *Virtual methods* allow programmers to design and implement systems that are more extensible. With virtual methods, programs can be written to process—as base-class objects—objects of all existing classes in a hierarchy. To view the method header for **ToString**, select **Help > Index...**, and enter **Object.ToString method** (filtered by **.Net Framework SDK**) in the search text box. The page displayed contains a description of method **ToString**, which includes the following header:

```
public: virtual String * ToString();
```

To illustrate the usefulness of the keyword **virtual**, suppose a set of shape classes such as **Circle**, **Triangle**, **Rectangle**, **Square**, etc. derive from base class **Shape**. In object-oriented programming, each of these classes might be endowed with the ability to draw itself. Although each class has its own **Draw** method, the **Draw** method for each shape is quite different. When drawing a shape, whatever that shape may be, it would be nice to be able to treat all these shapes generically as objects of the base class **Shape**. Then to draw any shape, we could simply call method **Draw** of base class **Shape** and let the program determine dynamically (i.e., at run time) which derived class **draw** method to use. To enable this kind of behavior, we declare **Draw** in the base class as a **virtual** method and we override **Draw** in each of the derived classes to draw the appropriate shape.

In the case of method **ToString**, any class can override class **Object**'s **ToString** method. When an object of a derived class calls method **ToString**, the correct **ToString** implementation is called. If the derived class does not override **ToString**, the derived class inherits its immediate base class's method definition. If the **Point** class did not override **ToString**, invoking method **ToString** on a **Point** object would call base class **Object**'s version of the method.

Software Engineering Observation 6.5

*Once a method is declared **virtual**, it remains **virtual** all the way down the inheritance hierarchy from that point even if it is not declared **virtual** when a class overrides it.*

Good Programming Practice 6.1

*Even though certain functions are implicitly **virtual** because of a declaration made higher in the class hierarchy, explicitly declare these methods **virtual** at every level of the hierarchy to promote program clarity.*

Software Engineering Observation 6.6

*When a derived class chooses not to define a **virtual** method, the derived class simply inherits its immediate base class's **virtual** method definition.*

PointTest (Fig. 6.6) tests class **Point**. Notice that we use function **WinMain** (lines 7–28) rather than **main** in this example. As discussed in Chapter 2, function **WinMain** is the appropriate entry point for GUI applications. We discuss function **WinMain** and keyword **__stdcall** further in Chapter 9, Graphical User Interface Concepts: Part 1. Line 11 instantiates an object of class **Point** and assigns **72** as the *x*-coordinate value and

115 as the *y*-coordinate value. Lines 14–16 use properties **X** and **Y** to retrieve these values, then append the values to **output**. Lines 18–19 change the values of properties **X** and **Y** (implicitly invoking their *set* accessors), and line 23 calls **Point**'s **ToString** method to obtain the **Point**'s string representation.

We now discuss the second part of our introduction to inheritance by creating and testing (a completely new) class **Circle** (Fig. 6.7–Fig. 6.8), which directly inherits from class **System::Object** and represents an *x-y* coordinate pair (representing the center of the circle) and a radius. Lines 60–61 (of Fig. 6.7) declare the instance variables **x, y** and **radius** as **private** data. The **public** services of class **Circle** include two **Circle** constructors (lines 17–18); properties **X**, **Y** and **Radius** (lines 21–52); and methods **Diameter**, **Circumference**, **Area** and **ToString** (lines 54–57). These properties and methods encapsulate all necessary features (i.e., the "analytic geometry") of a circle; in the next section, we show how this encapsulation enables us to reuse and extend this class.

```
1   // Fig. 6.7: Circle.h
2   // Circle class contains x-y coordinates pair and radius.
3
4   #pragma once
5
6   #using <mscorlib.dll>
7   #using <system.drawing.dll>
8   #using <system.windows.forms.dll>
9
10  using namespace System;
11  using namespace System::Windows::Forms;
12
13  // Circle class definition implicitly inherits from Object
14  public __gc class Circle
15  {
16  public:
17     Circle();                    // default constructor
18     Circle( int, int, double );  // constructor
19
20     // property X
21     __property int get_X()
22     {
23        return x;
24     }
25
26     __property void set_X( int value )
27     {
28        x = value;
29     }
30
31     // property Y
32     __property int get_Y()
33     {
34        return y;
35     }
36
```

Fig. 6.7   **Circle** class contains an *x-y* coordinate and a radius. (Part 1 of 2.)

```
37          __property void set_Y( int value )
38          {
39             y = value;
40          }
41
42          // property Radius
43          __property double get_Radius()
44          {
45             return radius;
46          }
47
48          __property void set_Radius( double value )
49          {
50             if ( value >= 0 )      // validation needed
51                radius = value;
52          }
53
54          double Diameter();        // calculate diameter
55          double Circumference();   // calculate circumference
56          double Area();            // calculate area
57          String *ToString();   // return string representation of Circle
58
59       private:
60          int x, y;                 // coordinates of Circle's center
61          double radius;            // Circle's radius
62       }; // end class Circle
```

Fig. 6.7   `Circle` class contains an *x-y* coordinate and a radius. (Part 2 of 2.)

```
1    // Fig. 6.8: Circle.cpp
2    // Method definitions for class Circle.
3
4    #include "Circle.h"
5
6    // default constructor
7    Circle::Circle()
8    {
9       // implicit call to Object constructor occurs here
10   }
11
12   // constructor
13   Circle::Circle( int xValue, int yValue, double radiusValue )
14   {
15
16      // implicit call to Object constructor occurs here
17      x = xValue;
18      y = yValue;
19      radius = radiusValue;
20   }
21
```

Fig. 6.8   `Circle` class method definitions. (Part 1 of 2.)

```
22   // calculate diameter
23   double Circle::Diameter()
24   {
25      return radius * 2;
26   }
27
28   // calculate circumference
29   double Circle::Circumference()
30   {
31      return Math::PI * Diameter();
32   }
33
34   // calculate area
35   double Circle::Area()
36   {
37      return Math::PI * Math::Pow( radius, 2 );
38   }
39
40   // return string representation of Circle
41   String *Circle::ToString()
42   {
43      return String::Concat( S"Center = [", x.ToString(),
44         S", ", y.ToString(), S"]; Radius = ", radius.ToString() );
45   }
```

Fig. 6.8   **Circle** class method definitions. (Part 2 of 2.)

CircleTest (Fig. 6.9) tests class **Circle**. Line 11 instantiates an object of class **Circle**, assigning **37** as the *x*-coordinate value, **43** as the *y*-coordinate value and **2.5** as the radius value. Lines 14–17 use properties **X**, **Y** and **Radius** to retrieve these values, then concatenate the values to **output**. Lines 20–22 use **Circle**'s **X**, **Y** and **Radius** properties to change the *x-y* coordinates and the radius, respectively. Property **Radius** ensures that member variable **radius** cannot be assigned a negative value. Lines 25–26 call **Circle**'s **ToString** method to obtain the **Circle**'s string representation, and lines 29–38 call **Circle**'s **Diameter**, **Circumference** and **Area** methods.

```
1    // Fig. 6.9: CircleTest.cpp
2    // Testing class Circle.
3
4    #include "Circle.h"
5
6    // main entry point for application
7    int __stdcall WinMain()
8    {
9
10      // instantiate Circle
11      Circle *circle = new Circle( 37, 43, 2.5 );
12
13      // get Circle's initial x-y coordinates and radius
14      String *output = String::Concat( S"X coordinate is ",
```

Fig. 6.9   **CircleTest** demonstrates **Circle** functionality. (Part 1 of 2.)

```
15            circle->X.ToString(), S"\nY coordinate is ",
16            circle->Y.ToString(), S"\nRadius is ",
17            circle->Radius.ToString() );
18
19      // set Circle's x-y coordinates and radius to new values
20      circle->X = 2;
21      circle->Y = 2;
22      circle->Radius = 4.25;
23
24      // display Circle's string representation
25      output = String::Concat( output, S"\n\nThe new location and "
26         S"radius of circle are \n", circle->ToString(), S"\n" );
27
28      // display diameter
29      output = String::Concat( output, S"Diameter is ",
30         circle->Diameter().ToString( S"F" ), S"\n" );
31
32      // display circumference
33      output = String::Concat( output, S"Circumference is ",
34         circle->Circumference().ToString( S"F" ), S"\n" );
35
36      // display area
37      output = String::Concat( output, S"Area is ",
38         circle->Area().ToString( S"F" ) );
39
40      MessageBox::Show( output, S"Demonstrating Class Circle" );
41
42      return 0;
43   } // end function WinMain
```

Fig. 6.9   **CircleTest** demonstrates **Circle** functionality. (Part 2 of 2.)

After writing all the code for class **Circle** (Fig. 6.7–Fig. 6.8), we note that a major portion of the code in this class is similar, if not identical, to much of the code in class **Point**. For example, the declaration in **Circle** of **private** variables **x** and **y** and properties **X** and **Y** are identical to those of class **Point**. In addition, the class **Circle** constructors and method **ToString** are almost identical to those of class **Point**, except that they also supply **radius** information. The only other additions to class **Circle** are **private** member variable **radius**, property **Radius** and methods **Diameter**, **Circumference** and **Area**.

It appears that we literally copied code from class **Point**, pasted this code in the code from class **Circle**, then modified class **Circle** to include a radius. This "copy-and-paste" approach is often error-prone and time-consuming. Worse yet, it can result in many physical copies of the code existing throughout a system, creating a code-maintenance "nightmare." Is there a way to "absorb" the attributes and behaviors of one class in a way that makes them part of other classes without duplicating code?

In the next examples we answer that question, using a more elegant class construction approach emphasizing the benefits of inheritance. Now, we create and test a class **Circle2** (Fig. 6.10–Fig. 6.11) that inherits variables **x** and **y** and properties **X** and **Y** from class **Point** (Fig. 6.4). This class **Circle2** "is a" **Point** (because inheritance absorbs the capabilities of class **Point**), but also contains its own member **radius** (line 33 of Fig. 6.10). The colon (**:**) symbol in the class declaration (line 9) indicates inheritance. As a derived class, **Circle2** inherits all the members of class **Point**, except for the constructors. Thus, the **public** services to **Circle2** include the two **Circle2** constructors (lines 12–13); the **public** methods inherited from class **Point**; property **Radius** (lines 16–25); and the **Circle2** methods **Diameter**, **Circumference**, **Area** and **ToString** (lines 27–30). We declare method **Area** as **virtual**. The derived classes (such as class **Cylinder**, as we will see in Section 6.5) override this method to provide a more appropriate implementation. The driver (Fig. 6.12) executes the application.

```
1   // Fig. 6.10: Circle2.h
2   // Circle2 class that inherits from class Point.
3
4   #pragma once
5
6   #include "Point.h"
7
8   // Circle2 class definition inherits from Point
9   public __gc class Circle2 : public Point
10  {
11  public:
12     Circle2();                       // default constructor
13     Circle2( int, int, double );    // constructor
14
15     // property Radius
16     __property double get_Radius()
17     {
18        return radius;
19     }
20
21     __property void set_Radius( double value )
22     {
23        if ( value >= 0 )
24           radius = value;
25     }
26
27     double Diameter();
28     double Circumference();
29     virtual double Area();
30     String *ToString(); // return string representation of Circle2
31
```

Fig. 6.10 **Circle2** class that inherits from class **Point**. (Part 1 of 2.)

```
32   private:
33      double radius;        // Circle2's radius
34   }; // end class Circle2
```

Fig. 6.10 `Circle2` class that inherits from class **Point**. (Part 2 of 2.)

```
1    // Fig. 6.11: Circle2.cpp
2    // Method definitions for class Circle2.
3
4    #include "Point.h"
5    #include "Circle2.h"
6
7    // default constructor
8    Circle2::Circle2()
9    {
10       // implicit call to Point constructor occurs here
11   }
12
13   // constructor
14   Circle2::Circle2( int xValue, int yValue, double radiusValue )
15   {
16
17       // implicit call to Point constructor occurs here
18       x = xValue;
19       y = yValue;
20       Radius = radiusValue;
21   }
22
23   // calculate diameter
24   double Circle2::Diameter()
25   {
26       return radius * 2;
27   }
28
29   // calculate circumference
30   double Circle2::Circumference()
31   {
32       return Math::PI * Diameter();
33   }
34
35   // calculate area
36   double Circle2::Area()
37   {
38       return Math::PI * Math::Pow( radius, 2 );
39   }
40
41   // return string representation of Circle2
42   String *Circle2::ToString()
43   {
44       return String::Concat( S"Center = [", x.ToString(),
45          y.ToString(), S"]; Radius = ", radius.ToString() );
46   }
```

Fig. 6.11 `Circle2` class method definitions.

```cpp
1   // Fig. 6.12: CircleTest2.cpp
2   // Testing class Circle2.
3
4   #include "Circle2.h"
5
6   // main entry point for application
7   int __stdcall WinMain()
8   {
9
10      // instantiate Circle2
11      Circle2 *circle = new Circle2( 37, 43, 2.5 );
12
13      // get Circle2's initial x-y coordinates and radius
14      String *output = String::Concat( S"X coordinate is ",
15         circle->X.ToString(), S"\nY coordinate is ",
16         circle->Y.ToString(), S"\nRadius is ",
17         circle->Radius.ToString() );
18
19      // set Circle2's x-y coordinates and radius to new values
20      circle->X = 2;
21      circle->Y = 2;
22      circle->Radius = 4.25;
23
24      // display Circle2's string representation
25      output = String::Concat( output, S"\n\nThe new location and "
26         S"radius of circle are \n", circle->ToString(), S"\n" );
27
28      // display diameter
29      output = String::Concat( output, S"Diameter is ",
30         circle->Diameter().ToString( S"F" ), S"\n" );
31
32      // display circumference
33      output = String::Concat( output, S"Circumference is ",
34         circle->Circumference().ToString( S"F" ), S"\n" );
35
36      // display area
37      output = String::Concat( output, S"Area is ",
38         circle->Area().ToString( S"F" ) );
39
40      MessageBox::Show( output, S"Demonstrating Class Circle2" );
41
42      return 0;
43   } // end function WinMain
```

!	☑	Description	File	Line
		Click here to add a new task		
!		error C2248: 'Point::x' : cannot access private member declared in class 'Point'	c:\Books\2002\VCPPhtp1\...\Fig09_10-12\CircleTest2\Circle2.cpp	17
!		error C2248: 'Point::y' : cannot access private member declared in class 'Point'	c:\Books\2002\VCPPhtp1\...\Fig09_10-12\CircleTest2\Circle2.cpp	18
!		error C2248: 'Point::x' : cannot access private member declared in class 'Point'	c:\Books\2002\VCPPhtp1\...\Fig09_10-12\CircleTest2\Circle2.cpp	43
!		error C2248: 'Point::y' : cannot access private member declared in class 'Point'	c:\Books\2002\VCPPhtp1\...\Fig09_10-12\CircleTest2\Circle2.cpp	44

Task List - 4 Build Error tasks shown (filtered)

Fig. 6.12 `CircleTest2` demonstrates `Circle2` functionality.

Lines 10 and 17 in the **Circle2** constructors (lines 8–21 of Fig. 6.11) demonstrate when the default **Point** constructor will be invoked, initializing the base-class portion (variables **x** and **y**, inherited from class **Point**) of a **Circle2** object to **0**. However, because the parameterized constructor (lines 14–21) should set the *x-y* coordinate to a specific value, lines 18–19 attempt to assign argument values to **x** and **y** directly. Even though lines 18–19 attempt to set **x** and **y** values explicitly, line 17 first calls the **Point** default constructor to initialize these variables to their default values. The compiler generates syntax errors for lines 18–19 (and lines 44–45, where **Circle2**'s method **ToString** attempts to use the values of **x** and **y** directly), because the derived class **Circle2** is not allowed to access the base class **Point**'s **private** members **x** and **y**. MC++ rigidly enforces restriction on accessing **private** data members, so that even a derived class (i.e., which is closely related to its base class) cannot access base-class **private** data.

To enable class **Circle2** to access **Point** member variables **x** and **y** directly, we can declare those variables as **protected**. As we discussed in Section 6.3, a base class's **protected** members can be accessed only in that base class or in any classes derived from that base class. Class **Point2** (Fig. 6.13–Fig. 6.14) modifies class **Point** (Fig. 6.4) to declare variables **x** and **y** as **protected** (Fig. 6.13, line 45) instead of **private**. The driver (Fig. 6.15) executes the application.

```
1   // Fig. 6.13: Point2.h
2   // Point2 class contains an x-y coordinate pair as protected data.
3
4   #pragma once
5
6   #using <mscorlib.dll>
7   #using <system.windows.forms.dll>
8
9   using namespace System;
10  using namespace System::Windows::Forms;
11
12  // Point2 class definition implicitly inherits from Object
13  public __gc class Point2
14  {
15  public:
16      Point2();              // default constructor
17      Point2( int, int );    // constructor
18
19      // property X
20      __property int get_X()
21      {
22          return x;
23      }
24
25      __property void set_X( int value )
26      {
27          x = value;
28      }
29
30      // property Y
31      __property int get_Y()
32      {
```

Fig. 6.13   **Point2** class represents an *x-y*-coordinate pair as **protected** data. (Part 1 of 2.)

```
33          return y;
34      }
35
36      __property void set_Y( int value )
37      {
38          y = value;
39      }
40
41      // return string representation of Point2
42      String *ToString();
43
44  protected:
45      int x, y;                    // point coordinate
46  }; // end class Point2
```

Fig. 6.13 **Point2** class represents an *x-y*-coordinate pair as **protected** data. (Part 2 of 2.)

```
1   // Fig. 6.14: Point2.cpp
2   // Method definitions for class Point2.
3
4   #include "Point2.h"
5
6   // default constructor
7   Point2::Point2()
8   {
9       // implicit call to Object constructor occurs here
10  }
11
12  // constructor
13  Point2::Point2( int xValue, int yValue )
14  {
15
16      // implicit call to Object constructor occurs here
17      x = xValue;
18      y = yValue;
19  }
20
21  // return string representation of Point2
22  String *Point2::ToString()
23  {
24      return String::Concat( S"[", x.ToString(),
25          S", ", y.ToString(), S"]" );
26  }
```

Fig. 6.14 **Point2** class method definitions.

```
1   // Fig. 6.15: PointTest2.cpp
2   // Testing class Point2.
3
4   #include "Point2.h"
```

Fig. 6.15 **PointTest2** demonstrates **Point2** functionality. (Part 1 of 2.)

```
5
6    // main entry point for application
7    int __stdcall WinMain()
8    {
9
10       // instantiate Point2 object
11       Point2 *point = new Point2( 72, 115 );
12
13       // display point coordinates via X and Y properties
14       String *output = String::Concat( S"X coordinate is ",
15          point->X.ToString(), S"\nY coordinate is ",
16          point->Y.ToString() );
17
18       point->X = 10;      // set x-coordinate via X property
19       point->Y = 10;      // set y-coordinate via Y property
20
21       // display new point value
22       output = String::Concat( output,
23          S"\n\nThe new location of point is ", point->ToString() );
24
25       MessageBox::Show( output, S"Demonstrating Class Point2" );
26
27       return 0;
28    } // end function WinMain
```

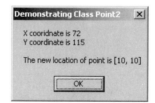

Fig. 6.15 `PointTest2` demonstrates `Point2` functionality. (Part 2 of 2.)

Class **Circle3** (Fig. 6.16–Fig. 6.17) modifies class **Circle2** (Fig. 6.10–Fig. 6.11) to inherit from class **Point2** rather than inheriting from class **Point**. Because class **Circle3** is a class derived from class **Point2**, class **Circle3** can access class **Point2**'s **protected** member variables **x** and **y** directly, and the compiler does not generate errors when compiling Fig. 6.18. This shows the special privileges that a derived class is granted to access **protected** base-class data members. A derived class also can access **protected** properties and methods in any of that derived class's base classes. The driver (Fig. 6.18) executes the application.

```
1    // Fig. 6.16: Circle3.h
2    // Circle2 class that inherits from class Point2.
3
4    #pragma once
5
6    #include "Point2.h"
7
```

Fig. 6.16 `Circle3` class that inherits from `Point2`. (Part 1 of 2.)

```
8   public __gc class Circle3 : public Point2
9   {
10  public:
11     Circle3();                        // default constructor
12     Circle3( int, int, double );      // constructor
13
14     // property Radius
15     __property double get_Radius()
16     {
17        return radius;
18     }
19
20     __property void set_Radius( double value )
21     {
22        if ( value >= 0 )
23           radius = value;
24     }
25
26     double Diameter();                // calculate diameter
27     double Circumference();           // calculate circumference
28     virtual double Area();            // calculate area
29
30     // return string representation of Circle3
31     String *ToString();
32
33  private:
34     double radius;                    // Circle3's radius
35  }; // end class Circle3
```

Fig. 6.16 `Circle3` class that inherits from `Point2`. (Part 2 of 2.)

```
1   // Fig. 6.17: Circle3.cpp
2   // Method definitions for class Circle3.
3
4   #include "Circle3.h"
5
6   // default constructor
7   Circle3::Circle3()
8   {
9      // implicit call to Point2 constructor occurs here
10  }
11
12  // constructor
13  Circle3::Circle3( int xValue, int yValue, double radiusValue )
14  {
15
16     // implicit call to Point2 constructor occurs here
17     x = xValue;
18     y = yValue;
19     Radius = radiusValue;
20  }
21
```

Fig. 6.17 `Circle3` class method definitions. (Part 1 of 2.)

```
22   // calculate diameter
23   double Circle3::Diameter()
24   {
25      return radius * 2;
26   }
27
28   // calculate circumference
29   double Circle3::Circumference()
30   {
31      return Math::PI * Diameter();
32   }
33
34   // calculate area
35   double Circle3::Area()
36   {
37      return Math::PI * Math::Pow( radius, 2 );
38   }
39
40   // return string representation of Circle3
41   String *Circle3::ToString()
42   {
43      return String::Concat( S"Center = [", x.ToString(),
44         S", ", y.ToString(), S"]; Radius = ", radius.ToString() );
45   }
```

Fig. 6.17 Circle3 class method definitions. (Part 2 of 2.)

```
1    // Fig. 6.18: CircleTest3.cpp
2    // Testing class Circle3.
3
4    #include "Circle3.h"
5
6    // main entry point for application
7    int __stdcall WinMain()
8    {
9
10      // instantiate Circle3
11      Circle3 *circle = new Circle3( 37, 43, 2.5 );
12
13      // get Circle3's initial x-y coordinates and radius
14      String *output = String::Concat( S"X coordinate is ",
15         circle->X.ToString(), S"\nY coordinate is ",
16         circle->Y.ToString(), S"\nRadius is ",
17         circle->Radius.ToString() );
18
19      // set Circle3's x-y coordinates and radius to new values
20      circle->X = 2;
21      circle->Y = 2;
22      circle->Radius = 4.25;
23
24      // display Circle3's string representation
25      output = String::Concat( output, S"\n\n",
```

Fig. 6.18 CircleTest3 demonstrates Circle3 functionality. (Part 1 of 2.)

```
26          S"The new location and radius of circle are\n",
27          circle, S"\n" );
28
29     // display diameter
30     output = String::Concat( output, S"Diameter is ",
31          circle->Diameter().ToString( S"F" ), S"\n" );
32
33     // display circumference
34     output = String::Concat( output, S"Circumference is ",
35          circle->Circumference().ToString( S"F" ), S"\n" );
36
37     // display area
38     output = String::Concat( output, S"Area is ",
39          circle->Area().ToString( S"F" ) );
40
41     MessageBox::Show( output, S"Demonstrating Class Circle3" );
42
43     return 0;
44 } // end function WinMain
```

Fig. 6.18 `CircleTest3` demonstrates `Circle3` functionality. (Part 2 of 2.)

CircleTest3 (Fig. 6.18) performs identical tests on class **Circle3** as **CircleTest** (Fig. 6.9) performed on class **Circle**. Note that the outputs of the two programs are identical. We created class **Circle** without using inheritance and created class **Circle3** using inheritance; however, both classes provide the same functionality. Also, there is now only one copy of the point functionality.

In the previous example, we declared the base-class instance variables as **protected**, so that a derived class could modify their values directly. The use of **protected** variables allows for a slight increase in performance, because we avoid incurring the overhead of a method call to a property's *set* or *get* accessor. However, in most MC++ applications, in which user interaction comprises a large part of the execution time, the optimization offered through the use of **protected** variables is negligible.

Using **protected** instance variables creates two major problems. First, the derived-class object does not have to use a property to set the value of the base-class's **protected** data. Therefore, a derived-class object can easily assign an inappropriate value to the **protected** data, thus leaving the object in an inconsistent state. For example, if we were to declare **Circle3**'s variable **radius** as **protected**, a derived-class object (e.g., **Cylinder**) could then assign a negative value to **radius**. The second problem with using **protected** data is that derived-class methods are more likely to be written to depend on base-class implementation. In practice, derived classes should depend only on the base-class services (i.e., non-**private** methods and properties) and not on base-class implementation. With **protected** data in the base class, if the base-class implementation changes, we may need to modify all derived classes of that base class. For example, if for some reason we were to change the names of variables **x** and **y** to **xCoordinate** and **yCoordinate**, then we would have to do so for all occurrences in which a derived class references these base-class variables directly. In such a case, the software is said to be *fragile* or *brittle*. The programmer should be able to change the base-class implementation freely, while still providing the same services to derived classes. (Of course, if the base-class services change, we must reimplement our derived classes. However, good object-oriented design attempts to prevent this.)

Software Engineering Observation 6.7

*The most appropriate time to use the **protected** access modifier is when a base class should provide a service only to its derived classes (i.e., the base class should not provide the service to other clients).*

Software Engineering Observation 6.8

*Declaring base-class instance variables **private** (as opposed to declaring them **protected**) enables programmers to change base-class implementation without having to change derived-class implementation.*

Testing and Debugging Tip 6.1

*When possible, avoid including **protected** data in a base class. Rather, include non-**private** properties and methods that access **private** data, ensuring that the object maintains a consistent state.*

We re-examine our point-circle hierarchy example once more; this time, attempting to use the best software engineering techniques. We use **Point3** (Fig. 6.19–Fig. 6.20), which declares variables **x** and **y** as **private** and uses properties in method **ToString** to access these values. We show how derived class **Circle4** (Fig. 6.21–Fig. 6.22) can invoke non-**private** base-class methods and properties to manipulate these variables. The driver (Fig. 6.23) executes the application.

```
1   // Fig. 6.19: Point3.h
2   // Point3 class represents an x-y coordinate pair.
3
4   #pragma once
5
6   #using <mscorlib.dll>
7   #using <system.windows.forms.dll>
8
9   using namespace System;
10  using namespace System::Windows::Forms;
11
12  public __gc class Point3
13  {
14  public:
15     Point3();            // default constructor
16     Point3( int, int );  // constructor
```

Fig. 6.19 **Point3** class uses properties to manipulate **private** data. (Part 1 of 2.)

```
17
18        // property X
19        __property int get_X()
20        {
21           return x;
22        }
23
24        __property void set_X( int value )
25        {
26           x = value;
27        }
28
29        // property Y
30        __property int get_Y()
31        {
32           return y;
33        }
34
35        __property void set_Y( int value )
36        {
37           y = value;
38        }
39
40        // return string representation of Point3
41        String *ToString();
42
43     private:
44        int x, y;                 // point coordinate
45     }; // end class Point3
```

Fig. 6.19 **Point3** class uses properties to manipulate **private** data. (Part 2 of 2.)

```
1     // Fig. 6.20: Point3.cpp
2     // Method definitions for class Point3.
3
4     #include "Point3.h"
5
6     using namespace System;
7
8     // default constructor
9     Point3::Point3()
10    {
11       // implicit call to Object constructor occurs here
12    }
13
14    // constructor
15    Point3::Point3( int xValue, int yValue )
16    {
17
18       // implicit call to Object constructor occurs here
19       x = xValue;               // use property X
```

Fig. 6.20 **Point3** class method definitions. (Part 1 of 2.)

```
20       y = yValue;                  // use property Y
21    }
22
23    // return string representation of Point3
24    String *Point3::ToString()
25    {
26       return String::Concat( S"[", X.ToString(), S", ",
27          Y.ToString(), S"]" );
28    }
```

Fig. 6.20 `Point3` class method definitions. (Part 2 of 2.)

```
1     // Fig. 6.21: Circle4.h
2     // Circle4 class that inherits from class Point3.
3
4     #pragma once
5
6     #include "Point3.h"
7
8     // Circle4 class definition inherits from Point3
9     public __gc class Circle4 : public Point3
10    {
11    public:
12       Circle4();                       // default constructor
13       Circle4( int, int, double );    // constructor
14
15       // property Radius
16       __property double get_Radius()
17       {
18          return radius;
19       }
20
21       __property void set_Radius( double value )
22       {
23          if ( value >= 0 )               // validation needed
24             radius = value;
25       }
26
27       double Diameter();              // calculate diameter
28       double Circumference();         // calculate circumference
29       virtual double Area();          // calculate area
30
31       // return string representation of Circle4
32       String *ToString();
33
34    private:
35       double radius;
36    }; // end class Circle4
```

Fig. 6.21 `Circle4` class that inherits from **Point3**, which does not provide **protected** data.

```
1   // Fig. 6.22: Circle4.cpp
2   // Method definitions for class Circle4.
3
4   #include "Circle4.h"
5
6   // default constructor
7   Circle4::Circle4()
8   {
9      // implicit call to Point3 constructor occurs here
10  }
11
12  // constructor
13  Circle4::Circle4( int xValue, int yValue, double radiusValue )
14     : Point3( xValue, yValue )
15  {
16     Radius = radiusValue;
17  }
18
19  // calculate diameter
20  double Circle4::Diameter()
21  {
22     return Radius * 2;    // use property Radius
23  }
24
25  // calculate circumference
26  double Circle4::Circumference()
27  {
28     return Math::PI * Diameter();
29  }
30
31  // calculate area
32  double Circle4::Area()
33  {
34     return Math::PI * Math::Pow( Radius, 2 ); // user property
35  }
36
37  // return string representation of Circle4
38  String *Circle4::ToString()
39  {
40
41     // return Point3 string representation
42     return String::Concat( S"Center= ", __super::ToString(),
43        S"; Radius = ", Radius.ToString() ); //use property Radius
44  }
```

Fig. 6.22 Circle4 class method definitions.

```
1   // Fig. 6.23: CircleTest4.cpp
2   // Testing class Circle4.
3
4   #include "Circle4.h"
5
```

Fig. 6.23 CircleTest4 demonstrates **Circle4** functionality. (Part 1 of 2.)

```
6    // main entry point for application
7    int __stdcall WinMain()
8    {
9
10       // instantiate Circle4
11       Circle4 *circle = new Circle4( 37, 43, 2.5 );
12
13       // get Circle4's initial x-y coordinates and radius
14       String *output = String::Concat( S"X coordinate is ",
15          circle->X.ToString(), S"\nY coordinate is ",
16          circle->Y.ToString(), S"\nRadius is ",
17          circle->Radius.ToString() );
18
19       // set Circle4's x-y coordinates and radius to new values
20       circle->X = 2;
21       circle->Y = 2;
22       circle->Radius = 4.25;
23
24       // display Circle4's string representation
25       output = String::Concat( output, S"\n\n",
26          S"The new location and radius of circle are\n",
27          circle, S"\n" );
28
29       // display diameter
30       output = String::Concat( output, S"Diameter is ",
31          circle->Diameter().ToString( S"F" ), S"\n" );
32
33       // display circumference
34       output = String::Concat( output, S"Circumference is ",
35          circle->Circumference().ToString( S"F" ), S"\n" );
36
37       // display area
38       output = String::Concat( output, S"Area is ",
39          circle->Area().ToString( S"F" ) );
40
41       MessageBox::Show( output, S"Demonstrating Class Circle4" );
42
43       return 0;
44    } // end function WinMain
```

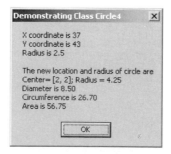

Fig. 6.23   `CircleTest4` demonstrates **Circle4** functionality. (Part 2 of 2.)

For the purpose of this example, to demonstrate both explicit and implicit calls to base-class constructors, we include a second constructor that calls the base-class constructor explicitly. Lines 13–17 (Fig. 6.22) declare the **Circle4** constructor that invokes the second **Point3** constructor explicitly (line 14). In this case, **xValue** and **yValue** are passed to initialize the **private** base-class members **x** and **y**. The colon symbol (**:**) followed by the class name accesses the base-class version explicitly. By making this call, we can initialize **x** and **y** in the base class to specific values, rather than to **0**.

Software Engineering Observation 6.9

When possible, use properties to alter and obtain the values of member variables, even if those values can be modified directly. A property's set *accessor can prevent attempts to assign an inappropriate value to that member variable, and a property's* get *accessor can help control the presentation of the data to clients.*

Performance Tip 6.1

Using a property to access a variable's value is slightly slower than accessing the data directly. However, attempting to optimize programs by referencing data directly often is unnecessary, because the compiler optimizes the programs implicitly. Today's so-called "optimizing compilers" are carefully designed to perform many optimizations implicitly, even if the programmer does not write what appears to be the most optimal code. A good rule is, "Do not second-guess the compiler."

Class **Circle4**'s **ToString** method (lines 38–44 of Fig. 6.22) overrides class **Point3**'s **ToString** method (lines 24–28 of Fig. 6.20). As we discussed earlier, we know that the appropriate **ToString** method will be invoked based on the calling object's type, because method **ToString** of class **System::Object** (class **Point3**'s base class) is declared **virtual**. Method **ToString** of class **Circle4** displays the **private** instance variables **x** and **y** of class **Point3** by calling the base class's **ToString** method (in this case, **Point3**'s **ToString** method). The call is made in line 42 via the expression **__super::ToString()** (discussed shortly) and causes the values of **x** and **y** to become part of the **Circle4**'s string representation. Using this approach is a good software engineering practice: If an object's method performs the actions needed by another object, call that method rather than duplicating its code body. Duplicate code creates code-maintenance problems. By having **Circle4**'s **ToString** method use the formatting provided by **Point3**'s **ToString** method, we avoid duplicating code.

Also, **Point3**'s **ToString** method performs part of the task of **Circle4**'s **ToString** method, so we call **Point3**'s **ToString** method from class **Circle4** using keyword **__super** (e.g., **__super::ToString()** in line 42). Keyword **__super** specifies that the base-class version of a method should be called. Thus, the expression **__super::ToString()** is equivalent to **Point3::ToString()**. Notice, however, that we do not use keyword **__super** in line 14, but specify class **Point3** explicitly. This is because keyword **__super** can appear only in the body of a method.

Software Engineering Observation 6.10

A redefinition in a derived class of a base-class method that uses a different signature than that of the base-class method is method overloading rather than method overriding.

Software Engineering Observation 6.11

*Although method **ToString** certainly could be overridden to perform arbitrary actions, the general understanding in the .NET community is that method **ToString** should be overridden to obtain an object's string representation.*

Common Programming Error 6.2

*When a base-class method is overridden in a derived class, the derived-class version often calls the base-class version to do additional work. Failure to use the __**super** keyword followed by the binary resolution operator (: :) when referencing the base class's method causes infinite recursion, because using the name of the method would cause the derived-class method to call itself.*

CircleTest4 (Fig. 6.23) performs identical manipulations on class **Circle4** (Fig. 6.21–Fig. 6.22) as did classes **CircleTest** (Fig. 6.9) and **CircleTest3** (Fig. 6.18). Note that the outputs of all three modules are identical. Therefore, although each "circle" class appears to behave identically, class **Circle4** is the most properly engineered. Using inheritance, we have efficiently and effectively constructed a well-engineered class.

6.5 Example: Three-Level Inheritance Hierarchy

Let us consider a more substantial inheritance example involving a three-level point-circle-cylinder hierarchy. In Section 6.4, we developed classes **Point3** (Fig. 6.19–Fig. 6.20) and **Circle4** (Fig. 6.21–Fig. 6.22). Now, we present an example in which we derive class **Cylinder** from class **Circle4**.

The first class that we use in our example is class **Point3** (Fig. 6.19–Fig. 6.20). We declared **Point3**'s instance variables as **private**. Class **Point3** also contains properties **X** and **Y** for accessing **x** and **y**, and method **ToString** (which **Point3** overrides from class **Object**) for obtaining a string representation of the *x-y* coordinate pair.

We also created class **Circle4** (Fig. 6.21–Fig. 6.22), which inherits from class **Point3**. Class **Circle4** inherits the **Point3** functionality, in addition to providing property **Radius**, which ensures that the **radius** data member cannot hold a negative value, and methods **Diameter**, **Circumference**, **Area** and **ToString**. Recall that method **Area** was declared **virtual** (line 29 of Fig. 6.21). Derived classes of class **Circle4** (such as class **Cylinder**, which we introduce momentarily) can override this method and provide specific implementations. A circle has an area that is calculated by the formula, πr^2, in which *r* represents the circle's radius. However, a cylinder has a surface area that is calculated by the formula, $(2\pi r^2) + (2\pi rh)$, in which *r* represents the cylinder's radius and *h* represents the cylinder's height. Therefore, class **Cylinder** must override method **Area** to include this calculation.

Figure 6.24–Fig. 6.25 presents class **Cylinder**, which inherits from class **Circle4** (line 9 of Fig. 6.24). Class **Cylinder**'s **public** services include the inherited **Circle4** functions **Diameter**, **Circumference**, **Area** and **ToString**; the inherited **Circle4** property **Radius**; the indirectly inherited **Point3** properties **X** and **Y**; the **Cylinder** constructor, property **Height** and method **Volume**. Method **Area** (lines 20–23 of Fig. 6.25) overrides method **Area** of class **Circle4**. Method **ToString** (lines 32–36) overrides method **ToString** of class **Circle4** to obtain a string representation for the cylinder. Class **Cylinder** also includes method **Volume** (lines 26–29) to calculate the cylinder's volume.

```
1   // Fig. 6.24: Cylinder.h
2   // Cylinder class that inherits from class Circle4.
3
4   #pragma once
5
6   #include "Circle4.h"
7
8   // Cylinder class definition inherits from Circle4
9   public __gc class Cylinder : public Circle4
10  {
11  public:
12     Cylinder();                                // default constructor
13     Cylinder( int, int, double, double );   // constructor
14
15     // property Height
16     __property double get_Height()
17     {
18        return height;
19     }
20
21     __property void set_Height( double value )
22     {
23        if ( value >= 0 )        // validate height
24           height = value;
25     }
26
27     // override Circle4 method Area to calculate Cylinder Area
28     double Area();                   // calculate area
29     double Volume();                 // calculate volume
30     String *ToString();              // convert Cylinder to string
31
32  private:
33     double height;
34  }; // end class Cylinder
```

Fig. 6.24 Cylinder class inherits from **Circle4** and overrides method **Area**.

```
1   // Fig. 6.25: Cylinder.cpp
2   // Method definitions for class Cylinder.
3
4   #include "Cylinder.h"
5
6   // default constructor
7   Cylinder::Cylinder()
8   {
9      // implicit call to Circle4 constructor occurs here
10  }
11
12  // constructor
13  Cylinder::Cylinder( int xValue, int yValue, double radiusValue,
14     double heightValue ) : Circle4( xValue, yValue, radiusValue )
15  {
```

Fig. 6.25 Cylinder class method definitions. (Part 1 of 2.)

```
16         height = heightValue;
17    }
18
19    // override Circle4 method Area to calculate Cylinder Area
20    double Cylinder::Area()
21    {
22         return 2 * __super::Area() + __super::Circumference() * Height;
23    }
24
25    // calculate volume
26    double Cylinder::Volume()
27    {
28         return __super::Area() * Height;
29    }
30
31    // convert Cylinder to string
32    String *Cylinder::ToString()
33    {
34         return String::Concat( __super::ToString(),
35             S"; Height = ", Height.ToString() );
36    }
```

Fig. 6.25   Cylinder class method definitions. (Part 2 of 2.)

CylinderTest (Fig. 6.26) tests class **Cylinder** class. Line 11 instantiates an object of class **Cylinder**. Lines 14–18 use properties **X**, **Y**, **Radius** and **Height** to obtain information about the **Cylinder** object, because **CylinderTest** cannot reference the **private** data of class **Cylinder** directly. Lines 21–24 use properties **X**, **Y**, **Radius** and **Height** to reset the **Cylinder**'s *x-y* coordinates (we assume the cylinder's *x-y* coordinates specify its position on the *x-y* plane), radius and height. Class **Cylinder** can use class **Point3**'s **X** and **Y** properties, because class **Cylinder** inherits them indirectly from class **Point3**—class **Cylinder** inherits properties **X** and **Y** directly from class **Circle4**, which inherited them directly from class **Point3**. Line 28 invokes method **ToString** implicitly to obtain the string representation of the **Cylinder** object. Lines 32–37 invoke methods **Diameter** and **Circumference** of the **Cylinder** object—because class **Cylinder** inherits these methods from class **Circle4** and does not override them, these functions, exactly as listed in **Circle4**, are invoked. Lines 40–45 invoke functions **Area** and **Volume**.

```
1    // Fig. 6.26: CylinderTest.cpp
2    // Tests class Cylinder.
3
4    #include "Cylinder.h"
5
6    // main entry point for application
7    int __stdcall WinMain()
8    {
9
```

Fig. 6.26   CylinderTest demonstrates **Cylinder** functionality. (Part 1 of 2.)

```
10     // instantiate object of class Cylinder
11     Cylinder *cylinder = new Cylinder( 12, 23, 2.5, 5.7 );
12
13     // properties get initial x-y coordinates, radius and height
14     String *output = String::Concat( S"X coordinate is ",
15        cylinder->X.ToString(), S"\nY coordinate is ",
16        cylinder->Y.ToString(), S"\nRadius is ",
17        cylinder->Radius.ToString(), S"\nHeight is ",
18        cylinder->Height.ToString() );
19
20     // properties set new x-y coordinate, radius and height
21     cylinder->X = 2;
22     cylinder->Y = 2;
23     cylinder->Radius = 4.25;
24     cylinder->Height = 10;
25
26     // get new x-y coordinate and radius
27     output = String::Concat( output, S"\n\nThe new location, ",
28        S"radius and height of cylinder are\n", cylinder,
29        S"\n\n" );
30
31     // display diameter
32     output = String::Concat( output, S"Diameter is ",
33        cylinder->Diameter().ToString( S"F" ), S"\n" );
34
35     // display circumference
36     output = String::Concat( output, S"Circumference is ",
37        cylinder->Circumference().ToString( S"F" ), S"\n" );
38
39     // display area
40     output = String::Concat ( output, S"Area is ",
41        cylinder->Area().ToString( S"F" ), S"\n" );
42
43     // display volume
44     output = String::Concat( output, S"Volume is ",
45        cylinder->Volume().ToString( S"F" ) );
46
47     MessageBox::Show( output, S"Demonstrating Class Cylinder" );
48
49     return 0;
50  } // end function WinMain
```

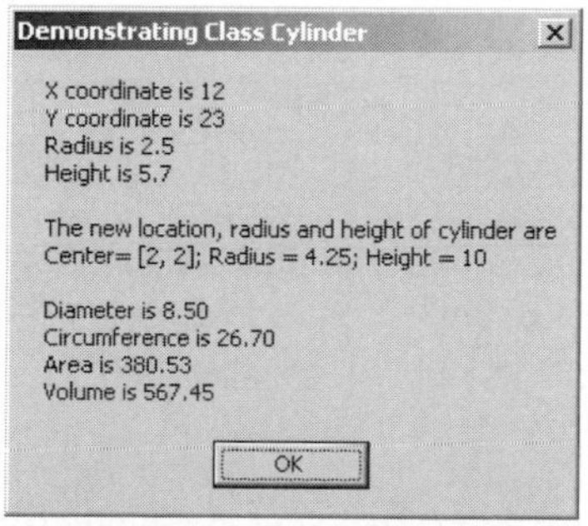

Fig. 6.26 **CylinderTest** demonstrates **Cylinder** functionality. (Part 2 of 2.)

Using the point-circle-cylinder example, we have shown the use and benefits of inheritance. We were able to develop classes **Circle4** and **Cylinder** using inheritance much faster than if we had developed these classes "from scratch." Inheritance avoids duplicating code and the associated code-maintenance problems.

6.6 Constructors and Destructors in Derived Classes

As we explained in the previous section, instantiating a derived-class object begins a chain of constructor calls in which the derived-class constructor, before performing its own tasks, invokes the base-class constructor either explicitly or implicitly. Similarly, if the base-class was derived from another class, the base-class constructor must invoke the constructor of the next class up in the hierarchy, and so on. The last constructor called in the chain is class **Object**'s constructor whose body actually finishes executing first—the original derived class's body finishes executing last. Each base-class constructor initializes the base-class instance variables that the derived-class object inherits. For example, consider the **Point3/Circle4** hierarchy. When a program creates a **Circle4** object, one of the **Circle4** constructors is called. That constructor calls class **Point3**'s constructor, which in turn calls class **Object**'s constructor. When class **Object**'s constructor completes execution, it returns control to class **Point3**'s constructor, which initializes the *x-y* coordinates of **Circle4**. When class **Point3**'s constructor completes execution, it returns control to class **Circle4**'s constructor, which initializes the **Circle4**'s radius.

Software Engineering Observation 6.12

When a program creates a derived-class object, the derived-class constructor immediately calls the base-class constructor, the base-class constructor's body executes, then the derived-class constructor's body executes.

When the garbage collector removes a derived-class object from memory, the garbage collector calls that object's destructor. This begins a chain of destructor calls in which the derived-class destructor and the destructors of the direct and indirect base classes execute in the reverse order of the order in which the constructors executed. Executing the destructors should free all the resources the object acquired before the garbage collector reclaims the memory for that object. When the garbage collector calls a derived-class object's destructor, the destructor performs its task, then invokes the destructor of the base class. This process repeats until class **Object**'s destructor is called.

MC++ actually implements destructors using class **Object**'s *Finalize* method (one of the eight methods that every __gc class inherits). When compiling a class definition that contains a destructor, the compiler translates a destructor definition into a **Finalize** method that performs the destructor's tasks, then invokes the base-class **Finalize** method as the last statement in the derived-class **Finalize** method. As mentioned in Chapter 5, Object-Based Programming, we cannot determine exactly when the destructor call will occur, because we cannot determine exactly when garbage collection occurs. However, by defining a destructor, we can specify code to execute before the garbage collector removes an object from memory.

Our next example revisits the point-circle hierarchy by defining class **Point4** (Fig. 6.27–Fig. 6.28) and class **Circle5** (Fig. 6.29–Fig. 6.30) that contain constructors and destructors, each of which prints a message when it runs.

```
1   // Fig. 6.27: Point4.h
2   // Point4 class represents an x-y coordinate pair.
3
4   #pragma once
5
6   #using <mscorlib.dll>
7   #using <system.windows.forms.dll>
8
9   using namespace System;
10  using namespace System::Windows::Forms;
11
12  // Point4 class definition
13  public __gc class Point4
14  {
15  public:
16     Point4();                  // default constructor
17     Point4( int, int );        // constructor
18     ~Point4();                 // destructor
19
20     // property X
21     __property int get_X()
22     {
23        return x;
24     }
25
26     __property void set_X( int value )
27     {
28        x = value;
29     }
30
31     // property Y
32     __property int get_Y()
33     {
34        return y;
35     }
36
37     __property void set_Y( int value )
38     {
39        y = value;
40     }
41
42     // return string representation of Point4
43     String *ToString();
44
45  private:
46     int x, y;                  // point coordinate
47  }; // end class Point4
```

Fig. 6.27 `Point4` base class contains constructors and finalizer.

```
1   // Fig. 6.28: Point4.cpp
2   // Method definitions for class Point4.
```

Fig. 6.28 `Point4` class method definitions. (Part 1 of 2.)

```
3
4   #include "Point4.h"
5
6   // default constructor
7   Point4::Point4()
8   {
9      // implicit call to Object constructor occurs here
10      Console::WriteLine( S"Point4 constructor: {0}", this );
11   }
12
13   // constructor
14   Point4::Point4( int xValue, int yValue )
15   {
16
17      // implicit call to Object constructor occurs here
18      x = xValue;
19      y = yValue;
20      Console::WriteLine( S"Point4 constructor: {0}", this );
21   }
22
23   // destructor
24   Point4::~Point4()
25   {
26      Console::WriteLine( S"Point4 destructor: {0}", this );
27   }
28
29   // return string representation of Point4
30   String *Point4::ToString()
31   {
32      return String::Concat( S"[", x.ToString(), S", ",
33         y.ToString(), S"]" );
34   }
```

Fig. 6.28   Point4 class method definitions. (Part 2 of 2.)

```
1   // Fig. 6.29: Circle5.h
2   // Circle5 class that inherits from class Point4.
3
4   #pragma once
5
6   #include "Point4.h"
7
8   // Circle5 class definition inherits from Point4
9   public __gc class Circle5 : public Point4
10   {
11   public:
12      Circle5();                          // default constructor
13      Circle5( int, int, double );   // constructor
14      ~Circle5();   // destructor overrides version in class Point4
15
```

Fig. 6.29   Circle5 class inherits from Point4 and overrides a finalizer method.
           (Part 1 of 2.)

```
16      // property Radius
17      __property double get_Radius()
18      {
19         return radius;
20      }
21
22      __property void set_Radius( double value )
23      {
24         if ( value >= 0 )
25            radius = value;
26      }
27
28      double Diameter();              // calculate diameter
29      double Circumference();         // calculate circumference
30      virtual double Area();          // calculate area
31
32      // return string representation of Circle5
33      String *ToString();
34
35   private:
36      double radius;
37   }; // end class Circle5
```

Fig. 6.29   Circle5 class inherits from **Point4** and overrides a finalizer method. (Part 2 of 2.)

```
1    // Fig. 6.30: Circle5.cpp
2    // Method definitions for class Circle5.
3
4    #include "Circle5.h"
5
6    // default constructor
7    Circle5::Circle5()
8    {
9
10      // implicit call to Point4 constructor occurs here
11      Console::WriteLine( S"Circle5 constructor: {0}", this );
12   }
13
14   // constructor
15   Circle5::Circle5( int xValue, int yValue, double radiusValue )
16      : Point4( xValue, yValue )
17   {
18      Radius = radiusValue;
19      Console::WriteLine( S"Circle5 constructor: {0}", this );
20   }
21
22   // destructor overrides version in class Point4
23   Circle5::~Circle5()
24   {
25      Console::WriteLine( S"Circle5 destructor: {0}", this );
26   }
27
```

Fig. 6.30   Circle5 class method definitions. (Part 1 of 2.)

```
28   // calculate diameter
29   double Circle5::Diameter()
30   {
31      return Radius * 2;
32   }
33
34   // calculate circumference
35   double Circle5::Circumference()
36   {
37      return Math::PI * Diameter();
38   }
39
40   // calculate area
41   double Circle5::Area()
42   {
43      return Math::PI * Math::Pow( Radius, 2 );
44   }
45
46   // return string representation of Circle5
47   String *Circle5::ToString()
48   {
49
50      // return Point4 string
51      return String::Concat( S"Center = ", __super::ToString(),
52         S"; Radius = ", Radius.ToString() );
53   }
```

Fig. 6.30 `Circle5` class method definitions. (Part 2 of 2.)

Class **Point4** (Fig. 6.27–Fig. 6.28) contains the features shown in Fig. 6.4. We modified the constructors (lines 7–21 of Fig. 6.28) to output a line of text when they are called and added a destructor (lines 24–27) that also outputs a line of text when it is called. Each output statement (lines 10, 20 and 26) adds pointer **this** to the output string. This implicitly invokes the class's **ToString** method to obtain the string representation of **Point4**'s coordinates. The driver (Fig. 6.31) executes that application.

```
1    // Fig. 6.31: ConstructorAndDestructor.cpp
2    // Display order in which base-class and derived-class
3    // constructors and destructors are called.
4
5    #include "Circle5.h"
6
7    // main entry point for application
8    int main()
9    {
10      Circle5 *circle1, *circle2;
11
12      // instantiate Circle5 objects
13      circle1 = new Circle5( 72, 29, 4.5 );
14      circle2 = new Circle5( 5, 5, 10 );
15
```

Fig. 6.31 Order in which constructors and destructors are called. (Part 1 of 2.)

```
16        Console::WriteLine();
17
18        // mark objects for garbage collection
19        circle1 = 0;
20        circle2 = 0;
21
22        // inform garbage collector to execute
23        GC::Collect();
24
25        return 0;
26   } // end function main
```

```
Point4 constructor: Center = [72, 29]; Radius = 0
Circle5 constructor: Center = [72, 29]; Radius = 4.5
Point4 constructor: Center = [5, 5]; Radius = 0
Circle5 constructor: Center = [5, 5]; Radius = 10

Circle5 destructor: Center = [5, 5]; Radius = 10
Point4 destructor: Center = [5, 5]; Radius = 10
Circle5 destructor: Center = [72, 29]; Radius = 4.5
Point4 destructor: Center = [72, 29]; Radius = 4.5
```

Fig. 6.31   Order in which constructors and destructors are called. (Part 2 of 2.)

Class **Circle5** (Fig. 6.29–Fig. 6.30) contains the features of **Circle4** (Fig. 6.21–Fig. 6.22), and we modified the two constructors (lines 7–20 of Fig. 6.30) to output a line of text when they are called. We also added a destructor (lines 23–26) that outputs a line of text when it is called. Each output statement (lines 11, 19 and 25) adds pointer **this** to the output string. This implicitly invokes the **Circle5**'s **ToString** method to obtain the string representation of **Circle5**'s coordinates and radius.

Figure 6.31 demonstrates the order in which constructors and destructors are called for objects of classes that are part of an inheritance class hierarchy. Function **main** (lines 8–26) begins by instantiating an object of class **Circle5**, then assigns it to pointer **circle1** (line 13). This invokes the **Circle5** constructor, which invokes the **Point4** constructor immediately. Then, the **Point4** constructor invokes the **Object** constructor. When the **Object** constructor (which does not print anything) returns control to the **Point4** constructor, the **Point4** constructor initializes the *x-y* coordinates, then outputs a string indicating that the **Point4** constructor was called. The output statement also calls method **ToString** implicitly (using pointer **this**) to obtain the string representation of the object being constructed. Then, control returns to the **Circle5** constructor, which initializes the radius and outputs the **Circle5**'s *x-y* coordinates and radius by calling method **ToString**.

Notice that the first two lines of the output from this program contain values for the *x-y* coordinates and the radius of **Circle5** object **circle1**. When constructing a **Circle5** object, the **this** pointer used in the body of both the **Circle5** and **Point4** constructors points to the **Circle5** object being constructed. When a program invokes method **ToString** on an object, the version of **ToString** that executes is always the version defined in that object's class. Because pointer **this** points to the current **Circle5** object being constructed, **Circle5**'s **ToString** method executes even when

ToString is invoked from the body of class **Point4**'s constructor. [*Note*: This would not be the case if the **Point4** constructor were called to initialize an object that was actually a new **Point4** object.] When the **Point4** constructor invokes method **ToString** for the **Circle5** being constructed, the program displays **0** for the **radius** value, because the **Circle5** constructor's body has not yet initialized the **radius**. Remember that **0.0** (displayed as **0**) is the default value of a **double** variable. The second line of the output shows the proper **radius** value (**4.5**), because that line is output after the **radius** is initialized.

Line 14 instantiates another object of class **Circle5**, then assigns it to pointer **circle2**. Again, this begins the chain of constructor calls in which the **Circle5** constructor, the **Point4** constructor and the **Object** constructor are called. In the output, notice that the body of the **Point4** constructor executes before the body of the **Circle5** constructor. This demonstrates that objects are constructed "inside out" (i.e., the base-class constructor is called first).

Lines 19–20 set pointers **circle1** and **circle2** to **0**. This removes the only pointers to these **Circle5** objects in the program. Thus, the garbage collector can release the memory that these objects occupy. Remember that we cannot guarantee when the garbage collector will execute, nor can we guarantee that it will collect all available objects when it does execute. To demonstrate the destructor invocations for the two **Circle5** objects, line 23 invokes class **GC**'s method **Collect** to request the garbage collector to run. Notice that each **Circle5** object's destructor outputs information before calling class **Point4**'s destructor. Objects are destroyed "outside in" (i.e., the derived-class destructor completes its tasks before invoking the base-class destructor).

6.7 Software Engineering with Inheritance

In this section, we discuss the use of inheritance to customize existing software. When we use inheritance to create a new class from an existing one, the new class inherits the data members, properties and functions of the existing class. We can customize the new class to meet our needs by including additional data members, properties and functions, and by overriding base-class members.

Sometimes, it is difficult for readers to appreciate the scope of problems faced by designers who work on large-scale software projects in industry. People experienced with such projects say that effective software reuse improves the software-development process. Object-oriented programming facilitates software reuse, thus shortening development times.

Visual C++ .NET encourages software reuse by providing the .NET Framework Class Library (FCL), which delivers the maximum benefits of software reuse through inheritance. As interest in .NET grows, interest in the FCL class libraries also increases. There is a worldwide commitment to the continued evolution of the FCL class libraries for a wide variety of applications. The FCL will grow as .NET matures.

Software Engineering Observation 6.13

At the design stage in an object-oriented system, the designer often determines that certain classes are closely related. The designer should "factor out" common attributes and behaviors and place these in a base class. Then use inheritance to form derived classes, endowing them with capabilities beyond those inherited from the base class.

Software Engineering Observation 6.14

The creation of a derived class does not affect its base class's source code. Inheritance preserves the integrity of a base class.

Software Engineering Observation 6.15

Just as designers of non-object-oriented systems should avoid proliferation of methods, designers of object-oriented systems should avoid proliferation of classes. Proliferation of classes creates management problems and can hinder software reusability, because it becomes difficult for a client to locate the most appropriate class of a huge class library. The alternative is to create fewer classes, in which each provides more substantial functionality, but such classes might provide too much functionality.

Performance Tip 6.2

If classes produced through inheritance are larger than they need to be (i.e., contain too much functionality), memory and processing resources might be wasted. Inherit from the class whose functionality is "closest" to what is needed.

Reading derived-class definitions can be confusing, because inherited members are not shown physically in the derived class, but nevertheless are present in the derived classes. A similar problem exists when documenting derived-class members.

In this chapter, we introduced inheritance—the ability to create classes by absorbing an existing class's data members and behaviors and embellishing these with new capabilities. In Chapter 7, we build upon our discussion of inheritance by introducing *polymorphism*—an object-oriented technique that enables us to write programs that handle, in a more general manner, a wide variety of classes related by inheritance. After studying Chapter 7, you will be familiar with encapsulation, inheritance and polymorphism—the most crucial aspects of object-oriented programming.

6.8 Summary

An "is-a" relationship represents inheritance. In an "is-a" relationship, an object of a derived class also can be treated as an object of its base class. A "has-a" relationship represents composition. In a "has-a" relationship, a class object contains one or more objects of other classes as members.

Inheritance relationships form tree-like hierarchical structures. A class exists in a hierarchical relationship with its derived classes. The direct base class of a derived class is the base class from which the derived class inherits [via the colon (**:**) symbol]. An indirect base class of a derived class is two or more levels up the class hierarchy from that derived class. With single inheritance, a class is derived from one base class. MC++ does not support multiple inheritance (i.e., deriving a class from more than one direct base class) of classes.

Because a derived class can include its own instance variables, properties and methods, a derived class is often larger than its base class. A derived class is more specific than its base class and represents a smaller group of objects. Every object of a derived class is also an object of that class's base class. However, base-class objects are not objects of that class's derived classes. It is possible to treat base-class objects and derived-class objects similarly; the commonality shared between the object types is expressed in the data members, properties and methods of the base class.

Derived-class methods and properties can access **protected** base-class members directly. A derived class cannot access **private** members of its base class directly. A derived class can access the **public** and **protected** members of its base class if the derived class is in the same assembly as the base class.

A base class's **public** members are accessible anywhere that the program has a pointer to an object of that base class or to an object of one of that base class's derived classes. A base class's **private** members are accessible only within the definition of that base class. A base class's **protected** members have an intermediate level of protection between **public** and **private** access. A base class's **protected** members can be accessed only in that base class or in any classes derived from that base class.

Unfortunately, the inclusion of **protected** instance variables often yields two major problems. First, the derived-class object does not have to use a property to set the value of the base-class's **protected** data. Second, derived-class methods are more likely to be written to depend on base-class implementation. MC++ rigidly enforces restriction on accessing **private** data members, so that even derived classes (i.e,. which are closely related to their base class) cannot access base-class **private** data. Declaring instance variables **private**, while providing non-**private** properties to manipulate and perform validation checking on this data, enforces good software engineering.

When a base-class member is inappropriate for a derived class, that member can be overridden (redefined) in the derived class with an appropriate implementation. A derived class also can redefine (override) a base-class method using the same signature. A base-class method is declared **virtual** if that method is to be overridden in a derived class and the programmer would like the compiler to determine the appropriate version to invoke based on the calling object's type. When a method is overridden in a derived class and that method is called on a derived-class object, the derived-class version (not the base-class version) is called.

When an object of a derived class is instantiated, the base class's constructor is called immediately (either explicitly or implicitly) to do any necessary initialization of the base-class instance variables in the derived-class object (before the derived class's instance variable are initialized). Base-class constructors and destructors are not inherited by derived classes.

Software reusability reduces program-development time. If an object's method/property performs the actions needed by another object, call that method/property rather than duplicating its code body. Duplicated code creates code-maintenance problems.

7

Object-Oriented Programming: Polymorphism

Objectives

- To understand the concept of polymorphism.
- To understand how polymorphism makes systems extensible and maintainable.
- To understand the distinction between abstract classes and concrete classes.
- To learn how to create __sealed classes, interfaces and delegates.

One Ring to rule them all, One Ring to find them,
One Ring to bring them all and in the darkness bind them.
John Ronald Reuel Tolkien,

General propositions do not decide concrete cases.
Oliver Wendell Holmes

A philosopher of imposing stature doesn't think in a vacuum.
Even his most abstract ideas are, to some extent, conditioned
by what is or is not known in the time when he lives.
Alfred North Whitehead

7.1 Introduction

The previous chapter's object-oriented programming (OOP) discussion focused on one of OOP's key component technologies, inheritance. In this chapter, we continue our study of OOP *polymorphism*. Both inheritance and polymorphism are crucial technologies in the development of complex software. Polymorphism enables us to write programs that handle a wide variety of related classes in a generic manner and facilitates adding new classes and capabilities to a system.

With polymorphism, it is possible to design and implement systems that are easily extensible. Programs can process objects of all classes in a class hierarchy generically as objects of a common base class. Furthermore, new classes can be added with little or no modification to the generic portions of the program, as long as those classes are part of the inheritance hierarchy that the program processes generically. The only parts of a program that must be altered to accommodate new classes are those program components that require direct knowledge of the new classes that the programmer adds to the hierarchy. In this chapter, we demonstrate two substantial class hierarchies and manipulate objects from those hierarchies polymorphically.

7.2 Derived-Class-Object to Base-Class-Object Conversion

In Chapter 6, we created a point-circle class hierarchy, in which class **Circle** inherited from class **Point**. The programs that manipulated objects of these classes always used **Point** pointers to refer to **Point** objects and **Circle** pointers to refer to **Circle** objects. In this section, we discuss the relationships between classes in a hierarchy that enable programs to assign derived-class objects to base-class pointers—a fundamental part of programs that process objects polymorphically. This section also discusses explicit casting between types in a class hierarchy.

An object of a derived class can be treated as an object of its base class. This enables various interesting manipulations. For example, a program can create an array of base-class pointers that refer to objects of many derived-class types. This is allowed despite the fact that the derived-class objects are of different data types. However, the reverse is not true—

a base-class object is not an object of any of its derived classes. For example, a **Point** is not a **Circle** in the hierarchy defined in Chapter 6, Object-Oriented Programming: Inheritance. If a base-class pointer refers to a derived-class object, it is possible to convert the base-class pointer to the object's actual data type and manipulate the object as that type.

The example in Fig. 7.1–Fig. 7.5 demonstrates assigning derived-class objects to base-class pointers and casting base-class pointers to derived-class pointers. Class **Point** (Fig. 7.1–Fig. 7.2), which we discussed in Chapter 6, represents an *x-y* coordinate pair. Class **Circle** (Fig. 7.3–Fig. 7.4), which we also discussed in Chapter 6, represents a circle and inherits from class **Point**. Each **Circle** object "is a" **Point** and also has a radius (represented via property **Radius**). **PointCircleTest.cpp** (Fig. 7.5) demonstrates the assignment and cast operations.

```
1    // Fig. 7.1: Point.h
2    // Point class represents an x-y coordinate pair.
3
4    #pragma once
5
6    #using <mscorlib.dll>
7    #using <system.dll>
8
9    using namespace System;
10
11   // Point class definition implicitly inherits from Object
12   public __gc class Point
13   {
14   public:
15      Point();              // default constructor
16      Point( int, int );    // constructor
17
18      // property X
19      __property int get_X()
20      {
21         return x;
22      }
23
24      __property void set_X( int value )
25      {
26         x = value;
27      }
28
29      // property Y
30      __property int get_Y()
31      {
32         return y;
33      }
34
35      __property void set_Y( int value )
36      {
37         y = value;
38      }
39
```

Fig. 7.1   **Point** class represents an *x-y* coordinate pair. (Part 1 of 2.)

```
40        // return string representation of Point
41        String *ToString();
42
43   private:
44        int x, y;                  // point coordinate
45   }; // end class Point
```

Fig. 7.1   **Point** class represents an *x-y* coordinate pair. (Part 2 of 2.)

```
1    // Fig. 7.2: Point.cpp
2    // Method definitions for class Point.
3
4    #include "Point.h"
5
6    // default constructor
7    Point::Point()
8    {
9        // implicit call to Object constructor occurs here
10   }
11
12   // constructor
13   Point::Point( int xValue, int yValue )
14   {
15
16        // implicit call to Object constructor occurs here
17        X = xValue;
18        Y = yValue;
19   }
20
21   // return string representation of Point
22   String *Point::ToString()
23   {
24        return String::Concat( S"[", X.ToString(), S", ",
25            Y.ToString(), S"]" );
26   }
```

Fig. 7.2   **Point** class method definitions.

```
1    // Fig. 7.3: Circle.h
2    // Circle class that inherits form class Point.
3
4    #pragma once
5
6    #using <mscorlib.dll>
7    #using <system.dll>
8
9    using namespace System;
10
11   #include "Point.h"
12
```

Fig. 7.3   **Circle** class that inherits from class **Point**. (Part 1 of 2.)

```
13   // Circle class definition inherits from Point
14   public __gc class Circle : public Point
15   {
16   public:
17      Circle();                          // default constructor
18      Circle( int, int, double );    // constructor
19
20      // property Radius
21      __property double get_Radius()
22      {
23         return radius;
24      }
25
26      __property void set_Radius( double value )
27      {
28         if ( value >= 0 )               // validate radius
29            radius = value;
30      }
31
32      double Diameter();
33      double Circumference();
34      virtual double Area();
35
36      // return string representation of Circle
37      String *ToString();
38
39   private:
40      double radius;                 // Circle's radius
41   }; // end class Circle
```

Fig. 7.3   `Circle` class that inherits from class **Point**. (Part 2 of 2.)

```
1    // Fig. 7.4: Circle.cpp
2    // Method definitions for class Circle.
3
4    #include "Circle.h"
5
6    // default constructor
7    Circle::Circle()
8    {
9       // implicit call to Point constructor occurs here
10   }
11
12   // constructor
13   Circle::Circle( int xValue, int yValue, double radiusValue )
14      : Point( xValue, yValue )
15   {
16      Radius = radiusValue;
17   }
18
```

Fig. 7.4   `Circle` class method definitions. (Part 1 of 2.)

```
19   // calculate diameter
20   double Circle::Diameter()
21   {
22      return Radius * 2;
23   }
24
25   // calculate circumference
26   double Circle::Circumference()
27   {
28      return Math::PI * Diameter();
29   }
30
31   // calculate area
32   double Circle::Area()
33   {
34      return Math::PI * Math::Pow( Radius, 2 );
35   }
36
37   // return string representation of Circle
38   String *Circle::ToString()
39   {
40      return String::Concat( S"Center = ", __super::ToString(),
41         S"; Radius = ", Radius.ToString() );
42   }
```

Fig. 7.4   `Circle` class method definitions. (Part 2 of 2.)

```
1    // Fig. 7.5: PointCircleTest.cpp
2    // Demonstrating inheritance and polymorphism.
3
4    #using <system.windows.forms.dll>
5
6    using namespace System::Windows::Forms;
7
8    #include "Circle.h"
9
10   // main entry point for application
11   int __stdcall WinMain()
12   {
13      Point *point1 = new Point( 30, 50 );
14      Circle *circle1 = new Circle( 120, 89, 2.7 );
15
16      String *output = String::Concat( S"Point point1: ",
17         point1->ToString(), S"\nCircle circle1: ",
18         circle1->ToString() );
19
20      // use 'is a' relationship to assign
21      // Circle *circle1 to Point pointer
22      Point *point2 = circle1;
23
```

Fig. 7.5   Derived-class pointers assigned to base-class pointers. (Part 1 of 2.)

```
24      output = String::Concat( output, S"\n\n",
25         S"Circle circle1 (via point2): ", point2->ToString() );
26
27      // downcast point2 to Circle *circle2
28      Circle *circle2 = __try_cast< Circle * >( point2 );
29
30      output = String::Concat( output, S"\n\n",
31         S"Circle circle1 (via circle2): ", circle2->ToString() );
32
33      output = String::Concat( output,
34         S"\nArea of circle1 (via circle2): ",
35         circle2->Area().ToString( "F" ) );
36
37      // attempt to assign point1 object to Circle pointer
38      if ( point1->GetType() == __typeof( Circle ) ) {
39         circle2 = __try_cast< Circle * >( point1 );
40         output = String::Concat( output, S"\n\ncast successful" );
41      }
42      else {
43         output = String::Concat( output,
44            S"\n\npoint1 does not refer to a Circle" );
45      }
46
47      MessageBox::Show( output,
48         S"Demonstrating the 'is a' relationship" );
49
50      return 0;
51   } // end function WinMain
```

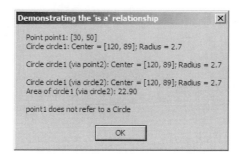

Fig. 7.5   Derived-class pointers assigned to base-class pointers. (Part 2 of 2.)

Figure 7.5 demonstrates assigning derived-class pointers to base-class pointers and casting base-class pointers to derived-class pointers. Lines 13–14 declare a **Point** pointer (**point1**) and a **Circle** pointer (**circle1**). Lines 16–18 append string representations of each object to **output** to show the values used to initialize these objects. Because **point1** is a pointer to a **Point** object, method **ToString** of **point1** prints the object as a **Point**. Similarly, because **circle1** is pointer to a **Circle** object, method **ToString** of **circle1** prints the object as a **Circle**.

Line 22 (Fig. 7.5) assigns **circle1** (a pointer to a derived-class object) to **point2** (a base-class pointer). It is acceptable to assign a derived-class object to a base-class pointer, because of the inheritance "is a" relationship. Class **Circle** inherits from class **Point**, because a **Circle** *is a* **Point** (in a structural sense, at least). However, assigning a base-class pointer to a derived-class pointer is potentially dangerous, as we will discuss.

Lines 24–25 invoke **point2->ToString** and append the result to **output**. When a **virtual** method invocation (such as method **ToString**) in encountered, the compiler determines which version of the method to call from the type of the object on which the method is called, not the type of the pointer that refers to the object. In this case, **point2** points to a **Circle** object, so **Circle** method **ToString** is called, rather than **Point** method **ToString** (as one might expect from the **point2** pointer, which was declared as type **Point ***). The decision about which method to call is an example of *polymorphism*, a concept that we discuss in detail throughout this chapter. Note that if **point2** pointed to a **Point** object rather than a **Circle** object, **Point**'s **ToString** method would be invoked instead.

Previous chapters used methods such as **Int32::Parse** and **Double::Parse** to convert between various built-in types. Now, we convert between object pointers of programmer-defined types. We use explicit casts to perform these conversions. Managed C++ supports five cast operators—**static_cast**, **dynamic_cast**, **reinterpret_cast**, **const_cast** and **__try_cast**. Operator **static_cast** performs a conversion between most fundamental data types during compile time. Operator **dynamic_cast** performs conversions of base-class objects to derived-class objects at runtime. If the cast is valid, the **dynamic_cast** operator returns a pointer to the derived-class object. However, if the cast is invalid, the operator returns **0** to indicate that a base-class object cannot be converted to the specified derived-class object. The *reinterpret_cast* operator performs *nonstandard casts* (e.g., casting from one pointer type to a different, unrelated pointer type). The **reinterpret_cast** operator can convert between pointer types not related by a hierarchy. Operator **reinterpret_cast** cannot be used to perform standard casts (i.e., **double** to **int**, etc.). The **const_cast** operator can be used to cast away (i.e., remove) a **const** or **volatile**[1] attribute of an object or pointer. Operator *__try_cast*, a new feature of MC++, is similar to **dynamic_cast** except that if the cast is invalid, the operator throws an *InvalidCastException*, which indicates that the cast operation is not allowed. Because of this inherent feature, we generally use operator **__try_cast** in our examples. Exceptions are discussed in detail in Chapter 8, Exception Handling.

Common Programming Error 7.1

Assigning a base-class object (or a base-class pointer) to a derived-class pointer (without an explicit cast) is a compilation error.

Software Engineering Observation 7.1

If a derived-class object has been assigned to a pointer of one of its direct or indirect base classes, it is acceptable to cast that base-class pointer back to a pointer of the derived-class type. In fact, this must be done to send that object messages that do not appear in the base class. [Note: We sometimes use the term "messages" to represent the invocation of methods and the use of object properties.]

---

1. The *volatile* type qualifier is applied to a definition of a variable that may be altered from outside the program (i.e., the variable is not completely under the control of the program and may be altered by the operating system, hardware, etc.).

Line 28 casts **point2**, which currently points to a **Circle** object (**circle1**), to a **Circle** and assigns the result to **circle2**. As we discuss momentarily, this cast would be dangerous if **point2** pointed to a **Point** object. Lines 30–31 invoke method **ToString** of the **Circle** object to which **circle2** now points (note that the fourth line of the output demonstrates that **Circle**'s **ToString** method is called). Lines 33–35 calculate and output **circle2**'s **Area**.

Line 39 explicitly casts pointer **point1** to a **Circle**. This is a dangerous operation, because **point** points to a **Point** object, and a **Point** is not a **Circle**. Objects can be cast only to their own type or to their base-class types. If this statement were to execute, the CLR would determine that **point1** points to a **Point** object, recognize the cast to **Circle** as dangerous and indicate an improper cast with an **InvalidCastException** message. However, we prevent this statement from executing by including an **if/else** structure (lines 38–45). The condition (line 38) uses the **GetType** method and **__typeof** keyword to determine whether the object to which **point1** points "is a" **Circle**. Method *GetType*, one of the eight methods defined in **System::Object**, returns the data type of an object. Similarly, the **__typeof** keyword returns the data type of a managed class, value class or managed interface. In our example, **GetType** returns **Point** and **__typeof** returns **Circle**. As a **Point** object is not a **Circle** object, the condition fails, and lines 43–44 append to **output** a string that indicates the result. Note that the **if** condition will be **true** if the left operand is a pointer to an instance of the right operand or if the left operarand is a pointer to an instance of a class that is derived from the right operand.

Common Programming Error 7.2

*Attempting to cast a base-class pointer to a derived-class type causes an **Invalid-CastException** (only when using the __try_cast operator) if the pointer points to a base-class object rather than an appropriate derived-class object.*

If we remove the **if** test and execute the program, a **MessageBox** similar to the one in Fig. 7.6 is displayed. We discuss how to deal with such situations in Chapter 8, Exception Handling.

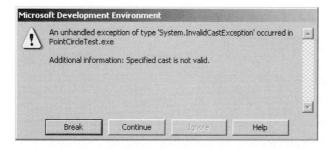

Fig. 7.6   `System.InvalidCastException` error message.

Despite the fact that a derived-class object also "is a" base-class object, the derived-class and base-class objects are different. As we have discussed previously, derived-class objects can be treated as if they were base-class objects. This is a logical relationship, because the derived class contains members that correspond to all members in the base class, but the derived class can have additional members. For this reason, assigning a base-class object to a derived-class pointer is not allowed without an explicit cast. Such an assignment would leave the additional derived-class members undefined.

There are four ways to mix base-class pointers and derived-class pointers with base-class objects and derived-class objects:

1. Referring to a base-class object with a base-class pointer is straightforward.

2. Referring to a derived-class object with a derived-class pointer is straightforward.

3. Referring to a derived-class object with a base-class pointer is safe, because the derived-class object *is an* object of its base class. However, this pointer can refer only to base-class members. If this code refers to derived-class-only members through the base-class pointer, the compiler reports an error.

4. Referring to a base-class object with a derived-class pointer generates a compiler error. To avoid this error, the derived-class pointer first must be cast to a base-class pointer explicitly. In this cast, the derived-class pointer must point to a derived-class object, or the .NET runtime generates a runtime error.

Common Programming Error 7.3

After assigning a derived-class object to a base-class pointer, attempting to reference derived-class-only members with the base-class pointer is a compilation error.

Common Programming Error 7.4

Treating a base-class object as a derived-class object can cause errors.

Though it is convenient to treat derived-class objects as base-class objects by manipulating derived-class objects with base-class pointers, doing so can cause significant problems. For example, a payroll system must be able to traverse an array of employees and calculate the weekly pay for each person. Intuition suggests that using base-class pointers would enable the program to call only the base-class payroll calculation routine (if there is such a routine in the base class). Using only base-class pointers, we can invoke the proper payroll calculation routine for each object, whether the object is a base-class object or a derived-class object. We learn how to create classes that exhibit this behavior as we introduce polymorphism throughout this chapter.

7.3 Type Fields and `switch` Statements

One way to determine the type of an object that is incorporated in a larger program is to use a `switch` structure. This allows us to distinguish among object types, then invoke an appropriate action for a particular object. For example, in a hierarchy of shapes in which each shape object has a `ShapeType` property, a `switch` structure could employ the object's `ShapeType` to determine which `Print` method to call.

However, using **switch** logic exposes programs to a variety of potential problems. For example, the programmer might forget to include a type test when one is warranted, or the programmer might forget to test all possible cases in a **switch** structure. When modifying a **switch**-based system by adding new types, the programmer might forget to insert the new cases in all relevant **switch** statements. Every addition or deletion of a class requires the modification of every **switch** statement in the system; tracking these statements down can be time consuming and error prone.

Software Engineering Observation 7.2

*Polymorphic programming can eliminate the need for unnecessary **switch** logic. Using the polymorphism mechanism to perform the equivalent logic, programmers can avoid the kinds of errors typically associated with **switch** logic.*

Testing and Debugging Tip 7.1

An interesting consequence of using polymorphism is that programs take on a simplified appearance. They contain less branching logic and more simple, sequential code. This simplification facilitates testing, debugging and program maintenance.

7.4 Polymorphism Examples

In this section, we discuss several examples of polymorphism. If class **Rectangle** is derived from class **Quadrilateral**, then a **Rectangle** object is a more specific version of a **Quadrilateral** object. Any operation (such as calculating the perimeter or the area) that can be performed on an object of class **Quadrilateral** also can be performed on an object of class **Rectangle**. Such operations also can be performed on other kinds of **Quadrilateral**s, such as **Square**s, **Parallelogram**s and **Trapezoid**s. When a program invokes a derived-class method through a base-class (i.e., **Quadrilateral**) pointer, the compiler polymorphically chooses the correct overriding method in the derived class from which the object was instantiated. We investigate this behavior in later examples.

Suppose that we design a video game that manipulates objects of many different types, including objects of classes **Martian**, **Venutian**, **Plutonian**, **SpaceShip** and **LaserBeam**. Also, imagine that each of these classes inherits from the common base class called **SpaceObject**, which contains method **DrawYourself**. Each derived class implements this method. A screen-manager program would maintain a container (such as a **SpaceObject** array) of pointers to objects of the various classes. To refresh the screen, the screen manager would periodically send each object the same message—namely, **DrawYourself**. However, each object responds in a unique way. For example, a **Martian** object would draw itself in red with the appropriate number of antennae. A **SpaceShip** object would draw itself as a bright silver flying saucer. A **LaserBeam** object would draw itself as a bright red beam across the screen. Thus, the same message sent to a variety of objects would have "many forms" of results—hence, the term *polymorphism*.

A polymorphic screen manager facilitates adding new classes to a system with minimal modifications to the system's code. Suppose that we want to add class **Mercurian**s to our video game. To do so, we must build a class **Mercurian** that inherits from **SpaceObject**, but provides its own definition of method **DrawYourself**. Then, when objects of class **Mercurian** appear in the container, the programmer does not need to modify the code for the screen manager. The screen manager invokes method **DrawYourself** on every object in the container, regardless of the object's type, so the new **Mercurian** objects simply "plug right in." Thus, without modifying the system (other than to build and include the classes themselves), programmers can use polymorphism to include additional types of classes that were not envisioned when the system was created.

With polymorphism, one method can cause different actions to occur, depending on the type of the object on which the method is invoked. This gives the programmer tremendous expressive capability. In the next several sections, we provide examples that demonstrate polymorphism.

Software Engineering Observation 7.3

With polymorphism, the programmer can deal in generalities and let the execution-time environment concern itself with the specifics. The programmer can command a wide variety of objects to behave in manners appropriate to those objects, even if the programmer does not know the objects' types.

Software Engineering Observation 7.4

Polymorphism promotes extensibility. Software used to invoke polymorphic behavior is written to be independent of the types of the objects to which messages (i.e., method calls) are sent. Thus, programmers can include into a system additional types of objects that respond to existing messages and can do this without modifying the base system.

7.5 Abstract Classes

When we think of a class as a type, we assume that programs will create objects of that type. However, there are cases in which it is useful to define classes for which the programmer never intends to instantiate any objects. Such classes are called *abstract classes*. We refer to such classes as *abstract base classes,* because such classes normally are used as base classes in inheritance hierarchies. These classes cannot be used to instantiate objects, since abstract classes are incomplete. Derived classes must define the "missing pieces." Abstract classes normally contain one or more *pure* **virtual** *methods* (sometimes called *abstract methods*), which we will discuss shortly. Derived classes must override inherited abstract methods and properties to enable objects of those derived classes to be instantiated. We discuss abstract classes extensively in Sections 7.6 and 7.8.

The purpose of an abstract class is to provide an appropriate base class from which other classes may inherit. Classes from which objects can be instantiated are called *concrete classes*. Such classes provide implementations of every method and property they define. We could have an abstract base class **TwoDimensionalObject** and derive such concrete classes as **Square**, **Circle** and **Triangle**. We could also have an abstract base class **ThreeDimensionalObject** and derive such concrete classes as **Cube**, **Sphere** and **Cylinder**. Abstract base classes are too generic to define real objects; we need to be more specific before we can think of instantiating objects. For example, if someone tells you to "draw the shape," what shape would you draw? Concrete classes provide the specifics that make it reasonable to instantiate objects.

A class is made abstract by declaring one or more of its **virtual** methods to be "pure," or by using the keyword **__abstract**. A *pure* **virtual** *method* is one with an *initializer* of **= 0** in its declaration as in

```
virtual double earnings() = 0; // pure virtual
```

We can also declare the *get* and *set* methods of properties as pure **virtual** methods as in

```
__property virtual String *get_Name() = 0; // pure virtual
```

For clarity, we explicitly declare abstract classes with the keyword `__abstract`. However, the `__abstract` keyword is optional if a `__gc` class contains one ore more pure `virtual` methods. [*Note*: Declaring an abstract class with keyword `__abstract` does not affect the methods or properties of the class. It simply ensures that the class cannot be instantiated. Methods and properties of `__abstract` classes are not implicitly `virtual`.]

An inheritance hierarchy does not need to contain any abstract classes, but, as we will see, many good object-oriented systems have class hierarchies headed by abstract base classes. In some cases, abstract classes constitute the top few levels of the hierarchy. A good example of this is the shape hierarchy in Fig. 6.3. The hierarchy begins with abstract base-class `Shape`. On the next level of the hierarchy, we have two more abstract base classes, namely `TwoDimensionalShape` and `ThreeDimensionalShape`. The next level of the hierarchy would define concrete classes for two-dimensional shapes, such as `Circle` and `Square`, and for three-dimensional shapes, such as `Sphere` and `Cube`.

Software Engineering Observation 7.5

An abstract class defines a common set of `public` *methods and properties for the various members of a class hierarchy. An abstract class typically contains one or more pure* `virtual` *methods that derived classes will override. All classes in the hierarchy can use this common set of* `public` *methods and properties.*

Abstract classes must specify signatures for their methods and properties. Concrete derived classes may override the virtual methods and properties of an abstract class and provide concrete implementations of those methods or properties. However, concrete derived classes must override all pure `virtual` methods of an abstract class.

Common Programming Error 7.5

Attempting to instantiate an object of an abstract class results in a compilation error.

Common Programming Error 7.6

Failure to override a pure `virtual` *method in a derived class is a syntax error, unless the derived class also is an abstract class.*

Software Engineering Observation 7.6

An abstract class can have instance data and non-virtual methods (including constructors), which are subject to the normal rules of inheritance by derived classes.

Software Engineering Observation 7.7

Concrete classes that indirectly inherit from an abstract class do not necessarily have to override the pure `virtual` *methods of the abstract class. If any class higher in the heirarchy has already provided an overridden version of a pure* `virtual` *method, the current class inherits that version and does not have to provide a separate implementation.*

Although we cannot instantiate objects of abstract base classes, we *can* use abstract base classes to declare pointers; these pointers can point to instances of any concrete classes derived from the abstract class. Programs can use such pointers to manipulate instances of the derived classes polymorphically.

Let us consider another application of polymorphism. A screen manager needs to display a variety of objects, including new types of objects that the programmer will add to the system after writing the screen manager. The system might need to display various shapes, such as **Circle**, **Triangle** or **Rectangle**, which are derived from abstract class **Shape**. The screen manager uses base-class pointers of type **Shape** to manage the objects that are displayed. To draw any object (regardless of the level at which that object's class appears in the inheritance hierarchy), the screen manager uses a base-class pointer to the object to invoke the object's **Draw** method. Method **Draw** is declared as pure **virtual** method in __**abstract** class **Shape**; therefore, each derived class should implement method **Draw**. Each **Shape** object in the inheritance hierarchy knows how to draw itself. The screen manager does not have to worry about the type of each object or whether the screen manager has ever encountered objects of that type.

Polymorphism is particularly effective for implementing layered software systems. In operating systems, for example, each type of physical device could operate quite differently from the others. Even so, commands to *read* or *write* data from and to devices may have a certain uniformity. The write message sent to a device-driver object needs to be interpreted specifically in the context of that device driver and how that device driver manipulates devices of a specific type. However, the write call itself really is no different from the write to any other device in the system—place some number of bytes from memory onto that device. An object-oriented operating system might use an abstract base class to provide an interface appropriate for all device drivers. Then, through inheritance from that abstract base class, derived classes are formed that all operate similarly. The capabilities (i.e., the **public** services) offered by the device drivers are provided as abstract methods in the abstract base class. The implementations of these abstract methods are provided in the derived classes that correspond to the specific types of device drivers.

It is common in object-oriented programming to define an *iterator class* that can traverse all the objects in a container (such as an array). For example, a program can print a list of objects in a linked list by creating an iterator object, then using the iterator to obtain the next element of the list each time the iterator is called. Iterators often are used in polymorphic programming to traverse an array or a linked list of objects from various levels of a hierarchy. The pointers in such a list are all base-class pointers. (See Chapter 19, Data Structures and Collections, to learn more about linked lists.) A list of objects of base class **TwoDimensionalShape** could contain objects from classes **Square**, **Circle**, **Triangle** and so on. Using polymorphism to send a **Draw** message to each object in the list would draw each object correctly on the screen.

7.6 Case Study: Inheriting Interface and Implementation

Our next example (Fig. 7.7–Fig. 7.15) reexamines the **Point**, **Circle**, **Cylinder** hierarchy that we explored in Chapter 6. In this example, the hierarchy begins with abstract base class **Shape** (Fig. 7.7–Fig. 7.8). This hierarchy mechanically demonstrates the power of polymorphism.

```
1   // Fig. 7.7: Shape.h
2   // Demonstrate a shape hierarchy using an abstract base class.
3
4   #pragma once
5
6   #using <mscorlib.dll>
7   #using <system.dll>
8
```

Fig. 7.7   **Shape** abstract base class. (Part 1 of 2.)

```
 9  using namespace System;
10
11  // __abstract classes cannot be instantiated
12  __abstract __gc class Shape
13  {
14  public:
15     virtual double Area();
16     virtual double Volume();
17
18     // property Name is a pure virtual method
19     __property virtual String *get_Name() = 0;
20  }; // end class Shape
```

Fig. 7.7   **Shape** abstract base class. (Part 2 of 2.)

```
 1  // Fig. 7.8: Shape.cpp
 2  // Method definitions for class Shape.
 3
 4  #include "Shape.h"
 5
 6  // return area
 7  double Shape::Area()
 8  {
 9     return 0;
10  }
11
12  // return volume
13  double Shape::Volume()
14  {
15     return 0;
16  }
```

Fig. 7.8   **Shape** class method definitions.

Abstract class **Shape** defines two concrete methods and one pure **virtual** method. All shapes have an area and a volume, so we include virtual methods **Area** (line 15 of Fig. 7.7) and **Volume** (line 16), which return the shape's area and volume, respectively. The volume of two-dimensional shapes is always zero, whereas three-dimensional shapes have a positive, nonzero volume. In class **Shape** (Fig. 7.8), methods **Area** and **Volume** return zero, by default. Programmers can override these methods in derived classes when those classes should have different area calculations [e.g., classes **Circle2** (Fig. 7.11–Fig. 7.12) and **Cylinder2** (Fig. 7.13–Fig. 7.14)] or different volume calculations (e.g., **Cylinder2**). Read-only property **Name** (line 19 of Fig. 7.7) is declared as a pure **virtual** method, so derived classes must implement this method to become concrete classes.

Class **Point2** (Fig. 7.9–Fig. 7.10) inherits from __abstract class **Shape** and overrides the property **Name**, which makes **Point2** a concrete class. A point's area and volume are zero, so class **Point2** does not override base-class methods **Area** and **Volume**. Lines 44–47 (Fig. 7.9) implement property **Name**. If we did not provide this implementation, class **Point2** would be an abstract class and we would not be able to instantiate **Point2** objects.

```
1   // Fig. 7.9: Point2.h
2   // Point2 inherits from abstract class Shape and represents
3   // an x-y coordinate pair.
4
5   #pragma once
6
7   #using <mscorlib.dll>
8   #using <system.dll>
9
10  using namespace System;
11
12  #include "Shape.h"
13
14  // Point2 inherits from abstract class Shape
15  public __gc class Point2: public Shape
16  {
17  public:
18     Point2();                    // default constructor
19     Point2( int, int );          // constructor
20
21     // property X
22     __property int get_X()
23     {
24        return x;
25     }
26
27     __property void set_X( int value )
28     {
29        x = value;
30     }
31
32     // property Y
33     __property int get_Y()
34     {
35        return y;
36     }
37
38     __property void set_Y( int value )
39     {
40        y = value;
41     }
42
43     // implement property Name of class Shape
44     __property virtual String *get_Name()
45     {
46        return S"Point2";
47     }
48
49     String *ToString();
50
51  private:
52     int x, y;                    // Point2 coordinates
53  }; // end class Point2
```

Fig. 7.9   Point2 class inherits from abstract class Shape.

```
1   // Fig. 7.10: Point2.cpp
2   // Method definitions for class Point2.
3
4   #include "Point2.h"
5
6   // default constructor
7   Point2::Point2()
8   {
9      // implicit call to Object constructor occurs here
10  }
11
12  // constructor
13  Point2::Point2( int xValue, int yValue )
14  {
15     X = xValue;
16     Y = yValue;
17  }
18
19  // return string representation of Point2 object
20  String *Point2::ToString()
21  {
22     return String::Concat( S"[", X.ToString(),
23        S", ", Y.ToString(), S"]" );
24  }
```

Fig. 7.10   **Point2** class method definitions.

Figure 7.11 defines class **Circle2**, which inherits from class **Point2**. Class **Circle2** contains property **Radius** (lines 21–32) for accessing the circle's radius. A circle has zero volume, so we do not override base-class method **Volume**. Rather, **Circle2** inherits this method from class **Point2**, which inherited the method from **Shape**. However, a circle does have an area, so **Circle2** overrides **Shape** method **Area** (lines 31–34 of Fig. 7.12). Property **Name** (lines 35–38 of Fig. 7.11) overrides property **Name** of class **Point2**. If **Circle2** did not override property **Name**, the class would inherit the **Point2** version of property **Name**. In that case, **Circle2**'s **Name** property would erroneously return "**Point2**."

```
1   // Fig. 7.11: Circle2.h
2   // Circle2 inherits from class Point2 and overrides key members.
3
4   #pragma once
5
6   #using <mscorlib.dll>
7   #using <system.dll>
8
9   using namespace System;
10
11  #include "Point2.h"
12
13  // Circle2 inherits from class Point2
14  public __gc class Circle2 : public Point2
```

Fig. 7.11   **Circle2** class that inherits from class **Point2**. (Part 1 of 2.)

```
15   {
16   public:
17      Circle2();                        // default constructor
18      Circle2( int, int, double );      // constructor
19
20      // property Radius
21      __property double get_Radius()
22      {
23         return radius;
24      }
25
26      __property void set_Radius( double value )
27      {
28
29         // ensure non-negative radius value
30         if ( value >= 0 )
31            radius = value;
32      }
33
34      // override property Name of class Point2
35      __property virtual String *get_Name()
36      {
37         return S"Circle2";
38      }
39
40      double Diameter();
41      double Circumference();
42      double Area();
43      String *ToString();
44
45   private:
46      double radius;                    // Circle2 radius
47   }; // end class Circle2
```

Fig. 7.11 `Circle2` class that inherits from class `Point2`. (Part 2 of 2.)

```
1    // Fig. 7.12: Circle2.cpp
2    // Method definitions for class Circle2.
3
4    #include "Circle2.h"
5
6    // default constructor
7    Circle2::Circle2()
8    {
9       // implicit call to Point2 constructor occurs here
10   }
11
12   Circle2::Circle2( int xValue, int yValue, double radiusValue )
13      : Point2( xValue, yValue )
14   {
15      Radius = radiusValue;
16   }
17
```

Fig. 7.12 `Circle2` class method definitions. (Part 1 of 2.)

```
18   // calculate diameter
19   double Circle2::Diameter()
20   {
21      return Radius * 2;
22   }
23
24   // calculate circumference
25   double Circle2::Circumference()
26   {
27      return Math::PI * Diameter();
28   }
29
30   // calculate area
31   double Circle2::Area()
32   {
33      return Math::PI * Math::Pow( Radius, 2 );
34   }
35
36   // return string representation of Circle2 object
37   String *Circle2::ToString()
38   {
39      return String::Concat( S"Center = ",
40         __super::ToString(), S"; Radius = ", Radius.ToString() );
41   }
```

Fig. 7.12 `Circle2` class method definitions. (Part 2 of 2.)

Figure 7.13 defines class **Cylinder2**, which inherits from class **Circle2**. Class **Cylinder2** contains property **Height** (lines 21–27) for accessing the cylinder's height. A cylinder has different area and volume calculations from those of a circle, so this class overrides method **Area** (lines 19–22 of Fig. 7.14) to calculate the cylinder's surface area (i.e., $2\pi r^2 + 2\pi rh$) and overrides method **Volume** (lines 25–28). Property **Name** (lines 35–38 of Fig. 7.13) overrides property **Name** of class **Circle2**. If this class did not override property **Name**, the class would inherit property **Name** of class **Circle2**, and this property would erroneously return "**Circle2**."

```
1    // Fig. 7.13: Cylinder2.h
2    // Cylinder2 inherits from class Circle2 and overrides key members.
3
4    #pragma once
5
6    #using <mscorlib.dll>
7    #using <system.dll>
8
9    using namespace System;
10
11   #include "Circle2.h"
12
13   // Cylinder2 inherits from class Circle2
14   public __gc class Cylinder2 : public Circle2
```

Fig. 7.13 `Cylinder2` class inherits from class `Circle2`. (Part 1 of 2.)

```
15  {
16  public:
17     Cylinder2();                              // default constructor
18     Cylinder2( int, int, double, double );   // constructor
19
20     // property Height
21     __property double get_Height()
22     {
23        return height;
24     }
25
26     __property void set_Height( double value )
27     {
28
29        // ensure non-negative height value
30        if ( value >= 0 )
31           height = value;
32     }
33
34     // override property Name of class Circle2
35     __property virtual String *get_Name()
36     {
37        return S"Cylinder2";
38     }
39
40     double Area();
41     double Volume();
42     String *ToString();
43
44  private:
45     double height;          // Cylinder2 height
46  }; // end class Cylinder2
```

Fig. 7.13 Cylinder2 class inherits from class **Circle2**. (Part 2 of 2.)

```
1   // Fig. 7.14: Cylinder2.cpp
2   // Cylinder2 inherits from class Circle2 and overrides key members.
3
4   #include "Cylinder2.h"
5
6   Cylinder2::Cylinder2()
7   {
8      // implicit call to Circle2 constructor occurs here
9   }
10
11  // constructor
12  Cylinder2::Cylinder2( int xValue, int yValue, double radiusValue,
13     double heightValue ) : Circle2( xValue, yValue, radiusValue )
14  {
15     Height = heightValue;
16  }
17
```

Fig. 7.14 Cylinder2 class method definitions. (Part 1 of 2.)

```
18   // calculate area
19   double Cylinder2::Area()
20   {
21      return 2 * __super::Area() + __super::Circumference() * Height;
22   }
23
24   // calculate volume
25   double Cylinder2::Volume()
26   {
27      return __super::Area() * Height;
28   }
29
30   // return string representation of Circle2 object
31   String *Cylinder2::ToString()
32   {
33      return String::Concat( __super::ToString(), S"; Height = ",
34         Height.ToString() );
35   }
```

Fig. 7.14 `Cylinder2` class method definitions. (Part 2 of 2.)

`AbstractShapesTest.cpp` (Fig. 7.15), creates an object of each of the three concrete classes and manipulates those objects polymorphically using an array of **Shape** pointers. Lines 14–16 instantiate **Point2** object **point**, **Circle2** object **circle** and **Cylinder2** object **cylinder**, respectively. Next, line 19 allocates array **arrayOfShapes**, which contains three **Shape** pointers. Line 22 assigns pointer **point** to the array element **arrayOfShapes[0]**, line 25 assigns pointer **circle** to the array element **arrayOfShapes[1]** and line 28 assigns pointer **cylinder** to the array element **arrayOfShapes[2]**. These assignments are possible because **Point2** is a **Shape**, **Circle2** is a **Shape** and **Cylinder2** is a **Shape**. Therefore, we can assign instances of derived classes **Point2**, **Circle2** and **Cylinder2** to base-class **Shape** pointers.

```
1    // Fig. 7.15: AbstractShapesTest.cpp
2    // Demonstrates polymorphism in Point-Circle-Cylinder hierarchy.
3
4    #using <system.windows.forms.dll>
5
6    using namespace System::Windows::Forms;
7
8    #include "Cylinder2.h"
9
10   int __stdcall WinMain()
11   {
12
13      // instantiates Point2, Circle2, Cylinder2 objects
14      Point2 *point = new Point2( 7, 11 );
15      Circle2 *circle = new Circle2( 22, 8, 3.5 );
16      Cylinder2 *cylinder = new Cylinder2( 10, 10, 3.3, 10 );
17
```

Fig. 7.15 **AbstractShapesTest** demonstrates polymorphism in point-circle-cylinder hierarchy. (Part 1 of 2.)

```
18      // create empty array of Shape base-class pointers
19      Shape *arrayOfShapes[] = new Shape *[ 3 ];
20
21      // arrayOfShapes[ 0 ] points to Point2 object
22      arrayOfShapes[ 0 ] = point;
23
24      // arrayOfShapes[ 1 ] points to Circle2 object
25      arrayOfShapes[ 1 ] = circle;
26
27      // arrayOfShapes[ 2 ] points to Cylinder2 object
28      arrayOfShapes[ 2 ] = cylinder;
29
30      String *output = String::Concat( point->Name, S": ", point,
31         S"\n", circle->Name, S": ", circle, S"\n",
32         cylinder->Name, S": ", cylinder );
33
34      // display Name, Area and Volume for each object
35      // in arrayOfShapes polymorphically
36      Shape *shape;
37
38      for ( int i = 0; i < arrayOfShapes->Length; i++ ) {
39         shape = arrayOfShapes[ i ];
40
41         output = String::Concat( output, S"\n\n",
42            shape->Name, S": ", shape, S"\nArea = ",
43            shape->Area().ToString( S"F" ), S"\nVolume = ",
44            shape->Volume().ToString( S"F" ) );
45      } // end for
46
47      MessageBox::Show( output, S"Demonstrating Polymorphism" );
48
49      return 0;
50   } // end function WinMain
```

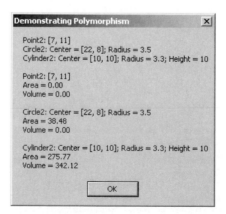

Fig. 7.15 `AbstractShapesTest` demonstrates polymorphism in point-circle-cylinder hierarchy. (Part 2 of 2.)

Lines 30–32 access property **Name** and invoke method **ToString** (implicitly) for objects **point**, **circle** and **cylinder**. Property **Name** returns the object's class name and method **ToString** returns the object's string representation (i.e., *x-y* coordinate pair, radius and height, depending on each object's type). Note that lines 30–32 use derived-class pointers to invoke each derived-class object's methods and properties.

By contrast, the **for** structure (lines 38–45) uses base-class **Shape** pointers to invoke each derived-class object's methods and properties. The **for** structure calls property **Name** and methods **ToString**, **Area** and **Volume** for each **Shape** pointer in **arrayOf-Shapes**. The property and methods are invoked on each object in **arrayOfShapes**. When the compiler looks at each method/property call, the compiler determines whether each **Shape** pointer (in **arrayOfShapes**) can make these calls. This is the case for property **Name** and methods **Area** and **Volume**, because they are defined in class **Shape**. However, class **Shape** does not define method **ToString**. For this method, the compiler proceeds to **Shape**'s base class (class **Object**) and determines that **Shape** inherited a no-argument **ToString** method from class **Object**. Once the compiler has determined that method **ToString** does, in fact, exist, the program can compile successfully. At runtime, however, the correct version of **ToString** will be called based on the type of the object (i.e., **Point2**, **Circle2** or **Cylinder2**).

The screen capture of Fig. 7.15 illustrates that the "appropriate" property **Name** and methods **ToString**, **Area** and **Volume** were invoked for each type of object in **array-OfShapes**. By "appropriate," we mean that each property and method call is mapped to the proper object. For example, in the **for** structure's first iteration, pointer **arrayOfShapes[0]** (which is a pointer to type **Shape**) points to the same object as **point** (which is a pointer to type **Point2**). Class **Point2** overrides property **Name** and method **ToString**, and inherits method **Area** and **Volume** from class **Shape**. At runtime, **arrayOfShapes[0]** accesses property **Name** and invokes methods **ToString**, **Area** and **Volume** of the **Point2** object. The compiler determines the correct object type, then uses that type to determine the appropriate version of each method to invoke. Through polymorphism, the call to property **Name** returns the string **"Point2:"**; the call to method **ToString** returns the string representation of **point**'s *x-y* coordinate pair; and methods **Area** and **Volume** each return **0.00** (as shown in the second group of outputs in Fig. 7.15).

Polymorphism occurs in the next two iterations of the **for** structure as well. Pointer **arrayOfShapes[1]** points to the same object as **circle** (which is a pointer to type **Circle2**). Class **Circle2** provides implementations for property **Name**, method **ToString** and method **Area**, and inherits method **Volume** from class **Point2** (which, in turn, inherited method **Volume** from class **Shape**). The compiler associates property **Name** and methods **ToString**, **Area** and **Volume** of the **Circle2** object to pointer **arrayOfShapes[1]**. As a result, property **Name** returns the string **"Circle2:"**; method **ToString** returns the string representation of **circle**'s *x-y* coordinate pair and radius; method **Area** returns the area (**38.48**); and method **Volume** returns **0.00**.

For the final iteration of the **for** structure, pointer **arrayOfShapes[2]** points to the same object as **cylinder** (which is a pointer to type **Cylinder2**). Class **Cylinder2** provides its own implementations for property **Name** and for methods **ToString**, **Area** and **Volume**. The compiler associates property **Name** and methods **ToString**, **Area** and **Volume** of the **Cylinder2** object to pointer **arrayOfShapes[2]**. Property **Name** returns the string **"Cylinder2:"**; method **ToString** returns the string representation of **cylinder**'s *x-y* coordinate pair, radius and height; method **Area** returns the cylinder's surface area (**275.77**); and method **Volume** returns the cylinder's volume (**342.12**).

7.7 __sealed Classes and Methods

In Chapter 5, Object-Based Programming, we saw that variables can be declared **const** to indicate that they cannot be modified after they are initialized. Variables declared with **const** must be initialized when they are declared.

The keyword **__sealed** is applied to methods and classes to prevent overriding and inheritance, respectively. A method that is declared **__sealed** cannot be overridden in a derived class.

Performance Tip 7.1

If the correct command line options are specified, the compiler can decide to inline a __sealed method call and will do so for small, simple __sealed methods. Inlining does not violate encapsulation or information hiding (but does improve performance, because it eliminates the overhead of making a method call).

Performance Tip 7.2

Pipelined processors can improve performance by executing portions of the next several instructions simultaneously, but not if those instructions follow a method call. Inlining (which the compiler can perform on a __sealed method) can improve performance in these processors as it eliminates the out-of-line transfer of control associated with a method call.

Software Engineering Observation 7.8

A class that is declared __sealed cannot be a base class (i.e., a class cannot inherit from a __sealed class). All methods in a __sealed class are __sealed implicitly.

Using the **__sealed** keyword with classes allows other runtime optimizations. For example, **virtual** method calls can be transformed into non-**virtual** method calls.

A **__sealed** class is the opposite of an **__abstract** class in certain ways. An **__abstract** class cannot be instantiated—other classes derive from the abstract base class and implement the base class's abstract members. A **__sealed** class, on the other hand, cannot have any derived classes. A class cannot be declared both **__sealed** and **__abstract**.

7.8 Case Study: Payroll System Using Polymorphism

Let us use **__abstract** classes and polymorphism to perform payroll calculations for various types of employees. We begin by creating abstract base class **Employee**. The derived classes of **Employee** are **Boss** (paid a fixed weekly salary, regardless of the number of hours worked), **CommissionWorker** (paid a flat base salary plus a percentage of the worker's sales), **PieceWorker** (paid a flat fee per item produced) and **HourlyWorker** (paid by the hour with "time-and-a-half" for overtime).

The application must determine the weekly earnings for all types of employees, so each class derived from **Employee** requires method **Earnings**. However, each derived class uses a different calculation to determine earnings for each specific type of employee. Therefore, we declare method **Earnings** as a pure **virtual** method in **Employee** and declare **Employee** to be an **__abstract** class. Each derived class overrides this method to calculate earnings for that employee type.

To calculate any employee's earnings, the program can use a base-class pointer to a derived-class object and invoke method **Earnings**. A real payroll system might reference the various **Employee** objects with individual elements in an array of **Employee** pointers. The program would traverse the array one element at a time, using the **Employee** pointers to invoke the appropriate **Earnings** method of each object.

Software Engineering Observation 7.9

*The ability to declare a pure **virtual** method gives the class designer considerable control over how derived classes are defined in a class hierarchy. Any class that inherits directly from a base class containing a pure **virtual** method must override the method. Otherwise, the new class also would be abstract, and attempts to instantiate objects of that class would fail.*

Let us consider class **Employee** (Fig. 7.16–Fig. 7.17). The **public** members include a constructor (lines 7–11 of Fig. 7.17) that takes as arguments the employee's first and last names; properties **FirstName** (lines 17–25 of Fig. 7.16) and **LastName** (lines 28–36); method **ToString** (lines 14–17 of Fig. 7.17), which returns the first name and last name separated by a space; and a pure **virtual** method **Earnings** (line 39 of Fig. 7.16). The **__abstract** keyword (line 11) indicates that class **Employee** is abstract; thus, it cannot be used to instantiate **Employee** objects. Method **Earnings** is defined as a pure **virtual** method, so the class does not provide a method implementation. All classes derived directly from class **Employee**— except for abstract derived classes—must implement this method. Method **Earnings** is defined as a **virtual** method in **Employee**, because we cannot calculate the earnings for a generic employee. To determine earnings, we first must know of the *type* of the employee. By declaring this method as a pure **virtual** method, we indicate that we will provide an implementation in each concrete derived class, but not in the base class itself.

```
1   // Fig. 7.16: Employee.h
2   // Abstract base class for company employees.
3
4   #pragma once
5
6   #using <mscorlib.dll>
7   #using <system.dll>
8
9   using namespace System;
10
11  __abstract __gc class Employee
12  {
13  public:
14     Employee( String *, String * );        // constructor
15
16     // property FirstName
17     __property String *get_FirstName()
18     {
19        return firstName;
20     }
21
```

Fig. 7.16 **Employee** abstract base class definition. (Part 1 of 2.)

```
22          __property void set_FirstName( String *value )
23          {
24              firstName = value;
25          }
26
27          // property LastName
28          __property String *get_LastName()
29          {
30              return lastName;
31          }
32
33          __property void set_LastName( String *value )
34          {
35              lastName = value;
36          }
37
38          String *ToString();
39          virtual Decimal Earnings() = 0;         // pure virtual method
40
41      private:
42          String *firstName;
43          String *lastName;
44      }; // end class Employee
```

Fig. 7.16 **Employee** abstract base class definition. (Part 2 of 2.)

```
1   // Fig. 7.17: Employee.cpp
2   // Method definitions for class Employee.
3
4   #include "Employee.h"
5
6   // constructor
7   Employee::Employee( String *firstNameValue, String *lastNameValue )
8   {
9       FirstName = firstNameValue;
10      LastName = lastNameValue;
11  }
12
13  // return string representation of Employee
14  String *Employee::ToString()
15  {
16      return String::Concat( FirstName, S" ", LastName );
17  }
```

Fig. 7.17 **Employee** class method definitions.

Class **Boss** (Fig. 7.18–Fig. 7.19) inherits from **Employee**. Class **Boss**'s constructor (lines 7–12 of Fig. 7.19) receives as arguments a first name, a last name and a salary. The constructor passes the first name and last name to the **Employee** constructor (line 9), which initializes the **FirstName** and **LastName** members of the base-class part of the derived-class object. Other **public** methods in class **Boss** include method **Earnings** (lines 15–18), which defines the calculation of a boss's earnings, and method **ToString** (lines 21–24), which returns a string that indicates the type of employee (i.e., **"Boss: "**) and the boss's name. Class **Boss** also includes property **WeeklySalary** (lines 19–30 of Fig. 7.18), which manipulates the value for member variable **salary**. Note that this property ensures only that **salary** cannot hold a negative value—in a real payroll system, this validation would be more extensive and carefully controlled.

```
1   // Fig. 7.18: Boss.h
2   // Boss class derived from Employee.
3
4   #pragma once
5
6   #using <mscorlib.dll>
7   #using <system.dll>
8
9   using namespace System;
10
11  #include "Employee.h"
12
13  public __gc class Boss: public Employee
14  {
15  public:
16     Boss( String *, String *, Decimal );     // constructor
17
18     // property WeeklySalary
19     __property Decimal get_WeeklySalary()
20     {
21        return salary;
22     }
23
24     __property void set_WeeklySalary( Decimal value )
25     {
26
27        // ensure positive salary value
28        if ( value >= 0 )
29           salary = value;
30     }
31
32     Decimal Earnings();
33     String *ToString();
34
35  private:
36     Decimal salary; // Boss's salary
37  }; // end class Boss
```

Fig. 7.18 **Boss** class inherits from class **Employee**.

```
1   // Fig. 7.19: Boss.cpp
2   // Method definitions for class Boss.
3
4   #include "Boss.h"
5
```

Fig. 7.19 **Boss** class method definitions. (Part 1 of 2.)

```
 6    // constructor
 7    Boss::Boss( String *firstNameValue, String *lastNameValue,
 8       Decimal salaryValue )
 9       : Employee ( firstNameValue, lastNameValue )
10    {
11       WeeklySalary = salaryValue;
12    }
13
14    // override base-class method to calculate Boss's earnings
15    Decimal Boss::Earnings()
16    {
17       return WeeklySalary;
18    }
19
20    // return string representation of Boss
21    String *Boss::ToString()
22    {
23       return String::Concat( S"Boss: ", __super::ToString() );
24    }
```

Fig. 7.19 **Boss** class method definitions. (Part 2 of 2.)

Class **CommissionWorker** (Fig. 7.20–Fig. 7.21) also inherits from class **Employee**. The constructor for this class (lines 7–15 of Fig. 7.21) receives as arguments a first name, a last name, a salary, a commission and a quantity of items sold. Line 10 passes the first name and last name to the base-class **Employee** constructor. Class **CommissionWorker** also provides properties **WeeklySalary** (lines 19–30 of Fig. 7.20), **Commission** (lines 33–44) and **Quantity** (lines 47–58); method **Earnings** (lines 19–22 of Fig. 7.21), which calculates the worker's wages; and method **ToString** (lines 25–29), which returns a string that indicates the employee type (i.e., **"CommissionWorker: "**) and the worker's name.

```
 1    // Fig. 7.20: CommissionWorker.h
 2    // CommissionWorker class derived from Employee.
 3
 4    #pragma once
 5
 6    #using <mscorlib.dll>
 7    #using <system.dll>
 8
 9    using namespace System;
10
11    #include "Employee.h"
12
13    public __gc class CommissionWorker : public Employee
14    {
15    public:
16       CommissionWorker( String *, String *, Decimal, Decimal, int );
17
```

Fig. 7.20 **CommissionWorker** class inherits from class **Employee**. (Part 1 of 2.)

```
18       // property WeeklySalary
19       __property Decimal get_WeeklySalary()
20       {
21          return salary;
22       }
23
24       __property void set_WeeklySalary( Decimal value )
25       {
26
27          // ensure non-negative salary value
28          if ( value >= 0 )
29             salary = value;
30       }
31
32       // property Commission
33       __property Decimal get_Commission()
34       {
35          return commission;
36       }
37
38       __property void set_Commission( Decimal value )
39       {
40
41          // ensure non-negative salary value
42          if ( value >= 0 )
43             commission = value;
44       }
45
46       // property Quantity
47       __property int get_Quantity()
48       {
49          return quantity;
50       }
51
52       __property void set_Quantity( int value )
53       {
54
55          // ensure non-negative salary value
56          if ( value >= 0 )
57             quantity = value;
58       }
59
60       Decimal Earnings();
61       String *ToString();
62
63    private:
64       Decimal salary;        // base weekly salary
65       Decimal commission;    // amount paid per item sold
66       int quantity;          // total items sold
67    }; // end class CommissionWorker
```

Fig. 7.20 CommissionWorker class inherits from class **Employee**. (Part 2 of 2.)

```
1   // Fig. 7.21: CommissionWorker.cpp
2   // Method definitions for class Employee.
3
4   #include "CommissionWorker.h"
5
6   // constructor
7   CommissionWorker::CommissionWorker( String *firstNameValue,
8      String *lastNameValue, Decimal salaryValue,
9      Decimal commissionValue, int quantityValue )
10     : Employee( firstNameValue, lastNameValue )
11  {
12     WeeklySalary = salaryValue;
13     Commission = commissionValue;
14     Quantity = quantityValue;
15  }
16
17  // override base-class method to calculate
18  // CommissionWorker's earnings
19  Decimal CommissionWorker::Earnings()
20  {
21     return WeeklySalary + Commission * Quantity;
22  }
23
24  // return string representation of CommissionWorker
25  String *CommissionWorker::ToString()
26  {
27     return String::Concat( S"CommissionWorker: ",
28        __super::ToString() );
29  }
```

Fig. 7.21   `CommissionWorker` class method definitions.

Class **PieceWorker** (Fig. 7.22–Fig. 7.23) inherits from class **Employee**. The constructor for this class (lines 7–13 of Fig. 7.23) receives as arguments a first name, a last name, a wage per piece and a quantity of items produced. Line 9 then passes the first name and last name to the base-class **Employee** constructor. Class **PieceWorker** also provides properties **WagePerPiece** (lines 17–28 of Fig. 7.22) and **Quantity** (lines 31–42); method **Earnings** (lines 16–19 of Fig. 7.23), which calculates a piece worker's earnings; and method **ToString** (lines 22–25), which returns a string that indicates the type of the employee (i.e., **"PieceWorker: "**) and the piece worker's name.

```
1   // Fig. 7.22: PieceWorker.h
2   // PieceWorker class derived from Employee.
3
4   #using <mscorlib.dll>
5   #using <system.dll>
6
7   using namespace System;
8
```

Fig. 7.22   `PieceWorker` class inherits from class **Employee**. (Part 1 of 2.)

```
9    #include "Employee.h"
10
11   public __gc class PieceWorker : public Employee
12   {
13   public:
14      PieceWorker( String *, String *, Decimal, int );
15
16      // property WagePerPiece
17      __property Decimal get_WagePerPiece()
18      {
19         return wagePerPiece;
20      }
21
22      __property void set_WagePerPiece( Decimal value )
23      {
24
25         // ensure non-negative salary value
26         if ( value >= 0 )
27            wagePerPiece = value;
28      }
29
30      // property Quantity
31      __property int get_Quantity()
32      {
33         return quantity;
34      }
35
36      __property void set_Quantity( int value )
37      {
38
39         // ensure non-negative salary value
40         if ( value >= 0  )
41            quantity = value;
42      }
43
44      Decimal Earnings();
45      String *ToString();
46
47   private:
48      Decimal wagePerPiece;  // wage per piece produced
49      int quantity;          // quantity of pieces produced
50   }; // end class PieceWorker
```

Fig. 7.22 `PieceWorker` class inherits from class **Employee**. (Part 2 of 2.)

```
1    // Fig.  7.23: PieceWorker.cpp
2    // Method definitions for class PieceWorker.
3
4    #include "PieceWorker.h"
5
```

Fig. 7.23 `PieceWorker` class method definitions. (Part 1 of 2.)

```
6    // constructor
7    PieceWorker::PieceWorker( String *firstNameValue,
8       String *lastNameValue, Decimal wagePerPieceValue,
9       int quantityValue ) : Employee( firstNameValue, lastNameValue )
10   {
11      WagePerPiece = wagePerPieceValue;
12      Quantity = quantityValue;
13   }
14
15   // override base-class method to calculate PieceWorker's earnings
16   Decimal PieceWorker::Earnings()
17   {
18      return Quantity * WagePerPiece;
19   }
20
21   // return string representation of PieceWorker
22   String *PieceWorker::ToString()
23   {
24      return String::Concat( S"PieceWorker: ", __super::ToString() );
25   }
```

Fig. 7.23 `PieceWorker` class method definitions. (Part 2 of 2.)

Class **HourlyWorker** (Fig. 7.24–Fig. 7.25) also inherits from class **Employee**. The constructor for this class (lines 7–14 of Fig. 7.25) receives as arguments a first name, a last name, a wage and the number of hours worked. Line 10 passes the first name and last name to the base-class **Employee** constructor. Class **HourlyWorker** also provides properties **Wage** (lines 17–28 of Fig. 7.24) and **HoursWorked** (lines 31–42); method **Earnings** (lines 17–35 of Fig. 7.25), which calculates an hourly worker's earnings; and method **ToString** (lines 38–41), which returns a string that indicates the type of the employee (i.e., **"HourlyWorker:"**) and the hourly worker's name. Note that hourly workers are paid "time-and-a-half" for "overtime" (i.e., hours worked in excess of 40 hours).

```
1    // Fig. 7.24: HourlyWorker.h
2    // HourlyWorker class derive from Employee.
3
4    #using <mscorlib.dll>
5    #using <system.dll>
6
7    using namespace System;
8
9    #include "Employee.h"
10
11   public __gc class HourlyWorker : public Employee
12   {
```

Fig. 7.24 `HourlyWorker` class inherits from class **Employee**. (Part 1 of 2.)

```
13   public:
14      HourlyWorker( String *, String *, Decimal, double );
15
16      // property Wage
17      __property Decimal get_Wage()
18      {
19         return wage;
20      }
21
22      __property void set_Wage( Decimal value )
23      {
24
25         // ensure non-negative wage value
26         if ( value >= 0)
27            wage = value;
28      }
29
30      // property HoursWorked
31      __property double get_HoursWorked()
32      {
33         return hoursWorked;
34      }
35
36      __property void set_HoursWorked( double value )
37      {
38
39         // ensure non-negative hoursWorked value
40         if ( value >= 0 )
41            hoursWorked = value;
42      }
43
44      Decimal Earnings();
45      String *ToString();
46
47   private:
48      Decimal wage;            // wage per hour of work
49      double hoursWorked;      // hours worked during week
50      static const int STANDARD_HOURS = 40;
51   }; // end class HourlyWorker
```

Fig. 7.24 `HourlyWorker` class inherits from class **Employee**. (Part 2 of 2.)

```
1   // Fig. 7.25: HourlyWorker.cpp
2   // Method definitions for class HourlyWorker.
3
4   #include "HourlyWorker.h"
5
6   // constructor
7   HourlyWorker::HourlyWorker( String *firstNameValue,
8      String *lastNameValue, Decimal wageValue,
9      double hoursWorkedValue )
```

Fig. 7.25 `HourlyWorker` class methods definitions. (Part 1 of 2.)

```
10        : Employee( firstNameValue, lastNameValue )
11    {
12        Wage = wageValue;
13        HoursWorked = hoursWorkedValue;
14    }
15
16    // override base-class method to calculate HourlyWorker earnings
17    Decimal HourlyWorker::Earnings()
18    {
19
20        // compensate for overtime (paid "time-and-a-half")
21        if ( HoursWorked <= STANDARD_HOURS ) {
22           return Wage * static_cast< Decimal >( HoursWorked );
23        }
24
25        else {
26
27           // calculate base and overtime pay
28           Decimal basePay = Wage *
29              static_cast< Decimal >( STANDARD_HOURS );
30           Decimal overtimePay = Wage * 1.5 *
31              static_cast< Decimal >( HoursWorked - STANDARD_HOURS );
32
33           return basePay + overtimePay;
34        }
35    } // end method Earnings
36
37    // return string representation of HourlyWorker
38    String *HourlyWorker::ToString()
39    {
40        return String::Concat( S"HourlyWorker: ", __super::ToString() );
41    }
```

Fig. 7.25 HourlyWorker class methods definitions. (Part 2 of 2.)

Function **WinMain** (lines 17–57) of class **EmployeesTest** (Fig. 7.26) declares **Employee** pointer **employee** (line 30). Each employee type is handled similarly in **WinMain**, so we discuss only the manipulations of the **Boss** object.

```
1    // Fig. 7.26: EmployeesTest.cpp
2    // Domesticates polymorphism by displaying earnings
3    // for various Employee types.
4
5    #using <system.windows.forms.dll>
6
7    using namespace System::Windows::Forms;
8
9    #include "PieceWorker.h"
10    #include "CommissionWorker.h"
11    #include "HourlyWorker.h"
12    #include "Boss.h"
```

Fig. 7.26 EmployeesTest class tests the Employee class hierarchy. (Part 1 of 3.)

```
13
14   // return string that contains Employee information
15   String *GetString( Employee *worker );
16
17   int __stdcall WinMain()
18   {
19      Boss *boss = new Boss( S"John", S"Smith", 800 );
20
21      CommissionWorker *commissionWorker =
22         new CommissionWorker( S"Sue", S"Jones", 400, 3, 150 );
23
24      PieceWorker *pieceWorker = new PieceWorker( S"Bob", S"Lewis",
25         static_cast< Decimal >( 2.5 ), 200 );
26
27      HourlyWorker *hourlyWorker = new HourlyWorker( S"Karen",
28         S"Price", static_cast< Decimal >( 13.75 ), 50 );
29
30      Employee *employee = boss;
31
32      String *output = String::Concat( GetString( employee ), boss,
33         S" earned ", boss->Earnings().ToString( "C" ), S"\n\n" );
34
35      employee = commissionWorker;
36
37      output = String::Concat( output, GetString( employee ),
38         commissionWorker, S" earned ",
39         commissionWorker->Earnings().ToString( "C" ), S"\n\n" );
40
41      employee = pieceWorker;
42
43      output = String::Concat( output, GetString( employee ),
44         pieceWorker, S" earned ",
45         pieceWorker->Earnings().ToString( "C" ), S"\n\n" );
46
47      employee = hourlyWorker;
48
49      output = String::Concat( output, GetString( employee ),
50         hourlyWorker, S" earned ",
51         hourlyWorker->Earnings().ToString( "C" ), S"\n\n" );
52
53      MessageBox::Show( output, S"Demonstrating Polymorphism",
54         MessageBoxButtons::OK, MessageBoxIcon::Information );
55
56      return 0;
57   } // end function WinMain
58
59   // return string that contains Employee information
60   String *GetString( Employee *worker )
61   {
62      return String::Concat( worker->ToString(), S" earned ",
63         worker->Earnings().ToString( "C" ), S"\n" );
64   } // end function GetString
```

Fig. 7.26 **EmployeesTest** class tests the **Employee** class hierarchy. (Part 2 of 3.)

Fig. 7.26   `EmployeesTest` class tests the `Employee` class hierarchy. (Part 3 of 3.)

Line 19 creates a new **Boss** object and passes to its constructor the boss's first name ("**John**"), last name ("**Smith**") and fixed weekly salary (**800**). Line 30 assigns the derived-class pointer **boss** to the base-class **Employee** pointer **employee**, so we can demonstrate the polymorphic determination of **boss**'s earnings. Lines 32–33 pass pointer **employee** as an argument to function **GetString** (lines 60–64), which polymorphically invokes methods **ToString** and **Earnings** on the **Employee** object the method receives as an argument. At this point, the compiler determines that the object passed to **GetString** is of type **Boss**, so lines 62–63 invoke **Boss** methods **ToString** and **Earnings**. These are classic examples of polymorphic behavior.

Method **Earnings** returns a **Decimal** object on which line 63 then calls method **ToString**. In this case, the string **"C"**, which is passed to an overloaded version of **Decimal** method **ToString**, stands for **Currency**, and **ToString** formats the string as a currency amount.

When function **GetString** returns to **WinMain**, lines 32–33 explicitly invoke methods **ToString** and **Earnings** through derived-class **Boss** pointer **boss** to show the method invocations that do not use polymorphic processing. The output generated in lines 32–33 is identical to that generated by methods **ToString** and **Earnings** through base-class pointer **employee** (i.e., the methods that use polymorphism), which verifies that the polymorphic methods invoke the appropriate methods in derived class **Boss**.

To prove that the base-class pointer **employee** can invoke the proper derived-class versions of methods **ToString** and **Earnings** for the other types of employees, lines 35, 41 and 47 assign to base-class pointer **employee** a different type of **Employee** object (**CommissionWorker**, **PieceWorker** and **HourlyWorker**, respectively). After each assignment, the application calls function **GetString** to return the results via the base-class pointer. Then the application calls methods **ToString** and **Earnings** of each derived-class pointer to show that the compiler correctly associates each method call to its corresponding derived-class object.

7.9 Case Study: Creating and Using Interfaces

We now present two more examples of polymorphism using *interfaces* that specify sets of **public** services (i.e., methods and properties) that classes must implement. An interface is used when there is no default implementation to inherit (i.e., no instance variables and no default-method implementations). Whereas an abstract class is best used for providing data and services for objects in a hierarchical relationship, an interface can be used for providing services that "bring together" disparate objects that relate to one another only through that interface.

An interface definition begins with the keyword **__interface** and contains a list of **public** methods and properties. All methods and properties of an interface must be pure **virtual** methods and must be declared **public**. Interfaces cannot contain data members. Interfaces can inherit from other interfaces, but not from base classes. To use an interface, a class must specify that it implements the interface and must provide implementations for every method and property specified in the interface definition. A class that implements an interface effectively signs a contract with the compiler that states, "this class will define all the methods and properties specified by the interface."

Common Programming Error 7.7

When a non-abstract class implements an **__interface***, leaving even a single* **__interface** *method or property undefined is an error. The class must define every method and property in the* **__interface***.*

Interfaces provide uniform sets of methods and properties for objects of disparate classes. These methods and properties enable programs to process the objects of those disparate classes polymorphically. For example, consider disparate objects that represent a person, a tree, a car and a file. These objects have "nothing to do" with one another—a person has a first name and last name; a tree has a trunk, a set of branches and a bunch of leaves; a car has wheels, gears and several other mechanisms that enable the car to move; and a file contains data. Due to the lack of commonality among these classes, modeling them via an inheritance hierarchy with a common base class seems illogical. However, these objects certainly have at least one common characteristic—an age. A person's age is represented by the number of years since that person was born; a tree's age is represented by the number of rings in its trunk; a car's age is represented by its manufacture date; and file's age is represented by its creation date. We can use an interface that provides a method or property that objects of these disparate classes can implement to return each object's age.

In this example, we use interface **IAge** (Fig. 7.27) to return the age information for classes **Person** (Fig. 7.28–Fig. 7.29) and **Tree** (Fig. 7.30–Fig. 7.31). The definition of interface **IAge** begins at line 11 with **public __gc __interface** and ends at line 16 with a closing curly brace. Lines 14–15 specify read-only properties **Age** and **Name**, for which every class that implements interface **IAge** must provide implementations. Declaring read-only properties is not required—an interface can also provide methods, write-only properties and properties with both *get* and *set* accessors. By containing these property declarations, interface **IAge** provides an opportunity for an object that implements **IAge** to return its age and name, respectively. However, the classes that implement these methods are not "required" to return an age and a name. On the other hand, classes implementing interface **IAge** are required to provide implementations for the interface's properties.

```
1   // Fig. 7.27: IAge.h
2   // Interface IAge declares property for setting and getting age.
3
4   #pragma once
5
6   #using <mscorlib.dll>
7   #using <system.dll>
8
9   using namespace System;
10
11  public __gc __interface IAge
12  {
13  public:
14     __property int get_Age() = 0;
15     __property String *get_Name() = 0;
16  }; // end interface IAge
```

Fig. 7.27   **IAge** interface for returning age of objects of disparate classes.

Line 11 (Fig. 7.28) uses MC++'s inheritance notation (i.e., *ClassName : Interface-Name*) to indicate that class **Person** implements interface **IAge**. In this example, class **Person** implements only one interface. A class can implement any number of interfaces in addition to inheriting from one class. To implement more than one interface or to implement interfaces in addition to inheriting from one class, the class definition must provide a comma-separated list of names after the semicolon such as

```
public __gc class MyClass2 : public IFace1, public IFace2,
       public MyClass1
```

Class **Person** (Fig. 7.28) has **private** data members **yearBorn**, **firstName** and **lastName** (lines 29–31), for which the constructor (lines 7–18 of Fig. 7.29) sets values. Because class **Person** (Fig. 7.28) implements interface **IAge**, class **Person** must implement properties **Age** and **Name**—defined on lines 17–20 and lines 23–26, respectively. Property **Age** allows the client to obtain the person's age, and property **Name** returns a string containing **firstName** and **lastName**. Note that property **Age** calculates the person's age by subtracting **yearBorn** from the current year (via property **Year** of property **DateTime::Now**, which returns the current date). These properties satisfy the implementation requirements defined in interface **IAge**, so class **Person** has fulfilled its "contract" with the compiler.

```
1   // Fig. 7.28: Person.h
2   // Class Person has a birthday.
3
4   #using <mscorlib.dll>
5   #using <system.dll>
6
7   using namespace System;
8
9   #include "IAge.h"
10
11  public __gc class Person : public IAge
12  {
```

Fig. 7.28   **Person** class implements **IAge** interface. (Part 1 of 2.)

```
13   public:
14      Person( String *, String *, int );
15
16      // property Age implementation of interface IAge
17      __property int get_Age()
18      {
19         return DateTime::Now.Year - yearBorn;
20      }
21
22      // property Name implementation of interface IAge
23      __property String *get_Name()
24      {
25         return String::Concat( firstName, S" ", lastName );
26      }
27
28   private:
29      String *firstName;
30      String *lastName;
31      int yearBorn;
32   }; // end class Person
```

Fig. 7.28 **Person** class implements **IAge** interface. (Part 2 of 2.)

```
1    // Fig. 7.29: Person.cpp
2    // Method definitions of class Person.
3
4    #include "Person.h"
5
6    // constructor
7    Person::Person( String *firstNameValue, String *lastNameValue,
8       int yearBornValue )
9    {
10      firstName = firstNameValue;
11      lastName = lastNameValue;
12
13      if ( ( yearBornValue > 0 ) &&
14         ( yearBornValue <= DateTime::Now.Year ) )
15            yearBorn = yearBornValue;
16      else
17         yearBorn = DateTime::Now.Year;
18   }
```

Fig. 7.29 **Person** class method definitions.

Class **Tree** (Fig. 7.30–Fig. 7.31) also implements interface **IAge**. Class **Tree** has **private** data member **rings** (line 30), which represents the number of rings inside the tree's trunk—this variable corresponds directly to the tree's age. The **Tree** constructor (lines 7–15 of Fig. 7.31) receives as an argument an **int** that specifies in which year the tree was planted. Class **Tree** also includes method **AddRing** (lines 18–21), which enables a program to increment the number of rings in the tree. Because class **Tree** implements interface **IAge**, class **Tree** (Fig. 7.30) must implement properties **Age** and **Name**— defined on lines 18–21 and lines 24–27, respectively. Property **Age** returns the value of **rings**, and property **Name** returns **"Tree"**.

```cpp
1   // Fig. 7.30: Tree.h
2   // Class Tree contains number of rings corresponding to its age.
3
4   #using <mscorlib.dll>
5   #using <system.dll>
6
7   using namespace System;
8
9   #include "IAge.h"
10
11  public __gc class Tree : public IAge
12  {
13  public:
14     Tree( int );                    // constructor
15     void AddRing();
16
17     // property Age implementation of interface IAge
18     __property int get_Age()
19     {
20        return rings;
21     }
22
23     // property Name implementation of interface IAge
24     __property String *get_Name()
25     {
26        return "Tree";
27     }
28
29  private:
30     int rings;      // number of rings in tree trunk
31  }; // end class Tree
```

Fig. 7.30   **Tree** class implements **IAge** interface.

```cpp
1   // Fig. 7.31: Tree.cpp
2   // Method definitions for class Tree.
3
4   #include "Tree.h"
5
6   // constructor
7   Tree::Tree( int yearPlanted )
8   {
9      if ( yearPlanted >= 0 && yearPlanted <= DateTime::Now.Year )
10
11        // count number of rings in Tree
12        rings = DateTime::Now.Year - yearPlanted;
13     else
14        rings = 0;
15  }
16
```

Fig. 7.31   **Tree** class method definitions. (Part 1 of 2.)

```
17   // increment rings
18   void Tree::AddRing()
19   {
20       rings++;
21   }
```

Fig. 7.31 **Tree** class method definitions. (Part 2 of 2.)

InterfacesTest.cpp (Fig. 7.32) demonstrates polymorphism on the objects of disparate classes **Person** and **Tree**. Line 13 instantiates pointer **tree** of type **Tree ***, and line 14 instantiates pointer **person** of type **Person ***. Line 17 declares **iAge-Array**—an array of two pointers to **IAge** objects. Lines 20 and 23 assign the address of **tree** and **person** to the first and second pointers in **iAgeArray**, respectively. Lines 26–27 invoke method **ToString** on **tree**, then invoke its properties **Age** and **Name** to return age and name information for object **tree**. Lines 30–31 invoke method **ToString** on **person**, then invoke its properties **Age** and **Name** to return age and name information for **person**. Next, we manipulate these objects polymorphically through the **iAgeArray** array of pointers to **IAge** objects. Lines 35–40 define a **for** structure that uses properties **Age** and **Name** to obtain age and name information for each **IAge** pointer in **iAgeArray**. Note that a program also can invoke class **Object**'s **public** methods (e.g., **ToString**) using any interface pointer. This is possible because every object inherits directly or indirectly from class **Object**. Therefore, every object is guaranteed to have the class **Object**'s **public** methods.

Software Engineering Observation 7.10

*In MC++, an interface pointer may invoke methods and properties that the interface declares and the **public** methods of class **Object**.*

Software Engineering Observation 7.11

*In MC++, an interface provides only those **public** services declared in the interface, whereas an abstract class provides the **public** services defined in the abstract class and those members inherited from the abstract class's base class.*

```
1    // Fig. 7.32: InterfacesTest.cpp
2    // Demonstrating polymorphism with interfaces.
3
4    #using <system.windows.forms.dll>
5
6    using namespace System::Windows::Forms;
7
8    #include "Person.h"
9    #include "Tree.h"
10
11   int __stdcall WinMain()
12   {
13       Tree *tree = new Tree( 1978 );
14       Person *person = new Person( S"Bob", S"Jones", 1971 );
15
```

Fig. 7.32 Polymorphism demonstrated on objects of disparate classes. (Part 1 of 2.)

```
16        // create array of IAge pointers
17        IAge *iAgeArray[] = new IAge *[ 2 ];
18
19        // IAgeArray[ 0 ] points to Tree object polymorphically
20        iAgeArray[ 0 ] = tree;
21
22        // IAgeArray[ 1 ] points to Person object polymorphically
23        iAgeArray[ 1 ] = person;
24
25        // display tree information
26        String *output = String::Concat( tree, S": ", tree->Name,
27           S"\nAge is ", tree->Age, S"\n\n" );
28
29        // display person information
30        output = String::Concat( output, person, S": ", person->Name,
31           S"\nAge is ", person->Age, S"\n\n" );
32
33        // display name and age for each IAge object in iAgeArray
34        IAge *agePtr;
35        for ( int i = 0; i < iAgeArray->Length; i++ ) {
36           agePtr = iAgeArray[ i ];
37
38           output = String::Concat( output, agePtr->Name,
39              S": Age is ", agePtr->Age.ToString(), S"\n" );
40        }
41
42        MessageBox::Show( output, S"Demonstrating Polymorphism" );
43
44        return 0;
45     } // end function WinMain
```

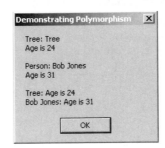

Fig. 7.32   Polymorphism demonstrated on objects of disparate classes. (Part 2 of 2.)

Our next example reexamines the **Point–Circle–Cylinder** hierarchy using an interface, rather than using an abstract class, to describe the common methods and properties of the classes in the hierarchy. We now show how a class can implement an interface, then act as a base class for derived classes to inherit the implementation. We create interface **IShape** (Fig. 7.33), which specifies methods **Area** and **Volume** and property **Name** (lines 16–20). Every class that implements interface **IShape** must provide implementations for these two methods and this read-only property. Note that, even though the methods in this example interface do not receive arguments, interface methods can receive arguments (just as regular methods can receive arguments).

Good Programming Practice 7.1

*By convention, begin the name of each interface with "**I**." This convention endures from the days when many developers used* Hungarian notation, *a naming style which involves prefixes. For example, a pointer would have prefix "p" (e.g.,* **pPoint**, **pCircle**, **pCylinder**). *Better editors and debuggers have rendered Hungarian notation outdated. Hungarian notation should only be used in the case of interface names.*

Class **Point3** (Fig. 7.34–Fig. 7.35) implements interface **IShape**; therefore, class **Point3** must implement all three **IShape** members. Lines 27–30 (Fig. 7.35) implement method **Area**, which returns **0**, because points have an area of zero. Lines 33–36 implement method **Volume**, which also returns **0**, because points have a volume of zero. Lines 46–49 (Fig. 7.34) implement read-only property **Name**, which returns the class name, or **"Point3"**.

```
1    // Fig. 7.33: IShape.h
2    // Interface IShape for Point, Circle, Cylinder Hierarchy.
3
4    #pragma once
5
6    #using <mscorlib.dll>
7    #using <system.dll>
8
9    using namespace System;
10
11   public __gc __interface IShape
12   {
13
14       // classes that implement IShape must implement these methods
15       // and this property
16       double Area();
17       double Volume();
18
19       // property Name
20       __property String *get_Name();
21   }; // end interface IShape
```

Fig. 7.33   **IShape** interface provides methods **Area** and **Volume** and property **Name**.

```
1    // Fig. 7.34: Point3.h
2    // Point3 implements interface IShape and represents
3    // an x-y coordinate pair.
4
5    #using <mscorlib.dll>
6    #using <system.dll>
7
8    using namespace System;
9
10   #include "IShape.h"
11
12   // Point3 implements IShape
13   public __gc class Point3 : public IShape
14   {
15   public:
```

Fig. 7.34   **Point3** class implements interface **IShape**. (Part 1 of 2.)

```
16        Point3();                        // default constructor
17        Point3( int, int );              // constructor
18
19     // property X
20     __property int get_X()
21     {
22        return x;
23     }
24
25     __property void set_X( int value )
26     {
27        x = value;
28     }
29
30     // property Y
31     __property int get_Y()
32     {
33        return y;
34     }
35
36     __property void set_Y( int value )
37     {
38        y = value;
39     }
40
41     String *ToString();
42     virtual double Area();
43     virtual double Volume();
44
45     // property Name
46     __property virtual String *get_Name()
47     {
48        return S"Point3";
49     }
50
51  private:
52     int x, y;                           // Point3 coordinates
53  }; // end class Point3
```

Fig. 7.34 **Point3** class implements interface **IShape**. (Part 2 of 2.)

```
1   // Fig. 7.35: Point3.cpp
2   // Method definitions for class Point3.
3
4   #include "Point3.h"
5
6   // default constructor
7   Point3::Point3()
8   {
9      // implicit call to Object constructor occurs here
10  }
11
```

Fig. 7.35 **Point3** class method definitions. (Part 1 of 2.)

```
12   // constructor
13   Point3::Point3( int xValue, int yValue )
14   {
15      X = xValue;
16      Y = yValue;
17   }
18
19   // return string representation of Point3 object
20   String *Point3::ToString()
21   {
22      return String::Concat( S"[", X.ToString(), S", ",
23         Y.ToString(), S"]" );
24   }
25
26   // implement interface IShape method Area
27   double Point3::Area()
28   {
29      return 0;
30   }
31
32   // implement interface IShape method Volume
33   double Point3::Volume()
34   {
35      return 0;
36   }
```

Fig. 7.35 `Point3` class method definitions. (Part 2 of 2.)

When a class implements an interface, the class enters the same kind of "is-a" relationship that inheritance establishes. In our example, class **Point3** implements interface **IShape**. Therefore, a **Point3** object *is an* **IShape**, and objects of any class that inherits from **Point3** are also **IShape**s. For example, class **Circle3** (Fig. 7.36–Fig. 7.37) inherits from class **Point3**; thus, a **Circle3** *is an* **IShape**. Class **Circle3** implements interface **IShape** implicitly and inherits the **IShape** methods that class **Point** implemented. Because circles do not have volume, class **Circle3** does not override class **Point3**'s **Volume** method, which returns zero. However, we do not want to use the class **Point3** method **Area** or property **Name** for class **Circle3**. Class **Circle3** should provide its own implementation for these, because the area and name of a circle differ from those of a point. Lines 32–35 (Fig. 7.37) override method **Area** to return the circle's area, and lines 40–43 (Fig. 7.36) override property **Name** to return **"Circle3"**.

```
1    // Fig. 7.36: Circle3.h
2    // Circle3 inherits from class Point3 and overrides key members.
3
4    #pragma once
5
6    #using <mscorlib.dll>
7    #using <system.dll>
8
9    using namespace System;
10
```

Fig. 7.36 `Circle3` class inherits from class `Point3`. (Part 1 of 2.)

```
11   #include "Point3.h"
12
13   // Circle3 inherits from class Point3
14   public __gc class Circle3 : public Point3
15   {
16   public:
17      Circle3();                          // default constructor
18      Circle3( int, int, double );    // constructor
19
20      // property Radius
21      __property double get_Radius()
22      {
23         return radius;
24      }
25
26      __property void set_Radius( double value )
27      {
28
29         // ensure non-negative radius value
30         if ( value >= 0 )
31            radius = value;
32      }
33
34      double Diameter();
35      double Circumference();
36      double Area();
37      String *ToString();
38
39      // override property Name from class Point3
40      __property String *get_Name()
41      {
42         return S"Circle3";
43      }
44
45   private:
46      double radius;                      // Circle3 radius
47   }; // end class Circle3
```

Fig. 7.36 `Circle3` class inherits from class **Point3**. (Part 2 of 2.)

```
1    // Fig. 7.37: Circle3.cpp
2    // Method definitions for class Circle3.
3
4    #include "Circle3.h"
5
6    // default constructor
7    Circle3::Circle3()
8    {
9       // implicit call to Point3 constructor occurs here
10   }
11
12   // constructor
```

Fig. 7.37 `Circle3` class method definitions. (Part 1 of 2.)

```
13   Circle3::Circle3( int xValue, int yValue, double radiusValue )
14   : Point3( xValue, yValue )
15   {
16      Radius = radiusValue;
17   }
18
19   // calculate diameter
20   double Circle3::Diameter()
21   {
22      return Radius * 2;
23   }
24
25   // calculate circumference
26   double Circle3::Circumference()
27   {
28      return Math::PI * Diameter();
29   }
30
31   // calculate area
32   double Circle3::Area()
33   {
34      return Math::PI * Math::Pow( Radius, 2 );
35   }
36
37   // return string representation of Circle3 object
38   String *Circle3::ToString()
39   {
40      return String::Concat( S"Center = ", __super::ToString(),
41         S"; Radius = ", Radius.ToString() );
42   }
```

Fig. 7.37   `Circle3` class method definitions. (Part 2 of 2.)

Class **Cylinder3** (Fig. 7.38–Fig. 7.39) inherits from class **Circle3**. **Cylinder3** implements interface **IShape** implicitly, because **Cylinder3** indirectly derives from **Point3**, which implements interface **IShape**. **Cylinder3** inherits method **Area** and property **Name** from **Circle3** and method **Volume** from **Point3**. However, **Cylinder3** overrides property **Name** and methods **Area** and **Volume** to perform **Cylinder3**-specific operations. Lines 20–23 (Fig. 7.39) override method **Area** to return the cylinder's surface area, lines 26–29 override method **Volume** to return the cylinder's volume, and lines 37–40 (Fig. 7.38) override property **Name** to return **"Cylinder3"**.

```
1   // Fig. 7.38: Cylinder3.h
2   // Cylinder3 inherits from class Circle3 and overrides key members.
3
4   #using <mscorlib.dll>
5   #using <system.dll>
6
7   using namespace System;
```

Fig. 7.38   `Cylinder3` class inherits from class `Circle3`. (Part 1 of 2.)

```
8
9  #include "Circle3.h"
10
11 // Cylinder3 inherits from class Circle3
12 public __gc class Cylinder3 : public Circle3
13 {
14 public:
15    Cylinder3();                               // default constructor
16    Cylinder3( int, int, double, double ); // constructor
17
18    // property Height
19    __property double get_Height()
20    {
21       return height;
22    }
23
24    __property void set_Height( double value )
25    {
26
27       // ensure non-negative height value
28       if ( value >= 0 )
29          height = value;
30    }
31
32    double Area();                            // calculate area
33    double Volume();                          // calculate volume
34    String *ToString();
35
36    // override property Name from class Cylinder3
37    __property String *get_Name()
38    {
39       return S"Cylinder3";
40    }
41
42 private:
43    double height;                            // Cylinder3 height
44 }; // end class Cylinder3
```

Fig. 7.38 Cylinder3 class inherits from class **Circle3**. (Part 2 of 2.)

```
1  // Fig. 7.39: Cylinder3.cpp
2  // Method definitions for class Cylinder3.
3
4  #include "Cylinder3.h"
5
6  // default constructor
7  Cylinder3::Cylinder3()
8  {
9     // implicit call to Circle3 constructor occurs here
10 }
11
```

Fig. 7.39 Cylinder3 class method definitions. (Part 1 of 2.)

```
12   // constructor
13   Cylinder3::Cylinder3( int xValue, int yValue, double radiusValue,
14      double heightValue ) : Circle3( xValue, yValue, radiusValue )
15   {
16      Height = heightValue;
17   }
18
19   // calculate area
20   double Cylinder3::Area()
21   {
22      return 2 * __super::Area() + __super::Circumference() * Height;
23   }
24
25   // calculate volume
26   double Cylinder3::Volume()
27   {
28      return __super::Area() * Height;
29   }
30
31   // return string representation of Circle3 object
32   String *Cylinder3::ToString()
33   {
34      return String::Concat( __super::ToString(),
35         S"; Height = ", Height.ToString() );
36   }
```

Fig. 7.39 `Cylinder3` class method definitions. (Part 2 of 2.)

Interfaces2Test.cpp (Fig. 7.40) demonstrates our point-circle-cylinder hierarchy that uses interfaces. Figure 7.40 has only two differences from the example in Fig. 7.15, which tested the class hierarchy created from the **__abstract** base class **Shape**. In Fig. 7.40, line 20 declares **arrayOfShapes** as an array of **IShape** interface pointers, rather than **Shape** base-class pointers.

```
1    // Fig. 7.40: Interfaces2Test.cpp
2    // Demonstrating polymorphism with interfaces in
3    // Point-Circle-Cylinder hierarchy.
4
5    #using <system.windows.forms.dll>
6
7    using namespace System::Windows::Forms;
8
9    #include "Cylinder3.h"
10
11   int __stdcall WinMain()
12   {
13
14      // instantiate Point3, Circle3 and Cylinder3 objects
15      Point3 *point = new Point3( 7, 11 );
16      Circle3 *circle = new Circle3( 22, 8, 3.5 );
```

Fig. 7.40 `Interfaces2Test` uses interfaces to demonstrate polymorphism in point-circle-cylinder hierarchy. (Part 1 of 2.)

```
17      Cylinder3 *cylinder = new Cylinder3( 10, 10 , 3.3, 10 );
18
19      // create array of IShape pointers
20      IShape *arrayOfShapes[] = new IShape*[ 3 ];
21
22      // arrayOfShapes[ 0 ] points to Point3 object
23      arrayOfShapes[ 0 ] = point;
24
25      // arrayOfShapes[ 1 ] points to Circle3 object
26      arrayOfShapes[ 1 ] = circle;
27
28      // arrayOfShapes[ 2 ] points to Cylinder3 object
29      arrayOfShapes[ 2 ] = cylinder;
30
31      String *output = String::Concat( point->Name, S": ",
32         point->ToString(), S"\n", circle->Name,
33         S": ", circle, S"\n", cylinder->Name,
34         S": ", cylinder->ToString() );
35
36      IShape *shape;
37
38      for ( int i = 0; i < arrayOfShapes->Length ; i++ ) {
39         shape = arrayOfShapes[ i ];
40
41         output = String::Concat( output, S"\n\n",
42            shape->Name, S": ", shape, S"\nArea = ",
43            shape->Area().ToString( S"F" ), S"\nVolume = ",
44            shape->Volume().ToString( S"F" ) );
45      }
46
47      MessageBox::Show( output, S"Demonstrating Polymorphism" );
48
49      return 0;
50   } // end function WinMain
```

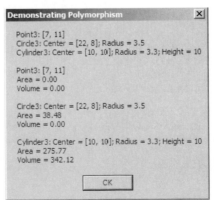

Fig. 7.40 `Interfaces2Test` uses interfaces to demonstrate polymorphism in point-circle-cylinder hierarchy. (Part 2 of 2.)

7.10 Delegates

In Chapter 6, Object-Oriented Programming: Inheritance, we discussed how objects can pass member variables as arguments to methods. However, sometimes, it is beneficial for objects to pass methods as arguments to other methods. For example, suppose that you wish to sort a series of values in ascending and descending order. Rather than provide separate ascending and descending sorting methods (one for each type of comparison), we could provide a single method that receives as an argument a pointer to the comparison method to use. To perform an ascending sort, we could pass to the sorting method the pointer to the ascending-sort-comparison method; to perform a descending sort, we could pass to the sorting method the pointer to the descending-sort-comparison method. The sorting method then would use this comparison method to sort the list—the sorting method would not need to know whether it is performing an ascending or a descending sort, or how the sorting string is implemented.

MC++ does not allow the passing of method pointers directly as arguments to other methods, but does provide *delegates*, which are classes that encapsulate sets of pointers to methods. A delegate object that contains method pointers can be passed to another method. Rather than send method pointers directly, objects can send delegate instances, which contain the pointers to the methods that we would like to send. The method that receives the pointer to the delegate then can invoke the methods the delegate contains.

A delegate that contains a single method is known as a *singlecast delegate* and is created or derived from class **Delegate**. Delegates that contain multiple methods are *multicast delegates* and are created or derived from class **MulticastDelegate**. Both delegate classes belong to namespace **System**.

To use a delegate, we first must declare one. The delegate's declaration specifies a method header (parameters and return value). Methods whose pointers will be contained within a delegate object must have the same method header as that defined in the delegate declaration. We then create methods that have this signature. The next step is to create a delegate instance that contains a pointer to that method. The delegate always accepts two parameters—a pointer to an object that encapsulates the method definition and a pointer to the method. After we create the delegate instance, we can invoke the method pointer that it contains. We show this process in our next example.

Class **DelegateBubbleSort** (Fig. 7.41–Fig. 7.42) uses delegates to sort an integer array in ascending or descending order. Line 14 (Fig. 7.41) provides the declaration for delegate **Comparator**. To declare a delegate, we declare a signature of a method— keyword **__delegate**, followed by the return type, the delegate name and parameter list. Delegate **Comparator** defines a method signature for methods that receive two **int** arguments and return a **bool**. Note that the body of delegate **Comparator** is not defined in Fig. 7.42. As we soon demonstrate, class **BubbleSort** (Fig. 7.43–Fig. 7.44) implements methods that adhere to delegate **Comparator**'s signature, then passes these methods (as arguments of type **Comparator**) to method **SortArray**. The declaration of a delegate does not define its intended role or implementation; our application uses this particular delegate when comparing two **int**s, but other applications might use it for different purposes.

```
1    // Fig. 7.41: DelegateBubbleSort.h
2    // Demonstrating delegates for sorting numbers.
3
4    #pragma once
5
6    #using <mscorlib.dll>
7    #using <system.dll>
8
9    using namespace System;
10
11   public __gc class DelegateBubbleSort
12   {
13   public:
14      __delegate bool Comparator( int, int );
15
16      // sort array using Comparator delegate
17      static void SortArray( int __gc[], Comparator * );
18
19   private:
20
21      // swap two elements
22      static void Swap( int __gc *, int __gc * );
23   }; // end class DelegateBubbleSort
```

Fig. 7.41   Delegates used in a bubble-sort program.

```
1    // Fig. 7.42: DelegateBubbleSort.cpp
2    // Method definitions for class DelegateBubbleSort.
3
4    #include "DelegateBubbleSort.h"
5
6    // sort array using Comparator delegate
7    void DelegateBubbleSort::SortArray( int array __gc[],
8       Comparator *Compare )
9    {
10      for ( int pass = 0; pass < array.Length; pass++ )
11
12         for ( int i = 0; i < array.Length - 1; i++ )
13
14            if ( Compare( array[ i ], array [ i + 1 ] ) )
15               Swap( &array[ i ], &array[ i + 1 ] );
16   }
17
18   // swap two elements
19   void DelegateBubbleSort::Swap( int __gc *firstElement,
20      int __gc *secondElement )
21   {
22      int hold = *firstElement;
23      *firstElement = *secondElement;
24      *secondElement = hold;
25   }
```

Fig. 7.42   DelegateBubbleSort class method definitions.

Lines 7–16 (Fig. 7.42) define method **SortArray**, which takes an array and a pointer to a **Comparator** delegate object as arguments. Method **SortArray** modifies the array by sorting its contents. Line 14 uses the delegate method to determine how to sort the array. Line 14 invokes the method enclosed within the delegate object by treating the delegate pointer as the method that the delegate object contains. MC++ invokes the enclosed method pointer directly, passing it parameters **array[i]** and **array[i + 1]**. The **Comparator** determines the sorting order for its two arguments. If the **Comparator** returns **true**, the two elements are out of order, so line 15 invokes method **Swap** (lines 19–25) to swap the elements. If the **Comparator** returns **false**, the two elements are in the correct order. To sort in ascending order, the **Comparator** returns **true** when the first element being compared is greater than the second element being compared. Similarly, to sort in descending order, the **Comparator** returns **true** when the first element being compared is less than the second element being compared.

Class **BubbleSort** (Fig. 7.43–Fig. 7.44) maintains the array to be sorted (line 23 of Fig. 7.43). The constructor (lines 6–9 of Fig. 7.44) calls method **PopulateArray**. Method **PopulateArray** (lines 24–33) fills the array with random integer values.

```
1   // Fig. 7.43: BubbleSort.h
2   // Demonstrates bubble sort using delegates to determine
3   // the sort order.
4
5   #pragma once
6
7   #include "DelegateBubbleSort.h"
8
9   public __gc class BubbleSort
10  {
11  public:
12     BubbleSort();    // constructor
13
14     void PopulateArray();
15
16     // sort the array
17     void SortArrayAscending();
18     void SortArrayDescending();
19
20     String *ToString();
21
22  private:
23     static int elementArray __gc[] = new int __gc[ 10 ];
24
25     // delegate implementation for ascending sort
26     bool SortAscending( int, int );
27
28     // delegate implementation for descending sort
29     bool SortDescending( int, int );
30  }; // end class BubbleSort
```

Fig. 7.43   **BubbleSort** class uses delegates to determine the sort order.

```cpp
1  // Fig. 7.44: BubbleSort.cpp
2  // Method definitions for class BubbleSort.
3
4  #include "BubbleSort.h"
5
6  BubbleSort::BubbleSort()
7  {
8     PopulateArray();
9  }
10
11  // delegate implementation for ascending sort
12  bool BubbleSort::SortAscending( int element1, int element2 )
13  {
14     return element1 > element2;
15  }
16
17  // delegate implementation for descending sort
18  bool BubbleSort::SortDescending( int element1, int element2 )
19  {
20     return element1 < element2;
21  }
22
23  // populate the array with random numbers
24  void BubbleSort::PopulateArray()
25  {
26
27     // create random-number generator
28     Random *randomNumber = new Random();
29
30     // populate elementArray with random integers
31     for ( int i = 0; i < elementArray->Length; i++ )
32        elementArray[ i ] = randomNumber->Next( 100 );
33  } // end method PopulateArray
34
35  // sort randomly generated numbers in ascending order
36  void BubbleSort::SortArrayAscending()
37  {
38     DelegateBubbleSort::SortArray( elementArray,
39        new DelegateBubbleSort::Comparator(
40        this, SortAscending ) );
41  }
42
43  // sort randomly generated numbers in descending order
44  void BubbleSort::SortArrayDescending()
45  {
46     DelegateBubbleSort::SortArray( elementArray,
47        new DelegateBubbleSort::Comparator(
48        this, SortDescending ) );
49  }
50
51  // return the contents of the array
52  String *BubbleSort::ToString()
53  {
54     int element;
```

Fig. 7.44 BubbleSort class method definitions. (Part 1 of 2.)

```
55      String *contents;
56
57      for( int i = 0; i < elementArray->Length; i++ ) {
58         element = elementArray[ i ];
59         contents = String::Concat( contents,
60            element.ToString(), S" " );
61      }
62
63      return contents;
64   } // end method ToString
```

Fig. 7.44 `BubbleSort` class method definitions. (Part 2 of 2.)

Methods **SortAscending** (lines 12–15 of Fig. 7.44) and **SortDescending** (lines 18–21) each have a signature that corresponds with the signature defined by the **Comparator** delegate declaration (i.e., each receives two **int**s and returns a **bool**). As we will see, the program passes to **DelegateBubbleSort** method **SortArray** delegates containing pointers to methods **SortAscending** and **SortDescending**, which will specify class **DelegateBubbleSort**'s sorting behavior.

Methods **SortArrayAscending** (lines 36–41) and **SortArrayDescending** (lines 44–49) sort the array in ascending and descending order, respectively. Method **SortArrayAscending** passes to **DelegateBubbleSort** method **SortArray** array **elementArray** and a pointer to method **SortAscending**. The syntax on lines 39–40

   new DelegateBubbleSort::Comparator(*this*, SortAscending)

creates a **Comparator** delegate that contains a pointer to method **SortAscending**. In method **SortArrayDescending**, lines 46–48 pass to method **SortArray** array **elementArray** and a delegate pointer to method **SortDescending**.

Figure 7.45 demonstrates class **BubbleSort** and displays the results in a **MessageBox**. We continue to explain and use delegates throughout the book.

```
1   // Fig. 7.45: DelegatesTest.cpp
2   // Demonstrates bubble-sort program.
3
4   #using <system.windows.forms.dll>
5
6   using namespace System::Windows::Forms;
7
8   #include "BubbleSort.h"
9
10  // main entry point for application
11  int __stdcall WinMain()
12  {
13     BubbleSort *sortPtr = new BubbleSort();
14
15     String *output = String::Concat( S"Unsorted array:\n",
16        sortPtr->ToString() );
17
18     sortPtr->SortArrayAscending();
19     output = String::Concat( output, S"\n\nSorted ascending:\n",
```

Fig. 7.45 Bubble-sort application demonstrates delegates. (Part 1 of 2.)

```
20          sortPtr->ToString() );
21
22     sortPtr->SortArrayDescending();
23     output = String::Concat( output, S"\n\nSorted descending:\n",
24          sortPtr->ToString() );
25
26     MessageBox::Show( output, S"Demonstrating delegates" );
27
28     return 0;
29  } // end function WinMain
```

Fig. 7.45   Bubble-sort application demonstrates delegates. (Part 2 of 2.)

7.11 Operator Overloading

Manipulations on class objects are accomplished by sending messages (in the form of method calls) to the objects. This method-call notation is cumbersome for certain kinds of classes, especially mathematical classes. For these classes, it would be convenient to use MC++'s rich set of built-in operators to specify object manipulations. In this section, we show how to enable MC++'s operators to work with class objects—via a process called *operator overloading*.

Software Engineering Observation 7.12

Use operator overloading when using an operator makes a program clearer than accomplishing the same operations with explicit method calls.

Software Engineering Observation 7.13

Avoid excessive or inconsistent use of operator overloading, as this can make a program cryptic and difficult to read.

MC++ enables the programmer to overload most operators to make them sensitive to the context in which they are used. Some operators are overloaded frequently, especially the assignment operator and various arithmetic operators, such as + and -. The job performed by overloaded operators also can be performed by explicit method calls, but operator notation often is more natural. The next several figures provide an example of using operator overloading with a complex-number class.

Class **ComplexNumber** (Fig. 7.46–Fig. 7.47) overloads the plus (+), minus (-) and multiplication (*) operators to enable programs to add, subtract and multiply instances of class **ComplexNumber** using common mathematical notation.

```
1   // Fig. 7.46: ComplexNumber.h
2   // Class that overloads operators for adding, subtracting
3   // and multiplying complex numbers.
4
5   #pragma once
6
7   #using <mscorlib.dll>
8   #using <system.dll>
9
10  using namespace System;
11
12  public __value class ComplexNumber
13  {
14  public:
15     ComplexNumber();                       // default constructor
16     ComplexNumber( int, int );             // constructor
17     String *ToString();
18
19     // property Real
20     __property int get_Real()
21     {
22        return real;
23     }
24
25     __property void set_Real( int value )
26     {
27        real = value;
28     }
29
30     // property Imaginary
31     __property int get_Imaginary()
32     {
33        return imaginary;
34     }
35
36     __property void set_Imaginary ( int value )
37     {
38        imaginary = value;
39     }
40
41     // overload the addition operator
42     static ComplexNumber op_Addition( ComplexNumber,
43        ComplexNumber );
44
45     // overload the subtraction operator
46     static ComplexNumber op_Subtraction( ComplexNumber,
47        ComplexNumber );
48
49     // overload the multiplication operator
50     static ComplexNumber op_Multiply( ComplexNumber,
51        ComplexNumber );
52
53  private:
54     int real;
```

Fig. 7.46 Overloading operators for complex numbers. (Part 1 of 2.)

```
55     int imaginary;
56  }; // end class ComplexNumber
```

Fig. 7.46 Overloading operators for complex numbers. (Part 2 of 2.)

```
1   // Fig. 7.47: ComplexNumber.cpp
2   // Method definitions for class ComplexNumber.
3
4   #include "ComplexNumber.h"
5
6   // default constructor
7   ComplexNumber::ComplexNumber() {}
8
9   // constructor
10  ComplexNumber::ComplexNumber( int a, int b )
11  {
12     Real = a;
13     Imaginary = b;
14  }
15
16  // return string representation of ComplexNumber
17  String *ComplexNumber::ToString()
18  {
19     return String::Concat( S"( ", real.ToString(),
20        ( imaginary < 0 ? S" - " : S" + " ),
21        ( imaginary < 0 ? ( imaginary * -1 ).ToString() :
22        imaginary.ToString() ), S"i )" );
23  }
24
25  // overload the addition operator
26  ComplexNumber ComplexNumber::op_Addition( ComplexNumber x,
27     ComplexNumber y )
28  {
29     return ComplexNumber( x.Real + y.Real,
30        x.Imaginary + y.Imaginary );
31  }
32
33  // overload the subtraction operator
34  ComplexNumber ComplexNumber::op_Subtraction( ComplexNumber x,
35     ComplexNumber y )
36  {
37     return ComplexNumber( x.Real - y.Real,
38        x.Imaginary - y.Imaginary );
39  }
40
41  // overload the multiplication operator
42  ComplexNumber ComplexNumber::op_Multiply( ComplexNumber x,
43     ComplexNumber y )
44  {
45     return ComplexNumber(
46        x.Real * y.Real - x.Imaginary * y.Imaginary,
47        x.Real * y.Imaginary + y.Real * x.Imaginary );
48  }
```

Fig. 7.47 **ComplexNumber** class method definitions.

Line 12 demonstrates the __value keyword. Unlike __gc classes, which are reference types, __value classes are value types.[2] For small objects with a short lifetime, creating __value classes improves program execution, because the overhead of passing objects (or classes) by reference is reduced. Using __value classes rather than __gc classes also allows us to access the objects directly, rather than using pointers. Members of __value classes are accessed using the dot operator (.). We will see the benefit of overloading operators in __value classes shortly.

Lines 26–31 (Fig. 7.47) overload the addition operator (+) to perform addition of ComplexNumbers. In MC++, specific method names are used to indicate overloaded operators. Method name op_Addition (line 26) indicates that a method will overload the addition operator. Similarly, method names op_Subtraction (line 34) and op_Multiply (line 42) indicate overloaded subtraction and multiplication operators, respectively.[3]

Methods that overload binary operators must take two arguments. The first argument is the left operand, and the second argument is the right operand. Class ComplexNumber's overloaded addition operator takes two ComplexNumbers as arguments and returns a ComplexNumber that represents the sum of the arguments. Note that this method is marked public and static (Fig. 7.46, line 42), which is required for overloaded operators. The body of the method (lines 29–30 of Fig. 7.47) performs the addition and returns the result as a new ComplexNumber. Lines 34–48 provide similar overloaded operators for subtracting and multiplying ComplexNumbers.

Software Engineering Observation 7.14

Overload operators to perform the same function or similar functions on class objects as the operators perform on objects of built-in types. Avoid non-intuitive use of operators.

Software Engineering Observation 7.15

At least one argument of an operator overload method must refer to an object of the class in which the operator is overloaded. This prevents programmers from changing how operators work on built-in types. (For example, if we were to define method op_Addition with two int arguments, we would be changing how the + operator works for int types.)

ComplexNumberTest.cpp (Fig. 7.48) demonstrates adding, subtracting and multiplying ComplexNumbers. Lines 14–20 create two ComplexNumbers and add their string representations to the output. Lines 23–24 perform an addition of the two ComplexNumbers using overloaded operator op_Addition. Because x and y are value types, rather than reference types, line 23 can use the familiar syntax of (x + y) to invoke method op_Addition. This syntax is equivalent to invoking method op_Addition directly (e.g., ComplexNumber::op_Addition(x, y)). Lines 27–32 perform similar operations for subtraction and multiplication of the two ComplexNumbers. Line 34 displays the results in a MessageBox.

---

2. More information about value types and reference types can be found in Chapter 4, Functions and Arrays.
3. For more operator method names, visit
   msdn.microsoft.com/library/default.asp?url=/library/en-us/
   cpgenref/html/cpconoperatoroverloadingusageguidelines.asp.

```cpp
1   // Fig. 7.48: ComplexNumberTest.cpp
2   // Example that uses operator overloading.
3
4   #using <system.windows.forms.dll>
5
6   using namespace System::Windows::Forms;
7
8   #include "ComplexNumber.h"
9
10  int __stdcall WinMain()
11  {
12
13     // create two ComplexNumbers
14     ComplexNumber x = ComplexNumber( 1, 2 );
15     String *output = String::Concat(
16        S"First Complex Number is: ", x.ToString() );
17
18     ComplexNumber y = ComplexNumber( 5, 9 );
19     output = String::Concat( output,
20        S"\nSecond Complex Number is: ", y.ToString() );
21
22     // perform addition
23     output = String::Concat( output, S"\n\n",
24        x.ToString(), S" + ", y.ToString(), S" = ", ( x + y ) );
25
26     // perform subtraction
27     output = String::Concat( output, S"\n",
28        x.ToString(), S" - ", y.ToString(), S" = ", ( x - y ) );
29
30     // perform multiplication
31     output = String::Concat( output, S"\n",
32        x.ToString(), S" * ", y.ToString(), S" = ", ( x * y ) );
33
34     MessageBox::Show( output, S"Operator Overloading" );
35
36     return 0;
37  } // end function WinMain
```

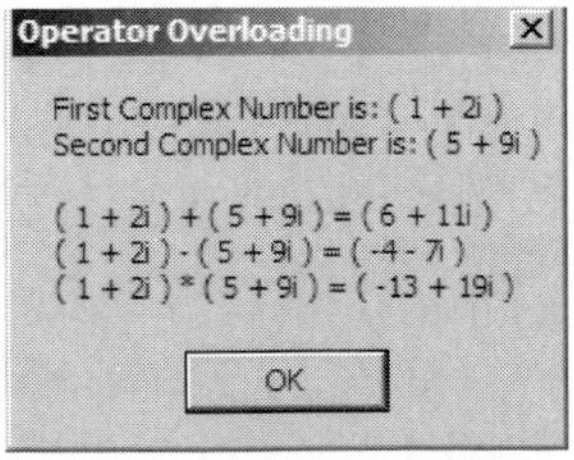

Fig. 7.48 `ComplexNumberTest` demonstrates operator overloading.

We now discuss the nature of operator overloading in __gc classes. If **Complex-Number** was a __gc class, we would have to use pointers to refer to **ComplexNumber**s (i.e., **x** and **y** would be of type **ComplexNumber ***). In this case, we would have to invoke method **op_Addition** as (***x + *y**) and modify **op_Addition** to accept and return references as

```
ComplexNumber& ComplexNumber::op_Addition ( ComplexNumber &x,
   ComplexNumber &y )
{
   return *( new ComplexNumber( x.Real + y.Real,
      x.Imaginary + y.Imaginary ) );
}
```

In this case, **op_Addition** would return a reference to a `__gc` type. Therefore, we would have to explicitly call method **ToString** in the call to **String::Concat** (e.g., `( *x + *y ).ToString()`).[4]

7.12 Summary

One means of processing objects of many different types is to use a **switch** structure to perform an appropriate action on each object based on that object's type. Polymorphic programming can eliminate the need for **switch** logic. With polymorphism, the programmer can deal in generalities and let the executing program concern itself with the specifics. Polymorphism enables us to write programs in a general fashion to handle a wide variety of existing and future related classes.

When we override a base class's method in a derived class, we hide the base class's implementation of that method. With polymorphism, new types of objects not even envisioned when a system is created may be added without modification to the system (other than the new class itself). Polymorphism allows one method call to perform different actions, depending on the type of the object receiving the call. The same message assumes "many forms"—hence, the term polymorphism.

This chapter introduced various types of classes and methods. Any class containing a pure **virtual** method becomes an abstract class. A program cannot instantiate objects of abstract classes, but can declare pointers to abstract classes. Such pointers can manipulate polymorphically instances of the derived classes. A `__sealed` class cannot be a base class (i.e., a class cannot inherit from a `__sealed` class).

An interface is used when there is no default implementation to inherit (i.e., no instance variables and no default-method implementations). Whereas an abstract class is best used for providing data and services for objects in a hierarchical relationship, an interface can be used for providing services that "bring together" disparate objects that relate to one another only through that interface.

An interface definition begins with the keyword `__interface` and contains a list of **public** methods and properties. To use an interface, a class must specify that it implements the interface and must provide implementations for every method and property specified in the interface definition. A class that implements an interface effectively signs a contract with the compiler that states, "this class will define all the methods and properties specified by the interface."

In MC++, it is impossible to pass a method pointer directly as an argument to another method. To address this problem, MC++ allows the creation of delegates, which are classes that encapsulate a set of pointers to methods.

---

4. It is possible to avoid this by having method **op_Addition** return a **ComplexNumber ***. However, it is preferable to have such overloaded operators return the same type as their arguments.

MC++ enables the programmer to overload most operators to make them sensitive to the context in which they are used. Methods that overload binary operators must take two arguments. The first argument is the left operand, and the second argument is the right operand. Method name **op_Addition** indicates that a method will overload the addition operator. Similarly, method names **op_Subtraction** and **op_Multiply** indicate overloaded subtraction and multiplication operators, respectively.

Exception Handling

Objectives

- To understand exceptions and error handling.
- To use **try** blocks to delimit code in which exceptions may occur.
- To **throw** exceptions.
- To use **catch** blocks to specify exception handlers.
- To use the **finally** block to release resources.
- To understand the .NET exception-class hierarchy.
- To create programmer-defined exceptions.

It is common sense to take a method and try it. If it fails, admit it frankly and try another. But above all, try something.
Franklin Delano Roosevelt

O! throw away the worser part of it,
And live the purer with the other half.
William Shakespeare

If they're running and they don't look where they're going
I have to come out from somewhere and catch them.
Jerome David Salinger

And oftentimes excusing of a fault
Doth make the fault the worse by the excuse.
William Shakespeare

I never forget a face, but in your case I'll make an exception.
Groucho (Julius Henry) Marx

Outline

8.1 Introduction

In this chapter, we introduce *exception handling*. An *exception* is an indication of a problem that occurs during a program's execution. The name "exception" comes from the fact that although a problem can occur, the problem occurs infrequently—if the "rule" is that a statement normally executes correctly, then the "exception to the rule" is that a problem occurs. Exception handling enables programmers to create applications that can resolve (or handle) exceptions. In many cases, handling an exception allows a program to continue executing as if no problem was encountered. A more severe problem may prevent a program from continuing normal execution, instead requiring the program to notify the user of the problem, then terminate in a controlled manner. The features presented in this chapter enable programmers to write clear, robust and more *fault-tolerant programs*.

The style and details of exception handling in MC++ are based in part on the work of Andrew Koenig and Bjarne Stroustrup, as presented in their paper, "Exception Handling for C++ (revised)."[1] MC++ designers extended the exception-handling mechanism used in standard C++.

This chapter begins with an overview of exception-handling concepts, then demonstrates basic exception-handling techniques. The chapter continues with an overview of the exception-handling class hierarchy. Programs typically request and release resources (such as files on disk) during program execution. Often, these resources are in limited supply or can be used by only one program at a time. We demonstrate a part of the exception-handling mechanism that enables a program to use a resource, then guarantees that the program releases the resource for use by other programs. The chapter continues with an example that demonstrates several properties of class **System::Exception** (the base class of all exception classes), followed by an example that shows programmers how to create and use their own exception classes.

8.2 Exception Handling Overview

The logic of the program frequently tests conditions that determine how program execution proceeds. We begin by performing a task. We then test whether that task executed correct-

---

1. Koenig, A. and B. Stroustrup, "Exception Handling for C++ (revised)," *Proceedings of the Usenix C++ Conference*, San Francisco, April 1990, 149–176.

ly. If not, we perform error processing. Otherwise we continue with the next task. Although this form of error-handling logic works, intermixing the logic of the program with the error-handling logic can make the program difficult to read, modify, maintain and debug—especially in large applications. In fact, if many of the potential problems occur infrequently, intermixing program logic and error handling can degrade the performance of the program, because the program must test extra conditions to determine whether the next task can be performed.

Exception handling enables the programmer to remove error-handling code (i.e., the code that resolves the error) from the "main line" of the program's execution. This improves program clarity and enhances modifiability. Programmers can decide to handle whatever exceptions they choose—all types of exceptions, all exceptions of a certain type or all exceptions of a group of related types. Such flexibility reduces the likelihood that errors will be overlooked and thereby increases a program's robustness.

Testing and Debugging Tip 8.1

Exception handling helps improve a program's fault tolerance. When it is easy to write error-processing code, programmers are more likely to use it.

Software Engineering Observation 8.1

Although it is possible to do so, do not use exception handling for conventional flow of control. It is difficult to keep track of a larger number of exception cases and programs with a large number of exception cases are hard to read and maintain.

Exception handling is designed to process *synchronous errors*—errors that occur during the normal program flow of control. Common examples of these errors are out-of-range array subscripts, arithmetic overflow (i.e., a value outside the representable range of values), division by zero, invalid method parameters and running out of available memory. Exception handling also can process certain *asynchronous* events, such as disk I/O completions.

Good Programming Practice 8.1

Avoid using exception handling for purposes other than error handling, because this can reduce program clarity.

With programming languages that do not support exception handling, programmers often delay the writing of error-processing code and sometimes simply forget to include it. This results in less robust software products. MC++ enables the programmer to deal with exception handling easily from the inception of a project. Still, the programmer must put considerable effort into incorporating an exception-handling strategy into software projects.

Software Engineering Observation 8.2

Try to incorporate the exception-handling strategy into a system from the inception of the design process. Adding effective exception handling after a system has been implemented can be difficult.

Software Engineering Observation 8.3

In the past, programmers used many techniques to implement error-processing code. Exception handling provides a single, uniform technique for processing errors. This helps programmers working on large projects to understand each other's error-processing code.

The exception-handling mechanism also is useful for processing problems that occur when a program interacts with software elements, such as methods, constructors, assemblies and classes. Rather than internally handling problems that occur, such software elements often use exceptions to notify programs when problems occur. This enables programmers to implement customized error handling for each application.

Common Programming Error 8.1

Aborting a program component could leave a resource—such as file stream or I/O device—in a state in which other programs are unable to acquire the resource. This is known as a "resource leak."

Performance Tip 8.1

When no exceptions occur, exception-handling code incurs little performance penalties. Thus, programs that implement exception handling operate more efficiently than programs that perform error handling throughout the program logic.

Performance Tip 8.2

Exception handling should be used only for problems that occur infrequently. As a "rule of thumb," if a problem occurs at least 30% of the time when a particular statement executes, the program should test for the error inline; otherwise, the overhead of exception handling will cause the program to execute more slowly.[2]

Software Engineering Observation 8.4

Methods with common error conditions should return NULL[3] (or another appropriate value) rather than throwing exceptions. A program calling such a method simply can check the return value to determine success or failure of the method call.[4]

Complex applications normally consist of predefined software components (such as those defined in the .NET Framework) and components specific to the application that use the predefined components. When a predefined component encounters a problem, that component needs a mechanism to communicate the problem to the application-specific component—the predefined component cannot know in advance how each application will process a problem that occurs. Exception handling simplifies combining software components and having them work together effectively by enabling predefined components to communicate problems that occur to application-specific components, which can then process the problems in an application-specific manner.

Exception handling is geared to situations in which the method that detects an error is unable to handle it. Such a method *throws an exception*. There is no guarantee that there will be an *exception handler*—code that executes when the program detects an exception—to process that kind of exception. If there is, the exception will be *caught* and *handled*. The result of an *uncaught exception* depends on whether the program executes in debug mode or standard execution mode. In debug mode, when the program detects an uncaught exception, a dialog box appears that enables the programmer to view the problem in the debugger

2. "Best Practices for Handling Exceptions," *.NET Framework Developer's Guide*, Visual Studio .NET Online Help. **<ms-help://MS.VSCC/MS.MSDNVS/cpguide/html/cpconbestpracticesforhandlingexceptions.htm>**
3. Symbolic constant **NULL** is defined in the header file **<tchar.h>**. Initializing a pointer to **NULL** is equivalent to initializing a pointer to **0**.
4. "Best Practices for Handling Exceptions."

or continue program execution by ignoring the problem that occurred. In standard execution mode, a Windows application presents a dialog that enables the user to continue or terminate program execution, and a console application presents a dialog that enables the user to open the program in the debugger or terminate program execution.

MC++ uses **try** *blocks* to enable exception handling. A **try** block consists of keyword **try** followed by braces (**{}**) that define a block of code in which exceptions may occur. The **try** block encloses statements that could cause exceptions. Immediately following the **try** block are zero or more **catch** *blocks* (also called **catch** *handlers*). Each **catch** handler specifies in parentheses an exception parameter that represents the type of exception the **catch** handler can handle. If an exception parameter includes an optional parameter name, the **catch** handler can use that parameter name to interact with a caught exception object. Optionally, programmers can include a *parameterless* **catch** *handler* (also called a "catch-all" handler) that catches all exception types. After the last **catch** handler, an optional **__finally** *block* contains code that always executes, regardless of whether an exception occurs.

Common Programming Error 8.2

*The parameterless **catch** handler must be the last **catch** handler following a particular **try** block; otherwise, a syntax error occurs.*

When a method called in a program detects an exception or when the CLR detects a problem, the method or CLR *throws an exception*. The point in the program at which an exception occurs is called the *throw point*—an important location for debugging purposes (as we demonstrate in Section 8.6). Exceptions are objects of classes that extend class **Exception** of namespace **System**. If an exception occurs in a **try** block, the **try** block *expires* (i.e., terminates immediately) and program control transfers to the first **catch** handler (if there is one) following the **try** block. MC++ is said to use the *termination model of exception handling*, because the **try** block enclosing a thrown exception expires immediately when that exception occurs.[5] As with any other block of code, when a **try** block terminates, local variables defined in the block go out of scope. Next, the CLR searches for the first **catch** handler that can process the type of exception that occurred. The CLR locates the matching **catch** by comparing the thrown exception's type to each **catch**'s exception-parameter type until the CLR finds a match. A match occurs if the types are identical or if the thrown exception's type is a derived class of the exception-parameter type. When a **catch** handler finishes processing, local variables defined within the **catch** handler (including the **catch** parameter) go out of scope. If a match occurs, code contained within the matching **catch** handler is executed. All remaining **catch** handlers that correspond to the **try** block are ignored and execution resumes at the first line of code after the **try**/**catch** sequence.

If no exceptions occur in a **try** block, the CLR ignores the exception handlers for that block. Program execution resumes with the next statement after the **try**/**catch** sequence. If an exception that occurs in a **try** block has no matching **catch** handler, or if an exception occurs in a statement that is not in a **try** block, the method containing that statement

---

5. Some languages use the *resumption model of exception handling*, in which, after the handling of the exception, control returns to the point at which the exception was thrown and execution resumes from that point.

terminates immediately and the CLR attempts to locate an enclosing **try** block in a calling method. This process is called *stack unwinding* (discussed in Section 8.6).

8.3 Example: `DivideByZeroException`

Let us consider a simple example of exception handling. The application in Fig. 8.1 uses **try** and **catch** to specify a block of code that might throw exceptions and to handle those exceptions if they occur. The application prompts the user to enter two integers. The program converts the input values to type **int** and divides the first number (**numerator**) by the second number (**denominator**). Assuming that the user provides integers as input and does not specify 0 as the denominator for the division, line 26 displays the division result. However, if the user inputs a non-integer value or supplies 0 as the denominator, an exception occurs. This program demonstrates how to catch these exceptions.

```cpp
1   // Fig. 8.1: DivideByZero.cpp
2   // Divide-by-zero exception handling.
3
4   #using <mscorlib.dll>
5   #using <system.windows.forms.dll>
6
7   using namespace System;
8   using namespace System::Windows::Forms;
9
10  int main()
11  {
12     try {
13        Console::Write( S"Enter an integral numerator: " );
14
15        // Convert::ToInt32 generates FormatException if
16        // argument is not an integer
17        int numerator = Convert::ToInt32( Console::ReadLine() );
18
19        Console::Write( S"Enter an integral denominator: " );
20        int denominator = Convert::ToInt32( Console::ReadLine() );
21
22        // division generates DivideByZeroException if
23        // denominator is 0
24        int result = numerator / denominator;
25
26        Console::WriteLine( result );
27     } // end try
28
29     // process invalid number format
30     catch ( FormatException * ) {
31        Console::WriteLine( S"You must enter two integers." );
32     }
33
34     // user attempted to divide by zero
35     catch ( DivideByZeroException *divideByZeroException ) {
36        Console::WriteLine( divideByZeroException->Message );
37     }
38
```

Fig. 8.1   Divide-by-zero exception handling example. (Part 1 of 2.)

```
39      return 0;
40  } // end function main
```

```
Enter an integral numerator: 100
Enter an integral denominator: 7
14
```

```
Enter an integral numerator: 10
Enter an integral denominator: hello
You must enter two integers.
```

```
Enter an integral numerator: 100
Enter an integral denominator: 0
Attempted to divide by zero.
```

Fig. 8.1   Divide-by-zero exception handling example. (Part 2 of 2.)

Before we discuss the program details, consider the sample outputs in Fig. 8.1. The first output shows a successful calculation in which the user inputs the numerator **100** and the denominator **7**. Note that the result (**14**) is an integer, because integer division always yields integer results. The second output shows the result of inputting a non-integer value—in this case, the user input **"hello"** at the second prompt. The program attempts to convert the string the user input into an **int** value with method **Convert::ToInt32**. If the argument to **Convert::ToInt32** is not a valid representation of an integer (in this case a valid string representation of an integer, such as **"14"**), the method generates a **FormatException** (namespace **System**). The program detects the exception and displays an error message, indicating that the user must enter two integers. The last output demonstrates the result after an attempt to divide by zero. In integer arithmetic, the CLR tests for division by zero and generates a **DivideByZeroException** (namespace **System**) if the denominator is zero. The program detects the exception and displays an error-message, indicating an attempt to divide by zero.[6]

Let us consider the user interactions and flow of control that yield the results shown in the sample outputs. The user inputs values that represent the numerator and denominator, then presses *Enter*. Lines 12–27 define a **try** block that encloses the code that can throw exceptions, as well as the code that should not execute if an exception occurs. For example, the program should not display a new result (line 26) unless the calculation (line 24) completes successfully. Remember that the **try** block terminates immediately if an exception occurs, so the remaining code in the **try** block will not execute.

---

6. The CLR allows floating-point division by zero, which produces a positive or negative infinity result, depending on whether the numerator is positive or negative. Dividing zero by zero is a special case that results in a value called "not a number." Programs can test for these results using constants for positive infinity (**PositiveInfinity**), negative infinity (**NegativeInfinity**) and not a number (**NaN**) that are defined in structures **Double** (for **double** calculations) and **Single** (for **float** calculations).

The two statements that read the integers (lines 13–20) each call method **Convert::ToInt32** to convert strings to **int** values. This method throws a **FormatException** if it cannot convert its **String *** argument to an integer. If lines 13–20 properly convert the values (i.e., no exceptions occur), then line 24 divides the **numerator** by the **denominator** and assigns the result to variable **result**. If the denominator is zero, line 24 causes the CLR to throw a **DivideByZeroException**. If line 24 does not cause an exception, then line 26 displays the result of the division. If no exceptions occur in the **try** block, the program successfully completes the **try** block and ignores the **catch** handlers at lines 30–32 and 35–37—the program execution continues with the first statement following the **try/catch** sequence.

Immediately following the **try** block are two **catch** handlers (also called *catch* blocks)—lines 30–32 define the exception handler for a **FormatException**, and lines 35–37 define the exception handler for the **DivideByZeroException**. Each **catch** handler begins with keyword **catch** followed by an exception parameter in parentheses that specifies the type of exception handled by the **catch** handler. The exception-handling code appears in the **catch** handler. In general, when an exception occurs in a **try** block, a **catch** handler catches the exception and handles it. In Fig. 8.1, the first **catch** handler specifies that it catches the type **FormatException**s (thrown by method **Convert::ToInt32**), and the second **catch** handler specifies that it catches type **DivideByZeroException**s (thrown by the CLR). Only the matching **catch** handler executes if an exception occurs. Both of the exception handlers in this example display an error-message to the user. When program control reaches the end of a **catch** handler, the program considers the exception as having been handled, and program control continues with the first statement after the **try/catch** sequence (the **return** statement of function **main** in this example).

In the second sample output, the user input **hello** as the denominator. When line 20 executes, **Convert::ToInt32** cannot convert this string to an **int**, so **Convert::ToInt32** creates a **FormatException** object and throws it to indicate that the method was unable to convert the **String *** to an **int**. When an exception occurs, the **try** block expires (terminates). Any local variables defined in the **try** block go out of scope; therefore, those variables are not available to the exception handlers. Next, the CLR attempts to locate a matching **catch** handler, starting with the **catch** at line 30. The program compares the type of the thrown exception (**FormatException**) with the type in parentheses following keyword **catch** (also **FormatException**). A match occurs, so that exception handler executes and the program ignores all other exception handlers following the corresponding **try** block. Once the **catch** handler finishes processing, local variables defined within the **catch** handler go out of scope. If a match did not occur, the program compares the type of the thrown exception with the next **catch** handler in sequence and repeats the process until a match is found.

Software Engineering Observation 8.5

*Enclose in a **try** block a significant logical section of the program in which several statements can throw exceptions, rather than using a separate **try** block for every statement that throws an exception. However, for proper exception-handling granularity, each **try** block should enclose a section of code small enough that when an exception occurs, the specific context is known and the **catch** handlers can process the exception properly.*

Common Programming Error 8.3

*Attempting to access a **try** block's local variables in one of that **try** block's associated **catch** handlers is a syntax error. Before a corresponding **catch** handler can execute, the **try** block expires, and its local variables go out of scope.*

Common Programming Error 8.4

*Specifying a comma-separated list of exception parameters in a **catch** handler is a syntax error. Each **catch** can have only one exception parameter.*

In the third sample output, the user input **0** as the denominator. When line 24 executes, the CLR throws a **DivideByZeroException** object to indicate an attempt to divide by zero. Once again, the **try** block terminates immediately upon encountering the exception, and the program attempts to locate a matching **catch** handler, starting from the **catch** handler at line 30. The program compares the type of the thrown exception (**DivideByZeroException**) with the type in parentheses following keyword **catch** (**FormatException**). In this case, there is no match, because they are not the same exception types and because **FormatException** is not a base class of **DivideByZeroException**. So the program proceeds to line 35 and compares the type of the thrown exception (**DivideByZeroException**) with the type in parentheses following keyword **catch** (also **DivideByZeroException**). A match occurs, so that exception handler executes. Line 36 in this handler uses property **Message** of class **Exception** to display the error message to the user. If there were additional **catch** handlers, the program would ignore them.

Notice that the **catch** handler that begins on line 35 specifies parameter name **divideByZeroException**. Line 36 uses this parameter (of type **DivideByZeroException ***) to interact with the caught exception. Meanwhile, the catch handler that begins on line 30 does not specify a parameter name. Thus, this **catch** handler cannot interact with the caught exception object.

8.4 .NET **Exception** Hierarchy

The exception-handling mechanism allows only objects of class **Exception** and its derived classes to be thrown and caught.[7] This section overviews several of the .NET Framework's exception classes. In addition, we discuss how to determine whether a particular method throws exceptions.

Class **Exception** of namespace **System** is the base class of the .NET Framework exception hierarchy. Two of the most important derived classes of **Exception** are **ApplicationException** and **SystemException**. **ApplicationException** is a base class that programmers can extend to create exception data types that are specific to their applications. We discuss creating programmer-defined exception classes in Section 8.7. Programs can recover from most **ApplicationException**s and continue execution.

---

7. Actually, it is possible to **catch** exceptions of types that are not derived from class **Exception** using the parameterless **catch** handler. This is useful for handling exceptions from code written in other languages that do not require all exception types to derive from class **Exception** in the .NET framework.

The CLR can generate **SystemException**s at any point during the execution of the program. Many of these exceptions can be avoided by coding properly. These are called *runtime exceptions* and they derive from class **SystemException**. For example, if a program attempts to access an out-of-range array subscript, the CLR throws an exception of type **IndexOutOfRangeException** (a class derived from **SystemException**). Similarly, a runtime exception occurs when a program uses an object pointer to manipulate an object that does not yet exist (i.e., the pointer has a **NULL** value). Attempting to use such a **NULL** pointer causes a *NullReferenceException* (another type of **SystemException**). Programs typically cannot recover from most exceptions the CLR throws. Therefore, programs generally should not throw or catch **SystemException**s. [*Note*: For a complete list of derived classes of **Exception**, look up "**Exception** class" in the **Index** of the Visual Studio .NET online documentation.]

A benefit of using the exception-class hierarchy is that a **catch** handler can catch exceptions of a particular type or can use a base-class type to catch exceptions in a hierarchy of related exception types. For example, a **catch** handler that specifies an exception parameter of type **Exception** also can catch exceptions of all classes that extend **Exception**, because **Exception** is the base class of all exception classes. This allows for polymorphic processing of related exceptions. The benefit of the latter approach is that the exception handler can use the exception parameter to manipulate the caught exception. If the exception handler does not need access to the caught exception, the exception parameter may be omitted. If no exception type is specified, the catch handler will catch all exceptions.

Using inheritance with exceptions enables an exception handler to catch related exceptions with a concise notation. An exception handler certainly could catch each derived-class exception type individually, but catching the base-class exception type is more concise. However, this makes sense only if the handling behavior is the same for a base class and derived classes. Otherwise, catch each derived-class exception individually.

At this point, we know that there are many different exception types. We also know that methods and the CLR can both throw exceptions. But, how do we determine that an exception could occur in a program? For methods in the .NET Framework classes, we can look at the detailed description of the methods in the online documentation. If a method throws an exception, its description contains a section called "Exceptions" that specifies the types of exceptions thrown by the method and briefly describes potential causes for the exceptions. For example, look up "**Convert.ToInt32** method" in the index of the Visual Studio .NET online documentation. In the document that describes the method, click the link "**public: static int ToInt32(String *);**." In the document that appears, the "Exceptions" section indicates that method **Convert.ToInt32** throws three exception types—**ArgumentException**, **FormatException** and **OverflowException**—and describes the conditions under which each exception type occurs.

Good Programming Practice 8.2

Inserting a comment header for each method that lists the explicit exceptions that the method can throw makes future maintenance of the code easier.

Software Engineering Observation 8.6

*If a method is capable of throwing exceptions, statements that invoke that method should be placed in **try** blocks and those exceptions should be caught and handled.*

8.5 __finally Block

Programs frequently request and release resources dynamically (i.e., at execution time). For example, a program that reads a file from disk first requests the opening of that file. If that request succeeds, the program reads the contents of the file. Operating systems typically prevent more than one program from manipulating a file at once. Therefore, when a program finishes processing a file, the program normally closes the file (i.e., releases the resource). This enables other programs to use the file. Closing the file helps prevent the *resource leak*, in which the file resource is unavailable to other programs because a program using the file never closed it. Programs that obtain certain types of resources (such as files) must return those resources explicitly to the system to avoid resource leaks.

In programming languages, like C and C++, in which the programmer is responsible for dynamic memory management, the most common type of resource leak is a *memory leak*. This happens when a program allocates memory (as we do with operator **new**), but does not deallocate the memory when the memory is no longer needed in the program. In MC++, this normally is not an issue, because the CLR performs "garbage collection" of memory no longer needed by an executing program. However, other kinds of resource leaks (such as the unclosed file mentioned previously) can occur in MC++.

Testing and Debugging Tip 8.2

The CLR does not completely eliminate memory leaks. The CLR will not garbage-collect an object until the program has no more pointers to that object. In addition, the CLR cannot claim unmanaged memory. Thus, memory leaks can occur if programmers erroneously keep pointers to unwanted objects.

Most resources that require explicit release have potential exceptions associated with the processing of the resource. For example, a program that processes a file might receive **IOException**s during the processing. For this reason, file-processing code normally appears in a **try** block. Regardless of whether a program successfully processes a file, the program should close the file when the file is no longer needed. Suppose that a program places all resource-request and resource-release code in a **try** block. If no exceptions occur, the **try** block executes normally and releases the resources after using them. However, if an exception occurs, the **try** block may expire before the resource-release code can execute. We could duplicate all resource-release code in the **catch** handlers, but this makes the code more difficult to modify and maintain.

The exception-handling mechanism provides the ___**finally** block, which is guaranteed to execute if program control enters the corresponding **try** block. The ___**finally** block executes regardless of whether that **try** block executes successfully or an exception occurs. This guarantee makes the ___**finally** block an ideal location to place resource deallocation code for resources acquired and manipulated in the corresponding **try** block. If the **try** block executes successfully, the ___**finally** block executes immediately after the **try** block terminates. If an exception occurs in the **try** block, the ___**finally** block executes immediately after a **catch** handler completes exception handling. If the exception is not caught by a **catch** handler associated with that **try** block or if a **catch** handler associated with that **try** block throws an exception, the ___**finally** block executes, then the exception is processed by the next enclosing **try** block (if there is one).

Testing and Debugging Tip 8.3

A __finally block typically contains code to release resources acquired in the corresponding try block; this makes the __finally block an effective way to eliminate resource leaks.

Testing and Debugging Tip 8.4

The only reason a __finally block will not execute if program control entered the corresponding try block is that the application terminates before __finally can execute.

Performance Tip 8.3

As a rule, resources should be released as soon as it is apparent that they are no longer needed in a program, to make those resources immediately available for reuse, thus enhancing resource utilization in the program.

If one or more **catch** handlers follow a **try** block, the **__finally** block is optional. If no **catch** handlers follow a **try** block, a **__finally** block must appear immediately after the **try** block. If any **catch** handlers follow a **try** block, the **__finally** block appears after the last **catch**. Only whitespace and comments can separate the blocks in a **try/catch/__finally** sequence.

Common Programming Error 8.5

Placing the __finally block before a catch handler is a syntax error.

The MC++ application in Fig. 8.2 demonstrates that the **__finally** block always executes, even if no exception occurs in the corresponding **try** block. The program contains four functions that **main** invokes to demonstrate **__finally**—**DoesNot-ThrowException** (lines 61–81), **ThrowExceptionWithCatch** (lines 84–107), **ThrowExceptionWithoutCatch** (lines 110–129) and **ThrowException-CatchRethrow** (lines 132–162).

```
1    // Fig. 8.2: UsingExceptionTest.cpp
2    // Demonstrating __finally blocks.
3
4    #using <mscorlib.dll>
5
6    using namespace System;
7
8    void DoesNotThrowException();
9    void ThrowExceptionWithCatch();
10   void ThrowExceptionWithoutCatch();
11   void ThrowExceptionCatchRethrow();
12
13   // main entry point for application
14   int main()
15   {
16
```

Fig. 8.2   Demonstrating that **__finally** blocks always execute regardless of whether an exception occurs. (Part 1 of 5.)

```
17      // Case 1: no exceptions occur in called method
18      Console::WriteLine( S"Calling DoesNotThrowException" );
19      DoesNotThrowException();
20
21      // Case 2: exception occurs and is caught
22      Console::WriteLine( S"\nCalling ThrowExceptionWithCatch" );
23      ThrowExceptionWithCatch();
24
25      // Case 3: exception occurs, but not caught
26      // in called method, because no catch handlers
27      Console::WriteLine(
28         S"\nCalling ThrowExceptionWithoutCatch" );
29
30      // calls ThrowExceptionWithoutCatch
31      try {
32         ThrowExceptionWithoutCatch();
33      }
34
35      // process exception returned from ThrowExceptionWithoutCatch
36      catch( ... ) {
37         Console::WriteLine( S"Caught exception from: "
38            S"ThrowExceptionWithoutCatch in main" );
39      }
40
41      // Case 4: exception occurs and is caught
42      // in called method, then rethrown to caller
43      Console::WriteLine(
44         S"\nCalling ThrowExceptionCatchRethrow" );
45
46      // call ThrowExceptionCachRethrow
47      try {
48         ThrowExceptionCatchRethrow();
49      }
50
51      // process exception returned from ThrowExceptionCatchRethrow
52      catch (...) {
53         Console::WriteLine( String::Concat ( S"Caught exception from ",
54            S"ThrowExceptionCatchRethrow in main" ) );
55      }
56
57      return 0;
58   } // end function main
59
60   // no exception thrown
61   void DoesNotThrowException()
62   {
63
64      // try block does not throw any exceptions
65      try {
66         Console::WriteLine( S"In DoesNotThrowException" );
67      }
68
```

Fig. 8.2   Demonstrating that __finally blocks always execute regardless of whether an exception occurs. (Part 2 of 5.)

```
69          // this catch never executes
70          catch( ... ) {
71             Console::WriteLine( S"This catch never executes" );
72          }
73
74          // __finally executes because corresponding try executed
75          __finally {
76             Console::WriteLine(
77                S"Finally executed in DoesNotThrowException" );
78          }
79
80          Console::WriteLine( S"End of DoesNotThrowException" );
81       } // end method DoesNotThrowException
82
83       // throw exception and catches it locally
84       void ThrowExceptionWithCatch()
85       {
86          // try block throws exception
87          try {
88             Console::WriteLine( S"In ThrowExceptionWithCatch" );
89
90             throw new Exception(
91                S"Exception in ThrowExceptionWithCatch" );
92          }
93
94          // catch exception thrown in try block
95          catch ( Exception *error ) {
96             Console::WriteLine( String::Concat( S"Message: ",
97                error->Message ) );
98          }
99
100         // __finally executes because of corresponding try executed
101         __finally {
102            Console::WriteLine(
103               S"Finally executed in ThrowExceptionWithCatch" );
104         }
105
106         Console::WriteLine( S"End of ThrowExceptionWithCatch" );
107      } // end function ThrowExceptionWithCatch
108
109      // throw exception and does not catch it locally
110      void ThrowExceptionWithoutCatch()
111      {
112
113         // throw exception, but do not catch it
114         try {
115            Console::WriteLine( S"In ThrowExceptionWithoutCatch" );
116
117            throw new Exception(
118               S"Exception in ThrowExceptionWithoutCatch" );
119         }
120
121         // __finally executes because of corresponding try executed
```

Fig. 8.2   Demonstrating that __**finally** blocks always execute regardless of whether an exception occurs. (Part 3 of 5.)

```
122      __finally {
123         Console::WriteLine( String::Concat( S"Finally executed in ",
124            S"ThrowExceptionWithoutCatch" ) );
125      }
126
127      // unreachable code; would generate logic error
128      Console::WriteLine( S"This will never be printed" );
129   } // end function ThrowExceptionWithoutCatch
130
131   // throws exception, catches it and rethrows it
132   void ThrowExceptionCatchRethrow()
133   {
134
135      // try block throws exception
136      try {
137         Console::WriteLine( S"In ThrowExceptionCatchRethrow" );
138
139         throw new Exception(
140            S"Exception in ThrowExceptionCatchRethrow" );
141      }
142
143      // catch any exception, place in object error
144      catch ( Exception *error ) {
145         Console::WriteLine( String::Concat( S"Message: ",
146            error->Message ) );
147
148         // rethrow exception for further processing
149         throw error;
150
151         // unreachable code; would generate logic error
152      }
153
154      // __finally executes because of corresponding try executed
155      __finally {
156         Console::WriteLine( String::Concat( S"Finally executed in ",
157            S"ThrowExceptionCatchRethrow" ) );
158      }
159
160      // unreachable code; would generate logic error
161      Console::WriteLine( S"This will never be printed" );
162   } // end function ThrowExceptionCatchRethrow
```

```
Calling DoesNotThrowException
In DoesNotThrowException
Finally executed in DoesNotThrowException
End of DoesNotThrowException

Calling ThrowExceptionWithCatch
In ThrowExceptionWithCatch
Message: Exception in ThrowExceptionWithCatch
Finally executed in ThrowExceptionWithCatch
End of ThrowExceptionWithCatch
```
Continued at the top of the next page

Fig. 8.2   Demonstrating that __finally blocks always execute regardless of whether an exception occurs. (Part 4 of 5.)

Continued from the previous page

```
Calling ThrowExceptionWithoutCatch
In ThrowExceptionWithoutCatch
Finally executed in ThrowExceptionWithoutCatch
Caught exception from: ThrowExceptionWithoutCatch in main

Calling ThrowExceptionCatchRethrow
In ThrowExceptionCatchRethrow
Message: Exception in ThrowExceptionCatchRethrow
Finally executed in ThrowExceptionCatchRethrow
Caught exception from ThrowExceptionCatchRethrow in main
```

Fig. 8.2   Demonstrating that __**finally** blocks always execute regardless of whether an exception occurs. (Part 5 of 5.)

Line 19 invokes method **DoesNotThrowException** (lines 61–81). The **try** block (lines 65–67) begins by outputting a message (line 66). The **try** block does not throw any exceptions, so program control reaches the closing brace of the **try** block. The program skips the **catch** handler (lines 70–72), because no exception is thrown; instead, the program executes the __**finally** block (lines 75–78), which outputs a message. At this point, program control continues with the first statement after the __**finally** block (line 80), which outputs a message indicating that the end of the method has been reached. Then, program control returns to **main**. Notice that line 70 specifies the parameterless catch handler by placing an ellipsis (**. . .**) within the parentheses following keyword **catch**. Recall that the parameterless catch handler matches any exception.

Line 23 of **main** invokes method **ThrowExceptionWithCatch** (lines 84–107), which begins in its **try** block (lines 87–92) by outputting a message. Next, the **try** block creates a new **Exception** object and uses a *throw statement* to throw the exception object (lines 90–91). The string passed to the constructor becomes the exception object's error message. When a **throw** statement in a **try** block executes, the **try** block expires immediately, and program control continues at the first **catch** (lines 95–98) following this **try** block. In this example, the type thrown (**Exception**) matches the type specified in the **catch**, so lines 96–97 output a message indicating the exception that occurred. Then, the **finally** block (lines 101–104) executes and outputs a message. At this point, program control continues with the first statement after the __**finally** block (line 106), which outputs a message indicating that the end of the method has been reached, then program control returns to **main**. Note that, in line 97, we use the exception object's **Message** property to access the error message associated with the exception—(the message passed to the **Exception** constructor). Section 8.6 discusses several properties of class **Exception**.

 Common Programming Error 8.6

*In MC++, the expression of a **throw**—an exception object—must be of either class **Exception** or one of its derived classes.*

Lines 31–33 of **main** define a **try** block in which **main** invokes method **ThrowExceptionWithoutCatch** (lines 110–129). The **try** block enables **main** to catch any exceptions thrown by **ThrowExceptionWithoutCatch**. The **try** block in lines 114–119 of **ThrowExceptionWithoutCatch** begins by outputting a message. Next, the **try** block throws an **Exception** (lines 117–118), and the **try** block expires immediately. Normally, program control would continue at the first **catch** following the **try** block. However, this **try** block does not have any corresponding **catch** handlers. Therefore, the exception is not caught in method **ThrowExceptionWithoutCatch**. Normal program control cannot continue until that exception is caught and processed. Thus, the CLR will terminate **ThrowExceptionWithoutCatch** and program control will return to **main**. Before control returns to **main**, the **__finally** block (lines 122–125) executes and outputs a message. At this point, program control returns to **main**—any statements appearing after the **__finally** block would not execute. In this example, because the exception thrown at lines 117–118 is not caught, method **ThrowExceptionWithoutCatch** always terminates after the **__finally** block executes. In **main**, the **catch** handler at lines 36–39 catches the exception and displays a message indicating that the exception was caught in **main**.

Lines 47–49 of **main** define a **try** block in which **main** invokes method **Throw-ExceptionCatchRethrow** (lines 132–162). The **try** block enables **main** to catch any exceptions thrown by **ThrowExceptionCatchRethrow**. The **try** block in lines 136–141 of **ThrowExceptionCatchRethrow** begins by outputting a message (line 137), then throwing an **Exception** (lines 139–140). The **try** block expires immediately, and program control continues at the first **catch** (lines 144–152) following the **try** block. In this example, the type thrown (**Exception**) matches the type specified in the **catch**, so lines 145–146 output a message indicating the exception that occurred. Line 149 uses the **throw** statement to *rethrow* the exception. This indicates that the **catch** handler performed partial processing (or no processing) of the exception and is now passing the exception back to the calling function (in this case **main**) for further processing. Note that the expression to the **throw** statement is the pointer to the exception that was caught. When rethrowing the original exception, you can also use the statement

> **throw;**

with no expression. Section 8.6 discusses the **throw** statement with an expression. Such a **throw** statement enables programmers to catch an exception, create an exception object, then throw a different type of exception from the **catch** handler. Class library designers often do this to customize the exception types thrown from methods in their class libraries or to provide additional debugging information.

Software Engineering Observation 8.7

Whenever possible, a method should handle exceptions that are thrown in that method, rather than passing the exceptions to another region of the program.

Software Engineering Observation 8.8

Before throwing an exception to a calling method, the method that throws the exception should release any resources acquired within the method before the exception occurred.[8]

The exception handling in method **ThrowExceptionCatchRethrow** did not complete, because the program cannot run code in the **catch** handler placed after the invocation of the **throw** statement (line 149). Therefore, method **ThrowExceptionCatchRethrow** will terminate and return control to **main**. Once again, the **__finally** block (lines 155–158) will execute and output a message before control returns to **main**. When control

---

8. "Best Practices for Handling Exceptions," *.NET Framework Developer's Guide*, Visual Studio .NET   Online   Help.   **<ms-help://MS.VSCC/MS.MSDNVS/cpguide/html/ cpconbestpracticesforhandlingexceptions.htm>**

returns to **main**, the **catch** handler at lines 52–55 catches the exception and displays a message indicating that the exception was caught.

Note that the point at which program control continues after the **__finally** block executes depends on the exception-handling state. If the **try** block successfully completes or if a **catch** handler catches and handles an exception, control continues with the next statement after the **__finally** block. If an exception is not caught or if a **catch** handler rethrows an exception, program control continues in the next enclosing **try** block. The enclosing **try** may be in the calling method or one of its callers. Nesting a **try/catch** sequence in a **try** block is also possible, in which case the outer **try** block's catch handlers would process any exceptions that were not caught in the inner **try/catch** sequence. If a **try** block has a corresponding **__finally** block, the **__finally** block executes even if the **try** block terminates due to a **return** statement; then the **return** occurs.

Common Programming Error 8.7

*Throwing an exception from a **__finally** block can be dangerous. If an uncaught exception is awaiting processing when the **__finally** block executes and the **__finally** block throws a new exception that is not caught in the **__finally** block, the first exception is lost, and the new exception is the one passed to the next enclosing **try** block.*

Testing and Debugging Tip 8.5

*When placing code that can throw an exception in a **__finally** block, always enclose that code in a **try/catch** sequence that catches the appropriate exception types. This prevents losing uncaught and rethrown exceptions that occur before the **__finally** block executes.*

Software Engineering Observation 8.9

*MC++'s exception-handling mechanism removes error-processing code from the main line of a program to improve program clarity. Do not place **try-catch-__finally** around every statement that could throw an exception. Doing so makes programs difficult to read. Rather, place one **try** block around a significant portion of your code. Follow this **try** block with **catch** handlers that handle each of the possible exceptions and follow the **catch** handlers with a single **__finally** block.*

Performance Tip 8.4

*Adding an excessive number of **try-catch-__finally** blocks in your code can result in reduced performance.*

8.6 **Exception** Properties

As we discussed in Section 8.4, exception data types derive from class **Exception**, which has several properties. These properties frequently are used to formulate error messages for a caught exception. Two important properties are *Message* and *StackTrace*. Property **Message** stores the error message associated with an **Exception** object. This message may be a default message associated with the exception type or a customized message passed to an exception object's constructor when the exception object is constructed. Property **StackTrace** contains a string that represents the *method call stack*. The runtime environment keeps a list of method calls that have been made up to a given moment. The **StackTrace** string represents this sequential list of methods that had not finished processing at the time the exception occurred. The exact location at which the exception occurs in the program is called the exception's *throw point*.

Testing and Debugging Tip 8.6

A stack trace shows the complete method call stack at the time an exception occurred. This lets the programmer view the series of method calls that led to the exception. Information in the stack trace includes names of the methods on the call stack at the time of the exception, names of the classes in which those methods are defined, names of the namespaces in which those classes are defined and line numbers. The first line number in the stack trace indicates the throw point. Subsequent line numbers indicate the locations from which each method in the stack trace was called.

Another property used frequently by class library programmers is **InnerException**. Typically, programmers use this property to "wrap" exception objects caught in their code, then throw new exception types that are specific to their libraries. For example, a programmer implementing an accounting system might have some account-number processing code in which account numbers are input as strings, but represented with integers in the code. As you know, a program can convert strings to **Int32** values with **Convert::ToInt32**, which throws a **FormatException** when it encounters an invalid number format. When an invalid account-number format occurs, the accounting-system programmer might wish either to indicate an error message different from the default one supplied by **FormatException** or to indicate a new exception type, such as **InvalidAccountNumberFormatException**. In these cases, the programmer would provide code to catch the **FormatException**, then create an exception object in the **catch** handler, passing the original exception as one of the constructor arguments. The original exception object becomes the **InnerException** of the new exception object. When an **InvalidAccountNumberFormatException** occurs in code that uses the accounting-system library, the **catch** handler that catches the exception can view the original exception via the property **InnerException**. Thus, the exception indicates that an invalid account number was specified and that the particular problem was an invalid number format.

Our next example (Fig. 8.3–Fig. 8.5) demonstrates properties **Message**, **StackTrace** and **InnerException**, as well as method **ToString**. In addition, this example demonstrates *stack unwinding*—the process that attempts to locate an appropriate **catch** handler for an uncaught exception. As we discuss this example, we keep track of the methods on the call stack, so we can discuss property **StackTrace** and the stack-unwinding mechanism.

```
1   // Fig. 8.3: Properties.h
2   // Stack unwinding and Exception class properties.
3
4   #pragma once
5
6   #using <mscorlib.dll>
7
8   using namespace System;
9
10  // demonstrates using the Message, StackTrace and
11  // InnerException properties
12  public __gc class Properties
13  {
```

Fig. 8.3   **Exception** properties and stack unwinding. (Part 1 of 2.)

```
14   public:
15      static void Method1();
16      static void Method2();
17      static void Method3();
18   }; // end class Properties
```

Fig. 8.3   Exception properties and stack unwinding. (Part 2 of 2.)

```
1    // Fig. 8.4: Properties.cpp
2    // Method definitions for class Properties.
3
4    #include "Properties.h"
5
6    // calls Method2
7    void Properties::Method1()
8    {
9       Method2();
10   } // end method Method1
11
12   // calls Method3
13   void Properties::Method2()
14   {
15      Method3();
16   } // end method Method2
17
18   // throws an Exception containing an InnerException
19   void Properties::Method3()
20   {
21
22      // attempt to convert non-integer string to int
23      try {
24         Convert::ToInt32( S"Not an integer" );
25      }
26
27      // catch FormatException and wrap it in new Exception
28      catch ( FormatException *error ) {
29         throw new Exception( S"Exception occurred in Method3",
30            error );
31      }
32   } // end method Method3
```

Fig. 8.4   Properties class method definitions.

```
1    // Fig. 8.5: PropertiesTest.cpp
2    // PropertiesTest demonstrates stack unwinding.
3
4    #include "Properties.h"
5
6    // entry point for application
7    int main()
8    {
9
```

Fig. 8.5   PropertiesTest demonstrates stack unwinding. (Part 1 of 3.)

```
10        // calls Method1, any Exception it generates will be
11        // caught in the catch handler that follows
12        try {
13            Properties::Method1();
14        }
15
16        // output string representation of Exception, then
17        // output values of InnerException, Message,
18        // and StackTrace properties
19        catch( Exception *exception ) {
20            Console::WriteLine(
21                S"exception->ToString(): \n{0}\n",
22                exception->ToString() );
23
24            Console::WriteLine( S"exception->Message: \n{0}\n",
25                exception->Message );
26
27            Console::WriteLine( S"exception->StackTrace: \n{0}\n",
28                exception->StackTrace );
29
30            Console::WriteLine(
31                S"exception->InnerException: \n{0}",
32                exception->InnerException );
33        } // end catch
34
35        return 0;
36    } // end function main
```

```
exception->ToString():
System.Exception: Exception occurred in Method3 ---> System.FormatEx-
ception: Input string was not in a correct format.
   at System.Number.ParseInt32(String s, NumberStyles style,
      NumberFormatInfo info)
   at System.Convert.ToInt32(String value)
   at Properties.Method3() in
      c:\books\2002\vcppfep\vcppfep_examples\ch08\
      fig08_05-07\propertiestest\properties.cpp:line 24
   --- End of inner exception stack trace ---
   at Properties.Method3() in c:\books\2002\vcppfep\
      vcppfep_examples\ch08\fig08_05-07\propertiestest\
      properties.cpp:line 30
   at Properties.Method2() in c:\books\2002\vcpfep\
      vcppfep_examples\ch08\fig08_05-07\propertiestest\
      properties.cpp:line 15
   at Properties.Method1() in c:\books\2002\vcpfep\
     vcppfep_examples\ch08\fig08_05-07\propertiestest\
      properties.cpp:line 9
   at main() in c:\books\2002\vcppfep\vcppfep_examples\ch08\
      fig08_05-07\propertiestest\propertiestest.cpp:line 13

exception->Message:
Exception occurred in Method3
```

Continued at the top of the next page

Fig. 8.5   **PropertiesTest** demonstrates stack unwinding. (Part 2 of 3.)

```
                                    Continued from the previous page
exception->StackTrace:
   at Properties.Method3() in c:\books\2002\vcppfep\
      vcppfep_examples\ch08\fig08_05-07\propertiestest\
      properties.cpp:line 30
   at Properties.Method2() in c:\books\2002\vcppfep\
      vcppfep_examples\ch08\fig08_05-07\propertiestest\
      properties.cpp:line 15
   at Properties.Method1() in c:\books\2002\vcppfep\
      vcppfep_examples\ch08\fig08_05-07\propertiestest\
      properties.cpp:line 9
   at main() in c:\books\2002\vcppfep\vcppfep_examples\ch08\
      fig08_05-07\propertiestest\propertiestest.cpp:line 13

exception->InnerException:
System.FormatException: Input string was not in a correct format.
   at System.Number.ParseInt32(String s, NumberStyles style,
      NumberFormatInfo info)
   at System.Convert.ToInt32(String value)
   at Properties.Method3() in c:\books\2002\vcppfep\
      vcppfep_examples\ch08\fig08_05-07\propertiestest\
      properties.cpp:line 24
```

Fig. 8.5   **PropertiesTest** demonstrates stack unwinding. (Part 3 of 3.)

Program execution begins with the invocation of **main** (Fig. 8.5), which becomes the first method on the method call stack. Line 13 of the **try** block in **main** invokes **Method1** (lines 7–10 of Fig. 8.4), which becomes the second method on the stack. If **Method1** throws an exception, the **catch** handler at lines 19–33 (Fig. 8.5) handles the exception and outputs information about the exception that occurred. Line 9 of **Method1** (Fig. 8.4) invokes **Method2** (lines 13–16), which becomes the third method on the stack. Then line 15 of **Method2** invokes **Method3** (defined at lines 19–32), which becomes the fourth method on the stack.

Testing and Debugging Tip 8.7

When reading a stack trace, start from the top of the stack trace and read the error message first. Then, read the remainder of the stack trace, looking for the first line that indicates code that you wrote in your program. Normally, this is the location that caused the exception.

At this point, the method call stack for the program is

```
Method3
Method2
Method1

main
```

with the last method called (**Method3**) at the top and the first method called (**main**) at the bottom. The **try** block (lines 23–25 of Fig. 8.4) in **Method3** invokes method **Convert::ToInt32** (line 24) and attempts to convert a string to an **int**. At this point, **Convert::ToInt32** becomes the fifth and final method on the call stack.

The argument to **Convert::ToInt32** is not in integer format, so line 24 throws a **FormatException** that is caught at line 28 in **Method3**. The exception terminates the call to **Convert::ToInt32**, so the method is removed from the method-call stack. The **catch** handler creates an **Exception** object, then throws it. The first argument to the **Exception** constructor is the custom error message for our example, "**Exception occurred in Method3**." The second argument is the **InnerException** object—the **FormatException** that was caught. Note that the **StackTrace** for this new exception object will reflect the point at which the exception was thrown (line 29). Now, **Method3** terminates, because the exception thrown in the **catch** handler is not caught in the method body. Thus, control will be returned to the statement that invoked **Method3** in the prior method in the call stack (**Method2**). This removes or *unwinds* **Method3** from the method-call stack.

Good Programming Practice 8.3

When catching and rethrowing an exception, provide additional debugging information in the rethrown exception. To do so, create an **Exception** *object with more specific debugging information and pass the original caught exception to the new exception object's constructor to initialize the* **InnerException** *property.*[9]

When control returns to line 15 in **Method2**, the CLR determines that line 15 is not in a **try** block. Therefore, the exception cannot be caught in **Method2**, and **Method2** terminates. This unwinds **Method2** from the method-call stack and returns control to line 9 in **Method1**. Here again, line 9 is not in a **try** block, so the exception cannot be caught in **Method1**. The method terminates and unwinds from the call stack, returning control to line 13 in **main** (Fig. 8.5), which is in a **try** block. The **try** block in **main** expires, and the **catch** handler at lines 19–33 catches the exception. The **catch** handler uses method **ToString** and properties **Message**, **StackTrace** and **InnerException** to produce the output. Note that stack unwinding continues until either a **catch** handler catches the exception or the program terminates.

The first block of output (reformatted for readability) in Fig. 8.5 shows the exception's string representation returned from method **ToString**. This begins with the name of the exception class followed by the **Message** property value. The next eight lines show the string representation of the **InnerException** object. The remainder of that block of output shows the **StackTrace** for the exception thrown in **Method3**. Note that the **StackTrace** represents the state of the method-call stack at the throw point of the exception, not at the point where the exception eventually is caught. Each of the **StackTrace** lines that begins with "**at**" represents a method on the call stack. These lines indicate the method in which the exception occurred, the file in which that method resides and the line number in the file. Also, note that the stack trace includes the inner-exception stack trace.

The next block of output (two lines) simply displays the **Message** property (**Exception occurred in Method3**) of the exception thrown in **Method3**.

The third block of output displays the **StackTrace** property of the exception thrown in **Method3**. Note that the **StackTrace** property includes the stack trace starting from

9. "Best Practices for Handling Exceptions," *.NET Framework Developer's Guide*, Visual Studio .NET Online Help. **<ms-help://MS.VSCC/MS.MSDNVS/cpguide/html/ cpconbestpracticesforhandlingexceptions.htm>**

line 29 in **Method3**, because that is the point at which the **Exception** object was created and thrown. The stack trace always begins from the exception's throw point.

Finally, the last block of output displays the **ToString** representation of the **Inner-Exception** property, which includes the namespace and class names of that exception object, its **Message** property and its **StackTrace** property.

8.7 Programmer-Defined Exception Classes

In many cases, programmers can use existing exception classes from the .NET Framework to indicate exceptions that occur in their programs. However, in some cases, programmers may wish to create exception types that are more specific to the problems that occur in their programs. *Programmer-defined exception classes* should derive directly or indirectly from class **ApplicationException** of namespace **System**.

Good Programming Practice 8.4

Associating each type of malfunction with an appropriately named exception class improves program clarity.

Software Engineering Observation 8.10

Before creating programmer-defined exception classes, investigate the existing exception classes in the .NET Framework to determine whether an appropriate exception type already exists.

Software Engineering Observation 8.11

Programmers should create exception classes only if they need to catch and handle the new exceptions differently from other existing exception types.

Software Engineering Observation 8.12

Always catch any exception class that you create and throw.

Good Programming Practice 8.5

Only handle one problem per exception class. Never overload an exception class to deal with several exceptions.

Good Programming Practice 8.6

Use significant and meaningful names for exception classes.

Figures 8.6–8.8 demonstrate defining and using a programmer-defined exception class. Class **NegativeNumberException** (Fig. 8.6–Fig. 8.7) is a programmer-defined exception class representing exceptions that occur when a program performs an illegal operation on a negative number, such as the square root of a negative number.

```
1   // Fig. 8.6: NegativeNumberException.h
2   // NegativeNumberException represents exceptions caused by illegal
3   // operations performed on negative numbers.
4
5   #pragma once
6
7   #using <mscorlib.dll>
8   #using <system.dll>
9
10  using namespace System;
11
12  // NegativeNumberException represents exceptions caused by
13  // illegal operations performed on negative numbers
14  public __gc class NegativeNumberException
15     : public ApplicationException
16  {
17  public:
18     NegativeNumberException();
19     NegativeNumberException( String * );
20     NegativeNumberException( String *, Exception * );
21  }; // end class NegativeNumberException
```

Fig. 8.6 **ApplicationException** subclass thrown when a program performs illegal operations on negative numbers.

```
1   // Fig. 8.7: NegativeNumberException.cpp
2   // Method definitions for class NegativeNumberException.
3
4   #include "NegativeNumberException.h"
5
6   // default constructor
7   NegativeNumberException::NegativeNumberException()
8      : ApplicationException( S"Illegal operation for "
9      S"a negative number" )
10  {
11  }
12
13  // constructor for customizing error message
14  NegativeNumberException::NegativeNumberException(
15     String *message ) : ApplicationException( message )
16  {
17  }
18
19  // constructor for customizing error message and
20  // specifying inner exception object
21  NegativeNumberException::NegativeNumberException(
22     String *message, Exception *inner )
23     : ApplicationException( message, inner )
24  {
25  }
```

Fig. 8.7 **NegativeNumberException** class method definitions.

According to Microsoft,[10] programmer-defined exceptions should extend class **ApplicationException**, should have a class name that ends with "Exception" and should define three constructors—a default constructor, a constructor that receives a string argument (the error message) and a constructor that receives a string argument and an **Exception** argument (the error message and the inner-exception object).

NegativeNumberExceptions most likely occur during arithmetic operations, so it seems logical to derive class **NegativeNumberException** from class **ArithmeticException**. However, class **ArithmeticException** derives from class **SystemException**—the category of exceptions thrown by the CLR. **ApplicationException** specifically is the base class for exceptions thrown by a user program, not by the CLR.

Figure 8.8 demonstrates our programmer-defined exception class. The application enables the user to input a numeric value, then invokes function **FindSquareRoot** (lines 44–54) to calculate the square root of that value. For this purpose, **FindSquare-Root** invokes class **Math**'s *Sqrt* method, which receives a positive **double** value as its argument. If the argument is negative, method **Sqrt** normally returns constant **NaN**—"not a number"—from class **Double**. In this program, we would like to prevent the user from calculating the square root of a negative number. If the numeric value received from the user is negative, **FindSquareRoot** throws a **NegativeNumberException** (lines 49–50). Otherwise, **FindSquareRoot** invokes class **Math**'s **Sqrt** method to compute the square root.

```cpp
1    // Fig. 8.8: SquareRoot.cpp
2    // Demonstrating a programmer-defined exception class.
3
4    #using <mscorlib.dll>
5    #using <system.windows.forms.dll>
6
7    using namespace System;
8    using namespace System::Windows::Forms;
9
10   #include "NegativeNumberException.h"
11
12   double FindSquareRoot( double );
13
14   // obtain user input, convert to double and calculate
15   // square root
16   int main()
17   {
18
19      // catch any NegativeNumberExceptions thrown
20      try {
21         Console::Write( S"Please enter a number: " );
22
```

Fig. 8.8   **FindSquareRoot** function throws exception if error occurs when calculating square root. (Part 1 of 2.)

10. "Best Practices for Handling Exceptions," *.NET Framework Developer's Guide*, Visual Studio .NET Online Help. **<ms-help://MS.VSCC/MS.MSDNVS/cpguide/html/ cpconbestpracticesforhandlingexceptions.htm>**

```
23          double result =
24              FindSquareRoot( Double::Parse( Console::ReadLine() ) );
25
26          Console::WriteLine( result );
27      }
28
29      // process invalid number format
30      catch ( FormatException *notInteger ) {
31          Console::WriteLine( notInteger->Message );
32      }
33
34      // display message if negative number input
35      catch ( NegativeNumberException *error ) {
36          Console::WriteLine( error->Message );
37      }
38
39      return 0;
40  } // end function main
41
42  // computes the square root of its parameter; throws
43  // NegativeNumberException if parameter is negative
44  double FindSquareRoot( double operand )
45  {
46
47      // if negative operand, throw NegativeNumberException
48      if ( operand < 0 )
49          throw new NegativeNumberException(
50              S"Square root of negative number not permitted" );
51
52      // compute the square root
53      return Math::Sqrt( operand );
54  } // end function FindSquareRoot
```

```
Please enter a number: 33
5.74456264653803
```

```
Please enter a number: hello
Input string was not in a correct format.
```

```
Please enter a number: -12.45
Square root of negative number not permitted
```

Fig. 8.8   **FindSquareRoot** function throws exception if error occurs when calculating square root. (Part 2 of 2.)

The **try** block (lines 20–27) attempts to invoke **FindSquareRoot** with the value input by the user. If the user input is not a valid number, a **FormatException** occurs, and the **catch** handler at lines 30–32 processes the exception. If the user inputs a negative number, method **FindSquareRoot** throws a **NegativeNumberException** (lines 49–50). The **catch** handler at lines 35–37 catches and handles that exception.

8.8 Summary

An exception is an indication of a problem that occurs during a program's execution. Exception handling enables programmers to create applications that can resolve exceptions, often allowing a program to continue execution as if no problems were encountered. Exception handling enables programmers to write clear, robust and more fault-tolerant programs. Exception handling enables the programmer to remove error-handling code from the "main line" of the program's execution. This improves program clarity and enhances modifiability. .NET exception handling is designed to process synchronous errors (e.g., out-of-range array subscripts, arithmetic overflow, division by zero, invalid method parameters and memory exhaustion) and asynchronous events, such as disk-I/O completions.

When a method called in a program or the CLR detects a problem, the method or CLR throws an exception. The point in the program at which an exception occurs is called the throw point. There is no guarantee that there will be an exception handler to process that kind of exception. If there is, the exception will be caught and handled.

A **try** block consists of keyword **try** followed by braces (**{}**) that delimit a block of code in which exceptions could occur. Immediately following the **try** block are zero or more **catch** handlers. Each **catch** specifies in parentheses an exception parameter representing the exception type the **catch** can handle. If an exception parameter includes an optional parameter name, the **catch** handler can use that parameter name to interact with a caught exception object. There can be one parameterless **catch** handler that catches all exception types. After the last **catch** handler, an optional **__finally** block contains code that always executes, regardless of whether an exception occurs.

MC++ uses the termination model of exception handling. If an exception occurs in a **try** block, the block expires and program control transfers to the first **catch** handler following the **try** block that can process the type of exception that occurred. The appropriate handler is the first one in which the thrown exception's type matches, or is derived from, the exception type specified by the **catch** handler's exception parameter. If no exceptions occur in a **try** block, the CLR ignores the exception handlers for that block. If no exceptions occur or if an exception is caught and handled, the program resumes execution with the next statement after the **try/catch/__finally** sequence. If an exception occurs in a statement that is not in a **try** block, the method containing that statement terminates immediately—a process called stack unwinding.

The exception-handling mechanism allows only objects of class **Exception** and its derived classes to be thrown and caught. Class **Exception** of namespace **System** is the base class of the .NET Framework exception hierarchy. Exceptions are objects of classes that inherit directly or indirectly from class **Exception**.

Graphical User Interface Concepts: Part 1

Objectives

- To understand the design principles of graphical user interfaces.
- To understand, use and create events.
- To understand the namespaces containing graphical user interface components and event-handling classes and interfaces.
- To create graphical user interfaces.
- To create and manipulate buttons, labels, lists, textboxes and panels.
- To be able to use mouse and keyboard events.

... the wisest prophets make sure of the event first.
Horace Walpole

...The user should feel in control of the computer; not the other way around. This is achieved in applications that embody three qualities: responsiveness, permissiveness, and consistency.
Inside Macintosh, Volume 1
Apple Computer, Inc. 1985

All the better to see you with my dear.
The Big Bad Wolf to Little Red Riding Hood

9.1 Introduction

A *graphical user interface (GUI)* allows users to interact with a program visually. A GUI (pronounced "GOO-EE") gives a program a distinctive "look" and "feel." By providing different applications with a consistent set of intuitive user-interface components, GUIs allow users to spend less time trying to remember which keystroke sequences perform what functions and spend more time using the program in a productive manner.

Look-and-Feel Observation 9.1

Consistent user interfaces enable users to learn new applications faster.

As an example of a GUI, Fig. 9.1 contains an Internet Explorer window with some of its *GUI components* labeled. In the window, there is a *menu bar* containing *menus*, including **File**, **Edit**, **View**, **Favorites**, **Tools** and **Help**. Below the menu bar is a set of *buttons*; each has a defined task in Internet Explorer. Below the buttons is a *textbox,* in which the user can type the location of a World Wide Web site to visit. To the left of the textbox is a *label* that indicates the textbox's purpose. On the far right and bottom there are *scrollbars*. Scrollbars are used when there is more information in a window than can be displayed at once. By moving the scrollbars back and forth, the user can view different portions of the Web page. The menus, buttons, textboxes, labels and scrollbars are part of Internet Explorer's GUI. They form a user-friendly interface through which the user interacts with the Internet Explorer Web browser.

Button   Label   Menu   Menu bar   Textbox   Scrollbar

Fig. 9.1   Sample Internet Explorer window with GUI components.

GUIs are built from *GUI components*. A GUI component is an object with which the user interacts via the mouse or keyboard. Several common .NET GUI component classes are listed in Fig. 9.2. In the sections that follow, we discuss these GUI components in detail. In the next chapter, we discuss more advanced GUI components.

Control	Description
Label	An area in which icons or uneditable text can be displayed.
TextBox	An area in which the user inputs data from the keyboard. The area also can display information.
Button	An area that triggers an event when clicked.
CheckBox	A GUI control that is either selected or not selected.
ComboBox	A drop-down list of items from which the user can make a selection, by clicking an item in the list or by typing into a box, if permitted.
ListBox	An area in which a list of items is displayed from which the user can make a selection by clicking once on any element. Multiple elements can be selected.
Panel	A container in which components can be placed.

Fig. 9.2   Some basic GUI components. (Part 1 of 2.)

Control	Description
HScrollBar	Allows the user to access a range of values that cannot normally fit in its container horizontally.
VScrollBar	Allows the user to access a range of values that cannot normally fit in its container vertically.

Fig. 9.2   Some basic GUI components. (Part 2 of 2.)

9.2 Windows Forms

Windows Forms (also called *WinForms*) create GUIs for programs. A form is a graphical element that appears on the desktop. A form can be a dialog, an *SDI window* (*single document interface window*) or an *MDI window* (*multiple document interface window*, discussed in Chapter 10, Graphical User Interface Concepts: Part 2). A *control*, such as a button or label, is a component with a graphical part.

When interacting with windows, we say that the *active window* has the *focus*. The active window is the frontmost window and has a highlighted title bar. A window becomes the active window when the user clicks somewhere inside it. When a window has focus, the operating system directs user input from the keyboard and mouse to that application.

The form acts as a *container* for components and controls. Controls must be added to the form using code. When the user interacts with a control by using the mouse or keyboard, events (discussed in Section 9.3) are generated, and *event handlers* process those events. Events typically cause something to happen in response. For example, clicking the **OK** button in a **MessageBox** generates an event. An event handler in class **MessageBox** closes the **MessageBox** in response to this event.

Each .NET Framework class we present in this chapter is in the ***System::Windows::Forms*** *namespace*. Class **Form**, the basic window used by Windows applications, is fully qualified as **System::Windows::Forms::Form**. Likewise, class **Button** is actually **System::Windows::Forms::Button**.

The general design process for creating Windows applications requires creating a Windows Form, setting its properties, adding controls, setting their properties and implementing the event handlers. This must all be done using code in contrast to the drag and drop method available in Visual Basic .NET and C#. Figure 9.3 lists common **Form** properties and events.

Form Properties and Events	Description / Delegate and Event Arguments
Common Properties	
AcceptButton	Which button will be clicked when *Enter* is pressed.

Fig. 9.3   Common **Form** properties and events. (Part 1 of 2.)

Form Properties and Events	Description / Delegate and Event Arguments
Common Properties (Cont.)	
`AutoScroll`	Whether scrollbars appear when needed (if data fill more than one screen).
`CancelButton`	Button that is clicked when the *Escape* key is pressed.
`FormBorderStyle`	Border of the form (e.g., **none**, **single**, **3D**, **sizable**).
`Font`	Font of text displayed on the form, as well as the default font of controls added to the form.
`Text`	Text in the form's title bar.
Common Methods	
`Close`	Closes form and releases all resources. A closed form cannot be reopened.
`Hide`	Hides form (does not release resources).
`Show`	Displays a hidden form.
Common Events	*(Delegate **EventHandler**, event arguments **EventArgs**)*
`Load`	Occurs before a form is shown.

Fig. 9.3   Common **Form** properties and events. (Part 2 of 2.)

9.3 Event-Handling Model

GUIs are *event driven* (i.e., they generate *events* when the program's user interacts with the GUI). Typical interactions include moving the mouse, clicking the mouse, clicking a button, typing in a textbox, selecting an item from a menu and closing a window. Event handlers are methods that process events and perform tasks. For example, consider a form that changes color when a button is clicked. When clicked, the button generates an event and passes it to the event handler, and the event-handler code changes the form's color.

Each control that can generate events has an associated delegate that defines the signature for that control's event handlers. Recall from Chapter 7, Object-Oriented Programming: Polymorphism, that delegates are objects that reference methods. Event delegates are *multicast* (class **MulticastDelegate**)—they contain lists of method references. Each method must have the same *signature* (i.e., the same list of parameters). In the event-handling model, delegates act as intermediaries between objects that generate events and methods that handle those events (Fig. 9.4).

Software Engineering Observation 9.1

*Delegates enable classes to specify methods that will not be named or implemented until the class is instantiated. This is extremely helpful in creating event handlers. For instance, the creator of the **Form** class does not need to name or define the method that will be invoked when a control is clicked. Using delegates, the class can specify when such an event handler would be called. The programmers that create their own forms then can name and define this event handler. As long as it has been registered with the proper delegate, the method will be called at the proper time.*

Fig. 9.4   Event-handling model using delegates.

Once an event is raised, every method that the delegate references is called. Every method in the delegate must have the same signature, because they are all passed the same information.

9.3.1 Basic Event Handling

Figures 9.5–9.7 introduce our first Windows application example and basic event handling. In most cases, we do not have to create our own events. Instead, we can handle the events generated by .NET controls such as buttons and textboxes. These controls already have delegates for every event they can raise. The programmer creates the event handler and registers it with the delegate. In the following example, we create a form that displays a message box when clicked.

In this example, the form will take some action when clicked. We create an event handler (lines 33–36 of Fig. 9.6). The event handler's and the event delegates's signatures must match. This event handler is passed two object pointers. The first is a pointer to the object that raised the event (**sender**), and the second is a pointer to an event arguments object (**e**). Argument **e** is of type **EventArgs** (namespace **System**). Class **EventArgs** is the base class for objects that contain event information.

The format of this event-handling method is

```
void ControlName_EventName( Object *sender, EventArgs *e )
{
    event-handling code
}
```

where the name of the event handler is by default the name of the control, followed by an underscore and the name of the event. Event handlers have return type **void**. The differences between the various **EventArgs** classes are discussed in the following sections.

 Good Programming Practice 9.1

Use the event-handler naming convention ControlName_EventName *to keep methods organized. This tells a user which event a method handles, and for which control.*

This is the method that will be called when the form is clicked. As a response, we will have the form display a message box. To do this, insert the statement

```
MessageBox::Show( S"Form was pressed" );
```

into the event handler to get

```
void FormName_Click( Object *sender, EventArgs *e )
{
    MessageBox::Show( S"Form was pressed" );
}
```

After creating the event handler, we must *register* it with the delegate, which contains a list of event handlers to call. Registering an event handler with a delegate involves adding the event handler to the delegate's invocation list. Controls have a *delegate* for each of their events—the delegate has the same name as the event. For example, if we are handling event *EventName* for object **myControl**, then the delegate pointer is **myControl->***Event-Name*. Line 27 registers an event handler for the **Click** event. The **Click** event is triggered when a control is clicked (e.g., selected with the mouse pointer).:

```
this->Click += new EventHandler( this, MyForm_Click );
```

The first argument to the **EventHandler** constructor is an object pointer because method **MyForm_Click** is an instance method of class **MyForm**. This parameter specifies the object that receives the method call. If **MyForm_Click** were a **static** method, the first parameter to the constructor would be **0**. The second argument specifies the method to call.

The lefthand side is the delegate **Click**. **this** points to an object of class **MyForm**. The delegate pointer is initially empty—we must assign to it an object pointer (the right-hand side). We must create a new delegate object for each event handler. We create a new delegate object by writing

```
new EventHandler( this, methodName )
```

which returns a delegate object initialized with method *methodName*. The *methodName* is the name of the event handler, in our case it is **MyForm_Click**. The **+=** operator adds an **EventHandler** delegate to the current delegate's invocation list. Because the delegate pointer is initially empty, registering the first event handler creates a delegate object. In general, to register an event handler, write

```
objectName->EventName += new EventHandler( this, MyEventHandler );
```

We can add more event handlers using similar statements. *Event multicasting* is the ability to have multiple handlers for one event. Each event handler is called when the event occurs, but the order in which the event handlers are called is indeterminate. Use the **-=** operator to remove an event handler from a delegate object.

Common Programming Error 9.1

Assuming that multiple event handlers registered for the same event are called in a particular order can lead to logic errors. If the order is important, register the first event handler and have it call the others in order, passing the sender and event arguments.

Software Engineering Observation 9.2

*Events for prepackaged .NET components usually have consistent naming schemes. If the event is named **EventName**, its delegate is **EventNameEventHandler**, and the event arguments class is **EventNameEventArgs**. However, events that use class **EventArgs** use delegate **EventHandler**.*

To review, the information needed to register an event is the **EventArgs** class (a parameter for the event handler) and the **EventHandler** delegate (to register the event handler). To find more information about a particular type of event, search the help documentation for *ClassName* **class**; the events will be described with the class's other members. In particular,

```
ms-help://MS.VSCC/MS.MSDNVS/cpref/html/frlrfSystemWindows-
Forms.htm
```

contains links to information about the **System::Windows::Forms** namespace classes. Select the class name and then the link to the class's members to see more information
about events associated with that class.

We can now compile and execute the program, which appears in Fig. 9.7. Whenever
the form is clicked, a message box appears.

We now discuss the details of the program. Class **myForm** inherits from class **Form**
(which represents a form) in the .NET Framework Class Library's **System::Win-
dows::Form** namespace (line 17 of Fig. 9.5). A key benefit of inheriting from class
Form is that someone else has previously defined "what it means to be a form." The Windows operating system expects every window (e.g., form) to have certain attributes and
behaviors. However, because class **Form** already provides those capabilities, programmers
do not need to "reinvent the wheel" by defining all those capabilities themselves. Class
Form has over 400 methods! Extending from class **Form** enables programmers to create
forms quickly.

The constructor (lines 6–9 of Fig. 9.6) calls method **InitializeComponent** (lines
11–31) to set up the form. Line 15 calls *Control* class method *SuspendLayout* to sup-
press (i.e., ignore) any layout events while the programmer changes the configuration of
controls. Class **Control** is the base class for components with visual representations (i.e.,
controls). Class **Form** and the classes listed in Fig. 9.2 inherit directly or indirectly from
class **Control**.

```
1   // Fig. 9.5: SimpleEvent.h
2   // MyForm class header file.
3
4   #pragma once
5
6   #using <mscorlib.dll>
7
8   // assemblies for Windows Forms applications
9   #using <system.dll>
10  #using <system.drawing.dll>
11  #using <system.windows.forms.dll>
12
13  using namespace System;
14  using namespace System::Windows::Forms;
15
16  // demonstrates a simple event handler
17  public __gc class MyForm : public Form
18  {
19  public:
20     MyForm();
21
22  private:
23     void InitializeComponent();
24     void MyForm_Click( Object *, EventArgs * );
25  }; // end class MyForm
```

Fig. 9.5   **SimpleEvent** class demonstrates event handling.

```
1   // Fig. 9.6: SimpleEvent.cpp
2   // Creating an event handler.
3
4   #include "SimpleEvent.h"
5
6   MyForm::MyForm()
7   {
8       InitializeComponent();
9   }
10
11  void MyForm::InitializeComponent()
12  {
13
14      // suspend layout event handling
15      this->SuspendLayout();
16
17      // set base size for autoscaling of form
18      this->AutoScaleBaseSize = Drawing::Size( 5, 13 );
19
20      // set size of form's client area
21      this->ClientSize = Drawing::Size( 200, 200 );
22
23      // set title of form
24      this->Text = S"SimpleEventExample";
25
26      // bind event handler
27      this->Click += new EventHandler( this, MyForm_Click );
28
29      // layout changes made
30      this->ResumeLayout();
31  } // end method InitializeComponent
32
33  void MyForm::MyForm_Click( Object *sender, EventArgs *e )
34  {
35      MessageBox::Show( S"Form was pressed" );
36  }
```

Fig. 9.6   `SimpleEvent` class method definitions.

Form property **AutoScaleBaseSize** (line 18) sets the base size of the form for *autoscaling*. Autoscaling refers to the form's ability to size itself and its components based on its current font. Line 10 (Fig. 9.5) enables the programmer to access all the types defined in the **System::Drawing** namespace. This namespace contains the **Size** structure, a value type. A **Size** object can be used to set a component's height and width in pixels (line 18). Line 21 sets the form's *client size* (i.e., the size of the form excluding the title bar and borders). Line 24 sets the caption of the form that appears in the title bar. Line 30 invokes **Control** class method **ResumeLayout**, enabling the application to handle layout events again.

Figure 9.7 presents the driver program for our Windows application. Function *Win-Main* (line 6) is the entry point for GUI programs. The function associates a *message loop* with the current application, which will be handled in this application by class **Form**. Keyword **__stdcall** specifies that the function follows the *standard calling convention* (i.e., it tells the compiler how to pass arguments, how to generate the function's name, etc.).

```
1   // Fig. 9.7: SimpleEventTest.cpp
2   // Demonstrating an event handler.
3
4   #include "SimpleEvent.h"
5
6   int __stdcall WinMain()
7   {
8      Application::Run( new MyForm() );
9
10     return 0;
11  } // end function WinMain
```

Fig. 9.7   Event-handling demonstration.

Namespace **System::Windows::Form** includes class *Application*. Class **Application** contains **static** methods used to managed Windows applications. Method **Run** (line 8) displays the Windows form and starts the message loop. Windows applications communicate using *messages*—event descriptions. The message loop places each message on a queue and removes one at a time to forward it to the appropriate handler. The .NET Framework hides the details of complex message processing from programmers for their convenience. Method **Run** also adds an event handler for the **Closed** event, which occurs when the user closes the window or the program calls method **Close**.

9.4 Control Properties and Layout

This section overviews properties that are common to many controls. Controls derive from class **Control** (namespace **System::Windows::Forms**). Figure 9.8 contains a list of common properties and events for class **Control**. The **Text** property specifies the text that appears on a control, which may vary depending on the context. For example, the text of a Windows Form is its title bar, and the text of a button appears on its face. The *Focus* method transfers the focus to a control. When the focus is on a control, it becomes the active control. When the *Tab* key is pressed, the *TabIndex* property determines the order in which controls are given focus. This is helpful for users with disabilities who cannot use a mouse and for the user who enters information in many different locations—the user can enter information and quickly select the next control by pressing the *Tab* key. The *Enabled* property indicates whether the control can be used. Programs can set property **Enabled** to false when an option is unavailable to the user. In most cases, the control's text will appear gray (rather than black), when a control is disabled. Without having to disable a control, the control can be hidden from the user by setting the *Visible* property to **false** or by calling method **Hide**. When a control's **Visible** property is set to **false**, the control still exists, but it is not shown on the form.

Visual Studio .NET allows the programmer to *anchor* and *dock* controls, which helps to specify the layout of controls inside a container (such as a form). Anchoring allows controls to stay a fixed distance from the sides of the container, even when the control is resized. Docking allows controls to extend themselves along the sides of their containers.

Class Control Properties and Methods	Description
Common Properties	
BackColor	Background color of the control.
BackgroundImage	Background image of the control.
Enabled	Whether the control is enabled (i.e., if the user can interact with it). A disabled control will still be displayed, but "grayed-out"—portions of the control will become gray.
Focused	Whether a control has focus.
Font	Font used to display control's **Text**.
ForeColor	Foreground color of the control. This is usually the color used to display the control's **Text** property.
TabIndex	Tab order of the control. When the *Tab* key is pressed, the focus is moved to controls in increasing tab order. This order can be set by the programmer if the **TabStop** property is true.
TabStop	If **true** (the default value), user can use the *Tab* key to select the control.
Text	Text associated with the control. The location and appearance varies with the type of control.
TextAlign	The alignment of the text on the control. One of three horizontal positions (left, center or right) and one of three vertical positions (top, middle or bottom).
Visible	Whether the control is visible.
Common Methods	
Focus	Transfers the focus to the control.
Hide	Hides the control (equivalent to setting **Visible** to **false**).
Show	Shows the control (equivalent to setting **Visible** to **true**).

Fig. 9.8   **Control** class properties and methods.

A user may want a control to appear in a certain position (top, bottom, left or right) in a form even when that form is resized. The user can specify this by *anchoring* the control to a side (top, bottom, left or right). The control then maintains a fixed distance from the side to its parent container. In most cases, the parent container is a form; however, other controls can act as a parent container.

When parent containers are resized, all controls move. Unanchored controls move relative to their original position on the form, while anchored controls move so that they will be the same distance from each side that they are anchored to. When the form is resized, the anchored button moves so that it remains a constant distance from the top and left sides of the form (its parent). The unanchored button changes position as the form is resized.

Sometimes a programmer wants a control to span the entire side of the form, even when the form is resized. This is useful when we want one control to remain prevalent on the form, such as the status bar that might appear at the bottom of a program. *Docking* allows a control to spread itself along an entire side (left, right, top or bottom) of its parent container. When the parent is resized, the docked control resizes as well. The **Fill** dock option effectively docks the control to all sides of its parent, which causes it to fill its entire parent. Windows Forms contain property **DockPadding**, which sets the distance from docked controls to the edge of the form. The default value is zero, causing the controls to attach to the edge of the form. The control layout properties are summarized in Fig. 9.9.

The docking and anchoring options refer to the parent container, which may or may not be the form. (We learn about other parent containers later this chapter.) The minimum and maximum form sizes can be set using properties **MinimumSize** and **MaximumSize**, respectively. Both properties use the **Size** structure, which has properties **Height** and **Width**, specifying the size of the form. These properties allow the programmer to design the GUI layout for a given size range. To set a form to a fixed size, set its minimum and maximum size to the same value. *Duh*

Common Layout Properties	Description
Common Properties	
Anchor	Side of parent container at which to anchor control—values can be combined, such as **Top**, **Left**.
Dock	Side of parent container to dock control—values cannot be combined.
DockPadding (for containers)	Sets the dock spacing for controls inside the container. Default is zero, so controls appear flush against the side of the container.
Common Properties, con't.	
Location	Location of the upper left corner of the control, relative to its container.
Size	Size of the control. Takes a **Size** structure, which has properties **Height** and **Width**.
MinimumSize, **MaximumSize** (for Windows Forms)	The minimum and maximum size of the form.

Fig. 9.9   **Control** class layout properties.

Look-and-Feel Observation 9.2

Allow Windows forms to be resized—this enables users with limited screen space or multiple applications running at once to use the application more easily. Check that the GUI layout appears consistent for all permissible form sizes.

9.5 Labels, TextBoxes and Buttons

Labels provide text instructions or information about the program. Labels are defined with class **Label**, which derives from class **Control**. A **Label** displays *read-only text*, or text that the user cannot modify. Once labels are created, programs rarely change their contents. Figure 9.10 lists common **Label** properties.

A *textbox* (class **TextBox**) is an area in which text can be either input by the user from the keyboard or displayed. The programmer can also make a textbox read only. The user may read, select and copy text from a read-only textbox, but the user cannot alter the text. A *password textbox* is a **TextBox** that hides what the user entered. As the user types in characters, the password textbox displays only a certain character (usually *****). Altering the **PasswordChar** property of a textbox makes it a password textbox and sets the appropriate character to be displayed. Figure 9.11 lists the common properties and events of **TextBox**es.

Label Properties	Description / Delegate and Event Arguments
Common Properties	
Font	The font used by the text on the **Label**.
Text	The text to appear on the **Label**.
TextAlign	The alignment of the **Label**'s text on the control. One of three horizontal positions (**left**, **center** or **right**) and one of three vertical positions (**top**, **middle** or **bottom**).

Fig. 9.10   **Label** properties.

TextBox Properties and Events	Description / Delegate and Event Arguments
Common Properties	
AcceptsReturn	If **true**, pressing *Enter* creates a new line in textbox, if that that textbox spans multiple lines. If **false**, pressing *Enter* clicks the default button of the form.
Multiline	If **true**, textbox can span multiple lines. Default is **false**.
PasswordChar	Single character to display instead of typed text, making the **TextBox** a password box. If no character is specified, **Textbox** displays the typed text.

Fig. 9.11   **TextBox** properties and events. (Part 1 of 2.)

TextBox Properties and Events	Description / Delegate and Event Arguments
Common Properties (Cont.)	
ReadOnly	If **true**, **TextBox** has a gray background and its text cannot be edited. Default is **false**.
ScrollBars	For multiline textboxes, indicates which scrollbars appear (**none**, **horizontal**, **vertical** or **both**).
Text	The text to be displayed in the textbox.
Common Events	*(Delegate **EventHandler**, event arguments **EventArgs**)*
TextChanged	Raised when text changes in **TextBox** (the user added or deleted characters).

Fig. 9.11 **TextBox** properties and events. (Part 2 of 2.)

A *button* is a control that the user clicks to trigger a specific action. A program can use several other types of buttons, such as *checkboxes* and *radio buttons*. All the button types are derived from **ButtonBase** (namespace **System::Windows::Forms**), which defines common button features. In this section, we concentrate on class **Button**, which is often used to initiate a command. The other button types are covered in subsequent sections. The text on the face of a **Button** is called a *button label*. Figure 9.12 lists the common properties and events of **Button**s.

Look-and-Feel Observation 9.3

*Although **Label**s, **TextBox**es and other controls can respond to mouse-button clicks, **Button**s naturally convey this meaning. Use **Button**s (e.g., **OK**), rather than other types of controls, to initiate user actions.*

The program in Fig. 9.13–Fig. 9.15 uses a **TextBox**, a **Button** and a **Label**. The user enters text into a password box and clicks the **Button**. The text then appears in the **Label**. Normally, we would not display this text—the purpose of password textboxes is to hide the text being entered by the user from anyone who may be looking over a person's shoulder.

Button properties and events	Description / Delegate and Event Arguments
Common Properties	
Text	Text displayed on the **Button** face.
Common Events	*(Delegate **EventHandler**, event arguments **EventArgs**)*
Click	Raised when user clicks the control.

Fig. 9.12 **Button** properties and events.

```
1  // Fig. 9.13: LabelTextBoxButton.h
2  // LabelTextBoxButton class header file.
```

Fig. 9.13 Using a password field. (Part 1 of 2.)

```
3
4    #pragma once
5
6    #using <mscorlib.dll>
7    #using <system.dll>
8    #using <system.drawing.dll>
9    #using <system.windows.forms.dll>
10
11   using namespace System;
12   using namespace System::Windows::Forms;
13   using namespace System::Drawing;
14
15   // form that creates a password textbox and
16   // a label to display textbox contents
17   public __gc class LabelTextBoxButton : public Form
18   {
19   public:
20      LabelTextBoxButton();
21
22   private:
23      Button *displayPasswordButton;
24      Label *displayPasswordLabel;
25      TextBox *inputPasswordTextBox;
26      void InitializeComponent();
27      void displayPasswordButton_Click( Object *, EventArgs * );
28   }; // end class LabelTextBoxButton
```

Fig. 9.13 Using a password field. (Part 2 of 2.)

The constructor (lines 7–10 of Fig. 9.14) calls method **InitializeComponent** (line 9). Method **InitializeComponent** (lines 12–59) creates the components and controls in the form and sets their properties.

```
1    // Fig. 9.14: LabelTextBoxButton.cpp
2    // Using a Textbox, Label and Button to display
3    // the hidden text in a password field.
4
5    #include "LabelTextBoxButton.h"
6
7    LabelTextBoxButton::LabelTextBoxButton()
8    {
9       InitializeComponent();
10   }
11
12   void LabelTextBoxButton::InitializeComponent()
13   {
14      this->SuspendLayout();
15      this->AutoScaleBaseSize = Drawing::Size( 5, 13 );
16      this->ClientSize = Drawing::Size( 300, 130 );
17      this->Text = S"LabelTextBoxButtonTest";
18
```

Fig. 9.14 **LabelTextBoxButton** class method defintions. (Part 1 of 2.)

```
19       // instantiate button, textbox and label objects
20       this->displayPasswordButton = new Button();
21       this->inputPasswordTextBox = new TextBox();
22       this->displayPasswordLabel = new Label();
23
24       // button
25       this->displayPasswordButton->Location = Point( 115, 96 );
26       this->displayPasswordButton->Name =
27          S"displayPasswordButton";
28       this->displayPasswordButton->TabIndex = 1;
29       this->displayPasswordButton->Text = S"Show Me";
30
31       // associate button click with event handler
32       this->displayPasswordButton->Click +=
33          new EventHandler( this, displayPasswordButton_Click );
34
35       // textbox
36       this->inputPasswordTextBox->Location = Point( 16, 16 );
37       this->inputPasswordTextBox->Name = S"inputPasswordTextBox";
38       this->inputPasswordTextBox->PasswordChar = '*';
39       this->inputPasswordTextBox->Size = Drawing::Size( 264, 20 );
40       this->inputPasswordTextBox->TabIndex = 0;
41       this->inputPasswordTextBox->Text = S"";
42
43       // label
44       this->displayPasswordLabel->BorderStyle =
45          BorderStyle::Fixed3D;
46       this->displayPasswordLabel->Location = Point( 16, 48 );
47       this->displayPasswordLabel->Name = S"displayPasswordLabel";
48       this->displayPasswordLabel->Size = Drawing::Size( 264, 23 );
49       this->displayPasswordLabel->TabIndex = 2;
50
51       // display form
52       this->ClientSize = Drawing::Size( 292, 133 );
53       this->Controls->Add( displayPasswordLabel );
54       this->Controls->Add( inputPasswordTextBox );
55       this->Controls->Add( displayPasswordButton );
56       this->Name = S"LabelTextBoxButtonText";
57       this->Text = S"LabelTextBoxButtonTest";
58       this->ResumeLayout();
59    } // end method InitializeComponent
60
61    // display user input on label
62    void LabelTextBoxButton::displayPasswordButton_Click(
63       Object *sender, EventArgs *e )
64    {
65       displayPasswordLabel->Text = inputPasswordTextBox->Text;
66    }
```

Fig. 9.14 **LabelTextBoxButton** class method defintions. (Part 2 of 2.)

```
1    // Fig. 9.15: LabelTextBoxButtonTest.cpp
2    // Displaying the hidden text in a password field.
```

Fig. 9.15 Displaying the hidden text in a password field. (Part 1 of 2.)

```
3
4   #include "LabelTextBoxButton.h"
5
6   int __stdcall WinMain()
7   {
8      Application::Run( new LabelTextBoxButton() );
9
10     return 0;
11  } // end function WinMain
```

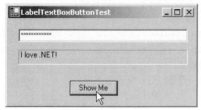 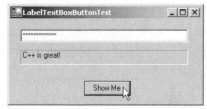

Fig. 9.15   Displaying the hidden text in a password field. (Part 2 of 2.)

The GUI contains a **Button**, a **Label** and a **TextBox** as controls of the form (lines 23–25 of Fig. 9.13). Lines 20–22 of Fig. 9.14 create the control objects and return pointers to them. Line 26 uses property **Location** (defined in namespace **System::Drawing**) to set the position of the **Button** control relative to the upper lefthand corner of the form (i.e., position (0,0)). The **Point** structure (defined in namespace **System::Drawing**) represents a pair of x- and y-coordinates. The ordered pair sets the position of the top left-hand corner of the control.

Once the components are positioned, we change their names by setting the **Name** property to **displayPasswordLabel**, **inputPasswordTextBox** and **display-PasswordButton**.

We set **displayPasswordButton**'s **Text** property to "**Show Me**" (line 29) and clear the **Text** of **inputPasswordTextBox** (line 41) so that it is initially blank when the program runs. The password character is set by assigning the asterisk character (*****) to the **PasswordChar** property (line 38). This property can take only one character.

The **BorderStyle** property of **displayPasswordLabel** is set to **Fixed3D**, to give our **Label** a three-dimensional appearance (lines 44–45). **Fixed3D** is a member of the **BorderStyle** enumeration (namespace **System::Windows::Forms**). An *enumeration* is a set of integer constants represented by identifiers. The members of enumeration **BorderStyle** are actually constants that have integer values; **Fixed3D** has the value **2**. However, we cannot replace **BorderStyle::Fixed3D** in line 45 with **2** because enumerations actually define types. The **BorderStyle** property of **dis-playPasswordLabel** has type **BorderStyle** and only accepts members of type **BorderStyle**.

Notice that we access enumeration values in the same way that we access static members of a class, using the scope resolution operator (**::**). Using enumerations rather than integer constants can make programs clearer. We demonstrate how to create enumerations in Chapter 13, Graphics and Multimedia.

Lines 53–55 add the label, textbox and button to the form. Class **Control**'s *Controls* property represents collection of controls in the parent control. Remember that class **Form** inherits indirectly from class **Control**. Each added control is a member of the **Control->ControlCollection** object assigned to the **Controls** property of the form. Class *Control::ControlCollection* includes method **Add**, which allows programmers to specify a **Control** object to insert into the collection.

Lines 32–33 add an event handler to the **Click** event, using the **EventHandler** delegate. This method, invoked whenever **displayPasswordButton** is clicked, displays **inputPasswordTextBox**'s text on **displayPasswordLabel**. Although **inputPasswordTextBox** displays all asterisks, it still retains its input text in its **Text** property. To show the text, we set **displayPasswordLabel**'s **Text** to **inputPasswordTextBox**'s **Text** (line 65). When **displayPasswordButton** is clicked, the **Click** event is triggered, and the event handler **displayPasswordButton_Click** runs (updating **displayPasswordLabel**).

9.6 GroupBoxes and Panels

*GroupBox*es and *Panel*s arrange components on a GUI. For example, buttons related to a particular task can be placed inside a **GroupBox** or **Panel**. All these buttons move together when the **GroupBox** or **Panel** is moved.

The main difference between the two classes is that **GroupBox**es can display a caption, and **Panel**s can have scrollbars. The scrollbars allow the user to view additional controls inside the **Panel** by scrolling the visible area. **GroupBox**es have thin borders by default, but **Panel**s can be set to have borders by changing their **BorderStyle** property.

Look-and-Feel Observation 9.4

Panels and GroupBoxes can contain other Panels and GroupBoxes.

Look-and-Feel Observation 9.5

Organize the GUI by anchoring and docking controls (of similar function) inside a Group-Box or Panel. The GroupBox or Panel then can be anchored or docked inside a form. This divides controls into functional "groups" that can be arranged easily.

To create a **GroupBox**, call the **GroupBox** constructor. Create new controls and use method **AddRange** to place them inside the **GroupBox**, causing them to become part of this class. These controls are added to the **GroupBox**'s **Controls** property. The **GroupBox**'s **Text** property determines its caption. The following tables list the common properties of **GroupBox**es (Fig. 9.16) and **Panel**s (Fig. 9.17).

GroupBox Properties	Description
Common Properties	
Controls	The controls that the **GroupBox** contains.

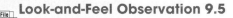

Fig. 9.16   **GroupBox** properties. (Part 1 of 2.)

GroupBox Properties	Description
Common Properties (Cont.)	
Text	Text displayed on the top portion of the **GroupBox** (its caption).

Fig. 9.16 **GroupBox** properties. (Part 2 of 2.)

Panel Properties	Description
Common Properties	
AutoScroll	Whether scrollbars appear when the **Panel** is too small to hold its controls. Default is **false**.
BorderStyle	Border of the **Panel** (default **None**; other options are **Fixed3D** and **FixedSingle**).
Controls	The controls that the **Panel** contains.

Fig. 9.17 **Panel** properties.

To create a **Panel**, call the **Panel** constructor. To enable the scrollbars, set the **Panel**'s **AutoScroll** property to **true**. If the **Panel** is resized and cannot hold its controls, scrollbars appear.

Look-and-Feel Observation 9.6

*Use **Panel**s with scrollbars to avoid cluttering a GUI and to reduce the GUI's size.*

The program in Fig. 9.18–Fig. 9.20 uses a **GroupBox** and a **Panel** to arrange buttons. These buttons change the text on a **Label**. Lines 13–14 (Fig. 9.19) initialize pointers to the two container controls—**mainGroupBox** and **mainPanel**. Method **Suspend-Layout** (lines 20–21) suppresses layout events for both containers and the main form.

```
1   // Fig. 9.18: GroupBoxPanel.h
2   // GroupBoxPanelExample class header file.
3
4   #pragma once
5
6   #using <mscorlib.dll>
7   #using <system.dll>
8   #using <system.drawing.dll>
9   #using <system.windows.forms.dll>
10
11  using namespace System;
12  using namespace System::Drawing;
13  using namespace System::Windows::Forms;
14
```

Fig. 9.18 **GroupBox** and **Panel** used to hold buttons. (Part 1 of 2.)

```
15   // form to display a groupbox versus a panel
16   public __gc class GroupBoxPanelExample : public Form
17   {
18   public:
19      GroupBoxPanelExample();
20
21   private:
22      Button *hiButton, *byeButton, *leftButton, *rightButton;
23      GroupBox *mainGroupBox;
24      Label *messageLabel;
25      Panel *mainPanel;
26      void InitializeComponent();
27      void hiButton_Click( Object *, EventArgs * );
28      void byeButton_Click( Object *, EventArgs * );
29      void leftButton_Click( Object *, EventArgs * );
30      void rightButton_Click( Object *, EventArgs * );
31   }; // end class GroupBoxPanelExample
```

Fig. 9.18   **GroupBox** and **Panel** used to hold buttons. (Part 2 of 2.)

```
1    // Fig. 9.19: GroupBoxPanel.cpp
2    // Using GroupBoxes and Panels to hold buttons.
3
4    #include "GroupBoxPanel.h"
5
6    GroupBoxPanelExample::GroupBoxPanelExample()
7    {
8       InitializeComponent();
9    }
10
11   void GroupBoxPanelExample::InitializeComponent()
12   {
13      this->mainGroupBox = new GroupBox();
14      this->mainPanel = new Panel();
15      this->messageLabel = new Label();
16      this->byeButton = new Button();
17      this->hiButton = new Button();
18      this->rightButton = new Button();
19      this->leftButton = new Button();
20      this->mainGroupBox->SuspendLayout();
21      this->mainPanel->SuspendLayout();
22      this->SuspendLayout();
23
24      // messageLabel
25      this->messageLabel->Location = Point( 24, 144 );
26      this->messageLabel->Name = S"messageLabel";
27      this->messageLabel->Size = Drawing::Size( 176, 32 );
28      this->messageLabel->TabIndex = 2;
29
30      // byeButton
31      this->byeButton->Location = Point( 96, 48 );
```

Fig. 9.19   **GroupBoxPanelExample** class method definitions. (Part 1 of 3.)

```
32      this->byeButton->Name = S"byeButton";
33      this->byeButton->Size = Drawing::Size( 72, 32 );
34      this->byeButton->TabIndex = 1;
35      this->byeButton->Text = S"Bye";
36
37      // register event handler
38      this->byeButton->Click += new EventHandler( this,
39         byeButton_Click );
40
41      // mainGroupBox
42      this->mainGroupBox->Controls->Add( byeButton );
43      this->mainGroupBox->Controls->Add( hiButton );
44      this->mainGroupBox->Location = Point( 24, 24 );
45      this->mainGroupBox->Name = S"mainGroupBox";
46      this->mainGroupBox->Size = Drawing::Size( 176, 104 );
47      this->mainGroupBox->Text = S"Main GroupBox";
48
49      // hiButton
50      this->hiButton->Location = Point( 8, 48 );
51      this->hiButton->Name = S"hiButton";
52      this->hiButton->Size = Drawing::Size( 72, 32 );
53      this->hiButton->TabIndex = 0;
54      this->hiButton->Text = S"Hi";
55      this->hiButton->Click += new EventHandler( this,
56         hiButton_Click );
57
58      // mainPanel
59      this->mainPanel->AutoScroll = true;
60      this->mainPanel->BorderStyle = BorderStyle::FixedSingle;
61      this->mainPanel->Controls->Add( rightButton );
62      this->mainPanel->Controls->Add( leftButton );
63      this->mainPanel->Location = Point( 24, 192 );
64      this->mainPanel->Name = S"mainPanel";
65      this->mainPanel->Size = Drawing::Size( 176, 112 );
66      this->mainPanel->TabIndex = 1;
67
68      // rightButton
69      this->rightButton->Location = Point( 264, 40 );
70      this->rightButton->Name = S"rightButton";
71      this->rightButton->Size = Drawing::Size( 80, 40 );
72      this->rightButton->TabIndex = 3;
73      this->rightButton->Text = S"Far Right";
74      this->rightButton->Click += new EventHandler( this,
75         rightButton_Click );
76
77      // leftButton
78      this->leftButton->Location = Point( 8, 40 );
79      this->leftButton->Name = S"leftButton";
80      this->leftButton->Size = Drawing::Size( 80, 40 );
81      this->leftButton->TabIndex = 2;
82      this->leftButton->Text = S"Far Left";
83      this->leftButton->Click += new EventHandler( this,
84         leftButton_Click );
85
```

Fig. 9.19 GroupBoxPanelExample class method definitions. (Part 2 of 3.)

```
86       // GroupBoxPanelExample
87       this->AutoScaleBaseSize = Drawing::Size( 5, 13 );
88       this->ClientSize = Drawing::Size( 224, 317 );
89       this->Controls->Add( messageLabel );
90       this->Controls->Add( mainPanel );
91       this->Controls->Add( mainGroupBox );
92       this->Name = S"GroupBoxPanelExample";
93       this->Text = S"GroupBoxPanelExample";
94       this->mainGroupBox->ResumeLayout();
95       this->mainPanel->ResumeLayout();
96       this->ResumeLayout();
97    } // end method InitializeComponent
98
99    // event handlers to change messageLabel
100
101   // event handler for hi button
102   void GroupBoxPanelExample::hiButton_Click( Object *sender,
103      EventArgs *e )
104   {
105      messageLabel->Text = S"Hi pressed";
106   }
107
108   // event handler for bye button
109   void GroupBoxPanelExample::byeButton_Click( Object *sender,
110      EventArgs *e )
111   {
112      messageLabel->Text = S"Bye pressed";
113   }
114
115   // event handler for far left button
116   void GroupBoxPanelExample::leftButton_Click( Object *sender,
117      EventArgs *e )
118   {
119      messageLabel->Text = S"Far left pressed";
120   }
121
122   // event handler for far right button
123   void GroupBoxPanelExample::rightButton_Click( Object *sender,
124      EventArgs *e )
125   {
126      messageLabel->Text = S"Far right pressed";
127   }
```

Fig. 9.19   GroupBoxPanelExample class method definitions. (Part 3 of 3.)

```
1    // Fig. 9.20: GroupBoxPanelTest.cpp
2    // GroupBox and Panel demonstration.
3
4    #include "GroupBoxPanel.h"
5
6    int __stdcall WinMain()
7    {
```

Fig. 9.20   GroupBox and **Panel** demonstration. (Part 1 of 2.)

```
8       Application::Run( new GroupBoxPanelExample() );
9
10      return 0;
11   } // end function WinMain
```

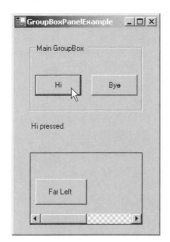 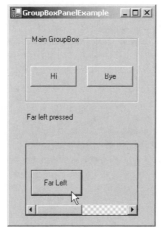 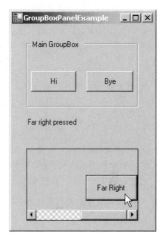

Fig. 9.20   **GroupBox** and **Panel** demonstration. (Part 2 of 2.)

The programmer can use method **Add** (lines 42–43, 61–62) to insert a control, such as a button, into a container control, like a **GroupBox** or a **Panel**. The **GroupBox** (named **mainGroupBox**) has two buttons, **hiButton** (labeled **Hi**) and **byeButton** (labeled **Bye**). The **Panel** (named **mainPanel**) has two buttons as well, **leftButton** (labeled **Far Left**) and **rightButton** (labeled **Far Right**). The **mainPanel** control also has its **AutoScroll** property set to **true**, allowing scrollbars to appear if needed (i.e., if the contents of the **Panel** take up more space than the **Panel** itself). The **Label** (named **messageLabel**) is initially blank.

The event handlers for the four buttons are located in lines 102–127. We add a line in each handler to change the text of **messageLabel**.

9.7 CheckBoxes and RadioButtons

MC++ has two types of *state buttons*—**CheckBox** and **RadioButton**—that can be in the on/off or true/false state. Classes **CheckBox** and **RadioButton** are derived from class **ButtonBase**. A group of **CheckBox**es allow the user to select combinations of choices. A **RadioButton** is different from a **CheckBox** in that there are normally several **RadioButton**s grouped together, and only one of the **RadioButton**s in the group can be selected (true) at any time.

A checkbox is a small white square that can be blank, can contain a checkmark or can be dimmed (i.e., the checkbox's state is indeterminate). When a checkbox is selected, a black checkmark appears in the box. There are no restrictions on how checkboxes are used: Any number may be selected at a time. The text that appears alongside a checkbox is referred to as the *checkbox label*. A list of common properties and events of class **Checkbox** appears in Fig. 9.21.

CheckBox events and properties	Description / Delegate and Event Arguments
Common Properties	
Checked	Whether the CheckBox has been checked.
CheckState	Whether the CheckBox is checked (contains a black checkmark) or unchecked (blank). An enumeration with values Checked, Unchecked or Indeterminate.
Text	Text displayed to the right of the CheckBox (called the label).
Common Events	*(Delegate EventHandler, event arguments EventArgs)*
CheckedChanged	Raised every time the CheckBox is either checked or unchecked. Default event when this control is double clicked in the designer.
CheckStateChanged	Raised when the CheckState property changes.

Fig. 9.21   CheckBox properties and events.

The program in Fig. 9.22–Fig. 9.24 allows the user to select a **CheckBox** to change the font style of a **Label**. One **CheckBox** applies a bold style, the other an italic style. If both checkboxes are selected, the style of the font is bold and italic. When the program initially executes, neither **CheckBox** is checked.

```
1   // Fig. 9.22: CheckBox.h
2   // Using CheckBoxes to toggle italic and bold styles.
3
4   #pragma once
5
6   #using <mscorlib.dll>
7   #using <system.dll>
8   #using <system.drawing.dll>
9   #using <system.windows.forms.dll>
10
11  using namespace System;
12  using namespace System::Drawing;
13  using namespace System::Windows::Forms;
14
15  public __gc class CheckBoxTest : public Form
16  {
17  public:
18     CheckBoxTest();
19
20  private:
21     CheckBox *boldCheckBox, *italicCheckBox;
22     Label *outputLabel;
23     void InitializeComponent();
```

Fig. 9.22   Using CheckBoxes to toggle italic and bold styles. (Part 1 of 2.)

```
24      void boldCheckBox_CheckedChanged( Object *, EventArgs * );
25      void italicCheckBox_CheckedChanged( Object *, EventArgs * );
26   }; // end class CheckBoxTest
```

Fig. 9.22   Using **CheckBox**es to toggle italic and bold styles. (Part 2 of 2.)

The first **CheckBox**, named **boldCheckBox**, has its **Text** property set to **Bold** (line 23 of Fig. 9.23). The other **CheckBox** is named **italicCheckBox** and is labeled **Italic** (line 38). The **Label**, named **outputLabel**, is labeled **Watch the font style change** (line 31).

```
1    // Fig. 9.23: CheckBox.cpp
2    // Using CheckBoxes to toggle italic and bold styles.
3
4    #include "CheckBox.h"
5
6    CheckBoxTest::CheckBoxTest()
7    {
8        InitializeComponent();
9    }
10
11   void CheckBoxTest::InitializeComponent()
12   {
13       this->boldCheckBox = new CheckBox();
14       this->italicCheckBox = new CheckBox();
15       this->outputLabel = new Label();
16       this->SuspendLayout();
17
18       // boldCheckBox
19       this->boldCheckBox->Location = Point( 72, 56 );
20       this->boldCheckBox->Name = S"boldCheckBox";
21       this->boldCheckBox->Size = Drawing::Size( 48, 24 );
22       this->boldCheckBox->TabIndex = 1;
23       this->boldCheckBox->Text = S"Bold";
24       this->boldCheckBox->CheckedChanged += new EventHandler(
25          this, boldCheckBox_CheckedChanged );
26
27       // outputLabel
28       this->outputLabel->Location = Point( 64, 24 );
29       this->outputLabel->Name = S"outputLabel";
30       this->outputLabel->Size = Drawing::Size( 152, 16 );
31       this->outputLabel->Text = S"Watch the font style change";
32
33       // italicCheckBox
34       this->italicCheckBox->Location = Point( 160, 56 );
35       this->italicCheckBox->Name = S"italicCheckBox";
36       this->italicCheckBox->Size = Drawing::Size( 48, 24 );
37       this->italicCheckBox->TabIndex = 0;
```

Fig. 9.23   **CheckBoxTest** class method definitions. (Part 1 of 2.)

```
38        this->italicCheckBox->Text = S"Italic";
39        this->italicCheckBox->CheckedChanged += new EventHandler(
40           this, italicCheckBox_CheckedChanged );
41
42        // CheckBoxTest
43        this->AutoScaleBaseSize = Drawing::Size( 5, 13 );
44        this->ClientSize = Drawing::Size( 264, 109 );
45        this->Controls->Add( italicCheckBox );
46        this->Controls->Add( boldCheckBox );
47        this->Controls->Add( outputLabel );
48        this->Name = S"CheckBoxTest";
49        this->Text = S"CheckBoxTest";
50        this->ResumeLayout();
51     } // end method InitializeComponent
52
53     // make text bold if not bold, if already bold make not bold
54     void CheckBoxTest::boldCheckBox_CheckedChanged( Object *sender,
55        EventArgs *e )
56     {
57        outputLabel->Font =
58           new Drawing::Font( outputLabel->Font->Name,
59           outputLabel->Font->Size, ( FontStyle )
60           ( outputLabel->Font->Style ^ FontStyle::Bold ) );
61     }
62
63     // make text italic if not italic, if already italic make not italic
64     void CheckBoxTest::italicCheckBox_CheckedChanged(
65        Object *sender, EventArgs *e )
66     {
67        outputLabel->Font =
68           new Drawing::Font( outputLabel->Font->Name,
69           outputLabel->Font->Size, ( FontStyle )
70           ( outputLabel->Font->Style ^ FontStyle::Italic ) );
71     }
```

Fig. 9.23   **CheckBoxTest** class method definitions. (Part 2 of 2.)

```
1     // Fig. 9.24: CheckBoxTest.cpp
2     // CheckBox demonstration.
3
4     #include "CheckBox.h"
5
6     int __stdcall WinMain()
7     {
8        Application::Run( new CheckBoxTest() );
9
10       return 0;
11    } // end function WinMain
```

Fig. 9.24   **CheckBox** demonstration. (Part 1 of 2.)

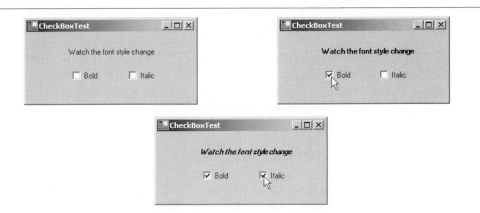

Fig. 9.24 **CheckBox** demonstration. (Part 2 of 2.)

After creating the components, we define their event handlers. To understand the code added to the event handler, we first discuss **outputLabel**'s **Font** property.

To change the font, the **Font** property must be set to a **Font** object. The **Font** constructor we use takes the font name, size and style. The first two arguments make use of **outputLabel**'s **Font** object, namely, **outputLabel->Font->Name** and **out-putLabel->Font->Size** (lines 58–59 of Fig. 9.23). The third argument specifies the font style. The style is a member of the *FontStyle* enumeration, which contains the font styles **Regular**, **Bold**, **Italic**, **Strikeout** and **Underline**. (The **Strikeout** style displays text with a line through it, the **Underline** style displays text with a line below it.) A **Font** object's *Style* property is set when the **Font** object is created—the **Style** property itself is read-only.

Styles can be combined using *bitwise operators*, or operators that perform manipulation on bits. All data are represented on the computer as a series of 0's and 1's. Each 0 or 1 is called a bit. Actions are taken and data are modified using these bit values. In this program, we need to set the font style so that the text will appear bold if it was not bold originally, and vice versa. Notice that on line 60 we use the bitwise XOR operator (^) to do this. Applying this operator to two bits does the following: If exactly one of the corresponding bits is 1, set the result to 1. By using the ^ operator as we did on line 60, we are setting the bit values for bold in the same way. The operand on the right (**FontStyle::Bold**) always has bit values set to bold. The operand on the left (**outputLabel->Font->Style**) must not be bold for the resulting style to be bold. (Remember for XOR, if one value is set to 1, the other must be 0, or the result will not be 1.) If **outputLabel->Font->Style** is bold, then the resulting style will not be bold. This operator also allows us to combine the styles. For instance, if the text were originally italicized, it would now be italicized and bold, rather than just bold.

We could have explicitly tested for the current style and changed it according to what we needed. For example, in the method **boldCheckBox_CheckChanged** we could have tested for the regular style, made it bold, tested for the bold style, made it regular, tested for the italic style, made it bold italic, or the italic bold style and made it italic. However, this method has a drawback—for every new style we add, we double the number of combinations. To add a checkbox for underline, we would have to test for eight possible styles. To add a checkbox for strikeout as well, we would have 16 tests in each event handler. By using the bitwise XOR operator, we save ourselves from this trouble. Each new style needs only a single statement in its event handler. In addition, styles can be removed easily, removing their handler. If we tested for every condition, we would have to remove the handler and all the unnecessary test conditions in the other handlers.

Radio buttons (defined with class **RadioButton**) are similar to checkboxes, because they also have two states—*selected* and *not selected* (also called *deselected*). However, radio buttons normally appear as a *group* in which only one radio button can be selected at a time. Selecting a different radio button in the group forces all other radio buttons in the group to be deselected. Radio buttons represent a set of *mutually exclusive* options (i.e., a set in which multiple options cannot be selected at the same time).

Look-and-Feel Observation 9.7
*Use **RadioButton**s when the user should choose only one option in a group.*

Look-and-Feel Observation 9.8
*Use **CheckBox**es when the user should be able to choose many options in a group.*

All radio buttons added to a container (such as a form) become part of the same group. To create new groups, radio buttons must be added to other containers such as **Group-Box**es or **Panel**s. The common properties and events of class **RadioButton** are listed in Fig. 9.25.

Software Engineering Observation 9.3
*Forms, **GroupBox**es, and **Panel**s can act as logical groups for radio buttons. The radio buttons within each group will be mutually exclusive to each other, but not to radio buttons in different groups.*

RadioButton properties and events	Description / Delegate and Event Arguments
Common Properties	
Checked	Whether the **RadioButton** is checked.
Text	Text displayed to the right of the **RadioButton** (called the label).
Common Events	*(Delegate **EventHandler**, event arguments **EventArgs**)*

Fig. 9.25 **RadioButton** properties and events. (Part 1 of 2.)

RadioButton properties and events	Description / Delegate and Event Arguments
Common Events (Cont.)	
Click	Raised when user clicks the control.
CheckedChanged	Raised every time the **RadioButton** is checked or unchecked.

Fig. 9.25 **RadioButton** properties and events. (Part 2 of 2.)

The program in Fig. 9.26–Fig. 9.28 uses radio buttons to select the options for a **MessageBox**. Users select the attributes they want then press the display button, which causes the **MessageBox** to appear. A **Label** in the lower-left corner shows the result of the **MessageBox** (**Yes**, **No**, **Cancel**, etc.). The different **MessageBox** icon and button types have been displayed in tables in Chapter 5, Object-Based Programming.

To store the user's choice of options, the objects **iconType** and **buttonType** are created and initialized (lines 29–30 of Fig. 9.26). Object **iconType** can be assigned an enumeration **MessageBoxIcon** value—**Asterisk**, **Error**, **Exclamation**, **Hand**, **Information**, **Question**, **Stop** or **Warning**. In this example, we use only **Error**, **Exclamation**, **Information** and **Question**.

```
1   // Fig. 9.26: RadioButton.h
2   // RadioButtonTest class header file.
3
4   #pragma once
5
6   #using <mscorlib.dll>
7   #using <system.dll>
8   #using <system.drawing.dll>
9   #using <system.windows.forms.dll>
10
11  using namespace System;
12  using namespace System::Drawing;
13  using namespace System::Windows::Forms;
14
15  public __gc class RadioButtonsTest : public Form
16  {
17  public:
18     RadioButtonsTest();
19
20  private:
21     Label *promptLabel, *displayLabel;
22     Button *displayButton;
23     RadioButton *questionButton, *informationButton,
```

Fig. 9.26 Using **RadioButton**s to set message window options. (Part 1 of 2.)

```
24            *exclamationButton, *errorButton,
25            *retryCancelButton, *yesNoButton,
26            *yesNoCancelButton, *okCancelButton,
27            *okButton, *abortRetryIgnoreButton;
28       GroupBox *iconTypeGroupBox, *buttonTypeGroupBox;
29       static MessageBoxIcon iconType = MessageBoxIcon::Error;
30       static MessageBoxButtons buttonType = MessageBoxButtons::OK;
31       void InitializeComponent();
32       void buttonType_CheckedChanged( Object *, EventArgs * );
33       void iconType_CheckedChanged( Object *, EventArgs * );
34       void displayButton_Click( Object *, EventArgs * );
35    }; // end class RadioButtonsTest
```

Fig. 9.26 Using **RadioButton**s to set message window options. (Part 2 of 2.)

Object **buttonType** can be assigned an enumeration **MessageBoxButton** value—**Abort-RetryIgnore**, **OK**, **OKCancel**, **RetryCancel**, **YesNo** or **YesNo-Cancel**. The name indicates which buttons will appear in the **MessageBox**. In this example, we use all **MessageBoxButton** enumeration values.

RadioButtons (lines 13–22 of Fig. 9.27) are created for the enumeration options, with their labels set appropriately. Two **GroupBox**es are created (lines 23–24), one for each enumeration. Their captions are **Button Type** and **Icon**. One label is used to prompt the user (**promptLabel**), while the other is used to display which button was pressed, once the custom **MessageBox** has been displayed (**displayLabel**). There is also a button (**displayButton**) that displays the text **Display**.

```
1    // Fig. 9.27: RadioButtons.cpp
2    // Using RadioButtons to set message window options.
3
4    #include "RadioButton.h"
5
6    RadioButtonsTest::RadioButtonsTest()
7    {
8       InitializeComponent();
9    }
10
11   void RadioButtonsTest::InitializeComponent()
12   {
13       this->informationButton = new RadioButton();
14       this->retryCancelButton = new RadioButton();
15       this->yesNoButton = new RadioButton();
16       this->yesNoCancelButton = new RadioButton();
17       this->abortRetryIgnoreButton = new RadioButton();
18       this->okCancelButton = new RadioButton();
19       this->okButton = new RadioButton();
20       this->questionButton = new RadioButton();
```

Fig. 9.27 **RadioButtonsTest** class method definitions. (Part 1 of 6.)

```
21      this->exclamationButton = new RadioButton();
22      this->errorButton = new RadioButton();
23      this->buttonTypeGroupBox = new GroupBox();
24      this->iconTypeGroupBox = new GroupBox();
25      this->displayLabel = new Label();
26      this->displayButton = new Button();
27      this->promptLabel = new Label();
28      this->buttonTypeGroupBox->SuspendLayout();
29      this->iconTypeGroupBox->SuspendLayout();
30      this->SuspendLayout();
31
32      // buttonTypeGroupBox
33      RadioButton *buttonBox[] = { this->retryCancelButton,
34         this->yesNoButton, this->yesNoCancelButton,
35         this->abortRetryIgnoreButton, this->okCancelButton,
36         this->okButton };
37      this->buttonTypeGroupBox->Controls->AddRange( buttonBox );
38      this->buttonTypeGroupBox->Location = Point( 16, 56 );
39      this->buttonTypeGroupBox->Name = S"buttonTypeGroupBox";
40      this->buttonTypeGroupBox->Size = Drawing::Size( 152, 272 );
41      this->buttonTypeGroupBox->TabIndex = 0;
42      this->buttonTypeGroupBox->Text = S"Button Type";
43
44      // retryCancelButton
45      this->retryCancelButton->Location = Point( 16, 224 );
46      this->retryCancelButton->Name = S"retryCancelButton";
47      this->retryCancelButton->Size = Drawing::Size( 100, 23 );
48      this->retryCancelButton->Text = S"RetryCancel";
49
50      // all radio buttons for button types are registered
51      // to buttonType_CheckedChanged event handler
52      this->retryCancelButton->CheckedChanged += new EventHandler(
53         this, buttonType_CheckedChanged );
54
55      // yesNoButton
56      this->yesNoButton->Location = Point( 16, 184 );
57      this->yesNoButton->Name = S"yesNoButton";
58      this->yesNoButton->Size = Drawing::Size( 100, 23 );
59      this->yesNoButton->Text = S"YesNo";
60      this->yesNoButton->CheckedChanged += new EventHandler(
61         this, buttonType_CheckedChanged );
62
63      // yesNoCancelButton
64      this->yesNoCancelButton->Location = Point( 16, 144 );
65      this->yesNoCancelButton->Name = S"yesNoCancelButton";
66      this->yesNoCancelButton->Size = Drawing::Size( 100, 23 );
67      this->yesNoCancelButton->Text = S"YesNoCancel";
68      this->yesNoCancelButton->CheckedChanged += new EventHandler(
69         this, buttonType_CheckedChanged );
70
71      // abortRetryIgnoreButton
72      this->abortRetryIgnoreButton->Location = Point( 16, 104 );
73      this->abortRetryIgnoreButton->Name =
```

Fig. 9.27 **RadioButtonsTest** class method definitions. (Part 2 of 6.)

```
74              S"abortRetryIgnoreButton";
75      this->abortRetryIgnoreButton->Size = Drawing::Size( 120, 23 );
76      this->abortRetryIgnoreButton->Text = S"AbortRetryIgnore";
77      this->abortRetryIgnoreButton->CheckedChanged +=
78          new EventHandler( this, buttonType_CheckedChanged );
79
80      // okCancelButton
81      this->okCancelButton->Location = Point( 16, 64 );
82      this->okCancelButton->Name = S"okCancelButton";
83      this->okCancelButton->Size = Drawing::Size( 100, 23 );
84      this->okCancelButton->Text = S"OKCancel";
85      this->okCancelButton->CheckedChanged += new EventHandler(
86          this, buttonType_CheckedChanged );
87
88      // okButton
89      this->okButton->Checked = true;
90      this->okButton->Location = Point( 16, 24 );
91      this->okButton->Name = S"okButton";
92      this->okButton->Size = Drawing::Size( 100, 23 );
93      this->okButton->Text = S"OK";
94      this->okButton->CheckedChanged += new EventHandler(
95          this, buttonType_CheckedChanged );
96
97      // iconTypeGroupBox
98      RadioButton *iconBox[] = { this->questionButton,
99          this->informationButton, this->exclamationButton,
100         this->errorButton };
101     this->iconTypeGroupBox->Controls->AddRange( iconBox );
102     this->iconTypeGroupBox->Location = Point( 200, 56 );
103     this->iconTypeGroupBox->Name = S"iconTypeGroupBox";
104     this->iconTypeGroupBox->Size = Drawing::Size( 136, 176 );
105     this->iconTypeGroupBox->Text = S"Icon";
106
107     // questionButton
108     this->questionButton->Location = Point( 16, 144 );
109     this->questionButton->Name = S"questionButton";
110     this->questionButton->Size = Drawing::Size( 100, 23 );
111     this->questionButton->Text = S"Question";
112
113     // all radio buttons for icon types are registered
114     // to iconType_CheckedChanged event handler
115     this->questionButton->CheckedChanged += new EventHandler(
116         this, iconType_CheckedChanged );
117
118     // informationButton
119     this->informationButton->Location = Point( 16, 104 );
120     this->informationButton->Name = S"informationButton";
121     this->informationButton->Size = Drawing::Size( 100, 23 );
122     this->informationButton->Text = S"Information";
123     this->informationButton->CheckedChanged += new EventHandler(
124         this, iconType_CheckedChanged );
125
126     // exclamationButton
```

Fig. 9.27   RadioButtonsTest class method definitions. (Part 3 of 6.)

```
127      this->exclamationButton->Location = Point( 16, 64 );
128      this->exclamationButton->Name = S"exclamationButton";
129      this->exclamationButton->Size = Drawing::Size( 104, 23 );
130      this->exclamationButton->Text = S"Exclamation";
131      this->exclamationButton->CheckedChanged += new EventHandler(
132         this, iconType_CheckedChanged );
133
134      // errorButton
135      this->errorButton->Checked = true;
136      this->errorButton->Location = Point( 16, 24 );
137      this->errorButton->Name = S"errorButton";
138      this->errorButton->Size = Drawing::Size( 100, 23 );
139      this->errorButton->Text = S"Error";
140      this->errorButton->CheckedChanged += new EventHandler(
141         this, iconType_CheckedChanged );
142
143      // displayLabel
144      this->displayLabel->Location = Point( 200, 304 );
145      this->displayLabel->Name = S"displayLabel";
146      this->displayLabel->Size = Drawing::Size( 136, 24 );
147
148      // displayButton
149      this->displayButton->Location = Point( 200, 240 );
150      this->displayButton->Name = S"displayButton";
151      this->displayButton->Size = Drawing::Size( 136, 48 );
152      this->displayButton->TabIndex = 2;
153      this->displayButton->Text = S"Display";
154      this->displayButton->Click += new EventHandler(
155         this, displayButton_Click );
156
157      // promptLabel
158      this->promptLabel->Font = new Drawing::Font(
159         S"Microsoft Sans Serif", 9.5, FontStyle::Regular,
160         GraphicsUnit::Point, 0 );
161      this->promptLabel->Location = Point( 8, 16 );
162      this->promptLabel->Name = S"promptLabel";
163      this->promptLabel->Size = Drawing::Size( 344, 24 );
164      this->promptLabel->Text =
165         S"Choose the type of MessageBox you would like "
166         S"to display!";
167
168      // RadioButtonsTest
169      this->AutoScaleBaseSize = Drawing::Size( 5, 13 );
170      this->ClientSize = Drawing::Size( 360, 341 );
171      Control *controls[] = { this->promptLabel,
172         this->displayLabel, this->displayButton,
173         this->iconTypeGroupBox, this->buttonTypeGroupBox };
174      this->Controls->AddRange( controls );
175      this->Name = S"RadioButtonsTest";
176      this->Text = S"Demonstrating RadioButtons";
177      this->buttonTypeGroupBox->ResumeLayout();
178      this->iconTypeGroupBox->ResumeLayout();
179      this->ResumeLayout();
```

Fig. 9.27   RadioButtonsTest class method definitions. (Part 4 of 6.)

```
180  } // end method InitializeComponent
181
182  // change button based on option chosen by sender
183  void RadioButtonsTest::buttonType_CheckedChanged(
184     Object *sender, EventArgs *e )
185  {
186     if ( sender == okButton ) // display OK button
187        buttonType = MessageBoxButtons::OK;
188
189     // display OK and Cancel buttons
190     else if ( sender == okCancelButton )
191        buttonType = MessageBoxButtons::OKCancel;
192
193     // display Abort, Retry and Ignore buttons
194     else if ( sender == abortRetryIgnoreButton )
195        buttonType = MessageBoxButtons::AbortRetryIgnore;
196
197     // display Yes, No and Cancel buttons
198     else if ( sender == yesNoCancelButton )
199        buttonType = MessageBoxButtons::YesNoCancel;
200
201     // display Yes and No buttons
202     else if ( sender == yesNoButton )
203        buttonType = MessageBoxButtons::YesNo;
204
205     // only one option left--display Retry and Cancel buttons
206     else
207        buttonType = MessageBoxButtons::RetryCancel;
208  } // end method buttonType_CheckedChanged
209
210  // change icon based on option chosen by sender
211  void RadioButtonsTest::iconType_CheckedChanged(
212     Object *sender, EventArgs *e )
213  {
214     if ( sender == errorButton ) // display error icon
215        iconType = MessageBoxIcon::Error;
216
217     // display exclamation point
218     else if ( sender == exclamationButton )
219        iconType = MessageBoxIcon::Exclamation;
220
221     // display information icon
222     else if ( sender == informationButton )
223        iconType = MessageBoxIcon::Information;
224
225     else // only one option left--display question mark
226        iconType = MessageBoxIcon::Question;
227  } // end method iconType_CheckedChanged
228
229  // display MessageBox and button user pressed
230  void RadioButtonsTest::displayButton_Click(
231     Object *sender, EventArgs *e )
```

Fig. 9.27 **RadioButtonsTest** class method definitions. (Part 5 of 6.)

```
232   {
233       DialogResult = MessageBox::Show(
234           S"This is Your Custom MessageBox.", S"Custom MessageBox",
235           buttonType, iconType );
236
237       // check for dialog result and display it in label
238       switch ( DialogResult )
239       {
240           case DialogResult::OK:
241               displayLabel->Text = S"OK was pressed.";
242               break;
243
244           case DialogResult::Cancel:
245               displayLabel->Text = S"Cancel was pressed.";
246               break;
247
248           case DialogResult::Abort:
249               displayLabel->Text = S"Abort was pressed.";
250               break;
251
252           case DialogResult::Retry:
253               displayLabel->Text = S"Retry was pressed.";
254               break;
255
256           case DialogResult::Ignore:
257               displayLabel->Text = S"Ignore was pressed.";
258               break;
259
260           case DialogResult::Yes:
261               displayLabel->Text = S"Yes was pressed.";
262               break;
263
264           case DialogResult::No:
265               displayLabel->Text = S"No was pressed.";
266               break;
267       } // end switch
268   } // end method displayButton_Click
```

Fig. 9.27 **RadioButtonsTest** class method definitions. (Part 6 of 6.)

```
1    // Fig. 9.28: RadioButtonTest.cpp
2    // RadioButton demonstration.
3
4    #include "RadioButton.h"
5
6    int __stdcall WinMain()
7    {
8        Application::Run( new RadioButtonsTest() );
9
10       return 0;
11   } // end function WinMain
```

Fig. 9.28 **RadioButton** demonstration. (Part 1 of 2.)

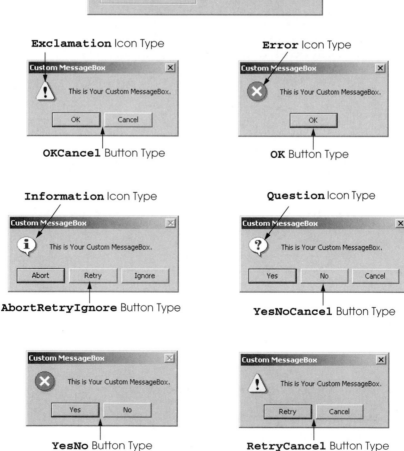

Fig. 9.28   **RadioButton** demonstration. (Part 2 of 2.)

The radio buttons are grouped; thus, only one option can be selected from each **GroupBox**. Rather than add each **RadioButton** individually to its **GroupBox**, we create an array of **RadioButton** pointers and use method **AddRange** to insert the array of controls into the **GroupBox**. For example, lines 33–36 create array **buttonBox**, which contains pointers to the **RadioButton**s for the button-type options. Method **AddRange** (line 37) inserts these radio buttons into the **buttonTypeGroupBox**. We use **AddRange** to insert the two **Label**s, the **Button** and the two **GroupBox**es onto the form (line 174), but we pass the method an array of **Control** pointers. We can place **Label**, **Button** and **GroupBox** pointers in an array of this type, because classes **Label**, **Button** and **GroupBox** are derived from class **Control**.

For event handling, one event handler exists for all the radio buttons in **buttonTypeGroupBox** and another for all the radio buttons in **iconTypeGroupBox**. Each radio button generates a **CheckedChanged** event when clicked. Each radio button that lists a button-type option is associated with **buttonType_CheckedChanged** (lines 183–208), while the ones that list the icon types are associated with **iconType_CheckedChanged** (lines 211–227).

Both handlers compare the **sender** object with every radio button to determine which button was selected. Notice that each **RadioButton** is referred to by the identifier assigned to its **Name** property when it is compared to the **sender** object (e.g., line 186). Depending on the radio button selected, either **iconType** or **buttonType** changes.

Method **displayButton_Click** (lines 230–268) creates a **MessageBox** (lines 233–235). Some of the **MessageBox** options are set by **iconType** and **buttonType**. The result of the message box is a **DialogResult** enumeration value—**Abort**, **Cancel**, **Ignore**, **No**, **None**, **OK**, **Retry** or **Yes**. The **switch** statement (lines 238–267) tests for the result and sets **displayLabel->Text** appropriately.

9.8 PictureBoxes

A picture box (class *PictureBox*) displays an image. The image, set by an object of class *Image*, can be in a bitmap (**.bmp**), **.gif**, **.jpg**, **.jpeg**, icon or metafile format (e.g., **.emf** (Enhanced Metafile Format) and **.mwf** (Microsoft Windows Metafile)). (Images and multimedia are discussed in Chapter 13, Graphics and Multimedia.) *GIF (Graphics Interchange Format)* and *JPEG (Joint Photographic Expert Group)* files are widely used file formats.

The *Image* property of class **PictureBox** sets the **Image** object to display, and the *SizeMode* property sets how the image is displayed (**Normal**, **StretchImage**, **AutoSize** or **CenterImage**). Figure 9.29 describes the important properties and events of class **PictureBox**.

PictureBox properties and events	Description / Delegate and Event Arguments
Common Properties	
Image	Image to display in the **PictureBox**.

Fig. 9.29 **PictureBox** properties and events. (Part 1 of 2.)

PictureBox properties and events	Description / Delegate and Event Arguments
Common Properties (Cont.)	
SizeMode	Gets value from enumeration `PictureBoxSizeMode` that controls image sizing and positioning. Values **Normal** (default), **Stretch-Image**, **AutoSize** and **CenterImage**. **Normal** puts image in top-left corner of **PictureBox**, and **CenterImage** puts image in middle. (Both cut off image if too large.) **StretchImage** resizes image to fit in **PictureBox**. **AutoSize** resizes **PictureBox** to hold image.
Common Events	*(Delegate **EventHandler**, event arguments **EventArgs**)*
Click	Raised when user clicks the control.

Fig. 9.29 `PictureBox` properties and events. (Part 2 of 2.)

The program in Fig. 9.30–Fig. 9.32 uses **PictureBox imagePictureBox** to display one of three bitmap images—**image0**, **image1** or **image2**. They are located in the directory **images** of our project folder, where the executable file is located. Whenever the **imagePictureBox** is clicked, the image changes. The **Label** (named **promptLabel**) on the top of the form includes the instructions **Click On Picture Box to View Images**.

```
1   // Fig. 9.30: PictureBox.h
2   // PictureBoxTest class header file.
3
4   #pragma once
5
6   #using <mscorlib.dll>
7   #using <system.dll>
8   #using <system.drawing.dll>
9   #using <system.windows.forms.dll>
10
11  using namespace System;
12  using namespace System::Drawing;
13  using namespace System::Windows::Forms;
14  using namespace System::IO;
15
16  public __gc class PictureBoxTest : public Form
17  {
18  public:
19     PictureBoxTest();
20
21  private:
22     PictureBox *imagePictureBox;
23     Label *promptLabel;
24     static int imageNum = -1;
25     void InitializeComponent();
26     void imagePictureBox_Click( Object *, EventArgs * );
27  }; // end class PictureBoxTest
```

Fig. 9.30 Using a **PictureBox** to display images.

Line 14 (Fig. 9.31) creates the **PictureBox**. Lines 30–33 sets **imagePictureBox**'s properties. Lines 36–37 associate the event handler
imagePictureBox_Click with the picture box. This program uses property **Text-
Align** (line 26–27) to set the horizontal and vertical placement of any text displayed on
label **promptLabel**. The property receives a value from enumeration ***Content-
Alignment*** (defined in namespace **System::Drawing**). This enumeration defines
constants like **BOTTOM**, **LEFT**, **MIDDLE**, **RIGHT**, **TOP**, **CENTER** and combinations such
as **MIDDLECENTER** and **TOPLEFT**, which is **TextAlign**'s default value.

```cpp
1   // Fig. 9.31: PictureBox.cpp
2   // Using a PictureBox to display images.
3
4   #include "PictureBox.h"
5
6   PictureBoxTest::PictureBoxTest()
7   {
8      InitializeComponent();
9   }
10
11  void PictureBoxTest::InitializeComponent()
12  {
13     this->promptLabel = new Label();
14     this->imagePictureBox = new PictureBox();
15     this->SuspendLayout();
16
17     // promptLabel
18     this->promptLabel->Font = new Drawing::Font(
19        S"Microsoft Sans Serif", 9, FontStyle::Bold,
20        GraphicsUnit::Point, 0 );
21     this->promptLabel->Location = Point( 22, 8 );
22     this->promptLabel->Name = S"promptLabel";
23     this->promptLabel->Size = Drawing::Size( 124, 56 );
24     this->promptLabel->Text =
25        S"Click On PictureBox to View Images";
26     this->promptLabel->TextAlign =
27        ContentAlignment::MiddleCenter;
28
29     // imagePictureBox
30     this->imagePictureBox->BorderStyle = BorderStyle::Fixed3D;
31     this->imagePictureBox->Location = Point( 34, 72 );
32     this->imagePictureBox->Name = S"imagePictureBox";
33     this->imagePictureBox->Size = Drawing::Size( 100, 100 );
34
35     // register event handler
36     this->imagePictureBox->Click += new EventHandler( this,
37        imagePictureBox_Click );
38
39     // PictureBoxTest
40     this->AutoScaleBaseSize = Drawing::Size( 5, 13 );
41     this->ClientSize = Drawing::Size( 168, 189 );
42     this->Controls->Add( imagePictureBox );
```

Fig. 9.31 **PictureBoxTest** class method definitions. (Part 1 of 2.)

```
43      this->Controls->Add( promptLabel );
44      this->Name = S"PictureBoxTest";
45      this->Text = S"PictureBoxTest";
46      this->ResumeLayout();
47   } // end method InitializeComponent
48
49   // change image whenever PictureBox clicked
50   void PictureBoxTest::imagePictureBox_Click( Object *sender,
51      EventArgs *e )
52   {
53      imageNum = ( imageNum + 1 ) % 3; // imageNum from 0 to 2
54
55      // create Image object from file, display on PictureBox
56      imagePictureBox->Image = Image::FromFile( String::Concat(
57         Directory::GetCurrentDirectory(), S"\\images\\image",
58         imageNum.ToString(), S".bmp" ) );
59   }
```

Fig. 9.31 **PictureBoxTest** class method definitions. (Part 2 of 2.)

```
1    // Fig. 9.32: PictureBoxTest.cpp
2    // PictureBox demonstration.
3
4    #include "PictureBox.h"
5
6    int __stdcall WinMain()
7    {
8       Application::Run( new PictureBoxTest() );
9
10      return 0;
11   } // end function WinMain
```

Fig. 9.32 **PictureBox** demonstration.

To respond to the user's clicks, we must handle the **Click** event (lines 50–59 of Fig. 9.31). Inside the event handler, we use an integer (**imageNum**) to store an integer representing the image we want to display. We then set the **Image** property of **imagePictureBox** to an **Image**. Class **Image** is discussed in Chapter 13, Graphics and Multimedia, but here we overview method *FromFile*, which takes a pointer to a **String** (the path to the image file) and creates an **Image** object.

To find the images, we use class ***Directory*** (namespace **System::IO**, specified on line 14 of Fig. 9.30) method ***GetCurrentDirectory*** (line 57 of Fig. 9.31). This returns the current directory of the executable file (usually **bin\Debug**) as a **String** pointer. To access the **images** subdirectory, we take the current directory and append "**\\images**" followed by "****" and the file name. We use a double slash because an escape sequence is needed to represent a single slash. We use **imageNum** to append the proper number, so we can load either **image0**, **image1** or **image2**. Integer **imageNum** stays between **0** and **2**, due to the modulus calculation (line 53). Finally, we append "**.bmp**" to the filename. Thus, if we want to load **image0**, the string becomes "*CurrentDir***images\image0.bmp**", where *CurrentDir* is the directory of the executable.

9.9 Mouse Event Handling

This section explains how to handle *mouse events,* such as *clicks*, *presses* and *moves*. Mouse events are generated when the mouse interacts with a control. They can be handled for any GUI control that derives from class **System::Windows::Forms::Control**. Mouse event information is passed using class ***MouseEventArgs***, and the delegate to create the mouse event handlers is ***MouseEventHandler***. Each mouse event-handling method must take an **object** and a **MouseEventArgs** object as arguments. The **Click** event, which we covered earlier, uses delegate **EventHandler** and event arguments **EventArgs**.

Class **MouseEventArgs** contains information about the mouse event, such as the *x*- and *y*-coordinates of the mouse pointer, the mouse button pressed, the number of clicks and the number of notches through which the mouse wheel turned. Note that the *x*- and *y*-coordinates of the **MouseEventArgs** object are relative to the control that raised the event. Point (0,0) is at the upper-left corner of the control. The various mouse events are described in Fig. 9.33.

Mouse Events, Delegates and Event Arguments	
*Mouse Events (Delegate **EventHandler**, event arguments **EventArgs**)*	
MouseEnter	Raised if the mouse cursor enters the area of the control.
MouseLeave	Raised if the mouse cursor leaves the area of the control.
*Mouse Events (Delegate **MouseEventHandler**, event arguments **MouseEventArgs**)*	
MouseDown	Raised if the mouse button is pressed while its cursor is over the area of the control.
MouseHover	Raised if the mouse cursor hovers over the area of the control.
MouseMove	Raised if the mouse cursor is moved while in the area of the control.
MouseUp	Raised if the mouse button is released when the cursor is over the area of the control.
*Class **MouseEventArgs** Properties*	
Button	Mouse button that was pressed (**left**, **right**, **middle** or **none**).

Fig. 9.33   Mouse events, delegates and event arguments. (Part 1 of 2.)

Mouse Events, Delegates and Event Arguments	

Class *MouseEventArgs* Properties (Cont.)	
`Clicks`	The number of times the mouse button was clicked.
`X`	The *x*-coordinate of the event, relative to the control.
`Y`	The *y*-coordinate of the event, relative to the control.

Fig. 9.33 Mouse events, delegates and event arguments. (Part 2 of 2.)

Figure 9.34–Fig. 9.36 uses mouse events to draw on the form. Whenever the user drags the mouse (i.e., moves the mouse while holding down a button), a line is drawn on the form.

Figure 9.34 (line 21) creates variable **shouldPaint**, which determines whether we should draw on the form. We want to draw only while the mouse button is pressed down. In the event handler for event **MouseDown**, **shouldPaint** is set to **true** (line 37 of Fig. 9.35). As soon as the mouse button is released the program stops drawing: **should-Paint** is set to **false** in the **MouseUp** event handler (line 44).

```
1   // Fig. 9.34: Painter.h
2   // Painter class header file.
3
4   #pragma once
5
6   #using <mscorlib.dll>
7   #using <system.dll>
8   #using <system.drawing.dll>
9   #using <system.windows.forms.dll>
10
11  using namespace System;
12  using namespace System::Drawing;
13  using namespace System::Windows::Forms;
14
15  public __gc class Painter : public Form
16  {
17  public:
18     Painter();
19
20  private:
21     static bool shouldPaint = false; // whether to paint
22     void InitializeComponent();
23     void Painter_MouseDown( Object *, MouseEventArgs * );
24     void Painter_MouseUp( Object *, MouseEventArgs * );
25     void Painter_MouseMove( Object *, MouseEventArgs * );
26  }; // end class Painter
```

Fig. 9.34 Mouse event handling.

```
1   // Fig. 9.35: Painter.cpp
2   // Using the mouse to draw on a form.
3
```

Fig. 9.35 **Painter** class method definitions. (Part 1 of 2.)

```
4   #include "Painter.h"
5
6   Painter::Painter()
7   {
8       InitializeComponent();
9   }
10
11  void Painter::InitializeComponent()
12  {
13      this->SuspendLayout();
14
15      // painter form
16      this->AutoScaleBaseSize = Drawing::Size( 5, 13 );
17      this->ClientSize = Drawing::Size( 144, 133 );
18      this->Name = S"Painter";
19      this->Text = S"Painter";
20
21      // register event handlers
22      this->MouseDown += new MouseEventHandler( this,
23         Painter_MouseDown );
24
25      this->MouseUp += new MouseEventHandler( this,
26         Painter_MouseUp );
27
28      this->MouseMove += new MouseEventHandler( this,
29         Painter_MouseMove );
30      this->ResumeLayout();
31  } // end method InitializeComponent
32
33  // should paint after mouse button has been pressed
34  void Painter::Painter_MouseDown( Object *sender,
35      MouseEventArgs *e )
36  {
37      shouldPaint = true;
38  }
39
40  // stop painting when mouse button released
41  void Painter::Painter_MouseUp( Object *sender,
42      MouseEventArgs *e )
43  {
44      shouldPaint = false;
45  }
46
47  // draw circle whenever mouse button moves (and mouse is down)
48  void Painter::Painter_MouseMove( Object *sender,
49      MouseEventArgs *e )
50  {
51      if ( shouldPaint ) {
52         Graphics *graphics = CreateGraphics();
53         graphics->FillEllipse( new SolidBrush(
54            Color::BlueViolet ), e->X, e->Y, 4, 4 );
55      }
56  }
```

Fig. 9.35 Painter class method definitions. (Part 2 of 2.)

```
1    // Fig. 9.36: PainterTest.cpp
2    // Mouse event handling demonstration.
3
4    #include "Painter.h"
5
6    int __stdcall WinMain()
7    {
8       Application::Run( new Painter() );
9
10      return 0;
11   } // end function WinMain
```

Fig. 9.36 Mouse event handling demonstration.

Whenever the mouse moves while the button is pressed down, the **MouseMove** event is generated. The event will be generated repeatedly. Inside the **Painter_MouseMove** event handler (lines 48–56), the program draws only if **shouldPaint** is **true** (indicating that the mouse button is down). Line 52 creates a *Graphics* object for the form, which provides methods for drawing various shapes. Method *FillEllipse* (lines 53–54) draws a circle at every point the mouse cursor moves over (while the mouse button is pressed). The first parameter to method **FillEllipse** is a *SolidBrush* object, which determines the color of the shape drawn. We create a new **SolidBrush** object by passing the constructor a *Color* value. Structure **Color** contains numerous predefined color constants—we selected **Color::BlueViolet** (line 54). The **SolidBrush** fills an elliptical region, which lies inside a bounding rectangle. The bounding rectangle is specified by the *x*- and *y*-coordinates of its upper-left corner, its height and its width. These four parameters are the final four arguments to method **FillEllipse**. The *x*- and *y*-coordinates are the location of the mouse event: They can be taken from the mouse event arguments (**e->X** and **e->Y**). To draw a circle, we set the height and width of the bounding rectangle equal—in this case, they are each four pixels.

9.10 Keyboard Event Handling

This section explains how to handle *key events*. Key events are generated when keys on the keyboard are pressed and released. These events can be handled by any control that inherits from **System::Windows::Forms::Control**. There are two types of key events. The first is event *KeyPress*, which fires when a key representing an ASCII character is pressed (determined by *KeyPressEventArgs* property *KeyChar*). ASCII is a 128-

character set of alphanumeric symbols. (The full listing can be found in Appendix C, ASCII Character Set.)

Using the **KeyPress** event, we cannot determine whether *modifier keys* (such as *Shift*, *Alt* and *Control*) were pressed. To determine such actions, handle the **KeyUp** or **KeyDown** events, which form the second type of key event. Class **KeyEventArgs** contains information about special modifier keys. The key's **Key** *enumeration* value can be returned, giving information about a wide range of non-ASCII keys. Modifier keys are often used in conjunction with the mouse to select or highlight information. The delegates for the two classes are **KeyPressEventHandler** (event argument class **KeyPressEventArgs**) and **KeyEventHandler** (event argument class **KeyEventArgs**). Figure 9.37 lists important information about key events.

Keyboard Events, Delegates and Event Arguments	
*Key Events (Delegate **KeyEventHandler**, event arguments **KeyEventArgs**)*	
KeyDown	Raised when key is initially pushed down.
KeyUp	Raised when key is released.
*Key Events (Delegate **KeyPressEventHandler**, event arguments **KeyPressEventArgs**)*	
KeyPress	Raised when key is pressed. Occurs repeatedly while key is held down, at a rate specified by the operating system.
*Class **KeyPressEventArgs** Properties*	
KeyChar	Returns the ASCII character for the key pressed.
Handled	Indicates whether the **KeyPress** event was handled (i.e., has an event handler associated with it).
*Class **KeyEventArgs** Properties*	
Alt	Indicates whether the *Alt* key was pressed.
Control	Indicates whether the *Control* key was pressed.
Shift	Indicates whether the *Shift* key was pressed.
Handled	Indicates whether the event was handled (i.e., has an event handler associated with it).
KeyCode	Returns the key code for the key, as a **Keys** enumeration. This does not include modifier key information. Used to test for a specific key.
KeyData	Returns the key code as a **Keys** enumeration, combined with modifier information. Used to determine all information about the key pressed.
KeyValue	Returns the key code as an **int**, rather than as a **Keys** enumeration. Used to obtain a numeric representation of the key pressed.

Fig. 9.37   Keyboard events, delegates and event arguments. (Part 1 of 2.)

Keyboard Events, Delegates and Event Arguments

Class ***KeyEventArgs*** *Properties (Cont.)*

Modifiers	Returns a **Keys** enumeration for any modifier keys pressed (*Alt*, *Control* and *Shift*). Used to determine modifier key information only.

Fig. 9.37 Keyboard events, delegates and event arguments. (Part 2 of 2.)

Figure 9.38–Fig. 9.40 demonstrate using the key event handlers to display the key that was pressed. The program's form contains two **Label**s. It displays the key pressed on one **Label** and modifier information on the other.

The two **Label**s (named **charLabel** and **keyInfoLabel**) are initially empty. The **KeyDown** and **KeyPress** events convey different information; thus, the form (**Key-Demo**) handles them both.

The **KeyPress** event handler (lines 53–58 of Fig. 9.39) accesses the **KeyChar** property of the **KeyPressEventArgs** object. This returns the key pressed as a **char** and displays it in **charLabel** (lines 56–57). If the key pressed was not an ASCII character, then the **KeyPress** event will not fire and **charLabel** remains empty. ASCII is a common encoding format for letters, numbers, punctuation marks and other characters. It does not support keys such as the *function keys* (like *F1*) or the modifier keys (*Alt*, *Control* and *Shift*)

```
1   // Fig. 9.38: KeyDemo.h
2   // KeyDemo class header file.
3
4   #pragma once
5
6   #using <mscorlib.dll>
7   #using <system.dll>
8   #using <system.drawing.dll>
9   #using <system.windows.forms.dll>
10
11  using namespace System;
12  using namespace System::Drawing;
13  using namespace System::Windows::Forms;
14
15  public __gc class KeyDemo : public Form
16  {
17  public:
18     KeyDemo();
19
20  private:
21     Label *charLabel, *keyInfoLabel;
22     void InitializeComponent();
23     void KeyDemo_KeyPress( Object *, KeyPressEventArgs * );
24     void KeyDemo_KeyDown( Object *, KeyEventArgs * );
25     void KeyDemo_KeyUp( Object *, KeyEventArgs * );
26  }; // end class KeyDemo
```

Fig. 9.38 Keyboard event handling.

```cpp
1   // Fig. 9.39: KeyDemo.cpp
2   // Displaying information about the key the user pressed.
3
4   #include "KeyDemo.h"
5
6   KeyDemo::KeyDemo()
7   {
8      InitializeComponent();
9   }
10
11  void KeyDemo::InitializeComponent()
12  {
13     this->charLabel = new Label();
14     this->keyInfoLabel = new Label();
15     this->SuspendLayout();
16
17     // charLabel
18     this->charLabel->Font = new Drawing::Font(
19        S"Microsoft Sans Serif", 12 );
20     this->charLabel->Location = Point( 8, 8 );
21     this->charLabel->Name = S"charLabel";
22     this->charLabel->Size = Drawing::Size( 168, 32 );
23
24     // keyInfoLabel
25     this->keyInfoLabel->Font = new Drawing::Font(
26        S"Microsoft Sans Serif", 12 );
27     this->keyInfoLabel->Location = Point( 8, 56 );
28     this->keyInfoLabel->Name = S"keyInfoLabel";
29     this->keyInfoLabel->Size = Drawing::Size( 168, 136 );
30
31     // KeyDemo
32     this->AutoScaleBaseSize = Drawing::Size( 15, 37 );
33     this->ClientSize = Drawing::Size( 184, 197 );
34     this->Controls->Add( keyInfoLabel );
35     this->Controls->Add( charLabel );
36     this->Font = new Drawing::Font( S"Microsoft Sans Serif", 24 );
37     this->Name = S"KeyDemo";
38     this->Text = S"KeyDemo";
39
40     // register event handlers (note different delegates)
41     this->KeyDown += new KeyEventHandler( this,
42        KeyDemo_KeyDown );
43
44     this->KeyPress += new KeyPressEventHandler( this,
45        KeyDemo_KeyPress );
46
47     this->KeyUp += new KeyEventHandler( this,
48        KeyDemo_KeyUp );
49
50     this->ResumeLayout();
51  } // end method InitializeComponent
52
```

Fig. 9.39 **KeyDemo** class method definitions. (Part 1 of 2.)

```
53   void KeyDemo::KeyDemo_KeyPress( Object *sender,
54      KeyPressEventArgs *e )
55   {
56      charLabel->Text = String::Concat( S"Key pressed: ",
57         ( e->KeyChar ).ToString() );
58   }
59
60   // display modifier keys, key code, key data and key value
61   void KeyDemo::KeyDemo_KeyDown( Object *sender, KeyEventArgs *e )
62   {
63      keyInfoLabel->Text = String::Concat(
64         S"Alt: ", ( e->Alt ? S"Yes" : S"No" ), S"\n",
65         S"Shift: ", ( e->Shift ? S"Yes" : S"No" ), S"\n",
66         S"Ctrl: ", ( e->Control ? S"Yes" : S"No" ), S"\n",
67         S"KeyCode: ", __box( e->KeyCode ), S"\n",
68         S"KeyData: ", __box( e->KeyData ), S"\n",
69         S"KeyValue: ", e->KeyValue );
70   }
71
72   // clear labels when key released
73   void KeyDemo::KeyDemo_KeyUp( Object *sender, KeyEventArgs *e )
74   {
75      keyInfoLabel->Text = S"";
76      charLabel->Text = S"";
77   }
```

Fig. 9.39   **KeyDemo** class method definitions. (Part 2 of 2.)

```
1    // Fig. 9.40: KeyDemoTest.cpp
2    // Keyboard event handling demonstration.
3
4    #include "KeyDemo.h"
5
6    int __stdcall WinMain()
7    {
8       Application::Run( new KeyDemo() );
9
10      return 0;
11   } // end function WinMain
```

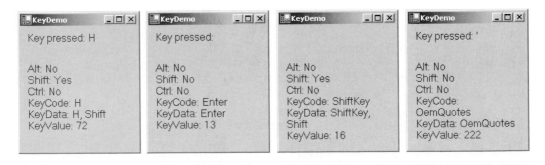

Fig. 9.40   Keyboard event handling demonstration.

The **KeyDown** event handler (lines 61–70) displays more information, all from its **KeyEventArgs** object. It tests for the *Alt*, *Shift* and *Control* keys (lines 64–66), using the **Alt**, **Shift** and **Control** properties, each of which returns **bool**. It then displays the **KeyCode**, **KeyData** and **KeyValue** properties.

The **KeyCode** property returns a **Keys** enumeration, which is converted to a string. The **KeyCode** property returns the key that was pressed, but does not provide any information about modifier keys. Thus, both a capital and a lowercase "a" are represented as the *A* key.

The **KeyData** property returns a **Keys** enumeration value as well, but includes data about modifier keys. Thus, if "A" is input, the **KeyData** shows that the *A* key and the *Shift* key were pressed. Lastly, **KeyValue** returns the key code for the key that was pressed as an integer. This integer is the *Windows virtual key code*, which provides an integer value for a wide range of keys and for mouse buttons. The Windows virtual key code is useful when testing for non-ASCII keys (such as *F12*).

Enumeration **Keys** is a value type. Method **String::Concat** (lines 63–69) expects to receive managed objects as its parameters. To use values from enumeration **Keys** enumeration (e.g., **KeyCode**) we need to convert the value types into reference types, or **__gc** objects.[1] We achieve this by *boxing* the values (lines 67–68). Boxing converts a value type into a managed object. Keyword **__box** creates a managed object, copies the value type's data into the new managed object and returns the address of the managed object.

Common Programming Error 9.2

The pointer returned by **__box** *is a copy of the original value. Modifying the boxed value does not alter the original unboxed object.*

The **KeyUp** event handler clears both labels when the key is released (lines 75–76). As we can see from the output, non-ASCII keys are not displayed in the upper **charLabel** because the **KeyPress** event was not generated. The **KeyDown** event is still raised, and **keyInfoLabel** displays information about the key. The **Keys** enumeration can be used to test for specific keys by comparing the key pressed to a specific **KeyCode**. The Visual Studio. NET documentation has a complete list of the **Keys** enumerations.

Software Engineering Observation 9.4

To cause a control to react when a certain key is pressed (such as Enter*), handle a key event and test for the key pressed. To cause a button to be clicked when the* Enter *key is pressed on a form, set the form's* **AcceptButton** *property.*

9.11 Summary

A graphical user interface (GUI) presents a pictorial interface to a program. A GUI (pronounced "GOO-EE") gives a program a distinctive "look" and "feel." By providing different applications with a consistent set of intuitive user interface components, GUIs allow the user to concentrate on using programs productively. GUIs are built from GUI components (sometimes called controls or widgets). A GUI control is a visual object with which the user interacts via the mouse or keyboard.

---

1. More information about value types and reference types can be found in Chapter 4, Functions and Arrays.

Windows Forms create GUIs. A form is a graphical element that appears on the desktop. A form can be a dialog or a window. A form acts as a container for components. A control is a graphical component, such as a button. Controls that are not visible usually are referred to simply as components. All forms, components and controls are classes. The general design process for creating Windows applications involves creating a Windows Form, setting its properties, adding controls, setting their properties and configuring event handlers.

GUIs are event driven. When the user interacts with a control, an event is generated. This event can trigger methods that respond to the user's actions. The event information is passed to event handlers.

Events are based on the notion of delegates. Delegates act as an intermediate step between the object creating (raising) the event and the method handling it. In many cases, the programmer will handle events generated by prepackaged controls. In this case, all the programmer needs to do is create and register the event handler.

Mouse events (clicks, presses and moves) can be handled for any GUI control that derives from **System::Windows::Forms::Control**. Mouse events use class **MouseEventArgs** (**MouseEventHandler** delegate) and **EventArgs** (**EventHandler** delegate). Class **MouseEventArgs** contains information about the *x*- and *y*-coordinates, the button used, the number of clicks and the number of notches through which the mouse wheel turned.

Key events are generated when keyboard's keys are pressed and released. These events can be handled by any control that inherits from **System::Windows::Forms::Control**. Event **KeyPress** can return a **char** for any ASCII character pressed. One cannot determine if special modifier keys (such as *Shift*, *Alt* and *Control*) were pressed. Events **KeyUp** and **KeyDown** test for special modifier keys (using **KeyEventArgs**). The delegates are **KeyPressEventHandler** (**KeyPressEventArgs**) and **KeyEventHandler** (**KeyEventArgs**). Class **KeyEventArgs** has properties **KeyCode**, **KeyData** and **KeyValue**. Property **KeyCode** returns the key pressed, but does not give any information about modifier keys. The **KeyData** property includes data about modifier keys. The **KeyValue** property returns the key code for the key pressed as an integer.

10

Graphical User Interface
Concepts: Part 2

Objectives

- To be able to use hyperlinks with the **LinkLabel** control.
- To be able to display lists using **ListBox**es and **ComboBox**es.
- To understand the use of the **ListView** and **TreeView** controls for displaying information.
- To be able to create menus, window tabs and multiple-document-interface (MDI) programs.
- To create custom controls.

I claim not to have controlled events, but confess plainly that events have controlled me.
Abraham Lincoln

A good symbol is the best argument, and is a missionary to persuade thousands.
Ralph Waldo Emerson

Capture its reality in paint!
Paul Cézanne

But, soft! what light through yonder window breaks?
It is the east, and Juliet is the sun!
William Shakespeare

An actor entering through the door, you've got nothing. But if he enters through the window, you've got a situation.
Billy Wilder

10.1 Introduction

This chapter continues our study of GUIs. We begin our discussion of more advanced topics with a commonly used GUI component, the *menu*, which presents a user with several logically organized options. We introduce **LinkLabel**s, powerful GUI components that enable the user to click the mouse to be taken to one of several destinations.

We consider GUI components that encapsulate smaller GUI components. We demonstrate how to manipulate a list of values via a **ListBox** and how to combine several checkboxes in a **CheckedListBox**. We also create drop-down lists using **ComboBox**es and display data hierarchically with a **TreeView** control. We present two important GUI components—tab controls and multiple-document-interface windows. These components enable developers to create real-world programs with sophisticated graphical user interfaces.

10.2 Menus

Menus are used to provide groups of related commands for Windows applications. Although these commands depend on the program, some—such as **Open** and **Save**—are common to many applications. Menus are an integral part of GUIs, because they make user actions possible without unnecessary "cluttering" of GUIs.

In Fig. 10.1, an expanded menu lists various commands (called *menu items*), plus *submenus* (menus within a menu). Notice that the top-level menus appear in the left portion of the figure, whereas any submenus are displayed to the right. A menu item that contains a submenu is considered to be the *parent menu* of that submenu.

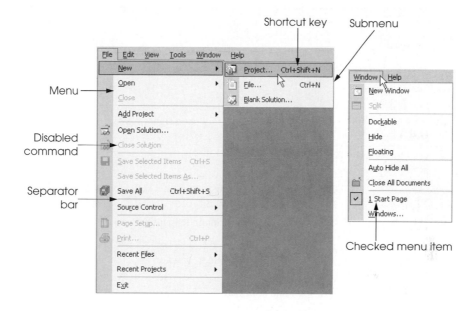

Fig. 10.1 Expanded and checked menus.

All menu items can have *Alt* key shortcuts (also called *access shortcuts* or *hot keys*), which are accessed by pressing *Alt* and the underlined letter (for example, *Alt + F* retrieves the **File** menu). This behavior can be established with property **Mnemonic** (Fig. 10.2). Property **Mnemonic** is read only, and the hot key is specified by inserting an ampersand before the character in the menu item's **Text** property. Menus that are not top-level menus can have shortcut keys as well (combinations of *Ctrl, Shift, Alt, F1, F2*, letter keys, etc.). Shortcut keys can be set with property **ShortCut**. Some menu items display checkmarks, usually indicating that multiple options on the menu can be selected at once.

Look-and-Feel Observation 10.1

*Button*s *also can have access shortcuts. Place the* **&** *symbol just before the character via which we wish to create a shortcut. To click the button, the user then presses Alt and the underlined character.*

MainMenu and MenuItem events and properties	Description / Delegate and Event Arguments
Common **MainMenu** *Properties*	
MenuItems	Represents the **MenuItem**s that are contained in the **MainMenu**.

Fig. 10.2 **MainMenu** and **MenuItem** properties and events. (Part 1 of 2.)

MainMenu and MenuItem events and properties	Description / Delegate and Event Arguments
Common **MainMenu** *Properties (Cont.)*	
RightToLeft	Causes menu text to display from right to left. Useful for languages that are read from right to left.
Common **MenuItem** *Properties*	
Checked	Indicates whether a menu item is checked. Default **false**, meaning that the menu item is not checked.
Index	Specifies an item's position in its parent menu.
MenuItems	Lists the submenu items for a particular menu item.
MergeOrder	Sets the position of a menu item when its parent menu is merged with another menu.
MergeType	Takes a value of the **MenuMerge** enumeration. Specifies how a parent menu merges with another menu. Possible values are **Add**, **MergeItems**, **Remove** and **Replace**.
Mnemonic	Indicates character associated with menu item (e.g., *Alt* + specified character is equivalent to clicking the item). Provides only a *get* accessor; set mnemonic character by preceding it with an ampersand (**&**) in menu item's **Text** property.
RadioCheck	Indicates whether a selected menu item appears as a radio button (black circle) or displays a checkmark. **true** creates radio button, **false** displays checkmark; default **false**.
Shortcut	Specifies the shortcut key for the menu item (e.g., *Ctrl + F9* can be equivalent to clicking a specific item).
ShowShortcut	Indicates whether a shortcut key is shown beside menu item text. Default is **true**, which displays the shortcut key.
Text	Specifies the text to appear in the menu item. To create an *Alt* access shortcut, precede a character with **&** (e.g., **&File** for <u>F</u>ile).
Common **MainMenu** *and* **MenuItem** *Event*	*(Delegate* **EventHandler**, *event arguments* **EventArgs**)
Click	Generated when a menu or menu item is clicked, or when a shortcut key is used.

Fig. 10.2   MainMenu and **MenuItem** properties and events. (Part 2 of 2.)

Each entry in the menu is of a **MenuItem** object (defined in namespace **System::Windows::Forms**). The menu itself is of type **MainMenu**. Menu items generate a **Click** event when selected. Menus can also display the names of open windows in multiple-document-interface (MDI) forms (see Section 10.9). Menu properties and events are summarized in Fig. 10.2.

Look-and-Feel Observation 10.2

It is conventional to place an ellipsis (...) after a menu item that brings up a dialog (such as **Save As...**). *Menu items that produce an immediate action without prompting the user (such as* **Save**) *should not have an ellipsis following their name.*

Class **MenuTest** (Fig. 10.3 and Fig. 10.4) creates a simple menu on a form. The form has a top-level **File** menu with menu items **About** (displays a message box) and **Exit** (terminates the program).The menu also includes a **Format** menu, which changes the text on a label. The **Format** menu has submenus **Color** and **Font**, which change the color and font of the text on a label. The driver program (Fig. 10.5) defines the entry point for the GUI application.

Look-and-Feel Observation 10.3

Using common Windows shortcuts (such as Ctrl+F for Find operations and Ctrl+S for Save operations) decreases an application's learning curve.

```cpp
1   // Fig. 10.3: Menus.h
2   // Header file for class UsingMenus.
3
4   #pragma once
5
6   #using <mscorlib.dll>
7   #using <system.dll>
8   #using <system.drawing.dll>
9   #using <system.windows.forms.dll>
10
11  using namespace System;
12  using namespace System::Drawing;
13  using namespace System::Windows::Forms;
14
15  public __gc class MenuTest : public Form
16  {
17  public:
18     MenuTest();
19
20  private:
21     Label *displayLabel;
22
23     // main menu (contains file and format menu)
24     MainMenu *mainMenu;
25
26     // file menu
27     MenuItem *fileMenuItem, *aboutMenuItem, *exitMenuItem;
28
29     // format menu
30     MenuItem *formatMenuItem;
31
```

Fig. 10.3   Menus for changing text and font color. (Part 1 of 2.)

```
32       // color submenu
33       MenuItem *colorMenuItem, *blackMenuItem, *blueMenuItem,
34          *redMenuItem, *greenMenuItem;
35
36       // font submenu
37       MenuItem *timesMenuItem, *courierMenuItem, *comicMenuItem,
38          *boldMenuItem, *italicMenuItem, *fontMenuItem;
39
40       MenuItem *separatorMenuItem;
41
42       void InitializeComponent();
43       void aboutMenuItem_Click( Object *, EventArgs * );
44       void exitMenuItem_Click( Object *, EventArgs * );
45       void ClearColor();
46       void blackMenuItem_Click( Object *, EventArgs * );
47       void blueMenuItem_Click( Object *, EventArgs * );
48       void greenMenuItem_Click( Object *, EventArgs * );
49       void redMenuItem_Click( Object *, EventArgs * );
50       void ClearFont();
51       void timesMenuItem_Click( Object *, EventArgs * );
52       void courierMenuItem_Click( Object *, EventArgs * );
53       void comicMenuItem_Click( Object *, EventArgs * );
54       void boldMenuItem_Click( Object *, EventArgs * );
55       void italicMenuItem_Click( Object *, EventArgs * );
56    }; // end class MenuTest
```

Fig. 10.3   Menus for changing text and font color. (Part 2 of 2.)

```
1     // Fig. 10.4: Menus.cpp
2     // Using menus to change font colors and styles.
3
4     #include "Menus.h"
5
6     MenuTest::MenuTest()
7     {
8        InitializeComponent();
9     }
10
11    void MenuTest::InitializeComponent()
12    {
13       this->displayLabel = new Label();
14       this->mainMenu = new MainMenu();
15       this->fileMenuItem = new MenuItem();
16       this->aboutMenuItem = new MenuItem();
17       this->exitMenuItem = new MenuItem();
18       this->formatMenuItem = new MenuItem();
19       this->colorMenuItem = new MenuItem();
20       this->blackMenuItem = new MenuItem();
21       this->blueMenuItem = new MenuItem();
22       this->redMenuItem = new MenuItem();
23       this->greenMenuItem = new MenuItem();
```

Fig. 10.4   **MenuTest** class method definitions. (Part 1 of 7.)

```
24      this->fontMenuItem = new MenuItem();
25      this->timesMenuItem = new MenuItem();
26      this->courierMenuItem = new MenuItem();
27      this->comicMenuItem = new MenuItem();
28      this->separatorMenuItem = new MenuItem();
29      this->boldMenuItem = new MenuItem();
30      this->italicMenuItem = new MenuItem();
31      this->SuspendLayout();
32
33      // displayLabel
34      this->displayLabel->Font = new Drawing::Font(
35         S"Times New Roman", 14 );
36      this->displayLabel->Location = Point( 16, 8 );
37      this->displayLabel->Name = S"displayLabel";
38      this->displayLabel->Size = Drawing::Size( 264, 88 );
39      this->displayLabel->Text = S"Use the Format menu to change "
40         S"the appearance of this text.";
41
42      // mainMenu
43      this->mainMenu->MenuItems->Add( this->fileMenuItem );
44      this->mainMenu->MenuItems->Add( this->formatMenuItem );
45
46      // fileMenuItem
47      this->fileMenuItem->Index = 0;
48      this->fileMenuItem->MenuItems->Add( this->aboutMenuItem );
49      this->fileMenuItem->MenuItems->Add( this->exitMenuItem );
50      this->fileMenuItem->Text = S"File";
51
52      // aboutMenuItem
53      this->aboutMenuItem->Index = 0;
54      this->aboutMenuItem->Text = S"About...";
55      this->aboutMenuItem->Click += new EventHandler( this,
56         aboutMenuItem_Click );
57
58      // exitMenuItem
59      this->exitMenuItem->Index = 1;
60      this->exitMenuItem->Text = S"Exit";
61      this->exitMenuItem->Click += new EventHandler( this,
62         exitMenuItem_Click );
63
64      // formatMenuItem
65      this->formatMenuItem->Index = 1;
66      this->formatMenuItem->MenuItems->Add( this->colorMenuItem );
67      this->formatMenuItem->MenuItems->Add( this->fontMenuItem );
68      this->formatMenuItem->Text = S"Format";
69
70      // colorMenuItem
71      this->colorMenuItem->Index = 0;
72      MenuItem *colorMenu[] = { this->blackMenuItem,
73         this->blueMenuItem, this->redMenuItem,
74         this->greenMenuItem };
75      this->colorMenuItem->MenuItems->AddRange( colorMenu );
76      this->colorMenuItem->Text = S"Color";
77
```

Fig. 10.4   MenuTest class method definitions. (Part 2 of 7.)

```
78      // blackMenuItem
79      this->blackMenuItem->Index = 0;
80      this->blackMenuItem->RadioCheck = true;
81      this->blackMenuItem->Text = S"Black";
82      this->blackMenuItem->Click += new EventHandler( this,
83          blackMenuItem_Click );
84
85      // blueMenuItem
86      this->blueMenuItem->Index = 1;
87      this->blueMenuItem->RadioCheck = true;
88      this->blueMenuItem->Text = S"Blue";
89      this->blueMenuItem->Click += new EventHandler( this,
90          blueMenuItem_Click );
91
92      // redMenuItem
93      this->redMenuItem->Index = 2;
94      this->redMenuItem->RadioCheck = true;
95      this->redMenuItem->Text = S"Red";
96      this->redMenuItem->Click += new EventHandler( this,
97          redMenuItem_Click );
98
99      // greenMenuItem
100     this->greenMenuItem->Index = 3;
101     this->greenMenuItem->RadioCheck = true;
102     this->greenMenuItem->Text = S"Green";
103     this->greenMenuItem->Click += new EventHandler( this,
104         greenMenuItem_Click );
105
106     // separatorMenuItem
107     this->separatorMenuItem->Index = 3;
108     this->separatorMenuItem->Text = S"-";
109
110     // fontMenuItem
111     this->fontMenuItem->Index = 1;
112     MenuItem *fontMenu[] = { this->timesMenuItem,
113         this->courierMenuItem, this->comicMenuItem,
114         this->separatorMenuItem, this->boldMenuItem,
115         this->italicMenuItem };
116     this->fontMenuItem->MenuItems->AddRange( fontMenu );
117     this->fontMenuItem->Text = S"Font";
118
119     // timesMenuItem
120     this->timesMenuItem->Index = 0;
121     this->timesMenuItem->Text = S"Times New Roman";
122     this->timesMenuItem->Click += new EventHandler( this,
123         timesMenuItem_Click );
124
125     // courierMenuItem
126     this->courierMenuItem->Index = 1;
127     this->courierMenuItem->Text = S"Courier";
128     this->courierMenuItem->Click += new EventHandler( this,
129         courierMenuItem_Click );
130
```

Fig. 10.4 **MenuTest** class method definitions. (Part 3 of 7.)

```
131        // comicMenuItem
132        this->comicMenuItem->Index = 2;
133        this->comicMenuItem->Text = S"Comic Sans";
134        this->comicMenuItem->Click += new EventHandler( this,
135           comicMenuItem_Click );
136
137        // boldMenuItem
138        this->boldMenuItem->Index = 4;
139        this->boldMenuItem->Text = S"Bold";
140        this->boldMenuItem->Click += new EventHandler( this,
141           boldMenuItem_Click );
142
143        // italicMenuItem
144        this->italicMenuItem->Index = 5;
145        this->italicMenuItem->Text = S"Italic";
146        this->italicMenuItem->Click += new EventHandler( this,
147           italicMenuItem_Click );
148
149        // MenuTest
150        this->AutoScaleBaseSize = Drawing::Size( 5, 13 );
151        this->ClientSize = Drawing::Size( 292, 97 );
152        this->Controls->Add( this->displayLabel );
153        this->Menu = this->mainMenu;
154        this->Name = S"MenuTest";
155        this->Text = S"MenuTest";
156        this->ResumeLayout();
157    } // end method InitializeComponent
158
159    // display MessageBox
160    void MenuTest::aboutMenuItem_Click( Object *sender,
161       EventArgs *e )
162    {
163       MessageBox::Show( S"This is an example\nof using menus.",
164          S"About", MessageBoxButtons::OK,
165          MessageBoxIcon::Information );
166    } // end method aboutMenuItem_Click
167
168    // exit program
169    void MenuTest::exitMenuItem_Click( Object *sender,
170       EventArgs *e )
171    {
172       Application::Exit();
173    } // end method exitMenuItem_Click
174
175    // reset color
176    void MenuTest::ClearColor()
177    {
178       // clear all checkmarks
179       blackMenuItem->Checked = false;
180       blueMenuItem->Checked = false;
181       redMenuItem->Checked = false;
182       greenMenuItem->Checked = false;
183    } // end method ClearColor
184
```

Fig. 10.4   MenuTest class method definitions. (Part 4 of 7.)

```
185    // update menu state and color display black
186    void MenuTest::blackMenuItem_Click( Object *sender,
187       EventArgs *e )
188    {
189       // reset checkmarks for color menu items
190       ClearColor();
191
192       // set color to black
193       displayLabel->ForeColor = Color::Black;
194       blackMenuItem->Checked = true;
195    } // end method blackMenuItem_Click
196
197    // update menu state and color display blue
198    void MenuTest::blueMenuItem_Click( Object *sender,
199       EventArgs *e )
200    {
201       // reset checkmarks for color menu items
202       ClearColor();
203
204       // set color to blue
205       displayLabel->ForeColor = Color::Blue;
206       blueMenuItem->Checked = true;
207    } // end method blueMenuItem_Click
208
209    // update menu state and color display red
210    void MenuTest::redMenuItem_Click( Object *sender, EventArgs *e )
211    {
212       // reset checkmarks for color menu items
213       ClearColor();
214
215       // set color to red
216       displayLabel->ForeColor = Color::Red;
217       redMenuItem->Checked = true;
218    } // end method redMenuItem_Click
219
220    // update menu state and color display green
221    void MenuTest::greenMenuItem_Click( Object *sender,
222       EventArgs *e )
223    {
224       // reset checkmarks for color menu items
225       ClearColor();
226
227       // set color to green
228       displayLabel->ForeColor = Color::Green;
229       greenMenuItem->Checked = true;
230    } // end method greenMenuItem_Click
231
232    // reset font types
233    void MenuTest::ClearFont()
234    {
235       // clear all checkmarks
236       timesMenuItem->Checked = false;
237       courierMenuItem->Checked = false;
```

Fig. 10.4 **MenuTest** class method definitions. (Part 5 of 7.)

```
238        comicMenuItem->Checked = false;
239  } // end method ClearFont
240
241  // update menu state and set font to Times
242  void MenuTest::timesMenuItem_Click( Object *sender,
243      EventArgs *e )
244  {
245      // reset checkmarks for font menu items
246      ClearFont();
247
248      // set Times New Roman font
249      timesMenuItem->Checked = true;
250      displayLabel->Font = new Drawing::Font(
251          S"Times New Roman", 14, displayLabel->Font->Style );
252  } // end method timesMenuItem_Click
253
254  // update menu state and set font to Courier
255  void MenuTest::courierMenuItem_Click( Object *sender,
256      EventArgs *e )
257  {
258      // reset checkmarks for font menu items
259      ClearFont();
260
261      // set Courier font
262      courierMenuItem->Checked = true;
263      displayLabel->Font = new Drawing::Font(
264          S"Courier New", 14, displayLabel->Font->Style );
265  } // end method courierMenuItem_Click
266
267  // update menu state and set font to Comic Sans MS
268  void MenuTest::comicMenuItem_Click( Object *sender,
269      EventArgs *e )
270  {
271      // reset checkmarks for font menu items
272      ClearFont();
273
274      // set Comic Sans font
275      comicMenuItem->Checked = true;
276      displayLabel->Font = new Drawing::Font(
277          S"Comic Sans MS", 14, displayLabel->Font->Style );
278  } // end method comicMenuItem_Click
279
280  // toggle checkmark and toggle bold style
281  void MenuTest::boldMenuItem_Click( Object *sender,
282      EventArgs *e )
283  {
284      // toggle checkmark
285      boldMenuItem->Checked = !boldMenuItem->Checked;
286
287      // use Xor to toggle bold, keep all other styles
288      displayLabel->Font = new Drawing::Font(
289          displayLabel->Font->FontFamily, 14, ( FontStyle )
290          ( displayLabel->Font->Style ^ FontStyle::Bold ) );
```

Fig. 10.4 MenuTest class method definitions. (Part 6 of 7.)

```
291  } // end method boldMenuItem_Click
292
293  // toggle checkmark and toggle italic style
294  void MenuTest::italicMenuItem_Click( Object *sender,
295     EventArgs *e )
296  {
297     // toggle checkmark
298     italicMenuItem->Checked = !italicMenuItem->Checked;
299
300     // use Xor to toggle bold, keep all other styles
301     displayLabel->Font = new Drawing::Font(
302        displayLabel->Font->FontFamily, 14, ( FontStyle )
303        ( displayLabel->Font->Style ^ FontStyle::Italic ) );
304  } // end method italicMenuItem_Click
```

Fig. 10.4 **MenuTest** class method definitions. (Part 7 of 7.)

```
1   // Fig. 10.5: MenusTest.cpp
2   // Demonstrating menus.
3
4   #include "Menus.h"
5
6   int __stdcall WinMain()
7   {
8      Application::Run( new MenuTest() );
9
10     return 0;
11  } // end WinMain
```

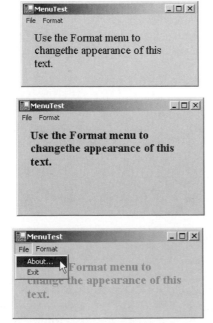

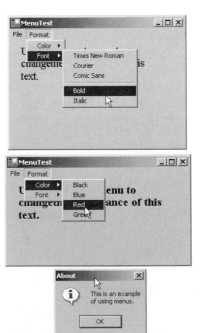

Fig. 10.5 Menu demonstration main application.

Line 14 of Fig. 10.4 instantiates a pointer to the **MainMenu** object (named **main-Menu**). A **MainMenu** control is the container for a form's menu. Lines 15–30 instantiate pointers to the **MenuItem** objects that will be added to this control. Property *MenuItems* represents a menu's menu items. Method **Add** (lines 43–44) adds the two top-level menus (**File** and **Format**) to the **mainMenu**'s menu items. Class **Form**'s property **Menu** (line 153) sets the menu (**mainMenu**) that the GUI displays.

We configure each **MenuItem** object. Property *Index* sets the position of the menu item; for instance, setting **fileMenuItem**'s **Index** property to **0** (line 47) indicates that menu **File** appears first in the menu bar. Property **Text** (e.g., line 50) sets each menu's caption. Setting property **Text** to **"-"** creates a separator bar (line 108), which we add as the fourth item of submenu **Font** (line 116).

Selecting a menu item generates a **Click** event. By default, selecting **File** and **Format** displays their child menus, and selecting **Color** and **Font** displays their submenus. We associate event handlers with the other menu items' **Click** event (e.g., lines 55–56).

Each **MenuItem** object has property **MenuItems**. For example, method **Add** (lines 48–49) appends menu items **About** and **Exit** to menu **File**. Adding menu items to a non-top-level menu item creates a submenu, such as submenu **Color** (lines 72–75).

We made the items in the **Color** submenu (**Black**, **Blue**, **Red** and **Green**) mutually exclusive—the user can select only one at a time. (We explain how we did this shortly.) To indicate this behavior to the user, we set the menu items' *RadioCheck* properties to **true**. This causes a radio button to appear (instead of a checkmark) when a user selects a color-menu item.

Each **Color** menu item has its own event handler. The event handler for color **Black** is **blackMenuItem_Click** (lincs 186–195). The event handlers for colors **Blue**, **Red** and **Green** are **blueMenuItem_Click** (lines 198–207), **redMenuItem_Click** (lines 210–218) and **greenMenuItem_Click** (lines 221–230), respectively. Each event handler uses the **Color** structure to assign a new value to **displayLabel**'s **Fore-Color** property (lines 193, 205, 216 and 228). The *Color* structure (located in namespace **System::Drawing**) contains several pre-defined colors as members. For instance, the color red can be specified using **Color::Red**. Thc **Color** structure will be discussed in more detail in Chapter 16, Graphics and Multimedia. Each **Color** menu item must be mutually exclusive, so each event handler calls method **ClearColor** (lines 176–183) before setting its corresponding **Checked** property to **true**. Method **ClearColor** sets the **Checked** property of each color **MenuItem** to **false**, effectively preventing more than one menu item from being checked at a time.

Software Engineering Observation 10.1

*The mutual exclusion of menu items is not enforced by the **MainMenu**, even when property **RadioCheck** is **true**. We must program this behavior.*

Look-and-Feel Observation 10.4

*Set the **RadioCheck** property to reflect the desired behavior of menu items. Use radio buttons (**RadioCheck** property set to **true**) to indicate mutually exclusive menu items. Use checkmarks (**RadioCheck** property set to **false**) for menu items that have no logical restriction.*

The **Font** menu contains three menu items for font types (**Courier**, **Times New Roman** and **Comic Sans**) and two menu items for font styles (**Bold** and **Italic**). We add a separator bar between the font-type and font-style menu items to indicate the distinction:

Font types are mutually exclusive; font styles are not. This means that a **Font** object can specify only one font face at a time, but can set multiple styles at once (e.g., a font can be both bold and italic). The font-type menu items display checks. As with the **Color** menu, we also must enforce mutual exclusion in our event handlers.

Event handlers for font-type menu items **TimesRoman**, **Courier** and **ComicSans** are **timesMenuItem_Click** (lines 242–252), **courierMenuItem_Click** (lines 255–265) and **comicMenuItem_Click** (lines 268–278), respectively. These event handlers behave in a manner similar to that of the event handlers for the **Color** menu items. Each event handler clears the **Checked** properties for all font-type menu items by calling method **ClearFont** (lines 233–239), then sets the **Checked** property of the menu item that generated the event to **true**. This enforces the mutual exclusion of the font-type menu items. As explained in Chapter 9, this program's event-handling structure allows us to add and remove menu entries while making minimal structural changes to the code.

The event handlers for the **Bold** and **Italic** menu items (lines 290–315) use the bitwise XOR operator. For each font style, the exclusive OR operator (**^**) changes the text to include the style or, if that style is already applied, to remove it. The toggling behavior provided by the XOR operator was explained in Chapter 9, Graphical User Interface Concepts: Part 1.

10.3 LinkLabels

The **LinkLabel** control displays links to other objects, such as files or Web pages (Fig. 10.6). A **LinkLabel** appears as underlined text (colored blue by default). When the mouse moves over the link, the pointer changes to a hand; this is similar to the behavior of a hyperlink in a Web page. The link can change color to indicate whether the link is new, visited or active. When clicked, the **LinkLabel** generates a **LinkClicked** event (see Fig. 10.7). Class **LinkLabel** is derived from class **Label** and therefore inherits all of class **Label**'s functionality.

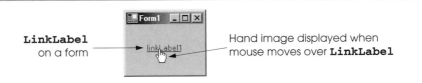

LinkLabel on a form

Hand image displayed when mouse moves over **LinkLabel**

Fig. 10.6   **LinkLabel** control in running program.

LinkLabel properties and events	Description / Delegate and Event Arguments
Common Properties	
ActiveLinkColor	Specifies the color of the active link when clicked. Default is red.
LinkArea	Specifies which portion of text in the **LinkLabel** is treated as part of the link.
LinkBehavior	Specifies the link's behavior, such as how the link appears when the mouse is placed over it.

Fig. 10.7   **LinkLabel** properties and events. (Part 1 of 2.)

LinkLabel properties and events	Description / Delegate and Event Arguments
Common Properties (Cont.)	
LinkColor	Specifies the original color of all links before they have been visited. Default is blue.
Links	Lists the **LinkLabel::Link** objects, which are the links contained in the **LinkLabel**.
LinkVisited	If **true**, link appears as if it were visited. (Its color is changed to that specified by property **VisitedLinkColor**.) Default **false**.
Text	Specifies the text to appear on the control.
UseMnemonic	If **true**, **&** character in **Text** property acts as a shortcut (similar to the *Alt* shortcut in menus).
VisitedLinkColor	Specifies the color of visited links. Default is purple.
Common Event	*(Delegate **LinkLabelLinkClickedEventHandler**, event arguments **LinkLabelLinkClickedEventArgs**)*
LinkClicked	Generated when link is clicked.

Fig. 10.7 **LinkLabel** properties and events. (Part 2 of 2.)

Class **LinkLabelTest** (Fig. 10.8 and Fig. 10.9) uses three **LinkLabel**s to link to the **C:** drive, the Deitel Web page (**www.deitel.com**) and the Notepad application, respectively. The **Text** properties of the **LinkLabel**s **driveLinkLabel** (line 23 of Fig. 10.9), **deitelLinkLabel** (lines 34–35) and **notepadLinkLabel** (line 46) are set to describe each link's purpose. The driver application (Fig. 10.10) demonstrates the GUI.

```
1    // Fig. 10.8: LinkLabels.h
2    // LinkLabelTest class header file.
3
4    #pragma once
5
6    #using <mscorlib.dll>
7    #using <system.dll>
8    #using <system.drawing.dll>
9    #using <system.windows.forms.dll>
10
11   using namespace System;
12   using namespace System::Drawing;
13   using namespace System::Windows::Forms;
14
15   public __gc class LinkLabelTest : public Form
16   {
17   public:
18      LinkLabelTest();
19
```

Fig. 10.8 **LinkLabel**s used to link to a folder, a Web page and an application. (Part 1 of 2.)

```
20    private:
21
22        // linklabels to C: drive, www.deitel.com and Notepad
23        LinkLabel *driveLinkLabel;
24        LinkLabel *deitelLinkLabel;
25        LinkLabel *notepadLinkLabel;
26
27        void InitializeComponent();
28        void driveLinkLabel_LinkClicked( Object *,
29           LinkLabelLinkClickedEventArgs * );
30        void deitelLinkLabel_LinkClicked( Object *,
31           LinkLabelLinkClickedEventArgs * );
32        void notepadLinkLabel_LinkClicked( Object *,
33           LinkLabelLinkClickedEventArgs * );
34    }; // end class LinkLabelTest
```

Fig. 10.8 **LinkLabel**s used to link to a folder, a Web page and an application. (Part 2 of 2.)

```
1    // Fig. 10.9: LinkLabels.cpp
2    // Using LinkLabels to create hyperlinks.
3
4    #include "LinkLabels.h"
5
6    LinkLabelTest::LinkLabelTest()
7    {
8        InitializeComponent();
9    }
10
11   void LinkLabelTest::InitializeComponent()
12   {
13       this->driveLinkLabel = new LinkLabel();
14       this->deitelLinkLabel = new LinkLabel();
15       this->notepadLinkLabel = new LinkLabel();
16       this->SuspendLayout();
17
18       // driveLinkLabel
19       this->driveLinkLabel->Location = Point( 64, 16 );
20       this->driveLinkLabel->Name = S"driveLinkLabel";
21       this->driveLinkLabel->TabIndex = 0;
22       this->driveLinkLabel->TabStop = true;
23       this->driveLinkLabel->Text = S"Click to browse C:\\";
24       this->driveLinkLabel->LinkClicked += new
25          LinkLabelLinkClickedEventHandler( this,
26          driveLinkLabel_LinkClicked );
27
28       // deitelLinkLabel
29       this->deitelLinkLabel->Location = Point( 64, 56 );
30       this->deitelLinkLabel->Name = S"deitelLinkLabel";
31       this->deitelLinkLabel->Size = Drawing::Size( 176, 24 );
32       this->deitelLinkLabel->TabIndex = 1;
33       this->deitelLinkLabel->TabStop = true;
34       this->deitelLinkLabel->Text =
```

Fig. 10.9 **LinkLabelTest** class method definitions. (Part 1 of 3.)

```
35            S"Click to visit www.deitel.com";
36    this->deitelLinkLabel->LinkClicked += new
37        LinkLabelLinkClickedEventHandler( this,
38        deitelLinkLabel_LinkClicked );
39
40    // notepadLinkLabel
41    this->notepadLinkLabel->Location = Point( 64, 96 );
42    this->notepadLinkLabel->Name = S"notepadLinkLabel";
43    this->notepadLinkLabel->Size = Drawing::Size( 128, 32 );
44    this->notepadLinkLabel->TabIndex = 2;
45    this->notepadLinkLabel->TabStop = true;
46    this->notepadLinkLabel->Text = S"Click to run Notepad";
47    this->notepadLinkLabel->LinkClicked += new
48        LinkLabelLinkClickedEventHandler( this,
49        notepadLinkLabel_LinkClicked );
50
51    // LinkLabelTest
52    this->AutoScaleBaseSize = Drawing::Size( 5, 13 );
53    this->ClientSize = Drawing::Size( 292, 149 );
54    this->Controls->Add( this->notepadLinkLabel );
55    this->Controls->Add( this->deitelLinkLabel );
56    this->Controls->Add( this->driveLinkLabel );
57    this->Name = S"LinkLabelTest";
58    this->Text = S"LinkLabelTest";
59    this->ResumeLayout();
60 } // end method InitializeComponent
61
62 // browse C:\ drive
63 void LinkLabelTest::driveLinkLabel_LinkClicked( Object *sender,
64    LinkLabelLinkClickedEventArgs *e )
65 {
66    driveLinkLabel->LinkVisited = true;
67
68    try {
69        Diagnostics::Process::Start( S"C:\\" );
70    }
71    catch ( ... ) {
72        MessageBox::Show( S"Error", S"No C:\\ drive" );
73    }
74 } // end method driveLinkLabel_LinkClicked
75
76 // load www.deitel.com in Web broswer
77 void LinkLabelTest::deitelLinkLabel_LinkClicked( Object *sender,
78    LinkLabelLinkClickedEventArgs *e )
79 {
80    deitelLinkLabel->LinkVisited = true;
81
82    try {
83        Diagnostics::Process::Start( S"IExplore",
84            S"http://www.deitel.com" );
85    }
86    catch ( ... ) {
87        MessageBox::Show( S"Error",
88            S"Unable to open Internet Explorer" );
```

Fig. 10.9 **LinkLabelTest** class method definitions. (Part 2 of 3.)

```
89        }
90   } // end method deitelLinkLabel_LinkClicked
91
92   // run application Notepad
93   void LinkLabelTest::notepadLinkLabel_LinkClicked(
94      Object *sender, LinkLabelLinkClickedEventArgs *e )
95   {
96      notepadLinkLabel->LinkVisited = true;
97
98      try {
99
100        // program called as if in run
101        // menu and full path not needed
102        Diagnostics::Process::Start( S"notepad" );
103     }
104     catch ( ... ) {
105        MessageBox::Show( S"Error", S"Unable to start Notepad" );
106     }
107  } // end method notepadLinkLabel_LinkClicked
```

Fig. 10.9 LinkLabelTest class method definitions. (Part 3 of 3.)

```
1    // Fig. 10.10: LinkLabelsTest.cpp
2    // LinkLabel demonstration.
3
4    #include "LinkLabels.h"
5
6    int __stdcall WinMain()
7    {
8       Application::Run( new LinkLabelTest() );
9
10      return 0;
11   } // end WinMain
```

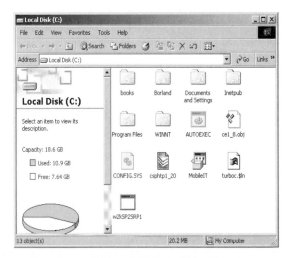

Fig. 10.10 LinkLabel demonstration. (Part 1 of 2.)

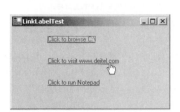

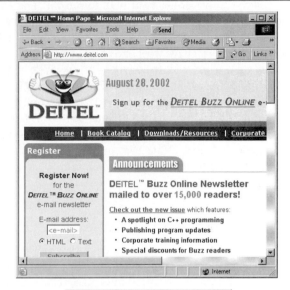

Fig. 10.10 **LinkLabel** demonstration. (Part 2 of 2.)

Look-and-Feel Observation 10.5

*Although other controls can perform actions similar to those of a **LinkLabel** (such as the opening of a Web page), **LinkLabel**s indicate that a link can be followed—a regular label or button does not necessarily convey that idea.*

The event handlers for the **LinkLabel** instances call **static** method **Start** of class **Process** (namespace **System::Diagnostics**). This method allows us to execute other programs from our application. Method **Start** can take as arguments either the file to open (a **String *** object) or the name of the application to run and its command-line arguments (two **String *** objects). Method **Start**'s arguments can be in the same form as if they were provided for input to the **Run** command in Windows. To open a file that has a file type that Windows recognizes, simply insert the file's full path name. The Windows operating system should be able to use the application associated with the given file's extension to open the file.

The event handler for **driveLinkLabel**'s **LinkClicked** events browses the **C:** drive (lines 63–74). Line 66 sets the **LinkVisited** property to **true**, which changes the link's color from blue to purple. The event handler then passes **"C:\"** to method **Start** line 69, which opens a **Windows Explorer** window.

The event handler for **deitelLinkLabel**'s **LinkClicked** events (lines 77–90) opens the Web page **www.deitel.com** in Internet Explorer. We achieve this by passing the string **"IExplore"** and the Web page address (lines 83–84), which opens Internet Explorer. Line 80 sets the **LinkVisited** property to **true**.

The event handler for **notepadLinkLabel**'s **LinkClicked** events opens the specified Notepad application (lines 93–107). Line 96 sets the link to appear as a visited link. Line 102 passes the argument **"notepad"** to method **Start**, which calls **notepad.exe**. Note that, in line 102, the **.exe** extension is not required—Windows can determine whether the argument given to method **Start** is an executable file.

10.4 `ListBox`es and `CheckedListBox`es

The *`ListBox`* control allows the user to view and select from multiple items in a list. (Users can select multiple items simultaneously from a **ListBox**, but not by default.) The *`CheckedListBox`* control extends a **ListBox** by including checkboxes next to each item in the list. This allows users to place checks on multiple items at once, as is possible in a **CheckBox** control. Figure 10.11 displays a sample **ListBox** and a sample **CheckedListBox**. In both controls, scrollbars appear if the number of items is too large to be displayed simultaneously in the component. Figure 10.12 lists common **ListBox** properties, methods and events.

The *`SelectionMode`* property determines the number of items that can be selected. This property has the possible values *`None`*, *`One`*, *`MultiSimple`* and *`MultiExtended`* (from the *`SelectionMode`* *enumeration*)—the differences among these settings are explained in Fig. 10.12. The *`SelectedIndexChanged`* event occurs when the user selects a new item.

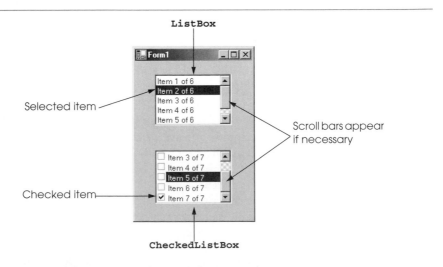

Fig. 10.11 `ListBox` and `CheckedListBox` on a form.

ListBox properties, methods and events	Description / Delegate and Event Arguments
Common Properties	
`Items`	Lists the items within the `ListBox`.
`MultiColumn`	Indicates whether the `ListBox` can break a list into multiple columns. Multiple columns are used to make vertical scrollbars unnecessary.
`SelectedIndex`	Returns the index of the currently selected item. If no items have been selected, the method returns `-1`.
`SelectedIndices`	Returns the indices of all currently selected items.
`SelectedItem`	Returns a pointer to the currently selected item. (If multiple items are selected, it returns the item with the lowest index number.)
`SelectedItems`	Returns the currently selected item(s).
`SelectionMode`	Determines the number of items that can be selected and the means through which multiple items can be selected. Values `None`, `One`, `MultiSimple` (multiple selection allowed) and `MultiExtended` (multiple selection allowed via a combination of arrow keys, mouse clicks and *Shift* and *Control* buttons).
`Sorted`	Indicates whether items appear in alphabetical order. `true` causes alphabetization; default is `false`.
Common Method	
`GetSelected`	Takes an index and returns `true` if the corresponding item is selected.
Common Event	*(Delegate `EventHandler`, event arguments `EventArgs`)*
`SelectedIndex-Changed`	Generated when selected index changes.

Fig. 10.12 `ListBox` properties, methods and events.

Both the `ListBox` and `CheckedListBox` have properties `Items`, `SelectedItem` and `SelectedIndex`. Property `Items` returns all the objects in the list as a collection. Collections are a common way of exposing lists of `Object`s in the .NET Framework. Many .NET GUI components (e.g., `ListBox`es) use collections to expose lists of internal objects (e.g., items contained within a `ListBox`). We discuss collections further in Chapter 19, Data Structures and Collections. Property `SelectedItem` returns the currently selected item. If the user can select multiple items, use collection `SelectedItems` to return all the selected items as a collection. Property `SelectedIndex` returns the index of the selected item—if there could be more than one, use property `SelectedIndices`. If no items are selected, property `SelectedIndex` returns `-1`. Method `GetSelected` takes an index and returns `true` if the corresponding item is selected.

To add items to the **ListBox** or the **CheckedListBox**, we must add objects to its **Items** collection. This can be accomplished by invoking method **Add** to add a **String *** to the **ListBox**'s or **CheckedListBox**'s **Items** collection. For example, we could write

*myListBox->***Items->Add(** *"myListItem"* **)**

to add **String *** *myListItem* to **ListBox** *myListBox*. To add multiple objects, programmers can either use method **Add** multiple times or use method **AddRange** to add an array of objects. Classes **ListBox** and **CheckedListBox** use each submitted object's **ToString** method to determine the label for the corresponding object's entry in the list.

10.4.1 ListBoxes

Class **ListBoxTest** (Fig. 10.13 and Fig. 10.14) enables the user to add, remove and clear items from **ListBox displayListBox** (line 13 of Fig. 10.14). Class **ListBox-Test** uses **TextBox inputTextBox** (line 14) to allow the user to type in a new item. When the user clicks button **addButton** (line 15), the new item appears in **display-ListBox**. Similarly, if the user selects an item and clicks **removeButton** (line 16), the item is deleted. Control **clearButton** (line 17) deletes all entries in **displayList-Box**. The user terminates the application by clicking button **exitButton** (line 18).

```
1   // Fig. 10.13: ListBox.h
2   // Header file for class ListBoxTest.
3
4   #pragma once
5
6   #using <mscorlib.dll>
7   #using <system.dll>
8   #using <system.drawing.dll>
9   #using <system.windows.forms.dll>
10
11  using namespace System;
12  using namespace System::Drawing;
13  using namespace System::Windows::Forms;
14
15  public __gc class ListBoxTest : public Form
16  {
17  public:
18     ListBoxTest();
19
20  private:
21
22     // contains user-input list of elements
23     ListBox *displayListBox;
24
25     // user input textbox
26     TextBox *inputTextBox;
27
```

Fig. 10.13 ListBox used in a program to add, remove and clear items. (Part 1 of 2.)

```
28      // add, remove, clear and exit command buttons
29      Button *addButton;
30      Button *removeButton;
31      Button *clearButton;
32      Button *exitButton;
33
34      void InitializeComponent();
35      void addButton_Click( Object *, EventArgs * );
36      void removeButton_Click( Object *, EventArgs * );
37      void clearButton_Click( Object *, EventArgs * );
38      void exitButton_Click( Object *, EventArgs * );
39   }; // end class ListBoxTest
```

Fig. 10.13 ListBox used in a program to add, remove and clear items. (Part 2 of 2.)

```
1    // Fig. 10.14: ListBox.cpp
2    // Program to add, remove and clear list box items.
3
4    #include "ListBox.h"
5
6    ListBoxTest::ListBoxTest()
7    {
8       InitializeComponent();
9    }
10
11   void ListBoxTest::InitializeComponent()
12   {
13      this->displayListBox = new ListBox();
14      this->inputTextBox = new TextBox();
15      this->addButton = new Button();
16      this->removeButton = new Button();
17      this->clearButton = new Button();
18      this->exitButton = new Button();
19      this->SuspendLayout();
20
21      // displayListBox
22      this->displayListBox->Location = Point( 16, 16 );
23      this->displayListBox->Name = S"displayListBox";
24      this->displayListBox->Size = Drawing::Size( 120, 290 );
25      this->displayListBox->TabIndex = 0;
26
27      // inputTextBox
28      this->inputTextBox->Location = Point( 168, 16 );
29      this->inputTextBox->Name = S"inputTextBox";
30      this->inputTextBox->TabIndex = 1;
31      this->inputTextBox->Text = S"";
32
33      // addButton
34      this->addButton->Font = new Drawing::Font(
35         S"Microsoft Sans Serif", 10, FontStyle::Regular,
36         GraphicsUnit::Point, 0 );
```

Fig. 10.14 ListBoxTest class methods definition. (Part 1 of 3.)

```
37       this->addButton->Location = Point( 168, 48 );
38       this->addButton->Name = S"addButton";
39       this->addButton->Size = Drawing::Size( 104, 48 );
40       this->addButton->TabIndex = 2;
41       this->addButton->Text = S"Add";
42       this->addButton->Click += new EventHandler( this,
43          addButton_Click );
44
45       // removeButton
46       this->removeButton->Font = new Drawing::Font(
47          S"Microsoft Sans Serif", 10, FontStyle::Regular,
48          GraphicsUnit::Point, 0 );
49       this->removeButton->Location = Point( 168, 112 );
50       this->removeButton->Name = S"removeButton";
51       this->removeButton->Size = Drawing::Size( 104, 48 );
52       this->removeButton->TabIndex = 3;
53       this->removeButton->Text = S"Remove";
54       this->removeButton->Click += new EventHandler( this,
55          removeButton_Click );
56
57       // clearButton
58       this->clearButton->Font = new Drawing::Font(
59          S"Microsoft Sans Serif", 10, FontStyle::Regular,
60          GraphicsUnit::Point, 0 );
61       this->clearButton->Location = Point( 168, 176 );
62       this->clearButton->Name = S"clearButton";
63       this->clearButton->Size = Drawing::Size( 104, 48 );
64       this->clearButton->TabIndex = 4;
65       this->clearButton->Text = S"Clear";
66       this->clearButton->Click += new EventHandler( this,
67          clearButton_Click );
68
69       // exitButton
70       this->exitButton->Font = new Drawing::Font(
71          S"Microsoft Sans Serif", 10, FontStyle::Regular,
72          GraphicsUnit::Point, 0 );
73       this->exitButton->Location = Point( 168, 240 );
74       this->exitButton->Name = S"exitButton";
75       this->exitButton->Size = Drawing::Size( 104, 48 );
76       this->exitButton->TabIndex = 5;
77       this->exitButton->Text = S"Exit";
78       this->exitButton->Click += new EventHandler( this,
79          exitButton_Click );
80
81       // ListBoxTest
82       this->AutoScaleBaseSize = Drawing::Size( 5, 13 );
83       this->ClientSize = Drawing::Size( 292, 325 );
84       Control *controls[] = { this->exitButton,
85          this->clearButton, this->removeButton,
86          this->addButton, this->inputTextBox,
87          this->displayListBox };
88       this->Controls->AddRange( controls );
89       this->Name = S"ListBoxTest";
```

Fig. 10.14 ListBoxTest class methods definition. (Part 2 of 3.)

```
90       this->Text = S"ListBoxTest";
91       this->ResumeLayout();
92  } // end method InitializeComponent
93
94  // add new item (text from input box) and clear input box
95  void ListBoxTest::addButton_Click( Object *sender,
96       EventArgs *e )
97  {
98       if ( inputTextBox->Text->Length > 0 ) {
99          displayListBox->Items->Add( inputTextBox->Text );
100         inputTextBox->Clear();
101      }
102  } // end method addButton_Click
103
104  // remove item if one selected
105  void ListBoxTest::removeButton_Click( Object *sender,
106      EventArgs *e )
107  {
108
109      // remove only if item selected
110      if ( displayListBox->SelectedIndex != -1 )
111         displayListBox->Items->RemoveAt(
112            displayListBox->SelectedIndex );
113  } // end method removeButton_Click
114
115  // clear all items
116  void ListBoxTest::clearButton_Click( Object *sender,
117      EventArgs *e )
118  {
119      displayListBox->Items->Clear();
120  } // end method clearButton_Click
121
122  // exit application
123  void ListBoxTest::exitButton_Click( Object *sender,
124      EventArgs *e )
125  {
126      Application::Exit();
127  } // end method exitButton_Click
```

Fig. 10.14 ListBoxTest class methods definition. (Part 3 of 3.)

```
1   // Fig. 10.15: ListBoxTest.cpp
2   // List box demonstration.
3
4   #include "ListBox.h"
5
6   int __stdcall WinMain()
7   {
8      Application::Run( new ListBoxTest() );
9
10     return 0;
11  } // end WinMain
```

Fig. 10.15 ListBox demonstration. (Part 1 of 2.)

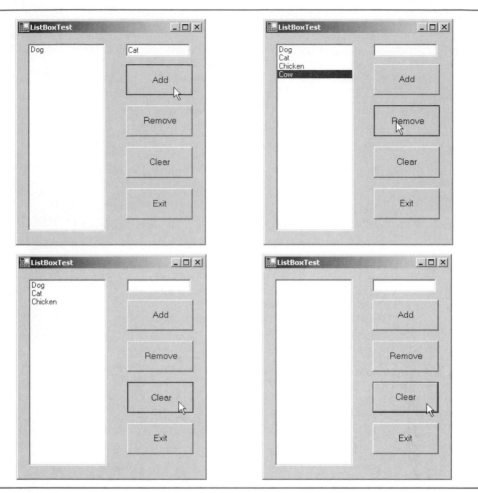

Fig. 10.15 ListBox demonstration. (Part 2 of 2.)

The **addButton_Click** event handler (lines 95–102) calls method **Add** of the **Items** collection in the **ListBox**. This method takes a **String *** to add to **display-ListBox**. In this case, the **String *** is the user-input text, or **inputTextBox->Text** (line 99). After the item is added, **inputTextBox->Text** is cleared (line 100).

The **removeButton_Click** event handler (lines 105–113) calls method *Remove* of the **Items** collection to remove an item from the **ListBox**. Event handler **removeButton_Click** first uses property **SelectedIndex** to check which index is selected. Unless **SelectedIndex** is **-1** (line 110), the handler removes the item that corresponds to the selected index.

The event handler for **clearButton_Click** (lines 116–120) calls method *Clear* of the **Items** collection (line 119). This removes all the entries in **displayListBox**. Finally, event handler **exitButton_Click** (lines 123–127) terminates the application, using method **Application::Exit** (line 126).

10.4.2 CheckedListBoxes

The **CheckedListBox** control derives from class **ListBox** and includes a checkbox next to each item in the list. **CheckedListBox**es imply that multiple items can be selected, and the only possible values for the **SelectionMode** property are **Selection-Mode::None** and **SelectionMode::One**. **SelectionMode::One** allows multiple selection, because checkboxes imply that there are no logical restrictions on the items—the user can select as many items as required. Thus, the only choice is whether to give the user multiple selection or no selection at all. This keeps the **CheckedListBox**'s behavior consistent with that of **CheckBox**es. The programmer should not use the last two **SelectionMode** values, **MultiSimple** and **MultiExtended**, because the only logical selection modes are handled by **None** and **One**. Common properties and events of **CheckedListBox**es appear in Fig. 10.16.

Common Programming Error 10.1

*If the programmer attempts to set the **SelectionMode** property to **MultiSimple** or **MultiExtended** for a **CheckedListBox**, a runtime error occurs.*

CheckedListBox properties, methods and events	Description / Delegate and Event Arguments
Common Properties	*(All the **ListBox** properties and events are inherited by **CheckedListBox**.)*
CheckedItems	Lists the collection of items that are checked. This is distinct from the selected items, which are highlighted (but not necessarily checked). [*Note: There can be at most one selected item at any given time.*]
CheckedIndices	Returns indices for the items that are checked. Not the same as the selected indices.
SelectionMode	Determines how many items can be checked. Only possible values are **One** (allows multiple checks to be placed) or **None** (does not allow any checks to be placed).
Common Method	
GetItemChecked	Takes an index, and returns **true** if corresponding item is checked.
Common Event	*(Delegate **ItemCheckEventHandler**, event arguments **Item-CheckEventArgs**)*
ItemCheck	Generated when an item is checked or unchecked.
ItemCheckEventArgs *Properties*	
CurrentValue	Indicates whether current item is checked or unchecked. Possible values are **Checked**, **Unchecked** and **Indeterminate**.
Index	Returns index of the item that changed.
NewValue	Specifies the new state of the item after the event was raised.

Fig. 10.16 CheckedListBox properties, methods and events.

Event **ItemCheck** is generated whenever a user checks or unchecks a **CheckedListBox** item. Event argument properties **CurrentValue** and **NewValue** return **CheckState** values for the current (i.e., the state before the event) and the new state of the item, respectively. Enumeration **CheckState** specifies the possible states of a **CheckedListBox** item (i.e., **Checked**, **Indeterminate**, **Unchecked**). A comparison of these values allows us to determine whether the **CheckedListBox** item was checked or unchecked. The **CheckedListBox** control retains the **SelectedItems** and **SelectedIndices** properties. (It inherits them from class **ListBox**.) However, it also includes properties **CheckedItems** and **CheckedIndices**, which return information about the checked items and indices.

Class **CheckedListBoxTest** (Fig. 10.17 and Fig. 10.18) uses a **CheckedListBox** and a **ListBox** to display a user's selection of books. The **CheckedListBox** named **inputCheckedListBox** (line 14 of Fig. 10.18) allows the user to select multiple titles. Items were added for some Deitel books: C++, Java, VB, Internet & WWW, Perl, Python, Wireless Internet and Advanced Java (the acronym HTP stands for "How to Program"). The **ListBox**, named **displayListBox** (line 13), displays the user's selection. In the screen shots accompanying this example, the **CheckedListBox** appears to the left, the **ListBox** to the right.

```
1   // Fig. 10.17: CheckedListBox.h
2   // Header file for class CheckedListBoxTest.
3
4   #pragma once
5
6   #using <mscorlib.dll>
7   #using <system.dll>
8   #using <system.drawing.dll>
9   #using <system.windows.forms.dll>
10
11  using namespace System;
12  using namespace System::Drawing;
13  using namespace System::Windows::Forms;
14
15  public __gc class CheckedListBoxTest : public Form
16  {
17  public:
18     CheckedListBoxTest();
19
20  private:
21
22     // list of available book titles
23     CheckedListBox *inputCheckedListBox;
24
25     // user selection list
26     ListBox *displayListBox;
27     void InitializeComponent();
28     void inputCheckedListBox_ItemCheck( Object *,
29        ItemCheckEventArgs * );
30  }; // end class CheckedListBox
```

Fig. 10.17 **CheckedListBox** and **ListBox** used in a program to display a user selection.

```
1    // Fig. 10.18: CheckedListBox.cpp
2    // Using the checked list boxes to add items to a list box.
3
4    #include "CheckedListBox.h"
5
6    CheckedListBoxTest::CheckedListBoxTest()
7    {
8       InitializeComponent();
9    }
10
11   void CheckedListBoxTest::InitializeComponent()
12   {
13      this->displayListBox = new ListBox();
14      this->inputCheckedListBox = new CheckedListBox();
15      this->SuspendLayout();
16
17      // displayListBox
18      this->displayListBox->Location = Point( 184, 16 );
19      this->displayListBox->Name = S"displayListBox";
20      this->displayListBox->Size = Drawing::Size( 128, 121 );
21      this->displayListBox->TabIndex = 4;
22
23      // inputCheckedListBox
24      this->inputCheckedListBox->HorizontalScrollbar = true;
25      String *options[] = { S"C++ HTP", S"Java HTP", S"VB HTP",
26         S"Internet & WWW", S"Perl HTP", S"Python HTP",
27         S"Wireless Internet HTP", S"Wireless Internet HTP" };
28      this->inputCheckedListBox->Items->AddRange( objectList );
29      this->inputCheckedListBox->Location = Point( 16, 16 );
30      this->inputCheckedListBox->Name = S"inputCheckedListBox";
31      this->inputCheckedListBox->Size = Drawing::Size( 152, 124 );
32      this->inputCheckedListBox->TabIndex = 3;
33      this->inputCheckedListBox->ItemCheck += new
34         ItemCheckEventHandler( this,
35            inputCheckedListBox_ItemCheck );
36
37      // CheckedListBoxTest
38      this->AutoScaleBaseSize = Drawing::Size( 5, 13 );
39      this->ClientSize = Drawing::Size( 344, 165 );
40      this->Controls->Add( this->displayListBox );
41      this->Controls->Add( this->inputCheckedListBox );
42      this->Name = S"CheckedListBoxTest";
43      this->Text = S"CheckedListBoxTest";
44      this->ResumeLayout();
45   } // end method InitializeComponent
46
47   // item about to change, add or remove from displayListBox
48   void CheckedListBoxTest::inputCheckedListBox_ItemCheck(
49      Object *sender, ItemCheckEventArgs *e )
50   {
51
52      // obtain pointer of selected item
53      String *item = inputCheckedListBox->SelectedItem->ToString();
54
```

Fig. 10.18 CheckedListBoxTest class method definitions. (Part 1 of 2.)

```
55      // if item checked add to listbox
56      // otherwise remove from listbox
57      if ( e->NewValue == CheckState::Checked )
58         displayListBox->Items->Add( item );
59      else
60         displayListBox->Items->Remove( item );
61   } // end method inputCheckedListBox_ItemCheck
```

Fig. 10.18 CheckedListBoxTest class method definitions. (Part 2 of 2.)

```
1    // Fig. 10.19: CheckListBoxTest.cpp
2    // Checked list boxes demonstration.
3
4    #include "CheckedListBox.h"
5
6    int __stdcall WinMain()
7    {
8       Application::Run( new CheckedListBoxTest() );
9
10      return 0;
11   } // end WinMain
```

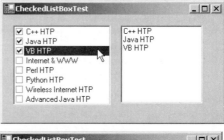

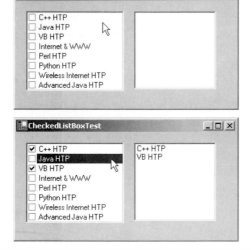

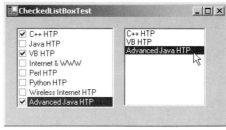

Fig. 10.19 CheckedListBox demonstration.

When the user checks or unchecks an item in **CheckedListBox input-CheckedListBox**, the system generates an **ItemCheck** event. Event handler **inputCheckedListBox_ItemCheck** (lines 48–61) handles the event. An **if/else** control structure (lines 57–60) determines whether the user checked or unchecked an item in the **CheckedListBox**. Line 57 uses the **NewValue** property to test for whether the item is being checked (**CheckState::Checked**). If the user checks an item, line 58 adds the checked entry to the **ListBox displayListBox**. If the user unchecks an item, line 60 removes the corresponding item from **displayListBox**.

10.5 ComboBoxes

The *ComboBox* control combines **TextBox** features with a *drop-down list*. A drop-down list is a GUI component that contains a list from which values can be chosen. It usually appears as a textbox with a down arrow to its right. By default, the user can enter text into the textbox or click the down arrow to display a list of predefined items. If a user chooses an element from this list, that element is displayed in the textbox. If the list contains more elements than can be displayed in the drop-down list, a scrollbar appears. The maximum number of items that a drop-down list can display at one time is set by property **MaxDrop-DownItems**. Figure 10.20 shows a sample **ComboBox** in three different states.

As with the **ListBox** control, the developer can add objects to collection **Items** programmatically, using methods **Add** and **AddRange**. Figure 10.21 lists common properties and events of class **ComboBox**.

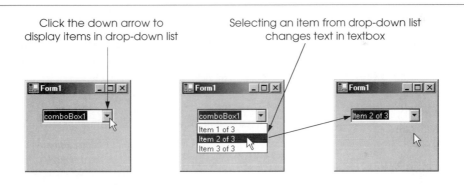

Click the down arrow to display items in drop-down list

Selecting an item from drop-down list changes text in textbox

Fig. 10.20 ComboBox demonstration.

ComboBox events and properties	Description / Delegate and Event Arguments
Common Properties	
DropDownStyle	Determines the type of combo box. Assigned a value from enumeration *ComboBoxStyle*. Value **Simple** means that the text portion is editable and the list portion is always visible. Value **DropDown** (the default) means that the text portion is editable, but the user must click an arrow button to see the list portion. Value **DropDownList** means that the text portion is not editable and the user must click the arrow button to see the list portion.
Items	The collection of items in the **ComboBox** control.
MaxDropDownItems	Specifies the maximum number of items (between **1** and **100**) that can display in the drop-down list. If the number of items exceeds the maximum number of items to display, a scroll bar appears.

Fig. 10.21 ComboBox properties and events. (Part 1 of 2.)

ComboBox events and properties	Description / Delegate and Event Arguments
Common Properties (Cont.)	
SelectedIndex	Returns index of currently selected item. If there is no currently selected item, **-1** is returned.
SelectedItem	Returns a pointer to the currently selected item.
Sorted	Specifies whether items in a list are alphabetized. If **true**, items appear in alphabetical order. Default is **false**.
Common Event	*(Delegate **EventHandler**, event arguments **EventArgs**)*
SelectedIndex-Changed	Generated when the selected index changes (such as when a check-box has been checked or unchecked).

Fig. 10.21 ComboBox properties and events. (Part 2 of 2.)

Property ***DropDownStyle*** determines the type of **ComboBox**. Style ***Simple*** does not display a drop-down arrow. Instead, a scrollbar appears next to the control, allowing the user to select a choice from the list. The user can also type in a selection. Style ***DropDown*** (the default) displays a drop-down list when the down arrow is clicked (or the down arrow key is pressed). The user can type a new item into the **ComboBox**. The last style is **DropDownList**, which displays a drop-down list, but does not allow the user to enter a new item. Drop-down lists save room, so a **ComboBox** should be used when GUI space is limited.

The **ComboBox** control has properties **Items** (a collection), **SelectedItem** and **SelectedIndex**, which are similar to the corresponding properties in **ListBox**. Users can select only one item at a time in a **ComboBox** (if zero, then **SelectedIndex** is **-1**). When the selected item changes, event **SelectedIndexChanged** is generated.

Class **ComboBoxTest** (Fig. 10.22 and Fig. 10.23) allows users to select a shape to draw—an empty or filled circle, ellipse, square or pie—by using a **ComboBox**. The combo box in this example is uneditable, so the user cannot input a custom item.

Look-and-Feel Observation 10.6

*Make lists (such as **ComboBox**es) editable only if the program is designed to accept user-submitted elements. Otherwise, the user might enter a custom item that is invalid.*

```
1   // Fig. 10.22: ComboBox.h
2   // Header file for class ComboBoxTest.
3
4   #pragma once
5
6   #using <mscorlib.dll>
7   #using <system.dll>
8   #using <system.windows.forms.dll>
9
10  using namespace System;
11  using namespace System::Windows::Forms;
12
```

Fig. 10.22 ComboBox used to draw a selected shape. (Part 1 of 2.)

```
13    public __gc class ComboBoxTest : public Form
14    {
15    public:
16        ComboBoxTest();
17
18    private:
19
20        // contains shape list (circle, square, ellipse, pie)
21        ComboBox *imageComboBox;
22
23        void InitializeComponent();
24        void imageComboBox_SelectedIndexChanged( Object *,
25            EventArgs * );
26    }; // end class ComboBoxTest
```

Fig. 10.22 ComboBox used to draw a selected shape. (Part 2 of 2.)

```
1     // Fig. 10.23: ComboBox.cpp
2     // Using ComboBox to select shape to draw
3
4     #include "ComboBox.h"
5
6     ComboBoxTest::ComboBoxTest()
7     {
8         InitializeComponent();
9     }
10
11    void ComboBoxTest::InitializeComponent()
12    {
13        this->imageComboBox = new ComboBox();
14        this->SuspendLayout();
15
16        // imageComboBox
17        this->imageComboBox->DropDownWidth = 121;
18        String *shapes[] = { S"Circle", S"Square", S"Ellipse",
19            S"Pie", S"Filled Circle", S"Filled Square",
20            S"Filled Ellipse", S"Filled Pie" };
21        this->imageComboBox->Items->AddRange( shapes );
22        this->imageComboBox->Location = Point( 8, 8 );
23        this->imageComboBox->Name = S"imageComboBox";
24        this->imageComboBox->DropDownStyle =
25            ComboBoxStyle::DropDownList;
26        this->imageComboBox->Size = Drawing::Size( 121, 21 );
27        this->imageComboBox->TabIndex = 1;
28        this->imageComboBox->SelectedIndexChanged += new
29            EventHandler( this, imageComboBox_SelectedIndexChanged );
30
31        // ComboBoxTest
32        this->AutoScaleBaseSize = Drawing::Size( 5, 13 );
33        this->ClientSize = Drawing::Size( 256, 229 );
34        this->Controls->Add( this->imageComboBox );
35        this->Name = S"ComboBoxTest";
```

Fig. 10.23 ComboBoxTest class methods definition. (Part 1 of 3.)

```
36        this->Text = S"ComboBoxTest";
37        this->ResumeLayout();
38     } // end method InitializeComponent
39
40     // get selected index, draw shape
41     void ComboBoxTest::imageComboBox_SelectedIndexChanged(
42        Object *sender, EventArgs *e )
43     {
44
45        // create graphics Object*, pen and brush
46        Graphics *myGraphics = CreateGraphics();
47
48        // create Pen using color DarkRed
49        Pen *myPen = new Pen( Color::DarkRed );
50
51        // create SolidBrush using color DarkRed
52        SolidBrush *mySolidBrush = new SolidBrush( Color::DarkRed );
53
54        // clear drawing area setting it to color White
55        myGraphics->Clear( Color::White );
56
57        // find index, draw proper shape
58        switch ( imageComboBox->SelectedIndex )
59        {
60
61           // case circle is selected
62           case 0:
63              myGraphics->DrawEllipse( myPen, 50, 50, 150, 150 );
64              break;
65
66           // case rectangle is selected
67           case 1:
68              myGraphics->DrawRectangle( myPen, 50, 50, 150, 150 );
69              break;
70
71           // case ellipse is selected
72           case 2:
73              myGraphics->DrawEllipse( myPen, 50, 85, 150, 115 );
74              break;
75
76           // case pie is selected
77           case 3:
78              myGraphics->DrawPie( myPen, 50, 50, 150, 150, 0, 45 );
79              break;
80
81           // case filled circle is selected
82           case 4:
83              myGraphics->FillEllipse( mySolidBrush, 50, 50, 150,
84                 150 );
85              break;
86
87           // case filled rectangle is selected
88           case 5:
```

Fig. 10.23 ComboBoxTest class methods definition. (Part 2 of 3.)

```
89              myGraphics->FillRectangle( mySolidBrush, 50, 50, 150,
90                 150 );
91              break;
92
93           // case filled ellipse is selected
94           case 6:
95              myGraphics->FillEllipse( mySolidBrush, 50, 85, 150,
96                 115 );
97              break;
98
99           // case filled pie is selected
100          case 7:
101             myGraphics->FillPie( mySolidBrush, 50, 50, 150, 150, 0,
102                45 );
103             break;
104
105          // good programming practice to include a default case
106          default:
107             break;
108       } // end switch
109 } // end method imageComboBox_SelectedIndexChanged
```

Fig. 10.23 ComboBoxTest class methods definition. (Part 3 of 3.)

```
1   // Fig. 10.24: ComboBoxTest.cpp
2   // ComboBox demonstration.
3
4   #include "ComboBox.h"
5
6   int __stdcall WinMain()
7   {
8      Application::Run( new ComboBoxTest() );
9
10     return 0;
11  } // end WinMain
```

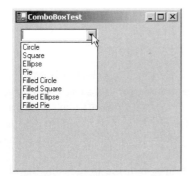 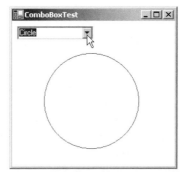

Fig. 10.24 ComboBox demonstration. (Part 1 of 2.)

 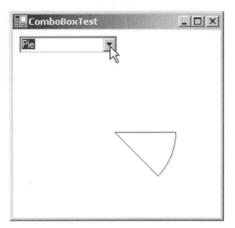

Fig. 10.24 ComboBox demonstration. (Part 2 of 2.)

After creating **ComboBox imageComboBox** (line 13 of Fig. 10.23), we add items **Circle**, **Square**, **Ellipse**, **Pie**, **Filled Circle**, **Filled Square**, **Filled Ellipse** and **Filled Pie** to collection **Items** (lines 18–21). Next, we make it uneditable by setting its **DropDownStyle** to **DropDownList** (lines 24–25). Whenever the user selects an item from **imageComboBox**, the system generates a **SelectedIndexChanged** event. Event handler **imageComboBox_SelectedIndexChanged** (lines 41–109) handles these events. Line 55 colors the entire form **White**, using method *Clear* of class **Graphics**. Lines 46–52 create a **Graphics** object, a *Pen* and a **SolidBrush**, with which the program draws on the form. The **Graphics** object (line 46) allows a pen or brush to draw on a component, using one of several **Graphics** methods. A **Pen** object can draw lines and curves. The **Pen** object is used by methods **DrawEllipse**, **DrawRectangle** and **DrawPie** (lines 63, 68, 73 and 78) to draw the outlines of their corresponding shapes. The **SolidBrush** object is used by methods **FillEllipse**, **FillRectangle** and **FillPie** (lines 83, 89, 95 and 101) to draw their corresponding solid shapes. Class **Graphics** is discussed in greater detail in Chapter 13, Graphics and Multimedia.

The application draws a particular shape specified by the selected item's index. The **switch** structure (lines 58–108) uses **imageComboBox->SelectedIndex** to determine which item the user selected. Method *DrawEllipse* of class **Graphics** (line 63) takes a **Pen**, the *x*- and *y*-coordinates of the ellipse's center and the width and height of the ellipse to draw. The origin of the coordinate system is in the upper-left corner of the form; the *x*-coordinate increases to the right, the *y*-coordinate increases downward. A circle is a special case of an ellipse in which the height and width are equal. Line 63 draws a circle. Line 73 draws an ellipse that has different values for height and width.

Method *DrawRectangle* of class **Graphics** (line 68) takes a **Pen**, the *x*- and *y*-coordinates of the upper-left corner and the width and height of the rectangle to draw. Method *DrawPie* (line 78) draws a pie as a portion of an ellipse. The ellipse is bounded by a rectangle. Method **DrawPie** takes a **Pen**, the *x*- and *y*-coordinates of the upper-left corner of the rectangle, its width and height, the start angle (in degrees), and the *sweep angle* (in degrees) of the pie. Method **DrawPie** draws a pie section of an ellipse beginning from the start angle and sweeping the number of degrees specified by the sweep angle. Angles increase clockwise. The *FillEllipse* (lines 83–84 and 95–96), *FillRect-angle* (lines 89–90) and *FillPie* (lines 101–102) methods are similar to their unfilled counterparts, except that they take a **SolidBrush** instead of a **Pen**. Some of the drawn shapes are illustrated in the screen shots at the bottom of Fig. 10.24.

10.6 TreeViews

The *TreeView* control displays *nodes* hierarchically on a *tree*. Traditionally, nodes are objects that contain values and can refer to other nodes. A *parent node* contains *child nodes*, and the child nodes can be parents to other nodes. Each child has only one parent. Two child nodes that have the same parent node are considered *sibling nodes*. A tree is a collection of nodes, usually organized in a hierarchical manner. The first parent node of a tree is the *root* node (a **TreeView** control can have multiple roots). For example, the file system of a computer can be represented as a tree. The top-level directory (perhaps **C:**) would be the root, each subfolder of **C:** would be a child node and each child folder could have its own children. **TreeView** controls are useful for displaying hierarchal information, such as the file structure that we just mentioned. We cover nodes and trees in greater detail in Chapter 19, Data Structures and Collections.

Figure 10.25 displays a sample **TreeView** control on a form. A parent node can be expanded or collapsed by clicking the plus or minus box to its left. Nodes without children do not have an expand or collapse box.

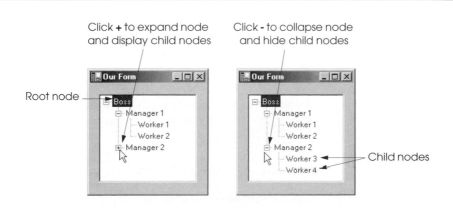

Fig. 10.25 **TreeView** displaying a sample tree.

The nodes displayed in a **TreeView** are instances of class ***TreeNode***. Each **TreeNode** has a ***Nodes*** collection (type ***TreeNodeCollection***), which contains a list of other **TreeNode**s—its children. The ***Parent*** property returns a pointer to the parent node (or **0** if the node is a root node). Figures 10.26 and 10.27 list the common properties of **TreeView**s and **TreeNode**s and an event of **TreeView**s.

TreeView properties and events	Description / Delegate and Event Arguments
Common Properties	
CheckBoxes	Indicates whether checkboxes appear next to nodes. If **true**, checkboxes are displayed. Default is **false**.
ImageList	Indicates the **ImageList** used to display icons by the nodes. An ***ImageList*** is a collection that contains a number of **Image** objects.
Nodes	Lists the collection of **TreeNode**s in the control. Contains methods **Add** (adds a **TreeNode** object), **Clear** (deletes the entire collection) and **Remove** (deletes a specific node). Removing a parent node deletes all its children.
SelectedNode	Currently selected node.
Common Event	*(Delegate **TreeViewEventHandler**, event arguments **TreeViewEventArgs**)*
AfterSelect	Generated after selected node changes.

Fig. 10.26 TreeView properties and events.

TreeNode properties and methods	Description / Delegate and Event Arguments
Common Properties	
Checked	Indicates whether the **TreeNode** is checked. (**CheckBoxes** property must be set to **true** in parent **TreeView**.)
FirstNode	Specifies the first node in the **Nodes** collection (i.e., first child in of current node).
FullPath	Indicates the path of the node, starting at the root of the tree.
ImageIndex	Specifies the index of the image to be shown when the node is deselected.
LastNode	Specifies the last node in the **Nodes** collection (i.e., last child in of current node).
NextNode	Next sibling node.
Nodes	The collection of **TreeNode**s contained in the current node (i.e., all the children of the current node). Contains methods **Add** (adds a **TreeNode** object), **Clear** (deletes the entire collection) and **Remove** (deletes a specific node). Removing a parent node deletes all its children.

Fig. 10.27 TreeNode properties and methods. (Part 1 of 2.)

TreeNode properties and methods	Description / Delegate and Event Arguments
PrevNode	Indicates the previous sibling node.
SelectedImageIndex	Specifies the index of the image to use when the node is selected.
Text	Specifies the text to display in the TreeView.
Common Methods	
Collapse	Collapses a node.
Expand	Expands a node.
ExpandAll	Expands all the children of a node.
GetNodeCount	Returns the number of child nodes.

Fig. 10.27 TreeNode properties and methods. (Part 2 of 2.)

To add nodes to the **TreeView** control, we first must create a root node. Make a new **TreeNode** object and pass it a **String *** to display. Then use method **Add** to add this new **TreeNode** to the **TreeView**'s **Nodes** collection. Thus, to add a root node to **TreeView** *myTreeView*, write

```
myTreeView->Nodes->Add( new TreeNode( RootLabel ) )
```

where *myTreeView* is the **TreeView** to which we are adding nodes and *RootLabel* is the text to display in *myTreeView*. To add children to a root node, add new **TreeNode**s to its **Nodes** collection. We select the appropriate root node from the **TreeView** by writing

```
myTreeView->Nodes->GetItem( myIndex )
```

where *myIndex* is the root node's index in *myTreeView*'s **Nodes** collection. We add nodes to child nodes through the same process by which we added root nodes to *myTreeView*. To add a child to the root node at index *myIndex*, write

```
myTreeView->Nodes->GetItem( myIndex )->Nodes->Add(
    new TreeNode( ChildLabel ) )
```

Class **TreeViewDirectoryStructureTest** (Fig. 10.28 and Fig. 10.29) uses a **TreeView** to display the directory file structure on a computer. The root node is the **C:** drive, and each subfolder of **C:** becomes a child. This layout is similar to that used in **Windows Explorer**. Folders can be expanded or collapsed by clicking the plus or minus boxes that appear to their left. Figure 10.30 presents the application's driver.

```
1   // Fig. 10.28: TreeViewDirectoryStructure.h
2   // Class TreeViewDirectoryStructureTest header file.
3
4   #pragma once
5
6   #using <mscorlib.dll>
7   #using <system.dll>
8   #using <system.drawing.dll>
9   #using <system.windows.forms.dll>
```

Fig. 10.28 TreeView used to display directories. (Part 1 of 2.)

```
10
11    using namespace System;
12    using namespace System::Drawing;
13    using namespace System::Windows::Forms;
14    using namespace System::IO;
15
16    public __gc class TreeViewDirectoryStructureTest : public Form
17    {
18    public:
19       TreeViewDirectoryStructureTest();
20       void PopulateTreeView( String *, TreeNode * );
21
22    private:
23
24       // contains view of c: drive directory structure
25       TreeView *directoryTreeView;
26       void InitializeComponent();
27       void TreeViewDirectoryStructureTest_Load( Object *,
28          EventArgs * );
29    }; // end class TreeViewDirectoryStructure
```

Fig. 10.28 TreeView used to display directories. (Part 2 of 2.)

```
1    // Fig. 10.29: TreeViewDirectoryStructure.cpp
2    // Using TreeView to display directory structure.
3
4    #include "TreeViewDirectoryStructure.h"
5
6    TreeViewDirectoryStructureTest::TreeViewDirectoryStructureTest()
7    {
8       InitializeComponent();
9    }
10
11   void TreeViewDirectoryStructureTest::InitializeComponent()
12   {
13      this->directoryTreeView = new TreeView();
14      this->SuspendLayout();
15
16      // directoryTreeView
17      this->directoryTreeView->Dock = DockStyle::Fill;
18      this->directoryTreeView->ImageIndex = -1;
19      this->directoryTreeView->Name = S"directoryTreeView";
20      this->directoryTreeView->SelectedImageIndex = -1;
21      this->directoryTreeView->Size = Drawing::Size( 292, 273 );
22      this->directoryTreeView->TabIndex = 1;
23
24      // TreeViewDirectoryStructureTest
25      this->AutoScaleBaseSize = Drawing::Size( 5, 13 );
26      this->ClientSize = Drawing::Size( 292, 273 );
27
28      this->Name = S"TreeViewDirectoryStructureTest";
29      this->Text = S"TreeViewDirectoryStructureTest";
```

Fig. 10.29 TreeViewDirectoryStructureTest class method definitions. (Part 1 of 3.)

```
30       this->Load += new EventHandler( this,
31          TreeViewDirectoryStructureTest_Load );
32       this->Controls->Add( this->directoryTreeView );
33       this->ResumeLayout();
34    } // end method InitializeComponent
35
36    void TreeViewDirectoryStructureTest::PopulateTreeView(
37       String *directoryValue, TreeNode *parentNode )
38    {
39
40       // populate current node with subdirectories
41       String *directoryArray[] =
42          Directory::GetDirectories( directoryValue );
43
44       // populate current node with subdirectories
45       if ( directoryArray.Length != 0 )
46       {
47
48          // for every subdirectory, create new TreeNode,
49          // add as child of current node and recursively
50          // populate child nodes with subdirectories
51          for ( int i = 0; i < directoryArray.Length; i++ ) {
52             try {
53
54                // create TreeNode for current directory
55                TreeNode *myNode = new TreeNode(
56                   directoryArray[ i ] );
57
58                // add current directory node to parent node
59                parentNode->Nodes->Add( myNode );
60
61                // recursively populate every subdirectory
62                PopulateTreeView( directoryArray[ i ], myNode );
63             } // end try
64
65             // catch exception
66             catch ( UnauthorizedAccessException *exception )
67             {
68                parentNode->Nodes->Add( String::Concat(
69                   S"Access denied\n", exception->Message ) );
70             }
71          } // end for
72       } // end if
73    } // end try
74    } // end method PopulateTreeView
75
76    // called by system when form loads
77    void TreeViewDirectoryStructureTest
78       ::TreeViewDirectoryStructureTest_Load(
79       Object *sender, EventArgs *e )
80    {
81
82       // add c:\ drive to directoryTreeView
83       // and insert its subfolders
```

Fig. 10.29 TreeViewDirectoryStructureTest class method definitions. (Part 2 of 3.)

```
84      directoryTreeView->Nodes->Add( S"C:\\" );
85      PopulateTreeView( S"C:\\",
86         directoryTreeView->Nodes->get_Item( 0 ) );
87  } // end method TreeViewDirectoryStructureTest_Load
```

Fig. 10.29 TreeViewDirectoryStructureTest class method definitions. (Part 3 of 3.)

```
1   // Fig. 10.30: TreeViewDirectoryStructureTest.cpp
2   // TreeView demonstration.
3
4   #include "TreeViewDirectoryStructure.h"
5
6   int __stdcall WinMain()
7   {
8      Application::Run( new TreeViewDirectoryStructureTest() );
9
10     return 0;
11  } // end WinMain
```

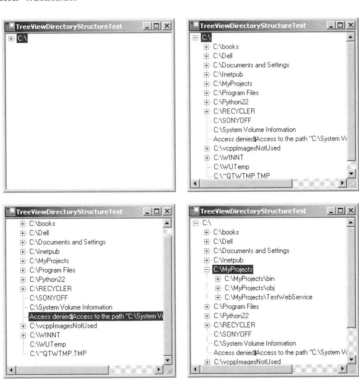

Fig. 10.30 TreeView demonstration.

When **TreeViewDirectoryStructureTest** loads, the system generates a **Load** event, which is handled by event handler **TreeViewDirectoryStruc-tureTest_Load** (lines 77–87). Line 84 adds a root node (**C:**) to our **TreeView**, named **directoryTreeView**. **C:** is the root folder for the entire directory structure. Lines 85–86 call method **PopulateTreeView** (lines 36–74), which takes a directory (a

String *) and a parent node. Method **PopulateTreeView** then creates child nodes corresponding to the subdirectories of the directory that was passed to it.

Method **PopulateTreeView** (lines 36–74) obtains a list of subdirectories, using method *GetDirectories* of class **Directory** (namespace **System::IO**) on line 42. Method **GetDirectories** takes a **String *** (the current directory) and returns an array of **String *** objects (the subdirectories), which is assigned to array **directoryArray**. If the specified directory is not accessible for security reasons, an **UnauthorizedAccessException** is thrown. Lines 66–70 catch this exception and add a node containing "**Access Denied**" instead of displaying the contents of the inaccessible directory. Note that the **try** and **catch** blocks are contained within the **for** loop; after an exception is handled, the **for** loop continues executing.

If there are accessible subdirectories, each **String *** in the **directoryArray** is used to create a new child node (lines 55–56). We use method **Add** (line 59) to add each child node to the parent. Then method **PopulateTreeView** is called recursively on every subdirectory (line 62) and eventually populates the entire directory structure. Our recursive algorithm causes our program to have a lengthy initial delay when it loads—it must create a tree for the entire **C:** drive. However, once the drive folder names are added to the appropriate **Nodes** collection, they can be expanded and collapsed without delay. In the next section, we present an alternative algorithm to solve this problem.

10.7 ListViews

The *ListView* control is similar to a **ListBox**, in that both display lists from which the user can select one or more items of type *ListViewItem* (to see an example of a **ListView** control, look ahead to the output of Fig. 10.34). The important difference between the two classes is that a **ListView** can display icons alongside the list items in a variety of ways (controlled by its **ImageList** property). Property *MultiSelect* (a boolean) determines whether multiple items can be selected. Checkboxes can be included by setting property **CheckBoxes** (a boolean) to **true**, making the **ListView**'s appearance similar to that of a **CheckedListBox**. Property *View* specifies the layout of the **ListBox**. Property *Activation* determines the method by which the user selects a list item. The details of these properties are explained in Fig. 10.31.

ListView events and properties	Description / Delegate and Event Arguments
Common Properties	
Activation	Determines the user action necessary to activate an item. This property takes a value in enumeration **ItemActivation**. Possible values are **OneClick** (single-click activation, item changes color when mouse cursor moves over item), **TwoClick** (double-click activation, item changes color when selected) and **Standard** (double-click activation, no associated color change).

Fig. 10.31 ListView properties and events. (Part 1 of 2.)

ListView events and properties	Description / Delegate and Event Arguments
CheckBoxes	Indicates whether items appear with checkboxes. If **true**, checkboxes are displayed. Default is **false**.
LargeImageList	Indicates the **ImageList** used when displaying large icons.
Items	Returns the collection of **ListViewItem**s in the control.
MultiSelect	Determines whether multiple selection is allowed. Default is **true**, which enables multiple selection.
SelectedItems	Lists the collection of currently selected items.
SmallImageList	Specifies the **ImageList** used when displaying small icons.
View	Determines appearance of **ListViewItem**s. Enumeration **View** values **LargeIcon** (large icon displayed, items can be in multiple columns), **SmallIcon** (small icon displayed), **List** (small icons displayed, items appear in a single column) and **Details** (like **List**, but multiple columns of information can be displayed per item).
Common Event	*(Delegate **EventHandler**, event arguments **EventArgs**)*
ItemActivate	Generated when an item in the **ListView** is activated. Does not specify which item is activated.

Fig. 10.31 ListView properties and events. (Part 2 of 2.)

ListView allows us to define the images used as icons for **ListView** items. To display images, we must use an **ImageList** component.

Class **ListViewTest** (Fig. 10.32 and Fig. 10.33) displays files and folders in a **ListView**, along with small icons representing each file or folder. If a file or folder is inaccessible because of permission settings, a message box appears. The program scans the contents of the directory as it browses, rather than indexing the entire drive at once. The driver (Fig. 10.34) demonstrates the functionality of **ListViewTest**.

```
1   // Fig. 10.32: ListView.h
2   // Displaying directories and their contents in ListView.
3
4   #pragma once
5
6   #using <mscorlib.dll>
7   #using <system.dll>
8   #using <system.drawing.dll>
9   #using <system.windows.forms.dll>
10
11  using namespace System;
12  using namespace System::Drawing;
```

Fig. 10.32 ListView displaying files and folders. (Part 1 of 2.)

```
13    using namespace System::Windows::Forms;
14    using namespace System::IO;
15
16    public __gc class ListViewTest : public Form
17    {
18    public:
19       ListViewTest();
20       void LoadFilesInDirectory( String * );
21
22    private:
23
24       // display labels for current location in directory tree
25       Label *currentLabel;
26       Label *displayLabel;
27
28       // display contents of current directory
29       ListView *browserListView;
30
31       // specifies images for file icons and folder icons
32       ImageList *fileFolder;
33
34       // get current directory
35       String *currentDirectory;
36       void InitializeComponent();
37       void browserListView_Click( Object *, EventArgs * );
38       void ListViewTest_Load( Object *, EventArgs * );
39    }; // end class ListViewTest
```

Fig. 10.32 ListView displaying files and folders. (Part 2 of 2.)

```
1     // Fig. 10.33: ListView.cpp
2     // Displaying directories and their contents in ListView.
3
4     #include "ListView.h"
5
6     ListViewTest::ListViewTest()
7     {
8        // get current directory
9        currentDirectory = Directory::GetCurrentDirectory();
10       InitializeComponent();
11    }
12
13    void ListViewTest::InitializeComponent()
14    {
15       this->browserListView = new ListView();
16       this->displayLabel = new Label();
17       this->currentLabel = new Label();
18       this->fileFolder = new ImageList();
19       this->SuspendLayout();
20
```

Fig. 10.33 ListViewTest class method definitions. (Part 1 of 5.)

```
21      // browserListView
22      this->browserListView->Location = Point( 24, 88 );
23      this->browserListView->Name = S"browserListView";
24      this->browserListView->Size = Drawing::Size( 448, 232 );
25      this->browserListView->SmallImageList = this->fileFolder;
26      this->browserListView->TabIndex = 5;
27      this->browserListView->View = View::List;
28      this->browserListView->Click += new EventHandler( this,
29         browserListView_Click );
30
31      // displayLabel
32      this->displayLabel->Font = new Drawing::Font(
33         S"Microsoft Sans Serif", 9.75, FontStyle::Regular,
34         GraphicsUnit::Point, 0 );
35      this->displayLabel->ForeColor = SystemColors::WindowText;
36      this->displayLabel->Location = Point( 136, 16 );
37      this->displayLabel->Name = S"displayLabel";
38      this->displayLabel->Size = Drawing::Size( 344, 56 );
39      this->displayLabel->TabIndex = 4;
40
41      // currentLabel
42      this->currentLabel->Font = new Drawing::Font(
43         S"Microsoft Sans Serif", 9.75, FontStyle::Regular,
44         GraphicsUnit::Point, 0 );
45      this->currentLabel->ForeColor = SystemColors::WindowText;
46      this->currentLabel->Location = Point( 24, 16 );
47      this->currentLabel->Name = S"currentLabel";
48      this->currentLabel->Size = Drawing::Size( 112, 23 );
49      this->currentLabel->TabIndex = 3;
50      this->currentLabel->Text = S"Now in Directory:";
51
52      // fileFolder
53      this->fileFolder->ColorDepth = ColorDepth::Depth8Bit;
54      this->fileFolder->ImageSize = Drawing::Size( 16, 16 );
55      this->fileFolder->TransparentColor = Color::Transparent;
56
57      // ListViewTest
58      this->AutoScaleBaseSize = Drawing::Size( 5, 13 );
59      this->ClientSize = Drawing::Size( 568, 349 );
60      this->Controls->Add( this->browserListView );
61      this->Controls->Add( this->displayLabel );
62      this->Controls->Add( this->currentLabel );
63      this->Name = S"ListViewTest";
64      this->Text = S"ListViewTest";
65      this->Load += new EventHandler( this, ListViewTest_Load );
66      this->ResumeLayout();
67   } // end method InitializeComponent
68
69   // display files/subdirectories of current directory
70   void ListViewTest::LoadFilesInDirectory(
71      String *currentDirectoryValue )
72   {
```

Fig. 10.33 ListViewTest class method definitions. (Part 2 of 5.)

```
73
74      // load directory information and display
75      try
76      {
77
78         // clear ListView and set first item
79         browserListView->Items->Clear();
80         browserListView->Items->Add( S"Go Up One Level" );
81
82         // update current directory
83         currentDirectory = currentDirectoryValue;
84         DirectoryInfo *newCurrentDirectory =
85            new DirectoryInfo( currentDirectory );
86
87         // put files and directories into arrays
88         DirectoryInfo *directoryArray[] =
89            newCurrentDirectory->GetDirectories();
90
91         FileInfo *fileArray[] =
92            newCurrentDirectory->GetFiles();
93
94         DirectoryInfo *dir;
95
96         // add directory names to ListView
97         for ( int i = 0; i < directoryArray.Length; i++ ) {
98
99            dir = directoryArray[ i ];
100
101           // add directory to ListView
102           ListViewItem *newDirectoryItem =
103              browserListView->Items->Add( dir->Name );
104
105           // set directory image
106           newDirectoryItem->ImageIndex = 0;
107        } // end for
108
109        FileInfo *file;
110
111        // add file names to ListView
112        for ( i = 0; i < fileArray.Length; i++ ) {
113
114           file = fileArray[ i ];
115
116           // add file to ListView
117           ListViewItem *newFileItem =
118              browserListView->Items->Add( file->Name );
119
120           newFileItem->ImageIndex = 1;  // set file image
121        } // end for
122     } // end try
123
124     // access denied
```

Fig. 10.33 **ListViewTest** class method definitions. (Part 3 of 5.)

```
125        catch ( UnauthorizedAccessException *exception )
126        {
127           MessageBox::Show( String::Concat(
128              S"Warning: Some fields may not be ",
129              S"visible due to permission settings.\n" ),
130              "Attention", MessageBoxButtons::OK,
131              MessageBoxIcon::Warning );
132        }
133  } // end method LoadFilesInDirectory
134
135  // browse directory user clicked or go up one level
136  void ListViewTest::browserListView_Click(
137     Object *sender, EventArgs *e )
138  {
139
140     // ensure item selected
141     if ( browserListView->SelectedItems->Count != 0 )
142     {
143
144        // if first item selected, go up one level
145        if ( browserListView->Items->get_Item( 0 )->Selected )
146        {
147
148           // create DirectoryInfo object for directory
149           DirectoryInfo *directoryObject =
150              new DirectoryInfo( currentDirectory );
151
152           // if directory has parent, load it
153           if ( directoryObject->Parent != 0 )
154              LoadFilesInDirectory(
155                 directoryObject->Parent->FullName );
156        } // end if
157
158        // selected directory or file
159        else
160        {
161
162           // directory or file chosen
163           String *chosen =
164              browserListView->SelectedItems->get_Item( 0 )->Text;
165
166           // if item selected is directory
167           if ( Directory::Exists( String::Concat(
168              currentDirectory, S"\\", chosen ) ) )
169           {
170
171              // load subdirectory
172              // if in c:\, do not need '\',
173              // otherwise we do
174              if ( currentDirectory == "C:\\" )
```

Fig. 10.33 ListViewTest class method definitions. (Part 4 of 5.)

```
175                    LoadFilesInDirectory( String::Concat(
176                        currentDirectory, chosen ));
177                else
178                    LoadFilesInDirectory( String::Concat(
179                        currentDirectory, S"\\", chosen ) );
180            } //end if
181         } // end else
182
183         // update displayLabel
184         displayLabel->Text = currentDirectory;
185      } // end if
186   } // end method browserListView_Click
187
188   // handle load event when Form displayed for first time
189   void ListViewTest::ListViewTest_Load(
190      Object *sender, EventArgs *e )
191   {
192
193      // set image list
194      Image *folderImage = Image::FromFile( String::Concat(
195         currentDirectory, S"\\images\\folder.bmp" ) );
196
197      Image *fileImage = Image::FromFile( String::Concat(
198         currentDirectory, S"\\images\\file.bmp" ));
199
200      fileFolder->Images->Add( folderImage );
201      fileFolder->Images->Add( fileImage );
202
203      // load current directory into browserListView
204      LoadFilesInDirectory( currentDirectory );
205      displayLabel->Text = currentDirectory;
206   } // end method ListViewTest_Load
```

Fig. 10.33 ListViewTest class method definitions. (Part 5 of 5.)

```
1   // Fig. 10.34: ListViewTest.cpp
2   // Displaying directories and their contents in ListView.
3
4   #include "ListView.h"
5
6   int __stdcall WinMain()
7   {
8      Application::Run( new ListViewTest() );
9
10      return 0;
11   } // end WinMain
```

Fig. 10.34 ListView demonstration. (Part 1 of 2.)

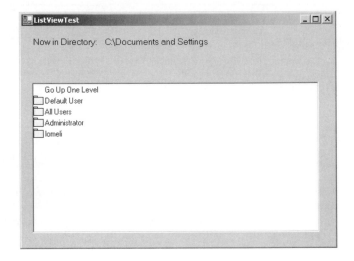

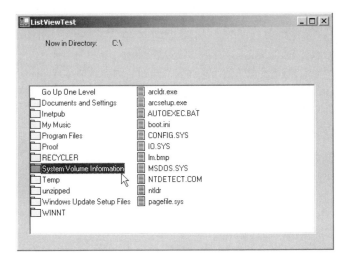

Fig. 10.34 ListView demonstration. (Part 2 of 2.)

To display icons beside list items, we must create an **ImageList** for the **ListView** **browserListView** (line 18 of Fig. 10.33). Developers can create such icons with any image software, such as Adobe® Photoshop™, Jasc® Paint Shop Pro™[1] or Microsoft® Paint. Developers can create bitmap images using Visual Studio. First, select **File** > **New** > **File...** which displays the **New File** dialog. Select **Bitmap File (.bmp)** which is listed in the **Visual C++** folder.

Method **LoadFilesInDirectory** (lines 70–133) is used to populate **browser-** **ListView** with the contents of the directory passed to it (**currentDirectory-** **Value**). It clears **browserListView** and adds the element **"Go Up One Level"**. When the user clicks this element, the program attempts to move up one level. (We see how shortly.) The method then creates a **DirectoryInfo** object initialized with the string **currentDirectory** (lines 84–85). If permission is not given to browse the directory, an exception is thrown (caught on lines 125–132). Method **LoadFilesInDirectory** works differently from method **PopulateTreeView** in the previous program (Fig. 10.29). Instead of loading all the folders in the entire hard drive, method **Load-** **FilesInDirectory** loads only the folders in the current directory.

Class *DirectoryInfo* (namespace **System::IO**) enables us to browse or manipulate the directory structure easily. Method *GetDirectories* (lines 88–89) of class **DirectoryInfo** returns an array of **DirectoryInfo** objects containing the subdirectories of the current directory. Similarly, method *GetFiles* (lines 91–92) returns an array of class *FileInfo* objects containing the files in the current directory. Property *Name* (of both class **DirectoryInfo** and class **FileInfo**) contains only the directory or file name, such as **temp** instead of **C:\myfolder\temp**. To access the full name (i.e., the full path of the file or directory), use property *FullName*.

Lines 97–107 and lines 112–121 iterate through the subdirectories and files of the current directory and add them to **browserListView**. Lines 106 and 120 set the **ImageIndex** properties of the newly created items. If an item is a directory, we set its icon to a directory icon (index **0**); if an item is a file, we set its icon to a file icon (index **1**).

Method **browserListView_Click** (lines 136–186) responds when the user clicks control **browserListView**. Line 141 checks on whether anything is selected. If a selection has been made, line 145 determines whether the user chose the first item in **browserListView**. The first item in **browserListView** is always **Go up one level**; if it is selected, the program attempts to go up a level. Lines 149–150 create a **DirectoryInfo** object for the current directory. Line 153 tests property **Parent** to ensure that the user is not at the root of the directory tree. Property *Parent* indicates the parent directory as a **DirectoryInfo** object; if it does not exist, **Parent** returns the value **0**. If a parent directory exists, then lines 154–155 pass the full name of the parent directory to method **LoadFilesIn-** **Directory**.

If the user did not select the first item in **browserListView**, lines 159–181 allow the user to continue navigating through the directory structure. Lines 163–164 create **String *** **chosen**, which receives the text of the selected item (the first item in collection **Selected-** **Items**). Lines 167–168 test whether the user's selection exists as valid directory (rather than a

---

1. Information about Adobe products can be found at **www.adobe.com**. Information about Jasc products and free trial downloads of the company's products are available at **www.jasc.com**.

file). The program combines variables **currentDirectory** and **chosen** (the new directory), separated by a slash (****), and passes this value to class **Directory**'s method ***Exists***. Method **Exists** returns **true** if its **String *** parameter is a directory. If this occurs, the program passes the **String *** to method **LoadFilesInDirectory**. The **C:** directory already includes a slash, so a slash is not needed when the current directory is the C drive (lines 175–176). However, other directories must include the slash (lines 178–179). Finally, **displayLabel** is updated with the new directory (line 184).

This program loads quickly, because it indexes only the files in the current directory. This means that, rather than having a large delay in the beginning, a small delay occurs whenever a new directory is loaded. In addition, changes in the directory structure can be shown by reloading a directory. The previous program (Fig. 10.28–Fig. 10.30) needs to be restarted to reflect any changes in the directory structure. This type of trade-off is typical in the software world. When designing applications that run for long periods of time, developers might choose a large initial delay to improve performance throughout the rest of the program. However, when creating applications that run for only short periods of time, developers often prefer fast initial loading times and a small delay after each action.

10.8 Tab Control

The ***TabControl*** control creates tabbed windows, such as those we have seen in the Visual Studio .NET IDE (Fig. 10.35). This allows the programmer to design user interfaces that fit a large number of controls or a large amount of data without using up valuable screen "real estate." **Tab-Control**s contain ***TabPage*** objects, which are similar to **Panel**s and **GroupBox**es in that **TabPage**s also can contain controls. The programmer adds controls to the **TabPage** objects, and adds the **TabPage**s to the **TabControl**. Only one **TabPage** is displayed at a time.

Note that clicking the tabs selects the **TabControl**—to select the **TabPage**, click the control area underneath the tabs. To view different **TabPage**s, click the appropriate tab. Common properties and events of **TabControl**s are described in Fig. 10.36.

Tab pages

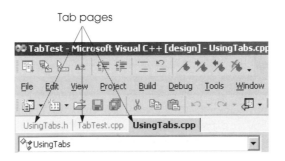

Fig. 10.35 Tabbed pages in Visual Studio .NET.

TabControl properties and events	Description / Delegate and Event Arguments
Common Properties	
ImageList	Specifies images to be displayed on a tab.
ItemSize	Specifies tab size.
MultiLine	Indicates whether multiple rows of tabs can be displayed.
SelectedIndex	Indicates index of **TabPage** that is currently selected
SelectedTab	Indicates the **TabPage** that is currently selected.
TabCount	Returns the number of tabs.
TabPages	Gets the collection of **TabPage**s within a **TabControl**.
Common Event	*(Delegate* **EventHandler**, *event arguments* **EventArgs***)*
SelectedIndexChanged	Generated when **SelectedIndex** changes (i.e., another **TabPage** is selected).

Fig. 10.36 TabControl properties and events.

Each **TabPage** generates its own **Click** event when its tab is clicked. Remember, events for controls can be handled by any event handler that is registered with the control's event delegate. This also applies to controls contained in a **TabPage**.

Class **UsingTabs** (Fig. 10.37 and Fig. 10.38) uses a **TabControl** to display various options relating to the text on a label (**Color**, **Size** and **Message**). The last **TabPage** displays an **About** message, which describes the use of **TabControl**s. The driver (Fig. 10.39) demonstrates the functionality of **UsingTabs**.

```
1   // Fig. 10.37: Tabs.h
2   // Class UsingTabs header file.
3
4   #pragma once
5
6   #using <mscorlib.dll>
7   #using <system.dll>
8   #using <system.drawing.dll>
9   #using <system.windows.forms.dll>
10
11  using namespace System;
12  using namespace System::Drawing;
13  using namespace System::Windows::Forms;
14
15  public __gc class UsingTabs : public Form
16  {
17  public:
18     UsingTabs();
19
```

Fig. 10.37 TabControl used to display various font settings. (Part 1 of 2.)

```
20   private:
21      Label *displayLabel;
22
23      // tab control containing table pages colorTabPage,
24      // sizeTabPage, messageTabPage and aboutTabPage
25      TabControl *optionsTabControl;
26
27      // tab page containing color options
28      TabPage *colorTabPage;
29      RadioButton *greenRadioButton;
30      RadioButton *redRadioButton;
31      RadioButton *blackRadioButton;
32
33      // tab page containing font size options
34      TabPage *sizeTabPage;
35      RadioButton *size20RadioButton;
36      RadioButton *size16RadioButton;
37      RadioButton *size12RadioButton;
38
39      // tab page containing text display options
40      TabPage *messageTabPage;
41      RadioButton *goodByeRadioButton;
42      RadioButton *helloRadioButton;
43
44      // tab page containing about message
45      TabPage *aboutTabPage;
46      Label *messageLabel;
47
48      void InitializeComponent();
49      void blackRadioButton_CheckedChanged( Object *,
50         EventArgs * );
51      void redRadioButton_CheckedChanged( Object *,
52         EventArgs * );
53      void greenRadioButton_CheckedChanged( Object *,
54         EventArgs * );
55      void size12RadioButton_CheckedChanged( Object *,
56         EventArgs * );
57      void size16RadioButton_CheckedChanged( Object *,
58         EventArgs * );
59      void size20RadioButton_CheckedChanged( Object *,
60         EventArgs * );
61      void helloRadioButton_CheckedChanged( Object *,
62         EventArgs * );
63      void goodByeRadioButton_CheckedChanged( Object *,
64         EventArgs * );
65   }; // end class UsingTabs
```

Fig. 10.37 **TabControl** used to display various font settings. (Part 2 of 2.)

```
1   // Fig. 10.38: TabTest.cpp
2   // Using TabControl to display various font settings.
3
```

Fig. 10.38 **UsingTabs** class method definitions. (Part 1 of 7.)

```
4    #include "Tabs.h"
5
6    UsingTabs::UsingTabs()
7    {
8       InitializeComponent();
9    }
10
11   void UsingTabs::InitializeComponent()
12   {
13      this->displayLabel = new Label();
14      this->optionsTabControl = new TabControl();
15      this->colorTabPage = new TabPage();
16      this->sizeTabPage = new TabPage();
17      this->messageTabPage = new TabPage();
18      this->aboutTabPage = new TabPage();
19      this->greenRadioButton = new RadioButton();
20      this->redRadioButton = new RadioButton();
21      this->blackRadioButton = new RadioButton();
22      this->size20RadioButton = new RadioButton();
23      this->size16RadioButton = new RadioButton();
24      this->size12RadioButton = new RadioButton();
25      this->goodByeRadioButton = new RadioButton();
26      this->helloRadioButton = new RadioButton();
27      this->messageLabel = new Label();
28      this->optionsTabControl->SuspendLayout();
29      this->colorTabPage->SuspendLayout();
30      this->sizeTabPage->SuspendLayout();
31      this->messageTabPage->SuspendLayout();
32      this->aboutTabPage->SuspendLayout();
33      this->SuspendLayout();
34
35      // displayLabel
36      this->displayLabel->Font = new Drawing::Font(
37         S"Microsoft Sans Serif", 12, FontStyle::Regular,
38         GraphicsUnit::Point, 0 );
39      this->displayLabel->Location = Point( 24, 192 );
40      this->displayLabel->Name = S"displayLabel";
41      this->displayLabel->Size = Drawing::Size( 272, 40 );
42      this->displayLabel->TabIndex = 3;
43      this->displayLabel->Text = S"Hello!";
44      this->displayLabel->TextAlign =
45         ContentAlignment::MiddleCenter;
46
47      // optionsTabControl
48      Control *controls[] = { this->colorTabPage, this->sizeTabPage,
49         this->messageTabPage, this->aboutTabPage };
50      this->optionsTabControl->Controls->AddRange( controls );
51      this->optionsTabControl->Location = Point( 16, 16 );
52      this->optionsTabControl->Name = S"optionsTabControl";
53      this->optionsTabControl->SelectedIndex = 0;
54      this->optionsTabControl->Size = Drawing::Size( 280, 168 );
55      this->optionsTabControl->TabIndex = 2;
56
```

Fig. 10.38 UsingTabs class method definitions. (Part 2 of 7.)

```
57     // colorTabPage
58     this->colorTabPage->Controls->Add( this->greenRadioButton );
59     this->colorTabPage->Controls->Add( this->redRadioButton );
60     this->colorTabPage->Controls->Add( this->blackRadioButton );
61     this->colorTabPage->Location = Point( 4, 22 );
62     this->colorTabPage->Name = S"colorTabPage";
63     this->colorTabPage->Size = Drawing::Size( 272, 142 );
64     this->colorTabPage->TabIndex = 0;
65     this->colorTabPage->Text = S"Color";
66
67     // greenRadioButton
68     this->greenRadioButton->Font = new Drawing::Font(
69        S"Microsoft Sans Serif", 9.75, FontStyle::Regular,
70        GraphicsUnit::Point, 0 );
71     this->greenRadioButton->Location = Point( 16, 104 );
72     this->greenRadioButton->Name = S"greenRadioButton";
73     this->greenRadioButton->TabIndex = 2;
74     this->greenRadioButton->Text = S"Green";
75     this->greenRadioButton->CheckedChanged += new EventHandler(
76        this, greenRadioButton_CheckedChanged );
77
78     // redRadioButton
79     this->redRadioButton->Font = new Drawing::Font(
80        S"Microsoft Sans Serif", 9.75, FontStyle::Regular,
81        GraphicsUnit::Point, 0 );
82     this->redRadioButton->Location = Point( 16, 64 );
83     this->redRadioButton->Name = S"redRadioButton";
84     this->redRadioButton->TabIndex = 1;
85     this->redRadioButton->Text = S"Red";
86     this->redRadioButton->CheckedChanged +=
87        new EventHandler( this, redRadioButton_CheckedChanged );
88
89     // blackRadioButton
90     this->blackRadioButton->Font = new Drawing::Font(
91        S"Microsoft Sans Serif", 9.75, FontStyle::Regular,
92        GraphicsUnit::Point, 0 );
93     this->blackRadioButton->Location = Point( 16, 24 );
94     this->blackRadioButton->Name = S"blackRadioButton";
95     this->blackRadioButton->TabIndex = 0;
96     this->blackRadioButton->Text = S"Black";
97     this->blackRadioButton->CheckedChanged += new
98        EventHandler( this, blackRadioButton_CheckedChanged );
99
100    // sizeTabPage
101    this->sizeTabPage->Controls->Add( this->size12RadioButton );
102    this->sizeTabPage->Controls->Add( this->size16RadioButton );
103    this->sizeTabPage->Controls->Add( this->size20RadioButton );
104    this->sizeTabPage->Location = Point( 4, 22 );
105    this->sizeTabPage->Name = S"sizeTabPage";
106    this->sizeTabPage->Size = Drawing::Size( 272, 142 );
107    this->sizeTabPage->TabIndex = 1;
108    this->sizeTabPage->Text = S"Size";
```

Fig. 10.38 UsingTabs class method definitions. (Part 3 of 7.)

```
109        this->sizeTabPage->Visible = false;
110
111        // size20RadioButton
112        this->size20RadioButton->Font = new Drawing::Font(
113           S"Microsoft Sans Serif", 9.75, FontStyle::Regular,
114           GraphicsUnit::Point, 0 );
115        this->size20RadioButton->Location = Point( 16, 104 );
116        this->size20RadioButton->Name = S"size20RadioButton";
117        this->size20RadioButton->TabIndex = 2;
118        this->size20RadioButton->Text = S"20 point";
119        this->size20RadioButton->CheckedChanged +=
120           new EventHandler( this, size20RadioButton_CheckedChanged );
121
122        // size16RadioButton
123        this->size16RadioButton->Font = new Drawing::Font(
124           S"Microsoft Sans Serif", 9.75, FontStyle::Regular,
125           GraphicsUnit::Point, 0 );
126        this->size16RadioButton->Location = Point( 16, 64 );
127        this->size16RadioButton->Name = S"size16RadioButton";
128        this->size16RadioButton->TabIndex = 1;
129        this->size16RadioButton->Text = S"16 point";
130        this->size16RadioButton->CheckedChanged += new
131           EventHandler( this, size16RadioButton_CheckedChanged );
132
133        // size12RadioButton
134        this->size12RadioButton->Font = new Drawing::Font(
135           S"Microsoft Sans Serif", 9.75, FontStyle::Regular,
136           GraphicsUnit::Point, 0 );
137        this->size12RadioButton->Location = Point( 16, 24 );
138        this->size12RadioButton->Name = S"size12RadioButton";
139        this->size12RadioButton->TabIndex = 0;
140        this->size12RadioButton->Text = S"12 point";
141        this->size12RadioButton->CheckedChanged += new
142           EventHandler( this, size12RadioButton_CheckedChanged );
143
144        // messageTabPage
145        this->messageTabPage->Controls->Add(
146           this->goodByeRadioButton );
147        this->messageTabPage->Controls->Add(
148           this->helloRadioButton );
149        this->messageTabPage->Location = Point( 4, 22 );
150        this->messageTabPage->Name = S"messageTabPage";
151        this->messageTabPage->Size = Drawing::Size( 272, 142 );
152        this->messageTabPage->TabIndex = 2;
153        this->messageTabPage->Text = S"Message";
154        this->messageTabPage->Visible = false;
155
156        // goodByeRadioButton
157        this->goodByeRadioButton->Font = new Drawing::Font(
158           S"Microsoft Sans Serif", 9.75, FontStyle::Regular,
159           GraphicsUnit::Point, 0 );
160        this->goodByeRadioButton->Location = Point( 16, 64 );
```

Fig. 10.38 UsingTabs class method definitions. (Part 4 of 7.)

```
161    this->goodByeRadioButton->Name = S"goodByeRadioButton";
162    this->goodByeRadioButton->TabIndex = 1;
163    this->goodByeRadioButton->Text = S"Goodbye!";
164    this->goodByeRadioButton->CheckedChanged += new
165       EventHandler( this, goodByeRadioButton_CheckedChanged );
166
167    // helloRadioButton
168    this->helloRadioButton->Font = new Drawing::Font(
169       S"Microsoft Sans Serif", 9.75, FontStyle::Regular,
170       GraphicsUnit::Point, 0 );
171    this->helloRadioButton->Location = Point( 16, 24 );
172    this->helloRadioButton->Name = S"helloRadioButton";
173    this->helloRadioButton->TabIndex = 0;
174    this->helloRadioButton->Text = S"Hello!";
175    this->helloRadioButton->CheckedChanged += new
176       EventHandler( this, helloRadioButton_CheckedChanged );
177
178    // aboutTabPage
179    this->aboutTabPage->Controls->Add( this->messageLabel );
180    this->aboutTabPage->Location = Point( 4, 22 );
181    this->aboutTabPage->Name = S"aboutTabPage";
182    this->aboutTabPage->Size = Drawing::Size( 272, 142 );
183    this->aboutTabPage->TabIndex = 3;
184    this->aboutTabPage->Text = S"About";
185    this->aboutTabPage->Visible = false;
186
187    // messageLabel
188    this->messageLabel->Font = new Drawing::Font(
189       S"Microsoft Sans Serif", 14.25, FontStyle::Regular,
190       GraphicsUnit::Point, 0 );
191    this->messageLabel->Location = Point( 16, 16 );
192    this->messageLabel->Name = S"messageLabel";
193    this->messageLabel->Size = Drawing::Size( 248, 104 );
194    this->messageLabel->TabIndex = 0;
195    this->messageLabel->Text =
196       S"Tabs organize controls and conserve screen space.";
197
198    // UsingTabs
199    this->AutoScaleBaseSize = Drawing::Size( 5, 13 );
200    this->ClientSize = Drawing::Size( 328, 245 );
201    this->Controls->Add( this->displayLabel );
202    this->Controls->Add( this->optionsTabControl );
203    this->Name = S"UsingTabs";
204    this->Text = S"UsingTabs";
205    this->optionsTabControl->ResumeLayout();
206    this->colorTabPage->ResumeLayout();
207    this->sizeTabPage->ResumeLayout();
208    this->messageTabPage->ResumeLayout();
209    this->aboutTabPage->ResumeLayout();
210    this->ResumeLayout();
211 } // end method InitializeComponent
212
```

Fig. 10.38 UsingTabs class method definitions. (Part 5 of 7.)

```
213  // event handler for black color radio button
214  void UsingTabs::blackRadioButton_CheckedChanged(
215     Object *sender, EventArgs *e )
216  {
217     displayLabel->ForeColor = Color::Black;
218  }
219
220  // event handler for red color radio button
221  void UsingTabs::redRadioButton_CheckedChanged(
222     Object *sender, EventArgs *e )
223  {
224     displayLabel->ForeColor = Color::Red;
225  }
226
227  // event handler for green color radio button
228  void UsingTabs::greenRadioButton_CheckedChanged(
229     Object *sender, EventArgs *e )
230  {
231     displayLabel->ForeColor = Color::Green;
232  }
233
234  // event handler for size 12 radio button
235  void UsingTabs::size12RadioButton_CheckedChanged(
236     Object *sender, EventArgs *e )
237  {
238     displayLabel->Font =
239        new Drawing::Font( displayLabel->Font->Name, 12 );
240  }
241
242  // event handler for size 16 radio button
243  void UsingTabs::size16RadioButton_CheckedChanged(
244     Object *sender, EventArgs *e )
245  {
246     displayLabel->Font =
247        new Drawing::Font( displayLabel->Font->Name, 16 );
248  }
249
250  // event handler for size 20 radio button
251  void UsingTabs::size20RadioButton_CheckedChanged(
252     Object *sender, EventArgs *e )
253  {
254     displayLabel->Font =
255        new Drawing::Font( displayLabel->Font->Name, 20 );
256  }
257
258  // event handler for message "Hello!" radio button
259  void UsingTabs::helloRadioButton_CheckedChanged(
260     Object *sender, EventArgs *e )
261  {
262     displayLabel->Text = S"Hello!";
263  }
264
```

Fig. 10.38 UsingTabs class method definitions. (Part 6 of 7.)

```
265   // event handler for message "Goodbye!" radio button
266   void UsingTabs::goodByeRadioButton_CheckedChanged(
267      Object *sender, EventArgs *e )
268   {
269      displayLabel->Text = S"Goodbye!";
270   }
```

Fig. 10.38 `UsingTabs` class method definitions. (Part 7 of 7.)

```
1    // Fig. 10.39: TabTest.cpp
2    // Using TabControl to display various font settings.
3
4    #include "Tabs.h"
5
6    int __stdcall WinMain()
7    {
8       Application::Run( new UsingTabs() );
9
10      return 0;
11   } // end WinMain
```

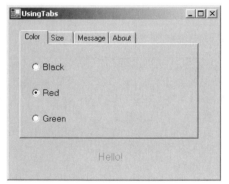
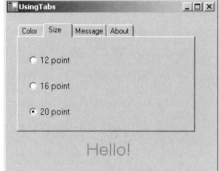
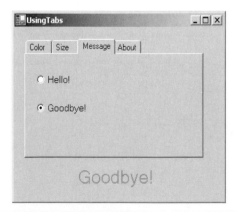

Fig. 10.39 `TabTest` demonstration.

The **TabControl optionsTabControl** (line 14 of Fig. 10.38) and **TabPage**s **color-TabPage** (line 15), **sizeTabPage** (line 16), **messageTabPage** (line 17) and **aboutTabPage** (line 18) are created by calling constructors **TabControl** and **TabPage**. **TabPage colorTabPage** contains three radio buttons for colors green (**greenRadioButton**, line 19), red (**redRadioButton**, line 20) and black (**blackRadioButton**, line 21). The **CheckChanged** event handler for each button updates the color of the text in **displayLabel** (lines 217, 224 and 231). **TabPage sizeTabPage** has three radio buttons, corresponding to font sizes 20 (**size20RadioButton**, line 22), 16 (**size16RadioButton**, line 23) and 12 (**size12RadioButton**, line 24), which change the font size of **displayLabel**—lines 238–239, 246–247 and 254–255, respectively. **TabPage messageTabPage** contains two radio buttons—for the messages **Goodbye!** (**goodbyeRadioButton**, line 25) and **Hello!** (**helloRadioButton**, line 26). The two radio buttons determine the text on **displayLabel** (lines 262 and 269).

Software Engineering Observation 10.2

*A **TabPage** can act as a container for a single logical group of radio buttons and enforces their mutual exclusivity. To place multiple radio-button groups inside a single **TabPage**, programmers should group radio buttons within **Panel**s or **GroupBox**es contained within the **TabPage**.*

The last **TabPage** (**aboutTabPage**, line 18 of Fig. 10.38) contains a **Label** (**messageLabel**, line 27) that describes the purpose of **TabControl**s.

10.9 Multiple-Document-Interface (MDI) Windows

In previous chapters, we have built only *single-document-interface (SDI)* applications. Such programs (including Notepad or Paint) support only one open window or document at a time. SDI applications usually have contracted abilities—Paint and Notepad, for example, have limited image- and text-editing features. To edit multiple documents, the user must create additional instances of the SDI application.

Multiple-document interface (MDI) programs (such as PaintShop Pro and Adobe Photoshop) enable users to edit multiple documents at once. MDI programs also tend to be more complex—PaintShop Pro and Photoshop have a greater number of image-editing features than does Paint. Until now, we had not mentioned that the applications we created were SDI applications. We define this here to emphasize the distinction between the two types of programs.

The application window of an MDI program is called the *parent window*, and each window inside the application is referred to as a *child window*. Although an MDI application can have many child windows, each has only one parent window. Furthermore, a maximum of one child window can be active at once. Child windows cannot be parents themselves and cannot be moved outside their parent. Otherwise, a child window behaves like any other window (with regard to closing, minimizing, resizing etc.). A child window's functionality can be different from the functionality of other child windows of the parent. For example, one child window might edit images, another might edit text and a third might display network traffic graphically, but all could belong to the same MDI parent. Figure 10.40 depicts a sample MDI application.

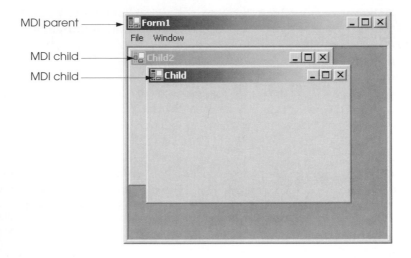

Fig. 10.40 MDI parent window and MDI child windows.

To create an MDI form, create a new form and set its *IsMDIContainer* property to **true**. Next, create a child form class to be added to the form. To add the child form to th4e parent, we must create a new child form object, set its MdiParent property to the parent form and call method Show. In general, to add a child form to a parent, write

```
Child *frmChild = new ChildFormClass();
frmChild->MdiParent = frmParent;
frmChild->Show();
```

Class **Form** property *MdiChildren* is an array of child **Form** pointers. This is useful if the parent window wants to check the status of all its children (such as to ensure that all are saved before the parent closes). Property *ActiveMdiChild* returns a pointer to the active child window; it returns **0** if there are no active child windows. Other features of MDI windows are described in Fig. 10.41.

MDI **Form** events and properties	Description / Delegate and Event Arguments
Common MDI Child Properties	
IsMdiChild	Indicates whether the **Form** is an MDI child. If **true**, **Form** is an MDI child (read-only property).
MdiParent	Specifies the MDI parent **Form** of the child.

Fig. 10.41 MDI parent and MDI child events and properties. (Part 1 of 2.)

MDI **Form** events and properties	Description / Delegate and Event Arguments
Common MDI Parent Properties	
`ActiveMdiChild`	Returns the **Form** that is the currently active MDI child (returns null reference if no children are active).
`IsMdiContainer`	Indicates whether a **Form** can be an MDI. If **true**, the **Form** can be an MDI parent. Default is **false**.
`MdiChildren`	Returns the MDI children as an array of **Form**s.
Common Method	
`LayoutMdi`	Determines the display of child forms on an MDI parent. Takes as a parameter an **MdiLayout** enumeration with possible values **ArrangeIcons**, **Cascade**, **TileHorizontal** and **TileVertical**. Figure 10.44 depicts the effects of these values.
Common Event	*(Delegate **EventHandler**, event arguments **EventArgs**)*
`MdiChildActivate`	Generated when an MDI child is closed or activated.

Fig. 10.41 MDI parent and MDI child events and properties. (Part 2 of 2.)

Child windows can be minimized, maximized and closed independently of each other and of the parent window. Figure 10.42 shows two images, one containing two minimized child windows and a second containing a maximized child window. When the parent is minimized or closed, the child windows are minimized or closed as well. Notice that the title bar in the second image of Fig. 10.42 is **Parent Window - [Child]**. When a child window is maximized, its title bar is inserted into the parent window's title bar. When a child window is minimized or maximized, its title bar displays a restore icon, which returns the child window to its previous size (its size before it was minimized or maximized).

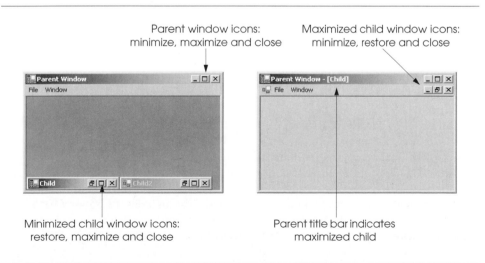

Parent window icons: minimize, maximize and close

Maximized child window icons: minimize, restore and close

Minimized child window icons: restore, maximize and close

Parent title bar indicates maximized child

Fig. 10.42 Minimized and maximized child windows.

The parent and child forms can have different menus, which are merged whenever a child window is selected. To specify how the menus merge, programmers can set the *MergeOrder* and the *MergeType* properties for each **MenuItem** (see Fig. 10.2). **MergeOrder** determines the order in which **MenuItem**s appear when two menus are merged. **MenuItem**s with a lower **MergeOrder** value will appear first. For example, if **Menu1** has items **File**, **Edit** and **Window** (and their orders are 0, 10 and 20) and **Menu2** has items **Format** and **View** (and their orders are 7 and 15), then the merged menu contains menu items **File**, **Format**, **Edit**, **View** and **Window**, in that order.

Each **MenuItem** instance has its own **MergeOrder** property. It is likely that, at some point in an application, two **MenuItem**s with the same **MergeOrder** value will merge. Property **MergeType** specifies the manner in which this conflict is resolved.

Property **MergeType** takes a *MenuMerge* enumeration value and determines which menu items will be displayed when two menu items with the same **MergeOrder** are merged. A menu item with value *Add* is added to its parent's menu as a new menu on the menu bar. (The parent's menu items come first.) If a child form's menu item has value *Replace*, it attempts to take the place of its parent form's corresponding menu item during merging. A menu with value *MergeItems* combines its items with that of its parent's corresponding menu. (If parent and child menus originally occupy the same space, their submenus will be brought together as one large menu.) A child's menu item with value *Remove* disappears when the menu is merged with that of its parent.

Value **MergeItems** acts passively—if the parent's menu has a **MergeType** that is different from the child menu's **MergeType**, the child's menu setting determines the outcome of the merge. When the child window is closed, the parent's original menu is restored.

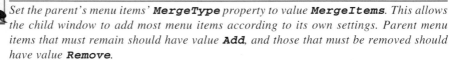

Software Engineering Observation 10.3

*Set the parent's menu items' **MergeType** property to value **MergeItems**. This allows the child window to add most menu items according to its own settings. Parent menu items that must remain should have value **Add**, and those that must be removed should have value **Remove**.*

The .NET Framework provides a property that facilitates the tracking of which child windows are opened in an MDI container. Property *MdiList* (a boolean) of class **MenuItem** determines whether a **MenuItem** displays a list of open child windows. The list appears at the bottom of the menu following a separator bar (first screen in Fig. 10.43). When a new child window is opened, an entry is added to the list. By default, if nine or more child windows are open, the list includes the option **More Windows...**, which allows the user to select a window from a list, using a scrollbar. Multiple **MenuItem**s can have their **MdiList** property set; each displays a list of open child windows.

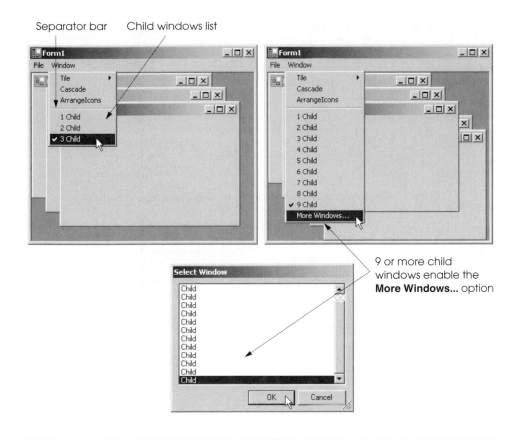

Fig. 10.43 MenuItem property **MdiList** example.

Good Programming Practice 10.1

*When creating MDI applications, include a menu item with its **MdiList** property set to **true**. This helps the user select a child window quickly, rather than having to search for it in the parent window. This feature normally appears on the **Window** menu.*

MDI containers allow developers to organize the placement of child windows. The child windows in an MDI application can be arranged by calling method **LayoutMdi** of the parent form. Method **LayoutMdi** takes an **MdiLayout** enumeration value—**ArrangeIcons**, **Cascade**, **TileHorizontal** or **TileVertical**. *Tiled windows* completely fill the parent and do not overlap; such windows can be arranged horizontally (value **TileHorizontal**) or vertically (value **TileVertical**). *Cascaded windows* (value **Cascade**) overlap—each is the same size and displays a visible title bar, if possible. Value **ArrangeIcons** arranges the icons for any minimized child windows. If minimized windows are scattered around the parent window, value **ArrangeIcons** orders them neatly at the bottom-left corner of the parent window. Figure 10.44 illustrates the values of the **MdiLayout** enumeration.

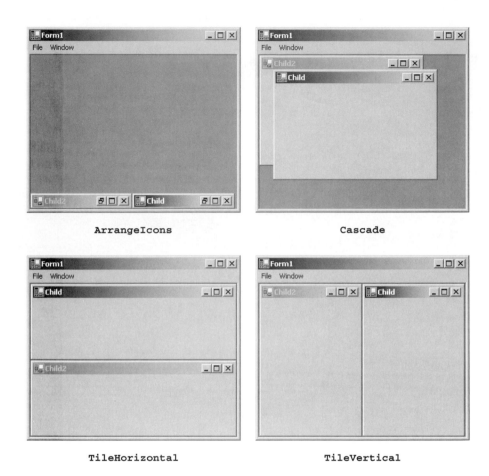

Fig. 10.44 **MdiLayout** enumeration values.

The next application demonstrates the use of MDI windows. The application contains classes **Child** (Fig. 10.45–Fig. 10.46) and **UsingMdi** (Fig. 10.47–Fig. 10.48) as well as a driver (Fig. 10.49). Class **UsingMdi** uses three instances of class **Child**, each of which contains a **PictureBox** and an image. The parent MDI form contains a menu that enables users to create and arrange child forms.

The MDI parent form contains two top-level menus. The first of these menus, **File** (**fileMenuItem**, line 14 of Fig. 10.48), contains both a **New** submenu (**newMenuItem**, line 15) and an **Exit** item (**exitMenuItem**, line 19). The second menu, **Format** (**formatMenuItem**, line 20), provides options for laying out the MDI children, plus a list of the active MDI children.

```
1   // Fig. 10.45: Child.h
2   // Child class header file.
3
```

Fig. 10.45 Child window of MDI parent. (Part 1 of 2.)

```
4   #pragma once
5
6   #using <mscorlib.dll>
7   #using <system.dll>
8   #using <system.drawing.dll>
9   #using <system.windows.forms.dll>
10
11  using namespace System;
12  using namespace System::Drawing;
13  using namespace System::Windows::Forms;
14  using namespace System::IO;
15
16  public __gc class Child : public Form
17  {
18  public:
19     Child( String *, String * );
20
21  private:
22     PictureBox *pictureBox;
23     void InitializeComponent();
24  }; // end class Child
```

Fig. 10.45 Child window of MDI parent. (Part 2 of 2.)

```
1   // Fig. 10.46: Child.cpp
2   // Child window of MDI parent.
3
4   #include "Child.h"
5
6   Child::Child( String *title, String *fileName )
7   {
8      this->pictureBox = new PictureBox();
9      Text = title;   // set title text
10     InitializeComponent();
11
12     // set image to display in pictureBox
13     pictureBox->Image = Image::FromFile( String::Concat(
14        Directory::GetCurrentDirectory(), fileName ) );
15  }
16
17  void Child::InitializeComponent()
18  {
19     this->SuspendLayout();
20     this->pictureBox->Location = Point( 8, 8 );
21     this->pictureBox->Name = S"pictureBox";
22     this->pictureBox->Size = Drawing::Size( 272, 256 );
23     this->pictureBox->TabIndex = 0;
24     this->pictureBox->TabStop = false;
25
26     // child
27     this->AutoScaleBaseSize = Drawing::Size( 5, 13 );
28     this->ClientSize = Drawing::Size( 292, 273 );
```

Fig. 10.46 Child class method definitions. (Part 1 of 2.)

```
29        this->Controls->Add( this->pictureBox );
30        this->ResumeLayout();
31    } // end method InitializeComponent
```

Fig. 10.46 Child class method definitions. (Part 2 of 2.)

```
1    // Fig. 10.47: UsingMDI.h
2    // UsingMDI class header file.
3
4    #pragma once
5
6    #include "Child.h"
7
8    public __gc class UsingMDI : public Form
9    {
10   public:
11       UsingMDI();
12
13   private:
14       MainMenu *mainMenu1;
15       MenuItem *fileMenuItem;
16       MenuItem *newMenuItem;
17       MenuItem *child1MenuItem;
18       MenuItem *child2MenuItem;
19       MenuItem *child3MenuItem;
20       MenuItem *exitMenuItem;
21       MenuItem *formatMenuItem;
22       MenuItem *cascadeMenuItem;
23       MenuItem *tileHorizontalMenuItem;
24       MenuItem *tileVerticalMenuItem;
25
26       void InitializeComponent();
27       void child1MenuItem_Click( Object *, EventArgs * );
28       void child2MenuItem_Click( Object *, EventArgs * );
29       void child3MenuItem_Click( Object *, EventArgs * );
30       void exitMenuItem_Click( Object *, EventArgs * );
31       void cascadeMenuItem_Click( Object *, EventArgs * );
32       void tileHorizontalMenuItem_Click( Object *, EventArgs * );
33       void tileVerticalMenuItem_Click( Object *, EventArgs * );
34   }; // end class UsingMDI
```

Fig. 10.47 Demonstrating use of MDI parent and child windows.

```
1    // Fig. 10.48: UsingMDI.cpp
2    // Demonstrating use of MDI parent and child windows.
3
4    #include "UsingMDI.h"
5
6    UsingMDI::UsingMDI()
7    {
8        InitializeComponent();
9    }
10
```

Fig. 10.48 UsingMDI class method definitions. (Part 1 of 4.)

```
11   void UsingMDI::InitializeComponent()
12   {
13       this->mainMenu1 = new MainMenu();
14       this->fileMenuItem = new MenuItem();
15       this->newMenuItem = new MenuItem();
16       this->child1MenuItem = new MenuItem();
17       this->child2MenuItem = new MenuItem();
18       this->child3MenuItem = new MenuItem();
19       this->exitMenuItem = new MenuItem();
20       this->formatMenuItem = new MenuItem();
21       this->cascadeMenuItem = new MenuItem();
22       this->tileHorizontalMenuItem = new MenuItem();
23       this->tileVerticalMenuItem = new MenuItem();
24       this->SuspendLayout();
25
26       // mainMenu1
27       this->mainMenu1->MenuItems->Add( this->fileMenuItem );
28       this->mainMenu1->MenuItems->Add( this->formatMenuItem );
29
30       // fileMenuItem
31       this->fileMenuItem->Index = 0;
32       this->fileMenuItem->MenuItems->Add( this->newMenuItem );
33       this->fileMenuItem->MenuItems->Add( this->exitMenuItem );
34       this->fileMenuItem->Text = S"File";
35
36       // newMenuItem
37       this->newMenuItem->Index = 0;
38       this->newMenuItem->MenuItems->Add( this->child1MenuItem );
39       this->newMenuItem->MenuItems->Add( this->child2MenuItem );
40       this->newMenuItem->MenuItems->Add( this->child3MenuItem );
41       this->newMenuItem->Text = S"New";
42
43       // child1MenuItem
44       this->child1MenuItem->Index = 0;
45       this->child1MenuItem->Text = S"Child1";
46       this->child1MenuItem->Click += new EventHandler( this,
47          child1MenuItem_Click );
48
49       // child2MenuItem
50       this->child2MenuItem->Index = 1;
51       this->child2MenuItem->Text = S"Child2";
52       this->child2MenuItem->Click += new EventHandler( this,
53          child2MenuItem_Click );
54
55       // child3MenuItem
56       this->child3MenuItem->Index = 2;
57       this->child3MenuItem->Text = S"Child3";
58       this->child3MenuItem->Click += new EventHandler( this,
59          child3MenuItem_Click );
60
61       // exitMenuItem
62       this->exitMenuItem->Index = 1;
63       this->exitMenuItem->Text = S"Exit";
64       this->exitMenuItem->Click += new EventHandler( this,
```

Fig. 10.48 UsingMDI class method definitions. (Part 2 of 4.)

```cpp
65            exitMenuItem_Click );
66
67      // formatMenuItem
68      this->formatMenuItem->Index = 1;
69      this->formatMenuItem->MdiList = true;
70      this->formatMenuItem->MenuItems->Add(
71         this->cascadeMenuItem );
72      this->formatMenuItem->MenuItems->Add(
73         this->tileHorizontalMenuItem );
74      this->formatMenuItem->MenuItems->Add(
75         this->tileVerticalMenuItem );
76      this->formatMenuItem->Text = S"Format";
77
78      // cascadeMenuItem
79      this->cascadeMenuItem->Index = 0;
80      this->cascadeMenuItem->Text = S"Cascade";
81      this->cascadeMenuItem->Click += new EventHandler( this,
82         cascadeMenuItem_Click );
83
84      // tileHorizontalMenuItem
85      this->tileHorizontalMenuItem->Index = 1;
86      this->tileHorizontalMenuItem->Text = S"Tile Horizontal";
87      this->tileHorizontalMenuItem->Click += new EventHandler(
88         this, tileHorizontalMenuItem_Click );
89
90      // tileVerticalMenuItem
91      this->tileVerticalMenuItem->Index = 2;
92      this->tileVerticalMenuItem->Text = S"Tile Vertical";
93      this->tileVerticalMenuItem->Click += new EventHandler( this,
94         tileVerticalMenuItem_Click );
95
96      // UsingMDI
97      this->AutoScaleBaseSize = Drawing::Size( 5, 13 );
98      this->ClientSize = Drawing::Size( 330, 320 );
99      this->IsMdiContainer = true;
100     this->Menu = this->mainMenu1;
101     this->Name = S"UsingMDI";
102     this->Text = S"UsingMDI";
103     this->ResumeLayout();
104  } // end method InitializeComponent
105
106  // create Child 1 when menu clicked
107  void UsingMDI::child1MenuItem_Click( Object *sender,
108     EventArgs *e )
109  {
110
111     // create new child
112     Child *formChild = new Child( S"Child 1",
113        S"\\images\\image0.jpg" );
114     formChild->MdiParent = this;     // set parent
115     formChild->Show();              // display child
116  } // end method child1MenuItem_Click
```

Fig. 10.48 UsingMDI class method definitions. (Part 3 of 4.)

```
117
118   // create Child 2 when menu clicked
119   void UsingMDI::child2MenuItem_Click( Object *sender,
120      EventArgs *e )
121   {
122
123      // create new child
124      Child *formChild = new Child( S"Child 2",
125         S"\\images\\image1.jpg" );
126      formChild->MdiParent = this;    // set parent
127      formChild->Show();              // display child
128   } // end method child2MenuItem_Click
129
130   // create Child 3 when menu clicked
131   void UsingMDI::child3MenuItem_Click( Object *sender,
132      EventArgs *e )
133   {
134
135      // create new child
136      Child *formChild = new Child( S"Child 3",
137         S"\\images\\image2.jpg" );
138      formChild->MdiParent = this;    // set parent
139      formChild->Show();              // display child
140   } // end method child3MenuItem_Click
141
142   // exit application
143   void UsingMDI::exitMenuItem_Click( Object *sender,
144      EventArgs *e )
145   {
146      Application::Exit();
147   } // end method exitMenuItem_Click
148
149   // set cascade layout
150   void UsingMDI::cascadeMenuItem_Click( Object *sender,
151      EventArgs *e )
152   {
153      this->LayoutMdi( MdiLayout::Cascade );
154   } // end method cascadeMenuItem_Click
155
156   // set TileHorizontal layout
157   void UsingMDI::tileHorizontalMenuItem_Click( Object *sender,
158      EventArgs *e )
159   {
160      this->LayoutMdi( MdiLayout::TileHorizontal );
161   } // end method tileHorizontalMenuItem_Click
162
163   // set TileVertical layout
164   void UsingMDI::tileVerticalMenuItem_Click( Object *sender,
165      EventArgs *e )
166   {
167      this->LayoutMdi( MdiLayout::TileVertical );
168   } // end method tileVerticalMenuItem_Click
```

Fig. 10.48 UsingMDI class method definitions. (Part 4 of 4.)

```
1   // Fig. 10.49: UsingMDITest.cpp
2   // Main application.
3
4   #include "UsingMDI.h"
5
6   int __stdcall WinMain()
7   {
8       Application::Run( new UsingMDI() );
9
10      return 0;
11  } // end WinMain
```

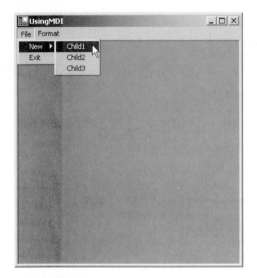

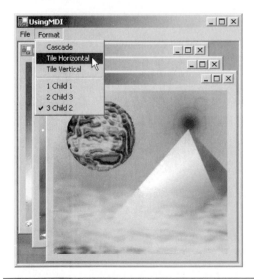

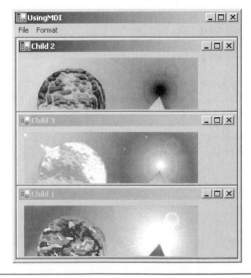

Fig. 10.49 MDI demonstration.

The **Cascade** menu item (**cascadeMenuItem**, line 21 of Fig. 10.48) has an event handler (**cascadeMenuItem_Click**, lines 150–154) that arranges the child windows in a cascading manner. The event handler calls method **LayoutMdi** with the argument **Cascade** from the **MdiLayout** enumeration (line 153).

The **Tile Horizontal** menu item (**tileHorizontalMenuItem**, line 22) has an event handler (**tileHorizontalMenuItem_Click**, lines 157–161) that arranges the child windows in a horizontal manner. The event handler calls method **LayoutMdi** with the argument **TileHorizontal** from enumeration **MdiLayout** (line 160).

Finally, the **Tile Vertical** menu item (**tileVerticalMenuItem**, line 23 has an event handler (**tileVerticalMenuItem_Click**, lines 164–168) that arranges the child windows in a vertical manner. The event handler calls method **LayoutMdi** with the argument **TileVertical** from enumeration **MdiLayout** (line 167).

In class **Child** (Fig. 10.45 and Fig. 10.46), we add a **PictureBox** (**pictureBox**, line 8) to form **Child**. The constructor invokes method **InitializeComponent** (line 10) and initializes the form's title (line 10) and the image to display in the **PictureBox** (lines 13–14).

The parent MDI form (Fig. 10.47 and Fig. 10.48) creates new instances of class **Child** each time the user selects a new child window from the **File** menu. The event handlers in lines 107–140 create new child forms that each contain an image. Each event handler creates a new instance of the child form, sets its **MdiParent** property to the parent form and calls method **Show** to display the child.

10.10 Visual Inheritance

In Chapter 6, Object-Oriented Programming: Inheritance, we discuss how to create classes by inheriting from other classes. We also can use inheritance to create **Form**s that display a GUI, because **Form**s are classes that derive from class **System::Windows::Forms::Form**. Visual inheritance allows us to create a new **Form** by inheriting from another **Form**. The derived **Form** class contains the functionality of its **Form** base class, including any base-class properties, methods, variables and controls. The derived class also inherits all visual aspects—such as sizing, component layout, spacing between GUI components, colors and fonts—from its base class.

Visual inheritance enables developers to achieve visual consistency across applications by reusing code. For example, a company could define a base form that contains a product's logo, a static background color, a predefined menu bar and other elements. Programmers then could use the base form throughout an application for purposes of uniformity and product branding.

Class **VisualInheritance** (Fig. 10.50 and Fig. 10.51) is a form that we use as a base class for demonstrating visual inheritance. The GUI contains two labels (one with text **Bugs, Bugs, Bugs** and one with **Copyright 2003, by Bug2Bug.com.**) and one button (displaying the text **Learn More**). When a user presses the **Learn More** button, method **learnMoreButton_Click** (lines 66–73 of Fig. 10.51) is invoked. This method displays a message box that provides some informative text. The driver (Fig. 10.52) starts the application.

```
1  // Fig. 10.50: VisualInheritance.h
2  // VisualInheritance class header file.
```

Fig. 10.50 Class **VisualInheritance**, which inherits from class **Form**, contains a button (**Learn More**). (Part 1 of 2.)

```
3
4    #pragma once
5
6    #using <mscorlib.dll>
7    #using <system.dll>
8    #using <system.drawing.dll>
9    #using <system.windows.forms.dll>
10
11   using namespace System;
12   using namespace System::Drawing;
13   using namespace System::Windows::Forms;
14
15   public __gc class VisualInheritance : public Form
16   {
17   public:
18      VisualInheritance();
19
20   private:
21      Label *bugsLabel;
22      Button *learnMoreButton;
23      Label *label1;
24      void InitializeComponent();
25      void learnMoreButton_Click( Object *, EventArgs * );
26   }; // end class VisualInheritance
```

Fig. 10.50 Class **VisualInheritance**, which inherits from class **Form**, contains a button (**Learn More**). (Part 2 of 2.)

```
1    // Fig. 10.51: VisualInheritance.cpp
2    // Base Form for use with visual inheritance.
3
4    #include "VisualInheritance.h"
5
6    VisualInheritance::VisualInheritance()
7    {
8       InitializeComponent();
9    }
10
11   void VisualInheritance::InitializeComponent()
12   {
13      this->bugsLabel = new Label();
14      this->learnMoreButton = new Button();
15      this->label1 = new Label();
16      this->SuspendLayout();
17
18      // bugsLabel
19      this->bugsLabel->BackColor = Color::White;
20      this->bugsLabel->Font = new Drawing::Font(
21         S"Microsoft Sans Serif", 20.25 );
22      this->bugsLabel->ForeColor = Color::MidnightBlue;
23      this->bugsLabel->Location = Point( 8, 8 );
24      this->bugsLabel->Name = S"bugsLabel";
25      this->bugsLabel->Size = Drawing::Size( 272, 80 );
```

Fig. 10.51 **VisualInheritance** class method definitions. (Part 1 of 2.)

```
26      this->bugsLabel->TabIndex = 0;
27      this->bugsLabel->Text = S"Bugs, Bugs, Bugs";
28      this->bugsLabel->TextAlign = ContentAlignment::MiddleCenter;
29
30      // learnMoreButton
31      this->learnMoreButton->BackColor = Color::White;
32      this->learnMoreButton->Font = new Drawing::Font(
33         S"Microsoft Sans Serif", 18.25 );
34      this->learnMoreButton->ForeColor = Color::MidnightBlue;
35      this->learnMoreButton->Location = Point( 8, 104 );
36      this->learnMoreButton->Name = S"learnMoreButton";
37      this->learnMoreButton->Size = Drawing::Size( 120, 88 );
38      this->learnMoreButton->TabIndex = 1;
39      this->learnMoreButton->Text = S"Learn More";
40      this->learnMoreButton->Click += new EventHandler( this,
41         learnMoreButton_Click );
42
43      // label1
44      this->label1->BackColor = Color::White;
45      this->label1->Font = new Drawing::Font(
46         S"Microsoft Sans Serif", 12 );
47      this->label1->ForeColor = Color::MidnightBlue;
48      this->label1->Location = Point( 8, 216 );
49      this->label1->Name = S"label1";
50      this->label1->Size = Drawing::Size( 272, 40 );
51      this->label1->TabIndex = 2;
52      this->label1->Text = S"Copyright 2003, by Bug2Bug.com";
53      this->label1->TextAlign = ContentAlignment::MiddleCenter;
54
55      // VisualInheritance
56      this->AutoScaleBaseSize = Drawing::Size( 5, 13 );
57      this->ClientSize = Drawing::Size( 292, 273 );
58      this->Controls->Add( this->label1 );
59      this->Controls->Add( this->learnMoreButton );
60      this->Controls->Add( this->bugsLabel );
61      this->Name = S"VisualInheritance";
62      this->Text = S"Visual Inheritance";
63      this->ResumeLayout();
64   } // end method InitializeComponent
65
66   void VisualInheritance::learnMoreButton_Click( Object *sender,
67      EventArgs *e )
68   {
69      MessageBox::Show(
70         S"Bugs, Bugs, Bugs is a product of Bug2Bug.com.",
71         S"Learn More", MessageBoxButtons::OK,
72         MessageBoxIcon::Information );
73   } // end method learnMoreButton_Click
```

Fig. 10.51 `VisualInheritance` class method definitions. (Part 2 of 2.)

```
1   // Fig. 10.52: VisualInheritanceTest.cpp
2   // Visual inheritance main application.
```

Fig. 10.52 Visual inheritance base class demonstration. (Part 1 of 2.)

```
3
4   #include "VisualInheritance.h"
5
6   int __stdcall WinMain()
7   {
8      Application::Run( new VisualInheritance() );
9
10     return 0;
11  }
```

Fig. 10.52 Visual inheritance base class demonstration. (Part 2 of 2.)

Class **VisualInheritanceTest** (Fig. 10.53 and Fig. 10.54) derives from class **VisualInheritance**. The GUI contains those components derived from class **VisualInheritance**, plus a button with text **Learn The Program** that we added in class **VisualInheritanceTest**. When a user presses this button, method **learnProgramButton_Click** (lines 38–45 of Fig. 10.54) is invoked. This method displays a simple message box.

Figure 10.55 demonstrates that the components, their layouts and the functionality of the base class **VisualInheritance** (Fig. 10.50 and Fig. 10.51) are inherited by **VisualInheritanceTest**. If a user clicks button **Learn More**, the base-class event handler **learnMoreButton_Click** displays a **MessageBox**.

```
1   // Fig. 10.53: VisualInheritanceTest.h
2   // VisualInheritanceTest class header file.
3
4   #using <mscorlib.dll>
5   #using <system.dll>
6   #using <system.drawing.dll>
7   #using <system.windows.forms.dll>
8
9   using namespace System;
10  using namespace System::Drawing;
```

Fig. 10.53 Class **VisualInheritanceTest**, which inherits from class **VisualInheritance**, contains an additional button. (Part 1 of 2.)

```
11    using namespace System::Windows::Forms;
12
13    #include "VisualInheritance.h"
14
15    public __gc class VisualInheritanceTest
16       : public VisualInheritance
17    {
18    public:
19       VisualInheritanceTest();
20
21    private:
22       Button *learnProgramButton;
23       void InitializeComponent();
24       void learnProgramButton_Click( Object *, EventArgs * );
25    }; // end class VisualInheritanceTest
```

Fig. 10.53 Class **VisualInheritanceTest**, which inherits from class **VisualInheritance**, contains an additional button. (Part 2 of 2.)

```
1    // Fig. 10.54: VisualInheritanceTest.cpp
2    // Derived Form using visual inheritance.
3
4    #include "VisualInheritanceTest.h"
5
6    VisualInheritanceTest::VisualInheritanceTest()
7    {
8       InitializeComponent();
9    }
10
11   void VisualInheritanceTest::InitializeComponent()
12   {
13      this->learnProgramButton = new Button();
14      this->SuspendLayout();
15
16      // learnProgramButton
17      this->learnProgramButton->BackColor = Color::White;
18      this->learnProgramButton->Font = new Drawing::Font(
19         S"Microsoft Sans Serif", 17 );
20      this->learnProgramButton->ForeColor = Color::MidnightBlue;
21      this->learnProgramButton->Location = Point( 152, 104 );
22      this->learnProgramButton->Name = S"learnProgramButton";
23      this->learnProgramButton->Size = Drawing::Size( 120, 88 );
24      this->learnProgramButton->TabIndex = 3;
25      this->learnProgramButton->Text = S"Learn the Program";
26      this->learnProgramButton->Click += new EventHandler( this,
27         learnProgramButton_Click );
28
29      // VisualInheritanceTest
30      this->AutoScaleBaseSize = Drawing::Size( 5, 13 );
31      this->ClientSize = Drawing::Size( 292, 273 );
32      this->Controls->Add( this->learnProgramButton );
33      this->Name = S"VisualInheritanceTest";
```

Fig. 10.54 **VisualInheritanceTest** class method definitions. (Part 1 of 2.)

```
34      this->ResumeLayout();
35   } // end method InitializeComponent
36
37   // invoke when user clicks Learn the Program Button
38   void VisualInheritanceTest::learnProgramButton_Click(
39      Object *sender, EventArgs *e )
40   {
41      MessageBox::Show(
42         S"This program was created by Deitel & Associates.",
43         S"Learn the Program", MessageBoxButtons::OK,
44         MessageBoxIcon::Information );
45   } // end method learnProgramButton_Click
```

Fig. 10.54 `VisualInheritanceTest` class method definitions. (Part 2 of 2.)

```
1    // Fig. 10.55: VisualInheritanceTestMain.cpp
2    // VisualInheritanceTest main application.
3
4    #include "VisualInheritanceTest.h"
5
6    int __stdcall WinMain()
7    {
8       Application::Run( new VisualInheritanceTest() );
9
10      return 0;
11   } // end WinMain
```

Fig. 10.55 Visual inheritance demonstration.

10.11 User-Defined Controls

The .NET Framework allows programmers to create *custom controls* that inherit from a variety of classes. The simplest way to create a custom control is to derive a class from an existing Windows Forms control, such as a **Label**. This is useful if the programmer wants to include functionality of an existing control, rather than having to reimplement the existing control in addition to including the desired new functionality. For example, we can create a new type of label that behaves like a normal **Label** but has a different appearance. We accomplish this by inheriting from class **Label** and overriding method **OnPaint**.

Look-and-Feel Observation 10.7

*To change the appearance of any control, override method **OnPaint**.*

All controls contain method **OnPaint**, which the system calls when a component must be redrawn (such as when the component is resized). Method **OnPaint** is passed a **PaintEventArgs** object, which contains graphics information—property **Graphics** is the graphics object used to draw on the control, and property **ClipRectangle** defines the rectangular boundary of the control. Whenever the system generates the **Paint** event (e.g., method **OnPaint** is invoked), our control's base class catches the event. Event **Paint** is generated when a control is redrawn. Through polymorphism, our control's **OnPaint** method is called. Our base class's **OnPaint** implementation is not called, so we must call it explicitly from our **OnPaint** implementation before we execute our custom-paint code. Alternatively, if we do not wish to let our base class paint itself, we should not call our base class's **OnPaint** method implementation.

To create a new control composed of existing controls, use class **UserControl**. Controls added to a custom control are called *constituent controls*. For example, a programmer could create a **UserControl** composed of a button, a label and a textbox, each associated with some functionality (such as that the button sets the label's text to that contained in the text box). The **UserControl** acts as a container for the controls added to it. The **UserControl** cannot determine how its constituent controls are drawn. Method **OnPaint** cannot be overridden in these custom controls—their appearance can be modified only by handling each constituent control's **Paint** event.

Using another technique, a programmer can create a brand-new control by inheriting from class **Control**. This class does not define any specific behavior; that task is left to the programmer. Instead, class **Control** handles the items associated with all controls, such as events and sizing handles. Method **OnPaint** should contain a call to the base class's **OnPaint** method, which calls the **Paint** event handlers. The programmer must then add code for custom graphics inside the overridden **OnPaint** method. This technique allows for the greatest flexibility, but also requires the most planning. All three approaches are summarized in Fig. 10.56.

Custom Control Techniques and **PaintEventArgs** Properties	Description
Inherit from Windows Forms control	Add functionality to a preexisting control. If overriding method **OnPaint**, call base class **OnPaint**. Can only add to the original control appearance, not redesign it.
Create a **UserControl**	Create a **UserControl** composed of multiple preexisting controls (and combine their functionality). Cannot override **OnPaint** methods of custom controls. Instead, add drawing code to a **Paint** event handler. Can only add to the original constituent control's appearance, not redesign it.
Inherit from class **Control**	Define a brand-new control. Override **OnPaint** method, call base-class method **OnPaint** and include methods to draw the control. Can customize control appearance and functionality.
PaintEventArgs *Properties*	*Use this object inside method* **OnPaint** *or* **Paint** *to draw on the control.*
Graphics	Indicates the graphics object of control. Used to draw on control.
ClipRectangle	Specifies the rectangle indicating boundary of control.

Fig. 10.56 Custom control creation.

We create a "clock" control in Fig. 10.57–Fig. 10.58. This is a **UserControl** composed of a label and a timer—whenever the timer generates an event, the label is updated to reflect the current time.

Figure 10.59 and Fig. 10.60 create a GUI that contains a **ClockUserControl**. The **ClockUserControl** object has a white background (line 24 of Fig. 10.58) to make it stand out in the form. Figure 10.61 shows the output of **ClockExample**, which is a simple form that contains our **ClockUserControl**.

```
1   // Fig. 10.57: ClockUserControl.h
2   // ClockUserControl class header file.
3
4   #pragma once
5
6   #using <mscorlib.dll>
7   #using <system.dll>
8   #using <system.drawing.dll>
9   #using <system.windows.forms.dll>
10
11  using namespace System;
12  using namespace System::Drawing;
13  using namespace System::Windows::Forms;
14
```

Fig. 10.57 Programmer-defined control that displays the current time. (Part 1 of 2.)

```
15    public __gc class ClockUserControl : public UserControl
16    {
17    public:
18       ClockUserControl();
19
20    private:
21       Timer *clockTimer;
22       Label *displayLabel;
23       void InitializeComponent();
24       void clockTimer_Tick( Object *, EventArgs * );
25    }; // end class ClockUserControl
```

Fig. 10.57 Programmer-defined control that displays the current time. (Part 2 of 2.)

```
1    // Fig. 10.58: ClockUserControl.cpp
2    // User-defined control with a timer and a label.
3
4    #include "ClockUserControl.h"
5
6    ClockUserControl::ClockUserControl()
7    {
8       InitializeComponent();
9    }
10
11   void ClockUserControl::InitializeComponent()
12   {
13      this->clockTimer = new Timer();
14      this->displayLabel = new Label();
15      this->SuspendLayout();
16
17      // clockTimer
18      this->clockTimer->Enabled = true;
19      this->clockTimer->Interval = 1000;
20      this->clockTimer->Tick += new EventHandler( this,
21         clockTimer_Tick );
22
23      // displayLabel
24      this->displayLabel->BackColor = Color::White;
25      this->displayLabel->Dock = DockStyle::Fill;
26      this->displayLabel->Font = new Drawing::Font(
27         "Microsoft Sans Serif", 12, FontStyle::Regular,
28         GraphicsUnit::Point, 0 );
29      this->displayLabel->Name = S"displayLabel";
30      this->displayLabel->Size = Drawing::Size( 150, 72 );
31      this->displayLabel->TabIndex = 1;
32      this->displayLabel->TextAlign =
33         ContentAlignment::MiddleCenter;
34
35      // ClockUserControl
36      this->Controls->Add( this->displayLabel );
37      this->Name = S"ClockUserControl";
38      this->Size = Drawing::Size( 150, 72 );
```

Fig. 10.58 ClockUserControl class method definitions. (Part 1 of 2.)

```
39        this->ResumeLayout();
40    }
41
42    // update label at every tick
43    void ClockUserControl::clockTimer_Tick( Object *sender,
44        EventArgs *e )
45    {
46
47        // get current time (Now), convert to string
48        displayLabel->Text = DateTime::Now.ToLongTimeString();
49    } // end method clockTimer_Tick
```

Fig. 10.58 `ClockUserControl` class method definitions. (Part 2 of 2.)

```
1    // Fig. 10.59: ClockExample.h
2    // clockForm class header file.
3
4    #pragma once
5
6    #include "ClockUserControl.h"
7
8    public __gc class ClockForm : public Form
9    {
10   public:
11       ClockForm();
12
13   private:
14       ClockUserControl *myClockUserControl;
15       void InitializeComponent();
16   }; // end class clockForm
```

Fig. 10.59 `ClockForm` class header file.

```
1    // Fig. 10.60: ClockExample.cpp
2    // Windows Form containing a ClockUserControl object.
3
4    #include "ClockExample.h"
5
6    ClockForm::ClockForm()
7    {
8        InitializeComponent();
9    }
10
11   void ClockForm::InitializeComponent()
12   {
13       this->myClockUserControl = new ClockUserControl();
14       this->SuspendLayout();
15
16       // myClockUserControl
17       this->myClockUserControl->Location = Point( 24, 24 );
```

Fig. 10.60 `ClockForm` class method definitions. (Part 1 of 2.)

```
18    this->myClockUserControl->Name = S"myClockUserControl";
19    this->myClockUserControl->Size = Drawing::Size( 96, 48 );
20    this->myClockUserControl->TabIndex = 0;
21
22    // clockForm
23    this->AutoScaleBaseSize = Drawing::Size( 5, 13 );
24    this->ClientSize = Drawing::Size( 144, 93 );
25    this->Controls->Add( this->myClockUserControl );
26    this->Name = S"clockForm";
27    this->Text = S"Clock";
28    this->ResumeLayout();
29 } // end method InitializeComponent
```

Fig. 10.60 ClockForm class method definitions. (Part 2 of 2.)

```
1    // Fig. 10.61: ClockExampleTest.cpp
2    // Clock main application.
3
4    #include "ClockExample.h"
5
6    int __stdcall WinMain()
7    {
8       Application::Run( new ClockForm() );
9
10      return 0;
11   } // end WinMain
```

Fig. 10.61 UserControl demonstration.

Line 13 (Fig. 10.60) instantiates the pointer to the **ClockUserControl**. Method **Add** (line 25) adds this constituent control to **ClockForm**.

*Timer*s (namespace **System::Windows::Forms**) are invisible components that reside on a form and generate *Tick* events at a set interval. This interval is set by the **Timer**'s *Interval* property, which defines the number of milliseconds (thousandths of a second) between events. By default, timers are disabled (i.e., they are not running). Line 18 of Fig. 10.58 enables the **Timer clockTimer** created in line 13.

We add a **Label** (**displayLabel**, line 14) and a **Timer** (**clockTimer**, line 13) to the **UserControl**. We set the **Timer** interval to 1000 milliseconds (line 19) and update **displayLabel**'s text with each event (lines 43–49).

Structure *DateTime* (namespace **System**) contains member **Now**, which is the current time. Method *ToLongTimeString* converts **Now** to a **String *** that contains the current hour, minute, and second (along with AM or PM). We use this to set **displayLabel**'s **Text** property on line 48.

Many of today's most successful commercial programs provide GUIs that are easy to use and manipulate. Because of this demand for user-friendly GUIs, the ability to design sophisticated GUIs is an essential programming skill. In the last two chapters, we have presented the basic techniques required to add various GUI components to a program. The next chapter explores a more behind-the-scenes topic, *multithreading*. In many programming languages, the programmer can create multiple *threads*, enabling several processes to occur at once. By learning to create and manage multithreading in MC++, readers will begin their study of a more robust type of software.

10.12 Summary

Menus are used to provide groups of related commands for Windows applications. Menus are an integral part of GUIs, because they enable user–application interaction without unnecessarily "cluttering" the GUI. Window's top-level menus appear on the top-left of the screen—any submenus or menu items are indented. Menu items can have *Alt* key shortcuts (also called access shortcuts or hot keys). Non-top-level menus can have shortcut keys (combinations of *Ctrl*, *Shift*, *Alt*, function keys *F1*, *F2*, letter keys etc.). Menus generate a **Click** event when selected.

The **LinkLabel** control is used to display links to other objects, such as files or Web pages. The links can change color to reflect whether each link is new, visited or active. When clicked, a **LinkLabel** generate a **LinkClicked** event.

The **ListBox** control allows the user to view and select multiple items from a list. The **CheckedListBox** control extends a **ListBox** by accompanying each item in the list with a checkbox. This allows multiple items to be selected with no logical restriction. The **SelectionMode** property determines how many items in a **CheckedListBox** can be selected. The **SelectedIndexChanged** event occurs when the user selects a new item in a **CheckedListBox**. **CheckBox**'s property **Items** returns all the objects in the list as a collection. Property **SelectedItem** returns the currently selected item. **SelectedIndex** returns the index of the selected item. Method **GetSelected** takes an index and returns **true** if the corresponding item is selected. **CheckedListBox**es imply that multiple items can be selected—the **SelectionMode** property can only have values **None** or **One**. **One** allows multiple selection. Event **ItemCheck** is generated whenever a **CheckedListBox** item is about to change.

The **ComboBox** control combines **TextBox** features with a drop-down list. The user can either select an option from the list or type one in (if allowed by the programmer). If the number of elements exceeds the maximum that can be displayed in the drop-down list, a scrollbar appears. Property **DropDownStyle** determines the type of **ComboBox**. The **ComboBox** control has properties **Items** (a collection), **SelectedItem** and **SelectedIndex**, which are similar to the corresponding properties in **ListBox**. When the selected item changes, event **SelectedIndexChanged** is generated.

The **TreeView** control can display nodes hierarchically on a tree. A node is an element that contains a value and pointers to other nodes. A parent node contains child nodes, and the child nodes can be parents themselves. A tree is a collection of nodes, usually organized in some manner. The first parent node of a tree is often called the root node. Each node has a **Nodes** collection, which contains a list of the **Node**'s children.

The **ListView** control is similar to a **ListBox**, in that both display lists from which the user can select one or more items of type **ListViewItem**. The important difference between the two classes is that a **ListView** can display icons alongside the list items in a variety of ways (controlled by its **ImageList** property).

The **TabControl** control creates tabbed windows. This allows the programmer to provide large quantities of information while saving screen space. **TabControl**s contain **TabPage** objects, which can contain controls. Each **TabPage** generates its own **Click** event when its tab is clicked. Events for controls inside the **TabPage** are still handled by the form.

Single-document-interface (SDI) applications can support only one open window or document at a time. Multiple-document-interface (MDI) programs allow users to edit multiple documents at a time. Each window inside an MDI application is called a child window, and the application window is called the parent window. To create an MDI form, set the form's **IsMDIContainer** property to **true**. The parent and child windows of an application can have different menus, which are merged (combined) whenever a child window is selected. Class **MenuItem** property **MdiList** (a boolean) allows a menu item to contain a list of open child windows. The child windows in an MDI application can be arranged by calling method **LayoutMdi** of the parent form.

The .NET Framework allows the programmer to create customized controls. The most basic way to create a customized control is to derive a class from an existing Windows Forms control. If we inherit from an existing Windows Forms control, we can add to its appearance, but not redesign it. To create a new control composed of existing controls, use class **UserControl**. To create a new control from the ground up, inherit from class **Control**.

11

Multithreading

Objectives

- To understand the concept of multithreading.
- To appreciate how multithreading can improve program performance.
- To understand how to create, manage and destroy threads.
- To understand the life cycle of a thread.
- To understand thread synchronization.
- To understand thread priorities and scheduling.

The spider's touch, how exquisitely fine!
Feels at each thread, and lives along the line.
Alexander Pope

A person with one watch knows what time it is; a person with
two watches is never sure.
Proverb

Learn to labor and to wait.
Henry Wadsworth Longfellow

The most general definition of beauty...Multeity in Unity.
Samuel Taylor Coleridge

Outline

11.1 Introduction

It would be nice if we could perform one action at a time and perform it well, but that is usually difficult to do. The human body performs a great variety of operations *in parallel*— or, as we will say throughout this chapter, *concurrently.* Respiration, blood circulation and digestion, for example, can occur concurrently. All the senses—sight, touch, smell, taste and hearing—can occur at once. Computers, too, can perform operations concurrently. It is common for desktop personal computers to be compiling a program, sending a file to a printer and receiving electronic mail messages over a network concurrently.

In the past, most programming languages did not enable programmers to specify concurrent activities. Rather, programming languages generally provided only a simple set of control structures that enabled programmers to perform one action at a time, proceeding to the next action after the previous one has finished. Historically, the type of concurrency that computers perform today generally has been implemented as operating system "primitives" available only to highly experienced "systems programmers."

The Ada programming language, developed by the United States Department of Defense, made concurrency primitives widely available to defense contractors building military command-and-control systems. However, Ada has not been widely used in universities and commercial industry.

The .NET Framework Class Library makes concurrency primitives available to the applications programmer. The programmer specifies that applications contain "threads of execution," each thread designating a portion of a program that may execute concurrently with other threads—this capability is called *multithreading*. Multithreading is available to all .NET programming languages, including MC++, C# and Visual Basic .NET.

Software Engineering Observation 11.1

The .NET Framework Class Library includes multithreading capabilities in namespace `System::Threading`. *This encourages the use of multithreading among a larger part of the applications-programming community.*

There are many applications of concurrent programming. For example, when programs download large files, such as audio clips or video clips from the World Wide Web, users do not want to wait until an entire clip downloads before starting the playback. To solve this problem, we can put multiple threads to work—one thread downloads a clip, and another plays the clip. These activities, or *tasks*, then may proceed concurrently. To avoid choppy playback, we *synchronize* the threads so that the player thread does not begin playing until there is a sufficient amount of the clip in memory to keep the player thread busy.

Another example of multithreading is MC++'s automatic *garbage collection*. C and traditional (i.e., unmanaged) C++ place with the programmer the responsibility of reclaiming dynamically allocated memory. The CLR provides a *garbage-collector thread* that reclaims dynamically allocated memory that is no longer needed.

Performance Tip 11.1

One of the reasons for the popularity of C and C++ over the years was that their memory-management techniques were more efficient than those of languages that used garbage collectors. In fact, memory management in managed C++ often is faster than in C or unmanaged C++.[1]

Good Programming Practice 11.1

*Set an object pointer to **0** (or **NULL**) when the program no longer needs that object. This enables the garbage collector to determine at the earliest possible moment that the object can be garbage collected. If such an object has other pointers to it, that object cannot be collected.*

Writing multithreaded programs can be tricky. Although the human mind can perform functions concurrently, people find it difficult to jump between parallel "trains of thought." To see why multithreading can be difficult to program and understand, try the following experiment: Open three books to page 1, and try reading the books concurrently. Read a few words from the first book, then read a few words from the second book, then read a few words from the third book, then loop back and read the next few words from the first book, etc. After this experiment, you will appreciate the challenges of multithreading—switching between books, reading briefly, remembering your place in each book, moving the book you are reading closer so you can see it, pushing books you are not reading aside—and amidst all this chaos, trying to comprehend the content of the books!

Performance Tip 11.2

A problem with single-threaded applications is that lengthy activities must complete before other activities can begin. In a multithreaded application, threads can share a processor (or set of processors), so that multiple tasks are performed in parallel.

11.2 Thread States: Life Cycle of a Thread

At any time, a thread is said to be in one of several *thread states* (illustrated in Fig. 11.1). This section discusses these states and the transitions between states. This section also discusses several methods of classes *Thread* and *Monitor* (each from namespace **System::Threading**) that cause state transitions.

---

1. E. Schanzer, "Performance Considerations for Run-Time Technologies in the .NET Framework," August 2001 <http://msdn.microsoft.com/library/default.asp?url= /library/en-us/dndotnet/html/dotnetperftechs.asp>.

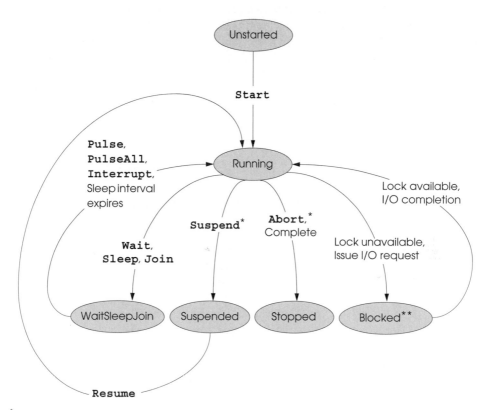

*A thread's **Suspend** and **Abort** methods may be called even if the thread is not in the *Running* state.

**The *Blocked* state is not an actual state in .NET. It is a conceptual state that describes a thread that is not *Running*. We discuss blocked threads in more detail later in this section.

Fig. 11.1   Thread life cycle.

A **Thread** object begins its life cycle in the *Unstarted* state when the program creates the object and passes a ***ThreadStart*** delegate to the object's constructor. The **Thread-Start** delegate, which specifies the actions the thread will perform during its life cycle, must be a method that returns **void** and takes no arguments. The thread remains in the *Unstarted* state until the program calls the **Thread**'s ***Start*** method, which places the thread in the *Running* state and immediately returns control to the part of the program that called **Start**. Then the newly *Running* thread and any other threads in the program can execute concurrently on a multiprocessor system or share the processor on a system with a single processor.

While in the *Running* state, the thread may not actually be executing all of the time. The thread executes in the *Running* state only when the operating system assigns a processor to the thread. (Section 11.3 discusses when different threads will be assigned the processor.) When a *Running* thread receives a processor for the first time, the thread begins executing its **ThreadStart** delegate.

A *Running* thread enters the *Stopped* (or *Aborted*) state when its **ThreadStart** delegate terminates. Note that a program can force a thread into the *Stopped* state by calling **Thread** method **Abort** on the appropriate **Thread** object. Method **Abort** throws a **ThreadAbortException** in the thread, normally causing the thread to terminate. When a thread is in the *Stopped* state and there are no pointers to the thread object, the garbage collector can remove the thread object from memory. [*Note*: Internally, when a thread's **Abort** method is called, the thread actually enters the *AbortRequested* state before entering the *Stopped* state. The thread remains in the *AbortRequested* state while waiting to receive the pending **ThreadAbortException**. When **Abort** is called, if the thread is in the *WaitSleepJoin*, *Suspended* or *Blocked* state, the thread resides in its current state and the *AbortRequested* state, and cannot receive the **ThreadAbortException** until it leaves its current state.]

A thread is considered to be *blocked* if it is unable to use a processor, even if there is a processor available. For example, a thread becomes blocked when the thread issues an input/output request or attempts to acquire an unavailable lock by calling **Monitor** method **Enter**.[2] The operating system blocks the thread from executing until the operating system can complete the I/O for which the thread is waiting or until the desired lock becomes available. At that point, the thread returns to the *Running* state so it can resume execution.

There are three ways by which a *Running* thread can enter the *WaitSleepJoin* state. If a thread encounters code that it cannot execute yet (normally because a condition is not satisfied), the thread can call **Monitor** method **Wait** to enter the *WaitSleepJoin* state. Once in this state, a thread returns to the *Running* state only when another thread invokes **Monitor** method **Pulse** or **PulseAll**. Method **Pulse** moves the next waiting thread back to the *Running* state. Method **PulseAll** moves all waiting threads back to the *Running* state.

A *Running* thread can call **Thread** method **Sleep** to enter the *WaitSleepJoin* state for a period of milliseconds specified as the argument to **Sleep**. A sleeping thread returns to the *Running* state when the designated sleep time expires. A sleeping thread cannot use a processor, even if one is available.

Any thread that enters the *WaitSleepJoin* state by calling **Monitor** method **Wait** or by calling **Thread** method **Sleep** can leave the *WaitSleepJoin* state and return to the *Running* state if that **Thread**'s **Interrupt** method is called by another thread in the program.

If a thread should not continue executing (we will call this the dependent thread) unless another thread terminates, the dependent thread calls the other thread's **Join** method to "join" the two threads and enters the *WaitSleepJoin* state. When two threads are "joined," the dependent thread leaves the *WaitSleepJoin* state when the other thread finishes execution (i.e., when it enters the *Stopped* state).

If a *Running* **Thread**'s **Suspend** method is called, the *Running* thread enters the *Suspended* state. A *Suspended* thread returns to the *Running* state when another thread in the program invokes the *Suspended* thread's **Resume** method. [*Note*: Internally, when a thread's **Suspend** method is called, the thread actually enters the *SuspendRequested* state before entering the *Suspended* state. The thread remains in the *SuspendRequested* state while waiting to respond to the **Suspend** request. If the thread is in the *WaitSleepJoin* state

---

2. Class **Monitor** is used to synchronize threads (see Section 11.4).

or is blocked when its **Suspend** method is called, the thread resides in its current state and the *SuspendRequested* state, and cannot respond to the **Suspend** request until it leaves its current state.]

If a thread's ***IsBackground*** property is set to **true**, the thread resides in the *Background* state (not shown in Fig. 11.1). A thread can reside in the *Background* state and any other state simultaneously. A process must wait for all *Foreground threads* (threads not in the *Background* state) to finish executing and enter the *Stopped* state before the process can terminate. However, if the only threads remaining in a process are *Background threads*, the CLR terminates those threads by invoking their **Abort** method and the process terminates.

11.3 Thread Priorities and Thread Scheduling

Every thread has a priority in the range between ***ThreadPriority::Lowest*** to ***ThreadPriority::Highest***. These two values come from the ***ThreadPriority*** enumeration (namespace **System::Threading**). The enumeration consists of the values **Lowest**, **BelowNormal**, **Normal**, **AboveNormal** and **Highest**. By default, each thread has priority **Normal**.

The Windows operating system supports a concept, called *timeslicing,* that enables threads of equal priority to share a processor. Without timeslicing, each thread in a set of equal-priority threads runs to completion (unless the thread leaves the *Running* state and becomes blocked) before the thread's peers get a chance to execute. With timeslicing, each thread receives a brief burst of processor time, called a *quantum*, during which the thread can execute. At the completion of the quantum, even if the thread has not finished executing, the processor is taken away from that thread and given to the next thread of equal priority, if one is available.

The job of the thread scheduler is to keep the highest-priority thread running at all times and, if there is more than one highest-priority thread, to ensure that all such threads execute for a quantum in round-robin fashion. Figure 11.2 illustrates the multilevel priority queue for threads. In Fig. 11.2, assuming a single-processor computer, threads A and B each execute for a quantum in round-robin fashion until both threads complete execution. This means that A gets a quantum of time to run. Then B gets a quantum. Then A gets another quantum. Then B gets another quantum. This continues until one thread completes. The processor then devotes all its power to the thread that remains (unless another thread of that priority is executing). Next, thread C runs to completion. Threads D, E and F each execute for a quantum in round-robin fashion until they all complete execution. This process continues until all threads run to completion. Note that, depending on the operating system, new higher-priority threads could postpone—possibly indefinitely—the execution of lower-priority threads. Such *indefinite postponement* often is referred to more colorfully as *starvation*.

A thread's priority can be adjusted with the ***Priority*** property, which accepts values from the **ThreadPriority** enumeration. If the argument is not one of the valid thread-priority constants, an **ArgumentException** occurs.

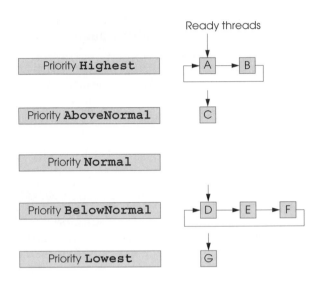

Fig. 11.2   Thread-priority scheduling.

A thread executes until it dies, becomes blocked for input/output (or some other reason), calls **Sleep**, **Join** or **Monitor** method **Wait**, is preempted by a thread of higher priority or has its quantum expire. A thread with a higher priority than the executing thread can start executing (and, hence, preempt the previously executing thread) if a sleeping thread wakes up, if I/O completes for a thread that blocked for that I/O, if either **Pulse** or **PulseAll** is called on an object on which **Wait** was called, or if a thread to which the high-priority thread was **Join**ed completes.

Figure 11.3–Fig. 11.5 demonstrate basic threading techniques, including the construction of a **Thread** object and using the **Thread** class's **static** method **Sleep**. The program creates three threads of execution, each with the default priority **Normal**. Each thread displays a message indicating that it is going to sleep for a random amount of time from 0 to 5000 milliseconds, then goes to sleep. When each thread awakens, the thread displays its name, indicates that it is done sleeping, terminates and enters the *Stopped* state. You will see that function **main** (i.e., the **main** *thread of execution*) terminates before the application terminates. The application consists of class **MessagePrinter** (Fig. 11.3–Fig. 11.4), which defines a **Print** method containing the actions each thread will perform, and main program **ThreadTester** (Fig. 11.5), which creates three threads.

```
1   // Fig. 11.3: MessagePrinter.h
2   // Multiple threads printing at different intervals.
3
4   #pragma once
5
6   #using <mscorlib.dll>
```

Fig. 11.3   Threads sleeping and printing. (Part 1 of 2.)

```
7
8   using namespace System;
9   using namespace System::Threading;
10
11  // Print method of this class used to control threads
12  public __gc class MessagePrinter
13  {
14  public:
15
16     // constructor to initialize a MessagePrinter object
17     MessagePrinter();
18
19     // method Print controls thread that prints messages
20     void Print();
21
22  private:
23     int sleepTime;
24     static Random *random = new Random();
25  }; // end class MessagePrinter
```

Fig. 11.3   Threads sleeping and printing. (Part 2 of 2.)

```
1   // Fig. 11.4: MessagePrinter.cpp
2   // Method definitions for class MessagePrinter.
3
4   #include "MessagePrinter.h"
5
6   // constructor to initialize a MessagePrinter object
7   MessagePrinter::MessagePrinter()
8   {
9
10     // pick random sleep time between 0 and 5 seconds
11     sleepTime = random->Next( 5001 );
12  }
13
14  // method Print controls thread that prints messages
15  void MessagePrinter::Print()
16  {
17
18     // obtain pointer to currently executing thread
19     Thread *current = Thread::CurrentThread;
20
21     // put thread to sleep for sleepTime amount of time
22     Console::WriteLine( String::Concat( current->Name,
23        S" going to sleep for ",  sleepTime.ToString() ) );
24
```

Fig. 11.4   MessagePrinter class method definitions. (Part 1 of 2.)

```
25        Thread::Sleep( sleepTime );
26
27        // print thread name
28        Console::WriteLine( S"{0} done sleeping", current->Name );
29    } // end method Print
```

Fig. 11.4 `MessagePrinter` class method definitions. (Part 2 of 2.)

```
1    // Fig. 11.5: ThreadTester.cpp
2    // Main program for MessagePrinter.
3
4    #include "MessagePrinter.h"
5
6    int main()
7    {
8
9        // Create and name each thread.  Use MessagePrinter's
10       // Print method as argument to ThreadStart delegate
11       MessagePrinter *printer1 = new MessagePrinter();
12       Thread *thread1 = new Thread ( new ThreadStart( printer1,
13          &MessagePrinter::Print ) );
14       thread1->Name = S"thread1";
15
16       MessagePrinter *printer2 = new MessagePrinter();
17       Thread *thread2 = new Thread ( new ThreadStart( printer2,
18          &MessagePrinter::Print ) );
19       thread2->Name = S"thread2";
20
21       MessagePrinter *printer3 = new MessagePrinter();
22       Thread *thread3 = new Thread ( new ThreadStart( printer3,
23          &MessagePrinter::Print ) );
24       thread3->Name = S"thread3";
25
26       Console::WriteLine( S"Starting threads" );
27
28       // call each thread's Start method to place each
29       // thread in Running state
30       thread1->Start();
31       thread2->Start();
32       thread3->Start();
33
34       Console::WriteLine( S"Threads started\n" );
35
36       return 0;
37    } // end function main
```

Fig. 11.5 `ThreadTester` demonstrates class `MessagePrinter`. (Part 1 of 2.)

```
Starting threads
Threads started

thread1 going to sleep for 2430
thread2 going to sleep for 311
thread3 going to sleep for 2779
thread2 done sleeping
thread1 done sleeping
thread3 done sleeping
```

```
Starting threads
Threads started

thread1 going to sleep for 4176
thread2 going to sleep for 3453
thread3 going to sleep for 327
thread3 done sleeping
thread2 done sleeping
thread1 done sleeping
```

Fig. 11.5 **ThreadTester** demonstrates class **MessagePrinter**. (Part 2 of 2.)

Objects of class **MessagePrinter** (Fig. 11.3–Fig. 11.4) control the life cycle of each of the three threads that function **main** creates. Class **MessagePrinter** consists of variable **sleepTime** (line 23 of Fig. 11.3), **static** variable **random** (line 24), a constructor (lines 7–12 of Fig. 11.4) and a **Print** method (lines 15–29). The **Message-Printer** constructor (lines 7–12) initializes **sleepTime** to a random integer from 0 up to, but not including, 5001 (i.e., from 0 to 5000). Each thread controlled by a **Message-Printer** object sleeps for the amount of time specified by the corresponding **Message-Printer** object's **sleepTime**.

Method **Print** begins by obtaining a pointer to the currently executing thread (line 19) via class **Thread**'s **static** property *CurrentThread*. The currently executing thread is the one that invokes method **Print**. Next, lines 22–23 display a message indicating the name of the currently executing thread and stating that the thread is going to sleep for a certain number of milliseconds. Note that line 22 uses the currently executing thread's *Name* property to obtain the thread's name (set in function **main** when each thread is created). Line 25 invokes **static Thread** method **Sleep** to place the thread into the *Wait-SleepJoin* state. At this point, the thread loses the processor and the system allows another thread to execute. When the thread awakens, it reenters the *Running* state again and waits until the system assigns a processor to the thread. When the **MessagePrinter** object begins executing again, line 28 displays the thread's name in a message that indicates the thread is done sleeping, and method **Print** terminates.

Function **main** (Fig. 11.5) creates three objects of class **MessagePrinter**, at lines 11, 16 and 21, respectively. Lines 12–13, 17–18 and 22–23 create and initialize three **Thread** objects. Lines 14, 19 and 24 set each **Thread**'s **Name** property, which we use for output purposes. Note that each **Thread**'s constructor receives a **ThreadStart** delegate as an argument. Remember that a **ThreadStart** delegate specifies the actions a thread performs during its life cycle. Lines 12–13 specify that the delegate for **thread1** will be **printer1**'s **Print** method. When **thread1** enters the *Running* state for the first time and begins executing, **thread1** will invoke **printer1**'s **Print** method to perform the tasks specified in method **Print**'s body. Thus, **thread1** will print its name, display the amount of time for which it will go to sleep, sleep for that amount of time, wake up and display a message indicating that the thread is done sleeping. At that point, method **Print** will terminate. A thread completes its task when the method specified by a **Thread**'s **ThreadStart** delegate terminates, placing the thread in the *Stopped* state. When **thread2** and **thread3** enter the *Running* state for the first time and begin executing, they invoke the **Print** methods of **printer2** and **printer3**, respectively. Threads **thread2** and **thread3** perform the same tasks as **thread1** by executing the **Print** methods of the objects to which **printer2** and **printer3** point (each of which has its own randomly chosen sleep time).

Testing and Debugging Tip 11.1

Naming threads helps in the debugging of a multithreaded program. Visual Studio .NET's debugger provides a **Threads** *window that displays the name of each thread and enables you to view the execution of any thread in the program.*

Lines 30–32 invoke each **Thread**'s **Start** method to place the threads in the *Running* state (sometimes called *launching a thread*). Method **Start** returns immediately from each invocation, then line 34 outputs a message indicating that the threads were started, and the **main** thread of execution terminates. The program itself does not terminate, however, because there are still threads that are alive (i.e., threads that were started have not reached the *Stopped* state yet). The program will not terminate until its last thread dies. When the system assigns a processor to a thread, the thread starts executing and calls the method specified by the thread's **ThreadStart** delegate. In this program, each thread invokes method **Print** of the appropriate **MessagePrinter** object to perform the tasks discussed previously.

Note that the sample outputs for this program show each thread and the thread's sleep time as the thread goes to sleep. The thread with the shortest sleep time normally awakens first, then indicates that it is done sleeping and terminates. In Section 11.7, we discuss multithreading issues that could prevent the thread with the shortest sleep time from awakening first.

11.4 Thread Synchronization and Class **Monitor**

Often, multiple threads of execution manipulate shared data. If threads with access to shared data simply read that data, then there is no need to prevent the data from being accessed by more than one thread at a time. However, when multiple threads share data and that data is modified by one or more of those threads, then indeterminate results may occur. If one thread is in the process of updating the data and another thread tries to update it too, the data will reflect the update that occurs second. If the data is an array or other data structure in which the threads could update separate parts of the data concurrently, it is possible that part of the data will reflect the information from one thread while another part of the data will reflect information from a different thread. When this happens, the program has difficulty determining when the data has been updated properly.

The problem can be solved by giving one thread at a time exclusive access to code that manipulates the shared data. During that time, other threads desiring to manipulate the data should be kept waiting. When the thread with exclusive access to the data completes its manipulation of the data, one of the threads waiting to manipulate the data should be allowed to proceed. In this fashion, each thread accessing the shared data excludes all other threads from doing so simultaneously. This is called *mutual exclusion* or *thread synchronization*.

MC++ uses the .NET Framework's monitors[3] to perform synchronization. Class **Monitor** provides the methods for *locking objects* to implement synchronized access to shared data. Locking an object means that only one thread can access that object at a time. When a thread wishes to acquire exclusive control over an object, the thread invokes **Monitor** method **Enter** to acquire the lock on that data object. After acquiring the lock for an object, a thread can manipulate that object's data. While the object is locked, all other threads attempting to acquire the lock on that object are blocked from acquiring the lock. When the thread that locked the shared object no longer requires the lock, that thread invokes **Monitor** method **Exit** to release the lock. At this point, if there is a thread that was previously blocked from acquiring the lock on the shared object, that thread acquires the lock to begin its processing of the object. If all threads with access to an object attempt to acquire the object's lock before manipulating the object, only one thread at a time will be allowed to manipulate the object. This helps ensure the integrity of the data.

Common Programming Error 11.1

Make sure that all code that updates a shared object locks the object before doing so. Otherwise, a thread calling a method that does not lock the object can make the object unstable even when another thread has acquired the lock for the object.

Performance Tip 11.3

*Placing the fewest number of statements necessary to update a shared object between calls to **Monitor** methods **Enter** and **Exit** minimizes the time that other threads must wait before updating the same object.*

Common Programming Error 11.2

*Deadlock occurs when a waiting thread (let us call this thread1) cannot proceed because it is waiting for another thread (let us call this thread2) to proceed. Similarly, thread2 cannot proceed because it is waiting for thread1 to proceed. The two threads are waiting for each other; therefore, the actions that would enable each thread to continue execution never occur. The document at **ms-help://MS.VSCC/MS.MSDNVS/cpguide/html/cpconthreading.htm** provides links to more information about threading and resolving deadlocks.*

If a thread determines that it cannot perform its task on a locked object, the thread can call **Monitor** method **Wait** and pass as an argument the object on which the thread will wait until the thread can perform its task. Invoking **Monitor::Wait** places that thread into the *WaitSleepJoin* state for that object. A thread in the *WaitSleepJoin* state for an object leaves the *WaitSleepJoin* state when a separate thread invokes **Monitor** method **Pulse** or **PulseAll** with the object as an argument. Method **Pulse** transitions the object's first waiting thread from the *WaitSleepJoin* state to the *Running* state. Method **PulseAll** tran-

---

3. Hoare, C. A. R., Monitors: An Operating System Structuring Concept, *Communications of the ACM*. Vol. 17, No. 10, October 1974: 549–557. *Corrigendum, Communications of the ACM*. Vol. 18, No. 2, February 1975: 95.

sitions all threads in the object's *WaitSleepJoin* state to the *Running* state. The transition to the *Running* state enables the thread (or threads) to get ready to continue executing.

Notice the difference between calling **Monitor** method **Enter** and calling **Monitor** method **Wait**. Threads that call **Monitor** method **Wait** with the object as an argument wait in an object's *WaitSleepJoin* state. However, threads that call **Monitor** method **Enter** while a lock is unavailable become blocked and wait there until the object's lock becomes available. Then, one of the blocked threads can acquire the object's lock.

Monitor methods **Enter**, **Exit**, **Wait**, **Pulse** and **PulseAll** all take a pointer to an object—usually the keyword **this**—as their argument.

Common Programming Error 11.3

A thread placed in the WaitSleepJoin *state by a call to method* **Wait** *cannot reenter the* Running *state to continue execution until a separate thread invokes* **Monitor** *method* **Pulse** *or* **PulseAll** *with the appropriate object as an argument or invokes* **Thread** *method* **Interrupt** *on the thread. If this does not occur, the waiting thread will wait forever and so can cause deadlock.*

Testing and Debugging Tip 11.2

When multiple threads manipulate a shared object, using monitors, ensure that if one thread calls **Monitor** *method* **Wait** *to enter the* WaitSleepJoin *state for the shared object, a separate thread eventually will call* **Monitor** *method* **Pulse** *to transition the thread waiting on the shared object back to the* Running *state. If multiple threads may be waiting for the shared object, a separate thread can call* **Monitor** *method* **PulseAll** *as a safeguard to ensure that all waiting threads have another opportunity to perform their tasks.*

Performance Tip 11.4

Synchronization to achieve correctness in multithreaded programs can make programs run more slowly, as a result of monitor overhead and the frequent transitioning of threads among the Running, WaitSleepJoin *and* Running *states. There is not much to say, however, for highly efficient, incorrect multithreaded programs!*

11.5 Producer/Consumer Relationship without Thread Synchronization

In a *producer/consumer relationship*, the *producer* portion of an application generates data and the *consumer* portion of an application uses that data. In a multithreaded producer/consumer relationship, a *producer thread* calls a *produce method* to generate data and place it into a shared region of memory, called a *buffer*. A *consumer thread* calls a *consume method* to read that data. If the producer waiting to put the next data into the buffer determines that the consumer has not yet read the previous data from the buffer, the producer thread should call **Wait**; otherwise, the consumer never sees the previous data and that data is lost to that application. When the consumer thread reads the message, it should call **Pulse** to allow a waiting producer to proceed. If a consumer thread finds the buffer empty or finds that the previous data has already been read, the consumer should call **Wait**; otherwise, the consumer might read "garbage" from the buffer or the consumer might process a previous data item more than once—each of these possibilities results in a logic error in the application. When the producer places the next data into the buffer, the producer should call **Pulse** to allow the consumer thread to proceed.

Let us consider how logic errors can arise if we do not synchronize access among multiple threads manipulating shared data. Consider a producer/consumer relationship in which a producer thread writes a sequence of numbers (we use 1–4) into a *shared buffer*—a memory location shared between multiple threads. The consumer thread reads this data from the shared buffer then displays the data. We display in the program's output the values that the producer writes (produces) and that the consumer reads (consumes). The next application demonstrates a producer and a consumer accessing a single shared cell (**int** variable **buffer**) of memory without any synchronization. Both the consumer and the producer threads access this single cell: The producer thread writes to the cell; the consumer thread reads from it. We would like each value the producer thread writes to the shared cell to be consumed exactly once by the consumer thread. However, the threads in this example are not synchronized. Therefore, data can be lost if the producer places new data into the slot before the consumer consumes the previous data. Also, data can be incorrectly repeated if the consumer consumes data again before the producer produces the next item. To show these possibilities, the consumer thread in the following example keeps a total of all the values it reads. The producer thread produces values from 1 to 4. If the consumer reads each value produced once and only once, the total would be 10. However, if you execute this program several times, you will see that the total is rarely, if ever, 10. Also, to emphasize our point, the producer and consumer threads in the example each sleep for random intervals of up to three seconds between performing their tasks. Thus, we do not know exactly when the producer thread will attempt to write a new value, nor do we know when the consumer thread will attempt to read a value.

The program consists of three classes—**HoldIntegerUnsynchronized** (Fig. 11.6), **Producer** (Fig. 11.7–Fig. 11.8) and **Consumer** (Fig. 11.9–Fig. 11.10)—and function **main** (Fig. 11.11).

Class **HoldIntegerUnsynchronized** (Fig. 11.6) consists of instance variable **buffer** (line 37) and property **Buffer** (lines 18–32), which provides both *get* and *set* accessors. Property **Buffer**'s accessors do not synchronize access to instance variable **buffer**. Note that each accessor uses class **Thread**'s **static** property **CurrentThread** to obtain a pointer to the currently executing thread, then uses that thread's property **Name** to obtain the thread's name.

```
1    // Fig. 11.6: Unsynchronized.h
2    // Showing multiple threads modifying a shared object without
3    // synchronization.
4
5    #pragma once
6
7    #using <mscorlib.dll>
8
9    using namespace System;
10   using namespace System::Threading;
11
12   // represents a single shared int
13   public __gc class HoldIntegerUnsynchronized
14   {
```

Fig. 11.6 **HoldIntegerUnsynchronized** class modifies as object without using synchronization. (Part 1 of 2.)

```
15   public:
16
17       // property Buffer
18       __property int get_Buffer()
19       {
20          Console::WriteLine( S"{0} reads {1}",
21             Thread::CurrentThread->Name, buffer.ToString() );
22
23          return buffer;
24       }
25
26       __property void set_Buffer( int value )
27       {
28          Console::WriteLine( S"{0} writes {1}",
29             Thread::CurrentThread->Name, value.ToString() );
30
31          buffer = value;
32       }
33
34   private:
35
36       // buffer shared by producer and consumer threads
37       static int buffer = -1;
38   }; // end class HoldIntegerUnsynchronized
```

Fig. 11.6 `HoldIntegerUnsynchronized` class modifies as object without using synchronization. (Part 2 of 2.)

Class **Producer** (Fig. 11.7–Fig. 11.8) consists of instance variable **sharedLocation** (line 20 of Fig. 11.7), instance variable **randomSleepTime** (line 21), a constructor (lines 8–13 of Fig. 11.8) to initialize the instance variables and a **Produce** method (lines 16–28). The constructor initializes instance variable **sharedLocation** to point to the **HoldIntegerUnsynchronized** object received from function **main** as the argument **shared**. The producer thread in this program executes the tasks specified in method **Produce** of class **Producer**. Method **Produce** contains a **for** structure (lines 21–24) that loops four times. Each iteration of the loop first invokes **Thread** method **Sleep** to place producer thread into the *WaitSleepJoin* state for a random time interval between 0 and 3000 milliseconds. When the thread awakens, line 23 assigns the value of control variable **count** to the **HoldIntegerUnsynchronized** object's **Buffer** property, which causes the *set* accessor of **HoldIntegerUnsynchronized** to modify the **buffer** instance variable of the **HoldIntegerUnsynchronized** object. When the loop completes, lines 26–27 display a line of text in the console window indicating that the thread finished producing data and that the thread is terminating, then the **Produce** method terminates and so places the producer thread in the *Stopped* state.

```
1   // Fig. 11.7: Producer.h
2   // Class Producer's Produce method controls a thread that
3   // stores values from 1 to 4 in sharedLocation.
```

Fig. 11.7 **Producer** class controls a thread that stores values in `sharedLocation`. (Part 1 of 2.)

```
4
5    #pragma once
6
7    #include "Unsynchronized.h"
8
9    public __gc class Producer
10   {
11   public:
12
13      // constructor
14      Producer( HoldIntegerUnsynchronized *, Random * );
15
16      // store values 1-4 in object sharedLocation
17      void Produce();
18
19   private:
20      HoldIntegerUnsynchronized *sharedLocation;
21      Random *randomSleepTime;
22   }; // end class Producer
```

Fig. 11.7 **Producer** class controls a thread that stores values in
          sharedLocation. (Part 2 of 2.)

```
1    // Fig. 11.8: Producer.cpp
2    // Method definitions for class Producer.
3
4    #include "Unsynchronized.h"
5    #include "Producer.h"
6
7    // constructor
8    Producer::Producer( HoldIntegerUnsynchronized *shared,
9       Random *random )
10   {
11      sharedLocation = shared;
12      randomSleepTime = random;
13   }
14
15   // store values 1-4 in object sharedLocation
16   void Producer::Produce()
17   {
18
19      // sleep for random interval up to 3000 milliseconds
20      // then set sharedLocation's Buffer property
21      for ( int count = 1; count <= 4; count++ ) {
22         Thread::Sleep( randomSleepTime->Next( 1, 3000 ) );
23         sharedLocation->Buffer = count;
24      }
25
26      Console::WriteLine( S"{0} done producing.\nTerminating {0}.",
27         Thread::CurrentThread->Name );
28   } // end method Produce
```

Fig. 11.8 **Producer** class method definitions.

Class **Consumer** (Fig. 11.9–Fig. 11.10) consists of instance variable **sharedLo-cation** (line 20 of Fig. 11.9), instance variable **randomSleepTime** (line 21), a constructor (lines 7–12 of Fig. 11.10) to initialize the instance variables and a **Consume** method (lines 15–29). The constructor initializes **sharedLocation** to point to the **HoldIntegerUnsynchronized** object received from **main** as the argument **shared**. The consumer thread in this program performs the tasks specified in class **Consumer**'s **Consume** method. The method contains a **for** structure (lines 21–24) that loops four times. Each iteration of the loop invokes **Thread** method **Sleep** to put the consumer thread into the *WaitSleepJoin* state for a random time interval between 0 and 3000 milliseconds. Next, line 23 gets the value of the **HoldIntegerUnsynchronized** object's **Buffer** property and adds the value to the variable **sum**. When the loop completes, lines 26–28 display a line in the console window indicating the sum of all values read, then the **Consume** method terminates, which places the consumer thread in the *Stopped* state.

```
1    // Fig. 11.9: Consumer.h
2    // Class Consumer's Consume method controls a thread that
3    // loops four times and reads a value from sharedLocation.
4
5    #pragma once
6
7    #include "Unsynchronized.h"
8
9    public __gc class Consumer
10   {
11   public:
12
13      // constructor
14      Consumer( HoldIntegerUnsynchronized *, Random * );
15
16      // read sharedLocation's value four times
17      void Consume();
18
19   private:
20      HoldIntegerUnsynchronized *sharedLocation;
21      Random *randomSleepTime;
22   }; // end class Consumer
```

Fig. 11.9 **Consumer** class that reads a value from **sharedLocation**.

```
1    // Fig. 11.10: Consumer.cpp
2    // Method definitions for class consumer.
3
4    #include "Consumer.h"
5
6    // constructor
7    Consumer::Consumer( HoldIntegerUnsynchronized *shared,
8       Random *random )
9    {
10      sharedLocation = shared;
```

Fig. 11.10 **Consumer** class method definitions. (Part 1 of 2.)

```
11      randomSleepTime = random;
12   }
13
14   // read sharedLocation's value four times
15   void Consumer::Consume()
16   {
17      int sum = 0;
18
19      // sleep for random interval up to 3000 milliseconds
20      // then add sharedLocation's Buffer property value to sum
21      for ( int count = 1; count <= 4; count++ ) {
22         Thread::Sleep( randomSleepTime->Next( 1, 3000 ) );
23         sum += sharedLocation->Buffer;
24      }
25
26      Console::WriteLine( S"{0} read values totaling: {1}.\n",
27         S"Terminating {0}.",
28         Thread::CurrentThread->Name, sum.ToString() );
29   } // end method Consume
```

Fig. 11.10 Consumer class method definitions. (Part 2 of 2.)

[*Note*: We use method **Sleep** in this example to emphasize the fact that, in multi-threaded applications, it is unclear when each thread will perform its task and for how long it will perform that task when it has the processor. Normally, these thread-scheduling issues are the job of the computer's operating system. In this program, our thread's tasks are quite simple—for the producer, loop four times, and perform an assignment statement; for the consumer, loop four times, and add a value to variable **sum**. Without the **Sleep** method call, and if the producer executes first, the producer would complete its task before the consumer ever gets a chance to execute. If the consumer executes first, it would consume **-1** four times, then terminate before the producer can produce the first real value.]

Function **main** (lines 8–38 of Fig. 11.11) instantiates a shared **HoldIntegerUnsynchronized** object (lines 12–13) and a **Random** object (line 16) for generating random sleep times and uses them as arguments to the constructors for the objects of classes **Producer** (lines 19) and **Consumer** (lines 21). The **HoldIntegerUnsynchronized** object contains the data that will be shared between the producer and consumer threads. Lines 25–27 create and name **producerThread**. The **ThreadStart** delegate for **producerThread** specifies that the thread will execute method **Produce** of object **producer**. Lines 29–31 create and name the **consumerThread**. The **ThreadStart** delegate for the **consumerThread** specifies that the thread will execute method **Consume** of object **consumer**. Finally, lines 34–35 place the two threads in the *Running* state by invoking each thread's **Start** method. Function **main** then terminates.

```
1   // Fig. 11.11: SharedCell.cpp
2   // Create and start producer and consumer threads.
```

Fig. 11.11 SharedCell demonstrates accessing a shared object without synchronization. (Part 1 of 3.)

```
3
4   #include "Unsynchronized.h"
5   #include "Producer.h"
6   #include "Consumer.h"
7
8   int main()
9   {
10
11      // create shared object used by threads
12      HoldIntegerUnsynchronized *holdInteger =
13         new HoldIntegerUnsynchronized();
14
15      // Random object used by each thread
16      Random *random = new Random();
17
18      // create Producer and Consumer objects
19      Producer *producer = new Producer( holdInteger, random );
20
21      Consumer *consumer = new Consumer( holdInteger, random );
22
23      // create threads for producer and consumer and set
24      // delegates for each thread
25      Thread *producerThread = new Thread( new ThreadStart(
26         producer, Producer::Produce ) );
27      producerThread->Name = S"Producer";
28
29      Thread *consumerThread = new Thread( new ThreadStart(
30         consumer, Consumer::Consume ) );
31      consumerThread->Name = S"Consumer";
32
33      // start each thread
34      producerThread->Start();
35      consumerThread->Start();
36
37      return 0;
38   } // end function main
```

```
Consumer reads -1
Consumer reads -1
Producer writes 1
Consumer reads 1
Consumer reads 1
Consumer read values totaling: 0.
Terminating Consumer.
Producer writes 2
Producer writes 3
Producer writes 4
Producer done producing.
Terminating Producer.
```

(Continued on top of next page)

Fig. 11.11 `SharedCell` demonstrates accessing a shared object without synchronization. (Part 2 of 3.)

(Continued from previous page)

```
Producer writes 1
Producer writes 2
Consumer reads 2
Consumer reads 2
Producer writes 3
Consumer reads 3
Producer writes 4
Producer done producing.
Terminating Producer.
Consumer reads 4
Consumer read values totaling: 11.
Terminating Consumer.
```

```
Producer writes 1
Producer writes 2
Consumer reads 2
Consumer reads 2
Producer writes 3
Consumer reads 3
Consumer reads 3
Consumer read values totaling: 10.
Terminating Consumer.
Producer writes 4
Producer done producing.
Terminating Producer.
```

Fig. 11.11 `SharedCell` demonstrates accessing a shared object without synchronization. (Part 3 of 3.)

Ideally, we would like every value produced by the **Producer** object to be consumed exactly once by the **Consumer** object. However, when we study the first output of Fig. 11.11, we see that the consumer retrieved a value (**-1**) before the producer ever placed a value in the shared buffer and that the value **1** was consumed twice. The consumer finished executing before the producer had an opportunity to produce the values **2**, **3** and **4**. Therefore, those three values were lost. In the second output, we see that the value **1** was lost, because the values **1** and **2** were produced before the consumer thread could read the value **1**. Also, the value **2** was consumed twice. The last sample output demonstrates that it is possible, with some luck, to get a proper output in which each value the producer produces is consumed once and only once by the consumer. This example clearly demonstrates that access to shared data by concurrent threads must be controled carefully; otherwise, a program might produce incorrect results.

To solve the problems of lost data and data consumed more than once in the previous example, we will (in Fig. 11.12–Fig. 11.18) synchronize access of the concurrent producer and consumer threads to the code that manipulates the shared data by using **Monitor** class methods **Enter**, **Wait**, **Pulse** and **Exit**. When a thread uses synchronization to access a shared object, the object is *locked*, so no other thread can acquire the lock for that shared object at the same time.

11.6 Producer/Consumer Relationship with Thread Synchronization

Figure 11.12–Fig. 11.18 demonstrate a producer and a consumer accessing a shared cell of memory with synchronization, so that the consumer consumes only after the producer produces a value and the producer produces a new value only after the consumer consumes the previous value produced. Classes **Producer** (Fig. 11.14–Fig. 11.15) and **Consumer** (Fig. 11.16–Fig. 11.17) and function **main** (Fig. 11.18) are identical to Fig. 11.6–Fig. 11.11, except that they use the class **HoldIntegerSynchronized** instead of **HoldIntenterUnsynchronized**.

Class **HoldIntegerSynchronized** (Fig. 11.12-Fig. 11.13) contains two instance variables—**buffer** (line 110 of Fig. 11.12) and **occupiedBufferCount** (line 113). Also, property **Buffer**'s *get* (lines 18–65) and *set* (lines 68–102) accessors now use methods of class **Monitor** to synchronize access to property **Buffer**. Instance variable **occupiedBufferCount** is known as a *condition variable*—property **Buffer**'s accessors use this **int** in conditions to determine whether it is the producer's turn to perform a task or the consumer's turn to perform a task. If **occupiedBufferCount** is 0, property **Buffer**'s *set* accessor can place a value into variable **buffer**, because the variable currently does not contain information. However, this means that property **Buffer**'s *get* accessor currently cannot read the value of **buffer**. If **occupiedBufferCount** is 1, the **Buffer** property's *get* accessor can read a value from variable **buffer**, because the variable currently does contain information. In this case, property **Buffer**'s *set* accessor currently cannot place a value into **buffer**.

```
1    // Fig. 11.12: Synchronized.h
2    // Showing multiple threads modifying a shared object with
3    // synchronization.
4
5    #pragma once
6
7    #using <mscorlib.dll>
8
9    using namespace System;
10   using namespace System::Threading;
11
12   // this class synchronizes access to an integer
13   public __gc class HoldIntegerSynchronized
14   {
15   public:
16
17       // property get_Buffer
18       __property int get_Buffer()
19       {
20
21           // obtain lock on this object
22           Monitor::Enter( this );
```

Fig. 11.12 HoldIntegerSynchronized class modifies an object using synchronization. (Part 1 of 3.)

```
23
24          // if there is no data to read, place invoking
25          // thread in WaitSleepJoin state
26          if ( occupiedBufferCount == 0 ) {
27             Console::WriteLine( S"{0} tries to read.",
28                Thread::CurrentThread->Name );
29
30             DisplayState( String::Concat( S"Buffer empty.",
31                Thread::CurrentThread->Name, S" waits." ) );
32
33             Monitor::Wait( this );
34          }
35
36          // indicate that producer can store another value
37          // because a consumer just retrieved buffer value
38          occupiedBufferCount--;
39
40          DisplayState( String::Concat(
41             Thread::CurrentThread->Name, S" reads ",
42             buffer.ToString() ) );
43
44          // tell waiting thread (if there is one) to
45          // become ready to execute (Running state)
46          Monitor::Pulse( this );
47
48          // Get copy of buffer before releasing lock.
49          // It is possible that the producer could be
50          // assigned the processor immediately after the
51          // monitor is released and before the return
52          // statement executes.  In this case, the producer
53          // would assign a new value to buffer before the
54          // return statement returns the value to the
55          // consumer.  Thus, the consumer would receive the
56          // new value.  Making a copy of buffer and
57          // returning the copy ensures that the
58          // consumer receives the proper value.
59          int bufferCopy = buffer;
60
61          // release lock on this object
62          Monitor::Exit( this );
63
64          return bufferCopy;
65       } // end property get_Buffer
66
67       // property set_Buffer
68       __property void set_Buffer( int value )
69       {
70
71          // acquire lock for this object
72          Monitor::Enter( this );
73
74          // if there are no empty locations, place invoking
```

Fig. 11.12 `HoldIntegerSynchronized` class modifies an object using synchronization. (Part 2 of 3.)

```
75        // thread in WaitSleepJoin state
76        if ( occupiedBufferCount == 1 ) {
77           Console::WriteLine( S"{0} tries to write.",
78              Thread::CurrentThread->Name );
79
80           DisplayState( String::Concat( S"Buffer full. ",
81              Thread::CurrentThread->Name, S" waits." ) );
82
83           Monitor::Wait( this );
84        }
85
86        // set new buffer value
87        HoldIntegerSynchronized::buffer = value;
88
89        // indicate producer cannot store another value
90        // until consumer retrieves current buffer value
91        occupiedBufferCount++;
92
93        DisplayState( String::Concat( Thread::CurrentThread->Name,
94           S" writes ", buffer.ToString() ) );
95
96        // tell waiting thread (if there is one) to
97        // become ready to execute (Running state)
98        Monitor::Pulse( this );
99
100       // release lock on this object
101       Monitor::Exit( this );
102    } // end property set_Buffer
103
104    // display current operation and buffer state
105    void DisplayState( String * );
106
107 private:
108
109    // buffer shared by producer and consumer threads
110    static int buffer = -1;
111
112    // occupiedBufferCount maintains count of occupied buffers
113    static int occupiedBufferCount = 0;
114 }; // end class HoldIntegerSynchronized
```

Fig. 11.12 `HoldIntegerSynchronized` class modifies an object using synchronization. (Part 3 of 3.)

```
1  // Fig. 11.13: Synchronized.cpp
2  // Method definitions for class HoldIntegerSynchronized
3
4  #include "Synchronized.h"
5
6  // display current operation and buffer state
7  void HoldIntegerSynchronized::DisplayState( String *operation )
8  {
```

Fig. 11.13 `HoldIntegerSynchronized` class method definitions. (Part 1 of 2.)

```
9        Console::WriteLine( S"{0,-35}{1,-9}{2}\n", operation,
10          buffer.ToString(), occupiedBufferCount.ToString() );
11    } // end method DisplayState
```

Fig. 11.13 `HoldIntegerSynchronized` class method definitions. (Part 2 of 2.)

The producer thread performs the tasks specified in the **producer** object's **Produce** method. When line 22 (Fig. 11.15) sets the value of **HoldIntegerSynchronized** property **Buffer**, the producer thread invokes the *set* accessor at lines 68–102 (Fig. 11.12). Line 72 invokes **Monitor** method **Enter** to acquire the lock on the **HoldIntegerSynchronized** object (**this**). The **if** structure at lines 76–84 determines whether **occupiedBufferCount** is **1**. If this condition is **true**, lines 77–78 output a message indicating that the producer thread tries to write a value, and lines 80–81 invoke method **DisplayState** (defined in Fig. 11.13) to output another message indicating that the buffer is full and that the producer thread waits. Line 83 (Fig. 11.12) invokes **Monitor** method **Wait** to place the calling thread (i.e., the producer) in the *WaitSleepJoin* state for the **HoldIntegerSynchronized** object and releases the lock on the object. Now another thread can invoke an accessor method of the **HoldIntegerSynchronized** object's **Buffer** property.

```
1    // Fig. 11.14: Producer.h
2    // Class Producer's Produce method controls a thread that
3    // stores values from 1 to 4 in sharedLocation.
4
5    #pragma once
6
7    #include "Synchronized.h"
8
9    public __gc class Producer
10   {
11   public:
12
13      // constructor
14      Producer( HoldIntegerSynchronized *, Random * );
15
16      // store values 1 - 4 in object sharedLocation
17      void Produce();
18
19   private:
20      HoldIntegerSynchronized *sharedLocation;
21      Random *randomSleepTime;
22   }; // end class Producer
```

Fig. 11.14 `Producer` class controls a thread that stores values in `sharedLocation`.

```
1    // Fig. 11.15: Producer.cpp
2    // Method definitions for class Producer.
3
4    #include "Producer.h"
```

Fig. 11.15 `Producer` class method definitions. (Part 1 of 2.)

```
 5
 6    // constructor
 7    Producer::Producer( HoldIntegerSynchronized *shared,
 8       Random *random )
 9    {
10       sharedLocation = shared;
11       randomSleepTime = random;
12    }
13
14    // store values 1 - 4 in object sharedLocation
15    void Producer::Produce()
16    {
17
18       // sleep for random interval up to 3000 milliseconds
19       // then set sharedLocation's Buffer property
20       for ( int count = 1; count <= 4 ; count++ ) {
21          Thread::Sleep( randomSleepTime->Next( 1, 3000 ) );
22          sharedLocation->Buffer = count;
23       }
24
25       Console::WriteLine( S"{0} done producing.\nTerminating {0}.",
26          Thread::CurrentThread->Name );
27    } // end method Produce
```

Fig. 11.15 Producer class method definitions. (Part 2 of 2.)

The producer thread remains in the *WaitSleepJoin* state until the thread is notified that it may proceed—at which point the thread returns to the *Running* state and waits for the system to assign a processor to the thread. When the thread begins executing, the thread implicitly reacquires the lock on the **HoldIntegerSynchronized** object and the *set* accessor continues executing with the next statement after **Wait**. Line 87 (Fig. 11.12) assigns **value** to **buffer**. Line 91 increments the **occupiedBufferCount** to indicate that the shared buffer now contains a value (i.e., a consumer can read the value, and a producer cannot yet put another value there). Lines 93–94 invoke method **Display-State** to output a line to the console window indicating that the producer is writing a new value into the **buffer**. Line 98 invokes **Monitor** method **Pulse** with the **HoldIntegerSynchronized** object as an argument. If there are any waiting threads, the first waiting thread enters the *Running* state, indicating that the thread can now attempt its task again (as soon as the thread is assigned a processor). The **Pulse** method returns immediately. Line 101 invokes **Monitor** method **Exit** to release the lock on the **Hold-IntegerSynchronized** object, and the *set* accessor returns to its caller.

Common Programming Error 11.4

Failure to release the lock on an object when that lock is no longer needed is a logic error. This will prevent the threads in your program that require the lock from acquiring the lock to proceed with their tasks. These threads will be forced to wait (unnecessarily, because the lock is no longer needed). Such waiting can lead to deadlock and indefinite postponement.

The *get* and *set* accessors are implemented similarly. The consumer thread performs the tasks specified in the **consumer** object's **Consume** method. The consumer thread gets the value of the **HoldIntegerSynchronized** object's **Buffer** property (line 26 of Fig. 11.17) by invoking the *get* accessor in Fig. 11.12. Line 22 (Fig. 11.12) invokes

Monitor method **Enter** to acquire the lock on the **HoldIntegerSynchronized** object.

```
1   // Fig. 11.16: Consumer.h
2   // Class Consumer's Consume method controls a thread that
3   // loops four times and reads a value from sharedLocaton.
4
5   #pragma once
6
7   #include "Synchronized.h"
8
9   public __gc class Consumer
10  {
11  public:
12
13     // constructor
14     Consumer( HoldIntegerSynchronized *, Random * );
15
16     // read sharedLocation's value four times
17     void Consume();
18
19  private:
20     HoldIntegerSynchronized *sharedLocation;
21     Random *randomSleepTime;
22  }; // end class Consumer
```

Fig. 11.16 Consumer class reads values from **sharedLocation**.

```
1   // Fig. 11.17: Consumer.cpp
2   // Method definitions for class Consumer.
3
4   #include "Consumer.h"
5
6   // constructor
7   Consumer::Consumer( HoldIntegerSynchronized *shared,
8      Random *random )
9   {
10     sharedLocation = shared;
11     randomSleepTime = random;
12  }
13
14  // read sharedLocation's value four times
15  void Consumer::Consume()
16  {
17     int sum = 0;
18
19     // get current thread
20     Thread *current = Thread::CurrentThread;
21
22     // sleep for random interval up to 3000 milliseconds
23     // then add sharedLocation's Buffer property value to sum
```

Fig. 11.17 Consumer class method definitions. (Part 1 of 2.)

```
24        for ( int count = 1; count <= 4; count++ ) {
25           Thread::Sleep( randomSleepTime->Next( 1, 3000 ) );
26           sum += sharedLocation->Buffer;
27        }
28
29        Console::WriteLine( S"{0} read values totaling: {1}.\n",
30           S"Terminating {0}.",
31           Thread::CurrentThread->Name, sum.ToString() );
32    } // end method Consume
```

Fig. 11.17 Consumer class method definitions. (Part 2 of 2.)

The **if** structure at lines 26–34 determines whether **occupiedBufferCount** is 0. If this condition is **true**, lines 27–28 output a message indicating that the consumer thread tries to read a value, and lines 30–31 invoke method **DisplayState** to output another message indicating that the buffer is empty and that the consumer thread waits. Line 33 invokes **Monitor** method **Wait** to place the calling thread (i.e., the consumer) in the *WaitSleepJoin* state for the **HoldIntegerSynchronized** object and releases the lock on the object. Now another thread can invoke an accessor method of the **HoldIntegerSynchronized** object's **Buffer** property.

The consumer thread object remains in the *WaitSleepJoin* state until the thread is notified that it may proceed—at which point, the thread returns to the *Running* state and waits for the system to assign a processor to the thread. When the thread begins executing, the thread implicitly reacquires the lock on the **HoldIntegerSynchronized** object, and the *get* accessor continues executing with the next statement after **Wait**. Line 38 decrements **occupiedBufferCount** to indicate that the shared buffer is now empty (i.e., a consumer cannot read the value, but a producer can place another value into the shared buffer), lines 40–42 output a line to the console window indicating the value the consumer is reading and line 46 invokes **Monitor** method **Pulse** with the **HoldIntegerSynchronized** object as an argument. If there are any waiting threads, the first waiting thread enters the *Running* state, indicating that the thread can now attempt its task again (as soon as the thread is assigned a processor). The **Pulse** method returns immediately. Line 59 gets a copy of **buffer** before releasing the lock. It is possible that the producer could be assigned the processor immediately after the lock is released (line 62) and before the **return** statement executes (line 64). In this case, the producer would assign a new value to **buffer** before the **return** statement returns the value to the consumer. Thus, the consumer would receive the new value. Making a copy of **buffer** and returning the copy ensures that the consumer receives the proper value. Line 62 invokes **Monitor** method **Exit** to release the lock on the **HoldIntegerSynchronized** object, and the *get* accessor returns **bufferCopy** to its caller.

Study the outputs in Fig. 11.18. Observe that every integer produced is consumed exactly once—no values are lost, and no values are consumed more than once. This occurs because the producer and consumer cannot perform tasks unless it is "their turn." The producer must go first; the consumer must wait if the producer has not produced since the consumer last consumed; and the producer must wait if the consumer has not yet consumed the value the producer most recently produced. Execute this program several times to confirm that every integer produced is consumed exactly once.

```
1   // Fig. 11.18: SharedCell.cpp
2   // Creates and starts producer and consumer threads.
3
4   #include "Synchronized.h"
5   #include "Producer.h"
6   #include "Consumer.h"
7
8   int main()
9   {
10
11      // create shared object used by threads
12      HoldIntegerSynchronized *holdInteger =
13         new HoldIntegerSynchronized();
14
15      // Random object used by each thread
16      Random *random = new Random();
17
18      // create Producer and Consumer objects
19      Producer *producer = new Producer( holdInteger, random );
20      Consumer *consumer = new Consumer( holdInteger, random );
21
22      // output column heads and initial buffer state
23      Console::WriteLine( S"{0,-35}{1,-9}{2}\n", S"Operation",
24         S"Buffer", S"Occupied Count" );
25      holdInteger->DisplayState( S"Initial state" );
26
27      // create threads for producer and consumer and set
28      // delegates for each thread
29      Thread *producerThread = new Thread( new ThreadStart(
30         producer, Producer::Produce ) );
31      producerThread->Name = S"Producer";
32
33      Thread *consumerThread = new Thread( new ThreadStart(
34         consumer, Consumer::Consume ) );
35      consumerThread->Name = S"Consumer";
36
37      // start each thread
38      producerThread->Start();
39      consumerThread->Start();
40
41      return 0;
42   } // end function main
```

Operation	Buffer	Occupied Count
Initial state	-1	0
Producer writes 1	1	1
Consumer reads 1	1	0
Producer writes 2	2	1

Fig. 11.18 SharedCell demonstrates the uses of classes Producer and Consumer. (Part 1 of 2.)

Operation	Buffer	Occupied Count
Producer tries to write. Buffer full. Producer waits.	2	1
Consumer reads 2	2	0
Producer writes 3	3	1
Consumer reads 3	3	0
Consumer tries to read. Buffer empty. Consumer waits.	3	0
Producer writes 4	4	1
Producer done producing. Terminating Producer.		
Consumer reads 4	4	0
Consumer read values totaling: 10. Terminating Consumer.		

Operation	Buffer	Occupied Count
Initial state	-1	0
Consumer tries to read. Buffer empty. Consumer waits.	-1	0
Producer writes 1	1	1
Consumer reads 1	1	0
Consumer tries to read. Buffer empty. Consumer waits.	1	0
Producer writes 2	2	1
Consumer reads 2	2	0
Producer writes 3	3	1
Consumer reads 3	3	0
Producer writes 4	4	1
Producer done producing. Terminating Producer.		
Consumer reads 4	4	0
Consumer read values totaling: 10. Terminating Consumer.		

Fig. 11.18 SharedCell demonstrates the uses of classes Producer and Consumer. (Part 2 of 2.)

11.7 Producer/Consumer Relationship: Circular Buffer

Figure 11.12–Fig.11.18 used thread synchronization to guarantee that two threads manipulated data in a shared buffer correctly. However, the application may not perform optimally. If the two threads operate at different speeds, one of the threads will spend more (or most) of its time waiting. For example, in Fig. 11.12–Fig. 11.18 we shared a single integer between the two threads. If the producer thread produces values faster than the consumer can consume those values, then the producer thread waits for the consumer, because there are no other locations in memory to place the next value. Similarly, if the consumer consumes faster than the producer can produce values, the consumer waits until the producer places the next value into the shared location in memory.

One solution is to change the priorities of the threads (discussed in Section 11.3) so that they produce or consume values at the same rate. However, even when we have threads that operate at the same relative speeds, over a period of time, those threads may become "out of sync," causing one of the threads to wait for the other. We cannot make assumptions about the relative speeds of asynchronous concurrent threads. There are too many interactions that occur with the operating system, the network, the user and other components, which can cause the threads to operate at different speeds. When this happens, threads wait. When threads wait, programs become less productive, user-interactive programs become less responsive and network applications suffer longer delays because the processor is not used efficiently.

To minimize the waiting for threads that share resources and operate at the same relative speeds, we can implement a *circular buffer* that provides extra buffers into which the producer can place values and from which the consumer can retrieve those values. Let us assume that the buffer is implemented as an array. The producer and consumer work from the beginning of the array. When either thread reaches the end of the array, it simply returns to the first element of the array to perform its next task. If the producer temporarily produces values faster than the consumer can consume them, the producer can write additional values into the extra buffers (if cells are available). This enables the producer to perform its task even though the consumer is not ready to receive the current value being produced. Similarly, if the consumer consumes faster than the producer produces new values, the consumer can read additional values from the buffer (if there are any). This enables the consumer to perform its task even though the producer is not ready to produce additional values.

Note that the circular buffer would be inappropriate if the producer and consumer operate at different speeds. If the consumer always executes faster than the producer, then a buffer at one location is enough. Additional locations would waste memory. If the producer always executes faster, a buffer with an infinite number of locations would be required to absorb the extra production.

The key to using a circular buffer is to define it with enough extra cells to handle the anticipated "extra" production. If, over a period of time, we determine that the producer often produces as many as three more values than the consumer can consume, we can define a buffer of at least three cells to handle the extra production. We do not want the buffer to be too small, because that would cause threads to wait more. On the other hand, we do not want the buffer to be too large, because that would waste memory.

Performance Tip 11.5

Even when using a circular buffer, it is possible that a producer thread could fill the buffer, which would force the producer thread to wait until a consumer consumes a value to free an element in the buffer. Similarly, if the buffer is empty at any given time, the consumer thread must wait until the producer produces another value. The key to using a circular buffer is optimizing the buffer size to minimize the amount of thread-wait time.

Figure 11.19–Fig. 11.27 demonstrate a producer and a consumer accessing a circular buffer (in this case, a shared array of three cells) with synchronization. In this version of the producer/consumer relationship, the consumer consumes a value only when the array is not empty and the producer produces a value only when the array is not full. This program is implemented as a Windows application that sends its output to a **TextBox**. Classes **Producer** (Fig. 11.21–Fig. 11.22) and **Consumer** (Fig. 11.23–Fig. 11.24) perform the same tasks as in the previous examples, except that they output messages to the **TextBox** in the application window. The statements that created and started the thread objects in function **main** of **SharedCell.cpp** in Fig. 11.11 and Fig. 11.18 now appear in class **CircularBuffer** (Fig. 11.26), where the **Load** event handler (lines 34–67) performs the statements.

The most significant changes from Fig. 11.12–Fig. 11.18 occur in class **HoldIntegerSynchronized** (Fig. 11.19). which now contains five instance variables. Array **buffers** is a three-element integer array that represents the circular buffer. Variable **occupiedBufferCount** is the condition variable that can be used to determine whether a producer can write into the circular buffer (i.e., **occupiedBufferCount** is less than the number of elements in array **buffers**) and whether a consumer can read from the circular buffer (i.e., **occupiedBufferCount** is greater than **0**). Variable **readLocation** indicates the position from which the next value can be read by a consumer. Variable **writeLocation** indicates the next location in which a value can be placed by a producer. The program displays output in **outputTextBox**.

```
1   // Fig. 11.19: HoldIntegerSynchronized.h
2   // Implementing the producer/consumer relationship with a
3   // circular buffer.
4
5   #pragma once
6
7   #using <mscorlib.dll>
8   #using <system.dll>
9   #using <system.drawing.dll>
10  #using <system.windows.forms.dll>
11
12  using namespace System;
13  using namespace System::Drawing;
14  using namespace System::Windows::Forms;
15  using namespace System::Threading;
16
```

Fig. 11.19 **HoldIntegerSynchronized** class accesses threads through a circular buffer. (Part 1 of 4.)

```
17   // implement the shared integer with synchronization
18   public __gc class HoldIntegerSynchronized
19   {
20   public:
21      HoldIntegerSynchronized( TextBox * );    // constructor
22
23      // property Buffer
24      __property int get_Buffer()
25      {
26
27         // lock this object while getting value
28         // from buffers array
29         Monitor::Enter( this );
30
31         // if there is no data to read, place invoking
32         // thread in WaitSleepJoin state
33         if ( occupiedBufferCount == 0 ) {
34            outputTextBox->Text = String::Concat(
35               outputTextBox->Text, S"\r\nAll buffers empty. ",
36               Thread::CurrentThread->Name, S" waits." );
37            outputTextBox->ScrollToCaret();
38
39            Monitor::Wait( this );
40         }
41
42         // obtain value at current readLocation, then
43         // add string indicating consumed value to output
44         int readValue = buffers[ readLocation ];
45
46         outputTextBox->Text = String::Concat(
47            outputTextBox->Text, S"\r\n",
48            Thread::CurrentThread->Name, S" reads ",
49            buffers[ readLocation ].ToString(), S" " );
50         outputTextBox->ScrollToCaret();
51
52         // just consumed a value, so decrement number of
53         // occupied buffers
54         occupiedBufferCount--;
55
56         // update readLocation for future read operation,
57         // then add current state to output
58         readLocation = ( readLocation + 1 ) % buffers.Length;
59         outputTextBox->Text = String::Concat(
60            outputTextBox->Text, CreateStateOutput() );
61         outputTextBox->ScrollToCaret();
62
63         // return waiting thread (if there is one)
64         // to Running state
65         Monitor::Pulse( this );
66
67         Monitor::Exit( this ); // end lock
68
```

Fig. 11.19 HoldIntegerSynchronized class accesses threads through a circular buffer. (Part 2 of 4.)

```
69          return readValue;        // end lock
70       } // end property get_Buffer
71
72       // property set_Buffer
73       __property void set_Buffer( int value )
74       {
75
76          // lock this object while setting value
77          // in buffers array
78          Monitor::Enter( this );
79
80          // if there are no empty locations, place invoking
81          // thread in WaitSleepJoin state
82          if ( occupiedBufferCount == buffers.Length ) {
83             outputTextBox->Text = String::Concat(
84                outputTextBox->Text, S"\r\nAll buffers full. ",
85                Thread::CurrentThread->Name, S" waits." );
86             outputTextBox->ScrollToCaret();
87
88             Monitor::Wait( this );
89          }
90
91          // place value in writeLocation of buffers, then
92          // add string indicating produced value to output
93          buffers[ writeLocation ] = value;
94
95          outputTextBox->Text = String::Concat(
96             outputTextBox->Text, S"\r\n",
97             Thread::CurrentThread->Name, S" writes ",
98             buffers[ writeLocation ].ToString(), S" " );
99          outputTextBox->ScrollToCaret();
100
101         // just produced a value, so increment number of
102         // occupied buffers
103         occupiedBufferCount++;
104
105         // update writeLocation for future write operation,
106         // then add current state to output
107         writeLocation = ( writeLocation + 1 ) % buffers.Length;
108         outputTextBox->Text = String::Concat(
109            outputTextBox->Text, CreateStateOutput() );
110         outputTextBox->ScrollToCaret();
111
112         // return waiting thread (if there is one)
113         // to Running state
114         Monitor::Pulse( this );
115
116         Monitor::Exit( this );        // end lock
117      } // end property set_Buffer
118
119      // create state output
120      String *CreateStateOutput();
```

Fig. 11.19 HoldIntegerSynchronized class accesses threads through a circular buffer. (Part 3 of 4.)

```
121
122  private:
123
124      // each array element is a buffer
125      static Int32 buffers[] = { -1, -1, -1 };
126
127      // occupiedBufferCount maintains count of occupied buffers
128      static int occupiedBufferCount = 0;
129
130      // variable that maintains read and write buffer locations
131      static int readLocation = 0, writeLocation = 0;
132
133      // GUI component to display output
134      TextBox *outputTextBox;
135  }; // end class HoldIntegerSynchronized
```

Fig. 11.19 HoldIntegerSynchronized class accesses threads through a circular buffer. (Part 4 of 4.)

The *set* accessor (lines 73–117 of Fig. 11.19) of property **Buffer** performs the same tasks that it did in Fig. 11.6, with a few modifications. As program control calls **Monitor** method **Enter** (line 78), the currently executing thread acquires the lock (assuming the lock is currently available) on the **HoldIntegerSynchronized** object (i.e., **this**). The **if** structure (lines 82–89) determines whether the producer must wait (i.e., all buffers are full). If the producer thread must wait, lines 83–85 append text to the **output-TextBox** indicating that the producer is waiting to perform its task, and line 88 invokes **Monitor** method **Wait** to place the producer thread in the *WaitSleepJoin* state of the **HoldIntegerSynchronized** object. When execution continues at line 93 after the **if** structure, the value written by the producer is placed in the circular buffer at location **writeLocation**. Next, lines 95–98 append a message containing the value produced to the **TextBox**. Line 103 increments **occupiedBufferCount**, because there is now at least one value in the buffer that the consumer can read. Then line 107 updates **writeLo-cation** for the next call to the *set* accessor of property **Buffer**. The output continues at lines 108–109 by invoking method **CreateStateOutput** (lines 14–54 of Fig. 11.20), which outputs the number of occupied buffers, the contents of the buffers and the current **writeLocation** and **readLocation**. Line 114 (Fig. 11.19) invokes **Monitor** method **Pulse** to indicate that a thread waiting on the **HoldIntegerSynchronized** object (if there is a waiting thread) should transition to the *Running* state. Finally, line 116 invokes **Monitor** method **Exit**, causing the thread to release the lock on the **HoldIn-tegerSynchronized** object.

Common Programming Error 11.5

*When using class **Monitor**'s **Enter** and **Exit** methods to manage an object's lock, **Exit** must be called explicitly to release the lock. If an exception occurs in a method before **Exit** can be called and that exception is not caught, the method could terminate without calling **Exit**. If so, the lock is not released. To avoid this error, place code that could throw exceptions in a **try** block, and place the call to **Exit** in the corresponding __finally block to ensure that the lock is released.*

```cpp
1   // Fig. 11.20: HoldIntegerSynchronized.cpp
2   // Method definitions for class HoldIntegerSynchronized.
3
4   #include "HoldIntegerSynchronized.h"
5
6   // constructor
7   HoldIntegerSynchronized::HoldIntegerSynchronized(
8       TextBox *output )
9   {
10      outputTextBox = output;
11  }
12
13  // create state output
14  String *HoldIntegerSynchronized::CreateStateOutput()
15  {
16
17      // display first line of state information
18      String *output = String::Concat ( S"(buffers occupied: ",
19         occupiedBufferCount.ToString(), S")\r\nbuffers: " );
20
21      for ( int i = 0; i < buffers.Length; i++ )
22         output = String::Concat( output, S" ",
23            buffers[ i ].ToString(), S"   " );
24
25      output = String::Concat( output, S"\r\n" );
26
27      // display second line of state information
28      output = String::Concat( output, S"           " );
29
30      for ( int i = 0; i < buffers.Length; i++ )
31         output = String::Concat( output, S"---- " );
32
33      output = String::Concat( output, S"\r\n" );
34
35      // display third line of state information
36      output = String::Concat( output, S"           " );
37
38      // display readLocation (R) and writeLocation (W)
39      // indicators below appropriate buffer locations
40      for ( int i = 0; i < buffers.Length; i++ )
41         if ( ( i == writeLocation ) &&
42            ( writeLocation == readLocation ) )
43               output = String::Concat( output, S" WR  " );
44         else if ( i == writeLocation )
45            output = String::Concat( output, S" W   " );
46         else if ( i == readLocation )
47            output = String::Concat( output, S"  R   " );
48         else
49            output = String::Concat( output, S"     " );
50
51      output = String::Concat( output, S"\r\n" );
52
53      return output;
54  } // end method CreateStateOutput
```

Fig. 11.20 HoldIntegerSynchronized class method definitions.

```
1    // Fig. 11.21: Producer.h
2    // Produce the integers from 11 to 20 and place them in buffer.
3
4    #pragma once
5
6    #include "HoldIntegerSynchronized.h"
7
8    public __gc class Producer
9    {
10   public:
11
12      // constructor
13      Producer( HoldIntegerSynchronized *, Random *, TextBox * );
14
15      // produce values from 11-20 and place them in
16      // sharedLocation's buffer
17      void Produce();
18
19   private:
20      HoldIntegerSynchronized *sharedLocation;
21      TextBox *outputTextBox;
22      Random *randomSleepTime;
23   }; // end class Producer
```

Fig. 11.21 Producer class places integers in a circular buffer.

```
1    // Fig. 11.22: Producer.cpp
2    // Method definitions for class Producer.
3
4    #include "Producer.h"
5
6    // constructor
7    Producer::Producer( HoldIntegerSynchronized *shared,
8       Random *random, TextBox *output )
9    {
10      sharedLocation = shared;
11      outputTextBox = output;
12      randomSleepTime = random;
13   }
14
15   // produce values from 11-20 and place them in
16   // sharedLocation's buffer
17   void Producer::Produce()
18   {
19
20      // sleep for random interval up to 3000 milliseconds
21      // then set sharedLocation's Buffer property
22      for ( int count = 11; count <= 20; count++ ) {
23         Thread::Sleep( randomSleepTime->Next( 1, 3000 ) );
24         sharedLocation->Buffer = count;
25      }
26
```

Fig. 11.22 Producer class method definitions. (Part 1 of 2.)

```
27        String *name = Thread::CurrentThread->Name;
28
29        outputTextBox->Text = String::Concat( outputTextBox->Text,
30           S"\r\n", name, S" done producing.\r\n", name,
31           S" terminated.\r\n" );
32        outputTextBox->ScrollToCaret();
33     } // end method Produce
```

Fig. 11.22 **Producer** class method definitions. (Part 2 of 2.)

```
1     // Fig. 11.23: Consumer.h
2     // Consume the integers 1 to 10 from circular buffer.
3
4     #pragma once
5
6     #include "HoldIntegerSynchronized.h"
7
8     public __gc class Consumer
9     {
10    public:
11
12       // constructor
13       Consumer( HoldIntegerSynchronized *, Random *, TextBox * );
14
15       // consume 10 integers from buffer
16       void Consume();
17
18    private:
19       HoldIntegerSynchronized *sharedLocation;
20       TextBox *outputTextBox;
21       Random *randomSleepTime;
22    }; // end class Consumer
```

Fig. 11.23 **Consumer** class to consume integers from circular buffer.

```
1     // Fig. 11.24: Consumer.cpp
2     // Method definitions for class Consumer.
3
4     #include "Consumer.h"
5
6     // constructor
7     Consumer::Consumer( HoldIntegerSynchronized *shared,
8        Random *random, TextBox *output )
9     {
10       sharedLocation = shared;
11       outputTextBox = output;
12       randomSleepTime = random;
13    }
14
15    // consume 10 integers from buffer
16    void Consumer::Consume()
17    {
```

Fig. 11.24 **Consumer** class method definitions. (Part 1 of 2.)

```
18        int sum = 0;
19
20        // loop 10 times and sleep for random interval up to
21        // 3000 milliseconds then add sharedLocation's
22        // Buffer property value to sum
23        for ( int count = 1; count <= 10; count++ ) {
24           Thread::Sleep( randomSleepTime->Next( 1, 3000 ) );
25           sum += sharedLocation->Buffer;
26        }
27
28        String *name = Thread::CurrentThread->Name;
29
30        outputTextBox->Text = String::Concat( outputTextBox->Text,
31           S"\r\nTotal ", name, S" consumed: ", sum.ToString(),
32           S".\r\n", name, S" terminated.\r\n" );
33        outputTextBox->ScrollToCaret();
34     } // end method Consume
```

Fig. 11.24 Consumer class method definitions. (Part 2 of 2.)

```
1     // Fig. 11.25: CircularBuffer.h
2     // Implementing the producer/consumer
3     // relationship with a circular buffer.
4
5     #pragma once
6
7     #include "Producer.h"
8     #include "Consumer.h"
9
10    public __gc class CircularBuffer : public Form
11    {
12    public:
13
14       // constructor
15       CircularBuffer();
16
17    private:
18
19       // start producer and consumer
20       void CircularBuffer_Load( Object *, EventArgs * );
21       TextBox *outputTextBox;
22    }; // end class CircularBuffer
```

Fig. 11.25 CircularBuffer class starts the producer and consumer threads.

```
1     // Fig. 11.26: CircularBuffer.cpp
2     // Method definitions for class CircularBuffer.
3
4     #include "CircularBuffer.h"
5
6     CircularBuffer::CircularBuffer()
```

Fig. 11.26 CircularBuffer class method definitions. (Part 1 of 3.)

```
 7  {
 8      this->outputTextBox = new TextBox();
 9      this->SuspendLayout();
10
11      // outputTextBox
12      this->outputTextBox->Dock = DockStyle::Fill;
13      this->outputTextBox->Font = new Drawing::Font(
14         S"Courier New", 11.0, FontStyle::Regular,
15         GraphicsUnit::Point, 0 );
16      this->outputTextBox->Multiline = true;
17      this->outputTextBox->Name = S"outputTextBox";
18      this->outputTextBox->ReadOnly = true;
19      this->outputTextBox->ScrollBars = ScrollBars::Vertical;
20      this->outputTextBox->Size = Drawing::Size( 304, 461 );
21      this->outputTextBox->TabIndex = 0;
22      this->outputTextBox->Text = S"";
23
24      // CircularBuffer
25      this->AutoScaleBaseSize = Drawing::Size( 5, 13 );
26      this->ClientSize = Drawing::Size( 304, 461 );
27      this->Controls->Add( this->outputTextBox );
28      this->Name = S"CircularBuffer";
29      this->Text = S"CircularBuffer";
30      this->Load += new EventHandler( this, CircularBuffer_Load );
31      this->ResumeLayout();
32  } // end method CircularBuffer
33
34  void CircularBuffer::CircularBuffer_Load( Object *sender,
35      EventArgs *e )
36  {
37
38      // create shared object
39      HoldIntegerSynchronized *sharedLocation =
40         new HoldIntegerSynchronized( outputTextBox );
41
42      // display sharedLocation state before producer
43      // and consumer threads begin execution
44      outputTextBox->Text = sharedLocation->CreateStateOutput();
45
46      // Random object used by each thread
47      Random *random = new Random();
48
49      // create Producer and Consumer objects
50      Producer *producer =
51         new Producer( sharedLocation, random, outputTextBox );
52      Consumer *consumer =
53         new Consumer( sharedLocation, random, outputTextBox );
54
55      // create and name threads
56      Thread *producerThread = new Thread( new ThreadStart(
57         producer, Producer::Produce ) );
58      producerThread->Name = S"Producer";
59
```

Fig. 11.26 CircularBuffer class method definitions. (Part 2 of 3.)

```
60        Thread *consumerThread = new Thread( new ThreadStart(
61           consumer, Consumer::Consume ) );
62        consumerThread->Name = S"Consumer";
63
64        // start threads
65        producerThread->Start();
66        consumerThread->Start();
67     } // end method CircularBuffer_Load
```

Fig. 11.26 `CircularBuffer` class method definitions. (Part 3 of 3.)

```
1     // Fig. 11.27: CircularBufferTest.cpp
2     // Driver file to run CircularBuffer application.
3
4     #include "CircularBuffer.h"
5
6     int __stdcall WinMain()
7     {
8        Application::Run( new CircularBuffer() );
9
10       return 0;
11    } // end function WinMain
```

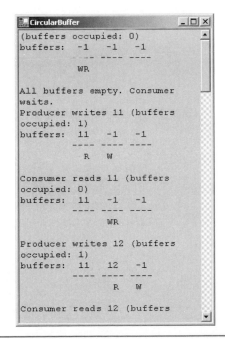
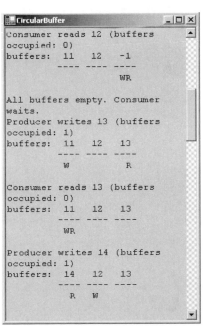

Fig. 11.27 `CircularBufferTest` demonstrates class `CircularBuffer`.
(Part 1 of 2.)

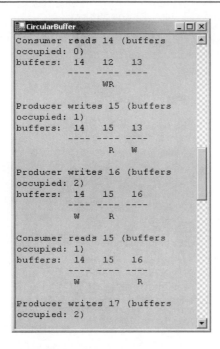

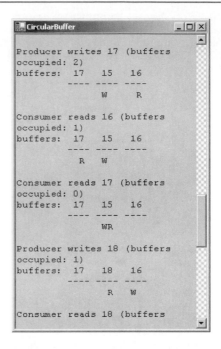

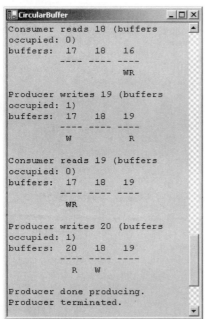

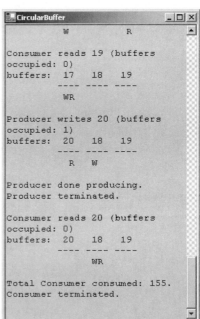

Fig. 11.27 `CircularBufferTest` demonstrates class `CircularBuffer`. (Part 2 of 2.)

The *get* accessor (lines 24–70 of Fig. 11.19) of property **Buffer** also performs the same tasks in this example that it did in Fig. 11.6, with a few minor modifications. Line 29 invokes **Monitor** method **Enter** to acquire the lock (assuming the lock is currently available). The **if** structure at lines 33–40 in the *get* accessor determines whether the consumer must wait (i.e., all buffers are empty). If the consumer thread must wait, lines 34–36 append text to the **outputTextBox** indicating that the consumer is waiting to perform its task, and line 39 invokes **Monitor** method **Wait** to place the consumer thread in the *WaitSleepJoin* state of the **HoldIntegerSynchronized** object. When execution continues at line 44 after the **if** structure, **readValue** is assigned the value at location **readLocation** in the circular buffer. Lines 46–49 append the value consumed to the **TextBox**. Line 53 decrements the **occupiedBufferCount**, because there is at least one open position in the buffer in which the producer thread can place a value. Then line 54 updates **readLocation** for the next call to the *get* accessor of **Buffer**. Lines 59–60 invoke method **CreateStateOutput** to output the number of occupied buffers, the contents of the buffers and the current **writeLocation** and **readLocation**. Line 65 invokes method **Pulse** to transition the next thread waiting for the **HoldIntegerSynchronized** object into the *Running* state. Finally, line 67 invokes **Monitor** method **Exit**, causing the thread to release the lock on the **HoldIntegerSynchronized** object, and line 69 returns the consumed value to the calling method.

In Fig. 11.27, the outputs include the current **occupiedBufferCount**, the contents of the buffers and the current **writeLocation** and **readLocation**. In the output, the letters **W** and **R** represent the current **writeLocation** and **readLocation**, respectively. Notice that, after the third value is placed in the third element of the buffer, the fourth value is inserted at the beginning of the array. This provides the circular buffer effect.

11.8 Summary

Computers perform operations concurrently, such as compiling programs, printing files and receiving electronic mail messages over a network. Programming languages generally provide only a simple set of control structures that enable programmers to perform one action at a time and proceed to the next action after the previous one finishes. Historically, the concurrency that computers perform generally has been implemented as operating system "primitives" available only to highly experienced "systems programmers."

The .NET Framework Class Library makes concurrency primitives available to the applications programmer. The programmer specifies that applications contain threads of execution, each thread designating a portion of a program that may execute concurrently with other threads—this capability is called multithreading.

A thread that was just created is in the *Unstarted* state. A thread is initialized using the **Thread** class's constructor, which receives a **ThreadStart** delegate. This delegate specifies the method that contains the tasks a thread will perform. A thread remains in the *Unstarted* state until the thread's **Start** method is called; this causes the thread to enter the *Running* state. A thread in the *Running* state starts executing when the system assigns a processor to the thread. The system assigns the processor to the highest-priority *Running* thread.

A thread enters the *Stopped* (or *Aborted*) state when its **ThreadStart** delegate completes or terminates. A thread is forced into the *Stopped* state when its **Abort** method is called (by itself or by another thread).

A *Running* thread becomes blocked when the thread issues an input/output request or attempts to acquire an unavailable lock by calling **Monitor** method **Enter**. A blocked thread becomes *Running* when the I/O it is waiting for completes or when the desired lock become available. A blocked thread cannot use a processor, even if one is available.

If a thread cannot continue executing (we will call this the dependent thread) unless another thread terminates, the dependent thread calls the other thread's **Join** method to "join" the two threads. When two threads are "joined," the dependent thread leaves the *WaitSleepJoin* state when the other thread finishes execution (enters the *Stopped* state). Any thread in the *WaitSleepJoin* state can leave that state if another thread invokes **Thread** method **Interrupt** on the thread in the *WaitSleepJoin* state.

If **Thread** method **Suspend** is called on a thread (by the thread itself or by another thread in the program), the thread enters the *Suspended* state. A thread leaves the *Suspended* state when a separate thread invokes **Thread** method **Resume** on the suspended thread.

Every thread has a priority of **ThreadPriority::Lowest**, **ThreadPriority::BelowNormal**, **ThreadPriority::Normal**, **ThreadPriority::AboveNormal** or **ThreadPriority::Highest**. The job of the thread scheduler is to keep the highest-priority thread running at all times and, if there is more than one highest-priority thread, to ensure that all equally high-priority threads execute for a quantum at a time in round-robin fashion. A thread's priority can be adjusted with the **Priority** property, which accepts an argument from the **ThreadPriority** enumeration.

In thread synchronization, when a thread encounters code that it cannot yet run, the thread can call **Monitor** method **Wait** until certain actions occur that enable the thread to continue executing. If a thread called **Monitor** method **Wait**, a corresponding call to the **Monitor** method **Pulse** or **PulseAll** by another thread in the program will transition the original thread from the *WaitSleepJoin* state to the *Running* state.

A thread that updates shared data calls **Monitor** method **Enter** to acquire the lock on that data. It updates the data and calls **Monitor** method **Exit** upon completion of the update. While that data is locked, all other threads attempting to acquire the lock on that data must wait.

12

Strings, Characters and Regular Expressions

Objectives

- To create and manipulate immutable character string objects of class **String**.
- To create and manipulate mutable character string objects of class **StringBuilder**.
- To use regular expressions in conjunction with classes **Regex** and **Match**.

The chief defect of Henry King
Was chewing little bits of string.
Hilaire Belloc

Vigorous writing is concise. A sentence should contain no
unnecessary words, a paragraph no unnecessary sentences.
William Strunk, Jr.

I have made this letter longer than usual, because I lack the
time to make it short.
Blaise Pascal

The difference between the almost-right word & the right
word is really a large matter—it's the difference between the
lightning bug and the lightning.
Mark Twain

Mum's the word.
Miguel de Cervantes

12.1 Introduction

In this chapter, we introduce the Framework Class Library's string and character processing capabilities and demonstrate the use of regular expressions to search for patterns in text. The techniques presented in this chapter can be employed to develop text editors, word processors, page-layout software, computerized typesetting systems and other kinds of text-processing software. Previous chapters have already presented several string-processing capabilities. In this chapter, we expand on this information by detailing the capabilities of class **String** and type **Char** from the **System** namespace, class **StringBuilder** from the **System::Text** namespace and classes **Regex** and **Match** from the **System::Text::RegularExpressions** namespace.

12.2 Fundamentals of Characters and Strings

Characters are the fundamental building blocks of MC++ source code. Every program is composed of characters that, when grouped together meaningfully, create a sequence that the compiler interprets as a series of instructions that describe how to accomplish a task. In addition to normal characters, a program also can contain *character constants*. A character constant is a character that is represented as an integer value, called a *character code*. For example, the integer value **122** corresponds to the character constant **'z'**. The integer value **10** corresponds to the newline character **'\n'**. In Windows NT based systems (Windows NT, 2000 and XP), character constants are established according to the *Unicode®* *character set*, an international character set that contains many more symbols and letters than does the ASCII character set (see Appendix C). To learn more about Unicode®, see Appendix D.

A string is a series of characters treated as a single unit. These characters can be uppercase letters, lowercase letters, digits and various *special characters,* such as +, -, *, /, $ and others. In MC++, a string is an object of class **String** in the **System** namespace. Because **String**s are a reference type, MC++ programs use **String *** objects (also called **String** pointers) to manipulate objects of type **String**. We write *string literals*, or *string constants* (often called *literal Strings*), as sequences of characters in double quotation marks, as follows:

```
"John Q. Doe"
"9999 Main Street"
"Waltham, Massachusetts"
"(201) 555-1212"
```

A declaration can assign a **String** literal to a **String** pointer. The declaration

```
String *color = "blue";
```

initializes **String** pointer **color** to point to the **String** literal object **"blue"**.

In MC++, **String** literals can also be prefixed by the letter **S** (e.g., **S"blue"**). **String** literals preceded by **S** are called managed **String** literals. Managed **String** literals are useful because they offer better performance than non-managed **String** literals.[1]

Performance Tip 12.1

If there are multiple occurrences of the same managed String literal object in an application, the program automatically points to a single copy of the managed String literal object from each location in the program that uses that managed String literal. It is possible for the program to share the object in this manner, because managed String literal objects are implicitly constant. Such sharing conserves memory.

Notice, however, that when we assign **"blue"** to **String** pointer **color** (above), we do not prefix it with the letter **S**. Thus, we are not creating a managed **String** literal. **String**s without prefixes are standard C++ **String** literals.

String literals prefixed by the letter **L** (e.g., **L"String literal"**) are standard C++ *wide-character string literals*. Wide-character **String** literals have a different internal representation than regular C++ **String** literals.[2] In MC++, both standard C++ **String** literals (with no prefix) and wide-character **String** literals (prefixed by **L**) may be assigned to **String** pointers without casting.

---

1. For more information about managed string literals, visit **msdn.microsoft.com/library/ en-us/vcmex/html/vcconStringLiteralsinMX.asp**.
2. For more information about standard C++ string literals, visit **www.zib.de/benger/C++/ clause2.html#s2.13.4** and **www.tempest-sw.com/cpp/ch01.html**.

Only managed **String** literals (prefixed by **S**) and standard C++ wide-character **String** literals (prefixed by **L**) can be used where **System::String** types are expected. However, managed **String** literals can not be used where standard C++ string types are expected.

12.3 String Constructors

Class **String** provides eight constructors for initializing **String**s in various ways. Figure 12.1 demonstrates the use of three of the constructors.

```
1   // Fig. 12.1: StringConstructor.cpp
2   // Demonstrating String class constructors.
3
4   #using <mscorlib.dll>
5   #using <system.windows.forms.dll>
6
7   using namespace System;
8   using namespace System::Windows::Forms;
9
10  int __stdcall WinMain()
11  {
12     String *output;
13     String *originalString;
14     String *string1, *string2, *string3, *string4;
15
16     __wchar_t characterArray __gc[] =
17        { 'b', 'i', 'r', 't', 'h', 'd', 'a', 'y' };
18
19     // string initialization
20     originalString = S"Welcome to Visual C++ .NET programming!";
21     string1 = originalString;
22     string2 = new String( characterArray );
23     string3 = new String( characterArray, 5, 3 );
24     string4 = new String( 'C', 5 );
25
26     output = String::Concat( S"string1 = ", S"\"", string1,
27        S"\"\n", S"string2 = ", S"\"", string2, S"\"\n",
28        S"string3 = ", S"\"", string3, S"\"\n",
29        S"string4 = ", S"\"", string4, S"\"\n" );
30
31     MessageBox::Show( output, S"String Class Constructors",
32        MessageBoxButtons::OK, MessageBoxIcon::Information );
33
34     return 0;
35  } // end function WinMain
```

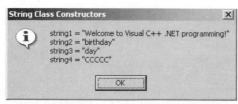

Fig. 12.1   String constructors.

Lines 12–14 declare **String** pointers **output, originalString, string1, string2, string3** and **string4**. Lines 16–17 allocate the **__wchar_t** array **characterArray**, which contains eight characters. Recall from Chapter 2, Visual Studio® .NET IDE and Visual C++ .NET Programming, that **__wchar_t** is an MC++ alias for .NET type **Char** and that we use MC++ aliases for the convenience of standard C++ programmers. We discuss type **Char** in detail in Section 12.15.

Line 20 assigns managed **String** literal **"Welcome to Visual C++ .NET programming!"** to **String** pointer **originalString**. Line 21 sets **string1** to point to the same **String** literal.

Line 22 assigns to **string2** a new **String**, using the **String** constructor that takes a **__wchar_t __gc** array (a managed character array) as an argument. The new **String** contains a copy of the characters in array **characterArray**.

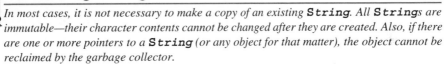

Software Engineering Observation 12.1

In most cases, it is not necessary to make a copy of an existing **String**. *All* **String**s *are immutable—their character contents cannot be changed after they are created. Also, if there are one or more pointers to a* **String** *(or any object for that matter), the object cannot be reclaimed by the garbage collector.*

Line 23 assigns to **string3** a new **String**, using the **String** constructor that takes a managed **__wchar_t** array and two **int** arguments. The second argument specifies the starting index position (the *offset*) from which characters in the array are copied. The third argument specifies the number of characters (the *count*) to be copied from the specified starting position in the array. The new **String** contains a copy of the specified characters in the array. If the specified offset or count indicates that the program should access an element outside the bounds of the character array, an *ArgumentOutOfRangeException* is thrown.

Line 24 assigns to **string4** a new **String**, using the **String** constructor that takes as arguments a character and an **int** specifying the number of times to repeat that character in the **String**.

12.4 String Chars Property, Length Property and CopyTo Method

The application in Fig. 12.2 presents the **String** indexed property, which facilitates the retrieval of any character in the **String**, and the **String** property *Length*, which returns the length of the **String**. The **String** method *CopyTo* copies a specified number of characters from a **String** into a **__wchar_t** array.

```
1   // Fig. 12.2: StringMethods.cpp
2   // Using String property Chars, property Length and method CopyTo.
3
4   #using <mscorlib.dll>
5   #using <system.windows.forms.dll>
6
7   using namespace System;
8   using namespace System::Windows::Forms;
9
```

Fig. 12.2   String Chars property , **Length** property and **CopyTo** method.
         (Part 1 of 2.)

```
10   // main entry point for application
11   int __stdcall WinMain()
12   {
13      String *string1, *output;
14      __wchar_t characterArray __gc[];
15
16      string1 = S"hello there";
17      characterArray = new __wchar_t __gc[ 5 ];
18
19      // output string
20      output = String::Concat( S"string1: \"", string1, S"\"" );
21
22      // test Length property
23      output = String::Concat( output, S"\nLength of string1: ",
24         string1->Length.ToString() );
25
26      // loop through character in string1 and display reversed
27      output = String::Concat( output,
28         S"\nThe string reversed is: " );
29
30      for ( int i = string1->Length - 1; i >= 0; i-- )
31         output = String::Concat( output,
32            string1->Chars[ i ].ToString() );
33
34      // copy characters from string1 into characterArray
35      string1->CopyTo( 0, characterArray, 0, 5 );
36      output = String::Concat( output,
37         S"\nThe character array is: " );
38
39      for ( int i = 0; i < characterArray->Length; i++ )
40         output = String::Concat( output,
41            characterArray[ i ].ToString() );
42
43      String *output2 = String::Concat( S"Demonstrating the String",
44         S" Chars Property, Length Property and CopyTo method" ); );
45
46      MessageBox::Show( output, output2, MessageBoxButtons::OK,
47         MessageBoxIcon::Information );
48
49      return 0;
50   } // end function WinMain
```

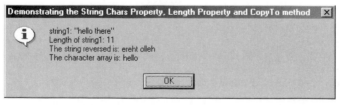

Fig. 12.2   **String Chars** property , **Length** property and **CopyTo** method.
(Part 2 of 2.)

In this example, we create an application that determines the length of a **String**, reverses the order of the characters in the **String** and copies a series of characters from the **String** into a character array.

Lines 23–24 use **String** property **Length** to determine the number of characters in the string pointed to by **string1**. Like arrays, **String**s always know their own size. Notice that in line 24, we use method **ToString** to convert the numerical length to a **String *** to be displayed. This is because method **String::Concat** does not automatically convert its arguments to **String** objects. We discuss method **Concat** in Section 12.9.

Lines 30–32 append to **output** the characters of the **string1** in reverse order. Indexed property *Chars* (of class **String**) returns the character at a specific position in the **String**. Property **Chars** is accessed as an array of **__wchar_t**s. The indexed property receives an integer argument as the *position number* and returns the character at that position. As with arrays, the first element of a **String** is considered to be at position 0.

Common Programming Error 12.1

*Attempting to access a character that is outside the bounds of a **String** (i.e., an index less than 0 or an index greater than or equal to the **String**'s length) results in an **IndexOutOfRangeException**.*

Line 35 uses **String** method **CopyTo** to copy the characters of **string1** into **characterArray**. The first argument given to method **CopyTo** is the index from which the method begins copying characters in **string1**. The second argument is the character array into which the characters are copied. The third argument is the index specifying the location at which the method places the copied characters in the character array. The last argument is the number of characters that the method will copy from **string1**. Lines 39–41 append the **__wchar_t** array contents to **output** one character at a time.

12.5 Comparing **Strings**

The next two examples demonstrate the various methods that MC++ provides for comparing **String**s. To understand how one **String** can be "greater than" or "less than" another **String**, consider the process of alphabetizing a series of last names. The reader would, no doubt, place **"Jones"** before **"Smith"**, because the first letter of **"Jones"** comes before the first letter of **"Smith"** in the alphabet. The alphabet is more than just a set of 26 letters—it is an ordered list of characters in which each letter occurs in a specific position. For example, **Z** is more than just a letter of the alphabet; **Z** is specifically the twenty-sixth letter of the alphabet.

Computers can order characters alphabetically because the characters are represented internally as numeric codes. When comparing two **String**s, MC++ simply compares the numeric codes of the characters in the **String**s.

Class **String** provides several ways to compare **String**s. The application in Fig. 12.3 demonstrates the use of method *Equals*, method *CompareTo* and the equality operator (**==**).

```
1    // Fig. 12.3: StringCompare.cpp
2    // Comparing strings.
3
4    #using <mscorlib.dll>
5    #using <system.windows.forms.dll>
6
7    using namespace System;
8    using namespace System::Windows::Forms;
9
10   int __stdcall WinMain()
11   {
12      String *string1 = S"hello";
13      String *string2 = S"goodbye";
14      String *string3 = S"Happy Birthday";
15      String *string4 = S"happy birthday";
16      String *output;
17
18      // output values of four strings
19      output = String::Concat( S"string1 = \"", string1, S"\"",
20         S"\nstring2 = \"", string2, S"\"", S"\nstring3 = \"",
21         string3, S"\"", S"\nstring4 = \"", string4, S"\"\n\n" );
22
23      // test for equality using Equals method
24      if ( string1->Equals( S"hello" ) )
25         output = String::Concat( output,
26            S"string1 equals \"hello\"\n" );
27      else
28         output = String::Concat( output,
29            S"string1 does not equal \"hello\"\n" );
30
31      // test for equality with ==
32      if ( string1 == S"hello" )
33         output = String::Concat( output,
34            S"string1 equals \"hello\"\n" );
35      else
36         output = String::Concat( output,
37            S"string1 does not equal \"hello\"\n" );
38
39      // test for equality comparing case
40      if ( String::Equals( string3, string4 ) )
41         output = String::Concat( output,
42            S"string3 equals string4\n" );
43      else
44         output = String::Concat( output,
45            S"string3 does not equal string4\n" );
46
47      // test CompareTo
48      output = String::Concat( output,
49         S"\nstring1.CompareTo( string2 ) is ",
50         string1->CompareTo( string2 ).ToString(), S"\n",
51         S"string2.CompareTo( string1 ) is ",
52         string2->CompareTo( string1 ), S"\n",
```

Fig. 12.3 **String** test to determine equality. (Part 1 of 2.)

```
53          S"string1.CompareTo( string1 ) is ",
54          string1->CompareTo( string1 ), S"\n",
55          S"string3.CompareTo( string4 ) is ",
56          string3->CompareTo( string4 ), S"\n",
57          S"string4.CompareTo( string3 ) is ",
58          string4->CompareTo( string3 ), S"\n" );
59
60       MessageBox::Show( output, S"Demonstrating String Comparisons",
61          MessageBoxButtons::OK, MessageBoxIcon::Information );
62
63       return 0;
64    } // end function WinMain
```

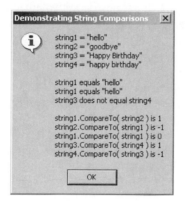

Fig. 12.3 **String** test to determine equality. (Part 2 of 2.)

The condition in the **if** structure (line 24) uses instance method **Equals** to compare **string1** and literal **String "hello"** to determine whether they are equal in content. Method **Equals** (inherited by **String** from class **Object**) tests any two objects for equality (i.e., checks whether the objects have identical contents). The method returns **true** if the objects are equal and **false** otherwise. In this instance, the preceding condition returns **true**, because **string1** points to **String** literal object **"hello"**. Method **Equals** uses a *lexicographical comparison*—the integer Unicode® values that represent each character in each **String** are compared. Method **Equals** compares the numeric Unicode® values that represent the characters in each **String**. A comparison of the **String "hello"** with the **String "HELLO"** would return **false**, because the numeric representations of lowercase letters are different from the numeric representations of corresponding uppercase letters.

The condition in the second **if** structure (line 32) uses the equality operator (**==**) to compare **string1** with the managed literal **"hello"** for equality. In MC++, the equality operator compares the pointers of two **Strings**. Thus, the condition in the **if** structure evaluates to **true**, because **string1** points to managed literal **String "hello"**.

We present the test for **String** equality between **string3** and **string4** (line 40) to illustrate that comparisons are indeed case sensitive. Here **static** method **Equals** (as opposed to the instance method in line 24) is used to compare the values of two **Strings**. **"Happy Birthday"** does not equal **"happy birthday"**, so the condition of the **if** structure fails, and the message **"string3 does not equal string4"** is added to the output message (lines 44–45).

Lines 48–58 use the **String** method **CompareTo** to compare **String**s. Method **CompareTo** returns **0** if the **String**s are equal, a **-1** if the **String** that invokes **CompareTo** is less than the **String** that is passed as an argument and a **1** if the **String** that invokes **CompareTo** is greater than the **String** that is passed as an argument. Method **CompareTo** uses a lexicographical comparison.

Notice that **CompareTo** considers **string3** to be larger than **string4**. The only difference between these two **String**s is that **string3** contains two uppercase letters. This example illustrates that an uppercase letter has a higher value in the Unicode® character set than its corresponding lowercase letter.

The application in Fig. 12.4 shows how to test whether a **String** instance begins or ends with a given string. Method **StartsWith** determines whether a **String** instance starts with the **String** literal passed to it as an argument. Method **EndsWith** determines whether a **String** instance ends with the **String** literal passed to it as an argument. Application **StringStartEnd**'s **WinMain** function defines an array of **String** pointers (called **strings**), which contains **"started"**, **"starting"**, **"ended"** and **"ending"**. The remainder of function **WinMain** tests the elements of the array to determine whether they start or end with a particular set of characters.

```
1   // Fig. 12.4: StringStartEnd.cpp
2   // Demonstrating StartsWith and EndsWith methods.
3
4   #using <mscorlib.dll>
5   #using <system.windows.forms.dll>
6
7   using namespace System;
8   using namespace System::Windows::Forms;
9
10  int __stdcall WinMain()
11  {
12     String *strings[] =
13        { S"started", S"starting", S"ended", S"ending" };
14
15     String *output = S"";
16
17     // test every string to see if it starts with "st"
18     for ( int i = 0; i < strings->Length; i++ )
19        if ( strings[ i ]->StartsWith( S"st" ) )
20           output = String::Concat( output, S"\"",
21              strings[ i ], S"\" starts with \"st\"\n" );
22
23     output = String::Concat( output, S"\n" );
24
25     // test every string to see if it ends with "ed"
26     for ( int i = 0; i < strings->Length; i++ )
27        if ( strings[ i ]->EndsWith( S"ed" ) )
28           output = String::Concat( output, S"\"",
```

Fig. 12.4 **StartsWith** and **EndsWith** methods demonstrated. (Part 1 of 2.)

```
29                      strings[ i ], S"\" ends with \"ed\"\n" );
30
31      MessageBox::Show( output,
32         S"Demonstrating StartsWith and EndsWith methods",
33         MessageBoxButtons::OK, MessageBoxIcon::Information );
34
35      return 0;
36  } // end function WinMain
```

Fig. 12.4   `StartsWith` and `EndsWith` methods demonstrated. (Part 2 of 2.)

Line 19 uses method **StartsWith**, which takes a **String *** argument. The condition in the **if** structure determines whether the **String *** at index **i** of the array starts with the characters **"st"**. If so, the method returns **true** and appends **strings[i]** to **output** for display purposes.

Line 27 uses method **EndsWith**, which also takes a **String *** argument. The condition in the **if** structure determines whether the **String *** at index **i** of the array ends with the characters **"ed"**. If so, the method returns **true**, and **strings[i]** is appended to **output** for display purposes.

12.6 String; Method GetHashCode

Often, it is necessary to store **String**s and other data types in a manner that enables the information to be found quickly. Onc of the best ways to make information easily accessible is to store it in a hash table. A *hash table* stores an object by performing a special calculation on that object, which produces a *hash code*. The object then is stored at a location in the hash table determined by the calculated hash code. When a program needs to retrieve the information, the same calculation is performed, generating the same hash code. Any object can be stored in a hash table. Class **Object** defines method *GetHashCode* to perform the hash-code calculation. Although all classes inherit this method from class **Object**, it is recommended that they override **Object**'s default implementation. Class **String** overrides method **GetHashCode** to provide a good hash-code distribution based on the contents of the **String**. We will discuss hashing in detail in Chapter 19, Data Structures and Collections.

The example in Fig. 12.5 demonstrates the application of the **GetHashCode** method to two **String**s (**"hello"** and "**Hello**"). Here, the hash-code value for each **String** is different. However, **String**s that are not identical can have the same hash-code value.

```
1    // Fig. 12.5: StringHashCode.cpp
2    // Demonstrating method GetHashCode of class String.
3
4    #using <mscorlib.dll>
5    #using <system.windows.forms.dll>
6
7    using namespace System;
8    using namespace System::Windows::Forms;
9
10   int __stdcall WinMain()
11   {
12      String *string1 = S"hello";
13      String *string2 = S"Hello";
14      String *output;
15
16      output = String::Concat( S"The hash code for \"", string1,
17         S"\" is ", string1->GetHashCode().ToString(), S"\n" );
18
19      output = String::Concat( output, S"The hash code for \"",
20         string2, S"\" is ", string2->GetHashCode().ToString(),
21         S"\n" );
22
23      MessageBox::Show( output,
24         S"Demonstrating String method GetHashCode",
25         MessageBoxButtons::OK, MessageBoxIcon::Information );
26
27      return 0;
28   } // end function WinMain
```

Fig. 12.5   GetHashCode method demonstration.

12.7 Locating Characters and Substrings in Strings

In many applications, it is necessary to search for a character or set of characters in a **String**. For example, a programmer creating a word processor would want to provide capabilities for searching through documents. The application in Fig. 12.6 demonstrates some of the many versions of **String** methods *IndexOf*, *IndexOfAny*, *LastIndexOf* and *LastIndexOfAny*, which search for a specified character or substring in a **String**. We perform all searches in this example on the **String** pointer **letters** (initialized with **"abcdefghijklmabcdefghijklm"**) located in function **WinMain**.

```
1    // Fig. 12.6: StringIndexMethods.cpp
2    // Using String searching methods.
3
4    #using <mscorlib.dll>
5    #using <system.windows.forms.dll>
6
7    using namespace System;
8    using namespace System::Windows::Forms;
9
10   int __stdcall WinMain()
11   {
12      String *letters = S"abcdefghijklmabcdefghijklm";
13      String *output = S"";
14      __wchar_t searchLetters __gc[] = { 'c', 'a', '$' };
15
16      // test IndexOf to locate a character in a string
17      output = String::Concat( output, S"'c' is located at index ",
18         letters->IndexOf( 'c' ).ToString() );
19
20      output = String::Concat( output, S"\n'a' is located at index ",
21         letters->IndexOf( 'a', 1 ).ToString() );
22
23      output = String::Concat( output, S"\n'$' is located at index ",
24         letters->IndexOf( '$', 3, 5 ).ToString() );
25
26      // test LastIndexOf to find a character in a string
27      output = String::Concat( output, S"\n\nlast 'c' is located at ",
28         S"index ", letters->LastIndexOf( 'c' ).ToString() );
29
30      output = String::Concat( output,
31         S"\nLast 'a' is located at index ",
32         letters->LastIndexOf( 'a', 25 ).ToString() );
33
34      output = String::Concat( output,
35         S"\nLast '$' is located at index ",
36         letters->LastIndexOf( '$', 15, 5 ).ToString() );
37
38      // test IndexOf to locate a substring in a string
39      output = String::Concat( output,
40         S"\n\n\"def\" is located at index ",
41         letters->IndexOf( "def" ).ToString() );
42
43      output = String::Concat( output,
44         S"\n\"def\" is located at index ",
45         letters->IndexOf( "def", 7 ).ToString() );
46
47      output = String::Concat( output,
48         S"\n\"hello\" is located at index ",
49         letters->IndexOf( "hello", 5, 15 ).ToString() );
50
```

Fig. 12.6 **StringIndexMethods** demonstrates **String** searching capabilities. (Part 1 of 3.)

```
51      // test LastIndexOf to find a substring in a string
52      output = String::Concat( output,
53         S"\n\nLast \"def\" is located at index ",
54         letters->LastIndexOf( "def" ).ToString() );
55
56      output = String::Concat( output,
57         S"\nLast \"def\" is located at index ",
58         letters->LastIndexOf( "def", 25 ).ToString() );
59
60      output = String::Concat( output,
61         S"\nLast \"hello\" is located at index ",
62         letters->LastIndexOf( "hello", 20, 15 ).ToString() );
63
64      // test IndexOfAny to find first occurrence of character
65      // in array
66      output = String::Concat( output,
67         S"\n\nFirst occurrence of 'c', 'a', '$' is ",
68         S"located at ",
69         letters->IndexOfAny( searchLetters ).ToString() );
70
71      output = String::Concat( output,
72         S"\nFirst occurrence of 'c', 'a' or '$' is ",
73         S"located at ",
74         letters->IndexOfAny( searchLetters, 7 ).ToString() );
75
76      output = String::Concat( output,
77         S"\nFirst occurrence of 'c', 'a' or '$' is ",
78         S"located at ",
79         letters->IndexOfAny( searchLetters, 20, 5 ).ToString() );
80
81      // test LastIndexOfAny to find last occurrence of character
82      // in array
83      output = String::Concat( output,
84         S"\n\nLast occurrence of 'c', 'a' or '$' is ",
85         S"located at ",
86         letters->LastIndexOfAny( searchLetters ).ToString() );
87
88      output = String::Concat( output,
89         S"\nLast occurrence of 'c', 'a' or '$' is ",
90         S"located at ",
91         letters->LastIndexOfAny( searchLetters, 1 ).ToString() );
92
93      output = String::Concat( output,
94         S"\nLast occurrence of 'c', 'a' or '$' is located at ",
95         letters->LastIndexOfAny( searchLetters, 25, 5 ).ToString() );
96
97      MessageBox::Show( output,
98         S"Demonstrating class index methods",
99         MessageBoxButtons::OK, MessageBoxIcon::Information );
100
101     return 0;
102  } // end function WinMain
```

Fig. 12.6 **StringIndexMethods** demonstrates **String** searching capabilities. (Part 2 of 3.)

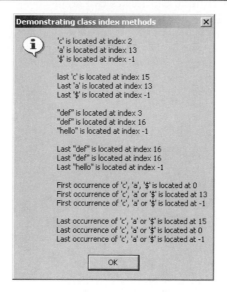

Fig. 12.6 `StringIndexMethods` demonstrates `String` searching capabilities. (Part 3 of 3.)

Lines 18, 21 and 24 use method **IndexOf** to locate the first occurrence of a character or substring in a **String**. If **IndexOf** finds a character, **IndexOf** returns the index of the specified character in the **String**; otherwise, **IndexOf** returns **–1**. The expression on line 21 uses a version of method **IndexOf** that takes two arguments—the character to search for and the starting index at which the search of the **String** should begin. The method does not examine any characters that occur prior to the starting index (in this case **1**). The expression in line 24 uses another version of method **IndexOf** that takes three arguments—the character to search for, the index at which to start searching and the number of characters to search.

Common Programming Error 12.2
Mixing up the order of arguments to **String** *methods is a common logic error.*

Common Programming Error 12.3
Be careful when specifying indices to **String** *methods. Specifying values that are off by one number is a common logic error.*

Lines 28, 32 and 36 use method **LastIndexOf** to locate the last occurrence of a character in a **String**. Method **LastIndexOf** performs the search from the end of the **String** toward the beginning of the **String**. If method **LastIndexOf** finds the character, **LastIndexOf** returns the index of the specified character in the **String**; otherwise, **LastIndexOf** returns **–1**. There are three versions of **LastIndexOf** that search for characters in a **String**. The expression in line 28 uses the version of method **LastIndexOf** that takes as an argument the character for which to search. The expression in line 32 uses the version of method **LastIndexOf** that takes two arguments—the character for which to search and the highest index from which to begin searching backward for the character. The expression in line 36 uses a third version of method **LastIndexOf** that takes three arguments—the character for which to search, the starting index from which to start searching backward and the number of characters (the portion of the **String**) to search.

Lines 41–62 use versions of **IndexOf** and **LastIndex Of** that take a **String *** instead of a character as the first argument. These versions of the methods perform identically to those described earlier, except that they search for sequences of characters (or substrings) that are specified by their **String *** arguments.

Lines 69–95 use methods **IndexOfAny** and **LastIndexOfAny**, which take an array of characters as the first argument. These versions of the methods also perform identically to those just described, except that they return the index of the first occurrence of any of the characters in the character array argument.

Common Programming Error 12.4

*In the overloaded methods **LastIndexOf** and **LastIndexOfAny** that take three parameters, the second argument must always be bigger than or equal to the third argument. This might seem counterintuitive, but remember that the search moves from the end of the string toward the start of the string.*

Common Programming Error 12.5

*Remember that **String** methods **IndexOf**, **IndexOfAny**, **LastIndexOf** and **LastIndexOfAny** return **-1** if the specified characters are not found in the **String**. Therefore, do not use the return values from these methods to directly access members of a **String**. In order to avoid an **IndexOutOfRangeException**, always check that the return value is not **-1** first.*

12.8 Extracting Substrings from `Strings`

Class **String** provides two *Substring* methods, which are used to create a new **String** by copying part of an existing **String**. Each method returns a new **String ***. The application in Fig. 12.7 demonstrates the use of both methods.

```
1   // Fig. 12.7: SubString.cpp
2   // Demonstrating the String Substring method.
3
4   #using <mscorlib.dll>
5   #using <system.windows.forms.dll>
6
7   using namespace System;
8   using namespace System::Windows::Forms;
9
10  int __stdcall WinMain()
11  {
12     String *letters = S"abcdefghijklmabcdefghijklm";
13     String *output = S"";
14
15     // invoke Substring method and pass it one parameter
16     output = String::Concat( output,
```

Fig. 12.7   Substrings generated from **String**s. (Part 1 of 2.)

```
17            S"Substring from index 20 to end is \"",
18            letters->Substring( 20 ), S"\"\n" );
19
20        // invoke Substring method and pass it two parameters
21        output = String::Concat( output,
22            S"Substring from index 0 to 6 is \"",
23            letters->Substring( 0, 6 ), S"\"" );
24
25        MessageBox::Show( output,
26            S"Demonstrating String method Substring",
27            MessageBoxButtons::OK, MessageBoxIcon::Information );
28
29        return 0;
30    } // end function WinMain
```

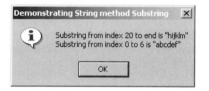

Fig. 12.7 Substrings generated from `String`s. (Part 2 of 2.)

The statement in line 18 uses method **SubString** that takes one **int** argument. The argument specifies the starting index from which the method copies characters in the original **String**. The substring returned contains a copy of the characters from the starting index to the end of the **String**. If the index specified in the argument is outside the bounds of the **String**, the program throws an **ArgumentOutOfRangeException**.

The second version of method **SubString** (line 23) takes two **int** arguments. The first argument specifies the starting index from which the method copies characters from the original **String**. The second argument specifies the length of the substring to be copied. The substring returned contains a copy of the specified characters from the original **String**.

12.9 Concatenating `Strings`

The **static** method *Concat* of class **String** (Fig. 12.8) concatenates two **String**s and returns a new **String *** containing the combined characters from both original **String**s. Line 21 appends the characters from **string2** to the end of **string1**, using method **Concat**. The statement on line 21 does not modify the original **String**s.

```
1    // Fig. 12.8: SubConcatenation.cpp
2    // Demonstrating String class Concat method.
3
4    #using <mscorlib.dll>
5    #using <system.windows.forms.dll>
6
7    using namespace System;
```

Fig. 12.8 `Concat static` method. (Part 1 of 2.)

```
8    using namespace System::Windows::Forms;
9
10   int __stdcall WinMain()
11   {
12      String *string1 = S"Happy ";
13      String *string2 = S"Birthday";
14      String *output;
15
16      output = String::Concat( S"string1 = \"",
17         string1, S"\"\nstring2 = \"", string2, S"\"" );
18
19      output = String::Concat( output, S"\n\nResult of ",
20         S"String::Concat( string1, string2 ) = ",
21         String::Concat( string1, string2 ) );
22
23      output = String::Concat( output, S"\nstring1 after ",
24         S"concatenation = ", string1 );
25
26      MessageBox::Show( output,
27         S"Demonstrating String method Concat",
28         MessageBoxButtons::OK, MessageBoxIcon::Information );
29
30      return 0;
31   } // end function WinMain
```

Fig. 12.8   Concat static method. (Part 2 of 2.)

12.10 Miscellaneous String Methods

Class **String** provides several methods that return modified copies of **String**s. The application in Fig. 12.9 demonstrates the use of these methods, which include **String** methods *Replace*, *ToLower*, *ToUpper*, *Trim* and *ToString*.

```
1    // Fig. 12.9: StringMiscellaneous2.cpp
2    // Demonstrating String methods Replace, ToLower, ToUpper, Trim
3    // and ToString.
4
5    #using <mscorlib.dll>
6    #using <system.windows.forms.dll>
7
```

Fig. 12.9   String methods Replace, ToLower, ToUpper, Trim and
         ToString. (Part 1 of 2.)

```
8    using namespace System;
9    using namespace System::Windows::Forms;
10
11   int __stdcall WinMain()
12   {
13      String *string1 = S"cheers!";
14      String *string2 = S"GOOD BYE ";
15      String *string3 = S"   spaces   ";
16      String *output;
17
18      output = String::Concat( S"string1 = \"", string1,
19         S"\"\n", S"string2 = \"", string2, S"\"\n",
20         S"string3 = \"", string3, S"\"" );
21
22      // call method Replace
23      output = String::Concat( output,
24         S"\n\nReplacing \"e\" with \"E\" in string1: \"",
25         string1->Replace( 'e', 'E' ), S"\"" );
26
27      // call methods ToLower and ToUpper
28      output = String::Concat( output,
29         S"\n\nstring1.ToUpper() = \"", string1->ToUpper(),
30         S"\"\nstring2.ToLower() = \"", string2->ToLower(), S"\"" );
31
32      // call method Trim
33      output = String::Concat( output,
34         S"\n\nstring3 after trim = \"", string3->Trim(), S"\"" );
35
36      // call method ToString
37      output = String::Concat( output, S"\n\nstring1 = \"",
38         string1->ToString(), S"\"" );
39
40      MessageBox::Show( output,
41         S"Demonstrating various String methods",
42         MessageBoxButtons::OK, MessageBoxIcon::Information );
43
44      return 0;
45   } // end function WinMain
```

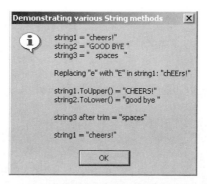

Fig. 12.9 `String` methods `Replace`, `ToLower`, `ToUpper`, `Trim` and `ToString`. (Part 2 of 2.)

Line 25 uses **String** method **Replace** to return a new **String ***, replacing every occurrence in **string1** of character **'e'** with character **'E'**. Method **Replace** takes two arguments—a character for which to search and another character with which to replace all matching occurrences of the first argument. There is another version of method **Replace** that takes **String** pointers instead of characters. The original **String** remains unchanged. If there are no occurrences of the first argument in the **String**, the method returns the original **String**.

String method **ToUpper** generates a new **String** (line 29) that replaces any lowercase letters in **string1** with their uppercase equivalent. The method returns a new **String *** containing the converted **String**; the original **String** remains unchanged. If there are no characters to convert to uppercase, the method returns the original **String ***. Line 30 uses **String** method **ToLower** to return a new **String *** in which any uppercase letters in **string2** are replaced by their lowercase equivalents. The original **String** is unchanged. As with **ToUpper**, if there are no characters to convert to lowercase, method **ToLower** returns the original **String ***.

Line 34 uses **String** method **Trim** to remove all whitespace characters that appear at the beginning and end of a **String**. Without otherwise altering the original **String**, the method returns a new **String *** that contains the **String**, but omits leading or trailing whitespace characters. Another version of method **Trim** takes a character array and returns a **String *** that does not contain the characters in the array argument.

Lines 37–38 use class **String**'s method **ToString** to show that the various other methods employed in this application have not modified **String1**. Why is the **ToString** method provided for class **String**? In MC++, all objects are derived from class **Object**, which defines **virtual** method **ToString**. Thus, method **ToString** can be called to obtain a **String** representation of any object. If a class that inherits from **Object** (such as **String**) does not override method **ToString**, the class uses the default version from class **Object**, which returns a **String *** consisting of the object's class name. Classes usually override method **ToString** to express the contents of an object as text. Class **String** overrides method **ToString** so that, instead of returning the class name, it simply returns the **String ***.

12.11 Class **StringBuilder**

The **String** class provides many capabilities for processing **String**s. However, a **String**'s contents can never change. Operations that seem to concatenate **String**s are in fact assigning **String** pointers to newly created **String**s (e.g., the method **Concat** creates a new **String** and assigns the initial **String** pointer to the newly created **String**).

The next several sections discuss the features of class *StringBuilder* (namespace **System::Text**), used to create and manipulate dynamic string information—i.e., *mutable* strings. Every **StringBuilder** object can store a certain number of characters, specified by its capacity. Exceeding the capacity of a **StringBuilder** causes the capacity to expand to accommodate the additional characters. As we will see, members of class **StringBuilder**, such as methods **Append** and **AppendFormat**, can be used for concatenation like method **Concat** for class **String**.

Software Engineering Observation 12.2

*Objects of class **String** are constant strings, whereas objects of class **StringBuilder** are mutable strings. MC++ can perform certain optimizations involving managed **String**s (such as the sharing of one **String** among multiple pointers), because it knows these objects will not change.*

Performance Tip 12.2

*When given the choice between using a **String** to represent a string and using a **String-Builder** object to represent that string, always use a **String** if the contents of the object will not change. When appropriate, using **String**s instead of **StringBuilder** objects improves performance.*

Class **StringBuilder** provides six overloaded constructors. Application **StringBuilderConstructor** (Fig. 12.10) demonstrates the use of three of these overloaded constructors.

```cpp
1   // Fig. 12.10: StringBuilderConstructor.cpp
2   // Demonstrating StringBuilder class constructors.
3
4   #using <mscorlib.dll>
5   #using <system.windows.forms.dll>
6
7   using namespace System;
8   using namespace System::Windows::Forms;
9   using namespace System::Text;
10
11  int __stdcall WinMain()
12  {
13     StringBuilder *buffer1, *buffer2, *buffer3;
14     String *output;
15
16     buffer1 = new StringBuilder();
17     buffer2 = new StringBuilder( 10 );
18     buffer3 = new StringBuilder( S"hello" );
19
20     output = String::Concat( S"buffer = \"", buffer1, S"\"\n" );
21
22     output = String::Concat( output, S"buffer2 = \"", buffer2,
23        S"\"\n" );
24
25     output = String::Concat( output, S"buffer3 = \"", buffer3,
26        S"\"\n" );
27
28     MessageBox::Show( output,
29        S"Demonstrating StringBuilder class constructors",
30        MessageBoxButtons::OK, MessageBoxIcon::Information );
31
```

Fig. 12.10 StringBuilder class constructors. (Part 1 of 2.)

```
32      return 0;
33  } // end function WinMain
```

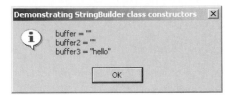

Fig. 12.10 `StringBuilder` class constructors. (Part 2 of 2.)

Line 16 employs the no-argument `StringBuilder` constructor to create a `StringBuilder` that contains no characters and has the default initial capacity (16 characters). Line 17 uses the `StringBuilder` constructor that takes an `int` argument to create a `StringBuilder` that contains no characters and has the initial capacity specified in the `int` argument (i.e., `10`). Line 18 uses the `StringBuilder` constructor that takes a `String *` argument to create a `StringBuilder` containing the characters referenced by the `String *` argument. The initial capacity is the smallest power of two greater than the number of characters in the `String` referenced by the `String *` argument. In this case, the capacity is eight, because eight is the smallest power of two greater than five, the number of characters in the `String "hello"`.

Lines 20–26 append the `StringBuilder`s to the output `String`. Notice that we do not need to use `StringBuilder` method `ToString` to obtain a `String *` representation of the `StringBuilder`s' contents (e.g., `buffer1->ToString`). This is because `String::Concat` can accept `StringBuilder`s as arguments.

12.12 `StringBuilder` `Length` and `Capacity` Properties, and `EnsureCapacity` Method

Class `StringBuilder` provides the *`Length`* and *`Capacity`* properties to return the number of characters currently in a `StringBuilder` and the number of characters that a `StringBuilder` can store without allocating more memory, respectively. These properties can also be used to increase or decrease the length or the capacity of the `StringBuilder`.

Method *`EnsureCapacity`* allows programmers to guarantee that a `StringBuilder` has a capacity that is larger than or equal to a specified value. This method can be helpful in reducing the number of times the capacity must be increased. Method `EnsureCapacity` takes an integer value and, if that value is larger than the `StringBuilder`'s current capacity, doubles the `StringBuilder`'s capacity. If the new capacity is still smaller than that of the argument specified, the `StringBuilder`'s capacity becomes one more than the argument provided. For example, if the current capacity is 17 and we wish to make it 40, 17 multiplied by 2 is not greater than 40, so the call will result in a new capacity of 41. If the current capacity is 23 and we wish to make it 40, 23 will be multiplied by 2 to result in a new capacity of 46. Both 41 and 46 are greater than 40, and so a capacity of 40 is indeed ensured by method **EnsureCapacity**. The program in Fig. 12.11 demonstrates the use of these methods and properties.

Good Programming Practice 12.1

*Accidentally specifying a **Capacity** below the **StringBuilder**'s current **Length** will result in an **ArgumentOutOfRangeException** exception. Always use **EnsureCapacity** to alter the **Capacity** property of a **StringBuilder** object.*

```cpp
1   // Fig. 12.11: StringBuilderFeatures.cpp
2   // Demonstrating some features of class StringBuilder.
3
4   #using <mscorlib.dll>
5   #using <system.windows.forms.dll>
6
7   using namespace System;
8   using namespace System::Windows::Forms;
9   using namespace System::Text;
10
11  int __stdcall WinMain()
12  {
13     StringBuilder *buffer =
14        new StringBuilder( S"Hello, how are you?" );
15
16     // use Length and Capacity properties
17     String *output = String::Concat( S"buffer = ",
18        buffer, S"\nLength = ",
19        buffer->Length.ToString(),
20        S"\nCapacity = ", buffer->Capacity.ToString() );
21
22     // use EnsureCapacity method
23     buffer->EnsureCapacity( 75 );
24
25     output = String::Concat( output, S"\n\nNew capacity = ",
26        buffer->Capacity.ToString() );
27
28     // truncate StringBuilder by setting Length property
29     buffer->Length = 10;
30
31     output = String::Concat( output, S"\n\nNew length = ",
32        buffer->Length.ToString(), S"\nbuffer = " );
33
34     // use StringBuilder indexed property
35     for ( int i = 0; i < buffer->Length; i++ )
36        output = String::Concat( output,
37           buffer->Chars[ i ].ToString() );
38
39     MessageBox::Show( output, S"StringBuilder features",
40        MessageBoxButtons::OK, MessageBoxIcon::Information );
41
42     return 0;
43  } // end function WinMain
```

Fig. 12.11 **StringBuilder** size manipulation. (Part 1 of 2.)

Fig. 12.11 `StringBuilder` size manipulation. (Part 2 of 2.)

The program contains one **StringBuilder**, called **buffer**. Lines 13–14 of the program use the **StringBuilder** constructor that takes a **String *** argument to instantiate the **StringBuilder** and initialize its value to **"Hello, how are you?"**. Lines 17–20 append to **output** the content, length and capacity of the **String-Builder**. In the output window, notice that the capacity of the **StringBuilder** is initially 32. Remember, the **StringBuilder** constructor that takes a **String *** argument creates a **StringBuilder** object with an initial capacity that is the smallest power of two greater than the number of characters in the **String *** passed as an argument.

Line 23 expands the capacity of the **StringBuilder** to a minimum of 75 characters. The current capacity (**32**) multiplied by two is less than 75, so method **Ensure-Capacity** increases the capacity to one greater than 75 (i.e., 76). If new characters are added to a **StringBuilder** so that its length exceeds its capacity, the capacity grows to accommodate the additional characters.

Line 29 uses **Length**'s *set* accessor to set the length of the **StringBuilder** to **10**. If the specified length is less than the current number of characters in the **String-Builder**, the contents of **StringBuilder** are truncated to the specified length (i.e., the program discards all characters in the **StringBuilder** that occur after the specified length). If the specified length is greater than the number of characters currently in the **StringBuilder**, null characters (that signal the end of a **String**) are appended to the **StringBuilder** until the total number of characters in the **StringBuilder** is equal to the specified length. Null characters have the numeric representation **0** and character constant representation **'\0'** (backslash followed by zero).

 Common Programming Error 12.6

*Assigning **NULL** to a **String** pointer can lead to logic errors. The keyword **NULL** is a null pointer, not a **String**. Do not confuse **NULL** with the empty string, **""** (the **String** that is of length 0 and contains no characters).*

12.13 StringBuilder Append and AppendFormat Methods

Class **StringBuilder** provides 19 overloaded *Append* methods that allow various data-type values to be added to the end of a **StringBuilder**. MC++ provides versions for each of the primitive data types and for character arrays, **String** pointers and **Object** pointers. Each of the methods takes an argument, converts it to a **String** and appends it to the **StringBuilder**. Figure 12.12 demonstrates the use of several **Append** methods.

```cpp
1   // Fig. 12.12: StringBuilderAppend.cpp
2   // Demonstrating StringBuilder Append methods.
3
4   #using <mscorlib.dll>
5   #using <system.windows.forms.dll>
6
7   using namespace System;
8   using namespace System::Windows::Forms;
9   using namespace System::Text;
10
11  int __stdcall WinMain()
12  {
13     Object *objectValue = S"hello";
14     String *stringValue = S"goodbye";
15     __wchar_t characterArray __gc[] = { 'a', 'b', 'c',
16        'd', 'e', 'f' };
17
18     bool booleanValue = true;
19     __wchar_t characterValue = 'Z';
20     int integerValue = 7;
21     long longValue = 1000000;
22     float floatValue = 2.5;
23     double doubleValue = 33.333;
24
25     StringBuilder *buffer = new StringBuilder();
26
27     // use method Append to add values to buffer
28     buffer->Append( objectValue );
29     buffer->Append( S"   " );
30     buffer->Append( stringValue );
31     buffer->Append( S"   " );
32     buffer->Append( characterArray );
33     buffer->Append( S"   " );
34     buffer->Append( characterArray, 0, 3 );
35     buffer->Append( S"   " );
36     buffer->Append( booleanValue );
37     buffer->Append( S"   " );
38     buffer->Append( characterValue );
39     buffer->Append( S"   " );
40     buffer->Append( integerValue );
41     buffer->Append( S"   " );
42     buffer->Append( longValue );
43     buffer->Append( S"   " );
44     buffer->Append( floatValue );
45     buffer->Append( S"   " );
46     buffer->Append( doubleValue );
47     buffer->Append( S"   " );
48
49     MessageBox::Show( String::Concat( S"buffer = ", buffer ),
50        S"Demonstrating StringBuilder Append method",
51        MessageBoxButtons::OK, MessageBoxIcon::Information );
52
```

Fig. 12.12 Append methods of **StringBuilder**. (Part 1 of 2.)

```
53        return 0;
54    } // end function WinMain
```

Fig. 12.12 Append methods of **StringBuilder**. (Part 2 of 2.)

Lines 28–47 use 10 different overloaded **Append** methods to attach the objects created in lines 13–23 to the end of the **StringBuilder**. **Append** behaves similarly to the **Concat** method, which is used with **String**s. Just as **Concat** seems to append objects to a **String**, method **Append** can append data types to a **StringBuilder**'s underlying string.

Class **StringBuilder** also provides method *AppendFormat*, which converts a **String** to a specified format and then appends it to the **StringBuilder**. The example in Fig. 12.13 demonstrates the use of this method.

```cpp
1    // Fig. 12.13: StringBuilderAppendFormat.cpp
2    // Demonstrating method AppendFormat.
3
4    #using <mscorlib.dll>
5    #using <system.windows.forms.dll>
6
7    using namespace System;
8    using namespace System::Windows::Forms;
9    using namespace System::Text;
10
11   int __stdcall WinMain()
12   {
13      StringBuilder *buffer = new StringBuilder();
14      String *string1, *string2;
15
16      // formatted string
17      string1 = S"This {0} costs: {1:C}.\n";
18
19      // string1 argument array
20      Object *objectArray[] = new Object*[ 2 ];
21
22      objectArray[ 0 ] = S"car";
23      objectArray[ 1 ] = __box( 1234.56 );
24
25      // append to buffer formatted string with argument
26      buffer->AppendFormat( string1, objectArray );
27
28      // formatted string
```

Fig. 12.13 **StringBuilder**'s **AppendFormat** method. (Part 1 of 2.)

```
29       string2 = String::Concat( S"Number: {0:d3}.\n",
30          S"Number right aligned with spaces:{0, 4}.\n",
31          S"Number left aligned with spaces:{0, -4}." );
32
33       // append to buffer formatted string with argument
34       buffer->AppendFormat( string2, __box( 5 ) );
35
36       // display formatted strings
37       MessageBox::Show( buffer->ToString(), S"Using AppendFormat",
38          MessageBoxButtons::OK, MessageBoxIcon::Information );
39
40       return 0;
41  } // end function WinMain
```

Fig. 12.13 `StringBuilder`'s `AppendFormat` method. (Part 2 of 2.)

Line 17 creates a **String *** that contains formatting information. The information enclosed within the braces determines how to format a specific piece of information. Formats have the form **{X[,Y][:FormatString]}**, where **X** is the number of the argument to be formatted, counting from zero. **Y** is an optional argument, which can be positive or negative, indicating how many characters should be in the result of formatting. If the resulting **String** is less than the number **Y**, the **String** will be padded with spaces to make up for the difference. A positive integer aligns the **String** to the right; a negative integer aligns it to the left. The optional **FormatString** applies a particular format to the argument (e.g., currency, decimal, scientific, etc.), "**{0}**" means the first argument will be printed out. "**{1:C}**" specifies that the second argument will be formatted as a currency value.

Line 20 creates array **objectArray**, and lines 22–23 insert two items into the **Object** array. Notice that line 23 must first use MC++ keyword **__box** to convert the value type (**1234.56**) to a managed **Object**. Refer to Chapter 9, Graphical User Interface Concepts: Part 1, for a discussion of keyword **__box**.

Line 26 shows a version of **AppendFormat**, which takes two parameters—a **String *** specifying the format and an array of objects to serve as the arguments to the format **String**. The argument indicated by "**{0}**" is in the object array at index **0**, and so on.

Lines 29–31 define another **String *** used for formatting. The first format "**{0:D3}**" specifies that the first argument will be formatted as a three-digit decimal, meaning any number that has fewer than three digits will have leading zeros placed in front to make up the difference. The next format "**{0, 4}**" specifies that the formatted **String** should have four characters and should be right aligned. The third format "**{0, -4}**" specifies that the **String**s should be aligned to the left. For more formatting options, please refer to the documentation.

Line 34 uses a version of **AppendFormat** that takes two parameters: a **String *** containing a format and an object to which the format is applied. In this case, the object is the number **5**. The output of Fig. 12.13 displays the result of applying these two versions of **AppendFormat** with their respective arguments.

12.14 `StringBuilder` Insert, Remove and Replace Methods

Class **StringBuilder** provides 18 overloaded *Insert* methods to allow various data-type values to be inserted at any position in a **StringBuilder**. The class provides versions for each of the primitive data types and for character arrays, **String** pointers and **Object** pointers. Each version of **Insert** takes its second argument, converts it to a **String** and inserts the **String** into the **StringBuilder** in front of the index specified by the first argument. The index specified by the first argument must be greater than or equal to **0** and less than the length of the **StringBuilder**; otherwise, the program throws an **ArgumentOutOfRangeException**.

Class **StringBuilder** also provides method *Remove* for deleting any portion of a **StringBuilder**. Method **Remove** takes two arguments—the index at which to begin deletion and the number of characters to delete. The sum of the starting subscript and the number of characters to be deleted must always be less than the length of the **String-Builder**; otherwise, the program throws an **ArgumentOutOfRangeException**. The **Insert** and **Remove** methods are demonstrated in Fig. 12.14.

Another useful method included with **StringBuilder** is *Replace*, which searches for a specified **String** or character and substitutes another **String** or character in its place. Figure 12.15 demonstrates this method.

```cpp
1   // Fig. 12.14: StringBuilderInsertRemove.cpp
2   // Demonstrating methods Insert and Remove of the
3   // StringBuilder class.
4
5   #using <mscorlib.dll>
6   #using <system.windows.forms.dll>
7
8   using namespace System;
9   using namespace System::Windows::Forms;
10  using namespace System::Text;
11
12  int __stdcall WinMain()
13  {
14      Object *objectValue = S"hello";
15      String *stringValue = S"good bye";
16      __wchar_t characterArray __gc[] = { 'a', 'b', 'c',
17          'd', 'e', 'f' };
18
19      bool booleanValue = true;
20      __wchar_t characterValue = 'K';
```

Fig. 12.14 `StringBuilder` text insertion and removal. (Part 1 of 2.)

```
21          int integerValue = 7;
22          long longValue = 10000000;
23          float floatValue = 2.5;
24          double doubleValue = 46.789;
25
26          StringBuilder *buffer = new StringBuilder();
27          String *output;
28
29          // insert value into buffer
30          buffer->Insert( 0, objectValue );
31          buffer->Insert( 0, "  " );
32          buffer->Insert( 0, stringValue );
33          buffer->Insert( 0, "  " );
34          buffer->Insert( 0, characterArray );
35          buffer->Insert( 0, "  " );
36          buffer->Insert( 0, booleanValue );
37          buffer->Insert( 0, "  " );
38          buffer->Insert( 0, characterValue );
39          buffer->Insert( 0, "  " );
40          buffer->Insert( 0, integerValue );
41          buffer->Insert( 0, "  " );
42          buffer->Insert( 0, longValue );
43          buffer->Insert( 0, "  " );
44          buffer->Insert( 0, floatValue );
45          buffer->Insert( 0, "  " );
46          buffer->Insert( 0, doubleValue );
47          buffer->Insert( 0, "  " );
48
49          output = String::Concat( S"buffer after inserts: \n",
50             buffer, S"\n\n" );
51
52          buffer->Remove( 10, 1 );  // delete 2 in 2.5
53          buffer->Remove( 2, 4 );   // delete 46.7 in 46.789
54
55          output = String::Concat( output,
56             S"buffer after Removes:\n", buffer );
57
58          MessageBox::Show( output, String::Concat(
59             S"Demonstrating StringBuilder Insert and Remove ",
60             S"methods" ), MessageBoxButtons::OK,
61             MessageBoxIcon::Information );
62
63       return 0;
64    } // end function WinMain
```

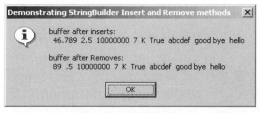

Fig. 12.14 StringBuilder text insertion and removal. (Part 2 of 2.)

```cpp
1   // Fig. 12.15: StringBuilderReplace.cpp
2   // Demonstrating method Replace.
3
4   #using <mscorlib.dll>
5   #using <system.windows.forms.dll>
6
7   using namespace System;
8   using namespace System::Windows::Forms;
9   using namespace System::Text;
10
11  int __stdcall WinMain()
12  {
13     StringBuilder *builder1 =
14        new StringBuilder( S"Happy Birthday Jane" );
15
16     StringBuilder *builder2 = new StringBuilder( S"goodbye greg" );
17
18     String *output = String::Concat( S"Before replacements:\n",
19        builder1, S"\n", builder2 );
20
21     builder1->Replace( S"Jane", S"Greg" );
22     builder2->Replace( 'g', 'G', 0, 5 );
23
24     output = String::Concat( output, S"\n\nAfter replacements:\n",
25        builder1, S"\n", builder2 );
26
27     MessageBox::Show( output,
28        S"Using StringBuilder method Replace",
29        MessageBoxButtons::OK, MessageBoxIcon::Information );
30
31     return 0;
32  } // end function WinMain
```

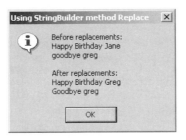

Fig. 12.15 `StringBuilder` text replacement.

Line 21 uses method **Replace** to replace all instances of the **String "Jane"** with the **String "Greg"** in **builder1**. Another overload of this method takes two characters as parameters and replaces each occurrence of the first with one of the second. Line 22 uses an overload of **Replace** that takes four parameters, the first two of which are characters and the second two of which are **int**s. The method replaces all instances of the first character with the second, beginning at the index specified by the first **int** and continuing for a count specified by the second. Thus, in this case, **Replace** looks through only five characters starting with the character at index **0**. As the outputs illustrates, this version of

Replace replaces **g** with **G** in the word **"goodbye"**, but not in **"greg"**. This is because the **g**s in **"greg"** do not fall in the range indicated by the **int** arguments (i.e., between indexes **0** and **4**).

12.15 Char Methods

MC++ provides a data type, called a *structure*, that is similar to a class. Like classes, structures include methods and properties. Both use the same modifiers (such as **public**, **private** and **protected**) and access members via the member access operator (**.**), the arrow member access operator (**->**) and the scope resolution operator (**::**). However, the default access specifier for classes is **private**, while the default access specifier for structures is **public**. Classes are created by using the keyword **class**, but structures are created using the keyword *struct*.

As discussed earlier in the book, many of the primitive data types that we have used in this book are actually aliases for different structures. For instance, in MC++, an **int** is defined by structure **System::Int32**, a **bool** by **System::Boolean**, and so on. These structures are derived from class *ValueType*, which in turn is derived from class **Object**. In this section, we present structure *Char*, which is the structure for characters. Recall that in MC++, **__wchar_t** is an alias for **Char**.

Most **Char** methods are **static**, take at least one character argument and perform either a test or a manipulation on the character. We present several of these methods in the next example. Figures 12.16–12.18 demonstrate **static** methods that test characters to determine whether they are of a specific character type and **static** methods that perform case conversions on characters.

```
1   // Fig. 12.16: StaticCharMethods.h
2   // Demonstrating static character testing methods
3   // from Char structure.
4
5   #pragma once
6
7   #using <system.dll>
8   #using <mscorlib.dll>
9   #using <system.drawing.dll>
10  #using <system.windows.forms.dll>
11
12  using namespace System;
13  using namespace System::Drawing;
14  using namespace System::Collections;
15  using namespace System::Windows::Forms;
16
17  public __gc class StaticCharMethods : public Form
18  {
19  public:
20     StaticCharMethods();
21
22  private:
23     Label *enterLabel;
```

Fig. 12.16 **Char**'s **static** character-testing methods and case-conversion methods. (Part 1 of 2.)

```
24       Button *analyzeButton;
25       TextBox *inputTextBox, *outputTextBox;
26
27       void InitializeComponent();
28       void analyzeButton_Click( Object *, EventArgs * );
29       void BuildOutput( __wchar_t );
30    }; // end class StaticCharMethods
```

Fig. 12.16 Char's static character-testing methods and case-conversion methods. (Part 2 of 2.)

```
1     // Fig. 12.17: StaticCharMethods.cpp
2     // Method definitions for class StaticCharMethods.
3
4     #include "StaticCharMethods.h"
5
6     StaticCharMethods::StaticCharMethods()
7     {
8        InitializeComponent();
9     }
10
11    void StaticCharMethods::InitializeComponent()
12    {
13       this->enterLabel = new Label();
14       this->inputTextBox = new TextBox();
15       this->analyzeButton = new Button();
16       this->outputTextBox = new TextBox();
17       this->SuspendLayout();
18
19       // enterLabel
20       this->enterLabel->Font = new Drawing::Font(
21          S"Microsoft Sans Serif", 9.75, FontStyle::Regular,
22          GraphicsUnit::Point, 0 );
23       this->enterLabel->Location = Point( 16, 16 );
24       this->enterLabel->Name = S"enterLabel";
25       this->enterLabel->Size = Drawing::Size( 120, 23 );
26       this->enterLabel->TabIndex = 0;
27       this->enterLabel->Text = S"Enter a character:";
28       this->enterLabel->TextAlign = ContentAlignment::MiddleLeft;
29
30       // inputTextBox
31       this->inputTextBox->Font = new Drawing::Font(
32          S"Microsoft Sans Serif", 9.75, FontStyle::Regular,
33          GraphicsUnit::Point, 0 );
34       this->inputTextBox->Location = Point( 144, 16 );
35       this->inputTextBox->MaxLength = 1;
36       this->inputTextBox->Name = S"inputTextBox";
37       this->inputTextBox->Size = Drawing::Size( 56, 24 );
38       this->inputTextBox->TabIndex = 1;
39       this->inputTextBox->Text = S"";
40
41       // analyzeButton
```

Fig. 12.17 StaticCharMethods class method definitions. (Part 1 of 3.)

```
42      this->analyzeButton->Location = Point( 40, 64 );
43      this->analyzeButton->Name = S"analyzeButton";
44      this->analyzeButton->Size = Drawing::Size( 136, 24 );
45      this->analyzeButton->TabIndex = 2;
46      this->analyzeButton->Text = S"Analyze Character";
47      this->analyzeButton->Click += new EventHandler( this,
48         analyzeButton_Click );
49
50      // outputTextBox
51      this->outputTextBox->Font = new Drawing::Font(
52         S"Microsoft Sans Serif", 9, FontStyle::Regular,
53         GraphicsUnit::Point, 0 );
54      this->outputTextBox->Location = Point( 24, 112 );
55      this->outputTextBox->Multiline = true;
56      this->outputTextBox->Name = S"outputTextBox";
57      this->outputTextBox->Size = Drawing::Size( 168, 152 );
58      this->outputTextBox->TabIndex = 3;
59      this->outputTextBox->Text = S"";
60
61      // StaticCharMethods
62      this->AutoScaleBaseSize = Drawing::Size( 5, 13 );
63      this->ClientSize = Drawing::Size( 224, 277 );
64      Control *control[] = { this->outputTextBox,
65         this->analyzeButton, this->inputTextBox,
66         this->enterLabel };
67      this->Controls->AddRange( control );
68      this->Name = S"StaticCharMethods";
69      this->Text = S"Static Character Methods";
70      this->ResumeLayout();
71   } // end method InitializeComponent
72
73   // handle analyzeButton_Click
74   void StaticCharMethods::analyzeButton_Click( Object *sender,
75      EventArgs *e )
76   {
77      __wchar_t character = Convert::ToChar( inputTextBox->Text );
78      BuildOutput( character );
79   } // end method analyzeButton_Click
80
81   // display character information in outputTextBox
82   void StaticCharMethods::BuildOutput( __wchar_t inputCharacter )
83   {
84      String *output;
85
86      output = String::Concat( S"is digit: ",
87         Char::IsDigit( inputCharacter ).ToString(), S"\r\n" );
88
89      output = String::Concat( output, S"is letter: ",
90         Char::IsLetter( inputCharacter ).ToString(), S"\r\n" );
91
92      output = String::Concat( output, S"is letter or digit: ",
93         Char::IsLetterOrDigit( inputCharacter ).ToString(),
94         S"\r\n" );
```

Fig. 12.17 `StaticCharMethods` class method definitions. (Part 2 of 3.)

```
95
96         output = String::Concat( output, S"is lower case: ",
97            Char::IsLower( inputCharacter ).ToString(), S"\r\n" );
98
99         output = String::Concat( output, S"is upper case: ",
100           Char::IsUpper( inputCharacter ).ToString(), S"\r\n" );
101
102        output = String::Concat( output, S"to upper case: ",
103           Char::ToUpper( inputCharacter ).ToString(), S"\r\n" );
104
105        output = String::Concat( output, S"to lower case: ",
106           Char::ToLower( inputCharacter ).ToString(), S"\r\n" );
107
108        output = String::Concat( output, S"is punctuation: ",
109           Char::IsPunctuation( inputCharacter ).ToString(),
110           S"\r\n" );
111
112        output = String::Concat( output, S"is symbol: ",
113           Char::IsSymbol( inputCharacter ).ToString() );
114
115        outputTextBox->Text = output;
116 } // end method BuildOutput
```

Fig. 12.17 StaticCharMethods class method definitions. (Part 3 of 3.)

```
1  // Fig. 12.18: CharMethodsTest.cpp
2  // Demonstrates Char methods.
3
4  #include "StaticCharMethods.h"
5
6  int __stdcall WinMain()
7  {
8     Application::Run( new StaticCharMethods() );
9
10    return 0;
11 } // end function WinMain
```

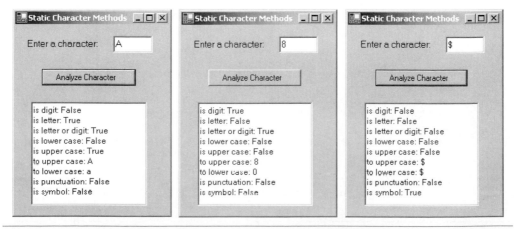

Fig. 12.18 CharMethodsTest demonstrates **Char** methods.

This Windows application contains a prompt, a **TextBox** into which the user can input a character, a button that the user can press after entering a character and a second **TextBox** that displays the output of our analysis. When the user clicks the **Analyze Character** button, event handler **analyzeButton_Click** (lines 74–79 of Fig. 12.17) is invoked. This method converts the entered data from a **String *** to a **Char**, using method **Convert::ToChar** (line 77). Line 78 calls method **BuildOutput**, which is defined in lines 82–116.

Line 87 uses **Char** method *IsDigit* to determine whether character **inputCharacter** is defined as a digit. If so, the method returns **true**; otherwise, it returns **false**. Line 90 uses **Char** method *IsLetter* to determine whether character **inputCharacter** is a letter. If so, the method returns **true**; otherwise, it returns **false**. Line 93 uses **Char** method *IsLetterOrDigit* to determine whether character **inputCharacter** is a letter or a digit. If so, the method returns **true**; otherwise, it returns **false**. Line 97 uses **Char** method *IsLower* to determine whether character **inputCharacter** is a lowercase letter. If so, the method returns **true**; otherwise, it returns **false**. Line 100 uses **Char** method *IsUpper* to determine whether character **inputCharacter** is an uppercase letter. If so, the method returns **true**; otherwise, it returns **false**. Line 103 uses **Char** method *ToUpper* to convert the character **inputCharacter** to its uppercase equivalent. The method returns the converted character if the character has an uppercase equivalent; otherwise, the method returns its original argument. Line 106 uses **Char** method *ToLower* to convert the character **inputCharacter** to its lowercase equivalent. The method returns the converted character if the character has a lowercase equivalent; otherwise, the method returns its original argument. Line 109 uses **Char** method *IsPunctuation* to determine whether character **inputCharacter** is a punctuation mark. If so, the method returns **true**; otherwise, it returns **false**. Line 113 uses **Char** method *IsSymbol* to determine whether character **inputCharacter** is a symbol. If so, the method returns **true**; otherwise it returns **false**.

Structure **Char** also contains other methods not shown in this example. Many of the **static** methods are similar; for instance, *IsWhiteSpace* is used to determine whether a certain character is a whitespace character (e.g., newline, tab or space). The structure also contains several **public** instance methods; many of these, such as methods **ToString** and **Equals**, are methods that we have seen before in other classes. This group includes method *CompareTo*, which is used to compare two character values with one another.

12.16 Card Shuffling and Dealing Simulation

In this section, we use random-number generation to develop a program that simulates the shuffling and dealing of cards. Once created, this program can be implemented in other applications that imitate specific card games.

Class **Card** (Fig. 12.19–Fig. 12.20) contains two **String *** instance variables— **face** and **suit**—that store the face name and suit name of a specific card. The constructor for the class receives two **String** pointers that it uses to initialize **face** and **suit**. Method **ToString** (lines 13–16 of Fig. 12.20) creates a **String *** consisting of the **face** of the card and the **suit** of the card.

```
1    // Fig. 12.19: Card.h
2    // Stores suit and face information of each card.
3
4    #pragma once
5
6    #using <mscorlib.dll>
7    #using <system.dll>
8
9    using namespace System;
10
11   // representation of a card
12   public __gc class Card
13   {
14   public:
15      Card( String *, String * );
16      String *ToString();
17
18   private:
19      String *face, *suit;
20   }; // end class Card
```

Fig. 12.19 Card class stores suit and face information.

```
1    // Fig. 12.20: Card.cpp
2    // Method definitions for class Card.
3
4    #include "Card.h"
5
6    Card::Card( String *faceValue, String *suitValue )
7    {
8       face = faceValue;
9       suit = suitValue;
10   }
11
12   // override ToString
13   String *Card::ToString()
14   {
15      return String::Concat( face, S" of ", suit );
16   } // end method ToString
```

Fig. 12.20 Card class method definitions.

We develop application **DeckForm** (Fig. 12.21–Fig. 12.22), which creates a deck of 52 playing cards, using **Card** objects. Users can deal each card by clicking the **Deal Card** button. Each dealt card is displayed in a **Label**. Users can also shuffle the deck at any time by clicking the **Shuffle Cards** button.

```
1    // Fig. 12.21: DeckOfCards.h
2    // Simulates card drawing and shuffling.
3
4    #pragma once
```

Fig. 12.21 DeckForm class simulates card drawing and shuffling. (Part 1 of 2.)

```
5
6   #using <system.dll>
7   #using <system.drawing.dll>
8   #using <system.windows.forms.dll>
9
10  using namespace System::Drawing;
11  using namespace System::Windows::Forms;
12
13  #include <tchar.h>
14  #include "Card.h"
15
16  // provides functionality for the form
17  public __gc class DeckForm : public Form
18  {
19  public:
20     DeckForm();
21
22  private:
23     Button *dealButton, *shuffleButton;
24     Label *displayLabel, *statusLabel;
25
26     static Card *deck[] = new Card *[ 52 ];
27     int currentCard;
28
29     void InitializeComponent();
30     void Shuffle();
31     Card *DealCard();
32     void DeckForm_Load( Object *, EventArgs * );
33     void dealButton_Click( Object *, EventArgs * );
34     void shuffleButton_Click( Object *, EventArgs * );
35  }; // end class DeckForm
```

Fig. 12.21 DeckForm class simulates card drawing and shuffling. (Part 2 of 2.)

```
1   // Fig. 12.22: DeckOfCards.cpp
2   // Method definitions for class DeckForm.
3
4   #include "DeckOfCards.h"
5
6   DeckForm::DeckForm()
7   {
8      InitializeComponent();
9   }
10
11  void DeckForm::InitializeComponent()
12  {
13     this->dealButton = new Button();
14     this->shuffleButton = new Button();
15     this->displayLabel = new Label();
16     this->statusLabel = new Label();
17     this->SuspendLayout();
18
```

Fig. 12.22 DeckForm class method definitions. (Part 1 of 4.)

```
19        // dealButton
20        this->dealButton->Font = new Drawing::Font(
21           S"Microsoft Sans Serif", 11.25, FontStyle::Regular,
22           GraphicsUnit::Point, 0 );
23        this->dealButton->Location = Point( 48, 24 );
24        this->dealButton->Name = S"dealButton";
25        this->dealButton->Size = Drawing::Size( 120, 56 );
26        this->dealButton->TabIndex = 0;
27        this->dealButton->Text = S"Deal Card";
28        this->dealButton->Click += new EventHandler( this,
29           this->dealButton_Click );
30
31        // shuffleButton
32        this->shuffleButton->Font = new Drawing::Font(
33           S"Microsoft Sans Serif", 11.25, FontStyle::Regular,
34           GraphicsUnit::Point, 0 );
35        this->shuffleButton->Location = Point( 248, 24 );
36        this->shuffleButton->Name = S"shuffleButton";
37        this->shuffleButton->Size = Drawing::Size( 120, 56 );
38        this->shuffleButton->TabIndex = 1;
39        this->shuffleButton->Text = S"Shuffle Cards";
40        this->shuffleButton->Click += new EventHandler( this,
41           this->shuffleButton_Click );
42
43        // displayLabel
44        this->displayLabel->BorderStyle = BorderStyle::Fixed3D;
45        this->displayLabel->Location = Point( 112, 96 );
46        this->displayLabel->Name = S"displayLabel";
47        this->displayLabel->Size = Drawing::Size( 168, 24 );
48        this->displayLabel->TabIndex = 2;
49        this->displayLabel->TextAlign =
50           ContentAlignment::MiddleCenter;
51
52        // statusLabel
53        this->statusLabel->BorderStyle = BorderStyle::Fixed3D;
54        this->statusLabel->Location = Point( 128, 144 );
55        this->statusLabel->Name = S"statusLabel";
56        this->statusLabel->Size = Drawing::Size( 136, 24 );
57        this->statusLabel->TabIndex = 3;
58        this->statusLabel->TextAlign = ContentAlignment::MiddleCenter;
59
60        // DeckForm
61        this->AutoScaleBaseSize = Drawing::Size( 5, 13 );
62        this->ClientSize = Drawing::Size( 408, 181 );
63        Control *control[] = { this->statusLabel, this->displayLabel,
64           this->shuffleButton, this->dealButton };
65        this->Controls->AddRange( control );
66        this->Name = "DeckForm";
67        this->Text = "Card Dealing Program";
68        this->Load += new EventHandler( this, this->DeckForm_Load );
69        this->ResumeLayout();
70     } // end method InitializeComponent
71
```

Fig. 12.22 DeckForm class method definitions. (Part 2 of 4.)

```
72    // handles form at load time
73    void DeckForm::DeckForm_Load( Object *sender, EventArgs *e )
74    {
75       String *faces[] = { S"Ace", S"Deuce", S"Three", S"Four",
76          S"Five", S"Six", S"Seven", S"Eight", S"Nine", S"Ten",
77          S"Jack", S"Queen", S"King" };
78
79       String *suits[] = { S"Hearts", S"Diamonds", S"Clubs",
80          S"Spades" };
81
82       // no cards have been drawn
83       currentCard = -1;
84
85       // initialize deck
86       for ( int i = 0; i < deck.Length; i++ )
87          deck[ i ] = new Card( faces[ i % 13 ], suits[ i % 4 ] );
88    } // end method DeckForm_Load
89
90    // handles dealButton_Click
91    void DeckForm::dealButton_Click( Object *sender, EventArgs *e )
92    {
93       Card *dealt = DealCard();
94
95       // if dealt card is null, then no cards left
96       // player must shuffle cards
97       if ( dealt != NULL ) {
98          displayLabel->Text = dealt->ToString();
99          statusLabel->Text = String::Concat( S"Card #: ",
100            currentCard.ToString() );
101      }
102      else {
103         displayLabel->Text = S"NO MORE CARDS TO DEAL";
104         statusLabel->Text = S"Shuffle cards to continue";
105      }
106   } // end method dealButton_Click
107
108   // shuffle cards
109   void DeckForm::Shuffle()
110   {
111      Random *randomNumber = new Random();
112      Card *temporaryValue;
113
114      currentCard = -1;
115
116      // swap each card with random card
117      for ( int i = 0; i < deck.Length; i++ ) {
118         int j = randomNumber->Next( 52 );
119
120         // swap cards
121         temporaryValue = deck[ i ];
122         deck[ i ] = deck[ j ];
123         deck[ j ] = temporaryValue;
124      }
```

Fig. 12.22 DeckForm class method definitions. (Part 3 of 4.)

```
125
126     dealButton->Enabled = true;
127  } // end method Shuffle
128
129  // deal the cards
130  Card *DeckForm::DealCard()
131  {
132
133     // if there is a card to deal, then deal it;
134     // otherwise, signal that cards need to be shuffled by
135     // disabling dealButton and returning null
136     if ( currentCard + 1 < deck.Length ) {
137        currentCard++;
138        return deck[ currentCard ];
139     }
140     else {
141        dealButton->Enabled = false;
142        return NULL;
143     }
144  } // end method DealCard
145
146  // handles shuffleButton_Click
147  void DeckForm::shuffleButton_Click( Object *sender, EventArgs *e )
148  {
149     displayLabel->Text = S"SHUFFLING...";
150     Shuffle();
151     displayLabel->Text = S"DECK IS SHUFFLED";
152     statusLabel->Text = S"";
153  } // end method shuffleButton_Click
```

Fig. 12.22 DeckForm class method definitions. (Part 4 of 4.)

Method **DeckForm_Load** (lines 73–88 of Fig. 12.22) uses the **for** structure (lines 86–87) to fill the **deck** array with **Card**s. Note that each **Card** is instantiated and initialized with two **String** pointers—one from the **faces** array (**"Ace"** through **"King"**) and one from the **suits** array (**"Hearts"**, **"Diamonds"**, **"Clubs"** or **"Spades"**). The calculation **i % 13** always results in a value from **0** to **12** (the thirteen subscripts of the **faces** array), and the calculation **i % 4** always results in a value from **0** to **3** (the four subscripts in the **suits** array). The initialized **deck** array contains the cards with faces ace through king for each suit.

When users click the **Deal Card** button, event handler **dealButton_Click** (lines 91–106) invokes method **DealCard** (defined in lines 130–144) to get the next card in the **deck** array. If the deck is not empty, the method returns a **Card** object pointer; otherwise, it returns **NULL**. If the pointer is not **NULL**, lines 98–100 display the **Card** in **display-Label** and display the card number in the **statusLabel**.

If **DealCard** returns a **NULL** pointer, the **String "NO MORE CARDS TO DEAL"** is displayed in **displayLabel**, and the **String "Shuffle cards to continue"** is displayed in **statusLabel** (lines 103–104).

When users click the **Shuffle Cards** button, its event-handling method **shuffleButton_Click** (lines 147–153) invokes method **Shuffle** (defined on lines 109–127) to shuffle the cards. The method loops through all 52 cards (array subscripts 0–

51). For each card, the method randomly picks a number between **0** and **51**. Then the current **Card** object and the randomly selected **Card** object are swapped in the array. To shuffle the cards, method **Shuffle** makes a total of only 52 swaps during a single pass of the entire array. When the shuffling is complete, **displayLabel** displays the **String** **"DECK IS SHUFFLED"**. Figure 12.23 executes the application.

```cpp
1   // Fig. 12.23: DeckOfCardsTest.cpp
2   // Demonstrates card-shuffling program.
3
4   #include "DeckOfCards.h"
5
6   int __stdcall WinMain()
7   {
8      Application::Run( new DeckForm() );
9
10     return 0;
11  } // end function WinMain
```

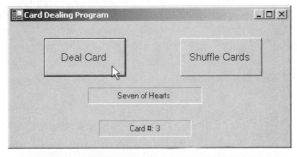

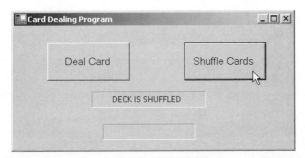

Fig. 12.23 DeckOfCardsTest demonstrates card-shuffling program. (Part 1 of 2.)

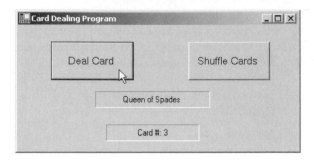

Fig. 12.23 `DeckOfCardsTest` demonstrates card-shuffling program. (Part 2 of 2.)

12.17 Regular Expressions and Class `Regex`

Regular expressions are specially formatted `String`s used to find patterns in text and can be useful during information validation, to ensure that data are in a particular format. For example, a ZIP code must consist of five digits, and a last name must start with a capital letter. One application of regular expressions is to facilitate the construction of a compiler. Often, a large and complex regular expression is used to validate the syntax of a program. If the program code does not match the regular expression, the compiler knows that there is a syntax error within the code.

The .NET Framework provides several classes to help developers recognize and manipulate regular expressions. Class *`Regex`* (`System::Text::RegularExpressions` namespace) represents an immutable regular expression. It contains static methods that allow use of the `Regex` class without explicitly instantiating objects of that class. Class *`Match`* represents the results of a regular expression matching operation.

Class `Regex` provides method *`Match`*, which returns an object of class `Match` that represents a single regular expression match. `Regex` also provides method *`Matches`*, which finds all matches of a regular expression in an arbitrary `String` and returns a *`MatchCollection`* object—i.e., a set of `Match`es.

 Common Programming Error 12.7

When using regular expressions, do not confuse class `Match` *with the method* `Match`*, which belongs to class* `Regex`*.*

The table in Fig. 12.24 specifies some *character classes* that can be used with regular expressions. A character class is an escape sequence that represents a group of characters.

Character	Matches	Character	Matches
\d	any digit	\D	any non-digit
\w	any word character	\W	any non-word character
\s	any whitespace	\S	any non-whitespace

Fig. 12.24 Character classes.

Common Programming Error 12.8

Be sure to use the correct case when specifying a character class. Mixing up the case of character classes will cause a search for the exact opposite of what you are trying to find.

A *word character* cause a any alphanumeric character or underscore. A *whitespace* character is a space, a tab, a carriage return, a newline or a form feed. A *digit* is any numeric character. Regular expressions are not limited to these character classes, however. The expressions employ various operators and other forms of notation to search for complex patterns. We discuss several of these techniques in the context of the next few examples.

Figure 12.25 presents a simple example that employs regular expressions. This program takes birthdays and tries to match them to a regular expression. The expression matches only birthdays that do not occur in April and that belong to people whose names begin with **"J"**.

```cpp
1   // Fig. 12.25: RegexMatches.cpp
2   // Demonstrating Class Regex.
3
4   #using <mscorlib.dll>
5   #using <system.dll>
6   #using <system.windows.forms.dll>
7
8   using namespace System;
9   using namespace System::Windows::Forms;
10  using namespace System::Text::RegularExpressions;
11
12  int __stdcall WinMain()
13  {
14      String *output = "";
15
16      // create regular expression
17      Regex *expression =
18          new Regex( S"(J.*\\d[0-35-9]-\\d\\d-\\d\\d)" );
19
20      String *string1 = String::Concat(
21          S"Jane's Birthday is 05-12-75\n",
22          S"Dave's Birthday is 11-04-68\n",
23          S"John's Birthday is 04-28-73\n",
24          S"Joe's Birthday is 12-17-77" );
25
26      // declare an object of Match
27      Match *myMatch = 0;
28
29      // match regular expression to string and
30      // print out all matches
31      for ( int i = 0; i < expression->Matches( string1 )->Count;
32          i++ ) {
33          myMatch = expression->Matches( string1 )->Item[ i ];
34          output = String::Concat( output, myMatch->ToString(),
35              S"\n" );
36      }
37
38      MessageBox::Show( output, S"Using class Regex",
```

Fig. 12.25 Regular expressions used to check birthdays. (Part 1 of 2.)

```
39          MessageBoxButtons::OK, MessageBoxIcon::Information );
40
41      return 0;
42  } // end function WinMain
```

Fig. 12.25 Regular expressions used to check birthdays. (Part 2 of 2.)

Lines 17–18 create an instance of class **Regex** and defines the regular expression pattern for which **Regex** will search. The first character in the regular expression, **"J"**, is treated as a literal character. This means that any **String** matching this regular expression is required to start with **"J"**.

In a regular expression, the dot character **"."** matches any single character except a newline character. However, when the dot character is followed by an asterisk, as in the expression **".*"**, it matches any number of unspecified characters. In general, when the operator **"*"** is applied to any expression, the expression will match zero or more occurrences of the expression. By contrast, the application of the operator **"+"** to an expression causes the expression to match one or more occurrences of that expression. For example, both **"A*"** and **"A+"** will match **"A"**, but only **"A*"** will match an empty **String**.

As indicated in Fig. 12.24, **"\d"** matches any numeric digit. Notice that to specify character classes in the **String *** passed to the **Regex** constructor, we must precede each class (e.g., \d) with the escape character (\). To specify sets of characters other than those that have a character class, characters can be listed in square brackets, **[]**. For example, the pattern **"[aeiou]"** can be used to match any vowel. Ranges of characters can be represented by placing a dash (-) between two characters. In the example, **"[0-35-9]"** matches only digits in the ranges specified by the pattern. In this case, the pattern matches any digit between **0** and **3** or between **5** and **9**; therefore, it matches any digit except **4**. If the first character in the brackets is the **"^"**, the expression accepts any character other than those indicated. However, it is important to note that **"[^4]"** is not the same as **"[0-35-9]"**; the former matches any nondigit, in addition to the digits other than **4**.

Although the **"-"** character indicates a range when it is enclosed in square brackets, instances of the **"-"** character outside grouping expressions are treated as literal characters. Thus, the regular expression in lines 17–18 searches for a **String** that starts with the letter **"J"**, followed by any number of characters, followed by a two-digit number (of which the second digit cannot be **4**), followed by a dash, another two-digit number, a dash and another two-digit number.

Lines 31–36 use a **for** loop to iterate through each **Match** obtained from **expression->Matches**, which used **string1** as an argument. The output in Fig. 12.25 indicates the two matches that were found in **string1**. Notice that both matches conform to the pattern specified by the regular expression.

The asterisk (*****) and plus (**+**) in the previous example are called *quantifiers*. Quantifiers can be used to match a number of instances of a pattern, rather than just one instance of a pattern. Figure 12.26 lists various quantifiers and their uses.

Quantifier	Matches
*	Matches zero or more occurrences of the pattern.
+	Matches one or more occurrences of the pattern.
?	Matches zero or one occurrences of the pattern.
{n}	Matches exactly **n** occurrences.
{n,}	Matches at least **n** occurrences.
{n,m}	Matches between **n** and **m** (inclusive) occurrences.

Fig. 12.26 Quantifiers used in regular expressions.

Common Programming Error 12.9

Be sure to use the correct quantifier in a regular expression. Mixing up quantifiers is a common mistake, and using the incorrect quantifier may produce undesirable results.

We have already discussed how the asterisk (*) and plus (+) work. The question mark (?) matches zero or one occurrences of the expression that it quantifies. A set of braces containing one number ({n}) matches exactly **n** occurrences of the expression it quantifies. We demonstrate this quantifier in the next example. Including a comma after the number enclosed in braces matches at least **n** occurrences of the quantified expression. The set of braces containing two numbers ({n,m}), matches between **n** and **m** occurrences of the expression that it qualifies. All of the quantifiers are *greedy*. This means that they will match as many occurrences as they can as long as the match is successful. However, if any of these quantifiers is followed by a question mark (?), the quantifier becomes *lazy*. It then will match as few occurrences as possible as long as the match is successful.

The Windows application in Fig. 12.27–Fig. 12.29 presents a more involved example that validates user input via regular expressions.

```
1   // Fig. 12.27: Validate.h
2   // Using regular expressions to validate user information.
3
4   #pragma once
5
6   #using <system.dll>
7   #using <mscorlib.dll>
8   #using <system.drawing.dll>
9   #using <system.windows.forms.dll>
10
11  using namespace System;
12  using namespace System::Drawing;
13  using namespace System::Windows::Forms;
14  using namespace System::Text::RegularExpressions;
15
```

Fig. 12.27 Validating user information using regular expressions. (Part 1 of 2.)

```
16    // use regular expressions to validate strings
17    public __gc class ValidateForm : public Form
18    {
19    public:
20       ValidateForm();
21
22    private:
23       Label *phoneLabel, *zipLabel, *stateLabel, *cityLabel,
24          *addressLabel, *firstLabel, *lastLabel;
25
26       Button *OkButton;
27
28       TextBox *phoneTextBox, *zipTextBox, *stateTextBox;
29          *cityTextBox, *addressTextBox, *firstTextBox;
30          *lastTextBox;
31
32       void InitializeComponent();
33       void OkButton_Click( Object *, EventArgs * );
34    }; // end class ValidateForm
```

Fig. 12.27 Validating user information using regular expressions. (Part 2 of 2.)

```
 1    // Fig. 12.28: Validate.cpp
 2    // Method definitions for clas ValidateForm.
 3
 4    #include "Validate.h"
 5
 6    ValidateForm::ValidateForm()
 7    {
 8       InitializeComponent();
 9    }
10
11    void ValidateForm::InitializeComponent()
12    {
13       this->phoneLabel = new Label();
14       this->zipLabel = new Label();
15       this->stateLabel = new Label();
16       this->cityLabel = new Label();
17       this->addressLabel = new Label();
18       this->firstLabel = new Label();
19       this->lastLabel = new Label();
20       this->OkButton = new Button();
21       this->phoneTextBox = new TextBox();
22       this->zipTextBox = new TextBox();
23       this->stateTextBox = new TextBox();
24       this->cityTextBox = new TextBox();
25       this->addressTextBox = new TextBox();
26       this->firstTextBox = new TextBox();
27       this->lastTextBox = new TextBox();
28       this->SuspendLayout();
```

Fig. 12.28 ValidateForm class method definitions. (Part 1 of 6.)

```
29
30     // phoneLabel
31     this->phoneLabel->Location = Point( 10, 240 );
32     this->phoneLabel->Name = S"phoneLabel";
33     this->phoneLabel->Size = Drawing::Size( 80, 24 );
34     this->phoneLabel->TabIndex = 29;
35     this->phoneLabel->Text = S"Phone";
36     this->phoneLabel->TextAlign = ContentAlignment::MiddleRight;
37
38     // zipLabel
39     this->zipLabel->Location = Point( 10, 205 );
40     this->zipLabel->Name = S"zipLabel";
41     this->zipLabel->Size = Drawing::Size( 80, 24 );
42     this->zipLabel->TabIndex = 28;
43     this->zipLabel->Text = S"Zip";
44     this->zipLabel->TextAlign = ContentAlignment::MiddleRight;
45
46     // stateLabel
47     this->stateLabel->Location = Point( 10, 170 );
48     this->stateLabel->Name = S"stateLabel";
49     this->stateLabel->Size = Drawing::Size( 80, 24 );
50     this->stateLabel->TabIndex = 27;
51     this->stateLabel->Text = S"State";
52     this->stateLabel->TextAlign = ContentAlignment::MiddleRight;
53
54     // cityLabel
55     this->cityLabel->Location = Point( 10, 135 );
56     this->cityLabel->Name = S"cityLabel";
57     this->cityLabel->Size = Drawing::Size( 80, 24 );
58     this->cityLabel->TabIndex = 26;
59     this->cityLabel->Text = S"City";
60     this->cityLabel->TextAlign = ContentAlignment::MiddleRight;
61
62     // addressLabel
63     this->addressLabel->Location = Point( 10, 100 );
64     this->addressLabel->Name = S"addressLabel";
65     this->addressLabel->Size = Drawing::Size( 80, 24 );
66     this->addressLabel->TabIndex = 25;
67     this->addressLabel->Text = S"Address";
68     this->addressLabel->TextAlign = ContentAlignment::MiddleRight;
69
70     // firstLabel
71     this->firstLabel->Location = Point( 10, 65 );
72     this->firstLabel->Name = S"firstLabel";
73     this->firstLabel->Size = Drawing::Size( 80, 24 );
74     this->firstLabel->TabIndex = 24;
75     this->firstLabel->Text = S"First Name";
76     this->firstLabel->TextAlign = ContentAlignment::MiddleRight;
77
78     // lastLabel
79     this->lastLabel->Location = Point( 10, 30 );
80     this->lastLabel->Name = S"lastLabel";
81     this->lastLabel->Size = Drawing::Size( 80, 24 );
```

Fig. 12.28 `ValidateForm` class method definitions. (Part 2 of 6.)

```
82       this->lastLabel->TabIndex = 23;
83       this->lastLabel->Text = S"LastName";
84       this->lastLabel->TextAlign = ContentAlignment::MiddleRight;
85
86       // OkButton
87       this->OkButton->Location = Point( 112, 296 );
88       this->OkButton->Name = S"OkButton";
89       this->OkButton->TabIndex = 30;
90       this->OkButton->Text = S"OK";
91       this->OkButton->Click += new EventHandler( this,
92          OkButton_Click );
93
94       // phoneTextBox
95       this->phoneTextBox->Location = Point( 100, 240 );
96       this->phoneTextBox->Name = S"phoneTextBox";
97       this->phoneTextBox->Size = Drawing::Size( 136, 20 );
98       this->phoneTextBox->TabIndex = 22;
99       this->phoneTextBox->Text = S"";
100
101      // zipTextBox
102      this->zipTextBox->Location = Point( 100, 205 );
103      this->zipTextBox->Name = S"zipTextBox";
104      this->zipTextBox->Size = Drawing::Size( 136, 20 );
105      this->zipTextBox->TabIndex = 21;
106      this->zipTextBox->Text = S"";
107
108      // stateTextBox
109      this->stateTextBox->Location = Point( 100, 170 );
110      this->stateTextBox->Name = S"stateTextBox";
111      this->stateTextBox->Size = Drawing::Size( 136, 20 );
112      this->stateTextBox->TabIndex = 20;
113      this->stateTextBox->Text = S"";
114
115      // cityTextBox
116      this->cityTextBox->Location = Point( 100, 135 );
117      this->cityTextBox->Name = S"cityTextBox";
118      this->cityTextBox->Size = Drawing::Size( 136, 20 );
119      this->cityTextBox->TabIndex = 19;
120      this->cityTextBox->Text = S"";
121
122      // addressTextBox
123      this->addressTextBox->Location = Point( 100, 100 );
124      this->addressTextBox->Name = S"addressTextBox";
125      this->addressTextBox->Size = Drawing::Size( 136, 20 );
126      this->addressTextBox->TabIndex = 18;
127      this->addressTextBox->Text = S"";
128
129      // firstTextBox
130      this->firstTextBox->Location = Point( 100, 65 );
131      this->firstTextBox->Name = S"firstTextBox";
132      this->firstTextBox->Size = Drawing::Size( 136, 20 );
133      this->firstTextBox->TabIndex = 17;
134      this->firstTextBox->Text = S"";
```

Fig. 12.28 ValidateForm class method definitions. (Part 3 of 6.)

```
135
136        // lastTextBox
137        this->lastTextBox->Location = Point( 100, 30 );
138        this->lastTextBox->Name = S"lastTextBox";
139        this->lastTextBox->Size = Drawing::Size( 136, 20 );
140        this->lastTextBox->TabIndex = 16;
141        this->lastTextBox->Text = S"";
142
143        // ValidateForm
144        this->AutoScaleBaseSize = Drawing::Size( 5, 13 );
145        this->ClientSize = Drawing::Size( 312, 341 );
146        Control *control[] = { this->phoneLabel, this->zipLabel,
147           this->stateLabel, this->cityLabel, this->addressLabel,
148           this->firstLabel, this->lastLabel, this->OkButton,
149           this->phoneTextBox, this->zipTextBox, this->stateTextBox,
150           this->cityTextBox, this->addressTextBox,
151           this->firstTextBox, this->lastTextBox };
152        this->Controls->AddRange( control );
153        this->Name = S"ValidateForm";
154        this->Text = S"Validate";
155        this->ResumeLayout();
156    } // end method InitializeComponent
157
158    // handles OkButton_Click event
159    void ValidateForm::OkButton_Click( Object *sender, EventArgs *e )
160    {
161
162        // ensures no textboxes are empty
163        if ( lastTextBox->Text->Equals( String::Empty ) ||
164           firstTextBox->Text->Equals( String::Empty ) ||
165           addressTextBox->Text->Equals( String::Empty ) ||
166           cityTextBox->Text->Equals( String::Empty ) ||
167           stateTextBox->Text->Equals( String::Empty ) ||
168           zipTextBox->Text->Equals( String::Empty ) ||
169           phoneTextBox->Text->Equals( String::Empty ) ) {
170
171           // display popup box
172           MessageBox::Show( S"Please fill in all fields.",
173              S"Error", MessageBoxButtons::OK,
174              MessageBoxIcon::Error );
175
176           // set focus to lastTextBox
177           lastTextBox->Focus();
178
179           return;
180        } // end if
181
182        // if last name format invalid show message
183        if ( !Regex::Match( lastTextBox->Text,
184           S"^[A-Z][a-zA-Z]+$" )->Success ) {
185
186           // last name was incorrect
187           MessageBox::Show( S"Invalid Last Name", S"Message",
```

Fig. 12.28 ValidateForm class method definitions. (Part 4 of 6.)

```
188                 MessageBoxButtons::OK, MessageBoxIcon::Error );
189           lastTextBox->Focus();
190
191           return;
192      } // end if
193
194      // if first name format invalid show message
195      if ( !Regex::Match( firstTextBox->Text,
196           S"^[A-Z][a-zA-Z]+$" )->Success ) {
197
198           // first name was incorrect
199           MessageBox::Show( S"Invalid First Name", S"Message",
200                 MessageBoxButtons::OK, MessageBoxIcon::Error );
201           firstTextBox->Focus();
202
203           return;
204      } // end if
205
206      // if address format invalid show message
207      if ( !Regex::Match( addressTextBox->Text, String::Concat(
208           S"^[0-9]+\\s+([a-zA-Z]+|[a-zA-Z]+",
209           S"\\s[a-zA-Z]+)$" ) )->Success ) {
210
211           // address was incorrect
212           MessageBox::Show( S"Invalid Address", S"Message",
213                 MessageBoxButtons::OK, MessageBoxIcon::Error );
214           addressTextBox->Focus();
215
216           return;
217      } // end if
218
219      // if city format invalid show message
220      if ( !Regex::Match( cityTextBox->Text,
221           S"^([a-zA-Z]+|[a-zA-Z]+\\s[a-zA-Z]+)$" )->Success ) {
222
223           // city was incorrect
224           MessageBox::Show( S"Invalid City", S"Message",
225                 MessageBoxButtons::OK, MessageBoxIcon::Error );
226           cityTextBox->Focus();
227
228           return;
229      } // end if
230
231      // if state format invalid show message
232      if ( !Regex::Match( stateTextBox->Text,
233           S"^([a-zA-Z]+|[a-zA-Z]+\\s[a-zA-Z]+)$" )->Success ) {
234
235           // state was incorrect
236           MessageBox::Show( S"Invalid State", S"Message",
237                 MessageBoxButtons::OK, MessageBoxIcon::Error );
238           stateTextBox->Focus();
239
```

Fig. 12.28 ValidateForm class method definitions. (Part 5 of 6.)

```
240        return;
241     } // end if
242
243     // if zip code format invalid show message
244     if ( !Regex::Match( zipTextBox->Text,
245        S"^\\d{5}$" )->Success ) {
246
247        // zip was incorrect
248        MessageBox::Show( S"Invalid Zip Code", S"Message",
249           MessageBoxButtons::OK, MessageBoxIcon::Error );
250        zipTextBox->Focus();
251
252        return;
253     } // end if
254
255     // if phone number format invalid show message
256     if ( !Regex::Match( phoneTextBox->Text,
257        S"^[1-9]\\d{2}-[1-9]\\d{2}-\\d{4}$" )->Success ) {
258
259        // phone number was incorrect
260        MessageBox::Show( S"Invalid Phone Number", S"Message",
261           MessageBoxButtons::OK, MessageBoxIcon::Error );
262        phoneTextBox->Focus();
263
264        return;
265     } // end if
266
267     // information is valid, signal user and exit application
268     this->Hide();
269     MessageBox::Show( S"Thank You!", S"Information Correct",
270        MessageBoxButtons::OK, MessageBoxIcon::Information );
271
272     Application::Exit();
273  } // end method OkButton_Click
```

Fig. 12.28 `ValidateForm` class method definitions. (Part 6 of 6.)

```
1   // Fig. 12.29: ValidateTest.cpp
2   // Demonstrates validation of user information.
3
4   #include "Validate.h"
5
6   int __stdcall WinMain()
7   {
8      Application::Run( new ValidateForm() );
9
10     return 0;
11  } // end function WinMain
```

Fig. 12.29 `ValidateTest` demonstrates validation of user information. (Part 1 of 2.)

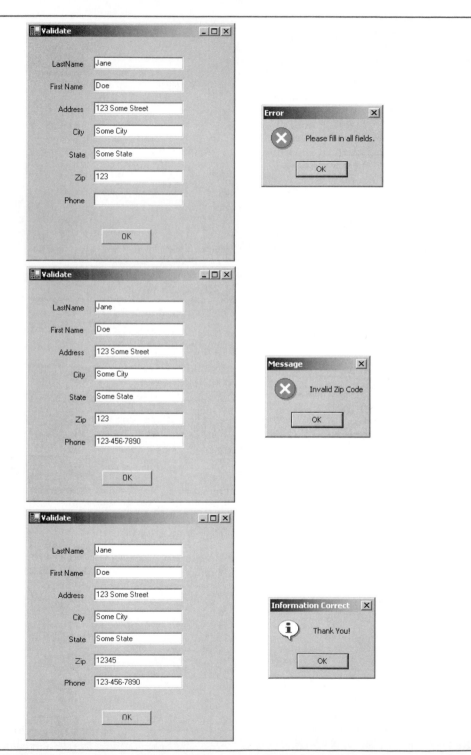

Fig. 12.29 ValidateTest demonstrates validation of user information. (Part 2 of 2.)

When a user clicks the **OK** button, the program uses **String** field *Empty* to ensure that none of the fields are empty (lines 163–169 of Fig. 12.28). **String::Empty** is a read-only field that has the value of the empty string, **""**. We could replace each instance of **String::Empty** with the empty string itself, and the program would still function in the same way.

If one or more fields are empty, the program signals the user that all fields must be filled before the program can validate the input information (lines 172–174). Line 177 calls instance method *Focus* of class **TextBox**. Method **Focus** places the cursor within the **TextBox** that made the call. The program then exits the event handler (line 179). If there are no empty fields, the user input is validated. The **Last Name** is validated first (lines 183–184). If it passes the test (i.e., if the *Success* property of the **Match** instance is **true**), control moves on to validate the **First Name** (lines 195–196). This process continues until all **TextBox**es are validated or until a test fails (**Success** is **false**) and the program sends an appropriate error message. If all fields contain valid information, success is signaled, and the program quits.

In the previous example, we searched for substrings that matched a regular expression. In this example, we want to check whether an entire **String** conforms to a regular expression. For example, we want to accept **"Smith"** as a last name, but not **"9@Smith#"**. We achieve this effect by beginning each regular expression with a **"^"** character and ending it with a **"$"** character. The **"^"** and **"$"** characters match the positions at the beginning and end of a **String**, respectively. This forces the regular expression to evaluate the entire **String** and not return a match if a substring matches successfully.

In this program, we use the **static** version of **Regex** method **Match**, which takes an additional parameter specifying the regular expression that we are trying to match. The expression in line 184 (of Fig. 12.28) uses the square bracket and range notation to match an uppercase first letter, followed by letters of any case—**a-z** matches any lowercase letter, and **A-Z** matches any uppercase letter. The **+** quantifier signifies that the second range of characters might occur one or more times in the **String**. Thus, this expression matches any **String** consisting of one uppercase letter, followed by one or more additional letters.

The notation **\s** matches a single whitespace character (lines 208–209, 221 and 233). The expression **\d{5}**, used in the **Zip** (zip code) field, matches any five digits (line 245). Recall that a set of braces containing one number (**{n}**) matches exactly **n** occurrences of the expression it quantifies. Thus, the expression **\d** with a positive integer **x** in curly braces (**\d{x}**) will match any **x** digits. (Notice the importance of the **"^"** and **"$"** characters to prevent zip codes with extra digits from being validated.)

The character "**|**" matches the expression to its left or to its right. For example, **Hi (John|Jane)** matches both **Hi John** and **Hi Jane**. Note the use of parentheses to group parts of the regular expression. Quantifiers may be applied to patterns enclosed in parentheses to create more complex regular expressions.

The **Last Name** and **First Name** fields both accept **String**s of any length, that begin with an uppercase letter. The **Address** field matches at least one digit, followed by at least one whitespace character and then either one or more letters or else one or more letters followed by a space and another series of one or more letters (lines 207–209). Therefore, **"10 Broadway"** and **"10 Main Street"** are both valid addresses. The **City** (lines 220–221) and **State** (lines 232–233) fields match any word of at least one character or, alternatively, any two words of at least one character if the words are separated by a single space. This means both **Waltham** and **West Newton** would match. As previously stated, the **Zip** code must be a five-digit number (lines 244–245). The **Phone** number must be of the form **xxx-yyy-yyyy**, where the **x**s represent the area code and **y**s the number (lines 256–257). The first **x** and the first **y** cannot be zero.

Sometimes it is useful to replace parts of a **String** with another, or split a **String** according to a regular expression. For this purpose, the **Regex** class provides **static** and instance versions of methods *Replace* and *Split*, which are demonstrated in Fig. 12.30.

```
1   // Fig. 12.30: RegexSubstitution.cpp
2   // Using Regex method Replace.
3
4   #using <system.dll>
5   #using <mscorlib.dll>
6   #using <system.windows.forms.dll>
7
8   using namespace System;
9   using namespace System::Windows::Forms;
10  using namespace System::Text::RegularExpressions;
11
12  int __stdcall WinMain()
13  {
14     String *testString1 = S"This sentence ends in 5 stars *****";
15     String *testString2 = S"1, 2, 3, 4, 5, 6, 7, 8";
16     Regex *testRegex1 = new Regex( S"stars" );
17     Regex *testRegex2 = new Regex( S"\\d" );
18     String *results[];
19     String *output = String::Concat( S"Original String 1\t\t\t",
20        testString1 );
21
22     testString1 = Regex::Replace( testString1, S"\\*", S"^" );
23
24     output = String::Concat( output, S"\n^ substituted for ",
25        S"*\t\t\t",testString1 );
26
27     testString1 = testRegex1->Replace( testString1, S"carets" );
28
29     output = String::Concat( output, S"\n\"carets\" ",
30        S"substituted for \"stars\"\t", testString1 );
31
32     output = String::Concat( output, S"\nEvery word replaced ",
33        S"by \"word\"\t", Regex::Replace(
34        testString1, S"\\w+", S"word" ) );
35
36     output = String::Concat( output, S"\n\nOriginal ",
37        S"String 2\t\t\t", testString2 );
38
39     output = String::Concat( output, S"\nFirst 3 digits ",
40        S"replaced by \"digit\"\t", testRegex2->Replace(
41        testString2, S"digit", 3 ) );
42
43     output = String::Concat( output, S"\nString split at ",
44        S"commas\t\t[" );
```

Fig. 12.30 **Regex** methods **Replace** and **Split**. (Part 1 of 2.)

```
45
46      results = Regex::Split( testString2, S",\\s*" );
47
48      String *resultString;
49
50      for ( int i = 0; i < results->Length; i++ ) {
51         resultString = results->Item[ i ]->ToString();
52
53         output = String::Concat( output, S"\"",
54            resultString, S"\", " );
55      }
56
57      output = String::Concat( output->Substring( 0,
58         output->Length - 2 ), S"]" );
59
60      MessageBox::Show( output,
61         S"Substitution Using Regular Expressions" );
62
63      return 0;
64   } // end function WinMain
```

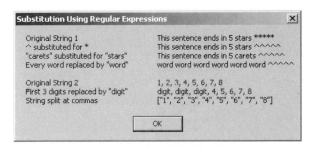

Fig. 12.30 Regex methods **Replace** and **Split**. (Part 2 of 2.)

Method **Replace** replaces text in a **String** with new text wherever the original **String** matches a regular expression. We present two versions of this method in Fig. 12.30. The first version (line 22) is **static** and takes three parameters—a pointer to the **String** to modify, the **String *** containing the regular expression to match and a pointer to the replacement **String**. Here **Replace** replaces every instance of **"*"** in **testString1** with **"^"**. Notice that the regular expression (**"*"**) precedes character ***** with a backslash, ****. Normally, ***** is a quantifier indicating that a regular expression should match any number of occurrences of a preceding pattern. However, in line 22, we want to find all occurrences of the literal character *****; to do this, we must escape character ***** with character ****. By escaping a special regular expression character with a ****, we inform the regular-expression matching engine to find the actual character, as opposed to what it represents in a regular expression. The second version of method **Replace** (line 27) is an instance method that uses the regular expression passed to the constructor for **testRegex1** (line 16) to perform the replacement operation. In this case, every match for the regular expression **"stars"** in **testString1** is replaced with **"carets"**. Notice that we have now supplied two arguments to method **Replace**—a pointer to the **String** to modify and a pointer to the replacement **String**. The regular expression to match is provided by **testRegex1**, which calls the method.

Line 17 instantiates **testRegex2** with argument **"\\d"**. This call to instance method **Replace** in lines 40–41 takes three arguments—a pointer to the **String** to modify, the **String *** containing the replacement text and an **int** specifying the number of replacements to make. In other words, this version of **Replace** replaces the first three instances of a digit (**"\d"**) in **testString2** with the text **"digit"** (lines 40–41). Lines 57-58 remove the final space and quote, and add a closing brace, signifying the end of the list of digits.

Method **Split** divides a **String** into several substrings. The original **String** is broken in any location that matches a specified regular expression. Method **Split** returns an array containing the substrings between matches for the regular expression. In line 46, we use the **static** version of method **Split** to separate a **String** of comma-separated integers. The first argument is a pointer to the **String** to split; the second argument is the regular expression. In this case, we use the regular expression **",\\s*"** to separate the substrings wherever a comma occurs. By matching any whitespace characters, we eliminate extra spaces from the resulting substrings.

12.18 Summary

Characters are the fundamental building blocks of MC++ program code. Every program is composed of a sequence of characters that is interpreted by the compiler as a series of instructions used to accomplish a task.

A **String** is a series of characters treated as a single unit. A **String** may include letters, digits and various special characters, such as +, -, *, /, \$ and others. All characters correspond to numeric codes.

When the computer compares two **String**s, it actually compares the numeric codes of the characters in the **String**s. Method **Equals** uses a lexicographical comparison, meaning that if a certain **String** has a higher value than another **String**, it would be found later in a dictionary. Method **Equals** compares the integer Unicode® values that represent each character in each **String**. Method **CompareTo** returns 0 if the **String**s are equal, a negative number if the **String** that invokes **CompareTo** is less than the **String** passed as an argument, a positive number if the **String** that invokes **CompareTo** is greater than the **String** passed as an argument. Method **CompareTo** uses a lexicographical comparison.

A hash table stores information, using a special calculation on the object to be stored that produces a hash code. The hash code is used to choose the location in the table at which to store the object. Class **Object** defines method **GetHashCode** to perform the hash-code calculation. This method is inherited by all subclasses of **Object**. Method **GetHashCode** is overridden by **String** to provide a good hash-code distribution based on the contents of the **String**.

Class **String** provides two **Substring** methods to enable a new **String** to be created by copying part of an existing **String**.

String method **IndexOf** locates the first occurrence of a character or a substring in a **String**. Method **LastIndexOf** locates the last occurrence of a character or a substring in a **String**.

String method **StartsWith** determines whether a **String** starts with the characters specified as an argument. **String** method **EndsWith** determines whether a **String** ends with the characters specified as an argument.

The **static** method **Concat** of class **String** concatenates two **String**s and returns a new **String *** containing the characters from both original **String**s. Once a **String** is created, its contents can never change. Class **StringBuilder** is available for creating and manipulating dynamic **String**s (i.e., **String**s that can change). Class **StringBuilder** provides **Length** and **Capacity** properties to return the number of characters currently in a **StringBuilder** and the number of characters that can be stored in a **StringBuilder** without allocating more memory, respectively. These properties also can be used to increase or decrease the length or the capacity of the **String-Builder**.

Method **EnsureCapacity** allows programmers to guarantee that a **String-Builder** has a minimum capacity. Method **EnsureCapacity** attempts to double the capacity. If this value is greater than the value that the programmer wishes to ensure, this will be the new capacity. Otherwise, **EnsureCapacity** alters the capacity to make it one more than the requested number.

Class **StringBuilder** provides 19 overloaded **Append** methods to allow various data-type values to be added to the end of a **StringBuilder**. Versions are provided for each of the primitive data types and for character arrays, **String** pointers and **Object** pointers. Class **StringBuilder** also provides method **AppendFormat**, which converts a **String** to a specified format and then appends it to the **StringBuilder**.

Class **StringBuilder** provides 19 overloaded **Insert** methods to allow various data-type values to be inserted at any position in a **StringBuilder**. Versions are provided for each of the primitive data types and for character arrays, **String** pointers and **Object** pointers. Class **StringBuilder** also provides method **Remove** for deleting any portion of a **StringBuilder**. Another useful method included with **String-Builder** is **Replace**. **Replace** searches for a specified **String** or character and substitutes another in its place.

Regular expressions find patterns in text. The .NET Framework provides class **Regex** to aid developers in recognizing and manipulating regular expressions. **Regex** provides method **Match**, which returns an object of class **Match**. This object represents a single match in a regular expression. **Regex** also provides the method **Matches**, which finds all matches of a regular expression in an arbitrary **String** and returns a **MatchCollection**—a set of **Match**es. Both classes **Regex** and **Match** are in namespace **System::Text::RegularExpressions**.

13

Graphics and Multimedia

Objectives

- To understand graphics contexts and graphics objects.
- To manipulate colors and fonts.
- To understand and be able to use GDI+ **Graphics** methods to draw lines, rectangles, **String**s and images.
- To use class **Image** to manipulate and display images.
- To draw complex shapes from simple shapes with class **GraphicsPath**.
- To use Windows Media Player and Microsoft Agent in an MC++ application.

One picture is worth ten thousand words.
Chinese proverb

Treat nature in terms of the cylinder, the sphere, the cone, all in perspective.
Paul Cezanne

Nothing ever becomes real till it is experienced—even a proverb is no proverb to you till your life has illustrated it.
John Keats

A picture shows me at a glance what it takes dozens of pages of a book to expound.
Ivan Sergeyevich

Outline

13.1 Introduction

In this chapter, we overview Visual C++ .NET's tools for drawing two-dimensional shapes and for controlling colors and fonts. Visual C++ .NET supports graphics that enable programmers to enhance their Windows applications visually. The FCL contains many sophisticated drawing capabilities as part of namespace **System::Drawing** and the other namespaces that make up the .NET resource *GDI+*. GDI+, an extension of the Graphical Device Interface, is an application programming interface (API) that provides classes for creating two-dimensional vector graphics (a way of describing graphics so that they may be easily manipulated with high-performance techniques), manipulating fonts and inserting images. GDI+ expands GDI by simplifying the programming model and introducing several new features, such as graphics paths, extended image-file format support and *alpha blending* (see Section 13.3). Using the GDI+ API, programmers can create images without worrying about the platform-specific details of their graphics hardware.

We begin with an introduction to the .NET framework's drawing capabilities. We then present more powerful drawing capabilities, such as changing the styles of lines used to draw shapes and controlling the colors and patterns of filled shapes.

Figure 13.1 depicts a portion of the **System::Drawing** class hierarchy, which includes several of the basic graphics classes and structures covered in this chapter. The most commonly used components of GDI+ reside in the **System::Drawing** and *System::Drawing::Drawing2D* namespaces.

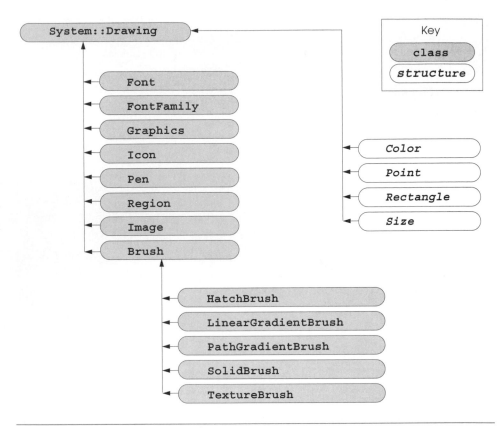

Fig. 13.1 `System::Drawing` namespace's classes and structures.

Class *Graphics* contains methods used for drawing **String**s, lines, rectangles and other shapes on a **Control**. The drawing methods of class **Graphics** usually require a *Pen* or *Brush* object to render a specified shape. The **Pen** draws shape outlines; the **Brush** draws solid objects.

Structure *Color* contains numerous **static** properties, which set the colors of various graphical components, plus methods that allow users to create new colors. Class *Font* contains properties that define unique fonts. Class *FontFamily* contains methods for obtaining font information.

To begin drawing in MC++, we first must understand GDI+'s *coordinate system* (Fig. 13.2), a scheme for identifying every point on the screen. By default, the upper-left corner of a GUI component (such as a **Panel** or a **Form**) has the coordinates (0, 0). A coordinate pair has both an *x-coordinate* (the *horizontal coordinate*) and a *y-coordinate* (the *vertical coordinate*). The *x*-coordinate is the horizontal distance (to the right) from the upper-left corner. The *y*-coordinate is the vertical distance (downward) from the upper-left corner. The *x-axis* defines every horizontal coordinate, and the *y-axis* defines every vertical coordinate. Programmers position text and shapes on the screen by specifying their (*x,y*) coordinates. Coordinate units are measured in *pixels* ("picture elements"), which are the smallest units of resolution on a display monitor.

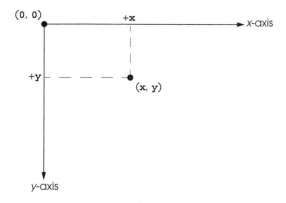

Fig. 13.2   GDI+ coordinate system. Units are measured in pixels.

The **System::Drawing** namespace provides structures **Rectangle** and **Point**. The *Rectangle structure* defines rectangular shapes and dimensions. The *Point structure* represents the (*x,y*) coordinates of a point on a two-dimensional plane.

 Portability Tip 13.1

Different display monitors have different resolutions, so the density of pixels on various monitors will vary. This might cause the sizes of graphics to appear different on different monitors.

In the remainder of this chapter, we explore techniques for manipulating images and creating smooth animations. We also discuss class *Image*, which can store and manipulate images from various file formats. Later, we explain how to combine the graphical rendering capabilities covered in the early sections of the chapter with those for image manipulation.

13.2 Graphics Contexts and Graphics Objects

A *graphics context* represents a drawing surface that enables drawing on the screen. A **Graphics** object manages a graphics context by controlling how information is drawn. **Graphics** objects contain methods for drawing, font manipulation, color manipulation and other graphics-related actions. Every Windows application that derives from class **System::Windows::Forms::Form** inherits a **virtual *OnPaint*** event handler, where most graphics operations are performed. The arguments to the **OnPaint** method include a **PaintEventArgs *** object from which we can obtain a **Graphics** object for the control. We must obtain the **Graphics** object on each call to the method, because the properties of the graphics context that the graphics object represents could change. The **OnPaint** method triggers the **Control**'s *Paint* event, which indicates that a control is being drawn or redrawn.

When displaying graphical information on a **Form**'s client area, programmers can override the **OnPaint** method to retrieve a **Graphics** object from argument **PaintEventArgs *** or to create a new **Graphics** object associated with the appropriate surface. We demonstrate these techniques of drawing later in the chapter.

To override the inherited **OnPaint** method, use the following method declaration in the header (**.h**) file:

```
protected:
   void OnPaint( PaintEventArgs * );
```

In the implementation (**.cpp**) file, begin the method definition as:

```
void className::OnPaint( PaintEventArgs *e )
```

Every overriden **OnPaint** method should call the **OnPaint** method of its base class (**__super**). Therefore, the first statement in the overridden **OnPaint** method should be:

```
__super::OnPaint( e );
```

Next, extract the incoming **Graphics** object from the **PaintEventArgs** argument:

```
Graphics *graphicsObject = e->Graphics;
```

Variable **graphicsObject** now is available to draw shapes and **String**s on the form.

Programmers seldom call the **OnPaint** method directly, because the drawing of graphics is an *event-driven process*. An event—such as the covering, uncovering or resizing of a window—calls the **OnPaint** method of that form.

If programmers need to cause method **OnPaint** to run explicitly, they should not call method **OnPaint**. Rather, they can call the *Invalidate* method (inherited from **Control**). This method refreshes a control's client area and implicitly invokes method **OnPaint**. Several overloaded **Invalidate** methods exist that allow programmers to update portions of the client area.

Common Programming Error 13.1

*Forgetting to call the **OnPaint** method of the base class in the **OnPaint** method of a derived class can cause errors. Specifically, the **Paint** event may not be raised.*

Performance Tip 13.1

*Calling the **Invalidate** method to refresh a **Control** often is inefficient. Instead, call **Invalidate** with a **Rectangle** parameter to refresh only the area designated by the rectangle. This improves program performance.*

Calling the **OnPaint** method raises the **Paint** event. Programmers can add an event handler for the **Paint** event instead of overriding the **OnPaint** method. The form of a **Paint** event handler is:

```
void className::controlName_Paint( Object *sender,
   PaintEventArgs *e )
```

where *controlName* is the name of the control for which we are defining a **Paint** event handler.

When any control (such as a **TextBox** or **Label**) is displayed, the program calls that control's **Paint** event handler. Thus, if we wish to define a method that only updates a certain control (rather than the entire **Form**, such as method **OnPaint**), we can simply provide an event handler for that control's **Paint** event. We demonstrate this in later examples.

Controls, such as **Label**s and **Button**s, do not have their own graphics contexts (i.e., they normally cannot be drawn on), but one can be created. To draw on a control, first create its graphics object by invoking the *CreateGraphics* method:

```
Graphics *graphicsObject = controlName->CreateGraphics();
```

where *graphicsObject* represents an instance of class **Graphics** and *controlName* is any control. Now, a programmer can use the methods provided in class **Graphics** to draw on the control.

13.3 Color Control

Colors can enhance a program's appearance and help convey meaning. For example, a red traffic light indicates stop, yellow indicates caution and green indicates go.

Structure **Color** defines methods and constants used to manipulate colors. Because it is a lightweight object that performs only a handful of operations and stores **static** fields, **Color** is implemented as a structure, rather than as a class.

Every color can be created from a combination of alpha, red, green and blue components. Together, these components are called *ARGB values*. All four ARGB components are **byte**s that represent integer values in the range from 0–255. The alpha value determines the opacity of the color. For example, the alpha value 0 specifies a transparent color, the value 255 an opaque color. Alpha values between 0 and 255 (inclusive) result in a weighted blending effect of the color's RGB value with that of any background color, causing a semitransparent effect. The first number in the RGB value defines the amount of red in the color, the second defines the amount of green and the third defines the amount of blue. The larger the value, the greater the amount of that particular color. Visual C++ .NET enables programmers to choose from almost 17 million colors. If a particular computer cannot display all these colors, it will display the color closest to the one specified or attempt to emulate it using *dithering* (using small dots of existing colors to form a pattern that simulates the desired color). Figure 13.3 summarizes some predefined **Color** constants, and Fig. 13.4 describes several **Color** methods and properties.

Constants in structure Color (all are public static)	RGB value	Constants in structure Color (all are public static)	RGB value
Orange	255, 200, 0	White	255, 255, 255
Pink	255, 175, 175	Gray	128, 128, 128
Cyan	0, 255, 255	DarkGray	64, 64, 64
Magenta	255, 0, 255	Red	255, 0, 0
Yellow	255, 255, 0	Green	0, 255, 0
Black	0, 0, 0	Blue	0, 0, 255

Fig. 13.3 **Color** structure **static** constants and their RGB values.

Structure Color methods and properties	Description
Common Methods	
static FromArgb	Creates a color based on red, green and blue values expressed as **int**s from 0 to 255. Overloaded version allows specification of alpha, red, green and blue values.
static FromName	Creates a color from a name, passed as a pointer to a **String**.

Fig. 13.4 **Color** structure members. (Part 1 of 2.)

Structure Color methods and properties	Description
Common Properties	
A	**byte** between 0 and 255 (inclusive), representing the alpha component.
R	**byte** between 0 and 255 (inclusive), representing the red component.
G	**byte** between 0 and 255 (inclusive), representing the green component.
B	**byte** between 0 and 255 (inclusive), representing the blue component.

Fig. 13.4 **Color** structure members. (Part 2 of 2.)

The table in Fig. 13.4 describes two **FromArgb** method calls. One takes three **int** arguments, and one takes four **int** arguments (all argument values must be between 0 and 255, inclusive). Both take **int** arguments specifying the amount of red, green and blue. The overloaded version takes four arguments and allows the user to specify alpha; the three-argument version defaults the alpha to 255. Both methods return a **Color** object representing the specified values. **Color** properties *A*, *R*, *G* and *B* return **byte**s that represent **int** values from 0 to 255, corresponding to the amounts of alpha, red, green and blue, respectively.

Programmers draw shapes and **String**s with **Brush**es and **Pen**s. A **Pen**, which functions similarly to the way an ordinary pen does, is used to draw lines. Most drawing methods require a **Pen** object. The overloaded **Pen** constructors allow programmers to specify the colors and widths of the lines that they wish to draw. The **System::Drawing** namespace also provides a **Pen**s collection containing predefined **Pen**s.

All classes derived from abstract class **Brush** define objects that color the interiors of graphical shapes; for example, the **SolidBrush** constructor takes a **Color** object—the color to draw. In most **Fill** methods, **Brush**es fill a space with a color, pattern or image. Figure 13.5 summarizes various **Brush**es and their functions.

Class	Description
HatchBrush	Uses a rectangular brush to fill a region with a pattern. The pattern is defined by a member of the **HatchStyle** enumeration, a foreground color (with which the pattern is drawn) and a background color.
LinearGradient-Brush	Fills a region with a gradual blend of one color into another. Linear gradients are defined along a line. They can be specified by the two colors, the angle of the gradient and either the width of a rectangle or two points.
SolidBrush	Fills a region with one color. Defined by a **Color** object.
TextureBrush	Fills a region by repeating a specified **Image** across the surface.

Fig. 13.5 Classes that derive from class **Brush**.

The application in Figs. 13.6–13.8 demonstrates several of the methods and properties described in Fig. 13.4. It displays two overlapping rectangles, allowing the user to experiment with color values and color names.

```cpp
1   // Fig. 13.6: ShowColors.h
2   // Using different colors in Visual C++ .NET.
3
4   #pragma once
5
6   #using <mscorlib.dll>
7   #using <system.dll>
8   #using <system.drawing.dll>
9   #using <system.windows.forms.dll>
10
11  using namespace System;
12  using namespace System::Drawing;
13  using namespace System::Windows::Forms;
14
15  public __gc class ShowColors : public Form
16  {
17  public:
18     ShowColors();
19
20  protected:
21     void OnPaint( PaintEventArgs * );
22
23  private:
24
25     // color for back rectangle
26     Color behindColor;
27
28     // color for front rectangle
29     Color frontColor;
30
31     GroupBox *nameGroup;
32     GroupBox *colorValueGroup;
33     TextBox *colorNameTextBox;
34     TextBox *alphaTextBox;
35     TextBox *redTextBox;
36     TextBox *greenTextBox;
37     TextBox *blueTextBox;
38     Button *colorValueButton;
39     Button *colorNameButton;
40
41     void InitializeComponent();
42     void colorValueButton_Click( Object *, EventArgs * );
43     void colorNameButton_Click( Object *, EventArgs * );
44  }; // end class ShowColors
```

Fig. 13.6 Color value and alpha demonstration.

```
1    // Fig. 13.7: ShowColors.cpp
2    // Method definitions for class ShowColors.
3
4    #include "ShowColors.h"
5
6    // default constructor
7    ShowColors::ShowColors()
8    {
9        InitializeComponent();
10   }
11
12   // override Form OnPaint method
13   void ShowColors::OnPaint( PaintEventArgs *paintEvent )
14   {
15       __super::OnPaint( paintEvent ); // call base OnPaint method
16
17       Graphics *graphicsObject = paintEvent->Graphics; // get graphics
18
19       // create text brush
20       SolidBrush *textBrush = new SolidBrush( Color::Black );
21
22       // create solid brush
23       SolidBrush *brush = new SolidBrush( Color::White );
24
25       // draw white background
26       graphicsObject->FillRectangle( brush, 4, 4, 275, 180 );
27
28       // display name of behindColor
29       graphicsObject->DrawString( this->behindColor.Name, Font,
30           textBrush, 40, 5 );
31
32       // set brush color and display back rectangle
33       brush->Color = this->behindColor;
34
35       graphicsObject->FillRectangle( brush, 45, 20, 150, 120 );
36
37       // display ARGB values of front color
38       graphicsObject->DrawString( String::Concat(
39           S"Alpha: ", frontColor.A.ToString(),
40           S" Red: ", frontColor.R.ToString(),
41           S" Green: ", frontColor.G.ToString(),
42           S" Blue: ", frontColor.B.ToString() ),
43           Font, textBrush, 55, 165 );
44
45       // set brush color and display front rectangle
46       brush->Color = frontColor;
47
48       graphicsObject->FillRectangle( brush, 65, 35, 170, 130 );
49   } // end method OnPaint
```

Fig. 13.7 ShowColors class method definitions. (Part 1 of 4.)

```
50
51    void ShowColors::InitializeComponent()
52    {
53        this->frontColor = Color::FromArgb( 100, 0 , 0, 255 );
54        this->behindColor = Color::Wheat;
55
56        this->nameGroup = new GroupBox();
57        this->colorValueGroup = new GroupBox();
58        this->colorNameTextBox = new TextBox();
59        this->alphaTextBox = new TextBox();
60        this->redTextBox = new TextBox();
61        this->greenTextBox = new TextBox();
62        this->blueTextBox = new TextBox();
63        this->colorValueButton = new Button();
64        this->colorNameButton = new Button();
65        this->nameGroup->SuspendLayout();
66        this->colorValueGroup->SuspendLayout();
67        this->SuspendLayout();
68
69        // nameGroup
70        Control *tempControl[] = { this->colorNameButton,
71            this->colorNameTextBox };
72        this->nameGroup->Controls->AddRange( tempControl );
73        this->nameGroup->Location = Point( 8, 184 );
74        this->nameGroup->Name = S"nameGroup";
75        this->nameGroup->Size = Drawing::Size( 320, 64 );
76        this->nameGroup->TabIndex = 0;
77        this->nameGroup->TabStop = false;
78        this->nameGroup->Text = S"Set Back Color Name";
79
80        // colorValueGroup
81        Control *tempControl2[] = { this->colorValueButton,
82            this->blueTextBox, this->greenTextBox, this->redTextBox,
83            this->alphaTextBox };
84        this->colorValueGroup->Controls->AddRange( tempControl2 );
85        this->colorValueGroup->Location = Point( 8, 264 );
86        this->colorValueGroup->Name = S"colorValueGroup";
87        this->colorValueGroup->Size = Drawing::Size( 320, 56 );
88        this->colorValueGroup->TabIndex = 1;
89        this->colorValueGroup->TabStop = false;
90        this->colorValueGroup->Text = S"Set Front Color Value";
91
92        // colorNameTextBox
93        this->colorNameTextBox->Location = Point( 16, 24 );
94        this->colorNameTextBox->Name = S"colorNameTextBox";
95        this->colorNameTextBox->Size = Drawing::Size( 152, 20 );
96        this->colorNameTextBox->TabIndex = 0;
97        this->colorNameTextBox->Text = S"";
98
99        // alphaTextBox
100       this->alphaTextBox->Location = Point( 16, 24 );
101       this->alphaTextBox->Name = S"alphaTextBox";
102       this->alphaTextBox->Size = Drawing::Size( 32, 20 );
```

Fig. 13.7   **ShowColors** class method definitions. (Part 2 of 4.)

```
103        this->alphaTextBox->TabIndex = 0;
104        this->alphaTextBox->Text = S"";
105
106        // redTextBox
107        this->redTextBox->Location = Point( 56, 24 );
108        this->redTextBox->Name = S"redTextBox";
109        this->redTextBox->Size = Drawing::Size( 32, 20 );
110        this->redTextBox->TabIndex = 1;
111        this->redTextBox->Text = S"";
112
113        // greenTextBox
114        this->greenTextBox->Location = Point( 96, 24 );
115        this->greenTextBox->Name = S"greenTextBox";
116        this->greenTextBox->Size = Drawing::Size( 32, 20 );
117        this->greenTextBox->TabIndex = 2;
118        this->greenTextBox->Text = S"";
119
120        // blueTextBox
121        this->blueTextBox->Location = Point( 136, 24 );
122        this->blueTextBox->Name = S"blueTextBox";
123        this->blueTextBox->Size = Drawing::Size( 32, 20 );
124        this->blueTextBox->TabIndex = 3;
125        this->blueTextBox->Text = S"";
126
127        // colorValueButton
128        this->colorValueButton->Location = Point( 192, 24 );
129        this->colorValueButton->Name = S"colorValueButton";
130        this->colorValueButton->Size = Drawing::Size( 104, 23 );
131        this->colorValueButton->TabIndex = 4;
132        this->colorValueButton->Text = S"Set Color Value";
133        this->colorValueButton->Click += new EventHandler( this,
134           colorValueButton_Click );
135
136        // colorNameButton
137        this->colorNameButton->Location = Point( 192, 24 );
138        this->colorNameButton->Name = S"colorNameButton";
139        this->colorNameButton->Size = Drawing::Size( 104, 23 );
140        this->colorNameButton->TabIndex = 1;
141        this->colorNameButton->Text = S"Set Color Name";
142        this->colorNameButton->Click += new EventHandler( this,
143           colorNameButton_Click );
144
145        // ShowColors
146        this->AutoScaleBaseSize = Drawing::Size( 5, 13 );
147        this->ClientSize = Drawing::Size( 344, 333 );
148        Control *tempControl3[] = { this->colorValueGroup,
149           this->nameGroup };
150        this->Controls->AddRange( tempControl3 );
151        this->Name = S"ShowColors";
152        this->Text = S"ShowColors";
153        this->nameGroup->ResumeLayout();
154        this->colorValueGroup->ResumeLayout();
155        this->ResumeLayout();
```

Fig. 13.7 ShowColors class method definitions. (Part 3 of 4.)

```
156  } // end method InitializeComponent
157
158  // handle colorValueButton click event
159  void ShowColors::colorValueButton_Click(
160     Object *sender, EventArgs *e )
161  {
162     try {
163
164        // obtain new front color from text boxes
165        frontColor = Color::FromArgb(
166           Convert::ToInt32( alphaTextBox->Text ),
167           Convert::ToInt32( redTextBox->Text ),
168           Convert::ToInt32( greenTextBox->Text ),
169           Convert::ToInt32( blueTextBox->Text ) );
170
171        Invalidate( Rectangle( 4, 4, 275, 180 ) ); // refresh Form
172     }
173     catch ( FormatException *formatException ) {
174        MessageBox::Show( formatException->Message, S"Error",
175           MessageBoxButtons::OK, MessageBoxIcon::Error );
176     }
177     catch ( ArgumentException *argumentException ) {
178        MessageBox::Show( argumentException->Message, S"Error",
179           MessageBoxButtons::OK, MessageBoxIcon::Error );
180     }
181  } // end method colorValueButton_Click
182
183  // handle colorNameButton click event
184  void ShowColors::colorNameButton_Click(
185     Object *sender, EventArgs *e )
186  {
187     // set behindColor to color specified in text box
188     behindColor = Color::FromName( colorNameTextBox->Text );
189
190     Invalidate( Rectangle( 4, 4, 275, 180 ) ); // refresh Form
191  } // end method colorNameButton_Click
```

Fig. 13.7   **ShowColors** class method definitions. (Part 4 of 4.)

```
1   // Fig. 13.8: ShowColorsTest.cpp
2   // Entry point for application.
3
4   #include "ShowColors.h"
5
6   int __stdcall WinMain()()
7   {
8      Application::Run( new ShowColors() );
9
10     return 0;
11  } // end function WinMain
```

Fig. 13.8   **ShowColors** class driver. (Part 1 of 2.)

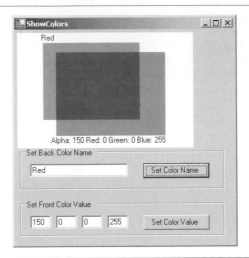

Fig. 13.8   `ShowColors` class driver. (Part 2 of 2.)

When the application begins its execution, it calls class **ShowColors**'s **OnPaint** method to paint the window. **Line 15 invokes __super::OnPaint(paint Event)** (as discussed in Section 13.2). Line 17 (of Fig. 13.7) gets a pointer to **Paint-EventArgs e**'s **Graphics** object and assigns it to **graphicsObject**. Lines 20 and 23 create black and white **SolidBrush**es for drawing on the form. Class **SolidBrush** derives from abstract base class **Brush**; programmers can draw solid shapes with the **SolidBrush**.

Graphics method *FillRectangle* draws a rectangle that is filled with the color or pattern of the **Brush** passed as the first argument to **FillRectangle**. Lines 26 calls method **FillRectangle** with **brush** as the first argument, specifying that we want a solid white rectangle to be drawn. Other parameters passed to this method are the *x*- and *y*-coordinates of a point and the width and height of the rectangle to draw. The point represents the upper-left corner of the rectangle. Lines 29–30 display the name of the **Brush**'s **Color** property with the **Graphics** *DrawString* method. The programmer has access to several overloaded **DrawString** methods; the version demonstrated in lines 29–30 takes a pointer to the **String** to display, the display **Font**, a **Brush** and the x- and y-coordinates of the location for the **String**'s first character.

Lines 33–35 assign **Color** value **behindColor**, which is initialized to **Color::Wheat** on line 54, to the **Brush**'s **Color** property and display a rectangle. Lines 38–43 extract and display the ARGB values of **Color frontColor** and then display a filled rectangle that overlaps the first.

Button event handler **colorValueButton_Click** (lines 159–181) uses **Color** method **FromArgb** to construct a new **Color** object from the ARGB values that a user specifies via text boxes. It then assigns the newly created **Color** to **frontColor**. The **catch** blocks in lines 173–180 notify the user if invalid values have been entered. **Button** event handler **colorNameButton_Click** (lines 184–191) uses the **Color**

method **FromName** to create a new **Color** object from the **colorName** that a user enters in a text box. This **Color** is assigned to **behindColor**. Valid color names for method **FromName** are any name described by the *KnownColor* enumeration[1] (namespace **System::Drawing**). If the user does not enter a valid color name, a default color with ARGB values of **0** is used.

Notice that both **colorValueButton_Click** and **colorNameButton_Click** call method **Invalidate** with a **Rectangle** argument. The coordinates of the **Rectangle** are the same as those used in line 26 to draw the white background. Thus, only the region containing the white background will be updated each time.

If the user assigns an alpha value between 0 and 255 (inclusive) for the **frontColor**, the effects of alpha blending are apparent. In the screenshot output, the red back rectangle blends with the blue front rectangle to create purple where the two overlap.

 Software Engineering Observation 13.1

*No methods in structure **Color** enable programmers to change the characteristics of the current color. To use a different color, create a new **Color** object.*

The predefined GUI component *ColorDialog* is a dialog box that allows users to select from a palette of available colors. It also offers the option of creating custom colors. The program in Fig. 13.9–Fig. 13.11 demonstrates the use of such a dialog. When a user selects a color and presses **OK**, the application retrieves the user's selection via the **ColorDialog**'s *Color* property.

The GUI for this application contains two **Button**s. The top one, **backgroundColorButton**, allows the user to change the form and button background colors. The bottom one, **textColorButton**, allows the user to change the button text colors.

```
1   // Fig. 13.9: ShowColorsComplex.h
2   // Change the background and text colors of a form.
3
4   #pragma once
5
6   #using <mscorlib.dll>
7   #using <system.dll>
8   #using <system.drawing.dll>
9   #using <system.windows.forms.dll>
10
11  using namespace System;
12  using namespace System::Drawing;
13  using namespace System::Windows::Forms;
14
15  public __gc class ShowColorsComplex : public Form
16  {
17  public:
18     ShowColorsComplex();
19
```

Fig. 13.9   Change the background and text colors of a form. (Part 1 of 2.)

---

1. A list of colors defined by the **KnownColor** enumeration can be found at
   `msdn.microsoft.com/library/default.asp?url=/library/en-us/cpref/`
   `html/frlrfsystemdrawingknowncolorclasstopic.asp`.

```
20    private:
21       Button *backgroundColorButton;
22       Button *textColorButton;
23
24       void InitializeComponent();
25       void textColorButton_Click( Object *, EventArgs * );
26       void backgroundColorButton_Click( Object *, EventArgs * );
27    }; // end class ShowColorsComplex
```

Fig. 13.9   Change the background and text colors of a form. (Part 2 of 2.)

```
1     // Fig. 13.10: ShowColorsComplex.cpp
2     // Method definitions for class ShowColorsComplex.
3
4     #include "ShowColorsComplex.h"
5
6     // default constructor
7     ShowColorsComplex::ShowColorsComplex()
8     {
9        InitializeComponent();
10    }
11
12    void ShowColorsComplex::InitializeComponent()
13    {
14       this->backgroundColorButton = new Button();
15       this->textColorButton = new Button();
16       this->SuspendLayout();
17
18       // backgroundColorButton
19       this->backgroundColorButton->Location = Point( 16, 16 );
20       this->backgroundColorButton->Name = S"backgroundColorButton";
21       this->backgroundColorButton->Size = Drawing::Size( 264, 32 );
22       this->backgroundColorButton->TabIndex = 0;
23       this->backgroundColorButton->Text =
24          S"Change Background Color";
25       this->backgroundColorButton->Click += new EventHandler( this,
26          backgroundColorButton_Click );
27
28       // textColorButton
29       this->textColorButton->Location = Point( 16, 64 );
30       this->textColorButton->Name = S"textColorButton";
31       this->textColorButton->Size = Drawing::Size( 264, 32 );
32       this->textColorButton->TabIndex = 1;
33       this->textColorButton->Text = S"Change Text Color";
34       this->textColorButton->Click += new EventHandler( this,
35          textColorButton_Click );
36
37       // ShowColorsComplex
38       this->AutoScaleBaseSize = Drawing::Size( 5, 13 );
39       this->ClientSize = Drawing::Size( 292, 109 );
40       Control *tempControl[] = { this->textColorButton,
```

Fig. 13.10 ShowColorsComplex class method definitions. (Part 1 of 2.)

```cpp
41            this->backgroundColorButton };
42        this->Controls->AddRange( tempControl );
43        this->Name = S"ShowColorsComplex";
44        this->Text = S"ShowColorsComplex";
45        this->ResumeLayout();
46    }
47
48    // change text color
49    void ShowColorsComplex::textColorButton_Click(
50        Object *sender, EventArgs *e )
51    {
52        // create ColorDialog object
53        ColorDialog *colorChooser = new ColorDialog();
54        Windows::Forms::DialogResult result;
55
56        // get chosen color
57        result = colorChooser->ShowDialog();
58
59        if ( result == DialogResult::Cancel )
60            return;
61
62        // assign forecolor to result of dialog
63        this->ForeColor = colorChooser->Color;
64    } // end method textColorButton_Click
65
66    // change background color
67    void ShowColorsComplex::backgroundColorButton_Click(
68        Object *sender, EventArgs *e )
69    {
70        // create ColorDialog object
71        ColorDialog *colorChooser = new ColorDialog();
72        Windows::Forms::DialogResult result;
73
74        // show ColorDialog and get result
75        colorChooser->FullOpen = true;
76        result = colorChooser->ShowDialog();
77
78        if ( result == DialogResult::Cancel )
79            return;
80
81        // set background color
82        this->BackColor = colorChooser->Color;
83    } // end method backgroundColorButton_Click
```

Fig. 13.10 ShowColorsComplex class method definitions. (Part 2 of 2.)

```cpp
1    // Fig. 13.11: ShowColorsComplexTest.cpp
2    // Entry point for application.
3
4    #include "ShowColorsComplex.h"
5
```

Fig. 13.11 ShowColorsComplex class driver. (Part 1 of 2.)

```
 6    int __stdcall WinMain()()
 7    {
 8       Application::Run( new ShowColorsComplex() );
 9
10       return 0;
11    } // end function WinMain
```

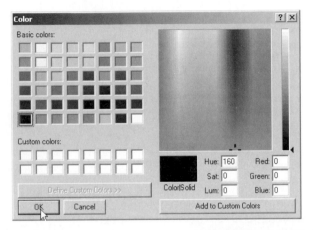

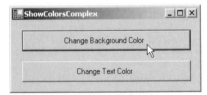 

Fig. 13.11 `ShowColorsComplex` class driver. (Part 2 of 2.)

Lines 49–64 (of Fig. 13.10) define the event handler that is called when the user clicks **Button textColorButton**. The event handler creates a new **ColorDialog** named **colorChooser** and invokes its *ShowDialog* method, which displays the window. Method **ShowDialog** returns a **DialogResult** (**result**) specifying whether the user selected **OK** (**DialogResult::OK**) or **Cancel** (**DialogResult::Cancel**). If the user selects **OK** after choosing a color, line 63 sets the text color of the form (including both buttons) to the selected color. Property **Color** of **colorChooser** stores users' selections.

Lines 67–83 define the event handler for button **backgroundColorButton**. The method modifies the background color of the form by setting **BackColor** equal to the dialog's **Color** property. The method creates a new **ColorDialog** and sets the dialog's *FullOpen* property to **true**. The dialog now displays all available colors, as shown in the screen capture in Fig. 13.11. The regular color display does not show the right-hand portion of the screen.

Users are not restricted to the **ColorDialog**'s 48 colors. To create a custom color, users can click anywhere in the **ColorDialog**'s large rectangle—this displays the various color shades. Adjust the slider, hue and other features to refine the color. When finished, click the **Add to Custom Colors** button, which adds the custom color to a square in the custom colors section of the dialog. Clicking **OK** sets the **Color** property of the

ColorDialog to that color. Selecting a color and pressing the dialog's **OK** button causes the application's background color to change.

13.4 Font Control

This section introduces methods and constants that are related to font control. Once a **Font** has been created, its properties cannot be modified. If programmers require a different **Font**, they must create a new **Font** object—there are many overloaded versions of the **Font** constructor for creating custom **Font**s. Some properties of class **Font** are summarized in Fig. 13.12.

Note that the **Size** property returns the font size as measured in design units, whereas **SizeInPoints** returns the font size as measured in points (a more common measurement). When we say that the **Size** property measures the size of the font in *design units*, we mean that the font size can be specified in a variety of ways, such as inches or millimeters. Some versions of the **Font** constructor accept a *GraphicsUnit* argument—an enumeration that allows users to specify the unit of measurement employed to describe the font size. Members of the **GraphicsUnit** enumeration include *Point* (1/72 inch), *Display* (1/75 inch), *Document* (1/300 inch), *Millimeter*, *Inch* and *Pixel*. If this argument is provided, the **Size** property contains the size of the font as measured in the specified design unit, and the **SizeInPoints** property converts the size of the font into points. For example, if we create a **Font** having size **1** and specify that **GraphicsUnit::Inch** be used to measure the font, the **Size** property will be **1**, and the **SizeInPoints** property will be **72**. If we employ a constructor that does not accept a member of **GraphicsUnit**, the default measurement for the font size is **GraphicsUnit::Point** (thus, the **Size** and **SizeInPoints** properties will be equal).

Class **Font** has a number of constructors. Most require a *font name*, which is a **String *** representing a font currently supported by the system. Common fonts include Microsoft *SansSerif* and *Serif*. Constructors also usually require the *font size* as an argument. Lastly, **Font** constructors usually require a *font style*, specified by the *FontStyle* enumeration: *Bold*, *Italic*, *Regular*, *Strikeout* and *Underline*. Font styles can be combined via the '**|**' operator (for example, **FontStyle::Italic | FontStyle::Bold** makes a font both italic and bold).

Property	Description
Bold	Tests a font for a bold font style. Returns **true** if the font is bold.
FontFamily	Represents the **FontFamily** of the **Font** (a grouping structure to organize fonts and define their similar properties).
Height	Represents the height of the font.
Italic	Tests a font for an italic font style. Returns **true** if the font is italic.
Name	Represents the font's name as a **String** pointer.
Size	Returns a **float** value indicating the current font size measured in design units (design units are any specified units of measurement for the font).

Fig. 13.12 Font class read-only properties. (Part 1 of 2.)

Property	Description
SizeInPoints	Returns a **float** value indicating the current font size measured in points.
Strikeout	Tests a font for a strikeout font style. Returns **true** if the font is in strikeout format.
Underline	Tests a font for a underline font style. Returns **true** if the font is underlined.

Fig. 13.12 **Font** class read-only properties. (Part 2 of 2.)

Common Programming Error 13.2

Specifying a font that is not available on a system is a logic error. If this occurs, that system's default font will be used instead.

Figures 13.13–13.15 display text in four different fonts, each of a different size. The program uses the **Font** constructor to initialize **Font** objects (lines 20–38 of Fig. 13.14). Each call to the **Font** constructor passes a font name (e.g., Arial, Times New Roman, Courier New or Tahoma) as a **String ***, a font size (a **float**) and a **FontStyle** object (**style**). **Graphics** method **DrawString** sets the font and draws the text at the specified location. Line 17 creates a **DarkBlue SolidBrush** object (**brush**), causing all **String**s drawn with that brush to appear in **DarkBlue**. Lines 30–31 set the font style to both bold and italic using the | operator. Notice that we must cast the result of this operation to a **FontStyle** object before using it.

Software Engineering Observation 13.2

There is no way to change the properties of a **Font** *object—to use a different font, the programmer must create a new* **Font** *object.*

```
1   // Fig. 13.13: UsingFonts.h
2   // Demonstrating various font settings.
3
4   #pragma once
5
6   #using <mscorlib.dll>
7   #using <system.dll>
8   #using <system.drawing.dll>
9   #using <system.windows.forms.dll>
10
11  using namespace System;
12  using namespace System::Drawing;
13  using namespace System::Windows::Forms;
14
15  public __gc class UsingFonts : public Form
16  {
17  public:
```

Fig. 13.13 **Font**s and **FontStyle**s. (Part 1 of 2.)

```
18        UsingFonts();
19
20   protected:
21      void OnPaint( PaintEventArgs *paintEvent );
22
23   private:
24      void InitializeComponent();
25   }; // end class UsingFonts
```

Fig. 13.13 Fonts and FontStyles. (Part 2 of 2.)

```
1    // Fig. 13.14: UsingFonts.cpp
2    // Method definitions for class UsingFonts.
3
4    #include "UsingFonts.h"
5
6    UsingFonts::UsingFonts()
7    {
8       InitializeComponent();
9    }
10
11   // demonstrate various font and style settings
12   void UsingFonts::OnPaint( PaintEventArgs *paintEvent )
13   {
14      __super::OnPaint( paintEvent ); // call base OnPaint method
15
16      Graphics *graphicsObject = paintEvent->Graphics;
17      SolidBrush *brush = new SolidBrush( Color::DarkBlue );
18
19      // arial, 12 pt bold
20      FontStyle style = FontStyle::Bold;
21      Drawing::Font *arial =
22         new Drawing::Font( S"Arial", 12, style );
23
24      // times new roman, 12 pt regular
25      style = FontStyle::Regular;
26      Drawing::Font *timesNewRoman =
27         new Drawing::Font( S"Times New Roman", 12, style );
28
29      // courier new, 16 pt bold and italic
30      style = static_cast< FontStyle >( FontStyle::Bold |
31         FontStyle::Italic );
32      Drawing::Font *courierNew =
33         new Drawing::Font( S"Courier New", 16, style );
34
35      // tahoma, 18 pt strikeout
36      style = FontStyle::Strikeout;
37      Drawing::Font *tahoma =
38         new Drawing::Font( S"Tahoma", 18, style );
39
40      graphicsObject->DrawString( String::Concat( arial->Name,
```

Fig. 13.14 UsingFonts class method definitions. (Part 1 of 2.)

```
41          S" 12 point bold." ), arial, brush, 10, 10 );
42
43      graphicsObject->DrawString( String::Concat(
44          timesNewRoman->Name, S" 12 point plain." ),
45          timesNewRoman, brush, 10, 30 );
46
47      graphicsObject->DrawString( String::Concat( courierNew->Name,
48          S" 16 point bold and italic." ), courierNew,
49          brush, 10, 54 );
50
51      graphicsObject->DrawString( String::Concat( tahoma->Name,
52          S" 18 point strikeout." ), tahoma, brush, 10, 75 );
53  } // end method OnPaint
54
55  void UsingFonts::InitializeComponent()
56  {
57      this->AutoScaleBaseSize = Drawing::Size( 5, 13 );
58      this->ClientSize = Drawing::Size( 504, 109 );
59      this->Name = S"UsingFonts";
60      this->Text = S"UsingFonts";
61  }
```

Fig. 13.14 UsingFonts class method definitions. (Part 2 of 2.)

```
 1  // Fig. 13.15: UsingFontsTest.cpp
 2  // Entry point for application.
 3
 4  #include "UsingFonts.h"
 5
 6  int __stdcall WinMain()()
 7  {
 8      Application::Run( new UsingFonts() );
 9
10      return 0;
11  } // end function WinMain
```

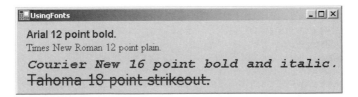

Fig. 13.15 UsingFonts class driver.

Programmers can define precise information about a font's *metrics* (or properties), such as *height*, *descent* (the amount that characters dip below the baseline), *ascent* (the amount that characters rise above the baseline) and *leading* (the difference between the ascent of one line and the descent of the previous line). Figure 13.16 illustrates these properties.

Class *FontFamily* defines characteristics common to a group of related fonts. Class **FontFamily** provides several methods used to determine the font metrics that are shared by members of a particular family. These methods are summarized in Fig. 13.17.

Figures 13.18–13.20 display the metrics of two fonts. Line 20 (Fig. 13.19) creates **Font arial** and sets it to 12-point Arial font. Line 21 uses class **Font** property **FontFamily** to obtain object **arial**'s **FontFamily** object. Lines 26–27 output the **String** representation of the font. Lines 29–43 then use methods of class **FontFamily** to return integers specifying the ascent, descent, height and leading of the font. Lines 46–65 repeat this process for font **sansSerif**, a **Font** object derived from the MS Sans Serif **FontFamily**.

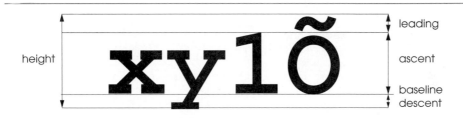

Fig. 13.16 Illustration of font metrics.

Method	Description
GetCellAscent	Returns an **int** representing the ascent of a font as measured in design units.
GetCellDescent	Returns an **int** representing the descent of a font as measured in design units.
GetEmHeight	Returns an **int** representing the height of a font as measured in design points.
GetLineSpacing	Returns an **int** representing the distance between two consecutive lines of text as measured in design units.

Fig. 13.17 **FontFamily** methods that return font-metric information.

```
1   // Fig. 13.18: UsingFontMetrics.h
2   // Displaying font metric information.
3
4   #pragma once
5
6   #using <mscorlib.dll>
7   #using <system.dll>
8   #using <system.drawing.dll>
9   #using <system.windows.forms.dll>
10
```

Fig. 13.18 **FontFamily** class used to obtain font-metric information. (Part 1 of 2.)

```
11   using namespace System;
12   using namespace System::Drawing;
13   using namespace System::Windows::Forms;
14
15   public __gc class UsingFontMetrics : public Form
16   {
17   public:
18      UsingFontMetrics();
19
20   protected:
21      void OnPaint( PaintEventArgs * );
22
23   private:
24      void InitializeComponent();
25   }; // end class UsingFontMetrics
```

Fig. 13.18 `FontFamily` class used to obtain font-metric information. (Part 2 of 2.)

```
1    // Fig. 13.19: UsingFontMetrics.cpp
2    // Method definitions for class UsingFontMetrics.
3
4    #include "UsingFontMetrics.h"
5
6    UsingFontMetrics::UsingFontMetrics()
7    {
8       InitializeComponent();
9    }
10
11   // displays font information
12   void UsingFontMetrics::OnPaint( PaintEventArgs *paintEvent )
13   {
14      __super::OnPaint( paintEvent ); // call base OnPaint method
15
16      Graphics *graphicsObject = paintEvent->Graphics;
17      SolidBrush *brush = new SolidBrush( Color::DarkBlue );
18
19      // Arial font metrics
20      Drawing::Font *arial = new Drawing::Font( S"Arial", 12 );
21      FontFamily *family = arial->FontFamily;
22      Drawing::Font *sanSerif = new Drawing::Font(
23         S"Microsoft Sans Serif", 14, FontStyle::Italic );
24
25      // display Arial font metrics
26      graphicsObject->DrawString( String::Concat
27         ( S"Current Font: ", arial ), arial, brush, 10, 10 );
28
29      graphicsObject->DrawString( String::Concat( S"Ascent: ",
30         family->GetCellAscent( FontStyle::Regular ).ToString() ),
31         arial, brush, 10, 30 );
32
```

Fig. 13.19 `UsingFontMetrics` class method definitions. (Part 1 of 2.)

```
33    graphicsObject->DrawString( String::Concat( S"Descent: ",
34       family->GetCellDescent( FontStyle::Regular ).ToString() ),
35       arial, brush, 10, 50 );
36
37    graphicsObject->DrawString( String::Concat( S"Height: ",
38       family->GetEmHeight( FontStyle::Regular ).ToString() ),
39       arial, brush, 10, 70 );
40
41    graphicsObject->DrawString( String::Concat( S"Leading: ",
42       family->GetLineSpacing( FontStyle::Regular ).ToString() ),
43       arial, brush, 10, 90 );
44
45    // display Sans Serif font metrics
46    family = sanSerif->FontFamily;
47
48    graphicsObject->DrawString( String::Concat( S"Current Font: ",
49       sanSerif ), sanSerif, brush, 10, 130 );
50
51    graphicsObject->DrawString( String::Concat( S"Ascent: ",
52       family->GetCellAscent( FontStyle::Regular ).ToString() ),
53       sanSerif, brush, 10, 150 );
54
55    graphicsObject->DrawString( String::Concat( S"Descent: ",
56       family->GetCellDescent( FontStyle::Regular ).ToString() ),
57       sanSerif, brush, 10, 170 );
58
59    graphicsObject->DrawString( String::Concat( S"Height: ",
60       family->GetEmHeight( FontStyle::Regular ).ToString() ),
61       sanSerif, brush, 10, 190 );
62
63    graphicsObject->DrawString( String::Concat( S"Leading: ",
64       family->GetLineSpacing( FontStyle::Regular ).ToString() ),
65       sanSerif, brush, 10, 210 );
66 } // end method OnPaint
67
68 void UsingFontMetrics::InitializeComponent()
69 {
70    this->AutoScaleBaseSize = Drawing::Size( 5, 13 );
71    this->ClientSize = Drawing::Size( 904, 237 );
72    this->Name = S"UsingFontMetrics";
73    this->Text = S"UsingFontMetrics";
74 }
```

Fig. 13.19 UsingFontMetrics class method definitions. (Part 2 of 2.)

```
1    // Fig. 13.20: UsingFontMetricsTest.cpp
2    // Entry point for application.
3
4    #include "UsingFontMetrics.h"
5
```

Fig. 13.20 UsingFontMetrics class driver. (Part 1 of 2.)

```
 6   int __stdcall WinMain()()
 7   {
 8       Application::Run( new UsingFontMetrics() );
 9
10       return 0;
11   } // end function WinMain
```

```
UsingFontMetrics                                                        _ □ ×
Current Font: [Font: Name=Arial, Size=12, Units=3, GdiCharSet=1, GdiVerticalFont=False]
Ascent: 1854
Descent: 434
Height: 2048
Leading: 2355


Current Font: [Font: Name=Microsoft Sans Serif, Size=14, Units=3, GdiCharSet=1, GdiVerticalFont=False]
Ascent: 1888
Descent: 430
Height: 2048
Leading: 2318
```

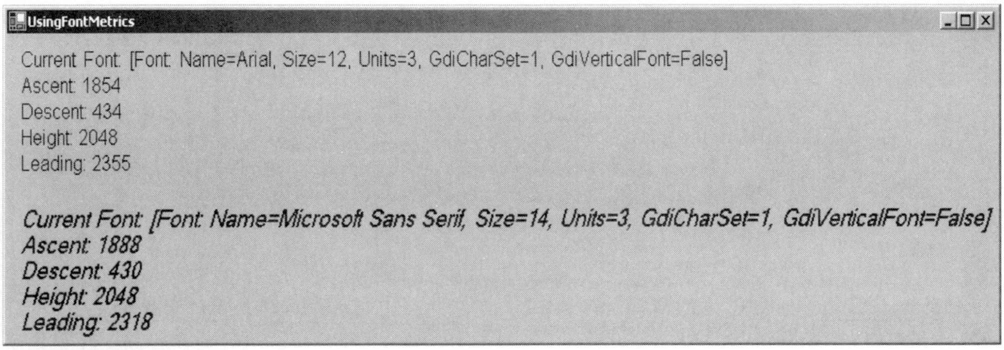

Fig. 13.20 `UsingFontMetrics` class driver. (Part 2 of 2.)

13.5 Drawing Lines, Rectangles and Ovals

This section presents a variety of **Graphics** methods for drawing lines, rectangles and ovals. Each of the drawing methods has several overloaded versions. When employing methods that draw shape outlines, we use versions that take a **Pen** and four **int**s; when employing methods that draw solid shapes, we use versions that take a **Brush** and four **int**s. In both instances, the first two **int** arguments represent the coordinates of the upper-left corner of the shape or its enclosing area, and the last two **int**s indicate the shape's width and height. Figure 13.21 summarizes various **Graphics** methods and their parameters.

The application in Fig. 13.22–Fig. 13.24 draws lines, rectangles and ellipses. In this application, we also demonstrate methods that draw filled and unfilled shapes.

Graphics Drawing Methods and Descriptions.

Note: Many of these methods are overloaded—consult the documentation for a full listing.

DrawLine(Pen p, int x1, int y1, int x2, int y2)
Draws a line from (**x1, y1**) to (**x2, y2**). The **Pen** determines the color, style and width of the line.

DrawRectangle(Pen p, int x, int y, int width, int height)
Draws a rectangle of the specified width and height. The top-left corner of the rectangle is at point (**x, y**). The **Pen** determines the color, style, and border width of the rectangle.

Fig. 13.21 `Graphics` methods that draw lines, rectangles and ovals. (Part 1 of 2.)

Graphics Drawing Methods and Descriptions.

FillRectangle(Brush b, *int* x, *int* y, *int* width, *int* height)
Draws a solid rectangle of the specified width and height. The top-left corner of the rectangle is at point (**x**, **y**). The **Brush** determines the fill pattern inside the rectangle.

DrawEllipse(Pen p, *int* x, *int* y, *int* width, *int* height)
Draws an ellipse inside a rectangle. The width and height of the rectangle are as specified, and its top-left corner is at point (**x**, **y**). The **Pen** determines the color, style and border width of the ellipse.

FillEllipse(Brush b, *int* x, *int* y, *int* width, *int* height)
Draws a filled ellipse inside a rectangle. The width and height of the rectangle are as specified, and its top-left corner is at point (**x**, **y**). The **Brush** determines the pattern inside the ellipse.

Fig. 13.21 **Graphics** methods that draw lines, rectangles and ovals. (Part 2 of 2.)

```
1   // Fig. 13.22: LinesRectanglesOvals.h
2   // Demonstrating lines, rectangles and ovals.
3
4   #pragma once
5
6   #using <mscorlib.dll>
7   #using <system.dll>
8   #using <system.drawing.dll>
9   #using <system.windows.forms.dll>
10
11  using namespace System;
12  using namespace System::Drawing;;
13  using namespace System::Windows::Forms;
14
15  public __gc class LinesRectanglesOvals : public Form
16  {
17  public:
18     LinesRectanglesOvals();
19
20  protected:
21     void OnPaint( PaintEventArgs * );
22
23  private:
24     void InitializeComponent();
25  }; // end class LinesRectanglesOvals
```

Fig. 13.22 Demonstration of methods that draw lines, rectangles and ellipses.

```
1   // Fig. 13.23: LinesRectanglesOvals.cpp
2   // Method definitions for class LinesRectanglesOvals.
3
4   #include "LinesRectanglesOvals.h"
5
6   LinesRectanglesOvals::LinesRectanglesOvals()
```

Fig. 13.23 **LinesRectanglesOvals** class method definitions. (Part 1 of 2.)

```
 7  {
 8      InitializeComponent();
 9  }
10
11  void LinesRectanglesOvals::OnPaint( PaintEventArgs *paintEvent )
12  {
13      __super::OnPaint( paintEvent ); // call base OnPaint method
14
15      // get graphics object
16      Graphics *graphicsObject = paintEvent->Graphics;
17      SolidBrush *brush = new SolidBrush( Color::Blue );
18      Pen *pen = new Pen( Color::AliceBlue );
19
20      // create filled rectangle
21      graphicsObject->FillRectangle( brush, 90, 30, 150, 90 );
22
23      // draw lines to connect rectangles
24      graphicsObject->DrawLine( pen, 90, 30, 110, 40 );
25      graphicsObject->DrawLine( pen, 90, 120, 110, 130 );
26      graphicsObject->DrawLine( pen, 240, 30, 260, 40 );
27      graphicsObject->DrawLine( pen, 240, 120, 260, 130 );
28
29      // draw top rectangle
30      graphicsObject->DrawRectangle( pen, 110, 40, 150, 90 );
31
32      // set brush to red
33      brush->Color = Color::Red;
34
35      // draw base Ellipse
36      graphicsObject->FillEllipse( brush, 280, 75, 100, 50 );
37
38      // draw connecting lines
39      graphicsObject->DrawLine( pen, 380, 55, 380, 100 );
40      graphicsObject->DrawLine( pen, 280, 55, 280, 100 );
41
42      // draw Ellipse outline
43      graphicsObject->DrawEllipse( pen, 280, 30, 100, 50 );
44  } // end method OnPaint
45
46  void LinesRectanglesOvals::InitializeComponent()
47  {
48      this->AutoScaleBaseSize = Drawing::Size( 5, 13 );
49      this->ClientSize = Drawing::Size( 488, 149 );
50      this->Name = S"LinesRectanglesOvals";
51      this->Text = S"LinesRectanglesOvals";
52  }
```

Fig. 13.23 `LinesRectanglesOvals` class method definitions. (Part 2 of 2.)

```
1  // Fig. 13.24: LinesRectanglesOvalsTest.cpp
2  // Entry point for application.
3
4  #include "LinesRectanglesOvals.h"
```

Fig. 13.24 `LinesRectanglesOvals` class driver. (Part 1 of 2.)

```
 5
 6   int __stdcall WinMain()()
 7   {
 8      Application::Run( new LinesRectanglesOvals() );
 9
10      return 0;
11   } // end function WinMain
```

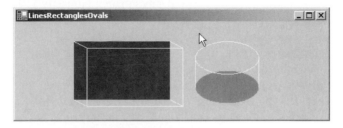

Fig. 13.24 LinesRectanglesOvals class driver. (Part 2 of 2.)

Methods *DrawRectangle* and *FillRectangle* (lines 30 and 21 of Fig. 13.23) draw rectangles on the screen. For each method, the first argument specifies the drawing object to use. The **DrawRectangle** method uses a **Pen** object, whereas the **FillRectangle** method uses a **Brush** object (in this case, an instance of **SolidBrush**, which derives from **Brush**). The next two arguments specify the coordinates of the upper-left corner of the *bounding rectangle*, which represents the area in which the rectangle will be drawn. The fourth and fifth arguments specify the rectangle's width and height. Method *DrawLine* (lines 24–27) takes a **Pen** and two pairs of **int**s, specifying the startpoint and endpoint of the line. The method then draws a line, using the **Pen** object passed to it.

Methods *DrawEllipse* and *FillEllipse* (lines 43 and 36 of Fig. 13.23) each provide overloaded versions that take five arguments. In both methods, the first argument specifies the drawing object to use. The next two arguments specify the upper-left coordinates of the bounding rectangle representing the area in which the ellipse will be drawn. The last two arguments specify the bounding rectangle's width and height, respectively.

Figure 13.25 depicts an ellipse bounded by a rectangle. The ellipse touches the midpoint of each of the four sides of the bounding rectangle. The bounding rectangle is not displayed on the screen.

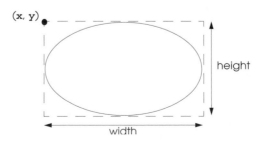

Fig. 13.25 Ellipse bounded by a rectangle.

13.6 Drawing Arcs

Arcs are portions of ellipses and are measured in degrees, beginning at a *starting angle* and continuing for a specified number of degrees called the *arc angle*. An arc is said to *sweep* (traverse) its arc angle, beginning from its starting angle. Arcs that sweep in a clockwise direction are measured in positive degrees; arcs that sweep in a counterclockwise direction are measured in negative degrees. Figure 13.26 depicts two arcs. Note that the arc in the left portion of the figure sweeps downward from zero degrees to approximately 110 degrees. Similarly, the arc in the right portion of the figure sweeps upward from zero degrees to approximately –110 degrees.

Notice the dashed boxes around the arcs in Fig. 13.26. We draw each arc as part of an oval (the rest of which is not visible). When drawing an oval, we specify the oval's dimensions in the form of a bounding rectangle that encloses the oval. The boxes in Fig. 13.26 correspond to these bounding rectangles. The **Graphics** methods used to draw arcs—**DrawArc**, **DrawPie** and **FillPie**—are summarized in Fig. 13.27.

The application in Fig. 13.28–Fig. 13.30 draws six images (three arcs and three filled pie slices) to demonstrate the arc methods listed in Fig. 13.27. To illustrate the bounding rectangles that determine the sizes and locations of the arcs, the arcs are displayed inside red rectangles that have the same *x*-coordinates, *y*-coordinates and width and height arguments as those that define the bounding rectangles for the arcs.

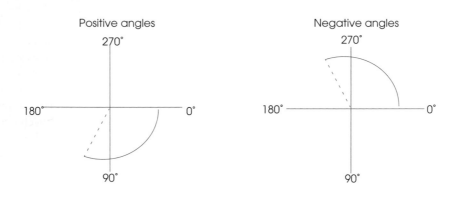

Fig. 13.26 Positive and negative arc angles.

Graphics Methods And Descriptions

Note: Many of these methods are overloaded—consult the documentation for a complete listing.

```
DrawArc( Pen *p, int x, int y, int width, int height,
    int startAngle, int sweepAngle )
```
Draws an arc of an ellipse, beginning from angle **startAngle** (in degrees) and sweeping **sweepAngle** degrees. The ellipse is defined by a bounding rectangle of width **w**, height **h** and upper-left corner **(x,y)**. The **Pen** determines the color, border width and style of the arc.

Fig. 13.27 **Graphics** methods for drawing arcs. (Part 1 of 2.)

Graphics Methods And Descriptions

`DrawPie( Pen *p, int x, int y, int width, int height,`
`    int startAngle, int sweepAngle )`
Draws a pie section of an ellipse, beginning from angle **startAngle** (in degrees) and sweeping **sweepAngle** degrees. The ellipse is defined by a bounding rectangle of width **w**, height **h** and upper-left corner (**x,y**). The **Pen** determines the color, border width and style of the arc.

`FillPie( Brush *b, int x, int y, int width, int height,`
`    int startAngle, int sweepAngle )`
Functions similarly to **DrawPie**, except draws a solid arc (i.e., a sector). The **Brush** determines the fill pattern for the solid arc.

Fig. 13.27 `Graphics` methods for drawing arcs. (Part 2 of 2.)

```
1   // Fig. 13.28:
2   // Drawing various arcs on a form.
3
4   #pragma once
5
6   #using <mscorlib.dll>
7   #using <system.dll>
8   #using <system.drawing.dll>
9   #using <system.windows.forms.dll>
10
11  using namespace System;
12  using namespace System::Drawing;
13  using namespace System::Windows::Forms;
14
15  public __gc class DrawArcs : public Form
16  {
17  public:
18     DrawArcs();
19     void OnPaint( PaintEventArgs * );
20
21  private:
22     void InitializeComponent();
23  }; // end class DrawArcs
```

Fig. 13.28 Arc-method demonstration.

```
1   // Fig. 13.29: DrawArcs.cpp
2   // Method definitions for class DrawArcs.
3
4   #include "DrawArcs.h"
5
6   // default constructor
7   DrawArcs::DrawArcs()
8   {
```

Fig. 13.29 `DrawArcs` class method definitions. (Part 1 of 2.)

```
 9        InitializeComponent();
10    }
11
12    void DrawArcs::InitializeComponent()
13    {
14        this->AutoScaleBaseSize = Drawing::Size( 5, 13 );
15        this->BackColor = SystemColors::ControlLight;
16        this->ClientSize = Drawing::Size( 292, 221 );
17        this->Name = S"arcForm";
18        this->Text = S"Drawing Arcs";
19    } // end method InitializeComponent
20
21    void DrawArcs::OnPaint( PaintEventArgs *paintEvent )
22    {
23        __super::OnPaint( paintEvent ); // call base OnPaint method
24
25        // get graphics object
26        Graphics *graphicsObject = paintEvent->Graphics;
27        Rectangle rectangle1 = Rectangle( 15, 35, 80, 80 );
28        SolidBrush *brush1 = new SolidBrush( Color::Firebrick );
29        Pen *pen1 = new Pen( brush1, 1 );
30        SolidBrush *brush2 = new SolidBrush( Color::DarkBlue );
31        Pen *pen2 = new Pen( brush2, 1 );
32
33        // start at 0 and sweep 360 degrees
34        graphicsObject->DrawRectangle( pen1, rectangle1 );
35        graphicsObject->DrawArc( pen2, rectangle1, 0, 360 );
36
37        // start at 0 and sweep 110 degrees
38        rectangle1.Location = Point( 100, 35 );
39        graphicsObject->DrawRectangle( pen1, rectangle1 );
40        graphicsObject->DrawArc( pen2, rectangle1, 0, 110 );
41
42        // start at 0 and sweep -270 degrees
43        rectangle1.Location = Point( 185, 35 );
44        graphicsObject->DrawRectangle( pen1, rectangle1 );
45        graphicsObject->DrawArc( pen2, rectangle1, 0, -270 );
46
47        // start at 0 and sweep 360 degrees
48        rectangle1.Location = Point( 15, 120 );
49        rectangle1.Size = Drawing::Size( 80, 40 );
50        graphicsObject->DrawRectangle( pen1, rectangle1 );
51        graphicsObject->FillPie( brush2, rectangle1, 0, 360 );
52
53        // start at 270 and sweep -90 degrees
54        rectangle1.Location = Point( 100, 120 );
55        graphicsObject->DrawRectangle( pen1, rectangle1 );
56        graphicsObject->FillPie( brush2, rectangle1, 270, -90 );
57
58        // start at 0 and sweep -270 degrees
59        rectangle1.Location = Point( 185, 120 );
60        graphicsObject->DrawRectangle( pen1, rectangle1 );
61        graphicsObject->FillPie( brush2, rectangle1, 0, -270 );
62    } // end method OnPaint
```

Fig. 13.29 DrawArcs class method definitions. (Part 2 of 2.)

```
1   // Fig. 13.30: DrawArcsTest.cpp
2   // Drawing various arcs on a form.
3
4   #include "DrawArcs.h"
5
6   int __stdcall WinMain()()
7   {
8      Application::Run( new DrawArcs() );
9
10     return 0;
11  } // end function WinMain
```

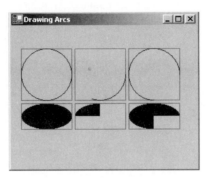

Fig. 13.30 DrawArcs class driver.

Lines 26–31 (Fig. 13.29) create the objects that we need to draw various arcs: **Graphics** objects, **Rectangle**s, **SolidBrush**es and **Pen**s. Lines 34–35 draw a rectangle and an arc inside the rectangle. The arc sweeps 360 degrees, forming a circle. Line 38 changes the location of the **Rectangle** by setting its **Location** property to a new **Point**. The **Point** constructor takes the *x-* and *y-*coordinates of the new point. The **Location** property determines the upper-left corner of the **Rectangle**. After drawing the rectangle, the program draws an arc that starts at 0 degrees and sweeps 110 degrees. Because angles in Visual C++ .NET increase in a clockwise direction, the arc sweeps downward.

Lines 43–45 perform similar functions, except that the specified arc sweeps -270 degrees. The **Size** property of a **Rectangle** determines the a49 sets the **Size** property to a new **Size** object, which changes the size of the rectangle.

The remainder of the program is similar to the portions described above, except that a **SolidBrush** is used with method **FillPie**, and the bounding rectangle has a different size. The resulting arcs, which are filled, can be seen in the bottom half of the screenshot in Fig. 13.30.

13.7 Drawing Polygons and Polylines

Polygons are multisided shapes. There are several **Graphics** methods used to draw polygons: *DrawLines* draws a series of connected points, *DrawPolygon* draws a closed polygon and *FillPolygon* draws a solid polygon. These methods are described in

Fig. 13.31. The program in Fig. 13.32–Fig. 13.34 allows users to draw polygons and connected lines via the methods listed in Fig. 13.31.

Method	Description
DrawLines	Draws a series of connected lines. The coordinates of each point are specified in an array of Points. If the last point is different from the first point, the figure is not closed.
DrawPolygon	Draws a polygon. The coordinates of each point are specified in an array of Point objects. This method draws a closed polygon, even if the last point is different from the first point.
FillPolygon	Draws a solid polygon. The coordinates of each point are specified in an array of Points. This method draws a closed polygon, even if the last point is different from the first point.

Fig. 13.31 Graphics methods for drawing polygons.

```
1   // Fig. 13.32: DrawPolygons.h
2   // Demonstrating polygons.
3
4   #pragma once
5
6   #using <mscorlib.dll>
7   #using <system.dll>
8   #using <system.drawing.dll>
9   #using <system.windows.forms.dll>
10
11  using namespace System;
12  using namespace System::Drawing;
13  using namespace System::Collections;
14  using namespace System::Windows::Forms;
15
16  public __gc class PolygonForm : public Form
17  {
18  public:
19     PolygonForm();
20
21  private:
22     Button *colorButton;
23     Button *clearButton;
24     GroupBox *typeGroup;
25     RadioButton *filledPolygonOption;
26     RadioButton *lineOption;
27     RadioButton *polygonOption;
28     Panel *drawPanel;
29
30     // contains list of polygon vertices
31     static ArrayList *points = new ArrayList();
32
```

Fig. 13.32 Polygon-drawing demonstration. (Part 1 of 2.)

```
33        // initialize default pen and brush
34        static Pen *pen = new Pen( Color::DarkBlue );
35        static SolidBrush *brush = new SolidBrush( Color::DarkBlue );
36
37        void InitializeComponent();
38        void drawPanel_MouseDown( Object *, MouseEventArgs * );
39        void drawPanel_Paint( Object *, PaintEventArgs * );
40        void clearButton_Click( Object *, EventArgs * );
41        void polygonOption_CheckedChanged( Object *,
42           EventArgs * );
43        void lineOption_CheckedChanged( Object *, EventArgs * );
44        void filledPolygonOption_CheckedChanged( Object *,
45           EventArgs * );
46        void colorButton_Click( Object *, EventArgs * );
47    }; // end class PolygonForm
```

Fig. 13.32 Polygon-drawing demonstration. (Part 2 of 2.)

```
1     // Fig. 13.33: DrawPolygons.cpp
2     // Method definitions for class PolygonForm.
3
4     #include "DrawPolygons.h"
5
6     PolygonForm::PolygonForm()
7     {
8        InitializeComponent();
9     }
10
11    void PolygonForm::InitializeComponent()
12    {
13       this->colorButton = new Button();
14       this->clearButton = new Button();
15       this->typeGroup = new GroupBox();
16       this->filledPolygonOption = new RadioButton();
17       this->lineOption = new RadioButton();
18       this->polygonOption = new RadioButton();
19       this->drawPanel = new Panel();
20       this->typeGroup->SuspendLayout();
21       this->SuspendLayout();
22
23       // colorButton
24       this->colorButton->Location = Point( 240, 192 );
25       this->colorButton->Name = S"colorButton";
26       this->colorButton->Size = Drawing::Size( 112, 24 );
27       this->colorButton->TabIndex = 7;
28       this->colorButton->Text = S"Change Color";
29       this->colorButton->Click += new EventHandler( this,
30          colorButton_Click );
31
32       // clearButton
33       this->clearButton->Location = Point( 240, 160 );
```

Fig. 13.33 `PolygonForm` class method definitions. (Part 1 of 5.)

```
34      this->clearButton->Name = S"clearButton";
35      this->clearButton->Size = Drawing::Size( 112, 24 );
36      this->clearButton->TabIndex = 6;
37      this->clearButton->Text = S"Clear";
38      this->clearButton->Click += new EventHandler( this,
39         clearButton_Click );
40
41      // typeGroup
42      Control *tempControl[] = { this->filledPolygonOption,
43         this->lineOption, this->polygonOption };
44      this->typeGroup->Controls->AddRange( tempControl );
45      this->typeGroup->Location = Point( 232, 8 );
46      this->typeGroup->Name = S"typeGroup";
47      this->typeGroup->Size = Drawing::Size( 128, 104 );
48      this->typeGroup->TabIndex = 4;
49      this->typeGroup->TabStop = false;
50      this->typeGroup->Text = S"Select Type";
51
52      // filledPolygonOption
53      this->filledPolygonOption->Location = Point( 8, 80 );
54      this->filledPolygonOption->Name = S"filledPolygonOption";
55      this->filledPolygonOption->Size = Drawing::Size( 112, 16 );
56      this->filledPolygonOption->TabIndex = 2;
57      this->filledPolygonOption->Text = S"Filled Polygon";
58      this->filledPolygonOption->CheckedChanged += new EventHandler(
59         this, filledPolygonOption_CheckedChanged );
60
61      // lineOption
62      this->lineOption->Location = Point( 8, 24 );
63      this->lineOption->Name = S"lineOption";
64      this->lineOption->Size = Drawing::Size( 112, 16 );
65      this->lineOption->TabIndex = 1;
66      this->lineOption->Text = S"Lines";
67      this->lineOption->CheckedChanged += new EventHandler(
68         this, lineOption_CheckedChanged );
69
70      // polygonOption
71      this->polygonOption->Location = Point( 8, 48 );
72      this->polygonOption->Name = S"polygonOption";
73      this->polygonOption->Size = Drawing::Size( 112, 24 );
74      this->polygonOption->TabIndex = 0;
75      this->polygonOption->Text = S"Polygon";
76      this->polygonOption->CheckedChanged += new EventHandler(
77         this, polygonOption_CheckedChanged );
78
79      // drawPanel
80      this->drawPanel->BackColor = SystemColors::Window;
81      this->drawPanel->BorderStyle = BorderStyle::Fixed3D;
82      this->drawPanel->Name = S"drawPanel";
83      this->drawPanel->Size = Drawing::Size( 232, 264 );
84      this->drawPanel->TabIndex = 5;
85      this->drawPanel->Paint += new PaintEventHandler(
```

Fig. 13.33 PolygonForm class method definitions. (Part 2 of 5.)

```
86            this, drawPanel_Paint );
87        this->drawPanel->MouseDown += new MouseEventHandler(
88            this, drawPanel_MouseDown );
89
90      // polygonForm
91      this->AutoScaleBaseSize = Drawing::Size( 5, 13 );
92      this->ClientSize = Drawing::Size( 360, 269 );
93      Control *tempControl2[] = { this->colorButton,
94          this->clearButton, this->typeGroup, this->drawPanel };
95      this->Controls->AddRange( tempControl2 );
96      this->Name = S"polygonForm";
97      this->Text = S"Drawing Polygons";
98      this->typeGroup->ResumeLayout();
99      this->ResumeLayout();
100 } // end method InitializeComponent
101
102 // draw panel mouse down event handler
103 void PolygonForm::drawPanel_MouseDown( Object *sender,
104    MouseEventArgs *e )
105 {
106    // add mouse position to vertex list
107    points->Add( __box( Point( e->X, e->Y ) ) );
108    drawPanel->Invalidate(); // refresh panel
109 } // end method drawPanel_MouseDown
110
111 void PolygonForm::drawPanel_Paint( Object *sender,
112    PaintEventArgs *e )
113 {
114    // get graphics object for panel
115    Graphics *graphicsObject = e->Graphics;
116
117    // if arraylist has 2 or more points, display shape
118    if ( points->Count > 1 ) {
119
120       // create array of points
121       Point pointArray[] = new Point[ points->Count ];
122
123       // add each point to the array
124       for( int i = 0; i < points->Count; i++ )
125          pointArray[ i ] = *(
126          dynamic_cast< Point* >( points->Item[ i ] ) );
127
128       if ( polygonOption->Checked )
129
130          // draw polygon
131          graphicsObject->DrawPolygon( pen, pointArray );
132
133       else if ( lineOption->Checked )
134
135          // draw lines
136          graphicsObject->DrawLines( pen, pointArray );
137
```

Fig. 13.33 PolygonForm class method definitions. (Part 3 of 5.)

```
138           else if ( filledPolygonOption->Checked )
139
140              // draw filled
141              graphicsObject->FillPolygon( brush, pointArray );
142        } //end if
143    } // end method drawPanel_Paint
144
145    // handle clearButton click event
146    void PolygonForm::clearButton_Click( Object *sender,
147       EventArgs *e )
148    {
149       points = new ArrayList(); // remove points
150
151       drawPanel->Invalidate(); // refresh panel
152    } // end method clearButton_Click
153
154    // handle polygon radio button CheckedChanged event
155    void PolygonForm::polygonOption_CheckedChanged(
156       Object *sender, EventArgs *e )
157    {
158       drawPanel->Invalidate(); // refresh panel
159    } // end method polygonOption_CheckedChanged
160
161    // handle line radio button CheckedChanged event
162    void PolygonForm::lineOption_CheckedChanged(
163       Object *sender, EventArgs *e )
164    {
165       drawPanel->Invalidate(); // refresh panel
166    } // end method lineOption_CheckedChanged
167
168    // handle filled polygon radio button
169    // CheckedChanged event
170    void PolygonForm::filledPolygonOption_CheckedChanged(
171       Object *sender, EventArgs *e )
172    {
173       drawPanel->Invalidate(); // refresh panel
174    } // end method filledPolygonOption_CheckedChanged
175
176    // handle colorButton click event
177    void PolygonForm::colorButton_Click(
178       Object *sender, EventArgs *e )
179    {
180       // create new color dialog
181       ColorDialog *dialogColor = new ColorDialog();
182
183       // show dialog and obtain result
184       Windows::Forms::DialogResult result =
185          dialogColor->ShowDialog();
186
187       // return if user cancels
188       if ( result == DialogResult::Cancel )
189          return;
```

Fig. 13.33 PolygonForm class method definitions. (Part 4 of 5.)

```
190
191     pen->Color = dialogColor->Color;   // set pen to color
192     brush->Color = dialogColor->Color; // set brush
193     drawPanel->Invalidate();           // refresh panel;
194  } // end method colorButton_Click
```

Fig. 13.33 `PolygonForm` class method definitions. (Part 5 of 5.)

```
1   // Fig. 13.34: DrawPolygonsTest.cpp
2   // Entry point for application.
3
4   #include "DrawPolygons.h"
5
6   int __stdcall WinMain()()
7   {
8       Application::Run( new PolygonForm() );
9
10      return 0;
11  } // end function WinMain
```

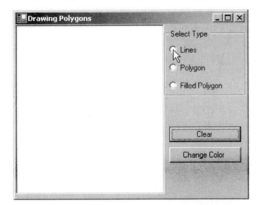

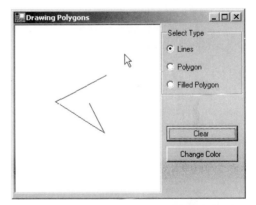

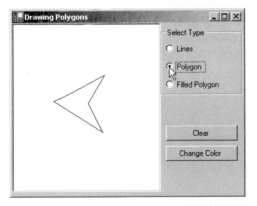

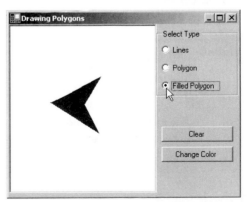

Fig. 13.34 `PolygonForm` class driver.

To allow the user to specify a variable number of points, line 31 (Fig. 13.32) declares **ArrayList points** as a container for our **Point** objects. Class **ArrayList** (namespace **System::Collections**) mimics the functionality of conventional arrays, yet provides dynamic resizing of the collection through the class's methods. **ArrayList**s store pointers to **Object**s. All classes derive from class **Object**, so an **ArrayList** can contain objects of any type. In this example, we use class **ArrayList** to store **Point** objects. We discuss class **ArrayList** in more detail in Chapter 19, Data Structures and Collections.

Lines 34–35 declare the **Pen** and **Brush** used to color our shapes. The **MouseDown** event handler (lines 103–109 of Fig. 13.33) for **Panel drawPanel** stores mouse-click locations in the **points ArrayList** using method *Add*. **ArrayList** method **Add** appends a new element at the end of an **ArrayList**.

Line 108 then calls method **Invalidate** of **drawPanel** to ensure that the panel refreshes to accommodate the new point. Notice that we call **Invalidate** of **draw-Panel** rather than the entire **Form** because we only wish to update the **drawPanel**. Method **drawPanel_Paint** (lines 111–143) handles the **Panel**'s **Paint** event. It obtains the panel's **Graphics** object (line 115) and, if the **ArrayList points** contains two or more **Points**, displays the polygon with the method that the user selected via the GUI radio buttons (lines 118–142). In lines 121–126, we extract the **Point** objects from the **ArrayList** using indexed property *Item*. **ArrayList** elements are accessed by following the **ArrayList** indexed property **Item** with the array subscript operator (**[]**) and the desired index of the element (e.g., **points->Item[i]**). However, notice that line 126 uses **dynamic_cast** to cast the returned item to type **Point ***. This is necessary because **ArrayList**s only store and return pointers to **Object**s. Thus, the **Object *** returned from indexed property **Item** must be cast to type **Point *** (line 126).

Method **clearButton_Click** (lines 146–152) handles the **Clear** button's click event, creates an empty **ArrayList** (causing the old list to be erased) and refreshes the display. Lines 155–174 define the event handlers for the radio buttons' **Checked-Changed** event. Each method refreshes **Panel drawPanel** to ensure that the panel display reflects the selected drawing type. Event method **colorButton_Click** (177–194) allows the user to select a new drawing color with a **ColorDialog**, using the same technique demonstrated in Fig. 13.10.

13.8 Advanced Graphics Capabilities

.NET offers many additional graphics capabilities. The **Brush** hierarchy, for example, also includes *HatchBrush*, *LinearGradientBrush*, *PathGradientBrush* and *TextureBrush*.

Figures 13.35–13.37 demonstrate several graphics features, such as dashed lines, thick lines and the ability to fill shapes with patterns. These represent just a few of the additional capabilities of the **System::Drawing** namespace.

```
1    // Fig. 13.35: DrawShapes.h
2    // Drawing various shapes on a form.
```

Fig. 13.35 Shapes drawn on a form. (Part 1 of 2.)

```
3
4    #pragma once
5
6    #using <mscorlib.dll>
7    #using <system.dll>
8    #using <system.drawing.dll>
9    #using <system.windows.forms.dll>
10
11   using namespace System;
12   using namespace System::Drawing;
13   using namespace System::Drawing::Drawing2D;
14   using namespace System::Windows::Forms;
15
16   public __gc class DrawShapesForm : public Form
17   {
18   public:
19      DrawShapesForm();
20      void OnPaint( PaintEventArgs * );
21
22   private:
23      void InitializeComponent();
24   }; // end class DrawShapesForm
```

Fig. 13.35 Shapes drawn on a form. (Part 2 of 2.)

```
1    // Fig. 13.36: DrawShapes.cpp
2    // Method definitions for class DrawShapesForm.
3
4    #include "DrawShapes.h"
5
6    // default constructor
7    DrawShapesForm::DrawShapesForm()
8    {
9       InitializeComponent();
10   }
11
12   void DrawShapesForm::InitializeComponent()
13   {
14      this->AutoScaleBaseSize = Drawing::Size( 5, 13 );
15      this->ClientSize = Drawing::Size( 520, 197 );
16      this->Name = S"drawShapesForm";
17      this->Text = S"Drawing Shapes";
18   } // end method InitializeComponent
19
20   // draw various shapes on form
21   void DrawShapesForm::OnPaint( PaintEventArgs *paintEvent )
22   {
23      __super::OnPaint( paintEvent ); // call base OnPaint method
24
```

Fig. 13.36 `DrawShapesForm` class method definitions. (Part 1 of 3.)

```
25       // pointer to object we will use
26       Graphics *graphicsObject = paintEvent->Graphics;
27
28       // ellipse rectangle and gradient brush
29       Rectangle drawArea1 = Rectangle( 5, 35, 30, 100 );
30       LinearGradientBrush *linearBrush =
31          new LinearGradientBrush( drawArea1, Color::Blue,
32          Color::Yellow, LinearGradientMode::ForwardDiagonal );
33
34       // pen and location for red outline rectangle
35       Pen *thickRedPen = new Pen( Color::Red, 10 );
36       Rectangle drawArea2 = Rectangle( 80, 30, 65, 100 );
37
38       // bitmap texture
39       Bitmap *textureBitmap = new Bitmap( 10, 10 );
40
41       // get bitmap graphics
42       Graphics *graphicsObject2 =
43          Graphics::FromImage( textureBitmap );
44
45       // brush and pen used throughout program
46       SolidBrush *solidColorBrush = new SolidBrush(
47          Color::Red );
48       Pen *coloredPen = new Pen( solidColorBrush );
49
50       // draw ellipse filled with a blue-yellow gradient
51       graphicsObject->FillEllipse(
52          linearBrush, 5, 30, 65, 100 );
53
54       // draw thick rectangle outline in red
55       graphicsObject->DrawRectangle(
56          thickRedPen, drawArea2 );
57
58       // fill textureBitmap with yellow
59       solidColorBrush->Color = Color::Yellow;
60       graphicsObject2->FillRectangle(
61          solidColorBrush, 0, 0, 10, 10 );
62
63       // draw small black rectangle in textureBitmap
64       coloredPen->Color = Color::Black;
65       graphicsObject2->DrawRectangle(
66          coloredPen, 1, 1, 6, 6 );
67
68       // draw small blue rectangle in textureBitmap
69       solidColorBrush->Color = Color::Blue;
70       graphicsObject2->FillRectangle(
71          solidColorBrush, 1, 1, 3, 3 );
72
73       // draw small red square in textureBitmap
74       solidColorBrush->Color = Color::Red;
75       graphicsObject2->FillRectangle(
76          solidColorBrush, 4, 4, 3, 3 );
```

Fig. 13.36 DrawShapesForm class method definitions. (Part 2 of 3.)

```
77
78        // create textured brush and
79        // display textured rectangle
80        TextureBrush *texturedBrush =
81           new TextureBrush( textureBitmap );
82        graphicsObject->FillRectangle(
83           texturedBrush, 155, 30, 75, 100 );
84
85        // draw pie-shaped arc in white
86        coloredPen->Color = Color::White;
87        coloredPen->Width = 6;
88        graphicsObject->DrawPie(
89           coloredPen, 240, 30, 75, 100, 0, 270 );
90
91        // draw lines in green and yellow
92        coloredPen->Color = Color::Green;
93        coloredPen->Width = 5;
94        graphicsObject->DrawLine(
95           coloredPen, 395, 30, 320, 150 );
96
97        // draw a rounded, dashed yellow line
98        coloredPen->Color = Color::Yellow;
99        coloredPen->DashCap = DashCap::Round;
100       coloredPen->DashStyle = DashStyle::Dash;
101       graphicsObject->DrawLine(
102          coloredPen, 320, 30, 395, 150 );
103    } // end method OnPaint
```

Fig. 13.36 `DrawShapesForm` class method definitions. (Part 3 of 3.)

```
1     // Fig. 13.37: DrawShapesTest.cpp
2     // Entry point for application.
3
4     #include "DrawShapes.h"
5
6     int __stdcall WinMain()()
7     {
8        Application::Run( new DrawShapesForm() );
9
10       return 0;
11    } // end function WinMain
```

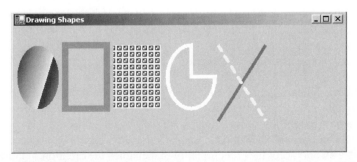

Fig. 13.37 `DrawShapesForm` class driver.

Lines 21–103 (Fig. 13.36) define method **OnPaint** for our form. Lines 30–32 create **LinearGradientBrush** object **linearBrush**, which resides in namespace **System::Drawing::Drawing2D**. A **LinearGradientBrush** enables users to draw with a color gradient. The **LinearGradientBrush** used in this example takes four arguments: A **Rectangle**, two **Color**s and a member of enumeration *Linear-GradientMode*. In Visual C++ .NET, all linear gradients are defined along a line that determines the gradient endpoint. This line can be specified either by starting and ending points or by the diagonal of a rectangle. The first argument, **Rectangle drawArea1**, specifies the defining line for **LinearGradientBrush linearBrush**. This **Rectangle** argument represents the endpoints of the linear gradient—the upper-left corner is the starting point, and the bottom-right corner is the ending point. The second and third arguments specify the colors that the gradient will use. In this case, the color of the ellipse will gradually change from **Color::Blue** to **Color::Yellow**. The last argument, a type from the enumeration *LinearGradientMode*, specifies the linear gradient's direction. In our case, we use *LinearGradientMode::ForwardDiagonal*, which creates a gradient from the upper-left to the lower-right corner. We then use **Graphics** method **FillEllipse** in lines 51–52 to draw an ellipse with **linearBrush**; the color gradually changes from blue to yellow, as described above.

In line 35, we create a **Pen** object **thickRedPen**. We pass to **thickRedPen**'s constructor **Color::Red** and the **int** argument **10**, indicating that we want **thickRedPen** to draw red lines that are 10 pixels wide.

Line 39 creates a new *Bitmap* image, which initially is empty. Class **Bitmap** can produce images in color and gray scale; this particular **Bitmap** is 10 pixels wide and 10 pixels tall. Method *FromImage* (line 43) is a **static** member of class **Graphics** and retrieves the **Graphics** object associated with an **Image**, which can be used to draw on an image. Lines 59–76 draw on the **Bitmap** a pattern consisting of black, blue, red and yellow rectangles and lines. A **TextureBrush** is a brush that fills the interior of a shape with an image, rather than with a solid color. In lines 82–83, **TextureBrush** object **textureBrush** fills a rectangle with our **Bitmap**. The **TextureBrush** constructor version that we use takes as an argument an image that defines its texture.

Next, we draw a pie-shaped arc with a thick white line. Lines 86–87 set **coloredPen**'s color to **White** and modify its width to be six pixels. We then draw the pie on the form by specifying the **Pen**, the *x*-coordinate, *y*-coordinate, length and width of the bounding rectangle and the start angle and sweep angle.

Finally, lines 99–100 make use of **System::Drawing::Drawing2D** enumerations *DashCap* and *DashStyle* to draw a diagonal dashed line. Line 99 sets the *DashCap* property of **coloredPen** (not to be confused with the **DashCap** enumeration) to a member of the **DashCap** enumeration. The **DashCap** enumeration specifies the styles for the start and end of a dashed line. In this case, we want both ends of the dashed line to be rounded, so we use *DashCap::Round*. Line 100 sets the *DashStyle* property of **coloredPen** (not to be confused with the **DashStyle** enumeration) to *Dash-Style::Dash*, indicating that we want our line to consist entirely of dashes.

Our next example demonstrates the use of a *general path*. A general path is a shape constructed from straight lines and complex curves. An object of class *GraphicsPath* (**System::Drawing::Drawing2D** namespace) represents a general path. The **GraphicsPath** class provides functionality that enables the creation of complex shapes from vector-based primitive graphics objects. A **GraphicsPath** object consists of fig-

ures defined by simple shapes. The start point of each vector-graphics object (such as a line
or arc) that is added to the path is connected by a straight line to the end point of the previous object. When called, **GraphicsPath** method *CloseFigure* method attaches the
final vector-graphic object endpoint to the initial starting point for the current figure by a
straight line, then starts a new figure. **GraphicsPath** method *StartFigure* begins a
new figure within the path without closing the previous figure.

Figures 13.38–13.40 draw general paths in the shape of five-pointed stars. Line 40
(Fig. 13.39) sets the origin of the **Graphics** object. The arguments to method *Trans-
lateTransform* indicate that the origin should be translated to the coordinates (150,
150). Lines 31–34 define two **int** arrays, representing the *x*- and *y*-coordinates of the
points in the star, and line 37 defines **GraphicsPath** object **star**. A **for** loop then creates lines to connect the points of the star and adds these lines to **star**. We use **GraphicsPath** method *AddLine* to append a line to the shape. The arguments of **AddLine**
specify the coordinates for the line's endpoints; each new call to **AddLine** adds a line from
the previous point to the current point. Line 48 uses **GraphicsPath** method **Close-
Figure** to complete the shape.

```
1    // Fig. 13.38: DrawStarsForm.h
2    // Using paths to draw stars on the form.
3
4    #pragma once
5
6    #using <mscorlib.dll>
7    #using <system.dll>
8    #using <system.drawing.dll>
9    #using <system.windows.forms.dll>
10
11   using namespace System;
12   using namespace System::Drawing;
13   using namespace System::Drawing::Drawing2D;
14   using namespace System::Windows::Forms;
15
16   public __gc class DrawStarsForm : public Form
17   {
18   public:
19      DrawStarsForm();
20      void OnPaint( PaintEventArgs * );
21
22   private:
23      void InitializeComponent();
24   }; // end class DrawStarsForm
```

Fig. 13.38 Paths used to draw stars on a form.

```cpp
1   // Fig. 13.39: DrawStarsForm.cpp
2   // Method definitions for class DrawStarsForm.
3
4   #include "DrawStarsForm.h"
5
6   DrawStarsForm::DrawStarsForm()
7   {
8      InitializeComponent();
9   }
10
11  void DrawStarsForm::InitializeComponent()
12  {
13     this->AutoScaleBaseSize = Drawing::Size( 5, 13 );
14     this->BackColor = Drawing::SystemColors::Info;
15     this->ClientSize = Drawing::Size( 304, 285 );
16     this->Name = S"DrawStarsForm";
17     this->Text = S"Drawing Stars";
18  }
19
20  // create path and draw stars along it
21  void DrawStarsForm::OnPaint( PaintEventArgs *paintEvent )
22  {
23     __super::OnPaint( paintEvent ); // call base OnPaint method
24
25     Graphics *graphicsObject = paintEvent->Graphics;
26     Random *random = new Random();
27     SolidBrush *brush =
28        new SolidBrush( Color::DarkMagenta );
29
30     // x and y points of the path
31     int xPoints[] =
32        { 55, 67, 109, 73, 83, 55, 27, 37, 1, 43 };
33     int yPoints[] =
34        { 0, 36, 36, 54, 96, 72, 96, 54, 36, 36 };
35
36     // create graphics path for star;
37     GraphicsPath *star = new GraphicsPath();
38
39     // translate the origin to (150, 150)
40     graphicsObject->TranslateTransform( 150, 150 );
41
42     // create star from series of points
43     for ( int i = 0; i <= 8; i += 2 )
44        star->AddLine( xPoints[ i ], yPoints[ i ],
45           xPoints[ i + 1 ], yPoints[ i + 1 ] );
46
```

Fig. 13.39 DrawStarsForm class method definitions. (Part 1 of 2.)

```
47       // close the shape
48       star->CloseFigure();
49
50       // rotate the origin and draw stars in random colors
51       for ( int i = 1; i <= 18; i++ ) {
52          graphicsObject->RotateTransform( 20 );
53
54          brush->Color = Color::FromArgb(
55             random->Next( 200, 256 ), random->Next( 256 ),
56             random->Next( 256 ), random->Next( 256 ) );
57
58          graphicsObject->FillPath( brush, star );
59       }
60    } // end method OnPaint
```

Fig. 13.39 DrawStarsForm class method definitions. (Part 2 of 2.)

The **for** structure in lines 51–59 draws the **star** 18 times, rotating it around the origin. Line 52 uses **Graphics** method *RotateTransform* to move to the next position on the form; the argument specifies the rotation angle in degrees. **Graphics** method **FillPath** (line 58) then draws a filled version of the **star** with the **Color** created on lines 54–56. The application determines the **SolidBrush**'s color randomly, using **Random** method **Next**.

```
1    // Fig. 13.40: DrawStarsFormTest.cpp
2    // Entry point for application.
3
4    #include "DrawStarsForm.h"
5
6    int __stdcall WinMain()()
7    {
8       Application::Run( new DrawStarsForm() );
9
10      return 0;
11   } // end function WinMain
```

Fig. 13.40 DrawStarsForm class driver.

13.9 Introduction to Multimedia

Visual C++ .NET offers many convenient ways to include images and animations in programs. People who entered the computing field decades ago used computers primarily to
perform arithmetic calculations. As the discipline evolves, we are beginning to realize the
importance of computers' data-manipulation capabilities. We are seeing a wide variety of
exciting new three-dimensional applications. Multimedia programming is an entertaining
and innovative field, but one that presents many challenges.

Multimedia applications demand extraordinary computing power. Until recently,
affordable computers with this amount of power were not available. However, today's
ultrafast processors are making multimedia-based applications commonplace. As the
market for multimedia explodes, users are purchasing the faster processors, larger memories and wider communications bandwidths needed to support multimedia applications.
This benefits the computer and communications industries, which provide the hardware,
software and services fueling the multimedia revolution.

In the remaining sections of this chapter, we introduce the use and manipulation of
images and other multimedia features and capabilities. Section 13.10 discusses how to
load, display and scale images; Section 13.11 demonstrates image animation;
Section 13.12 presents the video capabilities of the Windows Media Player control; and
Section 13.13 explores Microsoft Agent technology.

13.10 Loading, Displaying and Scaling Images

Visual C++ .NET's multimedia capabilities include graphics, images, animations and video. Previous sections demonstrated vector-graphics capabilities; this section concentrates
on image manipulation. The Windows form that we create in Fig. 13.41–Fig. 13.43 demonstrates the loading of an **Image** (**System::Drawing** namespace). The application allows users to enter a desired height and width for the **Image**, which then is displayed in
the specified size.

```
1   // Fig. 13.41: DisplayLogoForm.h
2   // Displaying and resizing an image.
3
4   #pragma once
5
6   #using <mscorlib.dll>
7   #using <system.dll>
8   #using <system.drawing.dll>
9   #using <system.windows.forms.dll>
10
11  using namespace System;
12  using namespace System::Drawing;
13  using namespace System::Windows::Forms;
14
15  public __gc class DisplayLogoForm : public Form
16  {
17  public:
```

Fig. 13.41 Image resizing. (Part 1 of 2.)

```
18        DisplayLogoForm();
19
20   private:
21        Button *setButton;
22        TextBox *heightTextBox;
23        Label *heightLabel;
24        TextBox *widthTextBox;
25        Label *widthLabel;
26        static Image *image = Image::FromFile( S"images/Logo.gif" );
27        Graphics *graphicsObject;
28
29        void InitializeComponent();
30        void setButton_Click( Object *, EventArgs * );
31   }; // end class DisplayLogoForm
```

Fig. 13.41 Image resizing. (Part 2 of 2.)

```
1    // Fig. 13.42: DisplayLogoForm.cpp
2    // Method definitions for class DisplayLogoForm.
3
4    #include "DisplayLogoForm.h"
5
6    DisplayLogoForm::DisplayLogoForm()
7    {
8        InitializeComponent();
9    }
10
11   void DisplayLogoForm::InitializeComponent()
12   {
13       this->setButton = new Button();
14       this->heightTextBox = new TextBox();
15       this->heightLabel = new Label();
16       this->widthTextBox = new TextBox();
17       this->widthLabel = new Label();
18       this->SuspendLayout();
19
20       // setButton
21       this->setButton->Location = Point( 456, 200 );
22       this->setButton->Name = S"setButton";
23       this->setButton->TabIndex = 9;
24       this->setButton->Text = S"Set";
25       this->setButton->Click += new EventHandler( this,
26           setButton_Click );
27
28       // heightTextBox
29       this->heightTextBox->Location = Point( 440, 160 );
30       this->heightTextBox->Name = S"heightTextBox";
31       this->heightTextBox->TabIndex = 8;
32       this->heightTextBox->Text = S"";
33
```

Fig. 13.42 `DisplayLogoForm` class method definitions. (Part 1 of 3.)

```
34       // heightLabel
35       this->heightLabel->Location = Point( 440, 128 );
36       this->heightLabel->Name = S"heightLabel";
37       this->heightLabel->TabIndex = 7;
38       this->heightLabel->Text = S"Height";
39
40       // widthTextBox
41       this->widthTextBox->Location = Point( 440, 88 );
42       this->widthTextBox->Name = S"widthTextBox";
43       this->widthTextBox->TabIndex = 6;
44       this->widthTextBox->Text = S"";
45
46       // widthLabel
47       this->widthLabel->Location = Point( 440, 56 );
48       this->widthLabel->Name = S"widthLabel";
49       this->widthLabel->TabIndex = 5;
50       this->widthLabel->Text = S"Width";
51
52       // DisplayLogoForm
53       this->AutoScaleBaseSize = Drawing::Size( 5, 13 );
54       this->ClientSize = Drawing::Size( 568, 273 );
55       Control *tempControl[] = { this->setButton,
56          this->heightTextBox, this->heightLabel,
57          this->widthTextBox, this->widthLabel };
58       this->Controls->AddRange( tempControl );
59       this->Name = S"DisplayLogoForm";
60       this->Text = S"Display Logo";
61       this->ResumeLayout();
62
63       graphicsObject = this->CreateGraphics();
64    } // end method InitializeComponent
65
66    void DisplayLogoForm::setButton_Click( Object *sender,
67       EventArgs *e )
68    {
69       int width, height;
70
71       try {
72
73          // get user input
74          width = Convert::ToInt32( widthTextBox->Text );
75          height = Convert::ToInt32( heightTextBox->Text );
76       }
77       catch ( FormatException *formatException ) {
78          MessageBox::Show( formatException->Message, S"Error",
79             MessageBoxButtons::OK, MessageBoxIcon::Error );
80
81          return;
82       }
83       catch ( OverflowException *overflowException ) {
84          MessageBox::Show( overflowException->Message, S"Error",
85             MessageBoxButtons::OK, MessageBoxIcon::Error );
```

Fig. 13.42 DisplayLogoForm class method definitions. (Part 2 of 3.)

```
86
87      return;
88   }
89
90   // if dimensions specified are too large
91   // display problem
92   if ( width > 375 || height > 225 ) {
93      MessageBox::Show( S"Height or Width too large" );
94
95      return;
96   }
97
98   // clear Windows Form
99   graphicsObject->Clear( this->BackColor );
100
101   // draw image
102   graphicsObject->DrawImage( image, 5, 5, width, height );
103 } // end method setButton_Click
```

Fig. 13.42 DisplayLogoForm class method definitions. (Part 3 of 3.)

```
1   // Fig. 13.43: DisplayLogoFormTest.cpp
2   // Entry point for application.
3
4   #include "DisplayLogoForm.h"
5
6   int __stdcall WinMain()()
7   {
8      Application::Run( new DisplayLogoForm() );
9
10      return 0;
11   } // end function WinMain
```

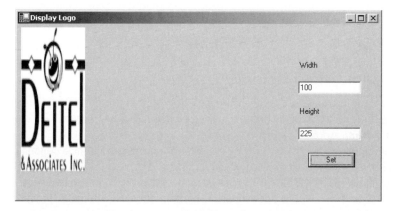

Fig. 13.43 DisplayLogoForm class driver. (Part 1 of 2.)

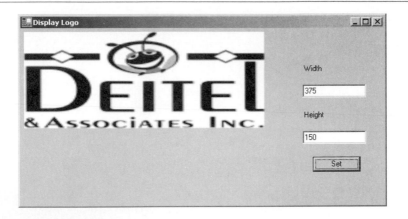

Fig. 13.43 `DisplayLogoForm` class driver. (Part 2 of 2.)

Line 26 (Fig. 13.41) declares **Image** pointer **image**. The **static Image** method *FromFile* then retrieves an image stored on disk and assigns it to **image** (line 26). Notice that we use a forward slash (/) as a separator character rather than two backslash characters (\\). We discuss separator characters in Chapter 14, Files and Streams.

Line 63 (Fig. 13.42) uses **Form** method **CreateGraphics** to create a **Graphics** object associated with the **Form**; we use this object to draw on the **Form**. Method **CreateGraphics** is inherited from class **Control**; all Windows controls, such as **Buttons** and **Panels**, also provide this method. When users click **Set**, the width and height parameters are parsed from the **TextBox**es (lines 74–75). The **catch** blocks in lines 77–88 inform the user if invalid values have been entered.

Line 92 then ensures that the dimensions are not too large. If the parameters are valid, line 99 calls **Graphics** method *Clear* to paint the entire **Form** in the current background color. Line 102 calls **Graphics** method *DrawImage* with the following parameters: the image to draw, the *x*-coordinate of the upper-left corner, the *y*-coordinate of the upper-left corner, the width of the image and the height of the image. If the width and height do not correspond to the image's original dimensions, the image is scaled to fit the new specifications.

13.11 Animating a Series of Images

The next example animates a series of images stored in an array. The application uses the same techniques to load and display **Image**s as those illustrated in Fig. 13.42. The images were created with Adobe Photoshop.

The animation in Fig. 13.44–Fig. 13.46 uses a **PictureBox**, which contains the images that we animate. We use a **Timer** to cycle through the images, causing a new image to display every 50 milliseconds. Variable **count** keeps track of the current image number and increases by one every time we display a new image. The array includes 30 images (numbered 0–29); when the application reaches image 29, it returns to image 0. The 30 images were prepared in advance and placed in the **images** folder inside the directory of the project.

```
1    // Fig. 13.44: LogoAnimator.h
2    // Program that animates a series of images.
3
4    #pragma once
5
6    #using <mscorlib.dll>
7    #using <system.dll>
8    #using <system.drawing.dll>
9    #using <system.windows.forms.dll>
10
11   using namespace System;
12   using namespace System::Drawing;
13   using namespace System::Collections;
14   using namespace System::ComponentModel;
15   using namespace System::Windows::Forms;
16
17   public __gc class LogoAnimator : public Form
18   {
19   public:
20      LogoAnimator();
21
22   private:
23      PictureBox *logoPictureBox;
24      Timer *Timer;
25      IContainer *components;
26      static ArrayList *images = new ArrayList();
27      static int count = -1;
28
29      void InitializeComponent();
30      void Timer_Tick( Object *, EventArgs * );
31   }; // end class LogoAnimator
```

Fig. 13.44 Animation of a series of images.

```
1    // Fig. 13.45: LogoAnimator.cpp
2    // Method definitions for class LogoAnimator.
3
4    #include "LogoAnimator.h"
5
6    LogoAnimator::LogoAnimator()
7    {
8       InitializeComponent();
9
10      for ( int i = 0; i < 30; i++ )
11         images->Add( Image::FromFile( String::Concat(
12         S"images/deitel", i.ToString(), S".gif" ) ) );
13
14      // load first image
15      logoPictureBox->Image = dynamic_cast< Image* >(
16         images->Item[ 0 ] );
17
```

Fig. 13.45 **LogoAnimator** class method definitions. (Part 1 of 2.)

```
18        // set PictureBox to be the same size as Image
19        logoPictureBox->Size = logoPictureBox->Image->Size;
20    } // end constructor
21
22    void LogoAnimator::InitializeComponent()
23    {
24        this->components = new System::ComponentModel::Container();
25        this->logoPictureBox = new PictureBox();
26        this->Timer = new Windows::Forms::Timer( this->components );
27        this->SuspendLayout();
28
29        // logoPictureBox
30        this->logoPictureBox->Location = Point( 32, 24 );
31        this->logoPictureBox->Name = S"logoPictureBox";
32        this->logoPictureBox->Size = Drawing::Size( 168, 88 );
33        this->logoPictureBox->TabIndex = 1;
34        this->logoPictureBox->TabStop = false;
35
36        // Timer
37        this->Timer->Enabled = true;
38        this->Timer->Tick += new EventHandler( this,
39           Timer_Tick );
40
41        // animatorForm
42        this->AutoScaleBaseSize = Drawing::Size( 5, 13 );
43        this->ClientSize = Drawing::Size( 232, 141 );
44        this->Controls->Add( this->logoPictureBox );
45        this->Name = S"animatorForm";
46        this->Text = S"LogoAnimator";
47        this->ResumeLayout();
48    } // end method InitializeComponent
49
50    void LogoAnimator::Timer_Tick( Object *sender, EventArgs *e )
51    {
52        // increment counter
53        count = ( count + 1 ) % 30;
54
55        // load next image
56        logoPictureBox->Image = dynamic_cast< Image* >(
57           images->Item[ count ] );
58    } // end method Timer_Tick
```

Fig. 13.45 LogoAnimator class method definitions. (Part 2 of 2.)

```
1    // Fig. 13.46: LogoAnimatorTest.cpp
2    // Entry point for application.
3
4    #include "LogoAnimator.h"
5
6    int __stdcall WinMain()()
7    {
```

Fig. 13.46 LogoAnimator class driver. (Part 1 of 2.)

```
8       Application::Run( new LogoAnimator() );
9
10      return 0;
11   } // end function WinMain
```

Fig. 13.46 LogoAnimator class driver. (Part 2 of 2.)

Lines 10–12 (Fig. 13.45) load each of 30 images and place them in an **ArrayList**. Lines 11–12 use **ArrayList** method **Add** to add each **Image**. Lines 15-16 retrieve the first image using **ArrayList** indexed property **Item** then place it in the **PictureBox**. Line 19 modifies the size of the **PictureBox** so that it is equal to the size of the **Image** it is displaying. The event handler for **timer**'s **Tick** event (line 50–58) then displays the next image from the **ArrayList**.

Performance Tip 13.2

*It is more efficient to load an animation's frames as one image than to load each image separately. (A painting program, such as Adobe Photoshop® (**www.adobe.com**) or Jasc® Paint Shop Pro™ (**www.jasc.com**) can be used to combine the animation's frames into one image.) If the images are being loaded separately from the Web, each loaded image requires a separate connection to the site on which the images are stored; this process can result in poor performance.[2]*

Performance Tip 13.3

Loading animation frames can cause program delays, because the program waits for all frames to load before displaying them.

The following chess example demonstrates the capabilities of GDI+ as they pertain to a chess-game application. These capabilities include techniques for two-dimensional *collision detection* and *regional invalidation* (refreshing only the required parts of the screen) to increase performance. Two-dimensional collision detection is the detection of an overlap between two shapes. In the next example, we demonstrate the simplest form of collision detection, which determines whether a point (the mouse-click location) is contained within a rectangle (a chess-piece image).

Class **ChessPiece** (Fig. 13.47) is a container class for the individual chess pieces. Lines 21–29 creates a *user-defined type* called an *enumeration*. This public enumeration, **Types**, identifies each chess-piece type and also serves to identify the location of each

---

2. For more information about Web animation options, visit **graphicssoft.about.com/library/weekly/aa000713a.htm**.

piece in the chess-piece image file. An enumeration, introduced by the MC++ keyword **enum** and followed by a *type name* (in this case, **Types**), is a set of integer constants represented by identifiers. The values of these *enumeration constants* start at **0**, unless specified otherwise, and are incremented by **1**. In lines 21–29, **KING** is assigned the value **0** and the value of each subsequent constant is incremented by **1** (with **PAWN** being assigned the value **5**). The identifiers in an **enum** must be unique, but separate enumeration constants can have the same integer value. Variables of user-defined type **Types** can only be assigned one of the six values declared in the enumeration.

```
1   // Fig. 13.47: ChessPiece.h
2   // Storage class for chess piece attributes.
3
4   #pragma once
5
6   #using <mscorlib.dll>
7   #using <system.dll>
8   #using <system.drawing.dll>
9   #using <system.windows.forms.dll>
10
11  using namespace System;
12  using namespace System::Drawing;
13  using namespace System::Collections;
14  using namespace System::Windows::Forms;
15
16  public __gc class ChessPiece
17  {
18  public:
19
20      // define chess-piece type constants (values 0-5)
21      __value enum Types
22      {
23          KING,
24          QUEEN,
25          BISHOP,
26          KNIGHT,
27          ROOK,
28          PAWN
29      };
30
31      ChessPiece( int, int, int, Bitmap * );
32      void Draw( Graphics * );
33      Rectangle GetBounds();
34      void SetLocation( int , int );
35
36  private:
37      int currentType;          // this object's type
38      Bitmap *pieceImage;       // this object's image
39      Rectangle targetRectangle; // default display location
40  }; // end class ChessPiece
```

Fig. 13.47 Container class for chess pieces.

Notice that we use MC++ keyword `__value` when declaring enumeration **Types** to ensure that the enumeration is a value type. For more information about keyword `__value`, refer to Chapter 7, Object-Oriented Programming: Polymorphism.

Good Programming Practice 13.1

Capitalize the first letter of an identifier used as a user-defined type name.

Common Programming Error 13.3

Assigning the integer equivalent of an enumeration constant to a variable of the enumeration type is a syntax error.

A popular enumeration is

```
__value enum Months { JAN = 1, FEB, MAR, APR, MAY, JUN, JUL,
                       AUG, SEP, OCT, NOV, DEC };
```

which creates a user-defined type **Months** with enumeration constants representing the months of the year. Because the first value in the preceding enumeration is explicitly set to **1**, the remaining values are incremented from **1**, resulting in the values **1** through **12**. Any enumeration constant can be assigned an integer value in the enumeration definition, and subsequent enumeration constants will each have a value 1 higher than the preceding constant.

Common Programming Error 13.4

After an enumeration constant has been defined, attempting to assign another value to the enumeration constant is a syntax error.

Good Programming Practice 13.2

Use only uppercase letters in the names of enumeration constants. This makes these constants stand out in a program and reminds the programmer that enumeration constants are not variables.

Good Programming Practice 13.3

Using enumerations rather than integer constants can make programs clearer.

Rectangle object **targetRectangle** (lines 13–14 of Fig. 13.48) identifies the image location on the chess board. The **x** and **y** properties of the rectangle are assigned in the **ChessPiece** constructor, and all chess-piece images have height and width **75**.

```
1   // Fig. 13.48: ChessPiece.cpp
2   // Method definitions for class ChessPiece.
3
4   #include "ChessPiece.h"
5
6   // construct piece
7   ChessPiece::ChessPiece( int type, int xLocation,
8      int yLocation, Bitmap *sourceImage )
9   {
10     currentType = type; // set current type
```

Fig. 13.48 **ChessPiece** class method definitions. (Part 1 of 2.)

```
11
12      // set current location
13      targetRectangle = Rectangle(
14         xLocation, yLocation, 75, 75 );
15
16      // obtain pieceImage from section of sourceImage
17      pieceImage = sourceImage->Clone(
18         Rectangle( type * 75, 0, 75, 75 ),
19         Drawing::Imaging::PixelFormat::DontCare );
20   } // end constructor
21
22   // draw chess piece
23   void ChessPiece::Draw( Graphics *graphicsObject )
24   {
25      graphicsObject->DrawImage( pieceImage, targetRectangle );
26   } // end method Draw
27
28   // obtain this piece's location rectangle
29   Rectangle ChessPiece::GetBounds()
30   {
31      return targetRectangle;
32   } // end method GetBounds
33
34   // set this piece's location
35   void ChessPiece::SetLocation( int xLocation, int yLocation )
36   {
37      targetRectangle.X = xLocation;
38      targetRectangle.Y = yLocation;
39   } // end method SetLocation
```

Fig. 13.48 ChessPiece class method definitions. (Part 2 of 2.)

The **ChessPiece** constructor (lines 7–20) requires that the calling class define a chess-piece type, its **x** and **y** location and the **Bitmap** containing all chess-piece images. Rather than loading the chess-piece image within the class, we allow the calling class to pass the image. This avoids the image-loading overhead for each piece. It also increases the flexibility of the class by allowing the user to change images; for example, in this case, we use the class for both black and white chess-piece images. Lines 17–19 extract a subimage that contains only the current piece's bitmap data. Our chess-piece images are defined in a specific manner: One image contains six chess-piece images, each defined within a 75-pixel block, resulting in a total image size of 450-by-75. We obtain a single image via **Bitmap**'s *Clone* method, which allows us to specify a rectangle image location and the desired pixel format. The location is a 75-by-75 pixel block with its upper-left corner **x** equal to **75 * type** and the corresponding **y** equal to **0**. For the pixel format, we specify constant **DontCare**, causing the format to remain unchanged.

Method **Draw** (lines 23–26) causes the **ChessPiece** to draw **pieceImage** in **targetRectangle** on the passed **Graphics** object. Method **GetBounds** returns the object **targetRectangle** for use in collision detection, and **SetLocation** allows the calling class to specify a new piece location.

Class **ChessGame** (Fig. 13.49) defines the game and graphics code for our chess game. Lines 23–34 define class-scope variables the program requires. **ArrayList**

chessTile (line 23) stores the board tile images. It contains four images: Two light tiles and two dark tiles (to increase board variety). **ArrayList chessPieces** (line 26) stores all active **ChessPiece** objects and **int selectedIndex** (line 29) identifies the index in **chessPieces** of the currently selected piece. The **board** (line 31) is an 8-by-8, two-dimensional **int** array corresponding to the squares of a chess board. Each board element is an integer from 0 to 3 that corresponds to an index in **chessTile** and is used to specify the chess-board-square image. **const int TILESIZE** (line 34) defines the size of each tile in pixels.

```
1   // Fig. 13.49: ChessGame.h
2   // Chess Game graphics code.
3
4   #pragma once
5
6   #include "ChessPiece.h"
7
8   public __gc class ChessGame : public Form
9   {
10  public:
11     ChessGame();
12
13  protected:
14     void OnPaint( PaintEventArgs * );
15
16  private:
17     PictureBox *pieceBox;
18     MainMenu *GameMenu;
19     MenuItem *gameItem;
20     MenuItem *newGameItem;
21
22     // ArrayList for board tile images
23     static ArrayList *chessTile = new ArrayList();
24
25     // ArrayList for chess pieces
26     static ArrayList *chessPieces = new ArrayList();
27
28     // define index for selected piece
29     static int selectedIndex = -1;
30
31     static int board[,] = new int __gc[ 8, 8 ]; // board array
32
33     // define chess tile size in pixels
34     static const int TILESIZE = 75;
35
36     void InitializeComponent();
37     void ChessGame_Load( Object *, EventArgs * );
38     void ResetBoard();
39     int CheckBounds( Point, int );
40     void pieceBox_Paint( Object *, PaintEventArgs * );
41     void pieceBox_MouseDown( Object *, MouseEventArgs * );
```

Fig. 13.49 Chess-game code. (Part 1 of 2.)

```
42        void pieceBox_MouseMove( Object *, MouseEventArgs * );
43        void pieceBox_MouseUp( Object *, MouseEventArgs * );
44        ChessPiece* GetPiece( int );
45        void newGameItem_Click( Object *, EventArgs * );
46    }; // end class ChessGame
```

Fig. 13.49 Chess-game code. (Part 2 of 2.)

The chess game GUI consists of **Form ChessGame**, the area in which we draw the tiles; **Panel pieceBox**, the window in which we draw the pieces (note that **pieceBox** background color is set to **"transparent"**); and a **Menu** that allows the user to begin a new game. Although the pieces and tiles could have been drawn on the same form, doing so would decrease performance. We would be forced to refresh the board as well as the pieces every time we refreshed the control.

The **ChessGame Load** event (lines 66–77 of Fig. 13.50) loads each tile image into **chessTile**. It then calls method **ResetBoard** to refresh the **Form** and begin the game. Method **ResetBoard** (lines 80–185) assigns **chessPieces** to a new **ArrayList**, loading images for both the black and the white chess-piece sets, and creates **Bitmap selected** to define the currently selected **Bitmap** set. Lines 105–184 loop through the 64 positions on the chess board, setting the tile color and piece for each tile. Lines 109–110 cause the currently selected image to switch to the **blackPieces** after the fifth row. If the row counter is on the first or last row, lines 117–154 add a new piece to **chessPieces**. The type of the piece is based on the current column we are initializing. Pieces in chess are positioned in the following order, from left to right: rook, knight, bishop, queen, king, bishop, knight and rook. Lines 157–163 add a new pawn at the current location if the current **row** is second or seventh (**1** or **6**).

```
1    // Fig. 13.50: ChessGame.cpp
2    // Method definitions for class ChessGame.
3
4    #include "ChessGame.h"
5
6    ChessGame::ChessGame()
7    {
8        InitializeComponent();
9    } // end constructor
10
11   void ChessGame::InitializeComponent()
12   {
13       this->pieceBox = new PictureBox();
14       this->GameMenu = new MainMenu();
15       this->gameItem = new MenuItem();
16       this->newGameItem = new MenuItem();
17       this->SuspendLayout();
18
19       // pieceBox
20       this->pieceBox->BackColor = Color::Transparent;
21       this->pieceBox->Name = S"pieceBox";
```

Fig. 13.50 ChessGame class method definitions. (Part 1 of 7.)

```
22      this->pieceBox->Size = Drawing::Size( 600, 600 );
23      this->pieceBox->TabIndex = 1;
24      this->pieceBox->TabStop = false;
25      this->pieceBox->Paint += new PaintEventHandler(
26         this, pieceBox_Paint );
27      this->pieceBox->MouseUp += new MouseEventHandler(
28         this, pieceBox_MouseUp );
29      this->pieceBox->MouseMove += new MouseEventHandler(
30         this, pieceBox_MouseMove );
31      this->pieceBox->MouseDown += new MouseEventHandler(
32         this, pieceBox_MouseDown );
33
34      // GameMenu
35      MenuItem *temp[] = { this->gameItem };
36      this->GameMenu->MenuItems->AddRange( temp );
37
38      // gameItem
39      this->gameItem->Index = 0;
40      MenuItem *temp2[] = { this->newGameItem };
41      this->gameItem->MenuItems->AddRange( temp2 );
42      this->gameItem->Text = S"Game";
43
44      // newGameItem
45      this->newGameItem->Index = 0;
46      this->newGameItem->Shortcut = Shortcut::F2;
47      this->newGameItem->Text = S"New Game";
48      this->newGameItem->Click += new EventHandler( this,
49         newGameItem_Click );
50
51      // ChessGame
52      this->AutoScaleBaseSize = Drawing::Size( 5, 13 );
53      this->ClientSize = Drawing::Size( 602, 595 );
54      Control *temp3[] = { this->pieceBox };
55      this->Controls->AddRange( temp3 );
56      this->FormBorderStyle = FormBorderStyle::Fixed3D;
57      this->Menu = this->GameMenu;
58      this->Name = S"ChessGame";
59      this->Text = S"Chess";
60      this->Load += new EventHandler( this,
61         ChessGame_Load );
62      this->ResumeLayout();
63   } // end method InitializeComponent
64
65   // load tile bitmaps and reset game
66   void ChessGame::ChessGame_Load(
67      Object *sender, EventArgs *e )
68   {
69      // load chess board tiles
70      chessTile->Add( Bitmap::FromFile( S"lightTile1.png" ) );
71      chessTile->Add( Bitmap::FromFile( S"lightTile2.png" ) );
72      chessTile->Add( Bitmap::FromFile( S"darkTile1.png" ) );
73      chessTile->Add( Bitmap::FromFile( S"darkTile2.png" ) );
74
```

Fig. 13.50 ChessGame class method definitions. (Part 2 of 7.)

```
75        ResetBoard(); // initialize board
76        Invalidate(); // refresh form
77     } // end method ChessGame_Load
78
79     // initialize pieces to start and rebuild board
80     void ChessGame::ResetBoard()
81     {
82        int current = -1;
83        ChessPiece *piece;
84        Random *random = new Random();
85        bool light = true;
86        int type;
87
88        // ensure empty arraylist
89        chessPieces = new ArrayList();
90
91        // load whitepieces image
92        Bitmap *whitePieces =
93           dynamic_cast < Bitmap * >(
94              Image::FromFile( S"whitePieces.png" ) );
95
96        // load blackpieces image
97        Bitmap *blackPieces =
98           dynamic_cast < Bitmap * >(
99              Image::FromFile( S"blackPieces.png" ) );
100
101       // set whitepieces drawn first
102       Bitmap *selected = whitePieces;
103
104       // traverse board rows in outer loop
105       for ( int row = 0;
106          row <= board->GetUpperBound( 0 ); row++ ) {
107
108          // if at bottom rows, set to black pieces images
109          if ( row > 5 )
110             selected = blackPieces;
111
112          // traverse board columns in inner loop
113          for ( int column = 0;
114             column <= board->GetUpperBound( 1 ); column++ ) {
115
116             // if first or last row, organize pieces
117             if ( row == 0 || row == 7 ) {
118
119                switch ( column ) {
120                   case 0:
121                   case 7: // set current piece to rook
122                      current = ChessPiece::Types::ROOK;
123                      break;
124
125                   case 1:
126                   case 6: // set current piece to knight
127                      current = ChessPiece::Types::KNIGHT;
```

Fig. 13.50 ChessGame class method definitions. (Part 3 of 7.)

```
128                    break;
129
130               case 2:
131               case 5: // set current piece to bishop
132                   current = ChessPiece::Types::BISHOP;
133                   break;
134
135               case 3: // set current piece to king
136                   current = ChessPiece::Types::KING;
137                   break;
138
139               case 4: // set current piece to queen
140                   current = ChessPiece::Types::QUEEN;
141                   break;
142
143               default:
144                   break;
145            } // end switch
146
147            // create current piece at start position
148            piece = new ChessPiece( current,
149               column * TILESIZE, row * TILESIZE,
150               selected );
151
152            // add piece to arraylist
153            chessPieces->Add( piece );
154         } // end if
155
156         // if second or seventh row, organize pawns
157         if ( row == 1 || row == 6 ) {
158            piece = new ChessPiece( ChessPiece::Types::PAWN,
159               column * TILESIZE, row * TILESIZE, selected );
160
161            // add piece to arraylist
162            chessPieces->Add( piece );
163         }
164
165         // determine board piece type
166         type = random->Next( 0, 2 );
167
168         if ( light ) {
169
170            // set light tile
171            board[ row, column ] = type;
172            light = false;
173         }
174         else {
175
176            // set dark tile
177            board[ row, column ] = type + 2;
178            light = true;
179         }
180      } // end inner for
```

Fig. 13.50 ChessGame class method definitions. (Part 4 of 7.)

```
181
182        // account for new row tile color switch
183        light = !light;
184     } // end outer for
185  } // end method ResetBoard
186
187  // display board in OnPaint method
188  void ChessGame::OnPaint( PaintEventArgs *e )
189  {
190     __super::OnPaint( e ); // call base OnPaint method
191
192     // obtain graphics object
193     Graphics *graphicsObject = e->Graphics;
194
195     for ( int row = 0;
196        row <= board->GetUpperBound( 0 ); row++ ) {
197
198        for ( int column = 0;
199           column <= board->GetUpperBound( 1 ); column++ ) {
200
201           // draw image specified in board array
202           graphicsObject->DrawImage(
203              dynamic_cast < Image * >(
204              chessTile->Item[ board[ row, column ] ] ),
205              Point( TILESIZE * column,
206              TILESIZE * row ) );
207        } // end inner for
208     } // end outer for
209  } // end method OnPaint
210
211  // return index of piece that intersects point
212  // optionally exclude a value
213  int ChessGame::CheckBounds( Point point, int exclude )
214  {
215     Rectangle rectangle; // current bounding rectangle
216
217     for ( int i = 0; i < chessPieces->Count; i++ ) {
218
219        // get piece rectangle
220        rectangle = GetPiece( i )->GetBounds();
221
222        // check if rectangle contains point
223        if ( rectangle.Contains( point ) && i != exclude )
224           return i;
225     }
226     return -1;
227  } // end method CheckBounds
228
229  // handle pieceBox paint event
230  void ChessGame::pieceBox_Paint(
231     Object *sender, PaintEventArgs *e )
232  {
233     // draw all pieces
```

Fig. 13.50 ChessGame class method definitions. (Part 5 of 7.)

```
234      for ( int i = 0; i < chessPieces->Count; i++ )
235          GetPiece( i )->Draw( e->Graphics );
236  } // end method pieceBox_Paint
237
238  void ChessGame::pieceBox_MouseDown(
239      Object *sender, MouseEventArgs *e )
240  {
241      // determine selected piece
242      selectedIndex =
243          CheckBounds( Point( e->X, e->Y ), -1 );
244  } // end method pieceBox_MouseDown
245
246  // if piece is selected, move it
247  void ChessGame::pieceBox_MouseMove(
248      Object *sender, MouseEventArgs *e )
249  {
250      if ( selectedIndex > -1 ) {
251          Rectangle region = Rectangle(
252              e->X - TILESIZE * 2, e->Y - TILESIZE * 2,
253              TILESIZE * 4, TILESIZE * 4 );
254
255          // set piece center to mouse
256          GetPiece( selectedIndex )->SetLocation(
257              e->X - TILESIZE / 2, e->Y - TILESIZE / 2 );
258
259          // refresh immediate are
260          pieceBox->Invalidate( region );
261      } // end if
262  } // end method pieceBox_MouseMove
263
264  // on mouse up deselect piece and remove taken piece
265  void ChessGame::pieceBox_MouseUp(
266      Object *sender, MouseEventArgs *e )
267  {
268      int remove = -1;
269      int maxLocation = 7 * TILESIZE;
270
271      //if chess piece was selected
272      if ( selectedIndex > -1 ) {
273          Point current = Point( e->X, e->Y );
274          Point newPoint = Point(
275              current.X - ( current.X % TILESIZE ),
276              current.Y - ( current.Y % TILESIZE ) );
277
278          // ensure that new point is within bounds of board
279          if ( newPoint.X < 0 )
280              newPoint.X = 0;
281          else if ( newPoint.X > maxLocation )
282              newPoint.X = maxLocation;
283
284          if ( newPoint.Y < 0 )
285              newPoint.Y = 0;
286          else if ( newPoint.Y > maxLocation )
```

Fig. 13.50 ChessGame class method definitions. (Part 6 of 7.)

```
287              newPoint.Y = maxLocation;
288
289        // check bounds with point, exclude selected piece
290        remove = CheckBounds( newPoint, selectedIndex );
291
292        // snap piece into center of closest square
293        GetPiece( selectedIndex )->SetLocation( newPoint.X,
294           newPoint.Y );
295
296        // deselect piece
297        selectedIndex = -1;
298
299        // remove taken piece
300        if ( remove > -1 )
301           chessPieces->RemoveAt( remove );
302     } // end if
303
304     // refresh pieceBox to ensure artifact removal
305     pieceBox->Invalidate();
306  } // end method pieceBox_MouseUp
307
308  // helper function to convert
309  // ArrayList object to ChessPiece
310  ChessPiece* ChessGame::GetPiece( int i )
311  {
312     return dynamic_cast < ChessPiece* >(
313        chessPieces->Item[ i ] );
314  } // end method GetPiece
315
316  // handle NewGame menu option click
317  void ChessGame::newGameItem_Click(
318     Object *sender, EventArgs *e )
319  {
320     ResetBoard(); // reinitialize board
321     Invalidate(); // refresh form
322  } // end method newGameItem_Click
```

Fig. 13.50 `ChessGame` class method definitions. (Part 7 of 7.)

A chess board is defined by alternating light and dark tiles across a row in a pattern where the color that starts each row is equal to the color of the last tile of the previous row. Lines 168–179 assign the current board-tile color as an index in the **board** array. Based on the alternating value of **bool** variable **light** and the results of the random operation on line 166, **0** and **1** are light tiles, whereas **2** and **3** are dark tiles. Line 183 inverts the value of **light** at the end of each row to maintain the staggered effect of a chess board.

Method **OnPaint** (lines 188–209) handles this class **Form**'s **Paint** event and draws the tiles according to their values in the board array. Method **pieceBox_Paint** (lines 230–236), which handles the **pieceBox Panel Paint** event, iterates through each element of the **chessPiece ArrayList** and calls its **Draw** method.

The **MouseDown** event handler (lines 238–244) calls method **CheckBounds** (lines 213–227) with the location of the user's click to determine whether the user selected a piece. **CheckBounds** returns an integer locating a collision from a given point.

The **MouseMove** event handler (lines 247–262) moves the currently selected piece with the mouse. Lines 256–257 set the selected piece location to the mouse-cursor position, adjusting the location by up to half a tile to center the image on the mouse. Line 260 defines and refreshes a region of the **Panel** that spans two tiles in every direction from the mouse. As mentioned earlier in the chapter, the **Invalidate** method is slow. This means that the **MouseMove** event handler might be called again several times before the **Invalidate** method completes. If a user working on a slow computer moves the mouse quickly, the application could leave behind *artifacts*. An artifact is any unintended visual abnormality in a graphical program. By causing the program to refresh a two-square rectangle, which should suffice in most cases, we achieve a significant performance enhancement over an entire component refresh during each **MouseMove** event.

Lines 265–306 define the **MouseUp** event handler. If a piece has been selected, lines 268–301 determine the index in **chessPieces** of any piece collision, remove the collided piece, snap (align) the current piece into a valid location and deselect the piece. We check for piece collisions to allow the chess piece to "take" other chess pieces. Lines 279–287 begin by checking whether the current position exists on the game board. If the current position is not in the valid range (**0** to **TILESIZE * 7**), the position is modified to fit within the bounds of the board. Line 290 then checks whether any piece (excluding the currently selected piece) is beneath the new location. If a collision is detected, the returned piece index is assigned to **int remove**. Lines 293–294 determine the closest valid chess tile and "snap" the selected piece to that location. If **remove** contains a positive value, line 301 removes the object at that index from the **chessPieces ArrayList**. Finally, the entire **Panel** is **Invalidate**d in line 305 to display the new piece location and remove any artifacts created during the move.

Method **CheckBounds** (lines 213–227) is a collision-detection helper method; it iterates through the **chessPieces ArrayList** and returns the index of any piece rectangle containing the point value passed to the method (the mouse location, in this example). Method **CheckBounds** optionally can exclude a single piece index (to ignore the selected index in the **MouseUp** event handler, in this example).

Lines 310–314 define helper function **GetPiece**, which simplifies the conversion from **Object**s in the **ArrayList chessPieces** to **ChessPiece** types. Method **newGameItem_Click** handles the **NewGame** menu item click event, calls **Refresh-Board** to reset the game and **Invalidate**s the entire form. Figure 13.51 executes the chess application.

```
1   // Fig. 13.51: ChessGameTest.cpp
2   // Entry point for application.
3
4   #include "ChessGame.h"
5
6   int __stdcall WinMain()()
7   {
8      Application::Run( new ChessGame() );
9
10     return 0;
11  } // end function WinMain
```

Fig. 13.51 ChessGameTest.cpp demonstrates a chess game. (Part 1 of 3.)

Fig. 13.51 ChessGameTest.cpp demonstrates a chess game. (Part 2 of 3.)

Fig. 13.51 `ChessGameTest.cpp` demonstrates a chess game. (Part 3 of 3.)

13.12 Windows Media Player

The Windows Media Player control enables an application to play video and sound in many multimedia formats. These include *MPEG (Motion Pictures Experts Group)* audio and video, *AVI (audio-video interleave)* video, *WAV (Windows wave-file format)* audio and *MIDI (Musical Instrument Digital Interface)* audio. Users can find preexisting audio and video on the Internet, or they can create their own files, using available sound and graphics packages.

The Windows Media Player control is an *ActiveX control*. ActiveX controls are reusable GUI components in Windows. Windows comes with a number of pre-installed ActiveX controls, such as the Windows Media Player control.

Figures 13.52–13.54 demonstrate the Windows Media Player control, which enables users to play multimedia files. To use the Windows Media Player control in MC++, programmers must create the necessary DLLs—**MediaPlayer.dll** and **AxMedia-Player.dll**—by running the command

```
aximp c:\winnt\system32\msdxm.ocx
```

from directory

```
c:\Program Files\Microsoft Visual Studio .NET\
frameworkSDK\bin
```

The *ActiveX Control Importer* (**aximp**) will create the DLLs in the same directory.[3] These DLLs can then be referenced relatively or copied into the project's **Debug** directory and referenced locally. We discuss ActiveX controls and **aximp** in more detail in Chapter 25, COM Interoperability Services.

```cpp
1   // Fig. 13.52: MediaPlayer.h
2   // Demonstrates the Windows Media Player control.
3
4   #pragma once
5
6   #using <mscorlib.dll>
7   #using <system.dll>
8   #using <system.drawing.dll>
9   #using <system.windows.forms.dll>
10
11  #using "MediaPlayer.dll"
12  #using "AxMediaPlayer.dll"
13
14  using namespace System;
15  using namespace System::Drawing;
16  using namespace System::Windows::Forms;
17
18  public __gc class MyMediaPlayer : public Form
19  {
20  public:
21     MyMediaPlayer();
22
23  private:
24     MainMenu *applicationMenu;
25     MenuItem *fileItem;
26     MenuItem *openItem;
27     MenuItem *exitItem;
28     MenuItem *aboutItem;
29     MenuItem *aboutMessageItem;
30     OpenFileDialog *openMediaFileDialog;
31     AxMediaPlayer::AxMediaPlayer *player;
32
33     void InitializeComponent();
34     void openItem_Click( Object *, EventArgs * );
35     void exitItem_Click( Object *, EventArgs * );
36     void aboutMessageItem_Click( Object *, EventArgs * );
37  }; // end class MyMediaPlayer
```

Fig. 13.52 Windows Media Player demonstration.

---

3. For more information about creating DLLs using **aximp**, visit **msdn.microsoft.com/ library/en-us/cptools/html/cpgrfwindowsformsactivexcontrol importeraximpexe.asp**.

```
1    // Fig. 13.53: MediaPlayer.cpp
2    // Method definitions for class MyMediaPlayer.
3
4    #include "MyMediaPlayer.h"
5
6    MyMediaPlayer::MyMediaPlayer()
7    {
8       InitializeComponent();
9    }
10
11   void MyMediaPlayer::InitializeComponent()
12   {
13      System::Resources::ResourceManager *resources =
14         new System::Resources::ResourceManager
15         ( __typeof( MyMediaPlayer ) );
16      this->player = new AxMediaPlayer::AxMediaPlayer();
17      this->applicationMenu = new MainMenu();
18      this->fileItem = new MenuItem();
19      this->openItem = new MenuItem();
20      this->exitItem = new MenuItem();
21      this->aboutItem = new MenuItem();
22      this->aboutMessageItem = new MenuItem();
23      this->openMediaFileDialog = new OpenFileDialog();
24
25      this->player->BeginInit();
26      this->SuspendLayout();
27
28      // player
29      this->player->Name = S"player";
30      this->player->Size = Drawing::Size( 312, 288 );
31      this->player->TabIndex = 0;
32
33      // applicationMenu
34      MenuItem *temp3[] = { this->fileItem, this->aboutItem };
35      this->applicationMenu->MenuItems->AddRange( temp3 );
36
37      // fileItem
38      this->fileItem->Index = 0;
39      MenuItem *temp4[] = { this->openItem, this->exitItem };
40      this->fileItem->MenuItems->AddRange( temp4 );
41      this->fileItem->Text = S"File";
42
43      // openItem
44      this->openItem->Index = 0;
45      this->openItem->Text = S"Open...";
46      this->openItem->Click += new EventHandler( this,
47         openItem_Click );
48
49      // exitItem
50      this->exitItem->Index = 1;
51      this->exitItem->Text = S"Exit";
52      this->exitItem->Click += new EventHandler( this,
53         exitItem_Click );
54
55      // aboutItem
```

Fig. 13.53 MyMediaPlayer class method definitions. (Part 1 of 2.)

```
56         this->aboutItem->Index = 1;
57         MenuItem *temp[] = { this->aboutMessageItem };
58         this->aboutItem->MenuItems->AddRange( temp );
59         this->aboutItem->Text = S"About";
60
61         // aboutMessageItem
62         this->aboutMessageItem->Index = 0;
63         this->aboutMessageItem->Text =
64            S"About Windows Media Player";
65         this->aboutMessageItem->Click += new EventHandler(
66            this, aboutMessageItem_Click );
67
68         // MediaPlayer
69         this->AutoScaleBaseSize = Drawing::Size( 5, 13 );
70         this->ClientSize = Drawing::Size( 312, 287 );
71         Control *temp2[] = { this->player };
72         this->Controls->AddRange( temp2 );
73         this->Menu = this->applicationMenu;
74         this->Name = S"MediaPlayer";
75         this->Text = S"MediaPlayer";
76
77         this->player->EndInit();
78
79         this->ResumeLayout();
80      } // end method InitializeComponent
81
82      // open new media file in Windows Media Player
83      void MyMediaPlayer::openItem_Click(
84         Object *sender, EventArgs *e )
85      {
86         openMediaFileDialog->ShowDialog();
87
88         player->FileName = openMediaFileDialog->FileName;
89
90         // adjust the size of the Media Player control and
91         // the Form according to the size of the image
92         player->Size.Width = player->ImageSourceWidth;
93         player->Size.Height = player->ImageSourceHeight;
94
95         this->Size.Width = player->Size.Width + 20;
96         this->Size.Height = player->Size.Height + 60;
97      } // end method openItem_Click
98
99      void MyMediaPlayer::exitItem_Click(
100        Object *sender, EventArgs *e )
101     {
102        Application::Exit();
103     } // end method exitItem_Click
104
105     void MyMediaPlayer::aboutMessageItem_Click(
106        Object *sender, EventArgs *e )
107     {
108        player->AboutBox();
109     } // end method aboutMessageItem_Click
```

Fig. 13.53 `MyMediaPlayer` class method definitions. (Part 2 of 2.)

```
1   // Fig. 13.54: MediaPlayerTest.cpp
2   // Entry point for application.
3
4   #include "MyMediaPlayer.h"
5
6   using namespace System::Threading;
7
8   int __stdcall WinMain()()
9   {
10      // set program to single threaded execution
11      Thread::CurrentThread->ApartmentState = ApartmentState::STA;
12
13      Application::Run( new MyMediaPlayer() );
14
15      return 0;
16  } // end function WinMain
```

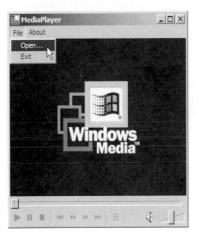

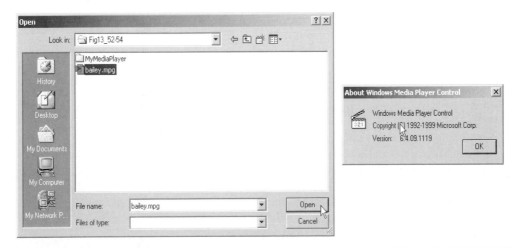

Fig. 13.54 MyMediaPlayer class driver.

Once the DLLs have been created, we can then use them to access the Windows Media Player control. Lines 11–12 (Fig. 13.52) include **MediaPlayer.dll** and **AxMedia-Player.dll**. Line 31 declares a Windows Media Player control object of type **AxMediaPlayer**. The Windows Media Player control provides several buttons that allow the user to play the current file, pause, stop, play the previous file, rewind, forward and play the next file. The control also includes a volume control and trackbars to select a specific position in the media file.

The application provides a **MainMenu**, which includes **File** and **About** menus. The **File** menu contains the **Open** and **Exit** menu items; the **About** menu contains the **About Windows Media Player** menu item.

When a user chooses **Open** from the **File** menu, event handler **openItem_Click** (lines 83–97 of Fig. 13.53) executes. Line 86 invokes *OpenFileDialog* method *ShowDialog*. Class **OpenFileDialog** represents a dialog box that allows a user to select a file; Method **ShowDialog** displays the dialog box.

The program then sets the *FileName* property of the **player** (the Windows Media Player control object of type **AxMediaPlayer**) to the name of the file chosen by the user. The **FileName** property specifies the file that Windows Media Player currently is using. Lines 92–96 adjust the size of **player** and the application to reflect the size of the media contained in the file.

The event handler that executes when the user selects **Exit** from the **File** menu (lines 99–103) simply calls **Application::Exit** to terminate the application. The event handler that executes when the user chooses **About Windows Media Player** from the **About** menu (lines 105–109) calls the *AboutBox* method of the player. **AboutBox** simply displays a preset message box containing information about Windows Media Player.

ActiveX controls are designed to run in a *single thread apartment (STA)* threading model. To initialize the control properly, the application must be run in a STA threading model. Thus, when Fig. 13.54 starts the application, line 11 obtains the current thread and explicitly sets the apartment model using enumeration *ApartmentState*.

13.13 Microsoft Agent

Microsoft Agent is a technology used to add *interactive animated characters* to Windows applications or Web pages. Interactivity is the key function of Microsoft Agent technology: Microsoft Agent characters can speak and respond to user input via speech recognition and synthesis. Microsoft employs its Agent technology in applications such as Word, Excel and PowerPoint. Agents in these programs aid users in finding answers to questions and in understanding how the applications function.

The Microsoft Agent control provides programmers with access to four predefined characters—*Genie* (a genie), *Merlin* (a wizard), *Peedy* (a parrot) and *Robby* (a robot). Each character has a unique set of animations that programmers can use in their applications to illustrate different points and functions. For instance, the Peedy character-animation set includes different flying animations, which the programmer might use to move Peedy on the screen. Microsoft provides basic information on Agent technology at its Web site,

`www.microsoft.com/msagent`

Microsoft Agent technology enables users to interact with applications and Web pages through speech, the most natural form of human communication. When the user speaks into a microphone, the control uses a *speech recognition engine,* an application that translates vocal sound input from a microphone into language that the computer understands. The Microsoft Agent control also uses a *text-to-speech engine*, which generates characters' spoken responses. A text-to-speech engine is an application that translates typed words into audio sound that users hear through headphones or speakers connected to a computer. Microsoft provides speech recognition and text-to-speech engines for several languages at its Web site,

        `www.microsoft.com/products/msagent/downloads.htm`

Programmers can even create their own animated characters with the help of the *Microsoft Agent Character Editor* and the *Microsoft Linguistic Sound Editing Tool*. These products are available free for download from

        `www.microsoft.com/products/msagent/devdownloads.htm`

This section introduces the basic capabilities of the Microsoft Agent control. For complete details on downloading this control, visit

        `www.microsoft.com/products/msagent/downloads.htm`

The following example, Peedy's Pizza Palace, was developed by Microsoft to illustrate the capabilities of the Microsoft Agent control. Peedy's Pizza Palace is an online pizza shop where users can place their orders via voice input. The Peedy character interacts with users by helping them choose toppings and then calculating the totals for their orders.
Readers can view this example at

        `agent.microsoft.com/agent2/sdk/samples/html/peedypza.htm`

To run this example, students must download the Peedy character file, a text-to-speech engine and a speech-recognition engine. When the page loads, the browser prompts for these downloads. Follow the directions provided by Microsoft to complete installation.
When the window opens, Peedy introduces himself (Fig. 13.55), and the words he speaks appear in a cartoon bubble above his head. Notice that Peedy's animations correspond to the words he speaks.
Programmers can synchronize character animations with speech output to illustrate a point or to convey a character's mood. For instance, Fig. 13.56 depicts Peedy's *Pleased* animation. The Peedy character-animation set includes eighty-five different animations, each of which is unique to the Peedy character.

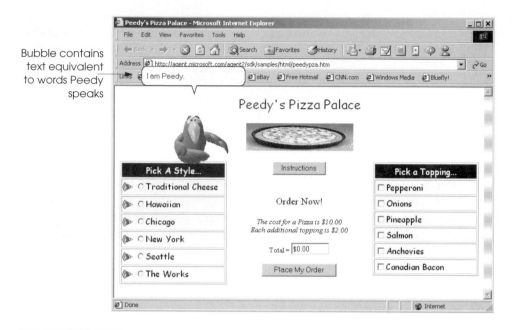

Bubble contains
text equivalent
to words Peedy
speaks

Fig. 13.55 Peedy introducing himself when the window opens.

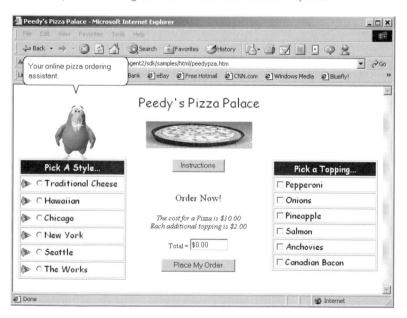

Fig. 13.56 Peedy's *Pleased* animation.

Look-and-Feel Observation 13.1

Agent characters remain on top of all active windows while a Microsoft Agent application is running. Their motions are not limited to the boundaries of the browser or application window.

Peedy also responds to input from the keyboard and mouse. Figure 13.57 shows what happens when a user clicks Peedy with the mouse pointer. Peedy jumps up, ruffles his feathers and exclaims, "Hey that tickles!" or, "Be careful with that pointer!" Users can relocate Peedy on the screen by clicking and dragging him with the mouse. However, even when the user moves Peedy to a different part of the screen, he continues to perform his preset animations and location changes.

Many location changes involve animations. For instance, Peedy can hop from one screen location to another, or he can fly (Fig. 13.58).

Once Peedy completes the ordering instructions, a text box appears beneath him indicating that he is listening for a voice command (Fig. 13.59). A user can enter the type of pizza to order either by speaking the style name into a microphone or by clicking the radio button corresponding to the choice.

If a user chooses speech input, a box appears below Peedy displaying the words that Peedy "heard" (i.e., the words translated to the program by the speech-recognition engine). Once he recognizes the user input, Peedy gives the user a description of the selected pizza. Figure 13.60 shows what happens when the user chooses **Seattle** as the pizza style.

Peedy then asks the user to choose additional toppings. Again, the user can either speak or use the mouse to make a selection. Check boxes corresponding to toppings that come with the selected pizza style are checked for the user. Figure 13.61 shows what happens when a user chooses anchovies as an additional topping. Peedy makes a wisecrack about the user's choice.

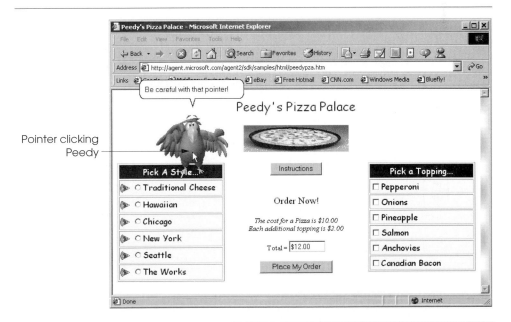

Fig. 13.57 Peedy's reaction when he is clicked.

Fig. 13.58 Peedy flying animation.

Fig. 13.59 Peedy waiting for speech input.

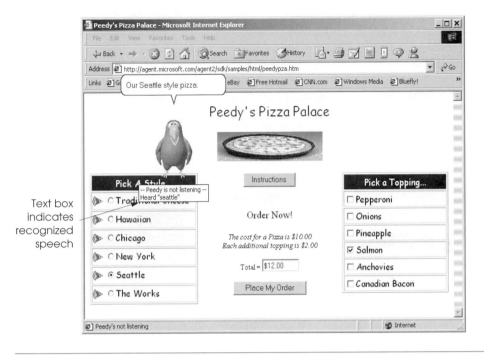

Fig. 13.60 Peedy repeating the user's request for Seattle-style pizza.

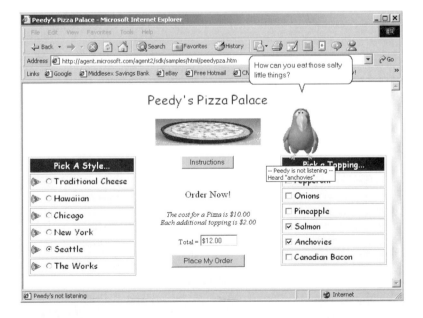

Fig. 13.61 Peedy repeating the user's request for anchovies as an additional topping.

The user can submit the order either by pressing the **Place My Order** button or by speaking "Place order" into the microphone. Peedy recounts the order while writing down the order items on his notepad (Fig. 13.62). He then calculates the figures on his calculator and reports the total to the user (Fig. 13.63).

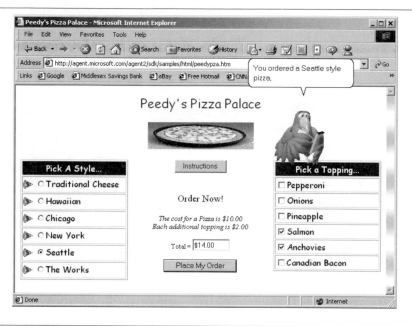

Fig. 13.62 Peedy recounting the order.

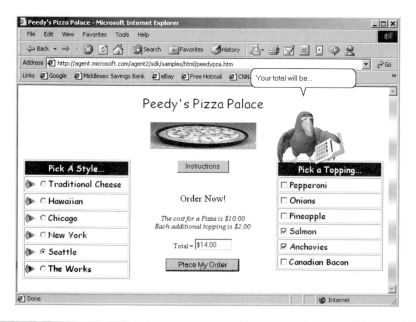

Fig. 13.63 Peedy calculating the total.

Figures 13.64–13.66 demonstrate how to build a simple application with the Microsoft Agent control. This application contains two drop-down lists from which the user can choose an Agent character and a character animation. When the user chooses from these lists, the chosen character appears and performs the chosen animation. The application uses speech recognition and synthesis to control the character animations and speech: Users can tell the character which animation to perform by pressing the *Scroll Lock* key and then speaking the animation name into a microphone.

```cpp
1   // Fig. 13.64: MicrosoftAgent.h
2   // Class AgentForm demonstrates Microsoft Agent.
3
4   #pragma once
5
6   #using <mscorlib.dll>
7   #using <system.dll>
8   #using <system.drawing.dll>
9   #using <system.windows.forms.dll>
10
11  #using "AgentObjects.dll"
12  #using "AxAgentObjects.dll"
13
14  using namespace System;
15  using namespace System::Drawing;
16  using namespace System::Collections;
17  using namespace System::Windows::Forms;
18  using namespace System::IO;
19  using namespace System::Threading;
20
21  public __gc class AgentForm : public Form
22  {
23  public:
24     AgentForm();
25
26  private:
27     ComboBox *actionsCombo;
28     ComboBox *characterCombo;
29
30     Button *speakButton;
31     GroupBox *characterGroup;
32     AxAgentObjects::AxAgent* mainAgent;
33
34     TextBox *speechTextBox;
35     TextBox *locationTextBox;
36
37     AgentObjects::IAgentCtlCharacter *speaker;
38
39     void InitializeComponent();
40     void locationTextBox_KeyDown( Object *sender,
41        KeyEventArgs *eventArgs );
42
43     void speakButton_Click( Object *sender,
44        EventArgs *eventArgs );
45
```

Fig. 13.64 Microsoft Agent demonstration. (Part 1 of 2.)

```
46        void mainAgent_ClickEvent( Object *sender,
47           AxAgentObjects::_AgentEvents_ClickEvent *eventArgs );
48
49        void characterCombo_SelectedIndexChanged(
50           Object *sender, EventArgs *eventArgs );
51
52        void ChangeCharacter( String *name );
53
54        void GetAnimationNames();
55        void actionsCombo_SelectedIndexChanged(
56           Object *sender, EventArgs *eventArgs );
57
58        void mainAgent_Command( Object *sender,
59           AxAgentObjects::_AgentEvents_CommandEvent *eventArgs );
60    }; // end class Agent
```

Fig. 13.64 Microsoft Agent demonstration. (Part 2 of 2.)

```
1     // Fig. 13.65: MicrosoftAgent.cpp
2     // Method definitions for class AgentForm.
3
4     #include "MicrosoftAgent.h"
5
6     AgentForm::AgentForm()
7     {
8        InitializeComponent();
9     }
10
11    void AgentForm::InitializeComponent()
12    {
13       System::Resources::ResourceManager *resources =
14          new System::Resources::ResourceManager(
15          __typeof( AgentForm ) );
16
17       this->actionsCombo = new ComboBox();
18       this->speechTextBox = new TextBox();
19       this->speakButton = new Button();
20       this->characterGroup = new GroupBox();
21       this->characterCombo = new ComboBox();
22       this->locationTextBox = new TextBox();
23       this->mainAgent = new AxAgentObjects::AxAgent();
24
25       this->characterGroup->SuspendLayout();
26
27       this->mainAgent->BeginInit();
28
29       this->SuspendLayout();
30
31       // actionsCombo
32       this->actionsCombo->Enabled = false;
33       this->actionsCombo->Location = Drawing::Point( 312, 72 );
34       this->actionsCombo->Name = S"actionsCombo";
35       this->actionsCombo->Size = Drawing::Size( 128, 21 );
```

Fig. 13.65 AgentForm class method definitions. (Part 1 of 6.)

```
36        this->actionsCombo->TabIndex = 11;
37        this->actionsCombo->Text = S"Select an Action";
38        this->actionsCombo->SelectedIndexChanged +=
39           new EventHandler( this,
40           actionsCombo_SelectedIndexChanged );
41
42        // speechTextBox
43        this->speechTextBox->Enabled = false;
44        this->speechTextBox->Location.X = 8;
45        this->speechTextBox->Location.Y = 16;
46        this->speechTextBox->Multiline = true;
47        this->speechTextBox->Name = S"speechTextBox";
48        this->speechTextBox->Size = Drawing::Size( 280, 80 );
49        this->speechTextBox->TabIndex = 10;
50        this->speechTextBox->Text = S"";
51
52        // speakButton
53        this->speakButton->Enabled = false;
54        this->speakButton->Location = Drawing::Point( 328, 24 );
55        this->speakButton->Name = S"speakButton";
56        this->speakButton->Size = Drawing::Size( 104, 32 );
57        this->speakButton->TabIndex = 9;
58        this->speakButton->Text = S"Speak";
59        this->speakButton->Click +=
60           new EventHandler( this, speakButton_Click );
61
62        // characterGroup
63        this->characterGroup->Location = Drawing::Point( 8, 104 );
64        this->characterGroup->Name = S"characterGroup";
65        this->characterGroup->Size = Drawing::Size( 440, 56 );
66        this->characterGroup->TabIndex = 8;
67        this->characterGroup->TabStop = false;
68        this->characterGroup->Text = S"Character Name/Location";
69
70        // characterCombo
71        this->characterCombo->Enabled = false;
72        String *temporary2[] = { S"Genie", S"Merlin",
73           S"Peedy", S"Robby" };
74        this->characterCombo->Items->AddRange( temporary2 );
75        this->characterCombo->Location = Drawing::Point( 304, 24 );
76        this->characterCombo->Name = S"characterCombo";
77        this->characterCombo->Size = Drawing::Size( 128, 21 );
78        this->characterCombo->TabIndex = 1;
79        this->characterCombo->Text = S"Select A Character";
80        this->characterCombo->SelectedIndexChanged +=
81           new EventHandler( this,
82           characterCombo_SelectedIndexChanged );
83
84        Control *temporary1[] = { this->characterCombo,
85           this->locationTextBox };
86
87        this->characterGroup->Controls->AddRange( temporary1 );
88
```

Fig. 13.65 `AgentForm` class method definitions. (Part 2 of 6.)

```
89        // locationTextBox
90        this->locationTextBox->Location = Drawing::Point( 16, 24 );
91        this->locationTextBox->Name = S"locationTextBox";
92        this->locationTextBox->Size = Drawing::Size( 272, 20 );
93        this->locationTextBox->TabIndex = 0;
94        this->locationTextBox->Text = S"C:\\WINNT\\msagent\\chars\\";
95        this->locationTextBox->KeyDown +=
96           new KeyEventHandler( this,
97           locationTextBox_KeyDown );
98
99        // mainAgent
100       this->mainAgent->Enabled = true;
101       this->mainAgent->Location = Drawing::Point( 304, 24 );
102       this->mainAgent->Name = S"mainAgent";
103       this->mainAgent->Size = Drawing::Size( 32, 32 );
104       this->mainAgent->TabIndex = 12;
105       this->mainAgent->ClickEvent +=
106           new AxAgentObjects::_AgentEvents_ClickEventHandler(
107           this, mainAgent_ClickEvent );
108       this->mainAgent->Command +=
109           new AxAgentObjects::_AgentEvents_CommandEventHandler(
110           this, mainAgent_Command );
111
112       // Agent
113       this->AutoScaleBaseSize = Drawing::Size( 5, 13 );
114       this->ClientSize = Drawing::Size( 448, 165 );
115
116       Control *temporary3 [] = { this->mainAgent,
117           this->actionsCombo, this->speechTextBox,
118           this->speakButton, this->characterGroup };
119
120       this->Controls->AddRange( temporary3 );
121       this->Name = S"Agent";
122       this->Text = S"Microsoft Agent";
123
124       this->characterGroup->ResumeLayout();
125       this->mainAgent->EndInit();
126       this->ResumeLayout();
127  } // end method InitializeComponent
128
129  // KeyDown event handler for locationTextBox
130  void AgentForm::locationTextBox_KeyDown(
131      Object *sender, KeyEventArgs *eventArgs )
132  {
133      if ( eventArgs->KeyCode == Keys::Enter ) {
134
135          // set character location to text box value
136          String *location = locationTextBox->Text;
137
138          // initialize the characters
139          try {
140
141              // load characters into agent object
```

Fig. 13.65 AgentForm class method definitions. (Part 3 of 6.)

```
142              mainAgent->Characters->Load( S"Genie",
143                 String::Concat( location, S"Genie.acs" ) );
144
145              mainAgent->Characters->Load( S"Merlin",
146                 String::Concat( location, S"Merlin.acs" ) );
147
148              mainAgent->Characters->Load( S"Peedy",
149                 String::Concat( location, S"Peedy.acs" ) );
150
151              mainAgent->Characters->Load( S"Robby",
152                 String::Concat( location, S"Robby.acs" ) );
153
154              // disable TextBox for entering the location
155              // and enable other controls
156              locationTextBox->Enabled = false;
157              speechTextBox->Enabled = true;
158              speakButton->Enabled = true;
159              characterCombo->Enabled = true;
160              actionsCombo->Enabled = true;
161
162              // set current character to Genie and show him
163              speaker = mainAgent->Characters->Item[ S"Genie" ];
164
165              // obtain an animation name list
166              GetAnimationNames();
167              speaker->Show( 0 );
168           } // end try
169           catch( FileNotFoundException * ) {
170              MessageBox::Show( S"Invalid character location",
171                 S"Error", MessageBoxButtons::OK,
172                 MessageBoxIcon::Error );
173           } // end catch
174        } // end if
175  } // end method locationTextBox_KeyDown
176
177  void AgentForm::speakButton_Click(
178     Object *sender, EventArgs *eventArgs)
179  {
180     // if textbox is empty, have the character ask
181     // user to type the words into textbox, otherwise
182     // have character say the words in textbox
183     if ( speechTextBox->Text->Equals( S"" ) )
184        speaker->Speak(
185           S"Please, type the words you want me to speak", S"" );
186     else
187        speaker->Speak( speechTextBox->Text, S"" );
188
189  } // end method speakButton_Click
190
191  // click event for agent
192  void AgentForm::mainAgent_ClickEvent( Object *sender,
193     AxAgentObjects::_AgentEvents_ClickEvent *eventArgs )
194  {
```

Fig. 13.65 AgentForm class method definitions. (Part 4 of 6.)

```
195        speaker->Play( S"Confused" );
196        speaker->Speak( S"Why are you poking me?", S"" );
197        speaker->Play( S"RestPose" );
198   } // end method mainAgent_ClickEvent
199
200   // combobox changed event, switch active agent
201   void AgentForm::characterCombo_SelectedIndexChanged(
202        Object *sender, EventArgs *eventArgs )
203   {
204        ChangeCharacter( characterCombo->Text );
205   } // end method characterCombo_SelectedIndexChanged
206
207   void AgentForm::ChangeCharacter( String *name )
208   {
209        speaker->Hide( 0 );
210        speaker = mainAgent->Characters->Item[ name ];
211
212        // regenerate animation name list
213        GetAnimationNames();
214        speaker->Show( 0 );
215   } // end method ChangeCharacter
216
217   // get animation names and store in arraylist
218   void AgentForm::GetAnimationNames()
219   {
220        Monitor::Enter( this );   // ensure thread safety
221
222        // get animation names
223        IEnumerator *enumerator = mainAgent->Characters->Item[
224           speaker->Name ]->AnimationNames->GetEnumerator();
225
226        String *voiceString;
227
228        // clear actionsCombo
229        actionsCombo->Items->Clear();
230        speaker->Commands->RemoveAll();
231
232        // copy enumeration to ArrayList
233        while ( enumerator->MoveNext() ) {
234
235           //remove underscores in speech string
236           voiceString = __try_cast< String * >(
237              enumerator->Current );
238           voiceString = voiceString->Replace(
239              S"_", S"underscore" );
240
241           actionsCombo->Items->Add( enumerator->Current );
242
243           // add all animations as voice enabled commands
244           speaker->Commands->Add(
245              __try_cast< String * >( enumerator->Current ),
246              enumerator->Current,
```

Fig. 13.65 AgentForm class method definitions. (Part 5 of 6.)

```
247              voiceString, __box( true ), __box( false ) );
248        } // end while
249
250        // add custom command
251        speaker->Commands->Add(
252           S"MoveToMouse", S"MoveToMouse",
253           S"MoveToMouse", __box( true ), __box( true ) );
254
255        Monitor::Exit( this );
256     } // end method GetAnimationNames
257
258     // user selects new action
259     void AgentForm::actionsCombo_SelectedIndexChanged(
260        Object *sender, EventArgs *eventArgs )
261     {
262        speaker->StopAll( S"Play" );
263        speaker->Play( actionsCombo->Text );
264        speaker->Play( S"RestPose" );
265     } // end method actionsCombo_SelectedIndexChanged
266
267     // handles agent commands
268     void AgentForm::mainAgent_Command( Object *sender,
269        AxAgentObjects::_AgentEvents_CommandEvent *eventArgs )
270     {
271        // get UserInput object
272        AgentObjects::IAgentCtlUserInput *command =
273           __try_cast< AgentObjects::IAgentCtlUserInput * >
274           ( eventArgs->userInput );
275
276        // change character if user speaks character name
277        if ( command->Voice->Equals( S"Peedy" ) ||
278           command->Voice->Equals( S"Robby" ) ||
279           command->Voice->Equals( S"Merlin" ) ||
280           command->Voice->Equals( S"Genie" ) ) {
281           ChangeCharacter( command->Voice );
282
283           return;
284        }
285
286        // send agent to mouse
287        if ( command->Voice->Equals( S"MoveToMouse" ) ) {
288           speaker->MoveTo(
289              Convert::ToInt16( Cursor->Position.X - 60 ),
290              Convert::ToInt16( Cursor->Position.Y - 60 ),
291              __box( 5 ) );
292
293           return;
294        }
295
296        // play new animation
297        speaker->StopAll( S"Play" );
298        speaker->Play( command->Name );
299     } // end method mainAgent_Command
```

Fig. 13.65 AgentForm class method definitions. (Part 6 of 6.)

```
1   // Fig. 13.66: MicrosoftAgentTest.cpp
2   // Entry point for application.
3
4   #include "MicrosoftAgent.h"
5
6   int __stdcall WinMain()
7   {
8      // set program to single threaded execution
9      Thread::CurrentThread->ApartmentState = ApartmentState::STA;
10
11     Application::Run( new AgentForm() );
12
13     return 0;
14  } // end function WinMain
```

Fig. 13.66 AgentForm class driver. (Part 1 of 2.)

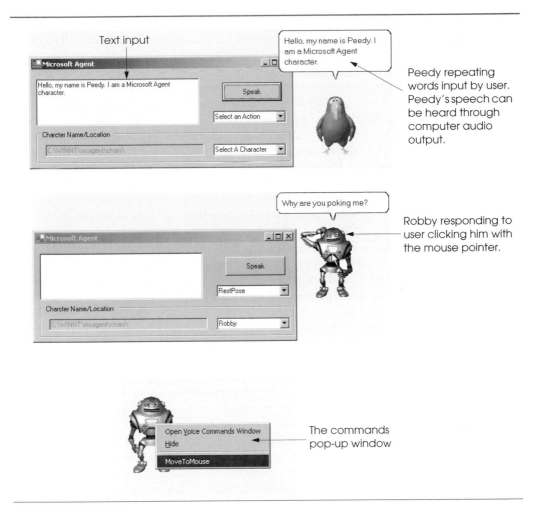

Fig. 13.66 `AgentForm` class driver. (Part 2 of 2.)

The example also allows the user to switch to a new character by speaking its name and also creates a custom command, **MoveToMouse**. In addition, the characters also speak any text that a user enters into the text box. Before running this example, readers first must download and install the control, speech-recognition engine, text-to-speech engine and character definitions from the Microsoft Agent Web site listed previously.

To use the Microsoft Agent control, the programmer first must create the necessary DLLs—**AgentObjects.dll** and **AxAgentObjects.dll**—by running the following command

```
aximp  c:\winnt\msagent\agentctl.dll
```

from directory

```
c:\Program Files\Microsoft Visual Studio .NET\frame-
workSDK\bin
```

The ActiveX Control Importer (**aximp**) will create the DLLs in the same directory.

Once the DLLs have been created, we can then use them to access the Microsoft Agent control. Lines 11–12 (Fig. 13.64) include **AgentObjects.dll** and **AxAgentObjects.dll**. Line 32 declares Microsoft Agent object (of type *AxAgent*) **mainAgent**. In addition to the Microsoft Agent object **mainAgent**, which manages all the characters, we also need an object (of type *IAgentCtlCharacter*) to represent the current character. We declare this object, named **speaker**, in line 37. When the program begins, the only enabled control is the **locationTextBox**. This text box contains the default location for the character files, but the user can change this location if the files are located elsewhere on the user's computer. Once the user presses *Enter* in the **TextBox**, event handler **locationTextBox_KeyDown** (lines 130–175 of Fig. 13.65) executes. Lines 142–152 load the character descriptions for the predefined animated characters. If the specified location of the characters is incorrect, or if any character is missing, a **FileNotFoundException** is thrown.

Lines 156–160 disable **locationTextBox** and enable the rest of the controls. Lines 163–167 set Genie as the default character, obtain all animation names via method **GetAnimationNames** and then call **IAgentCtlCharacter** method *Show* to display the character. We access characters through property *Characters* of **mainAgent**, which contains all characters that have been loaded. We use the indexer of the **Characters** property to specify the name of the character that we wish to load (**"Genie"**).

When a user pokes the character (i.e., clicks it with the mouse), event handler **mainAgent_ClickEvent** (lines 192–198) executes. First, **speaker** method *Play* plays an animation. This method accepts as an argument a **String *** representing one of the predefined animations for the character. (A list of animations for each character is available at the Microsoft Agent Web site; each character provides over 70 animations.) In our example, the argument to **Play** is **"Confused"**—this animation is defined for all four characters, each of which expresses this emotion in a unique way. The character then speaks, **"Why are you poking me?"** via a call to method *Speak*. Finally, the *RestPose* animation is played, which returns the character to its neutral, resting pose.

The list of valid commands for a character is contained in property *Commands* of the **IAgentCtlCharacter** object (**speaker**, in this example). The commands for an Agent character can be viewed in the **Commands** pop-up window, which displays when the user right-clicks an Agent character (the last screenshot in Fig. 13.66). Method *Add* (line 244–247) adds a new command to the command list. Method **Add** takes three **String *** arguments and two **bool** arguments. The first **String *** argument identifies the name of the command, which we use to identify the command programmatically. The second **String *** defines the command name as it appears in the **Commands** pop-up window. The third **String *** defines the voice input that triggers the command. The first **bool** specifies whether the command is active; the second **bool** indicates whether the command is visible in the **Commands** pop-up window. A command is triggered when the user selects the command from the **Commands** pop-up window or speaks the voice input into a microphone. Command logic is handled in the *Command* event of the **AxAgent** control (**mainAgent**, in this example). In addition, Agent defines several global commands that have predefined functions (for example, speaking a character name causes that character to appear).

Method **GetAnimationNames** (lines 218–256) fills the **actionsCombo** ComboBox with the current character's animation listing and defines the valid commands that can be used with the character. The method uses methods **Monitor::Enter** (line 220) and **Monitor::Exit** (line 255) to prevent errors resulting from rapid character changes.

Lines 223–224 obtain the current character's animations using interface ***IEnumerator*** (sometimes called an *enumerator* or an *iterator*). Interface **IEnmerator** (namespace **System::Collections**) can be used to iterate (traverse) through items in a collection one element at a time. After lines 229–230 clear the existing items in the **ComboBox** and character's **Commands** property, lines 233–248 iterate through all items in the animation-name enumerator. For each animation, in lines 236–237, we assign the animation name to **String * voiceString**. Lines 238–239 remove any underscore characters (_) and replaces them with the string **"underscore"**; this changes the string so that a user can pronounce and employ it as a command activator. The **Add** method (lines 244–247) adds a new command to the current character. The **Add** method adds all animations as commands by providing the following arguments: The animation name as the new command's **name** and caption, and **voiceString** for the voice activation string. The method's **bool** arguments enable the command, but make it unavailable in the **Commands** pop-up window. Thus, the command can be activated only by voice input. Lines 251–253 create a new command, named **MoveToMouse**, which is visible in the **Commands** pop-up window.

After the **GetAnimationNames** method has been called, the user can select a value from the **actionsCombo ComboBox**. Event handler **actionsCombo_SelectedIndexChanged** (lines 259–265) stops any current animation and then displays the animation that the user selected from the **ComboBox**.

The user also can type text into the **TextBox** and click **Speak**. This causes event handler **speakButton_Click** (line 177–189) to call **speaker**'s method **Speak**, supplying as an argument the text in **speechTextBox**. If the user clicks **Speak** without providing text, the character speaks, **"Please, type the words you want me to speak"**.

At any point in the program, the user can choose to display a different character from the **ComboBox**. When this happens, the **SelectedIndexChanged** event handler for **characterCombo** (lines 201–205) executes. The event handler calls method **ChangeCharacter** (line 204) with the text in the **characterCombo ComboBox** as an argument. Method **ChangeCharacter** calls the **Hide** method of **speaker** (line 209) to remove the current character from view. Line 210 assigns the newly selected character to **speaker**, line 213 generates the character's animation names and commands, and line 214 displays the character via a call to method **Show**.

Each time a user presses the *Scroll Lock* key and speaks into a microphone or selects a command from the **Commands** pop-up window, event handler **mainAgent_Command** (lines 268–299) is called. This method is passed an argument of type **AxAgentObjects::_AgentEvents_CommandEvent**, which contains a single property, **userInput**. The **userInput** property returns an **Object** that can be converted to type ***AgentObjects::IAgentCtlUserInput***, an interface that represents user input. The **userInput** object is assigned to a **IAgentCtlUserInput** object **command**, which is used to identify the command and then take appropriate action. Lines 277–284 use method **ChangeCharacter** to change the current Agent character if the user speaks a character name. Microsoft Agent always will show a character when a user speaks its name; however, by controlling the character change, we can ensure that only one

Agent character is displayed at a time. Lines 287–294 move the character to the current mouse location if the user invokes the **MoveToMouse** command. The Agent method *MoveTo* takes *x*- and *y*-coordinate arguments and moves the character to the specified screen position, applying appropriate movement animations. For all other commands, we **Play** the command name as an animation on line 298.

In this chapter, we explored various graphics capabilities of GDI+, including pens, brushes and images, and some multimedia capabilities of the .NET Framework Class Library. In the next chapter, we cover the reading, writing and accessing of sequential- and random-access files. We also explore several types of streams included in Visual Studio .NET.

13.14 Summary

A coordinate system is used to identify every possible point on the screen. The upper-left corner of a GUI component has coordinates (0, 0). A coordinate pair is composed of an *x*-coordinate (the horizontal coordinate) and a *y*-coordinate (the vertical coordinate). Coordinate units are measured in pixels. A pixel is the smallest unit of resolution on a display monitor.

A graphics context represents a drawing surface on the screen. A **Graphics** object provides access to the graphics context of a control. **Graphics** objects contain methods for drawing, font manipulation, color manipulation and other graphics-related actions.

Structure **Color** defines constants for manipulating colors in a program. **Color** properties **R**, **G** and **B** return **int** values from 0–255, representing the amounts of red, green and blue, respectively, that exist in a **Color**. The larger the value, the greater the amount of that particular color. .NET provides class **ColorDialog** to display a dialog that allows users to select colors. **Component** property **BackColor** (one of the many **Component** properties that can be called on most GUI components) changes the component's background color.

Class **Font**'s constructors all take at least three arguments—the font name, the font size and the font style. The font name is any font currently supported by the system. The font style is a member of the **FontStyle** enumeration. Class **FontMetrics** defines several methods for obtaining font metrics. Class **Font** provides the **Bold**, **Italic**, **Strikeout** and **Underline** properties, which return **true** if the font is bold, italic, strikeout or underlined, respectively. Class **Font** provides the **Name** property, which returns a **String *** representing the name of the font. Class **Font** provides the **Size** and **SizeInPoints** properties, which return the size of the font in design units and in points, respectively. The **FontFamily** class provides information about such font metrics as the family's spacing and height.

Using Visual Studio .NET and MC++, programmers can create applications that use components, such as Windows Media Player and Microsoft Agent. The Windows Media Player allows programmers to create applications that can play multimedia files. Microsoft Agent is a technology that allows programmers to include interactive animated characters in their applications.

Files and Streams

Objectives

- To create, read, write and update files.
- To understand the streams class hierarchy in the .NET Framework.
- To use classes **File** and **Directory**.
- To use the **FileStream** and **BinaryFormatter** classes to read objects from, and write objects to, files.
- To become familiar with sequential-access and random-access file processing.

I can only assume that a "Do Not File" document is filed in a "Do Not File" file.
Senator Frank Church
Senate Intelligence Subcommittee Hearing, 1975

Consciousness … does not appear to itself chopped up in bits. … A "river" or a "stream" are the metaphors by which it is most naturally described.
William James

I read part of it all the way through.
Samuel Goldwyn

Outline

14.1 Introduction

Variables and arrays offer only temporary storage of data—the data are lost when an object is garbage collected or when the program terminates. By contrast, *files* are used for long-term storage of data and can retain data even after the program that created the data terminates. Data maintained in files often are called *persistent data*. Computers can store files on *secondary storage devices*, such as magnetic disks, optical disks and magnetic tapes. In this chapter, we explain how to create, update and process data files in MC++ programs. We consider both "sequential-access" files and "random-access" files, indicating the kinds of applications for which each is best suited. We have two goals in this chapter: To introduce the sequential-access and random-access file-processing paradigms and to provide the reader with sufficient stream-processing capabilities to support the networking features that we introduce in Chapter 18, Networking: Streams-Based Sockets and Datagrams.

File processing is one of a programming language's most important capabilities, because it enables a language to support commercial applications that typically process massive amounts of persistent data. This chapter discusses the .NET Framework's powerful and abundant file-processing and stream-input/output features.

14.2 Data Hierarchy

Ultimately, all data items processed by a computer are reduced to combinations of zeros and ones. This is because it is simple and economical to build electronic devices that can assume two stable states—0 represents one state, and 1 represents the other. It is remarkable that the impressive functions performed by computers involve only the most fundamental manipulations of 0s and 1s.

The smallest data items that computers support are called *bits* (short for "*binary digit*"—a digit that can assume one of two values). Each data item, or bit, can assume either the value **0** or the value **1**. Computer circuitry performs various simple bit manipulations, such as examining the value of a bit, setting the value of a bit and reversing a bit (from **1** to **0** or from **0** to **1**).

Programming with data in the low-level form of bits is cumbersome. It is preferable to program with data in forms such as *decimal digits* (i.e., 0, 1, 2, 3, 4, 5, 6, 7, 8 and 9), *letters* (i.e., A through Z and a through z) and *special symbols* (i.e., $, @, %, &, *, (,), -, +, ", :, ?, / and many others). Digits, letters and special symbols are referred to as *characters.* The set of all characters used to write programs and represent data items on a particular computer is called that computer's *character set.* Because computers can process only **1**s and **0**s, every character in a computer's character set is represented as a pattern of **1**s and **0**s. *Bytes* are composed of eight bits. For example, characters in **System::String** objects are *Unicode*® characters, which are composed of 2 bytes, or 16 bits. Programmers create programs and data items with characters; computers manipulate and process these characters as patterns of bits. More information about Unicode® can be found in Appendix D, Unicode®.

The various kinds of data items processed by computers can form a *data hierarchy* (Fig. 14.1) in which data items become larger and more complex in structure as we progress from bits, to characters, to fields (discussed momentarily) and up to larger data structures. [*Note*: The structure we suggest in this section is not the only structure a file may have. We only supply this structure as an example that we can build upon throughout the chapter.]

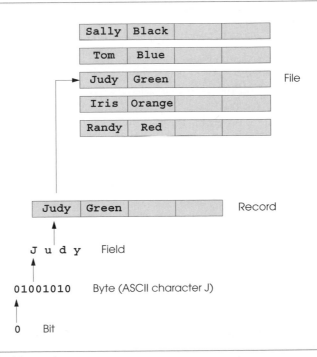

Fig. 14.1   Data hierarchy.

In the same way that characters are composed of bits, *fields* are composed of characters. A field is a group of characters that conveys some meaning. For example, a field consisting of uppercase and lowercase letters can represent a person's name.

Typically, a *record* is composed of several fields. In a payroll system, for example, a record for a particular employee might include the following fields:

1. Employee identification number

2. Name

3. Address

4. Hourly pay rate

5. Number of exemptions claimed

6. Year-to-date earnings

7. Amount of taxes withheld

Thus, a record is a group of related fields. In the preceding example, each field is associated with the same employee. A group of related records compose a *file*.[1] A company's payroll file normally contains one record for each employee. Thus, a payroll file for a small company might contain only 22 records, whereas a payroll file for a large company might contain 100,000 records. It is not unusual for a company to have many files, some containing millions, billions or even trillions of bits of information.

To facilitate the retrieval of specific records from a file, at least one field in each record is chosen as a unique *record key*. A record key identifies a record as belonging to a particular person or entity and distinguishes that record from all other records. In the payroll record described previously, the employee identification number normally would be chosen as the record key.

There are many ways of organizing records in a file. The most common type of organization is called a *sequential file*, in which records typically are stored in order by the record-key field. In a payroll file, records usually are placed in order by employee-identification numbers. The first employee record in the file contains the lowest employee-identification number, and subsequent records contain increasingly higher employee-identification numbers.

Most businesses use many different files to store data. For example, a company might have payroll files, accounts receivable files (listing money due from clients), accounts payable files (listing money due to suppliers), inventory files (listing facts about all the items handled by the business) and many other types of files. Sometimes, a group of related files is called a *database*. A collection of programs designed to create and manage databases is called a *database management system* (DBMS). We discuss databases in detail in Chapter 16, Databases, SQL and ADO .NET.

---

1. More generally, a file can contain arbitrary data in arbitrary formats. In most operating systems, a file is viewed as nothing more than a collection of bytes. In such an operating system, any organization of the bytes in a file (such as organizing the data into records) is a view created by the applications programmer.

14.3 Files and Streams

The .NET Framework views each file as a sequential *stream* of bytes (Fig. 14.2). Each file ends either with an *end-of-file marker* or at a specific byte number that is recorded in a system-maintained administrative data structure. When a file is *opened*, the Common Language Runtime (CLR) creates an object, then associates a stream with that object. The runtime environment creates three stream objects upon program execution, which are accessible via properties **Console::Out**, **Console::In** and **Console::Error**, respectively. These objects facilitate communication between a program and a particular file or device. Property **Console::In** returns the *standard input stream object*, which enables a program to input data from the keyboard. Property **Console::Out** returns the *standard output stream object*, which enables a program to output data to the screen. Property **Console::Error** returns the *standard error stream object*, which enables a program to output error messages to the screen. We have been using **Console::Out** and **Console::In** in our console applications—**Console** methods **Write** and **WriteLine** use **Console::Out** to perform output, and methods **Read** and **ReadLine** use **Console::In** to perform input.To perform file processing in MC++, namespace **System::IO** must be referenced. This namespace includes definitions for such stream classes as *StreamReader* (for text input from a stream), *StreamWriter* (for text output to a stream) and *FileStream* (for both input from and output to a file). Files are opened by creating objects of these stream classes, which inherit from **abstract** classes *TextReader*, *TextWriter* and *Stream*, respectively. Actually, properties **In** and **Out** of class **Console** are a **TextReader** and **TextWriter**, respectively.

The .NET Framework provides class *BinaryFormatter*, which is used in conjunction with a **Stream** object to perform input and output of objects. *Serialization* involves converting an object into a format that can be written to a file without losing any of that object's data. *Deserialization* consists of reading this format from a file and reconstructing the original object from it. A **BinaryFormatter** can serialize objects to, and deserialize objects from, a specified **Stream**.

Class *Stream* (namespace **System::IO**) provides functionality for representing streams as bytes. This class is **abstract**, so objects of this class cannot be instantiated. Classes *FileStream*, *MemoryStream* and *BufferedStream* (all from namespace **System::IO**) inherit from class **Stream**. Later in the chapter, we use **FileStream** to read data to, and write data from, sequential-access and random-access files. Class **MemoryStream** enables the transferal of data directly to and from memory—this type of transfer is much faster than are other types of data transfer (e.g., to and from disk). Class **BufferedStream** uses *buffering* to transfer data to or from a stream. Buffering is an I/O-performance-enhancement technique in which each output operation is directed to a region in memory, called a *buffer*, that is large enough to hold the data from many output operations. Then, actual transfer to the output device is performed in one large *physical output operation* each time the buffer fills. The output operations directed to the output buffer in memory often are called *logical output operations*.

The .NET Framework offers many classes for performing input and output. In this chapter, we use several key stream classes to implement a variety of file-processing programs that create, manipulate and destroy sequential-access files and random-access files. In Chapter 18, Networking: Streams-Based Sockets and Datagrams, we use stream classes extensively to implement networking applications.

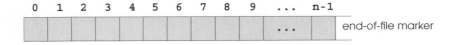

Fig. 14.2   .NET Framework's view of an *n*-byte file.

14.4 Classes `File` and `Directory`

Information on computers is stored in files, which are organized in directories. Class *File* is provided for manipulating files, and class *Directory* is provided for manipulating directories. Class **File** cannot write to or read from files directly; we discuss methods for reading and writing files in subsequent sections.

Note that the \ *separator character* separates directories and files in a path. On UNIX systems, the separator character is /. In Visual C++ .NET, both characters are actually processed identically in a path name. This means that, if we specified the path `c:\visual_cpp/README`, which uses one of each separator character, the file would still be processed properly. [*Note*: Remember that when specifying the path in a **String**, it is necessary to escape the backslash character (e.g., `c:\\visual_cpp/README`).]

Figure 14.3 lists some methods contained in class **File** for manipulating and determining information about particular files. Class **File** contains only **static** methods— you cannot instantiate objects of type **File**. We use several of these methods in the example of Fig. 14.5–Fig. 14.7.

`static` Method	Description
`AppendText`	Returns a **StreamWriter** that appends to an existing file or creates a file if one does not exist.
`Copy`	Copies a file to a new file.
`Create`	Creates a file and returns its associated **FileStream**.
`CreateText`	Creates a text file and returns its associated **StreamWriter**.
`Delete`	Deletes the specified file.
`Exists`	Returns **true** if the specified file exists (and the caller has the correct permissions); otherwise, it returns **false**.
`GetCreationTime`	Returns a **DateTime** object representing the time that the file was created.
`GetLastAccessTime`	Returns a **DateTime** object representing the time that the file was last accessed.
`GetLastWriteTime`	Returns a **DateTime** object representing the time that the file was last modified.

Fig. 14.3   `File` class methods (partial list). (Part 1 of 2.)

static Method	Description
Move	Moves the specified file to a specified location.
Open	Returns a **FileStream** associated with the specified file and equipped with the specified read/write permissions.
OpenRead	Returns a read-only **FileStream** associated with the specified file.
OpenText	Returns a **StreamReader** associated with the specified file.
OpenWrite	Returns a read/write **FileStream** associated with the specified file.

Fig. 14.3 **File** class methods (partial list). (Part 2 of 2.)

Class **Directory** provides capabilities for manipulating and iterating directories. Figure 14.4 lists some methods that can be used for directory manipulation. We employ several of these methods in the example of Fig. 14.5–Fig. 14.7.

static Method	Description
CreateDirectory	Creates a directory and returns its associated **Directory-Info**.
Delete	Deletes the specified directory.
Exists	Returns **true** if the specified directory exists; otherwise, it returns **false**.
GetLastWriteTime	Returns a **DateTime** object representing the time that the directory was last modified.
GetDirectories	Returns a **String *** array representing the names of the subdirectories in the specified directory.
GetFiles	Returns a **String *** array representing the names of the files in the specified directory.
GetCreationTime	Returns a **DateTime** object representing the time that the directory was created.
GetLastAccessTime	Returns a **DateTime** object representing the time that the directory was last accessed.
Move	Moves the specified directory to a specified location.
SetCreationTime	Sets the **DateTime** object representing the time that the directory was created.
SetLastAccessTime	Sets the **DateTime** object representing the time that the directory was last accessed.
SetLastWriteTime	Sets the **DateTime** object representing the time that items were last written to the directory.

Fig. 14.4 **Directory** class methods (partial list).

The *DirectoryInfo* object returned by method **CreateDirectory** contains information about a directory. Much of the information contained in this class also can be accessed via the methods of class **Directory**. Class **FileTest** (Fig. 14.5) uses methods described in Figs. 14.3 and 14.4 to access file and directory information. This class contains **TextBox inputTextBox** (line 25 of Fig. 14.5), which enables the user to input a file or directory name. For each key that the user presses in the text box, the program calls method **inputTextBox_KeyDown** (lines 72–135 of Fig. 14.6). If the user presses the *Enter* key (line 76), this method displays either file or directory contents, depending on the text the user input in the **TextBox**. (Note that, if the user does not press the *Enter* key, this method returns without displaying any content.) Line 84 uses method **Exists** of class **File** to determine whether the user-specified text is a name of an existing file. If the user specifies an existing file, line 88 invokes **private** method **GetInformation** (lines 138–162), which calls methods **GetCreationTime** (line 146), **GetLastWriteTime** (line 152) and **GetLastAccessTime** (line 158) of class **File** to access file information. When method **GetInformation** returns, line 94 instantiates a **StreamReader** for reading text from the file. The **StreamReader** constructor takes as an argument a **String *** containing the name of the file to open. Line 96 calls method *ReadToEnd* of the **StreamReader** to read the contents of the file, which are then displayed in the **outputTextBox**.

```
1    // Fig. 14.5: FileTest.h
2    // Using classes File and Directory.
3
4    #pragma once
5
6    #using <mscorlib.dll>
7    #using <system.dll>
8    #using <system.drawing.dll>
9    #using <system.windows.forms.dll>
10
11   using namespace System;
12   using namespace System::Drawing;
13   using namespace System::Windows::Forms;
14   using namespace System::IO;
15
16   // displays contents of files and directories
17   public __gc class FileTest : public Form
18   {
19   public:
20      FileTest();
21
22   private:
23      Label *directionsLabel;
24      TextBox *outputTextBox;
25      TextBox *inputTextBox;
26
27      void InitializeComponent();
28      void inputTextBox_KeyDown( Object *, KeyEventArgs * );
29      String *GetInformation( String * );
30   }; // end class FileTest
```

Fig. 14.5 **FileTest** class demonstrates classes **File** and **Directory**.

```cpp
1    // Fig. 14.6: FileTest.cpp
2    // Method definitions for class FileTest.
3
4    #include "FileTest.h"
5
6    FileTest::FileTest()
7    {
8       InitializeComponent();
9    }
10
11   void FileTest::InitializeComponent()
12   {
13      this->outputTextBox = new TextBox();
14      this->directionsLabel = new Label();
15      this->inputTextBox = new TextBox();
16
17      this->SuspendLayout();
18
19      // outputTextBox
20      this->outputTextBox->AutoSize = false;
21      this->outputTextBox->BackColor = SystemColors::Control;
22      this->outputTextBox->Font = new Drawing::Font(
23         S"Microsoft Sans Serif", 10, FontStyle::Regular,
24         GraphicsUnit::Point, 0 );
25      this->outputTextBox->Location = Point( 18, 103 );
26      this->outputTextBox->Multiline = true;
27      this->outputTextBox->Name = S"outputTextBox";
28      this->outputTextBox->ReadOnly = true;
29      this->outputTextBox->ScrollBars = ScrollBars::Vertical;
30      this->outputTextBox->Size = Drawing::Size( 375, 327 );
31      this->outputTextBox->TabIndex = 4;
32      this->outputTextBox->Text = S"";
33
34      // directionsLabel
35      this->directionsLabel->Font = new Drawing::Font(
36         S"Microsoft Sans Serif", 10, FontStyle::Regular,
37         GraphicsUnit::Point, 0 );
38      this->directionsLabel->Location = Point( 18, 19 );
39      this->directionsLabel->Name = S"directionsLabel";
40      this->directionsLabel->Size = Drawing::Size( 375, 18 );
41      this->directionsLabel->TabIndex = 5;
42      this->directionsLabel->Text = S"Enter file or directory:";
43      this->directionsLabel->TextAlign =
44         ContentAlignment::MiddleLeft;
45
46      // inputTextBox
47      this->inputTextBox->Font = new Drawing::Font(
48         S"Microsoft Sans Serif", 10, FontStyle::Regular,
49         GraphicsUnit::Point, 0 );
50      this->inputTextBox->Location = Point( 18, 56 );
51      this->inputTextBox->Name = S"inputTextBox";
52      this->inputTextBox->Size = Drawing::Size( 375, 23 );
53      this->inputTextBox->TabIndex = 3;
```

Fig. 14.6 **FileTest** class method definitions. (Part 1 of 4.)

```
54        this->inputTextBox->Text = S"";
55        this->inputTextBox->KeyDown += new KeyEventHandler( this,
56           inputTextBox_KeyDown );
57
58        // FileTest
59        this->AutoScaleBaseSize = Drawing::Size( 5, 13 );
60        this->ClientSize = Drawing::Size( 420, 444 );
61
62        Control *controls[] = { this->outputTextBox,
63           this->directionsLabel, this->inputTextBox };
64        this->Controls->AddRange( controls );
65        this->Name = S"FileTest";
66        this->Text = S"File Test";
67
68        this->ResumeLayout();
69     } // end method InitializeComponent
70
71     // invoked when user presses key
72     void FileTest::inputTextBox_KeyDown( Object *sender,
73        KeyEventArgs *e )
74     {
75        // determine whether user pressed Enter key
76        if ( e->KeyCode == Keys::Enter ) {
77
78           String *fileName; // name of file or directory
79
80           // get user-specified file or directory
81           fileName = inputTextBox->Text;
82
83           // determine whether fileName is a file
84           if ( File::Exists( fileName ) ) {
85
86              // get file's creation date,
87              // modification date, etc.
88              outputTextBox->Text = GetInformation( fileName );
89
90              // display file contents through StreamReader
91              try {
92
93                 // obtain reader and file contents
94                 StreamReader *stream = new StreamReader( fileName );
95                 outputTextBox->Text = String::Concat(
96                    outputTextBox->Text, stream->ReadToEnd() );
97              } // end try
98
99              // handle exception if StreamReader is unavailable
100             catch ( IOException * ) {
101                MessageBox::Show( S"File Error", S"File Error",
102                   MessageBoxButtons::OK, MessageBoxIcon::Error );
103             } // end catch
104          } // end if
105
106          // determine whether fileName is a directory
```

Fig. 14.6 **FileTest** class method definitions. (Part 2 of 4.)

```
107          else if ( Directory::Exists( fileName ) ) {
108
109             // get directory's creation date,
110             // modification date, etc.
111             outputTextBox->Text = GetInformation( fileName );
112
113             // obtain file/directory list of specified directory
114             String *directoryList[] =
115                Directory::GetDirectories( fileName );
116
117             outputTextBox->Text =
118                String::Concat( outputTextBox->Text,
119                S"\r\n\r\nDirectory contents:\r\n" );
120
121             // output directoryList contents
122             for ( int i = 0; i < directoryList->Length; i++ )
123                outputTextBox->Text =
124                   String::Concat( outputTextBox->Text,
125                   directoryList[ i ], S"\r\n" );
126          } // end if
127          else {
128
129             // notify user that neither file nor directory exists
130             MessageBox::Show( String::Concat( inputTextBox->Text,
131                S" does not exist" ), S"File Error",
132                MessageBoxButtons::OK, MessageBoxIcon::Error );
133          } // end else
134       } // end if
135 } // end method inputTextBox_KeyDown
136
137 // get information on file or directory
138 String *FileTest::GetInformation( String *fileName )
139 {
140    // output that file or directory exists
141    String *information =
142       String::Concat( fileName, S" exists\r\n\r\n" );
143
144    // output when file or directory was created
145    information = String::Concat( information, S"Created: ",
146       ( File::GetCreationTime( fileName ) ).ToString(),
147       S"\r\n" );
148
149    // output when file or directory was last modified
150    information = String::Concat( information,
151       S"Last modified: ",
152       ( File::GetLastWriteTime( fileName ) ).ToString(),
153       S"\r\n" );
154
155    // output when file or directory was last accessed
156    information = String::Concat( information,
157       S"Last accessed: ",
158       ( File::GetLastAccessTime( fileName ) ).ToString(),
159       S"\r\n\r\n" );
```

Fig. 14.6 `FileTest` class method definitions. (Part 3 of 4.)

```
160
161     return information;
162 } // end method GetInformation
```

Fig. 14.6 `FileTest` class method definitions. (Part 4 of 4.)

```
1  // Fig. 14.7: FileTestDriver.cpp
2  // Entry point for application.
3
4  #include "FileTest.h"
5
6  int __stdcall WinMain()
7  {
8      Application::Run( new FileTest() );
9
10     return 0;
11 } // end function WinMain
```

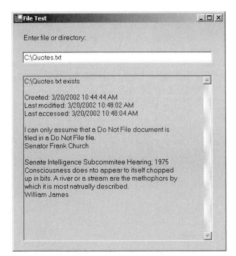
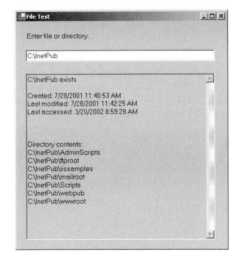
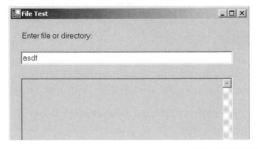

Fig. 14.7 `FileTest` class driver.

If line 84 determines that the user-specified text is not a file, line 107 determines whether it is a directory, using method **Exists** of class **Directory**. If the user specified an existing directory, line 111 invokes method **GetInformation** to access the directory information. Line 115 calls method **GetDirectories** of class **Directory** to obtain a

String * array containing the names of subdirectories in the specified directory. Lines 122–125 display each element in the String * array. Note that, if line 127 determines that the user-specified text is neither a file nor a directory, lines 130–132 notify the user (via a MessageBox) that the file or directory does not exist.

　　We now consider another example that uses the .NET Framework's file- and directory-manipulation capabilities. Class FileSearch (Fig. 14.8) uses classes File and Directory in conjunction with classes for performing regular expressions to report the number of files of each file type that exist in the specified directory path. The program also serves as a "clean-up" utility—when the program encounters a file that has the .bak extension (i.e., a backup file), the program displays a MessageBox asking whether that file should be removed, then responds appropriately to the user's input.

```
1   // Fig. 14.8: FileSearch.h
2   // Using regular expressions to determine file types.
3
4   #pragma once
5
6   #using <system.dll>
7   #using <mscorlib.dll>
8   #using <system.drawing.dll>
9   #using <system.windows.forms.dll>
10  #using <system.data.dll>
11
12  using namespace System;
13  using namespace System::Drawing;
14  using namespace System::Windows::Forms;
15  using namespace System::IO;
16  using namespace System::Text::RegularExpressions;
17  using namespace System::Collections::Specialized;
18
19  public __gc class FileSearch : public Form
20  {
21  public:
22     FileSearch();
23
24  private:
25     Label *directionsLabel;
26     Label *directoryLabel;
27     Button *searchButton;
28     TextBox *outputTextBox;
29     TextBox *inputTextBox;
30     String *searchDirectory;
31
32     // store extensions found and number found
33     NameValueCollection *found;
34
35     void InitializeComponent();
36     void inputTextBox_KeyDown( Object *, KeyEventArgs * );
37     void searchButton_Click( Object *, EventArgs * );
38     void SearchDirectory( String * );
39  }; // end class FileSearch
```

Fig. 14.8　Using regular expressions to determine file types.

When the user presses the *Enter* key or clicks the **Search Directory** button, the program invokes method **searchButton_Click** (lines 100–143 of Fig. 14.9), which searches recursively through the directory path that the user provides. If the user inputs text in the **TextBox**, line 107 calls method **Exists** of class **Directory** to determine whether that text indicates a valid directory. If the user specifies an invalid directory, lines 117–118 notify the user of the error and line 120 **return**s from the method.

```cpp
1   // Fig. 14.9: FileSearch.cpp
2   // Method definitions for class FileSearch.
3
4   #include "FileSearch.h"
5
6   FileSearch::FileSearch()
7   {
8      found = new NameValueCollection();
9      InitializeComponent();
10  }
11
12  void FileSearch::InitializeComponent()
13  {
14     this->outputTextBox = new TextBox();
15     this->inputTextBox = new TextBox();
16     this->searchButton = new Button();
17     this->directionsLabel = new Label();
18     this->directoryLabel = new Label();
19
20     this->SuspendLayout();
21
22     // outputTextBox
23     this->outputTextBox->AutoSize = false;
24     this->outputTextBox->BackColor = SystemColors::Control;
25     this->outputTextBox->Location = Point( 18, 211 );
26     this->outputTextBox->Multiline = true;
27     this->outputTextBox->Name = S"outputTextBox";
28     this->outputTextBox->ReadOnly = true;
29     this->outputTextBox->ScrollBars = ScrollBars::Vertical;
30     this->outputTextBox->Size = Drawing::Size( 421, 197 );
31     this->outputTextBox->TabIndex = 9;
32     this->outputTextBox->Text = S"";
33
34     // inputTextBox
35     this->inputTextBox->Location = Point( 18, 109 );
36     this->inputTextBox->Name = S"inputTextBox";
37     this->inputTextBox->Size = Drawing::Size( 421, 20 );
38     this->inputTextBox->TabIndex = 8;
39     this->inputTextBox->Text = S"";
40     this->inputTextBox->KeyDown += new KeyEventHandler( this,
41        inputTextBox_KeyDown );
42
43     // searchButton
```

Fig. 14.9 **FileSearch** class method definitions. (Part 1 of 5.)

```
44       this->searchButton->Font = new Drawing::Font(
45          S"Microsoft Sans Serif", 9.75, FontStyle::Regular,
46          GraphicsUnit::Point, 0 );
47       this->searchButton->Location = Point( 18, 155 );
48       this->searchButton->Name = S"searchButton";
49       this->searchButton->Size = Drawing::Size( 421, 38 );
50       this->searchButton->TabIndex = 7;
51       this->searchButton->Text = S"Search Directory";
52       this->searchButton->Click += new EventHandler( this,
53          searchButton_Click );
54
55       // directionsLabel
56       this->directionsLabel->Font = new Drawing::Font(
57          S"Microsoft Sans Serif", 10.0, FontStyle::Regular,
58          GraphicsUnit::Point, 0 );
59       this->directionsLabel->Location = Point( 18, 81 );
60       this->directionsLabel->Name = S"directionsLabel";
61       this->directionsLabel->Size = Drawing::Size( 412, 19 );
62       this->directionsLabel->TabIndex = 6;
63       this->directionsLabel->Text = S"Enter Path to Search:";
64
65       // directoryLabel
66       this->directoryLabel->Font = new Drawing::Font(
67          S"Microsoft Sans Serif", 10.0, FontStyle::Regular,
68          GraphicsUnit::Point, 0 );
69       this->directoryLabel->Location = Point( 18, 19 );
70       this->directoryLabel->Name = S"directoryLabel";
71       this->directoryLabel->Size = Drawing::Size( 412, 43 );
72       this->directoryLabel->TabIndex = 5;
73       this->directoryLabel->Text = S"Current Directory:";
74
75       // FileSearch
76       this->AutoScaleBaseSize = Drawing::Size( 5, 13 );
77       this->ClientSize = Drawing::Size( 457, 422 );
78
79       Control *controls[] = { this->outputTextBox,
80          this->inputTextBox, this->searchButton,
81          this->directionsLabel, this->directoryLabel };
82       this->Controls->AddRange( controls );
83       this->Name = S"FileSearch";
84       this->Text = S"Using Regular Expressions";
85
86       this->ResumeLayout();
87    } // end method InitializeComponent
88
89    // invoked when user types in text box
90    void FileSearch::inputTextBox_KeyDown( Object *sender,
91       KeyEventArgs *e )
92    {
93       // determine whether user pressed Enter
94       if ( e->KeyCode == Keys::Enter )
95          searchButton_Click( sender, e );
96
```

Fig. 14.9 `FileSearch` class method definitions. (Part 2 of 5.)

```
97    } // end method inputTextBox_KeyDown
98
99    // invoked when user clicks "Search Directory" button
100   void FileSearch::searchButton_Click( Object *sender,
101      EventArgs *e )
102   {
103      // check for user input; default is current directory
104      if ( inputTextBox->Text != S"" ) {
105
106         // verify that user input is valid directory name
107         if ( Directory::Exists( inputTextBox->Text ) ) {
108            searchDirectory = inputTextBox->Text;
109
110            // reset input text box and update display
111            directoryLabel->Text = String::Concat(
112               S"Current Directory:\r\n", searchDirectory );
113         }
114         else {
115
116            // show error if user does not specify valid directory
117            MessageBox::Show( S"Invalid Directory", S"Error",
118               MessageBoxButtons::OK, MessageBoxIcon::Error );
119
120            return;
121         } // end else
122      } // end if
123
124      // clear text boxes
125      inputTextBox->Text = S"";
126      outputTextBox->Text = S"";
127
128      Cursor::Current = Cursors::WaitCursor; // set wait cursor
129
130      SearchDirectory( searchDirectory ); // search directory
131
132      Cursor::Current = Cursors::Default; // set default cursor
133
134      // summarize and print results
135      for ( int current = 0; current < found->Count; current++ ) {
136         outputTextBox->Text = String::Concat( outputTextBox->Text,
137            S"* Found ", found->Get( current ), S" ",
138            found->GetKey( current ), S" files.\r\n" );
139      }
140
141      // clear output for new search
142      found->Clear();
143   } // end method searchButton_Click
144
145   // search directory using regular expression
146   void FileSearch::SearchDirectory( String *currentDirectory )
147   {
148      // for file name without directory path
```

Fig. 14.9 `FileSearch` class method definitions. (Part 3 of 5.)

```
149      try {
150         String *fileName = S"";
151
152         // regular expression for extensions matching pattern
153         Regex *regularExpression = new Regex(
154            S"[a-zA-Z0-9]+\\.(?<extension>\\w+)" );
155
156         // stores regular-expression-match result
157         Match *matchResult;
158
159         String *fileExtension; // holds file extensions
160
161         // number of files with given extension in directory
162         int extensionCount;
163
164         // get directories
165         String *directoryList[] =
166            Directory::GetDirectories( currentDirectory );
167
168         // get list of files in current directory
169         String *fileArray[] =
170            Directory::GetFiles( currentDirectory );
171
172         // iterate through list of files
173         for ( int myFile = 0; myFile < fileArray->Length;
174            myFile++ ) {
175
176            // remove directory path from file name
177            fileName = fileArray[ myFile ]->Substring(
178               fileArray[ myFile ]->LastIndexOf( S"\\" ) + 1 );
179
180            // obtain result for regular-expression search
181            matchResult = regularExpression->Match( fileName );
182
183            // check for match
184            if ( matchResult->Success )
185               fileExtension = matchResult->Result(
186                  S"${extension}" );
187            else
188               fileExtension = S"[no extension]";
189
190            // store value from container
191            if ( !( found->Get( fileExtension ) ) )
192               found->Add( fileExtension, S"1" );
193            else {
194               extensionCount = Int32::Parse(
195                  found->Get( fileExtension ) ) + 1;
196
197               found->Set( fileExtension,
198                  extensionCount.ToString() );
199            }
200
```

Fig. 14.9 FileSearch class method definitions. (Part 4 of 5.)

```
201            // search for backup(.bak) files
202            if ( fileExtension->Equals( S"bak" ) ) {
203
204                // prompt user to delete (.bak) file
205                Windows::Forms::DialogResult result =
206                    MessageBox::Show(
207                    String::Concat( S"Found backup file ",
208                    fileName, S". Delete?" ), S"Delete Backup",
209                    MessageBoxButtons::YesNo,
210                    MessageBoxIcon::Question );
211
212                // delete file if user clicked 'yes'
213                if ( result == DialogResult::Yes ) {
214                    File::Delete( fileArray[ myFile ] );
215
216                    extensionCount =
217                        Int32::Parse( found->Get( S"bak" ) ) - 1;
218
219                    found->Set( S"bak", extensionCount.ToString() );
220                } // end inner if
221            } // end outer if
222        } // end for
223
224        // recursive call to search files in subdirectory
225        for ( int i = 0; i < directoryList->Length; i++ )
226            SearchDirectory( directoryList[ i ] );
227    } // end try
228
229    // handle exception if files have unauthorized access
230    catch ( UnauthorizedAccessException * ) {
231        MessageBox::Show( String::Concat(
232            S"Some files may not be visible due to permission ",
233            S"settings\n" ), S"Warning",
234            MessageBoxButtons::OK, MessageBoxIcon::Information );
235    }
236 } // end method SearchDirectory
```

Fig. 14.9 FileSearch class method definitions. (Part 5 of 5.)

```
1  // Fig. 14.10: FileSearchTest.cpp
2  // Entry point for application.
3
4  #include "FileSearch.h"
5
6  int __stdcall WinMain()
7  {
8      Application::Run( new FileSearch() );
9
10     return 0;
11 } // end function WinMain
```

Fig. 14.10 FileSearch class driver. (Part 1 of 2.)

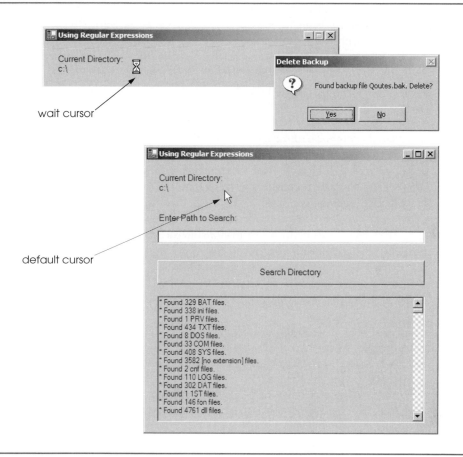

Fig. 14.10 `FileSearch` class driver. (Part 2 of 2.)

If the directory is valid, lines 125–126 clear the **TextBox**es. Line 128 then changes the user's mouse cursor using class *Cursor* (located in namespace **System::Windows::Forms**). Class **Cursor** represents the image used as the mouse cursor. Class *Cursors* (also located in namespace **System::Windows::Forms**), contains several **Cursor** objects that programmers can use. Line 128 sets **Cursor** property **Current** to **Cursors::*WaitCursor*. WaitCursor** is a **Cursor** object that represents the *wait cursor*—usually an hourglass symbol. Thus, while the program searches, an hourglass symbol will be used as the mouse cursor.[2] This is demonstrated in the screen captures at the end of Fig. 14.10.

Line 130 then passes the directory name as an argument to **private** method **SearchDirectory** (lines 146–236). This method locates files that match the regular expression defined in lines 153–154, which matches any sequence of numbers or letters fol-

---

2. For more information about changing the mouse cursor, visit **msdn.microsoft.com/ library/default.asp?url=/library/en-us/cpref/html/frlrfSystem WindowsFormsCursorClassTopic.asp**.

lowed by a period and one or more letters. Notice the substring of format (**?<exten-sion>***regular-expression*) in the argument to the **Regex** constructor (line 154). This causes all **String**s with the substring *regular-expression* to be tagged with the name **extension**. In this program, we assign to the variable **extension** any **String** matching one or more characters (i.e., **\w+**).

Lines 165–166 call method **GetDirectories** of class **Directory** to retrieve the names of all subdirectories that belong to the current directory. Lines 169–170 call method **GetFiles** of class **Directory** to store in **String *** array **fileArray** the names of files in the current directory. The **for** loop in lines 173–222 analyzes each file in the current directory; it then calls **SearchDirectory** recursively for each subdirectory in the current directory. Lines 177–178 eliminate the directory path, so the program can test only the file name when using the regular expression. Line 181 uses method **Match** of the **Regex** object to match the regular expression with the file name, then returns the result to object **matchResult** of type **Match**. If the match is successful, lines 185–186 use method **Result** of object **matchResult** to store the **extension** variable from object **matchResult** in **fileExtension** (recall that line 154 stores the **String** that will contain the current file's extension in variable **extension**). The syntax for retrieving a variable using method **Result** is **${***variable-name***}** (e.g., **${extension}**). If the match is unsuccessful, line 188 sets **fileExtension** to hold the value **"[no exten-sion]"**.

Class **FileSearch** uses an instance of class *NameValueCollection* (declared in line 33 of Fig. 14.8) to store each file-extension type and the number of files for each type. A **NameValueCollection** contains a collection of key/value pairs, each of which is a **String ***, and provides method *Add* to add a key/value pair. The indexer for this pair can index according to the order that the items were added or according to the entry key. Line 191 (Fig. 14.9) uses **NameValueCollection found** to determine whether this is the first occurrence of the file extension. If so, line 192 adds that extension to **found** as a key with the value **1**. If the extension is in **found** already, lines 194–198 increment the value associated with the extension in **found** to indicate another occurrence of that file extension.

Line 202 determines whether **fileExtension** equals "**bak**"—i.e., whether the file is a backup file. If so, lines 205–210 prompt the user to indicate whether the file should be removed; if the user clicks **Yes** (line 213), lines 214–219 delete the file and decrement the value for the "**bak**" file type in **found**.

Line 226 calls method **SearchDirectory** for each subdirectory. Using recursion, we ensure that the program performs the same logic for finding **bak** files on each subdirectory. After each subdirectory has been analyzed, method **SearchDirectory** completes. Line 132 then restores the user's mouse cursor to the *default cursor*—usually an arrow symbol—using class **Cursors::Default**. Finally, lines 135–138 display the search results in **outputTextBox**.

14.5 Creating a Sequential-Access File

The .NET Framework imposes no structure on files (i.e., concepts like that of a "record" do not exist). This means that the programmer must structure files to meet the requirements of applications. In the next example, we use text and special characters to organize our own concept of a "record."

The following examples demonstrate file processing in a bank-account maintenance application. These programs have similar user interfaces, so we created class **BankUI-Form** (Fig. 14.11–Fig. 14.12) to encapsulate a base-class GUI. (See the screen capture in Fig. 14.13.) Class **BankUIForm** contains four **Label**s (lines 32, 35, 38 and 41 of Fig. 14.11) and four **TextBox**es (lines 33, 36, 39 and 42). Methods **ClearTextBoxes** (lines 127–141 of Fig. 14.12), **SetTextBoxValues** (lines 144–168) and **GetText-BoxValues** (lines 171–186) clear, set the values of, and get the values of the text in the **TextBox**es, respectively.

Notice that line 185 of method **GetTextBoxValues** returns a managed array of **String *** objects (**values**). Recall from Chapter 4, Functions and Arrays, that any method that returns a managed array must suffix its definition with the dimensions of the array. For this reason, line 171 declares method **GetTextBoxValues** as

```
String *BankUIForm::GetTextBoxValues() []
```

The **[]** notation indicates that method **GetTextBoxValues** will return a managed array with one dimension.

```
1    // Fig. 14.11: BankUI.h
2    // A reusable windows form for the examples in this chapter.
3
4    #pragma once
5
6    #using <mscorlib.dll>
7    #using <system.dll>
8    #using <system.drawing.dll>
9    #using <system.windows.forms.dll>
10
11   using namespace System;
12   using namespace System::Drawing;
13   using namespace System::Windows::Forms;
14
15   namespace BankLibrary
16   {
17      public __gc class BankUIForm : public Form
18      {
19      public:
20         BankUIForm();
21
22         // enumeration constants specify TextBox indices
23         __value enum TextBoxIndices
24         {
25            ACCOUNT,
26            FIRST,
27            LAST,
28            BALANCE
29
30         }; // end enum
31
```

Fig. 14.11 Base class for GUIs in our file-processing applications. (Part 1 of 2.)

```
32          Label *accountLabel;
33          TextBox *accountTextBox;
34
35          Label *firstNameLabel;
36          TextBox *firstNameTextBox;
37
38          Label *lastNameLabel;
39          TextBox *lastNameTextBox;
40
41          Label *balanceLabel;
42          TextBox *balanceTextBox;
43
44          String *GetTextBoxValues() [];
45          void SetTextBoxValues( String *[] );
46          void ClearTextBoxes();
47
48       protected:
49
50          // number of TextBoxes on Form
51          static int TextBoxCount = 4;
52
53       private:
54          void InitializeComponent();
55       }; // end class BankUIForm
56    } // end namespace BankLibrary
```

Fig. 14.11 Base class for GUIs in our file-processing applications. (Part 2 of 2.)

```
1     // Fig. 14.12: BankUI.cpp
2     // Method definitions for class BankUIForm.
3
4     #include "stdafx.h"
5     #include "BankUI.h"
6
7     using namespace BankLibrary;
8
9     BankUIForm::BankUIForm()
10    {
11       InitializeComponent();
12    }
13
14    void BankUIForm::InitializeComponent()
15    {
16       this->balanceTextBox = new TextBox();
17       this->lastNameTextBox = new TextBox();
18       this->firstNameTextBox = new TextBox();
19       this->accountTextBox = new TextBox();
20       this->balanceLabel = new Label();
21       this->lastNameLabel = new Label();
22       this->firstNameLabel = new Label();
23       this->accountLabel = new Label();
24
```

Fig. 14.12 BankUI class method definitions. (Part 1 of 5.)

```
25        this->SuspendLayout();
26
27        // balanceTextBox
28        this->balanceTextBox->Font = new Drawing::Font(
29           S"Microsoft Sans Serif", 10.0, FontStyle::Regular,
30           GraphicsUnit::Point, 0 );
31        this->balanceTextBox->Location = Point( 184, 184 );
32        this->balanceTextBox->Name = S"balanceTextBox";
33        this->balanceTextBox->Size = Drawing::Size( 184, 26 );
34        this->balanceTextBox->TabIndex = 15;
35        this->balanceTextBox->Text = S"";
36
37        // lastNameTextBox
38        this->lastNameTextBox->Font = new Drawing::Font(
39           S"Microsoft Sans Serif", 10.0, FontStyle::Regular,
40           GraphicsUnit::Point, 0 );
41        this->lastNameTextBox->Location = Point( 184, 128 );
42        this->lastNameTextBox->Name = S"lastNameTextBox";
43        this->lastNameTextBox->Size = Drawing::Size( 184, 26 );
44        this->lastNameTextBox->TabIndex = 14;
45        this->lastNameTextBox->Text = S"";
46
47        // firstNameTextBox
48        this->firstNameTextBox->Font = new Drawing::Font(
49           S"Microsoft Sans Serif", 10.0, FontStyle::Regular,
50           GraphicsUnit::Point, 0 );
51        this->firstNameTextBox->Location = Point( 184, 72 );
52        this->firstNameTextBox->Name = S"firstNameTextBox";
53        this->firstNameTextBox->Size = Drawing::Size( 184, 26 );
54        this->firstNameTextBox->TabIndex = 13;
55        this->firstNameTextBox->Text = S"";
56
57        // accountTextBox
58        this->accountTextBox->Font = new Drawing::Font(
59           S"Microsoft Sans Serif", 10.0, FontStyle::Regular,
60           GraphicsUnit::Point, 0 );
61        this->accountTextBox->Location = Point( 184, 16 );
62        this->accountTextBox->Name = S"accountTextBox";
63        this->accountTextBox->Size = Drawing::Size( 184, 26 );
64        this->accountTextBox->TabIndex = 16;
65        this->accountTextBox->Text = S"";
66
67        // balanceLabel
68        this->balanceLabel->Font = new Drawing::Font(
69           S"Microsoft Sans Serif", 10.0, FontStyle::Regular,
70           GraphicsUnit::Point, 0 );
71        this->balanceLabel->Location = Point( 24, 184 );
72        this->balanceLabel->Name = S"balanceLabel";
73        this->balanceLabel->Size = Drawing::Size( 136, 23 );
74        this->balanceLabel->TabIndex = 12;
75        this->balanceLabel->Text = S"Balance";
76        this->balanceLabel->TextAlign = ContentAlignment::MiddleLeft;
77
```

Fig. 14.12 BankUI class method definitions. (Part 2 of 5.)

```
78      // lastNameLabel
79      this->lastNameLabel->Font = new Drawing::Font(
80         S"Microsoft Sans Serif", 10.0, FontStyle::Regular,
81         GraphicsUnit::Point, 0 );
82      this->lastNameLabel->Location = Point( 24, 128 );
83      this->lastNameLabel->Name = S"lastNameLabel";
84      this->lastNameLabel->Size = Drawing::Size( 136, 23 );
85      this->lastNameLabel->TabIndex = 11;
86      this->lastNameLabel->Text = S"Last Name";
87      this->lastNameLabel->TextAlign =
88         ContentAlignment::MiddleLeft;
89
90      // firstNameLabel
91      this->firstNameLabel->Font = new Drawing::Font(
92         S"Microsoft Sans Serif", 10.0, FontStyle::Regular,
93         GraphicsUnit::Point, 0 );
94      this->firstNameLabel->Location = Point( 24, 72 );
95      this->firstNameLabel->Name = S"firstNameLabel";
96      this->firstNameLabel->Size = Drawing::Size( 136, 23 );
97      this->firstNameLabel->TabIndex = 10;
98      this->firstNameLabel->Text = S"First Name";
99      this->firstNameLabel->TextAlign = ContentAlignment::MiddleLeft;
100
101     // accountLabel
102     this->accountLabel->Font = new Drawing::Font(
103        S"Microsoft Sans Serif", 10.0, FontStyle::Regular,
104        GraphicsUnit::Point, 0 );
105     this->accountLabel->Location = Point( 24, 16 );
106     this->accountLabel->Name = S"accountLabel";
107     this->accountLabel->Size = Drawing::Size( 136, 23 );
108     this->accountLabel->TabIndex = 17;
109     this->accountLabel->Text = S"Account";
110
111     // BankUIForm
112     this->AutoScaleBaseSize = Drawing::Size( 6, 15 );
113     this->ClientSize = Drawing::Size( 400, 231 );
114
115     Control *controls[] = { this->balanceTextBox,
116        this->lastNameTextBox, this->firstNameTextBox,
117        this->accountTextBox, this->balanceLabel,
118        this->lastNameLabel, this->firstNameLabel,
119        this->accountLabel };
120     this->Controls->AddRange( controls );
121     this->Name = S"BankUIForm";
122
123     this->ResumeLayout();
124  } // end method InitializeComponent
125
126  // clear all TextBoxes
127  void BankUIForm::ClearTextBoxes()
128  {
129     // iterate through every Control on form
130     for ( int i = 0; i < Controls->Count; i++ ) {
```

Fig. 14.12 BankUI class method definitions. (Part 3 of 5.)

```
131              Control *myControl =
132                 Controls->Item[ i ]; // get control
133
134              // determine whether Control is TextBox
135              if ( myControl->GetType() == __typeof( TextBox ) ) {
136
137                 // clear Text property (set to empty string)
138                 myControl->Text = S"";
139              } // end if
140           } // end for
141    } // end method ClearTextBoxes
142
143    // set text box values to String array values
144    void BankUIForm::SetTextBoxValues( String *values[] )
145    {
146        // determine whether String array has correct length
147        if ( values->Length != TextBoxCount ) {
148
149           // throw exception if not correct length
150           throw ( new ArgumentException( String::Concat(
151              S"There must be ", ( TextBoxCount + 1 ).ToString(),
152              S" strings in the array" ) ) );
153        }
154
155        // set array values if array has correct length
156        else {
157
158           // set array values to text box values
159           accountTextBox->Text =
160              values[ TextBoxIndices::ACCOUNT ];
161           firstNameTextBox->Text =
162              values[ TextBoxIndices::FIRST ];
163           lastNameTextBox->Text =
164              values[ TextBoxIndices::LAST ];
165           balanceTextBox->Text =
166              values[ TextBoxIndices::BALANCE ];
167        } // end else
168    } // end method SetTextBoxValues
169
170    // return text box values as string array
171    String *BankUIForm::GetTextBoxValues() []
172    {
173        String *values[] = new String*[ TextBoxCount ];
174
175        // copy text box fields to string array
176        values[ TextBoxIndices::ACCOUNT ] =
177           accountTextBox->Text;
178        values[ TextBoxIndices::FIRST ] =
179           firstNameTextBox->Text;
180        values[ TextBoxIndices::LAST ] =
181           lastNameTextBox->Text;
182        values[ TextBoxIndices::BALANCE ] =
183           balanceTextBox->Text;
```

Fig. 14.12 BankUI class method definitions. (Part 4 of 5.)

```
184
185     return values;
186 } // end method GetTextBoxValues
```

Fig. 14.12 **BankUI** class method definitions. (Part 5 of 5.)

```
1   // Fig. 14.13: BankUITest.cpp
2   // Entry point for application.
3
4   #include "stdafx.h"
5   #include "BankUI.h"
6
7   using namespace BankLibrary;
8
9   int __stdcall WinMain()
10  {
11      Application::Run( new BankUIForm() );
12
13      return 0;
14  } // end function WinMain
```

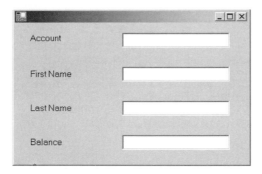

Fig. 14.13 **BankUIForm** class driver.

To reuse class **BankUIForm**, we compile the GUI into a DLL (dynamic link library) by creating a project of type **Managed C++ Class Library**. (The DLL we create is called **BankLibrary.dll**.) This library can be found at our Web site, **www.deitel.com**. We demonstrate how to create and reuse dynamic link libraries in Chapter 5.

Figure 14.14–Fig. 14.15 contain class **Record**, which Fig. 14.16–Fig. 14.18, Fig. 14.20–Fig. 14.22 and Fig. 14.23–Fig. 14.25 use for reading records from, and writing records to, a file sequentially. This class also belongs to the **BankLibrary** DLL, so it is located in the same project as is class **BankUIForm**.

```
1   // Fig. 14.14: Record.h
2   // Serializable class that represents a data record.
3
4   #pragma once
5
```

Fig. 14.14 Serializable class that represents a data record. (Part 1 of 3.)

```cpp
6    #using <system.dll>
7    #using <mscorlib.dll>
8
9    using namespace System;
10
11   namespace BankLibrary
12   {
13      [Serializable]
14      public __gc class Record
15      {
16      public:
17
18         // default constructor sets members to default values
19         Record();
20         Record( int, String *, String *, double );
21
22         // set method for property Account
23         __property void set_Account( int value )
24         {
25            account = value;
26         }
27
28         // get method for property Account
29         __property int get_Account()
30         {
31            return account;
32         }
33
34         // set method for property FirstName
35         __property void set_FirstName( String *value )
36         {
37            firstName = value;
38         }
39
40         // get method for property FirstName
41         __property String *get_FirstName()
42         {
43            return firstName;
44         }
45
46         // set method for property LastName
47         __property void set_LastName( String *value )
48         {
49            lastName = value;
50         }
51
52         // get method for property LastName
53         __property String *get_LastName()
54         {
55            return lastName;
56         }
57
58         // set method for property Balance
```

Fig. 14.14 Serializable class that represents a data record. (Part 2 of 3.)

```
59              __property void set_Balance( double value )
60              {
61                 balance = value;
62              }
63
64              // get method for property Balance
65              __property double get_Balance()
66              {
67                 return balance;
68              }
69
70        private:
71           int account;
72           String *firstName;
73           String *lastName;
74           double balance;
75        }; // end class Record
76     } // end namespace BankLibrary
```

Fig. 14.14 Serializable class that represents a data record. (Part 3 of 3.)

```
1    // Fig. 14.15: Record.cpp
2    // Method definitions for class Record.
3
4    #include "stdafx.h"
5    #include "Record.h"
6
7    using namespace BankLibrary;
8
9    // default constructor sets members to default values
10   Record::Record()
11   {
12      Account = 0;
13      FirstName = "";
14      LastName = "";
15      Balance = 0.0;
16   }
17
18   // overloaded constructor sets members to parameter values
19   Record::Record( int accountValue, String *firstNameValue,
20      String *lastNameValue, double balanceValue )
21   {
22      Account = accountValue;
23      FirstName = firstNameValue;
24      LastName = lastNameValue;
25      Balance = balanceValue;
26   } // end constructor
```

Fig. 14.15 Record class method definitions.

The **Serializable** attribute (line 13 of Fig. 14.14) indicates to the compiler that objects of class **Record** can be *serialized*, or stored to a stream—we can read and write to these streams. Objects that we wish to write to or read from a stream must include this attribute in their class definitions. Conversely, another available attribute, **NonSerialized**, can be used to indicate certain fields that should not be serialized.[3]

Class **Record** contains **private** data members **account**, **firstName**, **lastName** and **balance** (lines 71–74), which collectively represent all information necessary to store record data. The default constructor (lines 10–16 of Fig. 14.15) sets these members to their default (i.e., empty) values, and the overloaded constructor (lines 19–26) sets these members to specified parameter values. Class **Record** also provides properties **Account** (lines 23–32 of Fig. 14.14), **FirstName** (lines 35–44), **LastName** (lines 47–56) and **Balance** (lines 59–68) for accessing the account number, first name, last name and balance of each customer, respectively.

Class **CreateFileForm** (Fig. 14.16–Fig. 14.17) uses instances of class **Record** to create a sequential-access file that might be used in an accounts receivable system—a program that organizes data regarding money owed by a company's credit clients. For each client, the program obtains an account number and the client's first name, last name and balance (i.e., the amount of money that the client owes to the company for previously received goods or services). The data obtained for each client constitutes a record for that client. In this application, the account number represents the record key—files are created and maintained in account-number order. This program assumes that the user enters records in account-number order. However, a comprehensive accounts receivable system would provide a sorting capability. The user could enter the records in any order, and the records then could be sorted and written to the file in order. (Note that all outputs in this chapter should be read row by row, from left to right in each row.)

Figure 14.16–Fig. 14.17 contain the code for class **CreateFileForm**, which either creates or opens a file (depending on whether one exists), then allows the user to write bank information to that file. Line 22 (Fig. 14.16) imports the **BankLibrary** namespace; this namespace contains class **BankUIForm**, from which class **CreateFileForm** inherits (line 26). Because of this inheritance relationship, the **CreateFileForm** GUI is similar to that of class **BankUIForm** (shown in the Fig. 14.18 output), except that the inherited class contains buttons **Save As**, **Enter** and **Exit**.

```
1    // Fig. 14.16: CreateSequentialAccessFile.h
2    // Creating a sequential-access file.
3
4    #pragma once
5
6    #using <mscorlib.dll>
7    #using <system.dll>
8    #using <system.drawing.dll>
9    #using <system.windows.forms.dll>
10   #using <BankLibrary.dll>
11
12   // Visual C++ .NET namespaces
```

Fig. 14.16 **CreateFileForm** class creates a sequential-access file. (Part 1 of 2.)

---

3. For more information about serialization in .NET, visit **www.msdnaa.net/interchange/preview.asp?PeerID=1399**.

```
13   using namespace System;
14   using namespace System::Drawing;
15   using namespace System::Windows::Forms;
16   using namespace System::IO;
17   using namespace
18      System::Runtime::Serialization::Formatters::Binary;
19   using namespace System::Runtime::Serialization;
20
21   // Deitel namespace
22   using namespace BankLibrary;
23
24   #include <tchar.h>
25
26   public __gc class CreateFileForm : public BankUIForm
27   {
28   public:
29      CreateFileForm();
30
31   private:
32      Button *saveButton;
33      Button *enterButton;
34      Button *exitButton;
35
36      // serializes Record in binary format
37      static BinaryFormatter *formatter = new BinaryFormatter();
38
39      // stream through which serializable data is written to file
40      FileStream *output;
41
42      void InitializeComponent();
43      void saveButton_Click( Object *, EventArgs * );
44      void enterButton_Click( Object *, EventArgs * );
45      void exitButton_Click( Object *, EventArgs * );
46   }; // end class CreateFileForm
```

Fig. 14.16 `CreateFileForm` class creates a sequential-access file. (Part 2 of 2.)

```
1    // Fig. 14.17: CreateSequentialAccessFile.cpp
2    // Creating a sequential-access file.
3
4    #include "CreateSequentialAccessFile.h"
5
6    CreateFileForm::CreateFileForm()
7    {
8       InitializeComponent();
9    }
10
11   void CreateFileForm::InitializeComponent()
12   {
13      this->saveButton = new Button();
```

Fig. 14.17 `CreateFileForm` class method definitions. (Part 1 of 5.)

```
14      this->enterButton = new Button();
15      this-
16
17      this->SuspendLayout();
18
19      // set tab indices
20      this->accountTextBox->TabIndex = 1;
21      this->firstNameTextBox->TabIndex = 2;
22      this->lastNameTextBox->TabIndex = 3;
23      this->balanceTextBox->TabIndex = 4;
24
25      // saveButton
26      this->saveButton->Font = new Drawing::Font(
27         S"Microsoft Sans Serif", 10.0 );
28      this->saveButton->Location = Point( 16, 240 );
29      this->saveButton->Name = S"saveButton";
30      this->saveButton->Size = Drawing::Size( 112, 32 );
31      this->saveButton->TabIndex = 0;
32      this->saveButton->Text = S"Save As";
33      this->saveButton->Click += new EventHandler( this,
34         this->saveButton_Click );
35
36      // enterButton
37      this->enterButton->Enabled = false;
38      this->enterButton->Font = new Drawing::Font(
39         S"Microsoft Sans Serif", 10.0 );
40      this->enterButton->Location = Point( 144, 240 );
41      this->enterButton->Name = S"enterButton";
42      this->enterButton->Size = Drawing::Size( 112, 32 );
43      this->enterButton->TabIndex = 5;
44      this->enterButton->Text = S"Enter";
45      this->enterButton->Click += new EventHandler( this,
46         this->enterButton_Click );
47
48      // exitButton
49      this->exitButton->Font = new Drawing::Font(
50         S"Microsoft Sans Serif", 10 );
51      this->exitButton->Location = Point( 272, 240 );
52      this->exitButton->Name = S"exitButton";
53      this->exitButton->Size = Drawing::Size( 112, 32 );
54      this->exitButton->TabIndex = 6;
55      this->exitButton->Text = S"Exit";
56      this->exitButton->Click += new EventHandler(
57         this, this->exitButton_Click );
58
59      // CreateFileForm
60      this->AutoScaleBaseSize = Drawing::Size( 6, 15 );
61      this->ClientSize = Drawing::Size( 400, 287 );
62
63      Control *controls[] = { this->balanceTextBox,
64         this->lastNameTextBox, this->firstNameTextBox,
65         this->accountTextBox, this->balanceLabel,
66         this->lastNameLabel, this->firstNameLabel,
```

Fig. 14.17 `CreateFileForm` class method definitions. (Part 2 of 5.)

```
67              this->accountLabel, this->exitButton,
68              this->enterButton, this->saveButton };
69
70          this->Controls->AddRange( controls );
71          this->Name = S"CreateFileForm";
72          this->Text = S"Creating a Sequential File";
73
74          this->ResumeLayout();
75      } // end method InitializeComponent
76
77      // invoked when user clicks Save button
78      void CreateFileForm::saveButton_Click( Object *sender,
79          EventArgs *e )
80      {
81          // create dialog box enabling user to save file
82          SaveFileDialog *fileChooser = new SaveFileDialog();
83
84          Windows::Forms::DialogResult result =
85              fileChooser->ShowDialog();
86
87          String *fileName; // name of file to save data
88
89          // allow user to create file
90          fileChooser->CheckFileExists = false;
91
92          // exit event handler if user clicked "Cancel"
93          if ( result == DialogResult::Cancel )
94              return;
95
96          // get specified file name
97          fileName = fileChooser->FileName;
98
99          // show error if user specified invalid file
100         if ( ( fileName->Equals( S"" ) ) || ( fileName == NULL ) )
101             MessageBox::Show( S"Invalid File Name", S"Error",
102                 MessageBoxButtons::OK, MessageBoxIcon::Error );
103         else {
104
105             // save file via FileStream if user specified valid file
106             try {
107
108                 // open file with write access
109                 output = new FileStream( fileName,
110                     FileMode::OpenOrCreate, FileAccess::Write );
111
112                 // disable Save As button and enable Enter button
113                 saveButton->Enabled = false;
114                 enterButton->Enabled = true;
115             }
116
117             // handle exception if file does not exist
118             catch ( FileNotFoundException * ) {
119
```

Fig. 14.17 CreateFileForm class method definitions. (Part 3 of 5.)

```
120                 // notify user if file does not exist
121             MessageBox::Show( S"File Does Not Exist", S"Error",
122                MessageBoxButtons::OK, MessageBoxIcon::Error );
123          } // end catch
124       } // end else
125  } // end method saveButton_Click
126
127  // invoke when user clicks Enter button
128  void CreateFileForm::enterButton_Click( Object *sender,
129      EventArgs *e )
130  {
131      // store TextBox values string array
132      String *values[] = GetTextBoxValues();
133
134      // Record containing TextBox values to serialize
135      Record *record = new Record();
136
137      // determine whether TextBox account field is empty
138      if ( values[ TextBoxIndices::ACCOUNT ] != S"" ) {
139
140          // store TextBox values in Record and serialize Record
141          try {
142
143              // get account number value from TextBox
144              int accountNumber = Int32::Parse(
145                 values[ TextBoxIndices::ACCOUNT ] );
146
147              // determine whether accountNumber is valid
148              if ( accountNumber > 0 ) {
149
150                  // store TextBox fields in Record
151                  record->Account = accountNumber;
152                  record->FirstName =
153                     values[ TextBoxIndices::FIRST ];
154                  record->LastName =
155                     values[ TextBoxIndices::LAST ];
156                  record->Balance = Double::Parse( values[
157                     TextBoxIndices::BALANCE ] );
158
159                  // write Record to FileStream (serialize object)
160                  formatter->Serialize( output, record );
161              }
162              else {
163
164                  // notify user if invalid account number
165                  MessageBox::Show( S"Invalid Account Number",
166                     S"Error", MessageBoxButtons::OK,
167                     MessageBoxIcon::Error );
168              } // end else
169          } // end try
170
171          // notify user if error occurs in serialization
172          catch ( SerializationException * ) {
```

Fig. 14.17 CreateFileForm class method definitions. (Part 4 of 5.)

```
173                MessageBox::Show( S"Error Writing to File", S"Error",
174                    MessageBoxButtons::OK, MessageBoxIcon::Error );
175            }
176
177            // notify user if error occurs regarding parameter format
178            catch( FormatException * ) {
179                MessageBox::Show( S"Invalid Format", S"Error",
180                    MessageBoxButtons::OK, MessageBoxIcon::Error );
181            } // end catch
182        } // end if
183
184        ClearTextBoxes(); // clear TextBox values
185    } // end method enterButton_Click
186
187    // invoked when user clicks Exit button
188    void CreateFileForm::exitButton_Click( Object *sender,
189        EventArgs *e )
190    {
191        // determine whether file exists
192        if ( output != 0 ) {
193
194            // close file
195            try {
196                output->Close();
197            }
198
199            // notify user of error closing file
200            catch ( IOException * ) {
201                MessageBox::Show( S"Cannot close file", S"Error",
202                    MessageBoxButtons::OK, MessageBoxIcon::Error );
203            } // end catch
204        } // end if
205
206        Application::Exit();
207    } // end method exitButton_Click
```

Fig. 14.17 `CreateFileForm` class method definitions. (Part 5 of 5.)

```
1    // Fig. 14.18: CreateSequential.cpp
2    // Entry point for application.
3
4    #include "CreateSequentialAccessFile.h"
5
6    int __stdcall WinMain()
7    {
8        Application::Run( new CreateFileForm() );
9
10       return 0;
11   } // end function WinMain
```

Fig. 14.18 `CreateFileForm` class driver. (Part 1 of 3.)

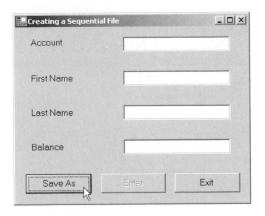

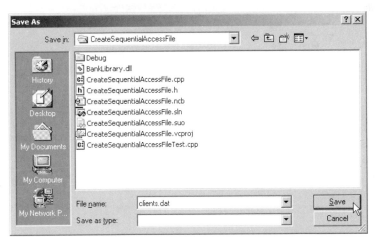

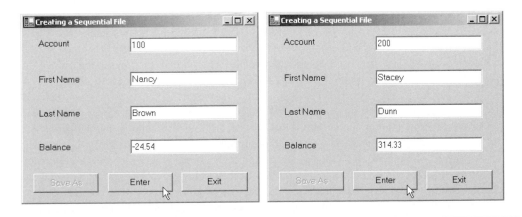

Fig. 14.18 `CreateFileForm` class driver. (Part 2 of 3.)

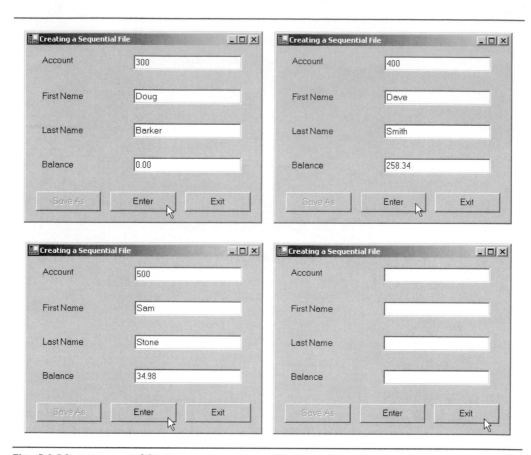

Fig. 14.18 `CreateFileForm` class driver. (Part 3 of 3.)

When the user clicks the **Save As** button, the program invokes method `saveButton_Click` (lines 78–125 of Fig. 14.17). Line 82 instantiates an object of class *SaveFileDialog*, which belongs to the `System::Windows::Forms` namespace. Objects of this class are used for selecting files (as shown in the second image in Fig. 14.18). Line 85 calls method *ShowDialog* of the `SaveFileDialog` object to display the `SaveFileDialog`. When displayed, a `SaveFileDialog` prevents the user from interacting with any other window in the program until the user closes the **Save-FileDialog** by clicking either **Save** or **Cancel**. Dialogs that behave in this fashion are called *modal dialogs*. The user selects the appropriate drive, directory and file name, then clicks **Save**. Method `ShowDialog` returns an integer specifying which button (**Save** or **Cancel**) the user clicked to close the dialog. In this example, the **Form** property **DialogResult** receives this integer. Line 93 tests for whether the user clicked **Cancel** by comparing the value returned by property `DialogResult` to constant *DialogResult::Cancel*. If the values are equal, method `saveButton_Click` returns (line

94). If the values are unequal (i.e., the user clicked **Save**, instead of clicking **Cancel**), line 97 uses property *FileName* of class `SaveFileDialog` to obtain the user-selected file.

As we stated previously in this chapter, we can open files for manipulation by creating objects of classes `FileStream`. In this example, we want the file to be opened for output, so lines 109–110 instantiate a `FileStream` object. The `FileStream` constructor that we use receives three arguments—a `String *` containing the name of the file to be opened, a constant describing how to open the file and a constant describing the file permissions. Line 110 passes constant `FileMode::OpenOrCreate` to the `FileStream` constructor as the constructor's second argument. This constant indicates that the `FileStream` object should open the file if the file exists or create the file if the file does not exist. The .NET Framework offers other `FileMode` constants describing how to open files; we introduce these constants as we use them in examples. Line 110 also passes constant `FileAccess::Write` to the `FileStream` constructor as the constructor's third argument. This constant ensures that the program can perform write-only operations on the `FileStream` object. The .NET Framework provides two other constants for this parameter—`FileAccess::Read` for read-only access and `FileAccess::ReadWrite` for both read and write access.

Good Programming Practice 14.1

When opening files, use the ***FileAccess*** *enumeration to control user access to these files.*

After the user types information in each `TextBox`, the user clicks the **Enter** button, which calls method `enterButton_Click` (lines 128–185) to save data from the `TextBox` in the user-specified file. If the user entered a valid account number (i.e., an integer greater than zero), lines 151–157 store the `TextBox` values in an object of type `Record`. If the user entered invalid data in one of the `TextBox`es (such as entering non-numeric characters in the **Balance** field), the program throws a `FormatException`. The `catch` block in lines 178–181 handles such an exception by notifying the user (via a `MessageBox`) of the improper format. If the user entered valid data, line 160 writes the record to the file by invoking method **Serialize** of the `BinaryFormatter` object (instantiated in line 38 of Fig. 14.16). Class `BinaryFormatter` uses methods *Serialize* and *Deserialize* to write and read objects into streams, respectively. Method **Serialize** writes the object's representation to a stream. Method **Deserialize** reads this representation from a stream and reconstructs the original object. Both methods throw a `Serialization-Exception` if an error occurs during serialization or deserialization (errors result when the methods attempt to access streams or records that do not exist). Both methods **Serialize** and **Deserialize** require a `Stream` object (e.g., the `FileStream`) as a parameter so that the `BinaryFormatter` can access the correct file; the `BinaryFormatter` must receive an instance of a class that derives from class **Stream**, because **Stream** is `abstract`. Class `BinaryFormatter` belongs to the *System::Runtime::Serialization::Formatters::Binary* namespace.

Common Programming Error 14.1

Failure to open a file before attempting to reference it in a program is a logic error.

When the user clicks the **Exit** button, the program invokes method **exitButton_Click** (lines 188–207 of Fig. 14.17) to exit the application. Line 196 closes the **FileStream** if one has been opened, and line 206 exits the program.

Performance Tip 14.1

Close each file explicitly when the program no longer needs to reference the file. This can reduce resource usage in programs that continue executing long after they finish using a specific file. The practice of explicitly closing files also improves program clarity.

Performance Tip 14.2

Releasing resources explicitly when they are no longer needed makes them immediately available for reuse by the program, thus improving resource utilization.

Common Programming Error 14.2

Files are not automatically closed when they are no longer referenced. Be sure to close each file when it is no longer needed by the program.

In the sample execution for the program in Fig. 14.16–Fig. 14.18, we entered information for five accounts (Fig. 14.19). The program does not depict how the data records are rendered in the file. To verify that the file has been created successfully, in the next section, we create a program to read and display the file.

Account Number	First Name	Last Name	Balance
100	Nancy	Brown	-25.54
200	Stacey	Dunn	314.33
300	Doug	Barker	0.00
400	Dave	Smith	258.34
500	Sam	Stone	34.98

Fig. 14.19 Sample data for the program of Fig. 14.16–Fig. 14.18.

14.6 Reading Data from a Sequential-Access File

Data are stored in files so that they can be retrieved for processing when they are needed. The previous section demonstrated how to create a file for use in sequential-access applications. In this section, we discuss how to read (or retrieve) data sequentially from a file.

Class **ReadSequentialAccessFileForm** (Fig. 14.20–Fig. 14.21) reads records from the file created by the program in Fig. 14.16–Fig. 14.18, then displays the contents of each record. Much of the code in this example is similar to that of Fig. 14.16–Fig. 14.18, so we discuss only the unique aspects of the application.

```
1    // Fig. 14.20: ReadSequentialAccessFile.h
2    // Reading a sequential-access file.
3
4    #pragma once
5
6    #using <mscorlib.dll>
7    #using <system.dll>
8    #using <system.drawing.dll>
9    #using <system.windows.forms.dll>
10   #using <BankLibrary.dll>
11
12   // Visual C++ .NET namespaces
13   using namespace System;
14   using namespace System::Drawing;
15   using namespace System::Windows::Forms;
16   using namespace System::IO;
17   using namespace
18      System::Runtime::Serialization::Formatters::Binary;
19   using namespace System::Runtime::Serialization;
20
21   // Deitel namespace
22   using namespace BankLibrary;
23
24   #include <tchar.h>
25
26   public __gc class ReadSequentialAccessFileForm : public BankUIForm
27   {
28   public:
29      Button *openButton;
30      Button *nextButton;
31      ReadSequentialAccessFileForm();
32
33   private:
34
35      // stream through which serializable data are read from file
36      FileStream *input;
37
38      // object for deserializing Record in binary format
39      static BinaryFormatter *reader = new BinaryFormatter();
```

Fig. 14.20 ReadSequentialAccessFileForm class reads a sequential-access file. (Part 1 of 2.)

```
40
41        void InitializeComponent();
42        void openButton_Click( Object *, EventArgs * );
43        void nextButton_Click( Object *, EventArgs * );
44    }; // end class ReadSequentialAccessFileForm
```

Fig. 14.20 `ReadSequentialAccessFileForm` class reads a sequential-access file. (Part 2 of 2.)

```
1     // Fig. 14.21: ReadSequentialAccessFile.cpp
2     // Method definitions for class ReadSequentialAccessFileForm.
3
4     #include "ReadSequentialAccessFile.h"
5
6     ReadSequentialAccessFileForm::ReadSequentialAccessFileForm()
7     {
8         InitializeComponent();
9     }
10
11    void ReadSequentialAccessFileForm::InitializeComponent()
12    {
13        this->openButton = new Button();
14        this->nextButton = new Button();
15
16        this->SuspendLayout();
17
18        // set tab indices
19        this->accountTextBox->TabIndex = 1;
20        this->firstNameTextBox->TabIndex = 2;
21        this->lastNameTextBox->TabIndex = 3;
22        this->balanceTextBox->TabIndex = 4;
23
24        // openButton
25        this->openButton->Font = new Drawing::Font(
26            S"Microsoft Sans Serif", 10 );
27        this->openButton->Location = Point( 32, 232 );
28        this->openButton->Name = S"openButton";
29        this->openButton->Size = Drawing::Size( 144, 32 );
30        this->openButton->TabIndex = 0;
31        this->openButton->Text = S"Open File";
32        this->openButton->Click += new EventHandler(
33            this, this->openButton_Click );
34
35        // nextButton
36        this->nextButton->Enabled = false;
37        this->nextButton->Font = new Drawing::Font(
38            S"Microsoft Sans Serif", 10 );
39        this->nextButton->Location = Point( 216, 232 );
40        this->nextButton->Name = S"nextButton";
41        this->nextButton->Size = Drawing::Size( 144, 32 );
42        this->nextButton->TabIndex = 5;
43        this->nextButton->Text = S"Next Record";
```

Fig. 14.21 `ReadSequentialAccessFileForm` class method definitions. (Part 1 of 3.)

```
44          this->nextButton->Click += new EventHandler(
45              this, this->nextButton_Click );
46
47          // ReadSequentialAccessFileForm
48          this->AutoScaleBaseSize = Drawing::Size( 6, 15 );
49          this->ClientSize = Drawing::Size( 400, 279 );
50
51          Control *controls[] = { this->balanceTextBox,
52              this->lastNameTextBox, this->firstNameTextBox,
53              this->accountTextBox, this->balanceLabel,
54              this->lastNameLabel, this->firstNameLabel,
55              this->accountLabel, this->nextButton, this->openButton };
56          this->Controls->AddRange( controls );
57          this->Name = S"ReadSequentialAccessFileForm";
58          this->Text = S"Reading a Sequential File";
59
60          this->ResumeLayout();
61      } // end method InitializeComponent
62
63      // invoked when user clicks Open File button
64      void ReadSequentialAccessFileForm::openButton_Click(
65          Object *sender, EventArgs *e )
66      {
67          // create dialog box enabling user to open file
68          OpenFileDialog *fileChooser = new OpenFileDialog();
69          Windows::Forms::DialogResult result =
70              fileChooser->ShowDialog();
71          String *fileName; // name of file containing data
72
73          // exit event handler if user clicked Cancel
74          if ( result == DialogResult::Cancel )
75              return;
76
77          // get specified file name
78          fileName = fileChooser->FileName;
79          ClearTextBoxes();
80
81          // show error if user specified invalid file
82          if ( ( fileName->Equals( S"" ) ) || ( fileName == NULL ) )
83              MessageBox::Show( S"Invalid File Name", S"Error",
84              MessageBoxButtons::OK, MessageBoxIcon::Error );
85          else {
86
87              // create FileStream to obtain read access to file
88              input = new FileStream( fileName, FileMode::Open,
89                  FileAccess::Read );
90
91              // enable next record button
92              nextButton->Enabled = true;
93          }
94      } // end method openButton_Click
95
```

Fig. 14.21 `ReadSequentialAccessFileForm` class method definitions.
(Part 2 of 3.)

```
96    // invoked when user clicks Next Record button
97    void ReadSequentialAccessFileForm::nextButton_Click(
98       Object *sender, EventArgs *e )
99    {
100      // deserialize Record and store data in TextBoxes
101      try {
102
103         // get next Record available in file
104         Record *record =
105            dynamic_cast< Record *>( reader->Deserialize( input ) );
106
107         // store Record values in temporary string array
108         String *values[] = { record->Account.ToString(),
109            record->FirstName->ToString(),
110            record->LastName->ToString(),
111            record->Balance.ToString() };
112
113         // copy string array values to TextBox values
114         SetTextBoxValues( values );
115      } // end try
116
117      // handle exception when no Records in file
118      catch ( SerializationException * ) {
119
120         // close FileStream if no Records in file
121         input->Close();
122
123         // enable Open File button
124         openButton->Enabled = true;
125
126         // disable Next Record button
127         nextButton->Enabled = false;
128
129         ClearTextBoxes();
130
131         // notify user if no Records in file
132         MessageBox::Show( S"No more records in file", S"",
133            MessageBoxButtons::OK, MessageBoxIcon::Information );
134      } // end catch
135   } // end method nextButton_Click
```

Fig. 14.21 `ReadSequentialAccessFileForm` class method definitions.
(Part 3 of 3.)

```
1    // Fig. 14.22: ReadSequential.cpp
2    // Entry point for application.
3
4    #include "ReadSequentialAccessFile.h"
5
6    int __stdcall WinMain()
7    {
8       Application::Run( new ReadSequentialAccessFileForm() );
```

Fig. 14.22 `ReadSequentialAccessFileForm` class driver. (Part 1 of 3.)

```
 9
10       return 0;
11    } // end function WinMain
```

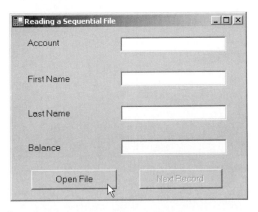

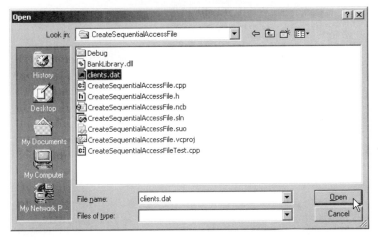

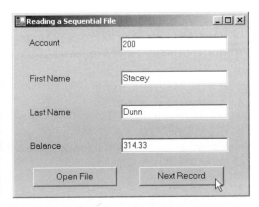

Fig. 14.22 `ReadSequentialAccessFileForm` class driver. (Part 2 of 3.)

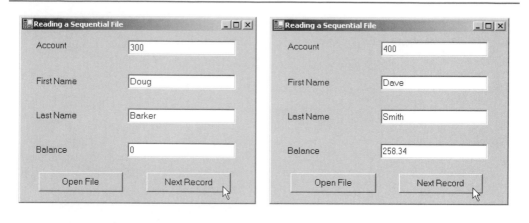

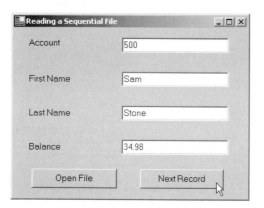

Fig. 14.22 `ReadSequentialAccessFileForm` class driver. (Part 3 of 3.)

When the user clicks the **Open File** button, the program calls method **open-Button_Click** (lines 64–94 of Fig. 14.21). Line 68 instantiates an object of class *OpenFileDialog*, and line 70 calls the object's *ShowDialog* method to display the **Open** dialog. (See the second screenshot in Fig. 14.22.) The behavior and GUI for this dialog and the **SaveFileDialog** are the same (except that **Save** is replaced by **Open**). If the user inputs a valid file name, lines 88–89 create a **FileStream** object and assign it to pointer **input**. We pass constant **FileMode::Open** as the second argument to the **FileStream** constructor. This constant indicates that the **FileStream** should open the file if the file exists or should throw a **FileNotFoundException** if the file does not exist. (In this example, the **FileStream** constructor will not throw a **FileNotFoundException**, because the **OpenFileDialog** requires the user to enter a name of a file that exists.) In the last example (Fig. 14.16–Fig. 14.18), we wrote text to the file, using a **FileStream** object with write-only access. In this example, (Fig. 14.20–Fig. 14.22), we specify read-only access to the file by passing constant **FileAccess::Read** as the third argument to the **FileStream** constructor.

Testing and Debugging Tip 14.1

Open a file with the **FileAccess::Read** *file-open mode if the contents of the file should not be modified. This prevents unintentional modification of the file's contents.*

When the user clicks the **Next Record** button, the program calls method **nextButton_Click** (lines 97–135), which reads the next record from the user-specified file. (The user must click **Next Record** after opening the file to view the first record.) Line 105 calls method **Deserialize** of the **BinaryFormatter** object to read the next record and casts the result to a **Record**—this cast is necessary, because **Deserialize** returns a pointer of type **Object**. Lines 108–114 then display the **Record** values in the **TextBox**es. When method **Deserialize** attempts to deserialize a record that does not exist in the file (i.e., the program has displayed all file records), the method throws a **SerializationException**. The **catch** block (lines 118–134) that handles this exception closes the **FileStream** object (line 121) and notifies the user that there are no more records (lines 132–133).

To retrieve data sequentially from a file, programs normally start from the beginning of the file, reading data consecutively until the desired data are found. It sometimes is necessary to process a file sequentially several times (from the beginning of the file) during the execution of a program. A **FileStream** object can reposition its *file-position pointer* (which contains the byte number of the next byte to be read from or written to the file) to any position in the file—we show this feature when we introduce random-access file-processing applications. When a **FileStream** object is opened, its file-position pointer is set to zero (i.e., the beginning of the file)

Performance Tip 14.3

It is time-consuming to close and reopen a file for the purpose of moving the file-position pointer to the file's beginning. Doing so frequently could slow program performance.

We now present a more substantial program (Fig. 14.23–Fig. 14.25) that builds on the concepts employed in Fig. 14.20–Fig. 14.22. Class **CreditInquiryForm** (Fig. 14.23–Fig. 14.24) is a credit-inquiry program that enables a credit manager to display account information for those customers with credit balances (i.e., customers to whom the company owes money), zero balances (i.e., customers who do not owe the company money) and debit balances (i.e., customers who owe the company money for previously received goods and services). Note that line 34 (Fig. 14.23) declares a *RichTextBox* that will display the account information. **RichTextBox**es provide more functionality than do regular **TextBox**es—for example, **RichTextBox**es offer method *Find* for searching individual strings and method *LoadFile* for displaying file contents. Class **RichTextBox** does not inherit from class **TextBox**; rather, both classes inherit directly from **abstract** class *System::Windows::Forms::TextBoxBase*. We use a **RichTextBox** in this example, because a **RichTextBox** displays multiple lines of text by default, whereas a regular **TextBox** displays only one. Alternatively, we could have specified that a **TextBox** object display multiple lines of text by setting its **Multiline** property to **true**.

The program in Fig. 14.23–Fig. 14.25 displays buttons that enable a credit manager to obtain credit information. The **Open File** button opens a file for gathering data. The **Credit Balances** button displays a list of accounts that have credit balances, the **Debit Balances** button displays a list of accounts that have debit balances, and the **Zero Balances** button displays a list of accounts that have zero balances. The **Done** button exits the application.

```cpp
1   // Fig. 14.23: CreditInquiry.h
2   // Read a file sequentially and display contents based on
3   // account type specified by user (credit, debit or zero balances).
4
5   #pragma once
6
7   #using <system.dll>
8   #using <mscorlib.dll>
9   #using <system.drawing.dll>
10  #using <system.windows.forms.dll>
11  #using <system.data.dll>
12  #using <BankLibrary.dll>
13
14  // Visual C++ .NET namespaces
15  using namespace System;
16  using namespace System::Drawing;
17  using namespace System::Windows::Forms;
18  using namespace System::IO;
19  using namespace
20     System::Runtime::Serialization::Formatters::Binary;
21  using namespace System::Runtime::Serialization;
22
23  // Deitel namespace
24  using namespace BankLibrary;
25
26  #include <tchar.h>
27
28  public __gc class CreditInquiryForm : public Form
29  {
30  public:
31     CreditInquiryForm();
32
33  private:
34     RichTextBox *displayTextBox;
35
36     Button *doneButton;
37     Button *zeroButton;
38     Button *debitButton;
39     Button *creditButton;
40     Button *openButton;
41
42     // stream through which serializable data are read from file
43     FileStream *input;
44
```

Fig. 14.23 `CreditInquiryForm` class demonstrates reading and displaying contents from a sequential-access file. (Part 1 of 2.)

```
45        // object for deserializing Record in binary format
46        static BinaryFormatter *reader = new BinaryFormatter();
47
48        // name of file that stores credit, debit and zero balances
49        String *fileName;
50
51        void InitializeComponent();
52        void openButton_Click( Object *, EventArgs * );
53        void get_Click( Object *, EventArgs * );
54        bool ShouldDisplay( double, String * );
55        void doneButton_Click( Object *, EventArgs * );
56     }; // end class CreditInquiryForm
```

Fig. 14.23 CreditInquiryForm class demonstrates reading and displaying contents from a sequential-access file. (Part 2 of 2.)

```
1     // Fig. 14.24: CreditInquiry.cpp
2     // Method definitions for class CreditInquiryForm.
3
4     #include "CreditInquiry.h"
5
6     CreditInquiryForm::CreditInquiryForm()
7     {
8        InitializeComponent();
9     }
10
11    void CreditInquiryForm::InitializeComponent()
12    {
13        this->doneButton = new Button();
14        this->zeroButton = new Button();
15        this->debitButton = new Button();
16        this->creditButton = new Button();
17        this->openButton = new Button();
18        this->displayTextBox = new RichTextBox();
19
20        this->SuspendLayout();
21
22        // doneButton
23        this->doneButton->Location = Point( 696, 216 );
24        this->doneButton->Name = S"doneButton";
25        this->doneButton->Size = Drawing::Size( 123, 40 );
26        this->doneButton->TabIndex = 12;
27        this->doneButton->Text = S"Done";
28        this->doneButton->Click += new EventHandler( this,
29           this->doneButton_Click );
30
31        // zeroButton
32        this->zeroButton->Enabled = false;
33        this->zeroButton->Location = Point( 532, 216 );
34        this->zeroButton->Name = S"zeroButton";
35        this->zeroButton->Size = Drawing::Size( 123, 40 );
```

Fig. 14.24 CreditInquiryForm class method definitions. (Part 1 of 5.)

```
36      this->zeroButton->TabIndex = 11;
37      this->zeroButton->Text = S"Zero Balances";
38      this->zeroButton->Click += new EventHandler( this,
39         this->get_Click );
40
41      // debitButton
42      this->debitButton->Enabled = false;
43      this->debitButton->Location = Point( 369, 216 );
44      this->debitButton->Name = S"debitButton";
45      this->debitButton->Size = Drawing::Size( 123, 40 );
46      this->debitButton->TabIndex = 10;
47      this->debitButton->Text = S"Debit Balances";
48      this->debitButton->Click += new EventHandler( this,
49         this->get_Click );
50
51      // creditButton
52      this->creditButton->Enabled = false;
53      this->creditButton->Location = Point( 205, 216 );
54      this->creditButton->Name = S"creditButton";
55      this->creditButton->Size = Drawing::Size( 123, 40 );
56      this->creditButton->TabIndex = 9;
57      this->creditButton->Text = S"Credit Balances";
58      this->creditButton->Click += new EventHandler( this,
59         this->get_Click );
60
61      // openButton
62      this->openButton->Location = Point( 41, 216 );
63      this->openButton->Name = S"openButton";
64      this->openButton->Size = Drawing::Size( 123, 40 );
65      this->openButton->TabIndex = 8;
66      this->openButton->Text = S"Open File";
67      this->openButton->Click += new EventHandler( this,
68         this->openButton_Click );
69
70      // displayTextBox
71      this->displayTextBox->Font = new Drawing::Font(
72         S"Microsoft Sans Serif", 10.0, FontStyle::Regular,
73         GraphicsUnit::Point, 0 );
74      this->displayTextBox->Location = Point( 10, 20 );
75      this->displayTextBox->Name = S"displayTextBox";
76      this->displayTextBox->Size = Drawing::Size( 830, 180 );
77      this->displayTextBox->TabIndex = 13;
78      this->displayTextBox->Text = S"";
79
80      // CreditInquiryForm
81      this->AutoScaleBaseSize = Drawing::Size( 6, 15 );
82      this->ClientSize = Drawing::Size( 849, 271 );
83
84      Control *controls[] = { this->doneButton, this->zeroButton,
85         this->debitButton, this->creditButton, this->openButton,
86         this->displayTextBox };
87      this->Controls->AddRange( controls );
88      this->Name = S"CreditInquiryForm";
```

Fig. 14.24 `CreditInquiryForm` class method definitions. (Part 2 of 5.)

```
89         this->Text = S"CreditInquiry";
90
91         this->ResumeLayout();
92    } // end method InitializeComponent
93
94    // invoked when user clicks Open File button
95    void CreditInquiryForm::openButton_Click( Object *sender,
96         EventArgs *e )
97    {
98         // create dialog box enabling user to open file
99         OpenFileDialog *fileChooser = new OpenFileDialog();
100        Windows::Forms::DialogResult result =
101           fileChooser->ShowDialog();
102
103        // exit event handler if user clicked Cancel
104        if ( result == DialogResult::Cancel )
105           return;
106
107        // get name from user
108        fileName = fileChooser->FileName;
109
110        // show error if user specified invalid file
111        if ( fileName->Equals( S"" ) || fileName == NULL )
112           MessageBox::Show( S"Invalid File Name", S"Error",
113           MessageBoxButtons::OK, MessageBoxIcon::Error );
114        else {
115
116           // enable all GUI buttons, disable Open File button
117           openButton->Enabled = false;
118           creditButton->Enabled = true;
119           debitButton->Enabled = true;
120           zeroButton->Enabled = true;
121        } // end else
122    } // end method openButton_Click
123
124    // invoked when user clicks Credit Balances,
125    // Debit Balances or Zero Balances button
126    void CreditInquiryForm::get_Click( Object *sender,
127         EventArgs *e )
128    {
129        // convert sender explicitly to object of type button
130        Button *senderButton = dynamic_cast< Button* >( sender );
131
132        // get text from clicked Button, which stores account type
133        String *accountType = senderButton->Text;
134
135        // read and display file information
136        try {
137
138           // close file from previous operation
139           if ( input != NULL )
140              input->Close();
141
```

Fig. 14.24 CreditInquiryForm class method definitions. (Part 3 of 5.)

```
142          // create FileStream to obtain read access to file
143          input = new FileStream( fileName, FileMode::Open,
144             FileAccess::Read );
145
146          displayTextBox->Text = S"The accounts are:\r\n";
147
148          // traverse file until end of file
149          while ( true ) {
150
151             // get next Record available in file
152             Record *record = dynamic_cast< Record * >(
153                reader->Deserialize( input ) );
154
155             // store record's last field in balance
156             double balance = record->Balance;
157
158             // determine whether to display balance
159             if ( ShouldDisplay( balance, accountType ) ) {
160
161                // display record
162                String *output = String::Concat(
163                   ( record->Account ).ToString(), S"\t",
164                   record->FirstName, S"\t", record->LastName,
165                   S"      ", S"\t" );
166
167                // display balance with correct monetary format
168                output = String::Concat( output, String::Format(
169                   S"{0:F}", balance.ToString() ), S"\r\n" );
170
171                // copy output to screen
172                displayTextBox->Text = String::Concat(
173                   displayTextBox->Text, output );
174             } // end if
175          } // end while
176       } // end try
177
178       // handle exception when file cannot be closed
179       catch ( IOException * ) {
180          MessageBox::Show( S"Cannot Close File", S"Error",
181             MessageBoxButtons::OK, MessageBoxIcon::Error );
182       }
183
184       // handle exception when no more records
185       catch ( SerializationException * ) {
186
187          // close FileStream if no Records in file
188          input->Close();
189       }
190    } // end method get_Click
191
192    // determine whether to display given record
193    bool CreditInquiryForm::ShouldDisplay( double balance,
194       String *accountType )
195    {
```

Fig. 14.24 `CreditInquiryForm` class method definitions. (Part 4 of 5.)

```
196        if ( balance > 0 ) {
197
198            // display credit balances
199            if ( accountType->Equals( S"Credit Balances" ) )
200                return true;
201        }
202        else if ( balance < 0 ) {
203
204            // display debit balances
205            if ( accountType->Equals( S"Debit Balances" ) )
206                return true;
207        }
208        else { // balance == 0
209
210            // display
211            if ( accountType->Equals( S"Zero Balances" ) )
212                return true;
213        }
214
215        return false;
216    } // end method ShouldDisplay
217
218    // invoked when user clicks Done button
219    void CreditInquiryForm::doneButton_Click( Object *sender,
220        EventArgs *e )
221    {
222        // determine whether file exists
223        if ( input != NULL ) {
224
225            // close file
226            try {
227                input->Close();
228            }
229
230            // handle exception if FileStream does not exist
231            catch ( IOException * ) {
232
233                // notify user of error closing file
234                MessageBox::Show( S"Cannot close file", S"Error",
235                    MessageBoxButtons::OK, MessageBoxIcon::Error );
236            } // end catch
237        } // end if
238
239        Application::Exit();
240    } // end method doneButton_Click
```

Fig. 14.24 CreditInquiryForm class method definitions. (Part 5 of 5.)

```
1    // Fig. 14.25: CreditInquiryTest.cpp
2    // Entry point for application.
3
4    #include "CreditInquiry.h"
5
```

Fig. 14.25 CreditInquiryForm class driver. (Part 1 of 3.)

```
6    int __stdcall WinMain()
7    {
8       Application::Run( new CreditInquiryForm() );
9
10      return 0;
11   } // end function WinMain
```

Fig. 14.25 `CreditInquiryForm` class driver. (Part 2 of 3.)

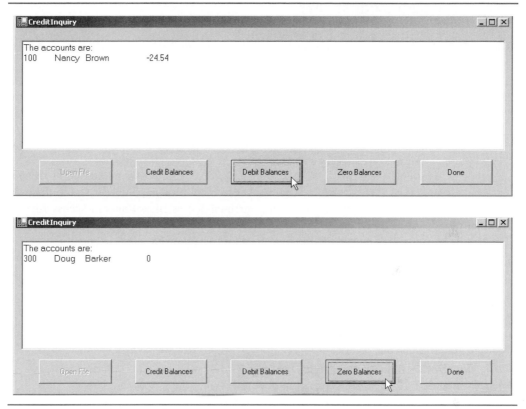

Fig. 14.25 `CreditInquiryForm` class driver. (Part 3 of 3.)

When the user clicks the **Open File** button, the program calls method `openButton_Click` (lines 95–122). Line 99 instantiates an object of class `Open-FileDialog`, and line 101 calls the object's `ShowDialog` method to display the **Open** dialog, in which the user inputs the name of the file to open.

When the user clicks **Credit Balances**, **Debit Balances** or **Zero Balances**, the program invokes method `get_Click` (lines 126–190). Line 130 casts the `sender` parameter, which is a pointer to the `Object` that sent the event, to a `Button` pointer. Line 133 can then extract the `Button` object's text into variable `accountType`, which the program uses to determine which GUI `Button` the user clicked. Lines 143–144 create a `FileStream` object with read-only file access and assign it to pointer `input`. Lines 149–175 define a `while` loop that uses `private` method `ShouldDisplay` (lines 193–216) to determine whether to display each record in the file. The `while` loop obtains each record by calling method `Deserialize` of the `FileStream` object repeatedly (lines 152–153). When the file-position pointer reaches the end of file, method `Deserialize` throws a `SerializationException`, which the `catch` block in lines 185–189 handles: Line 188 calls the `Close` method of `FileStream` to close the file, and method `get_Click` returns.

14.7 Random-Access Files

So far, we have explained how to create sequential-access files and how to search through such files to locate particular information. However, sequential-access files are inappropriate for so-called *"instant-access" applications*, in which a particular record of information must be located immediately. Popular instant-access applications include airline-reservation systems, banking systems, point-of-sale systems, automated-teller machines and other kinds of *transaction-processing systems* requiring rapid access to specific data. The bank at which an individual has an account might have hundreds of thousands or even millions of other customers; however, when that individual uses an automated teller machine, the appropriate account is checked for sufficient funds in seconds. This type of instant access can be made possible using *random-access files*. Individual records of a random-access file can be accessed directly (and quickly), without searching through potentially large numbers of other records, as is necessary with sequential-access files. Random-access files sometimes are called *direct-access files*.

As we discussed earlier in this chapter, the .NET Framework does not impose structure on files, so applications that use random-access files must implement the random-access capability. There are a variety of techniques for creating random-access files. Perhaps the simplest involves requiring that all records in a file be of a uniform, fixed length. The use of fixed-length records enables a program to calculate (as a function of the record size and the record key) the exact location of any record in relation to the beginning of the file. We soon demonstrate how this facilitates immediate access to specific records, even in large files.

Figure 14.26 illustrates the organization of a random-access file composed of fixed-length records (each record in this figure is 100 bytes long). Students can consider a random-access file as analogous to a railroad train with many cars, some of which are empty and some of which contain contents.

Data can be inserted into a random-access file without destroying other data in the file. In addition, previously stored data can be updated or dfile. In the following sections, we explain how to create a random-access file, write data to that file, read data both sequentially and randomly, update data and delete data that are no longer needed.

Figure 14.27–Fig. 14.28 contains class **RandomAccessRecord**, which is used in the random-access file-processing applications in this chapter. This class also belongs to the **BankLibrary** DLL—i.e., it is part of the project that contains classes **BankUIForm** and **Record**. (When adding class **RandomAccessRecord** to the project containing **BankUIForm** and **Record**, remember to rebuild the project.)

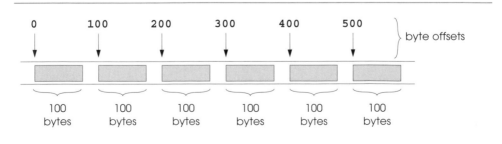

Fig. 14.26 Random-access file with fixed-length records.

```cpp
1    // Fig. 14.27: RandomAccessRecord.h
2    // Data-record class for random-access applications.
3
4    #pragma once
5
6    #using <system.dll>
7    #using <mscorlib.dll>
8
9    using namespace System;
10
11   // length of firstName and lastName
12   #define CHAR_ARRAY_LENGTH 15
13
14   #define SIZE_OF_CHAR sizeof( Char )
15   #define SIZE_OF_INT32 sizeof( Int32 )
16   #define SIZE_OF_DOUBLE sizeof( Double )
17
18   namespace BankLibrary
19   {
20      public __gc class RandomAccessRecord
21      {
22      public:
23
24         // length of record
25         static const int SIZE = ( SIZE_OF_INT32 + 2 * (
26            SIZE_OF_CHAR * CHAR_ARRAY_LENGTH ) + SIZE_OF_DOUBLE );
27
28         // default constructor sets members to default values
29         RandomAccessRecord();
30         RandomAccessRecord( int, String *, String *, double );
31
32         // get method of property Account
33         __property int get_Account()
34         {
35            return account;
36         }
37
38         // set method of property Account
39         __property void set_Account( int value )
40         {
41            account = value;
42         }
43
44         // get method of property FirstName
45         __property String *get_FirstName()
46         {
47            return new String( firstName );
48         }
49
50         // set method of property FirstName
51         __property void set_FirstName( String *value )
52         {
53            // determine length of string parameter
```

Fig. 14.27 Data-record class for random-access applications. (Part 1 of 3.)

```
54              int stringSize = value->Length;
55
56              // firstName string representation
57              String *firstNameString = value;
58
59              // append spaces to string parameter if too short
60              if ( stringSize <= CHAR_ARRAY_LENGTH ) {
61                  firstNameString = String::Concat( value,
62                      new String( ' ',
63                      CHAR_ARRAY_LENGTH - stringSize ) );
64              }
65              else {
66
67                  // remove characters from string parameter
68                  // if too long
69                  firstNameString =
70                      value->Substring( 0, CHAR_ARRAY_LENGTH );
71              }
72
73              // convert string parameter to char array
74              firstName = firstNameString->ToCharArray();
75
76          } // end set
77
78          // get method of property LastName
79          __property String *get_LastName()
80          {
81              return new String( lastName );
82          }
83
84          // set method of property LastName
85          __property void set_LastName( String *value )
86          {
87              // determine length of string parameter
88              int stringSize = value->Length;
89
90              // lastName string representation
91              String *lastNameString = value;
92
93              // append spaces to string parameter if too short
94              if ( stringSize <= CHAR_ARRAY_LENGTH ) {
95                  lastNameString = String::Concat( value,
96                      new String( ' ',
97                      CHAR_ARRAY_LENGTH - stringSize ) );
98              }
99              else {
100
101                 // remove characters from string parameter
102                 // if too long
103                 lastNameString =
104                     value->Substring( 0, CHAR_ARRAY_LENGTH );
105             }
106
```

Fig. 14.27 Data-record class for random-access applications. (Part 2 of 3.)

```
107                    // convert string parameter to char array
108                    lastName = lastNameString->ToCharArray();
109
110                } // end set
111
112                // get method of property Balance
113                __property double get_Balance()
114                {
115                    return balance;
116                }
117
118                // set method of property Balance
119                __property void set_Balance( double value )
120                {
121                    balance = value;
122                }
123
124            private:
125
126                // record data
127                int account;
128                __wchar_t firstName __gc[];
129                __wchar_t lastName __gc[];
130                double balance;
131        }; // end class RandomAccessRecord
132    } // end namespace BankLibrary
```

Fig. 14.27 Data-record class for random-access applications. (Part 3 of 3.)

```
1    // Fig. 14.28: RandomAccessRecord.cpp
2    // Method definitions for class RandomAccessRecord.
3
4    #include "stdafx.h"
5    #include "RandomAccessRecord.h"
6
7    using namespace BankLibrary;
8
9    // default constructor sets members to default values
10   RandomAccessRecord::RandomAccessRecord()
11   {
12       firstName = new __wchar_t __gc[ CHAR_ARRAY_LENGTH ];
13       lastName = new __wchar_t __gc[ CHAR_ARRAY_LENGTH ];
14       FirstName = "";
15       LastName = "";
16       Account = 0;
17       Balance = 0.0;
18   }
19
20   // overloaded counstructor sets members to parameter values
21   RandomAccessRecord::RandomAccessRecord( int accountValue,
22       String *firstNameValue, String *lastNameValue,
23       double balanceValue )
```

Fig. 14.28 RandomAccessRecord class method definitions. (Part 1 of 2.)

```
24   {
25      Account = accountValue;
26      FirstName = firstNameValue;
27      LastName = lastNameValue;
28      Balance = balanceValue;
29   } // end constructor
```

Fig. 14.28 `RandomAccessRecord` class method definitions. (Part 2 of 2.)

Like class **Record** (Fig. 14.14–Fig. 14.15), class **RandomAccessRecord** contains **private** data members (lines 127–130 of Fig. 14.27) for storing record information, two constructors for setting these members to default or to parameter-specified values, and properties for accessing these members. However, class **RandomAccessRecord** does not contain attribute **[Serializable]** before its class definition. We do not serialize this class, because the .NET Framework does not provide a means to obtain an object's size at runtime. This means that, if we serialize the class, we cannot guarantee a fixed-length record size.

Instead of serializing the class, we fix the length of the **private** data members, then write those data as a byte stream to the file. To fix this length, the **set** accessors of properties **FirstName** (lines 51–76) and **LastName** (lines 85–110) ensure that members **firstName** and **lastName** are **__wchar_t** arrays of exactly 15 elements. Each **set** accessor receives as an argument a **String *** representing the first name and last name, respectively. If the **String** referenced by the **String *** parameter contains fewer than 15 characters, the property's **set** accessor copies the **String**'s values to the **__wchar_t** array, then populates the remainder with spaces. If the **String** contains more than 15 characters, the **set** accessor stores only the first 15 characters of the **String** into the **__wchar_t** array. [*Note*: The **String** is truncated for convenience. In a commercial application, truncation of data may not be acceptable. One solution is to store any truncated data in another location. Another, more expensive, solution is to set the size of fields so large that data will never have to be truncated. If all else fails, alternative methods of data storage may have to be considered.]

Notice that rather than use the numeric constant **15** in the **set** accessors, we use *symbolic constant* **CHAR_ARRAY_LENGTH**, which is defined in line 12. We do this so that we can easily change this number in the future, if necessary. Symbolic constants—constants represented as symbols—are defined using *preprocessor directive* **#define**. The format for the **#define** preprocessor directive is

       #define *identifier replacement-text*

When this line appears in a file, all subsequent occurrences (except those inside a string) of *identifier* in that file will be replaced by *replacement-text* before the program is compiled. Thus, all occurrences of **CHAR_ARRAY_LENGTH** are replaced by numeric constant **15** before the program is compiled.

Lines 14–16 create symbolic constants **SIZE_OF_CHAR**, **SIZE_OF_INT32** and **SIZE_OF_DOUBLE** in a similar manner. The preprocessor will replace each constant with a call to *unary operator* **sizeof** that determines the size of its respective type (e.g., **sizeof(Int32)** returns the size, in bytes, of an object of type **Int32**). We use the **sizeof** operator to ensure that we use the correct number of bytes to store each record.

Lines 25–26 declare **const SIZE**, which specifies the record's length. Each record contains **account** (4-byte **int**, or **Int32**), **firstName** and **lastName** (two 15-element **__wchar_t** arrays, where each **__wchar_t**, or **Char**, occupies two bytes, resulting in a total of 60 bytes) and **balance** (8-byte **double**, or **Double**). In this example, each record (i.e., the four **private** data members that our programs will read to and write from files) occupies 72 bytes (4 bytes + 60 bytes + 8 bytes). [*Note*: We create **SIZE** as a **const** data member rather than a symbolic constant because we use this value multiple times in the following examples.]

14.8 Creating a Random-Access File

Consider the following problem statement for a credit-processing application:

> *Create a transaction-processing program capable of storing a maximum of 100 fixed-length records for a company that can have a maximum of 100 customers. Each record consists of an account number (which acts as the record key), a last name, a first name and a balance. The program can update an account, create an account and delete an account.*

The next several sections introduce the techniques necessary to create this credit-processing program. We now discuss the program used to create the random-access file that the remainder of the programs in this chapter use to manipulate data. Class **CreateRandomAccessFile** (Fig. 14.29–Fig. 14.30) creates a random-access file.

```
1   // Fig. 14.29: CreateRandomAccessFile.h
2   // Creating a random file.
3
4   #pragma once
5
6   #using <mscorlib.dll>
7   #using <system.dll>
8   #using <system.windows.forms.dll>
9   #using <BankLibrary.dll>
10
11  // Visual C++ .NET namespaces
12  using namespace System;
13  using namespace System::IO;
14  using namespace System::Windows::Forms;
15
16  // Deitel namespace
17  using namespace BankLibrary;
18
19  #include <tchar.h>
20
21  // number of records to write to disk
22  #define NUMBER_OF_RECORDS 100
23
24  public __gc class CreateRandomAccessFile : public Form
25  {
26  public:
27     void SaveFile();
28  }; // end class CreateRandomAccessFile
```

Fig. 14.29 Creating files for random-access file-processing applications.

```cpp
1   // Fig. 14.30: CreateRandomAccessFile.cpp
2   // Method definitions for class CreateRandomAccessFile.
3
4   #include "CreateRandomAccessFile.h"
5
6   // write records to disk
7   void CreateRandomAccessFile::SaveFile()
8   {
9      // record for writing to disk
10     RandomAccessRecord *blankRecord = new RandomAccessRecord();
11
12     // stream through which serializable data are written to file
13     FileStream *fileOutput = NULL;
14
15     // stream for writing bytes to file
16     BinaryWriter *binaryOutput = NULL;
17
18     // create dialog box enabling user to save file
19     SaveFileDialog *fileChooser = new SaveFileDialog();
20     Windows::Forms::DialogResult result =
21        fileChooser->ShowDialog();
22
23     // get file name from user
24     String *fileName = fileChooser->FileName;
25
26     // exit event handler if user clicked Cancel
27     if ( result == DialogResult::Cancel )
28        return;
29
30     // show error if user specified invalid file
31     if ( fileName->Equals( S"" ) || fileName == NULL )
32        MessageBox::Show( S"Invalid File Name", S"Error",
33        MessageBoxButtons::OK, MessageBoxIcon::Error );
34     else {
35
36        // write records to file
37        try {
38
39           // create FileStream to hold records
40           fileOutput = new FileStream( fileName,
41              FileMode::Create, FileAccess::Write );
42
43           // set length of file
44           fileOutput->SetLength( RandomAccessRecord::SIZE *
45              NUMBER_OF_RECORDS );
46
47           // create object for writing bytes to file
48           binaryOutput = new BinaryWriter( fileOutput );
49
50           // write empty records to file
51           for ( int i = 0; i < NUMBER_OF_RECORDS; i++ ) {
52
```

Fig. 14.30 `CreateRandomAccessFile` class method definitions. (Part 1 of 2.)

```
53              // set file position pointer in file
54              fileOutput->Position = i * RandomAccessRecord::SIZE;
55
56              // write blank record to file
57              binaryOutput->Write( blankRecord->Account );
58              binaryOutput->Write( blankRecord->FirstName );
59              binaryOutput->Write( blankRecord->LastName );
60              binaryOutput->Write( blankRecord->Balance );
61           }
62
63           // notify user of success
64           MessageBox::Show( S"File Created", S"Success",
65              MessageBoxButtons::OK, MessageBoxIcon::Information );
66        } // end try
67
68        // handle exception if error occurs during writing
69        catch ( IOException *fileException ) {
70
71           // notify user of error
72           MessageBox::Show( fileException->Message, S"Error",
73              MessageBoxButtons::OK, MessageBoxIcon::Error );
74        } // end catch
75     } // end else
76
77     // close FileStream
78     if ( fileOutput == NULL )
79        fileOutput->Close();
80
81     // close BinaryWriter
82     if ( binaryOutput == NULL )
83        binaryOutput->Close();
84  } // end method SaveFile
```

Fig. 14.30 `CreateRandomAccessFile` class method definitions. (Part 2 of 2.)

```
1   // Fig. 14.31: CreateRandom.cpp
2   // Entry point for application.
3
4   #include "CreateRandomAccessFile.h"
5
6   int __stdcall WinMain()
7   {
8      // create random file, then save to disk
9      CreateRandomAccessFile *file = new CreateRandomAccessFile();
10     file->SaveFile();
11
12     return 0;
13  } // end function WinMain
```

Fig. 14.31 Creating a new random-access file. (Part 1 of 2.)

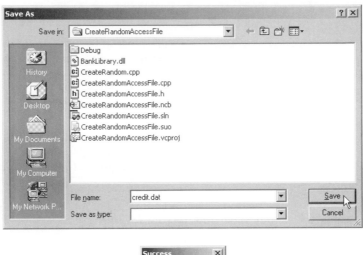

Fig. 14.31 Creating a new random-access file. (Part 2 of 2.)

Function **WinMain** (Fig. 14.31) starts the application, which creates a random-access file by calling the user-defined method **SaveFile** (lines 7–84 of Fig. 14.30). Method **SaveFile** populates a file with 100 copies of the default (i.e., empty) values for **private** data members **account**, **firstName**, **lastName** and **balance** of class **RandomAccessRecord**. Lines 19–21 create and display the **SaveFileDialog**, which enables a user to specify the file to which the program writes data. Lines 40–41 instantiate the **FileStream**. Note that line 41 passes constant **FileMode::Create**, which either creates the specified file (if the file does not exist), or overwrites the specified file (if it does exist). Lines 44–45 set the **FileStream**'s length, which is equal to the size of an individual **RandomAccessRecord** (obtained through constant **RandomAccessRecord::SIZE**) multiplied by the number of records we want to copy (obtained through constant **NUMBER_OF_RECORDS** (line 28 of Fig. 14.29), which we set to value **100**).

We now require a means to write bytes to a file. Class *BinaryWriter* of namespace **System::IO** provides methods for writing bytes to streams. The **BinaryWriter** constructor takes as an argument a pointer to an instance of class **Stream**, through which the **BinaryWriter** can write bytes. Class **FileStream** provides methods for writing streams to files and inherits from class **Stream**, so we can pass the **FileStream** pointer as an argument to the **BinaryWriter** constructor (line 48 of Fig. 14.30). Now, we can use the **BinaryWriter** to write bytes directly to the file.

Lines 51–61 populate the file with 100 copies of the empty record values (i.e., default values for **private** data members of class **RandomAccessRecord**). Line 54 changes the file-position pointer to specify the location in the file at which to write the next empty record. Now that we are working with a random-access file, we must set the file-pointer explicitly, using the **FileStream** object's **Position** property. This property receives as an argument a **long** value describing where to position the pointer relative to the beginning of the file—in this example, we set the pointer so that it advances a number of bytes that is equal to the record size (obtained by **RandomAccessRecord::SIZE**). Lines 57–60 call method **Write** of the **BinaryWriter** object to write the data. Method **Write** is an overloaded method that receives as an argument any primitive data type, then writes that type to a stream of bytes. After the **for** loop exits, lines 78–83 close the **FileStream** and **BinaryWriter** objects.

14.9 Writing Data "Randomly" to a Random-Access File

Now that we have created a random-access file, we use class **WriteRandomAccess-FileForm** (Fig. 14.32–Fig. 14.33) to write data to that file. When a user clicks the **Open File** button, the program invokes method **openButton_Click** (lines 66–108 of Fig. 14.33), which displays the **OpenFileDialog** for specifying the file in which to serialize data (lines 70–72); the program then uses the specified file to create a **FileStream** object with write-only access (lines 91–92). Line 95 uses the **FileStream** pointer to instantiate an object of class **BinaryWriter**, enabling the program to write bytes to files. We used the same approach when working with class **CreateRandomAccessFile** (Fig. 14.29–Fig. 14.30).

```
1    // Fig. 14.32: WriteRandomAccessFile.h
2    // Write data to a random-access file.
3
4    #pragma once
5
6    #using <system.dll>
7    #using <mscorlib.dll>
8    #using <system.drawing.dll>
9    #using <system.windows.forms.dll>
10   #using <BankLibrary.dll>
11
12   // Visual C++ .NET namespaces
13   using namespace System;
14   using namespace System::Drawing;
15   using namespace System::Windows::Forms;
16   using namespace System::IO;
17
18   // Deitel namespace
19   using namespace BankLibrary;
20
21   #include <tchar.h>
22
23   // number of RandomAccessRecords to write to disk
24   #define NUMBER_OF_RECORDS 100
```

Fig. 14.32 Writing records to random-access files. (Part 1 of 2.)

```
25
26   public __gc class WriteRandomAccessFileForm : public BankUIForm
27   {
28   public:
29      WriteRandomAccessFileForm();
30
31   private:
32      Button *openButton;
33      Button *enterButton;
34
35      // stream through which data are written to file
36      FileStream *fileOutput;
37
38      // stream for writing bytes to file
39      BinaryWriter *binaryOutput;
40
41      void InitializeComponent();
42      void openButton_Click( Object *, EventArgs * );
43      void enterButton_Click( Object *, EventArgs * );
44   }; // end class WriteRandomAccessFileForm
```

Fig. 14.32 Writing records to random-access files. (Part 2 of 2.)

```
1    // Fig. 14.33: WriteRandomAccessFile.cpp
2    // Method definitions for class WriteRandomAccessFileForm.
3
4    #include "WriteRandomAccessFile.h"
5
6    WriteRandomAccessFileForm::WriteRandomAccessFileForm()
7    {
8       InitializeComponent();
9    }
10
11   void WriteRandomAccessFileForm::InitializeComponent()
12   {
13      this->openButton = new Button();
14      this->enterButton = new Button();
15
16      this->SuspendLayout();
17
18      // set tab indices
19      this->accountTextBox->TabIndex = 1;
20      this->firstNameTextBox->TabIndex = 2;
21      this->lastNameTextBox->TabIndex = 3;
22      this->balanceTextBox->TabIndex = 4;
23
24      // openButton
25      this->openButton->Font = new Drawing::Font(
26         S"Microsoft Sans Serif", 10.0 );
```

Fig. 14.33 WriteRandomAccessFileForm class method definitions. (Part 1 of 4.)

```
27      this->openButton->ImageAlign = ContentAlignment::BottomCenter;
28      this->openButton->Location = Point( 32, 232 );
29      this->openButton->Name = S"openButton";
30      this->openButton->Size = Drawing::Size( 144, 32 );
31      this->openButton->TabIndex = 0;
32      this->openButton->Text = S"Open File";
33      this->openButton->Click += new EventHandler( this,
34         this->openButton_Click );
35
36      // enterButton
37      this->enterButton->Enabled = false;
38      this->enterButton->Font = new Drawing::Font(
39         S"Microsoft Sans Serif", 10.0 );
40      this->enterButton->ImageAlign = ContentAlignment::BottomCenter;
41      this->enterButton->Location = Point( 216, 232 );
42      this->enterButton->Name = S"enterButton";
43      this->enterButton->Size = Drawing::Size( 144, 32 );
44      this->enterButton->TabIndex = 5;
45      this->enterButton->Text = S"Enter";
46      this->enterButton->Click += new EventHandler( this,
47         this->enterButton_Click );
48
49      // WriteRandomAccessFileForm
50      this->AutoScaleBaseSize = Drawing::Size( 6, 15 );
51      this->ClientSize = Drawing::Size( 400, 279 );
52
53      Control *controls[] = { this->balanceTextBox,
54         this->lastNameTextBox, this->firstNameTextBox,
55         this->accountTextBox, this->balanceLabel,
56         this->lastNameLabel, this->firstNameLabel,
57         this->accountLabel, this->enterButton, this->openButton };
58      this->Controls->AddRange( controls );
59      this->Name = S"WriteRandomAccessFileForm";
60      this->Text = S"Write Random-Access File";
61
62      this->ResumeLayout();
63   } // end method InitializeComponent
64
65   // invoked when user clicks Open File button
66   void WriteRandomAccessFileForm::openButton_Click(
67      Object *sender, EventArgs *e )
68   {
69      // create dialog box enabling user to open file
70      OpenFileDialog *fileChooser = new OpenFileDialog();
71      Windows::Forms::DialogResult result =
72         fileChooser->ShowDialog();
73
74      // get file name from user
75      String *fileName = fileChooser->FileName;
76
77      // exit event handler if user clicked Cancel
78      if ( result == DialogResult::Cancel )
79         return;
```

Fig. 14.33 `WriteRandomAccessFileForm` class method definitions. (Part 2 of 4.)

```
80
81      // show error if user specified invalid file
82      if ( fileName->Equals( S"" ) || fileName == NULL )
83         MessageBox::Show( S"Invalid File Name", S"Error",
84            MessageBoxButtons::OK, MessageBoxIcon::Error );
85      else {
86
87         // open file if file already exists
88         try {
89
90            // create FileStream to hold records
91            fileOutput = new FileStream( fileName,
92               FileMode::Open, FileAccess::Write );
93
94            // create object for writing bytes to file
95            binaryOutput = new BinaryWriter( fileOutput );
96
97            // disable Open File button and enable Enter button
98            openButton->Enabled = false;
99            enterButton->Enabled = true;
100        } // end try
101
102        // notify user if file does not exist
103        catch ( IOException * ) {
104           MessageBox::Show( S"File Does Not Exits", S"Error",
105              MessageBoxButtons::OK, MessageBoxIcon::Error );
106        } // end catch
107     } // end else
108  } // end method openButton_Click
109
110  // invoked when user clicks Enter button
111  void WriteRandomAccessFileForm::enterButton_Click(
112     Object *sender, EventArgs *e )
113  {
114     // TextBox values string array
115     String *values[] = GetTextBoxValues();
116
117     // determine whether TextBox account field is empty
118     if ( values[ TextBoxIndices::ACCOUNT ] != S"" ) {
119
120        // write record to file at appropriate position
121        try {
122
123           // get account number value from TextBox
124           int accountNumber = Int32::Parse(
125              values[ TextBoxIndices::ACCOUNT ] );
126
127           // determine whether accountNumber is valid
128           if ( accountNumber > 0 &&
129              accountNumber <= NUMBER_OF_RECORDS ) {
130
```

Fig. 14.33 `WriteRandomAccessFileForm` class method definitions. (Part 3 of 4.)

```
131                      // move file position pointer
132                      fileOutput->Seek( ( accountNumber - 1 ) *
133                         RandomAccessRecord::SIZE, SeekOrigin::Begin );
134
135                      // write data to file
136                      binaryOutput->Write( accountNumber );
137                      binaryOutput->Write(
138                         values[ TextBoxIndices::FIRST ] );
139                      binaryOutput->Write(
140                         values[ TextBoxIndices::LAST ] );
141                      binaryOutput->Write( Double::Parse( values[
142                         TextBoxIndices::BALANCE ] ) );
143                   } // end if
144                   else {
145
146                      // notify user if invalid account number
147                      MessageBox::Show( S"Invalid Account Number",
148                         S"Error", MessageBoxButtons::OK,
149                         MessageBoxIcon::Error);
150                   } // end else
151                } // end try
152
153                // handle number-format exception
154                catch ( FormatException * ) {
155
156                   // notify user if error occurs when formatting numbers
157                   MessageBox::Show( S"Invalid Balance", S"Error",
158                      MessageBoxButtons::OK, MessageBoxIcon::Error );
159                } // end catch
160             } // end if
161
162          ClearTextBoxes(); // clear text box values
163       } // end method enterButton_Click
```

Fig. 14.33 `WriteRandomAccessFileForm` class method definitions. (Part 4 of 4.)

```
1    // Fig. 14.34: WriteRandom.cpp
2    // Entry point for application.
3
4    #include "WriteRandomAccessFile.h"
5
6    int __stdcall WinMain()
7    {
8       Application::Run( new WriteRandomAccessFileForm() );
9
10      return 0;
11   } // end function WinMain
```

Fig. 14.34 `WriteRandomAccessFileForm` class driver. (Part 1 of 3.)

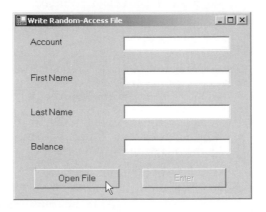

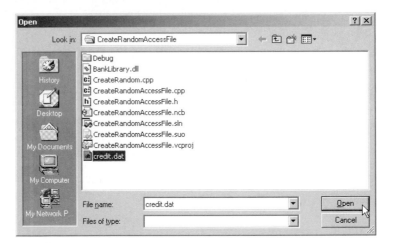

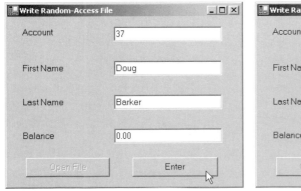
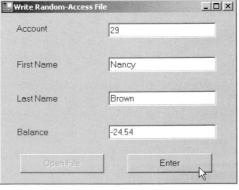

Fig. 14.34 WriteRandomAccessFileForm class driver. (Part 2 of 3.)

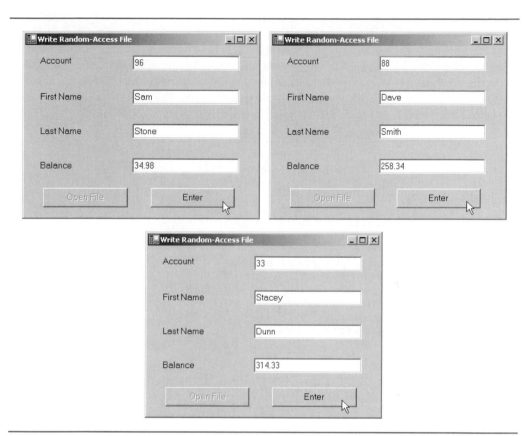

Fig. 14.34 `WriteRandomAccessFileForm` class driver. (Part 3 of 3.)

The user enters values in the **TextBox**es for the account number, first name, last name and balance. When the user clicks the **Enter** button, the program invokes method `enterButton_Click` (lines 111–163), which writes the data in the **TextBox**es to the file. Line 115 calls method `GetTextBoxValues` (provided by base class `BankUI-Form`) to retrieve the data. Lines 128–129 determine whether the **Account Number TextBox** holds valid information (i.e., the account number is in the range **1–100**).

Class `WriteRandomAccessFileForm` must calculate the location in the `FileStream` at which to insert the data from the **TextBox**es. Lines 132–133 use method `Seek` of the `FileStream` object to locate an exact point in the file. In this case, method `Seek` sets the position of the file-position pointer for the `FileStream` object to the byte location calculated by (`accountNumber - 1`) `* RandomAccessRecord::SIZE`. Because the account numbers range from **1** to **100**, we subtract **1** from the account number when calculating the byte location of the record. For example, our use of method `Seek` sets the first record's file-position pointer to byte 0 of the file (the file's beginning). The second argument to method `Seek` is a member of the enumeration `SeekOrigin` and specifies the location at which the method should begin seeking. We use `const SeekOrigin::Begin`, because we want the method to seek in relation to the beginning of the file. After the program determines the file location at which to place the record, lines 136–142 write the record to the file, using the `BinaryWriter` (discussed in the previous section).

14.10 Reading Data Sequentially from a Random-Access File

In the previous sections, we created a random-access file and wrote data to that file. Here, we develop a program (Fig. 14.35–Fig. 14.37) that opens the file, reads records from it and displays only the records that contain data (i.e., those records in which the account number is not zero). This program also provides an additional benefit. The reader should attempt to determine what it is—we will reveal it at the end of this section.

```cpp
1   // Fig. 14.35: ReadRandomAccessFile.h
2   // Reads and displays random-access file contents.
3
4   #pragma once
5
6   #using <system.dll>
7   #using <mscorlib.dll>
8   #using <system.drawing.dll>
9   #using <system.windows.forms.dll>
10  #using <BankLibrary.dll>
11
12  // Visual C++ .NET namespaces
13  using namespace System;
14  using namespace System::Drawing;
15  using namespace System::Windows::Forms;
16  using namespace System::IO;
17
18  // Deitel namespace
19  using namespace BankLibrary;
20
21  #include <tchar.h>
22
23  public __gc class ReadRandomAccessFileForm : public BankUIForm
24  {
25  public:
26     ReadRandomAccessFileForm();
27
28  private:
29     Button *openButton;
30     Button *nextButton;
31
32     // stream through which data are read from file
33     FileStream *fileInput;
34
35     // stream for reading bytes from file
36     BinaryReader *binaryInput;
37
38     // index of current record to be displayed
39     int currentRecordIndex;
40
41     void InitializeComponent();
42     void openButton_Click( Object *, EventArgs * );
43     void nextButton_Click( Object *, EventArgs * );
44  }; // end class ReadRandomAccessFileForm
```

Fig. 14.35 Reading records from random-access files sequentially.

```cpp
1    // Fig. 14.36: ReadRandomAccessFile.cpp
2    // Method definitions for class ReadRandomAccessFileForm.
3
4    #include "ReadRandomAccessFile.h"
5
6    ReadRandomAccessFileForm::ReadRandomAccessFileForm()
7    {
8       InitializeComponent();
9    }
10
11   void ReadRandomAccessFileForm::InitializeComponent()
12   {
13      this->openButton = new Button();
14      this->nextButton = new Button();
15
16      this->SuspendLayout();
17
18      // set tab indices
19      this->accountTextBox->TabIndex = 1;
20      this->firstNameTextBox->TabIndex = 2;
21      this->lastNameTextBox->TabIndex = 3;
22      this->balanceTextBox->TabIndex = 4;
23
24      // openButton
25      this->openButton->Font = new Drawing::Font(
26         S"Microsoft Sans Serif", 10.0 );
27      this->openButton->Location = Point( 32, 232 );
28      this->openButton->Name = S"openButton";
29      this->openButton->Size = Drawing::Size( 144, 32 );
30      this->openButton->TabIndex = 80;
31      this->openButton->Text = S"Open File";
32      this->openButton->Click += new EventHandler( this,
33         this->openButton_Click );
34
35      // nextButton
36      this->nextButton->Enabled = false;
37      this->nextButton->Font = new Drawing::Font(
38         S"Microsoft Sans Serif", 10.0 );
39      this->nextButton->Location = Point( 216, 232 );
40      this->nextButton->Name = S"nextButton";
41      this->nextButton->Size = Drawing::Size( 144, 32 );
42      this->nextButton->TabIndex = 5;
43      this->nextButton->Text = S"Next";
44      this->nextButton->Click += new EventHandler( this,
45         this->nextButton_Click );
46
47      // ReadRandomAccessFileForm
48      this->AutoScaleBaseSize = Drawing::Size( 6, 15 );
49      this->ClientSize = Drawing::Size( 400, 279 );
50
51      Control *controls[] = { this->balanceTextBox,
52         this->lastNameTextBox, this->firstNameTextBox,
53         this->accountTextBox, this->balanceLabel,
```

Fig. 14.36 ReadRandomAccessFileForm class method definitions. (Part 1 of 3.)

```
54            this->lastNameLabel, this->firstNameLabel,
55            this->accountLabel, this->nextButton, this->openButton };
56         this->Controls->AddRange( controls );
57         this->Name = S"ReadRandomAccessFileForm";
58         this->Text = S"Read Random-Access File";
59
60         this->ResumeLayout();
61      } // end method InitializeComponent
62
63      // invoked when user clicks Open File button
64      void ReadRandomAccessFileForm::openButton_Click(
65         Object *sender, EventArgs *e )
66      {
67         // create dialog box enabling user to open file
68         OpenFileDialog *fileChooser = new OpenFileDialog();
69         Windows::Forms::DialogResult result =
70            fileChooser->ShowDialog();
71
72         // get file name from user
73         String *fileName = fileChooser->FileName;
74
75         // exit eventhandler if user clicked Cancel
76         if ( result == DialogResult::Cancel )
77            return;
78
79         // show error if user specified invalid file
80         if ( fileName->Equals( S"" ) || fileName == NULL )
81            MessageBox::Show( S"Invalid File Name", S"Error",
82               MessageBoxButtons::OK, MessageBoxIcon::Error );
83         else {
84
85            // create FileStream to obtain read access to file
86            fileInput = new FileStream( fileName,
87               FileMode::Open, FileAccess::Read );
88
89            // use FileStream for BinaryWriter to read bytes from file
90            binaryInput = new BinaryReader( fileInput );
91
92            openButton->Enabled = false; // disable Open File button
93            nextButton->Enabled = true; // enable Next button
94
95            currentRecordIndex = 0;
96            ClearTextBoxes();
97         } // end else
98      } // end method openButton_Click
99
100     // invoked when user clicks Next button
101     void ReadRandomAccessFileForm::nextButton_Click(
102        Object *sender, EventArgs *e )
103     {
104        // record to store file data
105        RandomAccessRecord *record = new RandomAccessRecord();
106
```

Fig. 14.36 ReadRandomAccessFileForm class method definitions. (Part 2 of 3.)

```
107        // read record and store data in TextBoxes
108        try {
109
110           // get next record available in file
111           while( record->Account == 0 ) {
112
113              // set file position pointer to next record in file
114              fileInput->Seek(
115                 currentRecordIndex * RandomAccessRecord::SIZE,
116                 SeekOrigin::Begin );
117
118              currentRecordIndex += 1;
119
120              // read data from record
121              record->Account = binaryInput->ReadInt32();
122              record->FirstName = binaryInput->ReadString();
123              record->LastName = binaryInput->ReadString();
124              record->Balance = binaryInput->ReadDouble();
125           } // end while
126
127           // store record values in temporary string array
128           String *values[] = {
129              record->Account.ToString(),
130              record->FirstName->ToString(),
131              record->LastName->ToString(),
132              record->Balance.ToString() };
133
134           // copy string array values to TextBox values
135           SetTextBoxValues( values );
136        } // end while
137
138        // handle exception when no records in file
139        catch ( IOException * ) {
140
141           // close streams if no records in file
142           fileInput->Close();
143           binaryInput->Close();
144
145           openButton->Enabled = true; // enable Open File button
146           nextButton->Enabled = false; // disable Next button
147           ClearTextBoxes();
148
149           // notify user if no records in file
150           MessageBox::Show( S"No more records in file", S"",
151              MessageBoxButtons::OK, MessageBoxIcon::Information );
152        } // end catch
153     } // end method nextButton_Click
```

Fig. 14.36 `ReadRandomAccessFileForm` class method definitions. (Part 3 of 3.)

```
1    // Fig. 14.37: ReadRandom.cpp
2    // Entry point for application.
```

Fig. 14.37 `ReadRandomAccessFileForm` class driver. (Part 1 of 3.)

```
3
4   #include "ReadRandomAccessFile.h"
5
6   int __stdcall WinMain()
7   {
8      Application::Run( new ReadRandomAccessFileForm() );
9
10     return 0;
11  } // end WinMain
```

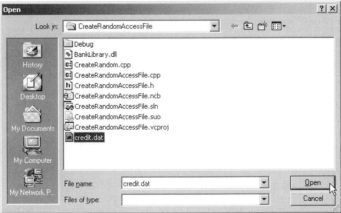

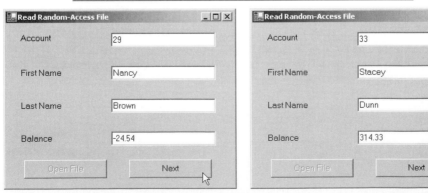

Fig. 14.37 ReadRandomAccessFileForm class driver. (Part 2 of 3.)

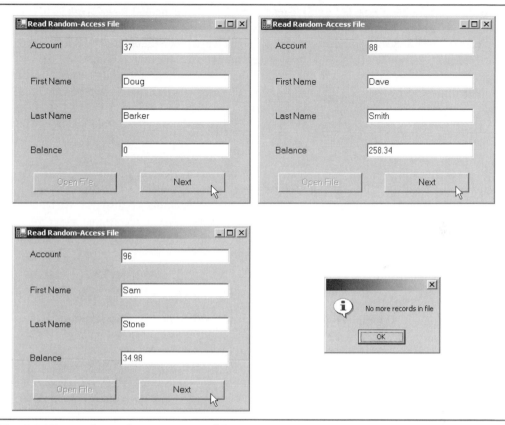

Fig. 14.37 `ReadRandomAccessFileForm` class driver. (Part 3 of 3.)

When the user clicks the **Open File** button, class `ReadRandomAccessFileForm` invokes method `openButton_Click` (lines 64–98 of Fig. 14.36), which displays the `OpenFileDialog` for specifying the file from which to read data. Lines 86–87 instantiate a `FileStream` object that opens a file with read-only access. Line 90 creates an instance of class *BinaryReader*, which reads bytes from a stream. We pass the `FileStream` pointer as an argument to the `BinaryReader` constructor, thus enabling the `BinaryReader` to read bytes from the file.

When the user clicks the **Next** button, the program calls method `nextButton_Click` (lines 101–153), which reads the next record from the file. Line 105 instantiates a **RandomAccessRecord** for storing the record data from the file. Lines 111–125 define a **while** loop that reads from the file until it reaches a record that has a non-zero account number (**0** is the initial value for the account number and indicates an empty record). Lines 114–116 call method **Seek** of the `FileStream` object, which moves the file-position pointer to the appropriate place in the file where the record must be read. To accomplish this, method **Seek** uses **int currentRecordIndex**, which stores the number of records that have been read. Lines 121–124 use the `BinaryReader` object to store the file data in the `RandomAccessRecord` object. Recall that class `BinaryWriter` provides overloaded **Write** methods for writing data. However, class `BinaryReader` does not provide overloaded **Read** methods to read data. This means that we must use method *ReadInt32* to read an **int**, method *ReadString* to read a **String *** and method *ReadDouble* to read a **double**. Note that the order of these method invocations must correspond to the order in which the **BinaryWriter** object wrote each data type. When the **BinaryReader** reads a valid account number (i.e., a non-zero value), the loop terminates, and lines 128–135 display the record values in the **TextBox**es. When the program has displayed all records, method **Seek** throws an **IOException** (because method **Seek** tries to position the file-position pointer to a location that is beyond the end-of-file marker). The **catch** block (lines 139–152) handles this exception by closing the **FileStream** and **BinaryReader** objects (lines 142–143) and notifying the user that no more records exist (lines 150–151).

What about that additional benefit we promised? If readers examine the GUI as the program executes, they will notice that the program displays the records in ascending order by account number! This is a simple consequence of using our direct-access techniques to store these records in the file. Sorting with direct-access techniques is also fast. We achieve this speed by making the file large enough to hold every possible record that a user might create. Of course, this means that the file could be sparsely occupied most of the time, resulting in a waste of storage. Here is yet another example of the space/time trade-off: By using large amounts of space, we are able to develop a fast sorting algorithm.

14.11 Case Study: A Transaction-Processing Program

We now develop a substantial transaction-processing program (Fig. 14.38–Fig. 14.51), using a random-access file to achieve "instant-access" processing. The program maintains a bank's account information. Users of this program can add new accounts, update existing accounts and delete accounts that are no longer needed. First, we discuss the transaction-processing behavior (i.e., the class that enables the addition, updating and removal of accounts). We then discuss the GUI, which contains windows that display the account information and enable the user to invoke the application's transaction-processing behavior. Note that this example is only a simple transaction-processing program. More information about processing transactions in .NET can be found at

> msdn.microsoft.com/library/default.asp?url=/library/en-us/
> cpguide/html/cpconprocessingtransactions.asp

Transaction-Processing Behavior
In this case study, we create class **Transaction** (Fig. 14.38–Fig. 14.39), which acts as a proxy to handle all transaction processing. Rather than providing the transaction-processing behavior themselves, the objects in this application use an instance of **Transaction** to provide the necessary functionality. By using a proxy, we can encapsulate transaction-processing behavior in only one class, enabling various other classes in our application to reuse this behavior. Furthermore, if we decide to modify this behavior, we need modify only the proxy (i.e., class **Transaction**), instead of having to modify the behavior of each class that uses the proxy.

```
1   // Fig. 14.38: Transaction.h
2   // Handles record transactions.
3
4   #pragma once
5
```

Fig. 14.38 Record-transaction class for the transaction-processor case study. (Part 1 of 2.)

```
6    #using <mscorlib.dll>
7    #using <system.dll>
8    #using <system.drawing.dll>
9    #using <system.windows.forms.dll>
10   #using <BankLibrary.dll>
11
12   // Visual C++ .NET namespaces
13   using namespace System;
14   using namespace System::IO;
15   using namespace System::Drawing;
16   using namespace System::Windows::Forms;
17   using namespace
18      System::Runtime::Serialization::Formatters::Binary;
19   using namespace System::Runtime::Serialization;
20
21   // Deitel namespace
22   using namespace BankLibrary;
23
24   #include <tchar.h>
25
26   // number of records to write to disk
27   #define NUMBER_OF_RECORDS 100
28
29   public __gc class Transaction
30   {
31   public:
32      void OpenFile( String * );
33      RandomAccessRecord *GetRecord( String * );
34      bool AddRecord( RandomAccessRecord *, int );
35
36   private:
37
38      // stream through which data moves to and from file
39      FileStream *file;
40
41      // stream for reading bytes from file
42      BinaryReader *binaryInput;
43
44      // stream for writing bytes to file
45      BinaryWriter *binaryOutput;
46   }; // end class Transaction
```

Fig. 14.38 Record-transaction class for the transaction-processor case study. (Part 2 of 2.)

```
1    // Fig. 14.39: Transaction.cpp
2    // Method definitions for class Transaction.
3
4    #include "Transaction.h"
5
6    // create/open file containing empty records
7    void Transaction::OpenFile( String *fileName )
8    {
```

Fig. 14.39 Transaction class handles record transactions. (Part 1 of 4.)

```cpp
 9      // write empty records to file
10      try {
11
12         // create FileStream from new file or existing file
13         file = new FileStream( fileName, FileMode::OpenOrCreate );
14
15         // use FileStream for BinaryWriter to read bytes from file
16         binaryInput = new BinaryReader( file );
17
18         // use FileStream for BinaryWriter to write bytes to file
19         binaryOutput = new BinaryWriter( file );
20
21         // determine whether file has just been created
22         if ( file->Length == 0 ) {
23
24            // record to be written to file
25            RandomAccessRecord *blankRecord =
26               new RandomAccessRecord();
27
28            // new record can hold NUMBER_OF_RECORDS records
29            file->SetLength( RandomAccessRecord::SIZE *
30               NUMBER_OF_RECORDS );
31
32            // write blank records to file
33            for ( int i = 1; i <= NUMBER_OF_RECORDS; i++ )
34               AddRecord( blankRecord, i );
35
36         } // end if
37      } // end try
38
39      // notify user of error during writing of blank records
40      catch ( IOException *fileException ) {
41         MessageBox::Show( fileException->Message, S"Error",
42            MessageBoxButtons::OK, MessageBoxIcon::Error );
43      } // end catch
44   } // end method OpenFile
45
46   // retrieve record depending on whether account is valid
47   RandomAccessRecord *Transaction::GetRecord(
48      String *accountValue )
49   {
50      // store file data associated with account in record
51      try {
52
53         // record to store file data
54         RandomAccessRecord *record = new RandomAccessRecord();
55
56         // get value from TextBox's account field
57         int accountNumber = Int32::Parse( accountValue );
58
59         // if account is invalid, do not read data
60         if ( accountNumber < 1 ||
61            accountNumber > NUMBER_OF_RECORDS ) {
```

Fig. 14.39 Transaction class handles record transactions. (Part 2 of 4.)

```
62
63                        // set record's account field with account number
64                        record->Account = accountNumber;
65              }
66
67          // get data from file if account is valid
68          else {
69
70              // locate position in file where record exists
71              file->Seek( ( accountNumber - 1 ) *
72                  RandomAccessRecord::SIZE, SeekOrigin::Begin );
73
74              // read data from record
75              record->Account = binaryInput->ReadInt32();
76              record->FirstName = binaryInput->ReadString();
77              record->LastName = binaryInput->ReadString();
78              record->Balance = binaryInput->ReadDouble();
79          } // end else
80
81          return record;
82      } // end try
83
84      // notify user of error during reading
85      catch ( IOException *fileException ) {
86          MessageBox::Show( fileException->Message, S"Error",
87              MessageBoxButtons::OK, MessageBoxIcon::Error );
88      } // end catch
89
90      return 0;
91  } // end method GetRecord
92
93  // add record to file at position determined by accountNumber
94  bool Transaction::AddRecord( RandomAccessRecord *record,
95      int accountNumber )
96  {
97      // write record to file
98      try {
99
100         // move file position pointer to appropriate position
101         file->Seek( ( accountNumber - 1 ) *
102             RandomAccessRecord::SIZE, SeekOrigin::Begin );
103
104         // write data to file
105         binaryOutput->Write( record->Account );
106         binaryOutput->Write( record->FirstName );
107         binaryOutput->Write( record->LastName );
108         binaryOutput->Write( record->Balance );
109     } // end try
110
111     // notify user if error occurs during writing
112     catch ( IOException *fileException ) {
113         MessageBox::Show( fileException->Message, S"Error",
114             MessageBoxButtons::OK, MessageBoxIcon::Error );
```

Fig. 14.39 Transaction class handles record transactions. (Part 3 of 4.)

```
115
116        return false; // failure
117    } // end catch
118
119    return true; // success
120 } // end method AddRecord
```

Fig. 14.39 `Transaction` class handles record transactions. (Part 4 of 4.)

Class **Transaction** contains methods **OpenFile**, **GetRecord** and **Add-Record**. Method **OpenFile** (lines 7–44 of Fig. 14.39) uses constant **FileMode::OpenOrCreate** (line 13) to create a **FileStream** object from either an existing file or one not yet created. Lines 16–19 use this **FileStream** to create **BinaryReader** and **BinaryWriter** objects for reading and writing bytes to the file, respectively. If the file is new, lines 25–34 populate the **FileStream** object with empty records. Lines 25–26 create a new **RandomAccessRecord** (with account number **0**). The **for** loop in lines 33–34 then adds this empty record to every position in the file (i.e., for account numbers in range **1–NUMBER_OF_RECORDS**).

Method **GetRecord** (lines 47–91) returns the record associated with the account-number parameter. Line 54 instantiates a **RandomAccessRecord** object that will store the file data. If the account parameter is valid, lines 71–72 call method **Seek** of the **FileStream** object, which uses the parameter to calculate the position of the specified record in the file. Lines 75–78 then call methods **ReadInt32**, **ReadString** and **Read-Double** of the **BinaryReader** object to store the file data in the **Random-AccessRecord** object. Line 89 returns the **RandomAccessRecord** object. We used these techniques in Section 14.10.

Method **AddRecord** (lines 94–120) inserts a record into the file. Lines 101–102 call method **Seek** of the **FileStream** object, which uses the **accountNumber** parameter to locate the position at which to insert the record in the file. Lines 105–108 call the overloaded **Write** methods of the **BinaryWriter** object to write the **RandomAccessRecord** object's data to the file. We used these techniques in Section 14.9. Note that, if an error occurs when adding the record (i.e., either the **FileStream** or the **BinaryWriter** throws an **IOException**), lines 113–116 notify the user of the error and return **false** (failure).

Transaction-Processor GUI

The GUI for this program uses a multiple-document interface. Class **Transaction-ProcessorForm** (Fig. 14.40–Fig. 14.41) is the parent window; it contains corresponding child windows **StartDialogForm** (Fig. 14.43–Fig. 14.44), **NewDialogForm** (Fig. 14.46–Fig. 14.47), **UpdateDialogForm** (Fig. 14.48–Fig. 14.49) and **Delete-DialogForm** (Fig. 14.50–Fig. 14.51). **StartDialogForm** allows the user to open a file containing account information and provides access to the **NewDialogForm**, **UpdateDialogForm** and **DeleteDialogForm** internal frames. These frames allow users to update, create and delete records, respectively.

Initially, **TransactionProcessorForm** displays the **StartDialogForm** object; this window provides the user with various options. It contains four buttons, which enable the user to create or open a file, create a record, update an existing record or delete an existing record.

```
1   // Fig. 14.40: TransactionProcessor.h
2   // MDI parent for transaction-processor application.
3
4   #pragma once
5
6   #include <tchar.h>
7   #include "StartDialog.h"
8
9   public __gc class TransactionProcessorForm : public Form
10  {
11  public:
12     TransactionProcessorForm();
13
14  private:
15     MdiClient *MdiClient1;
16
17     // pointer to StartDialog
18     StartDialogForm *startDialog;
19
20     void InitializeComponent();
21  }; // end class TransactionProcessorForm
```

Fig. 14.40 `TransactionProcessorForm` class demonstrates the transaction-processor application.

```
1   // Fig. 14.41: TransactionProcessor.cpp
2   // Method definitions for class TransactionProcessorForm.
3
4   #include "Transacti;onProcessor.h"
5
6   TransactionProcessorForm::TransactionProcessorForm()
7   {
8      InitializeComponent();
9
10     startDialog = new StartDialogForm();
11     startDialog->MdiParent = this;
12     startDialog->Show();
13  }
14
15  void TransactionProcessorForm::InitializeComponent()
16  {
17     this->MdiClient1 = new MdiClient();
18
19     this->SuspendLayout();
20
21     // MdiClient1
22     this->MdiClient1->Dock = DockStyle::Fill;
23     this->MdiClient1->Name = S"MdiClient1";
24     this->MdiClient1->TabIndex = 0;
25
26     // transactionProcessorForm
27     this->AutoScaleBaseSize = Drawing::Size( 6, 15 );
28     this->ClientSize = Drawing::Size( 675, 397 );
```

Fig. 14.41 `TransactionProcessorForm` class method definitions. (Part 1 of 2.)

```
29
30      Control *controls[] = { this->MdiClient1 };
31      this->Controls->AddRange( controls );
32      this->IsMdiContainer = true;
33      this->Name = S"transactionProcessorForm";
34      this->Text = S"Transaction Processor";
35
36      this->ResumeLayout();
37   } // end method InitializeComponent
```

Fig. 14.41 `TransactionProcessorForm` class method definitions. (Part 2 of 2.)

```
1    // Fig. 14.42: TransactionProcessorTest.cpp
2    // Entry point for application.
3
4    #include "TransactionProcessor.h"
5
6    int __stdcall WinMain()
7    {
8       Application::Run( new TransactionProcessorForm() );
9
10      return 0;
11   } // end function WinMain
```

Fig. 14.42 `TransactionProcessorForm` class driver.

Before the user can modify records, the user must either create or open a file. When the user clicks the **New/Open File** button, the program calls method **open-Button_Click** (lines 81–141 of Fig. 14.44), which opens a file that the application uses for modifying records. Lines 85–101 display the **OpenFileDialog** for specifying the file from which to read data, then use this file to create the **FileStream** object. Note that line 91 sets property **CheckFileExists** of the **OpenFileDialog** object to **false**—this enables the user to create a file if the specified file does not exist. If this property were **true** (its default value), the dialog would notify the user that the specified file does not exist, thus preventing the user from creating a file.

```
1    // Fig. 14.43: StartDialog.h
2    // Initial dialog box displayed to user. Provides buttons for
3    // creating/opening file and for adding, updating and removing
4    // records from file.
5
6    #pragma once
7
8    #include "NewDialog.h"
9    #include "DeleteDialog.h"
10   #include "UpdateDialog.h"
11   #include "MyDelegate.h"
```

Fig. 14.43 `StartDialogForm` class enables users to access dialog boxes associated with various transactions. (Part 1 of 2.)

```
12
13   public __gc class StartDialogForm : public Form
14   {
15   public:
16      StartDialogForm();
17
18   protected:
19      void ShowStartDialog();
20
21   private:
22      Button *updateButton;
23      Button *newButton;
24      Button *deleteButton;
25      Button *openButton;
26
27      // pointer to dialog box for adding record
28      NewDialogForm *newDialog;
29
30      // pointer to dialog box for updating record
31      UpdateDialogForm *updateDialog;
32
33      // pointer to dialog box for removing record
34      DeleteDialogForm *deleteDialog;
35
36      // pointer to object that handles transactions
37      Transaction *transactionProxy;
38
39      void InitializeComponent();
40      void openButton_Click( Object *, EventArgs * );
41      void newButton_Click( Object *, EventArgs * );
42      void updateButton_Click( Object *, EventArgs * );
43      void deleteButton_Click( Object *, EventArgs * );
44   }; // end class StartDialogForm
```

Fig. 14.43 `StartDialogForm` class enables users to access dialog boxes associated with various transactions. (Part 2 of 2.)

```
1    // Fig. 14.44: StartDialog.cpp
2    // Method definitions for class StartDialogForm.
3
4    #include "StartDialog.h"
5
6    StartDialogForm::StartDialogForm()
7    {
8       InitializeComponent();
9    }
10
11   void StartDialogForm::InitializeComponent()
12   {
13      this->updateButton = new Button();
14      this->newButton = new Button();
```

Fig. 14.44 `StartDialogForm` class method definitions. (Part 1 of 5.)

```
15      this->deleteButton = new Button();
16      this->openButton = new Button();
17
18      this->SuspendLayout();
19
20      // updateButton
21      this->updateButton->Enabled = false;
22      this->updateButton->Font = new Drawing::Font(
23         S"Microsoft Sans Serif", 10.0 );
24      this->updateButton->Location = Point( 16, 110 );
25      this->updateButton->Name = S"updateButton";
26      this->updateButton->Size = Drawing::Size( 150, 40 );
27      this->updateButton->TabIndex = 4;
28      this->updateButton->Text = S"Update Record";
29      this->updateButton->Click += new EventHandler( this,
30         this->updateButton_Click );
31
32      // newButton
33      this->newButton->Enabled = false;
34      this->newButton->Font = new Drawing::Font(
35         S"Microsoft Sans Serif", 10.0 );
36      this->newButton->Location = Point( 16, 60 );
37      this->newButton->Name = S"newButton";
38      this->newButton->Size = Drawing::Size( 150, 40 );
39      this->newButton->TabIndex = 5;
40      this->newButton->Text = S"New Record";
41      this->newButton->Click += new EventHandler( this,
42         this->newButton_Click );
43
44      // deleteButton
45      this->deleteButton->Enabled = false;
46      this->deleteButton->Font = new Drawing::Font(
47         S"Microsoft Sans Serif", 10.0 );
48      this->deleteButton->Location = Point( 16, 160 );
49      this->deleteButton->Name = S"deleteButton";
50      this->deleteButton->Size = Drawing::Size( 150, 40 );
51      this->deleteButton->TabIndex = 6;
52      this->deleteButton->Text = S"Delete Record";
53      this->deleteButton->Click += new EventHandler( this,
54         this->deleteButton_Click );
55
56      // openButton
57      this->openButton->Font = new Drawing::Font(
58         S"Microsoft Sans Serif", 10.0 );
59      this->openButton->Location = Point( 16, 10 );
60      this->openButton->Name = S"openButton";
61      this->openButton->Size = Drawing::Size( 150, 40 );
62      this->openButton->TabIndex = 7;
63      this->openButton->Text = S"New/Open File";
64      this->openButton->Click += new EventHandler( this,
65         this->openButton_Click );
```

Fig. 14.44 StartDialogForm class method definitions. (Part 2 of 5.)

```
66
67      // StartDialogForm
68      this->AutoScaleBaseSize = Drawing::Size( 6, 15 );
69      this->ClientSize = Drawing::Size( 184, 215 );
70   ;
71      Control *controls[] = { this->updateButton, this->newButton,
72         this->deleteButton, this->openButton };
73      this->Controls->AddRange( controls );
74      this->Name = S"StartDialogForm";
75      this->Text = S"Start Dialog";
76
77      this->ResumeLayout();
78   } // end method InitializeComponent
79
80   // invoked when user clicks New/Open File button
81   void StartDialogForm::openButton_Click(
82      Object *sender, EventArgs *e )
83   {
84      // create dialog box enabling user to create or open file
85      OpenFileDialog *fileChooser = new OpenFileDialog();
86      Windows::Forms::DialogResult result;
87      String *fileName;
88
89      // enable user to create file if file does not exist
90      fileChooser->Title = S"Create File / Open File";
91      fileChooser->CheckFileExists = false;
92
93      // show dialog box to user
94      result = fileChooser->ShowDialog();
95
96      // exit event handler if user clicked Cancel
97      if ( result == DialogResult::Cancel )
98         return;
99
100     // get file name from user
101     fileName = fileChooser->FileName;
102
103     // show error if user specified invalid file
104     if ( fileName == S"" || fileName == NULL )
105        MessageBox::Show( S"Invalid File Name", S"Error",
106           MessageBoxButtons::OK, MessageBoxIcon::Error );
107
108     // open or create file if user specified valid file
109     else {
110
111        // create Transaction with specified file
112        transactionProxy = new Transaction();
113        transactionProxy->OpenFile( fileName );
114
115        // enable GUI buttons except for New/Open File button
116        newButton->Enabled = true;
```

Fig. 14.44 StartDialogForm class method definitions. (Part 3 of 5.)

```
117            updateButton->Enabled = true;
118            deleteButton->Enabled = true;
119            openButton->Enabled = false;
120
121            // instantiate dialog box for creating records
122            newDialog = new NewDialogForm( transactionProxy,
123               new MyDelegate( this,
124               &StartDialogForm::ShowStartDialog ) );
125
126            // instantiate dialog box for updating records
127            updateDialog = new UpdateDialogForm( transactionProxy,
128               new MyDelegate( this,
129               &StartDialogForm::ShowStartDialog ) );
130
131            // instantiate dialog box for removing records
132            deleteDialog = new DeleteDialogForm( transactionProxy,
133               new MyDelegate( this,
134               &StartDialogForm::ShowStartDialog ) );
135
136            // set StartDialog as MdiParent for dialog boxes
137            newDialog->MdiParent = this->MdiParent;
138            updateDialog->MdiParent = this->MdiParent;
139            deleteDialog->MdiParent = this->MdiParent;
140       } // end else
141    } // end method openButton_Click
142
143    // invoked when user clicks New Record button
144    void StartDialogForm::newButton_Click(
145       Object *sender, EventArgs *e )
146    {
147       Hide(); // hide StartDialog
148       newDialog->Show(); // show NewDialog
149    } // end method newButton_Click
150
151    void StartDialogForm::updateButton_Click(
152       Object *sender, EventArgs *e )
153    {
154       Hide(); // hide StartDialog
155       updateDialog->Show(); // show UpdateDialog
156    } // end method updateButton_Click
157
158    void StartDialogForm::deleteButton_Click(
159       Object *sender, EventArgs *e )
160    {
161       Hide(); // hide StartDialog
162       deleteDialog->Show(); // show DeleteDialog
163    } // end method deleteButton_Click
164
165    void StartDialogForm::ShowStartDialog()
166    {
167       Show();
168    }
```

Fig. 14.44 StartDialogForm class method definitions. (Part 4 of 5.)

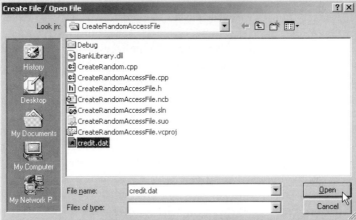

Fig. 14.44 `StartDialogForm` class method definitions. (Part 5 of 5.)

If the user specifies a file name, line 112 (of Fig. 14.44) instantiates an object of class **Transaction** (Fig. 14.38–Fig. 14.39), which acts as the proxy for creating, reading records from and writing records to random-access files. Line 113 calls **Transaction**'s method **OpenFile**, which either creates or opens the specified file, depending on whether the file does not exist or exists.

Class **StartDialogForm** also creates internal windows that enable the user to create, update and delete records. We do not use the default constructor; instead, we use an overloaded constructor that takes as arguments the **Transaction** object and a delegate object that points to method **ShowStartDialog** (lines 165–168). Each child window uses the second delegate parameter to display the **StartDialogForm** GUI when the user closes a child window. Lines 122–134 instantiate objects of classes **UpdateDialogForm**, **NewDialogForm** and **DeleteDialogForm**, which serve as the child windows.

When the user clicks the **New Record** button in the **Start Dialog**, the program invokes method **newButton_Click** of class **StartDialogForm** (lines 144–149 of Fig. 14.44), which displays the **NewDialogForm** internal frame (Fig. 14.46–Fig. 14.47). Class **NewDialogForm** enables the user to create records in the file that **StartDialogForm** opened (or created). Line 6 of Fig. 14.45 defines **MyDelegate** as a delegate to a method that does not return a value and has no parameters; method **ShowStartDialog** of class **StartDialogForm** (Fig. 14.44, lines 165–168) conforms to these requirements. Class **NewDialogForm** receives a **MyDelegate** pointer, which points to this method as a parameter—therefore, **NewDialogForm** can invoke this method to display the **StartDialogForm** when the user exits the **NewDialogForm**. Classes **UpdateDialogForm** and **DeleteDialogForm** also receive **MyDelegate** pointers as arguments, enabling them to display **StartDialogForm** after completing their tasks.

After the user enters data in the **TextBox**es of the **NewDialogForm** and clicks the **Save Record** button, the program invokes method **saveButton_Click** (lines 83–97 of Fig. 14.47) to write the record to disk. Lines 86–88 call method **GetRecord** of the **Transaction** object, which should return an empty **RandomAccessRecord**. If method **GetRecord** returns a **RandomAccessRecord** that contains data, the user is attempting to overwrite that **RandomAccessRecord** with a new one. Line 92 calls **private** method **InsertRecord** (lines 100–144). If the user is attempting to overwrite an existing record, lines 111–113 notify the user that the record already exists and return from the method. Otherwise, the **RandomAccessRecord** is empty, and method **InsertRecord** calls method **AddRecord** of the **Transaction** object (lines 130–131), which adds the newly created **RandomAccessRecord** to the file.

```
1   // Fig. 14.45: MyDelegate.h
2   // Declares MyDelegate as a delegate with no input or return values.
3
4   #pragma once
5
6   __delegate void MyDelegate();
```

Fig. 14.45 Delegate declaration used in transaction-processor case study.

```
1   // Fig. 14.46: NewDialog.h
2   // Enables user to insert new record into file.
3
```

Fig. 14.46 **NewDialogForm** class allows users to create new records. (Part 1 of 2.)

```
 4   #pragma once
 5
 6   #include "Transaction.h"
 7   #include "MyDelegate.h"
 8
 9   public __gc class NewDialogForm : public BankUIForm
10   {
11   public:
12      NewDialogForm();
13      NewDialogForm( Transaction *, MyDelegate * );
14
15      // delegate for method that displays previous window
16      MyDelegate *showPreviousWindow;
17
18   private:
19      Button *saveButton;
20      Button *cancelButton;
21
22      // pointer to object that handles transactions
23      Transaction *transactionProxy;
24
25      void InitializeComponent();
26      void cancelButton_Click( Object *, EventArgs * );
27      void saveButton_Click( Object *, EventArgs * );
28      void InsertRecord( RandomAccessRecord * );
29   }; // end class NewDialogForm
```

Fig. 14.46 NewDialogForm class allows users to create new records. (Part 2 of 2.)

```
 1   // Fig. 14.47: NewDialog.cpp
 2   // Method definitions for class NewDialogForm.
 3
 4   #include "NewDialog.h"
 5
 6   NewDialogForm::NewDialogForm()
 7   {
 8      InitializeComponent();
 9   }
10
11   NewDialogForm::NewDialogForm( Transaction *transactionProxyValue,
12      MyDelegate *delegateValue )
13   {
14      InitializeComponent();
15      showPreviousWindow = delegateValue;
16
17      // instantiate object that handles transactions
18      transactionProxy = transactionProxyValue;
19   }
20
```

Fig. 14.47 NewDialogForm class method definitions. (Part 1 of 4.)

```
21   void NewDialogForm::InitializeComponent()
22   {
23      this->saveButton = new Button();
24      this->cancelButton = new Button();
25
26      this->SuspendLayout();
27
28      // set tab indices
29      this->accountTextBox->TabIndex = 0;
30      this->firstNameTextBox->TabIndex = 1;
31      this->lastNameTextBox->TabIndex = 2;
32      this->balanceTextBox->TabIndex = 3;
33
34      // saveButton
35      this->saveButton->Font = new Drawing::Font(
36         S"Microsoft Sans Serif", 10.0 );
37      this->saveButton->Location = Point( 32, 232 );
38      this->saveButton->Name = S"saveButton";
39      this->saveButton->Size = Drawing::Size( 144, 32 );
40      this->saveButton->TabIndex = 4;
41      this->saveButton->Text = S"Save Record";
42      this->saveButton->Click += new EventHandler( this,
43         this->saveButton_Click );
44
45      // cancelButton
46      this->cancelButton->Font = new Drawing::Font(
47         S"Microsoft Sans Serif", 10.0 );
48      this->cancelButton->Location = Point( 216, 232 );
49      this->cancelButton->Name = S"cancelButton";
50      this->cancelButton->Size = Drawing::Size( 144, 32 );
51      this->cancelButton->TabIndex = 5;
52      this->cancelButton->Text = S"Cancel";
53      this->cancelButton->Click += new EventHandler( this,
54         this->cancelButton_Click );
55
56      // NewDialogForm
57      this->AutoScaleBaseSize = Drawing::Size( 6, 15 );
58      this->ClientSize = Drawing::Size( 400, 279 );
59
60      Control *control[] = { this->cancelButton,
61         this->balanceTextBox, this->lastNameTextBox,
62         this->firstNameTextBox, this->accountTextBox,
63         this->balanceLabel, this->lastNameLabel,
64         this->firstNameLabel, this->accountLabel,
65         this->saveButton };
66      this->Controls->AddRange( control );
67      this->Name = S"NewDialogForm";
68      this->Text = S"Create Record";
69
70      this->ResumeLayout();
71   } // end method InitializeComponent
72
73   // invoked when user clicks Cancel button
```

Fig. 14.47 NewDialogForm class method definitions. (Part 2 of 4.)

```
74   void NewDialogForm::cancelButton_Click( Object *sender,
75      EventArgs *e )
76   {
77      Hide();
78      ClearTextBoxes();
79      showPreviousWindow->Invoke();
80   } // end method cancelButton_Click
81
82   // invoked when user clicks Save Record button
83   void NewDialogForm::saveButton_Click( Object *sender,
84      EventArgs *e )
85   {
86      RandomAccessRecord *record =
87         transactionProxy->GetRecord( GetTextBoxValues()
88         [ TextBoxIndices::ACCOUNT ] );
89
90      // if record exists, add it to file
91      if ( record != NULL )
92         InsertRecord( record );
93
94      Hide();
95      ClearTextBoxes();
96      showPreviousWindow->Invoke();
97   } // end method saveButton_Click
98
99   // insert record in file at position specified by accountNumber
100  void NewDialogForm::InsertRecord( RandomAccessRecord *record )
101  {
102     //store TextBox values in string array
103     String *textBoxValues[] = GetTextBoxValues();
104
105     // store TextBox account field
106     int accountNumber = Int32::Parse(
107        textBoxValues[ TextBoxIndices::ACCOUNT ] );
108
109     // notify user and return if record account is not empty
110     if ( record->Account != 0 ) {
111        MessageBox::Show(
112           S"Record Already Exists or Invalid Number", S"Error",
113           MessageBoxButtons::OK, MessageBoxIcon::Error );
114
115        return;
116     }
117
118     // store values in record
119     record->Account = accountNumber;
120     record->FirstName =
121        textBoxValues[ TextBoxIndices::FIRST ];
122     record->LastName =
123        textBoxValues[ TextBoxIndices::LAST ];
124     record->Balance = Double::Parse(
125        textBoxValues[ TextBoxIndices::BALANCE ] );
126
```

Fig. 14.47 NewDialogForm class method definitions. (Part 3 of 4.)

```
127       // add record to file
128       try {
129
130          if ( transactionProxy->AddRecord(
131             record, accountNumber ) == false )
132
133             return; // if error
134       }
135
136       // notify user if error occurs in parameter mismatch
137       catch ( FormatException * ) {
138          MessageBox::Show( S"Invalid Balance", S"Error",
139             MessageBoxButtons::OK, MessageBoxIcon::Error );
140       }
141
142       MessageBox::Show( S"Record Created", S"Success",
143          MessageBoxButtons::OK, MessageBoxIcon::Information );
144 } // end method InsertRecord
```

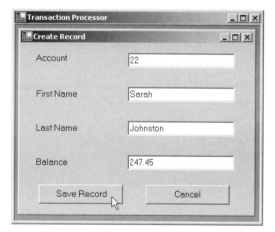

Fig. 14.47 `NewDialogForm` class method definitions. (Part 4 of 4.)

When the user clicks the **Update Record** button in the **Start Dialog**, the program invokes method **updateButton_Click** of class **StartDialogForm** (Fig. 14.44, lines 151–156), which displays the **UpdateDialogForm** internal frame (Fig. 14.48– Fig. 14.49). Class **UpdateDialogForm** enables the user to update existing records in the file.

To update a record, the user must enter the account number associated with that record. When the user presses *Enter*, **UpdateDialogForm** calls method **accountText-Box_KeyDown** (lines 103–139 of Fig. 14.49) to display the record contents. This method calls method **GetRecord** of the **Transaction** object (lines 110–112) to retrieve the specified **RandomAccessRecord**. If the record is not empty, lines 122–129 populate the **TextBox**es with the **RandomAccessRecord** values.

The **Transaction TextBox** initially contains the string **[Charge or Payment]**. The user should select this text, type the transaction amount (a positive value for a charge or a negative value for a payment), then press *Enter*. The program calls method **transactionTextBox_KeyDown** (lines 142–183) to add the user-specified transaction amount to the current balance.

```
1   // Fig. 14.48: UpdateDialog.h
2   // Enables user to update records in file.
3
4   #pragma once
5
6   #include "Transaction.h"
7   #include "MyDelegate.h"
8
9   public __gc class UpdateDialogForm: public BankUIForm
10  {
11  public:
12     UpdateDialogForm();
13     UpdateDialogForm( Transaction *transactionProxyValue,
14        MyDelegate *delegateValue );
15     void UpdateRecord( RandomAccessRecord *record );
16
17  private:
18     Label *transactionLabel;
19     TextBox *transactionTextBox;
20     Button *saveButton;
21     Button *cancelButton;
22
23     // pointer to object that handles transactions
24     Transaction *transactionProxy;
25
26     // delegate for method that displays previous window
27     MyDelegate *showPreviousWindow;
28
29     void InitializeComponent();
30     void accountTextBox_KeyDown( Object *, KeyEventArgs * );
31     void transactionTextBox_KeyDown( Object *, KeyEventArgs * );
32     void saveButton_Click( Object *, EventArgs * );
33     void cancelButton_Click( Object *, EventArgs * );
34  }; // end class UpdateDialogForm
```

Fig. 14.48 **UpdateDialogForm** class allows users to update records in transaction-processor case study.

```
1   // Fig. 14.49: UpdateDialog.cpp
2   // Method definitions for class UpdateDialogForm.
3
```

Fig. 14.49 **UpdateDialogForm** class method definitions. (Part 1 of 7.)

```
4   #include "UpdateDialog.h"
5
6   UpdateDialogForm::UpdateDialogForm()
7   {
8       InitializeComponent();
9   }
10
11  // initialize components and set members to parameter values
12  UpdateDialogForm::UpdateDialogForm(
13      Transaction *transactionProxyValue,
14      MyDelegate *delegateValue )
15  {
16      InitializeComponent();
17      showPreviousWindow = delegateValue;
18
19      // instantiate object that handles transactions
20      transactionProxy = transactionProxyValue;
21  }
22
23  void UpdateDialogForm::InitializeComponent()
24  {
25      this->saveButton = new Button();
26      this->transactionTextBox = new TextBox();
27      this->transactionLabel = new Label();
28      this->cancelButton = new Button();
29
30      this->SuspendLayout();
31
32      // accountTextBox
33      this->accountTextBox->TabIndex = 0;
34      this->accountTextBox->KeyDown += new KeyEventHandler( this,
35         this->accountTextBox_KeyDown );
36
37      // set tab stops
38      this->firstNameTextBox->TabStop = false;
39      this->lastNameTextBox->TabStop = false;
40      this->balanceTextBox->TabStop = false;
41
42      // saveButton
43      this->saveButton->Font = new Drawing::Font(
44         S"Microsoft Sans Serif", 10.0 );
45      this->saveButton->Location = Point( 32, 288 );
46      this->saveButton->Name = S"saveButton";
47      this->saveButton->Size = Drawing::Size( 144, 32 );
48      this->saveButton->TabIndex = 3;
49      this->saveButton->Text = S"Save Changes";
50      this->saveButton->Click += new EventHandler( this,
51         this->saveButton_Click );
52
53      // transactionTextBox
54      this->transactionTextBox->Font = new Drawing::Font(
55         S"Microsoft Sans Serif", 10.0 );
56      this->transactionTextBox->Location = Point( 184, 240 );
```

Fig. 14.49 UpdateDialogForm class method definitions. (Part 2 of 7.)

```
57        this->transactionTextBox->Name = S"transactionTextBox";
58        this->transactionTextBox->Size = Drawing::Size( 185, 26 );
59        this->transactionTextBox->TabIndex = 1;
60        this->transactionTextBox->Text = S"";
61        this->transactionTextBox->KeyDown += new KeyEventHandler(
62           this, this->transactionTextBox_KeyDown );
63
64        // transactionLabel
65        this->transactionLabel->Font = new Drawing::Font(
66           S"Microsoft Sans Serif", 10.0 );
67        this->transactionLabel->Location = Point( 24, 240 );
68        this->transactionLabel->Name = S"transactionLabel";
69        this->transactionLabel->Size = Drawing::Size( 136, 24 );
70        this->transactionLabel->TabIndex = 10;
71        this->transactionLabel->Text = S"Transaction";
72
73        // cancelButton
74        this->cancelButton->Font = new Drawing::Font(
75           S"Microsoft Sans Serif", 10.0 );
76        this->cancelButton->Location = Point( 216, 288 );
77        this->cancelButton->Name = S"cancelButton";
78        this->cancelButton->Size = Drawing::Size( 144, 32 );
79        this->cancelButton->TabIndex = 4;
80        this->cancelButton->Text = S"Cancel";
81        this->cancelButton->Click += new EventHandler( this,
82           this->cancelButton_Click );
83
84        // UpdateDialogForm
85        this->AutoScaleBaseSize = Drawing::Size( 6, 15 );
86        this->ClientSize = Drawing::Size( 400, 335 );
87
88        Control *controls[] = { this->balanceTextBox,
89           this->lastNameTextBox, this->firstNameTextBox,
90           this->accountTextBox, this->balanceLabel,
91           this->lastNameLabel, this->firstNameLabel,
92           this->accountLabel, this->cancelButton,
93           this->transactionLabel, this->transactionTextBox,
94           this->saveButton };
95        this->Controls->AddRange( controls );
96        this->Name = S"UpdateDialogForm";
97        this->Text = S"Update Record";
98
99        this->ResumeLayout();
100   } // end method InitializeComponent
101
102   // invoked when user enters text in account TextBox
103   void UpdateDialogForm::accountTextBox_KeyDown(
104      Object *sender, KeyEventArgs *e )
105   {
106      // determine whether user pressed Enter key
107      if ( e->KeyCode == Keys::Enter ) {
108
109         // retrieve record associated with account from file
```

Fig. 14.49 UpdateDialogForm class method definitions. (Part 3 of 7.)

```
110         RandomAccessRecord *record =
111            transactionProxy->GetRecord( GetTextBoxValues()
112            [ TextBoxIndices::ACCOUNT ] );
113
114         // return if record does not exist
115         if ( record == 0 )
116            return;
117
118         // determine whether record is empty
119         if ( record->Account != 0 ) {
120
121            // store record values in string array
122            String *values[] = { record->Account.ToString(),
123               record->FirstName->ToString(),
124               record->LastName->ToString(),
125               record->Balance.ToString() };
126
127            // copy string array value to TextBox values
128            SetTextBoxValues( values );
129            transactionTextBox->Text = S"[Charge or Payment]";
130
131         } // end if
132         else {
133
134            // notify user if record does not exist
135            MessageBox::Show( S"Record Does Not Exist", S"Error",
136               MessageBoxButtons::OK, MessageBoxIcon::Error );
137         } // end else
138      } // end if
139   } // end method accountTextBox_KeyDown
140
141   // invoked when user enters text in transaction TextBox
142   void UpdateDialogForm::transactionTextBox_KeyDown(
143      Object *sender, KeyEventArgs *e )
144   {
145      // determine whether user pressed Enter key
146      if ( e->KeyCode == Keys::Enter ) {
147
148         // calculate balance using transaction TextBox value
149         try {
150
151            // retrieve record associated with account from file
152            RandomAccessRecord *record =
153               transactionProxy->GetRecord( GetTextBoxValues()
154               [ TextBoxIndices::ACCOUNT ] );
155
156            // get transaction TextBox value
157            double transactionValue =
158               Double::Parse( transactionTextBox->Text );
159
160            // calculate new balance (old balance + transaction)
161            double newBalance =
162               record->Balance + transactionValue;
```

Fig. 14.49 UpdateDialogForm class method definitions. (Part 4 of 7.)

```
163
164            // store record values in string array
165            String *values[] = { record->Account.ToString(),
166               record->FirstName->ToString(),
167               record->LastName->ToString(),
168               newBalance.ToString() };
169
170            // copy string array value to TextBox values
171            SetTextBoxValues( values );
172
173            // clear transaction TextBox
174            transactionTextBox->Text = S"";
175         } // end try
176
177         // notify user if error occurs in parameter mismatch
178         catch ( FormatException * ) {
179            MessageBox::Show( S"Invalid Transaction", S"Error",
180               MessageBoxButtons::OK, MessageBoxIcon::Error );
181         } // end catch
182      } // end if
183 } // end method transactionTextBox_KeyDown
184
185 // invoked when user clicks Save Changes button
186 void UpdateDialogForm::saveButton_Click(
187      Object *sender, EventArgs *e )
188 {
189      RandomAccessRecord *record =
190         transactionProxy->GetRecord( GetTextBoxValues()
191         [ TextBoxIndices::ACCOUNT ] );
192
193      // if record exists, update in file
194      if ( record != 0 )
195         UpdateRecord( record );
196
197      Hide();
198      ClearTextBoxes();
199      showPreviousWindow->Invoke();
200 } // end method saveButton_Click
201
202 // invoked when user clicks Cancel button
203 void UpdateDialogForm::cancelButton_Click(
204      Object *sender, EventArgs *e )
205 {
206      Hide();
207      ClearTextBoxes();
208      showPreviousWindow->Invoke();
209 } // end method cancelButton_Click
210
211 // update record in file at position specified by accountNumber
212 void UpdateDialogForm::UpdateRecord( RandomAccessRecord *record )
213 {
214      // store TextBox values in record and write record to file
215      try {
```

Fig. 14.49 UpdateDialogForm class method definitions. (Part 5 of 7.)

```
216            int accountNumber = record->Account;
217            String *values[] = GetTextBoxValues();
218
219            // store values in record
220            record->Account = accountNumber;
221            record->FirstName =
222               values[ TextBoxIndices::FIRST ];
223            record->LastName = values[ TextBoxIndices::LAST ];
224            record->Balance =
225               Double::Parse(
226               values[ TextBoxIndices::BALANCE ] );
227
228            // add record to file
229            if ( transactionProxy->AddRecord(
230               record, accountNumber ) == false )
231
232               return; // if error
233         } // end try
234
235         // notify user if error occurs in parameter mismatch
236         catch ( FormatException * ) {
237            MessageBox::Show( S"Invalid Balance", S"Error",
238               MessageBoxButtons::OK, MessageBoxIcon::Error );
239            return;
240         }
241
242         MessageBox::Show( S"Record Updated", S"Success",
243            MessageBoxButtons::OK, MessageBoxIcon::Information );
244      } // end method UpdateRecord
```

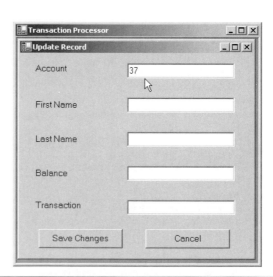

Fig. 14.49 UpdateDialogForm class method definitions. (Part 6 of 7.)

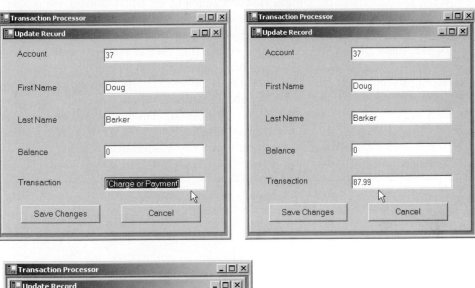

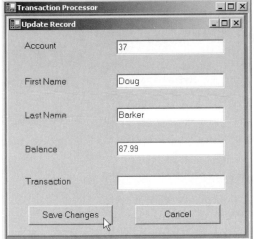

Fig. 14.49 UpdateDialogForm class method definitions. (Part 7 of 7.)

The user clicks the **Save Changes** button to write the altered contents of the **Text-Box**es to the file. (Note that pressing **Save Changes** does not update the **Balance** field—the user must press *Enter* to update this field before pressing **Save Changes**.) When the user clicks **Save Changes**, the program invokes method `saveButton_Click` (lines 186–200), which calls `private` method `UpdateRecord` (lines 212–244). This method calls method `AddRecord` of the `Transaction` object (lines 229–230) to store the `TextBox` values in a `RandomAccessRecord` and overwrite the existing file record with the `RandomAccessRecord` containing the new data.

When the user clicks the **Delete Record** button of the **Start Dialog**, the program invokes method **deleteButton_Click** of class **StartDialogForm** (Fig. 14.44, lines 158–163), which displays the **DeleteDialogForm** internal frame (Fig. 14.50–Fig. 14.51). Class **DeleteDialogForm** enables the user to remove existing records from the file. To remove a record, the user must enter the account number associated with that record. When the user clicks the **Delete Record** button (now, from the **DeleteDialogForm** internal frame), **DeleteDialogForm** calls method **deleteButton_Click** (lines 87–99 of Fig. 14.51). This method calls method **DeleteRecord** (lines 110–142), which ensures that the record to be deleted exists, then calls method **AddRecord** of the **Transaction** object (lines 128–129) to overwrite the file record with an empty one.

```
1    // Fig. 14.50: DeleteDialog.h
2    // Enables user to delete records in file.
3
4    #pragma once
5
6    #include "Transaction.h"
7    #include "MyDelegate.h"
8
9    public __gc class DeleteDialogForm : public Form
10   {
11   public:
12      DeleteDialogForm( Transaction *, MyDelegate * );
13      void DeleteRecord( RandomAccessRecord * );
14
15   private:
16      Label *accountLabel;
17      TextBox *accountTextBox;
18      Button *deleteButton;
19      Button *cancelButton;
20
21      // pointer to object that handles transactions
22      Transaction *transactionProxy;
23
24      // delegate for method that displays previous window
25      MyDelegate *showPreviousWindow;
26
27      void InitializeComponent();
28      void deleteButton_Click( Object *, EventArgs * );
29      void cancelButton_Click( Object *, EventArgs * );
30   }; // end class DeleteDialogForm
```

Fig. 14.50 **DeleteDialogForm** class allows users to delete records from files in the transaction-processor case study.

```
1    // Fig. 14.51: DeleteDialog.cpp
2    // Method definitions for class DeleteDialogForm.
3
```

Fig. 14.51 **DeleteDialogForm** class method definitions and program functionalities. (Part 1 of 4.)

```cpp
4    #include "DeleteDialog.h"
5
6    // initialize components and set members to parameter values
7    DeleteDialogForm::DeleteDialogForm(
8       Transaction *transactionProxyValue,
9       MyDelegate *delegateValue )
10   {
11      InitializeComponent();
12      showPreviousWindow = delegateValue;
13
14      // instantiate object that handles transactions
15      transactionProxy = transactionProxyValue;
16   }
17
18   void DeleteDialogForm::InitializeComponent()
19   {
20      this->accountLabel = new Label();
21      this->cancelButton = new Button();
22      this->accountTextBox = new TextBox();
23      this->deleteButton = new Button();
24
25      this->SuspendLayout();
26
27      // accountLabel
28      this->accountLabel->Font = new Drawing::Font(
29         S"Microsoft Sans Serif", 10.0, FontStyle::Regular,
30         GraphicsUnit::Point, 0 );
31      this->accountLabel->Location = Point( 24, 16 );
32      this->accountLabel->Name = S"accountLabel";
33      this->accountLabel->Size = Drawing::Size( 136, 20 );
34      this->accountLabel->TabIndex = 0;
35      this->accountLabel->Text = S"Account Number";
36      this->accountLabel->TextAlign = ContentAlignment::MiddleLeft;
37
38      // cancelButton
39      this->cancelButton->Font = new Drawing::Font(
40         S"Microsoft Sans Serif", 10.0, FontStyle::Regular,
41         GraphicsUnit::Point, 0 );
42      this->cancelButton->Location = Point( 176, 64 );
43      this->cancelButton->Name = S"cancelButton";
44      this->cancelButton->Size = Drawing::Size( 133, 32 );
45      this->cancelButton->TabIndex = 0;
46      this->cancelButton->Text = S"Cancel";
47      this->cancelButton->Click += new EventHandler( this,
48         this->cancelButton_Click );
49
50      // accountTextBox
51      this->accountTextBox->Font = new System::Drawing::Font(
52         S"Microsoft Sans Serif", 10.0, FontStyle::Regular,
53         GraphicsUnit::Point, 0 );
54      this->accountTextBox->Location = Point( 176, 16 );
55      this->accountTextBox->Name = S"accountTextBox";
```

Fig. 14.51 DeleteDialogForm class method definitions and program functionalities. (Part 2 of 4.)

```
56        this->accountTextBox->Size = Drawing::Size( 128, 26 );
57        this->accountTextBox->TabIndex = 3;
58        this->accountTextBox->Text = S"";
59
60        // deleteButton
61        this->deleteButton->Font = new Drawing::Font(
62           S"Microsoft Sans Serif", 10.0, FontStyle::Regular,
63           GraphicsUnit::Point, 0 );
64        this->deleteButton->Location = Point( 16, 64 );
65        this->deleteButton->Name = S"deleteButton";
66        this->deleteButton->Size = Drawing::Size( 133, 32 );
67        this->deleteButton->TabIndex = 1;
68        this->deleteButton->Text = S"Delete Record";
69        this->deleteButton->Click += new EventHandler( this,
70           this->deleteButton_Click);
71
72        // DeleteDialogForm
73        this->AutoScaleBaseSize = Drawing::Size( 6, 15 );
74        this->ClientSize = Drawing::Size( 328, 111 );
75
76        Control *controls[] = { this->cancelButton,
77           this->deleteButton, this->accountTextBox,
78           this->accountLabel };
79        this->Controls->AddRange( controls );
80        this->Name = S"DeleteDialogForm";
81        this->Text = S"Delete Record";
82
83        this->ResumeLayout();
84     } // end method InitializeComponent
85
86     // invoked when user clicks Delete Record button
87     void DeleteDialogForm::deleteButton_Click(
88        Object *sender, EventArgs *e )
89     {
90        RandomAccessRecord *record =
91           transactionProxy->GetRecord( accountTextBox->Text );
92
93        // if record exists, delete it in file
94        if ( record != NULL )
95           DeleteRecord( record );
96
97        this->Hide();
98        showPreviousWindow->Invoke();
99     } // end method deleteButton_Click
100
101    // invoked when user clicks Cancel button
102    void DeleteDialogForm::cancelButton_Click(
103       Object *sender, EventArgs *e)
104    {
105       this->Hide();
106       showPreviousWindow->Invoke();
```

Fig. 14.51 DeleteDialogForm class method definitions and program
functionalities. (Part 3 of 4.)

```
107  } // end method cancelButton_Click
108
109  // delete record in file at position specified by accountNumber
110  void DeleteDialogForm::DeleteRecord(
111     RandomAccessRecord *record )
112  {
113     int accountNumber = record->Account;
114
115     // display error message if record does not exist
116     if ( record->Account == 0 ) {
117        MessageBox::Show( S"Record Does Not Exist", S"Error",
118           MessageBoxButtons::OK, MessageBoxIcon::Error );
119        accountTextBox->Clear();
120
121        return;
122     }
123
124     // create blank record
125     record = new RandomAccessRecord();
126
127     // write over file record with empty record
128     if ( transactionProxy->AddRecord(
129        record, accountNumber ) == true )
130
131        // notify user of successful deletion
132        MessageBox::Show( S"Record Deleted", S"Success",
133           MessageBoxButtons::OK, MessageBoxIcon::Information );
134     else
135
136        // notify user of failure
137        MessageBox::Show( S"Record could not be deleted",
138           S"Error", MessageBoxButtons::OK,
139           MessageBoxIcon::Error );
140
141     accountTextBox->Clear();
142  } // end method DeleteRecord
```

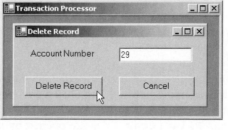

Fig. 14.51 `DeleteDialogForm` class method definitions and program functionalities. (Part 4 of 4.)

In this chapter, we demonstrated how to read data from files and write data to files via both sequential-access and random-access file-processing techniques. Using class **BinaryFormatter**, we serialized and deserialized objects to and from streams; we then employed **FileStream**, **BinaryWriter** and **BinaryReader** to transfer the objects' byte representation to and from files. In Chapter 15, we discuss *Extensible Markup Language (XML)*, a widely supported technology for describing data. Using XML, we can describe any type of data, such as mathematical formulas, music and financial reports.

14.12 Summary

All data items processed by a computer ultimately are reduced to combinations of zeros and ones. The smallest data items that computers support are called bits and can assume either the value **0** or the value **1**. Digits, letters and special symbols are referred to as characters. The set of all characters used to write programs and represent data items on a particular computer is called that computer's character set. Every character in a computer's character set is represented as a pattern of **1**s and **0**s (characters in **System::String** objects are Unicode® characters, which are composed of 2 bytes).

A record is a group of related fields. At least one field in a record is chosen as a record key, which identifies that record as belonging to a particular person or entity and distinguishes that record from all other records in the file. A file is a group of related records. Files are used for long-term retention of large amounts of data and can store those data even after the program that created the data terminates. Data maintained in files often are called persistent data. Sometimes, a group of related files is called a database. A collection of programs designed to create and manage databases is called a database management system (DBMS).

Class **File** enables programs to obtain information about a file. Class **Directory** enables programs to obtain information about a directory. Class **FileStream** provides method **Seek** for repositioning the file-position pointer (the byte number of the next byte in the file to be read or written) to any position in the file. The .NET Framework views each file as a sequential stream of bytes. Streams provide communication channels between files and programs. When a file is opened, an object is created, and a stream is associated with the object. To retrieve data sequentially from a file, programs normally start from the beginning of the file, reading all data consecutively until the desired data are found. Each file ends in some machine-dependent form of end-of-file marker.

Objects of classes **OpenFileDialog** and **SaveFileDialog** are used for selecting files to open and save, respectively. Method **ShowDialog** of these classes displays that dialog. When displayed, both an **OpenFileDialog** and a **SaveFileDialog** prevent the user from interacting with any other program window until the dialog is closed. Dialogs that behave in this fashion are called modal dialogs.

To perform file processing in MC++, the namespace **System::IO** must be referenced. This namespace includes definitions for stream classes such as **StreamReader**, **StreamWriter** and **FileStream**. Files are opened by instantiating objects of these classes. Programmers can use members of the **FileAccess** enumeration to control users' access to files.

The .NET Framework imposes no structure on files (i.e., concepts like that of a "record" do not exist). The programmer must structure each file appropriately to meet the requirements of an application. The most common type of file organization is the sequential file, in which records typically are stored in order by the record-key field. With a sequential-access file, each successive input/output request reads or writes the next consecutive set of data in the file.

Instant data access is possible with random-access files. A program can access individual records of a random-access file directly (and quickly) without searching through other records. Random-access files sometimes are called direct-access files. With a random-access file, each successive input/output request can be directed to any part of the file, which can be at any distance from the part of the file referenced in the previous request.

There are a variety of techniques for creating random-access files. Perhaps the simplest involves requiring that all records in a file be of the same fixed length. The use of fixed-length records makes it easy for a program to calculate (as a function of the record size and the record key) the exact location of any record in relation to the beginning of the file. Data can be inserted into a random-access file without destroying other data in the file. Users can also update or delete previously stored data without rewriting the entire file. Random-access file-processing programs rarely write a single field to a file. Normally, they write one object at a time.

BinaryFormatter uses methods **Serialize** and **Deserialize** to write and to read objects, respectively. Method **Serialize** writes the object's representation to a stream. Method **Deserialize** reads this representation from a stream and reconstructs the original object. Only classes with the **Serializable** attribute can be serialized to and deserialized from streams. Methods **Serialize** and **Deserialize** each require a **Stream** object as a parameter, enabling the **BinaryFormatter** to access the correct stream.

Class **BinaryReader** and **BinaryWriter** provide methods for reading and writing bytes to streams, respectively. The **BinaryReader** and **BinaryWriter** constructors receive as arguments pointers to instances of class **System::IO::Stream**. Class **FileStream** inherits from class **Stream**, so we can pass the **FileStream** object as an argument to either the **BinaryReader** or **BinaryWriter** constructor to create an object that can transfer bytes directly to or from a file.

Sorting with direct-access techniques is fast. This speed is achieved by making the file large enough to hold every possible record that might be created. Of course, this means that the file could be sparsely occupied most of the time, possibly wasting memory.

Extensible Markup Language (XML)

Objectives

- To mark up data using XML.
- To understand the concept of an XML namespace.
- To understand the relationship between DTDs, Schemas and XML.
- To create Schemas.
- To create and use simple XSLT documents.
- To transform XML documents into XHTML, using class **XslTransform**.

Knowing trees, I understand the meaning of patience.
Knowing grass, I can appreciate persistence.
Hal Borland

Like everything metaphysical, the harmony between thought
and reality is to be found in the grammar of the language.
Ludwig Wittgenstein

I played with an idea and grew willful, tossed it into the air;
transformed it; let it escape and recaptured it; made it
iridescent with fancy, and winged it with paradox.
Oscar Wilde

15.1 Introduction

The *Extensible Markup Language* (XML) was developed in 1996 by the *World Wide Web Consortium's (W3C's) XML Working Group*. XML is a portable, widely supported, *open* (i.e., non-proprietary) *technology* for describing data. XML is becoming the standard for storing data that is exchanged between applications. Using XML, document authors can describe any type of data, including mathematical formulas, software-configuration instructions, music, recipes and financial reports. XML documents are readable by both humans and machines.

The .NET Framework uses XML extensively. The Framework Class Library (FCL) provides an extensive set of XML-related classes. Mu;ch of Visual Studio .NET's internal implementation employs XML. Visual Studio .NET also includes an XML editor and validator.[1] In this chapter, we introduce XML, XML-related technologies and key classes for creating and manipulating XML documents.

15.2 XML Documents

In this section, we present our first XML document, which describes an article (Fig. 15.1). [*Note:* The line numbers shown are not part of the XML document.]

```
1   <?xml version = "1.0"?>
2
3   <!-- Fig. 15.1: article.xml      -->
4   <!-- Article structured with XML. -->
5
6   <article>
```

Fig. 15.1   XML used to mark up an article. (Part 1 of 2.)

1. For more information about XML in Visual Studio .NET, visit **msdn.microsoft.com/ library/default.asp?url=/library/en-us/vsintro7/html/ vxorixmlinvisualstudio.asp**.

```
7
8        <title>Simple XML</title>
9
10       <date>August 2002</date>
11
12       <author>
13           <firstName>Su</firstName>
14           <lastName>Fari</lastName>
15       </author>
16
17       <summary>XML is pretty easy.</summary>
18
19       <content>In this chapter, we present a wide variety of examples
20           that use XML.
21       </content>
22
23   </article>
```

Fig. 15.1   XML used to mark up an article. (Part 2 of 2.)

This document begins with an optional *XML declaration* (line 1), which identifies the document as an XML document. The **version** *information parameter* specifies the version of XML that is used in the document. XML comments (lines 3–4), which begin with **<!--** and end with **-->**, can be placed almost anywhere in an XML document. As in an MC++ program, comments are used in XML for documentation purposes.

Common Programming Error 15.1

The placement of any characters, including whitespace, before the XML declaration is a syntax error.

Portability Tip 15.1

Although the XML declaration is optional, documents should include the declaration to identify the version of XML used. Otherwise, in the future, a document that lacks an XML declaration might be assumed to conform to the latest version of XML, and errors could result.

In XML, data are marked up with *tags*, which are names enclosed in *angle brackets* (**<>**). Tags are used in pairs to delimit character data (e.g., **Simple XML** in line 8). A tag that begins *markup* (i.e., XML data) is called a *start tag*; a tag that terminates markup is called an *end tag*. Examples of start tags are **<article>** and **<title>** (lines 6 and 8, respectively). End tags differ from start tags in that they contain a *forward slash* (**/**) character immediately after the **<** character. Examples of end tags are **</title>** and **</article>** (lines 8 and 23, respectively). XML documents can contain any number of tags.

Common Programming Error 15.2

Failure to provide a corresponding end tag for a start tag is a syntax error.

Individual units of markup (i.e., everything included between a start tag and its corresponding end tag) are called *elements*. An XML document includes one element (called a *root element* or *document element*) that contains every other element. The root element must be the first element after the XML declaration. In Fig. 15.1, **article** (line 6) is the root element. Elements are *nested* within each other to form hierarchies—with the root element at the top of the hierarchy. This allows document authors to create explicit relationships between data. For example, elements **title**, **date**, **author**, **summary** and **content** are nested within **article**. Elements **firstName** and **lastName** are nested within **author**.

Common Programming Error 15.3

Attempting to create more than one root element in an XML document is a syntax error.

Element **title** (line 8) contains the title of the article, **Simple XML**, as character data. Similarly, **date** (line 10), **summary** (line 17) and **content** (lines 19–21) contain as character data the date, summary and content, respectively. XML element names can be of any length and may contain letters, digits, underscores, hyphens and periods—they must begin with a letter or an underscore.

Common Programming Error 15.4

XML is case sensitive. The use of the wrong case for an XML element name (in a begin tag, end tag, etc.) is a syntax error.

By itself, this document is simply a text file named **article.xml**. Although it is not required, most XML documents end in the file extension **.xml**. The processing of XML documents requires a program called an *XML parser* (also called an *XML processor*). Parsers are responsible for checking an XML document's syntax and making the XML document's data available to applications. Often, XML parsers are built into such applications as Visual Studio or are available for download over the Internet. Popular parsers include Microsoft's *msxml* (**msdn.microsoft.com/library/en-us/xmlsdk30/htm/xmmscxmloverview.asp**), the Apache Software Foundation's *Xerces* (**xml.apache.org**) and IBM's *XML4J* (**www-106.ibm.com/developerworks/library/xml4j**). In this chapter, we use msxml.

When the user loads **article.xml** into Internet Explorer (IE),[2] msxml parses the document and passes the parsed data to IE. IE then uses a built-in *style sheet* to format the data. Notice that the resulting format of the data (Fig. 15.2) is similar to the format of the XML document shown in Fig. 15.1. As we soon demonstrate, style sheets play an important and powerful role in the transformation of XML data into formats suitable for display.

Notice the minus (**−**) and plus (**+**) signs in Fig. 15.2. Although these are not part of the XML document, IE places them next to all *container elements* (i.e., elements that contain other elements). Container elements also are called *parent elements*. A minus sign indicates that the parent element's *child elements* (i.e., nested elements) are being displayed. When clicked, a minus sign becomes a plus sign (which collapses the container element and hides all children). Conversely, clicking a plus sign expands the container element and changes the plus sign to a minus sign. This behavior is similar to the viewing of the directory structure on a Windows system using Windows Explorer. In fact, a directory structure often is modeled as a series of tree structures, in which each drive letter (e.g., **C:**, etc.) represents the *root* of a tree. Each folder is a *node* in the tree. Parsers often place XML data into trees to facilitate efficient manipulation, as discussed in Section 15.4.

Common Programming Error 15.5

Nesting XML tags improperly is a syntax error. For example, `<x><y>hello</x></y>` is a error, because the `</y>` tag must precede the `</x>` tag.

---

2. IE 5 and higher.

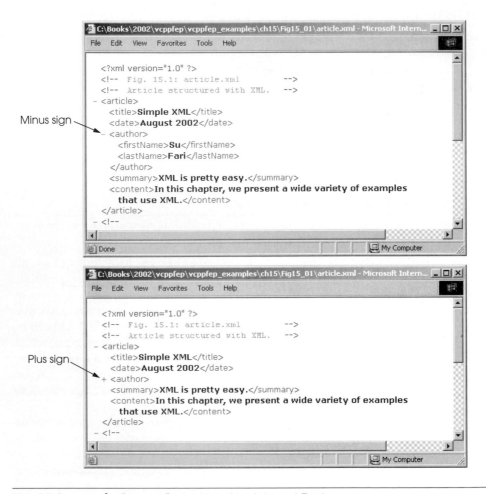

Minus sign

Plus sign

Fig. 15.2 `article.xml` displayed by Internet Explorer.

We now present a second XML document (Fig. 15.3), which marks up a business letter. This document contains significantly more data than did the previous XML document.

```
1   <?xml version = "1.0"?>
2
3   <!-- Fig. 15.3: letter.xml                 -->
4   <!-- Business letter formatted with XML. -->
5
6   <letter>
7      <contact type = "from">
8         <name>Jane Doe</name>
9         <address1>Box 12345</address1>
10        <address2>15 Any Ave.</address2>
11        <city>Othertown</city>
12        <state>Otherstate</state>
```

Fig. 15.3   XML used to mark up a business letter. (Part 1 of 2.)

```
13          <zip>67890</zip>
14          <phone>555-4321</phone>
15          <flag gender = "F" />
16      </contact>
17
18      <contact type = "to">
19          <name>John Doe</name>
20          <address1>123 Main St.</address1>
21          <address2></address2>
22          <city>Anytown</city>
23          <state>Anystate</state>
24          <zip>12345</zip>
25          <phone>555-1234</phone>
26          <flag gender = "M" />
27      </contact>
28
29      <salutation>Dear Sir:</salutation>
30
31          <paragraph>It is our privilege to inform you about our new
32              database managed with <technology>XML</technology>. This
33              new system allows you to reduce the load on
34              your inventory list server by having the client machine
35              perform the work of sorting and filtering the data.
36          </paragraph>
37
38          <paragraph>Please visit our Web site for availability
39              and pricing.
40          </paragraph>
41
42      <closing>Sincerely</closing>
43
44      <signature>Ms. Doe</signature>
45  </letter>
```

Fig. 15.3   XML used to mark up a business letter. (Part 2 of 2.)

Root element **letter** (lines 6–45) contains the child elements **contact** (lines 7–16 and 18–27), **salutation**, **paragraph** (lines 31–36 and 38–40), **closing** and **signature**. In addition to being placed between tags, data also can be placed in *attributes*, which are name-value pairs in start tags. Elements can have any number of attributes in their start tags. The first **contact** element (lines 7–16) has attribute **type** with attribute *value* **"from"**, which indicates that this **contact** element marks up information about the letter's sender. The second **contact** element (lines 18–27) has attribute **type** with value **"to"**, which indicates that this **contact** element marks up information about the letter's recipient. Like element names, attribute names are case sensitive; can be of any length; may contain letters, digits, underscores, hyphens and periods; and must begin with either a letter or underscore character. A **contact** element stores a contact's name, address, phone number and gender. Element **salutation** (line 29) marks up the letter's salutation. Lines 31–40 mark up the letter's body with **paragraph** elements. Elements **closing** (line 42) and **signature** (line 44) mark up the closing sentence and the signature of the letter's author, respectively.

Common Programming Error 15.6

Failure to enclose attribute values in either double (" ") or single (' ') quotes is a syntax error.

Common Programming Error 15.7

Attempting to provide two attributes with the same name for an element is a syntax error.

In line 15, we introduce *empty element* **flag**, which indicates the gender of the contact. Empty elements do not contain character data (i.e., they do not contain text between the start and end tags). Such elements are closed either by placing a slash at the end of the element (as shown in line 15) or by explicitly writing a closing tag, as in

> `<flag gender = "F"></flag>`

Notice that element **address2** in line 21 also contains no data. Thus, we could safely change line 21 to **<address2 />**. However, it probably would not be wise to omit the element entirely, as it may be required by some *DTD* or *Schema*. We discuss these in detail in Section 15.5.

15.3 XML Namespaces

The .NET Framework provides massive class libraries that groups its features into namespaces. These namespaces prevent *naming collisions* between programmer-defined identifiers and identifiers in class libraries. For example, we might use class **Book** to represent information on one of our publications; however, a stamp collector might use class **Book** to represent a book of stamps. A naming collision would occur if we use these two classes in the same assembly, without using namespaces to differentiate them.

Like the .NET Framework, XML also provides *namespaces*, which provide a means of uniquely identifying XML elements. In addition, XML-based languages—called *vocabularies*, such as XML Schema (Section 15.5) and Extensible Stylesheet Language (Section 15.6)—often use namespaces to identify their elements.

Elements are differentiated via *namespace prefixes*, which identify the namespace to which an element belongs. For example,

> `<deitel:book>Visual C++ .NET</deitel:book>`

qualifies element **book** with namespace prefix **deitel**. This indicates that element **book** is part of namespace **deitel**. Document authors can use any name for a namespace prefix except the reserved namespace prefix **xml**.

Common Programming Error 15.8

*Attempting to create a namespace prefix named **xml** in any mixture of case is a syntax error.*

The mark up in Fig. 15.4 demonstrates the use of namespaces. This XML document contains two **file** elements that are differentiated via namespaces.

```
1   <?xml version = "1.0"?>
2
3   <!-- Fig. 15.4: namespace.xml   -->
4   <!-- Demonstrating namespaces. -->
5
6   <text:directory xmlns:text = "urn:deitel:textInfo"
7      xmlns:image = "urn:deitel:imageInfo">
8
9      <text:file filename = "book.xml">
10        <text:description>A book list</text:description>
11     </text:file>
12
13     <image:file filename = "funny.jpg">
14        <image:description>A funny picture</image:description>
15        <image:size width = "200" height = "100" />
16     </image:file>
17
18  </text:directory>
```

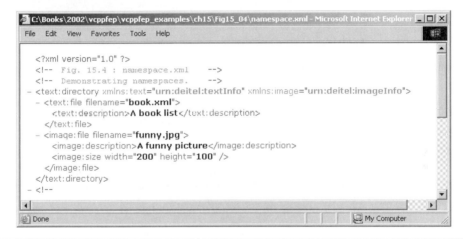

Fig. 15.4 XML namespaces demonstration.

Software Engineering Observation 15.1

A programmer has the option of qualifying an attribute with a namespace prefix. However, doing so is not required, because attributes always are associated with elements.

Lines 6–7 use attribute **xmlns** to create two namespace prefixes: **text** and **image**. Each namespace prefix is bound to a series of characters called a *uniform resource identifier (URI)* that uniquely identifies the namespace. Document authors create their own namespace prefixes and URIs.

To ensure that namespaces are unique, document authors must provide unique URIs. Here, we use the text **urn:deitel:textInfo** and **urn:deitel:imageInfo** as URIs. A common practice is to use *Universal Resource Locators (URLs)* for URIs, because the domain names (such as **www.deitel.com**) used in URLs are guaranteed to be unique. For example, lines 6–7 could have been written as

```
<text:directory xmlns:text =
    "http://www.deitel.com/xmlns-text"
    xmlns:image = "http://www.deitel.com/xmlns-image">
```

In this example, we use URLs related to the Deitel & Associates, Inc, domain name to identify namespaces. The XML parser never visits these URLs—they simply represent a series of characters used to differentiate names. The URLs need not refer to actual Web pages or be formed properly.

Lines 9–11 use the namespace prefix **text** to qualify elements **file** and **description** as belonging to the namespace **"urn:deitel:textInfo"**. Notice that the namespace prefix **text** is applied to the end tags as well. Lines 13–16 apply namespace prefix **image** to elements **file**, **description** and **size**.

To eliminate the need to precede each element with a namespace prefix, document authors can specify a *default namespace*. Figure 15.5 demonstrates the creation and use of default namespaces.

```
1   <?xml version = "1.0"?>
2
3   <!-- Fig. 15.5: defaultnamespace.xml   -->
4   <!-- Using default namespaces.         -->
5
6   <directory xmlns = "urn:deitel:textInfo"
7       xmlns:image = "urn:deitel:imageInfo">
8
9       <file filename = "book.xml">
10          <description>A book list</description>
11      </file>
12
13      <image:file filename = "funny.jpg">
14          <image:description>A funny picture</image:description>
15          <image:size width = "200" height = "100" />
16      </image:file>
17
18  </directory>
```

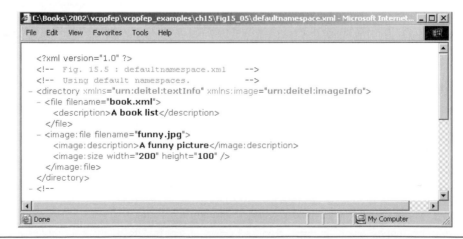

Fig. 15.5 Default namespaces demonstration.

Line 6 declares a default namespace using attribute **xmlns** with a URI as its value. Once we define this default namespace, child elements belonging to the namespace need not be qualified by a namespace prefix. Element **file** (line 9–11) is in the namespace **urn:deitel:textInfo**. Compare this to Fig. 15.4, where we prefixed **file** and **description** with **text** (lines 9–11).

The default namespace applies to the **directory** element and all elements that are not qualified with a namespace prefix. However, we can use a namespace prefix to specify a different namespace for particular elements. For example, the **file** element in line 13 is prefixed with **image** to indicate that it is in the namespace **urn:deitel:imageInfo**, rather than the default namespace.

15.4 Document Object Model (DOM)

Although XML documents are text files, retrieving data from them via sequential-file access techniques is neither practical nor efficient, especially in situations where data must be added or deleted dynamically.

Upon successful parsing of documents, some XML parsers store document data as tree structures in memory. Figure 15.6 illustrates the tree structure for the document **article.xml** discussed in Fig. 15.1. This hierarchical tree structure is called a *Document Object Model (DOM)* tree, and an XML parser that creates this type of structure is known as a *DOM parser*. The DOM tree represents each component of the XML document (e.g., **article**, **date**, **firstName**, etc.) as a node in the tree. Nodes (such as **author**) that contain other nodes (called *child nodes*) are called *parent nodes*. Nodes that have the same parent (such as **firstName** and **lastName**) are called *sibling nodes*. A node's *descendant nodes* include that node's children, its children's children and so on. Similarly, a node's *ancestor nodes* include that node's parent, its parent's parent and so on. Every DOM tree has a single *root node* that contains all other nodes in the document, such as comments and elements.

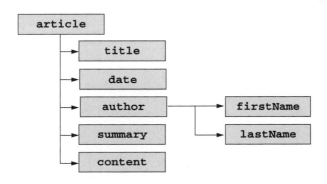

Fig. 15.6   Tree structure for Fig. 15.1.

Classes for creating, reading and manipulating XML documents are located in namespace **System::Xml**. This namespace also contains additional namespaces that contain other XML-related classes.

In this section, we present several examples that use DOM trees. Our first example, the program in Fig. 15.7–Fig. 15.9, loads the XML document presented in Fig. 15.1 and displays its data in a text box. This example uses class **XmlNodeReader** (derived from **XmlReader**), which iterates through each node in the XML document. Class **Xml-Reader** is an **abstract** class that defines the interface for reading XML documents.

```cpp
1   // Fig. 15.7: XmlReaderTest.h
2   // Reading an XML document.
3
4   #pragma once
5
6   #using <system.dll>
7   #using <mscorlib.dll>
8   #using <system.xml.dll>
9   #using <system.drawing.dll>
10  #using <system.windows.forms.dll>
11
12  using namespace System;
13  using namespace System::Xml;
14  using namespace System::Drawing;
15  using namespace System::Windows::Forms;
16
17  public __gc class XmlReaderTest : public Form
18  {
19  public:
20     XmlReaderTest();
21
22  private:
23     TextBox *outputTextBox;
24     void InitializeComponent();
25     void PrintXml();
26     void TabOutput( int );
27  }; // end class XmlReaderTest
```

Fig. 15.7   XmlNodeReader used to iterate through an XML document.

```cpp
1   // Fig. 15.8: XmlReaderTest.cpp
2   // Method definitions for class XmlReaderTest.
3
4   #include "XmlReaderTest.h"
5
6   XmlReaderTest::XmlReaderTest()
7   {
```

Fig. 15.8   XMLReaderTest class method definitions. (Part 1 of 4.)

```
 8        InitializeComponent();
 9        PrintXml();
10   } // end XmlReaderTest constructor
11
12   void XmlReaderTest::PrintXml()
13   {
14        // pointer to "XML document"
15        XmlDocument *document = new XmlDocument();
16        document->Load( S"article.xml" );
17
18        // create XmlNodeReader for document
19        XmlNodeReader *reader = new XmlNodeReader( document );
20
21        // show form before outputTextBox is populated
22        this->Show();
23
24        // tree depth is -1, no indentation
25        int depth = -1;
26
27        // display each node's content
28        while ( reader->Read() ){
29
30           switch ( reader->NodeType ){
31
32              // if Element, display its name
33              case XmlNodeType::Element:
34
35                 // increase tab depth
36                 depth++;
37                 TabOutput( depth );
38                 outputTextBox->Text = String::Concat(
39                    outputTextBox->Text, S"<", reader->Name,
40                    S">\r\n" );
41
42                 // if empty element, decrease depth
43                 if ( reader->IsEmptyElement )
44                    depth--;
45
46                 break;
47
48              // if Comment, display it
49              case XmlNodeType::Comment:
50                 TabOutput( depth );
51                 outputTextBox->Text = String::Concat(
52                    outputTextBox->Text, S"<!--", reader->Value,
53                    S"-->\r\n" );
54                 break;
55
56              // if Text, display it
57              case XmlNodeType::Text:
58                 TabOutput( depth );
59                 outputTextBox->Text = String::Concat(
60                    outputTextBox->Text, S"\t", reader->Value,
```

Fig. 15.8   **XMLReaderTest** class method definitions. (Part 2 of 4.)

```
61                   S"\r\n" );
62               break;
63
64           // if XML declaration, display it
65           case XmlNodeType::XmlDeclaration:
66               TabOutput( depth );
67               outputTextBox->Text = String::Concat(
68                   outputTextBox->Text, S"<?", reader->Name, S" ",
69                   reader->Value, S" ?>\r\n" );
70               break;
71
72           // if EndElement, display it and decrement depth
73           case XmlNodeType::EndElement:
74               TabOutput( depth );
75               outputTextBox->Text = String::Concat(
76                   outputTextBox->Text, S"</",
77                   reader->Name, S">\r\n" );
78               depth--;
79               break;
80
81       } // end switch
82   } // end while
83 } // end method PrintXml
84
85 void XmlReaderTest::InitializeComponent()
86 {
87     this->outputTextBox = new TextBox();
88     this->SuspendLayout();
89
90     // outputTextBox
91     this->outputTextBox->BackColor = Color::Honeydew;
92     this->outputTextBox->Font = new Drawing::Font(
93         S"Courier New", 8.25, FontStyle::Regular,
94         GraphicsUnit::Point, 0 );
95     this->outputTextBox->Location = Point( 8, 8 );
96     this->outputTextBox->Multiline = true;
97     this->outputTextBox->Name = S"outputTextBox";
98     this->outputTextBox->ReadOnly = true;
99     this->outputTextBox->ScrollBars = ScrollBars::Both;
100    this->outputTextBox->Size = Drawing::Size( 384, 376 );
101    this->outputTextBox->TabIndex = 1;
102    this->outputTextBox->Text = S"";
103    this->outputTextBox->WordWrap = false;
104
105    // XmlReaderTest
106    this->AutoScaleBaseSize = Drawing::Size( 5, 13 );
107    this->ClientSize = Drawing::Size( 400, 389 );
108    this->Controls->Add( this->outputTextBox );
109    this->Name = S"XmlReaderTest";
110    this->Text = S"XmlReaderTest";
111 } // end method InitializeComponent
112
113 // insert tabs
```

Fig. 15.8   XMLReaderTest class method definitions. (Part 3 of 4.)

```
114  void XmlReaderTest::TabOutput( int number )
115  {
116     for ( int i = 0; i < number; i++ )
117        outputTextBox->Text = String::Concat(
118           outputTextBox->Text, S"\t" );
119  } // end method TabOutput
```

Fig. 15.8 **XMLReaderTest** class method definitions. (Part 4 of 4.)

```
1   // Fig. 15.9: XmlReaderTestMain.cpp
2   // Entry point for application.
3
4   #include "XmlReaderTest.h"
5
6   int __stdcall WinMain()
7   {
8      Application::Run( new XmlReaderTest() );
9
10     return 0;
11  } // end WinMain
```

Fig. 15.9 Driver for class **XmlReaderTest**.

Line 13 (Fig. 15.7) includes the **System::Xml** namespace, which contains the XML classes used in this example. Line 15 (Fig. 15.8) creates a pointer to an *XmlDocument* object that conceptually represents an empty XML document. The XML document **article.xml** is parsed and loaded into this **XmlDocument** object when method *Load* is invoked in line 16. Once an XML document is loaded into an **XmlDocument**, its data can be read and manipulated programmatically. In this example, we read each node in the

XmlDocument, which is the DOM tree. In successive examples, we demonstrate how to manipulate node values.

Line 19 creates an **XmlNodeReader** and assign it to pointer **reader**, which enables us to read one node at a time from the **XmlDocument**. Method *Read* of **XmlNode-Reader** reads one node from the DOM tree. Placing this statement in the **while** loop (lines 28–82) makes **reader** read all the document nodes. The **switch** statement (lines 30–81) processes each node. Either the *Name* property (line 39), which contains the node's name, or the *Value* property (line 52), which contains the node's data, is formatted and concatenated to the **String** displayed in textbox **outputTextBox**. The *NodeType* property contains the node type (specifying whether the node is an element, comment, text, etc.). Notice that each **case** specifies a node type, using *XmlNodeType* enumeration constants.

Notice that the displayed output emphasizes the structure of the XML document. Variable **depth** (line 25) sets the number of tab characters used to indent each element. The depth is incremented each time an **Element** type is encountered and is decremented each time an **EndElement** or empty element is encountered. We use a similar technique in the next example to emphasize the tree structure of the XML document in the display.

Notice that our line breaks use the character sequence **"\r\n"**, which denotes a carriage return followed by a line feed. This is the standard line break for Windows-based applications and controls. Also notice that we set property **WordWrap** to **false** (line 103), which disables word wrapping in the multiline textbox (i.e., the textbox control does not break up long lines into multiple lines).

The program in Fig. 15.10–Fig. 15.12 demonstrates how to manipulate DOM trees programmatically. This program loads **letter.xml** (Fig. 15.3) into the DOM tree and then creates a second DOM tree that duplicates the DOM tree containing **letter.xml**'s contents. The GUI for this application contains a text box, a **TreeView** control and three buttons—**Build**, **Print** and **Reset**. When clicked, **Build** copies **letter.xml** and displays the document's tree structure in the **TreeView** control, **Print** displays the XML element values and names in a text box and **Reset** clears the **TreeView** control and text box content.

```
1   // Fig. 15.10: XmlDom.h
2   // Demonstrates DOM tree manipulation.
3
4   #pragma once
5
6   #using <system.dll>
7   #using <mscorlib.dll>
8   #using <system.xml.dll>
9   #using <system.drawing.dll>
10  #using <system.windows.forms.dll>
11
12  using namespace System;
13  using namespace System::Xml;
14  using namespace System::Drawing;
15  using namespace System::Windows::Forms;
16  using namespace System::IO;
```

Fig. 15.10 DOM structure of an XML document illustrated by a class. (Part 1 of 2.)

```
17
18   // contains TempFileCollection
19   using namespace System::CodeDom::Compiler;
20
21   // class XmlDom demonstrates the DOM
22   public __gc class XmlDom : public Form
23   {
24   public:
25      XmlDom();
26
27   private:
28      Button *buildButton;
29      Button *printButton;
30      TreeView *xmlTreeView;
31      TextBox *consoleTextBox;
32      Button *resetButton;
33
34      XmlDocument *source; // pointer to "XML document"
35
36      // pointer copy of source's "XML document"
37      XmlDocument *copy;
38
39      TreeNode *tree; // TreeNode pointer
40
41      void InitializeComponent();
42      void buildButton_Click( Object *, EventArgs * );
43      void printButton_Click( Object *, EventArgs * );
44      void resetButton_Click( Object *, EventArgs * );
45      void BuildTree( XmlNode *, XmlNode *, TreeNode * );
46   }; // end class XmlDom
```

Fig. 15.10 DOM structure of an XML document illustrated by a class. (Part 2 of 2.)

```
1    // Fig. 15.11: XmlDom.cpp
2    // Method definitions for class XmlDom.
3
4    #include "XmlDom.h"
5
6    XmlDom::XmlDom()
7    {
8       InitializeComponent();
9
10      // create XmlDocument and load letter.xml
11      source = new XmlDocument();
12      source->Load( S"letter.xml" );
13
14      // initialize pointers to 0
15      copy = 0;
16      tree = 0;
17   } // end constructor
18
```

Fig. 15.11 **XmlDom** class method definitions. (Part 1 of 6.)

```
19   void XmlDom::InitializeComponent()
20   {
21      this->resetButton = new Button();
22      this->buildButton = new Button();
23      this->xmlTreeView = new TreeView();
24      this->consoleTextBox = new TextBox();
25      this->printButton = new Button();
26      this->SuspendLayout();
27
28      // resetButton
29      this->resetButton->Enabled = false;
30      this->resetButton->Location = Point( 248, 8 );
31      this->resetButton->Name = S"resetButton";
32      this->resetButton->Size = Drawing::Size( 104, 23 );
33      this->resetButton->TabIndex = 4;
34      this->resetButton->Text = S"Reset";
35      this->resetButton->Click += new EventHandler(
36         this, resetButton_Click );
37
38      // buildButton
39      this->buildButton->Location = Point( 8, 8 );
40      this->buildButton->Name = S"buildButton";
41      this->buildButton->Size = Drawing::Size( 104, 23 );
42      this->buildButton->TabIndex = 0;
43      this->buildButton->Text = S"Build";
44      this->buildButton->Click += new EventHandler(
45         this, buildButton_Click );
46
47      // xmlTreeView
48      this->xmlTreeView->ImageIndex = -1;
49      this->xmlTreeView->Location = Point( 8, 40 );
50      this->xmlTreeView->Name = S"xmlTreeView";
51      this->xmlTreeView->SelectedImageIndex = -1;
52      this->xmlTreeView->Size = Drawing::Size( 344, 168 );
53      this->xmlTreeView->TabIndex = 2;
54
55      // consoleTextBox
56      this->consoleTextBox->BorderStyle = BorderStyle::FixedSingle;
57      this->consoleTextBox->Location = Point( 8, 224 );
58      this->consoleTextBox->Multiline = true;
59      this->consoleTextBox->Name = S"consoleTextBox";
60      this->consoleTextBox->ScrollBars = ScrollBars::Vertical;
61      this->consoleTextBox->Size = Drawing::Size( 344, 112 );
62      this->consoleTextBox->TabIndex = 3;
63      this->consoleTextBox->Text = S"";
64
65      // printButton
66      this->printButton->Enabled = false;
67      this->printButton->Location = Point( 128, 8 );
68      this->printButton->Name = S"printButton";
69      this->printButton->Size = Drawing::Size( 104, 23 );
70      this->printButton->TabIndex = 1;
71      this->printButton->Text = S"Print";
```

Fig. 15.11 XmlDom class method definitions. (Part 2 of 6.)

```
72      this->printButton->Click += new EventHandler(
73         this, printButton_Click );
74
75      // XmlDom
76      this->AutoScaleBaseSize = Drawing::Size( 5, 13 );
77      this->ClientSize = Drawing::Size( 360, 341 );
78      Control *control[] = { this->resetButton,
79         this->consoleTextBox, this->xmlTreeView,
80         this->printButton, this->buildButton };
81      this->Controls->AddRange( control );
82      this->Name = S"XmlDom";
83      this->Text = S"XmlDom";
84      this->ResumeLayout();
85   } // end method InitializeComponent
86
87   // event handler for buildButton click event
88   void XmlDom::buildButton_Click( Object *sender, EventArgs *e )
89   {
90      // determine if copy has been built already
91      if ( copy != 0 )
92         return;  // document already exists
93
94      // instantiate XmlDocument and TreeNode
95      copy = new XmlDocument();
96      tree = new TreeNode();
97
98      // add root node name to TreeNode and add
99      // TreeNode to TreeView control
100     tree->Text = source->Name;      // assigns #root
101     xmlTreeView->Nodes->Add( tree );
102
103     // build node and tree hierarchy
104     BuildTree( source, copy, tree );
105
106     printButton->Enabled = true;
107     resetButton->Enabled = true;
108  } // end method buildButton_Click
109
110  // event handler for printButton click event
111  void XmlDom::printButton_Click( Object *sender, EventArgs *e )
112  {
113     // exit if copy does not point to an XmlDocument
114     if ( copy == 0 )
115        return;
116
117     // create temporary XML file
118     TempFileCollection *file = new TempFileCollection();
119
120     // create file that is deleted at program termination
121     String *filename = file->AddExtension( S"xml", false );
122
123     // write XML data to disk
124     XmlTextWriter *writer = new XmlTextWriter( filename,
```

Fig. 15.11 **XmlDom** class method definitions. (Part 3 of 6.)

```
125            System::Text::Encoding::UTF8 );
126        copy->WriteTo( writer );
127        writer->Close();
128
129        // parse and load temporary XML document
130        XmlTextReader *reader = new XmlTextReader( filename );
131
132        // read, format and display data
133        while( reader->Read() ) {
134
135            if ( reader->NodeType == XmlNodeType::EndElement )
136                consoleTextBox->Text = String::Concat(
137                consoleTextBox->Text, S"/" );
138
139            if ( reader->Name != String::Empty )
140                consoleTextBox->Text = String::Concat(
141                consoleTextBox->Text, reader->Name, S"\r\n" );
142
143            if ( reader->Value != String::Empty )
144                consoleTextBox->Text = String::Concat(
145                consoleTextBox->Text, S"\t", reader->Value, S"\r\n" );
146        }
147
148        reader->Close();
149    } // end method printButton_Click
150
151    // handle resetButton click event
152    void XmlDom::resetButton_Click( Object *sender, EventArgs *e )
153    {
154        // remove TreeView nodes
155        if ( tree != 0 )
156            xmlTreeView->Nodes->Remove( tree );
157
158        xmlTreeView->Refresh(); // force TreeView update
159
160        // delete XmlDocument and tree
161        copy = 0;
162        tree = 0;
163
164        consoleTextBox->Text = S"";   // clear text box
165
166        printButton->Enabled = false;
167        resetButton->Enabled = false;
168    } // end method resetButton_Click
169
170    // construct DOM tree
171    void XmlDom::BuildTree( XmlNode *xmlSourceNode,
172        XmlNode *document, TreeNode *treeNode )
173    {
174        // create XmlNodeReader to access XML document
175        XmlNodeReader *nodeReader = new XmlNodeReader(
176            xmlSourceNode );
177
```

Fig. 15.11 XmlDom class method definitions. (Part 4 of 6.)

```
178       // represents current node in DOM tree
179       XmlNode *currentNode = 0;
180
181       // treeNode to add to existing tree
182       TreeNode *newNode = new TreeNode();
183
184       // points to modified node type for CreateNode
185       XmlNodeType modifiedNodeType;
186
187       while ( nodeReader->Read() ) {
188
189          // get current node type
190          modifiedNodeType = nodeReader->NodeType;
191
192          // check for EndElement, store as Element
193          if ( modifiedNodeType == XmlNodeType::EndElement )
194             modifiedNodeType = XmlNodeType::Element;
195
196          // create node copy
197          currentNode = copy->CreateNode( modifiedNodeType,
198             nodeReader->Name, nodeReader->NamespaceURI );
199
200          // build tree based on node type
201          switch ( nodeReader->NodeType ) {
202
203             // if Text node, add its value to tree
204             case XmlNodeType::Text:
205                newNode->Text = nodeReader->Value;
206                treeNode->Nodes->Add( newNode );
207
208                // append Text node value to currentNode data
209                dynamic_cast< XmlText * >( currentNode )->
210                   AppendData( nodeReader->Value );
211                document->AppendChild( currentNode );
212                break;
213
214             // if EndElement, move up tree
215             case XmlNodeType::EndElement:
216                document = document->ParentNode;
217                treeNode = treeNode->Parent;
218                break;
219
220             // if new element, add name and traverse tree
221             case XmlNodeType::Element:
222
223                // determine if element contains content
224                if ( !nodeReader->IsEmptyElement ) {
225
226                   // assign node text, add newNode as child
227                   newNode->Text = nodeReader->Name;
228                   treeNode->Nodes->Add( newNode );
229
```

Fig. 15.11 XmlDom class method definitions. (Part 5 of 6.)

```
230                        // set treeNode to last child
231                        treeNode = newNode;
232
233                        document->AppendChild( currentNode );
234                        document = document->LastChild;
235                     }
236
237                     // do not traverse empty elements
238                     else {
239
240                        // assign NodeType string to newNode
241                        newNode->Text =
242                           __box( nodeReader->NodeType )->ToString();
243
244                        treeNode->Nodes->Add( newNode );
245                        document->AppendChild( currentNode );
246                     }
247
248                     break;
249
250                  // all other types, display node type
251                  default:
252                     newNode->Text = __box( nodeReader->NodeType )->
253                        ToString();
254                     treeNode->Nodes->Add( newNode );
255                     document->AppendChild( currentNode );
256                     break;
257            } // end switch
258
259            newNode = new TreeNode();
260      } // end while
261
262      // update the TreeView control
263      xmlTreeView->ExpandAll();
264      xmlTreeView->Refresh();
265 } // end method BuildTree
```

Fig. 15.11 **XmlDom** class method definitions. (Part 6 of 6.)

```
1  // Fig. 15.12: XmlDomTest.cpp
2  // Entry point for application.
3
4  #include "XmlDom.h"
5
6  __stdcall WinMain()
7  {
8     Application::Run( new XmlDom() );
9
10     return 0;
11 } // end method WinMain
```

Fig. 15.12 Driver for class **XmlDom**. (Part 1 of 2.)

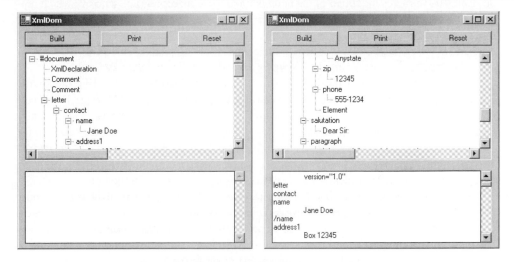

Fig. 15.12 Driver for class **XmlDom**. (Part 2 of 2.)

Lines 34 and 37 (Fig. 15.10) create pointers to **XmlDocument**s **source** and **copy**. Line 11 (Fig. 15.11) assigns a new **XmlDocument** object to pointer **source**. Line 12 then invokes method **Load** to parse and load **letter.xml**. We discuss pointer **copy** shortly.

Unfortunately, **XmlDocument**s do not provide any features for displaying their content graphically. In this example, we display the document's contents via a **TreeView** control. We use objects of class **TreeNode** to represent each node in the tree. Class **TreeView** and class **TreeNode** are part of namespace **System::Windows::Forms**. **TreeNode**s are added to the **TreeView** to emphasize the structure of the XML document.

When clicked, button **Build** triggers event handler **buildButton_Click** (lines 88–108), which copies **letter.xml** dynamically. The new **XmlDocument** and **TreeNode**s (i.e., the nodes used for graphical representation in the **TreeView**) are created in lines 95–

96. Line 100 retrieves the **Name** of the node pointed to by **source** (i.e., **#root**, which represents the document root) and assigns it to **tree**'s **Text** property. This **TreeNode** then is inserted into the **TreeView** control's node list. Method **Add** is called to add each new **TreeNode** to the **TreeView**'s **Nodes** collection. Line 104 calls method **BuildTree** to copy the **XMLDocument** pointed to by **source** and to update the **TreeView**.

Method **BuildTree** (line 171–265) receives an **XmlNode** representing the source node, an empty **XmlNode** and a **treeNode** to place in the DOM tree. Parameter **treeNode** points to the current location in the tree (i.e., the **TreeNode** most recently added to the **TreeView** control). Lines 175–176 instantiate a new **XmlNodeReader** for iterating through the DOM tree. Lines 179–182 declare **XmlNode** and **TreeNode** pointers that indicate the next nodes added to **document** (i.e., the DOM tree pointed to by **copy**) and **treeNode**. Lines 187–260 iterate through each node in the tree.

Lines 197–198 create a node containing a copy of the current **nodeReader** node. Method **CreateNode** of **XmlDocument** takes a **NodeType**, a **Name** and a **Name-spaceURI** as arguments. The **NodeType** cannot be an **EndElement** or method **CreateNode** raises **ArgumentOutOfRangeException**. If the **NodeType** is of type **EndElement**, lines 193–194 assign **modifiedNodeType** type **Element**.

The **switch** statement in lines 201–257 determines the node type, creates and adds nodes to the **TreeView** and updates the DOM tree. When a text node is encountered, the new **TreeNode**'s **newNode**'s **Text** property is assigned the current node's value. This **TreeNode** is added to the **TreeView** control. Lines 209–210 downcast **currentNode** to **XmlText** and append the node's value. The **currentNode** then is appended to the **document**. Lines 215–218 match an **EndElement** node type. This **case** moves up the tree, because the end of an element has been encountered. The **ParentNode** and **Parent** properties retrieve the **document**'s and **treeNode**'s parents, respectively.

Line 221 matches **Element** node types. Each nonempty **Element NodeType** (line 224) increases the depth of the tree; thus, we assign the current **nodeReader Name** to the **newNode**'s **Text** property and add the **newNode** to the **treeNode** node list. Lines 227–231 reorder the nodes in the node list to ensure that **newNode** is the last **TreeNode** in the node list. **XmlNode currentNode** is appended to **document** as the last child, and **document** is set to its **LastChild**, which is the child we just added. If it is an empty element (line 238), we assign to the **newNode**'s **Text** property the **String** representation of the **NodeType**. Next, the **newNode** is added to the **treeNode** node list. Line 245 appends the **currentNode** to the **document**. The **default** case assigns the string representation of the node type to the **NewNode Text** property, adds the **newNode** to the **TreeNode** node list and appends the **currentNode** to the **document**.

After building the DOM trees, the **TreeNode** node list displays in the **TreeView** control. Clicking the nodes (i.e., the **+** or **-** boxes) in the **TreeView** either expands or collapses them. Clicking **Print** invokes event handler **printButton_Click** (lines 111–149). Lines 118–121 create a temporary file for storing the XML. Line 118 creates an instance of class **TempFileCollection** (namespace **System::CodeDom::Compiler**). This class can be used to create and delete temporary files (i.e., files that store short-lived information). Line 121 calls **TempFileCollection** method **AddExtension**. We use a version of this method that accepts two arguments. The first argument is a **String *** that specifies the file extension of the file to create—in this case, **"xml"**. The second argument is a **bool** that specifies whether temporary files of this type (**xml**) should be kept after being used (i.e., when the **TempFileCollection** object is destroyed). We pass the value **false**, indicating that the temporary files (of type **xml**) should be deleted when the **TempFileCollection** is destroyed (i.e., goes out of scope). Method **AddExtension** returns the filename that it has just created, which we store in **String * filename**.

Lines 124–125 then create an **XmlTextWriter** for streaming the XML data to disk. The first argument to the **XmlTextWriter** constructor is the filename that it will use to output the data (**filename**). The second argument passed to the **XmlTextWriter** constructor specifies the encoding to use. We specify *UTF-8*, an 8-bit encoding for Unicode® characters. For more information about Unicode®, refer to Appendix D.

Line 126 calls method *WriteTo* to write the XML representation to the *XmlTextWriter* stream. Line 132 creates an *XmlTextReader* to read from the file. The **while** loop (line 138–146) reads each node in the DOM tree and writes tag names and character data to the text box. If it is an end element, a slash is concatenated. If the node has a **Name** or **Value**, that name or value is concatenated to the textbox text.

The **Reset** button's event handler, **resetButton_Click** (lines 152–168), deletes both dynamically generated trees and updates the **TreeView** control's display. Pointer **copy** is assigned **0** (to allow its tree to be garbage collected in line 161), and the **TreeNode** node list pointer **tree** is assigned **0**.

Although **XmlReader** includes methods for reading and modifying node values, it is not the most efficient means of locating data in a DOM tree. The .NET framework provides class *XPathNavigator* in namespace *System::Xml::XPath* for iterating through node lists that match search criteria, which are written as an *XPath expression*. XPath (XML Path Language) provides a syntax for locating specific nodes in XML documents effectively and efficiently. XPath is a string-based language of expressions used by XML and many of its related technologies (such as XSLT, discussed in Section 15.6).

Figure 15.13–Fig. 15.15 demonstrate how to navigate through an XML document with an **XPathNavigator**. Like Fig. 15.10–Fig. 15.12, this program uses a **TreeView** control and **TreeNode** objects to display the XML document's structure. However, instead of displaying the entire DOM tree, the **TreeNode** node list is updated each time the **XPathNavigator** is positioned to a new node. Nodes are added to and deleted from the **TreeView** to reflect the **XPathNavigator**'s location in the DOM tree. The XML document **sports.xml** that we use in this example is presented in Fig. 15.16.

```
1   // Fig. 15.13: PathNavigator.h
2   // Demonstrates Class XPathNavigator.
3
4   #pragma once
5
6   #using <system.dll>
7   #using <mscorlib.dll>
8   #using <system.xml.dll>
9   #using <system.drawing.dll>
10  #using <system.windows.forms.dll>
11
12  using namespace System;
13  using namespace System::Xml;
```

Fig. 15.13 **XPathNavigator** class used to navigate selected nodes. (Part 1 of 2.)

```
14   using namespace System::Drawing;
15   using namespace System::Windows::Forms;
16   using namespace System::Xml::XPath; // contains XPathNavigator
17
18   public __gc class PathNavigator : public Form
19   {
20   public:
21      PathNavigator();
22
23   private:
24      Button *firstChildButton;
25      Button *parentButton;
26      Button *nextButton;
27      Button *previousButton;
28      Button *selectButton;
29      TreeView *pathTreeViewer;
30      ComboBox *selectComboBox;
31      TextBox *selectTreeViewer;
32      GroupBox *navigateBox;
33      GroupBox *locateBox;
34
35      // navigator to traverse document
36      XPathNavigator *xpath;
37
38      // points to document for use by XPathNavigator
39      XPathDocument *document;
40
41      // points to TreeNode list used by TreeView control
42      TreeNode *tree;
43
44      void InitializeComponent();
45      void firstChildButton_Click( Object *, EventArgs * );
46      void parentButton_Click( Object *, EventArgs * );
47      void nextButton_Click( Object *, EventArgs * );
48      void previousButton_Click( Object *, EventArgs * );
49      void selectButton_Click( Object *, EventArgs * );
50      void DisplayIterator( XPathNodeIterator * );
51      void DetermineType( TreeNode *, XPathNavigator * );
52   }; // end class PathNavigator
```

Fig. 15.13 XPathNavigator class used to navigate selected nodes. (Part 2 of 2.)

```
1    // Fig. 15.14: PathNavigator.cpp
2    // Method definitions for class PathNavigator.
3
4    #include "PathNavigator.h"
5
6    PathNavigator::PathNavigator()
7    {
8       InitializeComponent();
9
```

Fig. 15.14 PathNavigator class method definitions. (Part 1 of 7.)

```
10      // load in XML document
11      document = new XPathDocument( S"sports.xml" );
12
13      // create navigator
14      xpath = document->CreateNavigator();
15
16      // create root node for TreeNodes
17      tree = new TreeNode();
18      tree->Text = __box( xpath->NodeType )->ToString();   // #root
19      pathTreeViewer->Nodes->Add( tree );        // add tree
20
21      // update TreeView control
22      pathTreeViewer->ExpandAll();
23      pathTreeViewer->Refresh();
24      pathTreeViewer->SelectedNode = tree;      // highlight root
25   } // end constructor
26
27   void PathNavigator::InitializeComponent()
28   {
29      this->selectButton = new Button();
30      this->nextButton = new Button();
31      this->parentButton = new Button();
32      this->firstChildButton = new Button();
33      this->pathTreeViewer = new TreeView();
34      this->previousButton = new Button();
35      this->selectComboBox = new ComboBox();
36      this->navigateBox = new GroupBox();
37      this->locateBox = new GroupBox();
38      this->selectTreeViewer = new TextBox();
39      this->navigateBox->SuspendLayout();
40      this->locateBox->SuspendLayout();
41      this->SuspendLayout();
42
43      // selectButton
44      this->selectButton->Location = Point( 8, 24 );
45      this->selectButton->Name = S"selectButton";
46      this->selectButton->Size = Drawing::Size( 80, 23 );
47      this->selectButton->TabIndex = 9;
48      this->selectButton->Text = S"Select";
49      this->selectButton->Click += new EventHandler( this,
50         selectButton_Click );
51
52      // nextButton
53      this->nextButton->Location = Point( 48, 88 );
54      this->nextButton->Name = S"nextButton";
55      this->nextButton->Size = Drawing::Size( 80, 23 );
56      this->nextButton->TabIndex = 3;
57      this->nextButton->Text = S"Next";
58      this->nextButton->Click += new EventHandler( this,
59         nextButton_Click );
60
61      // parentButton
62      this->parentButton->Location = Point( 8, 56 );
```

Fig. 15.14 PathNavigator class method definitions. (Part 2 of 7.)

```
63    this->parentButton->Name = S"parentButton";
64    this->parentButton->Size = Drawing::Size( 80, 23 );
65    this->parentButton->TabIndex = 2;
66    this->parentButton->Text = S"Parent";
67    this->parentButton->Click += new EventHandler( this,
68       parentButton_Click );
69
70    // firstChildButton
71    this->firstChildButton->Location = Point( 96, 56 );
72    this->firstChildButton->Name = S"firstChildButton";
73    this->firstChildButton->Size = Drawing::Size( 80, 24 );
74    this->firstChildButton->TabIndex = 1;
75    this->firstChildButton->Text = S"First Child";
76    this->firstChildButton->Click += new EventHandler( this,
77       firstChildButton_Click );
78
79    // pathTreeViewer
80    this->pathTreeViewer->FullRowSelect = true;
81    this->pathTreeViewer->HideSelection = false;
82    this->pathTreeViewer->ImageIndex = -1;
83    this->pathTreeViewer->Location = Point( 8, 264 );
84    this->pathTreeViewer->Name = S"pathTreeViewer";
85    this->pathTreeViewer->SelectedImageIndex = -1;
86    this->pathTreeViewer->Size = Drawing::Size( 328, 144 );
87    this->pathTreeViewer->TabIndex = 13;
88
89    // previousButton
90    this->previousButton->Location = Point( 48, 24 );
91    this->previousButton->Name = S"previousButton";
92    this->previousButton->Size = Drawing::Size( 80, 23 );
93    this->previousButton->TabIndex = 7;
94    this->previousButton->Text = S"Previous";
95    this->previousButton->Click += new EventHandler( this,
96       previousButton_Click );
97
98    // selectComboBox
99    String *object[] = { S"/sports", S"/sports/game/name",
100      S"/sports/game/paragraph",
101      S"/sports/game[name=\'Cricket\']" };
102   this->selectComboBox->DropDownWidth = 240;
103   this->selectComboBox->Items->AddRange( object );
104   this->selectComboBox->Location = Point( 96, 24 );
105   this->selectComboBox->Name = S"selectComboBox";
106   this->selectComboBox->Size = Drawing::Size( 240, 21 );
107   this->selectComboBox->TabIndex = 14;
108
109   // navigateBox
110   Button *buttons[] = { this->firstChildButton,
111      this->parentButton, this->previousButton,
112      this->nextButton };
113   this->navigateBox->Controls->AddRange( buttons );
114   this->navigateBox->Location = Point( 80, 136 );
115   this->navigateBox->Name = S"navigateBox";
```

Fig. 15.14 PathNavigator class method definitions. (Part 3 of 7.)

```
116      this->navigateBox->Size = Drawing::Size( 184, 120 );
117      this->navigateBox->TabIndex = 16;
118      this->navigateBox->TabStop = false;
119      this->navigateBox->Text = S"Navigation Controls";
120
121      // locateBox
122      this->locateBox->Controls->Add( this->selectTreeViewer );
123      this->locateBox->Controls->Add( this->selectComboBox );
124      this->locateBox->Controls->Add( this->selectButton );
125      this->locateBox->Location = Point( 8, 8 );
126      this->locateBox->Name = S"locateBox";
127      this->locateBox->Size = Drawing::Size( 336, 128 );
128      this->locateBox->TabIndex = 17;
129      this->locateBox->TabStop = false;
130      this->locateBox->Text = S"Locate Element";
131
132      // selectTreeViewer
133      this->selectTreeViewer->BackColor = Color::Honeydew;
134      this->selectTreeViewer->Location = Point( 16, 56 );
135      this->selectTreeViewer->Multiline = true;
136      this->selectTreeViewer->Name = S"selectTreeViewer";
137      this->selectTreeViewer->ReadOnly = true;
138      this->selectTreeViewer->Size = Drawing::Size( 304, 64 );
139      this->selectTreeViewer->TabIndex = 15;
140      this->selectTreeViewer->Text = S"";
141
142      // PathNavigator
143      this->AutoScaleBaseSize = Drawing::Size( 5, 13 );
144      this->ClientSize = Drawing::Size( 352, 413 );
145      this->Controls->Add( this->locateBox );
146      this->Controls->Add( this->navigateBox );
147      this->Controls->Add( this->pathTreeViewer );
148      this->Name = S"PathNavigator";
149      this->Text = S"PathNavigator";
150      this->navigateBox->ResumeLayout();
151      this->locateBox->ResumeLayout();
152      this->ResumeLayout();
153  } // end method InitializeComponent
154
155  // traverse to first child
156  void PathNavigator::firstChildButton_Click( Object *sender,
157      EventArgs *e )
158  {
159      TreeNode *newTreeNode;
160
161      // move to first child
162      if ( xpath->MoveToFirstChild() )   {
163         newTreeNode = new TreeNode(); // create new node
164
165         // set node's Text property to either
166         // navigator's name or value
167         DetermineType( newTreeNode, xpath );
168
```

Fig. 15.14 PathNavigator class method definitions. (Part 4 of 7.)

```
169          // add node to TreeNode node list
170          tree->Nodes->Add( newTreeNode );
171          tree = newTreeNode; // assign tree newTreeNode
172
173          // update TreeView control
174          pathTreeViewer->ExpandAll();
175          pathTreeViewer->Refresh();
176          pathTreeViewer->SelectedNode = tree;
177       }
178    else // node has no children
179          MessageBox::Show( S"Current Node has no children.",
180             S"", MessageBoxButtons::OK,
181             MessageBoxIcon::Information );
182  } // end method firstChildButton_Click
183
184  // traverse to node's parent on parentButton click event
185  void PathNavigator::parentButton_Click( Object *sender,
186     EventArgs *e )
187  {
188     // move to parent
189     if ( xpath->MoveToParent() ) {
190          tree = tree->Parent;
191
192          // get number of child nodes, not including subtrees
193          int count = tree->GetNodeCount( false );
194
195          // remove all children
196          tree->Nodes->Clear();
197
198          // update TreeView control
199          pathTreeViewer->ExpandAll();
200          pathTreeViewer->Refresh();
201          pathTreeViewer->SelectedNode = tree;
202       }
203    else // if node has no parent (root node)
204          MessageBox::Show( S"Current node has no parent.", S"",
205             MessageBoxButtons::OK,
206             MessageBoxIcon::Information );
207  } // end method parentButton_Click
208
209  // find next sibling on nextButton click event
210  void PathNavigator::nextButton_Click( Object *sender,
211     EventArgs *e )
212  {
213     TreeNode *newTreeNode = 0, *newNode = 0;
214
215     // move to next sibling
216     if ( xpath->MoveToNext() ) {
217          newTreeNode = tree->Parent; // get parent node
218
219          newNode = new TreeNode(); // create new node
220          DetermineType( newNode, xpath );
221          newTreeNode->Nodes->Add( newNode );
```

Fig. 15.14 PathNavigator class method definitions. (Part 5 of 7.)

```
222
223         // set current position for display
224         tree = newNode;
225
226         // update TreeView control
227         pathTreeViewer->ExpandAll();
228         pathTreeViewer->Refresh();
229         pathTreeViewer->SelectedNode = tree;
230      }
231   else // node has no additional siblings
232      MessageBox::Show( S"Current node is last sibling.",
233         S"", MessageBoxButtons::OK,
234         MessageBoxIcon::Information );
235 } // end method nextButton_Click
236
237 // get previous sibling on previousButton click
238 void PathNavigator::previousButton_Click( Object *sender,
239    EventArgs *e )
240 {
241    TreeNode *parentTreeNode = 0;
242
243    // move to previous sibling
244    if ( xpath->MoveToPrevious() ) {
245       parentTreeNode = tree->Parent; // get parent node
246
247       // delete current node
248       parentTreeNode->Nodes->Remove( tree );
249
250       // move to previous node
251       tree = parentTreeNode->LastNode;
252
253       // update TreeView control
254       pathTreeViewer->ExpandAll();
255       pathTreeViewer->Refresh();
256       pathTreeViewer->SelectedNode = tree;
257    }
258    else // if current node has no previous siblings
259       MessageBox::Show( S"Current node is first sibling.",
260          S"", MessageBoxButtons::OK,
261          MessageBoxIcon::Information );
262 } // end method previousButton_Click
263
264 // process selectButton click event
265 void PathNavigator::selectButton_Click( Object *sender,
266    EventArgs *e )
267 {
268    XPathNodeIterator *iterator; // enables node iteration
269
270    // get specified node from ComboBox
271    try {
272       iterator = xpath->Select( selectComboBox->Text );
273       DisplayIterator( iterator ); // print selection
274    }
```

Fig. 15.14 PathNavigator class method definitions. (Part 6 of 7.)

```
275
276     // catch invalid expressions
277     catch ( ArgumentException *argumentException ) {
278        MessageBox::Show( argumentException->Message,
279           S"Error", MessageBoxButtons::OK,
280           MessageBoxIcon::Error );
281     }
282
283     // catch empty expressions
284     catch ( XPathException * ) {
285        MessageBox::Show( S"Please select an expression",
286           S"Error", MessageBoxButtons::OK,
287           MessageBoxIcon::Error );
288     }
289  } // end method selectButton_Click
290
291  // print values for XPathNodeIterator
292  void PathNavigator::DisplayIterator(
293     XPathNodeIterator *iterator )
294  {
295     selectTreeViewer->Text = S"";
296
297     // prints selected node's values
298     while ( iterator->MoveNext() )
299        selectTreeViewer->Text = String::Concat(
300           iterator->Current->Value->Trim(),
301           selectTreeViewer->Text, S"\r\n" );
302  } // end method DisplayIterator
303
304  // determine if TreeNode should display current node name
305  // or value
306  void PathNavigator::DetermineType( TreeNode *node,
307     XPathNavigator *xPath )
308  {
309     // if Element, get its name
310     if ( xPath->NodeType == XPathNodeType::Element ) {
311
312        // get current node name, remove whitespace
313        node->Text = xPath->Name->Trim();
314     }
315     else {
316
317        // get current node value, remove whitespace
318        node->Text = xPath->Value->Trim();
319     }
320  } // end method DetermineType
```

Fig. 15.14 PathNavigator class method definitions. (Part 7 of 7.)

```
1    // Fig. 15.15: PathNavigatorTest.cpp
2    // Entry point for application.
3
```

Fig. 15.15 PathNavigator class driver. (Part 1 of 3.)

```
4   #include "PathNavigator.h"
5
6   int __stdcall WinMain()
7   {
8      Application::Run( new PathNavigator() );
9
10     return 0;
11  } // end WinMain
```

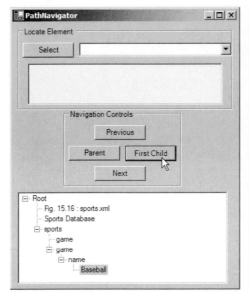

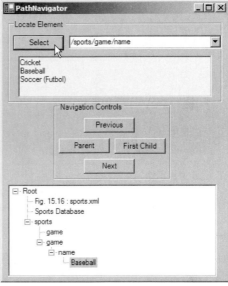

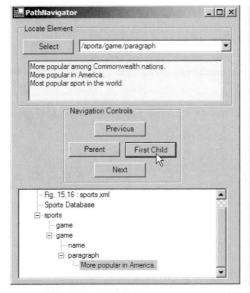

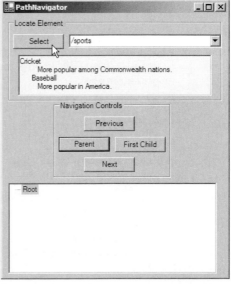

Fig. 15.15 PathNavigator class driver. (Part 2 of 3.)

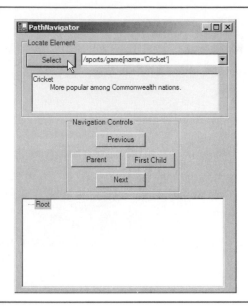

Fig. 15.15 PathNavigator class driver. (Part 3 of 3.)

```
1   <?xml version = "1.0"?>
2
3   <!-- Fig. 15.16: sports.xml   -->
4   <!-- Sports Database.         -->
5
6   <sports>
7
8      <game id = "783">
9         <name>Cricket</name>
10
11        <paragraph>
12           More popular among Commonwealth nations.
13        </paragraph>
14     </game>
15
16     <game id = "239">
17        <name>Baseball</name>
18
19        <paragraph>
20           More popular in America.
21        </paragraph>
22     </game>
23
24     <game id = "418">
25        <name>Soccer(Futbol)</name>
26        <paragraph>Most popular sport in the world</paragraph>
27     </game>
28  </sports>
```

Fig. 15.16 XML document that describes various sports.

This program loads XML document **sports.xml** into an *XPathDocument* object by passing the document's file name to the **XPathDocument** constructor (line 11 of Fig. 15.14). Method *CreateNavigator* (line 14) creates and returns an **XPathNavigator** pointer to the **XPathDocument**'s tree structure.

The navigation methods of **XPathNavigator** used in Fig. 15.14 are *MoveToFirstChild* (line 162), *MoveToParent* (line 189), *MoveToNext* (line 216) and *MoveToPrevious* (line 244). Each method performs the action that its name implies. Method **MoveToFirstChild** moves to the first child of the node pointed to by the **XPathNavigator**, **MoveToParent** moves to the parent node of the node pointed to by the **XPathNavigator**, **MoveToNext** moves to the next sibling of the node pointed to by the **XPathNavigator** and **MoveToPrevious** moves to the previous sibling of the node pointed to by the **XPathNavigator**. Each method returns a **bool** indicating whether the move was successful. In this example, we display a warning in a **MessageBox** whenever a move operation fails. Furthermore, each of these methods is called in the event handler of the button that matches its name (e.g., button **First Child** triggers **firstChildButton_Click**, which calls **MoveToFirstChild**).

Whenever we move forward via the **XPathNavigator**, as with **MoveToFirstChild** and **MoveToNext**, nodes are added to the **TreeNode** node list. Method **DetermineType** is a **private** method (defined in lines 306–320) that determines whether to assign the **Node**'s **Name** property or **Value** property to the **TreeNode** (lines 313 and 318). Whenever **MoveToParent** is called, all children of the parent node are removed from the display. Similarly, a call to **MoveToPrevious** removes the current sibling node. Note that the nodes are removed only from the **TreeView**, not from the tree representation of the document.

The other event handler corresponds to button **Select** (line 265–289). Method *Select* (line 272) takes search criteria in the form of either an *XPathExpression* or a **String *** that represents an XPath expression and returns as an **XPathNodeIterator** object any nodes that match the search criteria. The XPath expressions provided by this program's combo box are summarized in Fig. 15.17. The **catch** blocks in lines 277–288 catch any exceptions (**ArgumentException** or **XPathException**) that can occur if the user enters an invalid or empty expression.

Expression	Description
/sports	Matches the **sports** node that is a child node of the document root node. This node contains the root element.
/sports/game/name	Matches all **name** nodes that are child nodes of **game**. The **game** node must be a child of **sports** and **sports** must be a root element node.
/sports/game/paragraph	Matches all **paragraph** nodes that are child nodes of **game**. The **game** node must be a child of **sports**, and **sports** must be a root element node.

Fig. 15.17 XPath expressions and descriptions used in Fig. 15.13–Fig. 15.15. (Part 1 of 2.)

Expression	Description
`/sports/` `game[name='Cricket']`	Matches all **game** nodes that contain a child element **name** whose value is `Cricket`. The **game** node must be a child of **sports**, and **sports** must be a root element node.

Fig. 15.17 XPath expressions and descriptions used in Fig. 15.13–Fig. 15.15. (Part 2 of 2.)

Method **DisplayIterator** (defined in lines 292–302) appends the node values from the given **XPathNodeIterator** to the **selectTreeViewer** text box. Note that we call the **String** method **Trim** to remove unnecessary whitespace. Method *MoveNext* (line 298) advances to the next node, which can be accessed via property *Current* (line 300).

15.5 Document Type Definitions (DTDs), Schemas and Validation

XML documents can reference optional documents that specify how the XML documents should be structured. These optional documents are called *Document Type Definitions (DTDs)* and *Schemas*. When a DTD or Schema document is provided, some parsers (called *validating parsers*) can read the DTD or Schema and check the XML document's structure against it. If the XML document conforms to the DTD or Schema, then the XML document is *valid*. Parsers that cannot check for document conformity against the DTD or Schema are called *non-validating parsers*. If an XML parser (validating or non-validating) is able to process an XML document (that does not reference a DTD or Schema), the XML document is considered to be *well formed* (i.e., it is syntactically correct). By definition, a valid XML document is also a well-formed XML document. If a document is not well formed, parsing halts, and the parser issues an error.

Software Engineering Observation 15.2

DTD and Schema documents are essential components for XML documents used in business-to-business (B2B) transactions and mission-critical systems. These documents help ensure that XML documents are valid.

Software Engineering Observation 15.3

Because XML document content can be structured in many different ways, an application cannot determine whether the document it receives is complete, is missing data or is ordered properly. DTDs and Schemas solve this problem by providing an extensible means of describing a document's contents. An application can use a DTD or Schema document to perform a validity check on the document's contents.

15.5.1 Document Type Definitions

Document type definitions (DTDs) provide a means for type-checking XML documents and thus for verifying their *validity* (confirming that elements contain the proper attributes, elements are in the proper sequence, etc.). DTDs use *EBNF* (*Extended Backus-Naur Form*) *grammar* to describe an XML document's content. XML parsers need additional functionality to read EBNF grammar, because it is not XML syntax. Although DTDs are optional, they are recommended to ensure document conformity. The DTD in Fig. 15.18 defines the set of rules (i.e., the grammar) for structuring the business letter document contained in Fig. 15.19.

Portability Tip 15.2

DTDs can ensure consistency among XML documents generated by different programs.

Lines 4–5 use the ***ELEMENT*** *element type declaration* to define rules for element **letter**. In this case, **letter** contains one or more **contact** elements, one **salutation** element, one or more **paragraph** elements, one **closing** element and one **signature** element, in that sequence. The *plus sign* (**+**) *occurrence indicator* specifies that an element must occur one or more times. Other indicators include the *asterisk* (*****), which indicates an optional element that can occur any number of times, and the *question mark* (**?**), which indicates an optional element that can occur at most once. If an occurrence indicator is omitted, exactly one occurrence is expected.

The **contact** element definition (lines 7–8) specifies that it contains the **name**, **address1**, **address2**, **city**, **state**, **zip**, **phone** and **flag** elements—in that order. Exactly one occurrence of each is expected.

```
1    <!-- Fig. 15.18: letter.dtd        -->
2    <!-- DTD document for letter.xml. -->
3
4    <!ELEMENT letter ( contact+, salutation, paragraph+,
5       closing, signature )>
6
7    <!ELEMENT contact ( name, address1, address2, city, state,
8       zip, phone, flag )>
9    <!ATTLIST contact type CDATA #IMPLIED>
10
11   <!ELEMENT name ( #PCDATA )>
12   <!ELEMENT address1 ( #PCDATA )>
13   <!ELEMENT address2 ( #PCDATA )>
14   <!ELEMENT city ( #PCDATA )>
15   <!ELEMENT state ( #PCDATA )>
16   <!ELEMENT zip ( #PCDATA )>
17   <!ELEMENT phone ( #PCDATA )>
18   <!ELEMENT flag EMPTY>
19   <!ATTLIST flag gender (M | F) "M">
20
21   <!ELEMENT salutation ( #PCDATA )>
22   <!ELEMENT closing ( #PCDATA )>
23   <!ELEMENT paragraph ( #PCDATA )>
24   <!ELEMENT signature ( #PCDATA )>
```

Fig. 15.18 Document Type Definition (DTD) for a business letter.

Line 9 uses the ***ATTLIST*** *element type declaration* to define an attribute (i.e., **type**) for the **contact** element. Keyword ***#IMPLIED*** specifies that, if the parser finds a **con-tact** element without a **type** attribute, the application can provide a value or ignore the missing attribute. The absence of a **type** attribute cannot invalidate the document. Other types of default values include ***#REQUIRED*** and ***#FIXED***. Keyword ***#REQUIRED*** specifies that the attribute must be present in the document; keyword ***#FIXED*** specifies that the attribute (if present) must always be assigned a specific value. For example,

> `<!ATTLIST address zip #FIXED "01757">`

indicates that the value **01757** must be used for attribute **zip**; otherwise, the document is invalid. If the attribute is not present, then the parser, by default, uses the fixed value that is specified in the **ATTLIST** declaration. Flag ***CDATA*** specifies that attribute **type** contains a **String** that is not processed by the parser, but instead is passed to the application as is.

Software Engineering Observation 15.4

DTD syntax does not provide any mechanism for describing an element's (or attribute's) data type.

Flag ***#PCDATA*** (line 11) specifies that the element can store *parsed character data* (i.e., text). Parsed character data cannot contain markup. The characters *less than* (**<**) and *ampersand* (**&**) must be replaced by their *entities* (i.e., **<** and **&**). However, the ampersand character can be inserted when used with entities. See Appendix F, Introduction to XHTML: Part 2, for a list of predefined entities.

Line 18 defines an empty element named **flag**. Keyword ***EMPTY*** specifies that the element cannot contain character data. Empty elements commonly are used for their attributes.

Line 19 presents an *enumerated attribute types*, which declare a list of possible values an attribute can have. The attribute must be assigned a value from this list to conform to the DTD. Enumerated type values are separated by pipe characters (|). Line 19 contains an enumerated attribute type declaration that allows attribute **gender** to have either the value **M** or **F**. A default value of **"M"** is specified to the right of the element attribute type.

Common Programming Error 15.9

Any element, attribute or relationship not explicitly defined by a DTD results in an invalid document.

XML documents must explicitly reference a DTD against which they are going to be validated. Figure 15.19 is an XML document that conforms to **letter.dtd** (Fig. 15.18).

```
1   <?xml version = "1.0"?>
2
3   <!-- Fig. 15.19: letter2.xml              -->
4   <!-- Business letter formatted with XML. -->
5
6   <!DOCTYPE letter SYSTEM "letter.dtd">
7
8   <letter>
9       <contact type = "from">
```

Fig. 15.19 XML document referencing its associated DTD. (Part 1 of 2.)

```
10              <name>Jane Doe</name>
11              <address1>Box 12345</address1>
12              <address2>15 Any Ave.</address2>
13              <city>Othertown</city>
14              <state>Otherstate</state>
15              <zip>67890</zip>
16              <phone>555-4321</phone>
17              <flag gender = "F" />
18          </contact>
19
20          <contact type = "to">
21              <name>John Doe</name>
22              <address1>123 Main St.</address1>
23              <address2></address2>
24              <city>Anytown</city>
25              <state>Anystate</state>
26              <zip>12345</zip>
27              <phone>555-1234</phone>
28              <flag gender = "M" />
29          </contact>
30
31          <salutation>Dear Sir:</salutation>
32
33          <paragraph>It is our privilege to inform you about our new
34              database managed with XML. This new system
35              allows you to reduce the load on your inventory list
36              server by having the client machine perform the work of
37              sorting and filtering the data.
38          </paragraph>
39
40          <paragraph>Please visit our Web site for availability
41              and pricing.
42          </paragraph>
43          <closing>Sincerely</closing>
44          <signature>Ms. Doe</signature>
45      </letter>
```

Fig. 15.19 XML document referencing its associated DTD. (Part 2 of 2.)

This XML document is similar to that in Fig. 15.3. Line 6 references a DTD file. This markup contains three pieces: the name of the root element (**letter** in line 8) to which the DTD is applied, the keyword **SYSTEM** (which in this case denotes an *external DTD*—a DTD defined in a separate file) and the DTD's name and location (i.e., **letter.dtd** in the current directory). Though almost any file extension can be used, DTD documents typically end with the **.dtd** extension.

Various tools (many of which are free) check document conformity against DTDs and Schemas (discussed momentarily). The output in Fig. 15.20 shows the results of the validation of **letter2.xml** using Microsoft's *XML Validator*. Visit **www.w3.org/XML/Schema.html** for a list of validating tools. Microsoft's XML Validator is available free for download from

```
msdn.microsoft.com/downloads/samples/Internet/xml/
xml_validator/sample.asp
```

Microsoft's XML Validator can validate XML documents against DTDs locally or by uploading the documents to the XML Validator Web site. Here, **letter2.xml** and **letter.dtd** are placed in folder **C:\XML**. This XML document (**letter2.xml**) is well formed and conforms to **letter.dtd**.

XML documents that fail validation might still be well-formed documents. When a document fails to conform to a DTD or Schema, Microsoft XML Validator displays an error message. For example, the DTD in Fig. 15.18 indicates that the **contacts** element must contain child element **name**. If the document omits this child element, the document is well formed, but not valid. In such a scenario, Microsoft XML Validator displays the error message shown in Fig. 15.21.

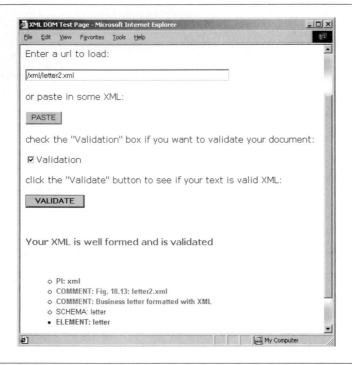

Fig. 15.20 XML Validator validates an XML document against a DTD.

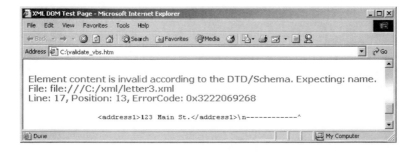

Fig. 15.21 XML Validator displaying an error message.

MC++ programs can use msxml to validate XML documents against DTDs. For information on how to accomplish this, visit:

**msdn.microsoft.com/library/en-us/cpguide/html/
cpconvalidationagainstdtdwithxmlvalidatingreader.asp**

Schemas are the preferred means of defining structures for XML documents in .NET. Although several types of Schema exist, the two most popular are Microsoft Schema and W3C Schema. We begin our discussion of Schemas in the next section.

15.5.2 Microsoft XML Schemas[3]

In this section, we introduce an alternative to DTDs—called Schemas—for defining an XML document's structure. Many developers in the XML community feel that DTDs are not flexible enough to meet today's programming needs. For example, DTDs cannot be manipulated (e.g., searched, programmatically modified, etc.) in the same manner that XML documents can, because DTDs are not XML documents. Furthermore, DTDs do not provide features for describing an element's (or attribute's) data type.

Unlike DTDs, Schemas do not use Extended Backus-Naur Form (EBNF) grammar. Instead, Schemas are XML documents which can be manipulated (e.g., elements can be added or removed, etc.) like any other XML document. As with DTDs, Schemas require validating parsers.

In this section, we focus on Microsoft's *XML Schema* vocabulary. Figure 15.22 presents an XML document that conforms to the Microsoft Schema document shown in Fig. 15.23. By convention, Microsoft XML Schema documents use the file extension **.xdr**, which is short for *XML-Data Reduced*. Line 6 (Fig. 15.22) references the Schema document **book.xdr**. A document using a Microsoft XML Schema uses attribute **xmlns** to reference its schema through a URI which begins with **x-schema** followed by a colon (**:**) and the name of the schema document.

```
1   <?xml version = "1.0"?>
2
3   <!-- Fig. 15.22: bookxdr.xml           -->
4   <!-- XML file that marks up book data. -->
5
6   <books xmlns = "x-schema:book.xdr">
7      <book>
8         <title>Visual C++ .NET: A Managed Code Approach for
9            Experienced Programmers</title>
10     </book>
11
12     <book>
13        <title>C# for Experienced Programmers</title>
14     </book>
```

Fig. 15.22 XML document that conforms to a Microsoft Schema document. (Part 1 of 2.)

---

3. W3C Schema, which we discuss in Section 15.5.3, is emerging as the industry standard for describing an XML document's structure. Within the next two years, we expect most developers will be using W3C Schema.

```
15
16      <book>
17        <title>Visual Basic .NET for Experienced Programmers
18        </title>
19      </book>
20
21      <book>
22        <title>Java Web Services for Experienced Programmers
23        </title>
24      </book>
25
26      <book>
27        <title>Web Services: A Technical Introduction</title>
28      </book>
29    </books>
```

Fig. 15.22 XML document that conforms to a Microsoft Schema document.
(Part 2 of 2.)

```
1    <?xml version = "1.0"?>
2
3    <!-- Fig. 15.23: book.xdr                         -->
4    <!-- Schema document to which book.xml conforms. -->
5
6    <Schema xmlns = "urn:schemas-microsoft-com:xml-data">
7      <ElementType name = "title" content = "textOnly"
8        model = "closed" />
9
10     <ElementType name = "book" content = "eltOnly" model = "closed">
11       <element type = "title" minOccurs = "1" maxOccurs = "1" />
12     </ElementType>
13
14     <ElementType name = "books" content = "eltOnly" model = "closed">
15       <element type = "book" minOccurs = "0" maxOccurs = "*" />
16     </ElementType>
17   </Schema>
```

Fig. 15.23 Microsoft Schema file that contains the structure to which **bookxdr.xml** conforms.

Software Engineering Observation 15.5

Schemas are XML documents that conform to DTDs, which define the structure of a Schema. These DTDs, which are bundled with the parser, are used to validate the Schemas that authors create.

Software Engineering Observation 15.6

Many organizations and individuals are creating DTDs and Schemas for a broad range of categories (e.g., financial transactions, medical prescriptions, etc.). Often, these collections—called repositories*—are available free for download from the Web.[4]*

---

4. See, for example, **opengis.net/schema.htm**.

In line 6 of Fig. 15.23, root element *Schema* begins the Schema markup. Microsoft Schemas use the namespace URI *"urn:schemas-microsoft-com:xml-data"*. Lines 7–8 use element *ElementType* to define element **title**. Attribute *content* specifies that this element contains parsed character data (i.e., text only). Element **title** is not permitted to contain child elements. Setting the *model* attribute to *"closed"* specifies that the element can only contain elements defined in the specified Schema. Line 10 defines element **book**; this element's **content** is "elements only" (i.e., *eltOnly*). This means that the element cannot contain mixed content (i.e., text and other elements). Within the **ElementType** element named **book**, the *element* element indicates that **title** is a **child** element of **book**. Attributes *minOccurs* and *maxOccurs* are set to *"1"*, indicating that a **book** element must contain exactly one **title** element. The asterisk (*) in line 15 indicates that the Schema permits any number of **book** elements in element **books**. We discuss how to validate **bookxdr.xml** against **book.xdr** in Section 15.5.4.

15.5.3 W3C XML Schema[5]

In this section, we focus on *W3C XML Schema*[6]—the schema that the W3C created. W3C XML Schema is a *Recommendation* (i.e., a stable release suitable for use in industry). Figure 15.24 shows a Schema-valid XML document named **bookxsd.xml** and Fig. 15.25 shows the W3C XML Schema document (**book.xsd**) that defines the structure for **bookxsd.xml**. Although Schema authors can use virtually any filename extension, W3C XML Schemas typically use the *.xsd* extension. We discuss how to validate **bookxsd.xml** against **book.xsd** in the next section.

```
1   <?xml version = "1.0"?>
2
3   <!-- Fig. 15.24: bookxsd.xml                    -->
4   <!-- Document that conforms to W3C XML Schema. -->
5
6   <deitel:books xmlns:deitel = "http://www.deitel.com/booklist">
7      <book>
8         <title>Perl How to Program</title>
9      </book>
10     <book>
11        <title>Python How to Program</title>
12     </book>
13  </deitel:books>
```

Fig. 15.24 XML document that conforms to W3C XML Schema.

```
1   <?xml version = "1.0"?>
2
```

Fig. 15.25 XSD Schema document to which **bookxsd.xml** conforms. (Part 1 of 2.)

---

5. We provide a detailed treatment of W3C Schema in *XML for Experienced Programmers* (late 2003).
6. For the latest on W3C XML Schema, visit **www.w3.org/XML/Schema**.

```
3    <!-- Fig. 15.25: book.xsd              -->
4    <!-- Simple W3C XML Schema document. -->
5
6    <xsd:schema xmlns:xsd = "http://www.w3.org/2001/XMLSchema"
7       xmlns:deitel = "http://www.deitel.com/booklist"
8       targetNamespace = "http://www.deitel.com/booklist">
9
10      <xsd:element name = "books" type = "deitel:BooksType"/>
11
12      <xsd:complexType name = "BooksType">
13         <xsd:sequence>
14            <xsd:element name = "book" type = "deitel:BookType"
15            minOccurs = "1" maxOccurs = "unbounded"/>
16         </xsd:sequence>
17      </xsd:complexType>
18
19      <xsd:complexType name = "BookType">
20         <xsd:sequence>
21            <xsd:element name = "title" type = "xsd:string"/>
22         </xsd:sequence>
23      </xsd:complexType>
24
25   </xsd:schema>
```

Fig. 15.25 XSD Schema document to which **bookxsd.xml** conforms. (Part 2 of 2.)

W3C XML Schemas use the namespace URI ***www.w3.org/2001/XMLSchema*** and often use *namespace prefix **xsd*** (line 6 in Fig. 15.25). Root element ***schema*** contains elements that define the XML document's structure. Line 7 binds the URI **http://www.deitel.com/booklist** to namespace prefix **deitel**. Line 8 specifies the ***targetNamespace***, which is the namespace for elements and attributes that this schema defines.

In W3C XML Schema, element ***element*** (line 10) defines an element. Attributes ***name*** and ***type*** specify the **element**'s name and data type, respectively. In this case, the name of the element is **books** and the data type is **deitel:BooksType**. Any element (e.g., **books**) that contains attributes or child elements must define a *complex type*, which defines each attribute and child element. Type **deitel:BooksType** (lines 12–17) is an example of a complex type. We prefix **BooksType** with **deitel**, because this is a complex type that we have created, not an existing W3C XML Schema complex type.

Lines 12–17 use element ***complexType*** to define type **BooksType** (used in line 10). Here, we define **BooksType** as an element type that has a child element named **book**. Because **book** also contains a child element, its type must be a complex type (e.g., **BookType**, which we define later). Attribute ***minOccurs*** specifies that **books** must contain a minimum of one **book** element. Attribute ***maxOccurs***, having value ***unbounded*** (line 15), specifies that **books** may have any number of **book** child elements. Element ***sequence*** specifies the order of elements in the complex type.

Lines 19–23 define the **complexType BookType**. Line 21 defines element **title** with **type *xsd:string***. When an element has a *simple type* such as **xsd:string**, it is prohibited from containing attributes and child elements. W3C XML Schema provides a large number of data types, such as *xsd:date* for dates, *xsd:int* for integers, *xsd:double* for floating-point numbers and *xsd:time* for time.

Good Programming Practice 15.1

*By convention, W3C XML Schema authors use namespace prefixes **xsd** or **xs** when referring to the URI **http://www.w3.org/2001/XMLSchema***

15.5.4 Schema Validation in Visual C++ .NET

In this section, we present an MC++ application (Fig. 15.26–Fig. 15.28) that uses classes from the .NET Framework Class Library to validate the XML documents presented in the last two sections against their respective Schemas. We use an instance of *XmlValidatingReader* to perform the validation.

```cpp
1   // Fig. 15.26: ValidationTest.h
2   // Validating XML documents against Schemas.
3
4   #pragma once
5
6   #using <system.dll>
7   #using <mscorlib.dll>
8   #using <system.xml.dll>
9   #using <system.drawing.dll>
10  #using <system.windows.forms.dll>
11
12  using namespace System;
13  using namespace System::Drawing;
14  using namespace System::Xml;
15  using namespace System::Windows::Forms;
16  using namespace System::Xml::Schema;  // contains Schema classes
17
18  // determines XML document Schema validity
19  public __gc class ValidationTest : public Form
20  {
21  public:
22     ValidationTest();
23
24  private:
25     ComboBox *filesComboBox;
26     Button *validateButton;
27     Label *consoleLabel;
28
29     XmlSchemaCollection *schemas;   // Schemas collection
30     bool valid;                     // validation result
31
32     void InitializeComponent();
33     void validateButton_Click( Object *, EventArgs * );
34     void ValidationError( Object *, ValidationEventArgs * );
35  }; // end class ValidationTest
```

Fig. 15.26 Schema-validation example.

```
1   // Fig. 15.27: ValidationTest.cpp
2   // Method definitions for class ValidationTest.
3
4   #include "ValidationTest.h"
5
6   ValidationTest::ValidationTest()
7   {
8      InitializeComponent();
9
10     valid = true;   // assume document is valid
11
12     // get Schema(s) for validation
13     schemas = new XmlSchemaCollection();
14     schemas->Add( S"book", S"book.xdr" );
15     schemas->Add( S"http://www.deitel.com/booklist", S"book.xsd" );
16  } // end constructor
17
18  void ValidationTest::InitializeComponent()
19  {
20     this->validateButton = new Button();
21     this->consoleLabel = new Label();
22     this->filesComboBox = new ComboBox();
23     this->SuspendLayout();
24
25     // validateButton
26     this->validateButton->Location = Point( 8, 48 );
27     this->validateButton->Name = S"validateButton";
28     this->validateButton->Size = Drawing::Size( 272, 23 );
29     this->validateButton->TabIndex = 1;
30     this->validateButton->Text = S"Validate";
31     this->validateButton->Click +=
32        new EventHandler( this, validateButton_Click );
33
34     // consoleLabel
35     this->consoleLabel->BackColor = Color::Honeydew;
36     this->consoleLabel->BorderStyle = BorderStyle::Fixed3D;
37     this->consoleLabel->Location = Point( 8, 88 );
38     this->consoleLabel->Name = S"consoleLabel";
39     this->consoleLabel->Size = Drawing::Size( 272, 64 );
40     this->consoleLabel->TabIndex = 2;
41
42     // filesComboBox
43     this->filesComboBox->DropDownWidth = 272;
44     String *files[] = { S"bookxsd.xml", S"bookxdr.xml",
45        S"bookxsdfail.xml", S"bookxdrfail.xml" };
46     this->filesComboBox->Items->AddRange( files );
47     this->filesComboBox->Location = Point( 8, 8 );
48     this->filesComboBox->Name = S"filesComboBox";
49     this->filesComboBox->Size = Drawing::Size( 272, 21 );
50     this->filesComboBox->TabIndex = 0;
51
52     // ValidationTest
53     this->AutoScaleBaseSize = Drawing::Size( 5, 13 );
```

Fig. 15.27 ValidationTest class method definitions. (Part 1 of 3.)

```
54      this->ClientSize = Drawing::Size( 292, 157 );
55      this->Controls->Add( this->consoleLabel );
56      this->Controls->Add( this->validateButton );
57      this->Controls->Add( this->filesComboBox );
58      this->Name = S"ValidationTest";
59      this->Text = S"ValidationTest";
60      this->ResumeLayout();
61   } // end method InitializeComponent
62
63   // handle validateButton click event
64   void ValidationTest::validateButton_Click( Object *sender,
65      EventArgs *e )
66   {
67      try {
68
69         // get XML document
70         XmlTextReader *reader =
71            new XmlTextReader( filesComboBox->Text );
72
73         // get validator
74         XmlValidatingReader *validator =
75            new XmlValidatingReader( reader );
76
77         // assign Schema(s)
78         validator->Schemas->Add( schemas );
79
80         // set validation type
81         validator->ValidationType = ValidationType::Auto;
82
83         // register event handler for validation error(s)
84         validator->ValidationEventHandler +=
85            new ValidationEventHandler( this, ValidationError );
86
87         // validate document node-by-node
88         while ( validator->Read() ) ; // empty body
89
90         // check validation result
91         if ( valid )
92            consoleLabel->Text = S"Document is valid";
93
94         valid = true; // reset variable
95
96         // close reader stream
97         validator->Close();
98      } // end try
99
100      // no filename has been specified
101      catch ( ArgumentException * ) {
102         MessageBox::Show( S"Please specify a filename",
103            S"Error", MessageBoxButtons::OK,
104            MessageBoxIcon::Error );
105      }
106
```

Fig. 15.27 ValidationTest class method definitions. (Part 2 of 3.)

```
107    // an invalid filename has been specified
108    catch ( System::IO::IOException *fileException ) {
109       MessageBox::Show( fileException->Message,
110          S"Error", MessageBoxButtons::OK,
111          MessageBoxIcon::Error );
112    }
113 } // end method validateButton_Click
114
115 // event handler for validation error
116 void ValidationTest::ValidationError( Object *sender,
117    ValidationEventArgs *arguments )
118 {
119    consoleLabel->Text = arguments->Message;
120    valid = false; // validation failed
121 } // end method ValidationError
```

Fig. 15.27 ValidationTest class method definitions. (Part 3 of 3.)

```
1    // Fig. 15.28: ValidationTestMain.cpp
2    // Entry point for application.
3
4    #include "ValidationTest.h"
5
6    int __stdcall WinMain()
7    {
8       Application::Run( new ValidationTest() );
9
10      return 0;
11   } // end WinMain
```

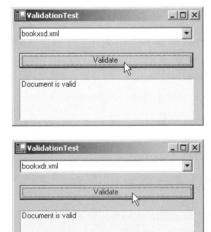

Fig. 15.28 Driver for class **ValidationTest**.

Line 13 (Fig. 15.27) creates an ***XmlSchemaCollection*** pointer named **schemas**. Line 14 calls method ***Add*** to add an ***XmlSchema*** object to the Schema collection. Method **Add** is passed a name that identifies the Schema (i.e., **"book"**) and the name of the Schema file (i.e., **"book.xdr"**). Line 15 calls method **Add** to add a W3C XML Schema. The first argument specifies the namespace URI (i.e., line 8 of Fig. 15.25) and the second argument identifies the schema file (i.e., **"book.xsd"**). This is the Schema that is used to validate **bookxsd.xml**.

Lines 70–71 create an **XmlTextReader** for the file that the user selected from **filesComboBox**. The XML document to be validated against a Schema contained in the **XmlSchemaCollection** must be passed to the **XmlValidatingReader** constructor (74–75). The **catch** blocks in lines 101–112 handle any exceptions (**ArgumentException** or **IOException**) that can occur if the user enters no filename or an invalid filename in **filesComboBox**.

Line 78 **Add**s the Schema collection pointed to by **schemas** to the ***Schemas*** property. This property sets the Schema used to validate the document. The ***ValidationType*** property (line 81) is set to the ***ValidationType*** enumeration constant for **Auto**matically identifying the Schema's type (i.e., XDR or XSD). Lines 84–85 register method **ValidationError** with ***ValidationEventHandler***. Method **ValidationError** (lines 116–121) is called if the document is invalid or if an error occurs, such as if the document cannot be found. Failure to register a method with **ValidationEventHandler** causes an exception to be thrown when the document is missing or invalid.

Validation is performed node-by-node, by calling the method ***Read*** (line 88). Each call to **Read** validates the next node in the document. The loop terminates either when all nodes have been validated successfully (and **valid** is still **true**) or a node fails validation (and **valid** has been set to **false** in line 120). When validated against their respective Schemas, the XML documents in Fig. 15.22 and Fig. 15.24 validate successfully.

Figure 15.29 and Fig. 15.30 list two XML documents that fail to conform to **book.xdr** and **book.xsd**, respectively. In both documents, an extra **title** element within a **book** element invalidates the documents. In Fig. 15.29, The extra elements in and are found on lines 10 and 21, respectively. Although both documents are invalid, they are well formed.

```
1    <?xml version = "1.0"?>
2
3    <!-- Fig. 15.29: bookxsdfail.xml                    -->
4    <!-- Document that does not conforms to W3C Schema. -->
5
6    <deitel:books xmlns:deitel = "http://www.deitel.com/booklist">
7       <book>
8          <title>Java Web Services for Experienced Programmers
9             </title>
10         <title>C# for Experienced Programmers</title>
11      </book>
12      <book>
13         <title>Visual C++ .NET: A Managed Code Approach</title>
```

Fig. 15.29 XML document that does not conform to the XSD schema of Fig. 15.25. (Part 1 of 2.)

```
14       </book>
15   </deitel:books>
```

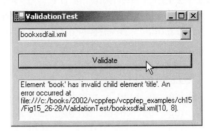

Fig. 15.29 XML document that does not conform to the XSD schema of Fig. 15.25. (Part 2 of 2.)

```
1   <?xml version = "1.0"?>
2
3   <!-- Fig. 15.30: bookxdrfail.xml                      -->
4   <!-- XML file that does not conform to Schema book.xdr. -->
5
6   <books xmlns = "x-schema:book.xdr">
7      <book>
8         <title>Web Services: A Technical Introduction</title>
9      </book>
10
11     <book>
12        <title>Java Web Services for Experienced Programmers
13        </title>
14     </book>
15
16     <book>
17        <title>Visual Basic .NET for Experienced Programmers
18        </title>
19     </book>
20
21     <book>
22        <title>C++ How to Program, 4/e</title>
23        <title>Python How to Program</title>
24     </book>
25
26     <book>
27        <title>C# for Experienced Programmers</title>
28     </book>
29   </books>
```

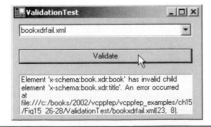

Fig. 15.30 XML file that does not conform to the Schema in Fig. 15.23.

15.6 Extensible Stylesheet Language and `XslTransform`

Extensible Stylesheet Language (XSL) is an XML vocabulary for formatting XML data. In this section, we discuss the portion of XSLcreates formatted text-based documents (including other XML documents) from XML documents. This process is called a *transformation* and involves two tree structures: the *source tree*, which is the XML document being transformed, and the *result tree*, which is the result (i.e., any text-based format such as XHTML or XML) of the transformation.[7] The source tree is not modified when a transformation occurs.

To perform transformations, an XSLT processor is required. Popular XSLT processors include Microsoft's msxml and the Apache Software Foundation's *Xalan* (**xml.apache.org**). The XML document, shown in Fig. 15.31, is transformed by msxml into an XHTML document (Fig. 15.32).

```
1   <?xml version = "1.0"?>
2
3   <!-- Fig. 15.31: sorting.xml                    -->
4   <!-- XML document containing book information. -->
5
6   <?xml:stylesheet type = "text/xsl" href = "sorting.xsl"?>
7
8   <book isbn = "999-99999-9-X">
9      <title>Bug2Bug&apos;s XML Primer</title>
10
11     <author>
12        <firstName>Observ</firstName>
13        <lastName>Ant</lastName>
14     </author>
15
16     <chapters>
17        <frontMatter>
18           <preface pages = "2" />
19           <contents pages = "5" />
20           <illustrations pages = "4" />
21        </frontMatter>
22
23        <chapter number = "3" pages = "44">
24           Advanced XML</chapter>
25
26        <chapter number = "2" pages = "35">
27           Intermediate XML</chapter>
28
29        <appendix number = "B" pages = "26">
30           Parsers and Tools</appendix>
31
32        <appendix number = "A" pages = "7">
33           Entities</appendix>
```

Fig. 15.31 XML document containing book information. (Part 1 of 2.)

---

7. Extensible Hypertext Markup Language (XHTML) is the W3C technical recommendation that replaces HTML for marking up content for the Web. For more information on XHTML, see the XHTML Appendices E and F, and visit **www.w3.org**.

```
34
35              <chapter number = "1" pages = "28">
36                 XML Fundamentals</chapter>
37           </chapters>
38
39           <media type = "CD" />
40        </book>
```

Fig. 15.31 XML document containing book information. (Part 2 of 2.)

Line 6 is a *processing instruction* (*PI*), which contains application-specific information that is embedded into the XML document. In this particular case, the processing
instruction is specific to IE and specifies the location of an XSLT document with which to
transform the XML document. The characters **<?** and **?>** delimit a processing instruction,
which consists of a *PI target* (e.g., **xml:stylesheet**) and *PI value* (e.g., **type =
"text/xsl" href = "sorting.xsl"**). The portion of this particular PI value that
follows **href** specifies the name and location of the style sheet to apply—in this case,
sorting.xsl, which is located in the same directory as this XML document.

Fig. 15.32 presents the XSLT document (**sorting.xsl**) that transforms
sorting.xml (Fig. 15.31) to XHTML.

Performance Tip 15.1

*Using Internet Explorer on the client to process XSLT documents conserves server resources
by using the client's processing power (instead of having the server process XSLT documents
for multiple clients).*

```
1    <?xml version = "1.0"?>
2
3    <!-- Fig. 15.32: sorting.xsl                        -->
4    <!-- Transformation of book information into XHTML. -->
5
6    <xsl:stylesheet version = "1.0"
7       xmlns:xsl = "http://www.w3.org/1999/XSL/Transform">
8
9       <!-- write XML declaration and DOCTYPE DTD information -->
10      <xsl:output method = "xml" omit-xml-declaration = "no"
11         doctype-system =
12            "http://www.w3.org/TR/xhtml1/DTD/xhtml1-strict.dtd"
13         doctype-public = "-//W3C//DTD XHTML 1.0 Strict//EN"/>
14
15      <!-- match document root -->
16      <xsl:template match = "/">
17         <html xmlns = "http://www.w3.org/1999/xhtml">
18            <xsl:apply-templates/>
19         </html>
20      </xsl:template>
21
22      <!-- match book -->
```

Fig. 15.32 XSL document that transforms **sorting.xml** (Fig. 15.31) into XHTML.
    (Part 1 of 3.)

```
23      <xsl:template match = "book">
24          <head>
25              <title>ISBN <xsl:value-of select = "@isbn" /> -
26                  <xsl:value-of select = "title" /></title>
27          </head>
28
29          <body>
30              <h1 style = "color: blue">
31                  <xsl:value-of select = "title"/></h1>
32
33              <h2 style = "color: blue">by <xsl:value-of
34                  select = "author/lastName" />,
35                  <xsl:value-of select = "author/firstName" /></h2>
36
37              <table style =
38                  "border-style: groove; background-color: wheat">
39
40                  <xsl:for-each select = "chapters/frontMatter/*">
41                      <tr>
42                          <td style = "text-align: right">
43                              <xsl:value-of select = "name()" />
44                          </td>
45
46                          <td>
47                              ( <xsl:value-of select = "@pages" /> pages )
48                          </td>
49                      </tr>
50                  </xsl:for-each>
51
52                  <xsl:for-each select = "chapters/chapter">
53                      <xsl:sort select = "@number" data-type = "number"
54                          order = "ascending" />
55                      <tr>
56                          <td style = "text-align: right">
57                              Chapter <xsl:value-of select = "@number" />
58                          </td>
59
60                          <td>
61                              ( <xsl:value-of select = "@pages" /> pages )
62                          </td>
63                      </tr>
64                  </xsl:for-each>
65
66                  <xsl:for-each select = "chapters/appendix">
67                      <xsl:sort select = "@number" data-type = "text"
68                          order = "ascending" />
69                      <tr>
70                          <td style = "text-align: right">
71                              Appendix <xsl:value-of select = "@number" />
72                          </td>
```

Fig. 15.32 XSL document that transforms **sorting.xml** (Fig. 15.31) into XHTML. (Part 2 of 3.)

```
73
74                            <td>
75                                ( <xsl:value-of select = "@pages" /> pages )
76                            </td>
77                        </tr>
78                    </xsl:for-each>
79                </table>
80
81                <br /><p style = "color: blue">Pages:
82                    <xsl:variable name = "pagecount"
83                        select = "sum(chapters//*/@pages)" />
84                    <xsl:value-of select = "$pagecount" />
85                <br />Media Type:
86                    <xsl:value-of select = "media/@type" /></p>
87            </body>
88        </xsl:template>
89
90    </xsl:stylesheet>
```

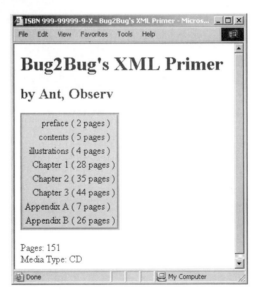

Fig. 15.32 XSL document that transforms `sorting.xml` (Fig. 15.31) into XHTML. (Part 3 of 3.)

Line 1 of Fig. 15.32 contains the XML declaration. Recall that an XSL document is an XML document. Lines 6–7 contain the **xsl:stylesheet** root element. Attribute **version** specifies the version of XSLT to which this document conforms. Namespace prefix **xsl** is defined and is bound to the XSLT URI defined by the W3C. When processed, lines 10–13 write the document type declaration to the result tree. Attribute **method** is assigned **"xml"**, which indicates that XML is being output to the result tree. Attribute **omit-xml-declaration** is assigned **"no"**, which outputs an XML declaration to the result tree.

Attribute **doctype-system** and **doctype-public** write the **Doctype** DTD information to the result tree.

XSLT documents contain one or more **xsl:template** elements that specify which information is output to the result tree. The template on line 16 **match**es the source tree's document root. When the document root is encountered, this template is applied, and any text marked up by this element that is not in the namespace pointed to by **xsl** is output to the result tree. Line 18 calls for all the **template**s that match children of the document root to be applied. Line 23 specifies a **template** that **match**es element **book**.

Lines 25–26 create the title for the XHTML document. We use the ISBN of the book from attribute **isbn** and the contents of element **title** to create the title string **ISBN 999-99999-9-X - Deitel's XML Primer**. Element **xsl:value-of** selects the **book** element's **isbn** attribute.

Lines 33–35 create a header element that contains the book's author. Because the *context node* (i.e., the current node being processed) is **book**, the XPath expression **author/ lastName** selects the author's last name, and the expression **author/firstName** selects the author's first name.

Line 40 selects each element (indicated by an asterisk) that is a child of element **frontMatter**. Line 43 calls *node-set function* **name** to retrieve the current node's element name (e.g., **preface**). The current node is the context node specified in the **xsl:for-each** (line 40).

Lines 53–54 sort **chapter**s by number in ascending order. Attribute **select** selects the value of context node **chapter**'s attribute **number**. Attribute **data-type**, having value **"number"**, specifies a numeric sort, and attribute **order** specifies **"ascending"** order. Attribute **data-type** also can be assigned the value **"text"** (line 67), and attribute **order** also may be assigned the value **"descending"**.

Lines 82–83 use an *XSL variable* to store the value of the book's page count and output it to the result tree. Attribute **name** specifies the variable's name, and attribute **select** assigns it a value. Function **sum** totals the values for all **page** attribute values. The two slashes between **chapters** and ***** indicate that all descendant nodes of **chapters** are searched for elements that contain an attribute named **pages**.

The **System::Xml::Xsl** namespace provides classes for applying XSLT style sheets to XML documents. Specifically, an object of class **XslTransform** can be used to perform the transformation.

Figure 15.33–Fig. 15.35 apply a style sheet (**sports.xsl**) to **sports.xml** (Fig. 15.16). The transformation result is written to a text box and to a file. We also show the transformation results rendered in IE.

```
1   // Fig. 15.33: TransformTest.h
2   // Applying a style sheet to an XML document.
3
4   #pragma once
5
6   #using <system.dll>
7   #using <mscorlib.dll>
8   #using <system.xml.dll>
9   #using <system.drawing.dll>
10  #using <system.windows.forms.dll>
```

Fig. 15.33 XSL style sheet applied to an XML document. (Part 1 of 2.)

```
11
12    using namespace System;
13    using namespace System::Xml;
14    using namespace System::Drawing;
15    using namespace System::Windows::Forms;
16    using namespace System::Xml::XPath;
17    using namespace System::Xml::Xsl;
18    using namespace System::IO;
19
20    // transforms XML document with style sheet
21    public __gc class TransformTest : public Form
22    {
23    public:
24       TransformTest();
25
26    private:
27       TextBox *consoleTextBox;
28       Button *transformButton;
29       XmlDocument *document;      // Xml document root
30       XPathNavigator *navigator; // navigate document
31       XslTransform *transformer; // transform document
32       StringWriter *output;       // display document
33       void InitializeComponent();
34       void transformButton_Click( Object *, EventArgs * );
35    }; // end class TransformTest
```

Fig. 15.33 XSL style sheet applied to an XML document. (Part 2 of 2.)

```
1    // Fig. 15.34: TransformTest.cpp
2    // Method definitions for class TransformTest.
3
4    #include "TransformTest.h"
5
6    TransformTest::TransformTest()
7    {
8       InitializeComponent();
9
10      // load XML data
11      document = new XmlDocument();
12      document->Load( S"sports.xml" );
13
14      // create navigator
15      navigator = document->CreateNavigator();
16
17      // load style sheet
18      transformer = new XslTransform();
19      transformer->Load( S"sports.xsl" );
20   } // end constructor
21
22   void TransformTest::InitializeComponent()
23   {
24      this->consoleTextBox = new TextBox();
```

Fig. 15.34 TransformTest class method definitions. (Part 1 of 2.)

```
25      this->transformButton = new Button();
26      this->SuspendLayout();
27
28      // consoleTextBox
29      this->consoleTextBox->BackColor = SystemColors::HighlightText;
30      this->consoleTextBox->Location = Point( 8, 48 );
31      this->consoleTextBox->Multiline = true;
32      this->consoleTextBox->Name = S"consoleTextBox";
33      this->consoleTextBox->ReadOnly = true;
34      this->consoleTextBox->ScrollBars = ScrollBars::Vertical;
35      this->consoleTextBox->Size = Drawing::Size( 280, 216 );
36      this->consoleTextBox->TabIndex = 0;
37      this->consoleTextBox->Text = S"";
38
39      // transformButton
40      this->transformButton->Location = Point( 8, 8 );
41      this->transformButton->Name = S"transformButton";
42      this->transformButton->Size = Drawing::Size( 280, 23 );
43      this->transformButton->TabIndex = 1;
44      this->transformButton->Text = S"Transform XML";
45      this->transformButton->Click +=
46         new EventHandler( this, transformButton_Click );
47
48      // TransformTest
49      this->AutoScaleBaseSize = Drawing::Size( 5, 13 );
50      this->ClientSize = Drawing::Size( 292, 273 );
51      this->Controls->Add( this->transformButton );
52      this->Controls->Add( this->consoleTextBox );
53      this->Name = S"TransformTest";
54      this->Text = S"TransformTest";
55      this->ResumeLayout();
56   } // end method InitializeComponent
57
58   // transformButton click event
59   void TransformTest::transformButton_Click( Object *sender,
60      EventArgs *e )
61   {
62      // transform XML data
63      output = new StringWriter();
64      transformer->Transform( navigator, 0, output );
65
66      // display transformation in text box
67      consoleTextBox->Text = output->ToString();
68
69      // write transformation result to disk
70      FileStream *stream = new FileStream( S"sports.html",
71         FileMode::Create );
72      StreamWriter *writer = new StreamWriter( stream );
73      writer->Write( output->ToString() );
74
75      // close streams
76      writer->Close();
77      output->Close();
78   } // end method transformButton_Click
```

Fig. 15.34 **TransformTest** class method definitions. (Part 2 of 2.)

```
1    // Fig. 15.35: TransformTestMain.cpp
2    // Entry point for application.
3
4    #include "TransformTest.h"
5
6    int __stdcall WinMain()
7    {
8       Application::Run( new TransformTest() );
9
10      return 0;
11   } // end WinMain
```

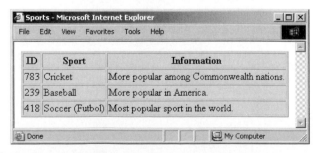

Fig. 15.35 Driver for class **TransformTest**.

Line 31 (Fig. 15.33) declares **XslTransform** pointer **transformer**. An object of this type is necessary to transform the XML data to another format. In line 12 (Fig. 15.34), the XML document is parsed and loaded into memory with a call to method **Load**. Method **CreateNavigator** is called in line 15 to create an **XPathNavigator** object, which is used to navigate the XML document during the transformation. A call to method *Load* of class **XslTransform** (line 19) parses and loads the style sheet that this application uses. The argument that is passed contains the name and location of the style sheet.

Event handler **transformButton_Click** (lines 59–78) calls method *Transform* of class **XslTransform** to apply the style sheet (**sports.xsl**) to **sports.xml** (line 64). This method takes three arguments: An **XPathNavigator** (created from **sports.xml**'s **XmlDocument**), an instance of class *XsltArgumentList*, which is a list of **String *** parameters that can be applied to a style sheet— **0**, in this case—and an instance of a derived class of **TextWriter** (in this example, an instance of class **StringWriter**). The results of the transformation are stored in the **StringWriter** object pointed to by **output**. Lines 70–73 write the transformation results to disk. The third screen shot depicts the created XHTML document when it is rendered in IE.

In this chapter, we studied the Extensible Markup Language and several of its related technologies. In Chapter 16, we begin our discussion of databases, which are crucial to the development of multi-tier Web-based applications.

15.7 Summary

XML is a widely supported, open (i.e., non-proprietary) technology for data exchange. XML is quickly becoming the standard by which applications maintain data. XML is highly portable. Any text editor that supports ASCII or Unicode® characters can render or display XML documents. Because XML elements describe the data they contain, they are both human and machine readable. XML permits document authors to create custom markup for virtually any type of information. This extensibility enables document authors to create entirely new markup languages, ones that describe specific types of data, including mathematical formulas, chemical molecular structures, music, recipes, etc.

The processing of XML documents—which programs typically store in files whose names end with the **.xml** extension—requires a program called an XML parser. A parser is responsible for identifying components of XML documents and for then storing those components in a data structure for manipulation. An XML document can reference another optional document that defines the XML document's structure. Two types of optional structure-defining documents are Document Type Definitions (DTDs) and Schemas.

An XML document begins with an optional XML declaration, which identifies the document as an XML document. The **version** information parameter specifies the version of XML syntax that is used in the document. Data is marked up with tags whose names are enclosed in angle brackets (**<>**). Tags are used in pairs to delimit markup. A tag that begins markup is called a start tag; a tag that terminates markup is called an end tag. End tags differ from start tags in that they contain a forward slash (**/**) character.

Individual units of markup are called elements, which are the most fundamental XML building blocks. XML documents contain one element, called a root element, that contains every other element in the document. Elements are embedded or nested within each other to form hierarchies, with the root element at the top of the hierarchy.

In addition to being placed between tags, data also can be placed in attributes, which are name–value pairs in start tags. Elements can have any number of attributes.

Because XML allows document authors to create their own tags, naming collisions. As in the .NET Framework, XML namespaces provide a means for document authors to prevent collisions. Namespace prefixes are prepended to elements to specify the namespace to which the element belongs. Each namespace prefix is bound to a uniform resource identifier (URI) that uniquely identifies the namespace. Document authors create their own namespace prefixes. Virtually any name can be used as a namespace prefix except the reserved namespace prefix **xml**. To eliminate the need to place a namespace prefix in each element, document authors can specify a default namespace for an element and its children.

When an XML parser successfully parses a document, the parser stores a tree structure containing the document's data in memory. This hierarchical tree structure is called a Document Object Model (DOM) tree. The DOM tree represents each component of the XML document as a node in the tree. The DOM tree has a single root node that contains all other nodes in the document.

Namespace **System::Xml** contains classes for creating, reading and manipulating XML documents. **XmlReader**-derived class **XmlNodeReader** iterates through each node in the XML document. Class **XmlReader** is an **abstract** class that defines the interface for reading XML documents. An **XmlDocument** object conceptually represents an empty XML document. Method **CreateNode** of **XmlDocument** takes a **NodeType**, a **Name** and a **NamespaceURI** as arguments. XML documents are parsed and loaded into an **XmlDocument** object when method **Load** is invoked. Once an XML document is loaded into an **XmlDocument**, its data can be read and manipulated programmatically. An **XmlNodeReader** allows us to read one node at a time from an **XmlDocument**. Method **Read** of **XmlReader** reads one node from the DOM tree. The **Name** property contains the node's name, the **Value** property contains the node's data and the **NodeType** property contains the node type (i.e., element, comment, text, etc.).

An **XmlTextWriter** streams XML data to a stream. Method **WriteTo** writes an XML representation to an **XmlTextWriter** stream. An **XmlTextReader** reads XML data from a stream.

Class **XPathNavigator** in the **System::Xml::XPath** namespace can iterate through node lists that match search criteria, written as an XPath expression. XPath (XML Path Language) provides a syntax for locating specific nodes in XML documents effectively and efficiently. XPath is a string-based language of expressions used by XML and many of its related technologies. Navigation methods of **XPathNavigator** are **MoveToFirstChild**, **MoveToParent**, **MoveToNext** and **MoveToPrevious**.

Whereas XML contains only data, XSLT is capable of converting XML into any text-based document (including another XML document). XSLT documents typically have the extension **.xsl**. When transforming an XML document via XSLT, two tree structures are involved: the source tree, which is the XML document being transformed, and the result tree, which is the result (e.g., XHTML) of the transformation.

XSLT specifies the use of element **value-of** to retrieve an attribute's value. The symbol **@** specifies an attribute node. The node-set function **name** retrieves the current node's element name. Attribute **select** selects the value of context node's attribute.

XML documents can be transformed programmatically through MC++. The **System::Xml::Xsl** namespace facilitates the application of XSLT style sheets to

XML documents. Class **XsltArgumentList** is a list of **String *** parameters that can be applied to a style sheet.

15.8 Internet and Web Resources

www.w3.org/xml
The W3C (World Wide Web Consortium) facilitates the development of common protocols to ensure interoperability on the Web. Their XML page includes information about upcoming events, publications, software and discussion groups. Visit this site to read about the latest developments in XML.

www.w3.org/TR/REC-xml
This W3C page contains a short introduction to XML as well as the most recent XML specification.

www.w3.org/XML/1999/XML-in-10-points
This W3C page describes the basics of XML in ten simple points. It is a useful page for those new to XML.

www.xml.org
xml.org is a reference for XML, DTDs, schemas and namespaces.

www.w3.org/style/XSL
This W3C page provides information on XSL, including such topics as XSL development, learning XSL, XSL-enabled tools, XSL specification, FAQs and XSL history.

www.w3.org/TR
This is the W3C technical reports and publications page. It contains links to working drafts, proposed recommendations and other resources.

www.xmlbooks.com
This site provides a list of XML books recommended by Charles Goldfarb, one of the original designers of GML (General Markup Language), from which SGML is derived.

www.xml-zone.com
The Development Exchange XML Zone is a complete resource for XML information. This site includes an FAQ, news, articles and links to other XML sites and newsgroups.

wdvl.internet.com/Authoring/Languages/XML
Web Developer's Virtual Library XML site includes tutorials, an FAQ, the latest news and extensive links to XML sites and software downloads.

www.xml.com
XML.com provides the latest news and information about XML, conference listings, links to XML Web resources organized by topic, tools and other resources.

msdn.microsoft.com/xml/default.asp
The MSDN Online XML Development Center features articles on XML, Ask the Experts chat sessions, samples and demos, newsgroups and other helpful information.

msdn.microsoft.com/downloads/samples/Internet/xml/xml_validator/ sample.asp
Microsoft's XML validator, which can be downloaded from this site, can validate both online and offline documents.

www.oasis-open.org/cover/xml.html
The SGML/XML Web Page is an extensive resource that includes links to several FAQs, online resources, industry initiatives, demos, conferences and tutorials.

www.gca.org/whats_xml/default.htm
The GCA site offers an XML glossary, list of books, brief descriptions of the draft standards for XML and links to online drafts.

www-106.ibm.com/developerworks/xml
The IBM XML Zone site is a great resource for developers. It provides news, tools, a library, case studies and information about events and standards.

developer.netscape.com/tech/xml
The XML and Metadata Developer Central site has demos, technical notes and news articles related to XML.

www.projectcool.com/developer/xmlz
The Project Cool Developer Zone site includes several tutorials covering introductory through advanced XML topics.

www.ucc.ie/xml
This site is a detailed XML FAQ. Developers can check out responses to some popular questions or submit their own questions through the site.

16

Database, SQL and ADO .NET

Objectives

- To understand the relational database model.
- To understand basic database queries that use Structured Query Language (SQL).
- To understand and use ADO .NET's disconnected model.
- To use the classes and interfaces of namespace **System::Data** to manipulate databases.
- To use the classes and interfaces of namespace **System::Data::OleDb**.

It is a capital mistake to theorize before one has data.
Arthur Conan Doyle

*Now go, write it before them in a table, and note it in a book,
that it may be for the time to come for ever and ever.*
The Holy Bible: The Old Testament

Let's look at the record.
Alfred Emanuel Smith

*Get your facts first, and then you can distort them as much as
you please.*
Mark Twain

I like two kinds of men: domestic and foreign.
Mae West

16.1 Introduction

A *database* is an integrated collection of data. Many different strategies exist for organizing data in databases to facilitate easy access to and manipulation of the data. A *database management system* (*DBMS*) provides mechanisms for storing and organizing data in a manner that is consistent with the database's format. Database management systems enable programmers to access and store data without worrying about the internal representation of databases.

Today's most popular database systems are *relational databases*. Almost universally, relational databases use a language called *Structured Query Language* (*SQL*—pronounced as its individual letters or as "sequel") to perform *queries* (i.e., to request information that satisfies given criteria) and to manipulate data. [*Note*: The writing in this chapter assumes that SQL is pronounced as its individual letters. For this reason, we often precede SQL with the article "an," as in "an SQL database" or "an SQL statement."]

Some popular enterprise-level relational database systems include Microsoft SQL Server, Oracle,™ Sybase,™ DB2,™ Informix™ and MySQL™. This chapter presents examples using Microsoft Access—a relational database system that is packaged with Microsoft Office. We provide the reader with links to more information about these products at the end of this chapter.

A programming language connects to, and interacts with, a relational database via an *interface*—software that facilitates communication between a database management system and a program. Many Visual C++ .NET programmers communicate with databases and manipulate their data through *Microsoft ActiveX Data Objects™* (ADO) or *ADO .NET*.

16.2 Relational Database Model

The *relational database model* is a logical representation of data that allows relationships among data to be considered without concern for the physical structure of the data.[1] A relational database is composed of *tables*. Figure 16.1 illustrates an example table that might be used in a personnel system. The table name is **Employee**, and its primary purpose is to illustrate the specific attributes of various employees. A particular row of the table is called a *record* (or *row*). This table consists of six records. The **number** *field* (or *column*) of each record in the table is the *primary key* for referencing data in the table. A primary key is a field (or combination of fields) in a table that contain(s) unique data—i.e, data that is not duplicated in other records of that table. This guarantees that each record can be identified by at least one distinct value. Examples of primary-key fields are columns that contain Social Security numbers, employee IDs and part numbers in an inventory system. The records of Fig. 16.1 are *ordered* by primary key. In this case, the records are listed in increasing order (they also could be listed in decreasing order).

Each column of the table represents a different field. Records normally are unique (by primary key) within a table, but other particular field values might be appear in multiple records. For example, three different records in the **Employee** table's **Department** field contain the number 413.

Often, different users of a database are interested in different data and different relationships among those data. Some users require only subsets of the table columns. To obtain table subsets, we use SQL statements to specify certain data we wish to *select* from a table. SQL provides a complete set of commands (including ***SELECT***) that enable programmers to define complex *queries* to select data from a table. The results of a query commonly are called *result sets* (or *record sets*). For example, we might select data from the table in Fig. 16.1 to create a new result set containing only the location of each department. This result set appears in Fig. 16.2. SQL queries are discussed in detail in Section 16.4.

---

1. The relational database model was developed in 1970 by Dr. Edgar F. Codd (also known as "Ted" Codd), a researcher for IBM. The following sites contain more information about E. F. Codd:
   `www.informatik.uni-trier.de/~ley/db/about/codd.html`
   `www.research.ibm.com/about/awards.shtml`
   `www.itworld.com/nl/db_mgr/05072001`

number	name	department	salary	location
23603	Jones	413	1100	New Jersey
24568	Kerwin	413	2000	New Jersey
34589	Larson	642	1800	Los Angeles
35761	Myers	611	1400	Orlando
47132	Neumann	413	9000	New Jersey
78321	Stephens	611	8500	Orlando

Record/Row — Primary key — Field/Column

Fig. 16.1   Relational-database structure of an **Employee** table.

department	location
413	New Jersey
611	Orlando
642	Los Angeles

Fig. 16.2   Result set formed by selecting **Department** and **Location** data from the **Employee** table.

16.3 Relational Database Overview: Books Database

The next section provides an overview of SQL in the context of a sample **Books** database that we created for this chapter. However, before we discuss SQL, we must explain the various tables of the **Books** database. We use this database to introduce various database concepts, including the use of SQL to manipulate and obtain useful information from the database.

The database consists of four tables: **Authors**, **Publishers**, **AuthorISBN** and **Titles**. The **Authors** table (described in that maintain each author's unique ID number, first name and last name. Figure 16.4 contains the data from the **Authors** table of the **Books** database.

The **Publishers** table (described in Fig. 16.5) consists of two fields, representing each publisher's unique ID and name. Figure 16.6 contains the data from the **Publishers** table of the **Books** database.

Field	Description
authorID	Author's ID number in the database. In the **Books** database, this integral field is defined as an *auto-incremented field* or *identity field*. For each new record inserted in this table, the database increments the **authorID** value, ensuring that each record has a unique **authorID**. This field represents the table's primary key.

Fig. 16.3   **Authors** table from **Books**. (Part 1 of 2.)

Field	Description
firstName	Author's first name (a string).
lastName	Author's last name (a string).

Fig. 16.3 Authors table from Books. (Part 2 of 2.)

authorID	firstName	lastName
1	Harvey	Deitel
2	Paul	,Deitel
3	Tem	Nieto
4	Kate	Steinbuhler
5	Sean	Santry
6	Ted	Lin
7	Praveen	Sadhu
8	David	McPhie
9	Cheryl	Yaeger
10	Marina	Zlatkina
11	Ben	Wiedermann
12	Jonathan	Liperi
13	Jeffrey	Listfield
14	Jeffrey	Hamm
15	Christina	Courtemarche

Fig. 16.4 Data from the Authors table of Books.

Field	Description
publisherID	The publisher's ID number in the database. This auto-incremented integral field is the table's primary-key field.
publisherName	The name of the publisher (a string).

Fig. 16.5 Publishers table from Books.

publisherID	publisherName
1	Prentice Hall
2	Prentice Hall PTG

Fig. 16.6 Data from the Publishers table of Books.

The **AuthorISBN** table (described in Fig. 16.7) consists of two fields that maintain the authors' ID numbers and the corresponding ISBN numbers of their books. This table helps associate the names of the authors with the titles of their books. To save space, Fig. 16.8 contains a portion of the data from the **AuthorISBN** table of the **Books** database. ISBN is an abbreviation for "International Standard Book Number"—a numbering scheme by which publishers worldwide assign every book a unique identification number. [*Note*: To save space, we have split the contents of this figure into two columns, each containing the **authorID** and **isbn** field.].

Field	Description
authorID	The author's ID number, which allows the database to associate each book with a specific author. The integer ID number in this field must also appear in the **Authors** table.
isbn	The ISBN number for a book (a string).

Fig. 16.7 AuthorISBN table from **Books**.

authorID	isbn	authorID	isbn
1	0130895725	2	0139163050
1	0132261197	2	013028419x
1	0130895717	2	0130161438
1	0135289106	2	0130856118
1	0139163050	2	0130125075
1	013028419x	2	0138993947
1	0130161438	2	0130852473
1	0130856118	2	0130829277
1	0130125075	2	0134569555
1	0138993947	2	0130829293
1	0130852473	2	0130284173
1	0130829277	2	0130284181
1	0134569555	2	0130895601
1	0130829293	2	0132261197
1	0130284173	2	0130895717
1	0130284181	2	0135289106
1	0130895601	3	013028419x
2	0130895725	3	0130161438

Fig. 16.8 Data from AuthorISBN table in **Books**. (Part 1 of 2.)

authorID	isbn	authorID	isbn
3	0130856118	3	0130284173
3	0134569555	3	0130284181
3	0130829293	4	0130895601

Fig. 16.8 Data from `AuthorISBN` table in `Books`. (Part 2 of 2.)

The **Titles** table (described in Fig. 16.9) consists of seven fields that maintain general information about the books in the database. This information includes each book's ISBN number, title, edition number, copyright year and publisher's ID number, as well as the name of a file containing an image of the book cover and, finally, each book's price. Figure 16.10 contains the data from the **Titles** table. [*Note*: Figure 16.10 contains a sample of the data contained in the **Titles** table. To conserve space in the text, we show only some of the most recent publications.]

Field	Description
isbn	ISBN number of the book (a string).
title	Title of the book (a string).
editionNumber	Edition number of the book (a string).
copyright	Copyright year of the book (an integer).
publisherID	Publisher's ID number (an integer). This value must correspond to an ID number in the **Publishers** table.
imageFile	Name of the file containing the book's cover image (a string).
price	Suggested retail price of the book (a real number). [*Note*: The prices shown in this database are for example purposes only.]

Fig. 16.9 `Titles` table from `Books`.

isbn	title	edition-Number	publish-erID	copy-right	imageFile	price
013045821X	Visual C++ .NET: A Managed Code Approach for Experienced Programmers	1	1	2003	vcppfxp.jpg	$69.95
0130923613	Python How to Program	1	1	2002	python.jpg	$69.95

Fig. 16.10 Data from the `Titles` table of `Books`. (Part 1 of 2.)

isbn	title	edition-Number	publish-erID	copy-right	imageFile	price
0130622214	C# How to Program	1	1	2002	`cshtp.jpg`	$69.95
0130341517	Java How to Program	4	1	2002	`jhtp4.jpg`	$69.95
0130649341	The Complete Java Training Course	4	2	2002	`javactc4.jpg`	$109.95
0130895601	Advanced Java 2 Platform How to Program	1	1	2002	`advjhtp1.jpg`	$69.95
0130308978	Internet and World Wide Web How to Program	2	1	2002	`iw3htp2.jpg`	$69.95
0130293636	Visual Basic .NET How to Program	2	1	2002	`vbnet.jpg`	$69.95
0130895725	C How to Program	3	1	2001	`chtp3.jpg`	$69.95
0130895717	C++ How to Program	3	1	2001	`cpphtp3.jpg`	$69.95
013028419X	e-Business and e-Commerce How to Program	1	1	2001	`ebechtp1.jpg`	$69.95
0130622265	Wireless Internet and Mobile Business How to Program	1	1	2001	`wireless.jpg`	$69.95
0130284181	Perl How to Program	1	1	2001	`perlhtp1.jpg`	$69.95
0130284173	XML How to Program	1	1	2001	`xmlhtp1.jpg`	$69.95

Fig. 16.10 Data from the **Titles** table of **Books**. (Part 2 of 2.)

Figure 16.11 illustrates the relationships among the tables in the **Books** database. The first line in each table is the table's name. The field whose name appears in italics contains that table's primary key. A table's primary key uniquely identifies each record in the table. Every record must have a value in the primary-key field, and the value must be unique. This is known as the *Rule of Entity Integrity*. Note that the **AuthorISBN** table contains two fields whose names are italicized. This indicates that these two fields form a *compound primary key*—each record in the table must have a unique **authorID–isbn** combination. For example, several records might have an **authorID** of **2**, and several records might have an **isbn** of **0130895601**, but only one record can have both an **authorID** of **2** and an **isbn** of **0130895601**.

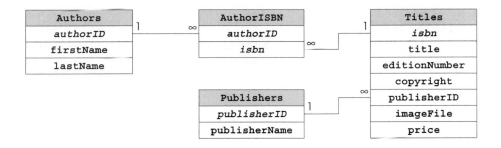

Fig. 16.11 Table relationships in **Books**.

Common Programming Error 16.1

Failure to provide a value for a primary-key field in every record breaks the Rule of Entity Integrity and causes the DBMS to report an error.

Common Programming Error 16.2

Providing duplicate values for the primary-key field of multiple records causes the DBMS to report an error.

The lines connecting the tables in Fig. 16.11 represent the *relationships* among the tables. Consider the line between the **Publishers** and **Titles** tables. On the **Publishers** end of the line, there is a **1**, and on the **T**end, there is an infinity (∞) symbol. This line indicates a *one-to-many relationship*, in which every publisher in the **Publishers** table can have an arbitrarily large number of books in the **Titles** table. Note that the relationship line links the **publisherID** field in the **Publishers** table to the **publisherID** field in **Titles** table. In the **Titles** table, the **publisherID** field is a *foreign key*—a field for which every entry has a unique value in another table and where the field in the other table is the primary key for that table (e.g., **publisherID** in the **Publishers** table). Programmers specify *foreign key constraints* when creating a table. The foreign key constraint helps maintain the *Rule of Referential Integrity*: Every foreign-key field value must appear as another table's primary-key field. Foreign keys enable information from multiple tables to be *joined* together for analysis purposes. There is a one-to-many relationship between a primary key and its corresponding foreign key. This means that a foreign-key field value can appear many times in its own table, but must appear exactly once as the primary key of another table. The line between the tables represents the link between the foreign key in one table and the primary key in another table.

Common Programming Error 16.3

Providing a foreign-key value that does not appear as a primary-key value in another table breaks the Rule of Referential Integrity and causes the DBMS to report an error.

The line between the **AuthorISBN** and **Authors** tables indicates that, for each author in the **Authors** table, the **AuthorISBN** table can contain an arbitrary number of ISBNs for books written by that author. The **authorID** field in the **AuthorISBN** table is a foreign key of the **authorID** field (the primary key) of the **Authors** table. Note, again, that the line between the tables links the foreign key in table **AuthorISBN** to the corresponding primary key in table **Authors**. The **AuthorISBN** table links information in the **Titles** and **Authors** tables.

The line between the **Titles** and **AuthorISBN** tables illustrates another one-to-many relationship; a title can be written by any number of authors. In fact, the sole purpose of the **AuthorISBN** table is to represent a many-to-many relationship between the **Authors** and **Titles** tables; an author can write any number of books, and a book can have any number of authors.

If we didn't create the **AuthorISBN** table, we would have to store redundant data in the **Titles** and **Authors** tables. For each book in **Titles**, we would have to store the **authorID** for all of its authors. Similarly, for each author in **Authors**, we would have to store the **isbn** of every book that author has written. If we then had to add another author to a book, we would have to update both the **Authors** and **Titles** tables. However, by storing the relationship between **Authors** and **Titles** in the **AuthorISBN** table, we achieve *normalization*. Normalization is the process of minimizing redundancy in a relational database to maximize the efficiency of modifications.[2]

16.4 Structured Query Language (SQL)

In this section, we provide an overview of Structured Query Language (SQL) in the context of our **Books** sample database. The SQL queries discussed here form the foundation for the SQL used in the chapter examples.

Figure 16.12 lists SQL keywords and provides a description of each. In the next several subsections, we discuss these SQL keywords in the context of complete SQL queries. Other SQL keywords exist, but are beyond the scope of this text. [*Note*: To locate additional information on SQL, please refer to the book's bibliography.]

SQL keyword	Description
SELECT	Selects (retrieves) fields from one or more tables.
FROM	Specifies tables from which to get fields or delete records. Required in every **SELECT** and **DELETE** statement.
WHERE	Specifies criteria that determine the rows to be retrieved.
INNER JOIN	Joins records from multiple tables to produce a single set of records.
GROUP BY	Specifies criteria for grouping records.
ORDER BY	Specifies criteria for ordering records.
INSERT	Inserts data into a specified table.
UPDATE	Updates data in a specified table.
DELETE	Deletes data from a specified table.

Fig. 16.12 SQL query keywords.

---

2. For more information about normalization, visit the following locations:
   `www.webopedia.com/TERM/N/normalization.html`
   `www.utexas.edu/cc/database/datamodeling/rm/rm7.html`

16.4.1 Basic SELECT Query

Let us consider several SQL queries that extract information from database **Books**. A typical SQL query "selects" information from one or more tables in a database. Such selections are performed by *SELECT queries*. The basic format for a **SELECT** query is

> *SELECT * FROM* tableName

In this query, the asterisk (*) indicates that all columns from the *tableName* table of the database should be selected. For example, to select the entire contents of the **Authors** table (i.e., all data depicted in Fig. 16.4), use the query

> *SELECT * FROM* Authors

To select specific fields from a table, replace the asterisk (*) with a comma-separated list of the field names to select. For example, to select only the fields **authorID** and **lastName** for all rows in the **Authors** table, use the query

> *SELECT* authorID, lastName *FROM* Authors

To save space, Fig. 16.13 presents only a portion of the data returned by the query. [*Note*: If a field name contains spaces, the entire field name must be enclosed in square brackets ([]) in the query. For example, if the field name is **first name**, it must appear in the query as **[first name]**.

Good Programming Practice 16.1

Not all DBMSs allow spaces to be used in field names. Some also do not allow dashes (–). To maximize the compatibility of your database, use underscores (_) rather than spaces or dashes to separate words in field names (as well as in table names, database names, etc.)

Common Programming Error 16.4

If a program assumes that an SQL statement using the asterisk (*) to select fields always returns those fields in the same order, the program could process the result set incorrectly. If the field order in the database table(s) changes, the order of the fields in the result set would change accordingly.

authorID	lastName	authorID	lastName
1	Deitel	9	Yaeger
2	Deitel	10	Zlatkina
3	Nieto	12	Wiedermann
4	Steinbuhler	12	Liperi
5	Santry	13	Listfield
6	Lin	14	Hamm
7	Sadhu	15	Courtemarche
8	McPhie		

Fig. 16.13 authorID and lastName from the Authors table.

Performance Tip 16.1

If a program does not know the order of fields in a result set, the program must process the fields by name. This could require a linear search of the field names in the result set. If users specify the field names that they wish to select from a table (or several tables), the application receiving the result set knows the order of the fields in advance. When this occurs, the program can process the data more efficiently, because fields can be accessed directly by column number.

16.4.2 WHERE Clause

In most cases, users search a database for records that satisfy certain *selection criteria*. Only records that match the selection criteria are selected. SQL uses the optional **WHERE** *clause* in a **SELECT** query to specify the selection criteria for the query. The simplest format for a **SELECT** query that includes selection criteria is

> **SELECT** *fieldName1*, *fieldName2*, … **FROM** *tableName* **WHERE** *criteria*

For example, to select the **title**, **editionNumber** and **copyright** fields from those rows of table **Titles** in which the **copyright** date is greater than **2001**, use the query

```
SELECT title, editionNumber, copyright
FROM Titles
WHERE copyright > 2001
```

Figure 16.14 shows the result set of the preceding query. [*Note*: When we construct a query for use in MC++, we simply create a **String *** containing the entire query. However, when we display queries in the text, we often use multiple lines and indentation to enhance readability.]

title	editionNumber	copyright
Visual C++ .NET: A Managed Code Approach for Experienced Programmers	1	2003
Internet and World Wide Web How to Program	2	2002
Java How to Program	4	2002
The Complete Java Training Course	4	2002
Advanced Java 2 Platform How to Program	1	2002
C# How To Program	1	2002
Python How to Program	1	2002
Visual Basic .NET How to Program	2	2002

Fig. 16.14 Titles with copyrights after 2001 from table **Titles**.

The **WHERE** clause condition can contain operators such as <, >, <=, >=, =, <> and *LIKE*.[3] Operator **LIKE** is used for *pattern matching* with wildcard characters *asterisk* (*****) and *question mark* (**?**). Pattern matching allows SQL to search for strings that "match a pattern."

A pattern that contains an asterisk (*****) searches for strings in which zero or more characters take the asterisk character's place in the pattern. For example, the following query locates the records of all authors whose last names start with the letter **D**:

```
SELECT authorID, firstName, lastName
FROM Authors
WHERE lastName LIKE 'D*'
```

The preceding query selects the two records shown in Fig. 16.15, because two of the authors in our database have last names that begin with the letter **D** (followed by zero or more characters). The ***** in the **WHERE** clause's **LIKE** pattern indicates that any number of characters can appear after the letter **D** in the **lastName** field. Notice that the pattern string is surrounded by single-quote characters

Portability Tip 16.1

*Not all database management systems support the **LIKE** operator, so be sure to read the DBMS's documentation carefully before employing this operator.*

Portability Tip 16.2

*Many database management systems use the **%** character in place of the ***** character in **LIKE** expressions.*

Portability Tip 16.3

In some database management systems, string data are case sensitive.

Portability Tip 16.4

In some database management systems, table names and field names are case sensitive..

authorID	firstName	lastName
1	Harvey	Deitel
2	Paul	Deitel

Fig. 16.15 Authors from the **Authors** table whose last names start with D.

---

3. Information about other operators available in **WHERE** clauses can be found at:
   www.baycongroup.com/sql_command_reference.htm
   www.firstsql.com/tutor2.htm

Good Programming Practice 16.2

By convention, SQL keywords should be written entirely in uppercase letters on database management systems that are not case sensitive. This emphasizes the SQL keywords in an SQL statement.

A pattern string including a question mark (**?**) character searches for strings in which exactly one character takes the question mark's place in the pattern. For example, the following query locates the records of all authors whose last names start with any character (specified with **?**), followed by the letter **i**, followed by any number of additional characters (specified with *****):

```
SELECT authorID, firstName, lastName
FROM Authors
WHERE lastName LIKE '?i*'
```

The preceding query produces the records listed in Fig. 16.16; five authors in our database have last names in which the letter **i** is the second letter.

Portability Tip 16.5

Many database management systems use the _ character in place of the ? character in LIKE expressions.

16.4.3 ORDER BY Clause

The results of a query can be arranged in ascending or descending order using the optional ***ORDER BY*** *clause*. The simplest forms for an **ORDER BY** clause are

```
SELECT fieldName1, fieldName2, ... FROM tableName ORDER BY field ASC
SELECT fieldName1, fieldName2, ... FROM tableName ORDER BY field DESC
```

where **ASC** specifies ascending order (lowest to highest), **DESC** specifies descending order (highest to lowest) and *field* specifies the field whose values determine the sorting order.

For example, to obtain a list of authors arranged in ascending order by last name (Fig. 16.17), use the query:

```
SELECT authorID, firstName, lastName
FROM Authors
ORDER BY lastName ASC
```

Note that the default sorting order is ascending; therefore, **ASC** is optional.

authorID	firstName	lastName
3	Tem	Nieto
6	Ted	Lin

Fig. 16.16 Authors from table **Authors** whose last names contain **i** as the second letter. (Part 1 of 2.)

authorID	firstName	lastName
11	Ben	Wiedermann
12	Jonathan	Liperi
13	Jeffrey	Listfield

Fig. 16.16 Authors from table **Authors** whose last names contain **i** as the second letter. (Part 2 of 2.)

authorID	firstName	lastName
15	Christina	Courtemarche
2	Paul	Deitel
1	Harvey	Deitel
14	Jeffrey	Hamm
6	Ted	Lin
12	Jonathan	Liperi
13	Jeffrey	Listfield
8	David	McPhie
3	Tem	Nieto
7	Praveen	Sadhu
5	Sean	Santry
4	Kate	Steinbuhler
11	Ben	Wiedermann
9	Cheryl	Yaeger
10	Marina	Zlatkina

Fig. 16.17 Authors from table **Authors** in ascending order by **lastName**.

To obtain the same list of authors arranged in descending order by last name (Fig. 16.18), use the query:

```
SELECT authorID, firstName, lastName
FROM Authors
ORDER BY lastName DESC
```

authorID	firstName	lastName
10	Marina	Zlatkina
9	Cheryl	Yaeger

Fig. 16.18 Authors from table **Authors** in descending order by **lastName**. (Part 1 of 2.)

authorID	firstName	lastName
11	Ben	Wiedermann
4	Kate	Steinbuhler
5	Sean	Santry
7	Praveen	Sadhu
3	Tem	Nieto
8	David	McPhie
13	Jeffrey	Listfield
12	Jonathan	Liperi
6	Ted	Lin
14	Jeffrey	Hamm
2	Paul	Deitel
1	Harvey	Deitel
15	Christina	Courtemarche

Fig. 16.18 Authors from table **Authors** in descending order by **lastName**. (Part 2 of 2.)

The **ORDER BY** clause also can be used to order records by multiple fields. Such queries are written in the form

ORDER BY *field1 sortingOrder*, *field2 sortingOrder*, ...

where *sortingOrder* is either **ASC** or **DESC**. Note that the *sortingOrder* does not have to be identical for each field.

For example, the query

```
SELECT authorID, firstName, lastName
FROM Authors
ORDER BY lastName, firstName
```

sorts all authors in ascending order by last name, then by first name. This means that, if any authors have the same last name, their records are returned sorted by first name (Fig. 16.19).

authorID	firstName	lastName
15	Christina	Courtemarche
1	Harvey	Deitel
2	Paul	Deitel
14	Jeffrey	Hamm
6	Ted	Lin

Fig. 16.19 Authors from table **Authors** in ascending order by **lastName** and by **firstName**. (Part 1 of 2.)

authorID	firstName	lastName
12	Jonathan	Liperi
13	Jeffrey	Listfield
8	David	McPhie
3	Tem	Nieto
7	Praveen	Sadhu
5	Sean	Santry
4	Kate	Steinbuhler
11	Ben	Wiedermann
9	Cheryl	Yaeger
10	Marina	Zlatkina

Fig. 16.19 Authors from table **Authors** in ascending order by **lastName** and by **firstName**. (Part 2 of 2.)

The **WHERE** and **ORDER BY** clauses can be combined in one query. For example, the query

```
SELECT isbn, title, editionNumber, copyright, price
FROM Titles
WHERE title
LIKE '*How to Program' ORDER BY title ASC
```

returns the ISBN, title, edition number, copyright and price of each book in the **Titles** table that has a **title** ending with "**How to Program**"; it lists these records in ascending order by **title**. The results of the query are depicted in Fig. 16.20.

isbn	title	edition-Number	copy-right	price
0130895601	Advanced Java 2 Platform How to Program	1	2002	$69.95
0131180436	C How to Program	1	1992	$69.95
0130895725	C How to Program	3	2001	$69.95
0132261197	C How to Program	2	1994	$49.95
0130622214	C# How To Program	1	2002	$69.95
0135289106	C++ How to Program	2	1998	$49.95
0131173340	C++ How to Program	1	1994	$69.95
0130895717	C++ How to Program	3	2001	$69.95

Fig. 16.20 Books from table **Titles** whose titles end with **How to Program**, in ascending order by **title**. (Part 1 of 2.)

isbn	title	edition-Number	copy-right	price
013028419X	e-Business and e-Commerce How to Program	1	2001	$69.95
0130308978	Internet and World Wide Web How to Program	2	2002	$69.95
0130161438	Internet and World Wide Web How to Program	1	2000	$69.95
0130341517	Java How to Program	4	2002	$69.95
0136325890	Java How to Program	1	1998	$49.95
0130284181	Perl How to Program	1	2001	$69.95
0130923613	Python How to Program	1	2002	$69.95
0130293636	Visual Basic .NET How to Program	2	2002	$69.95
0134569555	Visual Basic 6 How to Program	1	1999	$69.95
0130622265	Wireless Internet and Mobile Business How to Program	1	2001	$69.95
0130284173	XML How to Program	1	2001	$69.95

Fig. 16.20 Books from table **Titles** whose titles end with **How to Program**, in ascending order by **title**. (Part 2 of 2.)

16.4.4 Merging Data from Multiple Tables: INNER JOIN

Database designers often split related data into separate tables to ensure that a database does not store data redundantly. For example, the **Books** database has tables **Authors** and **Titles**. We use an **AuthorISBN** table to provide "links" between authors and their corresponding titles. If we did not separate this information into individual tables, we would need to include author information with each entry in the **Titles** table. This would result in the database storing duplicate author information for authors who wrote multiple books.

Often, it is necessary for analysis purposes to merge data from multiple tables into a single set of data. Referred to as *joining* the tables, this can be accomplished via an **INNER JOIN** operation in the **SELECT** query.[4] An **INNER JOIN** merges records from two or more tables by testing for matching values in a field that is common to the tables. The simplest format for an **INNER JOIN** clause is:

---

4. **INNER JOIN** is only one of a few different join operations available in SQL. For more information about **JOIN**, visit the following locations:
   www.w3schools.com/sql/sql_join.asp
   www.webreview.com/dd/2000/02_25_00_2.shtml
   www7b.boulder.ibm.com/dmdd/library/techarticle/purcell/0112purcell.html

```
SELECT fieldName1, fieldName2, ...
FROM table1
INNER JOIN table2
    ON table1.fieldName = table2.fieldName
```

The **ON** part of the **INNER JOIN** clause specifies the fields from each table that are compared to determine which records are joined. For example, the following query produces a list of authors accompanied by the ISBN numbers for books written by each author:

```
SELECT firstName, lastName, isbn
FROM Authors
INNER JOIN AuthorISBN
    ON Authors.authorID = AuthorISBN.authorID
ORDER BY lastName, firstName
```

The query merges the **firstName** and **lastName** fields from table **Authors** with the **isbn** field from table **AuthorISBN**, sorting the results in ascending order by **lastName** and **firstName**. Notice the use of the syntax *tableName.fieldName* in the **ON** part of the **INNER JOIN**. This syntax (called a *fully qualified name*) specifies the fields from each table that should be compared to join the tables. The "*tableName.*" syntax is required if the fields have the same name in both tables. The same syntax can be used in any query to distinguish among fields in different tables that have the same name. Fully qualified names that start with the database name can be used to perform cross-database queries.

Software Engineering Observation 16.1

If an SQL statement includes fields from multiple tables that have the same name, the statement must precede those field names with their table names and the dot operator (e.g., Authors.authorID).

Common Programming Error 16.5

In a query, failure to provide fully qualified names for fields that have the same name in two or more tables is an error.

As always, the query can contain an **ORDER BY** clause. Figure 16.21 depicts a sample of the results of the preceding query, ordered by **lastName** and **firstName**. [*Note*: To save space, we do not include all of the results from the query. We also split the results of the query into two columns, each containing the **firstName**, **lastName** and **isbn** fields.]

firstName	lastName	isbn	firstName	lastName	isbn
Harvey	Deitel	0130895601	Harvey	Deitel	0130852473
Harvey	Deitel	0130284181	Harvey	Deitel	0138993947
Harvey	Deitel	0130284173	Harvey	Deitel	0130856118

Fig. 16.21 Authors from table **Authors** and ISBN numbers of the authors' books, sorted in ascending order by **lastName** and **firstName**. (Part 1 of 2.)

firstName	lastName	isbn	firstName	lastName	isbn
Paul	Deitel	0130284181	Tem	Nieto	0130284181
Paul	Deitel	0130284173	Tem	Nieto	0130284173
Paul	Deitel	0130829293	Tem	Nieto	0130829293
Paul	Deitel	0134569555	Tem	Nieto	0134569555
Paul	Deitel	0130829277	Tem	Nieto	0130856118
Paul	Deitel	0130852473	Tem	Nieto	0130161438

Fig. 16.21 Authors from table **Authors** and ISBN numbers of the authors' books, sorted in ascending order by **lastName** and **firstName**. (Part 2 of 2.)

16.4.5 Joining Data from Tables Authors, AuthorISBN, Titles and Publishers

The **Books** database contains one predefined query (**TitleAuthor**), which selects as its results the title, ISBN number, author's first name, author's last name, copyright year and publisher's name for each book in the database. For books that have multiple authors, the query produces a separate composite record for each author. The **TitleAuthor** query is depicted in Fig. 16.22. Figure 16.23 contains a portion of the query results.

```
1   SELECT Titles.title, Titles.isbn, Authors.firstName,
2       Authors.lastName, Titles.copyright,
3        Publishers.publisherName
4   FROM
5   ( Publishers INNER JOIN Titles
6       ON Publishers.publisherID = Titles.publisherID )
7     INNER JOIN
8     ( Authors INNER JOIN AuthorISBN
9     ON Authors.authorID = AuthorISBN.authorID )
10   ON Titles.isbn = AuthorISBN.isbn
11   ORDER BY Titles.title
```

Fig. 16.22 **TitleAuthor** query of **Books** database.

Title	isbn	first-Name	last-Name	copy-right	publisher-Name
Advanced Java 2 Platform How to Program	0130895601	Paul	Deitel	2002	Prentice Hall
Advanced Java 2 Platform How to Program	0130895601	Harvey	Deitel	2002	Prentice Hall

Fig. 16.23 Portion of the result set produced by the query in Fig. 16.22. (Part 1 of 2.)

Title	isbn	first-Name	last-Name	copy-right	publisher-Name
Advanced Java 2 Platform How to Program	0130895601	Sean	Santry	2002	Prentice Hall
C How to Program	0131180436	Harvey	Deitel	1992	Prentice Hall
C How to Program	0131180436	Paul	Deitel	1992	Prentice Hall
C How to Program	0132261197	Harvey	Deitel	1994	Prentice Hall
C How to Program	0132261197	Paul	Deitel	1994	Prentice Hall
C How to Program	0130895725	Harvey	Deitel	2001	Prentice Hall
C How to Program	0130895725	Paul	Deitel	2001	Prentice Hall
C# How To Program	0130622214	Tem	Nieto	2002	Prentice Hall
C# How To Program	0130622214	Paul	Deitel	2002	Prentice Hall
C# How To Program	0130622214	Jeffrey	Listfield	2002	Prentice Hall
C# How To Program	0130622214	Cheryl	Yaeger	2002	Prentice Hall
C# How To Program	0130622214	Marina	Zlatkina	2002	Prentice Hall
C# How To Program	0130622214	Harvey	Deitel	2002	Prentice Hall
C++ How to Program	0130895717	Paul	Deitel	2001	Prentice Hall
C++ How to Program	0130895717	Harvey	Deitel	2001	Prentice Hall
C++ How to Program	0131173340	Paul	Deitel	1994	Prentice Hall
C++ How to Program	0131173340	Harvey	Deitel	1994	Prentice Hall
C++ How to Program	0135289106	Harvey	Deitel	1998	Prentice Hall
C++ How to Program	0135289106	Paul	Deitel	1998	Prentice Hall
e-Business and e-Commerce for Managers	0130323640	Harvey	Deitel	2000	Prentice Hall
e-Business and e-Commerce for Managers	0130323640	Kate	Stein-buhler	2000	Prentice Hall
e-Business and e-Commerce for Managers	0130323640	Paul	Deitel	2000	Prentice Hall
e-Business and e-Commerce How to Program	013028419X	Harvey	Deitel	2001	Prentice Hall
e-Business and e-Commerce How to Program	013028419X	Paul	Deitel	2001	Prentice Hall
e-Business and e-Commerce How to Program	013028419X	Tem	Nieto	2001	Prentice Hall

Fig. 16.23 Portion of the result set produced by the query in Fig. 16.22. (Part 2 of 2.)

We added indentation to the query in Fig. 16.22 to make the query more readable. Let us now break down the query into its various parts. Lines 1–3 contain a comma-separated list of the fields that the query returns; the order of the fields from left to right specifies the fields' order in the returned table. This query selects fields **title** and **isbn** from table **Titles**, fields **firstName** and **lastName** from table **Authors**, field **copyright** from table **Titles** and field **publisherName** from table **Publishers**. For purposes of clarity, we fully qualified each field name with its table name (e.g., **Titles.isbn**).

Lines 5–10 specify the **INNER JOIN** operations used to combine information from the various tables. There are three **INNER JOIN** operations. It is important to note that, although an **INNER JOIN** is performed on two tables, either of those two tables can be the result of another query or another **INNER JOIN**. We use parentheses to nest the **INNER JOIN** operations; SQL evaluates the innermost set of parentheses first and then moves outward. We begin with the **INNER JOIN**:

```
( Publishers INNER JOIN Titles
    ON Publishers.publisherID = Titles.publisherID )
```

which joins the **Publishers** table and the **Titles** table **ON** the condition that the **publisherID** numbers in each table match. The resulting temporary table contains information about each book and its publisher.

The other nested set of parentheses contains the **INNER JOIN**:

```
( Authors INNER JOIN AuthorISBN ON
    Authors.AuthorID = AuthorISBN.AuthorID )
```

which joins the **Authors** table and the **AuthorISBN** table **ON** the condition that the **authorID** fields in each table match. Remember that the **AuthorISBN** table has multiple entries for **ISBN** numbers of books that have more than one author. The third **INNER JOIN**:

```
( Publishers INNER JOIN Titles
    ON Publishers.publisherID = Titles.publisherID )
INNER JOIN
( Authors INNER JOIN AuthorISBN
    ON Authors.authorID = AuthorISBN.authorID )
ON Titles.isbn = AuthorISBN.isbn
```

joins the two temporary tables produced by the two prior inner joins **ON** the condition that the **Titles.isbn** field for each record in the first temporary table matches the corresponding **AuthorISBN.isbn** field for each record in the second temporary table. The result of all these **INNER JOIN** operations is a temporary table from which the appropriate fields are selected to produce the results of the query.

Finally, line 11 of the query,

```
ORDER BY Titles.title
```

indicates that all the records should be sorted in ascending order (the default) by title.

16.4.6 INSERT Statement

The *INSERT* statement inserts a new record in a table. The form for this statement is

```
INSERT INTO tableName ( fieldName1, fieldName2, ..., fieldNameN )
    VALUES ( value1, value2, ..., valueN )
```

where *tableName* is the table in which to insert the record. The *tableName* is followed by a comma-separated list of field names in parentheses. The list of field names is followed by the SQL keyword **VALUES** and a comma-separated list of values in parentheses. The specified values in this list must match the field names listed after the table name in both order and type (for example, if *fieldName1* is specified as the **firstName** field, then *value1* should be a string in single quotes representing the first name). The **INSERT** statement

```
INSERT INTO Authors ( firstName, lastName )
    VALUES ( 'Sue', 'Smith' )
```

inserts a record into the **Authors** table. The first comma-separated list indicates that the statement provides data for the **firstName** and **lastName** fields. The corresponding values to insert, which are contained in the second comma-separated list, are **'Sue'** and **'Smith'**. We do not specify an **authorID** in this example, because **authorID** is an auto-increment field in the database. Every new record that we add to this table is assigned a unique **authorID** value that is the next value in the auto-increment sequence (i.e., 1, 2, 3, etc.). In this case, **Sue Smith** would be assigned **authorID** number 16. Figure 16.24 shows the **Authors** table after we perform the **INSERT** operation.

authorID	firstName	lastName
1	Harvey	Deitel
2	Paul	Deitel
3	Tem	Nieto
4	Kate	Steinbuhler
5	Sean	Santry
6	Ted	Lin
7	Praveen	Sadhu
8	David	McPhie
9	Cheryl	Yaeger
10	Marina	Zlatkina
11	Ben	Wiedermann
12	Jonathan	Liperi
13	Jeffrey	Listfield
14	Jeffrey	Hamm
15	Christina	Courtemarche
16	Sue	Smith

Fig. 16.24 Authors after an **INSERT** operation to add a record.

Common Programming Error 16.6

SQL statements use the single-quote (') character as a delimiter for strings. To specify a string containing a single quote (such as O'Malley) in an SQL statement, the string must include two single quotes in the position where the single-quote character should appear in the string (e.g., **'O''Malley'** *). The first of the two single-quote characters acts as an escape character for the second. Failure to escape single-quote characters in a string that is part of an SQL statement is an SQL syntax error.*

Note that if the values being specified in the **INSERT** statement match the name and type of all required fields in the table (i.e., one value of the correct type is specified for each required field), it is possible to omit the list of field names. For example, the **INSERT** statement above can be also written as

```
INSERT INTO Authors VALUES ( 'Sue', 'Smith' )
```

Because the **authorID** field is an auto-increment field, it is not necessary to specify a value for it. The values in the list that follows keyword **VALUES** are then assigned to the remaining fields, **firstName** and **lastName**, in the order they occur (i.e., **'Sue'** is assigned to **firstName** and **'Smith'** is assigned to **lastName**).

Good Programming Practice 16.3

Although the shorthand version of **INSERT** *statements can be convenient, asvoid using it. Specifying a list of field names not only improves program clarity, but helps prevent program errors that could arise if the fields in a table are altered.*

16.4.7 UPDATE Statement

An **UPDATE** statement modifies data in a table. The simplest form for an **UPDATE** statement is

```
UPDATE tableName
   SET fieldName1 = value1, fieldName2 = value2, ..., fieldNameN = valueN
   WHERE criteria
```

where *tableName* is the table in which to update a record (or records). The *tableName* is followed by keyword **SET** and a comma-separated list of field name/value pairs written in the format, *fieldN*

ame = value. The **WHERE** clause specifies the criteria used to determine which record(s) to update. For example, the **UPDATE** statement:

```
UPDATE Authors
   SET lastName = 'Jones'
   WHERE lastName = 'Smith' AND firstName = 'Sue'
```

updates a record in the **Authors** table. The statement indicates that **lastName** will be assigned the new value **Jones** for the record in which **lastName** currently is equal to **Smith** and **firstName** is equal to **Sue**. If we know the **authorID** in advance of the

UPDATE operation (possibly because we searched for the record previously), the **WHERE** clause could be simplified as follows:

```
WHERE AuthorID = 16
```

Figure 16.25 depicts the **Authors** table after we perform the **UPDATE** operation.

Note that specifying a **WHERE** clause in an **UPDATE** statement is optional. If no **WHERE** clause is specified, the update will be performed on every record in the table. This is a convenient, but powerful, feature. For example, imagine that there is a 15% off sale for all Deitel books. The following query would update all book prices accordingly

```
UPDATE Titles
    SET price = 0.85 * price
```

Common Programming Error 16.7

*Failure to use a **WHERE** clause with an **UPDATE** statement could lead to logic errors. If an update does not apply to every record in the table, be sure to specify the correct **WHERE** clause.*

authorID	firstName	lastName
1	Harvey	Deitel
2	Paul	Deitel
3	Tem	Nieto
4	Kate	Steinbuhler
5	Sean	Santry
6	Ted	Lin
7	Praveen	Sadhu
8	David	McPhie
9	Cheryl	Yaeger
10	Marina	Zlatkina
11	Ben	Wiedermann
12	Jonathan	Liperi
13	Jeffrey	Listfield
14	Jeffrey	Hamm
15	Christina	Courtemarche
16	Sue	Jones

Fig. 16.25 Table **Authors** after an **UPDATE** operation to change a record.

16.4.8 DELETE Statement

An SQL *DELETE* statement removes data from a table. The simplest form for a **DELETE** statement is

> **DELETE FROM** *tableName* **WHERE** *criteria*

where *tableName* is the table from which to delete a record (or records). The **WHERE** clause specifies the criteria used to determine which record(s) to delete. For example, the **DELETE** statement

```
DELETE FROM Authors
    WHERE lastName = 'Jones' AND firstName = 'Sue'
```

deletes the record for **Sue Jones** from the **Authors** table.

Common Programming Error 16.8

WHERE clauses can match multiple records. When deleting records from a database, be sure to define a WHERE clause that matches only the records to be deleted.

Figure 16.26 depicts the **Authors** table after we perform the **DELETE** operation.

authorID	firstName	lastName
1	Harvey	Deitel
2	Paul	Deitel
3	Tem	Nieto
4	Kate	Steinbuhler
5	Sean	Santry
6	Ted	Lin
7	Praveen	Sadhu
8	David	McPhie
9	Cheryl	Yaeger
10	Marina	Zlatkina
11	Ben	Wiedermann
12	Jonathan	Liperi
13	Jeffrey	Listfield
14	Jeffrey	Hamm
15	Christina	Courtemarche

Fig. 16.26 Table **Authors** after a **DELETE** operation to remove a record.

As with **UPDATE** statements, the **WHERE** clause in a **DELETE** statement is optional. If no **WHERE** clause is specified, all records in the table will be deleted! This is a dangerously powerful feature. Use caution when creating **DELETE** statements.

16.5 ADO .NET Object Model

The ADO .NET object model provides an API for accessing database systems programmatically. ADO .NET was created for the .NET Framework and is an improvement to *ActiveX Data Objects*™ (ADO).

Namespace *System::Data* is the root namespace for the ADO .NET API. The primary namespaces for ADO .NET, *System::Data::OleDb* and *System::Data::SqlClient*, contain classes that enable programs to connect with and modify *data sources*. A data source is a location that contains data, such as a database. Namespace **System::Data::OleDb** contains classes that are designed to work with any data source, whereas the **System::Data::SqlClient** namespace contains classes that are optimized to work with Microsoft SQL Server 2000 databases.

Instances of class *System::Data::DataSet*, which consist of a set of **DataTable**s and relationships among those **DataTable**s, represent *caches* of data—data that a program stores temporarily in local memory. The structure of a **DataSet** mimics the structure of a relational database. An advantage of using class **DataSet** is that it is *disconnected*—the program does not need a persistent connection to the data source to work with data in a **DataSet**. The program connects to the data source only during the initial population of the **DataSet** and then to store any changes made in the **DataSet**. Hence, the program does not require any active, permanent connection to the data source.

Instances of class *OleDbConnection* (namespace **System::Data::OleDb**) represent connections to a data source. An instance of class *OleDbDataAdapter* connects to a data source through an instance of class **OleDbConnection** and can populate a **DataSet** with data from that data source. We discuss the details of creating and populating **DataSet**s later in this chapter. An instance of class *OleDbCommand* (namespace **System::Data::OleDb**) represents an arbitrary SQL command to be executed on a data source. A program can use instances of class **OleDbCommand** to manipulate a data source through an **OleDbConnection**. The programmer must close the active connection to the data source explicitly once no further changes are to be made. Unlike **DataSet**s, **OleDbCommand** objects do not cache data in local memory.

16.6 Programming with ADO .NET: Extracting Information from a Database

In this section, we present two examples that introduce how to connect to a database, query the database and display the results of the query. The database used in these examples is the Microsoft Access **Books** database that we have discussed throughout this chapter. It can be found in the project directory for the application of Fig. 16.27–Fig. 16.29. Each program must specify the location of this database on the computer's hard drive. When executing these examples, readers may need to update this location for each program. For example, before readers can run the application in Fig. 16.27–Fig. 16.29 on their computers, they may need to change lines 32–35 (Fig. 16.28) so that the code specifies the correct location of the database file.

16.6.1 Connecting to and Querying an Access Data Source

The first example (Fig. 16.27–Fig. 16.29) performs a simple query on the **Books** database that retrieves the entire **Authors** table and displays the data in a *DataGrid* (a **Sys-tem::Windows::Forms** component class that can display information from a data source, such as a table, in a GUI). The program illustrates the process of connecting to the database, querying the database and displaying the results in a **DataGrid**. The discussion following the example presents the key aspects of the program.

```
1   // Fig. 16.27: TableDisplay.h
2   // Displays data from a database table.
3
4   #pragma once
5
6   #using <system.dll>
7   #using <mscorlib.dll>
8   #using <system.data.dll>
9   #using <system.drawing.dll>
10  #using <system.windows.forms.dll>
11  #using <system.xml.dll>
12
13  using namespace System;
14  using namespace System::Drawing;
15  using namespace System::Windows::Forms;
16  using namespace System::Data;
17  using namespace System::Data::OleDb;
18  using namespace System::Xml;
19
20  public __gc class TableDisplay : public Form
21  {
22  public:
23     TableDisplay();
24
25  private:
26     DataSet *dataSet1;
27     OleDbDataAdapter *oleDbDataAdapter1;
28     DataGrid *dataGrid1;
29     OleDbCommand *oleDbSelectCommand1;
30     OleDbConnection *oleDbConnection1;
31
32     void InitializeComponent();
33     void SetupConnection();
34  }; // end class TableDisplay
```

Fig. 16.27 Accessing and displaying a database's data.

```
1   // Fig. 16.28: TableDisplay.cpp
2   // Method definitions for class TableDisplay.
3
4   #include "TableDisplay.h"
5
```

Fig. 16.28 TableDisplay class method definitions. (Part 1 of 3.)

```
 6   TableDisplay::TableDisplay()
 7   {
 8       SetupConnection();
 9
10       InitializeComponent();
11
12       // fill dataSet1 with data
13       oleDbDataAdapter1->Fill( dataSet1, S"Authors" );
14
15       // bind data in Users table in dataSet1 to dataGrid1
16       dataGrid1->SetDataBinding( dataSet1, S"Authors" );
17   } // end method SetupConnection
18
19   // setup database connection
20   void TableDisplay::SetupConnection()
21   {
22       this->dataSet1 = new DataSet( S"NewDataSet" );
23       this->oleDbDataAdapter1 = new OleDbDataAdapter();
24       this->oleDbSelectCommand1 = new OleDbCommand();
25       this->oleDbConnection1 = new OleDbConnection();
26
27       // specify command for adapter
28       this->oleDbDataAdapter1->SelectCommand =
29           this->oleDbSelectCommand1;
30
31       // create connection string
32       this->oleDbConnection1->ConnectionString =
33           S"Provider=Microsoft.Jet.OLEDB.4.0;Password=\"\";"
34           S"User ID=Admin;Data Source=Books.mdb;Mode=Share "
35           S"Deny None;Jet OLEDB:Database Password=\"\";";
36
37       this->oleDbConnection1->Open();   // open connection
38
39       // configure SELECT command
40       this->oleDbSelectCommand1->CommandText =
41           S"SELECT authorID, firstName, lastName FROM Authors";
42       this->oleDbSelectCommand1->Connection =
43           this->oleDbConnection1;
44   } // end method SetupConnection
45
46   void TableDisplay::InitializeComponent()
47   {
48       this->SuspendLayout();
49
50       // dataGrid1
51       this->dataGrid1 = new DataGrid();
52       this->dataGrid1->Location = Point( 16, 16 );
53       this->dataGrid1->Size = Drawing::Size( 264, 248 );
54
55       // TableDisplay
56       this->AutoScaleBaseSize = Drawing::Size( 5, 13 );
57       this->ClientSize = Drawing::Size( 292, 273 );
58       this->Controls->Add( this->dataGrid1 );
```

Fig. 16.28 TableDisplay class method definitions. (Part 2 of 3.)

```
59        this->Name = S"TableDisplay";
60        this->Text = S"TableDisplay";
61        this->ResumeLayout();
62   } // end method InitializeComponent
```

Fig. 16.28 `TableDisplay` class method definitions. (Part 3 of 3.)

```
1    // Fig. 16.29: TableDisplayTest.cpp
2    // Entry point for application.
3
4    #include "TableDisplay.h"
5
6    int __stdcall WinMain()
7    {
8        Application::Run( new TableDisplay() );
9
10       return 0;
11   } // end WinMain
```

Fig. 16.29 `TableDisplay` class driver.

Line 30 (Fig. 16.27) declares a `System::Data::OleDb::OleDbConnection` to the source, `oleDbConnection1`. Lines 32–35 (Fig. 16.28) initialize the `oleDbConnection` for this program. The `ConnectionString` property specifies the database file on the computer's hard drive. Note that if the database file did not exist in the current directory, it would be necessary to specify a path to the file. The `ConnectionString` also specifies `Microsoft.Jet.OLEDB.4.0`, the driver for Access databases, as the database driver. `ConnectionString`s can also specify other options. Some of the examples in this chapter use longer, more complicated `ConnectionString`s.[5]

---

5. For more information about `ConnectionString`s, visit `msdn.microsoft.com/library/default.asp?url=/library/en-us/cpref/html/frlrfSystemDataOleDbOleDbConnectionClassConnectionStringTopic.asp`.

Good Programming Practice 16.4

Use clear, descriptive variable names in code. This makes programs easier to understand.

Line 26 (Fig. 16.27) declares a **DataSet** to store the query results. An instance of class **OleDbDataAdapter** populates the **DataSet** in this example with data from the **Books** database. The instance property *SelectCommand* (lines 28–29 of Fig. 16.28) is an **OleDbCommand** object that specifies how the **OleDbDataAdapter** selects data in the database.

Each **OleDbCommand** object must have an **OleDbConnection** through which the **OleDbCommand** can communicate with the database. Property **Connection** is set to the **OleDbConnection** to the **Books** database. For **oleDbSelectCommand1**, lines 42–43 set the **Connection** property, and lines 40–41 set the **CommandText**. Property *CommandText* of class **OleDbCommand** is a **String *** representing the SQL statement that the **OleDbCommand** object executes.

Line 13 in the **TableDisplay** constructor populates **dataSet1** using an **OleDb-DataAdapter**. Line 13 calls **OleDbDataAdapter** method *Fill* to retrieve information from the database associated with the **OleDbConnection**, placing the information in the **DataSet** provided as an argument. This information will be stored in the **DataSet** in the form of a table. Because **DataSet**s can contain many tables, we provide a name for this table as the second argument to method **Fill**. We use the name **Authors** for simplicity, because this is the name of the table in the database that we are retrieving data from.

Line 16 invokes **DataGrid** method *SetDataBinding* to bind the **DataGrid** to a data source. The first argument is the **DataSet**—in this case, **dataSet1**—whose data the **DataGrid** should display. The second argument is a **String *** representing the name of the table within the **DataSet** we want to bind to the **DataGrid**. Once this line executes, the **DataGrid** is filled with the information in the **DataSet**—the number of rows and number of columns are set from the information in **dataSet1**.

Once the **DataGrid** is filled with the information, the data can be sorted in ascending or descending order by clicking a column name in the **DataGrid** (e.g., **firstName**). Note that this is simply a feature of **DataGrid**s. Each time the user performs such a sorting operation, the program is not performing another query on the database. Rather, it is simply sorting the data that has already been returned.

16.6.2 Querying the Books Database

The example in Fig. 16.30–Fig. 16.32 demonstrates how to execute SQL **SELECT** statements on database **Books.mdb** and display the results. Although Fig. 16.31 uses only **SELECT** statements to query the data, the same program could be used to execute many different SQL statements if we made a few modifications.

```
1   // Fig. 16.30: DisplayQueryResults.h
2   // Displays the contents of the authors database.
3
4   #pragma once
5
```

Fig. 16.30 Execute SQL statements on a database. (Part 1 of 2.)

```
 6    #using <system.dll>
 7    #using <mscorlib.dll>
 8    #using <system.data.dll>
 9    #using <system.drawing.dll>
10    #using <system.windows.forms.dll>
11    #using <system.xml.dll>
12
13    using namespace System;
14    using namespace System::Data;
15    using namespace System::Data::OleDb;
16    using namespace System::Drawing;
17    using namespace System::Windows::Forms;
18    using namespace System::Xml;
19
20    public __gc class DisplayQueryResults : public Form
21    {
22    public:
23       DisplayQueryResults();
24
25    private:
26       TextBox *queryTextBox;
27       Button *submitButton;
28       DataGrid *dataGrid1;
29
30       DataSet *dataSet1;
31       OleDbDataAdapter *oleDbDataAdapter1;
32       OleDbCommand *oleDbSelectCommand1;
33       OleDbConnection *oleDbConnection1;
34
35       void InitializeComponent();
36       void SetupConnection();
37
38       // perform SQL query on data
39       void submitButton_Click( Object *, EventArgs * );
40    }; // end class DisplayQueryResults
```

Fig. 16.30 Execute SQL statements on a database. (Part 2 of 2.)

```
 1    // Fig. 16.31: DisplayQueryResults.cpp
 2    // Method definitions for class DisplayQueryResults.
 3
 4    #include "DisplayQueryResults.h"
 5
 6    DisplayQueryResults::DisplayQueryResults()
 7    {
 8       SetupConnection();
 9       InitializeComponent();
10    }
11
12    // setup database connection
13    void DisplayQueryResults::SetupConnection()
14    {
```

Fig. 16.31 DisplayQueryResults class method definitions. (Part 1 of 3.)

```cpp
15        this->dataSet1 = new DataSet( S"NewDataSet" );
16        this->oleDbDataAdapter1 = new OleDbDataAdapter();
17        this->oleDbSelectCommand1 = new OleDbCommand();
18        this->oleDbConnection1 = new OleDbConnection();
19
20        // specify command for adapter
21        this->oleDbDataAdapter1->SelectCommand =
22           this->oleDbSelectCommand1;
23
24        // create connection string
25        this->oleDbConnection1->ConnectionString =
26           S"Provider=Microsoft.Jet.OLEDB.4.0;Password=\"\";"
27           S"User ID=Admin;Data Source=Books.mdb;Mode=Share "
28           S"Deny None;Jet OLEDB:Database Password=\"\";";
29
30        oleDbConnection1->Open();   // open connection
31
32        // configure SELECT command
33        this->oleDbSelectCommand1->CommandText =
34           S"SELECT authorID, firstName, lastName FROM Authors";
35        this->oleDbSelectCommand1->Connection =
36           this->oleDbConnection1;
37     } // end method SetupConnection
38
39     void DisplayQueryResults::InitializeComponent()
40     {
41        this->SuspendLayout();
42
43        this->queryTextBox = new TextBox();
44        this->submitButton = new Button();
45        this->dataGrid1 = new DataGrid();
46
47        // queryTextBox
48        this->queryTextBox->Location = Point( 8, 8 );
49        this->queryTextBox->Multiline = true;
50        this->queryTextBox->Name = S"queryTextBox";
51        this->queryTextBox->Size = Drawing::Size( 312, 64 );
52        this->queryTextBox->TabIndex = 0;
53        this->queryTextBox->Text = S"";
54
55        // submitButton
56        this->submitButton->Location = Point( 8, 80 );
57        this->submitButton->Name = S"submitButton";
58        this->submitButton->Size = Drawing::Size( 312, 24 );
59        this->submitButton->TabIndex = 1;
60        this->submitButton->Text = S"Submit Query";
61        this->submitButton->Click += new EventHandler( this,
62           submitButton_Click );
63
64        // dataGrid1
65        this->dataGrid1->Location = Point( 8, 112 );
66        this->dataGrid1->Name = S"dataGrid1";
67        this->dataGrid1->Size = Drawing::Size( 312, 184 );
```

Fig. 16.31 DisplayQueryResults class method definitions. (Part 2 of 3.)

```
68         this->dataGrid1->TabIndex = 2;
69
70         // DisplayQueryResults
71         this->AutoScaleBaseSize = Drawing::Size( 5, 13 );
72         this->ClientSize = Drawing::Size( 328, 301 );
73
74         Control *control[] = { this->dataGrid1, this->submitButton,
75            this->queryTextBox };
76         this->Controls->AddRange( control );
77         this->Name = S"DisplayQueryResults";
78         this->Text = S"DisplayQueryResults";
79         this->ResumeLayout();
80     } // end method InitializeComponent
81
82     // perform SQL query on data
83     void DisplayQueryResults::submitButton_Click(
84        Object *sender, EventArgs *e )
85     {
86        try {
87
88           // set the text of the SQL query to what the user typed in
89           oleDbDataAdapter1->SelectCommand->CommandText =
90              queryTextBox->Text;
91
92           // clear the DataSet from the previous operation
93           dataSet1->Clear();
94
95           // fill the data set with the information that results
96           // from the SQL query
97           oleDbDataAdapter1->Fill( dataSet1, S"Authors" );
98
99           // bind the DataGrid to the contents of the DatSet
100          dataGrid1->SetDataBinding( dataSet1, S"Authors" );
101       }
102       catch ( OleDbException *oleException ) {
103          MessageBox::Show( oleException->Message, S"Invalid query",
104             MessageBoxButtons::OK, MessageBoxIcon::Error );
105       }
106    } // end method submitButton_Click
```

Fig. 16.31 `DisplayQueryResults` class method definitions. (Part 3 of 3.)

```
1     // Fig. 16.32: DisplayQueryResults.cpp
2     // Entry point for application.
3
4     #include "DisplayQueryResults.h"
5
6     int __stdcall WinMain()
7     {
8        Application::Run( new DisplayQueryResults() );
9
10       return 0;
11    } // end WinMain
```

Fig. 16.32 `DisplayQueryResults` class driver. (Part 1 of 2.)

Fig. 16.32 `DisplayQueryResults` class driver. (Part 2 of 2.)

Method **submitButton_Click** is the key part of this program. When the program invokes this event handler, lines 89–90 (Fig. 16.31) assign the **SELECT** query entered by the user into **queryTextBox** to OleDbDataAdapter's **SelectCommand** property. This **String *** is parsed into an SQL query and executed on the database via the **OleDb-DataAdapter**'s **Fill** method (line 97). As we discussed in the previous section, method **Fill** places data from the database into **dataSet1**.

Notice that before calling **Fill** we first call **DataSet** method *Clear* (line 93). This method removes all the data stored in the **DataSet**. This ensures that the data currently displayed in the **DataGrid** is only from the most recently executed query. If we did not call method **Clear**, new data would simply be appended to the **DataGrid**.

> **Common Programming Error 16.9**
>
> *If a **DataSet** has been **Filled** at least once, forgetting to call a **DataSet**'s **Clear** method before calling method **Fill** again could lead to logic errors.*

To display, or redisplay, contents in the **DataGrid**, use method **SetData-Binding**. The first argument is the data source to be displayed in the table—a **DataSet**, in this case. The second argument is the **String *** name of the data source member to be displayed (line 100). Readers can try entering their own queries in the text box and then pressing the **Submit Query** button to execute the query.

16.7 Programming with ADO.NET: Modifying a Database

Our next example implements a simple address-book application that enables the user to insert, locate and update records in the Microsoft Access database **Addressbook**. The database contains one table (**addresses**) with 11 columns—**id, firstname, last-name, address, city, stateorprovince, postalcode, country, email-address, homephone** and **faxnumber**.

The **Addressbook** application (Fig. 16.33–Fig. 16.35) provides a GUI enabling users to execute SQL statements on the database. Earlier in the chapter, we presented examples demonstrating the use of **SELECT** statements to query a database. Here, that same functionality is provided.

```cpp
1    // Fig. 16.33: AddressBook.h
2    // Using SQL statements to manipulate a database.
3
4    #pragma once
5
6    #using <system.dll>
7    #using <mscorlib.dll>
8    #using <system.data.dll>
9    #using <system.drawing.dll>
10   #using <system.windows.forms.dll>
11   #using <system.xml.dll>
12
13   using namespace System;
14   using namespace System::Data;
15   using namespace System::Data::OleDb;
16   using namespace System::Drawing;
17   using namespace System::Windows::Forms;
18   using namespace System::Xml;
19
20   public __gc class AddressBook : public Form
21   {
22   public:
23      AddressBook();
24
25   private:
26      DataSet *dataSet1;
27      OleDbDataAdapter *oleDbDataAdapter1;
28      OleDbCommand *oleDbSelectCommand1;
29      OleDbCommand *oleDbInsertCommand1;
30      OleDbCommand *oleDbUpdateCommand1;
31      OleDbConnection *oleDbConnection1;
32
33      TextBox *homeTextBox, *firstTextBox, *lastTextBox, *idTextBox,
34         *stateTextBox, *statusTextBox, *postalTextBox, *faxTextBox,
35         *cityTextBox, *countryTextBox, *emailTextBox,
36         *addressTextBox;
37
38      Label *addressLabel, *cityLabel, *stateLabel, *idLabel,
39         *firstLabel, *lastLabel, *postalLabel, *countryLabel,
40         *emailLabel, *faxLabel, *homeLabel;
41
42      Button *clearButton, *helpButton, *findButton, *addButton,
43         *updateButton;
44
45      void InitializeComponent();
46      void SetupConnection();
47
48      void findButton_Click( Object *, EventArgs * );
49      void addButton_Click( Object *, EventArgs * );
50      void updateButton_Click( Object *, EventArgs * );
51      void clearButton_Click( Object *, EventArgs * );
52      void helpButton_Click( Object *, EventArgs * );
53      void Display( DataSet * );
54      void ClearTextBoxes();
55   }; // end class AddressBook
```

Fig. 16.33 Modifying a database.

```
1    // Fig. 16.34: AddressBook.cpp
2    // Method definitions for class AddressBook.
3
4    #include "AddressBook.h"
5
6    AddressBook::AddressBook()
7    {
8        SetupConnection();
9        InitializeComponent();
10   }
11
12   void AddressBook::InitializeComponent()
13   {
14       this->SuspendLayout();
15
16       this->countryLabel = new Label();
17       this->emailLabel = new Label();
18       this->addressLabel = new Label();
19       this->cityLabel = new Label();
20       this->stateLabel = new Label();
21       this->faxTextBox = new TextBox();
22       this->homeTextBox = new TextBox();
23       this->idLabel = new Label();
24       this->firstLabel = new Label();
25       this->lastLabel = new Label();
26       this->firstTextBox = new TextBox();
27       this->stateTextBox = new TextBox();
28       this->clearButton = new Button();
29       this->helpButton = new Button();
30       this->idTextBox = new TextBox();
31       this->lastTextBox = new TextBox();
32       this->findButton = new Button();
33       this->addButton = new Button();
34       this->updateButton = new Button();
35       this->postalTextBox = new TextBox();
36       this->addressTextBox = new TextBox();
37       this->cityTextBox = new TextBox();
38       this->postalLabel = new Label();
39       this->countryTextBox = new TextBox();
40       this->emailTextBox = new TextBox();
41       this->faxLabel = new Label();
42       this->homeLabel = new Label();
43       this->statusTextBox = new TextBox();
44
45       // findButton
46       this->findButton->Name = S"findButton";
47       this->findButton->Size = Drawing::Size( 72, 24 );
48       this->findButton->TabIndex = 0;
49       this->findButton->Text = S"Find";
50       this->findButton->Click += new EventHandler( this,
51          findButton_Click );
52
53       // addButton
54       this->addButton->Location = Point( 72, 0 );
```

Fig. 16.34 AddressBook class method definitons. (Part 1 of 11.)

```
55       this->addButton->Name = S"addButton";
56       this->addButton->Size = Drawing::Size( 80, 24 );
57       this->addButton->TabIndex = 1;
58       this->addButton->Text = S"Add";
59       this->addButton->Click += new EventHandler( this,
60          addButton_Click );
61
62       // updateButton
63       this->updateButton->Location = Point( 152, 0 );
64       this->updateButton->Name = S"updateButton";
65       this->updateButton->Size = Drawing::Size( 72, 24 );
66       this->updateButton->TabIndex = 2;
67       this->updateButton->Text = S"Update";
68       this->updateButton->Click += new EventHandler( this,
69          updateButton_Click );
70
71       // clearButton
72       this->clearButton->Location = Point( 224, 0 );
73       this->clearButton->Name = S"clearButton";
74       this->clearButton->Size = Drawing::Size( 80, 24 );
75       this->clearButton->TabIndex = 3;
76       this->clearButton->Text = S"Clear";
77       this->clearButton->Click += new EventHandler( this,
78          clearButton_Click );
79
80       // helpButton
81       this->helpButton->Location = Point( 304, 0 );
82       this->helpButton->Name = S"helpButton";
83       this->helpButton->Size = Drawing::Size( 80, 24 );
84       this->helpButton->TabIndex = 4;
85       this->helpButton->Text = S"Help";
86       this->helpButton->Click += new EventHandler( this,
87          helpButton_Click );
88
89       // idLabel
90       this->idLabel->Location = Point( 16, 40 );
91       this->idLabel->Name = S"idLabel";
92       this->idLabel->Size = Drawing::Size( 152, 16 );
93       this->idLabel->TabIndex = 15;
94       this->idLabel->Text = S"ID Number:";
95       this->idLabel->TextAlign = ContentAlignment::MiddleCenter;
96
97       // idTextBox
98       this->idTextBox->Location = Point( 184, 40 );
99       this->idTextBox->Name = S"idTextBox";
100      this->idTextBox->ReadOnly = true;
101      this->idTextBox->Size = Drawing::Size( 176, 20 );
102      this->idTextBox->TabIndex = 15;
103      this->idTextBox->Text = S"";
104
105      // firstLabel
106      this->firstLabel->Location = Point( 16, 72 );
107      this->firstLabel->Name = S"firstLabel";
```

Fig. 16.34 AddressBook class method definitons. (Part 2 of 11.)

```
108      this->firstLabel->Size = Drawing::Size( 152, 16 );
109      this->firstLabel->TabIndex = 15;
110      this->firstLabel->Text = S"First name:";
111      this->firstLabel->TextAlign = ContentAlignment::MiddleCenter;
112
113      // firstTextBox
114      this->firstTextBox->Location = Point( 184, 72 );
115      this->firstTextBox->Name = S"firstTextBox";
116      this->firstTextBox->Size = Drawing::Size( 176, 20 );
117      this->firstTextBox->TabIndex = 5;
118      this->firstTextBox->Text = S"";
119
120      // lastLabel
121      this->lastLabel->Location = Point( 16, 104 );
122      this->lastLabel->Name = S"lastLabel";
123      this->lastLabel->Size = Drawing::Size( 152, 16 );
124      this->lastLabel->TabIndex = 15;
125      this->lastLabel->Text = S"Last Name:";
126      this->lastLabel->TextAlign = ContentAlignment::MiddleCenter;
127
128      // lastTextBox
129      this->lastTextBox->Location = Point( 184, 104 );
130      this->lastTextBox->Name = S"lastTextBox";
131      this->lastTextBox->Size = Drawing::Size( 176, 20 );
132      this->lastTextBox->TabIndex = 6;
133      this->lastTextBox->Text = S"";
134
135      // addressLabel
136      this->addressLabel->Location = Point( 16, 136 );
137      this->addressLabel->Name = S"addressLabel";
138      this->addressLabel->Size = Drawing::Size( 152, 16 );
139      this->addressLabel->TabIndex = 15;
140      this->addressLabel->Text = S"Address:";
141      this->addressLabel->TextAlign = ContentAlignment::MiddleCenter;
142
143      // addressTextBox
144      this->addressTextBox->Location = Point( 184, 136 );
145      this->addressTextBox->Name = S"addressTextBox";
146      this->addressTextBox->Size = Drawing::Size( 176, 20 );
147      this->addressTextBox->TabIndex = 7;
148      this->addressTextBox->Text = S"";
149
150      // cityLabel
151      this->cityLabel->Location = Point( 16, 168 );
152      this->cityLabel->Name = S"cityLabel";
153      this->cityLabel->Size = Drawing::Size( 152, 16 );
154      this->cityLabel->TabIndex = 15;
155      this->cityLabel->Text = S"City:";
156      this->cityLabel->TextAlign = ContentAlignment::MiddleCenter;
157
158      // cityTextBox
159      this->cityTextBox->Location = Point( 184, 168 );
160      this->cityTextBox->Name = S"cityTextBox";
```

Fig. 16.34 AddressBook class method definitons. (Part 3 of 11.)

```
161     this->cityTextBox->Size = Drawing::Size( 176, 20 );
162     this->cityTextBox->TabIndex = 8;
163     this->cityTextBox->Text = S"";
164
165     // stateLabel
166     this->stateLabel->Location = Point( 16, 200 );
167     this->stateLabel->Name = S"stateLabel";
168     this->stateLabel->Size = Drawing::Size( 152, 16 );
169     this->stateLabel->TabIndex = 15;
170     this->stateLabel->Text = S"State/Province:";
171     this->stateLabel->TextAlign = ContentAlignment::MiddleCenter;
172
173     // stateTextBox
174     this->stateTextBox->Location = Point( 184, 200 );
175     this->stateTextBox->Name = S"stateTextBox";
176     this->stateTextBox->Size = Drawing::Size( 176, 20 );
177     this->stateTextBox->TabIndex = 9;
178     this->stateTextBox->Text = S"";
179
180     // postalLabel
181     this->postalLabel->Location = Point( 16, 232 );
182     this->postalLabel->Name = S"postalLabel";
183     this->postalLabel->Size = Drawing::Size( 152, 16 );
184     this->postalLabel->TabIndex = 15;
185     this->postalLabel->Text = S"Postal Code:";
186     this->postalLabel->TextAlign = ContentAlignment::MiddleCenter;
187
188     // postalTextBox
189     this->postalTextBox->Location = Point( 184, 232 );
190     this->postalTextBox->Name = S"postalTextBox";
191     this->postalTextBox->Size = Drawing::Size( 176, 20 );
192     this->postalTextBox->TabIndex = 10;
193     this->postalTextBox->Text = S"";
194
195     // countryLabel
196     this->countryLabel->Location = Point( 16, 264 );
197     this->countryLabel->Name = S"countryLabel";
198     this->countryLabel->Size = Drawing::Size( 152, 16 );
199     this->countryLabel->TabIndex = 15;
200     this->countryLabel->Text = S"Country:";
201     this->countryLabel->TextAlign = ContentAlignment::MiddleCenter;
202
203     // countryTextBox
204     this->countryTextBox->Location = Point( 184, 264 );
205     this->countryTextBox->Name = S"countryTextBox";
206     this->countryTextBox->Size = Drawing::Size( 176, 20 );
207     this->countryTextBox->TabIndex = 11;
208     this->countryTextBox->Text = S"";
209
210     // emailLabel
211     this->emailLabel->Location = Point( 16, 296 );
212     this->emailLabel->Name = S"emailLabel";
213     this->emailLabel->Size = Drawing::Size( 152, 16 );
```

Fig. 16.34 AddressBook class method definitons. (Part 4 of 11.)

```
214        this->emailLabel->TabIndex = 15;
215        this->emailLabel->Text = S"Email:";
216        this->emailLabel->TextAlign = ContentAlignment::MiddleCenter;
217
218        // emailTextBox
219        this->emailTextBox->Location = Point( 184, 296 );
220        this->emailTextBox->Name = S"emailTextBox";
221        this->emailTextBox->Size = Drawing::Size( 176, 20 );
222        this->emailTextBox->TabIndex = 12;
223        this->emailTextBox->Text = S"";
224
225        // homeLabel
226        this->homeLabel->Location = Point( 16, 328 );
227        this->homeLabel->Name = S"homeLabel";
228        this->homeLabel->Size = Drawing::Size( 152, 16 );
229        this->homeLabel->TabIndex = 15;
230        this->homeLabel->Text = S"Home Phone:";
231        this->homeLabel->TextAlign = ContentAlignment::MiddleCenter;
232
233        // homeTextBox
234        this->homeTextBox->Location = Point( 184, 328 );
235        this->homeTextBox->Name = S"homeTextBox";
236        this->homeTextBox->Size = Drawing::Size( 176, 20 );
237        this->homeTextBox->TabIndex = 13;
238        this->homeTextBox->Text = S"";
239
240        // faxLabel
241        this->faxLabel->Location = Point( 16, 360 );
242        this->faxLabel->Name = S"faxLabel";
243        this->faxLabel->Size = Drawing::Size( 152, 16 );
244        this->faxLabel->TabIndex = 15;
245        this->faxLabel->Text = S"Fax Number:";
246        this->faxLabel->TextAlign = ContentAlignment::MiddleCenter;
247
248        // faxTextBox
249        this->faxTextBox->Location = Point( 184, 360 );
250        this->faxTextBox->Name = S"faxTextBox";
251        this->faxTextBox->Size = Drawing::Size( 176, 20 );
252        this->faxTextBox->TabIndex = 14;
253        this->faxTextBox->Text = S"";
254
255        // statusTextBox
256        this->statusTextBox->Location = Point( 16, 400 );
257        this->statusTextBox->Multiline = true;
258        this->statusTextBox->Name = S"statusTextBox";
259        this->statusTextBox->ReadOnly = true;
260        this->statusTextBox->ScrollBars = ScrollBars::Vertical;
261        this->statusTextBox->Size = Drawing::Size( 344, 120 );
262        this->statusTextBox->TabIndex = 15;
263        this->statusTextBox->Text = S"";
264
265        this->AutoScaleBaseSize = Drawing::Size( 5, 13 );
266        this->ClientSize = Drawing::Size( 384, 533 );
```

Fig. 16.34 AddressBook class method definitons. (Part 5 of 11.)

```
267        Control *control[] = { this->statusTextBox, this->faxLabel,
268           this->homeLabel, this->emailLabel, this->countryLabel,
269           this->postalLabel, this->stateLabel, this->cityLabel,
270           this->addressLabel, this->lastLabel, this->firstLabel,
271           this->idLabel, this->faxTextBox, this->homeTextBox,
272           this->emailTextBox, this->countryTextBox,
273           this->postalTextBox, this->stateTextBox,
274           this->cityTextBox, this->addressTextBox,
275           this->lastTextBox, this->firstTextBox, this->idTextBox,
276           this->helpButton, this->clearButton, this->updateButton,
277           this->addButton, this->findButton };
278        this->Controls->AddRange( control );
279        this->Name = S"AddressBook";
280        this->Text = S"AddressBook";
281        this->ResumeLayout();
282    } // end method InitializeComponent
283
284    void AddressBook::SetupConnection()
285    {
286        this->dataSet1 = new DataSet( S"NewDataSet" );
287        this->oleDbDataAdapter1 = new OleDbDataAdapter();
288        this->oleDbConnection1 = new OleDbConnection();
289        this->oleDbInsertCommand1 = new OleDbCommand();
290        this->oleDbSelectCommand1 = new OleDbCommand();
291        this->oleDbUpdateCommand1 = new OleDbCommand();
292
293        // specify commands for adapter
294        this->oleDbDataAdapter1->InsertCommand =
295           this->oleDbInsertCommand1;
296        this->oleDbDataAdapter1->SelectCommand =
297           this->oleDbSelectCommand1;
298        this->oleDbDataAdapter1->UpdateCommand =
299           this->oleDbUpdateCommand1;
300
301        // create connection string
302        this->oleDbConnection1->ConnectionString =
303           S"Provider=Microsoft.Jet.OLEDB.4.0;Password=\"\";"
304           S"User ID=Admin;Data Source=addressbook.mdb;Mode=Share "
305           S"Deny None;Extended Properties=\"\";Jet OLEDB:"
306           S"System database=\"\";Jet OLEDB:Registry "
307           S"Path=\"\";Jet OLEDB:Database Password=\"\";"
308           S"Jet OLEDB:Engine Type=5;Jet OLEDB:Database "
309           S"Locking Mode=1;Jet OLEDB:Global Partial Bulk "
310           S"Ops=2;Jet OLEDB:Global Bulk Transactions=1;Jet "
311           S"OLEDB:New Database Password=\"\";Jet OLEDB:"
312           S"Create System Database=False;Jet OLEDB:Encrypt "
313           S"Database=False;Jet OLEDB:Don't Copy Locale on "
314           S"Compact=False;Jet OLEDB:Compact Without Replica "
315           S"Repair=False;Jet OLEDB:SFP=False";
316
317        oleDbConnection1->Open();  // open connection
318
```

Fig. 16.34 AddressBook class method definitons. (Part 6 of 11.)

```
319        // specify connection for commands
320        this->oleDbInsertCommand1->Connection = this->oleDbConnection1;
321        this->oleDbSelectCommand1->Connection = this->oleDbConnection1;
322        this->oleDbUpdateCommand1->Connection = this->oleDbConnection1;
323     }
324
325     void AddressBook::findButton_Click( Object *sender, EventArgs *e )
326     {
327        try {
328
329           if ( !lastTextBox->Text->Equals( String::Empty ) ) {
330
331              // clear the DataSet from the last operation
332              dataSet1->Clear();
333
334              // create SQL query to find the contact with the
335              // specified last name
336              oleDbDataAdapter1->SelectCommand->CommandText =
337                 String::Concat( S"SELECT * FROM addresses WHERE ",
338                 S"lastname = '", lastTextBox->Text, S"'" );
339
340              // fill dataSet1 with the rows resulting from the query
341              oleDbDataAdapter1->Fill( dataSet1 );
342
343              // display information
344              Display( dataSet1 );
345              statusTextBox->Text = String::Concat(
346                 statusTextBox->Text, S"\r\nQuery successful\r\n" );
347           } // end if
348           else
349              lastTextBox->Text =
350                 S"Enter last name here and press Find";
351        } // end try
352
353        catch ( OleDbException *oleException ) {
354           MessageBox::Show( oleException->Message, S"Error",
355              MessageBoxButtons::OK, MessageBoxIcon::Error );
356        } // end catch
357
358        catch ( InvalidOperationException *invalidException ) {
359           MessageBox::Show( invalidException->Message, S"Error",
360              MessageBoxButtons::OK, MessageBoxIcon::Error );
361        } // end catch
362     } // end method findButton_Click
363
364     void AddressBook::addButton_Click( Object *sender, EventArgs *e )
365     {
366        try {
367
368           if ( !lastTextBox->Text->Equals( String::Empty ) &&
369              !firstTextBox->Text->Equals( String::Empty ) &&
370              !addressTextBox->Text->Equals( String::Empty ) &&
```

Fig. 16.34 AddressBook class method definitons. (Part 7 of 11.)

```
371                !cityTextBox->Text->Equals( String::Empty ) &&
372                !stateTextBox->Text->Equals( String::Empty ) &&
373                !postalTextBox->Text->Equals( String::Empty ) &&
374                !countryTextBox->Text->Equals( String::Empty ) &&
375                !emailTextBox->Text->Equals( String::Empty ) &&
376                !homeTextBox->Text->Equals( String::Empty ) &&
377                !faxTextBox->Text->Equals( String::Empty ) ) {
378
379             // create the SQL query to insert a row
380             oleDbDataAdapter1->InsertCommand->CommandText =
381                String::Concat( S"INSERT INTO addresses (",
382                S"firstname, lastname, address, city, ",
383                S"stateorprovince, postalcode, country, ",
384                S"emailaddress, homephone, faxnumber",
385                S") VALUES ('",
386                firstTextBox->Text, S"', '",
387                lastTextBox->Text, S"', '",
388                addressTextBox->Text, S"', '",
389                cityTextBox->Text, S"', '",
390                stateTextBox->Text, S"', '",
391                postalTextBox->Text, S"', '",
392                countryTextBox->Text, S"', '",
393                emailTextBox->Text, S"', '",
394                homeTextBox->Text, S"', '",
395                faxTextBox->Text, S"')" );
396
397             // notify the user the query is being sent
398             statusTextBox->Text = String::Concat(
399                statusTextBox->Text, S"\r\nSending query: ",
400                oleDbDataAdapter1->InsertCommand->CommandText,
401                S"\r\n" );
402
403             // send query
404             oleDbDataAdapter1->InsertCommand->ExecuteNonQuery();
405
406             statusTextBox->Text = String::Concat(
407                statusTextBox->Text, S"\r\nQuery successful\r\n" );
408          } // end if
409          else
410             statusTextBox->Text = String::Concat(
411                statusTextBox->Text,
412                S"\r\nAll fields are required.\r\n" );
413       } // end try
414
415       catch ( OleDbException *oleException ) {
416          MessageBox::Show( oleException->Message, S"Error",
417             MessageBoxButtons::OK, MessageBoxIcon::Error );
418       } // end catch
419    } // end method addButton_Click
420
421    void AddressBook::updateButton_Click( Object *sender,
422       EventArgs *e )
```

Fig. 16.34 AddressBook class method definitons. (Part 8 of 11.)

```
423  {
424      try {
425
426          // make sure the user has already found the record
427          // he or she wishes to update
428          if ( !idTextBox->Text->Equals( String::Empty ) ) {
429
430              // make sure user has not left any other fields blank
431              if ( !lastTextBox->Text->Equals( String::Empty ) &&
432                   !firstTextBox->Text->Equals( String::Empty ) &&
433                   !addressTextBox->Text->Equals( String::Empty ) &&
434                   !cityTextBox->Text->Equals( String::Empty ) &&
435                   !stateTextBox->Text->Equals( String::Empty ) &&
436                   !postalTextBox->Text->Equals( String::Empty ) &&
437                   !countryTextBox->Text->Equals( String::Empty ) &&
438                   !emailTextBox->Text->Equals( String::Empty ) &&
439                   !homeTextBox->Text->Equals( String::Empty ) &&
440                   !faxTextBox->Text->Equals( String::Empty ) ) {
441
442                  // set the SQL query to update all the fields in
443                  // the table where the id number matches the id
444                  // in idTextBox
445                  oleDbDataAdapter1->UpdateCommand->CommandText =
446                      String::Concat( S"UPDATE addresses SET ",
447                      S"firstname ='", firstTextBox->Text,
448                      S"', lastname='", lastTextBox->Text,
449                      S"', address='", addressTextBox->Text,
450                      S"', city='", cityTextBox->Text,
451                      S"', stateorprovince='", stateTextBox->Text,
452                      S"', postalcode='", postalTextBox->Text,
453                      S"', country='", countryTextBox->Text,
454                      S"', emailaddress='", emailTextBox->Text,
455                      S"', homephone='", homeTextBox->Text,
456                      S"', faxnumber='", faxTextBox->Text,
457                      S"' WHERE id=", idTextBox->Text );
458
459                  // notify the user the query is being set
460                  statusTextBox->Text = String::Concat(
461                      statusTextBox->Text, S"\r\nSending query: ",
462                      oleDbDataAdapter1->UpdateCommand->CommandText,
463                      S"\r\n" );
464
465                  // execute query
466                  oleDbDataAdapter1->UpdateCommand->ExecuteNonQuery();
467
468                  statusTextBox->Text = String::Concat(
469                      statusTextBox->Text, S"\r\nQuery successful\r\n" );
470              }
471              else
472                  statusTextBox->Text = String::Concat(
473                      statusTextBox->Text,
474                      S"\r\nAll fields are required.\r\n" );
```

Fig. 16.34 AddressBook class method definitons. (Part 9 of 11.)

```
475
476        } // end if
477        else
478           statusTextBox->Text = String::Concat(
479              statusTextBox->Text,
480              S"\r\nYou may only update an existing record. ",
481              S"Use Find to locate the record, then modify the ",
482              S"information and press Update.\r\n" );
483     } // end try
484
485     catch ( OleDbException *oleException ) {
486        MessageBox::Show( oleException->Message, S"Error",
487           MessageBoxButtons::OK, MessageBoxIcon::Error );
488     } // end catch
489  } // end method updateButton_Click
490
491  void AddressBook::clearButton_Click( Object *sender,
492     EventArgs *e )
493  {
494     idTextBox->Clear();
495     ClearTextBoxes();
496  } // end method clearButton_Click
497
498  void AddressBook::helpButton_Click( Object *sender,
499     EventArgs *e )
500  {
501     statusTextBox->AppendText( String::Concat(
502        S"\r\nClick Find to locate a record\r\n",
503        S"Click Add to insert a new record.\r\n",
504        S"Click Update to update the information in a record ",
505        S"\r\nClick Clear to empty the textboxes" ) );
506  } // end method helpButton_Click
507
508  void AddressBook::Display( DataSet *dataSet )
509  {
510     try {
511
512        // get the first DataTable - there will always be one
513        DataTable *dataTable = dataSet->Tables->Item[ 0 ];
514
515        if ( dataTable->Rows->Count != 0 ) {
516
517           int recordNumber = Convert::ToInt32(
518              dataTable->Rows->Item[ 0 ]->Item[ 0 ] );
519
520           idTextBox->Text = recordNumber.ToString();
521           firstTextBox->Text = dataTable->Rows->Item[ 0 ]->
522              Item[ 1 ]->ToString();
523           lastTextBox->Text =  dataTable->Rows->Item[ 0 ]->
524              Item[ 2 ]->ToString();
525           addressTextBox->Text = dataTable->Rows->Item[ 0 ]->
526              Item[ 3 ]->ToString();
527           cityTextBox->Text = dataTable->Rows->Item[ 0 ]->
```

Fig. 16.34 AddressBook class method definitons. (Part 10 of 11.)

```
528                         Item[ 4 ]->ToString();
529                 stateTextBox->Text = dataTable->Rows->Item[ 0 ]->
530                     Item[ 5 ]->ToString();
531                 postalTextBox->Text = dataTable->Rows->Item[ 0 ]->
532                     Item[ 6 ]->ToString();
533                 countryTextBox->Text = dataTable->Rows->Item[ 0 ]->
534                     Item[ 7 ]->ToString();
535                 emailTextBox->Text = dataTable->Rows->Item[ 0 ]->
536                     Item[ 8 ]->ToString();
537                 homeTextBox->Text = dataTable->Rows->Item[ 0 ]->
538                     Item[ 9 ]->ToString();
539                 faxTextBox->Text = dataTable->Rows->Item[ 0 ]->
540                     Item[ 10 ]->ToString();
541            } // end if
542            else
543                statusTextBox->Text = String::Concat(
544                    statusTextBox->Text, S"\r\nNo record found\r\n" );
545        } // end try
546
547        catch ( OleDbException *oleException ) {
548            MessageBox::Show( oleException->Message, S"Error",
549                MessageBoxButtons::OK, MessageBoxIcon::Error );
550        } // end catch
551   } // end method Display
552
553   void AddressBook::ClearTextBoxes()
554   {
555        firstTextBox->Clear();
556        lastTextBox->Clear();
557        addressTextBox->Clear();
558        cityTextBox->Clear();
559        stateTextBox->Clear();
560        postalTextBox->Clear();
561        countryTextBox->Clear();
562        emailTextBox->Clear();
563        homeTextBox->Clear();
564        faxTextBox->Clear();
565   } // end method ClearTextBoxes
```

Fig. 16.34 AddressBook class method definitons. (Part 11 of 11.)

```
1    // Fig. 16.35: AddressBookTest.cpp
2    // Entry point for application.
3
4    #include "AddressBook.h"
5
6    int __stdcall WinMain()
7    {
8        Application::Run( new AddressBook() );
9
10       return 0;
11   } // end WinMain
```

Fig. 16.35 AddressBook class driver. (Part 1 of 3.)

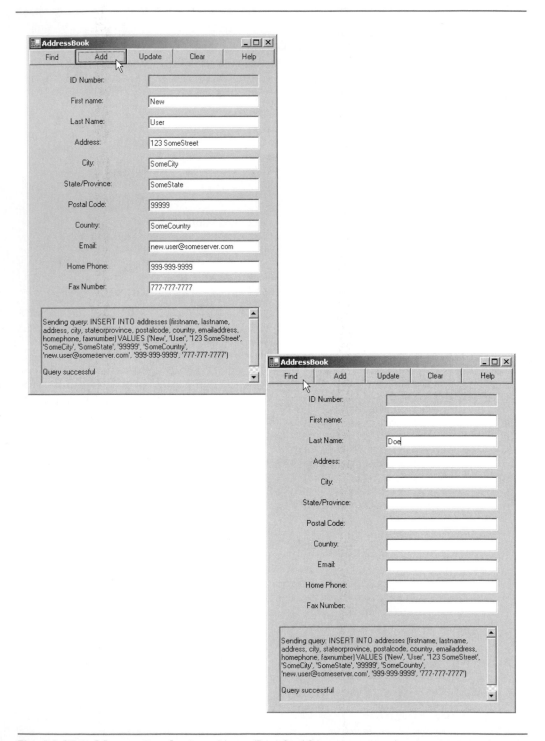

Fig. 16.35 `AddressBook` class driver. (Part 2 of 3.)

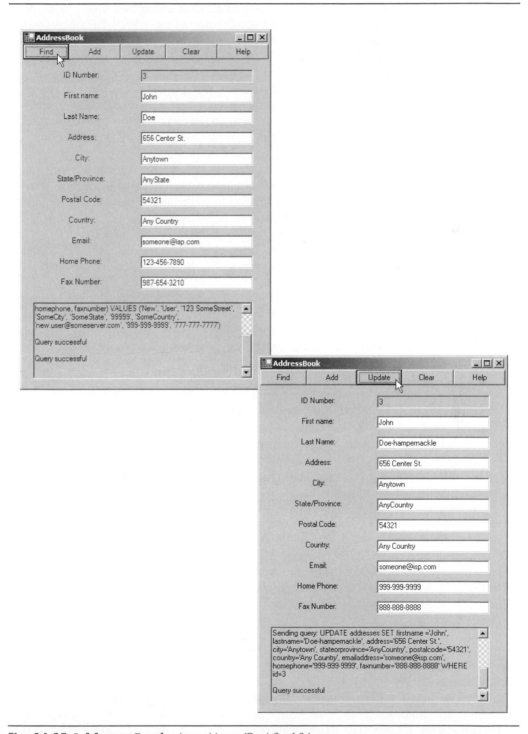

Fig. 16.35 AddressBook class driver. (Part 3 of 3.)

Instance **oleDbDataAdapter1** of class **OleDbDataAdapter** connects to the data source through an instance of class **OleDbConnection** (**oldDbConnection**) and can populate the **DataSet dataSet1** with data from that data source. Property *InsertCommand* (lines 294–295) specifies the SQL statement or stored procedure used to insert new records into the data source. Property *SelectCommand* (lines 296–297) specifies the SQL statement or stored procedure used (during a call to **Fill**) to select information from the data source. Similarly, property *UpdateCommand* (lines 298–299) specifies the SQL statement or stored procedure used to update records in the data source (that correspond to modified rows in the **DataSet**). Lines 320–322 specify the **OleDbConnection** used by each **OleDbCommand** to connect to the database.

Event handler **findButton_Click** (lines 325–362 of Fig. 16.34) performs the **SELECT** query on the database for the record associated with the string in **lastTextBox**. This represents the last name of the person whose record the user wishes to retrieve. Line 332 invokes method **Clear** of class **DataSet** to empty the **DataSet** of any prior data. Lines 336–338 then modify the text of the SQL query to perform the appropriate **SELECT** operation. This statement is executed by the **OleDbDataAdapter** method **Fill** (line 341), which is passed the **DataSet** as an argument. Finally, the **TextBox**es are updated with a call to method **Display** (line 344).

Methods **addButton_Click** (lines 364–419) and **updateButton_Click** (lines 421–489) perform **INSERT** and **UPDATE** operations, respectively. Each method uses members of class **OleDbCommand** to perform operations on a database. The instance properties **InsertCommand** and **UpdateCommand** of class **OleDbDataAdapter** are instances of class **OleDbCommand**.

Method **addButton_Click** sets property **CommandText** of **InsertCommand** to execute the appropriate **INSERT** statement on the database (lines 380–395). Method **updateButton_Click** sets this property of **UpdateCommand** to execute the appropriate **UPDATE** statement on the database (lines 445–457).

Method *ExecuteNonQuery* of class **OleDbCommand** performs the action specified by **CommandText**. Hence, the **INSERT** statement defined in lines 380–395 is executed when line 404 invokes method **ExecuteNonQuery**. Similarly, the **UPDATE** statement defined in lines 445–447 is executed by **ExecuteNonQuery** (line 466).

If the user specifies invalid input for any available command, the **OleDbException** exception that is raised is handled in a **catch** block (lines 353–356, 415–418 and 485–488). For simplicity, we simply display the error in a **MessageBox**.

Method **Display** (lines 508–551) updates the user interface with data from the newly retrieved address-book record. Line 513 obtains a **DataTable** from the **DataSet**'s **Tables** collection. This **DataTable** contains the results of our SQL query. Line 515 determines whether the query returned any rows. Property *Rows* of class **DataTable** provides access to all records retrieved by the query. Property **Rows** is similar to a two-dimensional rectangular array. Lines 517–518 retrieve the field with index *0, 0* (i.e., the first record's first column of data) and store the value in variable **recordNumber**. Lines 521–540 then retrieve the remaining fields of data from the **DataTable** to populate the user interface.

When clicked, the application's **Help** button prints instructions at the bottom of the application window (lines 498–506). The event handler for this button is **helpButton_Click**. The **Clear** button clears the text from the **TextBox**es. This event handler is defined in the method **clearButton_Click** (lines 491–496) and uses the utility method **ClearTextBoxes** (lines 553–565).

16.8 Reading and Writing XML Files

A powerful feature of ADO .NET is its ability to convert data stored in a data source to XML. Class **DataSet** of namespace **System::Data** provides methods *WriteXml*, *ReadXml* and *GetXml*, which enable developers to create XML documents from data sources and to convert data from XML into data sources. The application in Fig. 16.36– Fig. 16.38 populates a **DataSet** with statistics about baseball players and then writes the data to a file as XML. The application also displays the XML in a **TextBox**. For more information about XML, refer to Chapter 15, Extensible Markup Language (XML).

```
1   // Fig. 16.36: XMLWriter.h
2   // Demonstrates generating XML from an ADO.NET DataSet.
3
4   #pragma once
5
6   #using <system.dll>
7   #using <mscorlib.dll>
8   #using <system.data.dll>
9   #using <system.drawing.dll>
10  #using <system.windows.forms.dll>
11  #using <system.xml.dll>
12
13  using namespace System;
14  using namespace System::Data;
15  using namespace System::Data::OleDb;
16  using namespace System::Drawing;
17  using namespace System::Windows::Forms;
18
19  public __gc class DatabaseXMLWriter : public Form
20  {
21  public:
22     DatabaseXMLWriter();
23
24  private:
25     OleDbDataAdapter *playersDataAdapter;
26     OleDbConnection *baseballConnection;
27     OleDbCommand *oleDbSelectCommand1;
28     DataSet *playersDataSet;
29     DataGrid *playersDataGrid;
30     Button *writeButton;
31     TextBox *outputTextBox;
32
33     void InitializeComponent();
34     void SetupConnection();
35     void writeButton_Click( Object *, EventArgs * );
36  }; // end class DatabaseXMLWriter
```

Fig. 16.36 Application that writes **DataSet** XML representation to a file.

```cpp
1    // Fig. 16.37: XMLWriter.cpp
2    // Method definitions for class DatabaseXMLWriter.
3
4    #include "XMLWriter.h"
5
6    DatabaseXMLWriter::DatabaseXMLWriter()
7    {
8       SetupConnection();
9       InitializeComponent();
10
11      // fill DataSet with data from OleDbDataAdapter
12      playersDataAdapter->Fill( playersDataSet, S"Players" );
13
14      // bind DataGrid to DataSet
15      playersDataGrid->SetDataBinding( playersDataSet, S"Players" );
16   }
17
18   void DatabaseXMLWriter::InitializeComponent()
19   {
20      this->SuspendLayout();
21      this->writeButton = new Button();
22      this->outputTextBox = new TextBox();
23
24      // writeButton
25      this->writeButton->Location = Point( 60, 8 );
26      this->writeButton->Name = S"writeButton";
27      this->writeButton->Size = Drawing::Size( 208, 24 );
28      this->writeButton->TabIndex = 1;
29      this->writeButton->Text = S"Write to XML";
30      this->writeButton->Click += new EventHandler( this,
31         writeButton_Click );
32
33      // playersDataGrid
34      this->playersDataGrid = new DataGrid();
35      this->playersDataGrid->DataMember = S"";
36      this->playersDataGrid->Location = Point( 8, 40 );
37      this->playersDataGrid->Name = S"playersDataGrid";
38      this->playersDataGrid->Size = Drawing::Size( 312, 168 );
39      this->playersDataGrid->TabIndex = 0;
40
41      // outputTextBox
42      this->outputTextBox->BackColor = SystemColors::Window;
43      this->outputTextBox->Location = Point( 8, 216 );
44      this->outputTextBox->Multiline = true;
45      this->outputTextBox->Name = S"outputTextBox";
46      this->outputTextBox->ReadOnly = true;
47      this->outputTextBox->ScrollBars = ScrollBars::Both;
48      this->outputTextBox->Size = Drawing::Size( 312, 96 );
49      this->outputTextBox->TabIndex = 2;
50      this->outputTextBox->Text = S"";
51
```

Fig. 16.37 DatabaseXMLWriter class method definitions. (Part 1 of 3.)

```
52        this->AutoScaleBaseSize = Drawing::Size( 5, 13 );
53        this->ClientSize = Drawing::Size( 328, 325 );
54        Control *control[] = { this->outputTextBox,
55           this->writeButton, this->playersDataGrid };
56        this->Controls->AddRange( control );
57        this->Name = S"XMLWriter";
58        this->Text = S"XMLWriter";
59        this->ResumeLayout();
60    } // end method InitializeComponent
61
62    void DatabaseXMLWriter::SetupConnection()
63    {
64        this->playersDataSet = new DataSet( S"NewDataSet" );
65        this->playersDataAdapter = new OleDbDataAdapter();
66        this->baseballConnection = new OleDbConnection();
67        this->oleDbSelectCommand1 = new OleDbCommand();
68
69        // specify commands for adapter
70        this->playersDataAdapter->SelectCommand =
71           this->oleDbSelectCommand1;
72
73        // create connection string
74        this->baseballConnection->ConnectionString =
75           S"Provider=Microsoft.Jet.OLEDB.4.0;Password=\"\";"
76           S"User ID=Admin;Data Source=baseball.mdb;Mode=Share "
77           S"Deny None;Extended Properties=\"\";Jet OLEDB:"
78           S"System database=\"\";Jet OLEDB:Registry "
79           S"Path=\"\";Jet OLEDB:Database Password=\"\";"
80           S"Jet OLEDB:Engine Type=5;Jet OLEDB:Database "
81           S"Locking Mode=1;Jet OLEDB:Global Partial Bulk "
82           S"Ops=2;Jet OLEDB:Global Bulk Transactions=1;Jet "
83           S"OLEDB:New Database Password=\"\";Jet OLEDB:"
84           S"Create System Database=False;Jet OLEDB:Encrypt "
85           S"Database=False;Jet OLEDB:Don't Copy Locale on "
86           S"Compact=False;Jet OLEDB:Compact Without Replica "
87           S"Repair=False;Jet OLEDB:SFP=False";
88
89        this->baseballConnection->Open();   // open connection
90
91        // configure SELECT command
92        this->oleDbSelectCommand1->CommandText =
93           S"SELECT firstName, lastName, battingAverage, playerID "
94           S"FROM Players";
95        this->oleDbSelectCommand1->Connection =
96           this->baseballConnection;
97    } // end method SetupConnection
98
99    // write XML representation of DataSet when button clicked
100   void DatabaseXMLWriter::writeButton_Click( Object *sender,
101      EventArgs *e )
102   {
```

Fig. 16.37 DatabaseXMLWriter class method definitions. (Part 2 of 3.)

```
103     // write XML representation of DataSet to file
104     playersDataSet->WriteXml( S"Players.xml" );
105
106     // display XML in TextBox
107     outputTextBox->Text = String::Concat( outputTextBox->Text,
108        S"Writing the following XML:\n\n",
109        playersDataSet->GetXml(), S"\n\n" );
110  } // end method writeButton_Click
```

Fig. 16.37 `DatabaseXMLWriter` class method definitions. (Part 3 of 3.)

```
1    // Fig. 16.38: XMLWriterTest.cpp
2    // Entry point for application.
3
4    #include "XMLWriter.h"
5
6    int __stdcall WinMain()
7    {
8       Application::Run( new DatabaseXMLWriter() );
9
10      return 0;
11   } // end WinMain
```

Fig. 16.38 `DatabaseXMLWriter` class driver.

The **DatabaseXMLWriter** constructor (lines 6–16 of Fig. 16.37) establishes a connection to the **Baseball** database in line 8. Microsoft access database Baseball has one table (**Players**) that consists of 4 columns—**playerID**, **firstName**, **lastName** and **battingAverage**. Line 12 then calls method **Fill** of class **OleDbDataAdapter** to populate **playersDataSet** with data from the **Players** table in the **Baseball** database. Line 15 binds **playersDataGrid** to **playersDataSet** to display the information to the user.

Method **writeButton_Click** defines the event handler for the **Write to XML** button. When the user clicks this button, line 104 invokes **DataSet** method **WriteXml**, which generates an XML representation of the data contained in the **DataSet** and writes the XML to the specified file. Figure 16.39 depicts this XML representation. Each **Players** element represents a record in the **Players** table. The **firstName**, **lastName**, **battingAverage** and **playerID** elements correspond to the fields of the same names in the **Players** table. Method **GetXml** returns a **String *** representing the **DataSet**'s data in XML form. Lines 107–109 append the XML **String *** to **outputTextBox**.

In this chapter, we discussed the fundamentals of Structured Query Language (SQL) and Visual C++ .NET's database capabilities. We learned that Visual C++ .NET programmers can communicate with databases and manipulate their data through *Microsoft ActiveX Data Objects*™ (ADO), via *ADO .NET*. In Chapter 17, we introduce Web services, which allow remote software to interact with methods and objects on a Web server.

```
1   <?xml version="1.0" standalone="yes"?>
2   <NewDataSet>
3       <Players>
4           <firstName>John</firstName>
5           <lastName>Doe</lastName>
6           <battingAverage>0.375</battingAverage>
7           <playerID>1</playerID>
8       </Players>
9
10      <Players>
11          <firstName>Jack</firstName>
12          <lastName>Smith</lastName>
13          <battingAverage>0.223</battingAverage>
14          <playerID>2</playerID>
15      </Players>
16
17      <Players>
18          <firstName>George</firstName>
19          <lastName>O'Malley</lastName>
20          <battingAverage>0.444</battingAverage>
21          <playerID>3</playerID>
22      </Players>
23  </NewDataSet>
```

Fig. 16.39 XML document generated from **DataSet** in **DatabaseXMLWriter**.

16.9 Summary

A database is an integrated collection of data. A database management system (DBMS) provides mechanisms for storing and organizing data. Today's most popular database systems are relational databases. A language called Structured Query Language (SQL) is used almost universally with relational-database systems to perform queries and to manipulate data. SQL provides a complete set of commands, enabling programmers to define complex queries to select data from a table.

A programming language connects to, and interacts with, relational databases via an interface—software that facilitates communications between a database management system and a program. Visual C++ .NET programmers can communicate with databases and manipulate their data via ADO .NET.

A relational database is composed of tables. A row of a table is called a record. A primary key is a field that contains unique data, or data that is not duplicated in other records of that table. Each column in a table represents a different field (or attribute). A primary key can be composed of more than one column (or field) in the database. A one-to-many relationship between tables indicates that a record in one table can have many corresponding records in a separate table. A foreign key is a field for which every entry in one table has a unique value in another table and where the field in the other table is the primary key for that table.

The results of a query commonly are called result sets (or record sets). The basic format for a **SELECT** query is

> **SELECT * FROM** *tableName*

where the asterisk (*****) indicates that all columns from *tableName* should be selected, and *tableName* specifies the table in the database from which the data will be selected. To select specific fields from a table, replace the asterisk (*****) with a comma-separated list of the field names to select.

The optional **WHERE** clause in a **SELECT** query specifies the selection criteria for the query. The simplest format for a **SELECT** query with selection criteria is

> **SELECT** *fieldName1, fieldName2, ...* **FROM** *tableName* **WHERE** *criteria*

The **WHERE** clause condition can contain operators **<, >, <=, >=, =, <>** and **LIKE**. Operator **LIKE** is used for pattern matching with the wildcard characters, asterisk (*****) and question mark (**?**). A pattern string containing an asterisk character (*****) searches for strings in which zero or more characters appear in the asterisk character's location in the pattern. A pattern string containing a question mark (**?**) searches for strings in which exactly one character appears in the question mark's position in the pattern.

The results of a query can be arranged in ascending or descending order via the optional **ORDER BY** clause. The simplest form of an **ORDER BY** clause is

> **SELECT** *fieldName1, fieldName2, ...* **FROM** *tableName* **ORDER BY** *field* **ASC**
> **SELECT** *fieldName1, fieldName2, ...* **FROM** *tableName* **ORDER BY** *field* **DESC**

where **ASC** specifies ascending order, **DESC** specifies descending order and *field* specifies the field to be sorted.

A join merges records from two or more tables by testing for matching values in a field that is common to both tables. The simplest format of a join is

```
SELECT fieldName1, fieldName2, ...
    FROM table1 INNER JOIN table2
    ON table1.fieldName = table2.fieldName
```

in which the **WHERE** clause specifies the fields from each table that should be compared to determine which records are joined. These fields normally represent the primary key in one table and the corresponding foreign key in another table. If an SQL statement uses fields that have the same name in multiple tables, the statement must fully qualify the field name by preceding it with its table name and the dot operator (.).

An **INSERT** statement inserts a new record in a table. The simplest form for this statement is

```
INSERT INTO tableName ( fieldName1, fieldName2, ..., fieldNameN )
    VALUES ( value1, value2, ..., valueN )
```

where *tableName* is the table in which to insert the record. The *tableName* is followed by a comma-separated list of field names in parentheses. The list of field names is followed by the SQL keyword **VALUES** and a comma-separated list of values in parentheses.

An **UPDATE** statement modifies data in a table. The form for an **UPDATE** statement is

```
UPDATE tableName
    SET fieldName1 = value1, fieldName2 = value2, ..., fieldNameN = valueN
    WHERE criteria
```

where *tableName* is the table in which to update a record (or records). The *tableName* is followed by keyword **SET** and a comma-separated list of field-name/value pairs, written in the format *fieldName = value*. The **WHERE** *criteria* determine the record(s) to update.

A **DELETE** statement removes data from a table. The form for a **DELETE** statement is

```
DELETE FROM tableName WHERE criteria
```

where *tableName* is the table from which to delete a record (or records). The **WHERE** *criteria* determine which record(s) to delete.

System::Data, **System::Data::OleDb** and **System::Data::Sql-Client** are the three main namespaces in ADO .NET. Class **DataSet** is from the **System::Data** namespace. Instances of this class represent in-memory caches of data. The advantage of using class **DataSet** is that it is a way to modify the contents of a data source without having to maintain an active connection. Method **Clear** of class **DataSet** is called to empty the **DataSet** of any prior data.

One approach to ADO .NET programming uses **OleDbCommand** of the **System::Data::OleDb** namespace. In this approach, SQL statements are executed directly on the data source. **OleDbCommand** instance property **Connection** is set to the **OleDbConnection** that the command will be executed on, and the instance property **CommandText** is set to the SQL query that will be executed on the database. Property **CommandText** of class **OleDbCommand** is the **String *** representing the SQL statement to be executed. Method **ExecuteNonQuery** of class **OleDbCommand** is called to perform the action specified by **CommandText** on the database.

OleDbCommands commands are what the **OleDbDataAdapter** executes on the database in the form of SQL queries. **OleDbDataAdapter** method **Fill** retrieves information from the database associated with the **OleDbConnection** and places this information in the **DataSet** provided as an argument. The instance properties **InsertCommand** and **UpdateCommand** of class **OleDbDataAdapter** are instances of class **OleDbCommand**.

A **DataGrid** is a **System::Windows::Forms** component class that can display a data source in a GUI. **DataGrid** method **SetDataBinding** binds a **DataGrid** to a data source.

A powerful feature of ADO .NET is its ability to convert data stored in a data source to XML, and vice versa. Method **WriteXml** of class **DataSet** writes the XML representation of the **DataSet** instance to the first argument passed to it. Method **ReadXml** of class **DataSet** reads the XML representation of the first argument passed to it into its own **DataSet**.

16.10 Internet and Web Resources

www.microsoft.com/office/access
The Microsoft Access home page contains product information, purchase information and information about using the software.

www.microsoft.com/sql
The official Microsoft SQL Server home page contains information about this family of products.

msdn.microsoft.com/sqlserver
The MSDN Library contains additional developer information about Microsoft SQL Server.

www.oracle.com
The official Oracle Corporation home page contains information about the Oracle9*i* database.

www.sybase.com
The official Sybase Inc. home page contains information about their database servers.

www-3.ibm.com/software/data/db2
The official IBM DB2 home page contains product information, purchase information and support information for this family of products.

www-3.ibm.com/software/data/informix
The official IBM Informix home page contains product information, purchase information and support information for this family of products.

www.mysql.com
The official MySQL home page contains information about this open source database.

17

Web Services

Objectives

- To understand what a Web service is.
- To understand the elements that compose a Web service, such as service descriptions and discovery files.
- To create Web services.
- To create a client that uses a Web service.
- To understand session tracking in Web services.
- To pass user-defined data types between Web services and Web clients.

A client is to me a mere unit, a factor in a problem.
Sir Arthur Conan Doyle

...if the simplest things of nature have a message that you understand, rejoice, for your soul is alive.
Eleonora Duse

Protocol is everything.
Françoise Giuliani

They also serve who only stand and wait.
John Milton

Outline

17.1 Introduction[1]

Throughout this book, we have created dynamic link libraries (DLLs) to facilitate software reusability and modularity—the cornerstones of good object-oriented programming. However, without remoting technologies such as Distributed Component Object Model (DCOM), Remote Procedure Call (RPC) or .NET remoting, the use of DLLs is limited by the fact that DLLs must reside on the same machine as the programs that use them. This chapter introduces the use of Web services (sometimes called *XML Web services*) to promote software reusability in distributed systems. Distributed-systems technologies allow applications to execute across multiple computers on a network. A Web service is an application that enables distributed computing by allowing one machine to call methods on other machines via common data formats and protocols, such as XML (Chapter 15). In .NET, these method calls are implemented via the Simple Object Access Protocol (SOAP), an XML-based protocol describing how to mark up requests and responses so that they can be

---

1. Internet Information Services (IIS) must be running to create a Web service in Visual Studio .NET. Information on installing and running IIS can be found at our Web site (**www.deitel.com**).

transferred via protocols such as HyperText Transfer Protocol (HTTP). Using SOAP, applications represent and transmit data in a standardized format—XML. The underlying implementation of the Web service is irrelevant to clients using the Web service.

Microsoft is encouraging software vendors and e-businesses to deploy Web services. As more and more people worldwide connect to the Internet via networks, applications that call methods across a network become more practical. Earlier in this text, we discussed the merits of object-oriented programming. Web services represent the next step in object-oriented programming: Instead of developing software from a small number of class libraries provided at one location, programmers can access countless libraries in multiple locations.

This technology also makes it easier for businesses to collaborate and grow together. By purchasing Web services that are relevant to their businesses, companies that create applications can spend less time coding and more time developing new products from existing components. In addition, e-businesses can employ Web services to provide their customers with an enhanced shopping experience. As a simple example, consider an online music store that enables users to purchase music CDs or to obtain information about artists. Now, suppose that another company that sells concert tickets provides a Web service that reports the dates of upcoming concerts by various artists and allows users to buy concert tickets. By licensing the concert-ticket Web service for use on its site, the online music store can sell concert tickets to its customers, a service that likely will result in increased traffic at its site. The company that sells concert tickets also benefits from the business relationship. In addition to selling more tickets, the company receives revenue from the online music store in exchange for the use of its Web service. Visual Studio and the .NET Framework provide a simple way to create Web services like the one discussed in this example.

In this chapter, we begin with a brief introduction to Web content and Web protocols. We then explore the steps involved in both creating and accessing Web services. For each example, we provide the code for the Web service, then give an example of an application that might use the Web service. Our initial examples are designed to offer a brief introduction to Web services and how they work in Visual Studio .NET. In later sections, we move on to demonstrate more sophisticated Web services.

17.2 HTTP Request Types

HTTP defines several request types (also known as *request methods*), each of which specifies how a client makes requests from a server. The two most common are *get* and *post*. These request types retrieve and send client form data from and to a Web server. A form is an HTML element that may contain text fields, radio buttons, check boxes and other graphical user-interface (GUI) components that allow users to enter data into a Web page. Forms can also contain hidden fields, not exposed as GUI components. A *get* request is used to send data to the server. A *post* request also is used to send data to the server. A *get* request sends form data as part of the URL (e.g., **www.searchsomething.com/ search?query=**_userquery_). In this fictitious request, the information following the **?** (**query=**_userquery_) indicates user-specified input. For example, if the user performs a search on "Massachusetts," the last part of the URL would be **?query=Massachusetts**. A *get* request limits the *query string* (e.g., **query=Massachusetts**) to a predefined number of characters. This limit varies from server to server. If the query string exceeds this limit, a *post* request must be used.

Software Engineering Observation 17.1

The data sent in a post *request is not part of the URL and cannot be seen by users. Forms that contain many fields often are submitted via a* post *request. Sensitive form fields, such as passwords, usually are sent using this request type.*

An HTTP request often sends data to a *server-side form handler* that processes the data. For example, when a user participates in a Web-based survey, the Web server receives the information specified in the form as part of the request and processes the survey in the form handler.

Browsers often *cache* (save on a local disk) Web pages for quick reloading, to reduce the amount of data that the browser needs to download. However, browsers typically do not cache the responses to *post* requests, because subsequent *post* requests might not contain the same information. For example, users participating in a Web-based survey may request the same Web page. Each user's response changes the overall results of the survey; thus, the information presented in the resulting Web page is different for each request.

Web browsers often cache the server's responses to *get* requests. A static Web page, such as a course syllabus, is cached in the event that the user requests the same resource again.

17.3 Multi-Tier Architecture

A Web server is part of a *multi-tier application*, sometimes referred to as an *n*-tier application. Multi-tier applications divide functionality into separate tiers (i.e., logical groupings of functionality). Tiers can be located on the same computer or on separate computers. Figure 17.1 presents the basic structure of a three-tier application.

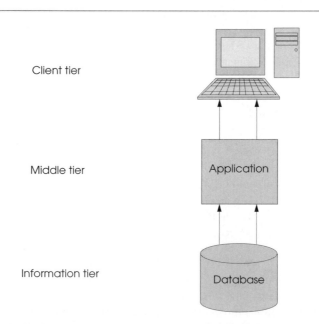

Client tier

Middle tier   Application

Information tier   Database

Fig. 17.1 Three-tier application model.

The *information tier* (also called the *data tier* or the *bottom tier*) maintains data for the application. This tier typically stores data in a *relational database management system (RDBMS)*. For example, a retail store might have a database of product information, such as descriptions, prices and quantities in stock. The same database also might contain customer information, such as user names for logging into the online store, billing addresses and credit-card numbers.

The *middle tier* implements *business logic* and *presentation logic* to control interactions between application clients and application data. The middle tier acts as an intermediary between data in the information tier and the application clients. The middle-tier *controller logic* processes client requests from the top tier (e.g., a request to view a product catalog) and retrieves data from the database. The middle-tier presentation logic then processes data from the information tier and presents the content to the client. In Web-based applications, the middle tier presentation logic typically presents content as HTML documents.

Business logic in the middle tier enforces *business rule*s and ensures that data is reliable before updating the database or presenting data to a user. Business rules dictate how clients can and cannot access application data and how applications process data.

The *client tier*, or *top tier*, is the application's user interface. Users interact directly with the application through the user interface. The client interacts with the middle tier to make requests and to retrieve data from the information tier. The client then displays to the user the data retrieved from the middle tier.

17.4 Accessing Web Servers

To request documents from Web servers, users must know the URLs at which those documents reside. A URL contains a machine name (called a *host name*) on which the Web server resides. Users can request documents from *local Web servers* (i.e., ones residing on user's machines) or *remote Web servers* (i.e., ones residing on machines across a network).

Local Web servers can be accessed in two ways: Through the machine name, or through `localhost`—a host name that references the local machine. We use `localhost` in this chapter. To determine the machine name in Windows 2000, right click **My Computer**, and select **Properties** from the context menu to display the **System Properties** dialog. In the dialog, click **Network Identification**. The **Full Computer Name:** field in the **System Properties** window displays the computer name. In Windows XP, select **Start > Control Panel > Switch to Classic View > System** to view the **System Properties** dialog. In the dialog, select the **Computer Name** tab.

A domain name represents a group of hosts on the Internet; it combines with a host name (e.g., **www**—World Wide Web) and a *top-level domain (TLD)* to form a *fully qualified host name*, which provides a user-friendly way to identify a site on the Internet. In a fully qualified host name, the TLD often describes the type of organization that owns the domain name. For example, the **com** TLD usually refers to a commercial business, whereas the **org** TLD usually refers to a nonprofit organization. In addition, each country has its own TLD, such as **cn** for China, **et** for Ethiopia, **om** for Oman and **us** for the United States.

Each fully qualified host name is assigned a unique address called an *IP address*, which is much like the street address of a house. Just as people use street addresses to locate houses or businesses in a city, computers use IP addresses to locate other computers on the Internet. A *domain name system (DNS) server*, a computer that maintains a database of host names and their corresponding IP addresses, translates fully qualified host names to IP addresses. This translation is referred to as a *DNS lookup*. For example, to access the Deitel Web site, type the hostname (`www.deitel.com`) into a Web browser. The DNS server translates `www.deitel.com` into the IP address of the Deitel Web server (i.e., `63.110.43.82`). The IP address of `localhost` is always `127.0.0.1`.

17.5 Simple HTTP Transaction

Before exploring Web-based applications development further, a basic understanding of networking and the World Wide Web is necessary. In this section, we examine the inner workings of the *HyperText Transfer Protocol (HTTP)* and discuss what occurs behind the scenes when a browser displays a Web page. HTTP is a protocol that specifies a set of *methods* and *headers* that allow clients and servers to interact and exchange information in a uniform and predictable way.

In their simplest form, Web pages are HTML documents—plain-text files that contain markings (*markup* or *tags*) describing the structures of the documents. For example, the HTML markup

```
<title>My Web Page</title>
```

indicates that the text contained between the `<title>` *start tag* and the `</title>` *end tag* is the Web page's title. HTML documents also can contain *hyperlinks*, which enable users to navigate their Web browsers to other Web pages. When the user activates a hyperlink (usually by clicking it with the mouse), the requested Web page (or different part of the same Web page) is loaded into the user's browser window.

Any HTML document available on the Web has a *Uniform Resource Locator (URL)*, which indicates the location of a resource. The URL contains information that directs Web browsers to the document. Computers that run *Web server* software provide such resources. Microsoft *Internet Information Services* (IIS) is the Web server that programmers use when developing Web services in Visual Studio .NET.

Let us examine the components of the following URL:

```
http://www.deitel.com/books/downloads.htm
```

The `http://` indicates that the resource is to be obtained via HTTP. The middle portion—`www.deitel.com`—is the fully qualified *hostname* of the server. The hostname is the name of the computer on which the resource resides. This computer usually is referred to as the *host*, because it houses and maintains resources. The hostname `www.deitel.com` is translated into an *IP address* (`63.110.43.82`) that identifies the server in a manner similar to that by which a telephone number uniquely defines a particular phone line. The translation of the hostname into an IP address normally is performed by a *domain name server (DNS)*—a computer that maintains a database of hostnames and their corresponding IP addresses. This translation operation is called a *DNS lookup*.

The remainder of the URL provides the name and location of the requested resource, `/books/downloads.htm` (an HTML document). This portion of the URL specifies both the name of the resource (`downloads.htm`) and its path, or location (`/books`), on the Web server. The path could specify the location of an actual directory on the Web server's file system. However, for security reasons, paths often specify the locations of a *virtual directory*. In such systems, the server translates the virtual directory into a real location on the server (or on another computer on the server's network), thus hiding the true location of the resource. Furthermore, some resources are created dynamically and do not reside anywhere on the server computer. The hostname in the URL for such a resource specifies the correct server, and the path and resource information identify the location of the resource with which to respond to the client's request.

When given a URL, a browser performs a simple HTTP transaction to retrieve and display a Web page. Figure 17.2 illustrates this transaction in detail. The transaction consists of interaction between the Web browser (the client side) and the Web-server application (the server side).

In Fig. 17.2, the Web browser sends an HTTP request to the server. The request (in its simplest form) is

```
GET /books/downloads.htm HTTP/1.1
```

The word **GET** is an *HTTP method* indicating that the client wishes to obtain a resource from the server. The remainder of the request provides the path name of the resource and the protocol's name and version number (**HTTP/1.1**).

Any server that understands HTTP (version 1.1) can translate this request and respond appropriately. Figure 17.3 depicts a Web server's response when it a successful request. The server first responds by sending a line of text that indicates the HTTP version, followed by a numeric code and phrase, both of which describe the status of the transaction. For example,

```
HTTP/1.1 200 OK
```

indicates success, whereas

```
HTTP/1.1 404 Not found
```

informs the client that the Web server could not locate the requested resource.

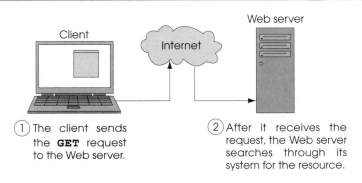

① The client sends the **GET** request to the Web server.

② After it receives the request, the Web server searches through its system for the resource.

Fig. 17.2 Web server/client interaction. Step 1: The **GET** request, **GET /books/downloads.htm HTTP/1.1**.

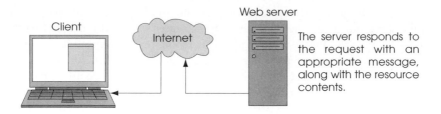

Fig. 17.3   Web server/client interaction. Step 2: The HTTP response, `HTTP/1.1 200 OK`.

The server then sends one or more *HTTP headers,* which provide information about the data that will be sent. In this case, the server is sending an HTML text document, so the HTTP header for this example reads

```
Content-type: text/html
```

This header specifies the *Multipurpose Internet Mail Extensions* (*MIME*) type of the content that the server is transmitting to the browser. MIME is an Internet standard used to identify various types of data so that programs can interpret those data correctly. For example, the MIME type `text/plain` indicates that the information is plain text, which a Web browser can display directly without any special formatting. Similarly, the MIME type `image/gif` indicates that the transmitted content is a GIF image, enabling the Web browser to display the image appropriately.

The set of headers is followed by a blank line, which indicates to the client that the server is finished sending HTTP headers. The server then sends the contents of the requested HTML document (`downloads.htm`). The server terminates the connection when the transfer of the resource is complete. At this point, the client-side browser parses the HTML it has received and *renders* (or displays) the results.

17.6 ASP (Active Server Pages) .NET

Microsoft's *Active Server Pages (ASP) .NET*, an integral part of the .NET initiative, is a technology for creating dynamic Web content marked up as HTML. Like Windows applications, Web pages built with ASP .NET are designed using Visual Studio .NET. ASP .NET developers can create multi-tier, database-intensive applications quickly by employing .NET's object-oriented languages and the FCL's *Web controls*. Web controls are similar to the controls in Windows applications, but are designed specifically for Web pages. ASP .NET is a sophisticated technology—it includes optimizations for performance, testing and security.

Unfortunately, Visual Studio .NET does not currently have the tools that allow developers to create ASP .NET Web applications easily in Visual C++ .NET. (We demonstrate creating Web applications with another technology, ATL Server, in Chapter 23.) However, tools *are* available that enable Visual C++ .NET developers to create Web services that use ASP .NET technology. Such Web services are sometimes referred to as *ASP .NET Web services*. Using ASP .NET to build a Web service provides several benefits. First, ASP .NET itself is built upon the .NET Framework, which allows the Web service to employ features of the CLR, such as memory management, interoperability and software reuse. The Web service also benefits from the ASP .NET optimizations mentioned earlier.

When a developer creates Web services using ASP .NET and Visual Studio .NET, many programming details are hidden. In the next section, we will see examples of this.

17.7 .NET Web Services Basics

As we mentioned earlier, a Web service is an application stored on one machine that can be accessed on another machine over a network. Due to the nature of this relationship, the machine on which the Web service resides commonly is referred to as a *remote machine*. The application that accesses the Web service sends a method call to the remote machine, which processes the call and sends a response to the application. This kind of distributed computing benefits various systems, including those without access to certain data and those lacking the processing power necessary to perform specific computations.

A Web service is, in its simplest form, a class. In previous chapters, when we wanted to include a class in a project, we would either define the class in our project or add a reference to the compiled DLL. This compiled DLL is placed in the **Debug** directory of an application by default. As a result, all pieces of our application reside on one machine. When a client uses a Web service, the class (and its compiled DLL) is stored on a remote machine— a compiled version of this class is not placed in the current application.

Most requests to and responses from Web services created with Visual Studio .NET are transmitted via SOAP. This means that any client capable of generating and processing SOAP messages can use a Web service, regardless of the language in which the Web service is written. SOAP will be discussed more in Section 17.8.

Web services have important implications for *business-to-business (B2B) transactions* (i.e., transactions that occur between two or more businesses). Now, instead of using proprietary applications, businesses can conduct transactions via Web services—a much simpler and more efficient means of conducting business. Because Web services and SOAP are platform independent, companies can collaborate and use Web services without worrying about the compatibility of various technologies or programming languages. In this way, Web services are an inexpensive, readily available solution to facilitate B2B transactions.

To create a Web service in Visual Studio .NET, a developer first creates a project of type **Managed C++ Web Service**. Visual Studio .NET, then generates files to contain the Web service code (which implements the Web service), an *ASMX file* (which provides documentation for the Web service) and a DISCO file (which potential clients use to discover the Web service) (Fig. 17.4). We discuss these files in more detail shortly. [*Note*: When a developer creates an application in Visual Studio .NET, the IDE typically generates several files. We have chosen to show only those files that are specific to Web-services applications.]

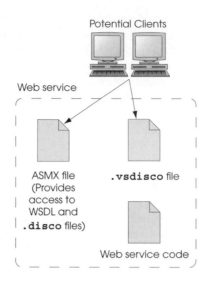

Fig. 17.4   Web service components.

When a developer creates a **Managed C++ Web Service** application, Visual Studio .NET provides code files to contain the Web service class and any other code that is part of the Web service implementation. The Web service class defines all methods that the Web service exposes to remote applications. Any methods (or additional classes) that the developer wants to incorporate in the Web service are added to this class. Developers must tag as a *Web method* each method that they want to expose. We demonstrate how to tag Web methods later in this chapter.

 Software Engineering Observation 17.2

> *By default, Visual Studio .NET creates only one* **.h** *and one* **.cpp** *file for the Web service implementation. More complex Web services can contain many code files.*

Once the developer adds the necessary programming logic to the Web service code file and successfully compiles the application, a client application can consume the Web service. However, clients must be able to find the Web service and learn about its capabilities. *Discovery of Web services (DISCO)* is a Microsoft-specific technology used to locate Web services in a particular directory on a server. There are three types of discovery files: **.disco** files, **.vsdisco** files and **.map** files. As we illustrate in Fig. 17.4, **.vsdisco** files are placed in the Web service application directory, whereas **.disco** files are accessed via the ASMX page. All three DISCO files contain XML that can help clients locate Web service files. A **.disco** file contains markup that specifies references to various Web services' documents. A **.vsdisco** file is slightly different. Rather than containing markup about Web services, this desired markup is generated when the file is requested. Markup containing references to Web services' documents will be generated and returned to the user. When a potential client requests a **.vsdisco** file, the .NET Framework analyzes the directory in which the **.vsdisco** file is located, as well as that directory's subdirectories. The .NET Framework then generates markup (using the same syntax as that of a **.disco** file) that contains references to all Web services in that direc-

tory and the directory's subdirectories. If this markup is generated, but not stored in the
`.vsdisco` file, then what information is contained in the `.vsdisco` file? Developers
can specify in the `.vsdisco` file certain directories that should not be searched when the
file is requested.[a] Normally, the `.vsdisco` file contains only markup specifying which
directories should not be searched. It is important to note that developers usually do not
view `.vsdisco` markup. Although a developer can open a `.vsdisco` file in a text editor
and examine its markup, `.vsdisco` files are intended to be requested (i.e., viewed in a
browser). Every time this occurs, new markup is generated and displayed.

The reader might be wondering why a developer would want to use one type of DISCO
file over another. Developers benefit from `.vsdisco` files, because the files contain a
small amount of data and provide up-to-date information on the Web service files provided
by a server. However, `.vsdisco` files generate more overhead than `.disco` files do,
because a search must be performed every time a `.vsdisco` file is accessed. Thus, some
developers find it more convenient to keep `.disco` files up-to-date manually. Many systems use both files. As we discuss later in this section, Web services created using
ASP .NET contain the functionality to generate a `.disco` file when it is requested. This
`.disco` file contains references to files in the current Web service only.[2] Thus, a developer typically places a `.vsdisco` file at the root of a server; when accessed, this file
locates the `.disco` files for Web services on the system and uses these `.disco` files'
markup to return information about the entire system.

Once a client locates a Web service, the client must access details regarding the Web
service's functionality and how to access that functionality. For this purpose, Web services
normally contain a *service description*. A service description is an XML document that
conforms to the *Web Service Description Language (WSDL),* an XML vocabulary that
defines the methods that the Web service makes available and the ways in which clients can
interact with those methods. The WSDL document also specifies lower-level information
that clients might need, such as the required formats for requests and responses.

Although WSDL documents supply this information, WSDL can be difficult to understand. Visual Studio .NET generates an ASMX file when a Web service is constructed to
offer a more understandable description of the Web service. Files with an *.asmx* extension
are ASP .NET Web service files. Such files can be viewed in a Web browser and contain
descriptions of Web service methods and ways to test these methods. The ASMX file also
indicates the compiled assembly, which contains the implementation of the Web service.
When the Web server receives a request for the Web service, it calls the ASMX file, which,
in turn, invokes the Web-service implementation. To view more technical information
about the Web service, developers can access the WSDL file (which also is generated by
ASP .NET). We will demonstrate how to do this shortly.

The ASMX file in Fig. 17.5 displays information about the **HugeInteger** Web service. This Web service, which we use as an example, is designed to perform calculations with
integers that contain a maximum of 100 digits. (Most programming languages cannot easily
perform calculations using integers this large.) The Web service provides client applications
with methods that take two "huge integers" and determine which one is larger or smaller,
whether the two numbers are equal, their sum and their difference. Notice that the top of the
page provides a link to the Web service's **Service Description**. Visual Studio .NET gen-

---

2. Although in this instance `.disco` files contain references to files in only one Web service, both
   `.disco` files can contain references to files in several Web services.

erates the WSDL service description. Client programs can use the service description to confirm the correctness of method calls when the client programs are compiled.

Rather than creating an actual WSDL file, ASP .NET generates WSDL information dynamically. If a client requests the Web service's WSDL file (either by appending *?WSDL* to the ASMX file's URL or by clicking the **Service Description** link), ASP .NET generates the WSDL description, which is then returned to the client and displayed in the Web browser. Because the WSDL file is generated when it is requested, clients can be sure that the WSDL contains the most current information.[b]

The programmer should not alter the service description, because it defines how a Web service works. When a user clicks the **Service Description** link at the top of the ASMX page, WSDL is displayed that defines the service description for this Web service (Fig. 17.6).

As mentioned earlier, the `.disco` file for the Web service is accessed via the ASMX page. Like WSDL data, the `.disco` information for an ASP .NET Web service is not a physical file.[3] The .NET Framework generates this file when a client requests it, by appending *?DISCO* to the ASMX's URL. Readers might be wondering why someone would access a `.disco` file this way—if potential clients know the URL of the Web service's ASMX file, then they have discovered the Web service already. However, `.disco` files also may be accessed when a client requests a `.vsdisco` file. For instance, recall that accessing a `.vsdisco` file causes the .NET Framework to search for Web services. When this occurs, the .NET Framework actually searches for ASMX files, `.disco` files and `.vsdisco` files.[c] This way, the information in a `.disco` file may be returned to a potential client that does *not* know the URL of any ASMX files on this machine.

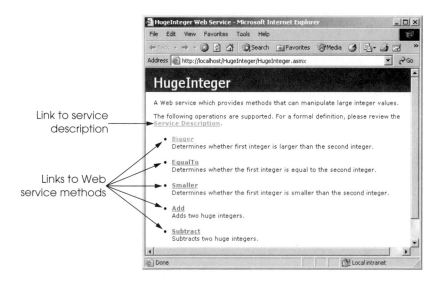

Fig. 17.5   ASMX file rendered in a Web browser.

---

3. It is common for XML documents to be created dynamically and manipulated programmatically, but never saved to disk.

Fig. 17.6 Service description for a Web service.

Below the **Service Description** link, the ASMX page shown in Fig. 17.5 lists the methods that the Web service offers. Clicking any method name requests a test page that describes the method (Fig. 17.7). After explaining the method's arguments, the test page allows users to test the method by entering the proper parameters and clicking **Invoke**. (We discuss the process of testing a Web service method shortly.) Below the **Invoke** button, the page displays sample request-and-response messages using SOAP, HTTP GET and HTTP POST. These protocols are the three options for sending and receiving messages in Web services. The protocol that transmits request and response messages also is known as the Web service's *wire format*, because it defines how information is sent "along the wire." SOAP is the more commonly used wire format, because both HTTP GET and HTTP POST are tied to HTTP, whereas SOAP can be sent along other transport protocols.

Figure 17.7 depicts the test page for the **HugeInteger** method **Bigger**. From this page, users can test the method by entering **Value**s in the **first:** and **second:** fields, then clicking **Invoke**. The method executes, and a new Web browser window opens to display an XML document that contains the result (Fig. 17.8).

Testing and Debugging Tip 17.1

Using the ASMX page of a Web service to test and debug methods makes that Web service more reliable and robust; it also reduces the likelihood that clients using the Web service will encounter errors.

Fig. 17.7 Invoking a Web service method from a Web browser.

Fig. 17.8 Results of invoking a Web service method from a Web browser.

Now that we have discussed the different files that compromise a .NET Web service, let us examine a .NET Web service client (Fig. 17.9). A .NET client can be any type of .NET application, such as a Windows program or a console application. Developers can consume Web services from their applications by the process of *adding a Web reference*. This process adds files to the client application that enable the client to access the Web service. To add a Web reference in Visual Studio .NET, the developer right-clicks the project name in the **Solution Explorer** and selects option **Add Web Reference...**. In the resulting dialog, the developer specifies the Web service to consume. Visual Studio .NET then adds an appropriate Web reference to the client application. We will demonstrate adding Web references in more detail in Section 17.9.

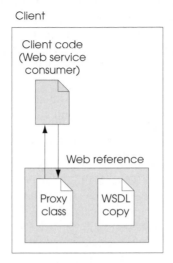

Fig. 17.9 .NET Web service client after Web reference has been added.

When developers specify the Web service they want to consume, Visual Studio .NET accesses the Web service's WSDL file and makes a copy of it, which will be stored as a file in the project folder.[4] The information in the WSDL file is used to create the *proxy class*, which handles all the "plumbing" required for Web service method calls. Whenever the client application calls a Web service method, the application actually calls a corresponding method in the proxy class. This method takes the name of the Web service method that is being called and its arguments, then formats them so that they can be sent as a request in a SOAP message. The Web service receives this request and executes the method call, sending back the result as another SOAP message. When the client application receives the SOAP message containing the response, the proxy class decodes it and formats the results so that the client application can access them. The information is then returned to the client. Figure 17.10 depicts interactions among the client code, proxy and Web service.

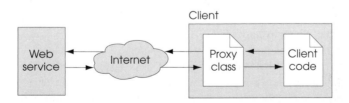

Fig. 17.10 Interaction between Web service and Web service client.

4. A copy of the WSDL file provides the client application with local access to the Web service's description. To ensure that the WSDL file is current, Visual Studio .NET provides an **Update Web Reference** option, which performs the process of updating the files in the **Web References** folder.

Just as .NET clients contain proxy classes to handle SOAP requests/responses, .NET Web services include their own proxy-like functionality. However, this functionality is provided by the .NET Framework, rather than being contained in a physical file (as is the proxy for the client)

It is important to note that the .NET environment hides from the programmer most of the details we have just discussed. Many aspects of Web service creation and consumption—such as generating WSDL, ASMX files, proxy classes and DISCO files—are handled by Visual Studio .NET and ASP .NET. Although developers are relieved of the tedious process of creating these files, they can still modify the files if necessary.

17.8 Simple Object Access Protocol (SOAP) and Web Services

The *Simple Object Access Protocol (SOAP)* is a platform-independent protocol that uses XML to make remote-procedure calls over HTTP. Each request and response is packaged in a *SOAP message*—an XML message that contains all the information necessary to process its contents. SOAP messages are quite popular, because they are written in the easy-to-understand and platform-independent XML. Similarly, HTTP was chosen to transmit SOAP messages, because HTTP is a standard protocol for sending information across the Internet. The use of XML and HTTP enables different operating systems to send and receive SOAP messages. Another benefit of HTTP is that it can be used with networks that contain *firewalls*—security barriers that restrict communication among networks.

SOAP supports an extensive set of data types. Readers should note that the wire format used to transmit requests and responses must support all data types passed between the applications. Web services that use SOAP support a wider variety of data types than do Web services that employ other wire formats. The data types supported by SOAP include most basic data types (such as **int**), plus **DataSet**, **DateTime**, **XmlNode** and several others. SOAP also permits the transmission of arrays of all these types. In addition, user-defined types can be used—we demonstrate how to do this in Section 17.13.

Applications send requests and responses to and from Web services via SOAP. When a program invokes a Web-service method, the request and all relevant information are packaged in a SOAP message and sent to the appropriate destination. When the Web service receives the SOAP message, it begins to process the contents (called the *SOAP envelope*), which specify the method that the client wishes to execute and any arguments the client is passing to that method. After the Web service receives this request and parses it, the proper method is called with the specified arguments (if there are any), and the response is sent back to the client in another SOAP message. The client parses the response to retrieve the result of the method call.

The SOAP request portrayed in Fig. 17.11 was taken directly from the **Bigger** method of the **HugeInteger** Web service (Fig. 17.7). This Web service provides programmers with several methods that manipulate integers larger than those that can be stored in a **long** variable. Most programmers do not manipulate SOAP messages, but instead allow the Web service to handle the details of transmission.

Figure 17.11 displays a standard SOAP request that is created when a client wishes to execute the **HugeInteger** Web service's method **Bigger**. When a request to a Web service causes such a SOAP request to be created, the elements **first** and **second**'s character data (**string**s) would contain the actual values that the user entered (lines 16–17). If this envelope contained the request from Fig. 17.7, element **first** and element **second** would contain the values entered in Fig. 17.7. Placeholder **length** (line 4) would contain the length of this SOAP message.

```
 1   POST /HugeIntegerWebService/HugeInteger.asmx HTTP/1.1
 2   Host: localhost
 3   Content-Type: text/xml; charset=utf-8
 4   Content-Length: length
 5   SOAPAction: "http://www.deitel.com/ch17/Bigger"
 6
 7   <?xml version="1.0" encoding="utf-8"?>
 8
 9   <soap:Envelope
10      xmlns:xsi="http://www.w3.org/2001/XMLSchema-instance"
11      xmlns:xsd="http://www.w3.org/2001/XMLSchema"
12      xmlns:soap="http://schemas.xmlsoap.org/soap/envelope/">
13
14      <soap:Body>
15         <Bigger xmlns="http://www.deitel.com/ch17/">
16            <first>string</first>
17            <second>string</second>
18         </Bigger>
19      </soap:Body>
20
21   </soap:Envelope>
```

Fig. 17.11 SOAP request for the **HugeInteger** Web service.

17.9 Publishing and Consuming Web Services

This section presents an example of creating (also known as *publishing*) and using (also known as *consuming*) a Web service. We will walk the reader through the creation of both a Web service and a Web service client. Figure 17.12 and Fig. 17.13 present the implementation files for the **HugeInteger** Web service (Fig. 17.5). The name of the Web service is based on the name of the class that defines it (in this case, **HugeInteger**). This Web service is designed to perform calculations with integers that contain a maximum of 100 digits. As we mentioned earlier, **long** variables cannot handle integers of this size (i.e., an overflow would occur). The Web service provides a client with methods that take two "huge integers" and determine which one is larger or smaller, whether the two numbers are equal, their sum or their difference. The reader can think of these methods as services that one application provides for the programmers of other applications (hence, the term "Web services"). Any programmer can access this Web service, use its methods and thus avoid writing over 200 lines of code.

```
1   // Fig. 17.12: HugeInteger.h
2   // HugeInteger Web service.
3
4   #pragma once
5
6   #using <system.dll>
7   #using <mscorlib.dll>
8   #using <System.Web.Services.dll>
9
```

Fig. 17.12 **HugeInteger** class header file. (Part 1 of 3.)

```cpp
10    using namespace System;
11    using namespace System::Text;
12    using namespace System::Web::Services;
13
14    namespace HugeInteger
15    {
16
17        // performs operations on large integers
18        [ WebServiceAttribute(
19           Namespace = "http://www.deitel.com/ch17/HugeInteger",
20           Description = "A Web service which provides methods that"
21           " can manipulate large integer values." ) ]
22        public __gc class HugeInteger : public WebService
23        {
24        public:
25           HugeInteger();
26
27           int number __gc[];
28
29           // indexed property that accepts an integer parameter
30           __property int get_Index( int index )
31           {
32              return number[ index ];
33           }
34
35           __property void set_Index( int index, int value )
36           {
37              number[ index ] = value;
38           }
39
40           String *ToString();
41
42           HugeInteger *FromString( String *integer );
43
44           [ WebMethod( Description = "Adds two huge integers." ) ]
45           String *Add( String *first, String *second );
46
47           [ WebMethod (
48              Description = "Subtracts two huge integers." ) ]
49           String *Subtract( String *first, String *second );
50
51           [ WebMethod( Description = "Determines whether the first"
52              "integer is larger than the second integer." ) ]
53           bool Bigger( String *first, String *second );
54
55           [ WebMethod( Description = "Determines whether the"
56              "first integer is smaller than the second integer." ) ]
57           bool Smaller( String *first, String *second );
58
59           [ WebMethod( Description = "Determines whether the"
60              "first integer is equal to the second integer." ) ]
61           bool EqualTo( String *first, String *second );
62
```

Fig. 17.12 HugeInteger class header file. (Part 2 of 3.)

```
63      private:
64         static const int MAXIMUM = 100;
65         void InitializeComponent();
66         void Borrow( HugeInteger *integer, int place );
67      };
68  } // end namespace HugeInteger
```

Fig. 17.12 `HugeInteger` class header file. (Part 3 of 3.)

```
1   // Fig. 17.13: HugeInteger.cpp
2   // HugeInteger Web service.
3
4   #include "stdafx.h"
5   #include "HugeInteger.h"
6   #include "Global.asax.h"
7
8   namespace HugeInteger
9   {
10     HugeInteger::HugeInteger()
11     {
12        InitializeComponent();
13        number = new int __gc[ MAXIMUM ];
14     }
15
16     void HugeInteger::InitializeComponent(){}
17
18     // returns String * representation of HugeInteger
19     String *HugeInteger::ToString()
20     {
21        StringBuilder *returnString = new StringBuilder();
22
23        int digit;
24
25        for ( int i = 0; i < number->Length; i++ ) {
26           digit = number[ i ];
27
28           returnString->Insert( 0, digit );
29        }
30
31        return returnString->ToString();
32     } // end method ToString
33
34     // creates HugeInteger based on argument
35     HugeInteger *HugeInteger::FromString( String *integer )
36     {
37        HugeInteger *parsedInteger = new HugeInteger();
38
39        for ( int i = 0; i < integer->Length; i++ )
40           parsedInteger->Index[ i ] = Int32::Parse( integer->
41              Chars[ integer->Length - i - 1 ].ToString() );
42
```

Fig. 17.13 `HugeInteger` Web service. (Part 1 of 4.)

```
43          return parsedInteger;
44     } // end method FromString
45
46     // WebMethod that performs integer addition
47     // represented by string * arguments
48     String *HugeInteger::Add( String *first, String *second )
49     {
50        int carry = 0;
51
52        HugeInteger *operand1 = FromString( first );
53        HugeInteger *operand2 = FromString( second );
54
55        // store result of addition
56        HugeInteger *result = new HugeInteger();
57
58        // perform addition algorithm for each digit
59        for ( int i = 0; i < MAXIMUM; i++ ) {
60
61           // add two digits in same columnresult is their sum,
62           // plus carry from previous operation modulus 10
63           result->Index[ i ] =
64              ( operand1->Index[ i ] + operand2->Index[ i ]
65              + carry ) % 10;
66
67           // store remainder of dividing sums of two digits by 10
68           carry = ( operand1->Index[ i ] + operand2->Index[ i ]
69              + carry ) / 10;
70        } // end for
71
72        return result->ToString();
73     } // end method Add
74
75     // WebMethod that performs the subtraction of integers
76     // represented by String * arguments
77     String *HugeInteger::Subtract( String *first, String *second )
78     {
79        HugeInteger *operand1 = FromString( first );
80        HugeInteger *operand2 = FromString( second );
81        HugeInteger *result = new HugeInteger();
82
83        // subtract top digit from bottom digit
84        for ( int i = 0; i < MAXIMUM; i++ ) {
85
86           // if top digit is smaller than bottom
87           // digit we need to borrow
88           if ( operand1->Index[ i ] < operand2->Index[ i ] )
89              Borrow( operand1, i );
90
91           // subtract bottom from top
92           result->Index[ i ] = operand1->Index[ i ]
93              - operand2->Index[ i ];
94        } // end for
95
```

Fig. 17.13 HugeInteger Web service. (Part 2 of 4.)

```
96           return result->ToString();
97        } // end method Subtract
98
99        // borrows 1 from next digit
100       void HugeInteger::Borrow( HugeInteger *integer, int place )
101       {
102
103          // if no place to borrow from, signal problem
104          if ( place >= MAXIMUM - 1 )
105             throw new ArgumentException();
106
107          // otherwise if next digit is zero, borrow left digit
108          else if ( integer->Index[ place + 1 ] == 0 )
109             Borrow( integer, place + 1 );
110
111          // add ten to current place because we borrowed and
112          // subtract one from previous digit
113          // - this is digit borrowed from
114          integer->Index[ place ] += 10;
115          integer->Index[ place + 1 ] -= 1;
116       } // end method Borrow
117
118       // WebMethod that returns true if first integer is
119       // bigger than second
120       bool HugeInteger::Bigger( String *first, String *second )
121       {
122          __wchar_t zeroes __gc[] = { '0' };
123
124          try {
125
126             // if elimination of all zeroes from result
127             // of subtraction is an empty string, numbers are equal,
128             // so return false, otherwise return true
129             if ( Subtract( first, second )->Trim( zeroes ) == "" )
130                return false;
131             else
132                return true;
133          }
134
135          // if ArgumentException occurs, first number
136          // was smaller, so return false
137          catch ( ArgumentException * ) {
138
139             return false;
140          }
141       } // end method Bigger
142
143       // WebMethod returns true if first integer is
144       // smaller than second
145       bool HugeInteger::Smaller( String *first, String *second )
146       {
147
148          // if second is bigger than first, then first is
```

Fig. 17.13 HugeInteger Web service. (Part 3 of 4.)

```
149            // smaller than second
150            return Bigger( second, first );
151        } // end method Smaller
152
153        // WebMethod that returns true if two integers are equal
154        bool HugeInteger::EqualTo( String *first, String *second )
155        {
156
157            // if either first is bigger than second, or first is
158            // smaller than second, they are not equal
159            if ( Bigger( first, second ) || Smaller( first, second ) )
160                return false;
161            else
162                return true;
163        } // end method EqualTo
164 } // end namespace HugeInteger
```

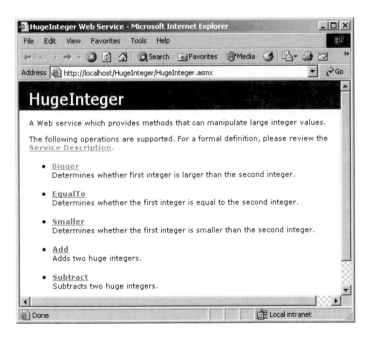

Fig. 17.13 HugeInteger Web service. (Part 4 of 4.)

In Fig. 17.12, line 19 assigns the Web service namespace to **www.deitel.com/ch17/HugeInteger**, to identify this Web service uniquely. The namespace is specified via the **Namespace** property of attribute **WebServiceAttribute**. Each Web service has a default namespace (**http://tempuri.org**), which is adequate for testing, but should be replaced before the Web service is deployed in real-world situations. In lines 20–21, we use property **Description** to provide information about our Web service that appears in the ASMX file. Line 22 specifies that our class derives from **WebService** (located in namespace **System::Web::Services**). By default, Visual Studio .NET defines our Web service so that it inherits from the **WebService** class. Although a Web-service class is not required to subclass **WebService**, class **WebService** provides members that are useful for obtaining information about the client and about the Web service itself. For instance, class **WebService** contains a **Session** object, which we will use later to store a user's information between Web service method calls. Several methods in class **HugeInteger** are tagged with *WebMethod* attributes, which *expose* the methods so that they can be called remotely. When this attribute is absent, the method is not accessible through the Web service. Notice that the **WebMethod** attribute, like attribute **WebServiceAttribute**, contains a **Description** property, which provides to the ASMX page information about the method. Readers can see these descriptions in the output of Fig. 17.13.

Good Programming Practice 17.1

Specify a namespace (e.g., a URL) for each Web service so that it can be uniquely identified.

Good Programming Practice 17.2

Specify descriptions for all Web services and Web-service methods so that clients can obtain additional information about the Web service and its contents.

Common Programming Error 17.1

Attempting to call a remote method from a Web service if the method is not declared with the **WebMethod** *attribute is a compilation error.*

Common Programming Error 17.2

Web-service methods cannot be declared **static***, or a compilation error. For a client to access a Web-service method, an instance of that Web service must exist.*

Lines 30–38 (Fig. 17.12) define an indexed property for our class. This enables us to access any digit in **HugeInteger** as if we were accessing it through array **number**. Lines 48–73 and 77–97 (Fig. 17.13) define **WebMethod**s **Add** and **Subtract**, which perform addition and subtraction, respectively. Method **Borrow** (lines 100–116) handles the case in which the digit in the left operand is smaller than the corresponding digit in the right operand. For instance, when we subtract 19 from 32, we usually go digit by digit, starting from the right. The number 2 is smaller than 9, so we add 10 to 2 (resulting in 12), which subtracts 9, resulting in 3 for the rightmost digit in the solution. We then subtract 1 from the next digit over (3), making it 2. The corresponding digit in the right operand is now the "1" in 19. The subtraction of 1 from 2 is 1, making the corresponding digit in the result 1. The final result, when both resulting digits are combined, is 13. Method **Borrow** adds 10 to the appropriate digit and subtracts 1 from the digit to its left. Because this is a utility method that is not intended to be called remotely, it is not qualified with attribute **WebMethod**.

The screen capture in Fig. 17.13 is identical to the one in Fig. 17.5. A client application can invoke only the five methods listed in the screen shot (i.e., the methods qualified with the **WebMethod** attribute).

Now, let us demonstrate how to create this Web service. To begin, we must create a project of type **Managed C++ Web Service**. By default, Web services are placed in the Web server's **wwwroot** directory on the server (**localhost**).

Visual Studio .NET generates a header file and a `.cpp` file named after the project. The Web service is defined in a namespace named after the project. The class in the header file is named **Class1** by default, but we changed this to the more descriptive **HugeInteger**. The `.cpp` file contains a sample method **HelloWorld**. We replaced this method with our own code for the **HugeInteger** project.

Note that the ASMX file contains only the line:

```
<%@ WebService Class="ProjectName.Class1" %>
```

indicating the class that defines our Web service.[5] This is the extent of the information that this file must contain. The programmer must insert the current project name and class name to create a working Web service. In this case, we changed the line to

```
<%@ WebService Class="HugeInteger.HugeInteger" %>
```

Now that we have defined our Web service, we demonstrate how to use it. First, a client application must be created. In this first example, we create a Windows application as our client. Once this application has been created, the client must add a proxy class for accessing the Web service. Recall that a proxy class (or proxy) is a class created from the Web service's WSDL file that enables the client to call Web-service methods over the Internet. The proxy class handles all the "plumbing" required for Web-service method calls. Whenever a call is made in the client application to a Web-service method, the application actually calls a corresponding method in the proxy class. This method takes the name of the method and its arguments; it then formats them so that they can be sent as a request in a SOAP message. The Web service receives this request and executes the method call, sending back the result as another SOAP message. When the client application receives the SOAP message containing the response, the proxy class decodes it and formats the results so that they are understandable to the client. This information then is returned to the client. It is important to note that the proxy class essentially is hidden from the programmer. We cannot, in fact, view it in the **Solution Explorer**. The purpose of the proxy class is to make it seem to clients that they are calling the Web-service methods directly. It is rarely necessary for the client to view or manipulate the proxy class.

The next example demonstrates how to create a Web-service client and its corresponding proxy class. We must begin by creating a project and adding a Web reference to that project. For simplicity, all of our applications are MC++ applications. When we add a Web reference to a client application, the proxy class is created. The client then creates an instance of the proxy class, which is used to call methods included in the Web service.

To create a proxy in Visual Studio .NET, right click the **References** folder in **Solution Explorer** and select **Add Web Reference** (Fig. 17.14). In the **Add Web Reference** dialog that appears (Fig. 17.15), enter the Web address of the Web service, and press *Enter*. In this chapter, we store the Web service in the root directory of our local Web server (`http://localhost`, whose physical path is `C:\Inetpub\wwwroot`). We now can add a Web reference by clicking the button **Add Reference** (Fig. 17.16). This adds **WebService.h** and a WSDL file to the **Solution Explorer** (Fig. 17.17). This header file defines **using** directives for the proxy class. The programmer needs to include this file

---

5. The `<%@` and `%>` symbols delimit an *ASP directive*. An ASP directive sets the environment used by the ASP script by assigning values to keywords (e.g., assigning the class name to keyword `Class`).

explicitly via **#include**. [*Note*: The Web-service class and the proxy class have the same name. Visual Studio .NET generates a proxy (a C# file with a **.cs** extension) for the Web service and a discovery file. Visual Studio .NET adds the proxy file to the project directory, but this file is not added to the **Solution Explorer**.]

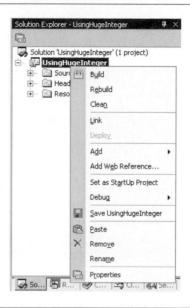

Fig. 17.14 Adding a Web-service reference to a project.

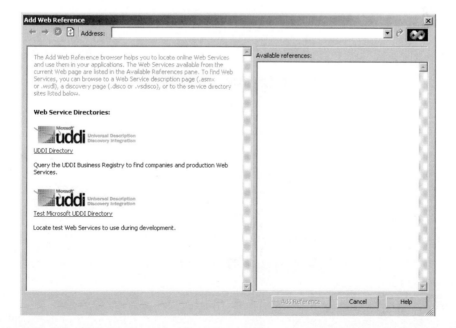

Fig. 17.15 Add Web Reference dialog.

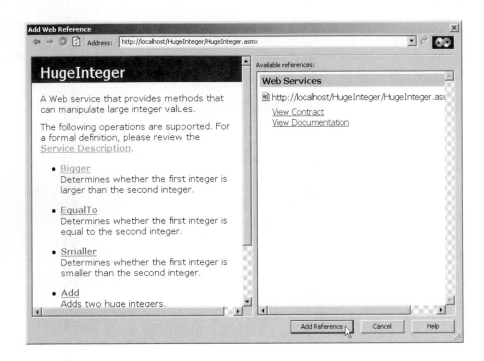

Fig. 17.16 Web reference selection and description.

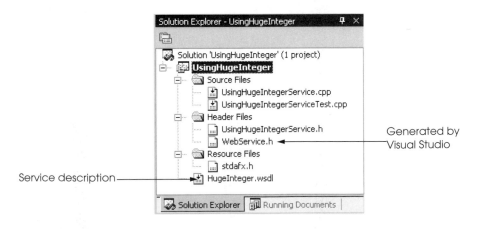

Fig. 17.17 Solution Explorer after adding a Web reference to a project.

Good Programming Practice 17.3

When creating a program that will use Web services, add the Web reference first. This will enable Visual Studio .NET to recognize an instance of the Web-service class, allowing Intellisense to help the developer use the Web service. IntelliSense is a Visual Studio .NET feature that lists a class's members. As the programmer types characters, the first member that matches all the characters typed is highlighted. The programmer can type the complete member name, double click the member name in the list or press the Tab key to complete the name. Once the complete name is provided, the IntelliSense window closes.

The steps that we described previously work well if the programmer knows the appropriate Web-services reference. However, what if we are trying to locate a new Web service? There are a few technologies that facilitate this process. Two common technologies are: *Universal Description, Discovery and Integration (UDDI)* and Discovery files (DISCO). We discussed DISCO in Section 17.7.[6] UDDI is a project for developing a set of specifications that define how Web services should be published so that programmers searching for Web services can find them. Microsoft and its partners are working on this ongoing project to help programmers at various companies locate Web services that conform to certain specifications, allowing developers to find different Web services through search engines. UDDI describes Web services; it then organizes this information in a central location. Although UDDI is beyond the scope of what we are teaching, the reader can learn more about this project and view a demonstration by visiting **www.uddi.org** and **uddi.microsoft.com**. These sites contain search tools that make finding Web services fast and easy.

Once the Web reference is added, the client can access the Web service through our proxy. The application in Fig. 17.18–Fig. 17.20 uses the **HugeInteger** Web service to perform computations with positive integers up to **100** digits long. [*Note:* If using the example downloaded from **www.deitel.com**, the reader might need to regenerate the proxy. This action can be performed by right-clicking the WSDL file in the **Solution Explorer** and selecting option **Update Web Reference**.]

```
1   // Fig. 17.18: UsingHugeIntegerService.h
2   // UsingHugeIntService class header file.
3
4   #pragma once
5
6   #using <mscorlib.dll>
7   #using <system.dll>
8   #using <system.drawing.dll>
9   #using <system.windows.forms.dll>
10  #using <system.web.dll>
11  #using <system.web.services.dll>
12
13  using namespace System;
```

Fig. 17.18 **UsingHugeIntService** class header file. (Part 1 of 2.)

---

6. One newer discovery technology, WS-Inspection, will be discussed in detail in Section 17.14.1.

```
14   using namespace System::Drawing;
15   using namespace System::Windows::Forms;
16   using namespace System::Web::Services::Protocols;
17
18   #include "WebService.h"
19
20   // allows user to perform operations on large integers
21   public __gc class UsingHugeIntService : public Form
22   {
23   public:
24      UsingHugeIntService();
25
26   protected:
27      void equalButton_Click( Object *sender, EventArgs *e );
28      void smallerButton_Click( Object *sender, EventArgs *e );
29      void biggerButton_Click( Object *sender, EventArgs *e );
30      void subtractButton_Click( Object *sender, EventArgs *e );
31      void addButton_Click( Object *sender, EventArgs *e );
32
33   private:
34      Label *promptLabel, *resultLabel;
35      TextBox *firstTextBox, *secondTextBox;
36      Button *addButton, *subtractButton, *biggerButton,
37         *smallerButton, *equalButton;
38
39      // declare a pointer to a Web service
40      HugeInteger *remoteInteger;
41
42      static __wchar_t zeroes __gc[] = { '0' };
43
44      void InitializeComponent();
45      bool CheckSize( TextBox *first, TextBox *second );
46   }; // end class UsingHugeIntegerService
```

Fig. 17.18 UsingHugeIntService class header file. (Part 2 of 2.)

```
1    // Fig. 17.19: UsingHugeIntegerService.cpp
2    // Using the HugeInteger Web service.
3
4    #include "UsingHugeIntegerService.h"
5
6    UsingHugeIntService::UsingHugeIntService()
7    {
8       InitializeComponent();
9
10      // instantiate remoteInteger
11      remoteInteger = new HugeInteger();
12   }
13
14   void UsingHugeIntService::InitializeComponent()
15   {
```

Fig. 17.19 Using the HugeInteger Web service. (Part 1 of 6.)

```
16        this->promptLabel = new Label();
17        this->firstTextBox = new TextBox();
18        this->secondTextBox = new TextBox();
19        this->addButton = new Button();
20        this->subtractButton = new Button();
21        this->biggerButton = new Button();
22        this->smallerButton = new Button();
23        this->equalButton = new Button();
24        this->resultLabel = new Label();
25        this->SuspendLayout();
26
27        // promptLabel
28        this->promptLabel->AutoSize = true;
29        this->promptLabel->Location = Point( 16, 24 );
30        this->promptLabel->Name = S"promptLabel";
31        this->promptLabel->Size = Drawing::Size( 287, 13 );
32        this->promptLabel->TabIndex = 0;
33        this->promptLabel->Text = S"Please enter ",
34           S"two positive numbers up to 100 digits each:";
35
36        // firstTextBox
37        this->firstTextBox->Font = new Drawing::Font(
38           S"Letter Gothic MT", 8.25, FontStyle::Regular,
39           GraphicsUnit::Point, 0 );
40        this->firstTextBox->Location = Point( 17, 56 );
41        this->firstTextBox->Name = S"firstTextBox";
42        this->firstTextBox->Size = Drawing::Size( 711, 21 );
43        this->firstTextBox->TabIndex = 1;
44        this->firstTextBox->Text = S"";
45
46        // secondTextBox
47        this->secondTextBox->Font = new Drawing::Font(
48           S"Letter Gothic MT", 8.25, FontStyle::Regular,
49           GraphicsUnit::Point, 0 );
50        this->secondTextBox->Location = Point( 17, 88 );
51        this->secondTextBox->Name = S"secondTextBox";
52        this->secondTextBox->Size = Drawing::Size( 711, 21 );
53        this->secondTextBox->TabIndex = 2;
54        this->secondTextBox->Text = S"";
55
56        // addButton
57        this->addButton->Location = Point( 84, 128 );
58        this->addButton->Name = S"addButton";
59        this->addButton->Size = Drawing::Size( 88, 23 );
60        this->addButton->TabIndex = 3;
61        this->addButton->Text = S"Add";
62        this->addButton->Click += new EventHandler( this,
63           addButton_Click );
64
65        // subtractButton
66        this->subtractButton->Location = Point( 212, 128 );
67        this->subtractButton->Name = S"subtractButton";
68        this->subtractButton->Size = Drawing::Size( 88, 23 );
```

Fig. 17.19 Using the **HugeInteger** Web service. (Part 2 of 6.)

```
69        this->subtractButton->TabIndex = 4;
70        this->subtractButton->Text = S"Subtract";
71        this->subtractButton->Click += new EventHandler( this,
72           subtractButton_Click );
73
74        // biggerButton
75        this->biggerButton->Location = Point( 332, 128 );
76        this->biggerButton->Name = S"biggerButton";
77        this->biggerButton->Size = Drawing::Size( 88, 23 );
78        this->biggerButton->TabIndex = 5;
79        this->biggerButton->Text = S"Larger Than";
80        this->biggerButton->Click += new EventHandler( this,
81           biggerButton_Click );
82
83        // smallerButton
84        this->smallerButton->Location = Point( 452, 128 );
85        this->smallerButton->Name = S"smallerButton";
86        this->smallerButton->Size = Drawing::Size( 88, 23 );
87        this->smallerButton->TabIndex = 6;
88        this->smallerButton->Text = S"Smaller Than";
89        this->smallerButton->Click += new EventHandler( this,
90           smallerButton_Click );
91
92        // equalButton
93        this->equalButton->Location = Point( 572, 128 );
94        this->equalButton->Name = S"equalButton";
95        this->equalButton->Size = Drawing::Size( 88, 23 );
96        this->equalButton->TabIndex = 7;
97        this->equalButton->Text = S"Equal";
98        this->equalButton->Click += new EventHandler( this,
99           equalButton_Click );
100
101       // resultLabel
102       this->resultLabel->BorderStyle = BorderStyle::FixedSingle;
103       this->resultLabel->Location = Point( 16, 176 );
104       this->resultLabel->Name = S"resultLabel";
105       this->resultLabel->Size = Drawing::Size( 712, 40 );
106       this->resultLabel->TabIndex = 8;
107
108       this->AutoScaleBaseSize = Drawing::Size( 5, 13 );
109       this->ClientSize = Drawing::Size( 744, 229 );
110       Control *control[] = { this->resultLabel,
111          this->equalButton, this->smallerButton,
112          this->biggerButton, this->subtractButton, this->addButton,
113          this->secondTextBox, this->firstTextBox,
114          this->promptLabel };
115       this->Controls->AddRange( control );
116       this->Name = S"UsingHugeIntService";
117       this->Text = S"UsingHugeInteger";
118       this->ResumeLayout();
119    } // end method InitializeComponent
120
121 // checks whether two numbers user input are equal
```

Fig. 17.19 Using the **HugeInteger** Web service. (Part 3 of 6.)

```
122   void UsingHugeIntService::equalButton_Click( Object *sender,
123       EventArgs *e )
124   {
125
126       // make sure HugeIntegers do not exceed 100 digits
127       if ( CheckSize( firstTextBox, secondTextBox ) )
128          return;
129
130       // call Web-service method to determine
131       // whether integers are equal
132       if ( remoteInteger->EqualTo(
133          firstTextBox->Text, secondTextBox->Text ) )
134
135          resultLabel->Text = String::Concat(
136              firstTextBox->Text->TrimStart( zeroes ),
137              S" is equal to ",
138              secondTextBox->Text->TrimStart( zeroes ) );
139
140       else
141          resultLabel->Text = String::Concat(
142              firstTextBox->Text->TrimStart( zeroes ),
143              S" is NOT equal to ",
144              secondTextBox->Text->TrimStart( zeroes ) );
145   } // end method equalButton_Click
146
147   // checks whether first integer input
148   // by user is smaller than second
149   void UsingHugeIntService::smallerButton_Click( Object *sender,
150       EventArgs *e )
151   {
152
153       // make sure HugeIntegers do not exceed 100 digits
154       if ( CheckSize( firstTextBox, secondTextBox ) )
155          return;
156
157       // call Web-service method to determine whether first
158       // integer is smaller than second
159       if ( remoteInteger->Smaller(
160          firstTextBox->Text, secondTextBox->Text ) )
161
162          resultLabel->Text = String::Concat(
163              firstTextBox->Text->TrimStart( zeroes ),
164              S" is smaller than ",
165              secondTextBox->Text->TrimStart( zeroes ) );
166       else
167          resultLabel->Text = String::Concat(
168              firstTextBox->Text->TrimStart( zeroes ),
169              S" is NOT smaller than ",
170              secondTextBox->Text->TrimStart( zeroes ) );
171   } // end method smallerButton_Click
172
173   // checks whether first integer input
174   // by user is bigger than second
```

Fig. 17.19 Using the **HugeInteger** Web service. (Part 4 of 6.)

```cpp
175  void UsingHugeIntService::biggerButton_Click( Object *sender,
176     EventArgs *e )
177  {
178
179     // make sure HugeIntegers do not exceed 100 digits
180     if ( CheckSize( firstTextBox, secondTextBox ) )
181        return;
182
183     // call Web-service method to determine whether first
184     // integer is larger than the second
185     if ( remoteInteger->Bigger( firstTextBox->Text,
186        secondTextBox->Text ) )
187
188        resultLabel->Text = String::Concat(
189           firstTextBox->Text->TrimStart( zeroes ),
190           S" is larger than ",
191           secondTextBox->Text->TrimStart( zeroes ) );
192     else
193        resultLabel->Text = String::Concat(
194           firstTextBox->Text->TrimStart( zeroes ),
195           S" is NOT larger than ",
196           secondTextBox->Text->TrimStart( zeroes ) );
197  } // end method biggerButton_Click
198
199  // subtract second integer from first
200  void UsingHugeIntService::subtractButton_Click( Object *sender,
201     EventArgs *e )
202  {
203
204     // make sure HugeIntegers do not exceed 100 digits
205     if ( CheckSize( firstTextBox, secondTextBox ) )
206        return;
207
208     // perform subtraction
209     try
210     {
211        String *result = remoteInteger->Subtract(
212           firstTextBox->Text,
213           secondTextBox->Text )->TrimStart( zeroes );
214
215        resultLabel->Text = ( ( result == S"" ) ? S"0" : result );
216     }
217
218     // if WebMethod throws an exception, then first
219     // argument was smaller than second
220     catch( SoapException * )
221     {
222        MessageBox::Show(
223           S"First argument was smaller than the second" );
224     }
225  } // end method subtractButton_Click
226
227  // adds two integers input by user
```

Fig. 17.19 Using the **HugeInteger** Web service. (Part 5 of 6.)

```
228  void UsingHugeIntService::addButton_Click( Object *sender,
229     EventArgs *e )
230  {
231
232     // make sure HugeInteger does not exceed 100 digits
233     // and is not situation where both integers are 100
234     // digits long--result in overflow
235     if ( firstTextBox->Text->Length > 100 ||
236        secondTextBox->Text->Length > 100 ||
237        ( firstTextBox->Text->Length == 100 &&
238        secondTextBox->Text->Length == 100 ) )
239     {
240        MessageBox::Show( String::Concat(
241           S"HugeIntegers must not be more ",
242           S"than 100 digits\nBoth integers cannot be of",
243           S" length 100: this causes an overflow",
244           S"Error", MessageBoxButtons::OK,
245           MessageBoxIcon::Information ) );
246
247        return;
248     }
249
250     // perform addition
251     resultLabel->Text = remoteInteger->Add( firstTextBox->Text,
252        secondTextBox->Text )->TrimStart( zeroes )->ToString();
253  } // end method addButton_Click
254
255  // determines whether size of integers is too big
256  bool UsingHugeIntService::CheckSize( TextBox *first,
257     TextBox *second )
258  {
259     if ( first->Text->Length > 100 || second->Text->Length > 100 ) {
260        MessageBox::Show( String::Concat( S"HugeIntegers must ",
261           S"be no more than 100 digits" ), S"Error",
262           MessageBoxButtons::OK, MessageBoxIcon::Information );
263        return true;
264     }
265
266     return false;
267  } // end method CheckSize
```

Fig. 17.19 Using the **HugeInteger** Web service. (Part 6 of 6.)

```
1  // Fig. 17.20: UsingHugeIntegerServiceTest.cpp
2  // Driver file for application.
3
4  #include "UsingHugeIntegerService.h"
5
6  int __stdcall WinMain()
7  {
8     Application::Run( new UsingHugeIntService() );
9
```

Fig. 17.20 **HugeInteger** Web-service demonstration. (Part 1 of 2.)

```
10      return 0;
11   } // end WinMain
```

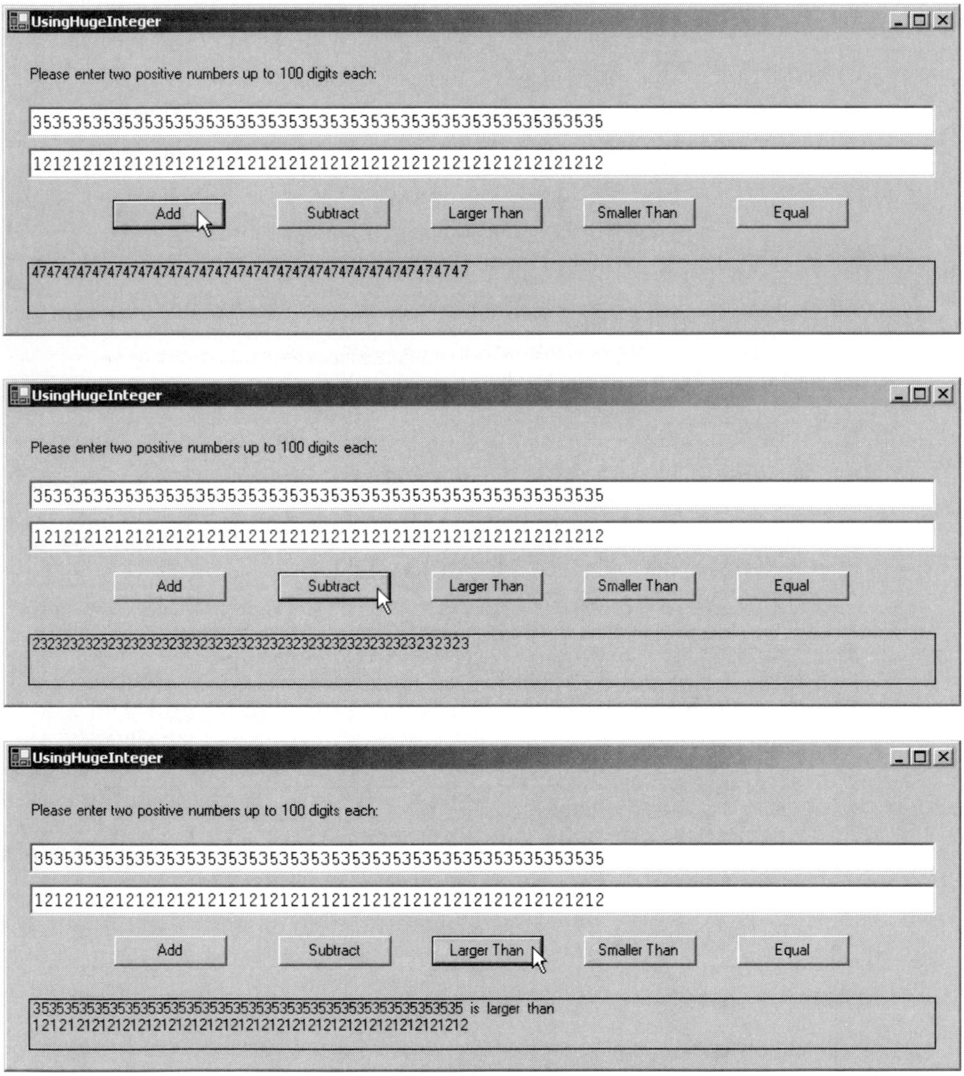

Fig. 17.20 HugeInteger Web-service demonstration. (Part 2 of 2.)

The user inputs two integers, each up to 100 digits long. The clicking of any button invokes a remote method to perform the appropriate calculation and return the result. The return value of each operation is displayed, and all leading zeroes are eliminated via **String** method **TrimStart**. Note that **UsingHugeInteger** does not have the capability to perform operations with 100-digit numbers. Instead, it creates **String *** representations of these numbers and passes them as arguments to Web-service methods that handle such tasks for us.

Line 18 of Fig. 17.18 includes our **WebService.h** header file. Line 11 of Fig. 17.19 instantiates **remoteInteger**, an instance of the proxy class. Method **equalButton_Click** (lines 122–145) uses **remoteInteger** to call Web-service method **EqualTo** to determine whether the integers are equal. Methods **smallerButton_Click** (lines 149–171), **biggerButton_Click** (lines 175–197), **subtractButton_Click** (lines 200–225) and **addButton_Click** (lines 228–253) invoke Web-service methods **Smaller** (line 159), **Bigger** (line 185), **Subtract** (line 211) and **Add** (line 251) using **remoteInteger**.

17.10 Session Tracking

Originally, critics accused the Internet and e-businesses of failing to provide the customized services typically experienced in brick-and-mortar stores. To address this problem, e-businesses began to establish mechanisms by which they could personalize users' browsing experiences, tailoring content to individual users while enabling them to bypass irrelevant information. Businesses achieve this level of service by tracking each customer's movement through the Internet and combining the collected data with information that the consumer provides, including billing information, personal preferences, interests and hobbies.

Personalization makes it possible for e-businesses to communicate effectively with their customers and improves users' ability to locate desired products and services. Companies that provide content of particular interest to users can establish relationships with customers and build on those relationships over time. Futhermore, by targeting consumers with personal offers, advertisements, promotions and services, e-businesses create customer loyalty. At Web sites such as **MSN.com** and **CNN.com**, sophisticated technology allows visitors to customize home pages to suit their individual needs and preferences. Similarly, online shopping sites often store personal information for customers and target them with notifications and special offers tailored to their interests. Such services can create customer bases that visit sites more frequently and make purchases from those sites more regularly.

A trade-off exists, however, between personalized e-business service and *privacy protection*. Whereas some consumers embrace the idea of tailored content, others fear the release of information that they provide to e-businesses or that is collected about them by tracking technologies will have adverse consequences on their lives. Consumers and privacy advocates ask: What if the e-businesses to which we give personal data sell or give that information to other organizations without our knowledge? What if we do not want our actions on the Internet—a supposedly anonymous medium—to be tracked and recorded by unknown parties? What if unauthorized parties gain access to sensitive private data, such as credit-card numbers or medical history? All of these are questions that must be debated and addressed by consumers, e-businesses and lawmakers, alike.

To provide personalized services to consumers, e-businesses must be able to recognize specific clients when they request information from a site. As we have discussed, HTTP enables the request/response system on which the Web operates. Unfortunately, HTTP is a stateless protocol—it does not support persistent connections that would enable Web servers to maintain state information for particular clients. This means that Web servers have no capacity to determine whether a request comes from a particular client or whether the same or different clients generate a series of requests. To circumvent this problem, sites such as **MSN.com** and **CNN.com** provide mechanisms by which they identify individual clients. A *session ID* represents a unique client on the Internet. If the client leaves a site and then returns later, the client will be recognized as the same user. To help the server distinguish among clients, each client must identify itself to the server. The tracking of individual clients, known as *session tracking*, can be achieved in one of a number of ways. One popular technique uses cookies (Section 17.10.1); another employs .NET's **HttpSession-State** object (Section 17.10.2). Additional session-tracking techniques include the use of hidden input form elements and URL rewriting. Using hidden form elements, the application writes its session-tracking data into a form in the Web page that it returns to the client in response to a prior request. When the user submits the form in the new Web page, all the form data, including the hidden fields, are sent to the form handler on the Web server. When a Web site employs URL rewriting, the site embeds session-tracking information directly in the URLs of the hyperlinks that the user clicks to send subsequent requests to the Web server.

17.10.1 Cookies

A popular way to customize Web pages for particular users is via *cookies*. A cookie is a text file that a Web site stores on an individual's computer to enable the site to track that individual's actions and preferences. The first time a user visits the Web site, the user's computer might receive a cookie that contains a unique identifier for that user. This cookie is reactivated each subsequent time the user visits that site. The Web site uses this cookie to identify the user and to store information, such as the user's zip code or other data that might facilitate the distribution of user-specific content. The collected information is intended to be an anonymous record for personalizing the user's future visits to the site. Cookies in a shopping application might store unique identifiers for users. When a user performs a task resulting in a request to the Web server, such as adding items to an online shopping cart, the server receives a cookie containing the user's unique identifier. The server then uses the unique identifier to locate the user's shopping cart and perform any necessary processing.

In addition to identifying users, cookies also can indicate a client's preferences. When a Web application receives a communication from a client, the application could examine the cookie(s) it sent to the client during previous communications, identify the client's preferences and immediately display products that are of interest to the client.

Every HTTP-based interaction between a client and a server includes a header that contains information either about the request (when the communication is from the client to the server) or about the response (when the communication is from the server to the client). When a Web application receives a request, the header includes such information as the request type (e.g., **GET**) and any cookies that the server has stored on the client machine. When the server formulates its response, the header information includes any cookies that the server wants to store on the client computer, as well as such information as the MIME type of the response.

Programmers can set an *expiration date* for a cookie—the Web browser maintains the cookie until the expiration date. The expiration date of a cookie can be set via the cookie's **Expires** property of class **HttpCookie**, which is used to implement cookies in .NET. When the browser requests a resource from a Web server, cookies previously sent to the client by that Web server are returned to the Web server as part of the request. Cookies are deleted when they expire. We summarize some commonly used **HttpCookie** properties in Fig. 17.21.

Properties	Description
Domain	Returns a string that contains the cookie's domain (i.e., the domain of the Web server from which the cookie was downloaded). This determines which Web servers can receive the cookie. By default, cookies are sent to the Web server that originally sent the cookie to the client.
Expires	Returns a DateTime object indicating when the browser can delete the cookie.
Name	Returns a string containing the cookie's name.
Path	Returns a string containing the URL prefix for the cookie. Cookies can be "targeted" to specific URLs that include directories on the Web server, enabling the programmer to specify the location of the cookie. By default, a cookie is returned to services that operate in the same directory as the service that sent the cookie or a subdirectory of that directory.
Secure	Returns a boolean value indicating whether the cookie should be transmitted using a secure protocol.
Value	Returns a string containing the cookie's value.

Fig. 17.21 HttpCookie properties.

17.10.2 Session Tracking with HttpSessionState

The .NET Framework provides session-tracking capabilities with the *HttpSession-State* class. Every Web-service application includes an HttpSessionState object, which is accessible through property *Session* of class WebService. When a Web service method is called, an HttpSessionState object is created and assigned to the Web service's Session property. We often refer to the property Session as the Session object.

 ### Software Engineering Observation 17.3

Visual C++ .NET Web-based applications must not use instance variables to maintain client-state information, because clients accessing that Web application in parallel might overwrite the shared instance variables. Web applications should maintain client-state information in HttpSessionState objects, because such objects are specific to each client.

An HttpSessionState object can store key-value pairs, where the key contains the name of a session attribute, and the value contains that attribute's value. In session terminology, these are called *session items*, and they are placed into an HttpSession-State object by calling method Add. One of the primary benefits of using HttpSessionState objects is that HttpSessionState objects can store any type of object as an attribute value. This provides programmers with increased flexibility in determining the type of state information they wish to maintain for their clients. If the application calls method Add to add an attribute that has the same name as an attribute previously stored in a session, the object associated with that attribute is replaced.

Figure 17.22 lists some common HttpSessionState properties. Property *SessionID* contains the *session's unique ID*. The first time a client connects to the Web server, the Web server generates the client's session ID. Property *Timeout* specifies the maximum amount of time that an HttpSessionState object can be inactive before it is discarded.

Properties	Description
Count	Specifies the number of key-value pairs in the **Session** object.
IsNewSession	Indicates whether this is a new session (i.e., whether the session was created when the page was loaded).
IsReadOnly	Indicates whether the **Session** object is read-only.
Keys	Returns a collection containing the **Session** object's keys.
SessionID	Returns the session's unique ID.
Timeout	Specifies the maximum number of minutes during which a session can be inactive (i.e., no requests are made) before the session expires. By default, this property is set to 20 minutes.

Fig. 17.22 `HttpSessionState` properties.

17.11 Session Tracking in Web Services

In this section, we incorporate session tracking into a Web service. Sometimes, it makes sense for client applications to call several methods from the same Web service or to call some methods several times. It would be beneficial for the Web service to maintain state information for the client. Using session tracking can be beneficial, because information that is stored as part of the session will not need to be passed back and forth between the Web service and the client. This will not only cause the client application to run faster, but it will require less effort on the part of the programmer (who likely will have to pass less information to a Web-service method).

Storing session information also can provide for a more intuitive Web service. In the following example, we create a Web service designed to assist with the computations involved in playing a game of Blackjack (Fig. 17.23–Fig. 17.27). We then use this Web service to create a dealer for a game of Blackjack. This dealer handles the details for our deck of cards. The information is stored as part of the session, so that one set of cards does not get mixed up with another deck of cards being used by another client application. Our example uses the subject of casino Blackjack rules that follows:

> The dealer and the player each receive two cards. The player's cards are dealt face up. Only one of the dealer's cards is dealt face up. Then, the player can begin taking additional cards, one at a time. These cards are dealt face up, and the player decides when to stop taking cards. If the sum of the player's cards exceeds 21, the game is over, and the player loses. When the player is satisfied with the current set of cards, the player "stays" (i.e., stops taking cards), and the dealer's hidden card is revealed. If the dealer's total is less than 17, the dealer must take another card; otherwise, the dealer must stay. The dealer must continue to take cards until the sum of the dealer's cards is greater than or equal to 17. If the dealer exceeds 21, the player wins. Otherwise, the hand with the higher point total wins. If both sets of cards have the same point total, the game is a "push" (i.e., a tie), and no one wins. Finally, if a player's first two cards total 21, the player immediately wins. This type of win is known as a "Blackjack."

The Web service that we create provides methods to deal a card and to count cards in a hand, determining a value for a specific hand. Each card is represented by a string in the form "`face suit`," where `face` is a digit that represents the face of the card, and `suit` is a digit that represents the suit of the card. After the Web service is created, we create a Windows application that uses these methods to implement a game of Blackjack.

```
1   // Fig. 17.23: BlackJackService.h
2   // BlackJackService class header file.
3
4   #pragma once
5
6   #using <mscorlib.dll>
7   #using <system.dll>
8   #using <system.windows.forms.dll>
9   #using <system.web.services.dll>
10
11  using namespace System;
12  using namespace System::Web::Services;
13
14  namespace BlackjackService
15  {
16     [ WebServiceAttribute(
17        Namespace = "http://www.deitel.com/ch17/BlackJack",
18        Description = "A Web service that provides methods "
19        "to manipulate a deck of cards." ) ]
20     public __gc class BlackjackService : public WebService
21     {
22     public:
23        BlackjackService();
24
25        [ WebMethod( EnableSession = true,
26           Description = "Deals the next card in the deck." ) ]
27        String *DealCard();
28
29        [ WebMethod( EnableSession = true,
30           Description = "Create and shuffle a deck of cards." ) ]
31        void Shuffle();
32
33        [ WebMethod( Description = "Compute a "
34           "numerical value for the current hand." ) ]
35        int CountCards( String *dealt );
36
37     private:
38        void InitializeComponent();
39     }; // end class BlackjackService
40  } // end namespace BlackjackService
```

Fig. 17.23 BlackjackService class header file.

```
1   // Fig. 17.24: BlackJackService.cpp
2   // Blackjack Web service which manipulates a deck of cards.
3
4   #include "stdafx.h"
5   #include "BlackJackService.h"
6   #include "Global.asax.h"
7
8   namespace BlackjackService
9   {
10     BlackjackService::BlackjackService()
```

Fig. 17.24 Blackjack Web service. (Part 1 of 3.)

```
11       {
12          InitializeComponent();
13       }
14
15       void BlackjackService::InitializeComponent() {}
16
17       // deal new card
18       String *BlackjackService::DealCard()
19       {
20          String *card = S"2 2";
21
22          // get client's deck
23          ArrayList* deck = dynamic_cast< ArrayList* >(
24             Session->Item[ S"deck" ] );
25          card = Convert::ToString( deck->Item[ 0 ] );
26          deck->RemoveAt( 0 );
27
28          return card;
29       } // end method DealCard
30
31       void BlackjackService::Shuffle()
32       {
33          Random *randomObject = new Random();
34
35          ArrayList *deck = new ArrayList();
36
37          // generate all possible cards
38          for ( int i = 1; i < 14; i++ ) {
39
40             for ( int j = 0; j < 4; j++ ) {
41                deck->Add( String::Concat( Convert::ToString( i ),
42                   S" ", Convert::ToString( j ) ) );
43             }
44          }
45
46          // swap each card with another card randomly
47          for ( int i = 0; i < deck->Count; i++ ) {
48             int newIndex = randomObject->Next( deck->Count );
49             Object *temporary = deck->Item[ i ];
50             deck->Item[ i ] = deck->Item[ newIndex ];
51             deck->Item[ newIndex ] = temporary;
52          }
53
54          // add this deck to user's session state
55          Session->Item[ S"deck" ] = deck;
56       } // end method Shuffle
57
58       // computes value of hand
59       int BlackjackService::CountCards( String *dealt )
60       {
61
62          // split string containing cards
63          __wchar_t tab __gc[] = { '\t' };
```

Fig. 17.24 Blackjack Web service. (Part 2 of 3.)

```
64          String *cards[] = dealt->Split( tab );
65          int total = 0, face, aceCount = 0;
66
67          String *drawn;
68
69          for ( int i = 0; i < cards->Length; i++ ) {
70             drawn = cards[ i ];
71
72             // get face of card
73             face = Int32::Parse(
74                drawn->Substring( 0, drawn->IndexOf( S" " ) ) );
75
76             switch( face ) {
77
78             // if ace, increment number of aces in hand
79             case 1:
80                aceCount++;
81                break;
82
83             // if Jack, Queen or King, add 10 to total
84             case 11: case 12: case 13:
85                total += 10;
86                break;
87
88             // otherwise, add value of face
89             default:
90                total += face;
91                break;
92             } // end switch
93          } // end for
94
95          // if any aces, calculate optimum total
96          if ( aceCount > 0 ) {
97
98             // if it is possible to count one ace as 11, and rest
99             // 1 each, do so; otherwise, count all aces as 1 each
100            if ( total + 11 + aceCount - 1 <= 21 )
101               total += 11 + aceCount - 1;
102            else
103               total += aceCount;
104         }
105
106         return total;
107      } // end method CountCards
108   } // end namespace BlackjackService
```

Fig. 17.24 Blackjack Web service. (Part 3 of 3.)

Lines 25–27 of Fig. 17.23 define method **DealCard** as a **WebMethod**, with property **EnableSession** set to **true** (line 25). This property needs to be set to **true** to maintain session information. This simple step provides an important advantage to our Web service. The Web service now can use the **HttpSessionState** object's property **Session** to maintain the deck of cards for each client application that wishes to use this Web service. We can use **Session** to store objects for a specific client between method calls.

As we discuss shortly, method **DealCard** removes a card from the deck and returns it to the client. If we were not using a session variable, the deck of cards would need to be passed back and forth with each method call. Not only does the use of session state make the method easier to call (it now requires no arguments), but we avoid the overhead that would occur from sending this information back and forth, making our Web service faster.

In our current implementation, we simply have methods that use session variables. The Web service, however, still cannot ascertain which session variables belong to which user. This is an important point—if the Web service cannot uniquely identify a user, it has failed to perform session tracking properly. If the same client called method **DealCard** twice, two different decks would be manipulated (as if two different users had called **Deal-Card**). To identify various users, the Web service creates a cookie for each user. Unfortunately, the Web service has no way of determining whether cookies are enabled on the client's machine. If the client application wishes to use this Web service, the client must accept this cookie in a *CookieContainer* object. We discuss this more when we look into the client application that uses the **Blackjack** Web service.

Method **DealCard** (lines 18–29 of Fig. 17.24) obtains the current user's deck as an *ArrayList* from the Web service's **Session** object (lines 23–24). You can think of an **ArrayList** as a dynamic array (i.e., its size can change at runtime). Class **ArrayList** is discussed in greater detail in Chapter 19, Data Structures and Collections. The class's method **Add** places an **Object *** in the **ArrayList**. Method **DealCard** then removes the top card from the deck (line 26) and returns the card's value as a **String** pointer (line 28).

Method **Shuffle** (lines 31–56) generates an **ArrayList** representing a card deck, shuffles it and stores the shuffled cards in the client's **Session** object. Lines 38–44 include **for** loops to generate **String**s in the form "**face suit**" to represent each possible card in a deck. Lines 47–52 shuffle the re-created deck by swapping each card with another card in the deck. Line 55 adds the **ArrayList** to the **Session** object to maintain the deck between method calls.

Method **CountCards** (lines 59–107) counts the values of the cards in a hand by trying to attain the highest score possible without going over 21. Precautions need to be taken when calculating the value of the cards, because an ace can be counted as either 1 or 11, and all face cards count as 10.

The string **dealt** is tokenized (i.e., broken up) into its individual cards by calling **String *** method **Split** and passing it an array that contains the tab character. The **for** loop (line 69–93) counts the value of each card. Lines 73–74 retrieve the first integer—the face—and use that value as input to the **switch** statement in line 76. If the card is 1 (an ace), the program increments variable **aceCount**. Because an ace can have two values, additional logic is required to process aces. If the card is a 13, 12 or 11 (King, Queen or Jack), the program adds 10 to the total. If the card is anything else, the program increases the total by that value.

In lines 96–104, the aces are counted after all the other cards. If several aces are included in a hand, only one can be counted as 11. (If two were counted as 11, we would already have a hand value of 22, which is a losing hand.) We then determine whether we can count an ace as 11 without exceeding 21. If this is possible, line 101 adjusts the total accordingly. Otherwise, line 103 adjusts the total by counting each ace as 1 point.

Method **CountCards** attempts to maximize the value of the current cards without exceeding 21. Imagine, for example, that the dealer has a 7 and then receives an ace. The new total could be either 8 or 18. However, **CountCards** always tries the maximize the value of the cards without going over 21, so the new total is 18.

Now we use the **Blackjack** Web service in a Windows application called **Game** (Fig. 17.25–Fig. 17.27). This program uses an instance of **BlackjackWebService** to represent the dealer, calling its **DealCard** and **CountCards** methods. The Web service keeps track of both the player's and the dealer's cards (i.e., all the cards that have been dealt).

```
1   // Fig. 17.25: Blackjack.h
2   // Blackjack class header file.
3
4   #pragma once
5
6   #using <mscorlib.dll>
7   #using <system.dll>
8   #using <system.drawing.dll>
9   #using <system.windows.forms.dll>
10
11  using namespace System;
12  using namespace System::Drawing;
13  using namespace System::Collections;
14  using namespace System::Windows::Forms;
15  using namespace System::Net;
16
17  #include "WebService.h"
18
19  // game that uses Blackjack Web service
20  public __gc class Blackjack : public Form
21  {
22  public:
23     __value enum GameStatus : int { PUSH, LOSE, WIN, BLACKJACK };
24
25     Blackjack();
26     void DisplayCard( int card, String *cardValue );
27     void GameOver( GameStatus winner );
28
29  protected:
30     void stayButton_Click( Object *sender, EventArgs *e );
31     void hitButton_Click( Object *sender, EventArgs *e );
32     void dealButton_Click( Object *sender, EventArgs *e );
33
34  private:
35     static const int PICTUREBOX_TOTAL = 22;
36     static PictureBox *pictureBoxArray[] =
37        new PictureBox*[ PICTUREBOX_TOTAL ];
38
39     Button *dealButton, *hitButton, *stayButton;
40
41     BlackjackService *dealer;
42     String *dealersCards, *playersCards;
43     ArrayList *cardBoxes;
44     int playerCard, dealerCard;
45
46     // labels displaying game status, dealer and player
```

Fig. 17.25 Blackjack class header file. (Part 1 of 2.)

```
47        Label *dealerLabel, *playerLabel, *statusLabel;
48
49        void InitializeComponent();
50        void DealerPlay();
51     }; // end class Blackjack
```

Fig. 17.25 Blackjack class header file. (Part 2 of 2.)

```
1    // Fig. 17.26: Blackjack.cpp
2    // Blackjack game that uses the Blackjack Web service.
3
4    #include "Blackjack.h"
5
6    Blackjack::Blackjack()
7    {
8       InitializeComponent();
9
10      dealer = new BlackjackService();
11
12      // allow session state
13      dealer->CookieContainer = new CookieContainer();
14
15      cardBoxes = new ArrayList();
16
17      // put PictureBoxes into cardBoxes
18      for ( int i = 0; i < PICTUREBOX_TOTAL; i++ )
19         cardBoxes->Add( pictureBoxArray[ i ] );
20   } // end method Blackjack
21
22   void Blackjack::InitializeComponent()
23   {
24      int i = 0;
25      this->hitButton = new Button();
26      this->dealButton = new Button();
27      this->stayButton = new Button();
28      this->statusLabel = new Label();
29      this->dealerLabel = new Label();
30      this->playerLabel = new Label();
31      this->SuspendLayout();
32
33      // y-coordinates for the four rows of picture boxes
34      int y1 = 56, y2 = 168, y3 = 336, y4 = 448;
35
36      // number of picture boxes in alternating rows
37      int row1 = 6, row2 = 5;
38
39      // x-values for the four rows of picture boxes
40      int xValues __gc[] = { 16, 104, 192, 280, 368, 456 };
41
42      // initialize picture boxes
43      for ( ; i < PICTUREBOX_TOTAL; i++ ) {
44         pictureBoxArray[ i ] = new PictureBox();
45         pictureBoxArray[ i ]->BackColor = Color::Green;
46         pictureBoxArray[ i ]->BorderStyle = BorderStyle::Fixed3D;
```

Fig. 17.26 Blackjack game that uses the Blackjack Web service. (Part 1 of 8.)

```
47          pictureBoxArray[ i ]->Size = Drawing::Size( 70, 90 );
48          pictureBoxArray[ i ]->TabStop = false;
49       }
50
51       // set positions of picture boxes in first row
52       for ( i = 0; i < row1; i++ ) {
53          pictureBoxArray[ i ]->Location =
54             Point( xValues[ i ], y1 );
55       }
56
57       // set picture boxes in second row
58       for ( ; i < row1 + row2; i++ ) {
59          pictureBoxArray[ i ]->Location =
60             Point( xValues[ i % row1 ], y2 );
61       }
62
63       // set picture boxes in third row
64       for ( ; i < PICTUREBOX_TOTAL - row1; i++ ) {
65          pictureBoxArray[ i ]->Location =
66             Point( xValues[ i % ( row1 + row2 ) ], y3 );
67       }
68
69       // set picture boxes in last row
70       for ( ; i < PICTUREBOX_TOTAL; i++ ) {
71          pictureBoxArray[ i ]->Location =
72             Point( xValues[ i % ( row1 + 2 * row2 ) ], y4 );
73       }
74
75       // hitButton
76       this->hitButton->BackColor = Color::Green;
77       this->hitButton->Font = new Drawing::Font(
78          S"Microsoft Sans Serif", 12, FontStyle::Bold,
79          GraphicsUnit::Point, 0 );
80       this->hitButton->ForeColor = Color::White;
81       this->hitButton->Location = Point( 560, 112 );
82       this->hitButton->Name = S"hitButton";
83       this->hitButton->Size = Drawing::Size( 112, 56 );
84       this->hitButton->TabIndex = 2;
85       this->hitButton->Text = S"Hit";
86       this->hitButton->Click += new EventHandler( this,
87          hitButton_Click );
88       this->hitButton->Enabled = false;
89
90       // dealButton
91       this->dealButton->BackColor = Color::Green;
92       this->dealButton->Font = new Drawing::Font(
93          S"Microsoft Sans Serif", 12, FontStyle::Bold,
94          GraphicsUnit::Point, 0 );
95       this->dealButton->ForeColor = Color::White;
96       this->dealButton->Location = Point( 560, 40 );
97       this->dealButton->Name = S"dealButton";
98       this->dealButton->Size = Drawing::Size( 112, 56 );
99       this->dealButton->TabIndex = 1;
100      this->dealButton->Text = S"Deal";
```

Fig. 17.26 Blackjack game that uses the **Blackjack** Web service. (Part 2 of 8.)

```
101      this->dealButton->Click += new EventHandler(
102         this, dealButton_Click );
103
104      // stayButton
105      this->stayButton->BackColor = Color::Green;
106      this->stayButton->Font = new Drawing::Font(
107         S"Microsoft Sans Serif", 12, FontStyle::Bold,
108         GraphicsUnit::Point, 0 );
109      this->stayButton->ForeColor = Color::White;
110      this->stayButton->Location = Point( 560, 184 );
111      this->stayButton->Name = S"stayButton";
112      this->stayButton->Size = Drawing::Size( 112, 56 );
113      this->stayButton->TabIndex = 3;
114      this->stayButton->Text = S"Stay";
115      this->stayButton->Click += new EventHandler( this,
116         stayButton_Click );
117      this->stayButton->Enabled = false;
118
119      // statusLabel
120      this->statusLabel->Font = new Drawing::Font(
121         S"Tahoma", 20.25, FontStyle::Bold,
122         GraphicsUnit::Point, 0 );
123      this->statusLabel->ForeColor = Color::Red;
124      this->statusLabel->Location = Point( 528, 280 );
125      this->statusLabel->Name = S"statusLabel";
126      this->statusLabel->Size = Drawing::Size( 160, 72 );
127      this->statusLabel->TabIndex = 4;
128
129      // dealerLabel
130      this->dealerLabel->Font = new Drawing::Font(
131         S"Microsoft Sans Serif", 17.5, FontStyle::Bold,
132         GraphicsUnit::Point, 0 );
133      this->dealerLabel->ForeColor = Color::White;
134      this->dealerLabel->Location = Point( 16, 16 );
135      this->dealerLabel->Name = S"dealerLabel";
136      this->dealerLabel->Size = Drawing::Size( 184, 32 );
137      this->dealerLabel->TabIndex = 5;
138      this->dealerLabel->Text = S"Dealer\'s Cards";
139
140      // playerLabel
141      this->playerLabel->Font = new Drawing::Font(
142         S"Microsoft Sans Serif", 17.5, FontStyle::Bold,
143         GraphicsUnit::Point, 0 );
144      this->playerLabel->ForeColor = Color::White;
145      this->playerLabel->Location = Point( 16, 296 );
146      this->playerLabel->Name = S"playerLabel";
147      this->playerLabel->Size = Drawing::Size( 184, 32 );
148      this->playerLabel->TabIndex = 6;
149      this->playerLabel->Text = S"Player\'s Cards";
150
151      // Blackjack
152      this->AutoScaleBaseSize = Drawing::Size( 5, 13 );
153      this->BackColor = Color::Green;
154      this->ClientSize = Drawing::Size( 704, 557 );
```

Fig. 17.26 Blackjack game that uses the **Blackjack** Web service. (Part 3 of 8.)

```
155      Control *controls[] = { this->playerLabel, this->dealerLabel,
156         this->statusLabel, this->stayButton, this->hitButton,
157         this->dealButton };
158      this->Controls->AddRange( controls );
159      this->Controls->AddRange( pictureBoxArray );
160      this->Name = S"Blackjack";
161      this->Text = S"Blackjack";
162      this->ResumeLayout();
163   } // end method InitializeComponent
164
165   // deals cards to dealer while dealer's total is
166   // less than 17, then computes value of each hand
167   // and determines winner
168   void Blackjack::stayButton_Click( Object *sender,
169      EventArgs *e )
170   {
171      stayButton->Enabled = false;
172      hitButton->Enabled = false;
173      dealButton->Enabled = true;
174      DealerPlay();
175   } // end method stayButton_Click
176
177   // process dealers turn
178   void Blackjack::DealerPlay()
179   {
180
181      // while value of dealer's hand is below 17,
182      // dealer must take cards
183      while ( dealer->CountCards( dealersCards ) < 17 ) {
184         dealersCards = String::Concat( dealersCards, S"\t",
185            dealer->DealCard() );
186         DisplayCard( dealerCard, S"" );
187         dealerCard++;
188         MessageBox::Show( S"Dealer takes a card" );
189      }
190
191      int dealersTotal = dealer->CountCards( dealersCards );
192      int playersTotal = dealer->CountCards( playersCards );
193
194      // if dealer busted, player wins
195      if ( dealersTotal > 21 ) {
196         GameOver( GameStatus::WIN );
197
198         return;
199      }
200
201      // if dealer and player have not exceeded 21,
202      // higher score wins; equal scores is a push.
203      if ( dealersTotal > playersTotal )
204         GameOver( GameStatus::LOSE );
205      else if ( playersTotal > dealersTotal )
206         GameOver( GameStatus::WIN );
207      else
208         GameOver( GameStatus::PUSH );
```

Fig. 17.26 Blackjack game that uses the **Blackjack** Web service. (Part 4 of 8.)

```
209  } // end method DealerPlay
210
211  // deal another card to player
212  void Blackjack::hitButton_Click( Object *sender,
213     EventArgs *e )
214  {
215
216     // get player another card
217     String *card = dealer->DealCard();
218     playersCards = String::Concat( playersCards, S"\t", card );
219     DisplayCard( playerCard, card );
220     playerCard++;
221
222     int total = dealer->CountCards( playersCards );
223
224     // if player exceeds 21, house wins
225     if ( total > 21 )
226        GameOver( GameStatus::LOSE );
227
228     // if player has 21, they cannot take more cards
229     // the dealer plays
230     if ( total == 21 ) {
231        hitButton->Enabled = false;
232        DealerPlay();
233     }
234  } // end method hitButton_Click
235
236  // deal two cards each to dealer and player
237  void Blackjack::dealButton_Click( Object *sender,
238     EventArgs *e )
239  {
240     String *card;
241
242     // clear card images
243     for ( int i = 0; i < cardBoxes->Count; i++ )
244        ( dynamic_cast< PictureBox* >(
245           cardBoxes->Item[ i ] ) )->Image = 0;
246
247     // clear status from previous game
248     statusLabel->Text = S"";
249
250     // shuffle cards
251     dealer->Shuffle();
252
253     // deal two cards to player
254     playersCards = dealer->DealCard();
255     DisplayCard( 11, playersCards );
256     card = dealer->DealCard();
257     DisplayCard( 12, card );
258     playersCards = String::Concat( playersCards, S"\t", card );
259
260     // deal two cards to dealer, only display face
261     // of first card
262     dealersCards = dealer->DealCard() ;
```

Fig. 17.26 Blackjack game that uses the **Blackjack** Web service. (Part 5 of 8.)

```
263     DisplayCard( 0, dealersCards );
264     card = dealer->DealCard();
265     DisplayCard( 1, S"" );
266     dealersCards = String::Concat( dealersCards, S"\t", card );
267
268     stayButton->Enabled = true;
269     hitButton->Enabled = true;
270     dealButton->Enabled = false;
271
272     int dealersTotal = dealer->CountCards( dealersCards );
273     int playersTotal = dealer->CountCards( playersCards );
274
275     // if hands equal 21, it is a push
276     if ( dealersTotal == playersTotal && dealersTotal == 21 )
277        GameOver( GameStatus::PUSH );
278
279     // if player has 21 player wins with blackjack
280     else if ( playersTotal == 21 )
281        GameOver( GameStatus::BLACKJACK );
282
283     // if dealer has 21, dealer wins
284     else if ( dealersTotal == 21 )
285        GameOver( GameStatus::LOSE );
286
287     dealerCard = 2;
288     playerCard = 13;
289  } // end method dealButton_Click
290
291  // displays card represented by cardValue in
292  // PictureBox with number card
293  void Blackjack::DisplayCard( int card, String *cardValue )
294  {
295
296     // retrieve appropriate PictureBox from ArrayList
297     PictureBox *displayBox = dynamic_cast< PictureBox* >(
298        cardBoxes->Item[ card ] );
299
300     // if string representing card is empty,
301     // set displayBox to display back of card
302     if ( cardValue == S"" ) {
303        displayBox->Image =
304           Image::FromFile( S"blackjack_images\\cardback.png" );
305
306        return;
307     }
308
309     // retrieve face value of card from cardValue
310     int faceNumber = Int32::Parse( cardValue->Substring( 0,
311        cardValue->IndexOf( S" " ) ) );
312
313     String *face = faceNumber.ToString();
314
315     // retrieve the suit of the card from cardValue
316     String *suit = cardValue->Substring(
```

Fig. 17.26 Blackjack game that uses the **Blackjack** Web service. (Part 6 of 8.)

```
317                cardValue->IndexOf( S" " ) + 1 );
318
319        char suitLetter;
320
321        // determine if suit is other than clubs
322        switch ( Convert::ToInt32( suit ) ) {
323
324            // suit is clubs
325            case 0:
326                suitLetter = 'c';
327                break;
328
329            // suit is diamonds
330            case 1:
331                suitLetter = 'd';
332                break;
333
334            // suit is hearts
335            case 2:
336                suitLetter = 'h';
337                break;
338
339            // else suit is spades
340            default:
341                suitLetter = 's';
342                break;
343        } // end switch
344
345        // set displayBox to display appropriate image
346        displayBox->Image = Image::FromFile(
347            String::Concat( S"blackjack_images\\", face,
348            Char::ToString( suitLetter ), S".png" ) );
349    } // end method DisplayCard
350
351    // displays all player cards and shows
352    // appropriate game status message
353    void Blackjack::GameOver( GameStatus winner )
354    {
355        __wchar_t tab __gc[] = { '\t' };
356        String *cards[] = dealersCards->Split( tab );
357
358        for ( int i = 0; i < cards->Length; i++ )
359            DisplayCard( i, cards[ i ] );
360
361        // push
362        if ( winner == GameStatus::PUSH )
363            statusLabel->Text = S"It's a tie!";
364
365        // player loses
366        else if ( winner == GameStatus::LOSE )
367            statusLabel->Text = S"You Lose Try Again!";
368
369        // player wins
370        else if ( winner == GameStatus::WIN )
```

Fig. 17.26 Blackjack game that uses the **Blackjack** Web service. (Part 7 of 8.)

```
371         statusLabel->Text = S"You Win!";
372
373     // player has won with blackjack
374     else
375         statusLabel->Text = S"BlackJack!";
376
377     stayButton->Enabled = false;
378     hitButton->Enabled = false;
379     dealButton->Enabled = true;
380 } // end method GameOver
```

Fig. 17.26 Blackjack game that uses the **Blackjack** Web service. (Part 8 of 8.)

```
1  // Fig. 17.27: BlackjackTest.cpp
2  // Driver file for application.
3
4  #include "Blackjack.h"
5
6  int __stdcall WinMain()
7  {
8     Application::Run( new Blackjack() );
9
10    return 0;
11 } // end function WinMain
```

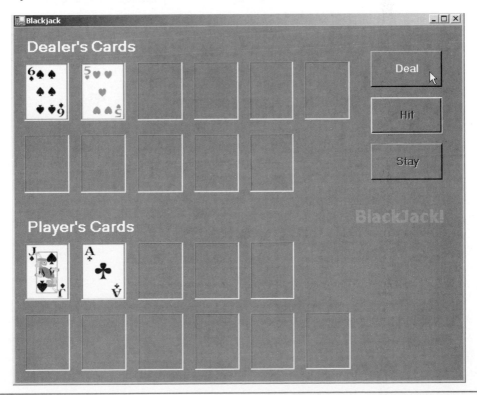

Fig. 17.27 Blackjack game demonstration. (Part 1 of 2.)

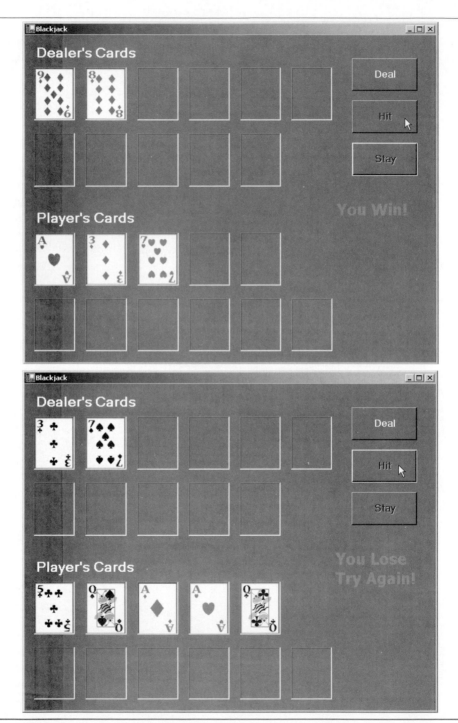

Fig. 17.27 Blackjack game demonstration. (Part 2 of 2.)

Each player has 11 **PictureBox**es—the maximum number of cards that can be dealt without exceeding 21. These **PictureBox**es are placed in an **ArrayList**, allowing us to index the **ArrayList** to determine which **PictureBox** displays the card image.

Previously, we mentioned that the client must provide a way to accept any cookies created by the Web service to identify users. Line 13 in the constructor (Fig. 17.26) creates a new **CookieContainer** object for the **CookieContainer** property of **dealer**. The **CookieContainer** property is a member of class *SoapHttpClientProtocol*, the base class of our proxy. Class *CookieContainer* (defined in namespace **System::Net**) acts as a storage space for an object of the **HttpCookie** class. Creating the **CookieContainer** allows the Web service to maintain session state for the current client. This **CookieContainer** stores a **Cookie** with a unique identifier that the server can use to recognize the client when that client makes future requests. By default, the **CookieContainer** is set to the null value (**NULL**), and a new **Session** object is created by the Web service for each client.

Method **GameOver** (lines 353–380) displays all the dealer's cards (many of which are turned face down during the game) and shows the appropriate message in the status **PictureBox**. Method **GameOver** receives as an argument a member of the **GameStatus** enumeration (defined in line 23 of Fig. 17.25). The enumeration represents whether the player tied, lost or won the game; its four members are **PUSH**, **LOSE**, **WIN** and **BLACKJACK**.

When the player clicks the **Deal** button (event handler on lines 237–289), all the **PictureBox**es are cleared, the deck is shuffled and the player and dealer receive two cards each. If both obtain scores of 21, method **GameOver** is called and is passed **GameStatus::PUSH**. If only the player has 21, **GameOver** is called and is passed **GameStatus::BLACKJACK**. If only the dealer has 21, method **GameOver** is called and is passed **GameStatus::LOSE**.

Finally, if **GameOver** is not called, the player can take additional cards by clicking the **Hit** button (event handler on lines 212–234). Each time a player clicks **Hit**, the player is dealt one card, which is displayed in the GUI. If the player exceeds 21, the game is over, and the player loses. If the player has exactly 21, the player is not allowed to take any more cards.

Players can click the **Stay** button to indicate that they do not want to risk being dealt another card. In the event handler for this event (lines 168–175), all three buttons are disabled, and method **DealerPlay** is called. This method (lines 178–209) causes the dealer to keep taking cards until the dealer's hand is worth 17 or more. If the dealer's hand exceeds 21, the player wins; otherwise, the values of the hands are compared, and **GameOver** is called with the appropriate argument.

Method **DisplayCard** (lines 293–349) retrieves the appropriate card image. It takes as arguments an integer representing the index of the **PictureBox** in the **ArrayList** that must have its image set and a string representing the card. An empty string indicates that we wish to display the back of a card; otherwise, the program extracts the face and suit from the **String** object and uses this information to find the correct image. The **switch** statement (lines 322–343) converts the number representing the suit into an integer and assigns the appropriate character to **suitLetter** (c for Clubs, d for Diamonds, h for Hearts and s for Spades). The character **suitLetter** completes the image's file name.

17.12 Case Study: Temperature-Information Application

This case study discusses both a Web service that presents weather forecasts for various cities around the United States and a Windows application that employs the Web service. The Web service uses networking capabilities to display the forecasts; it parses a Web page containing the required information and then extracts weather-forecast data.

First, we present Web service **TemperatureServer** in Fig. 17.28 and Fig. 17.29. This Web service reads a Web page and collects information about the temperature and weather conditions in several American cities. [*Note*: At the time of publication, this program runs in the manner that we describe. However, if changes are made to the Web page from which the program retrieves data, the program might work differently or not at all. Please check our Web site at **www.deitel.com** for updates.]

```cpp
1   // Fig. 17.28: TemperatureServer.h
2   // TemperatureServer class header file.
3
4   #using <mscorlib.dll>
5   #using <system.dll>
6   #using <system.windows.forms.dll>
7   #using <System.Web.Services.dll>
8
9   using namespace System;
10  using namespace System::Collections;
11  using namespace System::Web::Services;
12  using namespace System::IO;
13  using namespace System::Net;
14
15  #include "CityWeather.h"
16
17  namespace TemperatureServer
18  {
19     [ WebServiceAttribute( Namespace =
20        "http://www.deitel.com/ch20/TemperatureServer",
21        Description = "A Web service that provides information "
22        "from the National Weather Service." ) ]
23     public __gc class TemperatureServer : public WebService
24     {
25     public:
26        TemperatureServer();
27
28        [ WebMethod( EnableSession = true, Description = "Method "
29           "to read information from the weather service." ) ]
30        void UpdateWeatherConditions();
31
32        [ WebMethod( EnableSession = true, Description =
33           "Method to retrieve a list of cities." ) ]
34        String *Cities()[];
35
36        [ WebMethod( EnableSession = true, Description = "Method"
37           " to retrieve weather descriptions for a list "
38           "of cities." ) ]
```

Fig. 17.28 **TemperatureServer** class header file. (Part 1 of 2.)

```
39              String *Descriptions()[];
40
41              [ WebMethod( EnableSession = true, Description = "Method "
42                 "to retrieve the temperature for a list of cities." ) ]
43              String *Temperatures()[];
44
45         private:
46              void InitializeComponent();
47         }; // end class TemperatureServer
48    } // end namespace TemperatureServer
```

Fig. 17.28 TemperatureServer class header file. (Part 2 of 2.)

```
1     // Fig. 17.29: TemperatureServer.cpp
2     // TemperatureServer Web service that extracts weather
3     // information from a Web page.
4
5     #include "stdafx.h"
6     #include "Global.asax.h"
7     #include "TemperatureServer.h"
8
9     namespace TemperatureServer
10    {
11        TemperatureServer::TemperatureServer()
12        {
13            InitializeComponent();
14        }
15
16        void TemperatureServer::InitializeComponent() {}
17
18        void TemperatureServer::UpdateWeatherConditions()
19        {
20
21            // create WebClient to get access to Web page
22            WebClient *myClient = new WebClient();
23            ArrayList *cityList = new ArrayList();
24
25            // get StreamReader for response so we can read page
26            StreamReader *input = new StreamReader(
27               myClient->OpenRead(
28               S"http://iwin.nws.noaa.gov/iwin/us/traveler.html" ) );
29
30            String *separator = S"TAV12";
31
32            // locate line that starts with "TAV12"
33            while ( !input->ReadLine()->StartsWith( separator ) )
34               ; // do nothing
35
36            // day format and night format
37            String *dayFormat =
38               S"CITY              WEA     HI/LO   WEA     HI/LO";
```

Fig. 17.29 TemperatureServer Web service. (Part 1 of 3.)

```
39          String *nightFormat =
40             S"CITY              WEA      LO/HI   WEA      LO/HI";
41          String *inputLine = S"";
42
43          // locate header that begins weather information
44          do {
45             inputLine = input->ReadLine();
46          } while ( !inputLine->Equals( dayFormat ) &&
47             !inputLine->Equals( nightFormat ) );
48
49          // get first city's data
50          inputLine = input->ReadLine();
51
52          while ( inputLine->Length > 28 ) {
53
54             // create CityWeather object for city
55             CityWeather *weather = new CityWeather(
56                inputLine->Substring( 0, 16 ),
57                inputLine->Substring( 16, 7 ),
58                inputLine->Substring( 23, 7 ) );
59
60             // add to List
61             cityList->Add( weather );
62
63             // get next city's data
64             inputLine = input->ReadLine();
65          } // end while
66
67          // close connection to NWS server
68          input->Close();
69
70          // add city list to user session
71          Session->Add( S"cityList", cityList );
72       } // end method UpdateWeatherConditions
73
74       // gets all city names
75       String *TemperatureServer::Cities()[]
76       {
77          ArrayList *cityList = dynamic_cast< ArrayList * >(
78             Session->Item[ S"cityList" ] );
79          String *cities[] = new String*[ cityList->Count ];
80
81          // retrieve names for cities
82          for ( int i = 0; i < cityList->Count; i++ ) {
83             CityWeather* weather = dynamic_cast< CityWeather * >(
84                cityList->Item[ i ] );
85
86             cities[ i ] = weather->CityName;
87          }
88
89          return cities;
90       } // end method Cities
91
92       // gets all city descriptions
```

Fig. 17.29 TemperatureServer Web service. (Part 2 of 3.)

```
93      String *TemperatureServer::Descriptions()[]
94      {
95          ArrayList *cityList = dynamic_cast< ArrayList* >(
96              Session->Item[ S"cityList" ] );
97          String *descriptions[] = new String*[ cityList->Count ];
98
99          // retrieve weather descriptions for all cities
100         for ( int i = 0; i < cityList->Count; i++ ) {
101             CityWeather *weather = dynamic_cast< CityWeather* >(
102                 cityList->Item[ i ] );
103
104             descriptions[ i ] = weather->Description;
105         }
106
107         return descriptions;
108     } // end method Descriptions
109
110     // obtains each city temperature
111     String *TemperatureServer::Temperatures()[]
112     {
113         ArrayList *cityList = dynamic_cast< ArrayList* >(
114             Session->Item[ S"cityList" ] );
115         String *temperatures[] = new String*[ cityList->Count ];
116
117         // retrieve temperatures for all cities
118         for ( int i = 0; i < cityList->Count; i++ ) {
119
120             CityWeather *weather = dynamic_cast< CityWeather* >(
121                 cityList->Item[ i ] ) ;
122             temperatures[ i ] = weather->Temperature;
123         }
124
125         return temperatures;
126     } // end method Temperatures
127 } // end namespace TemperatureServer
```

Fig. 17.29 TemperatureServer Web service. (Part 3 of 3.)

Method **UpdateWeatherConditions**, which gathers weather data from a Web page, is the first **WebMethod** that a client must call from the Web service. The service also provides **WebMethod**s **Cities**, **Descriptions** and **Temperatures**, which return different kinds of forecast-related information. If one of these three methods is called before method **UpdateWeatherConditions** reads weather information from the Web page, no data will be returned to the client.

When **UpdateWeatherConditions** (lines 18–72 of Fig. 17.29) is invoked, the method connects to a Web site containing the traveler's forecasts from the National Weather Service (NWS). Line 22 creates a *WebClient* object, which we use because the **WebClient** class is designed for interaction with a source specified by a URL. In this case, the URL for the NWS page is **http://iwin.nws.noaa.gov/iwin/us/traveler.html**. Lines 27–28 call **WebClient** method *OpenRead*; the method retrieves a **Stream** from the URL containing the weather information and then uses this **Stream** to create a **StreamReader** object. Using a **StreamReader** object, the program can read the Web page's HTML markup line by line.

The section of the Web page in which we are interested starts with the string "**TAV12**." Therefore, lines 33–34 read the HTML markup one line at a time until this string is encountered. Once the string "**TAV12**" is reached, the **do/while** structure (lines 44–47) continues to read the page one line at a time until it finds the header line (i.e., the line at the beginning of the forecast table). This line starts with either **dayFormat**, indicating day format, or **nightFormat**, indicating night format. The line could be in either format; therefore, the structure checks for both. Line 50 reads the next line from the page, which is the first line containing temperature information.

The **while** structure (lines 52–65) creates a new **CityWeather** object to represent the current city. It parses the string containing the current weather data, separating the city name, the weather condition and the temperature. The **CityWeather** object is added to **cityList** (an **ArrayList** that contains a list of the cities, their descriptions and their current temperatures); then the next line from the page is read and stored in **inputLine** for the next iteration. This process continues until the length of the string read from the Web page is less than or equal to **28**. This signals the end of the temperature section. Line 71 adds **cityList** to the **Session** object so that the values are maintained between method calls.

Method **Cities** (lines 75–90) creates an array of strings that can contain as many string elements as there are elements in **cityList**. Line 77–78 obtains the list of cities from the **Session** object. Lines 82–87 iterate through each **CityWeather** object in **cityList** and insert the city name into the array, which is returned in line 89. Methods **Descriptions** (lines 93–108) and **Temperatures** (lines 111–126) behave similarly, except that they return weather descriptions and temperatures, respectively.

Figure 17.30 and Fig. 17.31 contain the code listing for the **CityWeather** class. The constructor takes three arguments: The city's name, the weather description and the current temperature. The class provides the read-only properties **CityName**, **Temperature** and **Description** so that these values can be retrieved by the Web service.

```
1   // Fig. 17.30: CityWeather.h
2   // CityWeather class header file.
3
4   #using <mscorlib.dll>
5   #using <system.dll>
6
7   using namespace System;
8
9   public __gc class CityWeather
10  {
11  public:
12     CityWeather( String *city, String *information,
13        String *degrees );
14
15     // city name
16     __property String *get_CityName()
17     {
```

Fig. 17.30 **CityWeather** class header file. (Part 1 of 2.)

```
18            return cityName;
19         }
20
21         // city temperature
22         __property String *get_Temperature()
23         {
24            return temperature;
25         }
26
27         // forecast description
28         __property String *get_Description()
29         {
30            return description;
31         }
32
33      private:
34         String *cityName;
35         String *temperature;
36         String *description;
37      }; // end class CityWeather
```

Fig. 17.30 `CityWeather` class header file. (Part 2 of 2.)

```
1    // Fig. 17.31: CityWeather.cpp
2    // Class representing the weather information for one city.
3
4    #include "stdafx.h"
5    #include "CityWeather.h"
6
7    CityWeather::CityWeather(
8       String *city, String *information, String *degrees )
9    {
10      cityName = city;
11      description = information;
12      temperature = degrees;
13   }
```

Fig. 17.31 Class that stores weather information about a city.

TemperatureClient (Fig. 17.32–Fig. 17.34) is a Windows application that uses the **TemperatureServer** Web service to display weather information in a graphical and easy-to-read manner. The application consists of 34 **Label**s, which are placed in two columns. Each **Label** displays the weather information for a different city.

```
1    // Fig. 17.32: Client.h
2    // Client class header file.
3
```

Fig. 17.32 `Client` class header file. (Part 1 of 2.)

```
4   #pragma once
5
6   #using <mscorlib.dll>
7   #using <system.dll>
8   #using <system.drawing.dll>
9   #using <system.windows.forms.dll>
10
11  using namespace System;
12  using namespace System::Drawing;
13  using namespace System::Collections;
14  using namespace System::Windows::Forms;
15  using namespace System::Net;
16
17  public __gc class Client : public Form
18  {
19  public:
20     Client();
21  private:
22     static int LABEL_COUNT = 36;
23     static Label *labelArray[] = new Label *[ LABEL_COUNT ];
24     static int yValues __gc[] = new int __gc[ LABEL_COUNT / 2 ];
25
26     void InitializeComponent();
27  }; // end class Client
```

Fig. 17.32 `Client` class header file. (Part 2 of 2.)

```
1   // Fig. 17.33: Client.cpp
2   // Class that displays weather information that it receives
3   // from a Web service.
4
5   #include "stdafx.h"
6   #include "Client.h"
7   #include "WebService.h"
8
9   Client::Client()
10  {
11     InitializeComponent();
12
13     TemperatureServer *server = new TemperatureServer();
14     server->CookieContainer = new CookieContainer();
15     server->UpdateWeatherConditions();
16
17     String *cities[] = server->Cities();
18     String *descriptions[] = server->Descriptions();
19     String *temperatures[] = server->Temperatures();
20
21     labelArray[ 0 ]->BackgroundImage = new Bitmap(
22        S"images\\header.png" );
23     labelArray[ 1 ]->BackgroundImage = new Bitmap(
24        S"images\\header.png" );
25
```

Fig. 17.33 Receiving temperature and weather data from a Web service. (Part 1 of 3.)

```
26        // create Hashtable and populate it with every label
27        Hashtable *cityLabels = new Hashtable();
28
29        for ( int i = 1; i < 35; i++ )
30           cityLabels->Add( __box( i ), labelArray[ i + 1 ] );
31
32        // create Hashtable and populate with all weather conditions
33        Hashtable *weather = new Hashtable();
34        weather->Add( S"SUNNY", S"sunny" );
35        weather->Add( S"PTCLDY", S"pcloudy" );
36        weather->Add( S"CLOUDY", S"mcloudy" );
37        weather->Add( S"MOCLDY", S"mcloudy" );
38        weather->Add( S"TSTRMS", S"rain" );
39        weather->Add( S"RAIN", S"rain" );
40        weather->Add( S"SNOW", S"snow" );
41        weather->Add( S"VRYHOT", S"vryhot" );
42        weather->Add( S"FAIR", S"fair" );
43        weather->Add( S"RNSNOW", S"rnsnow" );
44        weather->Add( S"SHWRS", S"showers" );
45        weather->Add( S"WINDY", S"windy" );
46        weather->Add( S"NOINFO", S"noinfo" );
47        weather->Add( S"MISG", S"noinfo" );
48        weather->Add( S"DRZL", S"rain" );
49        weather->Add( S"HAZE", S"noinfo" );
50        weather->Add( S"SMOKE", S"mcloudy" );
51
52        Bitmap *background = new Bitmap( "images/back.png" );
53        Drawing::Font *font = new Drawing::Font(
54           S"Courier New", 8, FontStyle::Bold );
55
56        // for every city
57        for ( int i = 0; i < cities->Length; i++ ) {
58
59           // use Hashtable cityLabels to find the next Label
60           Label *currentCity = dynamic_cast< Label* >(
61              cityLabels->Item[ __box( i + 1 ) ] );
62
63           try {
64
65              // set current Label's image to image
66              // corresponding to the city's weather condition -
67              // find correct image name in Hashtable weather
68              currentCity->Image = new Bitmap( String::Concat(
69                 S"images\\", dynamic_cast< String* >(
70                 weather->Item[ descriptions[ i ]->Trim() ] ),
71                 S".png" ) );
72
73           }
74           catch( Exception * ) {
75              currentCity->Image = new Bitmap( "images\\noinfo.png" );
76           }
77
78           // set background image, font and forecolor
```

Fig. 17.33 Receiving temperature and weather data from a Web service. (Part 2 of 3.)

```
79            // of Label
80            currentCity->BackgroundImage = background;
81            currentCity->Font = font;
82            currentCity->ForeColor = Color::White;
83
84            // set label's text to city name
85            currentCity->Text = String::Concat(
86                S"\r\n", cities[ i ], S" ", temperatures[ i ] );
87        } // end for
88    } // end constructor
89
90    void Client::InitializeComponent()
91    {
92        this->SuspendLayout();
93        int i = 0, temp = 0;
94
95        // y-coordinates of the top left hand corner of the labels
96        yValues[ 0 ] = 8;
97
98        for ( i = 1; i < LABEL_COUNT / 2; i++ )
99            yValues[ i ] = 40 * i;
100
101       // initialize 36 Label objects
102       for ( i = 0; i < LABEL_COUNT; i++ )
103           labelArray[ i ] = new Label();
104           labelArray[ i ]->BorderStyle = BorderStyle::FixedSingle;
105           labelArray[ i ]->ImageAlign = ContentAlignment::TopRight;
106       }
107
108       // set size of header labels
109       for ( i = 0; i < 2; i++ )
110           labelArray[ i ]->Size = Drawing::Size( 312, 32 );
111
112       // set size of city labels
113       for ( ; i < LABEL_COUNT; i++ )
114           labelArray[ i ]->Size = Drawing::Size( 312, 40 );
115
116       // set label positions
117       for ( i = 0; i < LABEL_COUNT; i += 2, temp++ ) {
118           labelArray[ i ]->Location = Point( 8,
119                 yValues[ temp ] );
120           labelArray[ i + 1 ]->Location = Point( 320,
121               yValues[ temp ] );
122       }
123
124       // Client
125       this->AutoScaleBaseSize = Drawing::Size( 5, 13 );
126       this->ClientSize = Drawing::Size( 640, 733 );
127       this->Controls->AddRange( labelArray );
128       this->Name = S"Client";
129       this->Text = S"Client";
130       this->ResumeLayout();
131   } // end method InitializeComponent
```

Fig. 17.33 Receiving temperature and weather data from a Web service. (Part 3 of 3.)

```
1   // Fig. 17.34: ClientTest.cpp
2   // Client driver.
3
4   #include "Client.h"
5
6   int __stdcall WinMain()
7   {
8      Application::Run( new Client() );
9
10     return 0;
11  } // end WinMain
```

Fig. 17.34 `Client` class driver.

Lines 13–15 of the constructor (Fig. 17.33) instantiate a **TemperatureServer** object, create a new **CookieContainer** object and update the weather data by calling method **UpdateWeatherConditions**. Lines 17–19 call **TemperatureServer** methods **Cities**, **Descriptions** and **Temperatures** to retrieve the city's weather and description information. Because the application presents weather data for so many cities, we must establish a way to organize the information in the **Label**s and to ensure that each weather description is accompanied by an appropriate image. To address these concerns, the program uses class **Hashtable** (discussed further in Chapter 19, Data Structures and Collections) to store all the **Label**s and weather descriptions and the names of their corresponding images. A **Hashtable** stores key-value pairs, in which both the key and the value can be any type of object. Method **Add** adds key-value pairs to a **Hashtable**. The class also provides an indexed array to return the key value on which the **Hashtable** is indexed. Line 27 creates a **Hashtable** object, and lines 29–30 add the **Label**s to the **Hashtable**, using the numbers 1 through 34 as keys. Then line 33 creates a second **Hashtable** object (**weather**) to contain pairs of weather conditions and the images associated with those conditions. Note that a given weather description does not necessarily correspond to the name of the PNG file containing the correct image. For example, both "**TSTRMS**" and "**RAIN**" weather conditions use the **rain.png** file.

Lines 57–87 set each **Label** so that it contains a city name, the current temperature in the city and an image corresponding to the weather condition for that city. Lines 60–61 use the indexed property of **Hashtable** to retrieve the next **Label** by passing as an argument the current value of **i** plus 1. We add 1 because the **Hashtable** indexed property begins at 0, despite the fact that both the labels and the **Hashtable** keys are numbered from 1–34.

Lines 68–71 set the **Label**'s image to the PNG image that corresponds to the city's weather condition. The application does this by retrieving the name of the PNG image from **Hashtable weather**. The program eliminates any spaces in the description string by calling **String** method **Trim**. Lines 80–86 set several **Label**s' properties to achieve the visual effect seen in the output. For each label, we specify a blue-and-black background image (line 80). Lines 85–86 set each label's text so that it displays the correct information for each city (i.e., the city's name and temperature).

17.13 User-Defined Types in Web Services

The Web service discussed in the previous section returns arrays of strings. It would be much more convenient if **TemperatureServer** could return an array of **CityWeather** objects, instead of an array of strings. Fortunately, it is possible to define and employ user-defined types (also known as *custom types*) in a Web service. These types can be passed into or returned from Web-service methods. Web-service clients also can use these user-defined types, because the proxy class created for the client contains these type definitions. There are, however, some subtleties to keep in mind when using user-defined types in Web services; we point these out as we encounter them in the next example.

The case study in this section presents a math-tutoring program. The Web service generates random equations of type **Equation**. The client inputs information about the kind of mathematical example that the user wants (addition, subtraction or multiplication) and the skill level of the user (1 creates equations using one-digit numbers, 2 specifies more difficult equations involving two-digit numbers and 3 specifies the most difficult equations, containing three-digit numbers). It then generates an equation consisting of random numbers that have the proper number of digits. The client receives the **Equation** and displays the sample questions to the user.

We mentioned earlier that all data types passed to and from Web services must be supported by SOAP. How, then, can SOAP support a type that is not even created yet? In Chapter 14, Files and Streams, we discussed the serializing of data types, which enables them to be written to files. Similarly, custom types that are sent to or from a Web service are serialized, enabling them to be passed in XML format. This process is referred to as *XML serialization*.

When defining objects to be returned from Web-service methods, there are several subtleties to understand. For example, any object returned by a Web-service method must have a default constructor. Although all objects can be instantiated via a default constructor (even if this constructor is not defined explicitly), a class returned from a Web service must have an explicitly defined constructor, even if its body is empty.

Common Programming Error 17.3

Failure to define explicitly a default constructor for a type being used in a Web service results in a runtime error.

A few additional requirements apply to custom types in Web services. Any members of our user-defined type that we wish to access on the client side must be declared `public`. We also must define both the *get* and the *set* accessors of any properties that we wish to access at runtime. The Web service needs to have ways both to retrieve and to manipulate such properties, because objects of the user-defined type will be converted into XML (when the objects are serialized), then converted back to objects (when they are deserialized). During serialization, the property value must be read (through the *get* accessor); during deserialization, the property value of the new object must be set (through the *set* accessor). If only one accessor is present, the client application will not have access to the property.

Common Programming Error 17.4

Defining only the get or the set accessor of a property for a user-defined type being used in a Web service results in a property that is inaccessible to the client.

Common Programming Error 17.5

Clients of a Web service can access only that service's `public` members. To allow access to `private` data, the programmer should provide `public` properties.

Figure 17.35 and Fig. 17.36 display class `Equation`. The constructor that is called (lines 16–37 of Fig. 17.36) takes three arguments—two integers representing the left and right operands and a string representing the algebraic operation to carry out. We define a default constructor (line 8–13) that assigns default values to the class data members. The constructor sets the `left`, `right` and `operation` fields; then it calculates the appropriate result. We do not use this default constructor, but it must be defined in the program.

```
1   // Fig. 17.35: Equation.h
2   // Equation class header file.
3
4   #pragma once
```

Fig. 17.35 `Equation` class header file. (Part 1 of 3.)

```
5
6   #using <mscorlib.dll>
7
8   using namespace System;
9
10  public __gc class Equation
11  {
12  public:
13     Equation();
14     Equation( int leftValue, int rightValue,
15        String *operationType );
16     String *ToString();
17
18     // property returning string representing left-hand side
19     __property String *get_LeftHandSide()
20     {
21        return String::Concat( Left.ToString(), S" ",
22           Operation, S" ", Right.ToString() );
23     }
24
25     __property void set_LeftHandSide( String *value ) {}
26
27     // property returning string representing right-hand side
28     __property String *get_RightHandSide()
29     {
30        return Result.ToString();
31     }
32
33     __property void set_RightHandSide( String *value ) {}
34
35     // left operand get and set property
36     __property int get_Left()
37     {
38        return left;
39     }
40
41     __property void set_Left( int value )
42     {
43        left = value;
44     }
45
46     // right operand get and set property
47     __property int get_Right()
48     {
49        return right;
50     }
51
52     __property void set_Right( int value )
53     {
54        right = value;
55     }
56
57     // get and set property of result of applying
```

Fig. 17.35 Equation class header file. (Part 2 of 3.)

```
58        // operation to left and right operands
59        __property int get_Result()
60        {
61           return result;
62        }
63
64        __property void set_Result( int value )
65        {
66           result = value;
67        }
68
69        // get and set property for operation
70        __property String *get_Operation()
71        {
72           return operation;
73        }
74
75        __property void set_Operation( String *value )
76        {
77           operation = value;
78        }
79
80   private:
81      int left, right, result;
82      String *operation;
83   }; // end class Equation
```

Fig. 17.35 Equation class header file. (Part 3 of 3.)

```
1    // Fig. 17.36: Equation.cpp
2    // Class Equation contains information about an equation.
3
4    #include "stdafx.h"
5    #include "Equation.h"
6
7    // required default constructor
8    Equation::Equation()
9    {
10      Left = 0;
11      Right = 0;
12      Operation = S"+";
13   }
14
15   // constructor for class Equation
16   Equation::Equation( int leftValue, int rightValue,
17      String *operationType )
18   {
19      Left = leftValue;
20      Right = rightValue;
```

Fig. 17.36 Class that stores equation information. (Part 1 of 2.)

```
21      Operation = operationType;
22
23      switch ( operationType->Chars[ 0 ] ) {
24
25         case '+':
26            Result = Left + Right;
27            break;
28         case '-':
29            Result = Left - Right;
30            break;
31         case '*':
32            Result = Left * Right;
33            break;
34         default:
35            break;
36      } // end switch
37   }
38
39   String *Equation::ToString()
40   {
41      return String::Concat( Left.ToString(), S" ", Operation,
42         S" ", Right.ToString(), S" = ", Result.ToString() );
43   }
```

Fig. 17.36 Class that stores equation information. (Part 2 of 2.)

Class **Equation** defines properties **LeftHandSide**, **RightHandSide**, **Left**, **Right**, **Operation** and **Result**. The program does not need to modify the values of some of these properties, but implementation for the *set* accessor must be provided. **LeftHandSide** returns a string representing everything to the left of the "=" sign, and **RightHandSide** returns a string representing everything to the right of the "=" sign. **Left** returns the **int** to the left of the operator (known as the left operand), and **Right** returns the **int** to the right of the operator (known as the right operand). **Result** returns the answer to the equation, and **Operation** returns the operator. The program does not actually need the **RightHandSide** property, but we have chosen to include it in case other clients choose to use it. Figure 17.38–Fig. 17.39 present the **Generator** Web service that creates random, customized **Equation**s.

Web service **Generator** contains only one Web-service method, **GenerateEquation**. This method takes as arguments a string representing the operation we wish to perform and an integer representing the desired difficulty level of the equation. Figure 17.37 demonstrates the result of executing a test call of this Web service. Notice that the return value from our Web-service method is marked up as XML. However, this example differs from previous ones in that the XML specifies the values for all **public** fields of the object that is being returned. The return object has been serialized into XML. Our proxy class takes this return value and deserializes it into an object (containing only the **public** data from the original object) that then is passed back to the client.

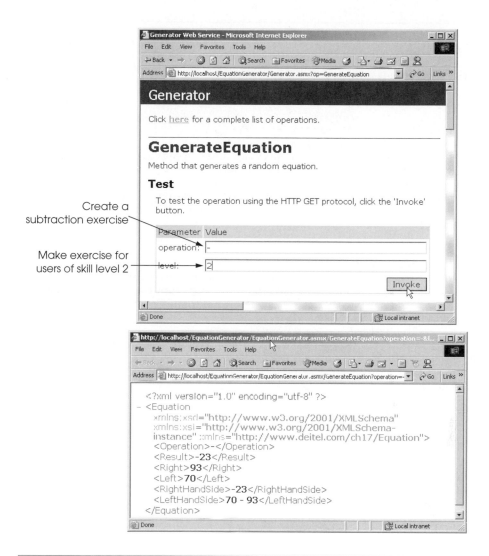

Create a subtraction exercise

Make exercise for users of skill level 2

Fig. 17.37 Returning an object from a Web-service method.

```
1   // Fig. 17.38: EquationGenerator.h
2   // Generator class header file.
3
4   #pragma once
5
6   #using <System.Web.Services.dll>
```

Fig. 17.38 Generator class header file. (Part 1 of 2.)

```
7
8   using namespace System::Web::Services;
9
10  #include "Equation.h"
11
12  namespace EquationGenerator
13  {
14     [ WebService( Namespace =
15        "http://www.deitel.com/ch17/Equation",
16        Description = "A Web service that generates questions "
17        "based on the specified mathematical operation and "
18        "level of difficulty chosen." ) ]
19     public __gc class Generator : public WebService
20     {
21     public:
22        Generator();
23
24        [ WebMethod ( Description =
25           "Method that generates a random equation." ) ]
26        Equation *GenerateEquation( String *operation, int level );
27
28     private:
29        void InitializeComponent();
30     }; // end class Generator
31  } // end namespace EquationGenerator
```

Fig. 17.38 Generator class header file. (Part 2 of 2.)

```
1   // Fig. 17.39: EquationGenerator.cpp
2   // Web service to generate random equations based on a
3   // specified operation and difficulty level.
4
5   #include "stdafx.h"
6   #include "EquationGenerator.h"
7   #include "Global.asax.h"
8
9   namespace EquationGenerator
10  {
11     Generator::Generator()
12     {
13        InitializeComponent();
14     }
15
16     void Generator::InitializeComponent() {}
17
18     Equation *Generator::GenerateEquation( String *operation,
19        int level )
20     {
21
22        // find maximum and minimum number to be used
23        int maximum = ( int ) Math::Pow( 10, level ),
24           minimum = ( int ) Math::Pow( 10, level - 1 );
```

Fig. 17.39 Web service that generates random equations. (Part 1 of 2.)

```
25
26              Random *random = new Random();
27
28              // create equation consisting of two random numbers
29              // between minimum and maximum parameters
30              Equation *equation = new Equation(
31                  random->Next( minimum, maximum ),
32                  random->Next( minimum, maximum ), operation );
33
34              return equation;
35          } // end method GenerateEquation
36      } // end namespace EquationGenerator
```

Fig. 17.39 Web service that generates random equations. (Part 2 of 2.)

Lines 23–24 (of Fig. 17.39) define the lower and upper bounds for the random numbers that the method generates. To set these limits, the program first calls **static** method **Pow** of class **Math**—this method raises its first argument to the power of its second argument. Integer **maximum** represents the upper bound for a randomly generated number. The program raises **10** to the power of the specified **level** argument and then passes this value as the upper bound. For instance, if **level** is **1**, **maximum** is **10**; if **level** is **2**, **maximum** is **100**; and so on. Variable **minimum**'s value is determined by raising **10** to a power one less than **level**. This calculates the smallest number with **level** digits. If **level** is **2**, **minimum** is **10**; if **level** is **3**, **minimum** is **100** and so on.

Lines 30–32 create a new **Equation** object. The program calls **Random** method **Next**, which returns an integer that is greater than or equal to a specified lower bound, but less than a specified upper bound. In this example, **Random** generates a left operand value that is greater than or equal to **minimum**, but less than **maximum** (i.e., a number with **level** digits). The right operand is another random number with the same characteristics. The operation passed to the **Equation** constructor is the **String * operation** that was received by **GenerateEquation**. The new **Equation** object is returned.

Figure 17.40–Fig. 17.42 list the math-tutoring application that uses the **Generator** Web service. The application calls **Generator**'s **GenerateEquation** method to create an **Equation** object. The application then displays the left-hand side of the **Equation** and waits for user input. In this example, the program accesses both class **Generator** and class **Equation** from within the **localhost** namespace—both are placed in this namespace when the proxy is generated.

```
1   // Fig. 17.40: Tutor.h
2   // Tutor class header file.
3
4   #pragma once
5
6   #using <mscorlib.dll>
7   #using <system.dll>
8   #using <system.drawing.dll>
```

Fig. 17.40 **Tutor** class header file. (Part 1 of 2.)

```
 9    #using <system.windows.forms.dll>
10
11    using namespace System;
12    using namespace System::Drawing;
13    using namespace System::ComponentModel;
14    using namespace System::Windows::Forms;
15
16    #include "stdafx.h"
17    #include "WebService.h"
18
19    public __gc class Tutor : public Form
20    {
21    public:
22       Tutor();
23
24    protected:
25       void generateButton_Click( Object *sender, EventArgs *e );
26       void okButton_Click( Object *sender, EventArgs *e );
27       void operationRadioButtons_Click( Object *Sender,
28          EventArgs *e );
29       void levelRadioButtons_Click( Object *sender,
30          EventArgs *e );
31
32    private:
33       Panel *panel1;
34       Panel *panel2;
35       Label *questionLabel;
36       TextBox *answerTextBox;
37       Button *okButton;
38       Button *generateButton;
39       RadioButton *oneRadioButton;
40       RadioButton *twoRadioButton;
41       RadioButton *threeRadioButton;
42       RadioButton *addRadioButton;
43       RadioButton *subtractRadioButton;
44       RadioButton *multiplyRadioButton;
45
46       static int level = 1;
47
48       Equation *equation;
49       Generator *generator;
50       static String *operation = S"+";
51       void InitializeComponent();
52    }; // end class Tutor
```

Fig. 17.40 Tutor class header file. (Part 2 of 2.)

```
1    // Fig. 17.41: Tutor.cpp
2    // Math-tutor program.
3
4    #include "Tutor.h"
5    #include "WebService.h"
```

Fig. 17.41 Math-tutor application. (Part 1 of 6.)

```
6
7   Tutor::Tutor()
8   {
9       generator = new Generator();
10      InitializeComponent();
11  }
12
13  void Tutor::InitializeComponent()
14  {
15      this->subtractRadioButton = new RadioButton();
16      this->answerTextBox = new TextBox();
17      this->threeRadioButton = new RadioButton();
18      this->generateButton = new Button();
19      this->panel1 = new Panel();
20      this->oneRadioButton = new RadioButton();
21      this->twoRadioButton = new RadioButton();
22      this->panel2 = new Panel();
23      this->multiplyRadioButton = new RadioButton();
24      this->addRadioButton = new RadioButton();
25      this->questionLabel = new Label();
26      this->okButton = new Button();
27      this->panel1->SuspendLayout();
28      this->panel2->SuspendLayout();
29      this->SuspendLayout();
30
31      // subtractRadioButton
32      this->subtractRadioButton->Location = Point( 88, 8 );
33      this->subtractRadioButton->Name = S"subtractRadioButton";
34      this->subtractRadioButton->Size = Drawing::Size( 80, 24 );
35      this->subtractRadioButton->TabIndex = 1;
36      this->subtractRadioButton->Text = S"Subtraction";
37      this->subtractRadioButton->CheckedChanged += new
38          EventHandler( this, this->operationRadioButtons_Click );
39
40      // answerTextBox
41      this->answerTextBox->Location = Point( 168, 24 );
42      this->answerTextBox->Name = S"answerTextBox";
43      this->answerTextBox->TabIndex = 3;
44      this->answerTextBox->Text = S"";
45
46      // threeRadioButton
47      this->threeRadioButton->Location = Point( 168, 8 );
48      this->threeRadioButton->Name = S"threeRadioButton";
49      this->threeRadioButton->Size = Drawing::Size( 40, 24 );
50      this->threeRadioButton->TabIndex = 3;
51      this->threeRadioButton->Text = S"3";
52      this->threeRadioButton->CheckedChanged += new
53          EventHandler( this, levelRadioButtons_Click );
54
55      // generateButton
56      this->generateButton->Location = Point( 288, 64 );
57      this->generateButton->Name = S"generateButton";
58      this->generateButton->Size = Drawing::Size( 96, 88 );
```

Fig. 17.41 Math-tutor application. (Part 2 of 6.)

```
59      this->generateButton->TabIndex = 5;
60      this->generateButton->Text = S"Generate Additon Example";
61      this->generateButton->Click += new EventHandler( this,
62         generateButton_Click );
63
64      // panel1
65      Control *control[] = { this->oneRadioButton,
66         this->twoRadioButton, this->threeRadioButton };
67      this->panel1->Controls->AddRange( control );
68      this->panel1->Location = Point( 16, 112 );
69      this->panel1->Name = S"panel1";
70      this->panel1->Size = Drawing::Size( 256, 40 );
71      this->panel1->TabIndex = 0;
72
73      // oneRadioButton
74      this->oneRadioButton->Checked = true;
75      this->oneRadioButton->Location = Point( 16, 8 );
76      this->oneRadioButton->Name = S"oneRadioButton";
77      this->oneRadioButton->Size = Drawing::Size( 32, 24 );
78      this->oneRadioButton->TabIndex = 1;
79      this->oneRadioButton->TabStop = true;
80      this->oneRadioButton->Text = S"1";
81      this->oneRadioButton->CheckedChanged += new
82         EventHandler( this, levelRadioButtons_Click );
83
84      // twoRadioButton
85      this->twoRadioButton->Location = Point( 88, 8 );
86      this->twoRadioButton->Name = S"twoRadioButton";
87      this->twoRadioButton->Size = Drawing::Size( 40, 24 );
88      this->twoRadioButton->TabIndex = 2;
89      this->twoRadioButton->Text = S"2";
90      this->twoRadioButton->CheckedChanged += new
91         EventHandler( this, levelRadioButtons_Click );
92
93      // panel2
94      Control *operationControl[] = { this->multiplyRadioButton,
95         this->subtractRadioButton, this->addRadioButton };
96      this->panel2->Controls->AddRange( operationControl );
97      this->panel2->Location = Point( 16, 64 );
98      this->panel2->Name = S"panel2";
99      this->panel2->Size = Drawing::Size( 256, 40 );
100     this->panel2->TabIndex = 1;
101
102     // multiplyRadioButton
103     this->multiplyRadioButton->Location = Point( 168, 8 );
104     this->multiplyRadioButton->Name = S"multiplyRadioButton";
105     this->multiplyRadioButton->Size = Drawing::Size( 88, 24 );
106     this->multiplyRadioButton->TabIndex = 2;
107     this->multiplyRadioButton->Text = S"Multiplication";
108     this->multiplyRadioButton->CheckedChanged += new
109        EventHandler( this, operationRadioButtons_Click );
110
```

Fig. 17.41 Math-tutor application. (Part 3 of 6.)

```
111      // addRadioButton
112      this->addRadioButton->Checked = true;
113      this->addRadioButton->Location = Point( 16, 8 );
114      this->addRadioButton->Name = S"addRadioButton";
115      this->addRadioButton->Size = Drawing::Size( 64, 24 );
116      this->addRadioButton->TabIndex = 0;
117      this->addRadioButton->TabStop = true;
118      this->addRadioButton->Text = S"Addition";
119      this->addRadioButton->CheckedChanged += new
120         EventHandler( this, operationRadioButtons_Click );
121
122      // questionLabel
123      this->questionLabel->BorderStyle = BorderStyle::FixedSingle;
124      this->questionLabel->Location = Point( 16, 24 );
125      this->questionLabel->Name = S"questionLabel";
126      this->questionLabel->Size = Drawing::Size( 136, 23 );
127      this->questionLabel->TabIndex = 2;
128
129      // okButton
130      this->okButton->Enabled = false;
131      this->okButton->Location = Point( 288, 24 );
132      this->okButton->Name = S"okButton";
133      this->okButton->Size = Drawing::Size( 96, 23 );
134      this->okButton->TabIndex = 4;
135      this->okButton->Text = S"OK";
136      this->okButton->Click += new EventHandler( this,
137         this->okButton_Click );
138
139      // Tutor
140      this->AutoScaleBaseSize = Drawing::Size( 5, 13 );
141      this->ClientSize = Drawing::Size( 416, 165 );
142      Control *control2[] = { this->generateButton,
143         this->okButton, this->answerTextBox, this->questionLabel,
144         this->panel2, this->panel1 };
145
146      this->Controls->AddRange( control2 );
147      this->Name = S"Tutor";
148      this->Text = S"Tutor";
149      this->panel1->ResumeLayout();
150      this->panel2->ResumeLayout();
151      this->ResumeLayout();
152   }
153
154   // generates new equation on click event
155   void Tutor::generateButton_Click( Object *sender, EventArgs *e )
156   {
157
158      // generate equation using current operation and level
159      equation = generator->GenerateEquation( operation,
160         level );
161
162      // display left-hand side of equation
```

Fig. 17.41 Math-tutor application. (Part 4 of 6.)

```
163      questionLabel->Text = equation->LeftHandSide;
164
165      okButton->Enabled = true;
166      answerTextBox->Enabled = true;
167 } // end method generateButton_Click
168
169 // check users answer
170 void Tutor::okButton_Click( Object *sender, EventArgs *e )
171 {
172
173      // determine correct result from Equation object
174      int answer = equation->Result;
175
176      // get user's answer
177      int myAnswer = Int32::Parse( answerTextBox->Text );
178
179      // test if user's answer is correct
180      if ( answer == myAnswer ) {
181         questionLabel->Text = S"";
182         answerTextBox->Text = S"";
183         okButton->Enabled = false;
184         MessageBox::Show( S"Correct! Good job!" );
185      }
186      else
187         MessageBox::Show( S"Incorrect. Try again." );
188 } // end method okButton_Click
189
190 // set the selected operation
191 void Tutor::operationRadioButtons_Click( Object *sender,
192      EventArgs *e )
193 {
194      RadioButton *item = dynamic_cast< RadioButton* >( sender );
195
196      // set the operation to be the appropriate symbol
197      if ( item == addRadioButton )
198         operation = S"+";
199      else if ( item == subtractRadioButton )
200         operation = S"-";
201      else
202         operation = S"*";
203
204      generateButton->Text = String::Concat( S"Generate ",
205         item->Text, S" Example" );
206 } // end method operationRadioButtons_Click
207
208 // set the current level
209 void Tutor::levelRadioButtons_Click( Object *sender,
210      EventArgs *e )
211 {
212      if ( sender == oneRadioButton )
213         level = 1;
214      else if ( sender == twoRadioButton )
```

Fig. 17.41 Math-tutor application. (Part 5 of 6.)

```
215        level = 2;
216     else
217        level = 3;
218 } // end method levelRadioButtons_Click
```

Fig. 17.41 Math-tutor application. (Part 6 of 6.)

```
1  // Fig. 17.42: TutorTest.cpp
2  // Math tutor driver.
3
4  #include "Tutor.h"
5
6  int __stdcall WinMain()
7  {
8     Application::Run( new Tutor() );
9
10    return 0;
11 } // end WinMain
```

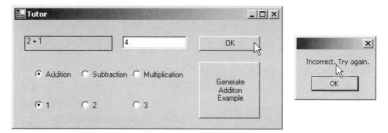

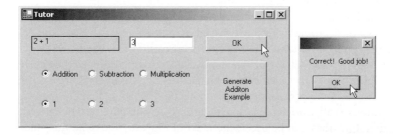

Fig. 17.42 Math-tutor driver. (Part 1 of 2.)

Fig. 17.42 Math-tutor driver. (Part 2 of 2.)

The math-tutoring application displays a question and waits for input. The default setting for the difficulty level is **1**, but the user can change this at any time by choosing a level from the bottom row of **RadioButton**s. Clicking any of the level options invokes **levelRadioButtons_Click** (lines 209–218), which sets integer **level** to the level selected by the user. Although the default setting for the question type is **Addition**, the user also can change this at any time by selecting one of the top row of **RadioButton**s. Doing so invokes the **operationRadioButtons_Click** (lines 191–206) event handler, which sets string **operation** so that it contains the symbol corresponding to the user's selection.

Event handler **generateButton_Click** (lines 155–167) invokes **Generator** method **GenerateEquation**. The left-hand side of the equation is displayed in **questionLabel** (line 163), and **okButton** is enabled so that the user can enter an answer. When the user clicks **OK**, **okButton_Click** (lines 170–188) checks for whether the user provided the correct answer.

17.14 Global XML Web Services Architecture (GXA)

Web-services technologies are designed to be simple and open, containing only the necessary features to transmit data between applications across a network. However, as organizations begin to use Web services in enterprise systems, core standards such as SOAP, WSDL and UDDI do not provide sufficient support for Web services. For example, how can Web-services transmissions be secured? How are SOAP messages routed from one location to another? How does one company locate another company's Web services? How are partner relationships and Web-services interactions managed electronically?

To address such problems, Microsoft and its partners have created the *Global XML Web Services Architecture (GXA)*, a series of specifications that extend SOAP and provide additional capabilities to Web services developers. Microsoft designed the specifications to supply the higher-level functionality that businesses require to implement complex Web services. GXA provides a general-purpose architecture, meaning that the specifications can be used in various Web service scenarios, regardless of complexity. The specifications are modular—therefore, they can be used separately or together to extend the functionality of

GXA as needed. Microsoft plans to submit the GXA specifications for standardization, which will establish GXA as an open architecture.[d]

GXA specifications include *WS-Security*, *WS-Inspection*, *WS-Routing* and *WS-Referral*. WS-Inspection is a specification that helps programmers locate Web services' WSDL files and UDDI descriptions. WS-Routing allows developers to define routing information for a SOAP message. Developers can use WS-Routing to indicate in a SOAP envelope the path that a SOAP message should take.[e] WS-Referral enables developers to modify routing information dynamically (i.e., a SOAP message's path may be changed as the SOAP message moves from one location to another).[f] WS-Security provides security for Web-services transmissions.

Figure 17.43 summarizes GXA's specifications, and Fig. 17.44 illustrates the relationships among the specifications. Notice that each specification enhances SOAP and that each specification is its own unit. The following sections discuss each specification in detail. New specifications are currently being developed and added to GXA. We will discuss some of these newer specifications in Section 17.14.4.

Specification	Description
WS-Inspection	Specification that facilitates the discovery of WSDL files and UDDI descriptions.
WS-Routing	Specification that allows developers to define routing information for a SOAP message statically.
WS-Referral	Specification that allows developers to define routing information for a SOAP message dynamically.
WS-Security	Specification that enables developers to secure Web-services transmissions.

Fig. 17.43 Current GXA specifications.

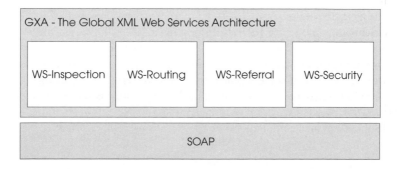

Fig. 17.44 SOAP provides the base for GXA specifications.

17.14.1 WS-Inspection[7]

WS-Inspection is a GXA specification created by Microsoft and IBM that addresses Web services discovery. WS-Inspection defines a syntax for creating *WS-Inspection documents*, which provide references to Web services available on a particular server. WS-Inspection's syntax is XML-based, so WS-Inspection documents contain references that are easy to understand, maintain and format into useful links.

UDDI allows developers to discover Web services by searching registries for services with specific capabilities. Why, then, would an organization want to use WS-Inspection? Whereas UDDI enables developers to discover Web services on the basis of functionality, WS-Inspection enables developers to discover Web services on the basis of location (i.e., Web services at a specific server). For example, some companies maintain relationships with partners that involve using each other's Web services. In these situations, a company might have access to a partner's server and might want to determine what Web services are available at that server. WS-Inspection is ideal for this purpose. Readers may notice that WS-Inspection provides a similar purpose to that of DISCO. WS-Inspection is, in fact, expected by some to replace DISCO in the future.

WS-Inspection information is stored in a document with a `.wsil` extension, known as a *WS-Inspection file* or a *WS-Inspection document*. WS-Inspection markup uses a `service` element to describe a Web service. The `service` element contains additional elements that provide further information about the Web service—including the `name` element, which identifies the service within the WSIL document; the `abstract` element, which provides a text description of the service; and a `description` element, which supplies references to service-description documents (usually WSDL files). In addition to the `service` element, a WSIL document can contain `link` elements, which supply links to other WSIL documents.

The WS-Inspection specification also includes *bindings*—i.e., extensions to WS-Inspection—that provide additional information to a `description` or a `link` element. Current bindings include the *WSDL binding* and the *UDDI binding*. The WSDL binding enables more specific referencing of a WSDL service description. For instance, a WSDL file can contain descriptions for several Web services; the WSDL binding enables the developer to specify one specific service within such a file. The UDDI binding enables the referencing of UDDI entries. Due to WS-Inspection's extensible nature, more bindings can be created as they are needed.

For WS-Inspection files to be useful, they must be easily accessible to developers searching for Web services. One way to make a WS-Inspection file available is to name the file `inspection.wsil` and place it in a standard location—this is usually the root directory of a Web server, which is the topmost folder on the server that contains the organization's Web services. Placing a WSIL file in the root directory is sometimes referred to as *publishing the file*. Another way of providing access to an inspection document is to include a link to the document on a company's Web site. This is sometimes referred to as the *Linked* technique.[g]

---

7. Information in this section is based primarily on K. Ballinger, et al., "Web Services Inspection Language (WS-Inspection) 1.0." `<msdn.microsoft.com/library/en-us/dnglobspec/html/ws-inspection.asp>`.

17.14.2 WS-Routing[8]

WS-Routing is a specification for defining the path of a SOAP message. A SOAP message may stop at many locations when going from the sender to the receiver. These locations can be quite different in nature, so we will use the general term *intermediary* to designate a stop on the SOAP message path. Some intermediaries are known as *SOAP nodes*, which are applications or programming components that understand and process SOAP messages. Using WS-Routing, developers can specify exactly where a SOAP message should go, where it should stop along the way and the order in which the stops should be made. WS-Routing also enables developers to define the paths of SOAP-message responses.

SOAP allows developers to indicate a series of intermediaries through which a SOAP message should pass, but it is difficult to specify the order in which the message reaches these intermediaries. This is because a SOAP message can be transmitted over various transport protocols, and each transport protocol defines its own way of specifying a message path. For example, a SOAP message might travel across HTTP from its sender to an intermediary, then travel across SMTP from the intermediary to the final recipient—it would be complex and difficult to define the SOAP message's path in relation to all possible transport protocols. A developer can specify the message path by "binding" a SOAP message to a particular transport protocol, then using that protocol to define the message's path. However, this means that the SOAP message can travel only over that particular protocol.

WS-Routing provides a solution to this problem by enabling developers to specify a message path, regardless of the transport mechanism. The WS-Routing specification defines a syntax that developers can include in the header of a SOAP message. The syntax's elements can specify the message's ultimate destination (using the **to** element), its point of origin (using the **from** element) and any intermediaries (using the **via** element). WS-Routing also provides the **fwd** and **rev** elements, which specify the forward and reverse message path, respectively, and the **id** and **relatesTo** elements, which enable a message to reference another message. This could be useful when an error message (known as a *fault message*, or *fault*) is being sent in response to another message. The **id** and **relatesTo** elements can be used in the fault message to reference the original message that caused the error. The **fwd** element contains a list of **via** elements, which specify intermediaries; the order of the **via** elements indicates the order in which the intermediaries should be reached.

When the message arrives at an intermediary (or its final destination), the receiver follows an algorithm to process the message. The receiver removes the first **via** element from the **fwd** element and determines whether the message has arrived at the proper intermediary. If so, the message is forwarded to the next receiver (specified by the next **via** element). If the removed **via** element does not reference the message's current location, an error message is returned to the original sender. If the removed **via** element was the last **via** element, the message is forwarded to the final destination, which is specified by the **to** element.

---

8. Information in this section is based primarily on H. Nielsen and S. Thatte, "Web Services Routing Protocol (WS-Routing)," October 2001 <**msdn.microsoft.com/library/en-us/ dnglobspec/html/ws-routing.asp**>.

If an intermediary receives a message with no **via** elements (or no **fwd** element), the intermediary analyzes the **to** element to determine whether the current location is the final destination. If it is, the message has reached its final destination. If not, a fault is generated.

The reverse message path is generated as the message travels from the sender to the receiver (provided that the **rev** element exists in the SOAP header). For example, when an intermediary removes the first **via** element from the **fwd** element, a corresponding **via** element is added to the **rev** element. Thus, the WS-Routing information for the return path is created as the message moves from intermediary to intermediary.

Figure 17.45 illustrates the actions of a SOAP message that contains WS-Routing information. [*Note*: The WS-Routing information in this figure is not displayed in its actual XML-based format.] The SOAP message begins at location **A**. Notice that **A** is specified in the **from** element, and **E**, the destination of this message, is specified in the **to** element. The path is specified in element **fwd**, which, in this case, indicates that the message should stop at intermediaries **B**, **C** and **D**, in that order. Notice that, as the message travels from one intermediary to the next, the current location is removed from the **fwd** element and added to the **rev** element. Keep in the mind that the SOAP header is, in fact, being modified as it moves from one intermediary to another.

17.14.3 WS-Referral[9]

The previous section discussed WS-Routing, which enables developers to specify the path of a SOAP message. However, it is not necessary to define a SOAP message's entire path before the message leaves its sender. When an intermediary receives a message that does

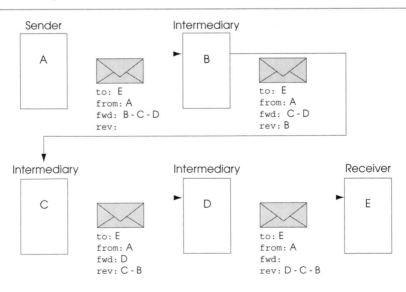

Fig. 17.45 SOAP message with WS-Routing information.

9. Information in this section is based primarily on H. Nielsen, et al., "Web Services Referral Protocol (WS-Referral)," October 2001 <**msdn.microsoft.com/library/en-us/ dnglobspec/html/ws-referral.asp**>. Note that this document is in draft form and is therefore likely to change in the future.

not have a specified next intermediary, that intermediary uses its own built-in routing information (referred to as *routing entries*), along with the ultimate destination indicated in the SOAP message, to determine the next intermediary. The message then is forwarded to the appropriate intermediary.

It is sometimes essential for a developer to modify an intermediary's routing entries. For instance, the developer might want to remove an unnecessary intermediary from the message path or inform other intermediaries of a new intermediary that can be used. WS-Referral is a specification for modifying routing entries and, thus, the paths of SOAP messages. WS-Referral can be used to modify only the routing entries of intermediaries known as SOAP routers. A *SOAP router* is a SOAP node that relays SOAP messages.[h] SOAP routers have the ability to process WS-Referral statements, which are discussed momentarily. WS-Referral can provide different SOAP routers with information about each other, which enables a SOAP message path to be changed dynamically.

The *WS-Referral Statement* is a statement used to modify routing entries. A WS-Referral statement contains a **for** element, which specifies the SOAP routers to which the statement should be applied. If a SOAP router receives a WS-Referral statement for which it is listed in the **for** element, the statement then is applied to that SOAP router. After the **for** element, an **if** element appears, which contains the conditions under which the statement should be applied. If the **if** element conditions are met, the message is sent to the next SOAP router, which is specified in a **go** element. WS-Referral statements are normally used to add or remove SOAP routers from a path.

WS-Referral statements can be delivered to a SOAP router in one of two ways. The first method, called a *WS-Referral Registration Message Exchange*, involves placing the WS-Referral statement in the body of a SOAP message, then sending the message to a SOAP router. In this scenario, the SOAP message is known as a *WS-Referral registration*. The SOAP router either can accept or reject the statement. The second method, known as *WS-Referral Header*, involves sending the WS-Referral statement in the header of a SOAP message.

In some situations, developers want to know what WS-Referral statements have been delivered to a SOAP router. For this purpose, WS-Referral provides the *WS-Referral Query Message Exchange*. Using WS-Referral Query Message Exchange, a query is sent (via a SOAP message) to a SOAP router. This query, which is stored in the body of the SOAP message, can be used to determine what WS-Referral statements are located at the SOAP router. The SOAP router returns a response message containing results of the query.

17.14.4 WS-Security[10]

WS-Security provides SOAP extensions that enable a developer to build secure Web services. Web services developers have numerous security options, but most do not address Web services-specific security issues. Low-level security options, such as firewall-based rules, Secure Sockets Layer (SSL) and Virtual Private Networks (VPN), do not provide ways of authenticating messages and are ill equipped to secure large numbers of SOAP

10. Information in this section is based primarily on B. Atkinson, et al., "Web Services Security (WS-Security)," April 2002 <**msdn.microsoft.com/library/en-us/dnglobspec/html/ws-security.asp**>.

18.1 Introduction

The Internet and the World Wide Web have generated a great deal of excitement in the business and computing communities. The Internet ties the "information world" together; the Web makes the Internet easy to use while providing the flair of multimedia. Organizations see both the Internet and the Web as crucial to their information-systems strategies. The .NET Framework offers a number of built-in networking capabilities that facilitate Internet-based and Web-based applications development. Visual C++ .NET not only can specify parallelism through multithreading, but also can enable programs to search the Web for information and collaborate with programs running on other computers internationally.

In Chapter 17, Web Services, we began our presentation of Visual C++ .NET's networking and distributed-computing capabilities. We discussed Web Services, a high-level networking technology that enables programmers to develop distributed applications in Visual C++ .NET. In this chapter, we focus on the networking technologies that support Visual C++ .NET's Web services capabilities and can be used to build distributed applications.

Our discussion of networking focuses on both sides of a *client/server relationship*. The *client* requests that some action be performed; the *server* performs the action and responds to the client. A common implementation of this request-response model is between Web browsers and Web servers. When users select Web sites that they wish to view through a browser (the client application), the browser makes a request to the appropriate Web server (the server application). The server normally responds to the client by sending the appropriate HTML Web pages.

The networking capabilities of the .NET Framework are grouped into several namespaces. The fundamental networking capabilities are defined by classes and interfaces of namespace **System::Net::Sockets**. Through this namespace, Visual C++ .NET offers *socket-based communications*, which enable developers to view networking as if it were file I/O. This means that a program can read from a *socket* (network connection) or write to a socket as easily as it can read from or write to a file. Sockets are the fundamental way to perform network communications in the .NET Framework. The term "socket" refers to the Berkeley Sockets Interface, which was developed in 1978 for network programming with UNIX and was popularized by C and C++ programmers.

The classes and interfaces of namespace **System::Net::Sockets** also offer *packet-based communications*, through which individual *packets* of information are transmitted. When data are sent across a network, the data are first broken up into *packets*—small amounts of data. Each packet contains a few bytes of the original data, as well as other information (called *header information*), including its origin and its destination. This is a common method of transmitting audio and video over the Internet. In this chapter, we show how to create and manipulate sockets and how to communicate via packets of data.

Socket-based communications in Visual C++ .NET employ *stream sockets*. With stream sockets, a *process* (running program) establishes a *connection* to another process (that is running on the same machine or on a different machine). While the connection is in place, data flows between the processes in continuous *streams*. For this reason, stream sockets are said to provide a *connection-oriented service*. The popular *TCP (Transmission Control Protocol)* facilitates stream-socket transmission.

By contrast, packet-based communications in Visual C++ .NET employ *datagram sockets*, through which individual packets of information are transmitted. Unlike TCP, the protocol used to enable datagram sockets—*UDP, the User Datagram Protocol*—is a *connectionless service* and does not guarantee that packets will arrive in any particular order. In fact, packets can be lost or duplicated and can arrive out of sequence. Applications that use UDP often require significant extra programming to deal with these problems. UDP is most appropriate for network applications that do not require the error checking and reliability of TCP. For example, several online multi-player games use UDP, because speed is more important than perfect accuracy in these types of applications. Stream sockets and the TCP protocol will be the most desirable method of communication for the vast majority of Visual C++ .NET programmers.

Performance Tip 18.1

Connectionless services generally offer better performance but less reliability than do connection-oriented services.

Portability Tip 18.1

The TCP protocol and its related set of protocols enable intercommunication among a wide variety of heterogeneous computer systems (i.e., computer systems with different processors and different operating systems).

18.2 Establishing a Simple Server (Using Stream Sockets)

Typically, with TCP and stream sockets, a server "waits" for a connection request from a client. Often, the server program contains a control structure or block of code that executes continuously until the server receives a request. On receiving a request, the server establishes a connection with the client. The server then uses this connection to handle future requests from that client and to send data to the client.

The establishment of a simple server with TCP and stream sockets in MC++ requires five steps. The first step is to create an object of class **TcpListener**, which belongs to namespace **System::Net::Sockets**. This class represents a TCP stream socket through which a server can listen for requests. A call to the **TcpListener** constructor, such as

```
TcpListener *server = new TcpListener( port );
```

binds (assigns) the server to the specified *port number*. A port number is a numeric identifier that a process uses to identify itself at a given *network address*, also known as an *Inter-*

net Protocol Address (*IP Address*). IP addresses identify computers on the Internet. In fact, Web-site names, such as **www.deitel.com**, are aliases for IP addresses. Any process that performs networking identifies itself via an *IP address/port number pair*. Hence, no two processes can have the same port number at a given IP address. The explicit binding of a socket to a port (using method ***Bind*** of class **Socket**) is usually unnecessary, because class **TcpListener** and other classes discussed in this chapter hide this binding (i.e., bind sockets to ports implicitly), plus they perform other socket-initialization operations.

Software Engineering Observation 18.1

Port numbers can have values between 0 and 65535. Many operating systems reserve port numbers below 1024 for system services (such as e-mail and Web servers). Applications must be granted special privileges to use these reserved port numbers. Usually, a server-side application should not specify port numbers below 1024 as connection ports, because some operating systems might reserve these numbers.

Common Programming Error 18.1

Attempting to bind an already assigned port at a given IP address is a logic error.

To receive requests, the **TcpListener** first must listen for them. The second step in our connection process is to call **TcpListener**'s ***Start*** method, which causes the **TcpListener** object to begin listening for connection requests. The third step establishes the connection between the server and client. The server listens indefinitely for a request—i.e., the execution of the server-side application waits until some client attempts to connect with it. The server creates a connection to the client upon receipt of a connection request. An object of class ***System::Net::Sockets::Socket*** manages each connection to the client. Method ***AcceptSocket*** of class **TcpListener** waits for a connection request, then creates a connection when a request is received. This method returns a **Socket** object upon connection, as in the statement

```
Socket *connection = server->AcceptSocket();
```

When the server receives a request, method **AcceptSocket** calls method ***Accept*** of the **TcpListener**'s underlying **Socket** to make the connection. This is an example of Visual C++ .NET's hiding of networking complexity from the programmer. The programmer can write the preceding statement into a server-side program, then allow the classes of namespace **System::Net::Sockets** to handle the details of accepting requests and establishing connections.

Step four is the processing phase, in which the server and the client communicate via methods ***Receive*** and ***Send*** of class **Socket**. Note that these methods, as well as TCP and stream sockets, can be used only when the server and client are connected. By contrast, through **Socket** methods ***SendTo*** and ***ReceiveFrom***, UDP and datagram sockets can be used when no connection exists.

The fifth step is the connection-termination phase. When the client and server have finished communicating, the server uses method ***Close*** of the **Socket** object to close the connection. Most servers then return to step two (i.e., wait for another client's connection request).

One problem associated with the server scheme described in this section is that step four *blocks* other requests while processing a client's request, so that no other client can connect with the server while the code that defines the processing phase is executing. The most common technique for addressing this problem is to use multithreaded servers, which place the processing-phase code in a separate thread. When the server receives a connection request, the server *spawns*, or creates, a **Thread** to process the connection, leaving its **TcpListener** (or **Socket**) free to receive other connections. This newly created **Thread** is also assigned a new **Socket** (with a different port number) that it can use to communicate with its client.

Software Engineering Observation 18.2
Using the .NET Framework's multithreading capabilities, we can create servers that can manage simultaneous connections with multiple clients. This multithreaded-server architecture is precisely what popular UNIX and Windows network servers use.

Software Engineering Observation 18.3
*A multithreaded server can be implemented to create a thread that manages network I/O across a pointer to a **Socket** object returned by method **AcceptSocket**. A multithreaded server also can be implemented to maintain a pool of threads that manage network I/O across newly created **Socket**s.*

Performance Tip 18.2
*In high-performance systems with abundant memory, a multithreaded server can be implemented to create a pool of threads. These threads can be assigned quickly to handle network I/O across each multiple **Socket**. Thus, when a connection is received, the server does not incur the overhead of thread creation.*

18.3 Establishing a Simple Client (Using Stream Sockets)

We create TCP-stream-socket clients via a process that requires four steps. In the first step, we create an object of class **TcpClient** (which belongs to namespace **System::Net::Sockets**) to connect to the server. This connection is established through method **Connect** of class **TcpClient**. One overloaded version of this method receives two arguments—the server's IP address and the port number—as in the following code:

```
TcpClient *client = new TcpClient();
client->Connect( serverAddress, serverPort );
```

Here, **serverPort** is an **int** that represents the server's port number; **serverAddress** can be either an **IPAddress** instance (that encapsulates the server's IP address) or a **String *** that specifies the server's hostname. Alternatively, the programmer could pass an object pointer of class **IPEndPoint**, which represents an IP address/port number pair, to a different overload of method **Connect**. Method **Connect** of class **TcpClient** calls method **Connect** of class **Socket** to establish the connection. If the connection is successful, method **TcpClient::Connect** returns a positive integer; otherwise, it returns **0** (i.e., **NULL**).

In step two, the **TcpClient** uses its method *GetStream* to get a *Network-Stream* so that it can write to and read from the server. **NetworkStream** methods *WriteByte* and *Write* can be used to output individual bytes or sets of bytes to the server, respectively; similarly, **NetworkStream** methods *ReadByte* and *Read* can be used to input individual bytes or sets of bytes from the server, respectively.

The third step is the processing phase, in which the client and the server communicate. In this phase, the client uses methods **Read**, **ReadByte**, **Write** and **WriteByte** of class **NetworkStream** to perform the appropriate communications. Using a process similar to that used by servers, a client can employ threads to prevent blocking of communications with other servers while processing data from one connection.

After the transmission is complete, step four requires the client to close the connection by calling method *Close* of the **NetworkStream** object. This closes the underlying **Socket** (if the **NetworkStream** has a pointer to that **Socket**). Then, the client calls method *Close* of class **TcpClient** to terminate the TCP connection. At this point, a new connection can be established through method **Connect**, as we have described.

Good Programming Practice 18.1

Leaving socket objects open after you have finished using them wastes resources. Remember to close each socket explicitly using method Close.

18.4 Client/Server Interaction with Stream-Socket Connections

The applications in Fig. 18.1–Fig. 18.3 and Fig. 18.4–Fig. 18.6 use the classes and techniques discussed in the previous two sections to construct a simple *client/server chat application*. The server waits for a client's request to make a connection. When a client application connects to the server, the server application sends an array of bytes to the client, indicating that the connection was successful. The client then displays a message notifying the user that a connection has been established.

Both the client and the server applications contain **TextBox**es that enable users to type messages and send them to the other application. When either the client or the server sends message "**TERMINATE**," the connection between the client and the server terminates. The server then waits for another client to request a connection. Fig. 18.1–Fig. 18.3 and Fig. 18.4–Fig. 18.6 provide the code for classes **Server** and **Client**, respectively. Fig. 18.6 also contains screen captures displaying the execution between the client and the server.

```
1   // Fig. 18.1: Server.h
2   // Set up a Server that will receive a connection from a client,
3   // send a string to the client, and close the connection.
4
5   #pragma once
6
7   #using <system.dll>
8   #using <mscorlib.dll>
9   #using <system.drawing.dll>
10  #using <system.windows.forms.dll>
11
```

Fig. 18.1   Server portion of a client/server stream-socket connection. (Part 1 of 2.)

```
12   using namespace System;
13   using namespace System::Drawing;
14   using namespace System::ComponentModel;
15   using namespace System::Windows::Forms;
16   using namespace System::Threading;
17   using namespace System::Net::Sockets;
18   using namespace System::IO;
19
20   #include <tchar.h>
21
22   // server that awaits client connections (one at a time) and
23   // allows a conversation between client and server
24   public __gc class Server : public Form
25   {
26   public:
27      Server();
28      void RunServer();
29
30   protected:
31      void Server_Closing( Object *, CancelEventArgs * );
32      void inputTextBox_KeyDown( Object *, KeyEventArgs * );
33
34   private:
35      TextBox *inputTextBox;
36      TextBox *displayTextBox;
37      Socket *connection;
38      Thread *readThread;
39
40      NetworkStream *socketStream;
41      BinaryWriter *writer;
42      BinaryReader *reader;
43
44      void InitializeComponent();
45   }; // end class Server
```

Fig. 18.1   Server portion of a client/server stream-socket connection. (Part 2 of 2.)

```
1    // Fig. 18.2: Server.cpp
2    // Method definitions for class Server.
3
4    #include "Server.h"
5
6    // default constructor
7    Server::Server()
8    {
9       InitializeComponent();
10
11      // create a new thread from the server
12      readThread = new Thread( new ThreadStart( this, RunServer ) );
13      readThread->Start();
14   }
```

Fig. 18.2   Server class method definitions. (Part 1 of 4.)

```
15
16   void Server::InitializeComponent()
17   {
18      this->displayTextBox = new TextBox();
19      this->inputTextBox = new TextBox();
20
21      this->SuspendLayout();
22
23      // displayTextBox
24      this->displayTextBox->Location = Point( 8, 40 );
25      this->displayTextBox->Multiline = true;
26      this->displayTextBox->Name = S"displayTextBox";
27      this->displayTextBox->ReadOnly = true;
28      this->displayTextBox->Size = Drawing::Size( 272, 208 );
29      this->displayTextBox->TabIndex = 1;
30      this->displayTextBox->Text = S"";
31
32      // inputTextBox
33      this->inputTextBox->Location = Point( 8, 8 );
34      this->inputTextBox->Name = S"inputTextBox";
35      this->inputTextBox->Size = Drawing::Size( 272, 20 );
36      this->inputTextBox->TabIndex = 0;
37      this->inputTextBox->Text = S"";
38      this->inputTextBox->KeyDown += new KeyEventHandler( this,
39         inputTextBox_KeyDown );
40
41      // server
42      this->AutoScaleBaseSize = Drawing::Size( 5, 13 );
43      this->ClientSize = Drawing::Size( 292, 261 );
44
45      Control *control[] = { this->displayTextBox,
46         this->inputTextBox };
47      this->Controls->AddRange( control );
48
49      this->Name = S"Server";
50      this->Text = S"Server";
51      this->Closing += new CancelEventHandler( this,
52         Server_Closing );
53
54      this->ResumeLayout();
55   } // end method InitializeComponent
56
57   void Server::Server_Closing( Object *sender, CancelEventArgs *e )
58   {
59      System::Environment::Exit( System::Environment::ExitCode );
60   }
61
62   // sends the text typed at the server to the client
63   void Server::inputTextBox_KeyDown(
64      Object *sender, KeyEventArgs *e )
65   {
66      // sends the text to the client
67      try {
```

Fig. 18.2   Server class method definitions. (Part 2 of 4.)

```
68
69              if ( e->KeyCode == Keys::Enter && connection != NULL ) {
70                 writer->Write( String::Concat( S"SERVER>>> ",
71                    inputTextBox->Text ) );
72
73                 displayTextBox->Text = String::Concat(
74                    displayTextBox->Text, S"\r\nSERVER>>> ",
75                    inputTextBox->Text );
76
77                 // if the user at the server signaled termination
78                 // sever the connection to the client
79                 if ( inputTextBox->Text->Equals( S"TERMINATE" ) )
80                    connection->Close();
81
82                 inputTextBox->Clear();
83              } // end if
84           } // end try
85           catch ( SocketException * ) {
86              displayTextBox->Text = String::Concat(
87                 displayTextBox->Text, S"\nError writing object" );
88           } // end catch
89        } // end method inputTextBox_KeyDown
90
91        // allows a client to connect and displays the text it sends
92        void Server::RunServer()
93        {
94           TcpListener *listener;
95           int counter = 1;
96
97           // wait for a client connection and display the text
98           // that the client sends
99           try {
100
101              // Step 1: create TcpListener
102              listener = new TcpListener( 4500 );
103
104              // Step 2: TcpListener waits for connection request
105              listener->Start();
106
107              // Step 3: establish connection upon client request
108              while ( true ) {
109                 displayTextBox->Text = S"Waiting for connection\r\n";
110
111                 // accept an incoming connection
112                 connection = listener->AcceptSocket();
113
114                 // create NetworkStream object associated with socket
115                 socketStream = new NetworkStream( connection );
116
117                 // create objects for transferring data across stream
118                 writer = new BinaryWriter( socketStream );
119                 reader = new BinaryReader( socketStream );
120
```

Fig. 18.2   Server class method definitions. (Part 3 of 4.)

```
121             displayTextBox->Text = String::Concat(
122                 displayTextBox->Text, S"Connection ",
123                 counter.ToString(), S" received.\r\n" );
124
125             // inform client that connection was successfull
126             writer->Write( S"SERVER>>> Connection successful" );
127
128             inputTextBox->ReadOnly = false;
129             String *theReply = S"";
130
131             // Step 4: read String data sent from client
132             do {
133
134                try {
135
136                   // read the string sent to the server
137                   theReply = reader->ReadString();
138
139                   // display the message
140                   displayTextBox->Text = String::Concat(
141                      displayTextBox->Text, S"\r\n", theReply );
142                } // end try
143
144                // handle exception if error reading data
145                catch ( Exception * ) {
146                   break;
147                } // end catch
148
149             } while ( !theReply->Equals( S"CLIENT>>> TERMINATE" )
150                && connection->Connected );
151
152             displayTextBox->Text = String::Concat(
153                displayTextBox->Text,
154                S"\r\nUser terminated connection" );
155
156             // Step 5: close connection
157             inputTextBox->ReadOnly = true;
158             writer->Close();
159             reader->Close();
160             socketStream->Close();
161             connection->Close();
162
163             ++counter;
164          } // end while
165       } // end try
166
167       catch ( Exception *error ) {
168          MessageBox::Show( error->ToString() );
169       }
170 } // end method RunServer
```

Fig. 18.2   **Server** class method definitions. (Part 4 of 4.)

```
1   // Fig. 18.3: ServerTest.cpp
2   // Entry point for application.
3
4   #include "Server.h"
5
6   int __stdcall WinMain()
7   {
8      Application::Run( new Server() );
9
10     return 0;
11  } // end function WinMain
```

Fig. 18.3 **Server** class driver.

```
1   // Fig. 18.4: Client.h
2   // Set up a Client that will read information sent
3   // from a Server and display the information.
4
5   #pragma once
6
7   #using <system.dll>
8   #using <mscorlib.dll>
9   #using <system.drawing.dll>
10  #using <system.windows.forms.dll>
11
12  using namespace System;
13  using namespace System::Drawing;
14  using namespace System::ComponentModel;
15  using namespace System::Windows::Forms;
16  using namespace System::Threading;
17  using namespace System::Net::Sockets;
18  using namespace System::IO;
19
20  // connects to a chat server
21  public __gc class Client : public Form
22  {
23  public:
24     Client();
25     void RunClient();
26
27  protected:
28     void Client_Closing( Object *, CancelEventArgs * );
29     void inputTextBox_KeyDown ( Object *, KeyEventArgs * );
30
31  private:
32     TextBox *inputTextBox;
33     TextBox *displayTextBox;
34
```

Fig. 18.4 Client portion of a client/server stream-socket connection. (Part 1 of 2.)

```
35        NetworkStream *output;
36        BinaryWriter *writer;
37        BinaryReader *reader;
38
39        String *message;
40
41        Thread *readThread;
42
43        void InitializeComponent();
44     }; // end class Client
```

Fig. 18.4 Client portion of a client/server stream-socket connection. (Part 2 of 2.)

```
1     // Fig. 18.5: Client.cpp
2     // Method defintions for class Client.
3
4     #include "Client.h"
5
6     // default constructor
7     Client::Client()
8     {
9        InitializeComponent();
10
11        readThread = new Thread( new ThreadStart( this, RunClient ) );
12        readThread->Start();
13     }
14
15     void Client::InitializeComponent()
16     {
17        this->inputTextBox = new TextBox();
18        this->displayTextBox = new TextBox();
19
20        this->SuspendLayout();
21
22        // inputTextBox
23        this->inputTextBox->Location = Point( 8, 8 );
24        this->inputTextBox->Name = S"inputTextBox";
25        this->inputTextBox->Size = Drawing::Size( 272, 20 );
26        this->inputTextBox->TabIndex = 0;
27        this->inputTextBox->Text = S"";
28        this->inputTextBox->KeyDown += new KeyEventHandler( this,
29           inputTextBox_KeyDown );
30
31        // displayTextBox
32        this->displayTextBox->Location = Point( 8, 40 );
33        this->displayTextBox->Multiline = true;
34        this->displayTextBox->Name = S"displayTextBox";
35        this->displayTextBox->ReadOnly = true;
36        this->displayTextBox->Size = Drawing::Size( 272, 208 );
37        this->displayTextBox->TabIndex = 1;
38        this->displayTextBox->Text = S"";
```

Fig. 18.5 Client class method definitions. (Part 1 of 4.)

```
39
40    // client
41    this->AutoScaleBaseSize = Drawing::Size( 5, 13 );
42    this->ClientSize = Drawing::Size( 292, 261 );
43
44    Control *control[] = { this->displayTextBox,
45       this->inputTextBox };
46    this->Controls->AddRange( control );
47
48    this->Name = S"Client";
49    this->Text = S"Client";
50    this->Closing += new CancelEventHandler( this,
51       Client_Closing );
52
53    this->ResumeLayout();
54 } // end method InitializeComponent
55
56 void Client::Client_Closing( Object *sender, CancelEventArgs *e )
57 {
58    System::Environment::Exit( System::Environment::ExitCode );
59 }
60
61 // sends text the user typed to server
62 void Client::inputTextBox_KeyDown (
63    Object *sender, KeyEventArgs *e )
64 {
65    try {
66
67       if ( e->KeyCode == Keys::Enter ) {
68
69          writer->Write( String::Concat(
70             S"CLIENT>>> ", inputTextBox->Text ) );
71
72          displayTextBox->Text = String::Concat(
73             displayTextBox->Text, S"\r\nCLIENT>>> ",
74             inputTextBox->Text );
75
76          inputTextBox->Clear();
77       } // end if
78    } // end try
79    catch ( SocketException * ) {
80       displayTextBox->Text = String::Concat(
81          displayTextBox->Text, S"\nError writing object" );
82    } // end catch
83 } // end method inputTextBox_KeyDown
84
85 // connect to server and display server-generated text
86 void Client::RunClient()
87 {
88    TcpClient *client;
89
90    // instantiate TcpClient for sending data to server
```

Fig. 18.5 Client class method definitions. (Part 2 of 4.)

```
 91        try {
 92           displayTextBox->Text = String::Concat(
 93              displayTextBox->Text, S"Attempting connection\r\n" );
 94
 95           // Step 1: create TcpClient and connect to server
 96           client = new TcpClient();
 97           client->Connect( S"localhost", 4500 );
 98
 99           // Step 2: get NetworkStream associated with TcpClient
100           output = client->GetStream();
101
102           // create objects for writing and reading across stream
103           writer = new BinaryWriter( output );
104           reader = new BinaryReader( output );
105
106           displayTextBox->Text = String::Concat(
107              displayTextBox->Text, S"\r\nGot I/O streams\r\n" );
108
109           inputTextBox->ReadOnly = false;
110
111           // loop until server signals termination
112           do {
113
114              // Step 3: processing phase
115              try {
116
117                 // read message from server
118                 message = reader->ReadString();
119                 displayTextBox->Text = String::Concat(
120                    displayTextBox->Text, S"\r\n", message );
121              } // end try
122
123              // handle exception if error in reading server data
124              catch ( Exception * ) {
125                 System::Environment::Exit(
126                    System::Environment::ExitCode );
127              } // end catch
128
129           } while ( !message->Equals( S"CLIENT>>> TERMINATE" ) );
130
131           displayTextBox->Text = String::Concat(
132              displayTextBox->Text,
133              S"\r\nClosing connection->\r\n" );
134
135           // Step 4: close connection
136           writer->Close();
137           reader->Close();
138           output->Close();
139           client->Close();
140
141           Application::Exit();
142        } // end try
143
144        // handle exception if error in establishing connection
```

Fig. 18.5 Client class method definitions. (Part 3 of 4.)

```
145       catch ( Exception *error ) {
146          MessageBox::Show( error->ToString() );
147
148          Application::Exit();
149       } // end catch
150    } // end method RunClient
```

Fig. 18.5 **Client** class method definitions. (Part 4 of 4.)

```
1    // Fig. 18.6: ClientTest.cpp
2    // Driver for application.
3
4    #include "Client.h"
5
6    int __stdcall WinMain()
7    {
8       Application::Run( new Client() );
9
10      return 0;
11   } // end function WinMain
```

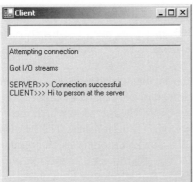

Fig. 18.6 **ClientTest.cpp** demonstrates a client/server stream-socket connection. (Part 1 of 2.)

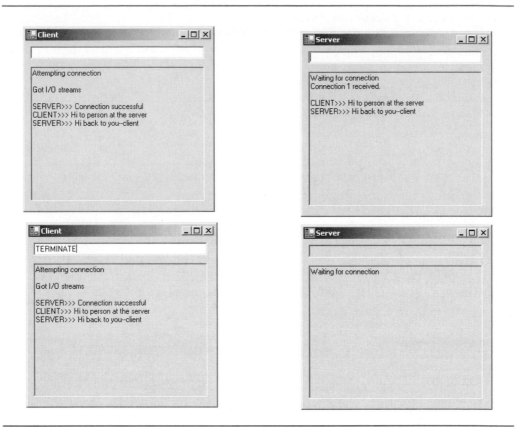

Fig. 18.6   ClientTest.cpp demonstrates a client/server stream-socket connection. (Part 2 of 2.)

As we analyze this example, we begin by discussing class **Server** (Fig. 18.1– Fig. 18.2). In the constructor, line 12 (Fig. 18.2) creates a **Thread** that will accept connections from clients. Line 13 starts the **Thread**, which invokes method **RunServer** (lines 92–170). Method **RunServer** initializes the server to receive connection requests and process connections. Line 102 instantiates the **TcpListener** to listen for a connection request from a client at port **4500** (Step 1). Line 105 then calls method **Start** of the **TcpListener** object, which causes the **TcpListener** to begin waiting for requests (Step 2).

Lines 108–164 declare an infinite **while** loop that establishes connections requested by clients (Step 3). Line 112 calls method **AcceptSocket** of the **TcpListener** object, which returns a **Socket** pointer upon successful connection. The thread in which method **AcceptSocket** is called stops executing until a connection is established. The **Socket** object will manage the connection. Line 115 passes this **Socket** pointer as an argument to the constructor of a **NetworkStream** object. Class **NetworkStream** provides access to streams across a network—in this example, the **NetworkStream** object provides access to the **Socket** connection. Lines 118–119 create instances of the *Binary-*

Writer and *BinaryReader* classes for writing and reading data. We pass the **NetworkStream** object as an argument to each constructor; **BinaryWriter** can write bytes to a **NetworkStream**, and **BinaryReader** can read bytes from a **Network-Stream**. Lines 121–123 append text to the **TextBox**, indicating that a connection was received.

BinaryWriter method *Write* has many overloaded versions, which enable the method to write various types to a stream. (You might remember that we used these over-loaded methods in Chapter 14, Files and Streams, to write record data to files.) Line 126 uses method **Write** to send to the client a **String *** notifying the user of a successful connec-tion. Lines 132–150 declare a **do/while** structure that executes until the server receives a message indicating connection termination (i.e., **CLIENT>>> TERMINATE**). Line 137 uses **BinaryReader** method *ReadString* to read a **String *** from the stream (Step 4). (You might remember that we also used this method in Chapter 14 to read records' first-names and last-names from files.) Method **ReadString** blocks until a **String *** is read. To prevent the whole server from blocking, we use a separate **Thread** to handle the transfer of information. The **while** statement loops until there is more information to read—this results in I/O blocking, which causes the program always to appear frozen. However, if we run this portion of the program in a separate **Thread**, the user can interact with the Windows Form and send messages while the program waits in the background for incoming messages.

When the chat is complete, lines 158–161 close the **BinaryWriter**, **Bina-ryReader**, **NetworkStream** and **Socket** (Step 5) by invoking their respective **Close** methods. The server then waits for another client connection request by returning to the beginning of the **while** loop (line 108).

When the user of the server application enters a string in the **TextBox** and presses the *Enter* key, event handler **inputTextBox_KeyDown** (lines 63–89) reads the string and sends it via method **Write** of class **BinaryWriter**. If a user terminates the server appli-cation, line 80 calls method **Close** of the **Socket** object to close the connection.

Lines 57–60 define the **Server_Closing** event handler for the **Closing** event. The event closes the application and uses **System::Environment::Exit** method with parameter **System::Environment::ExitCode** to terminate all threads. Method **Exit** of class **Environment** closes all threads associated with the application.

Figure 18.4–Fig. 18.5 list the code for the **Client** object. Like the **Server** object, the **Client** object creates a **Thread** (lines 11–12 of Fig. 18.5) in its constructor to handle all incoming messages. **Client** method **RunClient** (lines 86–150) connects to the **Server**, receives data from the **Server** and sends data to the **Server** (when the user presses *Enter*). Lines 96–97 instantiate a **TcpClient** object, then call its method **Con-nect** to establish a connection (Step 1). The first argument to method **Connect** is the name of the server—in our case, the server's name is *"localhost"*, meaning that the server is located on the same machine as the client. The **localhost** is also known as the *loopback IP address* and is equivalent to the IP address *127.0.0.1*. This value sends the data transmission back to the sender's IP address. [*Note*: We chose to demonstrate the client/server relationship by connecting between programs that are executing on the same computer (**localhost**). Normally, this argument would contain the Internet address of another computer.] The second argument to method **Connect** is the server port number. This number must match the port number at which the server waits for connections.

The **Client** uses a **NetworkStream** to send data to and receive data from the server. The client obtains the **NetworkStream** on line 100 through a call to **TcpClient** method **GetStream** (Step 2). The **do/while** structure in lines 112–129 loops until the client receives the connection-termination message (**SERVER>>> TERMINATE**). Line 118 uses **BinaryReader** method **ReadString** to obtain the next message from the server (Step 3). Lines 119–120 display the message, and lines 136–139 close the **BinaryWriter**, **BinaryReader**, **NetworkStream** and **TcpClient** objects (Step 4).

When the user of the client application enters a string in the **TextBox** and presses the *Enter* key, the event handler **inputTextBox_KeyDown** (lines 62–83) reads the string from the **TextBox** and sends it via **BinaryWriter** method **Write**. Notice that, here, the **Server** receives a connection, processes it, closes it and waits for the next one. In a real-world application, a server would likely receive a connection, set up the connection to be processed as a separate thread of execution and wait for new connections. The separate threads that process existing connections can continue to execute while the **Server** concentrates on new connection requests.

18.5 Connectionless Client/Server Interaction with Datagrams

Up to this point, we have discussed connection-oriented, streams-based transmission. Now, we consider connectionless transmission using datagrams.

Connection-oriented transmission is similar to interaction over a telephone system, in which a user dials a number and is *connected* to the telephone of the party desired. The system maintains the connection for the duration of the phone call, regardless of whether the users are speaking.

By contrast, connectionless transmission via *datagrams* more closely resembles the method by which the postal service carries and delivers mail. Connectionless transmission bundles and sends information in *packets* called datagrams, which can be thought of as similar to posted letters. If a large message will not fit in one envelope, that message is broken into separate message pieces and placed in separate, sequentially numbered envelopes. All the letters are mailed at once. The letters might arrive in order, out of order or not at all. The person at the receiving end reassembles the message pieces into sequential order before attempting to interpret the message. If the message is small enough to fit in one envelope, the sequencing problem is eliminated, but it is still possible that the message will never arrive. (Unlike with posted mail, duplicate of datagrams could reach receiving computers.) .NET provides the **UdpClient** class for connectionless transmission. Like **TcpListener** and **TcpClient**, **UdpClient** uses methods from class **Socket**. The **UdpClient** methods **Send** and **Receive** are used to transmit data with **Socket**'s **SendTo** method and to read data with **Socket**'s **ReceiveFrom** method, respectively.

The programs in Fig. 18.7–Fig. 18.9 and Fig. 18.10–Fig. 18.12 use datagrams to send *packets* of information between a client and server applications. In the **Client** application, the user types a message into a **TextBox** and presses *Enter*. The client converts the message to a **Byte** array and sends it to the server. The server receives the packet and displays the packet's information; it then *echoes*, or returns, the packet back to the client. When the client receives the packet, the client displays the packet's information. In this example (Fig. 18.7–Fig. 18.12), the implementations of the **Client** and **Server** classes are similar to the **Client** and **Server** classes created earlier (in Fig. 18.1–Fig. 18.6).

```
1   // Fig. 18.7: Server.h
2   // Set up a Server that will receive packets from a
3   // client and send packets to a client.
4
5   #pragma once
6
7   #using <system.dll>
8   #using <mscorlib.dll>
9   #using <system.drawing.dll>
10  #using <system.windows.forms.dll>
11  #using <system.data.dll>
12
13  using namespace System;
14  using namespace System::Drawing;
15  using namespace System::ComponentModel;
16  using namespace System::Windows::Forms;
17  using namespace System::Net;
18  using namespace System::Net::Sockets;
19  using namespace System::Threading;
20  using namespace System::Text;
21
22  // create the UDP server
23  public __gc class Server : public Form
24  {
25  public:
26     Server();
27     void WaitForPackets();
28
29  protected:
30     void Server_Closing( Object *, CancelEventArgs * );
31
32  private:
33     TextBox *displayTextBox;
34     UdpClient *client;
35     IPEndPoint *receivePoint;
36
37     void InitializeComponent();
38  }; // end class Server
```

Fig. 18.7   Server-side portion of connectionless client/server computing.

```
1   // Fig. 18.8: Server.cpp
2   // Method definitions for class Server.
3
4   #include "Server.h"
5
6   // no-argument constructor
7   Server::Server()
8   {
9      InitializeComponent();
10
```

Fig. 18.8   **Server** class method definitions. (Part 1 of 3.)

```
11       client = new UdpClient( 4500 );
12       receivePoint = new IPEndPoint( new IPAddress( 0 ), 0 );
13       Thread *readThread = new Thread(
14          new ThreadStart( this, WaitForPackets ) );
15
16       readThread->Start();
17    }
18
19    void Server::InitializeComponent()
20    {
21       this->displayTextBox = new TextBox();
22
23       this->SuspendLayout();
24
25       // displayTextBox
26       this->displayTextBox->Location = Point( 8, 8 );
27       this->displayTextBox->Multiline = true;
28       this->displayTextBox->Name = S"displayTextBox";
29       this->displayTextBox->ReadOnly = true;
30       this->displayTextBox->ScrollBars = ScrollBars::Vertical;
31       this->displayTextBox->Size = Drawing::Size( 264, 248 );
32       this->displayTextBox->TabIndex = 0;
33       this->displayTextBox->Text = S"";
34
35       // server
36       this->AutoScaleBaseSize = Drawing::Size( 5, 13 );
37       this->ClientSize = Drawing::Size( 280, 261 );
38
39       Control *control[] = { this->displayTextBox };
40       this->Controls->AddRange( control );
41
42       this->Name = S"Server";
43       this->Text = S"Server";
44       this->Closing += new CancelEventHandler( this,
45          Server_Closing );
46
47       this->ResumeLayout();
48    } // end method InitializeComponent
49
50    // shut down the server
51    void Server::Server_Closing( Object *sender, CancelEventArgs *e )
52    {
53       System::Environment::Exit( System::Environment::ExitCode );
54    }
55
56    // wait for a packet to arrive
57    void Server::WaitForPackets()
58    {
59       while ( true ) {
60
```

Fig. 18.8   **Server** class method definitions. (Part 2 of 3.)

```
61            // set up packet
62            Byte data __gc[] = client->Receive( &receivePoint );
63
64            displayTextBox->Text = String::Concat(
65               displayTextBox->Text, S"\r\nPacket received:",
66               S"\r\nLength: ", data->Length.ToString(),
67               S"\r\nContaining: ",
68               System::Text::Encoding::ASCII->GetString( data ) );
69
70            // echo information from packet back to client
71            displayTextBox->Text = String::Concat(
72               displayTextBox->Text,
73               S"\r\n\r\nEcho data back to client..." );
74
75            client->Send( data, data->Length, receivePoint );
76            displayTextBox->Text = String::Concat(
77               displayTextBox->Text, S"\r\nPacket sent\r\n" );
78         } // end while
79      } // end method WaitForPackets
```

Fig. 18.8 Server class method definitions. (Part 3 of 3.)

```
1   // Fig. 18.9: ServerTest.cpp
2   // Entry point for application.
3
4   #include "Server.h"
5
6   int __stdcall WinMain()
7   {
8      Application::Run( new Server() );
9
10     return 0;
11  } // end function WinMain
```

Fig. 18.9 Server class driver.

```
1   // Fig. 18.10: Client.h
2   // Set up a Client that sends packets to a server and receives
3   // packets from a server.
4
5   #pragma once
6
7   #using <system.dll>
8   #using <mscorlib.dll>
9   #using <system.drawing.dll>
10  #using <system.windows.forms.dll>
11  #using <system.data.dll>
12
13  using namespace System;
14  using namespace System::Drawing;
15  using namespace System::ComponentModel;
16  using namespace System::Windows::Forms;
17  using namespace System::Net;
18  using namespace System::Net::Sockets;
19  using namespace System::Threading;
20
21  // run the UDP client
22  public __gc class Client : public Form
23  {
24  public:
25     Client();
26     void WaitForPackets();
27
28  protected:
29     void Client_Closing( Object *, CancelEventArgs * );
30     void inputTextBox_KeyDown( Object *, KeyEventArgs * );
31
32  private:
33     TextBox *inputTextBox;
34     TextBox *displayTextBox;
35
36     UdpClient *client;
37     IPEndPoint *receivePoint;
38
39     void InitializeComponent();
40  }; // end class Client
```

Fig. 18.10 Client portion of connectionless client/server computing.

```
1   // Fig. 18.11: Client.cpp
2   // Method definitions for class Client.
3
4   #include "Client.h"
5
6   // no-argument constructor
7   Client::Client()
8   {
9      InitializeComponent();
```

Fig. 18.11 Client class method definitions. (Part 1 of 3.)

```
10
11      receivePoint = new IPEndPoint( new IPAddress( 0 ), 0 );
12      client = new UdpClient( 4501 );
13      Thread *thread =
14          new Thread( new ThreadStart( this, WaitForPackets ) );
15      thread->Start();
16   }
17
18   void Client::InitializeComponent()
19   {
20      this->displayTextBox = new TextBox();
21      this->inputTextBox = new TextBox();
22
23      this->SuspendLayout();
24
25      // displayTextBox
26      this->displayTextBox->Location = Point( 8, 40 );
27      this->displayTextBox->Multiline = true;
28      this->displayTextBox->Name = S"displayTextBox";
29      this->displayTextBox->ReadOnly = true;
30      this->displayTextBox->ScrollBars = ScrollBars::Vertical;
31      this->displayTextBox->Size = Drawing::Size( 264, 216 );
32      this->displayTextBox->TabIndex = 1;
33      this->displayTextBox->Text = S"";
34
35      // inputTextBox
36      this->inputTextBox->Location = Point( 8, 8 );
37      this->inputTextBox->Name = S"inputTextBox";
38      this->inputTextBox->Size = Drawing::Size( 264, 20 );
39      this->inputTextBox->TabIndex = 0;
40      this->inputTextBox->Text = S"";
41      this->inputTextBox->KeyDown += new KeyEventHandler( this,
42         inputTextBox_KeyDown );
43
44      // client
45      this->AutoScaleBaseSize = Drawing::Size( 5, 13 );
46      this->ClientSize = Drawing::Size( 280, 261 );
47
48      Control *control[] = { this->displayTextBox,
49         this->inputTextBox };
50      this->Controls->AddRange( control );
51
52      this->Name = S"Client";
53      this->Text = S"Client";
54      this->Closing += new CancelEventHandler( this,
55         Client_Closing );
56
57      this->ResumeLayout();
58   } // end method InitializeComponent
59
60   // shut down the client
61   void Client::Client_Closing( Object *sender, CancelEventArgs *e )
62   {
```

Fig. 18.11 Client class method definitions. (Part 2 of 3.)

```
63        System::Environment::Exit( System::Environment::ExitCode );
64    }
65
66    // send a packet
67    void Client::inputTextBox_KeyDown(
68        Object *sender, KeyEventArgs *e )
69    {
70        if ( e->KeyCode == Keys::Enter ) {
71
72            // create packet (datagram) as string
73            String *packet = inputTextBox->Text;
74
75            displayTextBox->Text = String::Concat(
76                displayTextBox->Text,
77                S"\r\nSending packet containing: ", packet );
78
79            // convert packet to byte array
80            Byte data __gc[] =
81                System::Text::Encoding::ASCII->GetBytes( packet );
82
83            // send packet to server on port 4500
84            client->Send( data, data->Length, S"localhost", 4500 );
85            displayTextBox->Text = String::Concat(
86                displayTextBox->Text, S"\r\nPacket sent\r\n" );
87            inputTextBox->Clear();
88        } // end if
89    } // end method inputTextBox_KeyDown
90
91    // wait for packets to arrive
92    void Client::WaitForPackets()
93    {
94        while ( true ) {
95
96            // receive byte array from server
97            Byte data __gc[]= client->Receive( &receivePoint );
98
99            // output packet data to TextBox
100           displayTextBox->Text = String::Concat(
101               displayTextBox->Text, S"\r\nPacket received:",
102               S"\r\nLength: ", data->Length.ToString(),
103               S"\r\nContaining: ",
104               System::Text::Encoding::ASCII->GetString( data ),
105               S"\r\n" );
106       } // end while
107   } // end method WaitForPackets
```

Fig. 18.11 `Client` class method definitions. (Part 3 of 3.)

```
1    // Fig. 18.12: ClientTest.cpp
2    // Entry point for application.
3
4    #include "Client.h"
```

Fig. 18.12 `Client` class driver. (Part 1 of 2.)

```
5
6    int __stdcall WinMain()
7    {
8        Application::Run( new Client() );
9
10       return 0;
11   } // end function WinMain
```

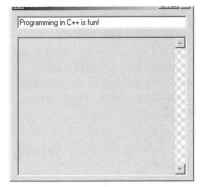
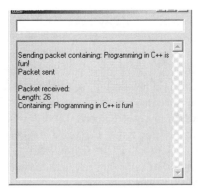

Fig. 18.12 Client class driver. (Part 2 of 2.)

The code in Fig. 18.7–Fig. 18.8 defines the **Server** for this application. Line 11 (Fig. 18.8) in the constructor for class **Server** creates an instance of the **UdpClient** class that receives data at port **4500**. This initializes the underlying **Socket** for communications. Line 12 creates an instance of class **IPEndPoint** to hold the IP address and port number of the client(s) that transmit to **Server**. The first argument to the constructor of **IPEndPoint** is an **IPAddress** object pointer; the second argument to the constructor for **IPEndPoint** is the port number of the endpoint. These values are both **0**, because we need only instantiate an empty **IPEndPoint** object. The IP addresses and port numbers of clients are copied into the **IPEndPoint** when datagrams are received from clients.

Server method **WaitForPackets** (lines 57–79) executes an infinite loop while waiting for data to arrive at the **Server**. When information arrives, the **UdpClient** method **Receive** (line 62) receives a **Byte** array from the client. We pass **Receive** a reference to the **IPEndPoint** object created in the constructor; this provides the method with an **IPEndPoint** into which the program copies the client's IP address and port number. This program will compile and run without an exception even if the pointer to the **IPEndPoint** object is **NULL**, because method **Receive** initializes the **IPEndPoint** if it is **NULL**.

Good Programming Practice 18.2

*Initialize all pointers to objects (with a value other than **NULL**). This protects code from methods that do not check their parameters for **NULL** pointers.*

Lines 64–73 update the **Server**'s display to include the packet's information and content. Line 75 echoes the data back to the client, using **UdpClient** method **Send**. This version of **Send** takes three arguments: the **Byte** array to send, an **int** representing the array's length and the **IPEndPoint** to which to send the data. We use array **data** returned by method **Receive** as the data, the length of array **data** as the length and the **IPEndPoint** passed to method **Receive** as the data's destination. The IP address and port number of the client that sent the data to **Server** are stored in **receivePoint**, so merely passing **receivePoint** to **Send** allows **Server** to respond to the client.

Class **Client** (Fig. 18.10–Fig. 18.11) works similarly to class **Server**, except that the **Client** object sends packets only when the user types a message in a **TextBox** and presses the *Enter* key. When this occurs, the program calls event handler **inputTextBox_KeyDown** (lines 67–89 of Fig. 18.11). Lines 80–81 convert the string that the user entered in the **TextBox** to a **Byte** array. Line 84 calls **UdpClient** method **Send** to send the **Byte** array to the **Server** that is located on **localhost** (i.e., the same machine). We specify the port as **4500**, which we know to be **Server**'s port.

Line 12 instantiates a **UdpClient** object to receive packets at port **4501**—we choose port **4501** because the **Server** already occupies port **4500**. Method **WaitFor-Packets** of class **Client** (lines 92–107) uses an infinite loop to wait for these packets. The **UdpClient** method **Receive** blocks until a packet of data is received (line 97). The blocking performed by method **Receive** does not prevent class **Client** from performing other services (e.g., handling user input), because a separate thread runs method **WaitForPackets**.

When a packet arrives, lines 100–105 display its contents in the **TextBox**. The user can type information into the **Client** window's **TextBox** and press the *Enter* key at any time, even while a packet is being received. The event handler for the **TextBox** processes the event and sends the data to the server.

18.6 Client/Server Tic-Tac-Toe Using a Multithreaded Server

In this section, we present our capstone networking example—the popular game Tic-Tac-Toe, implemented with stream sockets and client/server techniques. The program consists of a **Server** application (Fig. 18.13–Fig. 18.16) and two **Client** applications (Fig. 18.19–Fig. 18.21); **Server**, which inherits from interface **TicTacToeServer** (Fig. 18.13), allows the **Client**s to connect to the server and play Tic-Tac-Toe. We depict the output in Fig. 18.21. When the server receives a client connection, lines 66–77 of Fig. 18.15 create an instance of class **Player** (Fig. 18.17–Fig. 18.18) to process the client in a separate thread of execution. This enables the server to handle requests from both clients. The server assigns value **"X"** to the first client that connects (player **X** makes the first move), then assigns value **"O"** to the second client. Throughout the game, the server maintains information regarding the status of the board so that the server can validate players' requested moves. However, neither the server nor the client can establish whether a player has won the game—in this application, method **GameOver** (lines 142–145 of Fig. 18.15) always returns **false**. We leave it to the reader to implement functionality that enables the application to determine a winner. Each **Client** maintains its own GUI version of the Tic-Tac-Toe board to display the game. The clients can place marks only in empty squares on the board. Class **Square** (Fig. 18.22–Fig. 18.23) is used to define squares on the Tic-Tac-Toe board.

```
1    // Fig. 18.13: TicTacToeServer.h
2    // Interface that Server class implements.
3
4    #pragma once
5
6    #using <system.dll>
7    #using <mscorlib.dll>
8    #using <system.drawing.dll>
9    #using <system.windows.forms.dll>
10
11   using namespace System;
12   using namespace System::Drawing;
13   using namespace System::ComponentModel;
14   using namespace System::Windows::Forms;
15   using namespace System::Net::Sockets;
16   using namespace System::Threading;
17   using namespace System::IO;
18
19   __gc __interface TicTacToeServer
20   {
21   public:
22
23      // determine if the game is over
24      bool GameOver();
25
26      // appends the argument to text in displayTextBox
27      void Display( String * );
28
29      // determine if a move is valid
30      bool ValidMove( int, int );
31
32      __property bool get_IsDisconnected();
33   }; // end interface TicTacToeServer
```

Fig. 18.13 `TicTacToeServer` interface.

```
1    // Fig. 18.14: Server.h
2    // This class maintains a game of Tic-Tac-Toe for two
3    // client applications.
4
5    #pragma once
6
7    #include "TicTacToeServer.h"
8    #include "Player.h"
9
10   // awaits connections from two clients and allows them to
11   // play tic-tac-toe against each other
12   public __gc class Server : public Form, public TicTacToeServer
13   {
14   public:
```

Fig. 18.14 Server side of a client/server Tic-Tac-Toe program. (Part 1 of 2.)

```
15      Server();
16      void SetUp();
17      void Display( String * );
18      bool ValidMove( int , int );
19      bool IsOccupied( int );
20      bool GameOver();
21
22      __property bool get_IsDisconnected()
23      {
24         return disconnected;
25      }
26
27   protected:
28      void Server_Closing( Object *, CancelEventArgs * );
29
30   private:
31      TextBox *displayTextBox;
32
33      Byte board __gc[];
34
35      Player *players __gc[];
36      Thread *playerThreads __gc[];
37
38      TcpListener *listener;
39      int currentPlayer;
40      Thread *getPlayers;
41
42      static bool disconnected = false;
43
44      void InitializeComponent();
45   }; // end class Server
```

Fig. 18.14 Server side of a client/server Tic-Tac-Toe program. (Part 2 of 2.)

```
1    // Fig. 18.15: Server.cpp
2    // Method definitions for class Server.
3
4    #include "Server.h"
5
6    // default constructor
7    Server::Server()
8    {
9       InitializeComponent();
10
11      board = new Byte[ 9 ];
12
13      players = new Player *[ 2 ];
14      playerThreads = new Thread *[ 2 ];
15      currentPlayer = 0;
16
```

Fig. 18.15 Server class method definitions. (Part 1 of 4.)

```
17      // accept connections on a different thread
18      getPlayers = new Thread( new ThreadStart( this, SetUp ) );
19      getPlayers->Start();
20   } // end constructor
21
22   void Server::InitializeComponent()
23   {
24      this->displayTextBox = new TextBox();
25
26      this->SuspendLayout();
27
28      // displayTextBox
29      this->displayTextBox->Location = Point( 8, 8 );
30      this->displayTextBox->Multiline = true;
31      this->displayTextBox->Name = S"displayTextBox";
32      this->displayTextBox->ReadOnly = true;
33      this->displayTextBox->ScrollBars = ScrollBars::Vertical;
34      this->displayTextBox->Size = Drawing::Size( 272, 256 );
35      this->displayTextBox->TabIndex = 0;
36      this->displayTextBox->Text = S"";
37
38      // server
39      this->AutoScaleBaseSize = Drawing::Size( 5, 13 );
40      this->ClientSize = Drawing::Size( 292, 273 );
41
42      Control *control[] = { this->displayTextBox };
43      this->Controls->AddRange( control );
44
45      this->Name = S"Server";
46      this->Text = S"Tic Tac Toe Server";
47      this->Closing += new CancelEventHandler( this,
48        Server_Closing );
49
50      this->ResumeLayout();
51   } // end method InitializeComponent
52
53   void Server::Server_Closing( Object *sender, CancelEventArgs *e )
54   {
55      disconnected = true;
56   }
57
58   // accepts connections from 2 players
59   void Server::SetUp()
60   {
61      // set up Socket
62      listener = new TcpListener( 4500 );
63      listener->Start();
64
65      // accept first player and start a thread for him or her
66      players[ 0 ] =
67         new Player( listener->AcceptSocket(), this, 0 );
68      playerThreads[ 0 ] = new Thread(
```

Fig. 18.15 Server class method definitions. (Part 2 of 4.)

```
69            new ThreadStart( players[ 0 ], &Player::Run ) );
70        playerThreads[ 0 ]->Start();
71
72        // accept second player and start a thread for him or her
73        players[ 1 ] =
74            new Player( listener->AcceptSocket(), this, 1 );
75        playerThreads[ 1 ] =
76            new Thread( new ThreadStart( players[ 1 ], &Player::Run ) );
77        playerThreads[ 1 ]->Start();
78
79        // let the first player know that the other player has
80        // connected
81        Monitor::Enter( players[ 0 ] );
82        players[ 0 ]->ThreadSuspended = false;
83        Monitor::Pulse( players[ 0 ] );
84        Monitor::Exit( players[ 0 ] );
85    } // end method SetUp
86
87    // appends the argument to text in displayTextBox
88    void Server::Display( String *message )
89    {
90        displayTextBox->Text = String::Concat( displayTextBox->Text,
91            message, S"\r\n" );
92    }
93
94    // determine if a move is valid
95    bool Server::ValidMove( int location, int player )
96    {
97        // prevent another thread from making a move
98        Monitor::Enter( this );
99
100       // while it is not the current player's turn, wait
101       while ( player != currentPlayer )
102           Monitor::Wait( this );
103
104       // if the desired square is not occupied
105       if ( !IsOccupied( location ) ) {
106
107           // set the board to contain the current player's mark
108           board[ location ] = ( currentPlayer == 0 ? 'X' : 'O' );
109
110           // set the currentPlayer to be the other player
111           currentPlayer = ( currentPlayer + 1 ) % 2;
112
113           // notify the other player of the move
114           players[ currentPlayer ]->OtherPlayerMoved( location );
115
116           // alert the other player it's time to move
117           Monitor::Pulse( this );
118           Monitor::Exit( this );
119
120           return true;
121       } // end if
122       else {
```

Fig. 18.15 Server class method definitions. (Part 3 of 4.)

```
123
124         // allow another move attempt
125         Monitor::Pulse( this );
126         Monitor::Exit( this );
127
128         return false;
129      }
130  } // end method ValidMove
131
132  // determines whether the specified square is occupied
133  bool Server::IsOccupied( int location )
134  {
135      if ( board[ location ] == 'X' || board[ location ] == 'O' )
136         return true;
137      else
138         return false;
139  }
140
141  // determines if the game is over
142  bool Server::GameOver()
143  {
144      // place code here to test for a winner of the game
145      return false;
146  }
```

Fig. 18.15 Server class method definitions. (Part 4 of 4.)

```
1   // Fig. 18.16: ServerTest.cpp
2   // Entry point for application.
3
4   #include "Server.h"
5
6   int __stdcall WinMain()
7   {
8       Application::Run( new Server() );
9
10      return 0;
11  } // end function WinMain
```

Fig. 18.16 Server class driver.

```
1   // Fig. 18.17: Player.h
2   // This class processes a single Tic-Tac-Toe client
3   // in a separate thread of execution.
4
5   #pragma once
6
7   #include "TicTacToeServer.h"
```

Fig. 18.17 Player class represents a single player connected to the server.
(Part 1 of 2.)

```
8
9    public __gc class Player
10   {
11   public:
12      Player( Socket *, TicTacToeServer *, int );
13      void OtherPlayerMoved( int );
14      void Run();
15
16      __property bool get_ThreadSuspended()
17      {
18         return threadSuspended;
19      }
20
21      __property void set_ThreadSuspended( bool value )
22      {
23         threadSuspended = value;
24      }
25
26   private:
27      Socket *connection;
28      NetworkStream *socketStream;
29      TicTacToeServer *server;
30      BinaryWriter *writer;
31      BinaryReader *reader;
32
33      int number;
34      __wchar_t mark;
35      static bool threadSuspended = true;
36   }; // end class Player
```

Fig. 18.17 Player class represents a single player connected to the server.
(Part 2 of 2.)

```
1    // Fig. 18.18: Player.cpp
2    // Method definitions for class Player.
3
4    #include "Player.h"
5
6    Player::Player( Socket *socket, TicTacToeServer *serverValue,
7       int newNumber )
8    {
9       mark = ( newNumber == 0 ? 'X' : 'O' );
10
11      connection = socket;
12
13      server = serverValue;
14      number = newNumber;
15
16      // create NetworkStream object for Socket
17      socketStream = new NetworkStream( connection );
18
```

Fig. 18.18 Player class method definitions. (Part 1 of 3.)

```
19        // create Streams for reading/writing bytes
20        writer = new BinaryWriter( socketStream );
21        reader = new BinaryReader( socketStream );
22     } // end constructor
23
24     // signal other player of move
25     void Player::OtherPlayerMoved( int location )
26     {
27        // signal that opponent moved
28        writer->Write( S"Opponent moved" );
29        writer->Write( location ); // send location of move
30     }
31
32     // allows the players to make moves and receives moves
33     // from other player
34     void Player::Run()
35     {
36        bool done = false;
37
38        // display on the server that a connection was made
39        server->Display( String::Concat( S"Player ",
40           ( number == 0 ? S"X" : S"O" ), S" connected" ) );
41
42        // send the current player's mark to the server
43        writer->Write( mark );
44
45        // if number equals 0 then this player is X, so send
46        writer->Write( String::Concat( S"Player ", ( number == 0 ?
47           S"X connected\r\n" : S"O connected, please wait\r\n" ) ) );
48
49        // wait for another player to arrive
50        if ( mark == 'X' ) {
51           writer->Write( S"Waiting for another player" );
52
53           // wait for notification from server that another
54           // player has connected
55           Monitor::Enter( this );
56
57           while ( threadSuspended )
58              Monitor::Wait( this );
59
60           writer->Write( S"Other player connected. Your move" );
61           Monitor::Pulse( this );
62           Monitor::Exit( this );
63        } // end if
64
65        // play game
66        while ( !done ) {
67
68           // wait for data to become available
69           while ( connection->Available == 0 ) {
70              Thread::Sleep( 1000 );
71
```

Fig. 18.18 Player class method definitions. (Part 2 of 3.)

```
72              if ( server->IsDisconnected )
73                  return;
74          }
75
76          // receive data
77          int location = reader->ReadInt32();
78
79          // if the move is valid, display the move on the
80          // server and signal the move is valid
81          if ( server->ValidMove( location, number ) ) {
82              server->Display( String::Concat(
83                  S"loc: ", location.ToString() ) );
84              writer->Write( S"Valid move." );
85          }
86
87          // signal the move is invalid
88          else
89              writer->Write( S"Invalid move, try again" );
90
91          // if game is over, set done to true to exit while loop
92          if ( server->GameOver() )
93              done = true;
94      } // end while
95
96      // close the socket connection
97      writer->Close();
98      reader->Close();
99      socketStream->Close();
100     connection->Close();
101 } // end method Run
```

Fig. 18.18 Player class method definitions. (Part 3 of 3.)

```
1   // Fig. 18.19: Client.h
2   // Client for the TicTacToe program.
3
4   #pragma once
5
6   #using <system.dll>
7   #using <mscorlib.dll>
8   #using <system.drawing.dll>
9   #using <system.windows.forms.dll>
10  #using <system.data.dll>
11
12  using namespace System;
13  using namespace System::Drawing;
14  using namespace System::ComponentModel;
15  using namespace System::Windows::Forms;
16  using namespace System::Net::Sockets;
17  using namespace System::Threading;
```

Fig. 18.19 Client side of client/server Tic-Tac-Toe program. (Part 1 of 2.)

```cpp
18   using namespace System::IO;
19
20   #include "Square.h"
21
22   public __gc class Client : public Form
23   {
24   public:
25      Client();
26      void PaintSquares();
27      void Run();
28      void ProcessMessage( String * );
29      void SendClickedSquare( int );
30
31      // write-only property for the current square
32      __property void set_CurrentSquare( Square *value )
33      {
34         currentSquare = value;
35      }
36
37   protected:
38      void Client_Paint( Object *, PaintEventArgs * );
39      void Client_Closing( Object *, CancelEventArgs * );
40      void square_MouseUp( Object *, MouseEventArgs * );
41
42   private:
43      Label *idLabel;
44
45      TextBox *displayTextBox;
46
47      Panel *panel1, *panel2, *panel3, *panel4, *panel5, *panel6,
48         *panel7, *panel8, *panel9;
49
50      Square *board __gc[ , ];
51      Square *currentSquare;
52
53      Thread *outputThread;
54
55      TcpClient *connection;
56      NetworkStream *stream;
57      BinaryWriter *writer;
58      BinaryReader *reader;
59
60      __wchar_t myMark;
61      bool myTurn;
62
63      SolidBrush *brush;
64
65      static bool done = false;
66
67      void InitializeComponent();
68   }; // end class Client
```

Fig. 18.19 Client side of client/server Tic-Tac-Toe program. (Part 2 of 2.)

```
 1   // Fig. 18.20: Client.cpp
 2   // Method definitions for class Client.
 3
 4   #include "Client.h"
 5
 6   // default constructor
 7   Client::Client()
 8   {
 9      InitializeComponent();
10
11      board = new Square* __gc[ 3, 3 ];
12
13      // create 9 Square objects and place them on the board
14      board[ 0, 0 ] = new Square( panel1, ' ', 0 );
15      board[ 0, 1 ] = new Square( panel2, ' ', 1 );
16      board[ 0, 2 ] = new Square( panel3, ' ', 2 );
17      board[ 1, 0 ] = new Square( panel4, ' ', 3 );
18      board[ 1, 1 ] = new Square( panel5, ' ', 4 );
19      board[ 1, 2 ] = new Square( panel6, ' ', 5 );
20      board[ 2, 0 ] = new Square( panel7, ' ', 6 );
21      board[ 2, 1 ] = new Square( panel8, ' ', 7 );
22      board[ 2, 2 ] = new Square( panel9, ' ', 8 );
23
24      // create a SolidBrush for writing on the Squares
25      brush = new SolidBrush( Color::Black );
26
27      // Make connection to sever and get the associated
28      // network stream. Start separate thread to allow this
29      // program to continually update its output in textbox.
30      connection = new TcpClient( S"localhost", 4500 );
31      stream = connection->GetStream();
32
33      writer = new BinaryWriter( stream );
34      reader = new BinaryReader( stream );
35
36      // start a new thread for sending and receiving messages
37      outputThread = new Thread( new ThreadStart( this, Run ) );
38      outputThread->Start();
39   } // end constructor
40
41   void Client::InitializeComponent()
42   {
43      this->panel8 = new Panel();
44      this->panel9 = new Panel();
45      this->panel4 = new Panel();
46      this->panel5 = new Panel();
47      this->panel6 = new Panel();
48      this->panel7 = new Panel();
49      this->panel1 = new Panel();
50      this->panel2 = new Panel();
51      this->panel3 = new Panel();
52      this->displayTextBox = new TextBox();
53      this->idLabel = new Label();
```

Fig. 18.20 Client class method definitions. (Part 1 of 6.)

```
54
55        this->SuspendLayout();
56
57        // panel8
58        this->panel8->BorderStyle = BorderStyle::FixedSingle;
59        this->panel8->Location = Point( 136, 112 );
60        this->panel8->Name = S"panel8";
61        this->panel8->Size = Drawing::Size( 32, 32 );
62        this->panel8->TabIndex = 9;
63        this->panel8->MouseUp += new MouseEventHandler(
64           this, square_MouseUp );
65
66        // panel9
67        this->panel9->BorderStyle = BorderStyle::FixedSingle;
68        this->panel9->Location = Point( 168, 112 );
69        this->panel9->Name = S"panel9";
70        this->panel9->Size = Drawing::Size( 32, 32 );
71        this->panel9->TabIndex = 10;
72        this->panel9->MouseUp += new MouseEventHandler(
73           this, square_MouseUp );
74
75        // panel4
76        this->panel4->BorderStyle = BorderStyle::FixedSingle;
77        this->panel4->Location = Point( 104, 80 );
78        this->panel4->Name = S"panel4";
79        this->panel4->Size = Drawing::Size( 32, 32 );
80        this->panel4->TabIndex = 5;
81        this->panel4->MouseUp += new MouseEventHandler(
82           this, square_MouseUp );
83
84        // panel5
85        this->panel5->BorderStyle = BorderStyle::FixedSingle;
86        this->panel5->Location = Point( 136, 80 );
87        this->panel5->Name = S"panel5";
88        this->panel5->Size = Drawing::Size( 32, 32 );
89        this->panel5->TabIndex = 6;
90        this->panel5->MouseUp += new MouseEventHandler(
91           this, square_MouseUp );
92
93        // panel6
94        this->panel6->BorderStyle = BorderStyle::FixedSingle;
95        this->panel6->Location = Point( 168, 80 );
96        this->panel6->Name = S"panel6";
97        this->panel6->Size = Drawing::Size( 32, 32 );
98        this->panel6->TabIndex = 7;
99        this->panel6->MouseUp += new MouseEventHandler(
100          this, square_MouseUp );
101
102       // panel7
103       this->panel7->BorderStyle = BorderStyle::FixedSingle;
104       this->panel7->Location = Point( 104, 112 );
105       this->panel7->Name = S"panel7";
106       this->panel7->Size = Drawing::Size( 32, 32 );
```

Fig. 18.20 Client class method definitions. (Part 2 of 6.)

```
107        this->panel7->TabIndex = 8;
108        this->panel7->MouseUp += new MouseEventHandler(
109           this, square_MouseUp );
110
111        // panel1
112        this->panel1->BorderStyle = BorderStyle::FixedSingle;
113        this->panel1->Location = Point( 104, 48 );
114        this->panel1->Name = S"panel1";
115        this->panel1->Size = Drawing::Size( 32, 32 );
116        this->panel1->TabIndex = 2;
117        this->panel1->MouseUp += new MouseEventHandler(
118           this, square_MouseUp );
119
120        // panel2
121        this->panel2->BorderStyle = BorderStyle::FixedSingle;
122        this->panel2->Location = Point( 136, 48 );
123        this->panel2->Name = S"panel2";
124        this->panel2->Size = Drawing::Size( 32, 32 );
125        this->panel2->TabIndex = 3;
126        this->panel2->MouseUp += new MouseEventHandler(
127           this, square_MouseUp );
128
129        // panel3
130        this->panel3->BorderStyle = BorderStyle::FixedSingle;
131        this->panel3->Location = Point( 168, 48 );
132        this->panel3->Name = S"panel3";
133        this->panel3->Size = Drawing::Size( 32, 32 );
134        this->panel3->TabIndex = 4;
135        this->panel3->MouseUp += new MouseEventHandler(
136           this, square_MouseUp );
137
138        // displayTextBox
139        this->displayTextBox->Location = Point( 8, 184 );
140        this->displayTextBox->Multiline = true;
141        this->displayTextBox->Name = S"displayTextBox";
142        this->displayTextBox->ReadOnly = true;
143        this->displayTextBox->ScrollBars = ScrollBars::Vertical;
144        this->displayTextBox->Size = Drawing::Size( 272, 80 );
145        this->displayTextBox->TabIndex = 1;
146        this->displayTextBox->Text = S"";
147
148        // idLabel
149        this->idLabel->BorderStyle = BorderStyle::FixedSingle;
150        this->idLabel->Location = Point( 8, 8 );
151        this->idLabel->Name = S"idLabel";
152        this->idLabel->TabIndex = 0;
153
154        // client
155        this->AutoScaleBaseSize = Drawing::Size( 5, 13 );
156        this->ClientSize = Drawing::Size( 292, 273 );
157
158        Control *control[] = { this->panel9, this->panel8,
159           this->panel7, this->panel6, this->panel5, this->panel3,
```

Fig. 18.20 `Client` class method definitions. (Part 3 of 6.)

```
160            this->panel2, this->panel1, this->displayTextBox,
161            this->idLabel, this->panel4 };
162     this->Controls->AddRange( control );
163
164     this->Name = S"Client";
165     this->Text = S"Tic Tac Toe Client";
166     this->Closing += new CancelEventHandler( this,
167         Client_Closing );
168     this->Paint += new PaintEventHandler( this, Client_Paint );
169
170     this->ResumeLayout();
171  } // end method InitializeComponent
172
173  void Client::Client_Paint ( Object *sender, PaintEventArgs *e )
174  {
175     PaintSquares();
176  }
177
178  void Client::Client_Closing( Object *sender, CancelEventArgs *e )
179  {
180     done = true;
181  }
182
183  // draws the mark of each square
184  void Client::PaintSquares()
185  {
186     Graphics *g;
187
188     // draw the appropriate mark on each panel
189     for ( int row = 0; row < 3; row++ )
190
191        for ( int column = 0; column < 3; column++ ) {
192
193           // get the Graphics for each Panel
194           g = board[ row, column ]->SquarePanel->CreateGraphics();
195
196           // draw the appropriate letter on the panel
197           g->DrawString( __box( board[ row, column ]->Mark ),
198              this->Font, brush, 8, 8 );
199        }
200  } // end method PaintSquares
201
202  // send location of the clicked square to server
203  void Client::square_MouseUp( Object *sender, MouseEventArgs *e )
204  {
205     // for each square check if that square was clicked
206     for ( int row = 0; row < 3; row++ )
207
208        for ( int column = 0; column < 3; column++ )
209
210           if ( board[ row, column ]->SquarePanel == sender ) {
211              CurrentSquare = board[ row, column ];
```

Fig. 18.20 Client class method definitions. (Part 4 of 6.)

```
212
213                // send the move to the server
214                SendClickedSquare( board[ row, column ]->Location );
215           }
216    } // end method square_MouseUp
217
218    // control thread that allows continuous update of the
219    // textbox display
220    void Client::Run()
221    {
222       // first get players's mark (X or O)
223       myMark = reader->ReadChar();
224       idLabel->Text = String::Concat( S"You are player \"",
225          __box( myMark ), S"\"" );
226       myTurn = ( myMark == 'X' ? true : false );
227
228       // process incoming messages
229       try {
230
231          // receive messages sent to client
232          while ( true )
233             ProcessMessage( reader->ReadString() );
234       }
235       catch ( EndOfStreamException * ) {
236          MessageBox::Show( S"Server is down, game over", S"Error",
237             MessageBoxButtons::OK, MessageBoxIcon::Error );
238       }
239    } // end method Run
240
241    // process messages sent to client
242    void Client::ProcessMessage( String *message )
243    {
244       // if the move player sent to the server is valid
245       // update the display, set that square's mark to be
246       // the mark of the current player and repaint the board
247       if ( message->Equals( S"Valid move." ) ) {
248          displayTextBox->Text = String::Concat( displayTextBox->Text,
249             S"Valid move, please wait.\r\n" );
250          currentSquare->Mark = myMark;
251          PaintSquares();
252       }
253
254       // if the move is invalid, display that and it is now
255       // this player's turn again
256       else if ( message->Equals( S"Invalid move, try again" ) )   {
257          displayTextBox->Text = String::Concat(
258             displayTextBox->Text, message, S"\r\n" );
259          myTurn = true;
260       }
261
262       // if opponent moved
263       else if ( message->Equals( S"Opponent moved" ) ) {
```

Fig. 18.20 Client class method definitions. (Part 5 of 6.)

```
264
265          // find location of their move
266          int location = reader->ReadInt32();
267
268          // set that square to have the opponents mark and
269          // repaint the board
270          board[ location / 3, location % 3 ]->Mark =
271              ( myMark == 'X' ? 'O' : 'X' );
272          PaintSquares();
273
274          displayTextBox->Text = String::Concat( displayTextBox->Text,
275              S"Opponent moved.  Your turn.\r\n" );
276
277          // it is now this player's turn
278          myTurn = true;
279       } // end if
280
281       // display the message
282       else
283          displayTextBox->Text = String::Concat(
284              displayTextBox->Text, message, S"\r\n" );
285    } // end method ProcessMessage
286
287    // sends the server the number of the clicked square
288    void Client::SendClickedSquare( int location )
289    {
290       // if it is the current player's move right now
291       if ( myTurn ) {
292
293          // send the location of the move to the server
294          writer->Write( location );
295
296          // it is now the other player's turn
297          myTurn = false;
298       }
299    }
```

Fig. 18.20 Client class method definitions. (Part 6 of 6.)

```
1    // Fig. 18.21: ClientTest.cpp
2    // Entry point for application.
3
4    #include "Client.h"
5
6    int __stdcall WinMain()
7    {
8       Application::Run( new Client() );
9
10      return 0;
11   } // end function WinMain
```

Fig. 18.21 Client class driver. (Part 1 of 3.)

1.
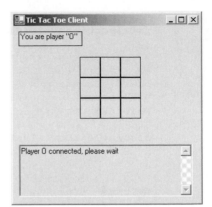

2.
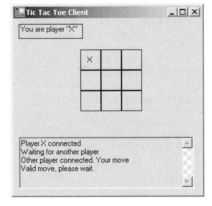
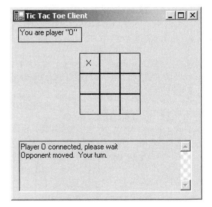

3.
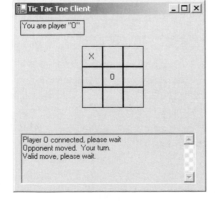
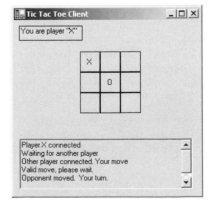

Fig. 18.21 Client class driver. (Part 2 of 3.)

4.

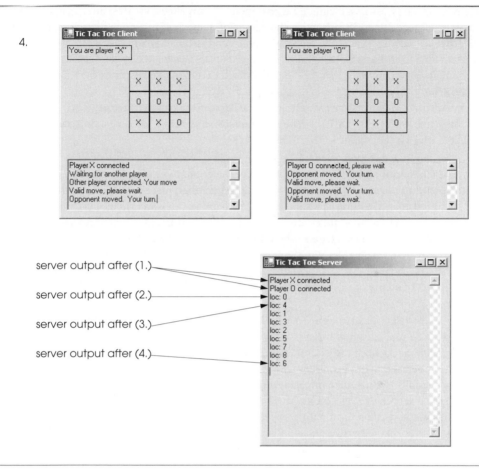

Fig. 18.21 Client class driver. (Part 3 of 3.)

Server (Fig. 18.14–Fig. 18.15) uses its constructor (lines 7–20 of Fig. 18.15) to create a **Byte** array to store the moves the players have made (line 11). The program creates an array of two pointers to **Player** objects (line 13) and an array of two pointers to **Thread** objects (line 14). Each element in both arrays corresponds to a Tic-Tac-Toe player. Variable **currentPlayer** is set to **0**, which corresponds to player **"X"** (line 15). In our program, player **"X"** makes the first move. Lines 18–19 create and start **Thread getPlayers**, which the **Server** uses to accept connections so that the current **Thread** does not block while awaiting players.

Thread **getPlayers** executes method **SetUp** (lines 59–85), which creates a **TcpListener** object to listen for requests on port **4500** (lines 62–63). This object then listens for connection requests from the first and second players. Lines 66–67 and 73–74 instantiate **Player** objects representing the players, and lines 68–69 and 75–76 create two **Thread**s that execute the **Run** methods of each **Player** object.

The **Player** constructor (Fig. 18.18, lines 6–22) receives as arguments a pointer to the **Socket** object (i.e., the connection to the client), a pointer to the **Server** object (as a **Tic-TacToeServer** pointer) and an **int** indicating the mark (**"X"** or **"O"**) used by that player.

In this case study, **Server** calls **Player** method **Run** (lines 34–103) after instantiating a **Player** object. Lines 39–47 notify the server of a successful connection and send to the client the **__wchar_t** that the client will place on the board when making a move. If **Run** is executing for **Player "X"**, lines 51–62 execute, causing **Player "X"** to wait for a second player to connect. Lines 57–58 define a **while** loop that suspends the **Player "X" Thread** until the server signals that **Player "O"** has connected. The server notifies the **Player** of the connection by setting the **Player**'s **threadSuspended** variable to **false** (line 82 of Fig. 18.15). When **threadSuspended** becomes **false**, **Player** exits the **while** loop in lines 57–58 (Fig. 18.18).

Method **Run** executes the **while** structure (lines 66–94), enabling the user to play the game. Each iteration of this structure waits for the client to send an **int** specifying where on the board to place the **"X"** or **"O"**—the **Player** then places the mark on the board, if the specified mark location is valid (e.g., that location does not already contain a mark). Note that the **while** structure continues execution only if **bool** variable **done** is **false**. This variable only becomes **true** when **Server** method **GameOver** returns **true** (lines 92–93). However, method **Run** may return prematurely if **Server** property **IsDisconnected** is **true** (line 72). This variable is set to **true** by event handler **Server_Closing** of class **Server**, which is invoked when the **Server**'s Form is closed.

Line 69 (Fig. 18.18) begins a **while** structure that loops until **Socket** property **Available** indicates that there is information to receive from the **Socket** (or until the server disconnects from the client). **Socket** property **Available** contains the amount of data, in bytes, that has been received. If there is no information, the thread goes to sleep for one second. Upon awakening, the thread uses property **IsDisconnected** to check for whether server variable **disconnect** is **true**. If the value is **true**, the **Thread** exits the method (thus terminating the **Thread**); otherwise, the **Thread** loops again. However, if property **Available** indicates that there is data to receive, the **while** loop of lines 69–74 terminates, enabling the information to be processed.

This information contains an **int** representing the location in which the client wants to place a mark. Line 77 calls method **ReadInt32** of the **BinaryReader** object (which reads from the **NetworkStream** created with the **Socket**) to read this **int** (or **Int32**). Line 81 then passes the **int** to **Server** method **ValidMove**. If this method validates the move, the **Player** places the mark in the desired location.

Method **ValidMove** (lines 95–130 of Fig. 18.15) sends to the client a message indicating whether the move was valid. Locations on the board correspond to numbers from **0–8** (**0–2** for the first row, **3–5** for the second and **6–8** for the third). All statements in method **ValidMove** are enclosed in **Monitor::Enter** and **Monitor::Exit** statements that allow only one move to be attempted at a time. This prevents two players from modifying the game's state information simultaneously. If the **Player** attempting to validate a move is not the current player (i.e., the one allowed to make a move), that **Player** is placed in a *wait* state until it is that **Player**'s turn to move (line 102). If the user attempts to place a mark in a location that already contains a mark, method **ValidMove** returns **false**. However, if the user has selected an unoccupied location (line 105), lines 108 places the mark on the local representation of the board. Line 114 notifies the other **Player** that a move has been made, and line 117 invokes the **Pulse** method so that the waiting **Player** can validate a move. The method then returns **true** to indicate that the move is valid.

When a **Client** application (Fig. 18.19–Fig. 18.21) executes, it creates a **TextBox** to display messages from the server and the Tic-Tac-Toe board representation. The board is created out of nine **Square** objects (Fig. 18.22–Fig. 18.23) that contain **Panel**s on which the user can click, indicating the position on the board in which to place a mark. The **Client**'s constructor (lines 7–39 of Fig. 18.20) opens a connection to the server (line 30) and obtains a pointer to the connection's associated **NetworkStream** object from **TcpClient** (line 31). Lines 37–38 start a thread to read messages sent from the server to the client. The server passes messages (e.g., whether each move is valid) to method **ProcessMessage** (lines 242–285). If the message indicates that a move is valid (line 247), the client sets its mark to the current square (the square that the user clicked) and repaints the board. If the message indicates that a move is invalid (line 256), the client notifies the user to click a different square. If the message indicates that the opponent made a move (line 263), line 266 reads from the server an **int** specifying where on the board the client should place the opponent's mark.

```
1    // Fig. 18.22: Square.h
2    // A Square on the TicTacToe board.
3
4    #pragma once
5
6    #using <system.dll>
7    #using <mscorlib.dll>
8    #using <system.windows.forms.dll>
9
10   using namespace System;
11   using namespace System::Windows::Forms;
12
13   // the representation of a square in a tic-tac-toe grid
14   public __gc class Square
15   {
16   public:
17      Square( Panel *, __wchar_t, int );
18
19      // property SquarePanel;
20      // the panel which the square represents
21      __property Panel *get_SquarePanel()
22      {
23         return panel;
24      } // end property SquarePanel
25
26      // property Mark; the mark of the square
27      __property __wchar_t get_Mark()
28      {
29         return mark;
30      }
31
32      __property void set_Mark( __wchar_t value )
33      {
34         mark = value;
```

Fig. 18.22 Square class represents a square on the Tic-Tac-Toe board. (Part 1 of 2.)

```
35      } // end property Mark
36
37      // property Location; the square's location on the board
38      __property int get_Location()
39      {
40         return location;
41      } // property Location
42
43   private:
44      Panel *panel;
45      __wchar_t mark;
46      int location;
47   }; // end class Square
```

Fig. 18.22 Square class represents a square on the Tic-Tac-Toe board. (Part 2 of 2.)

```
1    // Fig. 18.23: Square.cpp
2    // Method definitions for class Square.
3
4    #include "Square.h"
5
6    // constructor
7    Square::Square( Panel *newPanel, __wchar_t newMark,
8       int newLocation )
9    {
10      panel = newPanel;
11      mark = newMark;
12      location = newLocation;
13   }
```

Fig. 18.23 Square class method definitions.

In this chapter, we discussed how to use .NET Framework's networking technologies by providing both connection-oriented (i.e., streams-based) transmission and connectionless (i.e., packet-based) transmission. We showed how to create a simple server and client via stream sockets, then showed how to create a multithreaded server. In Chapter 19, Data Structures and Collections, we discuss how to store data dynamically, and we discuss several of the key classes that belong to the **System::Collections** namespace.

18.7 Summary

Sockets are the fundamental way to perform network communications in the .NET Framework. The term "socket" refers to the Berkeley Sockets Interface, which was developed in 1978 to facilitate network programming with UNIX and was popularized by C and C++ programmers. The two most popular types of sockets are stream sockets and datagram sockets. Stream sockets provide a connection-oriented service, meaning that one process establishes a connection to another process and that data can flow between the processes in continuous streams. Datagram sockets provide a connectionless service that uses messages to transmit data. Connectionless services generally offer greater performance but less reliability than connection-oriented services.

Transmission Control Protocol (TCP) is the preferred protocol for stream sockets. It is a reliable and relatively fast way to send data through a network. The User Datagram Protocol (UDP) is the preferred protocol for datagram sockets. UDP is unreliable. There is no guarantee that packets sent with UDP will arrive in the order in which they were sent or that they will arrive at all.

The establishment of a simple server with TCP and stream sockets in MC++ requires five steps. Step 1 is to create a **TcpListener** object. This class represents a TCP stream socket that a server can use to receive connections. To receive connections, the **TcpListener** must be listening for them. For the **TcpListener** to listen for client connections, its **Start** method must be called (Step 2). **TcpListener** method **AcceptSocket** blocks indefinitely until a connection is established, at which point it returns a **Socket** (Step 3). Step 4 is the processing phase, in which the server and the client communicate via methods **Read** and **Write** via a **NetworkStream** object. When the client and server have finished communicating, the server closes the connection with the **Close** method on the **Socket** (Step 5). Most servers will then, by means of a control loop, return to the **AcceptSocket** call step to wait for another client's connection. Multithreaded servers can manage many simultaneous connections with multiple clients.

A port number is a numeric ID number that a process uses to identify itself at a given network address, also known as an Internet Protocol Address (IP Address). An individual process running on a computer is identified by an IP address/port number pair. Hence, no two processes can have the same port number at a given IP address.

The establishment of a simple client requires four steps. In Step 1, we create a **TcpClient** to connect to the server. This connection is established through a call to the **TcpClient** method **Connect** containing two arguments—the server's IP address and the port number. In Step 2, the **TcpClient** uses method **GetStream** to get a **Stream** to write to and read from the server. Step 3 is the processing phase, in which the client and the server communicate. Step 4 has the client close the connection by calling the **Close** method on the **NetworkStream**.

NetworkStream methods **WriteByte** and **Write** can be used to output individual bytes or sets of bytes to the server, respectively. **NetworkStream** methods **ReadByte** and **Read** can be used to read individual bytes or sets of bytes from the server, respectively.

Class **UdpClient** is provided for connectionless transmission of data. Class **UdpClient** methods **Send** and **Receive** are used to transmit data. Class **IPAddress** represents an Internet Protocol address. Class **IPEndPoint** represents an endpoint on a network.

19

Data Structures and Collections

Objectives

- To form linked data structures that use pointers, self-referential classes and recursion.
- To create and manipulate dynamic data structures, such as linked lists, queues, stacks and binary trees.
- To understand various important applications of linked data structures.
- To understand how to create reusable data structures with classes, inheritance and composition.

Much that I bound, I could not free;
Much that I freed returned to me.
Lee Wilson Dodd

'Will you walk a little faster?' said a whiting to a snail,
'There's a porpoise close behind us, and he's treading on my
tail.'
Lewis Carroll

There is always room at the top.
Daniel Webster

Push on—keep moving.
Thomas Morton

I think that I shall never see
A poem lovely as a tree.
Joyce Kilmer

19.1 Introduction

The *data structures* that we have studied thus far have had fixed size, such as single- and double-subscripted arrays. This chapter introduces *dynamic data structures* that grow and shrink during execution time. *Linked lists* are collections of data items that are logically "lined up in a row"—users can make insertions and deletions anywhere in a linked list. *Stacks* are important in compilers and operating systems because insertions and deletions are made at only one end—the *top. Queues* represent waiting lines; insertions are made at the back (also referred to as the *tail*) of a queue, and deletions are made from the front (also referred to as the *head*) of a queue. *Binary trees* facilitate high-speed searching and sorting of data, efficient elimination of duplicate data items, representation of file system directories and compilation of expressions into machine language. These data structures have many other interesting applications as well.

We will discuss each of the major types of data structures and implement programs that create and manipulate them. We use classes, inheritance and composition to create and package these data structures for reusability and maintainability.

The chapter examples are practical programs that will be useful in more advanced courses and in industrial applications. The programs devote special attention to pointer manipulation and focus on it.

19.2 Self-Referential Classes

A *self-referential class* contains a pointer member that points to an object of the same class type. For example, the class definition in Fig. 19.1 defines a type, **Node**. This type has two **private** instance variables—integer member **data** and pointer member **next**. Member **next** points to an object of type **Node**, an object of the same type as the one being declared here—hence, the term "self-referential class." Member **next** is referred to as a *link* (i.e., **next** can be used to "tie" an object of type **Node** to another object of the same type). Class **Node** also has two properties: one for variable **data** (named **Data**), and another for variable **next** (named **Next**).Self-referential objects can be linked together to form useful data structures, such as lists, queues, stacks and trees. Figure 19.2 illustrates two self-referential objects linked together to form a list. A backslash (representing a **NULL** pointer) is placed in the link member of the second self-referential object to indicate that the link does not point to another object. The slash is for illustration purposes; it does not correspond to the backslash character. A **NULL** pointer normally indicates the end of a data structure. [*Note*: Readers should recall that in MC++, **0** represents a null pointer. However, throughout this chapter, we use **NULL** in place of **0**. **NULL** is defined in a number of headers, including **tchar.h**, and is interchangeable with **0**.]

```
1   // Fig. 19.1: NodeClass.cpp
2   // Example demonstrating a node class.
3
4   public __gc class Node
5   {
6   public:
7      Node( int d )
8      {
9         // constructor body
10     }
11
12     __property int get_Data()
13     {
14        // get body
15     }
16
17     __property void set_Data( int newData )
18     {
19        // set body
20     }
21
22     __property Node *get_Next()
23     {
24        // get body
25     }
26
27     __property void set_Next( Node *newNext )
28     {
29        // set body
30     }
31
32   private:
33      int data;
34      Node *next;
35   }; // end class Node
```

Fig. 19.1 Sample self-referential **Node** class definition.

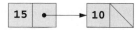

Fig. 19.2   Two self-referential class objects linked together.

Common Programming Error 19.1

*Not setting the link in the last node of a list (or other linear data structure) to **NULL** is a common logic error.*

Creating and maintaining dynamic data structures requires *dynamic memory allocation*—a program's ability to obtain more memory space at execution time to hold new nodes and to release space no longer needed. As we have already learned, MC++ programs do not explicitly release dynamically allocated memory. Rather, the CLR performs automatic garbage collection of managed objects.

The limit for dynamic memory allocation can be as large as the amount of available disk space in a virtual-memory system. Often, the limits are much smaller, because the computer's available memory must be shared among many users.

Operator **new** is essential to dynamic memory allocation. Operator **new** takes as an operand the type of the object being dynamically allocated and returns a pointer to a newly created object of that type. For example, the statement

```
Node *nodeToAdd = new Node( 10 );
```

allocates the appropriate amount of memory to store a **Node** and stores a pointer to this object in **nodeToAdd**. If no memory is available, **new** throws an **OutOfMemoryException**. The **10** is the **Node** object's data.

The following sections discuss lists, stacks, queues and trees. These data structures are created and maintained with dynamic memory allocation and self-referential classes.

Good Programming Practice 19.1

*When creating a very large number of objects, test for an **OutOfMemoryException** Perform appropriate error processing if the requested memory is not allocated.*

19.3 Linked; Lists

A *linked list* is a linear collection (i.e., a sequence) of self-referential class objects, called *nodes,* connected by pointer links—hence, the term "linked" list. A program accesses a linked list via a pointer to the first node of the list. Each subsequent node is accessed via the link-pointer member stored in the previous node. By convention, the link pointer in the last node of a list is set to **NULL** to mark the end of the list. Data are stored in a linked list dynamically—that is, each node is created as necessary. A node can contain data of any type, including objects of other classes. Stacks and queues are also linear data structures, and they are constrained versions of linked lists. Trees are nonlinear data structures.

Lists of data can be stored in arrays, but linked lists provide several advantages. A linked list is appropriate when the number of data elements to be represented in the data structure is unpredictable. Unlike a linked list, the size of a conventional array cannot be altered, because the array size is fixed at creation time. Conventional arrays can become full, but linked lists become full only when the system has insufficient memory to satisfy dynamic storage allocation requests.

Performance Tip 19.1

An array can be declared to contain more elements than the number of items expected, at the expense of wasting memory. Linked lists may provide better memory utilization in these situations and they allow the program to adapt at run time.

Performance Tip 19.2

After locating the insertion point for a new item in a sorted linked list, inserting an element in the list is fast—only two pointers have to be modified. All existing nodes remain at their current locations in memory.

Performance Tip 19.3

The elements of an array are stored contiguously in memory to allow immediate access to any array element—the address of any element can be calculated directly from its offset from the beginning of the array. Linked lists do not afford such immediate access to their elements—an element can be accessed only by traversing the list from the front.

Memory does not normally store linked list nodes contiguously. Rather, the nodes are logically contiguous. Figure 19.3 illustrates a linked list with several nodes. Variable **firstNode** is a pointer to the first node in the list (containing value **H**), and variable **lastNode** is a pointer to the last node in the list (containing value **Q**). A programmer would use pointers **firstNode** and **lastNode** to access the front and back of the list, respectively.

Performance Tip 19.4

Using dynamic memory allocation (instead of arrays) for data structures that grow and shrink at execution time can save memory. Keep in mind, however, that pointers occupy space, and that dynamic memory allocation incurs the overhead of method calls.

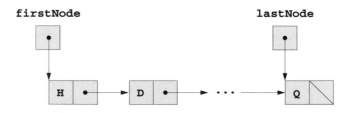

Fig. 19.3 Graphical representation of a linked list.

The program of Fig. 19.4–Fig. 19.10 uses an object of class **List** to manipulate a list of miscellaneous object types. Function **main** in **ListTest.cpp** (Fig. 19.10) creates a list of objects, inserts objects at the beginning of the list using **List** method **InsertAtFront**, inserts objects at the end of the list using **List** method **InsertAtBack**, deletes objects from the front of the list using **List** method **RemoveFromFront** and deletes objects from the end of the list using **List** method **RemoveFromBack**. Each insertion and deletion operation invokes **List** method **Print** to display the current list contents. A detailed discussion of the program follows. If an attempt is made to remove an item from an empty list, an **EmptyListException** occurs.

Performance Tip 19.5

Insertion and deletion in a sorted array can be time consuming—all the elements following the inserted or deleted element must be shifted appropriately.

The program contains three classes—**ListNode** (Fig. 19.4–Fig. 19.5), **List** (Fig. 19.6–Fig. 19.7) and **EmptyListException** (Fig. 19.8–Fig. 19.9). These classes create a linked-list library (defined in namespace **LinkedListLibrary**) that can be reused throughout this chapter.

Encapsulated in each **List** object is a linked list of **ListNode** objects. Class **ListNode** (Fig. 19.4–Fig. 19.5) consists of two member variables—**data** and **next**. Member **data** can point to any object. Member **next** stores a pointer to the next **ListNode** object in the linked list. A **List** accesses the **ListNode** member variables via the properties **Data** (lines 32–35 of Fig. 19.4) and **Next** (lines 22–30), respectively.

```
1   // Fig. 19.4: ListNode.h
2   // Class ListNode represents one node in a list.
3
4   #pragma once
5
6   #include <tchar.h>
7
8   #using <mscorlib.dll>
9   #using <system.dll>
10
11  using namespace System;
12
13  namespace LinkedListLibrary
14  {
15     // class to represent one node in a list
16     public __gc class ListNode
17     {
18     public:
19        ListNode( Object * );
20        ListNode( Object *, ListNode * );
21
```

Fig. 19.4 **ListNode** class represents one node in a list. (Part 1 of 2.)

```
22          __property ListNode *get_Next()
23          {
24             return next;
25          }
26
27          __property void set_Next( ListNode *value )
28          {
29             next = value;
30          }
31
32          __property Object *get_Data()
33          {
34             return data;
35          }
36
37       private:
38          Object *data;
39          ListNode *next;
40       }; // end class ListNode
41    } // end namespace LinkedListLibrary
```

Fig. 19.4 **ListNode** class represents one node in a list. (Part 2 of 2.)

```
1    // Fig. 19.5: ListNode.cpp
2    // Method definitions for class ListNode.
3
4    #include "stdafx.h"
5    #include "ListNode.h"
6
7    using namespace LinkedListLibrary;
8
9    // constructor to create ListNode that points to dataValue
10   // and is last node in list
11   ListNode::ListNode( Object *dataValue )
12   {
13      data = dataValue;
14      next = NULL;
15   }
16
17   // constructor to create ListNode that points to dataValue
18   // and points to next ListNode in List
19   ListNode::ListNode( Object *dataValue, ListNode *nextNode )
20   {
21      data = dataValue;
22      next = nextNode;
23   }
```

Fig. 19.5 **ListNode** class method definitions.

Common Programming Error 19.2

*Attempting to use the object pointed to by a link pointer without checking if the pointer is **NULL** first is a common mistake.*

Class **List** contains **private** members **firstNode** (a pointer to the first **List-Node** in a **List**) and **lastNode** (a pointer to the last **ListNode** in a **List**). The constructors (lines 10–14 and 17–21 of Fig. 19.7) initialize both pointers to **NULL**. **InsertAtFront** (lines 26–36), **InsertAtBack** (lines 41–53), **RemoveFromFront** (lines 56–74) and **RemoveFromBack** (lines 77–104) are the primary methods of class **List**. Each method uses **Monitor** methods **Enter** and **Exit** to ensure that **List** objects are *multithread safe* when used in a multithreaded program. If one thread is modifying the contents of a **List** object, no other thread can modify the same **List** object at the same time. Thus, these **List** methods are *reentrant*[1]—they can safely be entered from multiple points (or threads) at the same time. Method **IsEmpty** (lines 107–114) is a predicate method that determines whether the list is empty (i.e., the pointer to the first node of the list is **NULL**). Predicate methods typically test a condition and do not modify the object on which they are called. If the list is empty, method **IsEmpty** returns **true**; otherwise, it returns **false**. Method **Print** (lines 117–140) displays the list's contents. Both **IsEmpty** and **Print** also use methods **Monitor::Enter** and **Monitor::Exit** so that the state of the list does not change while those methods are performing their tasks.

Class **EmptyListException** (Fig. 19.8-Fig. 19.9) defines an exception class to handle illegal operations on an empty **List**.

```
1   // Fig. 19.6: List.h
2   // Class List represents a linked list of ListNodes.
3
4   #pragma once
5
6   #include "ListNode.h"
7   #include "EmptyListException.h"
8
9   namespace LinkedListLibrary
10  {
11     // class List definition
12     public __gc class List
13     {
14     public:
15        List( String * );
16        List();
17
18        void InsertAtFront( Object * );
19        void InsertAtBack( Object * );
20
21        Object *RemoveFromFront();
22        Object *RemoveFromBack();
23
24        bool IsEmpty();
25        virtual void Print();
26
```

Fig. 19.6 **List** class represents a linked list of **ListNode**s. (Part 1 of 2.)

---

1. More information about reentrant code can be found at
   www.mackido.com/Software/Reentrant.html.

```
27      private:
28         ListNode *firstNode;
29         ListNode *lastNode;
30         String *name;      // string like "list" to display
31      }; // end c
32   } // end namespace LinkedListLibrary
```

Fig. 19.6 **List** class represents a linked list of **ListNode**s. (Part 2 of 2.)

```
1    // Fig. 19.7: List.cpp
2    // Method definitions for class List.
3
4    #include "stdafx.h"
5    #include "List.h"
6
7    using namespace LinkedListLibrary;
8
9    // construct empty List with specified name
10   List::List( String *listName )
11   {
12      name = listName;
13      firstNode = lastNode = NULL;
14   }
15
16   // construct empty List with "list" as its name
17   List::List()
18   {
19      name = S"list";
20      firstNode = lastNode = NULL;
21   }
22
23   // Insert object at front of List. If List is empty,
24   // firstNode and lastNode will point to same object.
25   // Otherwise, firstNode points to the new node.
26   void List::InsertAtFront( Object *insertItem )
27   {
28      Monitor::Enter( this );
29
30      if( IsEmpty() )
31         firstNode = lastNode = new ListNode( insertItem );
32      else
33         firstNode = new ListNode( insertItem, firstNode );
34
35      Monitor::Exit( this );
36   } // end method InsertAtFront
37
38   // Insert object at end of List.  If List is empty,
39   // firstNode and lastNode will point to same object.
40   // Otherwise, lastNode's Next property points to new node.
41   void List::InsertAtBack( Object *insertItem )
42   {
```

Fig. 19.7 **List** class method definitions. (Part 1 of 3.)

```
43        Monitor::Enter ( this );
44
45        if ( IsEmpty() )
46            firstNode = lastNode = new ListNode( insertItem );
47        else {
48            lastNode->Next = new ListNode( insertItem );
49            lastNode = lastNode->Next;
50        }
51
52        Monitor::Exit( this );
53    } // end method InsertAtBack
54
55    // remove first node from List
56    Object *List::RemoveFromFront()
57    {
58        Monitor::Enter ( this );
59
60        if ( IsEmpty() )
61            throw new EmptyListException( name );
62
63        Object *removeItem = firstNode->Data; // retrieve data
64
65        // reset firstNode and lastNode pointers
66        if ( firstNode == lastNode )
67            firstNode = lastNode = NULL;
68        else
69            firstNode = firstNode->Next;
70
71        Monitor::Exit( this );
72
73        return removeItem; // return removed data
74    } // end method RemoveFromFront
75
76    // remove last node from List
77    Object *List::RemoveFromBack()
78    {
79        Monitor::Enter ( this );
80
81        if ( IsEmpty() )
82            throw new EmptyListException( name );
83
84        Object *removeItem = lastNode->Data; // retrieve data
85
86        // reset firstNode and lastNode pointers
87        if ( firstNode == lastNode )
88            firstNode = lastNode = NULL;
89        else {
90            ListNode *current = firstNode;
91
92            // loop while current node is not the new lastNode
93            while ( current->Next != lastNode )
94                current = current->Next; // move to next node
95
```

Fig. 19.7 List class method definitions. (Part 2 of 3.)

```
96            // current is now the new lastNode
97            lastNode = current;
98            current->Next = NULL;
99         }
100
101      Monitor::Exit( this );
102
103      return removeItem; // return removed data
104   } // end method RemoveFromBack
105
106   // return true if List is emtpy
107   bool List::IsEmpty()
108   {
109      Monitor::Enter( this );
110      bool isEmpty = ( firstNode == NULL );
111      Monitor::Exit( this );
112
113      return isEmpty;
114   } // end method IsEmpty
115
116   // output List contents
117   void List::Print()
118   {
119      Monitor::Enter( this );
120
121      if ( IsEmpty() ) {
122         Console::WriteLine( String::Concat( S"Empty ", name ) );
123         Monitor::Exit( this );
124         return;
125      }
126
127      Console::Write( String::Concat( S"The ", name, S" is: " ) );
128
129      ListNode *current = firstNode;
130
131      // output current node data while not at end of list
132      while ( current != NULL ) {
133         Console::Write( String::Concat( current->Data, S" " ) );
134         current = current->Next;
135      }
136
137      Console::WriteLine( S"\n" );
138
139      Monitor::Exit( this );
140   } // end method Print
```

Fig. 19.7 **List** class method definitions. (Part 3 of 3.)

```
1   // Fig. 19.8: EmpytListException.h
2   // Class EmptyListException declaration.
3
4   #pragma once
```

Fig. 19.8 **EmptyListException** is raised when the list is empty. (Part 1 of 2.)

```
 5
 6   #using <mscorlib.dll>
 7   #using <system.dll>
 8
 9   using namespace System;
10   using namespace System::Threading;
11
12   namespace LinkedListLibrary
13   {
14      // class EmptyListException definition
15      public __gc class EmptyListException :
16         public ApplicationException
17      {
18      public:
19         EmptyListException( String * );
20      }; // end class EmptyListExeption
21   } // end namespace LinkedListLibrary
```

Fig. 19.8 **EmptyListException** is raised when the list is empty. (Part 2 of 2.)

```
 1   // Fig. 19.9: EmptyListException.cpp
 2   // Class EmptyListException method definitions.
 3
 4   #include "stdafx.h"
 5   #include "EmptyListException.h"
 6
 7   using namespace LinkedListLibrary;
 8
 9   EmptyListException::EmptyListException( String *name ) :
10      ApplicationException( String::Concat(
11      S"The ", name, S" is empty" ) )
12   {
13   }
```

Fig. 19.9 **EmptyListException** class method definitions.

ListTest.cpp (Fig. 19.10) uses the linked-list library to create and manipulate a linked list. Line 13 creates a new instance of type **List** named **list**. Lines 16–19 create data to add to the list. Lines 22–29 use **List** insertion methods to insert these objects and use **List** method **Print** to output the contents of **list** after each insertion. Note that the primitive data types (i.e., **aBoolean**, **aCharacter** and **anInteger**) must be boxed as **Object**s before being passed to the **List** insertion methods.

```
 1   // Fig. 19.10: ListTest.cpp
 2   // Testing class List.
 3
 4   #using <mscorlib.dll>
 5   #using <system.dll>
 6   #using "LinkedListLibrary.dll"
```

Fig. 19.10 **ListTest.cpp** demonstrates the linked list. (Part 1 of 3.)

```
7
8    using namespace System;
9    using namespace LinkedListLibrary;
10
11   int main()
12   {
13      List *list = new List();    // create List container
14
15      // create data to store in List
16      bool aBoolean = true;
17      __wchar_t aCharacter = '$';
18      int anInteger = 34567;
19      String *aString = S"hello";
20
21      // use List insert methods
22      list->InsertAtFront( __box( aBoolean ) );
23      list->Print();
24      list->InsertAtFront( __box( aCharacter ) );
25      list->Print();
26      list->InsertAtBack( __box( anInteger ) );
27      list->Print();
28      list->InsertAtBack( aString );
29      list->Print();
30
31      // use List remove methods
32      Object *removedObject;
33
34      // remove data from list and print after each removal
35      try {
36         removedObject = list->RemoveFromFront();
37         Console::WriteLine( String::Concat( removedObject,
38            S" removed" ) );
39         list->Print();
40
41         removedObject = list->RemoveFromFront();
42         Console::WriteLine( String::Concat( removedObject,
43            S" removed" ) );
44         list->Print();
45
46         removedObject = list->RemoveFromBack();
47         Console::WriteLine( String::Concat( removedObject,
48            S" removed" ) );
49         list->Print();
50
51         removedObject = list->RemoveFromBack();
52         Console::WriteLine( String::Concat( removedObject,
53            S" removed" ) );
54         list->Print();
55      } // end try
56
57      // process exception if list empty when attempt is
58      // made to remove item
59      catch ( EmptyListException *emptyListException ) {
```

Fig. 19.10 ListTest.cpp demonstrates the linked list. (Part 2 of 3.)

```
60              Console::Error->WriteLine( String::Concat( S"\n",
61                 emptyListException ) );
62        }
63
64      return 0;
65    } // end function main
```

```
The list is: True

The list is: $ True

The list is: $ True 34567

The list is: $ True 34567 hello

$ removed
The list is: True 34567 hello

True removed
The list is: 34567 hello

hello removed
The list is: 34567

34567 removed
Emtpy list
```

Fig. 19.10 `ListTest.cpp` demonstrates the linked list. (Part 3 of 3.)

The code inside the **try** block (lines 35–55) removes objects via **List** deletion methods, outputs the object removed and outputs **list** after every deletion. If there is an attempt to remove an object from an empty list, this **try** block catches the **EmptyListException**. Note that **ListTest.cpp** uses namespace **LinkedListLibrary** (line 9); thus, **ListTest.cpp** must reference the DLL created by the **LinkedListLibrary** class library (line 6).

Over the next several pages, we discuss each of the methods of class **List** in detail. Method **InsertAtFront** (Fig. 19.7, lines 26–36) places a new node at the front of the list. The method consists of three steps (illustrated in Fig. 19.11):

1. Call **IsEmpty** to determine whether the list is empty (line 30).

2. If the list is empty, set both **firstNode** and **lastNode** to point to a new **ListNode** initialized with **insertItem** (line 31). The **ListNode** constructor at lines 11–15 (of Fig. 19.5) sets instance variable **data** to the **Object** pointer passed as the first argument and sets the **next** pointer to **NULL**.

3. If the list is not empty, the new node is "threaded" (not to be confused with *multi-threading*) into the list by setting **firstNode** to point to a new **ListNode** object initialized with **insertItem** and **firstNode** (line 33). When this **ListNode**

constructor (lines 19–23 of Fig. 19.5) executes, it sets instance variable **data** to point to the same object pointed to by the first argument and performs the insertion by setting the **next** pointer to the **ListNode** passed as the second argument.

Figure 19.11 illustrates method **InsertAtFront**. Part (a) of the figure shows the list and the new node during the **InsertAtFront** operation and before the threading of the new node into the list. The dotted arrows in part (b) illustrate step 3 of the **InsertAtFront** operation, which enables the node containing **12** to become the new list front.

Method **InsertAtBack** (Fig. 19.7, lines 41–53) places a new node at the back of the list. The method consists of three steps (illustrated in Fig. 19.12):

1. Call **IsEmpty** to determine whether the list is empty (line 45).

2. If the list is empty, set both **firstNode** and **lastNode** to point to a new **ListNode** initialized with **insertItem** (lines 46). The **ListNode** constructor at lines 11–15 (of Fig. 19.5) sets instance variable **data** to the **Object** pointer passed as the first argument and sets the **next** pointer to **NULL**.

3. If the list is not empty, thread the new node into the list by setting **lastNode** and **lastNode->next** to point to a new **ListNode** object initialized with **insertItem** (lines 48–49). When the **ListNode** constructor (lines 11–15 of Fig. 19.5) executes, it sets instance variable **data** to the **Object** pointer passed as an argument and sets the **next** pointer to **NULL**.

Figure 19.12 illustrates an **InsertAtBack** operation. Part a) of the figure shows the list and the new node during the **InsertAtBack** operation and before the new node has been threaded into the list. The dotted arrows in part b) illustrate the steps of method **InsertAtBack** that enable a new node to be added to the end of a list that is not empty.

Method **RemoveFromFront** (Fig. 19.7, lines 56–74) removes the front node of the list and returns a pointer to the removed data. The method throws an **EmptyListException** (line 61) if the programmer tries to remove a node from an empty list. Otherwise, the method returns a pointer to the removed data. The method consists of four steps (illustrated in Fig. 19.13):

1. Assign **firstNode->Data** (the data being removed from the list) to pointer **removeItem** (line 63).

2. If the objects to which **firstNode** and **lastNode** point are the same object (line 66), the list has only one element prior to the removal attempt. In this case, the method sets **firstNode** and **lastNode** to **NULL** (line 67) to "dethread" (remove) the node from the list (leaving the list empty).

3. If the list has more than one node prior to removal, then the method leaves pointer **lastNode** as is and simply assigns **firstNode->Next** to pointer **firstNode** (line 69). Thus, **firstNode** points to the node that was the second node prior to the **RemoveFromFront** call.

4. Return the **removeItem** pointer.

Notice that method **RemoveFromFront** returns a pointer to the object that has been removed from the list (**removeItem**). To delete the object, the programmer must do it explicitly (i.e., set **removeItem** to **NULL**). Figure 19.13 illustrates method **Remove-FromFront**. Part a) illustrates the list before the removal operation. Part b) shows actual pointer manipulations.

Common Programming Error 19.3

Forgetting to delete an object that has been removed from a linked list is a common error.

Method **RemoveFromBack** (Fig. 19.7, lines 77–104) removes the last node of a list and returns a pointer to the removed data. The method throws an **EmptyListException** (line 82) if the program attempts to remove a node from an empty list. The method consists of several steps (illustrated in Fig. 19.14):

1. Assign **lastNode->Data** (the data being removed from the list) to pointer **removeItem** (line 84).

2. If the objects to which **firstNode** and **lastNode** point are the same object (line 87), the list has only one element prior to the removal attempt. In this case, the method sets **firstNode** and **lastNode** to **NULL** (line 88) to dethread (remove) that node from the list (leaving the list empty).

3. If the list has more than one node prior to removal, create the **ListNode** pointer **current** and assign it **firstNode** (line 90).

4. Now "walk the list" with **current** until it points to the node before the last node. The **while** loop (lines 93–94) assigns **current->Next** to pointer **current** as long as **current->Next** is not equal to **lastNode**.

5. After locating the second-to-last node, assign **current** to **lastNode** (line 97) to dethread the last node from the list.

6. Set **current->Next** to **NULL** (line 98) in the new last node of the list to ensure proper list termination.

7. Return the **removeItem** pointer (line 103).

Notice that (as with method **RemoveFromFront**) method **RemoveFromBack** returns a pointer to the object that has been removed from the list (**removeItem**). To delete the object, the programmer must explicitly set **removeItem** to **NULL**. Figure 19.14 illustrates method **RemoveFromBack**. Part a) illustrates the list before the removal operation. Part b) shows the actual pointer manipulations.

Method **Print** (Fig. 19.7, lines 117–140) first checks for whether the list is empty (line 121). If so, **Print** displays output consisting of the string **"Empty "** and the list's **name**, then returns control to the calling method. Otherwise, **Print** outputs the data in the list. The method prints a string consisting of the string **"The "**, the **name** and the string **" is: "**. Then, line 129 creates **ListNode** pointer **current** and initializes it with **firstNode**. While **current** is not **NULL**, there are more items in the list. Therefore, the method prints **current->Data** (line 133), then assigns **current->Next** to **cur-**

rent (line 134) to move to the next node in the list. Note that, if the link in the last node of the list is not **NULL**, the printing algorithm will erroneously attempt to print past the end of the list. The printing algorithm is identical for linked lists, stacks and queues.

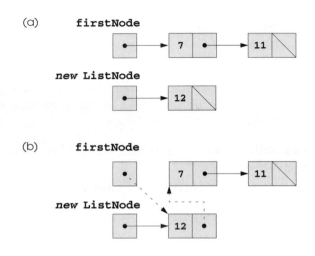

Fig. 19.11 Graphical representation of the **InsertAtFront** operation.

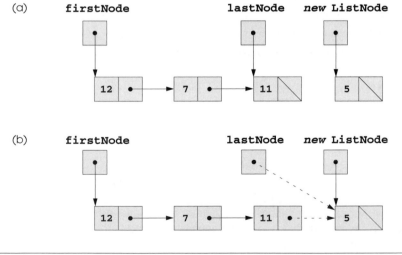

Fig. 19.12 Graphical representation of the **InsertAtBack** operation.

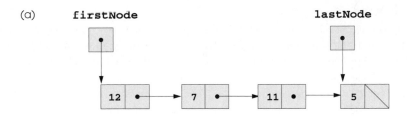

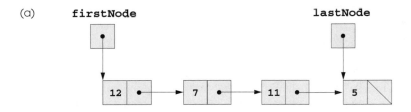

Fig. 19.13 Graphical representation of the **RemoveFromFront** operation.

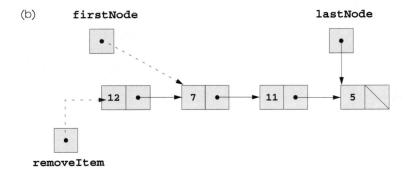

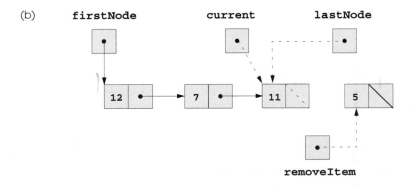

Fig. 19.14 Graphical representation of the **RemoveFromBack** operation.

19.4 Stacks

A *stack* is a constrained version of a linked list—a stack takes new nodes and releases nodes only at the top. For this reason, a stack is referred to as a *last-in, first-out (LIFO)* data structure. The link member in the bottom (i.e., last) node of the stack is set to **NULL** to indicate the bottom of the stack.

The primary operations to manipulate a stack are *push* and *pop*. Operation push adds a new node to the top of the stack. Operation pop removes a node from the top of the stack and returns the item from the popped node.

Stacks have many interesting applications. For example, when a program calls a method, the called method must know how to return to its caller, so the return address is pushed onto the *program execution stack*. If a series of method calls occurs, the successive return values are pushed onto the stack in last-in, first-out order so that each method can return to its caller. Stacks support recursive method calls in the same manner that they do conventional nonrecursive method calls.

The program-execution stack contains the space created for local variables on each invocation of a method during a program's execution. When the method returns to its caller, the space for that method's local variables is popped off the stack, and those variables are no longer known to the program.

The **System::Collections** namespace contains class **Stack** for implementing and manipulating stacks that can grow and shrink during program execution. Section 19.7 discusses class **Stack**.

We take advantage of the close relationship between lists and stacks to implement a stack class by reusing a list class. We demonstrate two different forms of reusability. First, we implement the stack class by inheriting from class **List** of Fig. 19.6–Fig. 19.7. Then, we implement an identically performing stack class through composition by including a **List** object as a **private** member of a stack class. This chapter implements list, stack and queue data structures to store **Object** pointers to encourage further reusability. Thus, any object type can be stored in a list, stack or queue.

The program of Fig. 19.15–Fig. 19.17 creates a stack class by inheriting from class **List** of Fig. 19.6–Fig. 19.7. We want the stack to have methods **Push**, **Pop**, **IsEmpty** and **Print**. Essentially, these are the methods **InsertAtFront**, **RemoveFromFront**, **IsEmpty** and **Print** of class **List**. Of course, class **List** contains other methods (such as **InsertAtBack** and **RemoveFromBack**) that we would rather not make accessible through the **public** interface of the stack. It is important to remember that all methods in the **public** interface of class **List** are also **public** methods of the derived class **StackInheritance** (Fig. 19.15–Fig. 19.16).

```
1   // Fig. 19.15: StackInheritance.h
2   // Implementing a stack by inheriting from class List.
3
4   #pragma once
5
6   #using <mscorlib.dll>
7   #using <system.dll>
8   #using "LinkedListLibrary.dll"
9
```

Fig. 19.15 **StackInheritance** extends class **List**. (Part 1 of 2.)

```
10   using namespace System;
11   using namespace LinkedListLibrary;
12
13   // class StackInheritance inherits class List's capabilities
14   public __gc class StackInheritance : public List
15   {
16   public:
17       StackInheritance();
18       void Push( Object * );
19       Object *Pop();
20   }; // end class StackInheritance
```

Fig. 19.15 **StackInheritance** extends class **List**. (Part 2 of 2.)

```
1    // Fig. 19.16: StackInheritance.cpp
2    // Method definitions for class StackInheritance.
3
4    #include "StackInheritance.h"
5
6    // pass name "stack" to List constructor
7    StackInheritance::StackInheritance() : List( S"stack" )
8    {
9    }
10
11   // place dataValue at top of stack by inserting
12   // dataValue at front of linked list
13   void StackInheritance::Push( Object *dataValue )
14   {
15       InsertAtFront( dataValue );
16   }
17
18   // remove item from top of stack by removing
19   // item at front of linked list
20   Object *StackInheritance::Pop()
21   {
22       return RemoveFromFront();
23   }
```

Fig. 19.16 **StackInheritance** class method definitions.

When we implement the stack's methods, we have each **StackInheritance** method call the appropriate **List** method—method **Push** calls **InsertAtFront**, method **Pop** calls **RemoveFromFront**. Class **StackInheritance** does not define methods **IsEmpty** and **Print**, because **StackInheritance** inherits these methods from class **List** into **StackInheritance**'s **public** interface. The methods in class **StackInheritance** do not use methods **Monitor::Enter** and **Monitor::Exit**. Each of the methods in this class calls a method from class **List** that uses **Monitor** methods **Enter** and **Exit**. If two threads call **Push** on the same stack object, only one of the threads at a time will be able to call **List** method **InsertAtFront**. Note that class **StackInheritance** uses namespace **LinkedListLibrary** (line 11 of Fig. 19.15); thus, the solution that defines **StackInheritance** must reference the DLL created by the **LinkedListLibrary** class library (line 8).

StackInheritanceTest.cpp's **main** function (Fig. 19.17) uses class **Stack-Inheritance** to instantiate a stack of **Object**s called **stack**. Lines 11–14 define the data that will be pushed onto the stack and popped off the stack. The program pushes onto the stack (at lines 17, 19, 21 and 23) a **bool** containing **true**, a **__wchar_t** containing **$**, an **int** containing **34567** and a **String *** containing **hello**. An infinite **while** loop (lines 29–34) pops the elements from the stack. The program uses method **Print** (inherited from class **List**) to output the contents of the stack after each operation (line 33). When there are no objects left to pop, the infinite loop forces method **Pop** to throw an **EmptyListException**. The program then displays the exception's stack trace (lines 39–40), which shows the program execution stack at the time the exception occurred.

```
1    // Fig. 19.17: StackInheritanceTest.cpp
2    // Testing class StackInheritance.
3
4    #include "StackInheritance.h"
5
6    int main()
7    {
8       StackInheritance *stack = new StackInheritance();
9
10      // create objects to store in the stack
11      bool aBoolean = true;
12      __wchar_t aCharacter = '$';
13      int anInteger = 34567;
14      String *aString = S"hello";
15
16      // use method Push to add items to stack
17      stack->Push( __box( aBoolean ) );
18      stack->Print();
19      stack->Push( __box( aCharacter ) );
20      stack->Print();
21      stack->Push( __box( anInteger ) );
22      stack->Print();
23      stack->Push( aString );
24      stack->Print();
25
26      // use method Pop to remove items from stack
27      try {
28
29         while ( true ) {
30            Object *removedObject = stack->Pop();
31            Console::WriteLine( String::Concat (
32               removedObject,S" popped" ) );
33            stack->Print();
34         }
35      }
36
37      // if exception occurs, print stack trace
38      catch ( EmptyListException *emptyListException ) {
39         Console::Error->WriteLine(
40            emptyListException->StackTrace );
41      }
```

Fig. 19.17 StackInheritance class driver. (Part 1 of 2.)

```
42
43      return 0;
44   } // end function main
```

```
The stack is: True

The stack is: $ True

The stack is: 34567 $ True

The stack is: hello 34567 $ True

hello popped
The stack is: 34567 $ True

34567 popped
The stack is: $ True

$ popped
The stack is: True

True popped
Empty stack
   at LinkedListLibrary.List.RemoveFromFront()
       in c:\ch19\fig19_04-09\linkedlistlibrary\list.cpp:line 61
   at StackInheritance.Pop()
       in c:\ch19\fig19_15-17\stackinheritancetest\
       stackinheritance.cpp:line 22
   at main()
       in c:\ch19\fig19_15-17\stackinheritancetest\
       stackinheritancetest.cpp:line 30
```

Fig. 19.17 `StackInheritance` class driver. (Part 2 of 2.)

Another way to implement a stack class is by reusing a list class through composition. The class in Fig. 19.18–Fig. 19.19 uses a **private** object of class **List** (line 23 of Fig. 19.18) in the definition of class **StackComposition**. Composition enables us to hide the methods of class **List** that should not be in our stack's **public** interface by providing **public** interface methods only to the required **List** methods. This class implements each stack method by delegating its work to an appropriate **List** method. In particular, **StackComposition** calls **List** methods **InsertAtFront**, **Remove-FromFront**, **IsEmpty** and **Print**. In this example, we do not show sample output for class **StackComposition**, because the only difference in the driver is that we change the type of the stack from **StackInheritance** to **StackComposition**. If you execute the application, you will see that the output (before the stack trace occurs) is identical.

```
1    // Fig. 19.18: StackComposition.h
2    // StackComposition definition with composed List object.
3
```

Fig. 19.18 `StackComposition` class encapsulates functionality of class `List`. (Part 1 of 2.)

```
4    #pragma once
5
6    #using <mscorlib.dll>
7    #using <system.dll>
8    #using "LinkedListLibrary.dll"
9
10   using namespace System;
11   using namespace LinkedListLibrary;
12
13   public __gc class StackComposition
14   {
15   public:
16      StackComposition();
17      void Push( Object * );
18      Object *Pop();
19      bool IsEmpty();
20      void Print();
21
22   private:
23      List *stack;
24   }; // end class StackComposition
```

Fig. 19.18 **StackComposition** class encapsulates functionality of class **List**. (Part 2 of 2.)

```
1    // Fig. 19.19: StackComposition.cpp
2    // Method definitions for class StackComposition.
3
4    #include "StackComposition.h"
5
6    // construct empty stack
7    StackComposition::StackComposition()
8    {
9       stack = new List( S"stack" );
10   }
11
12   // add object to stack
13   void StackComposition::Push( Object *dataValue )
14   {
15      stack->InsertAtFront( dataValue );
16   }
17
18   // remove object from stack
19   Object *StackComposition::Pop()
20   {
21      return stack->RemoveFromFront();
22   }
23
24   // determine wheater stack is empty
25   bool StackComposition::IsEmpty()
26   {
27      return stack->IsEmpty();
28   }
```

Fig. 19.19 **StackComposition** class method definitions. (Part 1 of 2.)

```
29
30    // output stack contents
31    void StackComposition::Print()
32    {
33        stack->Print();
34    }
```

Fig. 19.19 **StackComposition** class method definitions. (Part 2 of 2.)

19.5 Queues

Another common data structure is the *queue.* A queue is similar to a checkout line in a super-market—the first person in line is served first, customers enter the line only at the end, and they wait to be served. Queue nodes are removed only from the *head* of the queue and are inserted only at the *tail* of the queue. For this reason, a queue is a *first-in, first-out* (*FIFO*) data structure. The insert and remove operations are known as *enqueue* and *dequeue.*

Queues have many applications in computer systems. Most computers have only a single processor, so they cannot serve more than one user at a time. Entries for the other users are placed in a queue. The entry at the front of the queue receives the first available service. Each entry gradually advances to the front of the queue as users receive service.

Queues also support print spooling. A multiuser environment might have only one printer. Several users may send output to the printer. If the printer is busy, users may still generate other outputs, which are "spooled" to disk (much as thread is wound onto a spool), where they wait in a queue until the printer becomes available.

Information packets also wait in queues in computer networks. Each time a packet arrives at a network node, the routing node must route it to the next node on the network along the path to the packet's final destination. The routing node routes one packet at a time, so additional packets are enqueued until the router can route them.

A file server in a computer network handles file access requests from many clients throughout the network. Servers have a limited capacity to service requests from clients. When client requests exceed that capacity, the requests wait in queues.

The program of Fig. 19.20–Fig. 19.22 creates a queue class through inheritance from a list class. We want the **QueueInheritance** class (Fig. 19.20–Fig. 19.21) to have methods **Enqueue**, **Dequeue**, **IsEmpty** and **Print**. Note that these methods are essentially the **InsertAtBack**, **RemoveFromFront**, **IsEmpty** and **Print** methods of class **List**. Of course, the list class contains other methods (such as **InsertAtFront** and **RemoveFromBack**) that we would rather not make accessible through the **public** interface to the queue class. Remember that all methods in the **public** interface of the **List** class are also **public** methods of the derived class **QueueInheritance**.

```
1    // Fig. 19.20: QueueInheritance.h
2    // Implementing a queue by inheriting from class List.
3
4    #pragma once
5
```

Fig. 19.20 **QueueInheritance** extends class **List**. (Part 1 of 2.)

```
6    #using <mscorlib.dll>
7    #using <system.dll>
8    #using "LinkedListLibrary.dll"
9
10   #include <tchar.h>
11
12   using namespace System;
13   using namespace LinkedListLibrary;
14
15   // class QueueInheritance inherits List's capabilities
16   public __gc class QueueInheritance : public List
17   {
18   public:
19      QueueInheritance();
20      void Enqueue( Object * );
21      Object * Dequeue();
22   }; // end of QueueInheritance
```

Fig. 19.20 `QueueInheritance` extends class `List`. (Part 2 of 2.)

```
1    // Fig. 19.21: QueueInheritance.cpp
2    // Method definitions for class QueueInheritance.
3
4    #include "QueueInheritance.h"
5
6    // pass name "queue" to List constructor
7    QueueInheritance::QueueInheritance() : List( S"queue" )
8    {
9    }
10
11   // place dataValue at end of queue by inserting
12   // dataValue at end of linked list
13   void QueueInheritance::Enqueue( Object *dataValue )
14   {
15      InsertAtBack( dataValue );
16   }
17
18   // remove item from front of queue by removng
19   // item at front of linked list
20   Object* QueueInheritance::Dequeue()
21   {
22      return RemoveFromFront();
23   }
```

Fig. 19.21 `QueueInheritance` class method definitions.

When we implement the queue's methods, we have each **QueueInheritance** method call the appropriate **List** method—method **Enqueue** calls **InsertAtBack**, method **Dequeue** calls **RemoveFromFront**, and **IsEmpty** and **Print** calls invoke their base-class versions. Class **QueueInheritance** does not define methods **IsEmpty** and **Print**, because **QueueInheritance** inherits these methods from class **List** into **QueueInher-**

itance's **public** interface. Also, the methods in class **QueueInheritance** do not use methods **Monitor::Enter** and **Monitor::Exit**. Each of the methods in this class calls a method from class **List** that already uses **Monitor** methods **Enter** and **Exit**. Note that class **QueueInheritance** uses namespace **LinkedListLibrary** (line 13 of Fig. 19.20); thus, the solution that defines **QueueInheritance** must reference the DLL created by the **LinkedListLibrary** class library (line 8).

    QueueTest.cpp's **main** method (Fig. 19.22) uses class **QueueInheritance** to instantiate a queue of **Object**s called **queue**. Lines 11–14 define the data that will be enqueued and dequeued. The program enqueues (at lines 17, 19, 21 and 23) a **bool** containing **true**, a **__wchar_t** containing **$**, an **int** containing **34567** and a **String *** containing **hello**.

```
1   // Fig. 19.22: QueueTest.cpp
2   // Testing class QueueInheritance.
3
4   #include "QueueInheritance.h"
5
6   int main()
7   {
8      QueueInheritance *queue = new QueueInheritance();
9
10     // create objects to store in the stack
11     bool aBoolean = true;
12     __wchar_t aCharacter = '$';
13     int anInteger = 34567;
14     String *aString = S"hello";
15
16     // use method Enqueue to add items to queue
17     queue->Enqueue( __box( aBoolean ) );
18     queue->Print();
19     queue->Enqueue( __box( aCharacter ) );
20     queue->Print();
21     queue->Enqueue( __box( anInteger ) );
22     queue->Print();
23     queue->Enqueue( aString );
24     queue->Print();
25
26     // use method Dequeue to remove items from queue
27     Object *removedObject = NULL;
28
29     // remove items from queue
30     try {
31
32        while ( true ) {
33           removedObject = queue->Dequeue();
34           Console::WriteLine( String::Concat( removedObject,
35              S" dequeue" ) );
36           queue->Print();
37        } // end while
38     } // end try
39
```

Fig. 19.22 Inheritance used to create a queue. (Part 1 of 2.)

```
40        // if exception occurs, print stack trace
41        catch( EmptyListException *emptyListException) {
42            Console::Error->WriteLine(
43                emptyListException->StackTrace );
44        }
45
46        return 0;
47    } // end function main
```

```
The queue is: True

The queue is: True $

The queue is: True $ 34567

The queue is: True $ 34567 hello

True dequeue
The queue is: $ 34567 hello

$ dequeue
The queue is: 34567 hello

34567 dequeue
The queue is: hello

hello dequeue
Empty queue
    at LinkedListLibrary.List.RemoveFromFront()
        in c:\ch19\fig19_04-09\linkedlistlibrary\list.cpp:line 61
    at QueueInheritance.Dequeue()
        in c:\ch19\fig19_20-22\queuetest\queueinheritance.cpp:line 22
    at main()
        in c:\ch19\fig19_20-22\queuetest\queuetest.cpp:line 33
```

Fig. 19.22 Inheritance used to create a queue. (Part 2 of 2.)

An infinite **while** loop (lines 32–37) dequeues the elements from the queue in FIFO order. The program uses method **Print** (inherited from class **List**) to output the contents of the queue after each operation. When there are no objects left to dequeue, the infinite loop forces method **Dequeue** to throw an **EmptyListException**. The program then displays the exception's stack trace (lines 42–43), which shows the program execution stack at the time the exception occurred.

19.6 Trees

Linked lists, stacks and queues are *linear data structures* (i.e., *sequences*). A *tree* is a non-linear, two-dimensional data structure with special properties. Tree nodes contain two or more links. This section discusses *binary trees* (Fig. 19.23)—trees whose nodes all contain two links (of which none, one or both might be **NULL**). The *root node* is the first node in a tree. Each link in the root node points to a *child*. The *left child* is the first node in the *left subtree,* and the *right child* is the first node in the *right subtree.* The children of a specific node are called *siblings*. A node with no children is called a *leaf node*. Computer scientists normally draw trees from the root node down—exactly the opposite of the way most trees grow in nature.

Common Programming Error 19.4

*Not setting to **NULL** the links in leaf nodes of a tree is a common logic error.*

In our binary tree example, we create a special binary tree called a *binary search tree*. A binary search tree (with no duplicate node values) has the characteristic that the values in any left subtree are less than the value in the subtree's parent node, and the values in any right subtree are greater than the value in the subtree's parent node. Figure 19.24 illustrates a binary search tree with 12 integer values. Note that the shape of the binary search tree that corresponds to a set of data can depend on the order in which the values are inserted into the tree.

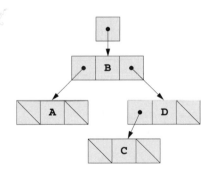

Fig. 19.23 Graphical representation of a binary tree.

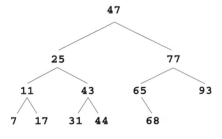

Fig. 19.24 Binary search tree containing 12 values.

19.6.1 Binary Search Tree of Integer Values

The application of Fig. 19.25–Fig. 19.29 creates a binary search tree of integers and traverses it (i.e., walks through all its nodes) in three ways—using recursive *inorder, preorder* and *postorder traversals*. The program generates 10 random numbers and inserts each into the tree. Fig. 19.27–Fig. 19.28 defines class **Tree**. Fig. 19.29 defines **TreeTest.cpp** to demonstrate class **Tr** instantiates an empty **Tree** object, then randomly generates 10 integers and inserts each value into the binary tree by calling **Tree** method **InsertNode**. The program then performs preorder, inorder and postorder traversals of the tree. We discuss these traversals shortly.

Class **TreeNode** (Fig. 19.25–Fig. 19.26) is a self-referential class containing three **private** data members—**leftNode** and **rightNode** (of type **TreeNode**) and **data** (of type **int**). Initially, every **TreeNode** is a leaf node, so the constructor (lines 7–11 of Fig. 19.26) initializes pointers **leftNode** and **rightNode** to **NULL**. Properties **LeftNode** (lines 20–28 of Fig. 19.25), **Data** (lines 31–39) and **RightNode** (lines 42–50) provide access to a **ListNode**'s **private** data members. We discuss **TreeNode** method **Insert** (lines 15–41 of Fig. 19.26) shortly.

```
1   // Fig. 19.25: TreeNode.h
2   // Definition of class TreeNode.
3
4   #pragma once
5
6   #using <mscorlib.dll>
7   #using <system.dll>
8
9   using namespace System;
10  using namespace System::Threading;
11
12  #include <tchar.h>
13
14  __gc class TreeNode
15  {
16  public:
17     TreeNode( int );
18
19     // LeftNode property
20     __property TreeNode *get_LeftNode()
21     {
22        return leftNode;
23     }
24
25     __property void set_LeftNode( TreeNode *value )
26     {
27        leftNode = value;
28     }
29
30     // Data property
31     __property int get_Data()
32     {
```

Fig. 19.25 TreeNode class represents one node in a binary tree. (Part 1 of 2.)

```
33          return data;
34       }
35
36       __property void set_Data( int value )
37       {
38          data = value;
39       }
40
41       // RightNode property
42       __property TreeNode *get_RightNode()
43       {
44          return rightNode;
45       }
46
47       __property void set_RightNode( TreeNode *value )
48       {
49          rightNode = value;
50       }
51
52       void Insert( int );
53
54    private:
55       TreeNode *leftNode;
56       int data;
57       TreeNode *rightNode;
58    }; // end class TreeNode
```

Fig. 19.25 TreeNode class represents one node in a binary tree. (Part 2 of 2.)

```
1     // Fig. 19.26: TreeNode.cpp
2     // Method definitions for class TreeNode.
3
4     #include "TreeNode.h"
5
6     // initialize data and make this a leaf node
7     TreeNode::TreeNode( int nodeData )
8     {
9        data = nodeData;
10       leftNode = rightNode = NULL; // node has no children
11    }
12
13    // insert TreeNode into Tree that contains nodes;
14    // ignore duplicate values
15    void TreeNode::Insert( int insertValue )
16    {
17       // insert in left subtree
18       if ( insertValue < data ) {
19
20          // insert new TreeNode
21          if ( leftNode == NULL )
22             leftNode = new TreeNode( insertValue );
23
```

Fig. 19.26 TreeNode class method definitions. (Part 1 of 2.)

```
24        // continue traversing left subtree
25        else
26            leftNode->Insert( insertValue );
27     }
28
29     // insert in right subtree
30     else if ( insertValue > data ) {
31
32        // insert new TreeNode
33        if ( rightNode == NULL )
34            rightNode = new TreeNode( insertValue );
35
36        // continue traversing right subtree
37        else
38            rightNode->Insert( insertValue );
39     }
40
41  } // end method Insert
```

Fig. 19.26 **TreeNode** class method definitions. (Part 2 of 2.)

Class **Tree** (Fig. 19.27–Fig. 19.28) manipulates objects of class **TreeNode**. Class **Tree** has as **private** member **root** (line 18 of Fig. 19.27)—a pointer to the root node of the tree. The class contains **public** method **InsertNode** (lines 15–24 of Fig. 19.28) to insert a new node in the tree and **public** methods **PreorderTraversal** (lines 27–32), **InorderTraversal** (lines 52–57) and **PostorderTraversal** (lines 77–82) to begin traversals of the tree. Each of these methods calls a separate recursive utility method to perform the traversal operations on the internal representation of the tree. The **Tree** constructor (lines 7–10) initializes **root** to **NULL** to indicate that the tree initially is empty.

```
1   // Fig. 19.27: Tree.h
2   // Definition of class Tree.
3
4   #pragma once
5
6   #include "TreeNode.h"
7
8   public __gc class Tree
9   {
10  public:
11     Tree();
12     void InsertNode( int );
13     void PreorderTraversal();
14     void InorderTraversal();
15     void PostorderTraversal();
16
17  private:
18     TreeNode *root;
19     void PreorderHelper( TreeNode * );
20     void InorderHelper( TreeNode * );
21     void PostorderHelper( TreeNode * );
22  }; // end class Tree
```

Fig. 19.27 **Tree** class represents a binary tree of **TreeNode**s.

```cpp
1   // Fig. 19.28: Tree.cpp
2   // Method definitions for class Tree.
3
4   #include "Tree.h"
5
6   // construct an empty Tree of integers
7   Tree::Tree()
8   {
9      root = NULL;
10  }
11
12  // Insert a new node in the binary search tree.
13  // If the root node is NULL, create the root node here.
14  // Otherwise, call the insert method of clas TreeNode.
15  void Tree::InsertNode( int insertValue )
16  {
17     Monitor::Enter( this );
18
19     if ( root == NULL )
20        root = new TreeNode( insertValue );
21     else root->Insert( insertValue );
22
23     Monitor::Exit( this );
24  } // end method InsertNode
25
26  // begin preorder traversal
27  void Tree::PreorderTraversal()
28  {
29     Monitor::Enter( this );
30     PreorderHelper( root );
31     Monitor::Exit( this );
32  } // end method PreorderTraversal
33
34  // recursive method to perform preorder traversal
35  void Tree::PreorderHelper( TreeNode *node )
36  {
37     if ( node == NULL )
38        return;
39
40     // output node data
41     Console::Write( String::Concat( node->Data.ToString(),
42        S" " ) );
43
44     // traverse left subtree
45     PreorderHelper( node->LeftNode );
46
47     // traverse right subtree
48     PreorderHelper( node->RightNode );
49  } // end method PreorderHelper
50
51  // begin inorder traversal
52  void Tree::InorderTraversal()
53  {
```

Fig. 19.28 Tree class method definitions. (Part 1 of 2.)

```
54        Monitor::Enter( this );
55        InorderHelper( root );
56        Monitor::Exit( this );
57     } // end method InorderTraversal
58
59     // recursive method to perform inorder traversal
60     void Tree::InorderHelper( TreeNode *node )
61     {
62        if ( node == NULL )
63           return;
64
65        // traverse left subtree
66        InorderHelper( node->LeftNode );
67
68        // output node data
69        Console::Write( String::Concat(
70           node->Data.ToString(), S" " ) );
71
72        // traverse right subtree
73        InorderHelper( node->RightNode );
74     } // end method InorderHelper
75
76     // begin postorder taversal
77     void Tree::PostorderTraversal()
78     {
79        Monitor::Enter( this );
80        PostorderHelper( root );
81        Monitor::Exit( this );
82     } // end method PostorderTraversal
83
84     // recursive method to perform postorder traversal
85     void Tree::PostorderHelper( TreeNode *node )
86     {
87        if ( node == NULL )
88           return;
89
90        // traverse left subtree
91        PostorderHelper( node->LeftNode );
92
93        // traverse right subtree
94        PostorderHelper( node->RightNode );
95
96        // output node data
97        Console::Write( String::Concat (
98           node->Data.ToString(), S" " ) );
99     } // end method PostorderHelper
```

Fig. 19.28 Tree class method definitions. (Part 2 of 2.)

```
1     // Fig. 19.29: TreeTest.cpp
2     // This program tests class Tree.
```

Fig. 19.29 TreeTest.cpp demonstrates creating and traversing a binary tree.
(Part 1 of 2.)

```
3
4    #include "Tree.h"
5
6    int main()
7    {
8        Tree *tree = new Tree();
9        int insertValue;
10
11       Console::WriteLine( S"Inserting values: " );
12       Random *random = new Random();
13
14       // insert 10 random integers from 0-99 in tree
15       for ( int i = 1; i <= 10; i++ ) {
16           insertValue = random->Next( 100 );
17           Console::Write( String::Concat(
18               insertValue.ToString(), S" " ) );
19
20           tree->InsertNode( insertValue );
21       } // end for
22
23       // perform preorder traversal of tree
24       Console::WriteLine( S"\n\nPreorder traversal" );
25       tree->PreorderTraversal();
26
27       // perform inorder traversal of tree
28       Console::WriteLine( S"\n\nInorder traversal" );
29       tree->InorderTraversal();
30
31       // perform postorder traversal of tree
32       Console::WriteLine( S"\n\nPostorder traversal" );
33       tree->PostorderTraversal();
34       Console::WriteLine();
35
36       return 0;
37   } // end function main
```

```
Inserting values:
70 90 75 23 98 76 19 98 96 56

Preorder traversal
70 23 19 56 90 75 76 98 96

Inorder traversal
19 23 56 70 75 76 90 96 98

Postorder traversal
19 56 23 76 75 96 98 90 70
```

Fig. 19.29 **TreeTest.cpp** demonstrates creating and traversing a binary tree.
(Part 2 of 2.)

The **Tree** class's method **InsertNode** (lines 15–24) first locks the **Tree** object for thread safety, then checks for whether the tree is empty. If so, line 20 allocates a new

TreeNode, initializes the node with the integer being inserted in the tree and assigns the new node to **root**. If the tree is not empty, **InsertNode** calls **TreeNode** method **Insert** (lines 15–41 of Fig. 19.26), which recursively determines the location for the new node in the tree and inserts the node at that location. *In a binary search tree, a node can be inserted only as a leaf node.*

The **TreeNode** method **Insert** compares the value to insert with the **data** value in the root node. If the insert value is less than the root-node data, the program checks for whether the left subtree is empty (line 21 of Fig. 19.26). If so, line 22 allocates a new **TreeNode**, initializes it with the integer being inserted and assigns the new node to pointer **leftNode**; otherwise, line 26 recursively calls **Insert** for the left subtree to insert the value into the left subtree. If the insert value is greater than the root-node data, the program checks for whether the right subtree is empty (line 33). If so, line 34 allocates a new **TreeNode**, initializes it with the integer being inserted and assigns the new node to pointer **rightNode**; otherwise, line 38 recursively calls **Insert** for the right subtree to insert the value in the right subtree.

Methods **InorderTraversal**, **PreorderTraversal** and **PostorderTraversal** call helper methods **InorderHelper** (lines 60–74 of Fig. 19.28), **PreorderHelper** (lines 35–49) and **PostorderHelper** (lines 85–99), respectively, to traverse the tree and print the node values. The purpose of the helper methods in class **Tree** is to allow the programmer to start a traversal without the need to obtain a pointer to the **root** node first, then call the recursive method with that pointer. Methods **InorderTraversal**, **PreorderTraversal** and **PostorderTraversal** simply take the **private** pointer **root** and pass it to the appropriate helper method to initiate a traversal of the tree. For the following discussion, we use the binary search tree shown in Fig. 19.30. Method **InorderHelper** (lines 60–74) defines the steps for an inorder traversal. Those steps are as follows:

1. If the argument is **NULL**, return immediately.

2. Traverse the left subtree with a call to **InorderHelper** (line 66).

3. Process the value in the node (line 69–70).

4. Traverse the right subtree with a call to **InorderHelper** (line 73).

The inorder traversal does not process the value in a node until the values in that node's left subtree are processed. The inorder traversal of the tree in Fig. 19.30 is

    6 13 17 27 33 42 48

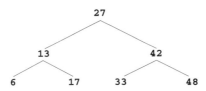

Fig. 19.30 Binary search tree.

Note that the inorder traversal of a binary search tree prints the node values in ascending order. The process of creating a binary search tree actually sorts the data—thus, this process is called the *binary tree sort*.

Method **PreorderHelper** (lines 35–49) defines the steps for a preorder traversal. Those steps are as follows:

1. If the argument is **NULL**, return immediately.

2. Process the value in the node (line 41–42).

3. Traverse the left subtree with a call to **PreorderHelper** (line 45).

4. Traverse the right subtree with a call to **PreorderHelper** (line 48).

The preorder traversal processes the value in each node as the node is visited. After processing the value in a given node, the preorder traversal processes the values in the left subtree, then the values in the right subtree. The preorder traversal of the tree in Fig. 19.30 is

```
27 13 6 17 42 33 48
```

Method **PostorderHelper** (lines 85–99) defines the steps for a postorder traversal. Those steps are as follows:

1. If the argument is **NULL**, return immediately.

2. Traverse the left subtree with a call to **PostorderHelper** (line 91).

3. Traverse the right subtree with a call to **PostorderHelper** (line 94).

4. Process the value in the node (line 97–98).

The postorder traversal processes the value in each node after the values of all that node's children are processed. The postorder traversal of the tree in Fig. 19.30 is

```
6 17 13 33 48 42 27
```

The binary search tree facilitates *duplicate elimination*. While building a tree, the insertion operation recognizes attempts to insert a duplicate value, because a duplicate follows the same "go left" or "go right" decisions on each comparison as the original value did. Thus, the insertion operation eventually compares the duplicate with a node containing the same value. At this point, the insertion operation might simply discard the duplicate value.

Searching a binary tree for a value that matches a key value is fast, especially for *tightly packed* trees. In a tightly packed tree, each level contains about twice as many elements as the previous level. Figure 19.30 shows a tightly packed binary tree. A binary search tree with n elements has a minimum of $\log_2 n$ levels. Thus, at most $\log_2 n$ comparisons are required either to find a match or to determine that no match exists. Searching a (tightly packed) 1000-element binary search tree requires at most 10 comparisons, because $2^{10} > 1000$. Searching a (tightly packed) 1,000,000-element binary search tree requires at most 20 comparisons, because $2^{20} > 1,000,000$.

19.6.2 Binary Search Tree of **IComparable** Objects

The binary tree example in Section 19.6.1 works nicely when all the data is of type **int**. Suppose that you want to manipulate a binary tree of double values. You could rewrite the **TreeNode** and **Tree** classes with different names and customize the classes to manipulate double values. Similarly, for each data type you could create customized versions of classes **TreeNode** and **Tree**. This results in a proliferation of code, which can become difficult to manage and maintain. The C++ programming language provides a technology, called *templates*, that enables us to write a class definition once, then have the compiler generate new versions of the class for any data type we choose.

Ideally, we would like to define the functionality of a binary tree once and reuse that functionality for many data types. Languages like Java™ and C++ provide polymorphic capabilities that enable all objects to be manipulated in a uniform manner. Using such capabilities enables us to design a more flexible data structure.

In our next example, we take advantage of C++'s polymorphic capabilities by implementing **TreeNode** and **Tree** classes that manipulate objects of any type that implements interface *IComparable* (namespace **System**). It is imperative that we be able to compare objects stored in a binary search, so that we can determine the path to the insertion point of a new node. Classes that implement **IComparable** define method *CompareTo*, which compares the object that invokes the method with the object that the method receives as an argument. The method returns an **int** value less than zero if the calling object is less than the argument object, zero if the objects are equal and a positive value if the calling object is greater than the argument object. Also, both the calling and argument objects must be of the same data type; otherwise, the method throws an **ArgumentException**. Many of the data types we have used throughout this book implement interface **IComparable**.

The program of Fig. 19.31–Fig. 19.35 enhances the program from Section 19.6.1 to manipulate **IComparable** objects. One restriction on the new versions of classes **TreeNode** and **Tree** in Fig. 19.31–Fig. 19.34 is that each **Tree** object can contain objects of only one data type (e.g., all **String** pointers or all **double**s). If a program attempts to insert multiple data types in the same **Tree** object, **ArgumentException**s will occur. We modified only nine lines of code in class **TreeNode** (lines 19, 33, 38, 54 and 58 of Fig. 19.31 and lines 7, 15, 18 and 30 of Fig. 19.32) and two lines of code in class **Tree** (line 12 of Fig. 19.33 and line 15 of Fig. 19.34) to enable processing of **IComparable** objects. With the exception of lines 18 and 30 (of Fig. 19.32), all other changes simply replaced the type **int** with the type **IComparable ***. Lines 18 and 30 previously used the **<** and **>** operators to compare the value being inserted with the value in a given node. These lines now compare **IComparable** objects via the interface's method **CompareTo**, then test the method's return value to determine whether it is less than zero (the calling object is less than the argument object) or greater than zero (the calling object is greater than the argument object), respectively.

```
1   // Fig. 19.31: TreeNode2.h
2   // Definition of class TreeNode for IComparable objects.
3
4   #pragma once
5
6   #using <mscorlib.dll>
7   #using <system.dll>
8
9   using namespace System;
```

Fig. 19.31 **TreeNode** class for manipulating **IComparable** objects. (Part 1 of 2.)

```
10   using namespace System::Threading;
11
12   #include <tchar.h>
13
14   public __gc class TreeNode
15   {
16   public:
17
18      // initialize data and make this a leaf node
19      TreeNode( IComparable * );
20
21      // property LeftNode
22      __property TreeNode *get_LeftNode()
23      {
24         return leftNode;
25      }
26
27      __property void set_LeftNode( TreeNode *value )
28      {
29         leftNode = value;
30      }
31
32      // property Data
33      __property IComparable *get_Data()
34      {
35         return data;
36      }
37
38      __property void set_Data( IComparable *value )
39      {
40         data = value;
41      }
42
43      // property RightNode
44      __property TreeNode *get_RightNode()
45      {
46         return rightNode;
47      }
48
49      __property void set_RightNode( TreeNode *value )
50      {
51         rightNode = value;
52      }
53
54      void Insert( IComparable * );
55
56   private:
57      TreeNode *leftNode;
58      IComparable *data;
59      TreeNode *rightNode;
60   }; // end class TreeNode
```

Fig. 19.31 TreeNode class for manipulating IComparable objects. (Part 2 of 2.)

```
1   // Fig. 19.32: TreeNode2.cpp
2   // Method definitions for class TreeNode.
3
4   #include "TreeNode2.h"
5
6   // initialize data and make this a leaf node
7   TreeNode::TreeNode( IComparable *nodeData )
8   {
9      data = nodeData;
10     leftNode = rightNode = NULL; // node has no children
11  }
12
13  // insert TreeNode into Tree that contains nodes;
14  // ignore duplicate values
15  void TreeNode::Insert( IComparable *insertValue )
16  {
17     // insert in left subtree
18     if ( insertValue->CompareTo( data ) < 0 ) {
19
20        // insert new TreeNode
21        if ( leftNode == NULL )
22           leftNode = new TreeNode( insertValue );
23
24        // continue traversing left subtree
25        else
26           leftNode->Insert( insertValue );
27     }
28
29     // insert in right subtree
30     else if ( insertValue->CompareTo( data ) > 0 ) {
31
32        // insert new TreeNOde
33        if ( rightNode == NULL )
34           rightNode = new TreeNode( insertValue );
35
36        // continue traversing right subtree
37        else
38           rightNode->Insert( insertValue );
39     }
40  } // end method Insert
```

Fig. 19.32 TreeNode class method definitions.

```
1   // Fig. 19.33: Tree2.h
2   // Definition of class Tree for IComparable objects.
3
4   #pragma once
5
6   #include "TreeNode2.h"
7
```

Fig. 19.33 Tree class for manipulating **IComparable** objects. (Part 1 of 2.)

```
8    public __gc class Tree
9    {
10   public:
11      Tree();
12      void InsertNode( IComparable * );
13      void PreorderTraversal();
14      void PreorderHelper( TreeNode * );
15      void InorderTraversal();
16      void InorderHelper( TreeNode * );
17      void PostorderTraversal();
18      void PostorderHelper( TreeNode * );
19
20   private:
21      TreeNode *root;
22   }; // end class Tree
```

Fig. 19.33 Tree class for manipulating **IComparable** objects. (Part 2 of 2.)

```
1    // Fig. 19.34: Tree2.cpp
2    // Method definitions for class Tree.
3
4    #include "Tree2.h"
5
6    // construct an empty Tree of integers
7    Tree::Tree()
8    {
9       root = NULL;
10   }
11
12   // Insert a new node in the binary search tree.
13   // If the root node is NULL, create the root node here.
14   // Otherwise, call the insert method of class TreeNode.
15   void Tree::InsertNode( IComparable *insertValue )
16   {
17      Monitor::Enter( this );
18
19      if ( root == NULL )
20         root = new TreeNode( insertValue );
21      else root->Insert( insertValue );
22
23      Monitor::Exit( this );
24   }
25
26   // begin preorder traversal
27   void Tree::PreorderTraversal()
28   {
29      Monitor::Enter( this );
30      PreorderHelper( root );
31      Monitor::Exit( this );
32   } // end method PreorderTraversal
33
34   // recursive method to perform preorder traversal
35   void Tree::PreorderHelper( TreeNode *node )
```

Fig. 19.34 Tree class method definitions. (Part 1 of 3.)

```
36   {
37      if ( node == NULL )
38         return;
39
40      // output node data
41      Console::Write( String::Concat(
42         node->Data->ToString(), S" " ) );
43
44      // traverse left subtree
45      PreorderHelper( node->LeftNode );
46
47      // traverse right subtree
48      PreorderHelper( node->RightNode );
49   } // end method PreorderHelper
50
51   // begin inorder traversal
52   void Tree::InorderTraversal()
53   {
54      Monitor::Enter( this );
55      InorderHelper( root );
56      Monitor::Exit( this );
57   } // end method InorderTraversal
58
59   // recursive method to perform inorder traversal
60   void Tree::InorderHelper( TreeNode *node )
61   {
62      if ( node == NULL )
63         return;
64
65      // traverse left subtree
66      InorderHelper( node->LeftNode );
67
68      // output node data
69      Console::Write( String::Concat(
70         node->Data->ToString(), S" " ) );
71
72      // traverse right subtree
73      InorderHelper( node->RightNode );
74   } // end method InorderHelper
75
76   // begin post order traversal
77   void Tree::PostorderTraversal()
78   {
79      Monitor::Enter( this );
80      PostorderHelper( root );
81      Monitor::Exit( this );
82   } // end method PostorderTraversal
83
84   // recursive method to perform postorder traversal
85   void Tree::PostorderHelper( TreeNode *node )
86   {
87      if ( node == NULL )
88         return;
89
```

Fig. 19.34 Tree class method definitions. (Part 2 of 3.)

```
90        // traverse left subtre
91        PostorderHelper( node->LeftNode );
92
93        // traverse right subtree
94        PostorderHelper( node->RightNode );
95
96        // output node data
97        Console::Write( String::Concat(
98           node->Data->ToString(), S" " ) );
99    } // end method PostorderHelper
```

Fig. 19.34 Tree class method definitions. (Part 3 of 3.)

TreeTest2.cpp (Fig. 19.35) creates three **Tree** objects to store **int**, **double** and **String *** values, all of which the .NET Framework defines as **IComparable** types. The program populates the trees with the values in arrays **intArray** (line 11), **double-Array** (lines 12–13) and **stringArray** (lines 14–15), respectively.

```
1    // Fig. 19.35: TreeTest2.cpp
2    // Entry point for application.
3
4    #include "Tree2.h"
5
6    void populateTree( Array *array, Tree *tree, String *name );
7    void traverseTree( Tree *, String * );
8
9    int main()
10   {
11      int intArray __gc[] = { 8, 2, 4, 3, 1, 7, 5, 6 };
12      double doubleArray __gc[] =
13         { 8.8, 2.2, 4.4, 3.3, 1.1, 7.7, 5.5, 6.6 };
14      String *stringArray[] = { S"eight", S"two", S"four",
15         S"three", S"one", S"seven", S"five", S"six" };
16
17      // create int Tree
18      Tree *intTree = new Tree();
19      populateTree( intArray, intTree, S"intTree" );
20      traverseTree( intTree, S"intTree" );
21
22      // create double Tree
23      Tree *doubleTree = new Tree();
24      populateTree( doubleArray, doubleTree, S"doubleTree" );
25      traverseTree( doubleTree, S"doubleTree" );
26
27      // create String Tree
28      Tree *stringTree = new Tree();
29      populateTree( stringArray, stringTree, S"stringTree" );
30      traverseTree( stringTree, S"stringTree" );
31
32      return 0;
```

Fig. 19.35 TreeTest2.cpp demonstrates class **Tree** with **IComparable** objects. (Part 1 of 3.)

```
33    } // end function main
34
35    // populate Tree with array elements
36    void populateTree( Array *array, Tree *tree, String *name )
37    {
38       Console::WriteLine( String::Concat( S"\nInserting into ",
39          name, S":" ) );
40
41       IComparable *data;
42
43       for ( int i = 0; i < array->Length; i++ ) {
44          data = dynamic_cast< IComparable * >( array->Item[ i ] );
45          Console::Write( String::Concat( data->ToString(), S" " ) );
46          tree->InsertNode( data );
47       }
48    } // end function populateTree
49
50    // perform traversals
51    void traverseTree( Tree *tree, String *treeType )
52    {
53       // perform preorder traversal of tree
54       Console::WriteLine( String::Concat(
55          S"\n\nPreorder traversal of ", treeType ) );
56       tree->PreorderTraversal();
57
58       // perform inorder traversal of tree
59       Console::WriteLine( String::Concat(
60          S"\n\nInorder traversal of ", treeType ) );
61       tree->InorderTraversal();
62
63       // perform postorder traversal of tree
64       Console::WriteLine( String::Concat(
65          S"\n\nPostorder traversal of ", treeType ) );
66       tree->PostorderTraversal();
67       Console::WriteLine( S"\n" );
68    } // end function traverseTree
```

```
Inserting into intTree:
8 2 4 3 1 7 5 6

Preorder traversal of intTree
8 2 1 4 3 7 5 6

Inorder traversal of intTree
1 2 3 4 5 6 7 8

Postorder traversal of intTree
1 3 6 5 7 4 2 8

Inserting into doubleTree:
8.8 2.2 4.4 3.3 1.1 7.7 5.5 6.6
```

Continued at the top of the next page

Fig. 19.35 `TreeTest2.cpp` demonstrates class `Tree` with `IComparable` objects. (Part 2 of 3.)

Continued from the previous page

```
Preorder traversal of doubleTree
8.8 2.2 1.1 4.4 3.3 7.7 5.5 6.6

Inorder traversal of doubleTree
1.1 2.2 3.3 4.4 5.5 6.6 7.7 8.8

Postorder traversal of doubleTree
1.1 3.3 6.6 5.5 7.7 4.4 2.2 8.8


Inserting into stringTree:
eight two four three one seven five six

Preorder traversal of stringTree
eight two four five three one seven six

Inorder traversal of stringTree
eight five four one seven six three two

Postorder traversal of stringTree
five six seven one three four two eight
```

Fig. 19.35 `TreeTest2.cpp` demonstrates class **Tree** with **IComparable** objects. (Part 3 of 3.)

Method **populateTree** (lines 36–48) receives an **Array** containing the initializer values for the **Tree**, a **Tree** into which the array elements will be placed and a **String *** representing the **Tree** name as arguments, then inserts each **Array** element into the **Tree**. Method **traverseTree** (lines 51–68) receives a **Tree** and a **String *** representing the **Tree** name as arguments, then outputs the preorder, inorder and postorder traversals of the **Tree**. Note that the inorder traversal of each **Tree** outputs the data in sorted order regardless of the data type stored in the **Tree**. Our polymorphic implementation of class **Tree** invokes the appropriate data type's **CompareTo** method to trace the path to each value's insertion point by using the standard binary search tree insertion rules. Also, notice that the **Tree** of **String** pointers appears in alphabetical order.

19.7 Collection Classes

The previous sections of this chapter discussed how to create and manipulate data structures. The discussion was "low level," in the sense that we painstakingly created each element of each data structure dynamically with **new** and modified the data structures by directly manipulating their elements and pointers to their elements. In this section, we consider the prepackaged data-structure classes provided by the .NET Framework. These classes are known as *collection classes*—they store collections of data. Each instance of one of these classes is known as a *collection*, which is a set of items.

With collection classes, instead of creating data structures, the programmer simply uses existing data structures, without concern for how the data structures are implemented. This methodology is a marvelous example of code reuse. Programmers can code faster and can expect excellent performance, maximizing execution speed and minimizing memory consumption.

Some examples of collections are the cards you hold in a card game, your favorite songs stored in your computer and the real-estate records in your local registry of deeds (which map book numbers and page numbers to property owners). The .NET Framework provides several collections. We demonstrate four collection classes—**Array**, **Array-List**, **Stack** and **Hashtable**—all from namespace **System::Collections**, plus built-in array capabilities. In addition, namespace **System::Collections** provides several other data structures, including **BitArray** (a collection of true/false values), **Queue** and **SortedList** (a collection of key/value pairs that are sorted by key and can be accessed either by key or by index).

The .NET Framework provides ready-to-go, reusable components; you do not need to write your own collection classes. The collections are standardized, so applications can share them easily, without having to be concerned with the details of their implementation. These collections are written for broad reuse. They are tuned for rapid execution and for efficient use of memory. As new data structures and algorithms are developed that fit this framework, a large base of programmers already will be familiar with the interfaces and algorithms implemented by those data structures.

19.7.1 Class **Array**

Chapter 4, Functions and Arrays, presented basic array-processing capabilities, and many subsequent chapters used the techniques shown there. We discussed briefly that all arrays inherit from class **Array** (namespace **System**) and how class **Array** can be used to construct jagged arrays. We also discussed **Array** property **Length** that specifies the number of elements in an array. In addition, class **Array** provides **static** methods that provide algorithms for processing arrays. Typically, class **Array** overloads these methods to provide multiple options for performing algorithms. For example, **Array** method *Reverse* can reverse the order of the elements in an entire array or can reverse the elements in a specified range of elements in an array. For a complete list of class **Array**'s **static** methods and their overloaded versions, see the online documentation for the class.[2] Figure 19.36–Figure 19.38 demonstrates several **static** methods of class **Array**.

Line 15 (of Fig. 19.37) uses **static Array** method *Sort* to sort an array of **double** values. When this method returns, the array contains its original elements, but sorted in ascending order.

Lines 18 uses **static Array** method *Copy* to copy elements from array **intValues** into array **intValuesCopy**. The first argument is the array to copy (**intValues**), the second argument is the destination array (**intValuesCopy**) and the third argument is an integer representing the number of elements to copy (in this case, **intValues.Length** specifies all elements).

```
1    // Fig. 19.36: UsingArray.h
2    // Using Array class to perform common array manipulations.
3
```

Fig. 19.36 **UsingArray** class demonstrates class **Array**. (Part 1 of 2.)

---

2. The online documentation for class **Array** can be found at
   msdn.microsoft.com/library/default.asp?url=/library/en-us/cpref/html/frlrfsystemarrayclasstopic.asp.

```
4    #pragma once
5
6    #using <mscorlib.dll>
7    #using <system.dll>
8    #using <system.drawing.dll>
9    #using <system.windows.forms.dll>
10
11   using namespace System;
12   using namespace System::Windows::Forms;
13   using namespace System::Collections;
14
15   public __gc class UsingArray
16   {
17   public:
18      void Start();
19
20   private:
21      static int intValues __gc[] = { 1, 2, 3, 4, 5, 6 };
22      static double doubleValues __gc[] =
23         { 8.4, 9.3, 0.2, 7.9, 3.4 };
24      int intValuesCopy __gc[];
25      String *output;
26      void PrintArray();
27   }; // end class UsingArray
```

Fig. 19.36 UsingArray class demonstrates class **Array**. (Part 2 of 2.)

```
1    // Fig. 19.37: UsingArray.cpp
2    // Method definitions for class UsingArray.
3
4    #include "UsingArray.h"
5
6    // method to build and display program output
7    void UsingArray::Start()
8    {
9       intValuesCopy = new int __gc[ intValues.Length ];
10
11      output = S"Initial Array values:\n";
12      PrintArray(); // output initial array contents
13
14      // sort doubleValues
15      Array::Sort( doubleValues );
16
17      // copy intValues into intValuesCopy
18      Array::Copy( intValues, intValuesCopy, intValues.Length );
19
20      output = String::Concat( output,
21         S"\nArray values after Sort and Copy:\n" );
22      PrintArray(); // output array contents
23      output = String::Concat( output, S"\n" );
24
```

Fig. 19.37 UsingArray class method definitions. (Part 1 of 2.)

```
25          // search for 5 in intValues
26          int result = Array::BinarySearch( intValues, __box( 5 ) );
27          output = String::Concat( output,
28              ( result >= 0 ? String::Concat( S"5 found at element ",
29              result.ToString() ) : S"5 not found" ),
30              S" in intValues\n" );
31
32          // search for 8763 in intValues
33          result = Array::BinarySearch( intValues, __box( 8763 ) );
34          output = String::Concat( output,
35              ( result >= 0 ? S"8763 found at element ",
36              result.ToString() ) : S"8763 not found" ),
37              S" in intValues\n" );
38
39          MessageBox::Show( output, S"Using Class Array",
40              MessageBoxButtons::OK, MessageBoxIcon::Information );
41      } // end method Start
42
43      // append array content to output string
44      void UsingArray::PrintArray()
45      {
46          output = String::Concat( output, S"doubleValues: " );
47
48          double element;
49
50          for ( int i = 0; i < doubleValues.Length; i++ ) {
51              element = doubleValues[ i ];
52              output = String::Concat( output, element.ToString(), S" " );
53          }
54
55          output = String::Concat( output, S"\nintValues: " );
56
57          int intElement;
58
59          for( int j = 0; j < intValues.Length; j++ ) {
60              intElement = intValues[ j ];
61              output = String::Concat( output, intElement.ToString(),
62                  S" " );
63          }
64
65          output = String::Concat( output, S"\nintValuesCopy: " );
66
67          int intCopy;
68
69          for( int n = 0; n < intValuesCopy.Length; n++ ) {
70              intCopy = intValuesCopy[ n ];
71              output = String::Concat( output, intCopy.ToString(),
72                  S" " );
73          }
74
75          output = String::Concat( output, S"\n" );
76      } // end method PrintArray
```

Fig. 19.37 UsingArray class method definitions. (Part 2 of 2.)

```
1   // Fig. 19.38: UsingArrayTest.cpp
2   // Entry point for application.
3
4   #include "UsingArray.h"
5
6   int __stdcall WinMain()
7   {
8      UsingArray *application = new UsingArray();
9      application->Start();
10
11     return 0;
12  } // end function WinMain
```

Fig. 19.38 **UsingArrayTest.cpp** demonstrates class Array.

Lines 26 and 33 invoke **static Array** method *BinarySearch* to perform binary searches on array **intValues**. Method **BinarySearch** receives the *sorted* array in which to search and the key for which to search. The method returns the index in the array at which it finds the key (or a negative number if the key was not found).

Other **static Array** methods include *Clear* (to set a range of elements to **0** or **NULL**), *CreateInstance* (to create a new array of a specified data type), *IndexOf* (to locate the first occurrence of an object in an array or portion of an array) and *LastIndexOf* (to locate the last occurrence of an object in an array or portion of an array).

19.7.2 Class **ArrayList**

In most programming languages, conventional arrays have a fixed size—they cannot be changed dynamically to conform to an application's execution-time memory requirements. In some applications, this fixed-size feature presents a problem for programmers. They must choose between using fixed-size arrays that are large enough to store the maximum number of elements the program could require and using dynamic data structures that can grow and shrink the amount of memory required to store data in response to the changing requirements of a program at execution time.

The .NET Framework's *ArrayList* collection mimics the functionality of conventional arrays, yet provides dynamic resizing of the collection through the class's methods. At any time an **ArrayList** contains a certain number of elements less than or equal to its *capacity*—the number of elements currently reserved for an **ArrayList**. A program can manipulate the capacity with **ArrayList** property *Capacity*. If an **ArrayList** needs to grow, it by default doubles its current **Capacity**.

Performance Tip 19.6

*As with linked lists, inserting additional elements into an **ArrayList** whose current size is less than its capacity is a fast operation.*

Performance Tip 19.7

*It is a slow operation to insert an element into an **ArrayList** that needs to grow larger to accommodate a new element.*

Performance Tip 19.8

*If storage is at a premium, use method **TrimToSize** of class **ArrayList** to trim an Ar-rayList to its exact size. This will optimize an **ArrayList**'s memory use. Be careful—if the program needs to insert additional elements, the process will be slower because the Ar-rayList must grow dynamically (trimming leaves no room for growth).*

Performance Tip 19.9

*The default capacity increment, doubling the size of the **ArrayList**, might seem to waste storage, but doubling is an efficient way for an **ArrayList** to grow quickly to "about the right size." This is a much more efficient use of time than growing the **ArrayList** by one element at a time in response to insert operations.*

ArrayLists store pointers to **Object**s. All classes derive from class **Object**, so an **ArrayList** can contain objects of any type. Figure 19.39 lists some useful methods of class **ArrayList**.

Method	Description
Add	Adds an **Object** to the **ArrayList**. Returns an **int** specifying the index at which the **Object** was added.
Clear	Removes all the elements from the **ArrayList**.
Contains	Returns **true** if the specified **Object** is in the **ArrayList**; otherwise, returns **false**.
IndexOf	Returns the index of the first occurrence of the specified **Object** in the **ArrayList**.
Insert	Inserts an **Object** at the specified index.
Remove	Removes the first occurrence of the specified **Object**.
RemoveAt	Removes an object at the specified index.
RemoveRange	Removes a specified number of elements starting at a specified index in the **ArrayList**.
Sort	Sorts the **ArrayList**.
TrimToSize	Sets the **Capacity** of the **ArrayList** to be the number of elements the **ArrayList** currently contains.

Fig. 19.39 Some methods of class **ArrayList**.

Figure 19.40–Fig. 19.42 demonstrates class **ArrayList** and several of its methods. Users can type a string into the user interface's **TextBox**, then press a button representing an **ArrayList** method to see that method's functionality. A **TextBox** displays messages indicating each operation's results.

```
1   // Fig. 19.40: ArrayListTest.h
2   // Demonstrating ArrayList functionality.
3
4   #pragma once
5
6   #using <mscorlib.dll>
7   #using <system.dll>
8   #using <system.data.dll>
9   #using <system.drawing.dll>
10  #using <system.windows.forms.dll>
11
12  using namespace System;
13  using namespace System::Drawing;
14  using namespace System::Collections;
15  using namespace System::Windows::Forms;
16  using namespace System::Text;
17
18  public __gc class ArrayListTest : public Form
19  {
20  public:
21     ArrayListTest();
22
23  private:
24     Button *addButton;
25     TextBox *inputTextBox;
26     Label *inputLabel;
27     Button *removeButton;
28     Button *firstButton;
29     Button *lastButton;
30     Button *isEmptyButton;
31     Button *containsButton;
32     Button *locationButton;
33     Button *trimButton;
34     Button *statisticsButton;
35     Button *displayButton;
36     TextBox *consoleTextBox;
37
38     // ArrayList for manipulating strings
39     static ArrayList *arrayList = new ArrayList( 1 );
40
41     void InitializeComponent();
42     void addButton_Click( Object *, EventArgs * );
43     void removeButton_Click( Object *, EventArgs * );
44     void firstButton_Click( Object *, EventArgs * );
45     void lastButton_Click( Object *, EventArgs * );
46     void isEmptyButton_Click( Object *, EventArgs * );
```

Fig. 19.40 ArrayListTest class demonstrates class **ArrayList**. (Part 1 of 2.)

```
47        void containsButton_Click( Object *, EventArgs * );
48        void locationButton_Click( Object *, EventArgs * );
49        void trimButton_Click( Object *, EventArgs * );
50        void statisticsButton_Click( Object *, EventArgs * );
51        void displayButton_Click( Object *, EventArgs * );
52    }; // end class ArrayListTest
```

Fig. 19.40 `ArrayListTest` class demonstrates class `ArrayList`. (Part 2 of 2.)

```
1    // Fig. 19.41: ArrayListTest.cpp
2    // Method definitions for class ArrayListTest.
3
4    #include "ArrayListTest.h"
5
6    ArrayListTest::ArrayListTest()
7    {
8        InitializeComponent();
9    }
10
11   void ArrayListTest::InitializeComponent()
12   {
13       this->addButton = new Button();
14       this->removeButton = new Button();
15       this->firstButton = new Button();
16       this->lastButton = new Button();
17       this->isEmptyButton = new Button();
18       this->containsButton = new Button();
19       this->locationButton = new Button();
20       this->trimButton = new Button();
21       this->statisticsButton = new Button();
22       this->displayButton = new Button();
23       this->inputTextBox = new TextBox();
24       this->consoleTextBox = new TextBox();
25       this->inputLabel = new Label();
26
27       this->SuspendLayout();
28
29       // addButton
30       this->addButton->Location = Point( 200, 8 );
31       this->addButton->Name = S"addButton";
32       this->addButton->Size = Drawing::Size( 80, 23 );
33       this->addButton->TabIndex = 0;
34       this->addButton->Text = S"Add";
35       this->addButton->Click += new EventHandler( this,
36          addButton_Click );
37
38       // removeButton
39       this->removeButton->Location = Point( 8, 56 );
40       this->removeButton->Name = S"removeButton";
41       this->removeButton->Size = Drawing::Size( 80, 23 );
42       this->removeButton->TabIndex = 1;
```

Fig. 19.41 `ArrayListTest` class method definitions. (Part 1 of 6.)

```
43      this->removeButton->Text = S"Remove";
44      this->removeBut;ton->Click += new EventHandler( this,
45          removeButton_Click );
46
47      // firstButton
48      this->firstButton->Location = Point( 104, 56 );
49      this->firstButton->Name = S"firstButton";
50      this->firstButton->Size = Drawing::Size( 80, 23 );
51      this->firstButton->TabIndex = 2;
52      this->firstButton->Text = S"First";
53      this->firstButton->Click += new EventHandler( this,
54          firstButton_Click );
55
56      // lastButton
57      this->lastButton->Location = Point( 200, 56 );
58      this->lastButton->Name = S"lastButton";
59      this->lastButton->Size = Drawing::Size( 80, 23 );
60      this->lastButton->TabIndex = 3;
61      this->lastButton->Text = S"Last";
62      this->lastButton->Click += new EventHandler( this,
63          lastButton_Click );
64
65      // isEmptyButton
66      this->isEmptyButton->Location = Point( 8, 104 );
67      this->isEmptyButton->Name = S"isEmptyButton";
68      this->isEmptyButton->Size = Drawing::Size( 80, 23 );
69      this->isEmptyButton->TabIndex = 4;
70      this->isEmptyButton->Text = S"Is Empty?";
71      this->isEmptyButton->Click += new EventHandler( this,
72          isEmptyButton_Click );
73
74      // containsButton
75      this->containsButton->Location = Point( 104, 104 );
76      this->containsButton->Name = S"containsButton";
77      this->containsButton->Size = Drawing::Size( 80, 23 );
78      this->containsButton->TabIndex = 5;
79      this->containsButton->Text = S"Contains";
80      this->containsButton->Click += new EventHandler( this,
81          containsButton_Click );
82
83      // locationButton
84      this->locationButton->Location = Point( 200, 104 );
85      this->locationButton->Name = S"locationButton";
86      this->locationButton->Size = Drawing::Size( 80, 24 );
87      this->locationButton->TabIndex = 6;
88      this->locationButton->Text = S"Location";
89      this->locationButton->Click += new EventHandler( this,
90          locationButton_Click );
91
92      // trimButton
93      this->trimButton->Location = Point( 8, 152 );
94      this->trimButton->Name = S"trimButton";
95      this->trimButton->Size = Drawing::Size( 80, 24 );
```

Fig. 19.41 **ArrayListTest** class method definitions. (Part 2 of 6.)

```
96      this->trimButton->TabIndex = 7;
97      this->trimButton->Text = S"Trim";
98      this->trimButton->Click += new EventHandler( this,
99         trimButton_Click );
100
101     // statisticsButton
102     this->statisticsButton->Location = Point( 104, 152 );
103     this->statisticsButton->Name = S"statisticsButton";
104     this->statisticsButton->Size = Drawing::Size( 80, 23 );
105     this->statisticsButton->TabIndex = 8;
106     this->statisticsButton->Text = S"Statistics";
107     this->statisticsButton->Click += new EventHandler( this,
108        statisticsButton_Click );
109
110     // displayButton
111     this->displayButton->Location = Point( 200, 152 );
112     this->displayButton->Name = S"displayButton";
113     this->displayButton->Size = Drawing::Size( 80, 23 );
114     this->displayButton->TabIndex = 9;
115     this->displayButton->Text = S"Display";
116     this->displayButton->Click += new EventHandler( this,
117        displayButton_Click );
118
119     // inputTextBox
120     this->inputTextBox->Location = Point( 88, 8 );
121     this->inputTextBox->Name = S"inputTextBox";
122     this->inputTextBox->TabIndex = 10;
123     this->inputTextBox->Text = S"";
124
125     // consoleTextBox
126     this->consoleTextBox->Location = Point( 8, 200 );
127     this->consoleTextBox->Multiline = true;
128     this->consoleTextBox->Name = S"consoleTextBox";
129     this->consoleTextBox->ReadOnly = true;
130     this->consoleTextBox->Size = Drawing::Size( 272, 64 );
131     this->consoleTextBox->TabIndex = 11;
132     this->consoleTextBox->Text = S"";
133
134     // inputLabel
135     this->inputLabel->Location = Point( 8, 16 );
136     this->inputLabel->Name = S"inputLabel";
137     this->inputLabel->Size = Drawing::Size( 72, 24 );
138     this->inputLabel->TabIndex = 12;
139     this->inputLabel->Text = S"Enter a string";
140
141     // ArrayListTest
142     this->AutoScaleBaseSize = Drawing::Size( 5, 13 );
143     this->ClientSize = Drawing::Size( 292, 273 );
144
145     Control *control[] = { this->inputLabel,
146        this->consoleTextBox, this->inputTextBox,
147        this->displayButton, this->statisticsButton,
148        this->trimButton, this->locationButton,
```

Fig. 19.41 ArrayListTest class method definitions. (Part 3 of 6.)

```
149            this->containsButton, this->isEmptyButton,
150            this->lastButton, this->firstButton,
151            this->removeButton, this->addButton };
152      this->Controls->AddRange( control );
153
154      this->Name = S"ArrayListTest";
155      this->Text = S"ArrayListTest";
156
157      this->ResumeLayout();
158 } // end method InitializeComponent
159
160 // add item to end of arrayList
161 void ArrayListTest::addButton_Click(
162      Object *sender, EventArgs *e )
163 {
164      arrayList->Add( inputTextBox->Text );
165      consoleTextBox->Text = String::Concat(
166         S"Added to end: ", inputTextBox->Text );
167      inputTextBox->Clear();
168 } // end method addButton_Click
169
170 // remove specified item from arrayList
171 void ArrayListTest::removeButton_Click(
172      Object *sender, EventArgs *e )
173 {
174      arrayList->Remove( inputTextBox->Text );
175      consoleTextBox->Text = String::Concat( S"Removed: ",
176         inputTextBox->Text );
177      inputTextBox->Clear();
178 } // end method removeButton_Click
179
180 // display first element
181 void ArrayListTest::firstButton_Click(
182      Object *sender, EventArgs *e )
183 {
184      // get first element
185      try {
186         consoleTextBox->Text = String::Concat(
187            S"First element: ", arrayList->Item[ 0 ] );
188      }
189
190      // show exception if no elements in arrayList
191      catch ( ArgumentOutOfRangeException *outOfRange ) {
192         consoleTextBox->Text = outOfRange->ToString();
193      }
194 } // end method firstButton_Click
195
196 // display last element
197 void ArrayListTest::lastButton_Click(
198      Object *sender, EventArgs *e )
199 {
200      // get last element
```

Fig. 19.41 ArrayListTest class method definitions. (Part 4 of 6.)

```
201     try {
202        consoleTextBox->Text = String::Concat( S"Last element: ",
203           arrayList->Item[ arrayList->Count - 1 ] );
204     }
205
206     // show exception if no elements in arrayList
207     catch ( ArgumentOutOfRangeException *outOfRange ) {
208        consoleTextBox->Text = outOfRange->ToString();
209     }
210  } // end method lastButton_Click
211
212  // determine whether arrayList is empty
213  void ArrayListTest::isEmptyButton_Click(
214     Object *sender, EventArgs *e )
215  {
216     consoleTextBox->Text = ( arrayList->Count == 0 ?
217        S"arrayList is empty" : S"arrayList is not empty" );
218  } // end method isEmptyButton_Click
219
220  // determine whether arrayList contains specified object
221  void ArrayListTest::containsButton_Click(
222     Object *sender, EventArgs *e )
223  {
224     if ( arrayList->Contains( inputTextBox->Text ) )
225        consoleTextBox->Text = String::Concat( S"arrayList contains ",
226        inputTextBox->Text );
227     else
228        consoleTextBox->Text = String::Concat( inputTextBox->Text,
229        S" not found" );
230  } // end method containsButton_Click
231
232  // determine location of specified object
233  void ArrayListTest::locationButton_Click(
234     Object *sender, EventArgs *e )
235  {
236     consoleTextBox->Text = String::Concat(
237        S"Element is at location ",
238        arrayList->IndexOf( inputTextBox->Text ).ToString() );
239  } // end method locationButton_Click
240
241  // trim arrayList to current size
242  void ArrayListTest::trimButton_Click(
243     Object *sender, EventArgs *e )
244  {
245     arrayList->TrimToSize();
246     consoleTextBox->Text = S"Vector trimmed to size";
247  } // end method trimButton_Click
248
249  // show arrayList current size and capacity
250  void ArrayListTest::statisticsButton_Click(
251     Object *sender, EventArgs *e )
252  {
```

Fig. 19.41 ArrayListTest class method definitions. (Part 5 of 6.)

```
253        consoleTextBox->Text = String::Concat( S"Size = ",
254           arrayList->Count.ToString(),
255           S"; capacity = ", arrayList->Capacity.ToString() );
256    } // end method statisticsButton_Click
257
258    // display contents of arrayList
259    void ArrayListTest::displayButton_Click(
260       Object *sender, EventArgs *e )
261    {
262       IEnumerator *enumerator = arrayList->GetEnumerator();
263       StringBuilder *buffer = new StringBuilder();
264
265       while ( enumerator->MoveNext() )
266          buffer->Append( String::Concat(
267          enumerator->Current, S"   " ) );
268
269       consoleTextBox->Text = buffer->ToString();
270    } // end method displayButton_Click
```

Fig. 19.41 ArrayListTest class method definitions. (Part 6 of 6.)

```
1    // Fig. 19.42: ArrayListTestMain.cpp
2    // Entry point for application.
3
4    #include "ArrayListTest.h"
5
6    int __stdcall WinMain()
7    {
8       Application::Run( new ArrayListTest() );
9
10      return 0;
11   } // end function WinMain
```

Fig. 19.42 ArrayListTestMain.cpp demonstrates the **ArrayList** class.
(Part 1 of 2.)

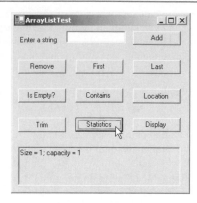

Fig. 19.42 `ArrayListTestMain.cpp` demonstrates the `ArrayList` class.
(Part 2 of 2.)

The **ArrayList** in this example stores **String** pointers that users input in the **TextBox**. Line 39 (of Fig. 19.40) creates an **ArrayList** with an initial capacity of one element. This **ArrayList** will double in size each time the user fills the array and attempts to add another element.

ArrayList method *Add* appends a new element at the end of an **ArrayList**. When the user clicks **Add**, event handler **addButton_Click** (lines 161–168 of Fig. 19.41) invokes method **Add** (line 164) to append the **String *** in the **input-TextBox** to the **ArrayList**.

ArrayList method *Remove* deletes a specified item from an **ArrayList**. When the user clicks **Remove**, event handler **removeButton_Click** (line 171–178) invokes **Remove** (line 174) to remove the **String *** specified in the **inputTextBox** from the **ArrayList**. If the object passed to **Remove** is in the **ArrayList**, the first occurrence of that object is removed, and all subsequent elements shift toward the beginning of the **ArrayList** to fill the empty position.

Note that MC++ programmers cannot access **ArrayList** elements as they do conventional array elements, by following the **ArrayList** pointer name with the array subscript operator (**[]**) and the desired index of the element (e.g., **arrayList[0]**). Rather, programmers can access **ArrayList** elements by following the **ArrayList** indexed property **Item** with the array subscript operator (**[]**) and the desired index of the element (e.g., **arrayList->Item[0]**).

Event handlers **firstButton_Click** (lines 181–194) and **lastButton_Click** (lines 197–210) use **ArrayList** property **Item** to retrieve the first element (line 187) and last element (line 203), respectively. An **ArgumentOutOfRangeException** occurs if the specified index is not both greater than **0** and less than the number of elements currently stored in the **ArrayList**.

Event handler **isEmptyButton_Click** (lines 213–218) uses **ArrayList** property *Count* (line 216) to determine whether the **ArrayList** is empty. Event handler **containsButton_Click** (lines 221–230) uses **ArrayList** method *Contains* (line 224) to determine whether the given object is currently in the **ArrayList**. If so, the method returns **true**; otherwise, it returns **false**.

Performance Tip 19.10

*ArrayList method **Contains** performs a linear search, which is a costly operation for large **ArrayLists**. If the **ArrayList** is sorted, use **ArrayList** method **Binary-Search** to perform a more efficient search.*

When the user clicks **Location**, event handler **locationButton_Click** (lines 233–239) invokes **ArrayList** method *IndexOf* (line 238) to determine the index of a particular object in the **ArrayList**. **IndexOf** returns **-1** if the element is not found.

When the user clicks **Trim**, event handler **trimButton_Click** (lines 242–247) invokes method *TrimToSize* (line 245) to set the **Capacity** property to equal the **Count** property. This reduces the storage capacity of the **ArrayList** to the exact number of elements currently in the **ArrayList**.

When the user clicks **Statistics**, **statisticsButton_Click** (lines 250–256) uses the **Count** and **Capacity** properties to display the current number of elements in the **ArrayList** and the maximum number of elements that can be stored without allocating more memory to the **ArrayList**.

When users click **Display**, **displayButton_Click** (lines 259–270) outputs the contents of the **ArrayList**. This event handler uses an *IEnumerator* (sometimes called an *enumerator* or an *iterator*) to traverse the elements of an **ArrayList** one element at a time. Interface **IEnumerator** defines methods *MoveNext* and *Reset* and property *Current*. **MoveNext** moves the enumerator to the next element in the **Array-List**. The first call to **MoveNext** positions the enumerator at the first element of the **ArrayList**. **MoveNext** returns **true** if there is at least one more element in the **ArrayList**; otherwise, the method returns **false**. Method **Reset** positions the enumerator before the first element of the **ArrayList**. Methods **MoveNext** and **Reset** throw an **InvalidOperationException** if the contents of the collection are modified in any way after the enumerator's creation. Property **Current** returns the object at the current location in the **ArrayList**.

Line 262 creates an **IEnumerator** called **enumerator** and assigns it the result of calling **ArrayList** method *GetEnumerator*. Lines 265–267 iterate while **MoveNext** returns **true**, retrieve the current item via property **Current** and append it to **buffer**. When the loop terminates, line 269 displays the contents of **buffer**.

19.7.3 Class Stack

The **Stack** class, as its name implies, implements a stack data structure. This class provides much of the functionality that we defined in our implementation in Section 19.4. Refer back to that section for a discussion of stack-data structure concepts. The application in Fig. 19.43–Fig. 19.45 provides a GUI that enables the user to test many **Stack** methods. Line 12 of the **StackTest** constructor (Fig. 19.44) creates a **Stack** with the default initial capacity (10 elements).

```
1   // Fig. 19.43: StackTest.h
2   // Demonstrates class Stack of namespace System::Collections.
3
4   #pragma once
5
6   #using <mscorlib.dll>
7   #using <system.dll>
8   #using <system.data.dll>
9   #using <system.drawing.dll>
10  #using <system.windows.forms.dll>
11
12  using namespace System;
13  using namespace System::Drawing;
14  using namespace System::Collections;
15  using namespace System::Windows::Forms;
16  using namespace System::Text;
17
18  #include <tchar.h>
19
20  public __gc class StackTest : public Form
21  {
22  public:
23     StackTest();
24
25  private:
26     Label *inputLabel;
27     TextBox *inputTextBox;
28     Button *pushButton;
29     Button *popButton;
30     Button *peekButton;
31     Button *isEmptyButton;
32     Button *searchButton;
33     Button *displayButton;
34     Label *statusLabel;
35
36     Stack *stack;
37
38     void InitializeComponent();
39     void pushButton_Click( Object *, EventArgs * );
40     void popButton_Click( Object *, EventArgs * );
41     void peekButton_Click( Object *, EventArgs * );
42     void isEmptyButton_Click( Object *, EventArgs * );
43
44     // determine whether specified element is on stack
45     void searchButton_Click( Object *, EventArgs * );
46
47     // display stack contents
48     void displayButton_Click( Object *, EventArgs * );
49  }; // end class StackTest
```

Fig. 19.43 StackTest class demonstrates class Stack.

```cpp
1   // Fig. 19.44: StackTest.cpp
2   // Method definitions for class StackTest.
3
4   #include "StackTest.h"
5
6   StackTest::StackTest()
7   {
8      // Required for Windows Form Designer support
9      InitializeComponent();
10
11     // create Stack
12     stack = new Stack();
13  }
14
15  void StackTest::InitializeComponent()
16  {
17     this->inputLabel = new Label();
18     this->inputTextBox = new TextBox();
19     this->pushButton = new Button();
20     this->popButton = new Button();
21     this->peekButton = new Button();
22     this->isEmptyButton = new Button();
23     this->searchButton = new Button();
24     this->displayButton = new Button();
25     this->statusLabel = new Label();
26
27     this->SuspendLayout();
28
29     // inputLabel
30     this->inputLabel->Location = Point( 8, 8 );
31     this->inputLabel->Name = S"inputLabel";
32     this->inputLabel->Size = Drawing::Size( 80, 23 );
33     this->inputLabel->TabIndex = 0;
34     this->inputLabel->Text = S"Enter a string:";
35     this->inputLabel->TextAlign = ContentAlignment::MiddleCenter;
36
37     // inputTextBox
38     this->inputTextBox->Location = Point( 88, 8 );
39     this->inputTextBox->Name = S"inputTextBox";
40     this->inputTextBox->Size = Drawing::Size( 112, 20 );
41     this->inputTextBox->TabIndex = 1;
42     this->inputTextBox->Text = S"";
43
44     // pushButton
45     this->pushButton->Location = Point( 208, 8 );
46     this->pushButton->Name = S"pushButton";
47     this->pushButton->TabIndex = 2;
48     this->pushButton->Text = S"Push";
49     this->pushButton->Click += new EventHandler( this,
50        pushButton_Click );
51
52     // popButton
53     this->popButton->Location = Point( 288, 8 );
```

Fig. 19.44 StackTest class method definitions. (Part 1 of 4.)

```
54     this->popButton->Name = S"popButton";
55     this->popButton->TabIndex = 3;
56     this->popButton->Text = S"Pop";
57     this->popButton->Click += new EventHandler( this,
58        popButton_Click );
59
60     // peekButton
61     this->peekButton->Location = Point( 368, 8 );
62     this->peekButton->Name = S"peekButton";
63     this->peekButton->TabIndex = 4;
64     this->peekButton->Text = S"Peek";
65     this->peekButton->Click += new EventHandler( this,
66        peekButton_Click );
67
68     // isEmptyButton
69     this->isEmptyButton->Location = Point( 448, 8 );
70     this->isEmptyButton->Name = S"isEmptyButton";
71     this->isEmptyButton->TabIndex = 5;
72     this->isEmptyButton->Text = S"Is Empty?";
73     this->isEmptyButton->Click += new EventHandler( this,
74        isEmptyButton_Click );
75
76     // searchButton
77     this->searchButton->Location = Point( 528, 8 );
78     this->searchButton->Name = S"searchButton";
79     this->searchButton->TabIndex = 6;
80     this->searchButton->Text = S"Search";
81     this->searchButton->Click += new EventHandler( this,
82        searchButton_Click );
83
84     // displayButton
85     this->displayButton->Location = Point( 608, 8 );
86     this->displayButton->Name = S"displayButton";
87     this->displayButton->TabIndex = 7;
88     this->displayButton->Text = S"Display";
89     this->displayButton->Click += new EventHandler( this,
90        displayButton_Click );
91
92     // statusLabel
93     this->statusLabel->Location = Point( 16, 48 );
94     this->statusLabel->Name = S"statusLabel";
95     this->statusLabel->Size = Drawing::Size( 664, 23 );
96     this->statusLabel->TabIndex = 8;
97
98     // StackTest
99     this->AutoScaleBaseSize = Drawing::Size( 5, 13 );
100    this->ClientSize = Drawing::Size( 688, 77 );
101
102    Control *control[] = { this->statusLabel,
103       this->displayButton, this->searchButton,
104       this->isEmptyButton, this->peekButton,
105       this->popButton, this->pushButton,
106       this->inputTextBox, this->inputLabel };
```

Fig. 19.44 StackTest class method definitions. (Part 2 of 4.)

```
107        this->Controls->AddRange( control );
108
109        this->Name = S"StackTest";
110        this->Text = S"StackTest";
111
112        this->ResumeLayout();
113    } // end method InitializeComponent
114
115    // push element onto stack
116    void StackTest::pushButton_Click( Object *sender, EventArgs *e )
117    {
118        stack->Push( inputTextBox->Text );
119        statusLabel->Text = String::Concat( S"Pushed: ",
120           inputTextBox->Text );
121    } // end method pushButton_Click
122
123    // pop element from stack
124    void StackTest::popButton_Click( Object *sender, EventArgs *e )
125    {
126        // pop element
127        try {
128           statusLabel->Text = String::Concat( S"Popped: ",
129              stack->Pop() );
130        }
131
132        // print message if stack is empty
133        catch ( InvalidOperationException *invalidOperation ) {
134           statusLabel->Text = invalidOperation->ToString();
135        }
136    } // end method popButton_Click
137
138    // peek at top element of stack
139    void StackTest::peekButton_Click( Object *sender, EventArgs *e )
140    {
141        // view top element
142        try {
143           statusLabel->Text = String::Concat( S"Top: ", stack->Peek() );
144        }
145
146        // print message if stack is empty
147        catch ( InvalidOperationException *invalidOperation ) {
148           statusLabel->Text = invalidOperation->ToString();
149        }
150    } // end method peekButton_Click
151
152    // determine whether stack is empty
153    void StackTest::isEmptyButton_Click( Object *sender, EventArgs *e )
154    {
155        statusLabel->Text = ( stack->Count == 0 ?
156           S"Stack is empty" : S"Stack is not empty" );
157    } // end method isEmptyButton_Click
158
```

Fig. 19.44 StackTest class method definitions. (Part 3 of 4.)

```
159   // determine whether specified element is on stack
160   void StackTest::searchButton_Click( Object *sender, EventArgs *e )
161   {
162      String *result = stack->Contains( inputTextBox->Text ) ?
163         S" found" : S" not found";
164
165      statusLabel->Text = String::Concat( inputTextBox->Text, result );
166   } // end method searchButton_Click
167
168   // display stack contents
169   void StackTest::displayButton_Click( Object *sender, EventArgs *e )
170   {
171      IEnumerator *enumerator = stack->GetEnumerator();
172      StringBuilder *buffer = new StringBuilder();
173
174      // while the enumerator can move on to the next element
175      // print that element out
176      while ( enumerator->MoveNext() )
177         buffer->Append( String::Concat( enumerator->Current, S" " ) );
178
179      statusLabel->Text = buffer->ToString();
180   } // end method displayButton_Click
```

Fig. 19.44 StackTest class method definitions. (Part 4 of 4.)

```
1    // Fig. 19.45: StackTestMain.cpp
2    // Entry point for application.
3
4    #include "StackTest.h"
5
6    int __stdcall WinMain()
7    {
8       Application::Run( new StackTest() );
9
10      return 0;
11   } // end function WinMain
```

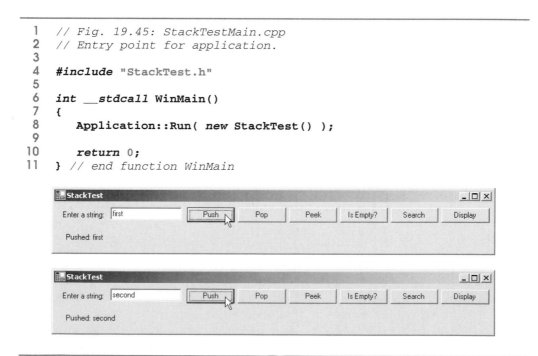

Fig. 19.45 StackTestMain.cpp demonstrates class **Stack**. (Part 1 of 2.)

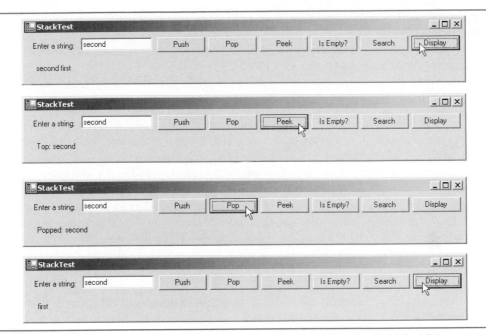

Fig. 19.45 `StackTestMain.cpp` demonstrates class `Stack`. (Part 2 of 2.)

As one might expect, class **Stack** has methods **Push** and **Pop** to perform the basic stack operations. Method ***Push*** takes an **Object** as an argument and adds it to the top of the **Stack**. If the number of items on the **Stack** (the **Count** property) is equal to the capacity at the time of the **Push** operation, the **Stack** grows to accommodate more **Object**s. Event handler **pushButton_Click** (lines 116–121 of Fig. 19.44) uses method **Push** to add a user-specified string to the stack (line 118).

Method ***Pop*** takes no arguments. This method removes and returns the object currently on top of the **Stack**. Event handler **popButton_Click** (lines 124–136) calls method **Pop** (line 129) to remove an object from the **Stack**. An **InvalidOperation-Exception** occurs if the **Stack** is empty when the program calls **Pop**.

Method ***Peek*** returns the value of the top stack element, but does not remove the element from the **Stack**. We use **Peek** at line 143 in event handler **peekButton_Click** (lines 139–150) to view the object on top of the **Stack**. As with **Pop**, an **InvalidOperationException** occurs if the **Stack** is empty when the program calls **Peek**.

> **Common Programming Error 19.5**
>
> *Attempting to* ***Peek*** *or* ***Pop*** *an empty* ***Stack*** *(a* ***Stack*** *whose* ***Count*** *property equals 0) causes an* ***InvalidOperationException***.

Event handler **isEmptyButton_Click** (lines 153–157) determines whether the **Stack** is empty by comparing the **Stack**'s **Count** property to 0. If it is 0, the **Stack** is empty; otherwise, it is not. Event handler **searchButton_Click** (lines 160–166) uses **Stack** method **Contains** (lines 162–163) to determine whether the **Stack** contains the object specified as its argument. **Contains** returns **true** if the **Stack** contains the specified object, **false** otherwise.

Event handler **displayButton_Click** (lines 169–180) uses an **IEnumerator** to traverse the **Stack** and display its contents.

19.7.4 Class **Hashtable**

Object-oriented programming languages facilitate the creating of new types. When a program creates objects of new or existing types, it then needs to manage those objects efficiently. This includes sorting and retrieving objects. Sorting and retrieving information with arrays is efficient if some aspect of your data directly matches the key value and if those keys are unique and tightly packed. If you have 100 employees with nine-digit Social Security numbers and you want to store and retrieve employee data by using the Social Security number as a key, it would nominally require an array with 999,999,999 elements, because there are 999,999,999 unique nine-digit numbers. This is impractical for virtually all applications that key on Social Security numbers. If you could have an array that large, you could get very high performance storing and retrieving employee records by simply using the Social Security number as the array index.

A large variety of applications have this problem—namely, that either the keys are of the wrong type (i.e., not nonnegative integers), or they are of the right type, but they are sparsely spread over a large range.

What is needed is a high-speed scheme for converting keys such as Social Security numbers and inventory part numbers into unique array subscripts. Then, when an application needs to store something, the scheme could convert the application key rapidly into a subscript and the record of information could be stored at that location in the array. Retrieval occurs the same way—once the application has a key for which it wants to retrieve the data record, the application simply applies the conversion to the key, which produces the array subscript where the data resides in the array and retrieves the data.

The scheme we describe here is the basis of a technique called *hashing*. Why the name? Because, when we convert a key into an array subscript, we literally scramble the bits, forming a kind of "mishmash" number. The number actually has no real significance beyond its usefulness in storing and retrieving this particular data record.

A glitch in the scheme occurs when *collisions* occur [i.e., two different keys "hash into" the same cell (or element) in the array]. We cannot sort two different data records into the same space, so we need to find an alternative home for all records beyond the first that hash to a particular array subscript. Many schemes exist for doing this. One is to "hash again" (i.e., to reapply the hashing transformation to the key to provide a next candidate cell in the array). The hashing process is designed to be quite random, so the assumption is that, with just a few hashes, an available cell will be found.

Another scheme uses one hash to locate the first candidate cell. If the cell is occupied, successive cells are searched linearly until an available cell is found. Retrieval works the same way—the key is hashed once, the resulting cell is checked for whether it contains the desired data. If it does, the search is complete. If it does not, successive cells are searched linearly until the desired item(s) are found.

The most popular solution to hash-table collisions is to have each cell of the table be a hash "bucket," typically a linked list of all the key/value pairs that hash to that cell. This is the solution that the .NET Framework's *Hashtable* class implements.

The *load factor* is one factor that affects the performance of hashing schemes. The load factor is the ratio of the number of occupied cells in the hash table to the size of the hash table. The closer the ratio gets to 1.0, the greater the chance of collisions.

Performance Tip 19.11

The load factor in a hash table is a classic example of a space/time trade-off: By increasing the load factor, we get better memory utilization, but the program runs slower due to increased hashing collisions. By decreasing the load factor, we get better program speed because of reduced hashing collisions, but we get poorer memory utilization because a larger portion of the hash table remains empty.

Programming hash tables properly is too complex for most casual programmers. Computer science students study hashing schemes thoroughly in courses called "Data Structures" and "Algorithms." Recognizing the value of hashing, .NET provides class **Hashtable** and some related features to enable programmers to take advantage of hashing without the complex details.

The preceding sentence is profoundly important in our study of object-oriented programming. Classes encapsulate and hide complexity (i.e., implementation details) and offer user-friendly interfaces. Crafting classes to do this properly is one of the most valued skills in the field of object-oriented programming.

A *hash function* performs a calculation that determines where to place data in the hashtable. The hash function is applied to the key in a key/value pair of objects. Class **Hashtable** can accept any object as a key. For this reason, class **Object** defines method **GetHashCode**, which all objects in MC++ inherit. Most classes that are candidates to be used as keys in a hash table override this method to provide one that performs efficient hashcode calculations for a specific data type. For example, a **String** has a hashcode calculation that is based on the contents of the **String**. Figure 19.46–Fig. 19.50 demonstrates several methods of class **Hashtable**.

```
1   // Fig. 19.46: Employee.h
2   // Employee class for hashtable demonstration.
3
4   #pragma once
5
6   #using <mscorlib.dll>
7   #using <System.dll>
8   #using <System.data.dll>
9   #using <System.drawing.dll>
10  #using <System.windows.forms.dll>
11
12  using namespace System;
13  using namespace System::Drawing;
14  using namespace System::Collections;
15  using namespace System::Windows::Forms;
16  using namespace System::Text;
17
18  #include <tchar.h>
19
20  public __gc class Employee
21  {
```

Fig. 19.46 Employee class represents a single employee. (Part 1 of 2.)

```
22   public:
23      Employee( String *, String * );
24      String *ToString();
25
26   private:
27      String *first, *last;
28   }; // end class Employee
```

Fig. 19.46 Employee class represents a single employee. (Part 2 of 2.)

```
1    // Fig. 19.47: Employee.cpp
2    // Method definitions for class Employee.
3
4    #include "Employee.h"
5
6    // constructor
7    Employee::Employee( String *fName, String *lName )
8    {
9       first = fName;
10      last = lName;
11   }
12
13   // return Employee first and last names as string
14   String *Employee::ToString()
15   {
16      return String::Concat( first, S" ", last );
17   }
```

Fig. 19.47 Employee class method definitions.

```
1    // Fig. 19.48: HashTableTest.h
2    // Demonstrate class Hashtable of namespace System::Collections.
3
4    #pragma once
5
6    #include "Employee.h"
7
8    public __gc class HashTableTest : public Form
9    {
10   public:
11      HashTableTest();
12
13   private:
14      Label *firstNameLabel;
15      Label *lastNameLabel;
16      Button *addButton;
17      TextBox *lastNameTextBox;
18      TextBox *consoleTextBox;
19      TextBox *firstNameTextBox;
```

Fig. 19.48 HashTableTest class demonstrates class **Hashtable**. (Part 1 of 2.)

```
20      Button *getButton;
21      Button *removeButton;
22      Button *emptyButton;
23      Button *containsKeyButton;
24      Button *clearTableButton;
25      Button *listObjectsButton;
26      Button *listKeysButton;
27      Label *statusLabel;
28
29      // Hashtable to demonstrate functionality
30      Hashtable *table;
31
32      void InitializeComponent();
33      void addButton_Click( Object *, EventArgs * );
34      void getButton_Click( Object *, EventArgs * );
35      void removeButton_Click( Object *, EventArgs * );
36      void emptyButton_Click( Object *, EventArgs * );
37      void containsKeyButton_Click( Object *, EventArgs * );
38      void clearTableButton_Click( Object *, EventArgs * );
39      void listObjectsButton_Click( Object *, EventArgs * );
40      void listKeysButton_Click( Object *, EventArgs * );
41   }; // end class HashTableTest
```

Fig. 19.48 **HashTableTest** class demonstrates class **Hashtable**. (Part 2 of 2.)

```
1    // Fig. 19.49: HashtableTest.cpp
2    // Method definitions for class HashTableTest.
3
4    #include "HashTableTest.h"
5
6    HashTableTest::HashTableTest()
7    {
8       InitializeComponent();
9
10      // create Hashtable object
11      table = new Hashtable();
12   }
13
14   void HashTableTest::InitializeComponent()
15   {
16      this->lastNameLabel = new Label();
17      this->addButton = new Button();
18      this->lastNameTextBox = new TextBox();
19      this->listKeysButton = new Button();
20      this->removeButton = new Button();
21      this->consoleTextBox = new TextBox();
22      this->containsKeyButton = new Button();
23      this->getButton = new Button();
24      this->firstNameLabel = new Label();
25      this->listObjectsButton = new Button();
26      this->statusLabel = new Label();
27      this->firstNameTextBox = new TextBox();
```

Fig. 19.49 **HashTableTest** class method definitions. (Part 1 of 6.)

```
28        this->clearTableButton = new Button();
29        this->emptyButton = new Button();
30
31        this->SuspendLayout();
32
33        // lastNameLabel
34        this->lastNameLabel->Location = Point( 216, 16 );
35        this->lastNameLabel->Name = S"lastNameLabel";
36        this->lastNameLabel->Size = Drawing::Size( 96, 24 );
37        this->lastNameLabel->TabIndex = 1;
38        this->lastNameLabel->Text = S"Last Name (key):";
39
40        // addButton
41        this->addButton->Location = Point( 448, 16 );
42        this->addButton->Name = S"addButton";
43        this->addButton->Size = Drawing::Size( 88, 23 );
44        this->addButton->TabIndex = 5;
45        this->addButton->Text = S"Add";
46        this->addButton->Click += new EventHandler( this,
47           addButton_Click );
48
49        // lastNameTextBox
50        this->lastNameTextBox->Location = Point( 320, 16 );
51        this->lastNameTextBox->Name = S"lastNameTextBox";
52        this->lastNameTextBox->Size = Drawing::Size( 96, 20 );
53        this->lastNameTextBox->TabIndex = 3;
54        this->lastNameTextBox->Text = S"";
55
56        // listKeysButton
57        this->listKeysButton->Location = Point( 560, 112 );
58        this->listKeysButton->Name = S"listKeysButton";
59        this->listKeysButton->Size = Drawing::Size( 88, 23 );
60        this->listKeysButton->TabIndex = 12;
61        this->listKeysButton->Text = S"List Keys";
62        this->listKeysButton->Click += new EventHandler( this,
63           listKeysButton_Click );
64
65        // removeButton
66        this->removeButton->Location = Point( 448, 48 );
67        this->removeButton->Name = S"removeButton";
68        this->removeButton->Size = Drawing::Size( 88, 23 );
69        this->removeButton->TabIndex = 7;
70        this->removeButton->Text = S"Remove";
71        this->removeButton->Click += new EventHandler( this,
72           removeButton_Click );
73
74        // consoleTextBox
75        this->consoleTextBox->Location = Point( 16, 56 );
76        this->consoleTextBox->Multiline = true;
77        this->consoleTextBox->Name = S"consoleTextBox";
78        this->consoleTextBox->ReadOnly = true;
79        this->consoleTextBox->ScrollBars = ScrollBars::Vertical;
80        this->consoleTextBox->Size = Drawing::Size( 400, 120 );
```

Fig. 19.49 HashTableTest class method definitions. (Part 2 of 6.)

```
81      this->consoleTextBox->TabIndex = 4;
82      this->consoleTextBox->Text = S"";
83
84      // containsKeyButton
85      this->containsKeyButton->Location = Point( 448, 80 );
86      this->containsKeyButton->Name = S"containsKeyButton";
87      this->containsKeyButton->Size = Drawing::Size( 88, 23 );
88      this->containsKeyButton->TabIndex = 9;
89      this->containsKeyButton->Text = S"Contains Key";
90      this->containsKeyButton->Click += new EventHandler( this,
91         containsKeyButton_Click );
92
93      // getButton
94      this->getButton->Location = Point( 560, 16 );
95      this->getButton->Name = S"getButton";
96      this->getButton->Size = Drawing::Size( 88, 23 );
97      this->getButton->TabIndex = 6;
98      this->getButton->Text = S"Get";
99      this->getButton->Click += new EventHandler( this,
100        getButton_Click );
101
102     // firstNameLabel
103     this->firstNameLabel->Location = Point( 16, 16 );
104     this->firstNameLabel->Name = S"firstNameLabel";
105     this->firstNameLabel->Size = Drawing::Size( 80, 24 );
106     this->firstNameLabel->TabIndex = 0;
107     this->firstNameLabel->Text = S"First Name:";
108
109     // listObjectsButton
110     this->listObjectsButton->Location = Point( 448, 112 );
111     this->listObjectsButton->Name = S"listObjectsButton";
112     this->listObjectsButton->Size = Drawing::Size( 88, 23 );
113     this->listObjectsButton->TabIndex = 11;
114     this->listObjectsButton->Text = S"List Objects";
115     this->listObjectsButton->Click += new EventHandler( this,
116        listObjectsButton_Click );
117
118     // statusLabel
119     this->statusLabel->Location = Point( 448, 152 );
120     this->statusLabel->Name = S"statusLabel";
121     this->statusLabel->Size = Drawing::Size( 192, 23 );
122     this->statusLabel->TabIndex = 13;
123
124     // firstNameTextBox
125     this->firstNameTextBox->Location = Point( 96, 16 );
126     this->firstNameTextBox->Name = S"firstNameTextBox";
127     this->firstNameTextBox->Size = Drawing::Size( 96, 20 );
128     this->firstNameTextBox->TabIndex = 2;
129     this->firstNameTextBox->Text = S"";
130
131     // clearTableButton
132     this->clearTableButton->Location = Point( 560, 80 );
133     this->clearTableButton->Name = S"clearTableButton";
```

Fig. 19.49 HashTableTest class method definitions. (Part 3 of 6.)

```
134     this->clearTableButton->Size = Drawing::Size( 88, 23 );
135     this->clearTableButton->TabIndex = 10;
136     this->clearTableButton->Text = S"Clear Table";
137     this->clearTableButton->Click += new EventHandler( this,
138        clearTableButton_Click );
139
140     // emptyButton
141     this->emptyButton->Location = Point( 560, 48 );
142     this->emptyButton->Name = S"emptyButton";
143     this->emptyButton->Size = Drawing::Size( 88, 23 );
144     this->emptyButton->TabIndex = 8;
145     this->emptyButton->Text = S"Empty";
146     this->emptyButton->Click += new EventHandler( this,
147        emptyButton_Click );
148
149     // HashTableTest
150     this->AutoScaleBaseSize = Drawing::Size( 5, 13 );
151     this->ClientSize = Drawing::Size( 656, 189 );
152
153     Control *control[] = { this->statusLabel,
154        this->listKeysButton, this->listObjectsButton,
155        this->clearTableButton, this->containsKeyButton,
156        this->emptyButton, this->removeButton,
157        this->getButton, this->addButton,
158        this->consoleTextBox, this->lastNameTextBox,
159        this->firstNameTextBox, this->lastNameLabel,
160        this->firstNameLabel };
161     this->Controls->AddRange( control );
162
163     this->Name = S"HashTableTest";
164     this->Text = S"HashTableTest";
165
166     this->ResumeLayout();
167  } // end method InitializeComponent
168
169  // add last name and Employee Object *to table
170  void HashTableTest::addButton_Click(
171     Object *sender, EventArgs *e )
172  {
173     Employee *employee = new Employee( firstNameTextBox->Text,
174        lastNameTextBox->Text );
175
176     // add new key/value pair
177     try {
178        table->Add( lastNameTextBox->Text, employee );
179        statusLabel->Text = String::Concat( S"Put: ",
180           employee->ToString() );
181     }
182
183     // if key is NULL or already in table, output message
184     catch ( ArgumentException *argumentException ) {
185        statusLabel->Text = argumentException->ToString();
186     }
```

Fig. 19.49 HashTableTest class method definitions. (Part 4 of 6.)

```
187  } // end method addButton_Click
188
189  // get
190  void HashTableTest::getButton_Click(
191     Object *sender, EventArgs *e )
192  {
193     Object *result = table->Item[ lastNameTextBox->Text ];
194
195     if ( result != NULL )
196        statusLabel->Text = String::Concat( S"Get: ",
197        result->ToString() );
198     else
199        statusLabel->Text = String::Concat( S"Get: ",
200        lastNameTextBox->Text, S" not in table" );
201  } // end method getButton_Click
202
203  // remove key/value pair from table
204  void HashTableTest::removeButton_Click(
205     Object *sender, EventArgs *e )
206  {
207     table->Remove( lastNameTextBox->Text );
208     statusLabel->Text = S"Object *Removed";
209  } // end method removeButton_Click
210
211  // determine whether table is empty
212  void HashTableTest::emptyButton_Click(
213     Object *sender, System::EventArgs *e )
214  {
215     statusLabel->Text = String::Concat( S"Table is ",
216        ( table->Count == 0 ? S"empty" : S"not empty" ) );
217  } // end method emptyButton_Click
218
219  // determine whether table contains specified key
220  void HashTableTest::containsKeyButton_Click(
221     Object *sender, EventArgs *e )
222  {
223     statusLabel->Text = String::Concat( S"Contains key: ",
224        table->ContainsKey( lastNameTextBox->Text ).ToString() );
225  } // end method containsKeyButton_Click
226
227  // discard all table contents
228  void HashTableTest::clearTableButton_Click(
229     Object *sender, EventArgs *e )
230  {
231     table->Clear();
232     statusLabel->Text = S"Clear: Table is now empty";
233  } // end method clearTableButton_Click
234
235  // display list of objects in table
236  void HashTableTest::listObjectsButton_Click(
237     Object *sender, EventArgs *e )
238  {
239     IDictionaryEnumerator *enumerator = table->GetEnumerator();
```

Fig. 19.49 HashTableTest class method definitions. (Part 5 of 6.)

```
240      StringBuilder *buffer = new StringBuilder();
241
242      while ( enumerator->MoveNext() )
243         buffer->Append( String::Concat( enumerator->Value,
244         S"\r\n" ) );
245
246      consoleTextBox->Text = buffer->ToString();
247      statusLabel->Text = S"";
248   } // end method listObjectsButton_Click
249
250   // display list of keys in table
251   void HashTableTest::listKeysButton_Click(
252      Object *sender, EventArgs *e )
253   {
254      IDictionaryEnumerator *enumerator = table->GetEnumerator();
255      StringBuilder *buffer = new StringBuilder();
256
257      while ( enumerator->MoveNext() )
258         buffer->Append( String::Concat( enumerator->Key,
259         S"\r\n" ) );
260
261      consoleTextBox->Text = buffer->ToString();
262      statusLabel->Text = S"";
263   } // end method listKeysButton_Click
```

Fig. 19.49 HashTableTest class method definitions. (Part 6 of 6.)

```
1    // Fig. 19.50: HashtableTestMain.cpp
2    // Entry point for application.
3
4    #include "HashTableTest.h"
5
6    int __stdcall WinMain()
7    {
8       Application::Run( new HashTableTest() );
9
10      return 0;
11   } // end function WinMain
```

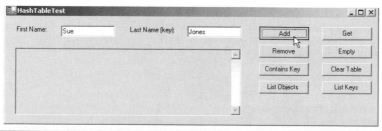

Fig. 19.50 HashtableTestMain.cpp demonstrates the **Hashtable** class.
(Part 1 of 2.)

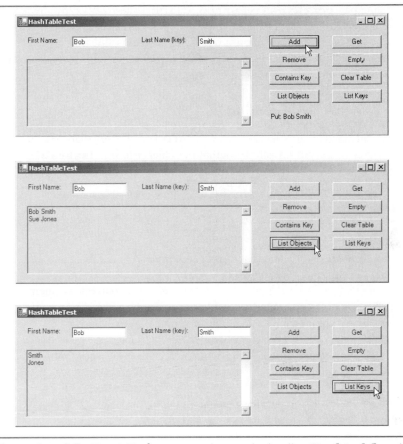

Fig. 19.50 HashtableTestMain.cpp demonstrates the **Hashtable** class.
(Part 2 of 2.)

Event handler **addButton_Click** (lines 170–187 of Fig. 19.49) reads the first name and last name of an employee from the user interface, creates an object of class **Employee** (Fig. 19.46–Fig. 19.47) and adds that **Employee** to the **Hashtable** with method **Add** (line 178). This method receives two arguments—a key object, and a value object. In this example, the key is the last name of the **Employee** (a **String *), and the value is the corresponding **Employee** pointer. An **ArgumentException** occurs if the **Hashtable** already contains the key or if the key is **NULL**.

Event handler **getButton_Click** (lines 190–201) retrieves the object associated with a specific key, using the **Hashtable**'s **Item** property as shown on line 193. The expression in parentheses is the key for which the **Hashtable** should return the corresponding object. If the key is not found, the result is **NULL**.

Event handler **removeButton_Click** (lines 204–209) invokes **Hashtable** method **Remove** to delete a key and its associated object from the **Hashtable**. If the key does not exist in the table, nothing happens.

Event handler **emptyButton_Click** (lines 212–217) uses **Hashtable** property **Count** to determine whether the **Hashtable** is empty (i.e., **Count** is **0**).

Event handler **containsKeyButton_Click** (lines 220–225) invokes **Hashtable** method *ContainsKey* to find out whether the **Hashtable** contains the specified key. If so, the method returns **true**; otherwise, it returns **false**.

Event handler **clearTableButton_Click** (lines 228–233) invokes **Hashtable** method *Clear* to delete all **Hashtable** entries.

Class **Hashtable** provides method **GetEnumerator**, which returns an enumerator of type *IDictionaryEnumerator*, which derives from **IEnumerator**. Such enumerators provide properties *Key* and *Value* to access the information for a key/value pair. The event handler at lines 236–248 (**listObjectsButton_click**) uses the **Value** property of the enumerator to output the objects in the **Hashtable**. The event handler at lines 251–263 (**listKeysButton_click**) uses the **Key** property of the enumerator to output the keys in the **Hashtable**.

19.8 Summary

Dynamic data structures can grow and shrink at execution time. Creating and maintaining dynamic data structures requires dynamic memory allocation—the ability for a program to obtain more memory at execution time (to hold new nodes) and to release memory no longer needed. The limit for dynamic memory allocation can be as large as the available physical memory in the computer or the amount of available disk space in a virtual-memory system. Memory can be allocated dynamically with operator **new**. Operator **new** takes as an operand the type of the object being dynamically allocated and returns a pointer to a newly created object of that type. If no memory is available, **new** throws an **OutOfMemoryException**.

Self-referential classes can be used to create dynamic data structures. A self-referential class contains a data member that points to an object of the same class type. Self-referential objects can be linked to form useful data structures, such as lists, queues, stacks and trees.

A linked list is a linear collection (i.e., a sequence) of self-referential class objects called nodes, connected by pointer links. A node can contain data of any type, including objects of other classes. A linked list is accessed via a pointer to the first node of the list. Each subsequent node is accessed via the link-pointer member stored in the previous node. By convention, the link pointer in the last node of a list is set to **NULL** to mark the end of the list.

Stacks are important in compilers and operating systems. A stack is a constrained version of a linked list—new nodes can be added to a stack and removed from a stack only at the top. A stack is referred to as a last-in, first-out (LIFO) data structure. The primary stack operations are push and pop. Operation push adds a new node to the top of the stack. Operation pop removes a node from the top of the stack and returns the data object from the popped node.

Queues represent waiting lines. Insertions occur at the back (also referred to as the tail) of a queue, and deletions occur from the front (also referred to as the head) of a queue. A queue is similar to a checkout line in a supermarket: The first person in line is served first; other customers enter the line only at the end and wait to be served. Queue nodes are removed only from the head of the queue and are inserted only at the tail of the queue. For this reason, a queue is referred to as a first-in, first-out (FIFO) data structure. The insert and remove operations for a queue are known as enqueue and dequeue.

Binary trees facilitate high-speed searching and sorting of data. Tree nodes contain two or more links. A binary tree is a tree whose nodes all contain two links. The root node is the first node in a tree. Each link in the root node points to a child. The left child is the first node in the left subtree and the right child is the first node in the right subtree. The children of a node are called siblings. A node with no children is called a leaf node. A binary search tree (with no duplicate node values) has the characteristic that the values in any left subtree are less than the values that subtree's parent node and the values in any right subtree are greater than the values in that subtree's parent node. In a binary search tree, a node can be inserted only as a leaf node.

An inorder traversal of a binary search tree processes the node values in ascending order. The process of creating a binary search tree actually sorts the data—hence, the term "binary tree sort." In a preorder traversal, the value in each node is processed as the node is visited. After the value in a given node is processed, the values in the left subtree are processed, then the values in the right subtree are processed. In a postorder traversal, the value in each node is processed after the node's left and right subtrees are processed. The binary search tree facilitates duplicate elimination. As the tree is created, attempts to insert a duplicate value are recognized because a duplicate follows the same "go left" or "go right" decisions on each comparison that the original value did. Thus, the duplicate eventually is compared with a node containing the same value. The duplicate value may simply be discarded at this point.

The .NET Framework provides ready-to-go, reusable components; you do not need to write your own collection classes. Class **ArrayList** can be used as a dynamically growing array. **ArrayList** method **Add** adds an **Object** to the **ArrayList**. **ArrayList** method **Remove** removes the first occurrence of the specified **Object** from the **ArrayList**. **ArrayList** elements can be accessed by following the **ArrayList** indexed property **Item** with the array subscript operator (**[]**) and the desired index of the element.

Class **Stack** is provided in the **System::Collections** namespace. **Stack** method **Push** performs the push operation on the **Stack**. **Stack** method **Pop** performs the pop operation on the **Stack**.

Class **Hashtable** is provided in the **System::Collections** namespace. **Hashtable** method **Add** adds a key/value pair to the **Hashtable**. Any class that implements the **IEnumerator** interface must define methods **MoveNext** and **Reset** and the **Current** property. Method **MoveNext** must be called before the **Current** property is accessed for the first time. Methods **MoveNext** and **Reset** throw an **InvalidOperationException** if the contents of the collection were modified in any way after the enumerator's creation.

20

Accessibility

Objectives

- To introduce the World Wide Web Consortium's Web Content Accessibility Guidelines 1.0 (WCAG 1.0).
- To understand how to use the **alt** attribute of the HTML **<img>** tag to describe images to people with visual impairments, mobile-Web-device users and others unable to view images.
- To understand how to make tables more accessible to page readers.
- To understand how to verify that XHTML tags are used properly and how to ensure that Web pages can be viewed on any type of display or reader.
- To understand how VoiceXML™ and CallXML™ are changing the way in which people with disabilities access information on the Web.
- To introduce the accessibility aids offered in Windows XP and Visual Studio .NET.

'Tis the good reader that makes the good book...
Ralph Waldo Emerson

I once was lost, but now am found,
Was blind, but now I see.
John Newton

Outline

20.1 Introduction

Throughout this book, we discuss the creation of Visual C++ .NET applications. Later chapters also introduce the development of Web-based content that uses XHTML and XML. In this chapter, we explore the topic of *accessibility*, which refers to the level of usability that an application or Web site provides to people with various disabilities. Disabilities that might affect an individual's computer or Internet usage are common; they include visual impairments, hearing impairments, other physical injuries (such as the inability to use a keyboard or a mouse) and learning disabilities. In today's computing environment, such impediments prevent many users from taking full advantage of applications and Web content.

The design of applications and sites to meet the needs of individuals with disabilities should be a priority for all software companies and e-businesses. People affected by disabilities represent a significant portion of the population, and legal ramifications could exist for companies that discriminate by failing to provide adequate and universal access to their resources. In this chapter, we explore the World Wide Web Consortium's *Web Accessibility Initiative* and its guidelines and review various laws regarding the availability of computing and Internet resources to people with disabilities. We also highlight companies that have developed systems, products and services that meet the needs of this demographic. As students use Visual C++ .NET and its related technologies to design applications and Web sites, they should keep in mind the accessibility requirements and recommendations that we discuss in this chapter.

20.2 Regulations and Resources

Over the past several years, the United States has taken legislative steps to ensure that people with disabilities are given the tools they need to use computers and access the Web. A wide variety of legislation, including the *Americans With Disabilities Act* (ADA) of 1990, governs the provision of computer and Web accessibility (Fig. 20.1). These laws have inspired significant legal action. For example, according to the ADA, companies are required to offer equal access to individuals with visual problems. The National Federation for the Blind (NFB) cited this law in a 1999 suit against AOL, alleging to the company's failure to make its services available to individuals with disabilities.

Act	Purpose
Americans with Disabilities Act	The ADA prohibits discrimination on the basis of disability in employment, state and local government, public accommodations, commercial facilities, transportation and telecommunications. More information can be found at **www.ada.gov**.
Telecommunications Act of 1996	The Telecommunications Act of 1996 contains two amendments to Section 255 and Section 251(a)(2) of the Communications Act of 1934. These amendments require that communication devices, such as cell phones, telephones and pagers, be accessible to individuals with disabilities. More information can be found at **www.fcc.gov/telecom.html**.
Individuals with Disabilities Education Act of 1997	The Individuals with Disabilities Education Act stipulates that education materials in schools must be made accessible to children with disabilities. More information can be found at **www.ed.gov/offices/OSERS/Policy/IDEA**.

Fig. 20.1   Acts designed to improve Internet and computer accessibility for people with disabilities. (Part 1 of 2.)

Act	Purpose
Rehabilitation Act	Section 504 of the Rehabilitation Act states that college sponsored activities receiving federal funding cannot discriminate against individuals with disabilities. Section 508 mandates that all government institutions receiving federal funding must design their Web sites so that they are accessible to individuals with disabilities. Businesses that sell services to the government also must abide by this act. More information can be found at **www.ed.gov/offices/OSERS/RSA**.

Fig. 20.1   Acts designed to improve Internet and computer accessibility for people with disabilities. (Part 2 of 2.)

There are 54 million Americans with disabilities, and these individuals represent an estimated $1 trillion in annual purchasing power. In addition to legislation, many organizations and resources focus on assisting individuals with disabilities to access computers and the Internet. **WeMedia.com**™(Fig. 20.2) is a Web site that provides news, information, products and services to the millions of people with disabilities and to their families, friends and caregivers.

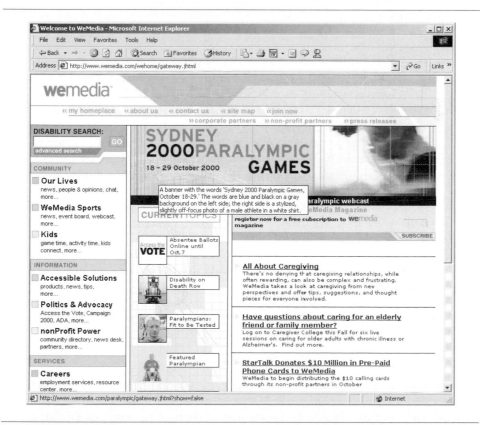

Fig. 20.2   Wemedia.com home page. (Courtesy of Wemedia, Inc.)

As these laws and resources exemplify, computer and Internet accessibility for individuals with disabilities is quickly becoming a reality. Such accessibility enables individuals with disabilities to work in a vast array of new fields. This is partly because the Internet provides a medium through which disabled people can telecommute to jobs and interact easily with others without traveling. Such technologies as voice activation, visual enhancers and auditory aids create additional employment opportunities. For example, people with visual impairments can use computer monitors with enlarged text, and people with physical impairments can use head pointers with on-screen keyboards. In the remaining sections of this chapter, we explore various organizations, techniques, products and services that help provide computer and Internet access to people with disabilities.

20.3 Web Accessibility Initiative

Currently, most Web sites are considered to be either partially or totally inaccessible to people with visual, learning or mobility impairments. Total accessibility is difficult to achieve, because of the variety of disabilities that must be accommodated and because of problems resulting from language barriers and hardware and software inconsistencies. However, a high level of accessibility is attainable. As more people with disabilities begin to use the Internet, it is imperative that Website designers increase the accessibility of their sites. Although computer and Web accessibility is the focus of some recent legislation, standards organizations also see the need for industry recommendations. In an attempt to address issues of accessibility, the World Wide Web Consortium (W3C) launched the *Web Accessibility Initiative* (WAI™) in April 1997. To learn more about the WAI or to read its mission statement, visit **www.w3.org/WAI**.

This chapter explains various techniques used to develop accessible Web sites. In 1999, the WAI published the *Web Content Accessibility Guidelines* (*WCAG*) *1.0* to help businesses ascertain whether their Web sites are universally accessible. The WCAG 1.0 (available at **www.w3.org/TR/WCAG10**) uses checkpoints to list specific accessibility requirements. Each checkpoint is accompanied by a corresponding priority rating that indicates the requirement's level of importance. *Priority-one checkpoints* are goals that must be met to ensure accessibility; we focus on these points in this chapter. *Priority-two checkpoints*, though not essential, are highly recommended. If these checkpoints are not satisfied, people with certain disabilities will experience difficulty accessing Web sites. *Priority-three checkpoints* improve accessibility slightly.

At the time of publication, the WAI was working on *WCAG 2.0*; a working draft of this publication can be found at **www.w3.org/TR/WCAG20**. A single checkpoint in the WCAG 2.0 Working Draft might encompass several checkpoints from WCAG 1.0. Once WCAG 2.0 has been reviewed and published by the W3C, its checkpoints will supersede those of WCAG 1.0. Furthermore, the new version can be applied to a wider range of markup languages (i.e., XML, WML, etc.) and content types than can its predecessor.

The WAI also presents a supplemental checklist of *quick tips*, which reinforce ten important points relating to accessible Web-site design. More information on the WAI Quick Tips can be found at **www.w3.org/WAI/References/Quicktips**.

20.4 Providing Alternatives for Images

One important WAI requirement specifies that every image on a Web page should be accompanied by a textual description that clearly defines the purpose of the image. To accomplish this task, Web developers can use the **alt** attribute of the **img** and **input** tags to include a textual equivalent for every image or graphic included on a site.

Web developers who do not use the **alt** attribute to provide text equivalents increase the difficulties that people with visual impairments experience in navigating the Web. Specialized *user agents* (or *accessibility aids*), such as *screen readers* (programs that allow users to hear all text that is displayed on their screens) and *braille displays* (devices that receive data from screen-reading software and then output the data as braille), enable people with visual impairments to access text-based information that normally is displayed on the screen. A user agent visually interprets Web-page source code and translates it into a format that is accessible to people with various disabilities. Web browsers, such as Microsoft Internet Explorer and Netscape Communicator, and the screen readers mentioned throughout this chapter are examples of user agents.

Similarly, Web pages that do not provide text equivalents for video and audio clips are difficult for people with visual and hearing impairments to access. Screen readers cannot interpret images, movies and most other non-XHTML content from these Web pages. However, by providing multimedia-based information in a variety of ways (e.g., by using the **alt** attribute, or by providing in-line descriptions of images), Web designers can help maximize the accessibility of their sites' content.

Web designers should provide useful and appropriate text equivalents in the **alt** attribute for use by nonvisual user agents. For example, if the **alt** attribute describes a sales-growth chart, it should provide a brief summary of the data, but should not describe the data in the chart. Instead, a complete description of the chart's data should be included in the *longdesc* (long description) *attribute*, which is intended to augment the **alt** attribute's description. The **longdesc** attribute contains a link to a Web page describing the image or multimedia content. Currently, most Web browsers do not support the **longdesc** attribute. An alternative to the **longdesc** attribute is *D-link*, which provides descriptive text about graphs and charts. More information on D-links can be obtained at the *CORDA Technologies* Web site (**www.corda.com**).

The use of a screen reader to facilitate Web-site navigation can be time-consuming and frustrating, because screen readers cannot interpret pictures and other graphical content. The inclusion of a link at the top of each Web page providing direct access to the page's content could allow disabled users to bypass long lists of navigation links and other irrelevant or inaccessible content. This jump can save time and eliminate frustration for individuals with visual impairments.

Emacspeak (**www.cs.cornell.edu/home/raman/emacspeak**) is a screen interface that improves the quality of Internet access for individuals with visual disabilities by translating text to voice data. The open-source product also implements auditory icons that play various sounds. Emacspeak can be customized with Linux operating systems and provides support for the IBM *ViaVoice* speech engine.

In March 2001, We Media introduced another user agent, the *WeMedia Browser*, which allows people with vision impairments and cognitive disabilities (such as dyslexia) to use the Internet more conveniently. The WeMedia Browser enhances traditional browser capabilities by providing oversized buttons and keystroke commands that assist in navigation. The browser "reads" text that the user selects, allowing the user to control the speed and volume at which the browser reads the contents of the Web page. The WeMedia Browser free download is available at **www.wemedia.com**.

IBM Home Page Reader (HPR) is another browser that "reads" text selected by the user. The HPR uses IBM ViaVoice technology to synthesize an audible voice. A trial version of HPR is available at **www-3.ibm.com/able/hpr.html**.

20.5 Maximizing Readability by Focusing on Structure

Many Web sites use XHTML tags for aesthetic purposes, ignoring the tags' intended functions. For example, the **`<h1>`** heading tag often is used erroneously to make text large and bold, rather than to indicate a major section head for content. This practice might create a desired visual effect, but it causes problems for screen readers. When the screen-reader software encounters the **`<h1>`** tag, it might verbally inform the user that a new section has been reached. If this is not in fact the case, the **`<h1>`** tag might confuse users. Therefore, developers should use the **`h1`** only in accordance with its XHTML specifications (e.g., to mark up a heading that introduces an important section of a document). Instead of using **`h1`** to make text large and bold, developers can use CSS (Cascading Style Sheets) or XSL (Extensible Stylesheet Language) to format and style the text. For further examples of this nature, refer to the WCAG 1.0 Web site at **`www.w3.org/TR/WCAG10`**. [*Note:* The **`<strong>`** tag also can be used to make text bold; however, screen readers emphasize bold text, which affects the inflection of what is spoken.]

Another accessibility issue is *readability*. When creating a Web page intended for the general public, it is important to consider the reading level (i.e., level of difficulty to read and understand) at which content is written. Web-site designers can make their sites easier to read by using shorter words. Furthermore, slang terms and other nontraditional language could be problematic for users from other countries, so developers should limit the use of such words.

WCAG 1.0 suggests using a paragraph's first sentence to convey its subject. When a Web site states the point of a paragraph in this paragraph's first sentence, it is easier for individuals with disabilities both to find crucial information and to bypass unwanted material.

The *Gunning Fog Index*, a formula that produces a readability grade when applied to a text sample, can evaluate a Web site's readability. To obtain more information about the Gunning Fog Index, visit **`www.trainingpost.org/3-2-inst.htm`**.

20.6 Accessibility in Visual Studio .NET

In the previous sections, we have outlined various accessibility guidelines presented in the W3C's Web Accessibility initiative. However, Visual Studio .NET provides its own guidelines for designing accessible software within its programming environment. For instance, one guideline recommends reserving the use of color for the enhancement or emphasis of information, instead of for aesthetic purposes. A second guideline recommends providing information about objects (e.g., desktop icons and open windows) to the accessibility aids (specialized software that renders applications to individuals with disabilities). Such information might include the name, location and size of a window. A third guideline recommends designing user interfaces so that they can accommodate user preferences. For example, people with visual disabilities should be able to modify the font size of a user interface. A fourth guideline recommends allowing users to adjust the time setting for applications that have time constraints. For example, users with mobility or speech disabilities might experience difficulty when using applications that require users to enter input within a predetermined period of time (such as 10 seconds). However, if such applications provide adjustable time settings, users can modify the settings to suit their needs.

In addition to suggesting guidelines thc help developers create accessible applications, Visual Studio .NET also offers features that enable disabled individuals to use the development environment itself. For example, users can enlarge icons and text, customize the toolbox and keyboard and rearrange windows. The next subsections illustrate these capabilities.

20.6.1 Enlarging Toolbar Icons

To enlarge icons in Visual Studio, select **Tools > Customize** . In the **Customize** window's **Options** tab, select the **Large Icons** check box (Fig. 20.3), and select **Close**. Figure 20.4 depicts the enlarged icons on the Visual Studio development window.

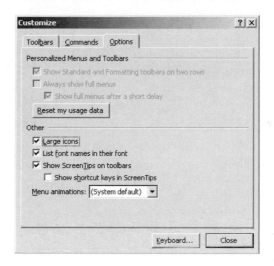

Fig. 20.3   Enlarging icons using the **Customize** feature.

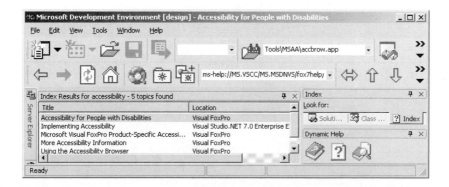

Fig. 20.4   Enlarged icons in the development window.

20.6.2 Enlarging the Text

Visual Studio uses the default operating-system font settings when displaying text. However, some individuals cannot read these default font settings, so the applications are inaccessible to them. To remedy this, Visual Studio allows users to modify the font size. Select **Tools > Options....** In the **Options** window, open the **Environment** folder, and choose **Fonts and Colors**. In the **Show settings for** drop-down box, select **Text Editor**. In the **Font** drop-down box, select a different style of font and, in the **Size** drop-down box, select a different font size. Figure 20.5 depicts the **Text Editor** before we modified the font size, Fig. 20.6 shows the **Options** window with the new font settings, and Fig. 20.7 displays the **Text Editor** after the changes have been applied.

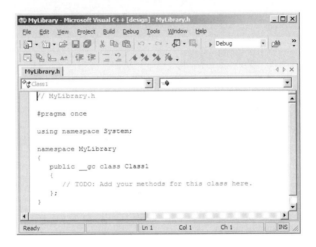

Fig. 20.5   Text Editor before modifying the font size.

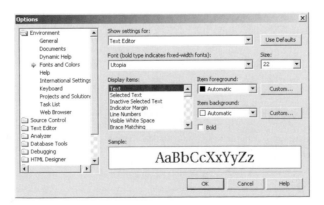

Fig. 20.6   Enlarging text in the **Options** window.

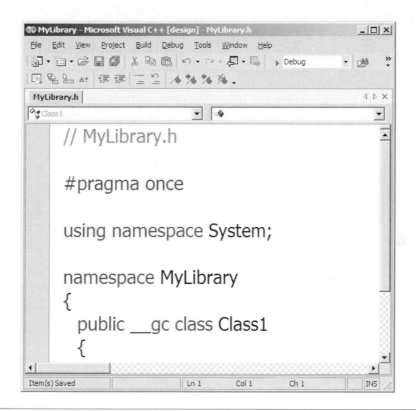

Fig. 20.7   Text Editor after the font size is modified.

20.6.3 Modifying the Keyboard

Another accessibility feature in Visual Studio .NET allows individuals with disabilities to customize their keyboards by creating *shortcut keys* (i.e., combinations of keyboard keys that, when pressed together, perform frequent tasks; for example, *Ctrl + V* causes text to be pasted from the clipboard). To create a shortcut key, begin by selecting **Tools > Options...**. In the **Options** window, select the **Keyboard** item from the **Environment** folder. From the **Keyboard mapping scheme** drop-down list, select a scheme, and click the **Save As** button. Then, assign a name to the scheme in the **Save Scheme** dialog box and click **OK**. Enter the task of the shortcut key in the **Show commands containing** text box. For example, if we were creating a shortcut key for the paste function, we would enter **Paste** in the text box, or we would select the proper task from the selection list directly below the text box. Then, in the **Use new shortcut in** drop-down list, select the applications that will use the shortcut key. If the shortcut key will be used in all applications, select **Global**. Finally, in the **Press shortcut key(s)** text box, assign a shortcut key to the task in the form *nontext key + text key*. Valid nontext keys include *Ctrl*, *Shift* and *Alt*; valid text keys include A–Z, inclusive. [*Note*: To enter a nontext key, select the key itself—do not type the word *Ctrl*, *Shift* or *Alt*. It is possible to include more than one nontext key as part of a shortcut key. Do not enter the + symbol.] Thus, a valid shortcut key might be *Ctrl+Alt+D*. After assigning a shortcut key, select **Assign** and then **OK**. Figure 20.8 illustrates the process of creating a shortcut key for the `NewBreakpoint` function. The shortcut key (*Ctrl+Alt+D*) is valid only in the **Text Editor**.

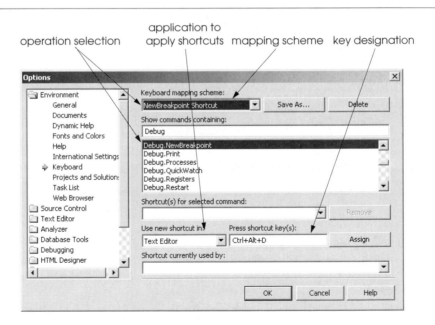

Fig. 20.8   Shortcut-key creation.

20.6.4 Rearranging Windows

Some screen readers have difficulty interpreting user interfaces that include multiple tabs; this is because most screen readers can read information on only one screen. To accommodate such screen readers, Visual Studio .NET allows developers to customize their user interfaces so that multiple document windows appear. To remove tabs, select **Tools > Options...** from the **Tools** menu. Then, in the **Options** window, select the **General** item from the **Environment** folder. In the **Settings** section, select the **MDI environment** radio button and click **OK**. Figure 20.9 depicts the **Options** window, and Fig. 20.10 illustrates a document window with and without tabs.

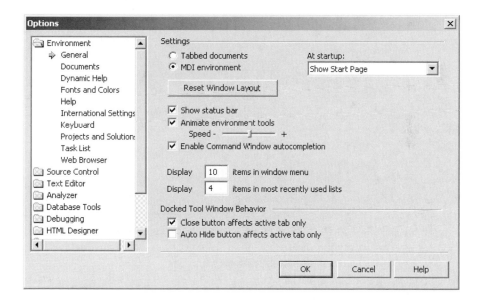

Fig. 20.9 Removing tabs from Visual Studio environment.

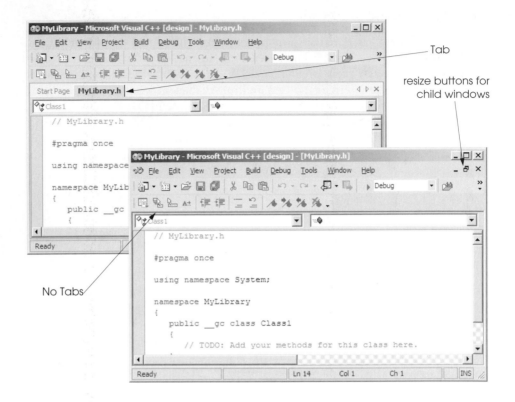

Fig. 20.10 Document windows with tabs and without tabs.

20.7 Accessibility in Visual C++ .NET

Visual Studio .NET provides extensive accessibility features and also presents guidelines for creating accessible applications in its development environment. Similar recommendations guide the development of MC++ applications that are accessible to people with disabilities. It is important that MC++ programmers gear applications toward as many potential users as possible, rather than toward only the average user. With some modifications, most applications can be made accessible to a wide variety of individuals. General guidelines for designing accessible applications are to

1. Use larger-sized fonts—this helps people with visual impairments see the text.

2. Create flexible applications that provide keyboard shortcuts for all features within the application—this allows people to use the application without employing a mouse.

3. Allow information to be conveyed to the user both in a visual and in an audio context.

4. Use graphics and images whenever helpful—visual cues can increase accessibility for people who have trouble reading text on the screen.

5. Never signal information with sound only—someone accessing the information might not have speakers or might have hearing impairments.[1]

6. Test the application without using either a mouse or a keyboard. Access to an application's functionality should not be limited to one input device.

For more information on these and other design guidelines for accessible applications, please refer to the Visual Studio .NET documentation under the **overview** subsection of the index topic **accessibility**.[2] This section provides links to discussions of how to design more accessible applications.

One specific way that programmers can make their applications more accessible is to use a *text-to-speech* control in their programs. A text-to-speech control can convert text into speech—a computerized voice speaks the words provided as text to the control. Text-to-speech controls facilitate access for people who cannot see the screen.

Another way to make applications more accessible is to use *tab stops*. A tab stop occurs when the user presses the *Tab* key, causing the focus to transfer to another control. The order in which the controls gain focus is called the *tab order*, which is determined by the **TabIndex** value of the controls (controls gain focus in ascending order). Each control also has a **TabStop** property—if this property is **true**, the control is included in the tab order; otherwise, it is not. Using the **TabIndex** and **TabStop** properties makes it simple to create more easily navigable applications. If these properties are set incorrectly, the logical ordering of the application might not be maintained. Consider an application that has **TextBox**es in which a user inputs a first name, a last name and an address. The logical tab order would take the user from the **TextBox** for the first name to the one for the last name and then to the one for the address.

A third and important way in which programmers can increase the accessibility of their applications is to use specific classes provided by .NET. Class **Control**, for example, has many properties designed for conveying information to users. These applications can then, in turn, find the required information stored as properties. Figure 20.11 lists some properties of class **Control** that are designed to provide information to users.

---

1. "Basic Principles of Accessible Design," *.NET Framework Developer's Guide*, Visual Studio .NET Online Help

2. This information is located at **ms-help://MS.VSCC/MS.MSDNVS/vsintro7/html/vxoriAccessibilityInVisualStudioNET.htm**

Property	Purpose
AccessibleDescription	Describes the control to an accessibility client application. For example, a **CheckBox** that says **"New User"** would not require more description, but a **CheckBox** with an image of a cat would have its **AccessibleDescription** property set to something like, **"A CheckBox with an image of a cat on it"**.
AccessibleName	Contains a short name or identifier for the control.
AccessibleRole	Member of the **AccessibleRole** enumeration. Represents the role of this control in the application—this information might help the accessibility client application determine what actions it should take.
IsAccessible	Contains a **bool** value specifying whether the control is visible to accessibility client applications.

Fig. 20.11 Properties of class **Control** related to accessibility.

The application in Fig. 20.12–Fig. 20.14 uses a text-to-speech control, tab stops and class **Control**'s accessibility-related properties. It consists of a form with three **Label**s, three **TextBox**es and a **Button**, enabling a user to submit the information. The program does not process the submitted information—the application is intended only to demonstrate the use of the text-to-speech control.[3]

The text-to-speech control used in Fig. 20.12–Fig. 20.14 is a Microsoft ActiveX Control. To use the text-to-speech control, programmers must create the necessary DLLs—**HTTSLib.dll** and **AxHTTSLib.dll**—by running the command

        aximp C:\winnt\speech\VText.dll

from directory

        **C:\Program Files\Microsoft Visual Studio .NET\
        frameworkSDK\bin**

The ActiveX Control Importer (**aximp**) will create the DLLs in the same directory.[4] These DLLs can then be referenced relatively or copied into the project's **Debug** directory and referenced locally (lines 10–11 of Fig. 20.12).

If **VText.dll** does not already exist on your system, download and execute the Speech SDK from

        www.microsoft.com/speech/download/

The executable downloaded will extract the necessary DLL into the correct directory (i.e., **C:\winnt\speech**).

---

3. At the time of publication, this program did not work on Windows XP. Please check the **Downloads/Resources** link of our Web site for updates to this application.
4. For more information about creating DLLs using **aximp**, visit **msdn.microsoft.com/library/en-us/cptools/html/cpgrfwindowsformsactivexcontrol importeraximpexe.asp**.

```
 1    // Fig. 20.12: TextToSpeech.h
 2    // Providing audio for people with visual impairments.
 3
 4    #pragma once
 5
 6    #using <mscorlib.dll>
 7    #using <system.dll>
 8    #using <system.drawing.dll>
 9    #using <system.windows.forms.dll>
10    #using <HTTSLib.dll>
11    #using <AxHTTSLib.dll>
12
13    using namespace System;
14    using namespace System::Drawing;
15    using namespace System::Windows::Forms;
16    using namespace System::Threading;
17
18    // helps users navigate a form with the aid of audio cues
19    public __gc class TextToSpeech : public Form
20    {
21    public:
22       TextToSpeech();
23
24    private:
25       Label *nameLabel;
26       Label *phoneLabel;
27       TextBox *nameTextBox;
28       TextBox *phoneTextBox;
29       TextBox *passwordTextBox;
30       Button *submitButton;
31       Label *passwordLabel;
32
33       AxHTTSLib::AxTextToSpeech *speaker;
34
35       void InitializeComponent();
36       void controls_MouseHover( Object *sender, EventArgs *e );
37       void submitButton_Click( Object *sender, EventArgs *e );
38    }; // end class TextToSpeech
```

Fig. 20.12 TextToSpeech class provides audio cues for navigating a form.

```
 1    // Fig. 20.13: TextToSpeech.cpp
 2    // Method definitions for clas TextToSpeech.
 3
 4    #include "TextToSpeech.h"
 5
 6    // default constructor
 7    TextToSpeech::TextToSpeech()
 8    {
 9       InitializeComponent();
10
11       // set Form to be visible to accessibility applications
```

Fig. 20.13 TextToSpeech class method definitions. (Part 1 of 5.)

```
12       this->IsAccessible = true;
13
14       // let all controls be visible to accessibility applications
15       Control *current;
16
17       for ( int i = 0; i < this->Controls->Count; i++ ){
18          current = Controls->Item[ i ];
19          current->IsAccessible = true;
20       }
21   } // end constructor
22
23   void TextToSpeech::InitializeComponent()
24   {
25       System::Resources::ResourceManager *resources =
26          new System::Resources::ResourceManager(
27          __typeof( TextToSpeech ) );
28
29       this->nameLabel = new Label();
30       this->phoneLabel = new Label();
31       this->nameTextBox = new TextBox();
32       this->phoneTextBox = new TextBox();
33       this->passwordTextBox = new TextBox();
34       this->submitButton = new Button();
35       this->passwordLabel = new Label();
36       this->speaker = new AxHTTSLib::AxTextToSpeech();
37       this->speaker->BeginInit();
38
39       this->SuspendLayout();
40
41       // nameLabel
42       this->nameLabel->AccessibleDescription = S"User Name";
43       this->nameLabel->AccessibleName = S"User Name";
44       this->nameLabel->BorderStyle = BorderStyle::FixedSingle;
45       this->nameLabel->Location = Point( 32, 32 );
46       this->nameLabel->Name = S"nameLabel";
47       this->nameLabel->Size = Drawing::Size( 96, 23 );
48       this->nameLabel->TabIndex = 5;
49       this->nameLabel->Text = S"Name";
50       this->nameLabel->MouseHover += new EventHandler( this,
51          controls_MouseHover );
52
53       // phoneLabel
54       this->phoneLabel->AccessibleDescription = S"Phone Number Label";
55       this->phoneLabel->AccessibleName = S"Phone Number Label";
56       this->phoneLabel->BorderStyle = BorderStyle::FixedSingle;
57       this->phoneLabel->Location = Point( 32, 64 );
58       this->phoneLabel->Name = S"phoneLabel";
59       this->phoneLabel->Size = Drawing::Size( 96, 23 );
60       this->phoneLabel->TabIndex = 6;
61       this->phoneLabel->Text = S"Phone Number";
62       this->phoneLabel->MouseHover += new EventHandler( this,
63          controls_MouseHover );
64
```

Fig. 20.13 TextToSpeech class method definitions. (Part 2 of 5.)

```
65        // nameTextBox
66        this->nameTextBox->AccessibleDescription = S"Enter User Name";
67        this->nameTextBox->AccessibleName = S"User Name TextBox";
68        this->nameTextBox->Location = Point( 152, 32 );
69        this->nameTextBox->Name = S"nameTextBox";
70        this->nameTextBox->TabIndex = 1;
71        this->nameTextBox->Text = S"";
72        this->nameTextBox->MouseHover += new EventHandler( this,
73           controls_MouseHover );
74
75        // phoneTextBox
76        this->phoneTextBox->AccessibleDescription =
77           S"Enter Phone Number";
78        this->phoneTextBox->AccessibleName = S"Phone Number TextBox";
79        this->phoneTextBox->Location = Point( 152, 64 );
80        this->phoneTextBox->Name = S"phoneTextBox";
81        this->phoneTextBox->TabIndex = 2;
82        this->phoneTextBox->Text = S"";
83        this->phoneTextBox->MouseHover += new EventHandler( this,
84           controls_MouseHover );
85
86        // passwordTextBox
87        this->passwordTextBox->AccessibleDescription =
88           S"Enter Password";
89        this->passwordTextBox->AccessibleName = S"Password TextBox";
90        this->passwordTextBox->Location = Point( 152, 96 );
91        this->passwordTextBox->Name = S"passwordTextBox";
92        this->passwordTextBox->PasswordChar = '*';
93        this->passwordTextBox->TabIndex = 3;
94        this->passwordTextBox->Text = S"";
95        this->passwordTextBox->MouseHover += new EventHandler( this,
96           controls_MouseHover );
97
98        // submitButton
99        this->submitButton->AccessibleDescription =
100          S"Submit the Information";
101       this->submitButton->AccessibleName = S"Submit Information";
102       this->submitButton->Location = Point( 112, 144 );
103       this->submitButton->Name = S"submitButton";
104       this->submitButton->TabIndex = 4;
105       this->submitButton->Text = S"&Submit";
106       this->submitButton->Click += new EventHandler( this,
107          submitButton_Click );
108       this->submitButton->MouseHover += new EventHandler( this,
109          controls_MouseHover );
110
111       // passwordLabel
112       this->passwordLabel->AccessibleDescription =
113          S"Password Label";
114       this->passwordLabel->AccessibleName = S"Password Label";

115       this->passwordLabel->BorderStyle = BorderStyle::FixedSingle;
116       this->passwordLabel->Location = Point( 32, 96 );
117       this->passwordLabel->Name = S"passwordLabel";
```

Fig. 20.13 TextToSpeech class method definitions. (Part 3 of 5.)

```
118      this->passwordLabel->Size = Drawing::Size( 96, 23 );
119      this->passwordLabel->TabIndex = 7;
120      this->passwordLabel->Text = S"Password";
121      this->passwordLabel->MouseHover += new EventHandler( this,
122         controls_MouseHover );
123
124      // speaker
125      this->speaker->AccessibleDescription =
126         S"Give Information about Form";
127      this->speaker->AccessibleName = S"Speaker";
128      this->speaker->Enabled = true;
129      this->speaker->Location = Point( 288, 40 );
130      this->speaker->Name = S"speaker";
131      this->speaker->Size = Drawing::Size( 112, 104 );
132      this->speaker->TabIndex = 8;
133      this->speaker->TabStop = false;
134
135      // TextToSpeech
136      this->AccessibleDescription = S"Registration Form";
137      this->AccessibleName = S"Registration Form";
138      this->AutoScaleBaseSize = Drawing::Size( 5, 13 );
139      this->ClientSize = Drawing::Size( 416, 181 );
140
141      Control *control[] = { this->speaker, this->passwordLabel,
142         this->submitButton, this->passwordTextBox,
143         this->phoneTextBox, this->nameTextBox, this->phoneLabel,
144         this->nameLabel };
145      this->Controls->AddRange( control );
146
147      this->Name = S"TextToSpeech";
148      this->Text = S"TextToSpeech";
149      this->speaker->EndInit();
150
151      this->ResumeLayout();
152   } // end method InitializeComponent
153
154   // tell user over which control the mouse is
155   void TextToSpeech::controls_MouseHover(
156      Object *sender, EventArgs *e )
157   {
158      // if mouse is over a Label, tell user to enter information
159      if ( sender->GetType() == nameLabel->GetType() ) {
160         Label *temporary = dynamic_cast< Label * >( sender );
161         speaker->Speak( String::Concat( S"Please enter your ",
162            temporary->Text, S" in the textbox to the right" ) );
163      }
164
165      // if mouse is over a TextBox, tell user what
166      // information was entered
167      else if ( sender->GetType() == nameTextBox->GetType() ) {
168         TextBox *temporary = dynamic_cast< TextBox * >( sender );
169         speaker->Speak(String::Concat( S"You have entered ",
170            ( temporary->Text == S"" ? S"nothing" :
```

Fig. 20.13 TextToSpeech class method definitions. (Part 4 of 5.)

```
171             temporary->Text ), S" in the ", temporary->Name ) );
172     }
173
174     // otherwise, user is over Button, so tell user to click
175     // it to submit the information
176     else
177        speaker->Speak(
178           S"Click on this button to submit your information" );
179  } // end method controls_MouseHover
180
181  // thank user for submitting information
182  void TextToSpeech::submitButton_Click(
183     Object *sender, EventArgs *e )
184  {
185     speaker->Speak(
186        S"Thank you, your information has been submitted." );
187
188     MessageBox::Show( S"Your information has been submitted.",
189        S"Thank you" );
190
191     Application::Exit();
192  } // end method submitButton_Click
```

Fig. 20.13 TextToSpeech class method definitions. (Part 5 of 5.)

```
1   // Fig. 20.14: TextToSpecchTest.cpp
2   // Entry point for TextToSpeech application.
3
4   #include "TextToSpeech.h"
5
6   int __stdcall WinMain()
7   {
8      Thread::CurrentThread->ApartmentState = ApartmentState::STA;
9      Application::Run( new TextToSpeech() );
10
11     return 0;
12  } // end function WinMain
```

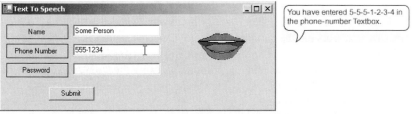

Fig. 20.14 Application with accessibility features.

The accessibility features in this program work as follows: When the mouse is over a label, the text-to-speech control prompts the user to enter the appropriate information in the textbox located to the right of the label. If the mouse is over a textbox, the contents of the textbox are spoken. Lastly, if the mouse is over button **Submit**, the user is told that the button should be clicked to submit the information. The tab order is the following: the textboxes where the user inputs the name, phone number and password, then the button. The labels and text-to-speech control are not included in the tab order, because the user cannot interact with them, and their inclusion would serve no purpose. The accessibility properties are set so that accessibility client applications will obtain appropriate information about the controls.

The application has three labels that prompt for the user's name, phone number and password. Three corresponding textboxes accept the user's input, and a button allows the user to submit the form. Line 33 (of Fig. 20.12) declares a pointer to a text-to-speech control of type **AxTextToSpeech** named **speaker**. We want the user to hear audio descriptions of controls when the mouse is located over those controls. Lines 155–179 (of Fig. 20.13) define the **controls_MouseHover** event handler—we attach this method to the three textboxes and the button as the event handler for the **MouseHover** event.

Method **controls_MouseHover** determines which type of control the mouse is hovering over and generates the appropriate audio. Line 159 checks for whether the type of the control calling the method is the same as that of **nameLabel**. Here, we use method **GetType** of class **Object**, which returns an instance of class *Type*; this class represents information about a particular class. We call method **GetType** on object **sender**. Event-handler argument **sender** is a pointer to the control that triggered the event. When the condition at line 159 evaluates to **true** (i.e., the control that triggered the event is the same type as **nameLabel**), lines 160–162 execute. Line 160 casts **sender** to a **Label** pointer (now that we know it is one) and assigns it to **Label** ***temporary**. Lines 161–162 call **speaker**'s method **Speak**, which provides the **String *** that should be converted to speech.

A similar process is performed to determine whether the mouse is over a **TextBox** (line 167) and to generate the appropriate audio (lines 168–171). Lastly, if the control over which the mouse is hovering is neither a **Label** nor a **TextBox**, it must be the **Button**; lines 177–178 tell the user to click the button to submit information. Method **submitButton_Click** (lines 182–192) executes when the user clicks the **Button**. This event handler calls **speaker**'s method **Speak**, providing as an argument a thank-you message, displays a similar message in a **MessageBox** and then exits the application.

Line 105 sets the **Text** property of **submitButton** to **"&Submit"**. This is an example of providing keyboard access to the functionality of the application. Recall that, in Chapter 10, Graphical User Interface Concepts: Part 2, we assigned shortcut keys by placing **"&"** in front of the letter that would become the shortcut key. Here, we do the same for **submitButton**—pressing **Alt+S** on the keyboard is equivalent to clicking the **submitButton**.

We establish the tab order in this application by setting the **TabIndex** and **TabStop** properties. The **TabIndex** properties of the controls are assigned in lines 48, 60, 70, 81, 93, 104, 119 and 132. The textboxes are assigned the tab indices 1–3, in order of their appearance (vertically) on the form. The button is assigned tab index 4, and the rest of the controls are given tab indices 5–8. We want the tab order to include only the textboxes and the button. The default setting for the **TabStop** property of labels is **false**—thus, we do not need to change it; the labels will not be included in the tab order. The **TabStop** property of textboxes and buttons is **true**, which means that we do not need to change the values for those controls either. The **TabStop** property of **speaker**, however, is **true** by default. We set it to **false**, indicating that we do not want **speaker** included in the tab order. In general, those controls with which the user cannot interact directly should have their **TabStop** properties set to **false**.

The last accessibility feature in this application involves setting the accessibility properties of the controls so that client accessibility applications can access and process the controls properly. Lines 42, 54, 66, 76–77, 87–88, 99–100, 112–113, 125–126 and 136 set the **AccessibleDescription** properties of all the controls (including the Form). Lines 43, 55, 67, 78, 89, 101, 114, 127 and 137 set the **AccessibleName** properties of all the controls (again including the Form). The **IsAccessible** property is not visible in the **Properties** window during design time, so we must write code to set it to **true**. Line 12 sets the **IsAccessible** property of **TextToSpeech** to **true**. Lines 17–20 loop through each control on the form and set each **IsAccessible** property to **true**. The Form and all its controls now will be visible to client accessibility applications.

20.8 Accessibility in XHTML Tables

Complex Web pages often contain tables that format content and present data. However, many screen readers are incapable of translating tables correctly unless developers design the tables with screen-reader requirements in mind. For example, the *CAST eReader*, a screen reader developed by the Center for Applied Special Technology (**www.cast.org**), starts at the top-left-hand cell and reads columns from left to right, top to bottom. This technique of reading data from a table is referred to as *linearized*. Figure 20.15 creates a simple table listing the costs of various fruits; later, we provide this table to the CAST eReader to demonstrate its linear reading of the table. The CAST eReader reads the table in Fig. 20.15 as follows:

> *Price of Fruit Fruit Price Apple $0.25 Orange $0.50 Banana $1.00 Pineapple $2.00*

This reading does not present the content of the table adequately: The reading neither specifies caption and header information nor links data contained in cells to the column headers that describe them. WCAG 1.0 recommends using Cascading Style Sheets (CSS) instead of tables, unless a table's content linearizes in an understandable manner.

```
1   <?xml version = "1.0"?>
2   <!DOCTYPE html PUBLIC "-//W3C//DTD XHTML 1.0 Strict//EN"
3       "http://www.w3.org/TR/xhtml1/DTD/xhtml1-strict.dtd">
4
5   <!-- Fig. 20.15: withoutheaders.html -->
6   <!-- Table without headers.          -->
7
8   <html xmlns = "http://www.w3.org/1999/xhtml">
9      <head>
10        <title>XHTML Table Without Headers</title>
11
12        <style type = "text/css">
13           body { background-color: #ccffaa;
14                  text-align: center }
15        </style>
16     </head>
17
```

Fig. 20.15 XHTML table without accessibility modifications. (Part 1 of 2.)

```
18      <body>
19
20         <p>Price of Fruit</p>
21
22         <table border = "1" width = "50%">
23
24            <tr>
25               <td>Fruit</td>
26               <td>Price</td>
27            </tr>
28
29            <tr>
30               <td>Apple</td>
31               <td>$0.25</td>
32            </tr>
33
34            <tr>
35               <td>Orange</td>
36               <td>$0.50</td>
37            </tr>
38
39            <tr>
40               <td>Banana</td>
41               <td>$1.00</td>
42            </tr>
43
44            <tr>
45               <td>Pineapple</td>
46               <td>$2.00</td>
47            </tr>
48
49         </table>
50
51      </body>
52   </html>
```

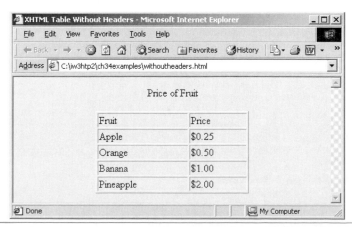

Fig. 20.15 XHTML table without accessibility modifications. (Part 2 of 2.)

If the table in Fig. 20.15 were large, the screen reader's linearized reading would be even more confusing to users. However, modifying the **<td>** tag with the **headers** attribute and modifying *header cells* (cells specified by the **<th>** tag) with the **id** attribute causes the table to be read as intended. Figure 20.16 demonstrates how these modifications change the way in which a screen reader interprets the table.

```
1   <?xml version = "1.0"?>
2   <!DOCTYPE html PUBLIC "-//W3C//DTD XHTML 1.0 Strict//EN"
3      "http://www.w3.org/TR/xhtml1/DTD/xhtml1-strict.dtd">
4
5   <!-- Fig. 20.16: withheaders.html   -->
6   <!-- Table with headers.            -->
7
8   <html xmlns = "http://www.w3.org/1999/xhtml">
9      <head>
10        <title>XHTML Table With Headers</title>
11
12        <style type = "text/css">
13           body { background-color: #ccffaa;
14                  text-align: center }
15        </style>
16     </head>
17
18     <body>
19
20     <!-- This table uses the id and headers attributes to    -->
21     <!-- ensure readability by text-based browsers. It also   -->
22     <!-- uses a summary attribute, used by screen readers to   -->
23     <!-- describe the table.                               -->
24
25        <table width = "50%" border = "1"
26           summary = "This table uses th elements and id and
27           headers attributes to make the table readable
28           by screen readers">
29
30           <caption><strong>Price of Fruit</strong></caption>
31
32           <tr>
33              <th id = "fruit">Fruit</th>
34              <th id = "price">Price</th>
35           </tr>
36
37           <tr>
38              <td headers = "fruit">Apple</td>
39              <td headers = "price">$0.25</td>
40           </tr>
41
42           <tr>
43              <td headers = "fruit">Orange</td>
44              <td headers = "price">$0.50</td>
45           </tr>
46
47           <tr>
48              <td headers = "fruit">Banana</td>
49              <td headers = "price">$1.00</td>
```

Fig. 20.16 Table optimized for screen reading, using attribute **headers**. (Part 1 of 2.)

```
50            </tr>
51
52            <tr>
53               <td headers = "fruit">Pineapple</td>
54               <td headers = "price">$2.00</td>
55            </tr>
56
57         </table>
58
59      </body>
60   </html>
```

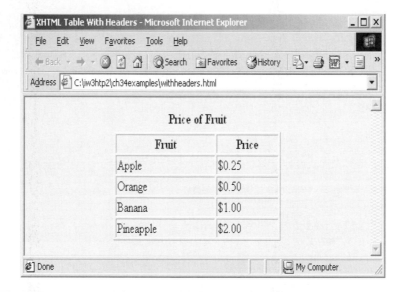

Fig. 20.16 Table optimized for screen reading, using attribute **headers**. (Part 2 of 2.)

This table does not appear to be different from the standard XHTML table shown in Fig. 20.15. However, the formatting of this table allows a screen reader to read the contained data more intelligently. A screen reader vocalizes the data from the table in Fig. 20.16 as follows:

```
Caption: Price of Fruit
Summary: This table uses th elements and id and headers
attributes to make the table readable by screen readers
Fruit: Apple, Price: $0.25
Fruit: Orange, Price: $0.50
Fruit: Banana, Price: $1.00
Fruit: Pineapple, Price: $2.00
```

Every cell in the table is preceded by its corresponding header when read by the screen reader. This format helps the listener understand the table. The **headers** *attribute* is intended specifically for use in tables that hold large amounts of data. Most small tables linearize fairly well, as long as the **<th>** tag is used properly. We also suggest using the

summary attribute and **caption** element to enhance clarity. To view additional examples that demonstrate how to make tables accessible, visit **www.w3.org/TR/WCAG**.

20.9 Accessibility in XHTML Frames

Web designers often use frames to display more than one XHTML file in a single browser window. Frames are a convenient way to ensure that certain content always displays on the screen. Unfortunately, frames often lack proper descriptions and thus hinder users with text-based browsers and users listening via speech synthesizers from navigating the Web site.

A site that uses frames must provide a meaningful description of each frame in the frame's **<title>** tag. Examples of good titles include "*Navigation Frame*" and "*Main Content Frame.*" Users navigating via text-based browsers, such as Lynx, must choose which frame they want to open; descriptive titles make this choice simpler. However, the assignment of titles to frames does not solve all the navigation problems associated with frames. Web designers also should use the **<noframes>** tag, which provides alternative content for browsers that do not support frames.

Look-and-Feel Observation 20.1

Always provide titles for frames to ensure that user agents that do not support frames have alternatives.

Look-and-Feel Observation 20.2

Include a title for each frame's contents with the **frame** *element; if possible, provide links to the individual pages within the frameset, so that users still can navigate through the Web pages. To provide alternative content to browsers that do not support frames, use the* **<noframes>** *tag. This also improves access for browsers that offer limited support for frames.*

WCAG 1.0 suggests using Cascading Style Sheets (CSS) as an alternative to frames, because CSS can provide similar functionality and is highly customizible. Unfortunately, the ability to display multiple XHTML documents in a single browser window requires the complete support of HTML 4, which is not widespread. However, the second generation of Cascading Style Sheets (CSS2) can display a single document as if it were several documents. CSS2 is not yet fully supported by many user agents.

20.10 Accessibility in XML

XML gives developers the freedom to create new markup languages. Although this feature provides many advantages, the new languages might not incorporate accessibility features. To prevent the proliferation of inaccessible languages, the WAI is developing guidelines—the *XML Guidelines (XML GL)*—to facilitate the creation of accessible XML documents. The XML Guidelines recommend including a text description, similar to XHTML's **<alt>** tag, for each nontext object on a page. To enhance accessibility further, element types should allow grouping and classification and should identify important content. Without an accessible user interface, other efforts to implement accessibility are less effective. Therefore, it is essential to create stylesheets that can produce multiple outputs, including document outlines.

Many XML languages, including Synchronized Multimedia Integration Language (SMIL) and Scalable Vector Graphics (SVG), have implemented several of the WAI guidelines. The WAI XML Accessibility Guidelines can be found at **www.w3.org/WAI/PF/xmlgl.htm.**

20.11 Using Voice Synthesis and Recognition with VoiceXML™

A joint effort by AT&T,® IBM,® Lucent™ and Motorola® has created an XML vocabulary that marks up information for use by *speech synthesizers*, or tools that enable computers to speak to users. This technology, called *VoiceXML*, can provide tremendous benefits to people with visual impairments and to people who are illiterate. VoiceXML-enabled applications read Web pages to the user and then employ *speech recognition* technology to understand words spoken into a microphone. An example of a speech-recognition tool is IBM's *ViaVoice* (**www-4.ibm.com/software/speech**). To learn more about speech recognition and synthesis, consult Chapter 16, Graphics and Multimedia.

The VoiceXML interpreter and the VoiceXML browser process VoiceXML. In the future, Web browsers might incorporate these interpreters. VoiceXML is derived from XML, so VoiceXML is platform independent. When a VoiceXML document is loaded, a *voice server* sends a message to the VoiceXML browser and begins a verbal conversation between the user and the computer.

The IBM *WebSphere Voice Server SDK 1.5* is a VoiceXML interpreter that can be used to test VoiceXML documents on the desktop. To download the VoiceServer SDK, visit **www.alphaworks.ibm.com/tech/voiceserversdk**. [*Note*: To run the VoiceXML program in Fig. 20.17, download *Java 2 Platform Standard Edition* (Java SDK) 1.3 from **www.java.sun.com/j2se/1.3**. Installation instructions for both the VoiceServerSDK and the Java SDK are located on the Deitel & Associates, Inc., Web site at **www.deitel.com**.]

Figure 20.17 and Fig. 20.18 depict examples of VoiceXML that could be included on a Web site. The computer speaks a document's text to the user, and the text embedded in the VoiceXML tags enables verbal interaction between the user and the browser. The output included in Fig. 20.18 demonstrates a conversation that might take place between a user and a computer after these documents have been loaded.

```
1   <?xml version = "1.0"?>
2   <vxml version = "1.0">
3
4   <!-- Fig. 20.17: main.vxml -->
5   <!-- Voice page.           -->
6
7   <link next = "#home">
8      <grammar>home</grammar>
9   </link>
10
11  <link next = "#end">
12     <grammar>exit</grammar>
13  </link>
14
15  <var name = "currentOption" expr = "'home'"/>
16
17  <form>
18     <block>
19        <emp>Welcome</emp> to the voice page of Deitel and
20        Associates. To exit any time say "exit".
```

Fig. 20.17 Home page written in VoiceXML. (Part 1 of 3.)

```
21          To go to the home page any time say "home".
22      </block>
23
24      <subdialog src = "#home"/>
25  </form>
26
27  <menu id = "home">
28      <prompt count = "1" timeout = "10s">
29          You have just entered the Deitel home page.
30          Please make a selection by speaking one of the
31          following options:
32          <break msecs = "1000" />
33          <enumerate/>
34      </prompt>
35
36      <prompt count = "2">
37          Please say one of the following.
38          <break msecs = "1000" />
39          <enumerate/>
40      </prompt>
41
42      <choice next = "#about">About us</choice>
43      <choice next = "#directions">Driving directions</choice>
44      <choice next = "publications.vxml">Publications</choice>
45  </menu>
46
47  <form id = "about">
48      <block>
49          About Deitel and Associates, Inc.
50          Deitel and Associates, Inc. is an internationally
51          recognized corporate training and publishing
52          organization, specializing in programming languages,
53          Internet and World Wide Web technology and object
54          technology education. Deitel and Associates, Inc. is a
55          member of the World Wide Web Consortium. The company
56          provides courses on Java, C++, Visual Basic, C, Internet
57          and World Wide Web programming and Object Technology.
58          <assign name = "currentOption" expr = "'about'"/>
59          <goto next = "#repeat"/>
60      </block>
61  </form>
62
63  <form id = "directions">
64      <block>
65          Directions to Deitel and Associates, Inc. We are located at
66          <sayas class = "digits">12</sayas>
67          Clock Tower Place, suite
68
69          <sayas class = "digits">200</sayas>,
70          in Maynard, Massachusetts.
71          <assign name = "currentOption" expr = "'directions'"/>
72          <goto next = "#repeat"/>
73      </block>
74  </form>
```

Fig. 20.17 Home page written in VoiceXML. (Part 2 of 3.)

```
74
75    <form id = "repeat">
76       <field name = "confirm" type = "boolean">
77          <prompt>
78             To repeat say "yes". To go back to home, say "no".
79          </prompt>
80
81          <filled>
82             <if cond = "confirm == true">
83                <goto expr = "'#' + currentOption"/>
84             <else/>
85                <goto next = "#home"/>
86             </if>
87          </filled>
88
89       </field>
90    </form>
91
92    <form id = "end">
93       <block>
94          Thank you for visiting Deitel and Associates voice page.
95          Have a nice day.
96          <exit/>
97       </block>
98    </form>
99
100   </vxml>
```

Fig. 20.17 Home page written in VoiceXML. (Part 3 of 3.)

```
101   <?xml version = "1.0"?>
102   <vxml version = "1.0">
103
104   <!-- Fig. 20.18: publications.vxml       -->
105   <!-- Voice page for various publications. -->
106
107   <link next = "main.vxml#home">
108      <grammar>home</grammar>
109   </link>
110
111   <link next = "main.vxml#end">
112      <grammar>exit</grammar>
113   </link>
114
115   <link next = "#publication">
116      <grammar>menu</grammar>
```

```
117   </link>
118
119   <var name = "currentOption" expr = "'home'"/>
120
121   <menu id = "publication">
122
```

Fig. 20.18 Publication page of Deitel and Associates' VoiceXML page. (Part 1 of 4.)

```
123    <prompt count = "1" timeout = "12s">
124        Following are some of our publications. For more
125        information visit our web page at www.deitel.com.
126        To repeat the following menu, say menu at any time.
127        Please select by saying one of the following books:
128        <break msecs = "1000" />
129        <enumerate/>
130    </prompt>
131
132    <prompt count = "2">
133        Please select from the following books.
134        <break msecs = "1000" />
135        <enumerate/>
136    </prompt>
137
138    <choice next = "#java">Java.</choice>
139    <choice next = "#c">C.</choice>
140    <choice next = "#cplus">C plus plus.</choice>
141 </menu>
142
143 <form id = "java">
144    <block>
145        Java How to program, third edition.
146        The complete, authoritative introduction to Java.
147        Java is revolutionizing software development with
148        multimedia-intensive, platform-independent,
149        object-oriented code for conventional, Internet,
150        Intranet and Extranet-based applets and applications.
151        This Third Edition of the world's most widely used
152        university-level Java textbook carefully explains
153        Java's extraordinary capabilities.
154        <assign name = "currentOption" expr = "'java'"/>
155        <goto next = "#repeat"/>
156    </block>
157 </form>
158
159 <form id = "c">
160    <block>
161        C How to Program, third edition.
162        This is the long-awaited, thorough revision to the
163        world's best-selling introductory C book! The book's
164        powerful "teach by example" approach is based on
165        more than 10,000 lines of live code, thoroughly
166        explained and illustrated with screen captures showing
167        detailed output.World-renowned corporate trainers and
168        best-selling authors Harvey and Paul Deitel offer the
169        most comprehensive, practical introduction to C ever
170        published with hundreds of hands-on exercises, more

171        than 250 complete programs written and documented for
172        easy learning, and exceptional insight into good
173        programming practices, maximizing performance, avoiding
174        errors, debugging, and testing. New features include
175        thorough introductions to C++, Java, and object-oriented
176        programming that build directly on the C skills taught
```

Fig. 20.18 Publication page of Deitel and Associates' VoiceXML page. (Part 2 of 4.)

```
177        in this book; coverage of graphical user interface
178        development and C library functions; and many new,
179        substantial hands-on projects.For anyone who wants to
180        learn C, improve their existing C skills, and understand
181        how C serves as the foundation for C++, Java, and
182        object-oriented development.
183        <assign name = "currentOption" expr = "'c'"/>
184        <goto next = "#repeat"/>
185     </block>
186  </form>
187
188  <form id = "cplus">
189     <block>
190        The C++ how to program, second edition.
191        With nearly 250,000 sold, Harvey and Paul Deitel's C++
192        How to Program is the world's best-selling introduction
193        to C++ programming. Now, this classic has been thoroughly
194        updated! The new, full-color Third Edition has been
195        completely revised to reflect the ANSI C++ standard, add
196        powerful new coverage of object analysis and design with
197        UML, and give beginning C++ developers even better live
198        code examples and real-world projects. The Deitels' C++
199        How to Program is the most comprehensive, practical
200        introduction to C++ ever published with hundreds of
201        hands-on exercises, roughly 250 complete programs written
202        and documented for easy learning, and exceptional insight
203        into good programming practices, maximizing performance,
204        avoiding errors, debugging, and testing. This new Third
205        Edition covers every key concept and technique ANSI C++
206        developers need to master: control structures, functions,
207        arrays, pointers and strings, classes and data
208        abstraction, operator overloading, inheritance, virtual
209        functions, polymorphism, I/O, templates, exception
210        handling, file processing, data structures, and more. It
211        also includes a detailed introduction to Standard
212        Template Library containers, container adapters,
213        algorithms, and iterators.
214        <assign name = "currentOption" expr = "'cplus'"/>
215        <goto next = "#repeat"/>
216     </block>
217  </form>
218
219  <form id = "repeat">
220     <field name = "confirm" type = "boolean">
221
222        <prompt>
223           To repeat say "yes". Say "no", to go back to home.
224        </prompt>
225
226        <filled>
227           <if cond = "confirm == true">
228              <goto expr = "'#' + currentOption"/>
229           <else/>
230              <goto next = "#publication"/>
```

Fig. 20.18 Publication page of Deitel and Associates' VoiceXML page. (Part 3 of 4.)

```
231               </if>
232            </filled>
233         </field>
234      </form>
235   </vxml>
```

Computer speaks:
**Welcome to the voice page of Deitel and Associates. To exit any time
say exit. To go to the home page any time say home.**

User speaks:
Home

Computer speaks:
**You have just entered the Deitel home page. Please make a selection
by speaking one of the following options: About us, Driving directions, Publications.**

User speaks:
Driving directions

Computer speaks:
**Directions to Deitel and Associates, Inc.
We are located at 12 Clock Tower Place,
suite 200, in Maynard, Massachusetts.
To repeat say yes. To go back to home, say no.**

Fig. 20.18 Publication page of Deitel and Associates' VoiceXML page. (Part 4 of 4.)

A VoiceXML document contains a series of dialogs and subdialogs, resulting in
spoken interaction between the user and the computer. The **<form>** and **<menu>** tags
implement the dialogs. A *form* element both presents information to the user and gathers
data from the user. A *menu* element provides the user with list options and then transfers
control to another dialog in response to the user's selection.

Lines 7–9 (of Fig. 20.17) use element *link* to create an active link to the home page.
Attribute *next* specifies the URL to which the browser is directed when a user selects the
link. Element *grammar* marks up the text that the user must speak to select the link. In the
link element, we navigate to the element containing **id home** when a user speaks the
word **home**. Lines 11–13 use element **link** to create a link to **id end** when a user speaks
the word **exit**.

Lines 17–25 create a form dialog, using element **form**, which collects information
from the user. Lines 18–22 present introductory text. Element **block**, which can exist only
within a **form** element, groups together elements that perform an action or an event. Element **emp** indicates that a section of text should be spoken with emphasis. If the level of
emphasis is not specified, then the default level—*moderate*—is used. Our example uses the
default level. [*Note*: To specify an emphasis level, use the **level** attribute. This attribute
accepts the following values: *strong*, *moderate*, *none* and *reduced*.]

The **menu** element in line 27 enables users to select the page to which they would like to
link. The *choice* element, which always is part of either a **menu** or a **form**, presents the

options. The **next** attribute indicates the page that is loaded when a user makes a selection. The user selects a **choice** element by speaking the text marked up between the tags into a microphone. In this example, the first and second **choice** elements in lines 42–43 transfer control to a *local dialog* (i.e., a location within the same document) when they are selected. The third **choice** element transfers the user to the document **publications.vxml**. Lines 28–34 use element **prompt** to instruct the user to make a selection. Attribute **count** maintains a record of the number of times that a prompt is spoken (i.e., each time the computer reads a prompt, **count** increments by one). The **count** attribute transfers control to another prompt once a certain limit has been reached. Attribute **timeout** specifies how long the program should wait, after outputting the prompt, for users to respond. In the event that the user does not respond before the timeout period expires, lines 36–40 provide a second, shorter prompt that reminds the user to make a selection.

When the user chooses the **publications** option, **publications.vxml** (Fig. 20.18) loads into the browser. Lines 107–113 define **link** elements that provide links to **main.vxml**. Lines 115–117 provide links to the **menu** element (lines 121–141), which asks users to select one of the following publications: Java, C or C++. The **form** elements in lines 143–217 describe books that correspond to these topics. Once the browser speaks the description, control transfers to the **form** element with an **id** attribute whose value equals **repeat** (lines 219–234).

Figure 20.19 provides a brief description of each VoiceXML tag that we used in the previous example (Fig. 20.18).

VoiceXML Tag	Description
<assign>	Assigns a value to a variable.
<block>	Presents information to users without any interaction between the user and the computer (i.e., the computer does not expect any input from the user).
<break>	Instructs the computer to pause its speech output for a specified period of time.
<choice>	Specifies an option in a *menu* element.
<enumerate>	Lists all the available options to the user.
<exit>	Exits the program.
<filled>	Contains elements that execute when the computer receives input for a *form* element from the user.
<form>	Gathers information from the user for a set of variables.
<goto>	Transfers control from one dialog to another.
<grammar>	Specifies grammar for the expected input from the user.
<if>, *<else>*, *<elseif>*	Indicates a control statement used for making logic decisions.

Fig. 20.19 VoiceXML tags. (Part 1 of 2.)

VoiceXML Tag	Description
`<link>`	Performs a transfer of control similar to the *goto* statement, but a *link* can be executed at any time during the program's execution.
`<menu>`	Provides user options and then transfers control to other dialogs on the basis of the selected option.
`<prompt>`	Specifies text to be read to users when they must make a selection.
`<subdialog>`	Calls another dialog. After executing the subdialog, the calling dialog resumes control.
`<var>`	Declares a variable.
`<vxml>`	Top-level tag that specifies that the document should be processed by a VoiceXML interpreter.

Fig. 20.19 VoiceXML tags. (Part 2 of 2.)

20.12 CallXML™

Another advancement benefiting people with visual impairments is *CallXML*, a voice technology created and supported by *Voxeo* (**www.voxeo.com**). CallXML creates phone-to-Web applications that control incoming and outgoing telephone calls. Examples of CallXML applications include voice mail, interactive voice-response systems and Internet call waiting. VoiceXML allows computers to read Web pages to users with visual impairments; CallXML reads Web content to users via a telephone. CallXML has important implications for individuals who do not have a computer, but do have a telephone.

When users access CallXML applications, a text-to-speech (TTS) engine converts text to an automated voice. The TTS engine then reads information contained within CallXML elements to the users. CallXML applications are tailored to respond to input from callers. [*Note*: Users must have a touch-tone phone to access CallXML applications.]

Typically, CallXML applications play prerecorded audio clips or text as output, requesting responses as input. An audio clip might contain a greeting that introduces callers to the application, or it might recite a menu of options, requesting that callers make a touch-tone entry. Certain applications, such as voice mail, might require both verbal and touch-tone input. Once the application receives the necessary input, it responds by invoking CallXML elements (such as **text**) that contain the information a TTS engine reads to users. If the application does not receive input within a designated time frame, it prompts the user to enter valid input.

When a user accesses a CallXML application, the incoming telephone call is referred to as a session. A CallXML application can support multiple sessions, so the application can process multiple telephone calls at once. Each session is independent of the others and is assigned a unique sessionID for identification. A session terminates either when the user hangs up the telephone or when the CallXML application invokes the **hangup** element.

Our first CallXML application demonstrates the classic "Hello World" example (Fig. 20.20). The **<callxml>** tag in line 6 declares that the content is a CallXML document. Line 7 contains the **Hello World text**. All text that is to be spoken by a text-to-speech (TTS) engine must be placed within **<text>** tags.

To deploy a CallXML application, register with the *Voxeo* Community (**community.voxeo.com**), a Web resource that facilitates the creation, debugging and deployment of phone applications. For the most part, Voxeo resources are free, but the company does charge fees when CallXML applications are deployed commercially. The Voxeo Community assigns a unique telephone number to each CallXML application so that external users can access and interact with the application. [*Note*: Voxeo assigns telephone numbers only to applications that reside on the Internet. If you have access to a Web server (such as IIS, PWS or Apache), use it to post your CallXML application. Otherwise, open an Internet account through one of the many Internet-service companies (e.g, **geocities.yahoo.com**, **angelfire.lycos.com**, **www.stormpages.com**, **www.freewebsites.com** or **www.brinkster.com**). These companies allow individuals to post documents on the Internet, using their Web servers.]

```
1   <?xml version = "1.0" encoding = "UTF-8"?>
2
3   <!-- Fig. 20.20: hello.xml          -->
4   <!-- The classic Hello World example. -->
5
6   <callxml>
7      <text>Hello World.</text>
8   </callxml>
```

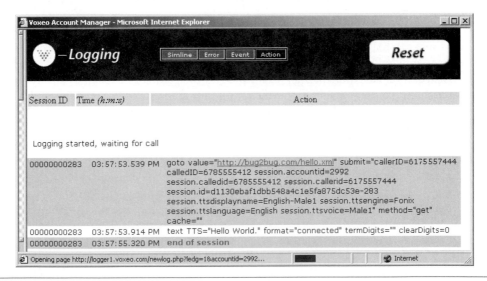

Fig. 20.20 Hello World CallXML example. (Courtesy of Voxeo, © Voxeo Corporation 2000–2002.)

Figure 20.20 also demonstrates the *logging* feature of the **Voxeo Account Manager**, which is accessible to registered members. The logging feature records and displays the "conversation" between the user and the application. The first row of the logging feature lists the URL of the CallXML application and the *global variables* associated with that session. When a session begins, the application creates and assigns values to global variables that the entire application can access and modify. The subsequent row(s) display the "conversation." This example demonstrates a one-way conversation (i.e., the application does not accept any input from the user) in which the TTS engine says **Hello World**. The last row displays the **end of session** message, which states that the phone call has terminated. The logging feature assists developers in the debugging of their applications. By observing a CallXML "conversation," a developer can determine the point at which the application terminates. If the application terminates abruptly ("crashes"), the logging feature displays information regarding the type and location of the error, pointing the developer toward the section of the application that is causing the problem.

The next example (Fig. 20.21) depicts a CallXML application that reads the ISBN numbers of three Deitel textbooks—*Internet and World Wide Web How to Program: Second Edition*, *XML How to Program* and *Java How to Program: Fourth Edition*—on the basis of a user's touch-tone input. [*Note*: The code has been formatted for presentation purposes.]

```
1   <?xml version = "1.0" encoding = "UTF-8"?>
2
3   <!-- Fig. 20.21: isbn.xml                          -->
4   <!-- Reads the ISBN value of three Deitel books -->
5
6   <callxml>
7      <block>
8         <text>
9            Welcome. To obtain the ISBN of the Internet and World
10           Wide Web How to Program: Second Edition, please enter 1.
11           To obtain the ISBN of the XML How to Program,
12           please enter 2. To obtain the ISBN of the Java How
13           to Program: Fourth Ediplease enter 3. To exit the
14           application, please enter 4.
15        </text>
16
17        <!-- Obtains the numeric value entered by the user and -->
18        <!-- stores it in the variable ISBN. The user has 60   -->
19        <!-- seconds to enter one numeric value               -->
20        <getDigits var = "ISBN"
21           maxDigits = "1"
22           termDigits = "1234"
23           maxTime = "60s" />
24
25        <!-- Requests that the user enter a valid numeric -->

26        <!-- value after the elapsed time of 60 seconds   -->
27        <onMaxSilence>
28           <text>
29              Please enter either 1, 2, 3 or 4.
30           </text>
```

Fig. 20.21 CallXML example that reads three ISBN values. (Part 1 of 3.) (Courtesy of Voxeo, © Voxeo Corporation 2000–2002.)

```
31
32            <getDigits var = "ISBN"
33                termDigits = "1234"
34                maxDigits = "1"
35                maxTime = "60s" />
36
37          </onMaxSilence>
38
39          <onTermDigit value = "1">
40              <text>
41                  The ISBN for the Internet book is 0130308978.
42                  Thank you for calling our CallXML application.
43                  Good-bye.
44              </text>
45          </onTermDigit>
46
47          <onTermDigit value = "2">
48              <text>
49                  The ISBN for the XML book is 0130284173.
50                  Thank you for calling our CallXML application.
51                  Good-bye.
52              </text>
53          </onTermDigit>
54
55          <onTermDigit value = "3">
56              <text>
57                  The ISBN for the Java book is 0130341517.
58                  Thank you for calling our CallXML application.
59                  Good-bye.
60              </text>
61          </onTermDigit>
62
63          <onTermDigit value = "4">
64              <text>
65                  Thank you for calling our CallXML application.
66                  Good-bye.
67              </text>
68          </onTermDigit>
69      </block>
70
71      <!-- Event handler that terminates the call -->
72      <onHangup />
73  </callxml>
```

Fig. 20.21 CallXML example that reads three ISBN values. (Part 2 of 3.) (Courtesy of Voxeo, © Voxeo Corporation 2000–2002.)

Fig. 20.21 CallXML example that reads three ISBN values. (Part 3 of 3.) (Courtesy of Voxeo, © Voxeo Corporation 2000–2002.)

The **<block>** tag (line 7) encapsulates other CallXML tags. Usually, sets of CallXML tags that perform similar tasks are enclosed within **<block>**...**</block>**. The **block** element in this example encapsulates the **<text>**, **<getDigits>**, **<onMaxSilence>** and **<onTermDigit>** tags. A **block** element also can be nested within other **block** elements.

Lines 20–23 contain some attributes of the **<getDigits>** tag. The **getDigits** element obtains the user's touch-tone response and stores it in the variable declared by the **var** attribute (i.e., **ISBN**). The **maxDigits** attribute (line 21) indicates the maximum number of digits that the application can accept. This application accepts only one character. If no maximum is stated, then the application uses the default value, *nolimit*.

The **termDigits** attribute (line 22) contains the list of characters that terminate user input. When a user inputs a character from this list, the application is notified that it has received the last acceptable input; any character entered after this point is invalid. These characters do not terminate the call; they simply notify the application to proceed to the next instruction, because the necessary input has been received. In our example, the values for **termDigits** are **1**, **2**, **3** and **4**. The default value for **termDigits** is the null value (**""**).

The **maxTime** attribute (line 23) indicates the maximum amount of time that the application will wait for a user response. If the user fails to enter input within the given time frame, then the CallXML application invokes the event handler **onMaxSilence**. The default value for this attribute is 30 seconds.

The *onMaxSilence* element (lines 27–37) is an event handler that is invoked when attribute **maxTime** (or **maxSilence**) expires. The event handler notifies the application of the appropriate action to perform when a user fails to respond. In this case, the application asks the user to enter a value, because the **maxTime** has expired. After receiving input, **getDigits** (line 32) stores the entered value in the **ISBN** variable.

The *onTermDigit* element (lines 39–68) is an event handler that notifies the application of the appropriate action to perform when a user selects one of the **termDigits** characters. At least one **<onTermDigit>** tag must be associated with (i.e., must appear after) the **get-Digits** element, even if the default value (**" "**) is used. We provide four actions that the application can perform in response to the specific **termDigits** value entered by the user. For example, if the user enters **1**, the application reads the ISBN value for the *Internet and World Wide Web How to Program: Second Edition* textbook.

Line 72 contains the **<onHangup/>** event handler, which terminates the telephone call when the user hangs up the telephone. Our **<onHangup>** event handler is an empty tag (i.e., no action is performed when this tag is invoked).

The logging feature (Fig. 20.21) displays the "conversation" between the application and the user. As in the previous example, the first row specifies the URL of the application and the global variables of the session. The subsequent rows display the "conversation": The application asks the caller which ISBN value to read; the caller enters **1** (*Internet and World Wide Web How to Program: Second Edition*), and the application reads the corresponding ISBN. The **end of session** message states that the application has terminated.

We provide brief descriptions of various logic and action CallXML elements in Fig. 20.22. *Logic elements* assign values to, and clear values from, the session variables; *action elements* perform specified tasks, such as answering and terminating a telephone call during the current session. A complete list of CallXML elements is available at

> **www.oasis-open.org/cover/callxmlv2.html**

Elements	Description
assign	Assigns a **value** to a variable, **var**.
clear	Clears the contents of the **var** attribute.
clearDigits	Clears all digits that the user has entered.
goto	Navigates to another section of the current CallXML application or to a different CallXML application. The **value** attribute specifies the URL of the invoked application. The **submit** attribute lists the variables that are passed to the invoked application. The **method** attribute states whether to use the HTTP *get* or *post* request type when sending and retrieving information. A *get* request retrieves data from a Web server without modifying the contents, whereas the *post* request receives modified data.

Fig. 20.22 CallXML elements. (Part 1 of 2.)

Elements	Description
run	Starts a new CallXML session for each call. The **value** attribute specifies the CallXML application to retrieve. The **submit** attribute lists the variables that are passed to the invoked application. The **method** attribute states whether to use the HTTP *get* or *post* request type. The **var** attribute stores the identification number of the session.
sendEvent	Allows multiple sessions to exchange messages. The **value** attribute stores the message, and the **session** attribute specifies the identification number of the session that receives the message.
answer	Answers an incoming telephone call.
call	Calls the URL specified by the **value** attribute. The **callerID** attribute contains the phone number that is displayed on a CallerID device. The **maxTime** attribute specifies the length of time to wait for the call to be answered before disconnecting.
conference	Connects multiple sessions so that individuals can participate in a conference call. The **targetSessions** attribute specifies the identification numbers of the sessions, and the **termDigits** attribute indicates the touch-tone keys that terminate the call.
wait	Waits for user input. The **value** attribute specifies how long to wait. The **termDigits** attribute indicates the touch-tone keys that terminate the **wait** element.
play	Plays an audio file or pronounces a value that is stored as a number, date or amount of money and is indicated by the **format** attribute. The **value** attribute contains the information (location of the audio file, number, date or amount of money) that corresponds to the **format** attribute. The **clearDigits** attribute specifies whether or not to delete the previously entered input. The **termDigits** attribute indicates the touch-tone keys that terminate the audio file, etc.
recordAudio	Records an audio file and stores it at the URL specified by **value**. The **format** attribute indicates the file extension of the audio clip. Other attributes include **termDigits**, **clearDigits**, **maxTime** and **maxSilence**.

Fig. 20.22 CallXML elements. (Part 2 of 2.)

20.13 JAWS® for Windows

JAWS (Job Access with Sound) is one of the leading screen readers currently on the market. Henter-Joyce, a division of Freedom Scientific,™ created this application to help people with visual impairments interact with technology.

To download a demonstration version of JAWS, visit **www.freedomscientific.com**. The JAWS demo is fully functional and includes an extensive, highly customized help system. Users can select the voice that "reads" Web content and the rate at which text is spoken. Users also can create keyboard shortcuts. Although the demo is in English, the full version of JAWS allows the user to choose any one of several supported languages.

JAWS also includes special key commands for popular programs, such as Microsoft Internet Explorer and Microsoft Word. For example, when browsing in Internet Explorer, JAWS' capabilities extend beyond the reading of content on the screen. If JAWS is enabled, pressing *Insert + F7* in Internet Explorer opens a **Links List** dialog, which displays all the links available on a Web page. For more information about JAWS and the other products offered by Henter-Joyce, visit **www.free-domscientific.com**.

20.14 Other Accessibility Tools

Many accessibility products are available to assist people with disabilities. One such technology, Microsoft's *Active Accessibility*®, establishes a protocol by which an accessibility aid can retrieve information about an application's user interface in a consistent manner. Accessibility aids require such information as the name, location and layout of particular GUI elements within an application, so that the accessibility aid can render the information properly to the intended audience. Active Accessibility also enables software developers and accessibility-aid developers to design programs and products that are compatible with each other. Moreover, Active Accessibility is packaged in two components, enabling both programmers and individuals who use accessibility aids to employ the software. The *Software Development Kit (SDK)* component is intended for programmers: It includes testing tools, programmatic libraries and header files. The *Redistribution Kit (RDK)* component is intended for those who use accessibility aids: It installs a runtime component into the Microsoft operating system. Accessibility aids use the Active Accessibility runtime component to interact with and obtain information from any application software. For more information on Active Accessibility, visit

```
www.msdn.microsoft.com/library/default.asp?url=/nhp/
Default.asp?contentid=28000544
```

Another important accessibility tool for individuals with visual impairments is the *braille keyboard*. In addition to providing keys labeled with the letters they represent, a braille keyboard also has the equivalent braille symbol printed on each key. Most often, braille keyboards are combined with a speech synthesizer or a braille display, enabling users to interact with the computer to verify that their typing is correct.

Speech synthesis also provides benefits to people with disabilities. *Speech synthesizers* have been used for many years to aid people who are unable to communicate verbally. However, the growing popularity of the Web has prompted a surge of interest in the fields of speech synthesis and speech recognition. Now, these technologies are allowing individuals with disabilities to use computers more than ever before. The development of speech synthesizers also is enabling the improvement of other technologies, such as VoiceXML and *AuralCSS* (**www.w3.org/TR/REC-CSS2/aural.html**). These tools allow people with visual impairments and illiterate people to access Web sites.

Despite the existence of adaptive software and hardware for people with visual impairments, the accessibility of computers and the Internet is still hampered by the high costs, rapid obsolescence and unnecessary complexity of current technology. Moreover, almost all software currently available requires installation by a person who can see. *Ocularis* is a project launched in the open-source community that aims to address these problems. (Open-source software for people with visual impairments already exists; although it often is superior to its proprietary, closed-source counterparts, it has not yet reached its full potential.) Ocularis ensures that the blind can access and use all aspects of the Linux operating system. Products that integrate with Ocularis include word processors, calculators, basic finance applications, Internet browsers and e-mail clients. In addition, a screen reader is included for use with programs that have a command-line interface. The official Ocularis Web site is located at

`ocularis.sourceforge.net`

People with visual impairments are not the only beneficiaries of efforts to improve markup languages. People with hearing impairments also have a number of tools to help them interpret auditory information delivered over the Web. One of these tools, *Synchronized Multimedia Integration Language* (*SMIL*™), is designed to add extra *tracks* (layers of content found within a single audio or video file) to multimedia content. The additional tracks can contain closed captioning.

Technologies are being designed to help people with severe disabilities, such as quadriplegia, a form of paralysis that affects the body from the neck down. One such technology, *EagleEyes*, developed by researchers at Boston College (**www.bc.edu/eagleeyes**), is a system that translates eye movements into mouse movements. A user moves the mouse cursor by moving his or her eyes or head and is thereby able to control the computer.

GW Micro, Henter-Joyce and Adobe Systems, Inc., also are working on software that assists people with disabilities. Adobe Acrobat 5.0 complies with Microsoft's application programming interface (API) to allow businesses to provide information to a wider audience. JetForm Corp is also accommodating the needs of people with disabilities by developing server-based XML software. The new software allows users to download information in a format that best meets their needs.

There are many services on the Web that assist e-businesses in designing Web sites so that they are accessible to individuals with disabilities. For additional information, the U.S. Department of Justice (**www.usdoj.gov**) provides extensive resources detailing legal and technical issues related to people with disabilities.

20.15 Accessibility in Microsoft® Windows® XP

Because of the prominence of the Windows operating system, it is crucial that this operating system provide proper accessibility to individuals with disabilities. Beginning with Microsoft *Windows 95*, Microsoft has included accessibility features in its operating systems and many of its applications, including *Office 97*, *Office 2000* and *Netmeeting*. In Microsoft *Windows 2000* and *Windows XP*, Microsoft significantly enhanced the operating system's accessibility features. All the accessibility options provided by Windows XP are available through the ***Accessibility Wizard***, which guides users through Windows XP accessibility features and then configures users' computers in accordance with the chosen specifications. This section uses the **Accessibility Wizard** to guide users through the configuration of their Windows XP accessibility options.

To access the **Accessibility Wizard**, users' computers must be equipped with Microsoft Windows XP. Click the **Start** button and select **Programs**, followed by **Accessories**, **Accessibility** and **Accessibility Wizard**. When the wizard starts, the **Welcome** screen displays. Click **Next**. The next dialog asks the user to select a font size. Modify the font size if necessary; then, click **Next**.

Figure 20.23 depicts the **Display Settings** dialog. This dialog allows the user to activate the font-size settings chosen in the previous window, change the screen resolution, enable the *Microsoft Magnifier* (a program that displays an enlarged section of the screen in a separate window) and disable personalized menus. Personalized menus hide rarely used programs from the start menu and can be a hindrance to users with disabilities. Make appropriate selection, and click **Next**.

The **Set Wizard Options** dialog (Fig. 20.24) asks questions about the user's disabilities; the answers to these questions allow the **Accessibility Wizard** to customize Windows to suit the user's needs better. For demonstration purposes, we selected every type of disability included in the dialogue. Click **Next** to continue.

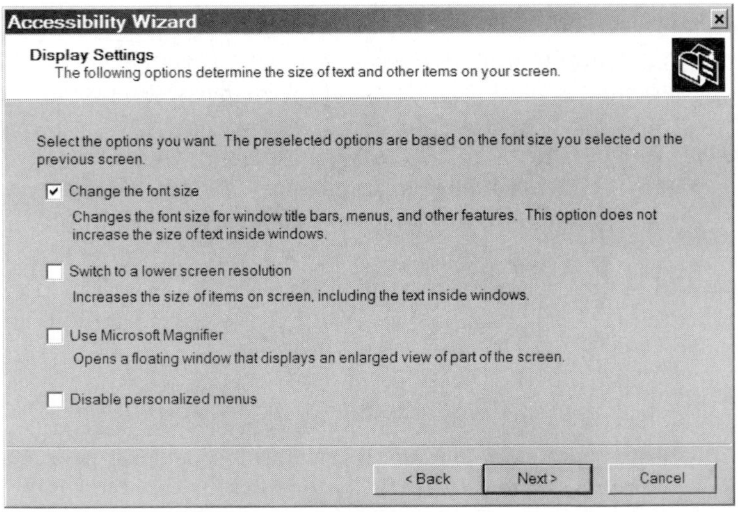

Fig. 20.23 Display Settings dialog.

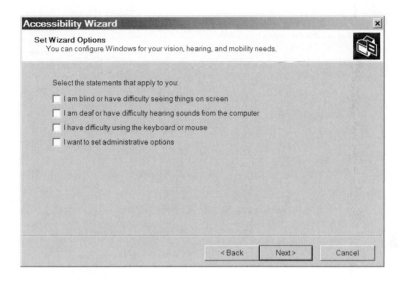

Fig. 20.24 Accessibility Wizard initialization options.

20.15.1 Tools for People with Visual Impairments

When we check all the options in Fig. 20.24, the wizard begins to configure Windows so that it is accessible to people with visual impairments. The dialog box shown in Fig. 20.25 allows the user to resize the scroll bars and window borders to increase their visibility. Click **Next** to proceed to the next dialog.

Figure 20.26 contains a dialog that allows the user to resize icons. Users with poor vision and users who are illiterate or have trouble reading benefit from large icons.

Clicking **Next** displays the **Display Color Settings** dialog (Fig. 20.27). These settings enable the user to change the Windows color scheme and resize various screen elements.

Click **Next** to view the dialog (Fig. 20.28) that enables customization of the mouse cursor. Anyone who has ever used a laptop computer knows how difficult it can be to see the mouse cursor. This is even more problematic for people with visual impairments. To address this problem, the wizard offers users the options of larger cursors, black cursors and cursors that invert the colors of objects underneath them. Click **Next**.

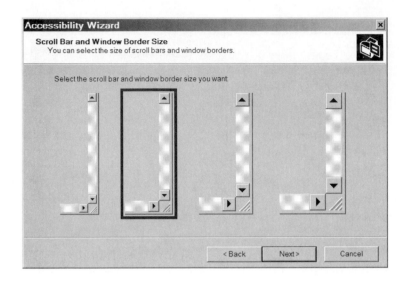

Fig. 20.25 Scroll Bar and Window Border Size dialog.

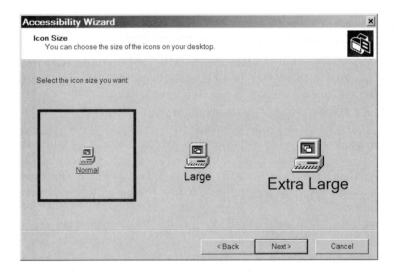

Fig. 20.26 Adjusting window-element sizes.

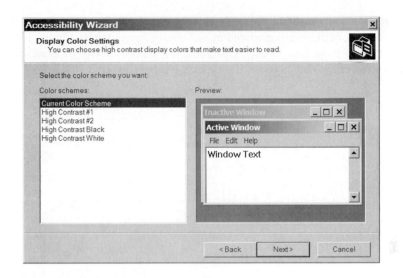

Fig. 20.27 **Display Color Settings** options.

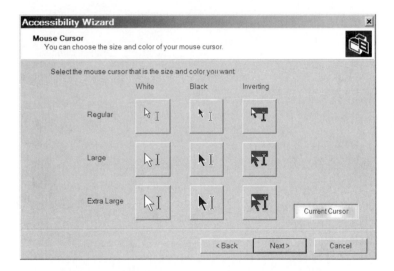

Fig. 20.28 **Accessibility Wizard** mouse-cursor adjustment tool.

20.15.2 Tools for People with Hearing Impairments

This section, which focuses on accessibility for people with hearing impairments, begins with the *SoundSentry* window (Fig. 20.29). **SoundSentry** is a tool that creates visual signals to notify users of system events. For example, people with hearing impairments are unable to hear the beeps that normally indicate warnings, so **SoundSentry** flashes the screen when a beep occurs. To continue on to the next dialog, click **Next**.

The next window is the *ShowSounds* window (Fig. 20.30). **ShowSounds** adds captions to spoken text and other sounds produced by today's multimedia-rich software. Note that, for **ShowSounds** to work in a specific application, developers must provide the captions and spoken text specifically within their software. Make selections and click **Next**.

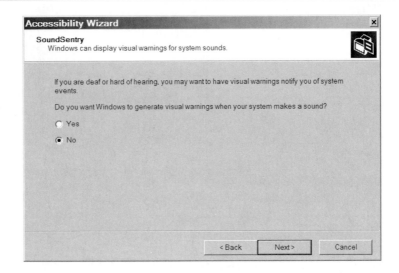

Fig. 20.29 SoundSentry dialog.

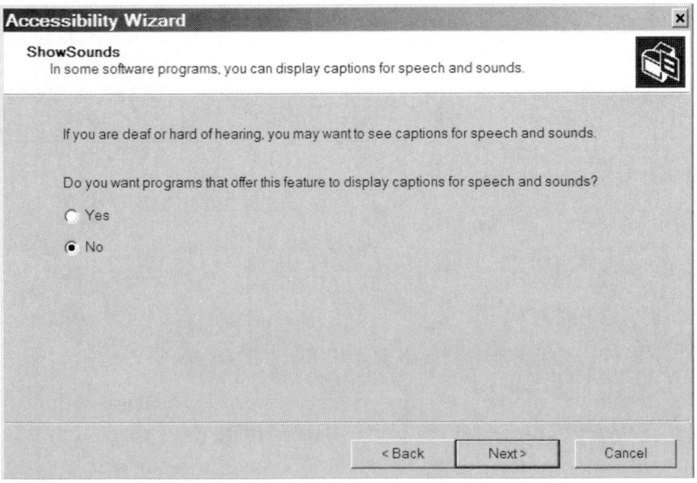

Fig. 20.30 ShowSounds dialog.

20.15.3 Tools for Users Who Have Difficulty Using the Keyboard and Mouse

The next dialog describes **StickyKeys** (Fig. 20.31). *StickyKeys* is a program that helps users who have difficulty pressing multiple keys at the same time. Many important computer commands can be invoked only by pressing specific key combinations. For example, the reboot command requires the user to press *Ctrl+Alt+Delete* simultaneously. **StickyKeys** enables the user to press key combinations in sequence, rather than at the same time. Click **Next** to continue to the **BounceKeys** dialog (Fig. 20.32).

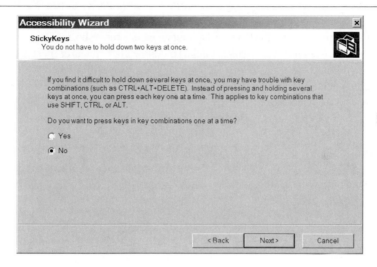

Fig. 20.31 StickyKeys window.

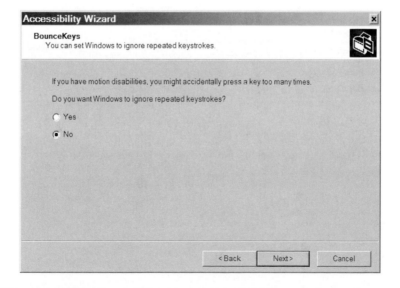

Fig. 20.32 BounceKeys dialog.

Another common problem that affects certain users with disabilities is the accidental pressing of the same key multiple times. This problem typically is caused by holding a key down too long. *BounceKeys* forces the computer to ignore repeated keystrokes. Click **Next**.

ToggleKeys (Fig. 20.33) alerts users that they have pressed one of the lock keys (i.e., *Caps Lock*, *Num Lock* or *Scroll Lock*) by sounding an audible beep. Make selections and click **Next**.

Next, the **Extra Keyboard Help** dialog (Fig. 20.34) is displayed. This dialog can activate a tool that displays such information as keyboard shortcuts and tool tips, when such information is available. Like **ShowSounds**, this tool requires that software developers provide the content to be displayed.

Clicking **Next** will load the **MouseKeys** (Fig. 20.35) customization window. *MouseKeys* is a tool that uses the keyboard to imitate mouse movements. The arrow keys direct the mouse, and the *5* key indicates a single click. To double click, the user must press the + key; to simulate the holding down of the mouse button, the user must press the *Ins* (Insert) key. To release the mouse button, the user must press the *Del* (Delete) key. Choose whether to enable **MouseKeys** and then click **Next.**

Today's computer tools, including most mice, are designed almost exclusively for right-handed users. Microsoft recognized this problem and added the *Mouse Button* **Settings** window (Fig. 20.36) to the **Accessibility Wizard**. This tool allows the user to create a virtual left-handed mouse by swapping the button functions. Click **Next**.

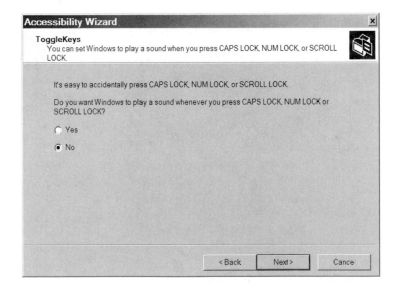

Fig. 20.33 ToggleKeys window.

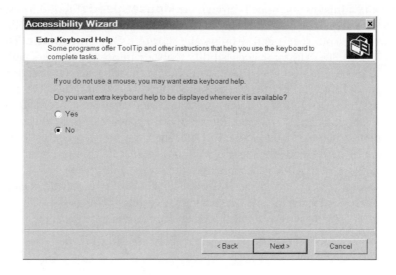

Fig. 20.34 Extra Keyboard Help dialog.

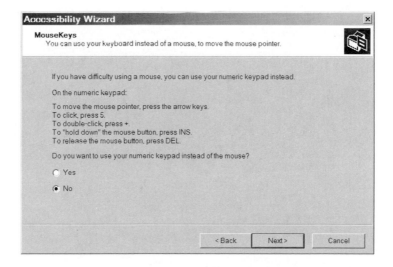

Fig. 20.35 MouseKeys window.

Users can adjust mouse speed through the **MouseSpeed** (Fig. 20.37) section of the **Accessibility Wizard**. Dragging the scroll bar changes the speed. Clicking the **Next** button sets the speed and displays the wizard's **Set Automatic Timeouts** window (Fig. 20.38). Although accessibility tools are important to users with disabilities, they can be a hindrance to users who do not need them. In situations where varying accessibility needs exist, it is important that the user be able to turn the accessibility tools on and off as necessary. The *Set Automatic Timeouts* window specifies a *timeout* period for enabling or disabling accessibility tools. A timeout either enables or disables a certain action after the computer has been idle for a specified amount of time. A screen saver is a common example of a program with a timeout period. Here, a timeout is set to toggle the accessibility tools.

After the user clicks **Next**, the **Default Accessibility Settings** dialog appears (Fig. 20.39). This dialog determines whether the accessibility settings should be used as the *default settings* for new user accounts. Set the accessibility settings as the default if the majority of new users will need them.

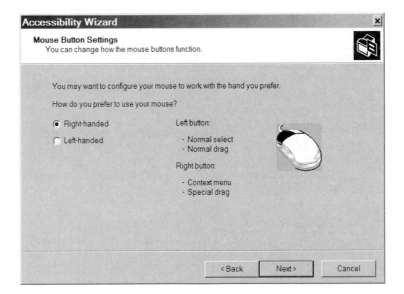

Fig. 20.36 **Mouse Button Settings** window.

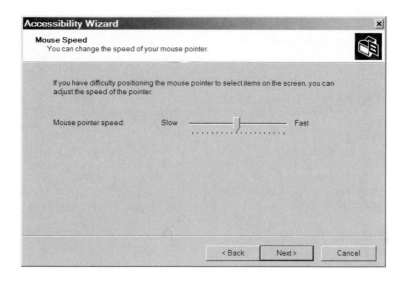

Fig. 20.37 Mouse Speed dialog.

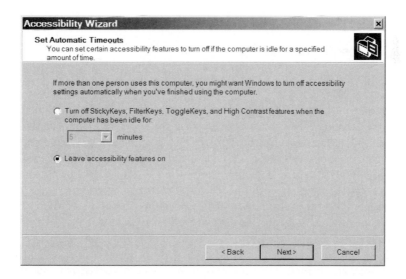

Fig. 20.38 Set Automatic Timeouts dialog.

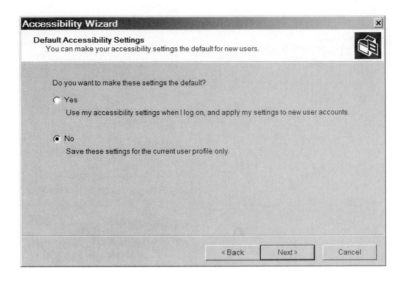

Fig. 20.39 Saving new accessibility settings.

20.15.4 Microsoft Narrator

Microsoft Narrator is a text-to-speech program designed for people with visual impairments. It reads text, describes the current desktop environment and alerts the user when certain Windows events occur. **Narrator** is intended to aid in the configuration of Microsoft Windows. It is a screen reader that works with Visual Studio .NET, Internet Explorer, Wordpad, Notepad and most programs in the **Control Panel**. Although its capabilities are limited outside these applications, **Narrator** is excellent at navigating the Windows environment.

To explore **Narrator**'s functionality, we explain how to use the program in conjunction with several Windows applications. Click the **Start** button and select **Programs > Accessories > Accessibility > Narrator**. Once **Narrator** is open, it describes the current foreground window. It then reads the text inside the window aloud to the user. When the user clicks **OK**, the dialog in Fig. 20.40 displays.

Checking the first option instructs **Narrator** to describe menus and new windows when they are opened. The second option instructs **Narrator** to speak the characters that users type as they type them. The third option moves the mouse cursor to the region currently being read by **Narrator**. Clicking the **Voice...** button enables the user to change the pitch, volume and speed of the narrator voice (Fig. 20.41).

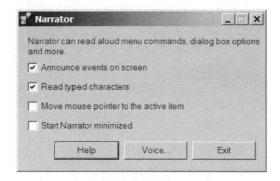

Fig. 20.40 Narrator window.

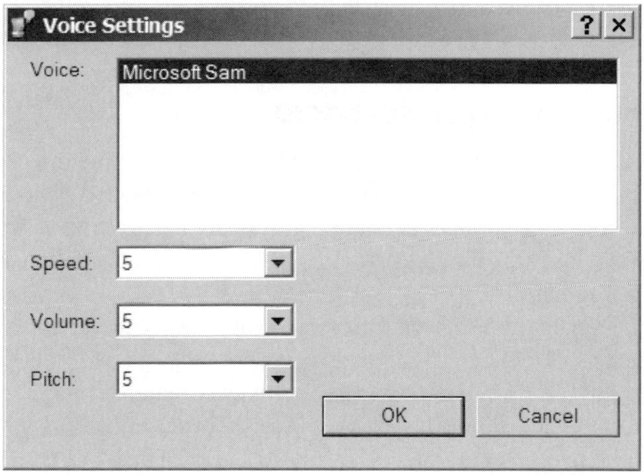

Fig. 20.41 Voice Settings window.

Now, we demonstrate **Narrator** in various applications. When **Narrator** is running, open **Notepad**, and click the **File** menu. **Narrator** announces the opening of the program and begins to describe the items in the **File** menu. As a user scrolls down the list, **Narrator** reads the item to which the mouse currently is pointing. Type some text and press *Ctrl-Shift-Enter* to hear **Narrator** read it (Fig. 20.42). If the **Read typed characters** option is checked, **Narrator** reads each character as it is typed. Users also can employ the keyboard's direction arrows to make **Narrator** read. The up and down arrows cause **Narrator** to speak the lines adjacent to the current mouse position, and the left and right arrows cause **Narrator** to speak the characters adjacent to the current mouse position.

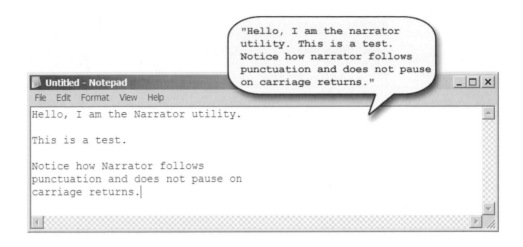

Fig. 20.42 Narrator reading **Notepad** text.

20.15.5 Microsoft On-Screen Keyboard

Some computer users lack the ability to use a keyboard, but are able to use a pointing device, such as a mouse. For these users, the ***On-Screen Keyboard*** is helpful. To access the On-Screen Keyboard, click the **Start** button and select **Programs > Accessories > Accessibility > On-Screen Keyboard**. Figure 20.43 depicts the layout of the Microsoft On-Screen Keyboard.

Users who have difficulty using the On-Screen Keyboard can purchase more sophisticated products, such as *Clicker 4*™ by Inclusive Technology. Clicker 4 is an aid designed for people who cannot use a keyboard effectively. Its best feature is that it can be customized. Keys can have letters, numbers, entire words or even pictures on them. For more information regarding Clicker 4, visit **www.inclusive.co.uk/catalog/clicker.shtml**.

Fig. 20.43 Microsoft **On-Screen Keyboard**.

20.15.6 Accessibility Features in Microsoft Internet Explorer 6

Internet Explorer 6 offers a variety of options that can improve usability. To access IE6's accessibility features, launch the program, click the **Tools** menu and select **Internet Options...**. Then, from the **Internet Options** dialog, press the button labeled **Accessibility...** to open the accessibility options (Fig. 20.44)

The accessibility options in IE6 are designed to improve the Web-browsing experiences of users with disabilities. Users are able to ignore Web colors, Web fonts and font-size tags. This eliminates accessibility problems arising from poor Web-page design and allows users to customize their Web browsing. Users can even specify a *style sheet,* which formats every Web site that users visit according to their personal preferences.

In the **Internet Options** dialog, click the **Advanced** tab. This opens the dialog depicted in Fig. 20.45. The first available option is labeled **Always expand ALT text for images**. By default, IE6 hides some of the `<alt>` text if the size of the text exceeds that of the image it describes. This option forces IE6 to show all the text. The second option reads **Move system caret with focus/selection changes**. This option is intended to make screen reading more effective. Some screen readers use the *system caret* (the blinking vertical bar associated with editing text) to choose what to read. If this option is not activated, screen readers might not read Web pages correctly.

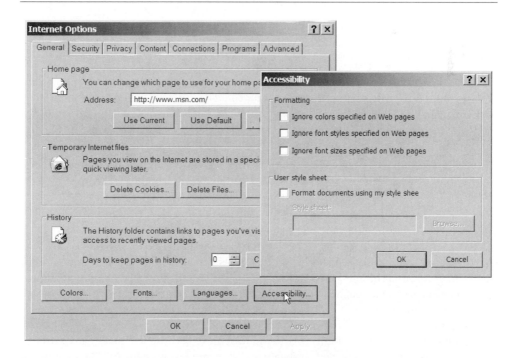

Fig. 20.44 Microsoft Internet Explorer 6's accessibility options.

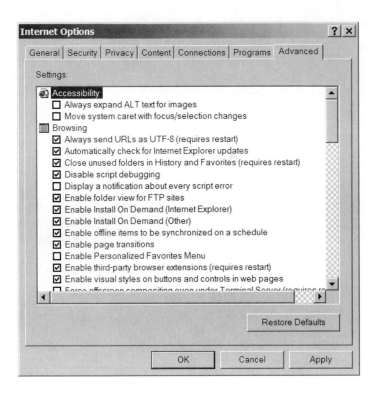

Fig. 20.45 Advanced accessibility settings in Microsoft Internet Explorer 6.

Web designers often forget to take accessibility into account when creating Web sites, and, in attempts to provide large amounts of content, they use fonts that are too small. Many user agents have addressed this problem by allowing the user to adjust the text size. Click the **View** menu and select **Text Size** to change the font size in pages rendered by IE6. By default, the text size is set to **Medium**.

In this chapter, we presented a wide variety of technologies that help people with various disabilities use computers and the Internet. We hope that all our readers will join us in emphasizing the importance of these capabilities in their schools and workplaces.

20.16 Summary

Enabling a Web site to meet the needs of individuals with disabilities is an important issue that is relevant to all business owners. Technologies such as voice activation, visual enhancers and auditory aids enable individuals with disabilities to have access to the Web and to software applications.

Accessibility refers to the level of usability of an application or Web site for people with disabilities. Total accessibility is difficult to achieve because there are many different disabilities, language barriers, and hardware and software inconsistencies. The majority of Web sites are considered to be either partially or totally inaccessible to people with visual, learning or mobility impairments. In 1997, the World Wide Web Consortium (W3C) launched the Web Accessibility Initiative (WAI). The WAI is an attempt to make the Web more accessible; its mission is described at **www.w3.org/WAI**. The WAI published the Web Content Accessibility Guidelines 1.0, which assign accessibility priorities to a three-tier structure of checkpoints. The WAI currently is working on a draft of the Web Content Accessibility Guidelines 2.0. One important WAI requirement is to ensure that every image, movie and sound on a Web site is accompanied by a description that clearly defines the item's purpose; the description is called an **<alt>** tag.

Specialized user agents, such as screen readers (programs that allow users to hear what is being displayed on their screen) and braille displays (devices that receive data from screen-reading software and output the data as braille), allow people with visual impairments to access text-based information that normally is displayed on the screen. Using a screen reader to navigate a Web site can be time consuming and frustrating, because screen readers are unable to interpret pictures and other graphical content that do not have alternative text. Including links at the top of each Web page provides easy access to the page's main content. Web pages with large amounts of multimedia content are difficult for user agents to interpret unless they are designed properly. Images, movies and most non-XHTML objects cannot be read by screen readers.

When creating a Web page for the general public, it is important to consider the reading level at which it is written. Web site designers can make their sites more readable through the use of shorter words; some users may have difficulty understanding slang and other nontraditional language. Misused heading tags (**<h1>**) also present challenges to some Web users—particularly those who cannot use a mouse. Web designers should also avoid misuse of the **alt** attribute; it is intended to provide a short description of an XHTML object that might not load properly on all user agents. The value of the **long-desc** attribute is a text-based URL, linked to a Web page, that describes the image associated with the attribute.

Web designers often use frames to display more than one XHTML file at a time. Unfortunately, frames often lack proper descriptions, thereby preventing users with text-based browsers and users with visual impairments from navigating the Web site. The **<noframes>** tag allows the designer to offer alternative content to users whose browsers do not support frames.

Speech synthesis is another area in which research is being done to help people with disabilities. VoiceXML has tremendous implications for people with visual impairments and for illiterate people. VoiceXML, a speech-recognition and -synthesis technology, reads Web pages to users and understands words spoken into a microphone. A VoiceXML document is composed of a series of dialogs and subdialogs, which result in spoken interaction between the user and the computer. VoiceXML is a voice-recognition technology.

CallXML, a language created and supported by Voxeo, creates phone-to-Web applications. These applications tailor themselves to the user's input. When a user accesses a CallXML application, the incoming telephone call is referred to as a session. A CallXML application can support multiple sessions that enable the application to receive multiple telephone calls at any given time. A session terminates either when the user hangs up the telephone or when the CallXML application invokes the **hangup** element. The contents of a CallXML application are inserted within the **<callxml>** tag. CallXML tags that perform similar tasks should be enclosed between the **<block>** and **</block>** tags. To deploy a CallXML application, register with the Voxeo Community, which assigns a telephone number to the application so that other users may access it. Voxeo's logging feature enables developers to debug their telephone application by observing the "conversation" between the user and the application.

Braille keyboards are similar to standard keyboards, except that in addition to having each key labeled with the letter it represents, braille keyboards have the equivalent braille symbol printed on the key. Most often, braille keyboards are combined with a speech synthesizer or a braille display, so users are able to interact with the computer to verify that their typing is correct.

Open-source software for people with visual impairments already exists and often is superior to most of its proprietary, closed-source counterparts. However, it still does not use the Linux OS to its full extent.

People with visual impairments are not the only beneficiaries of the effort being made to improve markup languages. Individuals with hearing impairments also have a great number of tools to help them interpret auditory information delivered over the Web. People with hearing impairments will soon benefit from what is called Synchronized Multimedia Integration Language (SMIL). This markup language is designed to add extra tracks— layers of content found within a single audio or video file. The additional tracks can contain such data as closed captioning.

EagleEyes, developed by researchers at Boston College (**www.bc.edu/ eagleeyes**), is a system that translates eye movements into mouse movements. Users move the mouse cursor by moving their eyes or head and are thereby able to control the computer.

All of the accessibility options provided by Windows XP are available through the **Accessibility Wizard**. The **Accessibility Wizard** takes a user step by step through all of the Windows accessibility features and configures his or her computer according to the chosen specifications. To solve problems seeing the mouse cursor, Microsoft offers the ability to use larger cursors, black cursors and cursors that invert objects underneath them. Microsoft Magnifier enlarges the section of your screen surrounding the mouse cursor. **SoundSentry** is a tool that creates visual signals when system events occur. **ShowSounds** adds captions to spoken text and other sounds produced by today's multimedia-rich software. **StickyKeys** is a program that helps users who have difficulty pressing multiple keys at the same time. **BounceKeys** forces the computer to ignore repeated keystrokes, solving the problem of accidentally pressing the same key more than once. **ToggleKeys** causes an audible beep to alert users that they have pressed one of the lock keys (i.e., *Caps Lock*, *Num Lock* or *Scroll Lock*). **MouseKeys** is a tool that uses the keyboard to emulate mouse movements. The **Mouse Button Settings** tool allows you to create a virtual left-handed mouse by swapping the button functions. Microsoft **Narrator** is a text-to-speech program for people with visual impairments. It reads text, describes the current desktop environment and alerts the user when certain Windows events occur.

A timeout either enables or disables a certain action after the computer has idled for a specified amount of time. A common use of a timeout is in a screen saver. Default settings are loaded when the computer is rebooted.

20.17 Internet and Web Resources

There are many accessibility resources available on the Internet and World Wide Web; this section lists a variety of these resources.

General Information, Guidelines and Definitions

www.w3.org/WAI
The World Wide Web Consortium's *Web Accessibility Initiative (WAI)* site promotes the design of universally accessible Web sites. This site contains the current guidelines and forthcoming standards for Web accessibility.

www.w3.org/TR/xhtml1
The *XHTML 1.0 Recommendation* contains XHTML 1.0 general information, compatibility issues, document type definition information, definitions, terminology and much more.

www.abledata.com/text2/icg_hear.htm
This page contains a consumer guide that discusses technologies designed for people with hearing impairments.

www.washington.edu/doit
The University of Washington's DO-IT (Disabilities, Opportunities, Internetworking and Technology) site provides information and Web-development resources for the creation of universally accessible Web sites.

www.webable.com
The *WebABLE* site contains links to many disability-related Internet resources; the site is geared towards those developing technologies for people with disabilities.

www.webaim.org
The *WebAIM* site provides a number of tutorials, articles, simulations and other useful resources that demonstrate how to design accessible Web sites. The site provides a screen-reader simulation.

deafness.about.com/health/deafness/msubvib.htm
This site provides information on vibrotactile devices, which allow individuals with hearing impairments to experience audio in the form of vibrations.

Developing Accessible Applications with Existing Technologies

msdn.microsoft.com/library/default.asp?url=/nhp/
Default.asp?contentid=28000544
This site contains information about Microsoft Active Accessibility, a COM-based technology that can be used to create accessible applications.

wdvl.com/Authoring/Languages/XML/XHTML
The Web Developers Virtual Library provides an introduction to XHTML. This site also contains articles, examples and links to other technologies.

www.w3.org/TR/1999/xhtml-modularization-19990406/DTD/doc
The XHTML 1.0 DTD documentation site provides links to DTD documentation for the strict, transitional and frameset document type definitions.

www.webreference.com/xml/reference/xhtml.html
This Web page contains a list of the frequently used XHTML tags, such as header tags, table tags, frame tags and form tags. It also provides a description of each tag.

www.w3.org/TR/REC-CSS2/aural.html
This site discusses Aural Style Sheets, outlining the purpose and uses of this new technology.

www.islandnet.com
Lynxit is a development tool that allows users to view any Web site as if they were using a text-only browser. The site's form allows you to enter a URL and returns the Web site in text-only format.

www.trill-home.com/lynx/public_lynx.html
This site allows users to browse the Web with a Lynx browser. Users can view how Web pages appear to users who are not using the most current technologies.

java.sun.com/products/java-media/speech/forDevelopers/JSML
This site outlines the specifications for JSML, Sun Microsystem's Java Speech Markup Language. This language, like VoiceXML, helps improve accessibility for people with visual impairments.

ocfo.ed.gov/coninfo/clibrary/software.htm
This is the U.S. Department of Education's Web site that outlines software accessibility requirements. The site helps developers produce accessible products.

www.speech.cs.cmu.edu/comp.speech/SpeechLinks.html
The *Speech Technology Hyperlinks* page has over 500 links to sites related to computer-based speech and speech-recognition tools.

www.islandnet.com/accessibility.html
This page provides a list of tips for creating accessible Web pages.

www.chantinc.com/technology
This page is the *Chant* Web site, which discusses speech technology and how it works. Chant also provides speech-synthesis and speech-recognition software.

www.oasis-open.org/cover/callxmlv2.html
This site provides a comprehensive list of the CallXML tags, complete with a description of each tag. The site also provides short examples on how to apply the tags in various applications.

web.ukonline.co.uk/ddmc/software.html
This site provides links to software designed for people with disabilities.

www.freedomscientific.com
Henter-Joyce is a division of Freedom Scientific that provides software for people with visual impairments. It is the homepage of JAWS (Job Access with Sound).

www-3.ibm.com/able/
This is the homepage of IBM's accessibility site. It provides information on IBM products and their accessibility and discusses hardware, software and Web accessibility.

www.w3.org/TR/voice-tts-reqs
This page explains the speech-synthesis markup requirements for voice markup languages.

www.cast.org
CAST (Center for Applied Special Technology) offers software, including a valuable accessibility checker, that can help individuals with disabilities use computers. The accessibility checker is a Web-based program that validates the accessibility of Web sites.

Information on Disabilities

deafness.about.com/health/deafness/msubmenu6.htm
This is the home page of **deafness.about.com**. It provides a wealth of information on the history of hearing loss, the current state of medical developments and other resources related to these topics.

www.trainingpost.org/3-2-inst.htm
This site presents a tutorial on the Gunning Fog Index. The Gunning Fog Index is a method of grading text according to its readability.

laurence.canlearn.ca/English/learn/accessibility2001/neads/index.shtml
INDIE stands for "Integrated Network of Disability Information and Education." This site is home to a search engine that helps users find information on disabilities.

www.wgbh.org/wgbh/pages/ncam/accesslinks.html
This page provides links to other accessibility pages across the Web.

21

Introduction to Unmanaged Code in Visual C++ .NET

Objectives

- To understand the differences between managed and unmanaged code.
- To understand the benefits and disadvantages of unmanaged code.
- To use the Unified Event Model.
- To learn some of the major and minor changes from the previous versions of Visual C++.
- To use unmanaged runtime checks.
- To understand the technologies introduced in Visual C++ .NET

Governments always tend to want not really a free press, but a managed or a well-conducted one.
Lord Radcliffe

A definition is the enclosing a wilderness of idea within a wall of words
Samuel Butler

The world is disgracefully managed, one hardly knows to whom to complain.
Ronald Firbank.

21.1 Introduction

Managed Extensions for C++ provide the capabilities to harness Microsoft's .NET platform and its Framework Class Library fully. In addition, Visual C++ .NET includes numerous additions and changes that simplify and expand existing frameworks and programming models. Perhaps the most powerful features of Visual C++ .NET are the services that allow for unparalleled interoperability between managed .NET code and existing native applications, DLLs and COM objects, including ActiveX controls.

In the remaining chapters in this book, we focus on the changes and additions to traditional Visual C++ as well as on the powerful interoperability features that separate Visual C++ .NET from other .NET languages. These chapters cover advanced material and will be most useful for readers that have prior knowledge of certain topics. The prerequisites for each chapter will be stated in each chapter's introduction. This chapter introduces the concept of unmanaged code and discusses some changes and features introduced to unmanaged code by Visual C++ .NET. A reader with prior knowledge of ANSI C++ will benefit most from this chapter.

21.2 Unmanaged Code

Simply stated, in .NET, *unmanaged code* is any code that cannot use the services provided by the *Common Language Runtime (CLR)*. As discussed earlier in this book, the CLR is the .NET environment that provides basic services such as garbage collection and array-bounds checking to .NET applications. Note that .NET provides services that allow unmanaged and managed code to transparently interact. The details of the differences between managed and unmanaged code is discussed more fully in Chapter 24, Managed and Unmanaged Code Interoperability.

21.2.1 Choosing Between Unmanaged and Managed Code

Choosing between developing with managed or unmanaged code is a crucial decision for any project manager. The decision affects many levels of design, development cycle planning and distribution. Many factors must be considered, such as development and testing time, performance requirements and legacy-code support.

Managed code often provides faster, easier development and typically results in fewer bugs. The Framework Class Library (FCL) provides a large set of reliable classes to perform most tasks, and the CLR handles many previously difficult-to-find, yet common programming mistakes, such as mismanaged memory and buffer overruns and underruns.

However, the CLR can be a detriment to certain performance-critical managed applications. The functions of the CLR require resources dedicated to managing the code, restricting the number of resources available for the application logic. In addition, .NET code is compiled into an intermediary, assembly-like, language—Microsoft Intermediate Language (MSIL). The just-in-time (JIT) compiler compiles MSIL to native code at runtime (or installation time). The JIT compiler compiles a routine into native code the first time the routine is called, then stores the compiled routine for future calls. JIT compilation could slow down applications, though the degree of the performance hit varies by application.

In some cases, the overhead from the combination of CLR routines and JIT compilation may result in lower performance. However, in many cases, the highly optimized algorithms used by the classes in the FCL can even increase the performance of an application—the FCL and modern powerful processors together often make the performance decrease between similar managed and unmanaged code applications unnoticeable.

Perhaps the most important reason to create a project in unmanaged code is to provide seamless integration with a large, well-tested, existing unmanaged code base, including the Win32 APIs. All existing pre-.NET C++ applications and libraries are written in unmanaged code, and it would not be practical to convert this enormous code base to a managed context. Visual C++ .NET provides facilities to harness .NET capabilities without sacrificing existing code.

It is in the migration from unmanaged to managed code that Visual C++ .NET shows its power and uniqueness. The flexibility of Visual C++ .NET not only allows easy integration of managed with unmanaged code, but also allows both types of code to work, side by side, in the same application. Visual C++ .NET allows the developer to provide fine-grained control over each managed and unmanaged interaction.

21.2.2 Future of Unmanaged Code

Despite the benefits provided by managed code, it is unlikely that unmanaged code will be disappearing for some time to come. For performance-critical applications such as games, scientific applications, device drivers and core operating system-components, it is unlikely that the benefits provided by the CLR will outweigh the performance cost and the sacrifice of low-level system control. However, applications that require the raw performance of unmanaged code make up a small minority of all applications. It is likely that most Windows developers will work at the managed level, while fewer developers work on unmanaged applications and technologies.

A concern of unmanaged Visual C++ developers is that the technology will stagnate in the face of .NET. The powerful additions and changes to traditional Visual C++ .NET by Microsoft prove that, despite the push towards .NET, the company is not abandoning unmanaged code and intends for unmanaged code to thrive as a separate entity from .NET. And, as long as unmanaged components exist, developers with the talent and knowledge to use, expand and debug those components will be required.

21.3 Changes in Visual C++ .NET

This section introduces some of the major and minor changes introduced to unmanaged code by Visual C++ .NET. The majority of the changes are designed to streamline and standardize common programming issues such as event handling and interfaces as well as to increase the ANSI compliance of Visual C++. [*Note*: Throughout this chapter and remaining chapters, we make use of Microsoft-specific data types, most of which are simply **typedefs** to standard C++ types. We use the Microsoft types to provide consistency with existing Win32 code and the Microsoft documentation.]

21.3.1 Unified Event Model

Visual C++ .NET introduces the *Unified Event Model*. The Unified Event Model standardizes events and event handling across unmanaged C++, COM and Managed extensions for C++. In previous editions of Visual C++, C++ programmers were forced to perform event handling via C-style function callbacks, and COM was restricted to a limited, but complex event model. The Unified Event Model provides common syntax and streamlined event processing to provide a simple and powerful event model. More information about event handling in Visual C++ .NET and the Unified Event Model can be found at

> **msdn.microsoft.com/library/default.asp?url=/library/en-us/**
> **vccore/html/vcconEventHandlingUsingAttributes.asp**

Figure 21.1 presents the class declarations for class **CTimerEventSource** (an event-source class), class **CTimer** (which runs a timer that fires events) and class **CTimerReceiver** (an event-receiver class). An *event-source* class defines events while an *event-receiver* (also known as an *event-sink*) class responds to the events.

```
1   // Fig. 21.1: Timer.h
2   // Class declarations for timer classes.
3
4   #pragma once
5
6   #include <iostream>
7   #include <time.h>
8   #include <windows.h>
9
10  using std::cout;
11
```

Fig. 21.1 Event handling in unmanaged code. (Part 1 of 2.)

```
12   // forward struct declaration
13   struct TimerArguments;
14
15   // attribute defines this class as an event handler class
16   [ event_source( native ) ]
17   class CTimerEventSource
18   {
19   public:
20
21      // event method
22      __event void TimerTick( time_t );
23   }; // end class CTimerEventSource
24
25   // class that simplifies timer creation
26   class CTimer
27   {
28   public:
29
30      // runs function RunTimer on its own thread
31      static HANDLE RunTimerThread( TimerArguments *timer );
32
33      // runs a timer which fires TimerTick events
34      static UINT WINAPI RunTimer( LPVOID argumentAddress );
35   }; // end class CTimer
36
37   // structure containing arguments to timer run method
38   struct TimerArguments
39   {
40      int tickTime;
41      CTimerEventSource *source;
42      bool running;
43   }; // end structure TimerArguments
44
45   // timer event receiver, displays the current time after each
46   // TimerTick event
47   [ event_receiver( native ) ]
48   class CTimerReceiver
49   {
50   public:
51
52      // constructor, hooks receiver to source
53      CTimerReceiver( CTimerEventSource *source );
54
55      // destructor, unhooks receiver from source
56      ~CTimerReceiver();
57
58      // TimerTick event handler
59      void TimerTick( time_t unformattedTime );
60
61   private:
62      CTimerEventSource *eventSource;
63   }; // end class CTimerReceiver
```

Fig. 21.1   Event handling in unmanaged code. (Part 2 of 2.)

Lines 17–23 declare event-source class **CTimerEventSource**, an event-source class that consists of events—methods designated by keyword **__event**—and is created by the ***event_source*** attribute. Attributes are a fundamental new feature in unmanaged Visual C++ .NET and will be covered in greater detail in Chapter 22, Attributed Programming in ATL/COM. In this case, the ***event_source*** attribute takes a single parameter that designates the type of event source; valid parameter values are **native** (for unmanaged C++), **com** (for COM) and **managed** (for MC++). Class **CTimerEventSource** declares a single event, **TimerTick**, that is intended to be raised after each "tick" of method **RunTimer**. Lines 26–35 declare class **CTimer**, which contains the two static methods **RunTimer** and **RunTimerThread**.

Method **RunTimer** is a threaded method (i.e., it is intended to run on its own thread); thus, it conforms to the Win32 thread function prototype **UINT WINAPI** *functionName* **(LPVOID)**. The method returns a *UINT* (the Windows **typedef** for **unsigned int**) that indicates the success or failure of the method. The method uses the *WINAPI* macro to define its calling convention; on a Windows PC, **WINAPI** is a macro for keyword **__stdcall**. The calling convention of a method determines the order and technique by which arguments are passed to the method, the internal naming convention and whether the caller or callee must manage the stack. In most cases, the programmer does not have to worry about the calling convention beyond specifying the desired type; the compiler handles the rest. Finally, the argument to method **RunTimer** is of type *LPVOID* (the Windows **typedef** for **void ***), which designates it may contain a pointer to any type. A threaded method (such as method **RunTimer**) may be passed only a single argument of any type—in most cases, this argument will be the address of a structure designed to contain the parameters required by the function. Method **RunTimer** expects to receive the address of a **TimerArguments** structure (lines 38 43), which contains the length of the timer tick, the event-source object and controls the duration of the timer, as an argument.

Method **RunTimerThread** is designed to simplify the process of creating a thread for method **RunTimer**. Method **RunTimerThread** returns a *HANDLE* (a **typedef** for type **void ***) to the created thread and expects a **TimerArguments** structure to pass to method **RunTimer**.

Lines 47–63 declare the event-receiver class **CTimerReceiver**, designated by the ***event_receiver*** attribute. Like attribute **event_source**, **event_receiver** takes a parameter—**native**, **com** or **managed**—that designates the event context. An event-receiver class usually contains one or more event handlers, methods that are triggered when an event is raised. Line 53 declares the class constructor; it takes a single argument, the **CTimerEventSource** object that contains the events to be handled. Line 59 declares the event handler method **TimerTick**, which handles the **CTimerEventSource** event **TimerTick**.

Figure 21.2 contains the method definitions for the classes in Fig. 21.1.

```
1   // Fig. 21.2: Timer.cpp
2   // Timer and receiver method definitions.
3
```

Fig. 21.2   Event timer classes method definitions. (Part 1 of 3.)

```
 4   #include "timer.h"
 5   #include <process.h>
 6
 7   // runs function RunTimer on own thread
 8   HANDLE CTimer::RunTimerThread( TimerArguments *arguments )
 9   {
10      UINT threadID;      // id number of timer thread
11      HANDLE handle;      // handle to timer thread
12
13      // run timer on separate thread
14      handle = ( HANDLE )_beginthreadex( NULL, 0,
15         &RunTimer, arguments, 0, &threadID );
16
17      // ensure thread creation success
18      if (handle == NULL) {
19         cout << "CreateThread failed.\n";
20
21         return 0;
22      }
23      else
24         return handle;
25   } // end method RunTimerThread
26
27   // static method runs timer
28   UINT WINAPI CTimer::RunTimer( LPVOID argumentAddress )
29   {
30
31      // receive timer argument list
32      TimerArguments *arguments = (TimerArguments *)argumentAddress;
33
34      // display tick time and duration of timer
35      cout << "Starting the timer. Will fire TimerTick every "
36         << arguments->tickTime << " seconds.\n";
37
38      time_t unformattedTime; // unformatted time variable
39
40      // continue looping until thread is stopped
41      while ( arguments->running ) {
42
43         // gets current time as number of seconds since
44         // January 1, 1970
45         time( &unformattedTime );
46
47         __raise arguments->source->TimerTick( unformattedTime );
48
49         // sleep for tickTime number of seconds
50         Sleep( arguments->tickTime * 1000 );
51      } // end while
52
53      _endthread();
54
```

Fig. 21.2   Event timer classes method definitions. (Part 2 of 3.)

```
55          return 0;
56       } // end method RunTimer
57
58       // constructor hooks this receiver to event source
59       CTimerReceiver::CTimerReceiver( CTimerEventSource *source )
60       {
61          eventSource = source;
62          __hook( &CTimerEventSource::TimerTick,
63             source, &CTimerReceiver::TimerTick );
64       } // end constructor
65
66       // destructor unhooks this receiver from event source
67       CTimerReceiver::~CTimerReceiver()
68       {
69          __unhook( &CTimerEventSource::TimerTick, eventSource,
70             &CTimerReceiver::TimerTick );
71       } // end destructor
72
73       // TimerTick event handler displays current time after
74       // each tick
75       void CTimerReceiver::TimerTick( time_t unformattedTime )
76       {
77
78          // store unformatted time in a tm structure containing
79          // formatted local time zone data
80          tm *time = localtime( &unformattedTime );
81
82          // display tick event and current time
83          cout << "Tick! " << time->tm_hour << ":"
84             << time->tm_min << ":" << time->tm_sec << "\n";
85       } // end method TimerTick
```

Fig. 21.2   Event timer classes method definitions. (Part 3 of 3.)

Lines 8–25 define **static** method **RunTimerThread**, which creates a thread running method **RunTimer**, using function _**beginthreadex** declared in header **process.h**. Lines 14–15 call function **_beginthreadex**, which takes six arguments. The first is a pointer to a structure containing the security permissions for the thread; the value **NULL** designates default security attributes. The second argument specifies the size in bytes of the stack to designate for the thread; the value **0** results in the stack size. The third argument is the pointer to the function to be executed by the thread; the designated method prototype must match the thread function prototype described in the previous paragraph. The fourth argument is a pointer to the argument to send to the threaded method; in this example, we pass the location of the **TimerArguments** structure. The fifth argument defines special flags for the created thread; the value **0** creates a thread that begins execution immediately. The sixth argument is a reference to a **UINT** that will contain the thread ID number when the function returns. Function **_beginthreadex** returns a **uintptr_t** that can be casted to type **HANDLE** to the created thread; if this value is **NULL**, the thread cannot be created. Lines 18–22 return **0** if the thread could not be created, the thread's **HANDLE** otherwise.

Method **RunTimer** (lines 28–56) runs a timer that fires a **TimerTick** event each time the designated number of seconds has passed. Line 32 obtains a pointer to the **TimerArguments** structure from the **LPVOID** address passed to the method. Lines 35–36 display the amount of time between each **TimerTick**. Lines 41–51 continue looping until the **running** value of the **TimerArguments** structure is set to false, which indicates that the calling method wishes to end the thread. Line 45 calls function **time**, which takes a reference to a **time_t** variable as an argument. When function **time** returns, the **time_t** variable contains the current time in terms of the number of seconds since January 1, 1970 (called the *epoch*). Line 47 then raises the **TimerTick** event in the **CTimer-Source** object specified in the passed **TimerArguments** structure with the current time as an argument. An event is raised with keyword __***raise*** followed by a call to the event method an object of an event-source class. Line 50 calls function **Sleep** to suspend the execution of the thread for the number of seconds equal to the time specified by the passed **TimerArguments** structure. Line 53 calls function _***endthread*** to terminate the current thread and release its resources.

Good Programming Practice 21.1

*Keyword __***raise*** is optional when triggering an event, but preceding an event call with the __***raise*** keyword greatly enhances the readability of your code.*

Lines 59–64 define the **CTimerReceiver** constructor, which hooks the event handler to an event source. Line 61 stores the passed **CTimerEventSource** pointer as a class member variable to allow the class destructor to unhook the event. Lines 62–63 use keyword __***hook***, which connects event sources and handlers and takes three arguments. The first argument is a pointer to an event-source method of an event-source class. The second argument is an instance of that event-source class and the third argument is a pointer to the event handler method for the specified event-source method. When an event handler is connected to an event source, the event handler will be called when the event is raised on the designated instance of the event-source class. Note that it is valid for a single event handler to be hooked to several event sources, and for a single event source to be hooked by several event handlers.

Lines 67–71 define the **CTimerReceiver** destructor, which unhooks the event handler from an event source. Line 69–70 use keyword __***unhook*** to disassociate the event handler from an event source. Keyword __***unhook*** takes three arguments: The first is a pointer to the event-source method from which the handler should be disconnected, the second is the event-source instance and the third is a pointer to the event handler method. An unhooked event handler no longer handles events from the specified event.

Good Programming Practice 21.2

Unhook all hooked events before destroying an event-receiver object.

Lines 75–85 define the event handler method for the **TimerTick** event. Line 80 uses function **localtime** to convert the unformatted **time_t** structure into a formatted **tm** structure. Lines 83–84 display the time at which the event handler method was called.

Figure 21.3 is the entry point for the application. The application combines the classes defined in Fig. 21.1 to demonstrate the Unified Event Model in native code.

```
1   // Fig. 21.3: Event Handling.cpp
2   // Timer class that fires events to a receiver class.
3
4   #include <tchar.h>
5   #include <iostream>
6   #include <time.h>
7   #include "timer.h"
8
9   using std::cout;
10
11  // entry point for application
12  int main( int argc, _TCHAR *argv[] )
13  {
14     CTimerEventSource source; // event source
15     HANDLE handle;            // handle to timer thread
16
17     // create event receiver
18     CTimerReceiver receiver( &source );
19
20     // build structure containing arguments to timer
21     TimerArguments timerArguments = { 2 , &source, true };
22
23     // instructions to stop timer
24     cout << "Press enter to stop the timer\n\n";
25
26     // create timer thread
27     handle = CTimer::RunTimerThread( &timerArguments );
28
29     // wait for user input, then close thread
30     getchar();
31
32     timerArguments.running = false;
33     WaitForSingleObject( handle, INFINITE );
34     CloseHandle( handle );
35
36     return 0;
37  } // end function main
```

```
Press enter to stop the timer

Starting the timer. Will fire TimerTick every 2 seconds.
Tick! 15:37:32
Tick! 15:37:34
Tick! 15:37:36
Tick! 15:37:38
Tick! 15:37:40
Tick! 15:37:42
Tick! 15:37:44
Tick! 15:37:46
```

Fig. 21.3 Event handling application entry point.

Line 18 creates a **CTimerReceiver** event-sink instance with a reference to the
CTimerEventSource object created in line 14. Line 21 constructs a **TimerArgu-**

ments structure specifying a tick length of two seconds and containing a reference to the event-source instance. Line 27 calls **CTimer** method **RunTimerThread** and obtains the handle to the created thread. Line 30 waits for user input; the **RunTimer** method will continue to fire events every two seconds while the main application is waiting for input. When the user enters any character, lines 32–33 indicate the timer thread should stop running and use Win32 function *WaitForSingleObject* to cause the application to wait until the thread completes. Win32 function *CloseHandle* is called in line 34 to release the **RunTimer** thread handle before the application exits.

The Unified Event Model provides an element of standardization that was previously missing from C++. Chapter 22, Attributed Programming in ATL/COM, will demonstrate the Unified Event Model as a simpler method to implement the COM connection-point event model.

21.3.2 Changes to Object-Oriented Capabilities

Visual C++ .NET includes new keywords and techniques designed to modernize C++'s object-oriented capabilities and simplify common tasks. Some of these new features increase Visual C++ .NET's ANSI/ISO compatibility.

Figure 21.4 shows the interface and class definitions for a simple word processor application (Fig. 21.6) that makes use of the new object-oriented programming features.

```
1   // Fig. 21.4: Document.h
2   // Document interface and class declarations.
3
4   #include <tchar.h>
5   #include <iostream>
6
7   using std::cout;
8   using std::endl;
9
10  // maximum document length, in characters
11  #define MAXIMUM_TEXT_LENGTH 5000
12
13  // IDocument interface, supports document printing
14  __interface IDocument
15  {
16  public:
17     IDocument *clone();
18     void AppendCharacter( char );
19     void print();
20  }; // end interface IDocument
21
22  // two dimensional shape interface
23  __interface ITwoDimensionalShape
24  {
25  public:
26     double area();
27     void printShapeName();
28     void print();
29  }; // end interface ITwoDimensionalShape
30
```

Fig. 21.4   **CRectangleDocument** interface and class declarations. (Part 1 of 2.)

```
31    // CRectanglePaper class implements both interfaces
32    class CRectangleDocument : public ITwoDimensionalShape,
33       public IDocument
34    {
35    public:
36
37       // construct new rectangular document
38       CRectangleDocument( int, int, char * );
39
40       double area(); // return area of page in characters
41       void printShapeName(); // print name of shape, rectangle
42       void ITwoDimensionalShape::print(); // print shape properties
43
44       // overrides IDocument clone function with covariant return type,
45       // makes clone of this document
46       CRectangleDocument *clone();
47
48       // adds specified character to document
49       void AppendCharacter( char );
50       void IDocument::print(); // prints document text
51
52    protected:
53
54       // adds newline to document, maintaining newline count
55       void addNewline();
56
57       int width, height, characterAfterNewline, newlineCount;
58       char text[ MAXIMUM_TEXT_LENGTH ];
59    }; // end class CRectangleDocument
```

Fig. 21.4 CRectangleDocument interface and class declarations. (Part 2 of 2.)

Line 11 defines the maximum size of the word processor document as **5000** characters. Lines 14–20 declare interface **IDocument**, a representation of a text document. Visual C++ .NET includes the **__interface** keyword to designate an interface. An **__interface** is roughly analogous to a class containing only pure virtual functions in traditional C++ and resembles a COM interface. An **__interface** could be implemented in traditional C++, but the keyword causes the compiler to enforce conventional interface rules. An interface defined with the **__interface** keyword must contain only **public** methods and properties and can inherit from other interfaces, but not from classes. An interface is restricted from containing data members, constructors, destructors, overloaded operators or **static** methods. The **IDocument** interface contains method **AppendCharacter** to add a character to the document, method **print** to display the document and method **clone** to create a copy of the document.

Lines 23–29 declare interface **ITwoDimensionalShape**, which represents a two-dimensional shape. Interface **ITwoDimensionalShape** contains method **area**, which returns the area of the shape, **printShapeName**, which displays the shape's name, and method **print**, which displays the shape's properties.

Lines 32–59 declare class **CRectangularDocument**, which represents a text document with rectangular margins. Class **CRectangularDocument** implements interface **ITwoDimensionalShape** and **IDocument** in lines 32–33. Line 38 declares the class constructor, intended to receive the document's margins, in characters as the first two arguments and the initial text as the third argument. Lines 40–50 implement the virtual methods defined in the interfaces.

Lines 42 and 50 demonstrate a new Visual C++ .NET feature called *explicit overrides*. Explicit overrides allow a derived class to override two inherited methods with the same name and method signature separately (rather than providing one override for both inherited methods). Explicitly overriding such methods uses the syntax

return-type interfaceName::*methodName* (*arguments*) ;

in the class declaration. In addition, the method definition must use the syntax:

return-type className::*interfaceName*::*methodName* (*arguments*)

Line 46 implements the **IDocument** method **clone** with a covariant return type. Visual C++ .NET now allows *covariant return types*, which means that a derived class can change the return type of an overridden base method to a derived type of the base return type.[1] Covariant return types are most commonly used, as in this example, in clone methods. In such classes, derived classes override the base-class clone method and change the return type to the derived type.

Lines 55–58 declare the class member variables and the helper method **addNewline**. Method **addNewline** adds a newline character to the end of the document and maintains the **newlineCount** and **characterAfterNewline** variables. Figure 21.5 contains the method definitions for class **CRectangleDocument**.

```
1   // Fig. 21.5: Document.cpp
2   // Rectangle document method definitions.
3
4   #include <tchar.h>
5   #include "Document.h"
6
7   // CRectangleDocument constructor
8   CRectangleDocument::CRectangleDocument( int widthValue,
9      int heightValue, char *initialText )
10  {
11
12     // initialize member variables
13     width = widthValue;
14     height = heightValue;
15     newlineCount = 0;
16     characterAfterNewline = 0;
17     text[ 0 ] = '\0';
18
19     int length = ( int )strlen( initialText );
20
21     // set initial page text
22     for ( int i = 0; i < length; i++ )
23        AppendCharacter( initialText[ i ] );
24  } // end constructor
25
```

Fig. 21.5 **CRectangleDocument** method definitions. (Part 1 of 4.)

---

1. More information about covariant return types can be found at
   msdn.microsoft.com/msdnmag/issues/02/02/ModernC/ModernC.asp.

```
26   // ITwoDimensionalShape area method
27   double CRectangleDocument::area()
28   {
29
30      // return character width and height
31      return width * height;
32   } // end method area
33
34   // ITwoDimensionalShape printShapeName method
35   void CRectangleDocument::printShapeName()
36   {
37
38      // print shape name
39      cout << "Rectangle\n";
40   } // end method printShapeName
41
42   // prints shape name and side values
43   void CRectangleDocument::ITwoDimensionalShape::print()
44   {
45      printShapeName();
46      cout << "width: " << width << "\nheight: " << height << endl;
47   } // end method print
48
49   // appends specified character to end of document
50   void CRectangleDocument::AppendCharacter( char newCharacter )
51   {
52
53      // obtain length of document
54      int textLength = ( int )strlen( text );
55
56      // check that new character will not overflow buffer
57      if ( textLength + 1 < MAXIMUM_TEXT_LENGTH ) {
58
59         // if newCharacter is newline character, use helper method
60         if ( newCharacter == '\n' )
61            addNewline();
62
63         // if new character would exceed specified bounds add
64         // newline before placing character
65         else if ( ( int )strlen(
66            &text[ characterAfterNewline ] ) > width ) {
67
68            addNewline();
69
70            // obtain new text length, if new character fits
71            // append newCharacter to document
72            textLength = ( int )strlen( text );
73            if ( textLength + 1 < MAXIMUM_TEXT_LENGTH ) {
74               text[ textLength ] = newCharacter;
75               text[ textLength + 1 ] = '\0';
76            } // end if
77         } // end else if
78         else {
```

Fig. 21.5 CRectangleDocument method definitions. (Part 2 of 4.)

```
79
80              // append newCharacter to end of document
81              text[ textLength ] = newCharacter;
82              text[ textLength + 1 ] = '\0';
83          } // end else
84      } // end outer if
85  } // end method AppendCharacter
86
87  // explicit override of IDocument print method to print page text
88  void CRectangleDocument::IDocument::print()
89  {
90      cout << text << endl;
91  } // end method print
92
93  // helper method to add newline character to text without disrupting
94  // newline count
95  void CRectangleDocument::addNewline()
96  {
97
98      // obtain length of document
99      int location = ( int )strlen( text );
100
101     // add newline character to end of document
102     text[ location ] = '\n';
103     text[ location + 1 ] = '\0';
104
105     // set last newline location
106     characterAfterNewline = location + 1;
107
108     // increment newline count
109     newlineCount++;
110
111     // check if newline pushed text past bottom of current page
112     if ( newlineCount >= height &&
113         strlen( text ) + 20 < MAXIMUM_TEXT_LENGTH ) {
114
115         // display page break text
116         strcat( text, "\n----------------\n\n" );
117
118         characterAfterNewline += 21;
119
120         // reset newline count
121         newlineCount = 0;
122     } // end if
123 } // end method addNewline
124
125 // creates copy of this document
126 CRectangleDocument *CRectangleDocument::clone()
127 {
128
129     // create document
130     CRectangleDocument *document =
131         new CRectangleDocument( width, height, text );
```

Fig. 21.5 CRectangleDocument method definitions. (Part 3 of 4.)

```
132
133     return document;
134 } // end method clone
```

Fig. 21.5 CRectangleDocument method definitions. (Part 4 of 4.)

Lines 8–24 define the constructor that initalizes the document margins and initial text. Method **area** in lines 27–32 returns the document's area in terms of characters. Method **printShapeName** in lines 35–40 displays the document's shape—rectangle.

Lines 43–47 define the explicitly overridden **ITwoDimensionalShape** method **print**. Linc 45 prints the shape name, and line 46 displays the document's width and height in terms of characters. Method **AppendCharacter** in lines 50–85 adds a single character to the end of the document. Line 54 uses standard library function *strlen* to return the length of the string. Line 57 ensures that adding a character will fit. Lines 78–83 execute if the character can be added to the buffer without adding any newlines.

Method **print** (lines 88–91) explicitly overrides the **IDocument print** method to display the document's text. Method **addNewline** in lines 95–123 adds a newline character to the end of the document. Line 99 obtains the length of the document, line 102 appends a newline character, and line 103 terminates the string with a null character. Line 106 sets the new location for variable **characterAfterNewline**, and line 109 increments the newline count. Lines 112–113 test for whether the newline character pushes text past the number of characters specified by document height, line 116 adds a page delimiter line to the document, line 118 sets variable **characterAfterNewline**, and line 121 resets the **newlineCount**.

Lines 126–134 demonstrate a covariant return type **clone** method. Lines 130–133 create a new **CRectangleDocument** with the current **Object**'s values and return the pointer. Figure 21.6 contains the application logic to use **CRectangleDocument** in a word-processor application.

```
1   // Fig. 21.6: WordProcessor.cpp
2   // Word processor application logic.
3
4   #include <tchar.h>
5   #include "Document.h"
6   #include <iostream>
7
8   using std::cout;
9   using std::endl;
10
11  // application entry point
12  int main( int argc, _TCHAR *argv[] )
13  {
14     char input = 0;
15
```

Fig. 21.6 Word-processor application logic. (Part 1 of 3.)

```
16      // create a paper 30 characters by 9 rows
17      CRectangleDocument paper( 30, 9, "" );
18
19      // obtain pointers to paper interfaces to allow proper print
20      // method resolution
21      IDocument *page = &paper;
22      ITwoDimensionalShape *shape = &paper;
23
24      // print page properties from ITwoDimensionalShape
25      cout << "Page Properties: ";
26      shape->print();
27      cout << endl;
28
29      // prompt user to begin input
30      cout << "Please begin typing.\n";
31
32      // continue until user enters end of file character
33      // ( ctrl + z in Windows )
34      while ( ( input = getchar() ) != EOF ) {
35
36         // if user presses ctrl + p in Windows, print document
37         if ( input == 0x10 ) {
38
39            cout << "-------------------------------\n"
40               << "Printing Page...\n\n";
41
42            // call IPage print method
43            page->print();
44            cout << "\nPage successfully printed\n"
45               << "-------------------------------\n"
46               << "Resume typing:\n";
47         }
48         else
49
50            // otherwise, append entered character to document
51            paper.AppendCharacter( input );
52      } // end while
53
54      // demonstrate covariance
55      cout << "Creating copy of document, displaying text\n";
56
57      // create copy of document
58      CRectangleDocument *document = paper.clone();
59
60      // get pointer to document as IDocument
61      page = document;
62      page->print();    // print text
63      delete document; // delete pointer
64
65      return 0;
66   } // end function main
```

Fig. 21.6   Word-processor application logic. (Part 2 of 3.)

```
Page Properties: Rectangle
width: 30
height: 9

Please begin typing.
MEMO
TO: ALL EMPLOYEES
FROM: Systems

We will be experiencing network downtime from May 1st to May 3rd as
we change service providers. We apologize for any inconvenience this
may cause.

Thank you for your patience,
-Systems^P
--------------------------------
Printing Page...

MEMO
TO: ALL EMPLOYEES
FROM: Systems

We will be experiencing network
 downtime from May 1st to May 3
rd as we change service provide
rs. We apologize for any incon
venience this may cause.

-----------------

Thank you for your patience,
-Systems

Page Successfully printed
--------------------------------
Resume typing:
^Z
Creating copy of document, displaying text
MEMO
TO: ALL EMPLOYEES
FROM: Systems

We will be experiencing network
 downtime from May 1st to May 3
rd as we change service provide
rs. We apologize for any incon
venience this may cause.

-----------------

Thank you for your patience,
-Systems
```

Fig. 21.6 Word-processor application logic. (Part 3 of 3.)

Line 17 creates a new **CRectangleDocument** object with page size of 30 x 9 characters and no initial text. Lines 21–22 obtain **IDocument** and **ITwoDimensionalShape** pointers to the **CRectangleDocument** object. Lines 25–27 display the document's shape properties by calling method **print** on the **ITwoDimensionalShape** pointer to the object. Lines 34–52 execute until the user presses *end of file* (*Ctrl+Z* in Windows). Lines 37–47 execute if the user presses *Ctrl+P* in Windows. Line 43 calls method **print** on the **IDocument** pointer to display the document. Line 51 executes if the user enters any other character and simply appends the character to the end of the document. Lines 58–63 create a copy of the document (using method **clone**) and display its text.

21.3.3 Minor Modifications and Changes to Unmanaged Code

The changes to unmanaged code in Visual C++ .NET are Microsoft's effort to increase the language's ANSI/ISO C++ standards compliance and to modernize the language. This section outlines some of the many minor changes to the language. A complete listing is available in the Microsoft documentation at

```
ms-help://MS.VSCC/MS.MSDNVS/vcedit/html/
vcrefwhatsnewcompilerandcplulangvisualc70.htm
```

ANSI C++ does not provide explicit Unicode® support (in fact, the specification does not specify any character set), and many implementations of the standard libraries only support the ANSI character set. Many industry leaders, including Microsoft, have been shifting their products to the Unicode® character set. (See Appendix D for more information on the Unicode® character set.) Visual C++ .NET provides extensions, including new library functions, to ease the shift from ANSI-based code to Unicode® two-byte characters. The extensions include the introduction of wide-character string-handling functions into the runtime libraries. A few of the new wide-character functions are listed in Fig. 21.7.

Function	Correlates to	Description
_cwprintf	printf	Prints a wide character string to standard output, allows formatting as **printf** using a wide-character string.
_putwch	putchar	Prints a wide character to standard output.
_putws	puts	Prints wide-character string to standard output.
_wtof	atof	Converts wide-character string to **double** value.
_getwch	getchar	Retrieves a character from standard input as a wide character.
_ungetwch	ungetc	Pushes a wide-character back onto a file stream.
cgetws	gets	Retrieves a wide character string from standard input.
_getwche	_getche	Retrieves a character from standard input as a wide character and echoes the value.

Fig. 21.7   Selected wide-character C runtime library functions. (Part 1 of 2.)

Function	Correlates to	Description
`_cwscanf`	`scanf`	Reads formatted data from input stream using wide character format string.

Fig. 21.7   Selected wide-character C runtime library functions. (Part 2 of 2.)

To increase Visual C++ .NET's ANSI/ISO C++ compliance, Microsoft has added support for **wchar_t** as a native type, function-**try** blocks, and templates that take template parameters.

The native **wchar_t** data type is a two-byte character ANSI C++ compliant type included by Microsoft in the current version of Visual C++. However, you must specifically enable the **/Zc:wchar_t** compiler option to obtain access to this type. Previously the type was defined in the **wchar.h** header, and was a **typedef** for **unsigned short**, the inclusion of **wchar_t** as a compiler recognized type gives benefits in the form of supporting overloading and better type safety.

*Function-***try** *blocks* allow a **try/catch** block to catch any exception in a function or method, including a constructor's initialization list. The syntax for a function-**try** block is as follows:

```
method-prototype
    try : initialization-list {

        // function body
    }
    catch( error-type ) {

        // error handler
    }
```

where *method-prototype* is the prototype for the method without the semicolon.[2]

Template functions and classes now may take template parameters using the following syntax:

```
template< template< class T > class T1 >
class-or-method-prototype {}
```

The templated template parameters expand the functionality of template classes to allow template classes and functions that can use and manipulate other templated classes.

In addition, several new classes have been introduced for both MFC and ATL. The MSDN documentation lists and describes each new class. Chapters 22 and 23 discuss some new classes in ATL and its new extension, ATL Server.

---

2. More information about function-**try** blocks can be found at
   msdn.microsoft.com/library/default.asp?url=/library/en-us/ vclang/html/vclrffunction-tryblocks.asp.

21.4 Additions to Visual C++ .NET

In addition to the minor tweaks and standards-compliance features discussed in the previous section, unmanaged Visual C++ .NET introduces several new technologies and concepts to the world of C++. These include basic managed features, simplified Web programming, COM and database programming as well as new features allowing unmanaged code to interact with managed code.

21.4.1 Runtime checks

Visual C++ .NET introduces several features to provide some basic runtime checks for unmanaged code. Figure 21.8 shows the property pages for our word-processor application in the previous section with all the runtime checks enabled. Access this property page by right clicking the project name, selecting **Properties**, navigating to the **C/C++** folder and selecting the **Code Generation** item.

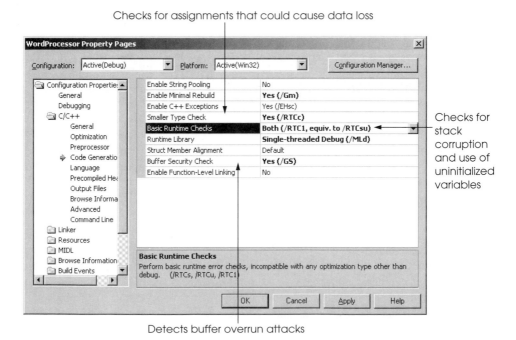

Checks for assignments that could cause data loss

Checks for stack corruption and use of uninitialized variables

Detects buffer overrun attacks

Fig. 21.8 Unmanaged runtime checks.

Of the four checks shown, three are termed runtime checks and one is a security check. The runtime checks—stack corruption, uninitialized variable use and data loss—work only if no compiler optimizations have been selected. Each check is designed for debug purposes and results in a small performance hit. The security check works in all build configurations and is designed to detect, at runtime, an attempt to exploit a common programming error called buffer overflow.

The **Smaller Type Check** option causes the code to throw an exception any time data are lost by assignment from a larger to a smaller type. In some cases the compiler will flag such instances as a warning, but in many cases it is unable to determine whether data are actually lost at compile time; this runtime check flags exactly where data loss occurs.

The **Basic Runtime Checks** option enables the stack-corruption check and the uninitialized-variable-use check. The stack, the memory that stores local variables and pointers, can be corrupted in a number of ways, but usually from the misuse of an array or a bad pointer. Writing to a bad location will often overwrite other data on the stack, or the stack pointer itself, resulting in stack corruption. The stack-corruption runtime check will flag an error any time an array or pointer writes to a location not allocated by the compiler for that data item. The uninitialized-variable check flags any location where a variable is used without initialization, which often results in unexpected program results.

In buffer-overrun attacks, a malicious user locates an area where the program allocates a variable to contain input on the stack, but does not ensure the length of the input. In such cases, the attacker can pass specifically formed bad input to the target program that overwrites the return address of a function with the address of malicious code. The buffer-security check places a security key in the memory preceding the return address for each function at runtime. When the function returns, the security key is checked; if the value is changed, the current thread of execution is halted. The buffer-security check is unique in that it runs in all build configurations, so it may be used in production applications to prevent attacks. While a program is executing with the stack-corruption runtime check enabled, the buffer-security check may not be raised, because the stack-corruption check detects many types of buffer overruns first.

Figure 21.9 demonstrates each of the runtime checks and the buffer-security check. Each program execution will raise a random check.

```
1   // Fig. 21.9: Runtime Checks.cpp
2   // Demonstrates native C++ runtime checks.
3
4   #include <tchar.h>
5   #include <time.h>
6   #include <stdlib.h>
7   #include <iostream>
8
9   void UninitializedVariable();
10  void LoseInformation();
11  void CorruptStack();
12  void BufferOverflow();
13
```

Fig. 21.9   Unmanaged runtime checks demonstration. (Part 1 of 5.)

```
14   using std::cin;
15   using std::cout;
16
17   // application entry point
18   int main( int argc, _TCHAR *argv[] )
19   {
20
21      // seed random number generator with current time
22      srand( time( NULL ) );
23
24      // get number from 0 to 3
25      int errorType = rand() % 4;
26
27      switch ( errorType ) {
28
29         case 0:
30
31            // cause uninitialized variable error
32            UninitializedVariable();
33            break;
34
35         case 1:
36
37            // cause loss of information error
38            LoseInformation();
39            break;
40
41         case 2:
42
43            // cause stack corruption
44            CorruptStack();
45            break;
46
47         case 3:
48
49            // cause buffer overflow
50            BufferOverflow();
51            break;
52      } // end switch
53
54      return 0;
55   } // end function main
56
57   // enable runtime checks for this section
58   #pragma runtime_checks( "scu", restore )
59
60   // uses an uninitialized variable
61   void UninitializedVariable()
62   {
63
64      // loop until runtime check flags uninitialized variable use
65      while ( true ) {
66         int variable;
```

Fig. 21.9 Unmanaged runtime checks demonstration. (Part 2 of 5.)

```
67
68          // satisfies compiler variable initialization check
69          if ( rand() == 1 )
70             variable = rand();
71
72          int variable2 = variable;     // error
73       }
74    } // end function UninitializedVariable
75
76    // assigns data to an item which cannot hold it all
77    void LoseInformation()
78    {
79       int nineBits = 256;
80       int eightBits = 255;
81       char item;
82
83       // 255 fits in char
84       item = eightBits;
85
86       // 256 causes error
87       item = nineBits;
88    } // end function LoseInformation
89
90    // clears the passed character string
91    void EmptyString( char *string )
92    {
93       char current;
94
95       // read until end of null terminated string
96       for ( int i = 0; ( current = string[ i ] ) != '\0'; i++ )
97          string[ i ] = 0;
98    } // end function EmptyString
99
100   // corrupts stack by passing address of character to
101   // function expecting null terminated character string
102   void CorruptStack()
103   {
104
105      // character on stack
106      char stackVariable;
107
108      // send address of character to string function
109      EmptyString( &stackVariable );
110
111      // corrupted stack will be detected when function returns
112   } // end function CorruptStack
113
114   // returns a password string
115   char *GetPassword()
116   {
117      return "This is a long password";
118   } // end function GetPassword
119
```

Fig. 21.9   Unmanaged runtime checks demonstration. (Part 3 of 5.)

```
120  // disable runtime checks, stack corruption check will flag overflow
121  // before the buffer overflow check
122  #pragma runtime_checks( "", off )
123
124  void BufferOverflow()
125  {
126
127      // buffer for password
128      char password[ 10 ];
129
130      // call password routine
131      char *getPassword = GetPassword();
132
133      // copy string, if getPassword is more than 10 characters
134      // function will overwrite return address.
135      strcpy( password, getPassword );
136  } // end function BufferOverflow
```

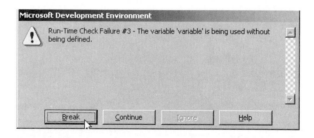

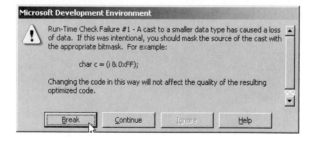

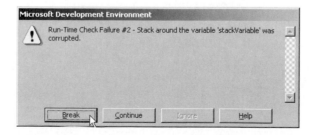

Fig. 21.9   Unmanaged runtime checks demonstration. (Part 4 of 5.)

Fig. 21.9   Unmanaged runtime checks demonstration. (Part 5 of 5.)

Line 22 calls standard library function **srand** to seed the **rand** function with the current time. Line 25 uses function **rand** and the modulus operator (**%**) to produce a pseudo-random number between 0 and 3. The **switch** structure (lines 27–52) uses the randomly generated number to select one of four functions to flag the runtime checks.

Line 58 enables all runtime checks. The **#pragma runtime_checks** enables, or disables, all the runtime checks set by the compiler for a particular block of code. A **#pragma** preprocessor directive supplies information to the compiler, often to perform functions similar to those of compiler flags. Note that the **runtime_checks #pragma** cannot enable a runtime check that was not set by the appropriate compiler flag when the application was compiled. The **#pragma runtime_checks** takes two arguments, a string describing the checks to enable or disable and either keyword **restore** or keyword **off**. The string can be empty or can be any combination of the letters **s**, **c** and **u**, which represent stack-corruption check, data-loss check and uninitialized-variable-assignment check, respectively. If keyword **restore** is used, the designated checks will be enabled. If an empty string is used, all checks set by the compiler flags are enabled. If keyword **off** is used, the designated checks are disabled, and, if an empty string is used, all checks are disabled.

Function **UninitializedVariable** (lines 61–74) demonstrates the uninitialized-variable-runtime check. The function contains an infinite loop that creates a new integer which is assigned only if the result of function **rand** is **1**; it is then used to initialize another variable. The compiler will not issue a warning at compilation time if it is at all possible for a variable to be initialized when it is used. The runtime check will halt the program and break into debug mode when the uninitialized variable is used, as shown in the first output.

Function **LoseInformation** (lines 77–88) creates two **ints**, **eightBits** and **nineBits**, and attempts to store them in a single-byte **char**. Integer **eightBits** is initialized to 255 (the largest possible single-byte value), and is assigned to the **char** in line 84 without a problem. However, line 87 attempts to store integer **nineBits**, which has the value **256**, in the **char**. The **char** data-type cannot hold the value **256**, so the assignment results in data loss. The runtime check detects the data loss, and program execution is halted to debug mode, as is shown in the second program output.

Function **CorruptStack** (lines 102–112) demonstrates the stack-corruption runtime check. Line 109 calls function **EmptyString**, which expects a null-terminated string, with a reference to a single character. Function **EmptyString** (lines 91–98) expects a character-string pointer and loops through each character of the string, setting its value to zero, until it reaches the null termination character. When **EmptyString** is passed the address to a single character, it instead interprets the address as a pointer to a null-terminated string. The function then reads bytes starting at the **char** location, over-writing arbitrary memory until it encounters zeroed memory, so any information between the address of the character and the first byte of zeroed memory is lost. The stack-corruption runtime check detects the error and breaks into debug mode when function **Corrupt-Stack** returns.

Line 122 disables runtime checks, to allow the buffer-overflow check to activate. The buffer-overflow check, unlike the runtime checks, works also when compiler optimizations are enabled; thus, we disable the runtime checks to prevent the stack-corruption check from discovering the buffer overflow before the security check does so. Function **Buffer-Overflow** (lines 124–136) creates a 10-character buffer to store a password and calls function **GetPassword** to obtain the user's password. Function **GetPassword** (lines 115–118) simply returns a string that is more than 10 characters. When the program calls function **strcpy**, the long password string overruns the designated 10-character buffer, into the function's return address. The buffer-security check will be triggered and will halt the program, as shown in the fourth program output.

21.4.2 Attributed Programming

Visual C++ .NET introduces a new programming model, *attributed programming*, based on attributes used in *Microsoft Interface Definition Language (MIDL)*, a language used to describe COM objects in a language-independent manner. Attributes are a powerful new feature designed primarily to simplify COM and database programming, but they may be used for several other purposes, such as the already demonstrated event-handling attributes. For a complete overview of attributed programming, see Chapter 22, Attributed Programming in ATL/COM.

21.4.3 ATL Server

ATL Server is a new set of classes designed to provide the power of native code with rapid Web-application and XML-Web-service development. Chapter 23 discusses ATL Server in detail.

21.4.4 .NET Interoperability

The focus of Chapters 24 and 25 is on combining managed and unmanaged code. The cornerstone of Visual C++ .NET is its services designed to smooth the transition from unmanaged to managed code. Chapter 24, Managed and Unmanaged Interoperability, discusses Microsoft's It Just Works (IJW) technology and the Platform Invoke service. Chapter 25, COM Interoperability Services, demonstrates COM and .NET component interoperability.

21.5 Summary

In .NET, unmanaged code is any code that does not target the Common Language Runtime (CLR). The CLR is the .NET environment that provides such basic services as garbage collection and array-bounds checking to .NET applications. The functions of the CLR require resources dedicated to managing the code, so fewer resources are available for the application logic.

.NET code is compiled into an intermediate, assembly-like, language: Microsoft Intermediate Language (MSIL). MSIL is compiled to native code at runtime (or installation time) by a Just-In-Time (JIT) compiler. The JIT compiler compiles a routine into native code the first time it is executed and stores the compiled code for future calls to the routine.

Virtually all pre-.NET applications and libraries are written with unmanaged code, and it would not be practical to convert the enormous code base to a managed context. Unmanaged Visual C++ .NET allows managed and unmanaged code to work side by side in the same application. For such performance-critical applications as games, scientific applications and core operating-system components, it is unlikely that the benefits provided by the CLR will outweigh the performance cost and the sacrifice of low-level system control.

The Unified Event Model standardizes events and event handling across unmanaged C++, COM and Managed extensions for C++. In previous editions of Visual C++, unmanaged C++ was forced to perform event handling via C-style function callbacks, and COM was restricted to a limited, through still complex, event model. The Unified Event Model uses common syntax and a streamlined event processing to provide a simple and powerful event model. The Unified Event Model promotes component reusability by allowing a server component to offer an event that clients may dynamically hook to, and unhook from, without the server component's requiring any knowledge of the implementation of the client component.

The **event_source** attribute takes a single parameter that designates the type of event source—valid parameter values are **native**, **com** and **managed**. An event-receiver (also known as an event-sink) class contains event-handling methods. Attribute **event_receiver** takes a parameter—**native**, **com** or **managed**—that designates the event context. An event-receiver class usually contains one or more event handlers (methods that are triggered when events are raised).

An event is raised with keyword **__raise** followed by a call to the event method of an object of an event-source class. Keyword **__raise** is optional when triggering an event, but preceding an event call with the **__raise** keyword greatly enhances the readability of your code.

Keyword **__hook** connects an event handler to an event source. When an event handler is hooked to an event, the event handler will be called when the event is raised on the specified instance of the event source. It is valid for a single event handler to be connected to several event sources and for a single event source to be hooked by several event handlers

Keyword **__unhook** disconnects an event handler from an event source. An unhooked event handler no longer handles events from the specified event. It is good practice to unhook all hooked events before the event-receiver object is destroyed

An **__interface** is roughly analogous to a class containing only pure virtual functions in traditional C++ and is designed after a COM interface. An interface defined with the **__interface** keyword must contain only **public** methods and properties and can inherit from other interfaces, but not from classes. An interface cannot contain data members, constructors, destructors, overloaded operators or **static** methods.

Explicit overrides allow a derived class to override two inherited methods with the same name and method signature. To explicitly override a method, scope the method name in the method declaration and definition, using the syntax *interface**::**methodName*. Visual C++ .NET now allows covariant return types, enabling a derived class to change the return type of an overridden base method to a derived type.

While ANSI C++ does not provide explicit Unicode® support and many implementations use the ANSI character set, many vendors, including Microsoft, have been shifting their products to the Unicode® character set. Visual C++ .NET provides extensions to ease the shift from ANSI-based code to Unicode® two-byte characters. The extensions include the introduction of wide-character string-handling functions into the runtime libraries.

The **wchar_t** data type was introduced in Visual C++ .NET as a native data type to increase ANSI compliance and enable overloading and increased type checking.

Function-**try** blocks allow a **try/catch** block to catch any exception in a function or method, including a constructor's initialization list.

Several runtime checks—stack corruption, uninitialized variable use and data loss—work only if no compiler optimizations have been selected. The security check works in all build configurations and is designed to detect, at runtime, an attempt to exploit a common programming error, the buffer overflow. The smaller-type check causes the code to throw an exception any time data is lost by assignment from a larger to a smaller type. The stack can be corrupted in a number of ways, but usually from the misuse of an array or a bad pointer. The uninitialized-variable check flags any location where a variable is used without initialization, which often results in unexpected program results.

In buffer-overrun attacks, a malicious user locates an area where the program allocates a variable to contain input on the stack, but does not check the length of the input. The buffer-security check detects vulnerable functions and places a security key in the memory preceding the return address at runtime. When the function returns, the security key is checked. If the value is changed; the program is halted.

Pragma runtime_checks enables, or disables, all the runtime checks set by the compiler for a particular block of code.

22

Attributed Programming in ATL/COM

Objectives

- To understand COM and ATL fundamentals.
- To understand how attributes and attribute providers work.
- To examine and debug injected code.
- To understand the Unified Event Model in COM.
- To create an attributed ATL COM Object.
- To create an attributed ATL ActiveX control.

Good order is the foundation of all good things.
Edmund Burke

Come and take choice of all my library,...
William Shakespeare

A library is thought in cold storage.
Lord Samuel

To every form of being is assigned,
Thus calmly spoke the venerable Sage,
An active Principle.
William Wordsworth

The movement of the progressive societies has hitherto been
a movement from Status to Contract.
Henry Maine

22.1 Introduction

Attributed programming is a new feature in Visual C++ .NET designed to simplify common programming tasks, most notably in the area of COM development. In this chapter we discuss how attributes simplify COM and ATL. This chapter (which is targeted towards developers with previous knowledge of unmanaged code, managed code, Win32 programming, COM and ATL) is designed to demonstrate the power of attributed programming in COM. While attributes simplify COM development, a solid understanding of COM basics is essential to use attributes correctly. The Internet and Web Resources section at the end of this chapter contains several resources for the developer looking to learn more about COM and ATL.

22.2 Attributes, COM and ATL

Before delving into attributed COM and ATL programming, this section provides a brief overview of each technology and concludes with a discussion of the purpose and technology behind COM attributed programming.

22.2.1 Introduction to COM

Initially, applications created for Windows or DOS were designed as single *monolithic executables*—i.e., complete applications packaged as single executable files. However, as software became more complex, developers began to experience difficulties constructing all the necessary components of an application. Furthermore, as the size of applications increased, it became impractical to package and deploy an entire application to accommodate each application upgrade or bug fix.

To address these problems, Microsoft incorporated *shared libraries* into Windows, enabling developers to reuse and modularize code easily. A shared library, or *dynamic link library (DLL)* in Windows, is a file containing compiled code that an application loads at execution time. The fact that these libraries are loaded at runtime allows developers to modify specific libraries and test the results without rebuilding an entire application. Multiple applications can use a single shared library, which reduces the overall memory requirements for running those applications. The partitioning of programs into small pieces also makes it easier to distribute application upgrades, because only the modified DLLs must be redistributed.

The introduction of shared libraries solved many problems that previously had restricted modularity and code reusability. However, the libraries also raised new concerns. Monolithic applications rarely created version conflicts—if an application vendor fixed a bug in one piece of software, it was unlikely that the upgrade would affect any other software on the system. With the establishment of system-wide shared libraries, a vendor's upgrade or modification of a library could "break" software that used an older version of that library. Often, developers packaged DLLs with their applications to ensure software compatibility. However, the packaged DLLs could overwrite preexisting libraries on users' systems, possibly affecting previously installed software. Problems introduced by shared libraries were so difficult to locate and fix that their effects became known as "DLL hell."

Microsoft developed the *Component Object Model (COM)* in an attempt to expand DLL functionality and correct DLL problems. COM is a binary standard that provides a platform-, language- and location-independent environment to develop reusable object-oriented software components. Microsoft defined the COM specification to be detailed and strict, thus ensuring that COM developers create compatible libraries. Microsoft also implemented the COM architecture on a large scale—virtually all Windows libraries adhere to the COM specification.

The COM specification is built on the concepts of *component objects* and *interfaces*. A component object provides a service that it exposes to the system via one or more interfaces. An interface simply provides a *contract* between the component object and other software that promises a set of functionality. COM is based on the client/server model—the component, or *server*, offers a service to another piece of software, the *client* (which may also be a server).

A fundamental element of the COM architecture is the restriction that prevents any component object from being accessed directly; it must always be accessed via a pointer to a supported interface. The extra level of indirection between the interface and component object allows the language independence and location independence features assured by COM and allows an elegant solution to the DLL-versioning problem.

Any language that allows indirect calls through *virtual function tables (vtables)*, such as C, C++, Visual Basic and Java may create and use COM objects. COM objects offer a language-independent interface to a client application; Any language that supports indirect calls can use the interface to access the component. And, because COM defines a binary standard, not a source standard, the client application can access the COM component in a standard fashion, without knowing the original component language.

The indirection between interface and component also allows a component to be used by other software *in-process*, *out-of-process* or even on a remote machine (using DCOM) without requiring a recompilation of the binary. In-process components are directly loaded into the client application's memory space, while out-of-process components reside in a separate memory space, either as a separate service or on a remote host. The connection between software components is controlled by COM; thus, it enables *remote procedure calls* (i.e., calls from a local process to a remote process), required to present software components with complete remote/local transparency. In each case, the client software component has only a pointer to the component interface; for an in-process COM object, calls on this pointer are directly referenced to the in-process component. For an out-of-process or remote call, a call on the interface pointer calls a local process proxy object provided by COM. The *proxy object* acts as a wrapper for the remote procedure and provides the function-call marshaling and connections required to reach the remote stub object. The remote *stub object* exists in the remote COM object process and unmarshals the function call, forwards the request to the COM object, then marshals and returns any return value. In a generic sense, *data marshaling* refers to the process of converting data types from one type to another, usually to facilitate data communication between applications or protocols with disparate type representations. In addition, *function-call marshaling* refers to the process of packaging a function call for a different communication standard, such as setting argument ordering and performing data marshaling on arguments and return types.

In addition, the interface model allows a component to add functionality without breaking backwards compatibility with existing software. Adding functionality to a COM component is as simple as implementing another interface—old software continues to use the old interface, while newer software can use newer interfaces. In addition, the interfaces provided by a COM component are dynamically exposed by a call to **QueryInterface**, which allows client code to dynamically determine if an object supports a selected interface.

Due to the complexity and rigidity of the COM specification, it requires significant developer resources to provide all the necessary functionality required of a full COM component. Microsoft has introduced several technologies to simplify COM component creation. The following section discusses Microsoft's Active Template Library as a technology to create COM components.

22.2.2 Introduction to ATL

The *Active Template Library (ATL)* was designed to provide a set of template classes to simplify the creation of small COM components and ActiveX controls. The primary design goal of the ATL team was to provide an efficient, low-overhead component implementation. Unlike the *Microsoft Foundation Classes (MFC)*, which are designed to simplify the creation of complex Windows applications and rely on a large runtime DLL, ATL provides small templated classes that are directly compiled into component code and require a significantly smaller runtime library.

As indicated by the name, ATL makes heavy use of templates to provide reusable, flexible code. A class uses ATL by inheriting from base classes and using itself as the template parameter. The template classes provide default COM interface implementations and use templates to provide general implementations that, when extended, are class specific.

The ATL classes provide a host of COM implementations to support COM tasks such as reference counting, object registration, ActiveX controls, error handling and much more. ATL is an evolving technology (the current version is 7.0, released with Visual C++ .NET), which replaces ATL 3.0, packaged with the previous version of Visual C++. ATL 7.0 provides various enhancements and changes to ATL that will be highlighted throughout this chapter.

The complexity of ATL deterred many programmers from learning and using the technology. The latest version of Visual C++ includes attributes that are used heavily by ATL to simplify component creation without sacrificing the efficiency.

22.2.3 Simplifying ATL with Attributes

Attributes are a new feature in Visual C++ .NET that use separate DLLs, called *attribute providers*, to inject code into an application. An attribute "marks up"—specifies a property of—a source file, class, interface, function or parameter. Attributes add or modify an item's functionality or describe the item to the compiler. When the Visual C++ .NET compiler encounters an attribute, it syntactically verifies the attribute and passes the attribute and its parameters off to an attribute provider. The attribute provider is a separate DLL that inserts, modifies or creates the necessary code for the attribute. The code from the attribute provider is incorporated into the application at link-time. Currently, Visual C++ ships with two attribute providers, **atlprov.dll** and **clxx.dll**.

Syntactically, attributes may be recognized in a source file as items contained in attribute blocks by square brackets and separated by commas. An attribute may take zero or more parameters, specified in parentheses. Attributes accept two types of input, named and unnamed parameters. *Named attribute parameters* are specified by a parameter name, followed by an equal sign and a value. In many cases, these parameters are optional. *Unnamed parameters* are specified by simply placing the argument value in parenthesis after the attribute name. These parameters are often required. In addition, many attributes have default values for several parameters, which are used if no alternate parameter value is supplied. Use the MSDN documentation to obtain a full listing of attributes, their named and unnamed parameters and their default arguments. A typical attribute block could look as follows:

```
[
    // attribute with no arguments
    attribute1_name,

    // attribute with single, unnamed argument
    attribute2_name( value ),

    // attribute with multiple, named arguments
    attribute3_name( parameter1 = value, parameter2 = value )
]
modified_element_name
```

Attributes were created, in part, as a solution to the difficulties involved in creating and maintaining COM objects, type libraries and registration scripts. However, attributes are used in Visual C++ .NET for many tasks. There are five attribute categories: IDL, COM, ATL Server, OLE DB and compiler attributes. This chapter will focus on IDL, COM and compiler attributes, while Chapter 23 discusses ATL Server and OLE DB attributes. Attributes in the IDL category are used by the compiler to generate the IDL file, and attributes in the COM category simplify COM component development.

A fundamental difficulty in COM component development has been maintenance of component description and registration information across several source files. In ATL 3.0, any change to a component, such as adding a method to the interface or altering the threading model, required altering the project's **.idl** and **.rgs** files. Correctly maintaining these separate files was an error-prone procedure. In addition, the developer was forced to learn the IDL syntax or become reliant on Visual Studio wizards. While previous versions of Visual Studio provided tools and wizards for COM components, these wizards did not eliminate much of the problems inherent with maintaining multiple description files and tended to slow down development time.

In Visual C++ .NET, attributes replace the separate **.idl** and **.rgs** files and cause the attribute providers to generate these files at compile time. In addition, while Visual Studio .NET still provides wizards for COM component creation, the programmer's reliance on wizards may be drastically reduced for simple tasks.

The second problem with implementing COM interfaces is providing for the derived class's object maps, object identification, class factories, threading and common-base-interface method implementations. COM attribute objects provide solutions for each of these tasks as well as performance monitoring capabilities. While it remains possible to provide custom implementations for COM component responsibilities, in most cases the default implementations provide the necessary functionality.

Compiler attributes provide functionality for the Unified Event Model, in addition to providing flags that control the generation and functionality of the project's libraries, IDL file and attributed code.

In some cases, it is helpful to view the code that is injected by the attribute providers. In most cases, the injected code is never written to a file, but the Visual C++ .NET compiler does include the option to write the merged code to disk at compile time. The compiler flag (**/Fx**) may be enabled in the project properties in Visual Studio .NET as shown in Fig. 22.1. The **/Fx** *compiler option* generates the attributed source and writes it to disk as a file in the form of *filename***.mrg.***extension*. Thus, a file named **myApplication.cpp** that contained attributes causes a generated file named **myApplication.mrg.cpp** to be created in the application directory. The generated merged source file may not contain exactly the code that is compiled for the attributes, but contains a representation of the compiled code.

22.3 Creating an Attributed COM DLL

The first example demonstrates COM attributes by creating a simple ATL COM+ 1.0 linked list library. The following steps guide the reader through the creation of the project and COM object using Visual Studio .NET Wizards:

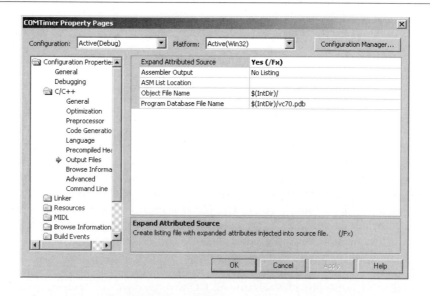

Fig. 22.1 Expand Attributed Source compiler option.

1. Create a new **Visual C++ Project** of type **ATL Project**, named `LinkedList` as show in Fig. 22.2.
2. Modify the **ATL Project Wizard** to ensure the **Application Settings** are as shown in Fig. 22.3. This will create an attributed DLL project with support for COM+ 1.0 and component registration.
3. In the project's **Solution Explorer**, right click the project name, and choose **Add > Add Class...** to display the dialog box shown in Fig. 22.4. Select **ATL COM+ 1.0 Component** and click **Open**
4. In the **ATL COM+ 1.0 Component Wizard**, enter the component's **Short Name** as **COMLinkedList**. Note that all other fields will be filled in for you, as shown in Fig. 22.5. Click **Finish**.

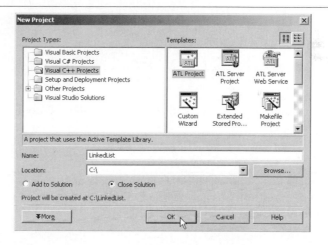

Fig. 22.2 **New Project** dialog creating an **ATL Project**.

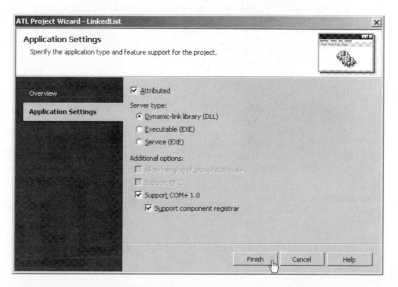

Fig. 22.3 **ATL Project Wizard** dialog.

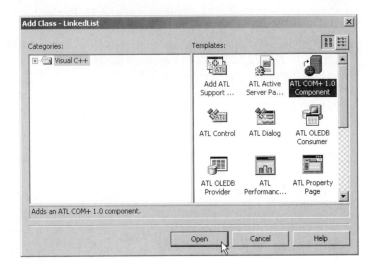

Fig. 22.4   **Add Class** dialog creating an **ATL COM+ 1.0 Component**.

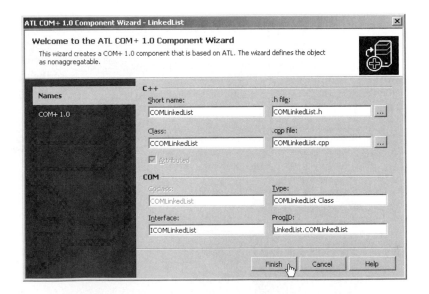

Fig. 22.5   **ATL COM+ 1.0 Component Wizard** for class **CCOMLinkedList**.

After completing these steps, the project will contain each of the files shown and described in Fig. 22.6.

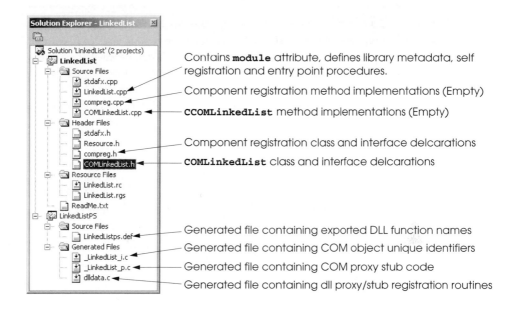

Fig. 22.6   LinkedList project files and descriptions.

Figure 22.7 shows the generated file **LinkedList.cpp**, which demonstrates the **module** attribute.

The **module** attribute (lines 10–15) is one of the most important attributes in the IDL category. Not only does it create the IDL library block used to describe the COM library, but it causes the compiler to inject default implementations of entry-point and library registration functions. The parameters to the **module** attribute, and their default values, are listed in Fig. 22.8.

```
1    // Fig. 22.7: LinkedList.cpp
2    // Generated module attribute for LinkedList application.
3
4    #include "stdafx.h"
5    #include "resource.h"
6    #include "compreg.h"
7
8    // module attribute causes injected implementations of DllMain,
9    // DllRegisterServer and DllUnregisterServer
10   [ module(dll, uuid = "{38030524-8230-462D-8EFD-24065193AD95}",
11       name = "LinkedList",
12       helpstring = "LinkedList 1.0 Type Library",
13       resource_name = "IDR_LINKEDLIST",
14       custom = { "a817e7a1-43fa-11d0-9e44-00aa00b6770a",
15           "{23AD707F-C566-4C40-91E7-23209A1AD172}"}) ];
```

Fig. 22.7   COM linked list library module attribute.

Parameter Name	Value	Description
type	dll, exe or service	(Optional) Defines whether module is to be in-process, out-of-process or Windows NT Service (Default value: dll).
name	string	(Optional) Human readable module name.
uuid	string	(Optional) Unique ID, generated if omitted.
version	floating-point value	(Optional) Specifies module version number (Default value: 1.0).
lcid	integer	(Optional) The locale identifier, an integer that specifies the country and language of the component.
control	boolean	(Optional) Specifies whether COM object is a control.
helpstring	string	(Optional) Specifies the type library name.
helpstringdll	string	(Optional) Specifies a .dll module file name to display in object viewer.
helpfile	string	(Optional) Name of module help file.
helpcontext	integer	(Optional) Unique ID that is used to map a module to its help text.
helpstringcontext	integer	(Optional) Unique ID that is used to map.
hidden	boolean	(Optional) A hidden module will not be displayed in a user-oriented browser.
restricted	boolean	(Optional) Specifies that the module's methods may not be called arbitrarily.
custom	string	(Optional) Allows custom data to be placed in the IDL file; takes two parameters: a unique ID for the custom data, and the custom data as a string.
resource_name	string	Specifies the module resource name for use in the .rgs file.

Fig. 22.8   module attribute parameters.

The **type** parameter value may be *dll*, *exe* or *service*; the value determines the entry-point and registration code injected by the **module** attribute; the default value is **dll**. The **dll** parameter causes the module to be implemented as a service intended to be run as part of another process; the injected code includes implementations of **DLLMain**, **DllRegisterServer** and **DllUnRegisterServer**. The **exe** parameter causes the module to be implemented as a COM server intended to be run as its own process; the injected code includes an implementation of **WinMain**. The **service** parameter causes the module to be implemented as a standalone Windows NT service; the injected code provides an implementation of **WinMain**. The remaining parameters directly correspond to the IDL library block attributes in an unattributed COM module **.idl** file.

Class **ListNode** (Fig. 22.9) represents a node in a linked list. Each **ListNode** stores a data item and a pointer to the next item in the list. For more information on the linked list data structure, consult Chapter 19, Data Structures and Collections.

```
 1   // Fig. 22.9: ListNode.h
 2   // Represents a node in a list; contains variant data and
 3   // a pointer to the next node in the list.
 4
 5   #pragma once
 6
 7   class ListNode
 8   {
 9   public:
10
11      // declare class CCOMLinkedList as friend
12      friend class CCOMLinkedList;
13      ListNode( const VARIANT * );   // constructor
14      VARIANT getData() const;       // return data in node
15
16   private:
17      VARIANT data;                  // data
18      ListNode *nextPtr;             // next node in list
19   }; // end class ListNode
```

Fig. 22.9 **ListNode** class stores **CCOMLinkedList** data.

Line 12 declares class **CCOMLinkedList** as a friend of **ListNode**; this allows **CCOMLinkedList** direct access to **ListNode**'s data members. The **ListNode** constructor (line 13) initializes the **VARIANT** data member to the constructor argument. Method **getData** (line 14) returns the data item of the **ListNode**. The private data members (lines 17–18) store the node data and a pointer to the next node in the list.

Class **ListNode**'s method definitions (Fig. 22.10) initialize and provide access to the class data members.

Figure 22.11 contains the attributed COM linked list interface declaration. While the project wizards place the object interface and implementation class in the same file we have moved the interface definition to **LinkedListInterface.h** to separate the list interface from its implementation. Note the similarity between the attributed interface declaration and a non-attributed project's **.idl** file.

```
 1   // Fig. 22.10: ListNode.cpp
 2   // ListNode class method implementations.
 3
 4   #include "stdafx.h"
 5   #include "listnode.h"
 6
 7   // constructor
 8   ListNode::ListNode( const VARIANT *info ) :
 9      data( *info ), nextPtr( 0 ) { }
10
11   // return copy of data in node
12   VARIANT ListNode::getData() const
13   {
14      return data;
15   }
```

Fig. 22.10 ListNode class method definitions.

```
1    // Fig. 22.11: LinkedInterface.h
2    // Contains COM Linked list interface definition.
3
4    #pragma once
5
6    // (generated) interface attributes
7    [
8       object,
9       uuid( "B32AE10B-C857-428D-99E5-091B1869B0C5" ),
10      dual, helpstring( "ICOMLinkedList Interface" ),
11      pointer_default( unique )
12   ]
13
14   // interface declaration
15   __interface ICOMLinkedList : IDispatch
16   {
17
18      // inserts VARIANT item at front of list
19      [ id( 1 ), helpstring( "Insert VARIANT at font of list" ) ]
20      HRESULT insertAtFront( [ in ] VARIANT *item );
21
22      // inserts VARIANT item at back of list
23      [ id( 2 ), helpstring( "Insert VARIANT at back of list" ) ]
24      HRESULT insertAtBack( [ in ] VARIANT *item );
25
26      // removes item at back of list
27      [ id( 3 ), helpstring( "Remove VARIANT from back of list" ) ]
28      HRESULT removeFromBack( [ out ] VARIANT *item );
29
30      // removes item at from of list
31      [ id( 4 ), helpstring( "Remove VARIANT from front of list" ) ]
32      HRESULT removeFromFront( [ out ] VARIANT *item );
33
34      // determines if list is empty
35      [ id( 5 ), helpstring( "Determine if list is empty" ) ]
36      HRESULT isEmpty( void );
37
38      // displays items in list
39      [ id( 6 ), helpstring( "Displays all items in list" ) ]
40      HRESULT print( void );
41   }; // end interface ICOMLinkedList
42
43   // declare object interface implementation class
44   class DECLSPEC_UUID( "CB0E7FFD-CD1E-4EF7-986B-BFC0B18C3D46" )
45      CCOMLinkedList;
```

Fig. 22.11 `ICOMLinkedList` interface declaration.

The interface attributes (lines 7–12) allow the programmer to define the interface's COM properties in the source file without maintaining a separate `.idl` file describing the interface. The **object** attribute (line 8) causes the interface to be placed in the component's `.idl` file as a custom interface. When an interface is marked by the **object** attribute, the compiler will force the interface to inherit from **IUnknown**. Attribute **uuid** (line 9) defines the interface GUID to uniquely identify the interface. Attribute **dual** (line 10) defines the interface as a *dual interface* (i.e., an interface that supports both **IDispatch** and VTBL binding). Attribute **helpstring** takes a string parameter to describe the modified COM interface. Attribute **pointer_default** (line 11) takes a single parameter, **ptr**, **ref** or **unique** and defines the default pointer type for the interface. Figure 22.12 compares the three COM pointer types.

Interface **ICOMLinkedList** (lines 15–41) uses attributes to specify the interface method properties. Attribute **id** (line 19) takes a single parameter defining the method ID; a method's ID must be unique within the interface and is traditionally numbered with consecutive integers, starting with **1**. Attribute **helpstring** (line 19) is a plain text description of the method. Methods **insertAtFront** (line 20) and **insertAtBack** (line 24) each take a single parameter, modified by attribute *in*, a **VARIANT** to add to the list. Methods **removeFromBack** (line 28) and **removeFromFront** (line 32) remove an item from the list. Each method takes a **VARIANT** argument modified by the *out* attribute that contains the removed item when the function returns. Method **isEmpty** (line 36) takes no arguments and is used to determine whether the list is full. Method **print** (line 40) takes no arguments and displays the contents of the list. Lines 44–45 use macro **DECLSPEC_UUID** to provide a forward declaration of the unique ID and name of the **CCOMLinkedList** class. The forward declaration allows any class which includes the header file to locate the implementation class.

Figure 22.13 presents the class declaration for class **CCOMLinkedList**, which implements **ICOMLinkedList**. The skeleton of this class is generated by the ATL COM+ component wizard.

Pointer Type	Allows NULL Pointers	May be Reassigned within Method	Allows Multiple Pointers to Same Memory Location
ptr	Yes	Yes	Yes
ref	No	No	No
unique	Yes	Yes	No

Fig. 22.12 COM pointer types and properties.

```
1   // Fig. 22.13: COMLinkedList.h
2   // Attributed ATL COM Linked List Interface and class
3   // definitions.
4
5   #pragma once
6
7   #include "resource.h"
8   #include <comsvcs.h>
9   #include <iostream>
10
```

Fig. 22.13 **CCOMLinkedList** class declaration. (Part 1 of 3.)

```
11   // node class for list
12   #include "ListNode.h"
13
14   // LinkedList interface
15   #include "LinkedInterface.h"
16
17   using std::cout;
18
19   // CCOMLinked List attributes
20   [
21      coclass,           // defines this class as COM class
22
23      // specifies that class uses single thread
24      threading( "single" ),
25
26      // indicates that class may not be aggregated
27      aggregatable( "never" ),
28
29      // version independent class id
30      vi_progid( "LinkedList.COMLinkedList" ),
31      progid( "LinkedList.COMLinkedList.1" ),  // version class id
32      version( 1.0 ),                          // class version
33      uuid( "CB0E7FFD-CD1E-4EF7-986B-BFC0B18C3D46" ), // unique ID
34      helpstring( "COMLinkedList Class" )      // class description
35   ]
36   class ATL_NO_VTABLE CCOMLinkedList : public ICOMLinkedList
37   {
38   public:
39
40      // member initialization
41      CCOMLinkedList()
42         : firstPtr( NULL )
43         , lastPtr( NULL )
44      {
45         // no other initialization required
46      }
47
48      // prevents object deletion inside FinalConstruct
49      DECLARE_PROTECT_FINAL_CONSTRUCT()
50
51      // called immediately following object construction
52      HRESULT FinalConstruct()
53      {
54         return S_OK;
55      }
56
57      // called when object is released, displays and deletes
58      // all remaining nodes in list
59      void FinalRelease();
60
61      // list method prototypes
62      STDMETHOD( insertAtFront )( VARIANT *item );
63      STDMETHOD( insertAtBack )( VARIANT *item );
```

Fig. 22.13 CCOMLinkedList class declaration. (Part 2 of 3.)

```
64        STDMETHOD( removeFromBack )( VARIANT *item);
65        STDMETHOD( removeFromFront )( VARIANT *item );
66        STDMETHOD( isEmpty )( void );
67        STDMETHOD( print )( void );
68
69   private:
70
71        // pointer to first node
72        ListNode *firstPtr;
73
74        // pointer to last node
75        ListNode *lastPtr;
76
77        // utility function to allocate new node
78        ListNode *getNewNode( VARIANT *item );
79   }; // end class CCOMLinkedList
```

Fig. 22.13 CCOMLinkedList class declaration. (Part 3 of 3.)

Attribute **coclass** (line 21) declares this class as a COM component. Attribute *coclass* injects a large amount of code into the class. The injected code includes automatic registration routines, the COM class factory implementation and the class's **IUnknown** implementations. In addition, the injected code includes the following methods in the class: *UpdateRegistry*, which registers the class in the registry; *GetObjectCLSID*, which returns the class's ID; *GetObjectFriendlyName*, which returns the object's name as a string in the form "*classname* Object;" *GetProgID*, which returns the value specified in the class's **progid** attribute; and *GetVersionIndependentProgID*, which returns the value specified in the class's **vi_progid** attribute. Finally, attribute **coclass** provides the COM object map between the COM interface and the class. Attribute **coclass** causes the modified class to implement **CComCoClass** for its class factory and **CComObjectRootEx** to maintain the object's reference counting and threading model. Attribute **threading** (line 24) supplies the template parameter for the **CComObjectRootEx** to specify the object's threading model; possible values are **apartment**, **free**, **single**, **neutral** and **both**. A discussion of COM threading models is beyond the scope of this chapter; for an in-depth treatment, reference the Internet and Web Resources section at the end of the chapter.

Attribute **aggregatable** (line 27) corresponds the IDL aggregatable attribute and takes a single, unnamed parameter as its value, which may be **never**, **allowed** or **always**. The **aggregatable** attribute sets the value of the IDL **aggregatable** attribute and, in ATL projects, injects the appropriate macro into compiled code. Attributes **vi_progid** and **progid** (lines 30–31) set the corresponding **.idl** file attributes, which are used to identify the class in a human readable format. Attribute **version** (line 32) specifies the class version number; the default value is **1.0**. Attribute **uuid** (line 33) sets the unique ID of the component used to register and identify the class. Attribute **helpstring** (line 34) sets the class description to display in an object browser.

Class **CCOMLinkedList** (lines 36–79) implements the **ICOMLinkedList** interface to create a COM object linked list. The constructor (line 41–46) initializes the first and last pointers of the list to **NULL**. Macro **DECLARE_PROTECT_FINAL_CONSTRUCT** is inserted by the class wizard to prevent the object from being destroyed during method **FinalConstruct**. Method **FinalConstruct** (lines 52–55) is inserted by the class wizard to contain any final component initialization code. Method **FinalRelease** (line 59) is called just before the component is released and is inserted by the class wizard to contain any final cleanup code. In this example, method **FinalRelease** will display all remaining list members and deallocate any dynamically allocated memory. Lines 62–67 declare the method prototypes for the **ICOMLinkedList** interface methods. Line 72 contains a pointer to a **ListNode** class that will be initialized to the first item in the list. Line 75 contains a pointer to a **ListNode** class that will be initialized to the last node in the list. Private helper function **getNewNode** (line 78) dynamically creates a new **ListNode** containing the passed **VARIANT** as its data value.

The **CCOMLinkedList** method definitions (Fig. 22.14) create and maintain a linked list of **ListNode**s.

```
1   // Fig. 22.14: COMLinkedList.cpp
2   // Method implementation for COM linked list.
3
4   #include "stdafx.h"
5   #include "COMLinkedList.h"
6
7   // inserts VARIANT at front of list
8   STDMETHODIMP CCOMLinkedList::insertAtFront( VARIANT *item )
9   {
10     ListNode *newPtr = getNewNode( item );
11
12     if ( isEmpty() == S_OK )   // list is empty
13        firstPtr = lastPtr = newPtr;
14     else {                     // list is not empty
15        newPtr->nextPtr = firstPtr;
16        firstPtr = newPtr;
17     }
18
19     return S_OK;
20  } // end method insertAtFront
21
22  // inserts variant at back of list
23  STDMETHODIMP CCOMLinkedList::insertAtBack( VARIANT *item )
24  {
25     ListNode *newPtr = getNewNode( item );
26
27     if ( isEmpty() == S_OK ) // list is empty
28        firstPtr = lastPtr = newPtr;
29     else {                     // list is not empty
30        lastPtr->nextPtr = newPtr;
31        lastPtr = newPtr;
32     }
33
34     return S_OK;
35  } // end method insertAtBack
36
37  // removes item from back of list
```

Fig. 22.14 CCOMLinkedList class method definitions. (Part 1 of 4.)

```
38    STDMETHODIMP CCOMLinkedList::removeFromBack( VARIANT *item )
39    {
40       if ( isEmpty() == S_OK )
41          return E_FAIL;    // delete unsuccessful
42       else {
43          ListNode *tempPtr = lastPtr;
44
45          if ( firstPtr == lastPtr )
46             firstPtr = lastPtr = 0;
47          else {
48             ListNode *currentPtr = firstPtr;
49
50             while ( currentPtr->nextPtr != lastPtr )
51                currentPtr = currentPtr->nextPtr;
52
53             lastPtr = currentPtr;
54             currentPtr->nextPtr = 0;
55          }
56
57          item = &tempPtr->data;
58          delete tempPtr;
59       } // end else
60
61       return S_OK;
62    } // end method removeFromBack
63
64    // removes item from front of list
65    STDMETHODIMP CCOMLinkedList::removeFromFront( VARIANT *item )
66    {
67       if ( isEmpty() == S_OK ) // list is empty
68          return E_FAIL;         // delete unsuccessful
69       else {
70          ListNode *tempPtr = firstPtr;
71
72          if ( firstPtr == lastPtr )
73             firstPtr = lastPtr = 0;
74          else
75             firstPtr = firstPtr->nextPtr;
76
77          item = &tempPtr->data; // store removed data
78          delete tempPtr;
79       } // end else
80
81       return S_OK;
82    } // end method removeFromFront
83
84    // determines if list is empty
85    STDMETHODIMP CCOMLinkedList::isEmpty( void )
86    {
87       if ( firstPtr == NULL )
88          return S_OK;
89       else
90          return S_FALSE;
```

Fig. 22.14 CCOMLinkedList class method definitions. (Part 2 of 4.)

```
91    } // end method isEmpty
92
93    // displays contents of list
94    STDMETHODIMP CCOMLinkedList::print( void )
95    {
96       if ( isEmpty() == S_OK ) {
97          cout << "Error: The list is empty\n\n";
98          return E_FAIL;
99       }
100
101      ListNode *currentPtr = firstPtr;
102
103      cout << "The list is: ";
104      HRESULT hr;
105
106      // convert each item to string and display
107      CComVariant variantString;
108      while ( currentPtr != 0 ) {
109         hr = VariantChangeType( &variantString,
110            &currentPtr->data, 0, VT_BSTR );
111
112         if ( SUCCEEDED( hr ) )
113            cout << ( const char* )CW2A( variantString.bstrVal )
114               << ", ";
115         else
116            cout << "Unable to display Item, ";
117
118         currentPtr = currentPtr->nextPtr;
119      } // end while
120
121      cout << "\n\n";
122
123      return S_OK;
124   } // end method print
125
126   // clean up allocated memory and display remaining items
127   void CCOMLinkedList::FinalRelease()
128   {
129      if ( isEmpty() == S_FALSE ) {     // list is not empty
130         cout << "Destroying nodes ...\n";
131
132         ListNode *currentPtr = firstPtr, *tempPtr;
133         HRESULT result;
134
135         // loop through all remaining nodes, delete each node
136         while ( currentPtr != 0 ) {
137            tempPtr = currentPtr;
138
139            // convert variant to string, display value
140            CComVariant stringVariant;
141            result = VariantChangeType( &stringVariant,
142               &currentPtr->data, 0, VT_BSTR );
143
```

Fig. 22.14 CCOMLinkedList class method definitions. (Part 3 of 4.)

```
144              if ( SUCCEEDED( result ) )
145                 cout << "Deleted: "
146                         << ( const char* )CW2A( stringVariant.bstrVal )
147                         << '\n';
148              else
149                 cout << "Unable to display Item \n";
150
151              // get next pointer
152              currentPtr = currentPtr->nextPtr;
153
154              // delete old pointer
155              delete tempPtr;
156          } // end while
157       } // end if
158
159       cout << "All nodes destroyed\n\n";
160    } // end method FinalRelease
161
162    // utility function to allocate new node
163    ListNode *CCOMLinkedList::getNewNode( VARIANT *item )
164    {
165       ListNode *ptr = new ListNode( item );
166
167       return ptr;
168    } // end method getNewNode
```

Fig. 22.14 **CCOMLinkedList** class method definitions. (Part 4 of 4.)

Method **insertAtFront** (lines 8–20) inserts an item at the front of the linked list. Line 10 creates a new **ListNode** object from the **VARIANT** type passed to the method. Line 12 uses method **isEmpty** to determine whether the list is currently empty. If the list is empty, line 13 initializes **firstPtr** and **lastPtr** to the newly created pointer **newPtr**. If the list is not empty, line 15 initializes **newPtr**'s **nextPtr** to the **firstPtr** of the list; line 16 sets **firstPtr** to **newPtr**, causing **newPtr** to become the first node in the list.

Method **insertAtBack** (lines 23–35) inserts an item at the back of the linked list. Line 25 creates a new **ListNode** object from the **VARIANT** type passed to the method. Line 27 uses method **isEmpty** to determine whether the list is currently empty. If the list is empty, line 28 initializes **firstPtr** and **lastPtr** to the newly created pointer **newPtr**. If the list is not empty, line 30 initializes **lastPtr**'s **nextPtr** to the **newPtr**; line 31 sets **lastPtr** to **newPtr**, causing **newPtr** to become the last node in the list.

Method **removeFromBack** (lines 38–62) removes the item at the tail of the linked list. If the list is empty, line 41 indicates an error and exits from the function. If the list is not empty, lines 42–59 execute to remove the last node of the list. Line 43 obtains a temporary pointer to the last node in the list. Lines 45–46 determine whether there is only a single node in the list, which occurs when the first pointer equals the last pointer, and sets both first and last pointers to **0**. Lines 47–55 execute if there is more than one node in the list; the first node is assigned to a pointer, and the list is traversed using the **ListNode**'s **nextPtr** member until the current **ListNode**'s

nextPtr member equals **lastPtr**. Line 53 sets the **lastPtr** pointer to the second-to-last node, and line 54 sets **nextPtr** value to **0**. Line 57 sets the **VARIANT** pointer item's data value to the data of the last node in the list. Finally, line 58 deletes the last node in the list.

Method **removeFromFront** (lines 65–82) removes the front node from the linked list. If the list is empty, the method returns **E_FAIL** (line 68). Otherwise, the method sets the **firstPtr** value to the second item in the list (line 75), stores the first item's data value to return to the calling function (line 77) and deletes the first node (line 78).

Method **isEmpty** (lines 85–91) returns **S_OK** if **firstPtr** is equal to **NULL** (lines 87–88) and returns **S_FALSE** otherwise.

Method **print** (lines 94–124) converts and displays each **VARIANT** as a string. If an empty list is printed, lines 96–99 display an error message and return **E_FAIL**. Lines 108–118 traverse each node in the list and display each node's data item. Function **VariantChangeType** (lines 109–110) converts a variant of one type to another type; the function takes four arguments. The first argument is a reference to a **VARIANT** structure to store the converted data, the second argument is the source **VARIANT** that contains the data to be converted, the third argument allows options to specify how the **VARIANT** is converted, and the fourth argument determines the data type to which the source data should be changed. If function **VariantChangeType** successfully converts the **ListNode**'s data to a **BSTR** character string, its value is converted to an ANSI C++ string (using the new **CW2A** class), cast to a **const char *** and displayed (line 113).

ATL 7.0 introduces a new set of string-conversion classes to perform the functions of the string macros from ATL 3.0. The ATL 3.0 string-conversion macros required the **USES_CONVERSION** macro and only allocated memory on the stack. The macros could cause an application to fail if the string was too large to fit on the stack, or the conversion macros executed enough times in a loop to fill the stack. The new ATL 7.0 classes do not require the **USES_CONVERSION** macro, allocate memory on the heap or stack as appropriate for the size of the string and deallocate memory when the object goes out of scope. The memory used by the classes is deallocated during each iteration of a loop, rather than only at the end of the function, providing better memory utilization. The new classes have the same names as their ATL 3.0 counterparts, but are preceded by a **C**. Thus, the ATL 7.0 string-conversion class name convention is **C**sourceType**2[C]**targetType**[Ex]**. The optional **C** designates a constant return string, and **Ex** allows the developer to specify the size of the buffer as a template parameter. The sourceType and targetType can equal **W** (Wide-character), **A** (ANSI-character), **T** (the applications default character type) or **OLE** (Wide Character). [Note: The ATL 7.0 string-conversion classes release the converted string when the class goes out of scope; thus, to maintain the converted string across multiple lines of code, create an instance of the string-conversion class and use the constructor to convert the source string.]

Method **FinalRelease** (lines 127–160) is called as the object is destroyed to display all remaining nodes in the list and free any dynamic memory. If the list is not empty, lines 130–156 execute. Lines 136–156 loop through each node in the list, display its data and delete the pointer.

Figure 22.15 presents the client application that tests our attributed COM object. Note that the project in Fig. 22.7–Fig. 22.14 must be built successfully before Fig. 22.15 will execute properly.

```cpp
1   // Fig. 22.15: ListClient.cpp
2   // COM client to test ATL COM Linked List object.
3
4   // required for CComVariant type
5   #include <atlbase.h>
6
7   #include <iostream>
8
9   // contains COMLinkedList interface definitions
10  #include "..\..\Fig22_07-14\linkedlist\_linkedlist.h"
11
12  using std::cout;
13
14  // linked list test application
15  int main()
16  {
17
18      // attempts to initialize COM
19      if ( SUCCEEDED( CoInitialize( NULL ) ) ) {
20
21          // pointer to COM timer object
22          ICOMLinkedList *list;
23
24          // create instance of COM object
25          HRESULT result = CoCreateInstance(
26              __uuidof( CCOMLinkedList ), NULL, CLSCTX_INPROC,
27              __uuidof( ICOMLinkedList ), ( void ** ) &list );
28
29          // use COM methods
30          if ( SUCCEEDED( result ) ) {
31              CComVariant object[] = {
32                  "Hello", 4.33, true, 'd', 13, L"Hello Wide"
33              };
34
35              // add each variant object to list
36              for ( int i = 0; i < 6; i++ ) {
37                  list->insertAtBack( &object[ i ] );
38                  list->insertAtFront( &object[ ++i ] );
39                  cout << "Added Two Objects.\n";
40                  list->print();
41              }
42
43              // remove 4 objects from list
44              for ( int i = 0; i < 4; i += 2 ) {
45                  VARIANT item;
46                  if ( !SUCCEEDED( list->removeFromFront( &item ) ) ) {
47                      cout << "Error: Unable to remove front item.\n";
48                      break;
49                  }
```

Fig. 22.15 CCOMLinkedList object test application. (Part 1 of 2.)

```
50
51                 if ( !SUCCEEDED( list->removeFromBack( &item ) ) ) {
52                     cout << "Error: Unable to remove back item.\n";
53                     break;
54                 }
55
56                 cout << "Removed Two Objects.\n";
57                 list->print();
58             } // end for
59
60             cout << "Releasing COM object.\n";
61
62             // release COM linked list; remaining list items
63             // are destroyed
64             list->Release();
65         } // end if
66
67         // uninitialize COM
68         CoUninitialize();
69     } // end if
70
71     return 0;
72 } // end function main
```

```
Added Two Objects.
The list is: 4.33, Hello,

Added Two Objects.
The list is: 100, 4.33, Hello, -1,

Added Two Objects.
The list is: Hello Wide, 100, 4.33, Hello, -1, 13,

Removed Two Objects.
The list is: 100, 4.33, Hello, -1,

Removed Two Objects.
The list is: 4.33, Hello,

Releasing COM object.
Destroying nodes ...
Deleted: 4.33
Deleted: Hello
All nodes destroyed
```

Fig. 22.15 **CCOMLinkedList** object test application. (Part 2 of 2.)

Line 5 includes header file **<atlbase.h>** to allow use of the **CComVariant** type, which is a wrapper around the **VARIANT** type. Line 10 includes the linked-list interface definitions. Function **main** (lines 15–72) instantiates the linked-list COM object, inserts and removes items from the list, and releases the object. Lines 22–68 execute if the call to **CoInitialize** succeeds in initializing the COM libraries.

Function **CoCreateInstance** initializes an in-process instance of the COM object **CCOMLinked** list (lines 25–27). The Microsoft-specific keyword **__uuidof** obtains the unique ID of an object declared with the **uuid** attribute. The **__uuidof** keyword allows COM clients to use COM objects without including the generated unique identifier file (i.e., **_LinkedList_i.c**) or relying on **CLSID**_name and **IID**_name macros. If function **CoCreateInstance** succeeds in creating the **CCOM-LinkedList** object, lines 31–64 add six **VARIANT** items to the list, remove four and release the list object. Finally, line 68 uninitializes the COM libraries using **CoUninitialize** before the program exits.

22.4 COM Event-Handling Attributes

The Unified Event Model, discussed for native events in Chapter 21, was introduced into COM to provide common event syntax and abstract the COM connection-point event model. The event attributes allow seamless implementation of event sources, event sinks, and event hooking and unhooking; the event attribute provider injects the necessary connection-point code during component compilation.

The next example demonstrates the COM Unified Event Model by creating a COM timer class similar to the example presented in Chapter 21, Introduction to Unmanaged Code in Visual C++ .NET. To generate this example, use Visual Studio .NET to create a new C++ attributed **ATL Project** named **COMTimer**, which supports COM+ 1.0. Add a new COM+ 1.0 class named **ComTimer** to the project, using the **ATL COM+ 1.0 Wizard** as explained in the previous section. While the generated project creates interface **IComTimer** and **CComTimer** in the same header file, we move the interface definition to a separate file; this makes it easier for an event-receiver class to use the event-source interface.

The COM Unified Event Model consists of three components—an *event interface*, an *event-source class*, and an *event-receiver class* (or *event-sink class*). An event interface specifies one or more event names and their parameters. An event-source class raises the events in an event receiver and an event-receiver class handles the events in an event receiver.

Figure 22.16 presents the event interface (**ITimerEvents**) and the COM interface definition for the event source class (**IComTimer**).

```
1   // Fig. 22.16: COMTimer.h
2   // Defines COM object and event interfaces. Acts as common
3   // header for object implementation and event receiver.
4
5   #pragma once
6
7   // IComTimer attributes
8   [
9      object,
10     uuid( "182A890F-8A47-40E4-BAAF-68691A2AC0D9" ),
11     dual, helpstring( "ICComTimer Interface" ),
12     pointer_default( unique )
13  ]
```

Fig. 22.16 **IComTimer** and **ITimerEvents** interfaces. (Part 1 of 2.)

```
14
15    // IComTimer interface
16    __interface IComTimer : IDispatch
17    {
18
19       // runs timer
20       [ id( 1 ), helpstring( "Runs the timer" ) ]
21       HRESULT Run( [ in ] int tickLength );
22    }; // interface IComTimer
23
24    // ITimerEvents event source interface attributes
25    [
26       dual,
27       uuid( "9BDA3657-8EEB-4a31-AF3C-21F4CAF874D7" ),
28       helpstring( "ITimer Events Interface" ),
29       pointer_default( unique )
30    ]
31    __interface ITimerEvents
32    {
33
34       // tick event
35       [ id( 1 ) , helpstring( "TimerTick event" ) ]
36       HRESULT TimerTick( [ in ] __int64 time );
37    }; // end interface ITimerEvents
38
39    // declare object interface implementation class
40    class DECLSPEC_UUID( "F01C8D77-37EF-4396-9F74-D1BC100EE390" )
41       CComTimer;
```

Fig. 22.16 `IComTimer` and `ITimerEvents` interfaces. (Part 2 of 2.)

Interface **IComTimer** (lines 16–22) is the COM interface for the event-source class. Attribute **object** (line 9) declares **IComTimer** as a custom interface (i.e., a non-OLE interface). The interface contains a single method **Run**, which takes in-parameter **tickLength** that specifies the time in seconds between "ticks" of the timer. Interface **ITimerEvents** (lines 31–37) is the event interface for the timer object, and contains a single event method, **TimerTick**, which takes an **__int64** argument specifying the time of the tick. Note that data types **time_t** and **__int64** are equivalent in Windows. Lines 40–41 contain the forward declaration of class **CComTimer** and an unique ID.

Class **CComItem** (Fig. 22.17) implements **IComTimer** to run a timer and is an event source that fires the **TimerTick** event in the event interface.

```
1    // Fig. 22.17: CComTimer.h
2    // COM timer class declaration.
3
4    #pragma once
5
6    #include "COMTimer.h"
7    #include "resource.h"
8    #include <comsvcs.h>
9    #include <iostream>
```

Fig. 22.17 `CComTimer` event-source class. (Part 1 of 2.)

```
10    #include <time.h>
11
12    using std::cout;
13
14    // CComTimer class attributes
15    [
16
17       // COM event source
18       event_source( com ),
19       coclass,
20       threading( "single" ),
21       aggregatable( "never" ),
22       vi_progid( "COMTimer.CComTimer" ),
23       progid( "COMTimer.CComTimer.1" ),
24       version( 1.0 ),
25       uuid( "F01C8D77-37EF-4396-9F74-D1BC100EE390" ),
26       helpstring( "CComTimer Class" )
27    ]
28    class ATL_NO_VTABLE CComTimer : public IComTimer
29    {
30    public:
31
32       // event interface
33       __event __interface ITimerEvents;
34
35       // default constructor
36       CComTimer()
37       {
38       }
39
40       // protects object from deletion during
41       // FinalConstruct method
42       DECLARE_PROTECT_FINAL_CONSTRUCT()
43
44       // called immediately following object
45       // construction
46       HRESULT FinalConstruct()
47       {
48          return S_OK;
49       }
50
51       // called as object is released
52       void FinalRelease()
53       {
54       }
55
56       // run method implementation
57       STDMETHOD( Run )( int tickLength );
58    }; // end class CComTimer
```

Fig. 22.17 CComTimer event-source class. (Part 2 of 2.)

Attribute **event_source** (line 18) uses the parameter **com** to declare this class as a COM connection-point event source. Keyword **__event** (line 33) works in conjunction with keyword **__interface** to designate an event-source interface. Keyword **__event** is an intrinsic function that injects the appropriate connection-point mapping code. Keyword **__event** causes attributes **default** and **source** to be inserted in the generated **.idl** file to indicate that the designated interface acts as a source of events. Method **Run** (line 57) executes a timer that fires events after each designated **tickLength**.

Figure 22.18 presents the implementation of method **Run**, which fires the **TimerTick** event each **tickLength** seconds until sent a **WM_QUIT** message.

```cpp
1   // Fig. 22.18: CComTimer.cpp
2   // CComTimer method implementation.
3
4   #include "stdafx.h"
5   #include "CComTimer.h"
6
7   // runs timer with specified duration and ticklength
8   STDMETHODIMP CComTimer::Run( int tickLength )
9   {
10
11     // display tick time and duration of timer
12     cout << "Starting the timer. Will fire TimerTick every "
13         << tickLength << " seconds.\n";
14
15     time_t unformattedTime; // unformatted time variable
16
17     HANDLE threadHandle;
18     DWORD result;
19
20     // get true handle to current thread
21     DuplicateHandle( GetCurrentProcess(), GetCurrentThread(),
22        GetCurrentProcess(), &threadHandle, 0, FALSE,
23        DUPLICATE_SAME_ACCESS );
24
25     // continue looping until timer is stopped
26     while ( true ) {
27
28        // stop thread for tickLength seconds without disrupting
29        // windows message queue
30        result = MsgWaitForMultipleObjects( 1, &threadHandle,
31           FALSE, tickLength * 1000, QS_POSTMESSAGE );
32
33        // check if MsgWaitForMultipleObjects returned by postmessage
34        if ( result == WAIT_OBJECT_0 + 1 ) {
35          MSG message;
36
37          // get message
38          GetMessage( &message, NULL, NULL, NULL );
39
40          // end loop if message was WM_QUIT
41          if ( message.message == WM_QUIT )
42             break;
43        } // end if
44
45        // get current time in seconds since January 1, 1970
```

Fig. 22.18 **CComTimer** class event-source method definitions. (Part 1 of 2.)

```
46          time( &unformattedTime );
47
48          // fire TimerTick event
49          __raise TimerTick( unformattedTime );
50       } // end while
51
52       return S_OK;
53    } // end method Run
```

Fig. 22.18 CComTimer class event-source method definitions. (Part 2 of 2.)

Method **Run** first displays the duration between each **TimerTick** event (lines 12–13). Then, lines 21–23 call Win32 function **DuplicateHandle** to obtain a true copy of the handle to the current thread. Function *DuplicateHandle* takes six arguments: the source process, the source thread, the target process, the location to store the duplicated thread, the security permissions and options for the duplicated handle. Unlike function **GetCurrent-Thread**, which returns a constant that always represents the current thread, **Duplicate-Handle** returns a true copy of the current thread handle that can be used by any function. Lines 26–50 loop until a **WM_QUIT** message is sent to the thread.

Win32 function *MsgWaitForMultipleObjects* (lines 30–31) causes the thread to sleep for the specified amount of time or until a message of the designated type is sent to the thread. There are several reasons for using **MsgWaitForMultip-leObjects** over Win32 function **Sleep**. First, it allows an application to stop the timer instantly by sending a **WM_QUIT** message. Second, calling **CoInitialize** on a thread opens a hidden window on the thread that receives messages from the message queue; if these messages are not properly received and dispatched, which does not happen in function **Sleep**, the message queue will continue to fill and other windows applications may be unable to dispatch and process windows messages, which can slow or stop the entire system. Function **MsgWaitForMultipleObjects** stops the thread, but continues to properly dispatch window messages. The function takes five arguments: The first specifies the number of handles sent in argument two; the second argument expects an array of handles to suspend; the third argument is a **BOOL** that determines whether one (**FALSE**) or all (**TRUE**) handles must receive the specified message type before the function returns. The fourth argument designates the maximum time, in milliseconds before returning, and the fifth argument defines the type of message which activates the suspended object. Function **MsgWaitForMultipleOb-jects** returns **WAIT_OBJECT_0** + *numberOfHandles* if it returns due to an incoming message of the type specified in the fifth argument of the function.

Lines 34–43 test for this return type and retrieve the message with function **Get-Message**. If the received message is **WM_QUIT**, line 42 **break**s the loop. Line 46 returns the current time, and line 49 uses keyword **__raise** to fire the **TimerTick** event. Keyword **__raise** is an intrinsic function that causes the attribute provider to create (in the COM class) a function that fires the specified event.

The examples in Fig. 22.19–Fig. 22.21 test whether the timer COM object contains an event sink class that handles the fired events. Before running this example, use Visual Studio .NET wizards to create an empty Win32 console application with ATL support named **COMTimerTest**.

Class **CTimerReceiver** (Fig. 22.19) is the event-sink class for the COM **Tim-erTick** event. Note that although it is not a COM object, it does receive a COM event.

```
1    // Fig. 22.19: TimerReceiver.h
2    // Timer event receiver class declaration.
3
4    #pragma once
5
6    #include "..\..\Fig22_16-18\COMTimer\COMTimer.h"
7    #include <time.h>
8    #include <iostream>
9
10   using std::cout;
11
12   [ event_receiver( com ) ]
13   class CTimerReceiver
14   {
15   public:
16
17       // constructor hooks this receiver to event source
18       CTimerReceiver();
19
20       // hooks event source to sink
21       void HookSource( IComTimer *source );
22
23       // unhooks event source from sink
24       void UnhookSource();
25
26       // TimerTick event handler displays current time after
27       // each tick
28       void TimerTick( __int64 unformattedTime );
29
30   private:
31       IComTimer *timer;
32   }; // end class CTimerReceiver
```

Fig. 22.19 CTimerReceiver COM event-sink class.

Attribute **event_receiver** (line 12) causes an attribute provider to inject code that enables the object to handle COM connection-point events. In addition to the type parameter discussed in Chapter 21, Introduction to Unmanaged Code in Visual ++ .NET, **event_receiver** takes a boolean parameter that determines whether the COM event receiver uses *layout-dependent* event handlers. The layout-dependent parameter is valid only for **com event_receiver**s and defaults to **false**. When the layout-dependent parameter is set to **true**, the method signature of each event handler must match the signature of the event it handles exactly, and the sink class must use the **coclass** attribute. If the layout-dependent parameter is **true**, events resolve faster, because less work is required to map the event interface method to the event handler.

Method **HookSource** (line 21) and method **UnhookSource** (line 24) attach or detach the **TimerTick** event handler to the **IComTimer** event source, respectively. Event-handler method **TimerTick** handles the **TimerTick** event raised by the **IComTimer**'s **Run** method. Figure 22.20 presents the method definitions for class **CTimerReceiver**.

```
1   // Fig. 22.20: TimerReceiver.cpp
2   // Method implementations for class CTimerReceiver.
3
4   #include "stdafx.h"
5   #include "TimerReceiver.h"
6
7   // constructor initializes tick value
8   CTimerReceiver::CTimerReceiver() {}
9
10  // method hooks this receiver to event source
11  void CTimerReceiver::HookSource( IComTimer *source )
12  {
13     timer = source;
14     __hook( &ITimerEvents::TimerTick,
15        source, &CTimerReceiver::TimerTick );
16  } // end method HookSource
17
18  // method unhooks this receiver from event source
19  void CTimerReceiver::UnhookSource()
20  {
21     __unhook( &ITimerEvents::TimerTick, timer,
22        &CTimerReceiver::TimerTick );
23  } // end method UnHookSource
24
25  // TimerTick event handler displays current time after
26  // each tick
27  void CTimerReceiver::TimerTick( __int64 unformattedTime )
28  {
29     time_t longTime = ( time_t )unformattedTime;
30
31     // store unformatted time in tm structure containing
32     // organized local time zone data
33     tm *time = localtime( &longTime );
34
35     // display tick event and current time
36     cout << "Tick! " << time->tm_hour << ":"
37        << time->tm_min << ":" << time->tm_sec << "\n";
38  } // end method TimerTick
```

Fig. 22.20 CTimerReceiver event-source class method definitions.

Method **HookSource** (lines 11–16) uses keyword **__hook**, which is an intrinsic function that creates a connection between the client event sink and the server connection point. The keyword **__hook** is an intrinsic function that contains the appropriate logic to call **AtlAdvise**, which provides the connection between the event source and sink. Keyword **__hook** takes three arguments—the address of the event interface method, an **event_source** object and the address of the event-handler method.

Method **UnhookSource** (lines 19–23) uses keyword **__unhook** to remove the connection between the server and client. Like keyword **__hook**, **__unhook** is an intrinsic function, and it provides the necessary logic to call **AtlUnadvise**, which breaks the client/server connection.

Event-handler method **TimerTick** receives the event and displays the time at which the timer "ticked." Line 29 converts the passed **__int64** value to a **time_t** value. Line

33 uses function **localtime** to convert the **time_t** value into a formatted **tm** structure containing the localized time.

Figure 22.21 contains the application logic to test the event source and event sink in a multithreaded application.

```cpp
1   // Fig. 22.21: COMTimerTest.cpp
2   // Tests CCOMTimer and CTimerReceiver.
3
4   #include "stdafx.h"
5   #include "TimerReceiver.h"
6
7   // places timer in COM module
8   [ module( name="TimerReceiver" ) ];
9   struct TimerArguments
10  {
11     int tickLength;
12     CTimerReceiver *receiver;
13  };
14
15  // initializes COM apartment thread and runs timer
16  DWORD WINAPI RunTimerThread( LPVOID timerArguments )
17  {
18
19     // attempt to initialize COM
20     if ( SUCCEEDED( CoInitialize( NULL ) ) ) {
21
22        // pointer to COM timer object
23        IComTimer *timer;
24
25        // create instance of COM object
26        HRESULT result = CoCreateInstance( __uuidof( CComTimer ),
27           NULL, CLSCTX_INPROC,__uuidof( IComTimer ),
28           ( void ** ) &timer );
29
30        // use COM methods
31        if ( SUCCEEDED( result ) ) {
32           TimerArguments arguments =
33              *( TimerArguments * )timerArguments;
34
35           // hook event to event receiver
36           arguments.receiver->HookSource( timer );
37           timer->Run( arguments.tickLength );
38
39           // unhook source from receiver
40           arguments.receiver->UnhookSource();
41
42           // release COM timer
43           timer->Release();
44        } // end if
45
46        // uninitialize COM
47        CoUninitialize();
48     } // end if
```

Fig. 22.21 COM event application entry point. (Part 1 of 2.)

```
49
50      return 0;
51   } // end function RunTimerThread
52
53   // entry point for application
54   int main( int argc, _TCHAR *argv[] )
55   {
56      HANDLE threadHandle;
57      DWORD threadID;
58      CTimerReceiver receiver;
59      TimerArguments arguments = { 2, &receiver };
60
61      cout << "Press Enter to halt timer.\n";
62
63      // create thread to run timer
64      threadHandle = CreateThread( NULL, 0, RunTimerThread,
65         &arguments, NULL, &threadID );
66
67      // wait for user input
68      getchar();
69
70      // stop timer
71      PostThreadMessage( threadID, WM_QUIT, 0, 0 );
72
73      // wait for thread to finish
74      WaitForSingleObject( threadHandle, INFINITE );
75
76      // close thread
77      CloseHandle( threadHandle );
78
79      return 0;
80   } // end function main
```

```
Press Enter to halt timer.
Starting the timer. Will fire TimerTick every 2 seconds.
Tick! 16:51:11
Tick! 16:51:13
Tick! 16:51:15
Tick! 16:51:17
Tick! 16:51:19
Tick! 16:51:21
```

Fig. 22.21 COM event application entry point. (Part 2 of 2.)

Line 8 declares attribute **module**, which is required for applications using COM events. Although the testing project does not include any COM objects, keywords **__hook** and **__unhook** insert a default implementation of the event interface using COM; thus, an application using these keywords in the COM event model must include attribute **module**.

Structure **TimerArguments** (lines 9–13) contains the arguments that are passed to the thread that runs the timer.

Function **RunTimerThread** (lines 16–51) initializes the COM libraries, creates an instance of the **CComTimer** class and hooks the event sink to the event source. Function **RunTimerThread** matches the function signature that is required for the Win32 **Cre-**

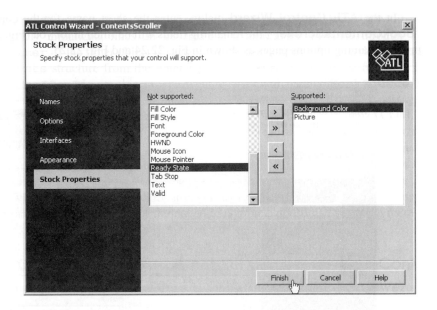

Fig. 22.25 BookContentsScroller stock properties.

The wizards generate two interfaces—**IBookContentsScroller** and **_IBookContentsScrollerEvents**—as well as an implementation class—**CBookContentsScroller** in a file called **BookContentsScroller.h**. The wizards also provide default implementations for the stock properties **BackColor** and **Picture**.

Figure 22.26 presents interfaces **IBookContentsScroller** and **_IBookContentsScrollerEvents**. Although the Visual Studio .NET Wizards generate both interfaces in **BookContentsScroller.h** (Fig. 22.27), we have chosen to place them in a separate file called **Interface.h** (Fig. 22.26).

```
1    // Fig. 22.26: Interface.h
2    // Defines the controls interfaces.
3
4    #pragma once
5
6    // maximum size of table of contents
7    #define CONTENTS_SIZE 100
8
9    // IBookContentsScroller
10   [
11      object,
12      uuid( "B6734743-3FB2-4A29-9C62-86F3F7D6E9A8" ),
13      dual,
14      helpstring( "IBookContentsScroller Interface" ),
15      pointer_default( unique )
```

Fig. 22.26 Interfaces **IBookContentsScroller** and **_IBookContentsScrollerEvents**. (Part 1 of 2.)

```
16  ]
17  __interface IBookContentsScroller : IDispatch
18  {
19
20      // background color property
21      [ propput, bindable, requestedit, id( DISPID_BACKCOLOR ) ]
22      HRESULT BackColor( [ in ]OLE_COLOR clr );
23      [ propget, bindable, requestedit, id( DISPID_BACKCOLOR ) ]
24      HRESULT BackColor( [ out,retval ]OLE_COLOR *pclr );
25
26      // picture stock property
27      [ propput, bindable, requestedit, id( DISPID_PICTURE ) ]
28      HRESULT Picture( [ in ]IPictureDisp *pPicture );
29      [ propget, bindable, requestedit, id( DISPID_PICTURE ) ]
30      HRESULT Picture( [ out, retval ]IPictureDisp **ppPicture );
31
32      // ContentsTable property
33      [ propput, bindable, requestedit, id( 1 ),
34          helpstring( "property ContentsTable" ) ]
35      HRESULT ContentsTable( [ in,out ]LONG *length,
36          [ in ] char *newVal[ CONTENTS_SIZE ] );
37
38      [ propget, bindable, requestedit, id( 1 ),
39          helpstring( "property ContentsTable" ) ]
40      HRESULT ContentsTable( [ in,out ]LONG *length,
41          [ out, retval ]char *pVal[ CONTENTS_SIZE ] );
42  }; // end interface IBookContentsScroller
43
44  // event interface, implemented by control to provide
45  // connection point to its container
46  [
47      uuid( "3B64BCA2-E383-4CDA-B1C5-EB7A66C828A1" ),
48      dispinterface,
49      helpstring( "_IBookContentsScrollerEvents Interface" )
50  ]
51  __interface _IBookContentsScrollerEvents
52  {
53
54      // event fired after each scrolling "tick" of table
55      // of contents
56      [ id( 1 ), helpstring( "method ScrollTick" ) ]
57      void ScrollTick( [ in ] LONG direction );
58  }; // end interface _IBookContentsScrollerEvents
```

Fig. 22.26 Interfaces **IBookContentsScroller** and
          _IBookContentsScrollerEvents. (Part 2 of 2.)

Line 7 declares the maximum number and size of each string in the table of contents. Interface **IBookContentsScroller** contains the control's properties, including two generated stock properties, **Picture** and **BackColor**, and the **ContentsTable** property which sets or gets the table of contents displayed on the control.

Lines 21 and 23 demonstrate attributes **propput**, **propget**, **bindable** and **requestedit**, each of which operate identically to the IDL attributes they replace.

Attributes **propput** and **propget** declare the method as a *set* or *get* property, respectively. Attribute **bindable** enables notification to be sent to an event sink any time the property changes. Attribute **requestedit** allows the property to request permission to change a property from a sink. Line 30 demonstrates the *retval* attribute, which causes the modified parameter to act as the return value for the method.

Attribute *dispinterface* (line 48) specifies the interface **_IBookContentsScrollerEvents** as a dispatch interface and causes the interface to inherit from **IDispatch**. The interface contains a single event method, **ScrollTick**, which is fired each time the control's table of contents is scrolled.

Class **CBookContentsScroller** (Fig. 22.27) implements the **IBookContentsScroller** interface, which defines the property and event mappings as well as the method declarations for the ActiveX control.

```
1    // Fig. 22.27: BookContentsScroller.h
2    // Control class definition and drawing function.
3
4    #pragma once
5
6    #include "resource.h"
7    #include <atlctl.h>
8    #include "Interface.h"
9    #include "ContentsScrollerProperties.h"
10
11   // defines direction of text scrolling
12   #define UP 1
13   #define DOWN -1
14
15   // control attributes
16   [
17       coclass,
18       threading( "apartment" ),
19       vi_progid( "ContentsScroller.BookContentsScroller" ),
20       progid( "ContentsScroller.BookContentsScroller.1" ),
21       version( 1.0 ),
22       uuid( "BB13E377-96A6-46A3-9770-B9D5E0182D00" ),
23       helpstring( "BookContentsScroller Class" ),
24       event_source( "com" ),
25       support_error_info( IBookContentsScroller ),
26       registration_script( "control.rgs" )
27   ]
28   class ATL_NO_VTABLE CBookContentsScroller :
29       public CStockPropImpl
30           <CBookContentsScroller, IBookContentsScroller>,
31       public IPersistStreamInitImpl<CBookContentsScroller>,
32       public IOleControlImpl<CBookContentsScroller>,
33       public IOleObjectImpl<CBookContentsScroller>,
34       public IOleInPlaceActiveObjectImpl<CBookContentsScroller>,
35       public IViewObjectExImpl<CBookContentsScroller>,
36       public IOleInPlaceObjectWindowlessImpl<CBookContentsScroller>,
37       public IPersistStorageImpl<CBookContentsScroller>,
38       public ISpecifyPropertyPagesImpl<CBookContentsScroller>,
```

Fig. 22.27 **CBookContentsScroller** ATL ActiveX control. (Part 1 of 4.)

```
39      public IQuickActivateImpl<CBookContentsScroller>,
40      public IDataObjectImpl<CBookContentsScroller>,
41      public CComControl<CBookContentsScroller>
42   {
43   public:
44
45      // constructor initializes members
46      CBookContentsScroller() : picture( NULL ), offset( 0 ),
47         scroll( 0 ), lastY( 0 ), start( 0 ), end( 0 )
48      {
49
50         // set default control size
51         m_sizeExtent.cx = 12000;
52         m_sizeExtent.cy = 6000;
53
54         // designates that this control must have its own window
55         m_bWindowOnly = true;
56
57         // initialize outlineRectangle to zero
58         ZeroMemory( ( void * ) &outlineRectangle,
59            sizeof( outlineRectangle ) );
60      } // end constructor
61
62      // defines control properties
63      DECLARE_OLEMISC_STATUS( OLEMISC_RECOMPOSEONRESIZE |
64         OLEMISC_ACTSLIKEBUTTON | OLEMISC_CANTLINKINSIDE |
65         OLEMISC_INSIDEOUT | OLEMISC_ACTIVATEWHENVISIBLE |
66         OLEMISC_SETCLIENTSITEFIRST )
67
68      // property mappings
69      BEGIN_PROP_MAP( CBookContentsScroller )
70
71         // control size properties
72         PROP_DATA_ENTRY( "_cx", m_sizeExtent.cx, VT_UI4 )
73         PROP_DATA_ENTRY( "_cy", m_sizeExtent.cy, VT_UI4 )
74
75         // stock property mappings
76         PROP_ENTRY( "Picture", DISPID_PICTURE,
77            CLSID_StockPicturePage )
78         PROP_ENTRY( "BackColor", DISPID_BACKCOLOR,
79            CLSID_StockColorPage )
80
81         // custom property mapping
82         PROP_ENTRY( "ContentsTable", 1,
83            __uuidof( CContentsScrollerProperties ) )
84      END_PROP_MAP()
85
86      // message map, link window messages to methods
87      BEGIN_MSG_MAP( CBookContentsScroller )
88         MESSAGE_HANDLER( WM_MOUSEMOVE, OnMouseMove )
89         CHAIN_MSG_MAP( CComControl<CBookContentsScroller> )
90         DEFAULT_REFLECTION_HANDLER()
91      END_MSG_MAP()
```

Fig. 22.27 CBookContentsScroller ATL ActiveX control. (Part 2 of 4.)

```
92
93      // declares COM event interface
94      __event __interface _IBookContentsScrollerEvents;
95
96      // control's view status
97      DECLARE_VIEW_STATUS( VIEWSTATUS_SOLIDBKGND |
98         VIEWSTATUS_OPAQUE )
99
100     // overridden OnDraw method to draw on control
101     HRESULT OnDraw( ATL_DRAWINFO& di );
102
103     // method invoked when background color changes
104     OLE_COLOR m_clrBackColor;
105     void OnBackColorChanged()
106     {
107        ATLTRACE( _T( "OnBackColorChanged\n" ) );
108     }
109
110     // method invoked when picture property is changed
111     CComPtr< IPictureDisp > m_pPicture;
112     void OnPictureChanged()
113     {
114        HRESULT result;
115
116        // obtain IPicture interface from IPictureDisp interface
117        if ( SUCCEEDED( ( result = m_pPicture->QueryInterface(
118           IID_IPicture, ( void ** )&picture) ) ) ) {
119
120           // refresh view
121           SetDirty( true );
122           FireViewChange();
123
124        }
125        ATLTRACE( _T( "OnPictureChanged\n" ) );
126     } // end method OnPictureChanged
127
128     // prevents object from deletion
129     // inside FinalConstruct
130     DECLARE_PROTECT_FINAL_CONSTRUCT()
131
132     // (generated) cleanup method
133     HRESULT FinalConstruct()
134     {
135        return S_OK;
136     }
137
138     // final release method
139     void FinalRelease()
140     {
141     }
142
143     // member variables
144     IPicture *picture;
```

Fig. 22.27 CBookContentsScroller ATL ActiveX control. (Part 3 of 4.)

```
145      char *contents[ CONTENTS_SIZE ];
146      long start, end;
147      int offset, scroll, lastY;
148      RECT outlineRectangle;
149
150      // ContentsTable property
151      STDMETHOD( put_ContentsTable )( LONG *length,
152         char *newVal[ CONTENTS_SIZE ] );
153
154      STDMETHOD( get_ContentsTable )( LONG *length,
155         char *pVal[ CONTENTS_SIZE ] );
156
157      LRESULT OnMouseMove( UINT uMsg, WPARAM wParam,
158         LPARAM lParam, BOOL& bHandled );
159
160   private:
161      void DrawLogic( HDC device, RECT bounds );
162   }; // end class CBookContentsScroller
```

Fig. 22.27 CBookContentsScroller ATL ActiveX control. (Part 4 of 4.)

Attribute **registration_script** (line 26) takes a single unnamed parameter that designates the path to a custom registration script (**.rgs**). If this attribute is not specified, Visual Studio .NET generates an **.rgs** file for the project. The control's constructor (lines 46–60) provides necessary initialization of member variables, most notably setting the default size to .01 millimeters (lines 51–52) and locking the control into a windowed-only state (line 55). Lines 82–83 provide the property map between the contents table array and a custom property page. Line 94 declares the **_IBookContentsScrollerEvents** interface as an event interface of **CBook-ContentsScroller**. Method **OnPictureChange** (lines 112–126) is a new notification feature introduced with the ATL 7.0 default property implementations. The method is fired after the property is set; in this case, we extract the **IPicture** interface from the **IPictureDisp** interface stored in the default property implementation. Figure 22.28 presents the method definitions for **CBookContentsScroller**.

```
1    // Fig. 22.28: BookContentsScroller.cpp
2    // Handles contents property and mouse-move event.
3
4    #include "stdafx.h"
5    #include "BookContentsScroller.h"
6
7    HRESULT CBookContentsScroller::OnDraw( ATL_DRAWINFO &di )
8    {
9
10       // obtain control drawing boundaries
11       RECT& controlBounds = *( RECT * )di.prcBounds;
12
13       // set boundaries for bitmap with 0, 0 origin
14       RECT bitmapBounds = { 0, 0, controlBounds.right -
15          controlBounds.left, controlBounds.bottom -
```

Fig. 22.28 CBookContentsScroller control method definitions. (Part 1 of 6.)

```
16              controlBounds.top };
17
18       // creates new context based on existing context
19       HDC bitmapContext = CreateCompatibleDC( di.hdcDraw );
20
21       // create bitmap as memory back-buffer for drawing operations
22       HBITMAP backBuffer = CreateCompatibleBitmap(
23          di.hdcDraw, bitmapBounds.right, bitmapBounds.bottom );
24
25       // set context drawing bitmap
26       HBITMAP saved = (HBITMAP)
27          SelectObject( bitmapContext, backBuffer );
28
29       // execute drawing logic on memory buffer
30       DrawLogic( bitmapContext, bitmapBounds );
31
32       // draw back-buffer to screen
33       BOOL result = BitBlt( di.hdcDraw,
34          controlBounds.left, controlBounds.top,
35          controlBounds.right- controlBounds.left,
36          controlBounds.bottom - controlBounds.top,
37          bitmapContext, 0, 0, SRCCOPY );
38
39       // clean up
40       SelectObject( bitmapContext, saved );
41       DeleteObject( backBuffer );
42       DeleteDC( bitmapContext );
43
44       return S_OK;
45    } // end method OnDraw
46
47    // contains control drawing logic
48    void CBookContentsScroller::DrawLogic( HDC device, RECT bounds )
49    {
50
51       // background color
52       COLORREF backColor;
53
54       // location of image
55       RECT imageLocation;
56
57       // set clip region to rectangle specified by bounds
58       HRGN oldRegion = NULL;
59       if ( GetClipRgn( device, oldRegion ) != 1)
60          oldRegion = NULL;
61
62       bool selectOldRegion = false;
63
64       // create new clip region from bounds
65       HRGN newRegion = CreateRectRgn(
66          bounds.left, bounds.top, bounds.right, bounds.bottom );
67
68       if ( newRegion != NULL ) {
69
```

Fig. 22.28 CBookContentsScroller control method definitions. (Part 2 of 6.)

```
70          // set new clip region
71          selectOldRegion = (
72              SelectClipRgn( device, newRegion ) != ERROR );
73      }
74
75      // convert BackColor property variable to COLORREF
76      // variable
77      OleTranslateColor( m_clrBackColor, NULL, &backColor );
78
79      // create background brush and stock gray brush
80      HBRUSH backgroundBrush =
81          ( HBRUSH ) CreateSolidBrush( backColor );
82      HBRUSH grayBush =
83          ( HBRUSH ) GetStockObject( GRAY_BRUSH );
84
85      // fill control with selected background color
86      FillRect( device, &bounds, backgroundBrush );
87
88      if ( picture != NULL ) {
89
90          // image width and height in HIMETRIC (.01 mm)
91          OLE_XSIZE_HIMETRIC width;
92          OLE_YSIZE_HIMETRIC height;
93
94          picture->get_Width( &width );
95          picture->get_Height( &height );
96
97          // convert HIMETRIC values into pixel values
98          int pixelWidth = MulDiv( width,
99              GetDeviceCaps( device, LOGPIXELSX ), 2540 );
100         int pixelHeight = MulDiv( height,
101             GetDeviceCaps( device, LOGPIXELSY ), 2540 );
102
103         // ensure image is centered on control
104         int centerX = ( ( bounds.right + bounds.left ) / 2) -
105             ( pixelWidth / 2 );
106
107         // set image location rectangle
108         imageLocation.left = centerX;
109         imageLocation.top = bounds.top;
110         imageLocation.right = centerX + pixelWidth;
111         imageLocation.bottom = bounds.top + pixelHeight;
112
113         // draw image
114         picture->Render( device, centerX,
115             bounds.top, pixelWidth, pixelHeight,
116             0, height, width, -height, NULL );
117     } // end if
118     else        // no picture present
119
120         //  initialize imageLocation bottom to top of control
121         imageLocation.bottom = bounds.top;
122
123     // sets color to draw behind text, 128, 128, 128 matches
```

Fig. 22.28 CBookContentsScroller control method definitions. (Part 3 of 6.)

```
124      // color specified in GRAY_BRUSH
125      SetBkColor( device, RGB( 128, 128, 128 ) );
126
127      // area to hold next line of text
128      RECT textLine;
129
130      // initialize to values for first line of text
131      textLine.top = imageLocation.bottom + 5;
132      textLine.left = bounds.left + 10;
133      textLine.right = bounds.right - 10;
134      textLine.bottom = textLine.top + 20;
135
136      // set values for outer bounds of text area
137      outlineRectangle.top = textLine.top - 2;
138      outlineRectangle.left = textLine.left - 2;
139      outlineRectangle.right = textLine.right + 2;
140      outlineRectangle.bottom = textLine.bottom + 42;
141
142      // create sunken-edged box at outlineRect
143      FillRect( device, &outlineRectangle, grayBush );
144      DrawEdge( device, &outlineRectangle,
145         EDGE_SUNKEN, BF_RECT );
146
147      if ( end > 0 ) {
148
149         // Create region to prevent text from being drawn outside
150         // gray box. Set bottom of clipping region to either
151         // 60 pixels from top, or bottom of control, whichever
152         // is smaller
153         HRGN region = CreateRectRgn( textLine.left, textLine.top,
154            textLine.right, ( textLine.top + 60 ) < bounds.bottom ?
155            textLine.top + 60 : bounds.bottom );
156
157         // set new clipping region
158         SelectClipRgn( device, region );
159
160         // reposition first text line by offset
161         textLine.top -= offset;
162
163         // copy start variable for modification
164         int startCopy = start;
165
166         // loop through and display 4 chapter titles
167         for ( int i = 0; i < 4 ; i++ ) {
168
169            // ensure buffer does not overflow
170            if ( startCopy + i >= end )
171               startCopy = -i;
172
173            // display current item in table of contents
174            DrawText( device, contents[ startCopy + i ],
175               -1, &textLine, DT_CENTER | DT_SINGLELINE );
176
```

Fig. 22.28 CBookContentsScroller control method definitions. (Part 4 of 6.)

```
177           // move down one row
178           textLine.top += 20;
179           textLine.bottom += 20;
180        } // end for
181
182        // change offset up or down depending on scroll value
183        offset += 5 * scroll;
184
185        // Prevent offset from exceeding 20 or dropping below 0.
186        // Offset 20 means item has scrolled off top of
187        // clipping region. Offset 0 means item has
188        // scrolled below bottom of clipping region
189        if ( offset > 20 ) {
190           start = ( start + 1 ) % end;
191           offset = 0;
192        }
193        else
194           if ( offset < 0 ) {
195              start = start - 1 < 0 ? end - 1 : start - 1;
196              offset = 20;
197           }
198
199        // fire ScrollTick event
200        __raise _IBookContentsScrollerEvents_ScrollTick( scroll );
201        scroll = 0;
202     } // end if
203
204     // restore previous clipping region
205     if ( selectOldRegion )
206        SelectClipRgn( device, oldRegion );
207
208     DeleteObject( backgroundBrush );
209  } // end method DrawLogic
210
211  // loads passed parameter into contents property
212  STDMETHODIMP CBookContentsScroller::put_ContentsTable(
213     LONG *length, char *newVal[ CONTENTS_SIZE ] )
214  {
215     for ( int i = 0; i < end; i++ )
216        delete[] contents[ i ];
217
218     // load each char pointer into contents array
219     for ( int i = 0; i < *length; i++ )
220        contents[ i ] = newVal[ i ];
221
222     start = 0;
223     end = *length;
224
225     return S_OK;
226  } // end method put_ContentsTable
227
228  // returns current table of contents and length
229  STDMETHODIMP CBookContentsScroller::get_ContentsTable(
```

Fig. 22.28 CBookContentsScroller control method definitions. (Part 5 of 6.)

```
230     LONG *length, char *pVal[ CONTENTS_SIZE ] )
231  {
232
233     // load each character string into pVal
234     for ( int i = 0; i < end; i++ )
235        pVal[i] = contents[ i ];
236
237     // set length equal to end
238     *length = end;
239
240     return S_OK;
241  } // end method get_ContentsTable
242
243  // MouseMove event handler scrolls book contents
244  // in direction of mouse
245  LRESULT CBookContentsScroller::OnMouseMove(UINT uMsg,
246     WPARAM wParam, LPARAM lParam, BOOL &bHandled )
247  {
248
249     // retrieve mouse y coordinate
250     long newY = HIWORD( lParam );
251
252     // set scroll variable if user is holding left mouse button
253     if ( wParam == MK_LBUTTON ) {
254        if ( newY < lastY )
255           scroll = UP;
256        else
257           scroll = DOWN;
258
259        // refresh text area
260        InvalidateRect( &outlineRectangle, FALSE );
261     }
262
263     // store mouse y location
264     lastY = newY;
265
266     return 0;
267  } // end method OnMouseMove
```

Fig. 22.28 `CBookContentsScroller` control method definitions. (Part 6 of 6.)

Method **OnDraw** (lines 7–45) provides double buffering to the control by redrawing the control on an off-screen bitmap and using GDI function *bitblt* to write the bitmap to the screen, eliminating flickering as the control is redrawn. Method **DrawLogic** (lines 48–209) is called by method **OnDraw** to draw the control on the off-screen buffer. Lines 88–117 draw the book cover image at the top center of the control. Lines 125–145 draw a sunken, gray box beneath the book cover image. Lines 147–202 draw four chapter headings from the **contentsTable** variable inside the sunken gray box. The headings are repositioned and clipped to simulate scrolling inside the gray box.

Methods **put_ContentsTable** (lines 212–226) and **get_ContentsTable** (lines 229–241) set and get the displayed table of contents as an array of strings.

Method **OnMouseMove** (lines 245–267) handles the mouse-moved event. If the user presses the left mouse button and moves the mouse, the rectangle containing the displayed table of contents will be refreshed and the contents scrolled in the specified direction.

Property **ContentsTable** uses a custom property sheet to set its values. To add a custom property sheet to the application, right click the project in the **Solution Explorer** window and select **Add > Add Class**. Choose **ATL Property Page** as shown in Fig. 22.29.

In the **ATL Property Page Wizard** screen (Fig. 22.30), enter **ContentsScrollerProperties** as the **Short Name** for the new class. The wizard will complete the remaining fields.

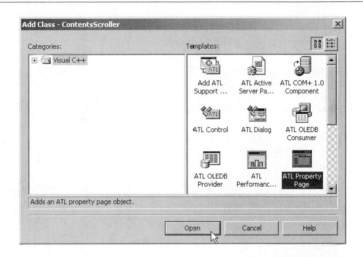

Fig. 22.29 Adding an ATL Property Page.

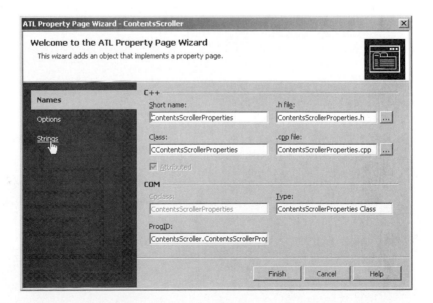

Fig. 22.30 ATL Property Page Wizard names screen.

In the **Strings** screen (Fig. 22.31) of the **ATL Property Page Wizard**, enter the **Title** of the page **Table Of Contents** and leave the remaining fields blank. The title string on the **Strings** page indicates the title string for the custom property page.

When the wizard creates the property page, it also creates a dialog resource called **IDD_CONTENTSSCROLLERPROPERTIES**. Access this resource with the resource viewer (**View > Resource View**) and create the page layout using the dialog editor (Fig. 22.32).

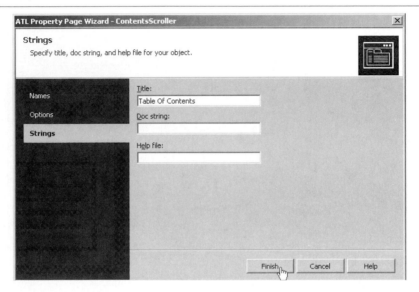

Fig. 22.31 ATL Property Page Wizard strings screen.

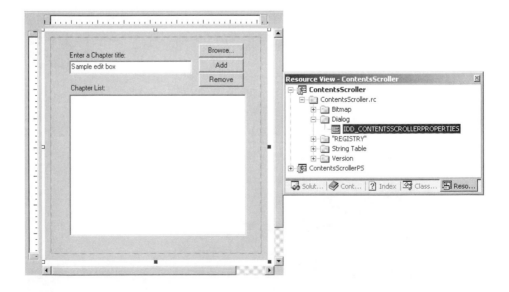

Fig. 22.32 Contents scroller custom property page dialog design.

Figure 22.33 presents the class definition for the table of contents custom property page. The property page allows the user to specify or open a file containing a set of chapter titles to display in the control's chapter heading box.

```
1   // Fig. 22.33: ContentsScrollerProperties.h
2   // Property page class.
3
4   #pragma once
5
6   #include "resource.h"
7   #include "Interface.h"
8
9   // class attributes
10  [
11     coclass,
12     threading( "apartment" ),
13     vi_progid( "ContentsScroller.ContentsScrollerProper" ),
14     progid( "ContentsScroller.ContentsScrollerProp.1" ),
15     version( 1.0 ),
16     uuid( "3A8ED90C-6196-4BF8-AAFE-722CF0D2996E" ),
17     helpstring( "ContentsScrollerProperties Class" )
18  ]
19  class ATL_NO_VTABLE CContentsScrollerProperties :
20     public IPropertyPageImpl< CContentsScrollerProperties >,
21     public CDialogImpl< CContentsScrollerProperties >
22  {
23  public:
24
25     // initialization constructor
26     CContentsScrollerProperties()
27     {
28
29        // gets basic properties from resource file
30        m_dwTitleID = IDS_TITLEContentsScrollerProperties;
31        m_dwHelpFileID = IDS_HELPFILEContentsScrollerProperties;
32        m_dwDocStringID = IDS_DOCSTRINGContentsScrollerProperties;
33     }
34
35     // ensures object will not be deleted during
36     // final construct
37     DECLARE_PROTECT_FINAL_CONSTRUCT()
38
39     // final construction method
40     HRESULT FinalConstruct()
41     {
42        return S_OK;
43     }
44
45     // release method
46     void FinalRelease()
47     {
48     }
49
```

Fig. 22.33 CContentsScrollerProperties custom property page. (Part 1 of 2.)

```
50        // stores objects IDD
51        enum { IDD = IDD_CONTENTSSCROLLERPROPERTIES };
52
53        // event handler mappings
54        BEGIN_MSG_MAP(CContentsScrollerProperties)
55           COMMAND_HANDLER( IDC_ADD_BUTTON, BN_CLICKED,
56              OnBnClickedAddButton )
57
58           COMMAND_HANDLER( IDC_CHAPTER_LIST, LBN_SELCHANGE,
59              OnLbnSelchangeChapterList )
60
61           COMMAND_HANDLER( IDC_REMOVE_BUTTON, BN_CLICKED,
62              OnBnClickedRemoveButton )
63
64           COMMAND_HANDLER( IDC_BROWSE_BUTTON, BN_CLICKED,
65              OnBnClickedBrowseButton )
66
67           MESSAGE_HANDLER( WM_INITDIALOG, OnInitDialog )
68
69           CHAIN_MSG_MAP(
70              IPropertyPageImpl< CContentsScrollerProperties > )
71
72        END_MSG_MAP()
73
74        // method called when user clicks OK or Apply in property
75        // window
76        STDMETHOD( Apply )( void );
77
78        // event handling method prototypes
79        LRESULT OnBnClickedAddButton( WORD wNotifyCode, WORD wID,
80           HWND hWndCtl, BOOL &bHandled );
81
82        LRESULT OnLbnSelchangeChapterList( WORD wNotifyCode,
83           WORD wID, HWND hWndCtl, BOOL &bHandled );
84
85        LRESULT OnBnClickedRemoveButton( WORD wNotifyCode,
86           WORD wID, HWND hWndCtl, BOOL &bHandled );
87
88        LRESULT OnBnClickedBrowseButton( WORD wNotifyCode,
89           WORD wID, HWND hWndCtl, BOOL &bHandled );
90
91        LRESULT OnInitDialog( UINT uMsg, WPARAM wParam,
92           LPARAM lParam, BOOL &bHandled );
93     }; // end class CContentsScrollerProperties
```

Fig. 22.33 `CContentsScrollerProperties` custom property page. (Part 2 of 2.)

Lines 54–72 define the message map between control events and their appropriate event handlers. Lines 79–92 declare the event-handler methods for each control event.

Figure 22.34 contains the method definitions for class **CContentsScroller-Properties**. The method definitions include adding and removing a chapter heading, loading chapter headings from a file and saving the chapter headings to the control.

```
1   // Fig. 22.34: ContentsScrollerProperties.cpp
2   // Event handler method for property page.
3
4   #include "stdafx.h"
5   #include "ContentsScrollerProperties.h"
6
7   HRESULT CContentsScrollerProperties::Apply( void )
8   {
9      ATLTRACE( _T( "CContentsScrollerProperties::Apply\n" ) );
10
11     // loop through each IBookContentsScroller object
12     // associated to this property page
13     for ( UINT i = 0; i < m_nObjects; i++ ) {
14        if ( IsPageDirty() == S_FALSE )
15           continue;
16
17        // obtain IBookContentsScroller object
18        CComQIPtr< IBookContentsScroller,
19           &__uuidof( IBookContentsScroller ) >
20           scroller( m_ppUnk[ i ] );
21
22        // get number of items in list box
23        long length = ( long )SendDlgItemMessage(
24           IDC_CHAPTER_LIST, LB_GETCOUNT );
25
26        // ensure that number of items is within bounds
27        if ( length < CONTENTS_SIZE && length > 0 ) {
28
29           // pointer to 2D array
30           char *contents[ CONTENTS_SIZE ];
31
32           // loop through each item in list box
33           for ( int i = 0; i < length; i++ ) {
34              contents[ i ] = new char[ CONTENTS_SIZE ];
35
36              // get each item in list box, store in contents
37              SendDlgItemMessage( IDC_CHAPTER_LIST, LB_GETTEXT,
38                 ( WPARAM )i, ( LPARAM )contents[ i ] );
39           }
40
41           // set ContentsTable property
42           if ( FAILED( scroller->put_ContentsTable(
43              &length, contents ) ) ) {
44
45              // error handling procedures
46              CComPtr< IErrorInfo > pError;
47              CComBSTR strError;
48              GetErrorInfo( 0, &pError );
49              pError->GetDescription( &strError );
50              MessageBox( COLE2T( strError ), _T( "Error" ),
51                 MB_ICONEXCLAMATION );
```

Fig. 22.34 CContentsScrollerProperties property page method definitions. (Part 1 of 5.)

```
52
53              return E_FAIL;
54           } // end if
55
56           // reset dirty status
57           SetDirty( FALSE );
58        } // end if
59        else
60           MessageBox( "Invalid number of chapter headings. "
61              "Add or remove some and try again", "Error", MB_OK );
62     } // end for
63
64     return S_OK;
65  } // end method Apply
66
67  // adds text from input box to list box
68  LRESULT CContentsScrollerProperties::OnBnClickedAddButton(
69     WORD wNotifyCode, WORD wID, HWND hWndCtl, BOOL& bHandled )
70  {
71     TCHAR chapter[ CONTENTS_SIZE ] = { 0 };
72
73     // retrieve text from input box
74     GetDlgItemText( IDC_ADD_BOX, chapter, 100 );
75
76     // check if input box contained value and add value to list box
77     if ( strlen( chapter ) > 0 ) {
78        SendDlgItemMessage(
79           IDC_CHAPTER_LIST, LB_ADDSTRING, 0, ( LPARAM )chapter );
80        SetDirty( TRUE );
81     }
82     else
83        MessageBox( "Please enter a chapter title", "Error" );
84
85     return 0;
86  } // end method OnBnClickedAddButton
87
88  // list box selection change event handler loads selected item
89  // into input box
90  LRESULT CContentsScrollerProperties::OnLbnSelchangeChapterList(
91     WORD wNotifyCode, WORD wID, HWND hWndCtl, BOOL &bHandled )
92  {
93     TCHAR chapter[ CONTENTS_SIZE ];
94
95     // get selected index
96     long index = ( long )SendDlgItemMessage(
97        IDC_CHAPTER_LIST, LB_GETCARETINDEX );
98
99     // get chapter title at selected index
100    SendDlgItemMessage( IDC_CHAPTER_LIST, LB_GETTEXT,
101       ( WPARAM )index, ( LPARAM )chapter );
102
103    // add chapter title to input box
```

Fig. 22.34 CContentsScrollerProperties property page method definitions. (Part 2 of 5.)

```
104        SetDlgItemText( IDC_ADD_BOX, chapter );
105
106        return 0;
107    } // end method OnLbnSelchangeChapterList
108
109    // remove list box item with text equal to input box value
110    LRESULT CContentsScrollerProperties::OnBnClickedRemoveButton(
111        WORD wNotifyCode, WORD wID, HWND hWndCtl, BOOL &bHandled )
112    {
113        TCHAR chapter[ CONTENTS_SIZE ];
114
115        // retrieve text from input box
116        GetDlgItemText( IDC_ADD_BOX, chapter, 100 );
117
118        if ( strlen( chapter ) > 0 ) {
119
120            // locate input string in list box
121            long index = ( long )SendDlgItemMessage( IDC_CHAPTER_LIST,
122                LB_FINDSTRING, 0 , ( LPARAM )chapter );
123
124            // if value was found, delete item at index from list box
125            if ( index != LB_ERR ) {
126                SendDlgItemMessage( IDC_CHAPTER_LIST, LB_DELETESTRING,
127                    ( WPARAM )index, 0 );
128                SetDirty( TRUE );
129            }
130            else
131                MessageBox( "Cannot find the given entry", "Error" );
132        } // end if
133        else
134            MessageBox( "Please enter a chapter title", "Error" );
135
136        return 0;
137    } // end method OnBnClickedRemoveButton
138
139    // BrowseButton event handler opens OpenFile dialog to choose
140    // table of contents file
141    LRESULT CContentsScrollerProperties::OnBnClickedBrowseButton(
142        WORD wNotifyCode, WORD wID, HWND hWndCtl, BOOL &bHandled )
143    {
144        char fileName[ 100 ] = { 0 };
145
146        // structure defining Open File dialog properties
147        OPENFILENAME file;
148
149        // clear memory in structure
150        memset( &file, 0, sizeof( file ) );
151        file.lStructSize = sizeof( OPENFILENAME );
152
153        // limit user to .CNTS files
154        file.lpstrFilter = "Table Of Contents (*.toc)\0*.toc\0";
155
```

Fig. 22.34 CContentsScrollerProperties property page method definitions. (Part 3 of 5.)

```
156      // buffer to contain selected file name
157      file.lpstrFile = fileName;
158      file.nMaxFile = 100;
159
160      // dialog title string
161      file.lpstrTitle = "Select a table of contents";
162
163      // dialog flags
164      file.Flags = OFN_LONGNAMES;
165
166      // create OpenFile dialog
167      BOOL result = GetOpenFileName( &file );
168      int read = 0;
169
170      // if user clicks OK, load file into list box
171      if ( result ) {
172         FILE *chapters = fopen( fileName, "rw" );
173         char chapterTitle[ 1000 ];
174
175         while( ( read = fscanf( chapters, "%[^\n]\n",
176            chapterTitle ) ) != -1 )
177
178            SendDlgItemMessage( IDC_CHAPTER_LIST, LB_ADDSTRING, 0,
179            ( LPARAM )chapterTitle );
180
181         SetDirty( TRUE );
182      }
183
184      return 0;
185   } // end method OnBnClickedBrowseButton
186
187   // reload table of contents list from ContentScroller
188   // object
189   LRESULT CContentsScrollerProperties::OnInitDialog( UINT uMsg,
190      WPARAM wParam, LPARAM lParam, BOOL &bHandled )
191   {
192
193      // loop through each object
194      if ( m_nObjects > 0 ) {
195
196         // obtain COM pointer to IBookContentsScroller object
197         CComQIPtr< IBookContentsScroller,
198            &__uuidof( IBookContentsScroller ) >
199            scroller( m_ppUnk[ 0 ] );
200
201         char *contents[ CONTENTS_SIZE ];
202         LONG length;
203
204         // access ContentsTable property
205         if ( FAILED( scroller->get_ContentsTable(
206            &length, contents ) ) ) {
207
```

Fig. 22.34 CContentsScrollerProperties property page method
definitions. (Part 4 of 5.)

```
208                CComPtr< IErrorInfo > pError;
209                CComBSTR strError;
210                GetErrorInfo( 0, &pError );
211                pError->GetDescription( &strError );
212                MessageBox( COLE2T( strError ), _T( "Error" ),
213                   MB_ICONEXCLAMATION );
214
215                return E_FAIL;
216             } // end if
217
218             // write each returned value into list box
219             for ( int j = 0; j < length; j++ ) {
220                SendDlgItemMessage( IDC_CHAPTER_LIST, LB_ADDSTRING, 0,
221                   ( LPARAM )contents[ j ] );
222             }
223          } // end if
224
225       return TRUE;
226    } // end method OnInitDialog
```

Fig. 22.34 `CContentsScrollerProperties` property page method definitions. (Part 5 of 5.)

Method **Apply** (lines 7–65) writes the table of contents to the client if the table has changed. It retrieves each item from the property page list box, constructs an array of strings and passes the array to the control via the **put_ContentsTable** property method.

Method **OnBnClickedAddButton** (lines 68–86) adds the text from the input box into the list box. Method **OnLbnSelchangeChapterList** (lines 90–107) handles the list box **LBN_SELCHANGE** message, which is triggered when the user selects an item in the list box. The method obtains the text from the selected item and adds the text to the page's input box. Method **OnBnClickedRemoveButton** (lines 110–137) handles the remove button's **BN_CLICKED** message. The method removes the list box item that matches the text entered in the page's input box. Method **OnBnClickedBrowse-Button** (lines 141–185) handles the browse button **BN_CLICKED** message. The method uses the common **GetOpenFileName** dialog to allow the user to select a file with the **.toc** extension that contains a list of chapter headings, which it then loads into the list box containing chapter titles. Method **OnInitDialog** (lines 189–226) handles the page's **WM_INITDIALOG** message, which is sent when the page is opened to initialize the control. **OnInitDialog** uses method **get_ContentsTable** to load the current contents table from the control and initialize the contents table list box.

Figure 22.35 displays the output of the **BookContentsScroller** control inside the ActiveX control test container. The test container may be accessed in Visual Studio .NET under the **Tools** menu as an **ActiveX Control Test Container**. To load the control, select **Edit > Insert New Control**, and select the **CBookContents-Scroller Object** control (shown in the first image of Fig. 22.35). When the page loads, it will display a white square with a gray box in the upper center (shown in the second image of Fig. 22.35). To access the control's property pages, select the control and use the **Edit > Properties...** command. The next four images in Fig. 22.35 demonstrate setting the control's properties pages, including the custom **Table of Contents** page. The final image displays the control after its properties have been set. Notice that the ActiveX Control Test Container displays the values fired by the events, as well as the **ATLTRACE** macro values.

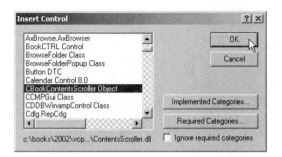

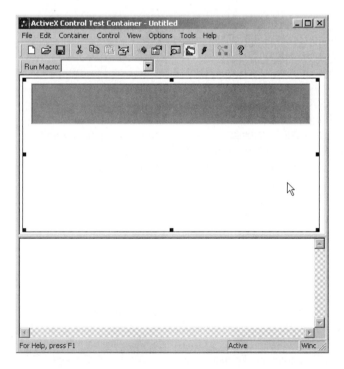

Fig. 22.35 `CBookContentsScroller` control output. (Part 1 of 3.)

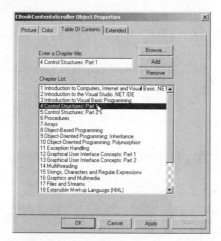

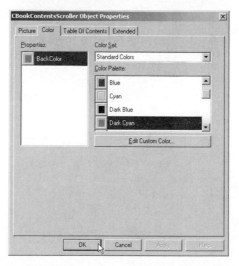

Fig. 22.35 CBookContentsScroller control output. (Part 2 of 3.)

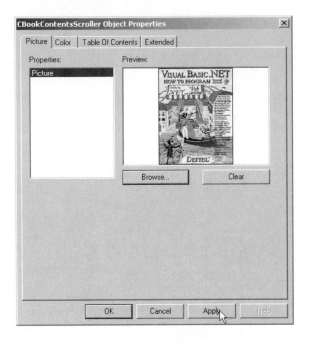

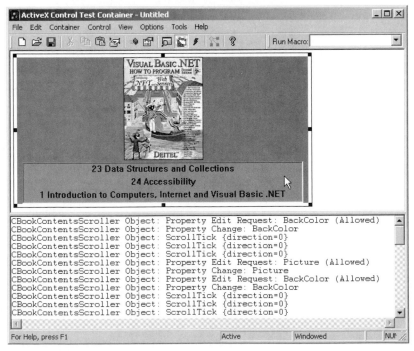

Fig. 22.35 `CBookContentsScroller` control output. (Part 3 of 3.)

This chapter introduced COM and ATL and demonstrated attributed programming in the ATL COM libraries and ActiveX controls. The next chapter demonstrates the new set of classes called ATL Server that enable simplified native Web applications and Web services. In addition to demonstrating the power of ATL server, the next chapter demonstrates attributes in the context of database and ATL server development.

22.6 Summary

The Component Object Model (COM) is an attempt to expand DLL functionality and correct many DLL problems. COM is a binary standard introduced by Microsoft to provide a platform-, language- and location-independent environment to develop reusable, object-oriented software components. Many Windows libraries adhere to the COM specification.

The COM specification is built on the concept of component objects and interfaces. A component object provides a service that it exposes to the system via one or more interfaces. An interface simply provides a contract between the component object and other software that promises a set of functionality. COM defines a binary standard, not a source standard, so the compiled code of any language may be used by any client application. The connection between software components is controlled by COM; thus, it provides the remote procedure calls required to present software components with complete remote/local transparency. The interface model allows a component to add functionality without breaking backwards compatibility with existing software, and the interfaces provided by a COM component are dynamically exposed, which allows client code to dynamically determine if an object supports a selected interface.

The Active Template Library (ATL) was designed to provide a set of template classes to simplify the creation of small, lightweight COM components and ActiveX controls. The primary design goal of the ATL team was to provide an efficient, low-overhead component implementation. ATL makes heavy use of templates to provide reusable, flexible code. A class uses ATL by inheriting from base classes and using itself as the template parameter.

The latest version of Visual C++ includes attributes, which are used heavily by ATL to simplify component creation without sacrificing the efficiency of ATL. Attributed programming is a new feature in Visual C++ .NET designed to simplify common programming tasks, most notably in the area of COM development. An attribute "marks up" a source file, class, interface, method or parameter and specifies a property of the item it modifies. Attributes were created, in part, as a solution to difficult coding involved in creating and maintaining COM objects, type libraries and registration scripts.

A fundamental difficulty in COM component development has been maintaining component description and registration information across several source files. Attributes replace the separate `.idl` and `.rgs` files and cause the attribute providers to generate these files at compile time, rather than forcing the programmer to maintain them. COM attributes provide solutions to create object maps, object identification, class factories, threading and common base interface method implementations.

Compiler attributes provide functionality for the Unified Event Model, in addition to providing flags pertaining to the generation and use of various library, IDL and attributed code.

The `/Fx` compiler option generates the attributed source and writes it to disk as a file. This allows you to review generated code to assist in debugging an application.

Attribute **module** is one of the most important attributes in the IDL category. Not only does it create the IDL library block used to describe the COM library, but it causes the compiler to inject default implementations of entry-point and library-registration functions.

Interface attributes allow the programmer to define the interface's COM properties in the source file without maintaining a separate **.idl** file describing the interface.

Component class attributes allow the programmer to specify specific component properties without maintaining a separate .idl file. Attribute **coclass** declares this class as a COM component. Attribute **threading** supplies the template parameter for the **CComObjectRootEx** to determine the object's threading model. Attribute **aggregatable** sets the value of the MIDL **aggregatable** attribute and, in ATL projects, injects the appropriate macro into compiled code. Attributes **vi_progid** and **progid** identify the class in a human-readable format. Attribute **version** specifies the class version number.

The new Microsoft-specific keyword __**uuidof** obtains the unique ID of an object declared with the **uuid** attribute, which is often used in functions such as **CoCreateInstance**.

Attribute **event_source** takes the parameter **com** to declare this class as a COM connection point event source. Keyword __**event** works in conjunction with the __**interface** keyword to designate an event-source interface. Keyword __**raise** modifies a method to fire an event. Attribute **event_receiver** causes an attribute provider to inject code that enables the object to handle COM connection point events. In addition to the type parameter, **event_receiver** takes a boolean parameter that determines whether the COM event receiver uses layout-dependent event handlers. Keyword __**hook**, which is treated as an attribute, creates a connection between the client event sink and the server-connection point. Keyword __**unhook** removes the connection between the server and client.

ATL ActiveX controls use a set of attributes to simplify property display and notification. Attributes **propput** and **propget** declare the method as a set or get property, respectively. Attribute **bindable** enables notification to be sent to an event sink any time the property changes. Attribute **requestedit** allows the property to request permission to change a property from a sink before allowing a property change.

Attribute **retval** causes the modified parameter to act as the return value for the method. Attribute **dispinterface** declares an interface as a dispatch interface and causes the interface to inherit from **IDispatch**. Attribute **registration_script** takes a single unnamed parameter that designates the path to a custom registration script (**.rgs**). If this attribute is not specified, Visual Studio .NET generates an **.rgs** file for the project.

22.7 Internet and Web Resources

**msdn.microsoft.com/library/default.asp?url=/library/en-us/com/
com_757w.asp**
This site contains an introduction and overview of the Component Object Model (COM) standard and implementation.

www.codeproject.com/atl/atl_underthehood_.asp
Here you will find the first of a series of articles that introduce the underlying technologies and techniques used by templates and the Active Template Library (ATL).

msdn.microsoft.com/msdnmag/issues/01/04/attributes/attributes.asp
This site provides an overview of COM and IDL attributes, and contains several examples and technical details of attributed programming model.

www.codeproject.com/atl/newinatl7.asp
This site introduces and provides examples for the new ATL 7.0 classes.

ATL Server Web Applications

Objectives

- To become familiar with Server Replacement Files in ATL Server.
- To create Web applications.
- To create an ATL Server application that consists of multiple Server Replacement Files.
- To control user access to Web applications through forms authentication.
- To use files and databases in ATL Server applications.
- To create XML Web services using ATL Server.

If any man will draw up his case, and put his name at the foot of the first page, I will give him an immediate reply. Where he compels me to turn over the sheet, he must wait my leisure.
Lord Sandwich

Rule One: Our client is always right
Rule Two: If you think our client is wrong, see Rule One.
Anonymous

A fair question should be followed by a deed in silence.
Dante Alighieri

One must have a good memory to be able to keep the promises one makes.
Friedrich Wilhelm Nietzsche

There can be no true response without responsibility; there can be no responsibility without response.
Arthur Vogel

23.1 Introduction

In Chapters 9 and 10, Graphical User Interface Concepts: Part 1 and Graphical User Interface Concepts: Part 2, we used Windows Forms and Windows controls to develop Windows applications. In this chapter (which is targeted towards developers with previous knowledge of unmanaged code, managed code and Win32 programming), we introduce *Web-based application development* with Microsoft's *ATL Server* technology. Web-based applications create content for Web-browser clients. This Web content can include Hyper-Text Markup Language (HTML) documents, client-side scripting, images and binary data.

We present several examples that demonstrate Web-based applications development, using *Server Response File*s (*SRF*) (or *stencils*), C++ programming and ATL server classes. Server Response Files have the file extension **.srf** and usually contain static HTML and *replacement tags* for dynamic content. The C++ applications use a set of templated classes and attributes that make up ATL Server to provide the logic for dynamic content creation.

ATL Server also provides support for unmanaged XML Web services. ATL Server provides an easy-to-use set of classes that allow developers to create XML Web services with the compatibility and efficiency of native code. At the end of this chapter we discuss the ATL Server Web services architecture and present a simple case-study to demonstrate a native XML Web service.

23.2 ATL Server Architecture

ATL Server is a set of classes designed to simplify Web development while providing the ability to call unmanaged C++ from within a Web page. The ATL Server architecture consists of three main components: Server Response Files (SRFs), Web Application DLLs and ISAPI Extension DLLs.[1]

A *Server Response File (SRF)* is a text file that usually contains static HTML and *replacement tags*. A replacement tag is a tag that is not displayed to the client, but must be handled by either an ISAPI extension DLL or a Web Application DLL.

The main purpose of the *ISAPI Extension DLL* is to delegate Web requests for `.srf` files to the appropriate Web Application DLL. The extension DLL is registered with Internet Information Services (IIS) as the handler for `.srf` requests. When a Web client requests an `.srf` file, IIS forwards the request to the ISAPI extension DLL. The extension DLL loads and parses the requested `.srf` file and looks for the **handler** tag specifying a Web Application DLL. It then forwards the content to the designated application DLL for processing. The ISAPI extension provides the Web application with methods and services to access and manage the current HTTP request. In addition, the ISAPI extension often provides additional functionality such as session tracking, thread management and performance caching.

A *Web application DLL* contains the application logic for parsing the `.srf` file. The Web application consists of one or more *request-handler classes* composed of replacement methods. A *replacement method* is a method in a request-handler class that corresponds to a specific tag name in the `.srf` file. As the request-handler class reads and processes stencil logic, it resolves all replacement tags with the appropriate replacement method. The replacement method produces the dynamic content by reading information from the request and writing HTML to the response stream. When the Web application has completed its response, the ISAPI extension sends the response buffer to the Web client via IIS.

23.3 Creating and Running a Simple ATL Server Example

In this section, we present our first example of an ATL Server application. When run, this program displays the text **A Simple ATL Server Example**, followed by the Web server's time. The program consists of an `.srf` file (Fig. 23.1) and a request-handler class (Fig. 23.3). We present the markup in the `.srf` file, the code in the request-handler class and the output of the application first; then, we carefully guide the reader through the step-by-step process of creating this program. [*Note*: The markup in Fig. 23.1 and other `.srf` file listings in this chapter has been modified slightly for presentation purposes.]

```
1   <!-- Fig. 23.1: WebTime.srf                              -->
2   <!-- Displays the current time on a label using the Time -->
3   <!-- replacement tag.                                     -->
4
5   <html>
6      <HEAD>
7         <meta name="vs_targetSchema"
8            content="http://schemas.microsoft.com/intellisense/ie5">
9         <META http-equiv="Content-Type"
10           content="text/html; charset=utf-8">
```

Fig. 23.1   SRF that displays the Web server's time. (Part 1 of 2.)

1. More information about ATL Server, including information about the ATL Server architecture, can be found at **msdn.microsoft.com/library/default.asp?url=/library/ en-us/vccore/html/vcconAtlServer.asp**.

```
11        </HEAD>
12
13        <BODY ms_positioning="GridLayout">
14           {{ handler WebTime.dll/Default }}
15
16           <DIV style="DISPLAY: inline; FONT-SIZE: xx-large;
17              Z-INDEX: 101; LEFT: 45px; WIDTH: 175px;
18              COLOR: lime; POSITION: absolute; TOP: 73px;
19              HEIGHT: 59px; BACKGROUND-COLOR: black"
20              ms_positioning="FlowLayout" id="timeLabel">
21              {{ Time }}</DIV>
22
23           <DIV style="DISPLAY: inline; FONT-SIZE: medium;
24              Z-INDEX: 102; LEFT: 45px; WIDTH: 233px;
25              POSITION: absolute; TOP: 35px; HEIGHT: 20px"
26              ms_positioning="FlowLayout" id="promptLabel">
27              A Simple ATL Server example</DIV>
28        </BODY>
29     </html>
```

Fig. 23.1   SRF that displays the Web server's time. (Part 2 of 2.)

Visual Studio .NET generates the markup shown in Fig. 23.1 when the programmer drags two **Label**s onto an **.srf** file and sets their properties (the Visual Studio .NET HTML designer is discussed later in this section). Notice that the **.srf** file contains other information, in addition to HTML. In an **.srf** file, replacement tags are enclosed within double curly braces ({{...}}). When the Web application encounters a replacement tag, it will attempt to locate the replacement method specified by the given tag name.

Line 14 contains tag **handler** that designates the path to the Web application DLL and the name of the request-handler class. There must be exactly one *handler tag* present in every SRF; the ISAPI Extension DLL forwards the request to the Web application class specified by this tag. Line 14 specifies that requests in this SRF will be handled by a request-handler class called **Default** located in **WebTime.dll** (discussed shortly).

Line 21 contains tag **Time**, which references a method defined in the request-handler class. At runtime this tag will be replaced by the output from the replacement method in the request-handler class.

Before presenting the request-handler class that handles the replacement tags of the **.srf** file, we briefly discuss ATL Server classes and attributes. There are well over one hundred ATL Server classes that assist the developer in a broad range of tasks including threading, session state management, caching, SOAP messaging and parsing.[2] Of these classes, some of the most important include **CRequestHandlerT**, **CHttpResponse**, **CHttpRequest** and **CStencil**.

ATL Server request-handler classes usually inherit from class *CRequestHandlerT*. This class receives the request from the ISAPI Extension DLL and parses the **.srf** file. In addition, it provides method *ValidateAndExchange*, which is called after each page request, and is usually overridden in the request-handler child class for initialization.

---

2. A full listing of the ATL Server classes can be found at
   msdn.microsoft.com/library/default.asp?url=/library/en-us/vclib/
   html/vclrfATLServerClasses.asp.

It also contains variables *m_HttpRequest* and *m_HttpResponse* of type **CHttpRequest** and **CHttpResponse**, respectively. These members provide information about the current request and allow access to the response stream.

Class **CRequestHandlerT** uses classes **CStencil** and **CHtmlStencil** to handle a set of predefined tags. The predefined tags, shown in Fig. 23.2, provide locale, comment and resources information. Developers can provide their own implementations for these tags, but in most cases the default implementation is sufficient.

Figure 23.3 presents the request-handler class for our example. Note that this class is a part of the **WebTime.dll** referenced on line 14 of Fig. 23.1.

Tag	Syntax	Comment
codepage tag	{{ **codepage** *characterSet* }}	Defines the character set of the page. Example Value: **utf-8**.
comment tag	{{ **//** *Comment* }} or {{ **!--** *Comment* }}	Places a comment in the **.srf** file, which will not be processed.
handler tag	{{ **handler** *Application*.**dll**/*HandlerName* }}	Defines the default Web Application DLL, all replacement tags that do not specify a Subhandler DLL will be resolved in the specified DLL.
Include tag	{{ **include** *file*.**srf** }}	Inserts the specified file into the current **.srf**.
locale tag	{{ **locale** *languageCode* }}	Specifies the language and country of the current page. Example Value: **us-en**.
subhandler tag	{{ **subhandler** *name* *Application*.**dll**/*ClassName* }}	Allows more than one Web Application DLL in a single **.srf** file. The Subhandler DLL is referenced by a replacement tag with the following syntax: *name*.*tagName*.

Fig. 23.2 Predefined tags handled by Class **CStencil** and **CHttpStencil**.

```
1   // Fig. 23.3: WebTime.h
2   // Displays current system time.
3
4   #pragma once
5
6   #include <time.h>
7
8   [ request_handler( "Default" ) ]
9   class CWebTimeHandler
10  {
11  public:
```

Fig. 23.3 Request-handler class that displays the Web server's time. (Part 1 of 2.)

```
12
13      // method called when page loads
14      HTTP_CODE ValidateAndExchange()
15      {
16         m_HttpResponse.SetContentType( "text/html" );
17
18         return HTTP_SUCCESS;
19      } // end method ValidateAndExchange
20
21   protected:
22
23      // Time tag replacement handler
24      [ tag_name( name="Time" ) ]
25      HTTP_CODE OnTime( void )
26      {
27         time_t currentTime;
28         tm *processedTime;
29
30         // obtain the current time
31         currentTime = time( NULL );
32         processedTime = localtime( &currentTime );
33
34         // display the current time
35         m_HttpResponse << processedTime->tm_hour << ":"
36            << processedTime->tm_min << ":"
37            << processedTime->tm_sec;
38
39         return HTTP_SUCCESS;
40      } // end method OnTime
41   }; // end class CWebTimeHandler
```

Fig. 23.3   Request-handler class that displays the Web server's time. (Part 2 of 2.)

ATL Server includes attributes that further simplify the mapping between SRF references and the classes and methods in the Web application DLL. Attribute **request_handler** on line 8 takes a single argument, the string **"Default"**. The attribute injects code into the class that causes the class to inherit from class **CRequest-HandlerT** and map to the request-handler name **Default**. The injected code allows the ISAPI Extension DLL to recognize this class as designated in the SRF **handler** tag:

```
{{ handler WebTime.dll/Default }}
```

The value after the forward slash (/) designates the class name as defined in the **request_handler** attribute,

Lines 9–41 define request-handler class **CWebTimeHandler**. Method *Validate-AndExchange* (lines 14–19) overrides the base-class method to provide initialization code. Method **ValidateAndExchange** is called once for each page request by a client. Line 16 uses the base-class member object **m_HttpResponse** method *SetContent-Type* to notify the client of the MIME type for our response, **text/html**. Line 18 returns enumeration *HTTP_CODE* member *HTTP_SUCCESS*, which designates that there were no errors during the method. A return value of *HTTP_FAILURE* would halt processing of the page and present an HTTP error 500 to the client. A return value of *HTTP_S_FALSE* indicates the method was successful, but returned a false value.

Lines 25–40 contain our tag-replacement method. Attribute **tag_name** (line 24) injects code into the class to map the string argument to the method name. This allows the request-handler class to match SRF replacement tags to the appropriate methods. Lines 28–32 obtain the current system time and store it in a **tm** structure. Finally, lines 35–37 use base member object **m_HttpResponse** overloaded **<<** operator to write the time into the response stream. In the processed SRF that is returned to the client, the call to tag replacement method **Time** will be replaced by the current system time.

Now that we have presented the SRF and the request-handler class, we outline the process by which we created this application:

1. *Create the project.* Select **File > New > Project...** to display the **New Project** dialog (Fig. 23.4). In this dialog, select **Visual C++ Projects** in the left pane and then *ATL Server Project* in the right pane. Specify **WebTime** in the **Name** field. IIS must be running to run the project successfully. IIS can be started by executing **inetmgr.exe**, right clicking **Default Web Site** in the dialog that appears and selecting **Start**. [*Note:* Programmers might need to expand the node representing their computer to display the **Default Web Site**.] Press the **OK** button to proceed to the **ATL Server Project Wizard**.

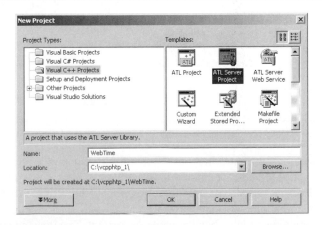

Fig. 23.4 Creating an **ATL Server Project** in Visual Studio .NET.

2. *Complete the ATL Server Project Wizard.* Visual Studio .NET allows the developer to customize the project with the **ATL Server Project Wizard** shown in Fig. 23.5. Click on **Project Settings** on the left side of the wizard and check the box **Generate Combined DLL**. This option makes it easier to manage both the ISAPI Extension DLL and the Web Application in the same project. Next, click **Developer Support Options**, and uncheck the **Generate TODO Comments** option to reduce the number of generated comments. Finally, click **Finish** at the bottom of the Wizard dialog box.

3. *Examine the newly created project.* The next several figures describe the new project's content; we begin with the **Solution Explorer**, shown in Fig. 23.6. Visual Studio .NET creates several files when a new **ATL Server Project** is created. **WebTime.srf** is the Server Response File. Double clicking the file in the **Solution Explorer** opens up VisualStudio .NET's HTML designer.

   The next figure (Fig. 23.7), shows the **HTML** controls listed in the **Toolbox** (**View > Toolbox**).[3] It contains the selection of HTML controls that may be dragged onto the **.srf** file.

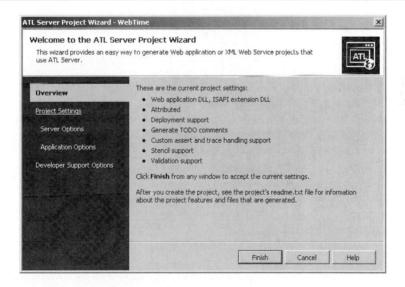

Fig. 23.5   ATL Server Project Wizard in Visual Studio .NET.

---

3. More information about the Visual Studio .NET **Toolbox** can be found at
   `ms-help://MS.VSCC/MS.MSDNVS/vsintro7/html/vxurfToolboxS.htm`

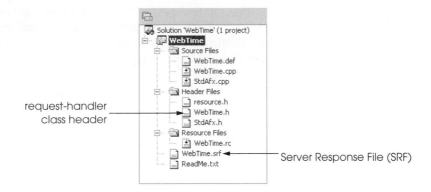

request-handler
class header

Server Response File (SRF)

Fig. 23.6   Solution Explorer window for project **WebTime**.

Fig. 23.7   HTML menu in the **Toolbox**.

Figure 23.10 shows the HTML designer for **WebTime.srf**. It consists of a window on which users drag and drop components, such as buttons and labels, from the **Toolbox**.

The HTML designer's *HTML* mode (Fig. 23.8) allows the programmer to view the markup that represents the user interface. Clicking the **HTML** button in the lower-left corner of the HTML designer switches the HTML designer to **HTML** mode. Similarly, clicking the *Design* button (to the left of the **HTML** button) returns the HTML designer to **Design** mode.

The next figure (Fig. 23.9) displays **WebTime.h**—the generated request-handler class file for **WebTime.srf**. Recall that Visual Studio .NET generates this request-handler class file when the project is created.

Fig. 23.8   HTML mode of HTML designer.

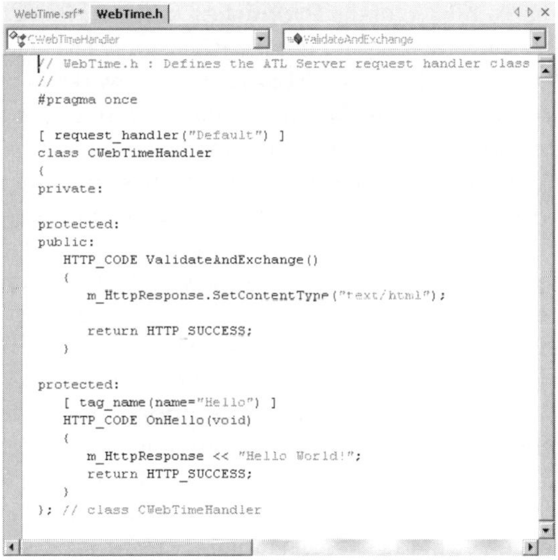

Fig. 23.9   Request-handler class file **WebTime.h** generated by Visual Studio .NET.

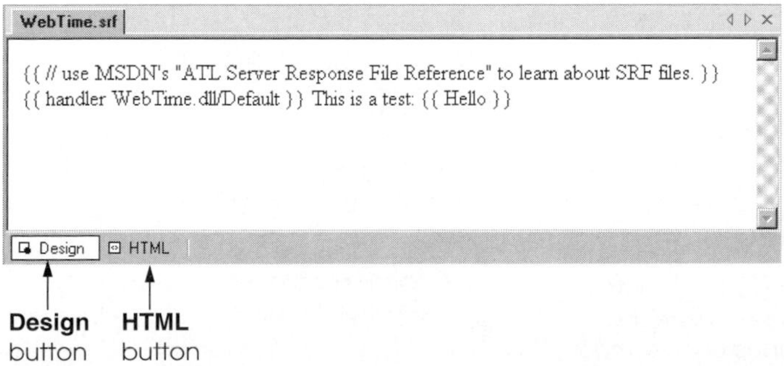

Fig. 23.10 Design mode of HTML designer.

4. *Design the page*. Designing an HTML page in Visual Studio .NET is as simple as dragging controls to the page from the **Toolbox** and dropping them onto the page. Like the HTML page itself, each control is an object that has properties. Developers can set these properties and events using the **Properties** window.

The *PageLayout* property determines how controls are arranged on the form (Fig. 23.11). By default, property `PageLayout` is set to *FlowLayout*, which causes controls to be placed sequentially on the Web page. This is called *relative positioning*, because the controls' positions are relative to the Web page's upper-left corner. Alternatively, the developer can set the Web page's **PageLayout** property to **GridLayout**, which specifies that all controls are located exactly where they are dropped on the Web page. This is called *absolute positioning*. We use both layouts in our examples; for each example, we will state beforehand which layout is being used. To view the page's properties, select *Document* from the drop-down list in the **Properties** window; **Document** is the name used to represent the Web page in the **Properties** window. Property `targetSchema` specifies the Web browser our page is designed for. The default schema, **Internet Explorer 3.02 / Navigator 3.0**, works in the largest number of browsers, but provides limited functionality. For all examples in this chapter we select **Internet Explorer 5.0** as our target schema.

In the **WebTime** example, we use a **GridLayout** page containing two **Label**s, which developers can place on the page either by drag-and-drop or by double-clicking the **Toolbox**'s **Label** control. Set the **id** property on the first **Label** to **promptLabel** and the second **id** to **timeLabel**. We replace the **timeLabel**'s text with **{{Time}}**, which will cause the label text to be set by the tag-replacement method. We set the text for **promptLabel** to **A Simple ATL Server Example**. Select the style property of **timeLabel** and click the ellipsis(**...**) button to open the **Style Builder** dialog. In the **Style Builder** dialog, set **timeLabel**'s background color, font color and font size attributes to **Black**, **LimeGreen** and **XX-Large**, respectively. We also set the labels' locations and sizes by dragging the controls. Once the **Label**s' properties are set in the **Properties** window, Visual Studio .NET updates the SRF's contents. Figure 23.12 shows the IDE after these properties are set.

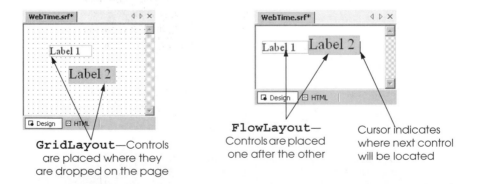

Fig. 23.11 `GridLayout` and `FlowLayout` illustration.

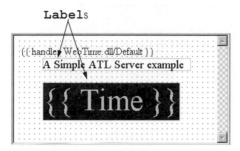

Fig. 23.12 `WebTime.srf` after adding two **Label**s and setting their properties.

5. *Add page logic*. Once the user interface has been designed, C++ code must be added to the request-handler class. In this example, lines 23–40 of Fig. 23.3 are added to the request-handler class file to replace the sample response method generated by the ATL Server Wizard.

6. *Run the program*. Select **Debug > Start**. An Internet Explorer window opens and loads the Web page (the `.srf` file). Notice that the URL is `http://local-host/WebTime/WebTime.srf` (Fig. 23.3), indicating that our SRF is located within the directory `WebTime`, which is located in the Web server's root directory.

23.4 AdRotator Example

Web pages often contain product and service advertisements that usually consist of images. Although Web site authors want to sell advertisements to as many sponsors as possible, Web pages can display only a limited number of advertisements at once. To address this problem, we will create an ATL Server example that demonstrates advertisement rotation.

Figure 23.13 demonstrates the SRF for our advertisement rotator, or **AdRotator**, example. The images that we rotate in this example include the flags of eleven countries. When a user clicks the displayed flag image, the browser is redirected to a Web page containing information about the country that the flag represents. If a user refreshes or re-requests the page, the next of the eleven flags is chosen displayed. [*Note*: For the remainder of this chapter, we present a screenshot of the page as displayed in the Visual Studio .NET HTML designer following each SRF.]

```
1   <!-- Fig. 23.13: AdRotatorTest.srf                         -->
2   <!-- Displays an image of a countries flag which varies -->
3   <!-- with each request.                                    -->
4
5   <html>
6      <HEAD>
7         <meta name="vs_targetSchema"
8            content="http://schemas.microsoft.com/intellisense/ie5">
9      </HEAD>
```

Fig. 23.13 `AdRotatorTest.srf` displays one of eleven flags on each page request. (Part 1 of 2.)

```
10
11       <BODY background="images\background.png">
12          {{ handler AdRotatorTest.dll/Default }}<br>
13
14          <DIV style="DISPLAY: inline; WIDTH: 161px; HEIGHT: 21px"
15             ms_positioning="FlowLayout">Ad Rotator Example:</DIV>
16
17          <P>{{ DisplayNextAd }}</P>
18       </BODY>
19    </html>
```

```
{{ handler AdRotatorTest.dll/Default }}
Ad Rotator Example:

{{ DisplayNextAd }}
```

Fig. 23.13 `AdRotatorTest.srf` displays one of eleven flags on each page request. (Part 2 of 2.)

The SRF in Fig. 23.13 contains a single **Label** and the replacement tag **DisplayNextAd**. The **background** property for our page is set to display the image **background.png**. To specify this file, click the ellipsis button provided next to the **Background** property and use the resulting dialog to browse for **background.png**.

Figure 23.14 shows the request-handler class file. The output depicts two different requests—the first time the page is requested, the American flag is shown, and, in the second request, the French flag is displayed. The last image depicts the Web page that loads when a user clicks the French flag. [*Note*: This example will not run correctly unless the images folder is copied from the project directory to **inetpub\wwwroot\AdRotatorTest**.]

```
1    // Fig. 23.14: AdRotatorTest.h
2    // Demonstrates advertisement rotation.
3
4    #pragma once
5
6    [ request_handler( "Default" ) ]
7    class CAdRotatorTestHandler
8    {
9    private:
10
11      // static member variables
12      static char *images[ 11 ];
13      static char *links[ 11 ];
14      static int selected;
15
```

Fig. 23.14 `AdRotator` request-handler file. (Part 1 of 3.)

```
16  public:
17
18      // method called when page loads
19      HTTP_CODE ValidateAndExchange()
20      {
21          m_HttpResponse.SetContentType( "text/html" );
22
23          return HTTP_SUCCESS;
24      } // end method ValidateAndExhange
25
26  protected:
27
28      // DisplayNextAd tag replacement handler
29      [ tag_name( name="DisplayNextAd" ) ]
30      HTTP_CODE OnDisplayNextAd( void )
31      {
32
33          // write rotated HTML
34          m_HttpResponse << "<A HREF=" << links[ selected ] << ">"
35              << "<IMG SRC=" << images[ selected ] << "></A>";
36
37          // move to the next ad
38          selected = ( selected + 1 ) % 11;
39
40          return HTTP_SUCCESS;
41      } // end method OnDisplayNextAd
42  }; // class CAdRotatorTestHandler
43
44  // image links, used by all clients
45  char *CAdRotatorTestHandler::links[] = {
46      "http://www.odci.gov/cia/publications/factbook/geos/us.html",
47      "http://www.odci.gov/cia/publications/factbook/geos/fr.html",
48      "http://www.odci.gov/cia/publications/factbook/geos/gm.html",
49      "http://www.odci.gov/cia/publications/factbook/geos/it.html",
50      "http://www.odci.gov/cia/publications/factbook/geos/sp.html",
51      "http://www.odci.gov/cia/publications/factbook/geos/lg.html",
52      "http://www.odci.gov/cia/publications/factbook/geos/pe.html",
53      "http://www.odci.gov/cia/publications/factbook/geos/sg.html",
54      "http://www.odci.gov/cia/publications/factbook/geos/sw.html",
55      "http://www.odci.gov/cia/publications/factbook/geos/th.html",
56      "http://www.odci.gov/cia/publications/factbook/geos/us.html"
57  };
58
59  // image filenames, used by all clients
60  char *CAdRotatorTestHandler::images[] = {
61      "images/us.png", "images/france.png", "images/germany.png",
62      "images/italy.png", "images/spain.png", "images/latvia.png",
63      "images/peru.png", "images/senegal.png", "images/sweden.png",
64      "images/thailand.png","images/unitedstates.png"
65  };
66
67  // currently selected image, used by all clients
68  int CAdRotatorTestHandler::selected = 0;
```

Fig. 23.14 AdRotator request-handler file. (Part 2 of 3.)

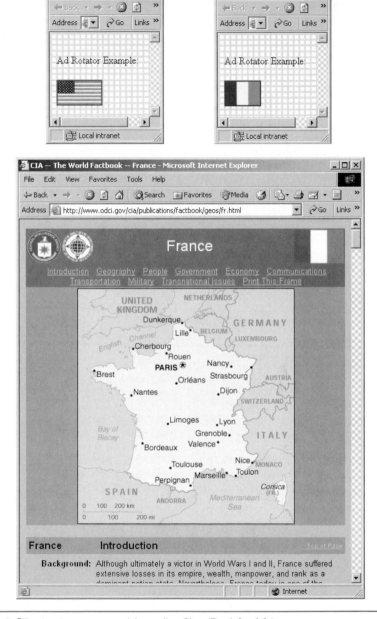

Fig. 23.14 `AdRotator` request-handler file. (Part 3 of 3.)

Lines 12–14 contain **static** member variables that are initialized on lines 45–68 to contain the link URL, image name and current index for which there is a single instance among all page requests.

Lines 30–41 contain the tag-replacement method **OnDisplayNextAd**, which maps to the replacement tag **DisplayNextAd** in Fig. 23.13. This method writes the HTML for an image link to the response buffer (lines 34–35) for the image and hyperlink at index **selected**. Then, it increments variable **selected**, so the next page request will result in the next image in the list (line 38).

23.5 Session Tracking

In this section we are going to demonstrate the various session-tracking techniques discussed in Chapter 17, Web Services. ATL Server provides support for both cookie-based and memory-backed or database-backed session tracking techniques.

23.5.1 Cookies

ATL Server supports cookies through use of the **CCookie** class. Class **CCookie** represents a cookie name-value pair and provides a set of methods that set the properties of a given cookie. Class **CCookie** is discussed in greater detail later in this section.

The next Web application demonstrates the use of cookies. The example contains two pages with corresponding request handling classes. In the first page (Fig. 23.15 with the handler in Fig. 23.16), users select their favorite programming language from a group of radio buttons, then submit the HTML **form** to the Web server for processing. The Web server responds by creating a cookie that stores a record of the chosen language, as well as the ISBN number for a book on that topic. The server then returns a page to the browser, allowing the user either to select another programming language or to view the second page in the application (Fig. 23.17 with the handler in Fig. 23.18), which lists recommended books pertaining to the programming language that the user selected previously. When the user clicks the hyperlink, the cookies previously stored on the client are read and used to form the list of book recommendations.

```
1    <!-- Fig. 23.15: Cookies.srf                                       -->
2    <!-- Displays language options for user book recommendations. -->
3
4    <html>
5       <HEAD>
6          <meta name="vs_targetSchema"
7             content="http://schemas.microsoft.com/intellisense/ie5">
8       </HEAD>
9
10      <BODY>
11         {{ handler Cookies.dll/Default }}
12         <P>{{ if CheckPost }}
13            <A href="Cookies.srf">
14               Click here to choose another language.</A>
15
16            <BR>
17
18            <A href="recommend.srf">
19               Click here to get book recommendations.</A></P>
20
21         <P>
```

Fig. 23.15 SRF that uses cookies to store programming language preferences. (Part 1 of 2.)

```
20   protected:
21
22      // CheckPost tag replacement handler
23      [ tag_name( name="CheckPost" ) ]
24      HTTP_CODE OnCheckPost( void )
25      {
26
27         // checks if current request is post
28         if ( (m_HttpRequest.GetMethod() ==
29            CHttpRequest::HTTP_METHOD::HTTP_METHOD_POST  ) ) {
30
31            // obtain the selected language
32            LPCSTR language =
33               m_HttpRequest.GetFormVars().Lookup( "RadioGroup" );
34
35            // write the selected language and ISBN number to a
36            // cookie
37            m_HttpResponse.AppendCookie(
38               language, findISBN( language ) );
39
40            return HTTP_SUCCESS;
41         } // end if
42
43         // return false if method is not "POST"
44         else
45            return HTTP_S_FALSE;
46      } // end method OnCheckPost
47
48   private:
49
50      // finds the ISBN of a Deitel book given a
51      // programming language
52      LPCSTR findISBN( LPCSTR language )
53      {
54         if ( strcmp( language, "C#" ) == 0 )
55            return "0-13-062221-4";
56
57         if ( strcmp( language, "C++") == 0 )
58            return "0-13-089571-7";
59
60         if ( strcmp(language, "C") == 0 )
61            return "0-13-089572-5";
62
63         if ( strcmp( language, "Python" ) == 0 )
64            return "0-13-092361-3";
65
66         if ( strcmp( language, "Visual Basic .NET" ) == 0 )
67            return "0-13-456955-5";
68
69         return NULL;
70      } // end method findISBN
71   }; // end class CCookiesHandler
```

Fig. 23.16 Replacement method that stores information using cookies. (Part 2 of 3.)

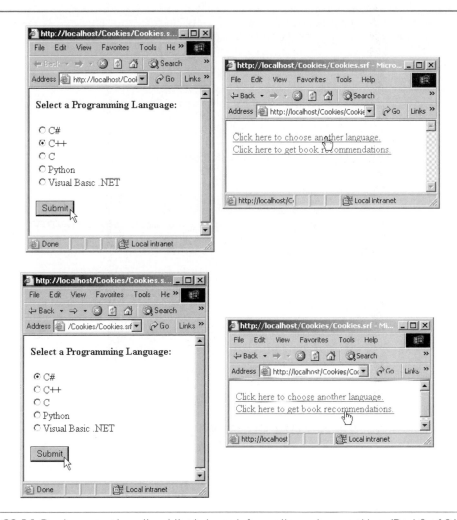

Fig. 23.16 Replacement method that stores information using cookies. (Part 3 of 3.)

As mentioned earlier, clicking the **Submit** button causes a *post* request to occur and the **CheckPost** tag to be evaluated. As a result, the condition in the **if** structure of lines 28–29 evaluates to **true**, and lines 32–40 execute. Lines 32–33 access the value of the selected radio button sent with the *post* request from the form in Fig. 23.15. Method **Get-FormVars** returns an object of type **CHttpRequestParms** that stores the collection of ID-value pairs from a submitted form. Method **Lookup** of class **CHttpRequestParms** retrieves the value in the collection that corresponds to the ID passed as an argument. In this case, the value returned is the **value** attribute of the selected radio button.

Lines 37–38 append a new cookie object (of type *CCookie*) to the response. The cookie contains the **language** and its corresponding **ISBN** number. The ISBN number is located by the **findISBN** method (lines 52–70), which returns the ISBN of the Deitel book for the given language.

When the user clicks the link to get book recommendations the **recommend.srf** (Fig. 23.17) is parsed and returned.

```
1   <!-- Fig. 23.17: recommend.srf                              -->
2   <!-- Recommends books based on user's language selection. -->
3
4   <html>
5      <head>
6         <meta name="vs_targetSchema"
7            content="http://schemas.microsoft.com/intellisense/ie5">
8      </head>
9
10     <BODY>
11        <P>{{ handler Cookies.dll/Recommend }}
12        </P>
13
14        <DIV style="DISPLAY: inline; FONT-WEIGHT: bold;
15           FONT-SIZE: x-large; WIDTH: 70px; HEIGHT: 15px"
16           ms_positioning="FlowLayout">Recommendations:</DIV>
17
18        <P></P>
19
20        <P><SELECT id="Select1" style="WIDTH: 361px;
21           HEIGHT: 241px" size="15" name="Select1">
22              {{ ListBooks }}
23           </SELECT></P>
24
25     </BODY>
26  </html>
```

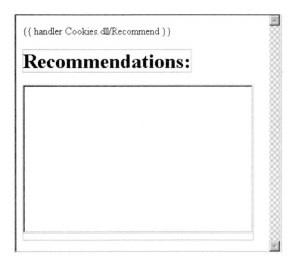

Fig. 23.17 SRF that returns book recommendations from information in a cookie.

Recommend.srf contains a label (lines 14–16) and a list box (lines 20–23). The label displays the text **Recommendations**, and the list box displays the recommendations created by the tag-replacement method **ListBooks** from the request-handler class shown in Fig. 23.18. [*Note*: The **recommend.h** header will not be included in the Web application DLL if it is not **#include**d in **Cookies.cpp**.]

```cpp
1   // Fig. 23.18: Recommend.h
2   // Displays book recommendations.
3
4   #pragma once
5
6   [ request_handler( "Recommend" ) ]
7   class CRecommendHandler
8   {
9   public:
10
11      // method called when page loads
12      HTTP_CODE ValidateAndExchange()
13      {
14         m_HttpResponse.SetContentType( "text/html" );
15
16         return HTTP_SUCCESS;
17      } // end method ValidateAndExchange
18
19   protected:
20
21      // ListBooks tag replacement handler
22      [ tag_name( name="ListBooks" ) ]
23      HTTP_CODE OnListBooks( void )
24      {
25
26         // pointer to the current cookie
27         const CCookie *currentCookie;
28         LPCSTR name;
29         POSITION cookieLocation;
30
31         // return the first client cookie
32         cookieLocation = m_HttpRequest.GetFirstCookie(
33            &name, &currentCookie );
34
35         // display recommendations
36         m_HttpResponse << "We Recommend:";
37
38         while ( cookieLocation != NULL ) {
39            m_HttpResponse << "<OPTION>" << name
40               << " How To Program. ISBN# "
41               << currentCookie->m_strValue
42               << "</OPTION>";
43
44            // get the next client cookie
45            cookieLocation =
46               m_HttpRequest.GetNextCookie(
47               cookieLocation, &name, &currentCookie );
48         } // end while
49
```

Fig. 23.18 Request-handler class that reads client cookies and displays book recommendations. (Part 1 of 2.)

```
50              return HTTP_SUCCESS;
51      } // end method OnListBooks
52   }; // end class CRecommendHandler
```

Fig. 23.18 Request-handler class that reads client cookies and displays book recommendations. (Part 2 of 2.)

Method **OnListBooks** (lines 23–51) retrieves the cookies from the client using the **CHttpRequest** object's cookie methods. Cookies can be read by an application only if they were created by a Web server in the domain in which that application is running—a Web server can never access cookies created outside the domain associated with that server. For example, a cookie created by a Web server in the **deitel.com** domain cannot be downloaded by a Web server in the **bug2bug.com** domain.

Method *GetFirstCookie* (lines 32–33) requires a **LPCSTR** to store the first cookie's name and a **CCookie** reference that contains the returned cookie when the method returns. All get cookie methods return a variable of type **POSITION**, which stores the location of the returned cookie. Method *GetNextCookie* (lines 46–47) requires the **POSITION** variable returned by a previous get cookie call to determine the next cookie in the list.

Lines 38–48 loop through each **CCookie** returned by the client and write the HTML to display the value as an option in the **recommend.srf** option list control. The **CCookie** object contains the **m_strName** and **m_strValue** member variables to allow access to the cookie's data. A cookie contains additional information called *attributes*, which allow the cookie creator to customize the cookie for its use. Class **CCookie** allows the programmer to set various attributes using the methods shown in Fig. 23.19.

Method	Argument Types	Comment
SetComment	LPCSTR	Adds plain text comment to cookie; describes the cookie to users if their browser is set to prompt before accepting a cookie.
SetCommentUrl	LPCSTR	Adds a link to the cookie that should describe the use of the cookie to users if their browser is set to prompt before accepting a cookie.
SetDiscard	bool	Adds the discard attribute to the cookie. The discard attribute causes a browser to discard a cookie when the browser exits, regardless of the values set in other attributes such as **MaxAge**.
SetDomain	LPCSTR	Specifies the domain attribute of the cookie to names of the servers to which this cookie should be set. By default, the domain attribute is set to the name of the server that wrote the cookie.
SetExpires	SYSTEM-TIME or LPCSTR	Sets the expires attribute to the provided date and time. Used in older browsers that do not support the maximum age cookie attribute to define when the cookie should be discarded by the browser.
SetMaxAge	UINT	Sets the maximum age attribute value of the cookie to define the time, in seconds that a cookie should persist before being discarded by the browser. The default value causes the browser to discard the cookie when it is closed.
SetPath	LPCSTR	Sets the cookies path attribute value, which defines the path of the URL to which the cookie applies. The cookie will be delivered only to pages at addresses that contain the path.
SetPort	LPCSTR	Sets the cookies port attribute value. The cookie will only be delivered with requests to a server on the provided port.
SetSecure	bool	Adds or removes the secure attribute from the cookie. If a cookie has the secure attribute, it will only be delivered over SSL connections.
SetVersion	UINT	Sets the cookie version attribute. The default value is **1** and should not be changed.

Fig. 23.19 Cookie attribute methods.

23.5.2 Session Tracking with a Memory-Backed Session State

ATL server provides memory-backed and database-backed session-tracking capabilities with interfaces **ISessionService** and **ISession**. A *memory-backed session-state* is a service, provided by the Web server, that maintains a unique identifier for each client and can store data in server memory for any particular client. A *database-backed session-state* is similar to memory-backed, but session data is written to a database to provide greater data persistence and allow multiple servers to access the same session data. To demonstrate basic session-tracking techniques, we modified Fig. 23.15–Fig. 23.18 to employ a memory-backed session state.

You may have noticed the **Session Services** checkbox in the **Server Options** page of the ATL Server Project Wizard (Fig. 23.20). Check the **Session Services** box and select the **Memory-backed session-state services**. This will enable the ISAPI extension DLL to maintain session variables for each client between page requests.

Figure 23.21 and Fig. 23.22 present the `.srf` files for the application, and Fig. 23.23 presents the request handler for both pages. The `.srf` files are similar to that presented in Fig. 23.15.

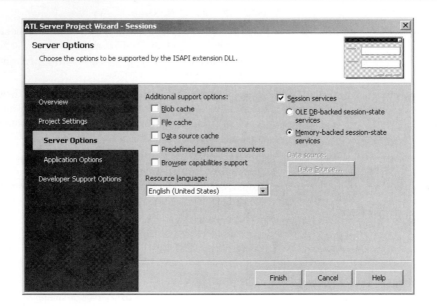

Fig. 23.20 **Session Services** option in **ATL Server Project Wizard**.

```
1   <!-- Fig. 23.21: Sessions.srf                            -->
2   <!-- Displays a list of programming languages and displays -->
3   <!-- the client's session ID.                             -->
4
5   <html>
6      <HEAD>
7         <meta name="vs_targetSchema"
8            content="http://schemas.microsoft.com/intellisense/ie5">
9      </HEAD>
10
11     <BODY>
```

Fig. 23.21 Memory-backed session-state SRF. (Part 1 of 3.)

```
12          {{ handler Sessions.dll/Default }}
13          <P>{{ if CheckPost }}
14              <A href="Sessions.srf">
15                  Click here to choose another language.</A>
16              <BR>
17              <A href="recommend.srf">
18                  Click here to get book recommendations.</A></P>
19
20          <P>{{ else }}
21          </P>
22
23          <DIV style="DISPLAY: inline; FONT-WEIGHT: bold;
24              WIDTH: 228px; HEIGHT: 20px" ms_positioning="FlowLayout">
25              Select a Programming Language:</DIV>
26
27          <P></P>
28          <P></P>
29
30          <FORM id="OptionsPage" method="post" runat="server">
31              <P>
32                  <INPUT id="C#" type="radio" value="C#"
33                      name="RadioGroup">C#<BR>
34
35                  <INPUT id="C++" type="radio" value="C++"
36                      name="RadioGroup">C++<BR>
37
38                  <INPUT id="C" style="WIDTH: 21px; HEIGHT: 20px"
39                      type="radio" value="C" name="RadioGroup">C<BR>
40
41                  <INPUT id="Python" type="radio" value="Python"
42                      name="RadioGroup">Python<BR>
43
44                  <INPUT id="Visual Basic .NET" type="radio"
45                      value="Visual Basic .NET" name="RadioGroup">
46                      Visual Basic .NET</P>
47              <P>
48                  <INPUT id="SubmitButton" type="submit"
49                      value="Submit" name="SubmitButton" runat="server"></P>
50          </FORM>
51
52          <P>{{endif}}
53          </P>
54
55          <P>
56          </P>
57
58          <DIV style="DISPLAY: inline; WIDTH: 355px; HEIGHT: 19px"
59              ms_positioning="FlowLayout">{{ SessionID }}</DIV>
60      </BODY>
61  </html>
```

Fig. 23.21 Memory-backed session-state SRF. (Part 2 of 3.)

Fig. 23.21 Memory-backed session-state SRF. (Part 3 of 3.)

```
1   <!-- Fig. 23.22: recommend.srf                          -->
2   <!-- Displays list of recommendations based on user -->
3   <!-- language selection.                               -->
4
5   <html>
6      <head>
7         <meta name="vs_targetSchema"
8            content="http://schemas.microsoft.com/intellisense/ie5">
9      </head>
10
11     <BODY>
12        <P>{{ handler Sessions.dll/Default }}
13        </P>
14
15        <P></P>
16
17        <DIV style="DISPLAY: inline; FONT-WEIGHT: bold;
18           FONT-SIZE: x-large; WIDTH: 70px; HEIGHT: 15px"
19           ms_positioning="FlowLayout">Recommendations:</DIV>
20
21        <P><SELECT id="Select1" style="WIDTH: 368px;
22           HEIGHT: 241px" size="15" name="Select1">
23              {{ ListBooks }}
```

Fig. 23.22 SRF that displays recommendations stored in session state. (Part 1 of 2.)

```
24            </SELECT></P>
25         </BODY>
26      </html>
```

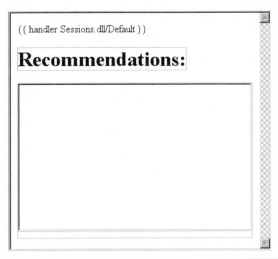

{{ handler Sessions.dll/Default }}

Recommendations:

Fig. 23.22 SRF that displays recommendations stored in session state. (Part 2 of 2.)

```
1    // Fig. 23.23: Sessions.h
2    // Demonstrates memory-resident session state variables.
3
4    #pragma once
5
6    #include <atlsession.h>
7
8    [ request_handler( "Default" ) ]
9    class CSessionsHandler
10   {
11   private:
12
13      // finds the ISBN of a deitel book given a
14      // programming language
15      LPCSTR findISBN( LPCSTR language )
16      {
17         if ( strcmp( language, "C#" ) == 0 )
18            return "0-13-062221-4";
19
20         if ( strcmp( language, "C++") == 0 )
21            return "0-13-089571-7";
22
23         if ( strcmp(language, "C") == 0 )
24            return "0-13-089572-5";
25
26         if ( strcmp( language, "Python" ) == 0 )
27            return "0-13-092361-3";
28
```

Fig. 23.23 Request-handler class that maintains session state. (Part 1 of 5.)

```
29          if ( strcmp( language, "Visual Basic .NET" ) == 0 )
30              return "0-13-456955-5";
31
32          return NULL;
33      } // end method findISBN
34
35      // COM object to store Session Service
36      CComPtr< ISessionStateService > sessionService;
37
38      // COM object to store session
39      CComPtr< ISession > session;
40
41  protected:
42
43      // CheckPost tag replacement handler
44      [ tag_name( name="CheckPost" ) ]
45      HTTP_CODE OnCheckPost( void )
46      {
47
48          // check for HTTP post method
49          if ( ( m_HttpRequest.GetMethod() ==
50              CHttpRequest::HTTP_METHOD::HTTP_METHOD_POST ) ) {
51
52              // get the selected language
53              LPCSTR language =
54                  m_HttpRequest.GetFormVars().Lookup( "RadioGroup" );
55
56              // store the results
57              CComVariant value = findISBN( language );
58              session->SetVariable( language, value );
59
60              return HTTP_SUCCESS;
61          } // end if
62          else
63              return HTTP_S_FALSE;
64      } // end method OnCheckPost
65
66      // SessionID tag replacement handler
67      [ tag_name( name = "SessionID" ) ]
68      HTTP_CODE OnSessionID( void )
69      {
70          CStringA sessionID;
71
72          // get the current session ID
73          m_HttpRequest.GetSessionCookie().GetValue( sessionID );
74          m_HttpResponse << "Your current session ID is: "
75              << ( sessionID.GetLength() ? sessionID :
76              "Not yet stored" );
77
78          return HTTP_SUCCESS;
79      } // end method OnSessionID
80
81      // ListBooks tag replacement handler
```

Fig. 23.23 Request-handler class that maintains session state. (Part 2 of 5.)

```
82        [ tag_name( name="ListBooks" ) ]
83        HTTP_CODE OnListBooks( void )
84        {
85           POSITION variablePosition;
86           HSESSIONENUM sessionEnumeration;
87           CComVariant value;
88           char name[ 64 ];
89           DWORD length = 65;
90           BSTR stringValue;
91
92           // obtain a reference to the first session variable
93           session->BeginVariableEnum( &variablePosition,
94              &sessionEnumeration );
95
96           // recommend books
97           m_HttpResponse << "We Recommend:";
98
99           // loop through session variables
100          while ( SUCCEEDED( session->GetNextVariable(
101             &variablePosition, &value, sessionEnumeration,
102             name, length ) ) ) {
103
104             value.CopyTo( &stringValue );
105             m_HttpResponse << "<OPTION>" << name
106                << " How To Program. ISBN# "
107                << stringValue << "</OPTION>";
108          } // end while
109
110          return HTTP_SUCCESS;
111       } // end method OnListBooks
112
113   public:
114
115       // method called when page loads
116       HTTP_CODE ValidateAndExchange()
117       {
118          m_HttpResponse.SetContentType( "text/html" );
119
120          // create an instance of the session service
121          HRESULT result = m_spServiceProvider->QueryService(
122             __uuidof( ISessionStateService ), &sessionService );
123
124          // get the current client session ID
125          CStringA sessionID;
126          m_HttpRequest.Cookies( SESSION_COOKIE_NAME ).GetValue(
127             sessionID );
128
129          // if session already exists load session variable
130          // into session
131          if ( sessionID.GetLength()  )
132             result = sessionService->GetSession(
133                sessionID, &session );
134
```

Fig. 23.23 Request-handler class that maintains session state. (Part 3 of 5.)

```
135        // otherwise, create a new session
136        else {
137
138            // variable to contain session ID
139            char id[ 65 ] = { 0 };
140            DWORD idLength = 64;
141
142            // create a new session
143            result = sessionService->CreateNewSession(
144                id, &idLength, &session );
145
146            // append session cookie to client
147            if ( SUCCEEDED( result ) ) {
148                CSessionCookie sessionCookie( id );
149                m_HttpResponse.AppendCookie( &sessionCookie );
150            }
151        } // end else
152
153        return HTTP_SUCCESS;
154    } // end method ValidateAndExchange
155 }; // end class CSessionsHandler
```

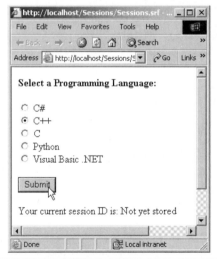

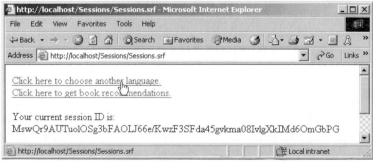

Fig. 23.23 Request-handler class that maintains session state. (Part 4 of 5.)

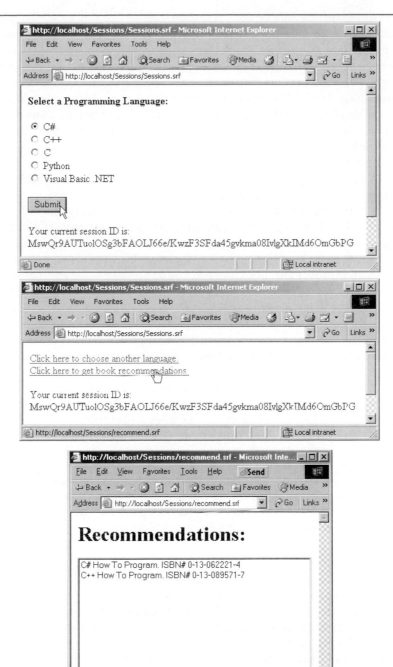

Fig. 23.23 Request-handler class that maintains session state. (Part 5 of 5.)

The ISAPI Extension DLL provides a session-state service that allows the Web application developer to create session objects for each client. This session-state service is accessed by interface **ISessionStateService**, which can create **ISession** objects for each client. In this Web application, we store the session state and session interfaces in **CComPtr**s **sessionService** and **session**, respectively. Method **ValidateAnd Exchange** (lines 116–154) ensures that each client that requests a page has a corresponding session object stored in **session**. Lines 121–122 obtain the **ISessionStateService** object maintained by the ISAPI extension DLL and store it in variable **sessionService**. Lines 126–127 attempt to obtain the session cookie from the client request. Users who have corresponding session objects maintained on the server will have session cookies that uniquely identify them to the server. The session cookie value is obtained from the request's cookie list by locating the value of the cookie that matches macro **SESSION_COOKIE_NAME**. Lines 131–133 determine whether the session cookie contained a value; if it did, we call **ISessionStateService** method *GetSession* with the session ID to store the session object in variable **session**. If the session cookie did not contain a session ID, the client is new, so we must create a new session to maintain that client's information. Lines 143–144 use **ISessionStateService** method **CreateNewSession** to create a new **ISession** object and store the session object in **session** and the session ID in variable **id**. Lines 147–150 check that method **CreateNewSession** was successful and append a **CSessionCookie** containing the session ID to the client, for retrieval in later page requests. When method **ValidateAnd Exchange** completes, the **ISession** object **session** will contain a reference to the current clients session object.

When the user clicks **Submit**, the **CheckSubmit** tag-replacement method adds the selected language and ISBN to the session object (line 58). Because much of this example is similar to the last example, we concentrate on the new features.

Software Engineering Observation 23.1

*A request handler must not use static instance variables to maintain client-state information, because clients accessing that request handler in parallel might overwrite the shared instance variables. Request handlers should maintain client-state information in **ISession** objects, because such objects are specific to each client.*

Like a cookie, an **ISession** object can store name-value pairs. In session terminology, these are called *session items*, and they are placed into an **ISession** object by calling method *SetVariable*. Line 58 calls **SetVariable** to place the language and its corresponding recommended book's ISBN number into the **ISession** object. One of the primary benefits of using **ISession** objects (rather than cookies) is that **ISession** objects can store any type of object (not just strings) as an attribute value. The information is stored in an object of type **CComVariant**, which may hold any data type. This provides C++ programmers with increased flexibility in determining the type of state information they wish to maintain for their clients. If the application calls method **SetVariable** to add an attribute that has the same name as an attribute previously stored in a session, the object associated with that attribute is replaced.

Method **OnSessionID** (lines 68–79) retrieves and displays the client's session ID on the **Sessions.srf**.

When the user chooses a language and selects the link to see recommendations, the **recommend.srf** page is loaded and method **OnListBooks** is called to fill the recommendations list. Lines 93–94 call **ISession** method *BeginVariableEnum*, which takes a **POSITION** and a **HSESSIONENUM** instance as arguments and stores the session variables in the **HSESSIONENUM** object and the position of the first value in the **POSITION** argument. Lines 100–108 loop through each value in object **HSESSIONENUM** and display its contents. Object **HSESSIONENUM** is navigated by calling method *GetNextVariable* of interface **ISession**, which requires the current **POSITION**, a **CComVariant** object to hold the session value, variable **HSESSIONENUM** created by **BeginVariableEnum**, a string buffer to hold the session object name and the length of the string buffer as arguments. When **GetNextVariable** returns, object **CComVariant** holds the value of the next session object in the list. We call method **CopyTo** of class **CComVariant** to store the session value in a string that we write to the response buffer in lines 105–107.

23.6 Case Study: Online Guest Book

Many Web sites allow users to provide feedback about the Web site in a *guest book*. Typically, users click a link on the Web site's homepage to request the guest-book page. This page usually consists of an HTML **form** that contains fields for the user's name, e-mail address, and a message. Data submitted to the guest book often are stored in a database located on the Web server's machine. In this section, we create a guest-book Web application.

The HTML **form** presented to the user consists of a user-name field, an e-mail address field and a message field. Figure 23.24 presents the SRF, and Fig. 23.25 presents the tag-replacement handler class for the guest-book application. For simplicity, we write the guest-book information to a text file.

```
1   <!-- Fig. 23.24: Guestbook.srf                       -->
2   <!-- Allows users to enter comments into a web guestbook. -->
3
4   <html>
5       <HEAD>
6           <meta name="vs_targetSchema"
7               content="http://schemas.microsoft.com/intellisense/ie5" >
8       </HEAD>
9
10      <BODY>
11          <P>{{ handler Guestbook.dll/Default }}
12          </P>
13
```

Fig. 23.24 Guest-book case study SRF. (Part 1 of 3.)

```
14          <DIV style="DISPLAY: inline; FONT-SIZE: x-large;
15             WIDTH: 531px; COLOR: blue; HEIGHT: 35px"
16             ms_positioning="FlowLayout">
17             Please leave a message in our guest book.</DIV>
18
19          <P></P>
20
21          <FORM method="post">
22             <DIV style="DISPLAY: inline; WIDTH: 149px;
23                HEIGHT: 19px" ms_positioning="FlowLayout">
24                Your Name:</DIV>
25
26             <INPUT id="nameBox" type="text" name="nameBox">
27
28             <P></P>
29             <P></P>
30
31             <DIV id="DIV1" style="DISPLAY: inline; WIDTH: 148px;
32                HEIGHT: 22px" ms_positioning="FlowLayout">
33                Your e-mail Address:</DIV>
34
35             <INPUT id="emailBox" type="text" name="emailBox">
36
37             <P></P>
38             <P></P>
39
40             <DIV style="DISPLAY: inline; WIDTH: 110px;
41                HEIGHT: 21px" ms_positioning="FlowLayout">
42                Tell the world:</DIV>
43
44             <BR>
45             <INPUT id="commentBox" style="WIDTH: 500px;
46                HEIGHT: 222px" type="text" size="78"
47                name="commentBox">
48
49             <P><INPUT id="Submit1" type="submit" value="Submit"
50                name="Submit1">     
51
52             <INPUT id="Reset1" type="reset" value="Reset"
53                name="Reset1"></P>
54          </FORM>
55          <P>{{ if Posted }}</P>
56          <P>{{ FillTable }}</P>
57          <P>
58          </P>
59          <P>{{ endif }}</P>
60       </BODY>
61    </html>
```

Fig. 23.24 Guest-book case study SRF. (Part 2 of 3.)

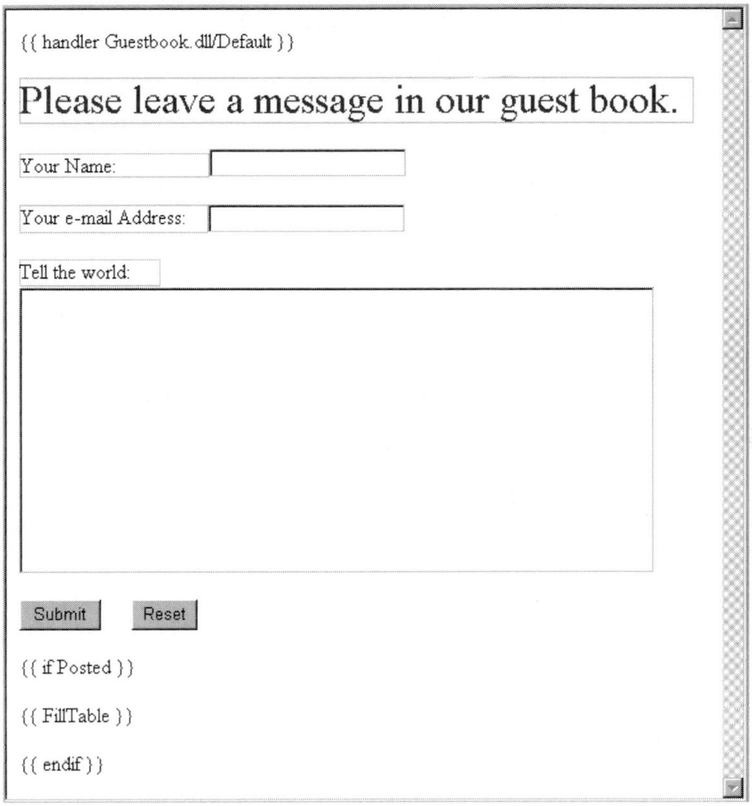

Fig. 23.24 Guest-book case study SRF. (Part 3 of 3.)

```
1   // Fig. 23.25: Guestbook.h
2   // Maintains a guestbook for web site visitors.
3
4   #pragma once
5
6   #include <fstream>
7
8   [ request_handler( "Default" ) ]
9   class CGuestbookHandler
10  {
11  public:
12
13      // method called on each page load
14      HTTP_CODE ValidateAndExchange()
15      {
16          m_HttpResponse.SetContentType( "text/html" );
17
```

Fig. 23.25 Guest-book case study handler class reads and writes guest-book entries. (Part 1 of 4.)

```
18              // check for HTTP POST
19              if ( m_HttpRequest.GetMethod() ==
20                 CHttpRequest::HTTP_METHOD_POST ) {
21
22                 // append to, or create file
23                 FILE *log = fopen( "c:\\guestbook.txt", "a+" );
24
25                 // obtain variables from input form
26                 LPCSTR name =
27                    m_HttpRequest.GetFormVars().Lookup( "nameBox" );
28
29                 LPCSTR email =
30                    m_HttpRequest.GetFormVars().Lookup( "emailBox" );
31
32                 LPCSTR comment =
33                    m_HttpRequest.GetFormVars().Lookup( "commentBox" );
34
35                 // write variables to file
36                 fprintf( log, "%s\t%s\t%s\n", name, email, comment );
37                 fclose( log );
38              } // end if
39
40              return HTTP_SUCCESS;
41          } // end method ValidateAndExchange
42
43      protected:
44
45          // OnPosted tag replacement handler
46          [ tag_name( name="Posted" ) ]
47          HTTP_CODE OnPosted( void )
48          {
49
50              // check for HTTP POST method
51              if ( m_HttpRequest.GetMethod() ==
52                 CHttpRequest::HTTP_METHOD_POST )
53
54                 return HTTP_SUCCESS;
55              else
56                 return HTTP_S_FALSE;
57          } // end method OnPosted
58
59          // FillTable tag replacement hander
60          [ tag_name( name="FillTable" ) ]
61          HTTP_CODE OnFillTable( void )
62          {
63
64              // write HTML to begin a table
65              m_HttpResponse << "<TABLE id=\"GuestTable\""
66                 << " cellSpacing=\"1\" cellPadding=\"1\""
67                 << " width=\"600\" border=\"1\">";
68
69              // open the guestbook log file
```

Fig. 23.25 Guest-book case study handler class reads and writes guest-book entries. (Part 2 of 4.)

```
70          FILE *log = fopen( "c:\\guestbook.txt", "r" );
71
72      char name[ 20 ], email[ 20 ], comment[ 256 ];
73
74      m_HttpResponse << "<TR style=\"FONT-WEIGHT: bold;\">\
75          <TD>Name</TD><TD>EMail</TD><TD>Comment</TD></TR>";
76
77      // read all guestbook entries and display in table
78      while ( fscanf( log, "%[^\t] %s %[^\n]\n",
79          name, email, comment ) != - 1 )
80
81          m_HttpResponse << "<TR><TD>" << name << "</TD><TD>"
82              << email << "</TD><TD>" << comment << "</TD></TR>\n";
83
84      // close table
85      m_HttpResponse << "</TABLE>\n";
86      fclose( log );
87
88      return HTTP_SUCCESS;
89  } // end method OnFillTable
90 }; // end class CGuestbookHandler
```

Fig. 23.25 Guest-book case study handler class reads and writes guest-book entries. (Part 3 of 4.)

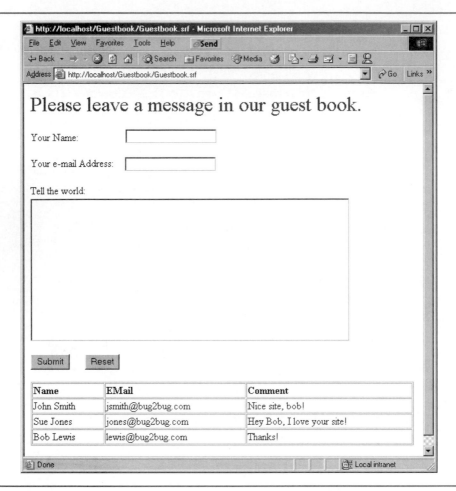

Fig. 23.25 Guest-book case study handler class reads and writes guest-book entries. (Part 4 of 4.)

The SRF generated by the GUI is shown in the output of Fig. 23.24. Lines 21–54 contain the form, which consists of three labels that correspond to the three input text boxes. The tag-replacement handler on line 55 determines whether the form has been posted. When tag-replacement handler **Posted** returns **HTTP_SUCCESS**, the tag-replacement handler **FillTable** will execute and create a table containing all guest-book entries. Figure 23.25 presents the replacement handler class for the guest-book application.

Method **ValidateAndExchange** (lines 14–41) is called at the start of each page request. This method is used to capture the form *post* and immediately write the form values to a text file. Lines 23–37 execute if the request method is *post*. Line 23 opens a the file **guestbook.txt** to append. [*Note*: Web applications require an absolute path for any file operations (e.g., **c:\guestbook.txt**).] Lines 26–36 read each form value and write the data to the file.

Method **OnPosted** (lines 47–57) handles the **Posted** replacement tag and simply returns **HTTP_SUCCESS** if the request method is *post* and **HTTP_S_FALSE** otherwise.

Method **OnFillTable** (lines 61–89) writes the guest-book entries into an HTML table. Lines 65–67 write the opening tag for the HTML table to the response stream. Line 70 opens the guest-book text file for reading, and lines 74–75 write the heading row for the guest-book table. The loop on lines 78–82 reads each guest-book entry and displays it as a row in the HTML table, halting when no more records can be read. Finally, lines 85–86 close the HTML table tag and the file stream.

23.7 Case Study: Connecting to a Database in ATL Server

This case study presents a Web-based application in which a user can view a list of publications by a specified author. This application uses a technique known as *forms authentication*, which protects a page so that only authenticated users can access that page. Authentication is a crucial tool for sites. This program contains two **.srf** files. The first page that a user requests is **Login.srf** (Fig. 23.26). After accessing this page, users select their names from the drop-down list and enter their passwords. If their passwords are valid, they are redirected to **DisplayBooks.srf** (Fig. 23.31), which provides a list of authors. When the user chooses an author and clicks the **Select** button, the data is posted, and the updated page displays a table that contains the titles, ISBNs and publishers of books written by the selected author.

```
1   <!-- Fig. 23.26: Login.srf                           -->
2   <!-- Page requesting login information from user. -->
3
4   <html>
5      <HEAD>
6         <meta name="vs_targetSchema"
7            content="http://schemas.microsoft.com/intellisense/ie5">
8      </HEAD>
9
10     <BODY bgColor="#ffebff" ms_positioning="GridLayout">
11        <P>{{ handler AuthorDatabase.dll/Default }}
12        {{ include ImageHeader.srf }}
13
14        <FORM method="post" runat="server" ID="Form1">
15           <P> </P>
16           <P> </P>
17
18           <DIV style="DISPLAY: inline; Z-INDEX: 101;
19              LEFT: 210px; WIDTH: 373px; POSITION: absolute;
20              TOP: 158px; HEIGHT: 22px" ms_positioning="FlowLayout">
21              Please select your name and enter your password
22              to log in:</DIV>
23
24           <DIV style="DISPLAY: inline; Z-INDEX: 102;
25              LEFT: 232px; WIDTH: 70px; POSITION: absolute;
26              TOP: 189px; HEIGHT: 15px"
27              ms_positioning="FlowLayout">Name:</DIV>
28
```

Fig. 23.26 Login SRF for database Web application. (Part 1 of 2.)

```
29              <P><SELECT id="nameList" style="Z-INDEX: 103;
30                 LEFT: 314px; POSITION: absolute; TOP: 187px"
31                 name="nameList">
32                    {{ Names }}
33                 </SELECT></P>
34
35              <DIV id="DIV1" style="DISPLAY: inline; Z-INDEX: 104;
36                 LEFT: 233px; WIDTH: 70px; POSITION: absolute;
37                 TOP: 223px; HEIGHT: 15px"
38                 ms_positioning="FlowLayout">Password</DIV>
39
40              <P>
41                 <INPUT id="passwordBox" style="Z-INDEX: 105;
42                    LEFT: 315px; POSITION: absolute; TOP: 220px"
43                    type="password" name="passwordBox">
44
45                 <INPUT id="Submit1" style="Z-INDEX: 106;
46                    LEFT: 342px; POSITION: absolute; TOP: 252px"
47                    type="submit" value="Submit" runat="server"
48                    name="Submit1"></P>
49
50              <DIV id="DIV2" style="DISPLAY: inline; Z-INDEX: 108;
51                 LEFT: 487px; WIDTH: 70px; COLOR: red;
52                 POSITION: absolute; TOP: 219px; HEIGHT: 15px"
53                 ms_positioning="FlowLayout">{{ Validate }}</DIV>
54           </FORM>
55        </BODY>
56     </html>
```

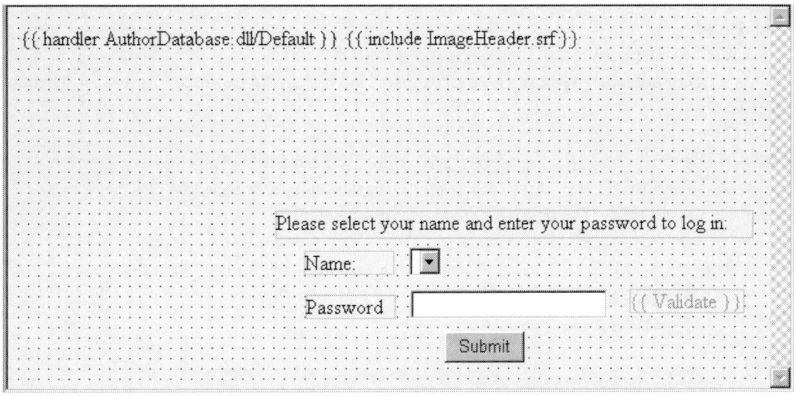

Fig. 23.26 Login SRF for database Web application. (Part 2 of 2.)

Much of the information provided by this Web page is accessed through databases stored in our project. **Login.srf** retrieves valid usernames for this site through **Login.mdb**, whereas all author information is retrieved from the **Books.mdb** database (also used in Chapter 16, Database, SQL and ADO .NET). The reader can view these databases by downloading the examples for this book from **www.deitel.com** and opening the **Database** directory for this chapter. After compiling this project, be sure to copy both databases into the **inetpub\wwwroot\authordatabase** directory for the application to accurately locate the databases.

Line 12 imports another SRF to the file; The **include** tag copies the contents of the referenced page to replace the **include** tag. For example, a programmer might want to include a *navigation bar* on every page of a site. If the site consists of a large number of pages, adding markup to create the navigation bar for each page could be time consuming. Moreover, if the programmer subsequently modifies the navigation bar, every page on the site that uses the navigation bar must be updated. By importing the page, the programmer can specify with only a few lines of markup where on each page the navigation bar is placed. If the navigation bar changes, the pages that use it are updated when those pages are requested in the future. The SRF for our simple **ImageHeader** SRF is show in Fig. 23.27.

The form (Fig. 23.26) includes several **label**s, an input **TextBox** (**passwordBox**) and an input **Select** element (**nameList**), which is populated by the tag-replacement method **Names** with usernames retrieved from a database. The validate replacement tag (line 53) will redirect the user to the next page if a password is entered and correct, and displays an error message if an invalid password is entered.

Visual Studio .NET provides a wizard to generate a class to easily add database connectivity to an application. In the **Solution Explorer**, right-click on the project name and select **Add > Add Class**. In the **Add Class** dialog box, select **ATL OLEDB Consumer** from the right pane and click **Open** as shown in Fig. 23.28.

```
1    <!-- Fig. 23.27: ImageHeader.srf                    -->
2    <!-- Image header for each application page.         -->
3
4    {{ handler AuthorDatabase.dll/Default }}
5    <IMG alt="" src="bug2bug.png">
```

Fig. 23.27 Image header for database Web application.

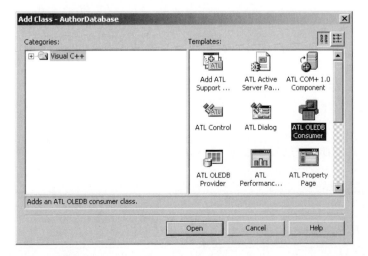

Fig. 23.28 Add Class dialog box.

The **ATL OLEDB Consumer Wizard** dialog box (Fig. 23.29) allows you to select a database and configure the capabilities of the generated class. Click the **Data Source...** button to open a new dialog box that allows you to select a database. In the new dialog box under the **Provider** tab, click **Microsoft Jet 4.0 OLE DB Provider**, then **Next**. Under the **Connection** tab, click the ellipsis button (**...**) to locate and add the `login.mdb` database. Click **OK** at the bottom of the **Data Link Properties** dialog box to finalize your selection. A dialog will pop up prompting you to select a database object—choose **Users** under **Tables** and click **OK**. In the main wizard dialog, ensure that the **Attributed** check box and **Command** radio button are selected and all other options are not. When you click **Finish**, the wizard will generate a class named **CUsers** that can connect to the database and contains a default query, which will return all values in the **Users** table of the `login.mdb` database.

The generated database consumer class contains methods to open and close the database or default query, as well as methods and properties to navigate and view the results returned by the query. The class contains a member variable for each database column of the type defined in the database schema. The member variables are named **m_***columnName*.

Figure 23.30 presents the replacement handler class for the login SRF. We include the header for the OLE DB Consumer Wizard generated class **CUsers** on line 6.

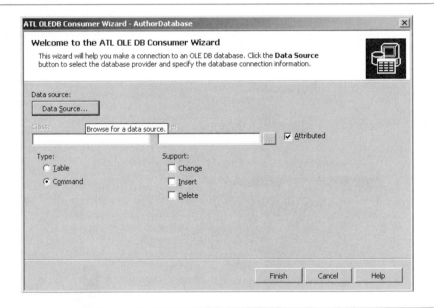

Fig. 23.29 **ATL OLEDB Consumer Wizard** dialog box.

```
1   // Fig. 23.30: Login.h
2   // Login name and validation code using a database.
3
```

Fig. 23.30 Login request-handler class populates a Select input from database.
   (Part 1 of 4.)

```
4    #pragma once
5
6    #include "Users.h"
7
8    #define LOGIN_COOKIE "allowaccess"
9
10   [ request_handler( "Default" ) ]
11   class CAuthorDatabaseHandler
12   {
13   private:
14      CUsers users;
15   public:
16
17      // method called for each page load
18      HTTP_CODE ValidateAndExchange()
19      {
20         m_HttpResponse.SetContentType( "text/html" );
21
22         return HTTP_SUCCESS;
23      } // end method ValidateAndExchange
24
25   protected:
26
27      // Names tag replacement handler-displays all usernames
28      [ tag_name( name="Names" ) ]
29      HTTP_CODE OnNames( void )
30      {
31
32         // open database and default query
33         users.OpenAll();
34
35         // move to first returned row
36         HRESULT result = users.MoveFirst();
37
38         // loop until error, or end of rowset
39         while ( SUCCEEDED( result ) && result != DB_S_ENDOFROWSET )
40         {
41
42            // print out each loginID
43            m_HttpResponse << "<OPTION value=\""
44               << users.m_loginID << "\">" << users.m_loginID
45               << "</OPTION>";
46
47            // move to the next row
48            result = users.MoveNext();
49         } // end while
50
51         // close database and default query
52         users.CloseAll();
53
54         return HTTP_SUCCESS;
55      } // end method OnNames
56
```

Fig. 23.30 Login request-handler class populates a Select input from database. (Part 2 of 4.)

```
57      // Validate tag replacement handler, validates password
58      [ tag_name( name="Validate" ) ]
59      HTTP_CODE OnValidate( void )
60      {
61
62          // only check if HTTP POST method
63          if ( m_HttpRequest.GetMethod() ==
64              CHttpRequest::HTTP_METHOD::HTTP_METHOD_POST ) {
65
66              // get entered password
67              LPCSTR password =
68                  m_HttpRequest.GetFormVars().Lookup( "passwordBox" );
69
70              // get entered username
71              LPCSTR userName =
72                  m_HttpRequest.GetFormVars().Lookup( "nameList" );
73
74              // open database and default query
75              users.OpenAll();
76
77              // move to first row of results
78              HRESULT result = users.MoveFirst();
79
80                  while ( SUCCEEDED( result ) && result != DB_S_ENDOFROWSET )
81              {
82
83                  // compare username and password
84                  if ( strcmp( users.m_password, password ) == 0 &&
85                      strcmp( users.m_loginID, userName ) == 0 ) {
86
87                      // Write authorization cookie to client
88                      m_HttpResponse.AppendCookie("AccessLevel",
89                          LOGIN_COOKIE );
90
91                      // redirect client to book display page
92                      m_HttpResponse.Redirect( "DisplayBooks.srf" );
93                      users.CloseAll();
94
95                      return HTTP_SUCCESS;
96                  } // end if
97
98                  // move to next row
99                  result = users.MoveNext();
100             } // end while
101
102             m_HttpResponse << "Invalid Password";
103         } // end if
104
105         users.CloseAll();
106
107         return HTTP_SUCCESS;
108     } // end method OnValidate
109 }; // end class CAuthorDatabaseHandler
```

Fig. 23.30 Login request-handler class populates a Select input from database.
(Part 3 of 4.)

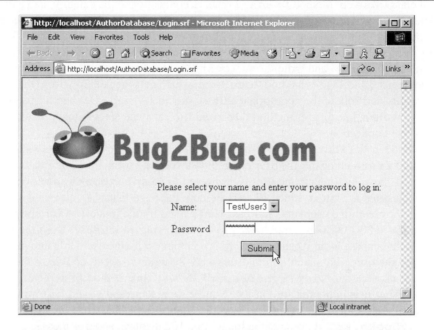

Fig. 23.30 Login request-handler class populates a Select input from database. (Part 4 of 4.)

Line 14 declares an object of the gencrated database consumer class **CUsers**. Replacement method **OnNames** on lines 28–53 populates the drop-down list from the SRF page with the username values in the database. Line 33 uses the generated method **Open-**

All of class **CUsers**. Method *OpenAll* opens a connection to the database and executes the default query. (Recall that the default query returns all rows from the table selected in the OLE DB consumer wizard.) Line 36 calls method *MoveFirst*, which stores the first row of results from the default query in the **CUser** member variables. Lines 39–49 loop through each query row and write the **m_loginID** value for each row as an option in the drop-down list. Line 48 uses method **MoveNext**, which gets the next row from the default query results and fills in the appropriate **CUser** member variables. When all usernames have been written, line 52 uses method *CloseAll* to close the default query result set and the database connection.

Method **OnValidate** (lines 59–108) is the replacement method for the **Validate** tag; **OnValidate** compares the user-entered password and username to the values in the database. If the values match, the user is redirected to **DisplayBooks.srf**, otherwise an error message is written. Lines 67–102 execute the page that was requested via *post*. Lines 67–72 obtain the username and password passed by the request. After opening the database, lines 80–100 loop through each row of the returned result set from the default query. Each database login ID and password is compared with the username and password entered by the user. If a match is found, lines 88–89 write a special cookie to the client, which allows access to **DisplayBooks.srf**. [*Note*: This method of authentication is not secure, but it is presented for clarity. A more secure method would be to transmit a random unique cookie to the client over a secure connection.] Line 92 redirects the user to **DisplayBooks.srf**. If no match is found, line 102 displays an error message.

After users have been authenticated, they will be redirected to **DisplayBooks.srf** (Fig. 23.31). This page provides a list of authors from which the user can choose one. After a choice has been made, a table of that author's books is displayed.

```
1   <!-- Fig. 23.31: DisplayBooks.srf                          -->
2   <!-- Allows user to choose an author and displays books    -->
3   <!-- published by the selected author.                      -->
4
5   <html>
6      <head>
7         <meta name="vs_targetSchema"
8            content="http://schemas.microsoft.com/intellisense/ie5">
9      </head>
10
11     <BODY bgColor="#ffebff">
12        <P>
13           {{ handler AuthorDatabase.dll/Display }}
14           <IMG alt="" src="bug2bug.png">
15        </P>
16
17        <P>{{ if NotPost }}
18        </P>
19        <P></P>
20
21        <FORM runat="server" id="Form1" method="post">
22           <DIV style="DISPLAY: inline; WIDTH: 109px;
23              HEIGHT: 23px" ms_positioning="FlowLayout">
24              Select an Author:</DIV>
```

Fig. 23.31 Displays a list of authors and their books. (Part 1 of 2.)

```
25
26              <SELECT id="nameList" name="nameList"
27                 runat="server">
28                 {{ ListAuthors }}
29              </SELECT>
30
31              <P></P>
32              <P>  <INPUT id="Submit1" type="submit"
33                 value="Submit" name="Submit1"></P>
34
35          </FORM>
36          <P>{{ else }}</P>
37
38          <DIV style="DISPLAY: inline; WIDTH: 159px; HEIGHT: 22px"
39             ms_positioning="FlowLayout">You Chose {{ Selected }}
40          </DIV>
41
42          <P>{{ DisplayBooks }}</P>
43          <P>{{ endif }}</P>
44      </BODY>
45  </html>
```

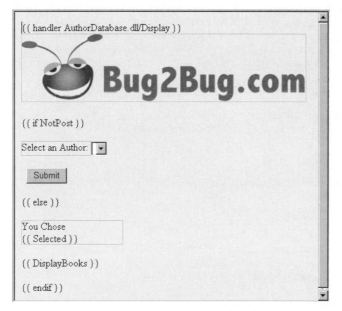

Fig. 23.31 Displays a list of authors and their books. (Part 2 of 2.)

The SRF (Fig. 23.31) for this page creates a number of controls: a drop-down box, two labels, a **Submit** button and three replacement tags. Users select an author from the drop-down box and click **Submit**, causing a *post* request to occur. When the **NotPost** tag returns false, the user is shown their selected author and the author's books are displayed. Figure 23.32 presents the request-handler class for this SRF. Use the **OLE DB Consumer Class wizard** to create class **CTitleAuthor** which connects to the **books.mdb** and the **TitleAuthor** view.

```
1    // Fig. 23.32: DisplayBooks.h
2    // Allows the user to choose and author and displays all
3    // published books.
4
5    #pragma once
6
7    #include "TitleAuthor.h"
8
9    // Display request handler
10   [ request_handler( "Display" ) ]
11   class CDisplayBooks
12   {
13   private:
14      CTitleAuthor authors;
15
16   public:
17
18      // method invoked on each page load
19      HTTP_CODE ValidateAndExchange()
20      {
21         CStringA value;
22         m_HttpResponse.SetContentType( "text/html" );
23         m_HttpRequest.Cookies( "AccessLevel" ).GetValue( value );
24
25         if ( strcmp( value, LOGIN_COOKIE ) == 0 )
26            return HTTP_SUCCESS;
27         else
28            m_HttpResponse.Redirect("Login.srf");
29
30         return HTTP_SUCCESS;
31      } // end method ValidateAndExchange
32
33   protected:
34
35      // NotPost tag replacement handler, determines HTTP Post
36      // request
37      [ tag_name( name="NotPost" ) ]
38      HTTP_CODE OnNotPost( void )
39      {
40         if ( m_HttpRequest.GetMethod() ==
41            CHttpRequest::HTTP_METHOD::HTTP_METHOD_POST )
42            return HTTP_S_FALSE;
43
44         return HTTP_SUCCESS;
45      } // end method OnNotPost
46
47      // ListAuthors tag replacement handler, lists all authors
48      // stored in database
49      [ tag_name( name="ListAuthors" ) ]
50      HTTP_CODE OnListAuthors( void )
51      {
52         char firstName[ 51 ], lastName[ 51 ];
53
```

Fig. 23.32 Request-handler class that displays a list of authors and their books.
(Part 1 of 4.)

```
54          // open data source, we will define the query
55          authors.OpenDataSource();
56
57          // db_command attribute allows definition of custom
58          // SQL query
59          [ db_command(
60
61              // db_command defines the SQL command and binding
62              // variables
63              db_command="SELECT firstName( [ bindto ] firstName ), \
64              lastName( [ bindto ] lastName ) FROM Authors",
65
66              // name defines the name of the created class
67              // source_name designates the data connection to use
68              name="authorCommand", source_name="authors" ) ];
69
70          // move to first result of SQL command
71          HRESULT result = authorCommand.MoveFirst();
72
73          // loop through results, display author names
74          while ( SUCCEEDED( result ) && result != DB_S_ENDOFROWSET )
75          {
76              m_HttpResponse << "<OPTION value=\"" << firstName
77                  << " " << lastName << "\">" << firstName << " "
78                  << lastName << "</OPTION>";
79              result = authorCommand.MoveNext();
80          }
81
82          // close data source
83          authors.CloseDataSource();
84
85          return HTTP_SUCCESS;
86      } // end method OnListAuthors
87
88      // Selected tag replacement handler, displays selected
89      // author
90      [ tag_name( name="Selected" ) ]
91      HTTP_CODE OnSelected( void )
92      {
93          m_HttpResponse
94              << m_HttpRequest.GetFormVars().Lookup( "nameList" );
95
96          return HTTP_SUCCESS;
97      } // end method OnSelected
98
99      // DisplayBooks tag replacement handler, displays
100     // published books of selected author
101     [ tag_name( name = "DisplayBooks" ) ]
102     HTTP_CODE OnDisplayBooks( void )
103     {
104         char firstName[ 51 ], lastName[ 51 ], title[ 51 ],
105             ISBN[ 51 ], publisher[51];
```

Fig. 23.32 Request-handler class that displays a list of authors and their books.
(Part 2 of 4.)

```
106
107        // read selected author into char arrays
108        sscanf( m_HttpRequest.GetFormVars().Lookup( "nameList" ),
109           "%s%s", firstName, lastName );
110
111        // open data source
112        authors.OpenDataSource();
113
114        [ db_command(
115
116           // bindings specifies binding parameters before
117           // defining SQL command
118           bindings="( [ bindto ] title, ISBN, publisher); \
119           ( [ in ] firstName, lastName)", name="authorCommand",
120           source_name="authors")
121           {
122              SELECT Title, ISBN, PublisherName
123              FROM TitleAuthor
124              WHERE firstName = ? AND lastName = ?
125           } ];
126
127        // move to first returned result
128        HRESULT result = authorCommand.MoveFirst();
129
130        // HTML to begin table
131        m_HttpResponse << "<table cellspacing=1 cellpadding=1\
132                          width=800 border=1>";
133
134        // display all table headings in bold
135        m_HttpResponse << "<TR style=\"FONT-WEIGHT: bold\">\
136                          <TD>Name</TD><TD>Title</TD><TD>\
137                          ISBN</TD><TD>Publisher</TD></TR>";
138
139        // loop through rows displaying results in table form
140        while ( SUCCEEDED( result ) && result != DB_S_ENDOFROWSET )
141        {
142           m_HttpResponse << "<TR><TD>" << firstName
143              << " " << lastName << "</TD><TD>"
144              << title << "</TD><TD>" << ISBN
145              << "</TD><TD>" << publisher << "</TD></TR>";
146
147           result = authorCommand.MoveNext();
148        }
149
150        // close HTML table
151        m_HttpResponse << "</TABLE>";
152
153        authors.CloseDataSource();
154
155        return HTTP_SUCCESS;
156     } // end method OnDisplayBooks
157  }; // end class CDisplayBooks
```

Fig. 23.32 Request-handler class that displays a list of authors and their books. (Part 3 of 4.)

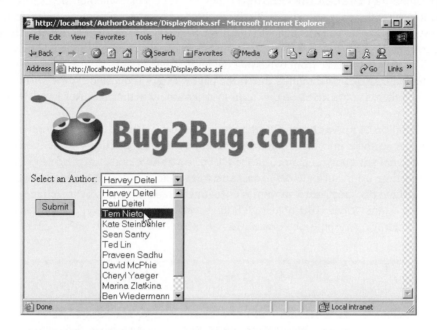

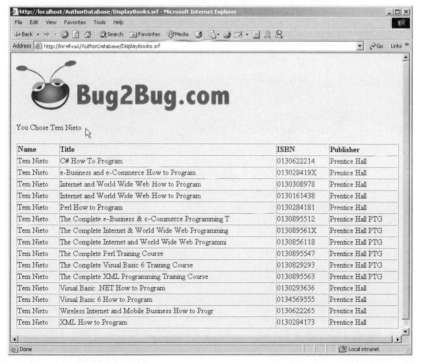

Fig. 23.32 Request-handler class that displays a list of authors and their books.
(Part 4 of 4.)

Method **ValidateAndExchange** (lines 19–31) checks whether the user is authorized to access the page. Lines 23–28 obtain the **AccessLevel** cookie value from the request; if the cookie value is equal to the **LOGIN_COOKIE** macro, **ValidateAndExchange** returns successful. If the values do not match, the user is redirected to the login page. This prevents a user from bypassing the login page.

Method **OnNotPost** returns true if the page was not requested by the *post* method, and false otherwise. **OnNotPost** is used to determine whether the user has selected an author.

Method **OnListAuthors** fills the drop-down box with the authors as options. Line 55 calls the attribute injected method *OpenDataSource*, which opens the data source, but not the default query contained in the **CTitleAuthor** object **authors**. Lines 59–68 demonstrate using attribute **db_command** to execute a custom query on an open database. Attribute **db_command** simplifies executing database queries by injecting code that creates a custom **CCommand** object with the specified, name, query, open database and variable bindings. Attribute **db_command** parameters are described in Fig. 23.33.

Parameter	Example	Comment
db_command	db_command="SELECT last-Name, firstName FROM Customers WHERE ID = ?"	Specifies the SQL query to execute on the database defined by parameter source_name.
name	name="results"	Specifies the name of the instance of the **CCommand** object created by the command.
source_name	source_name="dataSource"	Specifies the name of an object instance with an open database connection.
hresult	hresult="hresultVariable"	Specifies the name of an **HRESULT** variable to determine any errors that may have occurred.
bindings	bindings="([bindto] firstNameVar, lastNameVar); ([in] customerID)"	Defines the names of the variables used to store the result returned by the query. The specified variables receive the results returned by the query in the { *command* } parameter.
bulk_fetch	bulk_fetch=10	Defines the number of results returned at a time, the default is 1.
{ *command* }	{ SELECT lastName, firstName FROM Customers WHERE ID = ? }	Specifies the SQL query to execute on the database defined by parameter source_name. This block follows the closing attribute parenthesis and is usually clearer for longer queries.

Fig. 23.33 db_command attribute parameters.

Line 71 calls method **MoveFirst** on the object created by the **db_command** attribute. The method gets the first result of the query and places the results into the variables specified in the **db_command** parameter. Lines 74–80 loop through all rows returned by the query displaying each author last name/first name as an option in the drop-down box.

Method **OnSelected** (lines 91–97) is called after the user has submitted the author list with a *post* method. **OnSelected** displays the author selected from the drop-down list on the page.

Method **OnDisplayBooks** (lines 100–156) displays all books in the database written by the author selected from the drop-down box. Lines 107–108 read the selected author name into variables **firstName** and **lastName**. Lines 111–123 open the database and define a custom query that will return the book title, ISBN and publisher name of all rows with the given first and last name. Lines 131–137 write the open tag and heading row for the table. Lines 140–148 loop through the results returned by the query and display them in a table row. Lines 151 and 153 close the table tag and the database connection.

23.8 ATL Server Web Services

In addition to Web Applications, ATL Server provides a set of template classes and attributes designed to simplify the creation of XML Web Services in unmanaged code. The ATL Server Web-service classes are unique because they provide the only popular unmanaged Web-service implementation, and they deliver XML web services with the efficiency of native code. In Chapter 17, Web Services, we discussed Web-service architecture and implemented several Web Services using ASP .NET and managed C++. In this section, we introduce the ATL Server Web-service implementation and create an unmanaged huge integer Web-service client and server. This section assumes you understand the fundamentals of Web services; for more information on Web Services, HTTP, SOAP and XML, refer to Chapter 17.

23.8.1 Introduction to ATL Server Web-Services Architecture

The ATL Server Web Services architecture consists primarily of the same components as an ATL Server Web Application—IIS, and ISAPI extension DLL and a user-created DLL containing at least one request-handler class. The set components work together in the following sequence of events to receive and respond to a client's Web-service method request. [*Note*: This sequence of events applies only when the client calls a specific Web-service method; other cases, such as a request for the WSDL document, are handled slightly differently.]

    1. A client sends a request to the server that specifies the Web Service DLL and the request-handler class in the URL. The request includes an HTTP header indicating the Web-method name and a SOAP envelope describing the method arguments. The request URL is in the following form:

        http://*serverAddress*/*Path*/*WebService*.**dll?Handler=***handlerName*

2. IIS receives the request for the DLL, then forwards the request and its data to the ISAPI extension DLL registered for the Web Service.

3. The extension DLL parses the request for the **Handler** parameter; it then forwards the request data to the request-handler class identified by the **Handler** parameter value.

4. The request-handler class uses functionality provided by the ATL Server classes to match the request to the exposed Web-service method; it then calls the method and provides the SOAP envelope.

5. The Web-service method extracts the data from the SOAP envelope, executes the logic for the request and returns the result data as a SOAP envelope. The ATL Server classes provide the SOAP marshaling and unmarshaling functionality, using attributes.

While ATL Server provides an extensive set of classes and attributes for both Web Applications and Web Services, however, only a few are necessary to create a basic Web-service request-handler class. In the following section, we demonstrate and describe classes and attributes used to create a basic Web-service server and client, using ATL Server.

23.8.2 Creating an ATL Server Web Service

In Chapter 17, Web Services, we created a **HugeInteger** Web service using ASP .NET and managed C++. In this section, we will demonstrate how to use the wizards to create a basic Web Service, which we will use in the next section to recreate the **HugeInteger** Web service, using ATL Server Web Services.

Visual Studio .NET provides wizards that simplify Web-service creation. The wizards generate the ISAPI extension DLL and build a basic Web service. Use the following steps to create a Web service on your machine:

1. Open Visual Studio .NET and choose **File** > **New** > **Project**. In the **New Project** dialog box (Fig. 23.34), select the **Visual C++ Projects** folder from the left pane and **ATL Server Web Service** from the right pane. Enter **HugeInteger** in the **Name** input box and click **OK**.

2. By default, the project wizard will create an attributed project that includes a Web Service DLL and an ISAPI extension DLL. In addition, the generated project would include deployment support (automatic setup of the Web Service in IIS), extra comments and additional error checking and debugging code. The wizard defaults are shown in Fig. 23.35.

3. Select **Project Settings** on the left of the wizard. Then enable the **Generate combined DLL** checkbox and click **OK** (Fig. 23.36).

The wizard will then create a project containing the files shown in Fig. 23.37. The files of particular interest are **HugeInteger.h**, **HugeInteger.cpp**, **HugeInteger.disco** and **HugeInteger.htm**.

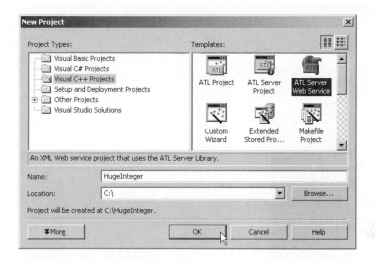

Fig. 23.34 New Project dialog box to create an ATL Server Web Service.

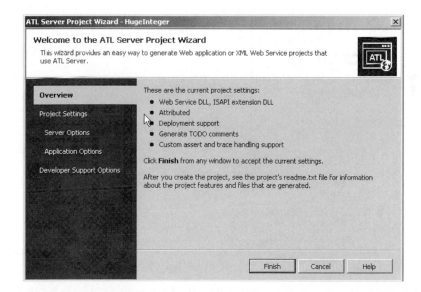

Fig. 23.35 ATL Server Project Wizard dialog that shows ATL Server Web-Service project defaults.

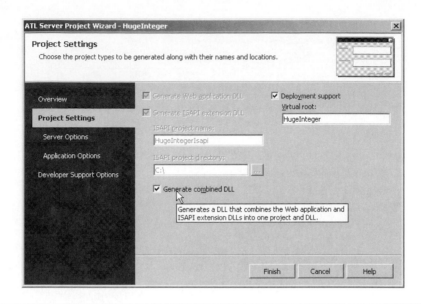

Fig. 23.36 ATL Server Web-service wizard Project Settings page.

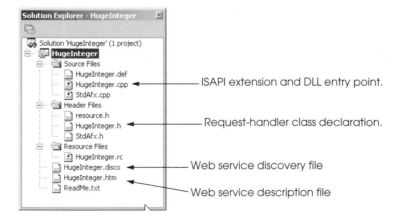

Fig. 23.37 Wizard-generated files for **HugeInteger** ATL Server Web service.

Before we create our own Web service, we will examine the sample code generated by the ATL Server Web Service wizard in the **HugeInteger.h** file. Figure 23.38 shows the sample request-handler class.

```
// HugeIntegerService - web service implementation
//
[
    request_handler(name="Default", sdl="GenHugeIntegerWSDL"),
    soap_handler(
        name="HugeIntegerService",
        namespace="urn:HugeIntegerService",
        protocol="soap"
    )
]
class CHugeIntegerService :
    public IHugeIntegerService
{
public:
    // This is a sample web service method that shows how to use the
    // soap_method attribute to expose a method as a web method
    [ soap_method ]
    HRESULT HelloWorld(/*[in]*/ BSTR bstrInput, /*[out, retval]*/ BSTR *bstrOutput)
    {
        CComBSTR bstrOut(L"Hello ");
        bstrOut += bstrInput;
        bstrOut += L"!";
        *bstrOutput = bstrOut.Detach();

        return S_OK;
    }
    // TODO: Add additional web service methods here
}; // class CHugeIntegerService
```

Fig. 23.38 Generated Web-service request-handler class.

The class is marked by both attributes ***request_handler*** and ***soap_handler***. As in a Web application, attribute **request_handler** exposes the class to the ISAPI extension as a class capable of handling Web requests. However, attribute **soap_handler** enables WSDL generation, and the functionality to parse SOAP envelopes and call the Web-service method.

Attribute **request_handler** takes parameter **name**, which is used by the ISAPI extension to resolve a client's request to the correct handler. The attribute may also take parameter **sdl**, which causes the ATL attribute provider to create a new request-handler class with the designated name; the generated class can be requested by a client to provide a WSDL description for the Web service from the information provided by the **soap_handler** attribute. [*Note*: You must specify attribute **soap_handler** to use the **sdl** parameter of attribute **request_handler**.]

Attribute **soap_handler** takes several parameters, including **name**, **namespace** and **protocol**. Parameter **name** sets the Web-service name as it would appear in the WSDL file. Parameter **namespace** sets the Web-service namespace; it defaults to **urn:***class name*. The **protocol** parameter serves to identify the Web-service protocol; the only protocol currently available is **soap**. In addition to providing WSDL information, attribute **soap_handler** causes the handler class to extend the **CSoapHandler** class.

Common Programming Error 23.1

*Do not confuse the Web service namespace, designated with the **namespace** parameter of the **soap_handler** attribute, with the C++ language construct **namespace**. Setting the Web service namespace does not place the class in a C++ **namespace**.*

Class **CSoapHandler** contains method **HandleRequest**, which is used to call the appropriate Web-service method (a method modified by attribute **soap_method**).

In addition, each method that is to be exposed by the Web service must be marked by attribute **soap_method**. When the compiler encounters attribute **soap_method**, it injects code to extract the arguments from the SOAP request and to marshal the method's return type as a SOAP envelope. In addition, the **soap_method** attribute marks a method for inclusion in the service's WSDL description.

23.8.3 Case Study: HugeIntegerService Web Service

This case study recreates the **HugeInteger** Web service from Chapter 17, Web Services. Use the project generated in the previous section to create this Web Service. We have modified the generated code to fit our coding conventions and have moved the **soap_method** definitions to a separate file, **HugeIntegerImpl.cpp**.

Figure 23.39 presents the **HugeIntergerService** Web Service interface and class declarations as well as class **HugeInteger**, which performs most of the logic for the application. This Web service is designed to perform calculations with integers that contain a maximum of 100 digits. As we mentioned earlier, **long** variables cannot handle integers of this size (i.e., an overflow would occur). The Web service provides a client with methods that take two "huge integers" and determine which one is larger or smaller, whether the two numbers are equal, their sum or their difference.

```
1   // Fig. 23.39: HugeInteger.h
2   // HugeIntergerService interface, implementation and helper
3   // class declarations.
4
5   #pragma once
6
7   // maximum integer length
8   #define MAXIMUM 100
9
10  // exception numbers
11  #define BORROW_ERROR 0
12  #define SUBTRACT_ERROR 1
13
14  // header for ComSafeArray
15  #include <atlsafe.h>
16
17  namespace HugeIntergerService
18  {
19
20      // Web service interface, IHugeIntegerService
21      [
22          uuid("9FAF0017-454E-404F-9585-959E4B2D8750"),
23          object
24      ]
25      __interface IHugeIntegerService
26      {
```

Fig. 23.39 **HugeIntegerService** ATL Server Web-service class declaration. (Part 1 of 4.)

```
27
28          // determines if first and second huge integers are equal
29          [ id( 1 ) ] HRESULT EqualTo( [ in ] BSTR first,
30             [ in ] BSTR second, [ out, retval ] VARIANT_BOOL
31             *output );
32
33          // determines if first huge integer is smaller than second
34          [ id( 2 ) ] HRESULT Smaller( [ in ] BSTR first,
35             [ in ] BSTR second, [ out, retval ] VARIANT_BOOL
36             *output );
37
38          // determines if first huge integer is larger than second
39          [ id( 3 ) ] HRESULT Bigger( [ in ] BSTR first,
40             [ in ] BSTR second, [ out, retval ] VARIANT_BOOL
41             *output );
42
43          // subtract first huge integer from second
44          [ id( 4 ) ] HRESULT Subtract( [ in ] BSTR first,
45             [ in ] BSTR second, [ out, retval ] BSTR *output );
46
47          // add first huge integer to second
48          [ id( 5 ) ] HRESULT Add( [ in ] BSTR first,
49             [ in ] BSTR second, [ out, retval ] BSTR *output );
50       }; // end interface IHugeIntegerService
51
52       // Web service implementation class
53       [
54
55          // request_handler attribute allows class to handle
56          // Web requests
57          request_handler(name="Default", sdl="GenHugeIntegerWSDL"),
58
59          // soap_handler attribute provides methods to handle
60          // and send soap messages
61          soap_handler(
62             name="HugeIntegerService",
63             namespace="urn:HugeIntegerService",
64             protocol="soap"
65          )
66       ]
67       class CHugeIntegerService : public IHugeIntegerService
68       {
69       public:
70
71          // class initialization method
72          HTTP_CODE InitializeHandler(AtlServerRequest *,
73             IServiceProvider * );
74
75          // interface implementation Web methods
76          [ soap_method ]
77          HRESULT EqualTo( BSTR first, BSTR second,
78             VARIANT_BOOL *result );
```

Fig. 23.39 HugeIntegerService ATL Server Web-service class declaration.
(Part 2 of 4.)

```
79
80          [ soap_method ]
81          HRESULT Smaller( BSTR first, BSTR second,
82             VARIANT_BOOL *result );
83
84          [ soap_method ]
85          HRESULT Bigger( BSTR first, BSTR second,
86             VARIANT_BOOL *result );
87
88          [ soap_method ]
89          HRESULT Subtract( BSTR first, BSTR second,
90             BSTR *result );
91
92          [ soap_method ]
93          HRESULT Add( BSTR first, BSTR second,
94             BSTR *result );
95      }; // end class CHugeIntegerService
96
97      // stores huge integer as int array, provides methods
98      // to convert to and from string representation
99      class HugeInteger
100     {
101     public:
102
103         // initializes values
104         HugeInteger();
105
106         // get digit at given index
107         int get_Digit( int );
108
109         // set digit to given value at given index
110         void  set_Digit( int, int  );
111
112         // returns string representation of HugeInteger
113         BSTR ToString();
114
115         // creates HugeInteger based on argument
116         static HugeInteger *FromString( BSTR );
117
118         // get integer length
119         int Length();
120
121         // arithmetic operators
122         HugeInteger operator+( HugeInteger & );
123         HugeInteger operator-( HugeInteger & );
124
125     private:
126
127         // borrows 1 from next digit for use in subtraction
128         static void Borrow( HugeInteger *, int );
129
130         // store number as array
```

Fig. 23.39 `HugeIntegerService` ATL Server Web-service class declaration.
(Part 3 of 4.)

```
131              int number[ MAXIMUM ];
132      }; // end class HugeInteger
133 } // end namespace HugeIntegerService
```

Fig. 23.39 `HugeIntegerService` ATL Server Web-service class declaration. (Part 4 of 4.)

The Web service consists of three components inside the `HugeIntegerService` namespace: interface `IHugeIntegerService` (lines 25–50), class `CHugeIntegerService` (lines 67–95) and class `HugeInteger` (lines 99–132).

Interface `IHugeIntegerService` acts as the default interface for the Web service—all `soap_method`s must be declared in an interface. ATL Server builds Web services using COM-style conventions; thus, a service's methods are available only through a COM interface.

Class `CHugeIntegerService` implements the interface and uses the ATL Server attributes `request_handler`, `soap_handler` and `soap_method`, as described in the previous section.

Class `HugeInteger` provides most of the logic for the `HugeInteger` application. It contains methods to create a `HugeInteger` from a string and to access individual digits, as well as addition and subtraction operators. Figure 23.40 contains the method definitions for classes `HugeInteger` and `CHugeIntegerService`.

```
1  // Fig. 23.40: HugeIntegerImpl.cpp
2  // Provides definitions for HugeInteger class and the
3  // Web service implementation.
4
5  #include "stdafx.h"
6  #include "HugeInteger.h"
7
8  // Web service namespace
9  using namespace HugeIntergerService;
10
11 // constructor clears number array memory
12 HugeInteger::HugeInteger()
13 {
14    ZeroMemory( number, sizeof( number ) );
15 } // end method HugeInteger
16
17 // gets a digit from the specified index of number array
18 int HugeInteger::get_Digit( int index )
19 {
20    return number[ index ];
21 } // end method get_Digit
22
23 // sets a digit at index to the specified value
24 void HugeInteger::set_Digit( int index, int value )
25 {
26    number[ index ] = value;
27 } // end method set_Digit
```

Fig. 23.40 `HugeInteger` and Web-service class method definitions. (Part 1 of 6.)

```
28
29   // returns string representation of HugeInteger
30   BSTR HugeInteger::ToString()
31   {
32      CAtlString returnString = "";
33      char nextNumber[ 2 ];
34      int length = this->Length();
35
36      // loop through number backwards, append each
37      // digit to returnString
38      for ( int i = length; i > 0; i-- )
39         returnString += itoa( number[ i - 1 ], nextNumber, 10 );
40
41      return returnString.AllocSysString();
42   } // end method ToString
43
44   // creates HugeInteger based on value
45   HugeInteger *HugeInteger::FromString( BSTR value )
46   {
47
48      // length of string
49      UINT length = SysStringLen( value );
50
51      // constrict ANSI string from BSTR
52      CW2A ansiString( value );
53
54      HugeInteger *parsedInteger = new HugeInteger();
55
56      char digitString[ 2 ] = { '\0' };
57
58      // construct number array from reverse order of string
59      for ( UINT i = 0; i < length; i++ ) {
60         digitString[ 0 ] = ansiString.m_szBuffer[ i ];
61         parsedInteger->set_Digit( length - i - 1,
62            atoi( digitString ) );
63      }
64
65      return parsedInteger;
66   } // end method FromString
67
68   // addition operator adds two HugeIntegers
69   HugeInteger HugeInteger::operator+( HugeInteger &value )
70   {
71
72      // storage value for addition remainders
73      int carry = 0;
74
75      // store result of addition
76      HugeInteger result;
77
78      // perform addition algorithm for each digit
79      for ( int i = 0; i < MAXIMUM; i++ ) {
80
```

Fig. 23.40 HugeInteger and Web-service class method definitions. (Part 2 of 6.)

```
81              // add two digits in same column
82              // result is their sum, plus carry from
83              // previous operation modulus 10
84              result.set_Digit( i,
85                  ( this->get_Digit( i ) + value.get_Digit( i )
86                  + carry ) % 10 );
87
88              // store remainder of dividing
89              // sums of two digits by 10
90              carry = ( this->get_Digit( i ) + value.get_Digit( i )
91                  + carry ) / 10;
92          } // end for
93
94          return result;
95      } // end operator+
96
97      // subtraction operator
98      HugeInteger HugeInteger::operator-( HugeInteger &value )
99      {
100         HugeInteger result;
101
102         // determine longest HugeInteger
103         int longest = this->Length() > value.Length()
104             ? this->Length() : value.Length();
105
106         // subtract this HugeInteger from value
107         for ( int i = 0; i < longest; i++ ) {
108
109             // if this digit is smaller than value
110             // digit we need to borrow. If borrow throws an
111             // exception, catch it and throw SUBTRACT_ERROR
112             try {
113                 if ( this->get_Digit( i ) < value.get_Digit( i ) )
114                     HugeInteger::Borrow( this, i );
115             }
116             catch ( int ) {
117                 throw SUBTRACT_ERROR;
118             }
119
120             // subtract this from value
121             result.set_Digit( i, this->get_Digit( i ) -
122                 value.get_Digit( i ) );
123         } // end for
124
125         return result;
126     } // end operator-
127
128     // borrows 1 from next digit place
129     void HugeInteger::Borrow( HugeInteger *integer, int place )
130     {
131
132         // if no place to borrow from, signal problem
133         if ( place >= integer->Length() )
```

Fig. 23.40 HugeInteger and Web-service class method definitions. (Part 3 of 6.)

```
134           throw BORROW_ERROR;
135
136      // otherwise if next digit is zero,
137      // borrow from next digit
138      else if ( integer->get_Digit( place + 1 ) == 0 )
139         Borrow( integer, place + 1 );
140
141      // add ten to current place because we borrowed
142      // and subtract one from previous digit -
143      // this is digit borrowed from
144      integer->set_Digit( place, integer->get_Digit( place ) + 10 );
145      place++;
146      integer->set_Digit( place, integer->get_Digit( place ) - 1 );
147   } // end method Borrow
148
149   // determines number length
150   int HugeInteger::Length()
151   {
152      int current = 0;
153      int count = MAXIMUM;
154
155      // loop from end of array until first non-zero value
156      for ( int i = MAXIMUM - 1; current == 0; i-- ) {
157         count--;
158         current = number[ count ];
159      }
160
161      // return last index, + 1 to account for 0 based array
162      return count + 1;
163   } // end method Length
164
165   // method to initialize SOAP services
166   HTTP_CODE CHugeIntegerService::InitializeHandler(
167      AtlServerRequest *pRequestInfo, IServiceProvider *pProvider)
168   {
169      if ( HTTP_SUCCESS !=
170         CSoapHandler<CHugeIntegerService>::InitializeHandler(
171         pRequestInfo, pProvider ) )
172         return HTTP_FAIL;
173
174      return HTTP_SUCCESS;
175   } // end method InitializeHandler
176
177   // construct and add HugeIntegers
178   HRESULT CHugeIntegerService::Add( BSTR first, BSTR second,
179      BSTR *result )
180   {
181
182      // construct operands from passed strings
183      HugeInteger *operand1 = HugeInteger::FromString( first );
184      HugeInteger *operand2 = HugeInteger::FromString( second );
185      HugeInteger resultValue;
186
```

Fig. 23.40 HugeInteger and Web-service class method definitions. (Part 4 of 6.)

```
187        // add and return HugeInteger as string
188        resultValue = *operand1 + *operand2;
189        *result = resultValue.ToString();
190
191        delete operand1;
192        delete operand2;
193
194        return S_OK;
195    } // end method Add
196
197    // subtract constructs HugeIntegers from strings and
198    // uses HugeInteger's subtract operator
199    HRESULT CHugeIntegerService::Subtract( BSTR first, BSTR second,
200        BSTR *result )
201    {
202
203        // construct operands from passed strings
204        HugeInteger *operand1 = HugeInteger::FromString( first );
205        HugeInteger *operand2 = HugeInteger::FromString( second );
206        HugeInteger resultValue;
207
208        // attempt to subtract first from second
209        try {
210            resultValue = *operand1 - *operand2;
211            *result = resultValue.ToString();
212
213            // delete allocated memory
214            delete operand1;
215            delete operand2;
216        }
217
218        // if subtraction fails, return error
219        catch ( int ) {
220
221            // delete allocated memory
222            delete operand1;
223            delete operand2;
224            return E_FAIL;
225        }
226
227        return S_OK;
228    } // end method Subtract
229
230    // determines if first is larger than second
231    HRESULT CHugeIntegerService::Bigger( BSTR first, BSTR second,
232        VARIANT_BOOL *output )
233    {
234        CComBSTR result;
235
236        // if subtract does not throw exception, either values
237        // are equal or first is bigger
238        if ( SUCCEEDED( Subtract( first, second, &result ) ) ) {
239
```

Fig. 23.40 HugeInteger and Web-service class method definitions. (Part 5 of 6.)

```
240          // if values are equal, return false, otherwise
241          // return true
242          if ( result == "" )
243             *output = VARIANT_FALSE;
244          else
245             *output = VARIANT_TRUE;
246       }
247
248       // if subtract returns an error, first value is smaller
249       else
250          *output = VARIANT_FALSE;
251
252       return HTTP_SUCCESS;
253    } // end method Bigger
254
255    // determines if first is smaller than second
256    HRESULT CHugeIntegerService::Smaller( BSTR first, BSTR second,
257       VARIANT_BOOL *output )
258    {
259       VARIANT_BOOL result;
260
261       // first is smaller than second when second is bigger
262       // than first
263       Bigger( second, first, &result );
264       *output = result;
265
266       return HTTP_SUCCESS;
267    } // end method Smaller
268
269    // determines HugeInteger equality
270    HRESULT CHugeIntegerService::EqualTo( BSTR first, BSTR second,
271       VARIANT_BOOL *output )
272    {
273       VARIANT_BOOL result1, result2;
274
275       Bigger( first, second, &result1 );
276       Smaller( first, second, &result2 );
277
278       // if either first is bigger than second, or first is
279       // smaller than second, they are not equal
280       if ( result1 || result2 )
281          *output = VARIANT_FALSE;
282       else
283          *output = VARIANT_TRUE;
284
285       return HTTP_SUCCESS;
286    } // end method EqualTo
```

Fig. 23.40 `HugeInteger` and Web-service class method definitions. (Part 6 of 6.)

Class **HugeInteger** method definitions (lines 12–163) define the core set of logic for the Web service. Lines 18–27 define get and set methods that allow access to any given digit in the **HugeInteger**. Method **ToString** (lines 30–42) builds a **BSTR** from the **HugeInteger** by building a string from each digit of array **number**, in reverse order.

The method uses **CAtlString** to build the string for performance reasons, then uses method **SysAllocString** to return a **BSTR**. Method **FromString** (lines 45–66) converts a **BSTR** into a **HugeInteger** by converting each character of the string into an **int** and storing the values in array number, in reverse order. The addition operator (lines 69–95) adds two **HugeInteger**s; the method adds each digit from the **HugeInteger**s, then returns a **HugeInteger** containing the new value. The subtraction operator (lines 98–126) performs digit-by-digit subtraction on two **HugeIntegers**. Method **Borrow** (lines 129–147) handles the case in subtraction when the digit in the first operand is smaller than the corresponding digit in the second operand. For instance, when we subtract 19 from 32, we usually go digit by digit, startiWng from the right. The number 2 is smaller than 9, so we add 10 to 2 (resulting in 12), which subtracts 9, resulting in 3 for the rightmost digit in the solution. We then subtract 1 from the next digit over (3), making it 2. The corresponding digit in the right operand is now the "1" in 19. The subtraction of 1 from 2 is 1, making the corresponding digit in the result 1. The final result, when both resulting digits are combined, is 13. Method **Borrow** adds 10 to the appropriate digit and subtracts 1 from the digit to its left. If the left digit is zero, the method will continue to move left until it finds a non-zero digit. If there are no remaining digits, the first operand is smaller than the second and method **Borrow** will throw an exception.

Class **CHugeIntegerService** method definitions (lines 166–286) use class **HugeInteger** to provide a set of publicly accessible SOAP methods. Method **InitializeHandler** (lines 166–175) calls **CSoapHandler** method *InitializeHandler* implementation to set up the ATL Server SOAP services; in addition, the method provides error handling to ensure the services are initialized correctly. Method **Add** (lines 178–195) uses **HugeInteger** method **FromString** to construct a **HugeInteger** instance from the **BSTR** arguments (lines 183–184); lines 188–189 add the **HugeInteger**s, using the addition operator, and return the result as a **BSTR** value. Method **Subtract** (lines 199–228) constructs **HugeIntegers** from the **BSTR** arguments, then uses the subtraction operator and **ToString** method to return the result as a **BSTR**. In addition, if the subtraction operator fails, the first number is smaller than the second, and method **Subtract** returns **E_FAIL**. Method **Bigger** (lines 231–253) uses method **Subtract** to determine if the first number is larger than the second. If **Subtract** fails or returns an empty string, the first is not larger than the second; otherwise, the first number is larger. Method **Smaller** (lines 256–267) simply uses method **Bigger** to determine if the second number is larger than the first; if the second number is larger, the first number is smaller. Method **EqualTo** (lines 270–286) uses methods **Bigger** and **Smaller** to determine equality. If the first number is neither larger or smaller than the second, the numbers are equal.

After building the example, simply ensure that IIS is running, and compile the solution. Visual Studio .NET provides deployment support and will build a virtual directory and enable access to the Web service.

23.8.4 Case Study: Unmanaged Web-Service Client

In this section, we build an unmanaged Web-service client for the **HugeIntegerService**. An unmanaged Web-service client uses Visual Studio .NET tools and ATL Server classes to access a Web service with the same level of simplicity afforded to managed .NET Web-service clients. Recall, from Chapter 17, that Web services are built on Internet stan-

```
67              // if error, display error message
68              if ( SUCCEEDED( hugeInteger.Subtract( input1BSTR,
69                 input2BSTR, &stringResult ) ) )
70
71                 result = CW2A( stringResult );
72              else
73                 result = "Error: Unable to subtract.\n";
74              break;
75
76          // determine if first integer is larger than second
77          // set result string to true or false
78          case 3:
79              hugeInteger.Bigger( input1BSTR, input2BSTR,
80                 &boolResult );
81              result = boolResult == 0 ? "False" : "True";
82              break;
83
84          // determine if first integer is smaller than second
85          // set result string to true or false
86          case 4:
87              hugeInteger.Smaller( input1BSTR, input2BSTR,
88                 &boolResult );
89              result = boolResult == 0 ? "False" : "True";
90              break;
91
92          // determine if entered integers are equal
93          case 5:
94              hugeInteger.EqualTo( input1BSTR, input2BSTR,
95                 &boolResult );
96              result = boolResult == 0 ? "False" : "True";
97              break;
98
99          // return if user chooses Quit
100         case 6:
101             return;
102             break;
103
104         // display error for all other inputs
105         default:
106             result = "Invalid operation, try again.";
107             break;
108      } // end switch
109
110      cout << result << endl << endl;
111    } // end while
112 } // end function AccessService
113
114 // entry point for application
115 int main()
116 {
117
118    // initialize COM
```

Fig. 23.41 UsingHugeIntegerService unmanaged Web-client application.
(Part 3 of 5.)

```
119        CoInitialize( NULL );
120
121        // use Web service
122        AccessService();
123
124        // release COM
125        CoUninitialize();
126
127        return 0;
128 } // end function main
```

```
Please input the first huge integer.
874235092340585858884399820
Please input the second huge integer. (Must be smaller than first)
23904449234444442233322
Choose one of the following:
1. Add the integers.
2. Subtract the integers.
3. Determine if the first integer is larger than the second.
4. Determine if the first integer is smaller than the second.
5. Determine if the first integer is equal to the second.
6. Quit.
1
874237482785509303026633142

Please input the first huge integer.
12893749844848889827398919992828347
Please input the second huge integer. (Must be smaller than first)
11233
Choose one of the following:
1. Add the integers.
2. Subtract the integers.
3. Determine if the first integer is larger than the second.
4. Determine if the first integer is smaller than the second.
5. Determine if the first integer is equal to the second.
6. Quit.
2
12893749844848889827398919992817114

Please input the first huge integer.
412333333333333321412
Please input the second huge integer. (Must be smaller than first)
123498720987098098882
Choose one of the following:
1. Add the integers.
2. Subtract the integers.
3. Determine if the first integer is larger than the second.
4. Determine if the first integer is smaller than the second.
5. Determine if the first integer is equal to the second.
6. Quit.
3
```

Fig. 23.41 `UsingHugeIntegerService` unmanaged Web-client application.
(Part 4 of 5.)

```
False

Please input the first huge integer.
342223482798728717777772364718
Please input the second huge integer. (Must be smaller than first)
123648777238648128384882737461B
Choose one of the following:
1. Add the integers.
2. Subtract the integers.
3. Determine if the first integer is larger than the second.
4. Determine if the first integer is smaller than the second.
5. Determine if the first integer is equal to the second.
6. Quit.
4
True

Please input the first huge integer.
3338928763459872992983B7465
Please input the second huge integer. (Must be smaller than first)
3338928763459872992983B7465
Choose one of the following:
1. Add the integers.
2. Subtract the integers.
3. Determine if the first integer is larger than the second.
4. Determine if the first integer is smaller than the second.
5. Determine if the first integer is equal to the second.
6. Quit.
5
True

Please input the first huge integer.
0
Please input the second huge integer. (Must be smaller than first)
0
Choose one of the following:
1. Add the  integers.
2. Subtract the integers.
3. Determine if the first integer is larger than the second.
4. Determine if the first integer is smaller than the second.
5. Determine if the first integer is equal to the second.
6. Quit.
6
```

Fig. 23.41 `UsingHugeIntegerService` unmanaged Web-client application.
(Part 5 of 5.)

Function **AccessService** (lines 13–112) contains the core application logic. Line 17 constructs the Web-service proxy object. By default, the proxy object exists in the namespace specified by the Web-service WSDL document and has the same name as the true Web service. Lines 24–29 prompt for a huge integer and store the input in a character array. Lines 32–42 display the available operations and store the user's choice. Lines 52–

108 call the appropriate method on the Web-service proxy object for the user's choice and stores the result in a string. Line 110 displays the result of the chosen operation.

Function **main** (lines 115–128) initializes COM; the Web service proxy class uses COM objects and requires that COM be initialized before it is created. In addition, the proxy class must be destroyed before uninitializing COM; to simplify this management, we created the proxy instance as a stack variable in method **AccessService**, forcing object destruction when the function returns.

In this chapter, we discussed ATL Server and its role in both Web applications and Web services. You now should be able to create dynamic SRFs that respond to user input, track and maintain a user's session information, and interact with a back-end database from a request-handler class. In addition, we discussed and presented unmanaged Web applications and clients that use ATL Server. In the next chapter, we introduce managed and unmanaged code interoperability services, which allow seamless integration of managed with unmanaged code.

23.9 Summary

ATL Server is a set of classes designed to simplify Web development while providing the power of unmanaged C++. The ATL Server architecture consists of three main components: Server Response Files (SRFs), Web Application DLLs and an ISAPI Extension DLL. A Server Response File (SRF) is a text file that usually contains static HTML and replacement tags. A replacement tag is not displayed to the client, but must be handled by either the ISAPI extension DLL or a Web Application DLL. The main purpose of the ISAPI Extension DLL is to delegate Web requests for **.srf** files to the appropriate Web Application DLL. A Web application DLL contains the application logic for parsing the **.srf** file. The Web application consists of one or more request-handler classes consisting of replacement methods.

In an SRF, replacement tags are enclosed within double curly braces ({{...}}). When the Web application encounters a replacement tag, it will attempt to locate the replacement method specified by the given name. The **handler** tag designates the path to the Web application DLL and the name of the request-handler class. This tag must be present in every SRF; the ISAPI Extension DLL forwards the request to the Web-application class specified by this tag.

ATL Server request-handler classes usually inherit from class **CRequestHandlerT**. This class receives the request from the ISAPI Extension DLL and parses the **.srf** file. Class **CRequestHandlerT** uses classes **CStencil** and **CHtmlStencil** to handle a set of predefined tags. The predefined tags provide locale, comment and resources information.

ATL Server includes attributes that further simplify the mapping between SRF references and the classes and methods in the Web-application DLL. Attribute **request_handler** takes a single parameter, the string **"Default"**. The attribute injects code into the class that causes the class to inherit from class **CRequestHandlerT** and map to the request-handler name **Default**. Method **ValidateAndExchange** overrides the base-class method to provide initialization code. Attribute **tag_name** injects code into the class to map the string argument to the method name.

SRFs can make use of control structures **if/else/endif** and **while/endwhile**. These structures behave as you would expect—the **if** and **while** structures operate on a conditional statement to control document rendering. A tag-replacement method may return **HTTP_SUCCESS** to designate true or **HTTP_S_FALSE** to designate a false condition to a control structure.

Method **GetFormVars** returns an object of type **CHttpRequestParms** that stores the collection of ID-value pairs from a submitted form. Method **Lookup** of class **CHttpRequestParms** retrieves the value in the collection that corresponds to the ID passed as an argument.

Class **CCookie** represents a single cookie, or a collection of cookies, and exposes the following methods: Method **GetFirstCookie** returns the first cookie in the collection; method **GetNextCookie** retrieves the next **CCookie** object in the cookie collection.

The ISAPI Extension DLL provides a session-state service that allows the Web application developer to create session objects for each client; this session-state service is accessed by interface **ISessionStateService**, which can create **ISession** objects for each client. Users who have corresponding session objects maintained on the server will have a session cookie that uniquely identifies them to the server. **ISessionStateService** method **GetSession**, with a session ID, stores the session object in an **ISession** pointer. **ISessionStateService** method **CreateNewSession** creates a new **ISession** object.

An **ISession** object can store name-value pairs. In session terminology, these are called session items, and they are placed into an **ISession** object by calling method **SetVariable**. **ISession** method **BeginVariableEnum** stores the session variables in a **HSESSIONENUM** object and the position of the first value in a **POSITION** argument. Method **GetNextVariable** of interface **ISession** returns the next variable in the **HSESSIONENUM** variable created by **BeginVariableEnum**,

Visual Studio .NET provides a wizard to generate a class to easily add database connectivity to an application. The **ATL OLEDB Consumer Wizard** dialog box allows you to select a database and configure the capabilities of the generated class. The generated database consumer class contains methods to open and close the database or default query, plus methods and properties to navigate and view the results returned by the query. The class contains a member variable for each database column of the type defined in the database schema. The member variables are named **m_***columnName*. Method **OpenAll** opens a connection to the database and executes the default query—which returns all rows from the table selected in the OLE DB consumer wizard. Method **MoveFirst** stores the first row of results from the default query in the **CUser** member variables. Method **MoveNext** gets the next row from the default query results and fills the appropriate member variables. Method **CloseAll** closes the default query result set and the database connection.

Attribute **db_command** executes a custom query on an open database. Attribute **db_command** simplifies executing database queries by injecting code that creates a custom **CCommand** object with the specified, name, query, open database and variable bindings.

ATL Server provides a set of template classes and attributes designed to simplify the creation of XML Web Services in unmanaged code. The ATL Server Web Services architecture consists primarily of the same components as an ATL Server Web Application—

IIS, and ISAPI extension DLL and a user-created DLL containing at least one request-handler class. The flow of a request is as follows: A client sends a request to the server for a given method. IIS receives the request for the DLL, then forwards the request and its data to the ISAPI extension DLL. The extension DLL parses the request then forwards the request data to the request-handler class. The request-handler class matches the request to the exposed Web-service method, then calls the method and provides the SOAP envelope.

Attribute **request_handler** exposes the class to the ISAPI extension as a class capable of handling Web requests. Attribute **soap_handler** enables WSDL generation and the functionality to parse SOAP envelopes and call the Web-service method. In addition to providing WSDL information, attribute **soap_handler** causes the handler class to extend **CSoapHandler** class. When the compiler encounters attribute **soap_method**, it injects code to extract the arguments from the SOAP request and to marshal the method's return type as a SOAP envelope.

An unmanaged Web-service client uses Visual Studio .NET tools and ATL Server classes to access a Web service with the same level of simplicity afforded to managed .NET Web-service clients. An unmanaged Web-service client is not restricted to an unmanaged Web service; because of the language abstraction provided by SOAP, an unmanaged client may use a managed Web service, and vice versa.

Managed and Unmanaged Interoperability

Objectives

- To understand the Visual C++ .NET compiler's It Just Works (IJW) feature.
- To marshal data types explicitly between managed and unmanaged code.
- To understand the difference between the managed and unmanaged heap.
- To provide wrappers for managed and unmanaged objects.
- To use the Platform Invoke Service for system libraries.
- To use delegates and managed structures with unmanaged callbacks and library functions.

Science is built up with facts, as a house is with stones. But a collection of facts is no more a science than a heap of stones is a house.
Jules Henri Poincaré

No particular results then, so far, but only an attitude of orientation, is what the pragmatic method means. The attitude of looking away from first things, principles, "categories," supposed necessities; and of looking toward last things, fruits, consequences, facts.
William James

It was, of course, a grand and impressive thing to do, to mistrust the obvious, and to pin one's faith in things which could not be seen!
Galen

Outline

24.1 Introduction

This chapter focuses on the differences between managed and unmanaged code contexts, and the technologies used to surmount the differences and allow interoperability between the context. Unlike other .NET languages, Visual C++ .NET allows side-by-side execution of managed and unmanaged code within the same application. The separation of execution into managed and unmanaged contexts, and the management of communication between these contexts make this side-by-side execution possible. A large part of the managed communication is the conversion (or marshaling) between native and .NET data types. The interoperability features of Visual C++ .NET may be split into three technologies—the It Just Works (IJW) compiler feature, the Platform Invoke Services and the COM Interop Services. This chapter (which is targeted towards developers with previous knowledge of unmanaged code and managed code) discusses IJW (Section 24.2) and the Platform Invoke Service (Section 24.5), and Chapter 25 discusses the COM interoperability features.

At a fundamental level this chapter discusses the differences between managed (`__gc`) and unmanaged (`__nogc`) classes, as well as the differences between managed (MSIL) code and unmanaged (native) code. It is important to note the distinction between the class and code, an unmanaged class may contain managed methods and a managed class may contain unmanaged methods.

24.2 It Just Works (IJW)

Microsoft's push towards .NET hinges on the ability to harness managed code without sacrificing existing unmanaged code. Thus, a primary goal of the Visual C++ .NET compiler team was ensuring that all existing C++ code could be compiled into MSIL without modification. This requirement was dubbed *It Just Works (IJW)* and allows developers to easily port existing code to the .NET Framework with a simple recompilation.

Most existing C++ code compiles into MSIL without errors or warnings, testifying to the large degree of success in IJW development. However, some code, such as functions containing inline assembly or functions with a variable number of arguments, cannot be compiled into MSIL. In addition, IJW will not compile any unmanaged classes as managed classes. Fortunately, Visual C++ .NET allows a single module to contain both MSIL and native code; thus, the compiler will embed code that cannot be compiled to MSIL as a native block within the .NET assembly. Additional IJW limitations prohibit unmanaged classes from inheriting, or being inherited by, a managed class and require the user to install the .NET runtime on their machine.

24.2.1 Managed vs. Unmanaged Code Revisited

When IJW converts most functions and methods to MSIL, the converted code gains access to the FCL and managed runtime features. However, IJW does not convert unmanaged C++ classes to managed classes. IJW leaves the classes unmanaged because it cannot convert many classes, such as those that use templates and multiple inheritance. In addition, IJW cannot determine the desired modifiers for a class, such as the access level (**public** or **private**) or the class type (**__gc** or **__value**). The unmanaged classes may contain managed methods, but only can be created dynamically on the unmanaged heap thus requiring explicit memory management. In addition, none of the CLR type checks and security features are available to the unmanaged class.

Despite its limitations, IJW provides essential functionality to the developer looking to port existing unmanaged code to a managed context. IJW makes the code .NET aware; that is, the converted methods and functions can recognize and use .NET data types, and the unmanaged classes can create certain managed value types as data members, reducing costly data type marshaling for calls with managed code. IJW also handles all data marshaling between the converted code and existing native functions. This enables incremental porting of native code to MSIL and transparent use of existing libraries and frameworks, such as the Win32 API, MFC or ATL.

The only change required to compile code as MSIL is including the **/clr** switch in the compiler command line. The switch enables IJW and changes the compilation target from a native code module to a MSIL assembly. To enable the **/clr** compiler switch in Visual Studio .NET, set the **Use Managed Extensions** option in the project property pages (Fig. 24.1) to **Yes**.

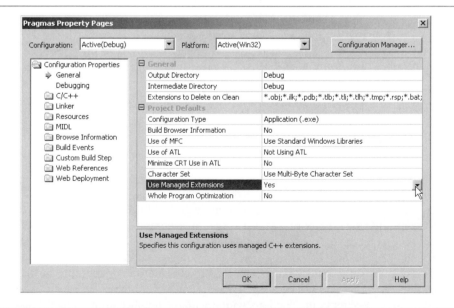

Fig. 24.1   Use Managed Extensions project property option.

Visual C++ .NET allows managed and unmanaged code and classes to coexist in the same code file. Classes that contain the __gc keyword are compiled as managed classes, and classes that contain either the __nogc keyword or no keyword at all are compiled as unmanaged data types. In addition, methods and functions are compiled as managed code when possible.

Visual C++ .NET introduces two new #pragma preprocessor directives for developers that require more control over the compilation target of methods and functions. The #pragma unmanaged causes all following method and function definitions to be compiled as native code. The #pragma managed terminates a #pragma unmanaged block and causes all following code to be compiled using IJW, as explained earlier. If the /clr compiler flag is not enabled, the managed and unmanaged #pragmas are ignored—all code is natively compiled. [*Note*: Using or defining a __gc class in a #pragma unmanaged block causes a compiler error.]

Fig. 24.2 uses #pragma managed and #pragma unmanaged to create managed and unmanaged code, respectively.

```
1   // Fig. 24.2: Pragmas.cpp
2   // Demonstrates the use of managed and unmanaged pragmas.
3   // Compares Managed, IJW converted and unmanaged classes.
4
5   #include <stdio.h>
6
7   #using <mscorlib.dll>
8
9   using namespace System;
10
11  // ManagedWelcome Class
12  public __gc class ManagedWelcome
13  {
14  public:
15     void Welcome()
16     {
17        Console::Write( S"Welcome to managed code!\n" );
18     } // end method Welcome
19  }; // end class ManagedWelcome
20
21  // IJWWelcome class, compiled as unmanaged class
22  __nogc class IJWWelcome
23  {
24  public:
25
26     // managed method
27     void WelcomeConsoleWrite()
28     {
29        Console::Write( "Welcome to managed code!\n" );
30     } // end method WelcomeConsoleWrite
```

Fig. 24.2 #pragma managed and unmanaged demonstration. (Part 1 of 3.)

```
31
32      // managed method using IJW marshaling
33      void WelcomePrintf()
34      {
35         printf( "Welcome to unmanaged code!\n" );
36      } // end method WelcomePrintf
37   }; // end class IJWWelcome
38
39   #pragma unmanaged
40
41   // UnmanagedWelcome class, compiled as unmanaged class
42   class UnmanagedWelcome
43   {
44   public:
45
46      // unmanaged method
47      void Welcome()
48      {
49         printf( "Welcome to unmanaged code!\n" );
50      } // end method Welcome
51   }; // end class UnmanagedWelcome
52
53   #pragma managed
54
55   // entry point for application, demonstrates each class
56   int main()
57   {
58      ManagedWelcome *managedWelcome = new ManagedWelcome();
59      IJWWelcome *nogcWelcome = new IJWWelcome();
60      UnmanagedWelcome unmanagedWelcome;
61
62      Console::WriteLine(
63         S"ManagedWelcome method Welcome:" );
64      managedWelcome->Welcome();
65
66      Console::WriteLine(
67         S"\nIJWWelcome method WelcomeConsoleWrite:" );
68      nogcWelcome->WelcomeConsoleWrite();
69
70      Console::WriteLine(
71         S"\nIJWWelcome method WelcomePrintf:" );
72      nogcWelcome->WelcomePrintf();
73
74      Console::WriteLine(
75         S"\nUnmanagedWelcome method Welcome:" );
76      unmanagedWelcome.Welcome();
77
78      delete nogcWelcome;
79
80      return 0;
81   } // end function main
```

Fig. 24.2   **#pragma managed** and **unmanaged** demonstration. (Part 2 of 3.)

```
ManagedWelcome method Welcome:
Welcome to managed code!

IJWWelcome method WelcomeConsoleWrite:
Welcome to managed code!

IJWWelcome method WelcomePrintf:
Welcome to unmanaged code!

UnmanagedWelcome method Welcome:
Welcome to unmanaged code!
```

Fig. 24.2   `#pragma managed` and `unmanaged` demonstration. (Part 3 of 3.)

Class **ManagedWelcome** (lines 12–19) contains method **Welcome** (lines 15–18) that uses managed method **Write** to print the string **"Welcome to managed code!"**. Class **IJWWelcome** (lines 22–37) contains two methods, **WelcomeConsoleWrite** (lines 27–30) and **WelcomePrintf** (lines 33–36). This class demonstrates how IJW enables **__nogc** classes to access FLC classes without requiring the removal of native calls. Method **WelcomeConsoleWrite** uses managed method **Write** to display the string **"Welcome to managed code!"**. Note that we do not prefix the string with **S**—this causes the compiler to create the string as an unmanaged value class, and the runtime will construct a **String** object from the value class. It is less efficient to rely on the compiler and runtime to convert ANSI strings; thus, it is good practice to always prefix managed strings with **S**. Method **WelcomePrintf** uses native function **printf** to display the string **"Welcome to unmanaged code!"**. IJW performs all the work required to call the native function from the managed method.

Line 39 demonstrates the **unmanaged pragma**—all code between the **unmanaged pragma** and **managed pragma** is compiled into native code. Class **UnmanagedWelcome** (lines 42–51) contains a single method **Welcome** that uses native function **printf** to print the string **"Welcome to unmanaged code!"**. The **Welcome** method in class **UnmanagedWelcome** is compiled into native code and cannot call methods of managed types (i.e., **Console::WriteLine**).

Line 53 uses **pragma managed** to re-enable MSIL compilation. Function **main** (lines 56–81) instantiates each class and calls each method. Line 59 uses keyword **new** to instantiate the **__nogc** class on the unmanaged heap; as such, the memory must be released with the **delete** keyword as shown in line 78.

To assist in demonstrating exactly how each class is compiled, we use Microsoft's *MSIL Disassembler* (*ildasm.exe*) to examine the project output file; **Pragmas.exe**. The **ildasm** tool (included in the *VisualStudio_Directory***\FrameworkSDK\Bin** directory) presents a tree view of the code and metadata in a .NET assembly. The **ildasm** tool also allows the user to view the MSIL code of any method contained in an assembly by double clicking the method name.[1]

Fig. 24.3 shows the MSIL Disassembler tree view of the **pragma**s application obtained by executing the following command:

---

1. More information about the MSIL Disassembler can be found at
   `msdn.microsoft.com/library/default.asp?url=/library/en-us/`
   `cptools/html/cpconmsildisassemblerildasmexe.asp`.

ildasm *Project_Directory***Debug\Pragmas.exe**

from the *VisualStudio_Directory***FrameworkSDK\Bin** directory. Each class is represented as a node in the tree. **__value** classes (the type used to represent unmanaged classes) are represented with a brown square and three outputs, while managed classes are represented as a blue square with three outputs. Notice that managed classes list their member functions as child nodes of the class. Unmanaged methods and managed methods that belong to **__nogc** classes are listed as static methods (denoted by the purple box containing an **S**) and are placed as top-level nodes in the tree. In addition, the compiler generates a set of stub (or *thunk*) methods for each native function called in the application. These proxy methods call the native method and perform any required argument or return type data marshaling between managed and native types. Currently, in Windows, the .NET primitive data types map directly to their native counterparts; thus, in many cases, the programmer does not need to marshal data types explicitly. The native type's size cannot be assumed, because .NET is designed as a cross-platform runtime. IJW's generated proxy classes allow programmers to transparently call unmanaged code from managed code.

Managed **Welcome** method   Unmanaged **Welcome** method

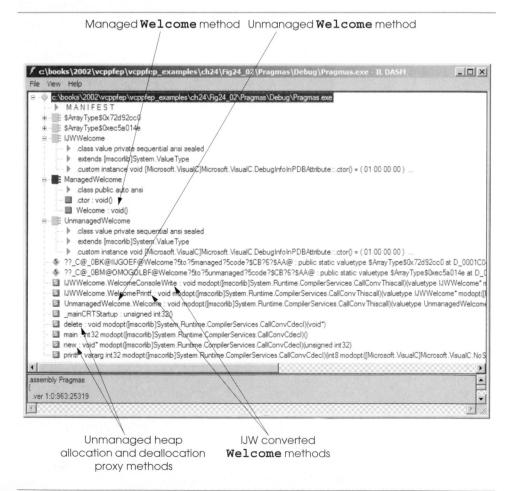

Unmanaged heap
allocation and deallocation
proxy methods

IJW converted
Welcome methods

Fig. 24.3   MSIL Disassembler showing **Pragmas.exe** .NET assembly.

Double clicking the managed **Welcome** method in **ildasm** displays the window shown in Fig. 24.4. This window contains the compiled MSIL code for the selected function. The logic and syntax of MSIL are beyond the scope of this book; however, the MSIL for each method is used to compare managed and unmanaged code.

The __**nogc** class **IJWWelcome** method disassembly (Fig. 24.5–Fig. 24.6) demonstrates IJW at work. Method **WelcomeConsoleWrite** converts the single-byte character string to a **String** class object before calling method **Write**. Method **WelcomePrintf** stores the ANSI string andcalls the generated **printf** proxy method, which then delegates the call to the unmanaged **printf** function.

In contrast to the other two classes, **ildasm** is unable to show the code for class **UnmanagedWelcome** method **Welcome** (Fig. 24.7). It does not have the capabilities to display unmanaged code. The .NET assembly contains a valid MSIL method prototype for the unmanaged method that managed code can use to call the method.

```
ManagedWelcome::Welcome : void()                            _ □ ×
.method public instance void  Welcome() cil managed
{
  // Code size       11 (0xb)
  .maxstack  1
  IL_0000:  ldstr      "Welcome to managed code!\n"
  IL_0005:  call       void [mscorlib]System.Console::Write(string)
  IL_000a:  ret
} // end of method ManagedWelcome::Welcome
```

Fig. 24.4   Disassembly for managed method **Welcome**.

```
Global Functions::IJWWelcome.WelcomeConsoleWrite : void modopt([mscorlib]System.Runtime.C...  _ □ ×
.method public static void modopt([mscorlib]System.Runtime.CompilerServices.C
          IJWWelcome.WelcomeConsoleWrite(valuetype IJWWelcome* modopt([Microsof
{
  .vtentry 2 : 1
  // Code size       16 (0x10)
  .maxstack  1
  IL_0000:  ldsflda    valuetype $ArrayType$0x72d92cc0 ??_C@_0BK@IIJGOEF@Welc
  IL_0005:  newobj     instance void [mscorlib]System.String::.ctor(int8*)
  IL_000a:  call       void [mscorlib]System.Console::Write(string)
  IL_000f:  ret
} // end of method 'Global Functions'::IJWWelcome.WelcomeConsoleWrite
```

Fig. 24.5   Disassembly for method **WelcomeConsoleWrite**.

```
Global Functions::IJWWelcome.WelcomePrintf : void modopt([mscorlib]System.Runtime.Compile...  _ □ ×
.method public static void modopt([mscorlib]System.Runtime.CompilerServices.
          IJWWelcome.WelcomePrintf(valuetype IJWWelcome* modopt([Microsoft.Vis
{
  .vtentry 3 : 1
  // Code size       12 (0xc)
  .maxstack  1
  IL_0000:  ldsflda    valuetype $ArrayType$0xec5a014e ??_C@_0BM@OMOGOLBF@We
  IL_0005:  call       vararg int32 modopt([mscorlib]System.Runtime.Compiler
  IL_000a:  pop
  IL_000b:  ret
} // end of method 'Global Functions'::IJWWelcome.WelcomePrintf
```

Fig. 24.6   Disassembly for method **WelcomePrintf**.

```
 Global Functions::UnmanagedWelcome.Welcome : void modopt([mscorlib]Syste...  _ □ ×
.method public static pinvokeimpl(/* No map */)
        void modopt([mscorlib]System.Runtime.CompilerServices.Cal
        UnmanagedWelcome.Welcome(valuetype UnmanagedWelcome* modo
{
  .custom instance void [mscorlib]System.Security.SuppressUnmanag
  // Embedded native code
  //  Disassembly of native methods is not supported.
  //  Managed TargetRVA = 0x1120
} // end of method 'Global Functions'::UnmanagedWelcome.Welcome
```

Fig. 24.7 Disassembly for unmanaged method **Welcome**.

24.2.2 Type Marshaling

In many cases, IJW is able to transparently perform data type marshaling between managed value types and unmanaged types. However, it is unable to perform data marshaling between managed objects from the managed heap and unmanaged types. The most notable instance where this becomes a problem is in the case of the **String** object. **String** objects consist of two-byte characters, while many unmanaged functions require single-byte ANSI character strings. Fortunately, the **System::Runtime::InteropServices** namespace includes class **Marshal**, which contains a large number of methods to assist in **String**, structure and COM interoperability issues. [*Note*: In many cases, IJW provides the correct data marshaling for **String**s without requiring the explicit use of class **Marshal**.]

The Sound Player application (Fig. 24.8–Fig. 24.11) demonstrates using IJW to call Win32 functions and class **Marshal** string conversion methods. The application displays a list of **.wav** files in a list box and allows the user to play the selected **.wav** file. Fig. 24.8 presents the class definition for class **SoundPlayer**.

```
1   // Fig. 24.8: SoundPlayer.h
2   // Class definition for SoundPlayer.
3
4   #pragma once
5
6   #include <windows.h>
7
8   // required libraries
9   #using <mscorlib.dll>
10  #using <system.dll>
11  #using <system.windows.forms.dll>
12  #using <system.drawing.dll>
13
14  // required namespaces
15  using namespace System;
16  using namespace System::Drawing;
17  using namespace System::Runtime::InteropServices;
18  using namespace System::Windows::Forms;
19
20  // contains PlaySound function
21  #pragma comment( lib, "winmm.lib" )
```

Fig. 24.8 **SoundPlayer** class method definitions. (Part 1 of 2.)

```
22
23   // contains messagebox function
24   #pragma comment( lib, "user32.lib" )
25
26   // inherits from Form, plays user selected .wav file
27   public __gc class SoundPlayer : public Form
28   {
29   public:
30      SoundPlayer();
31
32   private:
33
34      // GUI components
35      ComboBox *soundList;
36      Label *ChooseLabel;
37      Button *PlayButton;
38      System::ComponentModel::Container *components;
39      void InitializeComponent();
40
41      // click event handler
42      void PlayButton_Click( Object *, EventArgs * );
43   }; // end class SoundPlayer
```

Fig. 24.8 `SoundPlayer` class method definitions. (Part 2 of 2.)

Line 6 includes **<windows.h>**, which contains the function prototypes for Win32 API functions. Line 21 uses the comment **pragma** to include **winmm.lib** in the project. Library **winmm.lib** contains Windows multimedia functions, including **PlaySound**. Line 24 includes **user32.lib**, which defines function **MessageBoxW**. Class **Sound-Player** (lines 27–43) is a managed **Form** control that consists of a **ComboBox**, a **Label**, a **Button** and a **Button Click** event handler. Fig. 24.9 contains the method definitions for class **SoundPlayer**.

```
1    // Fig. 24.9: SoundPlayer.cpp
2    // Method definitions for class SoundPlayer.
3
4    #include "SoundPlayer.h"
5
6    // constructor
7    SoundPlayer::SoundPlayer()
8    {
9       components = 0;
10      InitializeComponent();
11   } // end constructor
12
13   // initialize GUI components
14   void SoundPlayer::InitializeComponent()
15   {
16
17      // create components and begin layout
18      soundList = new ComboBox();
19      ChooseLabel = new Label();
```

Fig. 24.9 `SoundPlayer` class method definitions. (Part 1 of 3.)

```
20      PlayButton = new Button();
21      SuspendLayout();
22
23      // populate list with available sounds
24      String *sounds[] = { S"applause.wav", S"collision.wav",
25          S"energy.wav", S"toneup.wav", S"tonedown.wav" };
26      soundList->Items->AddRange( sounds );
27
28      // initialize soundList ComboBox
29      soundList->Location = Point( 16, 32 );
30      soundList->Name = S"soundList";
31      soundList->Size = Drawing::Size( 216, 21 );
32      soundList->TabIndex = 0;
33
34      // label prompting user to select file
35      ChooseLabel->Location = Point( 16, 8 );
36      ChooseLabel->Name = S"ChooseLabel";
37      ChooseLabel->Size = Drawing::Size( 100, 16 );
38      ChooseLabel->TabIndex = 1;
39      ChooseLabel->Text = S"Choose A Sound";
40
41      // playButton plays selected sound file when pressed
42      PlayButton->Location = Drawing::Point( 16, 72 );
43      PlayButton->Name = S"PlayButton";
44      PlayButton->Size = Drawing::Size( 40, 23 );
45      PlayButton->TabIndex = 2;
46      PlayButton->Text = S"Play";
47      PlayButton->Click +=
48          new System::EventHandler(this, this->PlayButton_Click);
49
50      // setup form variables
51      AutoScaleBaseSize = Drawing::Size( 5, 13 );
52      ClientSize = Drawing::Size( 240, 101 );
53      Name = S"SoundPlayer";
54      Text = S"Sound Player";
55
56      // add controls
57      Control *controls[] = { PlayButton, ChooseLabel,
58          soundList };
59
60      Controls->AddRange( controls );
61
62      // apply layout changes
63      ResumeLayout( false );
64   } // end method InitializeComponent
65
66   // PlayButton click event handler
67   void SoundPlayer::PlayButton_Click( Object *sender,
68      EventArgs *event )
69   {
70
71      // obtain selected string from soundList
72      String *sound =
73          dynamic_cast< String * >( soundList->SelectedItem );
```

Fig. 24.9   **SoundPlayer** class method definitions. (Part 2 of 3.)

```
74
75        // ensure song was selected
76        if ( sound != NULL ) {
77
78            // obtain pointer to ANSI string
79            IntPtr stringPointer =
80                Marshal::StringToHGlobalAnsi( sound );
81
82            // cast pointer to LPCSTR, call Win32 PlaySound function
83            PlaySoundA(
84                static_cast< LPCSTR >( stringPointer.ToPointer() ),
85                NULL, SND_FILENAME | SND_ASYNC );
86
87            // free allocated unmanaged heap memory
88            Marshal::FreeHGlobal( stringPointer );
89        }
90        else // display Win32 MessageBox, IJW performs conversion
91            MessageBoxW( 0, L"Please Select a wav file from the list",
92                L"Error", MB_OK );
93    } // end method PlayButton_Click
```

Fig. 24.9   SoundPlayer class method definitions. (Part 3 of 3.)

Method **InitializeComponent** (lines 14–64) initializes the **Form** and GUI components to construct an interface consisting of a **ComboBox** containing **.wav** file names, a **Button** with a **Click** event handler **PlayButton_Click** and a **Label**.

Event handler method **PlayButton_Click** (lines 67–93) is fired when the form's button is pressed. Lines 72–73 extract the selected **String *** from **ComboBox soundlist**. If a valid **String *** is returned, lines 79–80 use class **Marshal** static method **StringToHGlobalAnsi**, which copies the referenced **String** object onto the unmanaged heap as an array of ANSI characters and returns an **IntPtr** to the location of the first character. Lines 83–85 execute to call Win32 function **PlaySoundA**. Function **PlaySoundA** receives a pointer to an ANSI string (of Win32 type **LPCSTR**) containing the file name, an optional argument to a sound resource and the playing options. Method **ToPointer** of class **IntPtr** returns a **void** pointer, which can be casted to **LPCSTR** and used as the function's first argument. Static method **FreeHGlobal** (line 88) frees the memory at the passed location, preventing a memory leak in our application. The string was copied to unmanaged memory on the unmanaged heap and must be released before the pointer to the memory falls out of scope. Function **MessageBoxW** (lines 91–92) is called if the user does not select a **.wav** file from the **ComboBox**. Function **MessageBoxW** requires no explicit marshaling because the strings are never placed in a **String** object and can be marshalled by IJW. Fig. 24.10 contains a list of class **Marshal**'s string marshaling methods.

Marshal String Method	Description
FreeBSTR	De-allocates memory allocated by method **StringToBSTR**.
FreeHGlobal	De-allocates memory allocated for ANSI and Unicode® strings by **StringToHGlobal**type methods.

Fig. 24.10 Marshal class string marshaling methods. (Part 1 of 2.)

Marshal String Method	Description
PtrToStringAnsi	Creates a **String** object from a ANSI character string pointer. Widens characters to Unicode® and constructs **String** object on managed heap.
PtrToStringAuto	Creates a **String** object from characters on the unmanaged heap. Determines whether the unmanaged memory contains ANSI or Unicode® characters and delegates method call to appropriate method.
PtrToStringBSTR	Creates a **String** object from a pointer to an unmanaged BSTR. Copies characters to managed heap and constructs a **String** object on the managed heap.
PtrToStringUni	Creates a **String** object from a pointer to an unmanaged Unicode® character string. Copies characters to a managed heap and constructs a **String** object on the managed heap.
StringToBSTR	Copies a **String** object character string to the unmanaged heap as a **BSTR** value and returns a pointer to the allocated memory.
StringToHGlobalAnsi	Copies a **String** object character string to the unmanaged heap as an ANSI character string and returns a pointer to the allocated memory.
StringToHGlobalAuto	Copies a **String** object character string to the unmanaged heap as the platform default type character string and returns a pointer to the allocated memory.
StringToHGlobalUni	Copies a **String** object character string to the unmanaged heap as a Unicode® character string and returns a pointer to the allocated memory.

Fig. 24.10 **Marshal** class string marshaling methods. (Part 2 of 2.)

Fig. 24.11 presents the application entry point for the sound-player application. Function **WinMain** simply runs a new instance of class **SoundPlayer**. This example uses the Win32 style arguments for function **WinMain**. Function **WinMain** is forward referenced in **winbase.h**, which is included by **windows.h**. The forward reference forces us to use the shown arguments. The first argument, of type **HINSTANCE**, contains a handle to the current application. The current application's **HINSTANCE** is used in many Win32 functions. The second argument is maintained for backwards compatibility, and is always a **NULL** handle. The third argument is a **char *** that contains the arguments passed to the application. The fourth argument is an integer designating how to show the window (e.g., maximized or minimized). We can ignore these parameters in our managed application because the **Form** class handles window creation and management.

```
1   // Fig. 24.11: IJWTypemarshaling.cpp
2   // Demonstrates IJW marshaling and explicit marshaling.
3
```

Fig. 24.11 Sound-player application entry point. (Part 1 of 2.)

```
4   #include "SoundPlayer.h"
5
6   #using <mscorlib.dll>
7
8   // entry point for application
9   int __stdcall WinMain( HINSTANCE instance, HINSTANCE oldInstance,
10     LPSTR commandLine, int showState )
11  {
12     Application::Run( new SoundPlayer() );
13
14     return 0;
15  } // end function WinMain
```

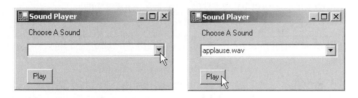

Fig. 24.11 Sound-player application entry point. (Part 2 of 2.)

24.3 Managed and Unmanaged Memory

An application that combines managed and unmanaged code uses a heap space that is logically divided into a *managed heap* and an *unmanaged heap*. While the heaps share a physical address space, the fundamental differences in managed and unmanaged code necessitate separate heaps.

The unmanaged heap—a large block of free memory—can store any type of dynamically allocated data. The heap is used in unmanaged applications for dynamically sized arrays, for blocks of data too large to fit on the stack and as storage for objects and data in memory that will not fall out of scope. However, unlike data on the stack, which has a definite lifetime and scope, unmanaged code does not know when data on the heap is no longer needed or usable. Thus, the programmer is required to free allocated memory.

The managed heap stores all managed objects, with the exception of __**value** types (unless the __**value** type is boxed, or is a member of a __**gc** class). The CLR runs in the managed heap and provides a set of services to the contained objects, including memory management and array bounds checking. Memory management is performed by the garbage collector: When the managed heap is running low on memory, the garbage collector traces all active pointers to the managed heap and frees any unreachable memory. As the garbage collector frees memory, it relocates valid objects to compact the memory space. If memory is compacted, the garbage collector makes any necessary corrections to the application's managed pointers.

For the programmer, the main difference between the managed and unmanaged heaps is the deterministic nature of the memory. An unmanaged code developer knows exactly when an object is destroyed and can directly manipulate memory based on an exact memory location—the data does not move. A managed code developer does not know when the garbage collector destroys an object and does not have any guarantees regarding an object's location in memory. In most cases, managed objects do not need an absolute memory address; the runtime adjusts pointers as memory moves. A problem arises when the programmer attempts to pass data on the managed heap to an unmanaged function. The runtime is unable to adjust the unmanaged function's pointers; thus, if the garbage collector moves the managed data, the unmanaged function will no longer have a valid pointer.

Microsoft introduced pinning pointers into MC++ to "lock" an object on the managed heap into a static memory location. Keyword **__pin** declares a *pinning pointer*. Any object pointed to by a pinning pointer is considered "pinned." If any member of a managed object is pinned, the entire object will be ignored by the garbage collector until the pinning pointer falls out of scope or is set to **0**. When the managed pinning pointer falls out of scope, the pinned object is no longer locked in place. Thus, any remaining unmanaged pointers to the object may point to an invalid memory location.

Common Programming Error 24.1

Be careful while using pinning pointers and large objects. If you forget to unpin pinned objects, resource exhaustion will result.

Figures 24.12 and 24.13 demonstrate pinning pointers to store a managed data item in a unmanaged collection class. Fig. 24.12 presents a templated queue class, which will be created on the unmanaged heap.

```
1   // Fig. 24.12: tqueue.h
2   // Unmanaged templated queue.
3
4   #pragma once
5
6   #include <iostream>
7   #include <cassert>
8
9   using std::cout;
10
11  template< class T > class Queue; // forward declaration
12
13  // class QueueNode represents each element in queue
14  template< class T >
15  class QueueNode
16  {
17     friend class Queue< T >;
18
19  public:
20     QueueNode( T * = 0 );
21     T getData() const;
22
23  private:
24     T data;
25     QueueNode *nextPtr;
26  }; // end class QueueNode
27
28  // initializes QueueNode data member
29  template< class T >
```

Fig. 24.12 Unmanaged templated classes **Queue** and **QueueNode**. (Part 1 of 4.)

```
30   QueueNode< T >::QueueNode( T *d )
31   {
32      data = *d;
33      nextPtr = 0;
34   } // end constructor
35
36   // returns contained item
37   template < class T >
38   T QueueNode< T >::getData() const
39   {
40      return data;
41   } // end method getData
42
43   // templated unmanaged Queue data structure class
44   template< class T >
45   class Queue
46   {
47   public:
48      Queue();              // constructor
49      ~Queue();             // destructor
50      void enqueue( T * );  // insert item in queue
51      T dequeue();          // remove item from queue
52      int isEmpty() const;  // determine if queue is empty
53      void print() const;   // output queue
54
55   private:
56      QueueNode< T > *headPtr;  // pointer to first QueueNode
57      QueueNode< T > *tailPtr;  // pointer to last QueueNode
58   }; // end class Queue
59
60   // constructor initializes queue pointer values
61   template< class T >
62   Queue< T >::Queue()
63   {
64      headPtr = tailPtr = 0;
65   } // end constructor
66
67   // destructor deletes remaining nodes from queue
68   template< class T >
69   Queue< T >::~Queue()
70   {
71      QueueNode< T > *tempPtr, *currentPtr = headPtr;
72
73      while ( currentPtr != 0 ) {
74         tempPtr = currentPtr;
75         currentPtr = currentPtr->nextPtr;
76         delete tempPtr;
77      }
78   } // end destructor
79
80   // inserts given item into queue
81   template < class T >
```

Fig. 24.12 Unmanaged templated classes **Queue** and **QueueNode**. (Part 2 of 4.)

```
82   void Queue< T >::enqueue( T *d )
83   {
84      QueueNode< T > *newPtr = new QueueNode< T >( d );
85      assert( newPtr != 0 );   // determine if memory was allocated
86
87      if ( isEmpty() )
88         headPtr = tailPtr = newPtr;
89      else {
90         tailPtr->nextPtr = newPtr;
91         tailPtr = newPtr;
92      }
93   } // end method enqueue
94
95   // removes front item from queue
96   template < class T >
97   T Queue< T >::dequeue()
98   {
99      assert( !isEmpty() );
100
101     QueueNode< T > *tempPtr = headPtr;
102
103     headPtr = headPtr->nextPtr;
104     T value = tempPtr->data;
105     delete tempPtr;
106
107     if ( headPtr == 0 )
108        tailPtr = 0;
109
110     return value;
111  } // end method dequeue
112
113  // determines if queue is empty
114  template < class T >
115  int Queue< T >::isEmpty() const
116  {
117     return headPtr == 0;
118  }
119
120  // displays values of items in queue
121  template < class T >
122  void Queue< T >::print() const
123  {
124     QueueNode< T > *currentPtr = headPtr;
125
126     if ( isEmpty() )              // queue is empty
127        cout << "Queue is empty" << endl;
128     else {                       // queue is not empty
129        cout << "The queue is:" << endl;
130
131        while ( currentPtr != 0 ) {
132           cout << currentPtr->data << ' ';
133           currentPtr = currentPtr->nextPtr;
```

Fig. 24.12 Unmanaged templated classes **Queue** and **QueueNode**. (Part 3 of 4.)

```
134          }
135
136          cout << endl;
137      } // end else
138  } // end method print
```

Fig. 24.12 Unmanaged templated classes `Queue` and `QueueNode`. (Part 4 of 4.)

Class `QueueNode` (lines 14–26) represents a single node in a queue. It is a templated class and stores a single data item and a pointer to the next `QueueNode` in the queue. The `QueueNode` constructor (lines 29–34) stores a copy of the passed data item and clears the pointer.

Class `Queue` (lines 44–58) is a templated implementation of a queue data structure. The class constructor (lines 61–65) sets the head and tail pointers to `0`. The class destructor (lines 68–78) releases the dynamically allocated `QueueNodes` before the `Queue` object is destroyed. Method `enqueue` (lines 81–93) allocates a new `QueueNode` object to store the passed data and adds the `QueueNode` to the tail of the `Queue`. Method `dequeue` (lines 96–111) removes the head `QueueNode` from the `Queue` and returns its contained data item. Method `isEmpty` (lines 114–118) returns a `bool` value indicating whether the `Queue` contains any `QueueNodes`. Method `print` (lines 121–138) displays the data item of each `QueueNode` in the `Queue`.

Fig. 24.13 contains enumeration `Products`, which represents all available items in a store. This figure also contains class `Shoppers`, which represents a single shopper in a store and maintains a shopper number and the shopper's selected items.

```
1    // Fig. 24.13: Shopper.h
2    // Contains store product enumeration and managed Shopper
3    // class declaration.
4
5    #pragma once
6
7    #using <mscorlib.dll>
8
9    using namespace System;
10
11   // store product enumeration
12   __value enum Products
13   {
14       MILK = 0,
15       EGGS = 1,
16       CHIPS = 2,
17       SODA = 3,
18       APPLES = 4,
19       GRAPES = 5
20   }; // end enum Products
21
22   // managed Shopper class maintains number for each shopper
23   public __gc class Shopper
24   {
25   public:
```

Fig. 24.13 `Shopper` class stores a customer number and selected products. (Part 1 of 2.)

```
26        Shopper( int );
27        void CheckoutCustomer();
28        int number;
29        int items __gc[];
30     }; // end class Shopper
```

Fig. 24.13 Shopper class stores a customer number and selected products. (Part 2 of 2.)

Enumeration **Products** (lines 12–20) represents the products available at the grocery store. Managed class **Shopper** (lines 23–30) contains an **int** data member **number** that stores a unique customer number and an array of **int**s (**items**) that represents each customer's purchases. In addition, it contains method **CheckoutCustomer** that displays each item in the **items** array. Fig. 24.14 contains the shopper class method definitions.

The class constructor (lines 6–9) initializes the **Shopper**'s **number** and **items** data members. Function **CheckoutCustomer** (lines 12–31) displays the name of each item selected by the **Shopper** object. Lines 20–28 test whether the **Shopper** object's **items** array contains any items with a value of **1**; if so, lines 24–26 convert the array index into a **Products** enumeration and display the appropriate **Product** item name.

```
1    // Fig. 24.14: Shopper.cpp
2    // Provides Shopper class method definitions.
3
4    #include "Shopper.h"
5
6    Shopper::Shopper( int numberValue ) : number( numberValue )
7    {
8       items = new int __gc[ 6 ];
9    } // end constructor
10
11   // display customer's purchases
12   void Shopper::CheckoutCustomer()
13   {
14
15      // enumeration instance
16      Products purchases;
17      Console::Write( String::Concat( S"Customer ",
18         number.ToString(), S" purchased: " ) );
19
20      for ( int i = 0; i < 6; i++ ) {
21
22         // display item name if customer purchased
23         if ( items[ i ] == 1 ) {
24            purchases = ( Products ) i;
25            Console::Write( __box( purchases ) );
26            Console::Write( S" " );
27         }
28      }
29
30      Console::WriteLine( S"" );
31   } // end method CheckoutCustomer
```

Fig. 24.14 Shopper class method definitions.

Fig. 24.15 presents the managed application that uses the unmanaged **Queue** class to store data from the managed heap. The program simulates a grocery store line—it creates an array of shoppers and randomly selects items and places them into line. Each shopper leaves the line after being serviced. [*Note*: A more realistic simulation would use threads. For simplicity, all shoppers enter the line before any are serviced.]

```cpp
1   // Fig. 24.15: pinning.cpp
2   // Demonstrates pinning a managed value type to pass
3   // to an unmanaged method.
4
5   #include "tqueue.h"
6   #include "Shopper.h"
7
8   #using <mscorlib.dll>
9
10  using namespace System;
11  using namespace System::Runtime::InteropServices;
12
13  // entry point for application
14  int main()
15  {
16
17     // create array of managed shoppers
18     Shopper *shoppers[] = new Shopper *[ 10 ];
19
20     // create unmanaged queue in unmanaged heap
21     Queue< int > *groceryLine = new Queue< int >();
22
23     Random *random = new Random();
24
25     // initialize shopper array
26     for ( int i = 0; i < 10; i++ ) {
27        shoppers[ i ] = new Shopper( i );
28
29        bool gotAnItem = false;
30
31        // select at least one random item
32        while( !gotAnItem )
33           for ( int j = 0; j < 6; j++ ) {
34              if ( random->Next( 2 ) == 1 ) {
35                 shoppers[ i ]->items[ j ] = 1;
36                 gotAnItem = true;
37              }
38           }
39     } // end for
40
41     // randomize shopper array
42     for ( int i = 0; i < 10; i++ ) {
43        Shopper *temporary = shoppers[ i ];
44
```

Fig. 24.15 Pinning pointer example uses unmanaged queue to store managed heap data. (Part 1 of 3.)

```
45            int index = random->Next( 10 );
46            shoppers[ i ] = shoppers[ index ];
47            shoppers[ index ] = temporary;
48        } // end for
49
50        // enqueue each shopper in grocery line
51        for ( int i = 0; i < 10; i++ ) {
52            int __pin *pinnedNumber = &shoppers[ i ]->number;
53            groceryLine->enqueue( pinnedNumber );
54            Console::WriteLine( String::Concat( S"Shopper number ",
55                shoppers[ i ]->number.ToString(),
56                S" has entered the line." ) );
57        }
58
59        int counter = 0;
60
61        // remove each shopper from grocery line
62        while ( !groceryLine->isEmpty() ) {
63            int number = groceryLine->dequeue();
64
65            // service customer
66            shoppers[ counter ]->CheckoutCustomer();
67            Console::WriteLine( String::Concat( S"Shopper number ",
68                number.ToString(), S" has been serviced.\n" ) );
69
70            counter++;
71        } // end while
72
73        // delete unmanaged queue
74        delete groceryLine;
75
76        return 0;
77    } // end function main
```

```
Shopper number 0 has entered the line.
Shopper number 4 has entered the line.
Shopper number 3 has entered the line.
Shopper number 6 has entered the line.
Shopper number 8 has entered the line.
Shopper number 7 has entered the line.
Shopper number 9 has entered the line.
Shopper number 1 has entered the line.
Shopper number 5 has entered the line.
Shopper number 2 has entered the line.
Customer 0 purchased: EGGS CHIPS SODA APPLES GRAPES
Shopper number 0 has been serviced.

Customer 4 purchased: CHIPS SODA APPLES
Shopper number 4 has been serviced.
```

(continued on next page)

Fig. 24.15 Pinning pointer example uses unmanaged queue to store managed heap data. (Part 2 of 3.)

(continued from previous page)

```
Customer 3 purchased: EGGS GRAPES
Shopper number 3 has been serviced.

Customer 6 purchased: EGGS SODA APPLES
Shopper number 6 has been serviced.

Customer 8 purchased: GRAPES
Shopper number 8 has been serviced.

Customer 7 purchased: EGGS SODA
Shopper number 7 has been serviced.

Customer 9 purchased: MILK CHIPS SODA APPLES
Shopper number 9 has been serviced.

Customer 1 purchased: CHIPS SODA
Shopper number 1 has been serviced.

Customer 5 purchased: CHIPS SODA APPLES GRAPES
Shopper number 5 has been serviced.

Customer 2 purchased: CHIPS SODA
Shopper number 2 has been serviced.
```

Fig. 24.15 Pinning pointer example uses unmanaged queue to store managed heap data. (Part 3 of 3.)

Function **main** (lines 14–77) provides the application's logic. Line 21 creates a new **Queue** data structure on the unmanaged heap. Lines 26–39 initialize 10 **Shopper**s and their purchased items. Lines 42–48 shuffle the order of the **Shopper**s array and randomly set each shopper's selected products. Lines 51–57 fill the unmanaged **Queue** with each shopper's identifying number. Line 52 obtains a pinning pointer to a **Shopper**'s **number** member variable. The **Shopper** object sits on the managed heap; thus, any call to an unmanaged function requires pinning the entire object, preventing the garbage collector from moving the passed data member. Using keyword **__pin** on a pointer to any internal member of a managed class forces the garbage collector to ignore the entire outer object. Line 53 passes the pinned pointer to the unmanaged **Queue** class **enqueue** method. Note that the pinning pointer will fall out of scope on line 57, releasing the managed object back to the garbage collector. However, the unmanaged **Queue** class makes a copy of the passed data item before the **enqueue** method returns; it does not maintain any pointer to the managed heap and will not be affected if the original data item changes location. Lines 62–71 execute until the unmanaged **Queue** object is empty, displaying each purchased item and removing each customer from the line with **Queue** method **dequeue**. Line 74 cleans the unmanaged heap by deleting unmanaged object **groceryLine**.

24.4 Wrappers

A large element of managed and unmanaged interoperability is the construction of *wrapper classes*. Wrapper classes facilitate the use of managed objects in an unmanaged context and unmanaged objects in a managed context. Wrapper classes generally provide an interface into an object of a separate context. The wrapper embeds an object, or a pointer to an object, of a separate context inside a custom class and exposes the embedded object's methods. Wrappers are required to use a managed class in an unmanaged context and are a helpful aid to using an unmanaged class in a managed context.

24.4.1 Wrapping Managed Objects

The fundamental difficulty in accessing managed objects from unmanaged code is maintaining an accurate pointer into the managed heap from unmanaged code. Unmanaged code does not have pointers that are adjustable by the CLR; thus, it can only use a managed object that has been pinned in the heap, as shown in the previous example. However, pinning an object in the heap is not an optimal solution. The garbage collector is designed to work on an unfragmented heap, and it is considerably less efficient when the heap contains a pinned object. In addition, an unmanaged object cannot arbitrarily create and use an object in the managed heap because only a managed object can maintain a pinning pointer to another managed object.

Fortunately, Microsoft has included the __value class *GCHandle* that can maintain a pointer to an object in the managed heap, as well as providing a pinning pointer. The CLR can maintain its pointer to the managed heap, and an unmanaged class can create and use a **GCHandle**. (Because **GCHandle** is managed and is a sequentially ordered __value class, we discuss structure ordering in more detail in Section 24.5.2.) However, class **GCHandle** requires the programmer to allocate and free the handle to the managed object. In addition, it requires the managed object to be accessed and cast through its **Target** property. Note that a **GCHandle** can maintain a normal or pinned pointer to the object. A normal pointer cannot be resolved to an address, but allows the garbage collector to reposition the object. A pinning pointer can be resolved to an address, but locks the object in the managed heap, slowing the garbage collector.

To simplify the use of **GCHandle** in unmanaged code, Microsoft provides a smart wrapper around a **GCHandle** object—templated class *gcroot* (contained in header **gcroot.h**). Class **gcroot** handles object allocation and de-allocation as well as object resolution via the **GCHandle**.

Fig. 24.16 presents an application that uses **gcroot** to create a wrapper class accessible from an unmanaged function. The application allows the unmanaged function to fill a managed **ArrayList** with data.

```
1   // Fig. 24.16: gcroot.cpp
2   // Demonstrates wrapping a managed object in a __nogc
3   // class for use in unmanaged functions.
4
5   #include <gcroot.h>
6   #include <windows.h>
7   #include <cmath>
8   #include <iostream>
9
10  #using <mscorlib.dll>
11  #using <System.dll>
12
```

Fig. 24.16 gcroot class wrapper demonstration. (Part 1 of 3.)

```cpp
13    using std::cout;
14    using std::endl;
15
16    using namespace System;
17    using namespace System::Collections;
18
19    // wraps managed ArrayList object in __nogc class
20    __nogc class DoubleListWrapper
21    {
22    public:
23
24       // unmanaged pointer to managed value class
25       gcroot< ArrayList * > list;
26
27       // constructs new ArrayList
28       DoubleListWrapper()
29       {
30          list = new ArrayList();
31       } // end constructor
32
33       // adds double to list
34       void Add( double item )
35       {
36          list->Add( __box( item ) );
37       } // end method Add
38
39       // removes specified double from list
40       void Remove( double item )
41       {
42          list->Remove( __box( item ) );
43       } // end method Remove
44
45       // returns item as unmanaged type
46       double get_Item( int index )
47       {
48
49          //
50          return *dynamic_cast< __box double * >
51             ( list->Item[ index ] );
52       } // end method get_Item
53
54       // returns number of items in list
55       int get_Count()
56       {
57          return list->Count;
58       }; // end method get_Count
59
60       // sorts list
61       void Sort()
62       {
63          list->Sort();
64       } // end method Sort
65    }; // end class DoubleListWrapper
```

Fig. 24.16 gcroot class wrapper demonstration. (Part 2 of 3.)

```
66
67   #pragma unmanaged
68
69   // unmanaged function fills managed ArrayList via wrapper
70   void FillDoubleList( DoubleListWrapper wrapper )
71   {
72      wrapper.Add( 3.14159265358979 );
73      wrapper.Add( 2.71828182845905 );
74      wrapper.Add( 343.37 );
75      wrapper.Add( 9.81 );
76      wrapper.Add( 299792458 );
77   } // end function FillDoubleList
78
79   // unmanaged function prints values of ArrayList
80   void PrintDoubleList( DoubleListWrapper wrapper )
81   {
82      for ( int i = 0; i < wrapper.get_Count(); i++ )
83         cout << wrapper.get_Item( i ) << endl;
84   } // end function PrintDoubleList
85
86   #pragma managed
87
88   // demonstrates ArrayListWrapper in managed code
89   int main()
90   {
91      DoubleListWrapper wrapper;
92      FillDoubleList( wrapper );
93      wrapper.Sort();
94      PrintDoubleList( wrapper );
95
96      return 0;
97   } // end function main
```

```
2.71828
3.14159
9.81
343.37
2.99792e+008
```

Fig. 24.16 gcroot class wrapper demonstration. (Part 3 of 3.)

Class **DoubleListWrapper** (lines 20–65) provides a __nogc wrapper class for common functions of managed collection class **ArrayList**. Line 25 creates a gcroot object to store an **ArrayList**. In the class constructor (lines 28–31), the gcroot handle is set to a new instance of an **ArrayList**. Lines 34–64 simply wrap class **ArrayList** methods **Add**, **Remove** and **Sort** and the properties **Items** and **Count**.

Lines 67–84 represent an unmanaged block, and the compiler stores the contained functions in the assembly as embedded native code. Function **FillDoubleList** (lines 70–77) uses the __nogc class **DoubleListWrapper** to fill the **ArrayList** with well-known math and physics constants. Function **PrintDoubleList** (lines 80–84) accesses the **DoubleListWrapper** properties **Count** and **Item** to display the contents of the **ArrayList**.

Function **main** (lines 89–97) creates a **DoubleListWrapper** and uses each of the native functions through IJW.

24.4.2 Wrapping Unmanaged Objects

Why provide a managed wrapper around an unmanaged object? After all, IJW does an excellent job allowing managed C++ to use unmanaged classes. However, unmanaged code is not as readily accessible to other managed .NET languages, including C# and Visual Basic .NET. Managed wrappers provide memory management so the programmer does not have to worry whether an object was allocated on the managed or unmanaged heap.

Fig. 24.17 presents the header containing the declaration for managed class **Queue-Wrapper**, which embeds an unmanaged pointer to an unmanaged **Queue** object (Fig. 24.12) and provides access to its methods. In addition, it enables a managed object of any type to be stored in the unmanaged queue using native type **VARIANT**.

```
1   // Fig. 24.17: Queue.h
2   // Managed class definitions, queue wrapper and Shopper.
3
4   #pragma once
5
6   #include <oaidl.h>    // header for VARIANT type
7   #include "tqueue.h"
8
9   #using <mscorlib.dll>
10
11  using namespace System;
12  using namespace System::Runtime::InteropServices;
13
14  // store product enumeration
15  __value enum Products
16  {
17      MILK = 0,
18      EGGS = 1,
19      CHIPS = 2,
20      SODA = 3,
21      APPLES = 4,
22      GRAPES = 5
23  }; // end enum Products
24
25  // wraps unmanaged queue class in managed context
26  public __gc class QueueWrapper
27  {
28  public:
29      QueueWrapper(); // initialize underlying queue
30      void enqueue( Object * ); // adds item to underlying queue
31      Object *dequeue(); // removes item from underlying queue
32      ~QueueWrapper();    // destroy remaining items
33
34      // property IsEmpty
35      __property int get_IsEmpty()
36      {
37          return queue->isEmpty();
```

Fig. 24.17 QueueWrapper class definition. (Part 1 of 2.)

```
38        }
39
40    private:
41
42        // unmanaged int queue
43        Queue< VARIANT > __nogc *queue;
44    }; // end class QueueWrapper
45
46    // managed Shopper class maintains number for each shopper
47    public __gc class Shopper
48    {
49    public:
50        Shopper( int );
51        void CheckoutCustomer();
52
53        // property Number
54        __property int get_Number()
55        {
56           return number;
57        }
58
59        __property void set_Number( int value )
60        {
61           number = value;
62        }
63
64        // property Item
65        __property int get_Item( int index )
66        {
67           if ( index < 6 && index >= 0 )
68              return items[ index ];
69           else
70              return -1;
71        }
72
73        __property void set_Item( int index, int value )
74        {
75           items[ index ] = value;
76        }
77
78    private:
79        int number;
80        int items __gc[];
81    }; // end class Shopper
```

Fig. 24.17 QueueWrapper class definition. (Part 2 of 2.)

Class **QueueWrapper** (lines 26–39) contains an embedded **__nogc** pointer to an unmanaged **Queue** (line(lines 30–31), and wraps the **isEmpty** method (lines 35–38).

Fig. 24.18 provides the method definitions for class **QueueWrapper**. Notice that it must perform the conversions between the managed **Object** type and the native **VARIANT** type.

```cpp
1   // Fig. 24.18: Queue.cpp
2   // QueueWrapper and shopper method implementations.
3
4   #include "Queue.h"
5
6   // constructs new unmanaged queue object
7   QueueWrapper::QueueWrapper()
8   {
9      queue = new Queue< VARIANT >();
10  } // end method QueueWrapper
11
12  // adds item to underlying queue
13  void QueueWrapper::enqueue( Object *item )
14  {
15
16     // convert passed Object to native VARIANT type
17     VARIANT variantItem;
18     IntPtr variantPointer( &variantItem );
19     Marshal::GetNativeVariantForObject( item, variantPointer );
20     queue->enqueue( &variantItem );
21  } // end method enqueue
22
23  // removes item from underlying queue
24  Object *QueueWrapper::dequeue()
25  {
26
27     // convert returned VARIANT to Object
28     IntPtr variantPointer( &queue->dequeue() );
29
30     return Marshal::GetObjectForNativeVariant( variantPointer );
31  } // end method dequeue
32
33  // deletes unmanaged, dynamically allocated memory
34  QueueWrapper::~QueueWrapper()
35  {
36     delete queue;
37  } // end destructor
38
39  // display each customer purchase
40  void Shopper::CheckoutCustomer()
41  {
42
43     // enumeration instance
44     Products purchases;
45     Console::Write( String::Concat( S"Customer ",
46       number.ToString(), S" purchased: " ) );
47
48     for ( int i = 0; i < 6; i++ ) {
49
50        // display item name if customer purchased
51        if ( items[ i ] == 1 ) {
52           purchases = ( Products ) i;
53           Console::Write( __box( purchases ) );
```

Fig. 24.18 QueueWrapper class method definitions. (Part 1 of 2.)

```
54            Console::Write( S" " );
55         }
56      } // end for
57
58      Console::WriteLine( S"" );
59   } // end method CheckoutCustomer
60
61   Shopper::Shopper( int numberValue ) : number( numberValue )
62   {
63      items = new int __gc[ 6 ];
64   }
```

Fig. 24.18 QueueWrapper class method definitions. (Part 2 of 2.)

The class constructor (lines 7–10) simply creates a new underlying unmanaged **Queue** object. Method **enqueue** (lines 13–21) stores an **Object** in the unmanaged queue by storing it as a **VARIANT** type. Lines 17–18 create an **IntPtr** to a **VARIANT** variable. **static** method **GetNativeVariantForObject** of class **Marshal** (line 19) takes two arguments, an **Object** pointer and an **IntPtr** that points to a valid **VARIANT** type. Method **GetNativeVariantForObject** converts the **Object** instance into the appropriate **VARIANT** type. Line 20 **enqueue**s the created **VARIANT** object in the unmanaged **Queue** instance.

Method **dequeue** (lines 24–31) dequeues an item from the unmanaged **Queue** and converts and returns the native **VARIANT** into a managed **Object** instance. Line 28 constructs an **IntPtr** that points to the **VARIANT** returned by the unmanaged queue's dequeue method. Method **GetObjectForNativeVariant** (line 30) takes an **IntPtr** pointer to a **VARIANT** as an argument and returns a managed **Object** equivalent of the **VARIANT**'s data item. The class destructor (lines 34–37) deletes the allocated unmanaged queue from the unmanaged heap.

Common Programming Error 24.2

*The programmer cannot predict when the garbage collector calls the managed class destructor. Programmers should not rely on the garbage collector to release resources in a timely fashion. However, you may implement the **IDisposable** interface to provide deterministic resource management.*

Fig. 24.19 presents an application similar to Fig. 24.13 that demonstrates the **Queue-Wrapper** class. The application is identical to the pinning application; however, it does not require the deletion of the **Queue** object or creation of a pinning variable for the **enqueue**d data item.

```
1   // Fig. 24.19: Embedding.cpp
2   // Tests the embedded linked list.
3
4   #using <mscorlib.dll>
5
6   #include "Queue.h"
7
```

Fig. 24.19 QueueWrapper class test application. (Part 1 of 3.)

```
 8   using namespace System;
 9
10   // entry point for application
11   int main()
12   {
13
14       // create array of managed shoppers
15       Shopper *shoppers[] = new Shopper *[ 10 ];
16
17       // create queue wrapper
18       QueueWrapper *groceryLine = new QueueWrapper();
19
20       Random *random = new Random();
21
22       // initialize shopper array
23       for ( int i = 0; i < 10; i++ ) {
24          shoppers[ i ] = new Shopper( i );
25
26          // select random items
27          bool gotAnItem = false;
28
29          while ( !gotAnItem )
30             for ( int j = 0; j < 6; j++ ) {
31                if ( random->Next( 2 ) == 1 )
32                   shoppers[ i ]->Item[ j ] = 1;
33                   gotAnItem = true;
34             }
35       } // end for
36
37       // randomize shopper array
38       for ( int i = 0; i < 10; i++ ) {
39          Shopper *temporary = shoppers[ i ];
40
41          int index = random->Next( 10 );
42          shoppers[ i ] = shoppers[ index ];
43          shoppers[ index ] = temporary;
44       } // end for
45
46       // enqueue each shopper in grocery line
47       for ( int i = 0; i < 10; i++ ) {
48          groceryLine->enqueue( __box( shoppers[ i ]->Number ) );
49          Console::WriteLine( String::Concat( S"Shopper number ",
50             shoppers[ i ]->Number.ToString(),
51             S" has entered the line." ) );
52       }
53
54       int counter = 0;
55
56       // remove each shopper from grocery line
57       while ( !groceryLine->IsEmpty ) {
58
59          // unbox Object
60          int number = *dynamic_cast< __box int * >(
```

Fig. 24.19 QueueWrapper class test application. (Part 2 of 3.)

```
61              groceryLine->dequeue() );
62
63          // service customer
64          shoppers[ counter ]->CheckoutCustomer();
65          Console::WriteLine( String::Concat( S"Shopper number ",
66              number.ToString(), S" has been serviced.\n" ) );
67
68          counter++;
69      } // end while
70
71      return 0;
72  } // end function main
```

```
Shopper number 7 has entered the line.
Shopper number 3 has entered the line.
Shopper number 8 has entered the line.
Shopper number 4 has entered the line.
Shopper number 6 has entered the line.
Shopper number 9 has entered the line.
Shopper number 5 has entered the line.
Shopper number 2 has entered the line.
Shopper number 0 has entered the line.
Shopper number 1 has entered the line.
Customer 7 purchased: MILK EGGS GRAPES
Shopper number 7 has been serviced.

Customer 3 purchased: CHIPS SODA GRAPES
Shopper number 3 has been serviced.

Customer 8 purchased: MILK EGGS
Shopper number 8 has been serviced.

Customer 4 purchased: CHIPS GRAPES
Shopper number 4 has been serviced.

Customer 6 purchased: MILK EGGS
Shopper number 6 has been serviced.

Customer 9 purchased: MILK SODA APPLES
Shopper number 9 has been serviced.

Customer 5 purchased: SODA GRAPES
Shopper number 5 has been serviced.

Customer 2 purchased: MILK SODA
Shopper number 2 has been serviced.

Customer 0 purchased: MILK SODA
Shopper number 0 has been serviced.

Customer 1 purchased: MILK EGGS CHIPS SODA
Shopper number 1 has been serviced.
```

Fig. 24.19 QueueWrapper class test application. (Part 3 of 3.)

24.5 Platform Invoke

Platform Invoke (or *PInvoke*) is a service that allows managed applications to easily call and marshal data contained in native DLLs. The Platform Invoke service is a critical feature that is primarily used to access Win32 API functions as managed functions or **static** members of a managed class. PInvoke handles loading the library, making the function call and data type marshaling.

So what advantages does PInvoke provide over calling native DLL functions via IJW? PInvoke provides a simpler and more powerful layer between managed and unmanaged code. To use a native library via IJW, the developer must explicitly load the library and provide any non-default data marshaling with application code as shown in Fig. 24.8–Fig. 24.11. Alternatively, PInvoke loads the library at the first DLL method invocation and uses attributes to provide correct non-default data marshaling and calling convention, without any additional application code. In addition, native DLL function calls can be placed as **static** methods in managed classes or namespaces to provide an extra level of organization over global functions. PInvoke also allows a native DLL function to be mapped to a managed method with a different name to prevent naming conflicts. However, while PInvoke provides more functionality than IJW, it generally requires more work on the part of the runtime and is slower.

24.5.1 DllImport Attribute

The functionality of Platform Invoke is accessed through attribute *DllImport* contained in namespace **System::Runtime::InteropServices**. Attribute **DllImport** modifies a function or **static** method declaration and designates that the modified item is, in fact, a proxy to a native DLL function. Attribute **DllImport** always specifies the native library name and may customize the native call via optional parameters.

Fig. 24.20 demonstrates attribute **DllImport** in a managed class. The example uses the attribute to call the Win32 API functions **PlaySound**, **MessageBoxW** and **SearchPath**. Notice how PInvoke eliminates the need to load the libraries explicitly and to marshal the strings in the application code as in the example shown in Fig. 24.8–Fig. 24.11.

Attribute **DllImport** (line 30) takes a required unnamed parameter designating the DLL name, in this case **winmm.dll**, and one of several optional parameters that customize the behavior of the native call. Fig. 24.21 shows the complete listing of **DllImport** attribute parameters.

Method **PlaySound** (line 31) maps to the Win32 function of the same name. PInvoke loads the **winmm.dll** library and marshals the first **String** class parameter as an ANSI string.

Method **Win32MessageBox** (lines 35–37) maps to the Win32 function **MessageBoxW**, in **user32.dll** using the **DllImport** parameter **EntryPoint**. Attribute **DllImport** for this method does not specify a **CharSet** value and defaults to **Ansi**. However, function **MessageBoxW** expects a Unicode® string. If we do not provide custom marshaling, the **MessageBox** displays the string incorrectly. Lines 36–37 use attribute **MarshalAs** to specify the exact marshaling required for the string parameter. Attribute *MarshalAs*, contained in the **System::Runtime::InteropServices** namespace, takes a single unnamed parameter from the **UnmanagedType** enumeration. Platform Invoke attempts to convert the attributed parameter at runtime to the **Unmanaged Type** item specified as parameter **MarshalAs**.

```
1    // Fig. 24.20: SoundPlayer.h
2    // Class definition for SoundPlayer.
3
4    #pragma once
5
6    #include <windows.h>
7
8    // required libraries
9    #using <mscorlib.dll>
10   #using <System.dll>
11   #using <System.Windows.Forms.dll>
12   #using <System.drawing.dll>
13
14   // required namespaces
15   using namespace System;
16   using namespace System::Text;
17   using namespace System::Drawing;
18   using namespace System::Windows::Forms;
19   using namespace System::Runtime::InteropServices;
20
21   // inherits from Form, plays user selected wav file
22   public __gc class SoundPlayer : public Form
23   {
24   public:
25      SoundPlayer();
26
27   private:
28
29      // maps function to PlaySound function in winmm.dll
30      [ DllImport( "winmm.dll", CharSet=Ansi ) ]
31      static bool PlaySound( String *, void *, int );
32
33      // maps function to MessageBoxW function in user32.dll
34      [ DllImport( "user32.dll", EntryPoint="MessageBoxW" ) ]
35      static unsigned int Win32MessageBox( int,
36         [ MarshalAs( UnmanagedType::LPWStr ) ] String *,
37         [ MarshalAs( UnmanagedType::LPWStr ) ] String *, int );
38
39      // maps method to SearchPath function in Kernel32.dll
40      [ DllImport( "kernel32.dll", SetLastError=true,
41         CharSet=Ansi ) ]
42      static unsigned int SearchPath(
43         String *, String *, String *, unsigned int,
44         StringBuilder *, StringBuilder ** );
45
46      // GUI components
47      ComboBox *soundList;
48      Label *ChooseLabel;
49      Button *PlayButton;
50      System::ComponentModel::Container *components;
51      void InitializeComponent();
52
53      // click event handler
```

Fig. 24.20 SoundPlayer class demonstrating attribute DllImport. (Part 1 of 2.)

```
54        void PlayButton_Click( Object *, EventArgs * );
55   }; // end class SoundPlayer
```

Fig. 24.20 `SoundPlayer` class demonstrating attribute `DllImport`. (Part 2 of 2.)

DllImport Parameter	Description
`CallingConvention`	Sets the calling convention for the imported function. The default value is `StdCall`; alternate values include `Cdecl` and `ThisCall`. A function's calling convention determines how the compiler manages the stack and the order of arguments.
`CharSet`	Determines the default character set used for `String` class marshaling; valid values are `Unicode`, `Ansi` and `Auto`. The `CharSet` parameter also affects function `EntryPoint` name resolution. If `CharSet` is `Ansi` and PInvoke cannot find the function specified in `EntryPoint`, PInvoke will add an `'A'` to the entry point string and search again. In contrast, if `CharSet` is `Unicode`, PInvoke appends a `'W'` character to the `EntryPoint` string and searches the library. If it cannot find such a function, it then searches for the original `EntryPoint`. The default value is `Ansi`.
`EntryPoint`	A string that designates the name of the DLL function to be called. The default value is the name of the managed proxy method.
`ExactSpelling`	A boolean value that prevents or allows the `CharSet` parameter from appending an `'A'` or `'W'` character to the end of the `EntryPoint` string. The default value is `false`.
`PreserveSig`	A boolean value that specifies that the designated method signature should not be changed. When this parameter is false, PInvoke converts the specified method signature into a `HRESULT` signature that uses [`out`, `retval`] for a return value. The default value is `true`.
`SetLastError`	A boolean value that indicates whether the called function may call Win32 function `SetLastError`. If this value is set to true, PInvoke calls function `GetLastError` before returning to managed code. The return value of `GetLastError` is stored and is accessible using static method `GetLastWin32Error` of class `Marshal`.

Fig. 24.21 `DllImport` attribute parameters and descriptions.

Managed data types can be divided into two groups—*blittable types* and *non-blittable types*. Blittable types are the data types with identical representations on the managed and native platforms. These types do not need to be explicitly marshalled. The default marshaling for blittable types is always correct because they can be directly copied to unmanaged code. In contrast, managed data types that can map to more than one native type are called non-blittable types. The default marshaling for non-blittable types may incorrectly convert the argument for the native function. Fig. 24.22 lists some non-blittable types and their corresponding `UnmanagedType`s.

Non-Blittable Type	UnmanagedType Member	Description
Array	LPArray	Converts from a managed array to a C-Style array.
Array	SafeArray	Converts from managed array to COM-Style **SAFEARRAY** type.
bool	Bool	Converts from **bool** to four-byte boolean.
bool	U1	Converts from managed **bool** to single-byte C-Style **bool**.
bool	VariantBool	Converts from managed bool to two-byte COM-Style **BOOL**.
Object	IDispatch	Converts from **Object** to COM **IDispatch** interface.
Object	Interface	Converts from **Object** to COM **IDispatch** interface if possible, otherwise converts to **IUnknown** interface.
Object	IUnknown	Converts from **Object** to COM **IUnknown** interface.
Object	Struct	Converts from **Object** to COM-Style **VARIANT**.
String	AnsiBStr	Converts from **String** to COM-Style ANSI **BSTR**.
String	BStr	Converts from **String** to COM-Style Unicode® **BSTR**.
String	LPStr	Converts from **String** to ANSI character string.
String	LPTStr	Converts from **String** to platform native string encoding (ANSI or Unicode®).
String	LPWStr	Converts from **String** to null-terminated Unicode® character array.
String	TBStr	Converts from **String** to COM-Style **BSTR** using platform native string encoding (ANSI or Unicode®).

Fig. 24.22 Some **UnmanagedType** enumeration members.

Method **SearchPath** (lines 42–44 of Fig. 24.20) maps to the Win32 API function of the same name (found in **kernel32.dll**) that searches a directory path for a designated filename and stores the full file path and filename in a string buffer. The **DllImport** attribute for this method allows subsequent use of **Marshal::GetLastWin32Error**, and that the method should use the ANSI version of function **SearchPath**. Parameter **CharSet** (line 41) defines the default marshaling for the **String** arguments as null-terminated ANSI character strings. The final two arguments to the native **SearchPath** function are **out** parameters. The function expects to receive a pointer to an allocated buffer of memory that it fills with the full file path and filename. Class **String** does not provide the functionality to allocate a block of memory that can be filled later, class **String** objects are immutable. They cannot be changed once allocated. To preserve **String** arguments when they are passed to native functions, Platform Invoke makes a copy of the string before sending the value to the native function; any changes made by the native function will not be reflected in the managed **String** object. The solution to the problem is to use class **StringBuilder**, which can be constructed to an explicit buffer size and is not immutable.

Fig. 24.23 presents the **SoundPlayer** method definitions. This file is identical to Fig. 24.9 except for method **PlayButton_Click**.

```cpp
1   // Fig. 24.23: SoundPlayer.cpp
2   // Method definitions for SoundPlayer application.
3
4   #include "SoundPlayer.h"
5
6   // constructor
7   SoundPlayer::SoundPlayer()
8   {
9       components = NULL;
10      InitializeComponent();
11  } // end constructor
12
13  // initialize GUI components
14  void SoundPlayer::InitializeComponent()
15  {
16
17      // create components and begin layout
18      soundList = new ComboBox();
19      ChooseLabel = new Label();
20      PlayButton = new Button();
21      SuspendLayout();
22
23      // populate list with available sounds
24      String *sounds[] = { S"applause.wav", S"collision.wav",
25          S"energy.wav", S"toneup.wav", S"tonedown.wav" };
26      soundList->Items->AddRange( sounds );
27
28      // initialize soundList ComboBox
29      soundList->Location = Point( 16, 32 );
30      soundList->Name = S"soundList";
31      soundList->Size = Drawing::Size( 216, 21 );
32      soundList->TabIndex = 0;
33
34      // label prompting user to select file
35      ChooseLabel->Location = Point( 16, 8 );
36      ChooseLabel->Name = S"ChooseLabel";
37      ChooseLabel->Size = Drawing::Size( 100, 16 );
38      ChooseLabel->TabIndex = 1;
39      ChooseLabel->Text = S"Choose A Sound";
40
```

Fig. 24.23 SoundPlayer class method definitions using **PInvoke**. (Part 1 of 3.)

```
41      // PlayButton plays selected sound file when pressed
42      PlayButton->Location = Point( 16, 72 );
43      PlayButton->Name = S"PlayButton";
44      PlayButton->Size = Drawing::Size( 40, 23 );
45      PlayButton->TabIndex = 2;
46      PlayButton->Text = S"Play";
47      PlayButton->Click +=
48         new System::EventHandler( this, this->PlayButton_Click );
49
50      // setup form variables
51      AutoScaleBaseSize = Drawing::Size( 5, 13 );
52      ClientSize = Drawing::Size( 240, 101 );
53      Name = S"SoundPlayer";
54      Text = S"Sound Player";
55
56      // add controls
57      Control *controls[] = { PlayButton, ChooseLabel, soundList };
58
59      Controls->AddRange( controls );
60
61      // apply layout changes
62      ResumeLayout();
63  } // end method InitializeComponent
64
65  // PlayButton click event handler
66  void SoundPlayer::PlayButton_Click( Object *sender,
67      EventArgs *event )
68  {
69
70      // obtain selected string from soundList
71      String *sound = this->soundList->Text;
72
73      // ensure song was selected
74      if ( sound != NULL && sound->Length > 0 ) {
75         StringBuilder *filePath = new StringBuilder( _MAX_PATH );
76         StringBuilder *foundFileName;
77
78         unsigned int result = this->SearchPath( NULL, sound, NULL,
79            _MAX_PATH, filePath, &foundFileName );
80
81         // search for selected file name
82         if ( result == 0 )
83
84            // display error number if function returns error
85            Win32MessageBox( 0, String::Concat(
86               S"Error while searching for file,",
87               S" windows returned error number: ",
88               Marshal::GetLastWin32Error().ToString() ),
89               S"Error", 0 );
90         else if ( result > _MAX_PATH )
91
92            // display required buffer size
93            Win32MessageBox( 0, String::Concat(
```

Fig. 24.23 SoundPlayer class method definitions using PInvoke. (Part 2 of 3.)

```
94                        S"Error while searching for file, ",
95                        S"insufficient buffer space for file path." ),
96                        S"Error", 0 );
97            else {
98
99                // display file path
100               Win32MessageBox( 0, String::Concat( 0,
101                   S"Playing sound located at ",
102                   filePath->ToString() ), S"Sound Location", 0 );
103
104               // play sound
105               this->PlaySound( sound, NULL, SND_ASYNC | SND_FILENAME );
106           }
107       } // end if
108       else // call PInvoke Win32 MessageBox function
109           Win32MessageBox( 0,
110               S"Please Select a wav file from the list", S"Error", 0 );
111 } // end method PlayButton_Click
```

Fig. 24.23 `SoundPlayer` class method definitions using `PInvoke`. (Part 3 of 3.)

Method **PlayButton_Click** (lines 66–111) retrieves the current text from the Form's **ComboBox** and attempts to locate the specified **.wav** file. If it finds the file, it plays the sound. Line 71 retrieves the current text from the combo box and stores the value in **sound**. If **sound** is not empty, line 75 constructs a new **StringBuilder** object with a buffer size of **_MAX_PATH** characters. The **_MAX_PATH** macro defines the maximum size of the systems file path length. Lines 78–79 call Platform Invoke proxy method **SearchPath** using the default search path and **sound** as the filename. If **SearchPath** returns **0**, the function encountered an error, and lines 85–89 display an error number using method **GetLastWin32Error** of class **Marshal**. If **SearchPath** returned a value larger than **_MAX_PATH**, the function could not fit the path string inside the designated buffer, lines 93–96 display an error message. If **SearchPath** found the designated file, lines 100–105 display a message box listing the file location and play the sound using function **PlaySound**.

Fig. 24.24 presents the application entry point for the sound-player application. The main method simply runs a new instance of class **SoundPlayer**.

```
1  // Fig. 24.24: PInvoke.cpp
2  // Runs soundPlayer application.
3
4  #include "SoundPlayer.h"
5
6  #using <mscorlib.dll>
7
8  // entry point for application
9  int __stdcall WinMain( HINSTANCE thisInstance,
10     HINSTANCE oldInstance, LPSTR arguments, int showCommand )
11 {
12    Application::Run( new SoundPlayer() );
13
14    return 0;
15 } // end function WinMain
```

Fig. 24.24 `PInvoke` application entry point. (Part 1 of 2.)

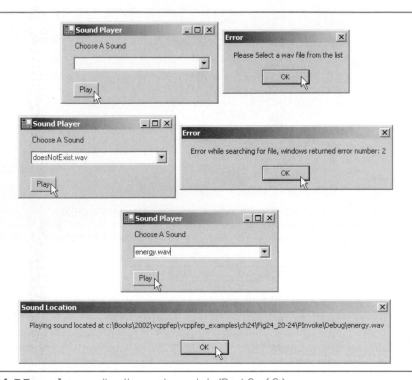

Fig. 24.24 `PInvoke` application entry point. (Part 2 of 2.)

24.5.2 Callbacks and Structures

A large number of functions in the Win32 API use structures as a method of passing arguments and *callbacks* as a method of event notification. Fortunately, PInvoke provides services that allow managed callback functions and structure marshaling.

Callbacks are based on function pointers—a callback-handler function is registered with a callback-notification function by a function pointer. However, managed code does not support direct function pointers, but managed code does have delegates. Recall that delegates are classes declared using __**delegate** keywords that act as intermediaries for methods. Platform Invoke allows the use of __**delegate**s as callback function pointers.

The next example demonstrates using PInvoke to register a managed callback handler and demonstrates how to construct and pass a managed object as an unmanaged structure. The example Fig. 24.25 presents the **ChooserOptions __value** type and the **ColorChooser** form class declaration.

```
1   // Fig. 24.25: ColorChooser.h
2   // Contains Class and Structure definitions for
3   // ColorChooser application.
4
5   #pragma once
6
```

Fig. 24.25 `ColorChooser` class declaration demonstrates PInvoke, structures and delegates. (Part 1 of 3.)

```
 7   #include <tchar.h>
 8   #include <time.h>
 9   #include <windows.h>
10
11   #using <mscorlib.dll>
12   #using <system.dll>
13   #using <system.windows.forms.dll>
14   #using <system.drawing.dll>
15
16   using namespace System;
17   using namespace System::Windows::Forms;
18   using namespace System::Drawing;
19   using namespace System::Runtime::InteropServices;
20
21   // undefine unmanaged messagebox macro
22   #undef MessageBox
23
24   // delegate, used as CALLBACK method
25   __delegate UINT ColorCallback( IntPtr, UINT, WPARAM, LPARAM );
26
27   // managed ChooserOptions structure, duplicate of
28   // unmanaged structure with same name
29   [ StructLayout( LayoutKind::Sequential ) ]
30   __value class ChooserOptions
31   {
32   public:
33      DWORD structureSize;    // size, in bytes of structure
34      IntPtr ownerHandle;      // handle to owner window
35      IntPtr hInstance;        // handle to template window
36      COLORREF resultColor;   // contains user selected color
37      COLORREF *customColors;// stores array of custom colors
38      DWORD flags;             // stores Color Dialog options
39      LPARAM customData;       // stores custom data for callback
40      ColorCallback *functionHook; // stores callback delegate
41      LPCTSTR templateName;   // stores name of template window
42   }; // end class ChooserOptions
43
44   // wrapper class for native ChooseColor dialog
45   public __gc class ColorChooser
46   {
47   public:
48
49      // creates and displays ChooseColor dialog
50      static Color PickColor( IntPtr, ColorCallback * );
51
52   private:
53
54      // do not allow instances of this class
55      ColorChooser() { }
56
```

Fig. 24.25 ColorChooser class declaration demonstrates PInvoke, structures and delegates. (Part 2 of 3.)

```
57       // PInvoke for Win32 common dialog ChooseColor function
58       [ DllImport( "comdlg32.dll" ) ]
59       static bool ChooseColor( ChooserOptions * );
60    }; // end class ColorChooser
61
62    // displays single button that uses ColorChooser
63    // wrapper class to allow user to change form background color
64    public __gc class Colors : public Form
65    {
66    public:
67
68       // constructor initializes GUI
69       Colors()
70       {
71          components = NULL;
72          InitializeComponents();
73       } // end constructor
74
75       // LoadTime property allows ColorChooser function
76       // to display native dialog loading time
77       __property void set_LoadTime( int value )
78       {
79          loadTime = value;
80
81          // display forms load time
82          MessageBox::Show( String::Concat( "Form loaded in ",
83             loadTime.ToString(), " milliseconds."), "Info",
84             MessageBoxButtons::OK, MessageBoxIcon::Information );
85       } // end property set_LoadTime
86
87    protected:
88
89       // delegate Chooser dialog message handler method
90       UINT MessageHandler( IntPtr, UINT, WPARAM, LPARAM );
91
92       // initialize GUI components
93       void InitializeComponents();
94
95       // ColorButton event handler
96       void ColorButton_Click( Object *, EventArgs * );
97
98    private:
99
100      // GUI button
101      Button *ColorButton;
102      System::ComponentModel::Container *components;
103
104      // dialog open time storage variable
105      int loadTime;
106   }; // end class Colors
```

Fig. 24.25 ColorChooser class declaration demonstrates PInvoke, structures and delegates. (Part 3 of 3.)

Line 9 includes **windows.h**, this will allow us to use the Windows macros for basic types and constants. Line 22 undefines the **MessageBox** macro, we must undefine the macro to use the managed **MessageBox** class. Undefining the macro prevents a naming collision between the unmanaged macro and the managed **MessageBox** class name. Line 25 declares delegate **ColorCallback**, with an identical signature to callback function **CCHookProc** (defined in the platform SDK), that we use as our callback function pointer.

Lines 29–42 define **__value** class **ChooserOptions**, created as a managed duplicate of the native structure **COLORCHOOSER**. The primary distinction between native **struct**s and managed **__value** classes is the layout of the data members. A native **struct**'s data members are laid out in memory sequentially, and many native functions manipulate structures based upon their size and layout. Managed **__value** classes are inappropriate for use as native structures, because they make no promise of sequential layout. However, attribute **StructLayout** (line 39) allows the programmer to specify the exact internal layout of the structure when it is exported to native code. Attribute **StructLayout** takes an unnamed parameter from the **LayoutKind** enumeration. Possible values are **Auto**, **Explicit** and **Sequential**. **Auto StructLayout** provides no guarantees of the structures layout. **Explicit** layout allows the programmer to define the exact byte layout of each data member. **Sequential** layout places each data member sequentially in memory in the order which they are declared.

Portability Tip 24.1

*Be careful when using **StructLayout** on code that should be portable to 64-bit architectures. Depending on how the structure layout members are referenced, you may need to align them on 8-byte boundaries using **StructLayout::Explicit** to avoid runtime alignment faults.*

Class **ColorChooser** (lines 45–60) wraps the native **ChooseColor** method, it contains a single **static** method **PickColor**, which calls the native **ChooseColor** method using a default set of arguments and hooks the passed delegate as a callback handler for the **ChooseColor** dialog.

Class **Colors** (lines 64–106) tests the **ColorChooser** class. Lines 77–85 declare property **set_LoadTime**, which displays the time in milliseconds that elapses before the native dialog is initialized. Method **MessageHandler** (line 90) is assigned to delegate **ColorCallback** as the callback message handler for the native **ChooseColor** dialog's windows message queue. Fig. 24.26 presents the method definitions for the classes in Fig. 24.25.

```cpp
1   // Fig. 24.26: ColorChooser.cpp
2   // Method definitions for classes defined in
3   // ColorChooser.h.
4
5   #include "ColorChooser.h"
6
7   // displays Win32 Common dialog ChooseColor
8   Color ColorChooser::PickColor( IntPtr windowHandle,
9      ColorCallback *delegate )
10  {
11
```

Fig. 24.26 **ColorChooser** and **Colors** class method definitions. (Part 1 of 4.)

```
12        // custom colors
13        COLORREF customColors[ 16 ];
14
15        // initialize custom color array to white
16        for ( int i = 0; i < 16; i++ )
17           customColors[ i ] = 0xFFFFFF;
18
19        // colorProperty structure, stores properties and
20        // contains color selected in dialog
21        ChooserOptions colorProperties;
22
23        // marshal SizeOf obtains size, in bytes of boxed value
24        colorProperties.structureSize =
25           Marshal::SizeOf( __box( colorProperties ) );
26
27        // sets structure default color to blue
28        colorProperties.resultColor = 0xFF0000;
29
30        // initialize dialog's custom colors to black
31        colorProperties.customColors = customColors;
32
33        // request ColorChooser box with fully extended custom
34        // color selector, callback message handler and initialized
35        // default value
36        colorProperties.flags = CC_FULLOPEN | CC_ENABLEHOOK |
37           CC_RGBINIT;
38
39        // create delegate to MessageHandler function to handle window
40        // messages
41        if ( delegate != NULL )
42           colorProperties.functionHook = delegate;
43
44        // if user supplied handler value, set specified handle
45        // as dialog owner, and store window handle as custom data
46        if ( windowHandle != NULL )
47           colorProperties.ownerHandle = windowHandle;
48
49        // store current time in milliseconds
50        colorProperties.customData =
51           DateTime::get_Now().get_Millisecond();
52
53        // call native ChooseColor function with ChooserOptions structure
54        if ( ChooseColor( &colorProperties ) )
55
56           // if user selects color and presses OK, convert returned
57           // value to .NET color structure
58           return ColorTranslator::FromWin32(
59              colorProperties.resultColor );
60
61        else
62           return Color::Empty; // return empty color
63     } // end method PickColor
64
```

Fig. 24.26 ColorChooser and Colors class method definitions. (Part 2 of 4.)

```
65    // managed delegate acts as Windows CALLBACK message hander
66    UINT Colors::MessageHandler( IntPtr windowHandle,
67       UINT message, WPARAM wParam, LPARAM lParam )
68    {
69
70       // check for dialog initialization
71       if ( message == WM_INITDIALOG && lParam != NULL ) {
72          IntPtr unmanagedChooseColor( lParam );
73
74          // obtain current system time in milliseconds
75          int currentTime = DateTime::get_Now().get_Millisecond();
76
77          // read customData member from unmanaged memory
78             customData = Marshal::ReadInt32( unmanagedChooseColor,
79             Marshal::OffsetOf( Type::GetType( S"ChooserOptions" ),
80             "customData" ).ToInt32() );
81
82          // set load time property in Colors form
83             LoadTime = currentTime - customData;
84       } // end if
85
86       return 0;
87    } // end delegate method MessageHandler
88
89    // colors form GUI code
90    void Colors::InitializeComponents()
91    {
92
93       // create button and chooser dialog
94       ColorButton = new Button();
95
96       SuspendLayout();
97
98       // initialize button properties
99       ColorButton->Location = Point( 20,20 );
100      ColorButton->Size = Drawing::Size( 200, 50 );
101      ColorButton->Text = S"Choose A Color";
102      ColorButton->Click += new EventHandler( this,
103         this->ColorButton_Click );
104
105      // initialize form properties
106      AutoScaleBaseSize = Drawing::Size( 5, 13 );
107      ClientSize = Drawing::Size( 240, 101 );
108      Name = S"Colors";
109      Text = S"Color Chooser";
110      Controls->Add( ColorButton );
111
112      ResumeLayout( false );
113   } // end method InitializeComponents
114
115   // ColorButton click event handler, displays ColorChooser and
116   // displays time taken to select color
117   void Colors::ColorButton_Click( Object *sender,
```

Fig. 24.26 ColorChooser and Colors class method definitions. (Part 3 of 4.)

```
118       EventArgs *event )
119   {
120
121       // pick color and store as background
122       BackColor = ColorChooser::PickColor( this->Handle,
123          new ColorCallback( this, MessageHandler ) );
124
125       // refresh form
126       Invalidate();
127   }; // end method ColorButton_Click
```

Fig. 24.26 `ColorChooser` and `Colors` class method definitions. (Part 4 of 4.)

Method **PickColor** (lines 8–63) builds a **ChooserOptions** structure, calls the native **ChooseColor** function and converts the selected color from an unmanaged Win32 format to a managed **Color** object. Lines 13–17 construct and initialize an array of 16 **COLORREFS** to white, the array used to specify the initial color of the 16 custom color boxes at the bottom of the color dialog. Lines 21–37 create a **ChooserOptions** structure and initialize its default color, custom color array, option flags and size variable. Many Win32 API structures require the size of the structure as one of the parameters. **static** method *SizeOf* of class **Marshal** determines the size in bytes of the designated structure. Lines 41–42 attach the delegate argument to the **functionHook** member of the **ChooserOptions** structure. Platform Invoke handles the differences between the __delegate and a true function pointer at runtime. Thus, the programmer does not need to make the distinction. Lines 50–51 set the **customData** member of the **ChooserOptions** object to the current time, in milliseconds. The **customData** member is sent to the **ColorCallback** with the **WM_INITDIALOG** message. We store the time to determine the time, in milliseconds, that it takes to load the native dialog. Line 54 calls the native function with a reference to the **ChooserOptions** structure, this will create and display the dialog. If the user chooses a color and clicks **OK**, the function stores the color in the Win32 color format in the **resultColor** member of the **ChooserOptions** structure. **static** method *FromWin32* of class **ColorTranslator** converts the Win32 color to a managed **Color** structure (lines 58–59).

Method **MessageHandler** (lines 66–87) implements the delegate method signature and is designed to process the **ColorDialog**'s window message queue. When **MessageHandler** receives the **WM_INITDIALOG** message, the **LPARAM** argument contains the location, in unmanaged memory, of the **ChooserOptions** structure used to initialize the **ColorDialog**. Line 72 creates a managed **IntPtr** that points to the unmanaged memory location. Lines 78–80 copy the **customData** member from the unmanaged memory location to a managed **int**. Static method **ReadInt32** of class **Marshal** reads a 32-bit integer from an unmanaged memory location into a managed **int**. The selected **ReadInt32** overload takes an **IntPtr** to unmanaged memory and an **int** that specifies the reading offset. We obtain the correct offset value with a call to **static** method **OffsetOf**, which takes a **Type** and a **String *** name of a data member and returns the number byte offset of the data member argument. Line 83 determines the difference between the time stored in **customData** and **currentTime** and sets value of the **LoadTime** property. Fig. 24.27 presents the **Colors** application entry point.

```
1   // Fig. 24.27: PInvokeStructCallback.cpp
2   // Application entry point for ColorChooser.
3
4   #include "ColorChooser.h"
5
6   #using <mscorlib.dll>
7
8   // runs Colors form
9   int __stdcall WinMain( HINSTANCE thisInstance,
10      HINSTANCE oldInstance, LPSTR arguments, int showCommand )
11  {
12      Application::Run( new Colors() );
13
14      return 0;
15  } // end function WinMain
```

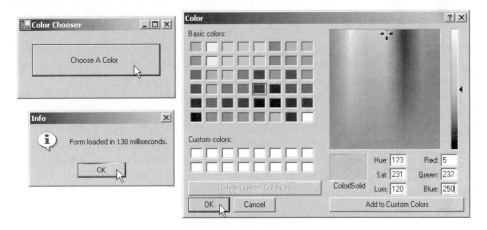

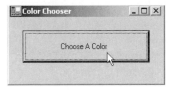

Fig. 24.27 `Colors` application entry point.

This chapter demonstrated managed and unmanaged interoperability using IJW for same-application marshaling and Platform Invoke for system libraries. Chapter 25 explores the second essential area of .NET interoperability services—COM Interop. The COM Interop services enable managed applications to use COM objects, expanding .NET to harness ActiveX, ATL and MFC. In addition, COM Interop allows COM-aware software to use .NET components as COM objects.

24.6 Summary

Visual C++ .NET allows side-by-side execution of managed and unmanaged code within an application. This is possible due to the separation of execution into a managed and unmanaged context and managing all communication between the contexts. A large part of the managed communication is the conversion (or marshaling) between native and .NET data types. The interoperability features of Visual C++ .NET may be split into three technologies—the It Just Works (IJW) compiler feature, the Platform Invoke Services and COM Interop Services.

A primary goal of the Visual C++ .NET compiler team was ensuring that all existing C++ code could be compiled into MSIL without modification. This requirement was dubbed It Just Works (IJW). Most existing C++ code compiles into MSIL without errors or warnings, testifying to the large degree of success in IJW development. However, some code, such as inline assembly or functions with a variable number of arguments, cannot be compiled into MSIL.

IJW will not compile any unmanaged classes as managed classes. IJW limitations prohibit unmanaged classes from inheriting, or being inherited by, a managed class.

When IJW converts most functions and methods to MSIL, the converted code gains access to the FCL and managed runtime features. Unmanaged classes may contain managed methods, but must still be dynamically created on the unmanaged heap, thus requiring explicit memory management. IJW makes code .NET aware; that is, the converted methods and functions can recognize and use .NET data types, and the unmanaged classes can create certain managed **value** types as data members,

IJW is unable to perform perfect data marshaling between managed objects from the managed heap and native types. The most notable instance where this becomes a problem is in the case of the **String** object. **String** objects consist of two-byte characters, while many native functions require single-byte ANSI character strings. Fortunately, the **Marshal** class contains a large number of methods to assist in **String**, structure and COM interoperability issues.

An application that combines managed and unmanaged code uses a heap space that is logically divided into a managed heap and an unmanaged heap. While the heaps share a physical address space, the fundamental differences in managed and unmanaged code necessitate separate heaps.

The unmanaged heap stores dynamically allocated memory. It is simply a large block of free memory that can store any type of data. The managed heap stores all managed objects, with the exception of __**value** classes. Managed object cannot be created on the application's stack. The CLR runs in the managed heap and provides a set of services to the contained objects.

Microsoft introduced pinning pointers into MC++ to "lock" an object on the managed heap into a static memory location. Keyword __**pin** declares a pinning pointer; any object pointed to by a pinning pointer is considered "pinned."

Wrapper classes facilitate the use of managed objects in an unmanaged context and unmanaged objects in a managed context. Wrapper classes generally provide an interface into an object of a separate context by embedding an object, or a pointer to an object, of a separate context inside a custom class and exposing the embedded object's methods.

The fundamental difficulty in accessing managed objects from unmanaged code is maintaining an accurate pointer into the managed heap from unmanaged or native code. Microsoft provides the __**value** class **GCHandle** that can maintain a pointer to an object in the managed heap, as well as provide a pinning pointer. Because **GCHandle** is managed and is a **value** class, the CLR can maintain its pointer to the managed heap and a __**nogc** class can create and use a **GCHandle**. Microsoft provides templated class **gcroot** (contained in header **gcroot.h**) as a smart wrapper around a **GCHandle** object. Class **gcroot** handles object allocation and de-allocation as well as object resolution via the **GCHandle**.

Providing a managed C++ wrapper to an unmanaged class allows other .NET languages to use the unmanaged class and removes the need to manage the unmanaged memory explicitly.

Platform Invoke (or PInvoke) is a service that allows managed applications to easily call and marshal data contained in native DLLs. The Platform Invoke service is a critical feature that is primarily used to access Win32 API functions as managed functions or static members of a managed class. PInvoke handles loading the library, making the function call and data type marshaling. The functionality of Platform Invoke is accessed through the **DllImport** attribute contained in the **System::Runtime::InteropServices** namespace. Attribute **DllImport** modifies a function or static method declaration and designates that the modified item is, in fact, a proxy stub to a native DLL function. The **DllImport** attribute always specifies the native library name and may customize the native call via optional parameters.

Managed data types can be divided into two groups—blittable types and non-blittable types. Blittable types are the data types with only one representation on the native platform. These types do not need to be explicitly marshalled. Managed data types that can map to more than one native type are called non-blittable types. The default marshaling for each of these types may incorrectly convert the argument for the native function.

Callbacks are based on function pointers—a callback handler function is registered with a callback notification function by a function pointer. Managed code does not support direct function pointers, but managed code does have delegates. Recall that delegates are classes declared using the **__delegate** keyword that act as intermediaries for methods. Platform Invoke allows the use of **__delegates** as callback function pointers.

COM Interoperability Services

Objectives

- To understand some key differences between the .NET and COM architectures.
- To understand how interop assemblies and the Runtime Callable Wrapper enables the use of COM components from .NET.
- To use the tools provided with the .NET Framework SDK to provide COM interoperability.
- To host an ActiveX control in a managed container.
- To understand how the COM Callable Wrapper uses .NET components from COM-aware applications.

Sometimes give your services for nothing.
Hippocrates

The greatness of art is not to find what is common but what is unique.
Isaac Bashevis Singer

Too early seen unknown, and known too late!
William Shakespeare

There is one thing stronger than all the armies in the world; an idea whose time has come.
Victor Hugo

There is a strong shadow where there is much light.
Johann Wolfgang von Goethe

Call things by their right names.
Robert Hall

25.1 Introduction

The .NET component architecture was designed to resolve most of the problems presented by COM. It eliminates reference counting, simplifies component deployment and resolves versioning issues. However, existing COM components cannot be replaced easily with managed counterparts. In fact, a large portion of Windows functionality is available only through COM objects and will not be available as .NET components for some time. The .NET and COM architectures are fundamentally different; however, Microsoft has included a set of *COM interoperability services* in .NET. These services allow .NET components to use COM components, and vice versa.

This chapter explains some of the key differences between the COM and .NET architectures and demonstrates the tools and technology that allows COM and .NET interoperability. This chapter (which is targeted towards developers with previous knowledge of unmanaged code, managed code, ATL and COM) requires that the reader is knowledgeable in the areas of COM architecture and implementation.

25.2 COM as .NET Components

COM interoperability services primarily exist to allow access to COM components from managed code. To use COM components, .NET must be able to locate and identify COM interfaces and methods. The runtime also must handle data marshaling between managed components and COM objects and reference counting. This section explains some of the differences between the COM and .NET architectures and how to compensate for these differences.

25.2.1 Type Libraries and Assemblies

The COM and .NET component architectures have different location techniques and layout of their respective component files.

A *COM component* consists of three distinct parts—the binary executable code, the *type library* description of the component and the registered unique IDs in the system registry. In many cases, the type library and binary code coexist in the same **.dll**, which is registered in the system registry to be located by COM clients.

A *.NET component* consists of a single entity, the *assembly*. An assembly contains all the component's type descriptions, identification and versioning information in addition to one or more modules, which contain the component's executable code. .NET clients do not rely on the system registry. Instead, they locate assemblies based on the application's directory or the global assembly cache.

As demonstrated in Chapter 24, Managed and Unmanaged Interoperability, .NET includes services that can overcome the differences between managed and unmanaged contexts. Thus, COM services must provide functionality to identify only the COM component and convert its type library to a format readable by .NET. The Framework SDK includes a *Type Library Importer* (**tlbimp.exe**) that can convert COM type libraries into .NET *interop assemblies*. The **tlbimp** tool (included in the *VisualStudio_Directory* **\FrameworkSDK\Bin** directory) produces an assembly that contains .NET metadata to describe the types, interfaces, methods and properties defined in the specified type library.[1]

Figure 25.1 declares a simple ATL COM component that provides a simple stack data structure implementation. In Section 25.2.3 and Section 25.2.4, we use this component to demonstrate the **tlbimp** tool and binding. The project is created using the **ATL project** Visual Studio .NET wizard to create an attributed ATL project with COM+ 1.0 support. The object was created using the **ATL COM+ 1.0 Component** wizard to create the **IStack** and **CStack** declaration. For more information on the wizards and attributes used in this example, refer to Chapter 22, Attributed Programming in ATL/COM.

```
1   // Fig. 25.1: Stack.h
2   // COM Stack data structure implementation.
3
4   #pragma once
5
6   #include "resource.h"
7   #include <comsvcs.h>
8
9   // stores VARIANT item and pointer to next item in stack
10  class StackNode
11  {
12  public:
13     StackNode( VARIANT item ) : data( item ) {}
14     VARIANT data;
15     StackNode *nextNode;
16  }; // end class StackNode
17
```

Fig. 25.1   **CStack** COM class declaration. (Part 1 of 2.)

---

1. More information about the Type Library Importer can be found at
   msdn.microsoft.com/library/default.asp?url=/library/en-us/
   cptools/html/cpgrftypelibraryimportertlbimpexe.asp.

```
18   // IStack interface
19   [
20      object,
21      uuid( "65464E68-C03C-49AF-9AD1-16B4C76028A4" ),
22      dual, helpstring( "IStack Interface" ),
23      pointer_default( unique )
24   ]
25   __interface IStack : IDispatch
26   {
27
28      // push item onto stack
29      [ id( 1 ) ] HRESULT Push( [ in ] VARIANT );
30
31      // pop item off stack
32      [ id( 2 ) ] HRESULT Pop( [ out, retval ] VARIANT * );
33   }; // end interface IStack
34
35   // stack implementation class
36   [
37      coclass,
38      threading( "single" ),
39      aggregatable( "never" ),
40      vi_progid( "COMStack.Stack" ),
41      progid( "COMStack.Stack.1" ),
42      version( 1.0 ),
43      uuid( "AE56EC8A-4315-40FA-B75B-0B9337BD4FEA" ),
44      helpstring( "Stack Class" )
45   ]
46   class ATL_NO_VTABLE CStack : public IStack
47   {
48   public:
49
50      // initialize stack pointer
51      CStack() : topItem( NULL ) {}
52
53      // destroy object
54      ~CStack();
55
56      // stack method implementations
57      STDMETHOD( Push( VARIANT ) );
58      STDMETHOD( Pop( VARIANT * ) );
59
60   private:
61
62      // stack pointer
63      StackNode *topItem;
64   }; // end class CStack
```

Fig. 25.1 CStack COM class declaration. (Part 2 of 2.)

Class **StackNode** (lines 10–16) represents an item in the stack, which maintains a **VARIANT** data item and a pointer to the next **StackNode** in the stack. Interface **IStack** (lines 19–33) is a dual interface that declares two methods—**Push** and **Pop**. Method **Push** adds the passed **VARIANT** argument to the top of the stack. Method **Pop** removes the top node from the stack and returns the **VARIANT** data member. Class **CStack** (lines 46–64) is a COM object that provides the **IStack** class implementation. Lines 57–58 declare method **Push** and method **Pop**. Line 63 declares a **StackNode** pointer that is used to point to the top item on the stack. Figure 25.2 contains the **CStack** COM class method definitions.

```cpp
1   // Fig. 25.2: Stack.cpp
2   // CStack class method definitions.
3
4   #include "stdafx.h"
5   #include "Stack.h"
6
7   // push item onto stack
8   STDMETHODIMP CStack::Push( VARIANT item )
9   {
10
11      // create new node for stack
12      StackNode *newNode = new StackNode( item );
13
14      // place new node in stack
15      if ( topItem == NULL ) {
16         topItem = newNode;
17         newNode->nextNode = NULL;
18      }
19      else {
20         newNode->nextNode = topItem;
21         topItem = newNode;
22      }
23
24      return S_OK;
25   } // end method Push
26
27   // pop item off stack
28   STDMETHODIMP CStack::Pop( VARIANT *returnValue )
29   {
30
31      // if stack is empty, return empty VARIANT
32      if ( topItem == NULL ) {
33         returnValue->vt = VT_EMPTY;
34         return S_FALSE;
35      }
36
37      // store top item and data
38      StackNode *temporary = topItem;
39      *returnValue = temporary->data;
40
41      // reposition stack pointer
42      topItem = topItem->nextNode;
43
```

Fig. 25.2   **CStack** COM class method definitions. (Part 1 of 2.)

```
44        // delete item
45        delete temporary;
46
47        return S_OK;
48    } // end method Pop
49
50    // destroy allocated stack nodes
51    CStack::~CStack() {
52
53        // loop to bottom of stack
54        while ( topItem != NULL ) {
55
56            // release top item, reposition stack pointer
57            StackNode *temporary = topItem;
58            topItem = topItem->nextNode;
59            delete temporary;
60        }
61    } // end destructor
```

Fig. 25.2 **CStack** COM class method definitions. (Part 2 of 2.)

Method **Push** (lines 8–25) places the **VARIANT** argument onto the stack. Line 12 constructs a new **StackNode** object using the passed **VARIANT** argument as data. Lines 15–22 adjust the newly created **StackNode**'s **nextNode** pointer to point to the previous top node and reassigns the **topItem StackNode** pointer to the new **StackNode**.

Method **Pop** (lines 28–48) removes the top item from the stack and returns its data member using the **retval** argument. Lines 32–35 return an empty **VARIANT** object if the stack is empty. Lines 38–47 retrieve the data item from the top node, reposition the stack pointer to the next node on the stack and delete the previous top node.

The class destructor (lines 51–61) traverses the stack and deletes each remaining node in the class to release all allocated memory before the object is destroyed.

Executing **tlbimp.exe** on the DLL generated by the stack application produces the following output:

```
>tlbimp COMStack.dll /out:InteropCOMStack.dll

Microsoft (R) .NET Framework Type Library to Assembly Con-
verter 1.0.3705.0

Copyright (C) Microsoft Corporation 1998-2001.  All rights
reserved.

Type library imported to InteropCOMStack.dll
```

The command creates an interop assembly in the application directory named **InteropCOMStack.dll**. The generated assembly can be examined using the Framework MSIL Disassembler (**ildasm.exe**) discussed in Chapter 24, Managed and Unmanaged Interoperability. Figure 25.3 shows the output of the MSIL Disassembler.

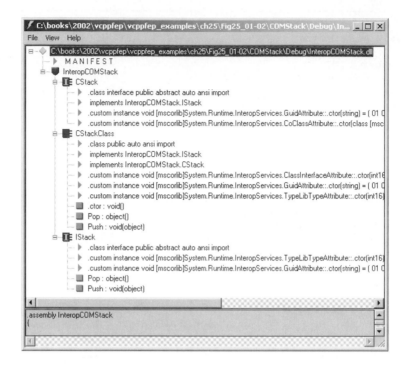

Fig. 25.3   MSIL Disassembler showing **COMStack** COM component.

The **tlbimp** tool converts each COM interface into a managed interface and each COM class into a managed **coclass** interface and implementation class. Managed interface **IStack** is a duplicate of the COM interface; in addition, it contains attributes **TypeLibType** and **Guid** that maintain the COM interface information. Managed **coclass** interface **CStack** stores the *Globally Unique Identifier (GUID)* of the COM **CStack** object's default interface (e.g., **IStack**). A GUID is a universally unique number used to identify and locate COM components and interfaces. The **coclass** interface is used in other .NET languages to provide a mapping between the default interface and implementation class. Class **CStackClass** is the managed COM object implementation class, the **tlbimp** tool appends **"Class"** to the COM object name for the implementation class name. In Visual C++ .NET, create an instance of the implementation class to access the native object.

25.2.2 The Runtime Callable Wrapper

A managed COM implementation class provides method implementations that delegate managed calls to the *Runtime Callable Wrapper (RCW)* . The RCW performs the majority of the COM interoperability work. To support COM objects successfully, an application must have a means of locating and instantiating the object, maintaining a reference count on the object, marshaling data-types to COM types and handling COM errors. The RCW provides each of these services.

To perform a registry lookup, the RCW locates the COM object using the metadata in the interop assembly or at runtime provided by the application. It then instantiates the COM object and begins reference counting. Once the object is created, the RCW performs native **QueryInterface** calls to identify the functionality of the COM object. The RCW then serves as an intermediary between managed and unmanaged code, delegating calls through the correct interface pointers and providing default marshaling for arguments and return types. The RCW also intercepts all COM **HRESULT** return values. If a method returns the error **HRESULT**, the RCW maps the native error to a managed exception and throws it. When the garbage collector destroys the RCW the garbage collector decrements the COM object's reference count before being destroyed. However, due to the unpredictable nature of the garbage collector, it is not possible to rely on the garbage collector to release the COM object in a timely manner. **static** method **ReleaseComObject** of class **Marshal** explicitly decrements the reference count of the passed object. This method should be used in combination with the **IDisposable** interface to gain control over the exact time of a COM objects release.

25.2.3 Early Binding

The **tlbimp** utility generates the interop assembly for early binding of COM objects. In *early binding*, the location, identifiers and type metadata is generated for a COM object beforehand. A project that uses early binding needs to include only the interop assembly: it then may use the COM implementation class as any other .NET object.

Figure 25.4 presents a simple managed application that creates a **CStack** COM object, pushes several objects onto the stack and pops each item off the stack.

```cpp
1   // Fig. 25.4: EarlyStack.cpp
2   // Uses CStack COM object with early binding.
3
4   #using <mscorlib.dll>
5
6   // imported interop assembly
7   #using "InteropCOMStack.dll"
8
9   #include <tchar.h>
10
11  using namespace System;
12  using namespace System::Collections;
13  using namespace InteropCOMStack;
14
15  // entry point for application
16  int main()
17  {
18
19      // create CStack instance
20      CStack *stack = new CStackClass();
21      IStack *stackInterface;
22
```

Fig. 25.4   Early binding **CStack** COM object. (Part 1 of 2.)

Fig. 25.5

```
27      }
28
29      // box items for stack
30      Object *data[] = { __box( 5 ), S"Hello",
31         __box( true ), __box( 12.45 ), new ArrayList() };
32
33      // argument array
34      Object *arguments[] = new Object *[ 1 ];
35
36      // place each boxed item into stack
37      for ( int i = 0; i < data->Length; i++ ) {
38         arguments[ 0 ] = data[ i ];
39
40         // call COM method
41         stackType->InvokeMember( S"Push",
42            BindingFlags::InvokeMethod, NULL, stack, arguments );
43      }
44
45      Object *returnValue;
46
47      // pop items off stack until empty
48      while ( ( returnValue = stackType->InvokeMember( "Pop",
49         BindingFlags::InvokeMethod, NULL, stack, NULL ) ) != NULL )
50         Console::WriteLine( returnValue );
51
52      return 0;
53   } // end function main
```

```
System.Collections.ArrayList
12.45
True
Hello
5
```

Fig. 25.5   Late-binding **CStack** COM object. (Part 2 of 2.)

Lines 17–18 call **static** method **GetTypeFromProgId** of class **Type**, which returns a **Type** instance that describes the COM object. **static** method **CreateInstance** of class **Activator** (line 21) creates an instance of the specified type and returns the type as an **Object**. The created COM object is managed by an RCW that handles reference counting and type marshaling. Lines 24–27 ensure that the object was successfully created. Lines 30–31 construct an **Object** array to hold the data pushed onto the stack. Lines 37–43 loop through each argument and call method **Push** to push the data on the stack.

To access a member on a late-bound COM object, use method **InvokeMember** of object **Type**. Method **InvokeMember** takes five arguments—a **String *** representing the name of the method to invoke, a member of enumeration **BindingFlags**, a **Binder**, an instance of the object on which to call the method and an object array containing the method arguments. Enumeration **BindingFlags** specifies the type of the class data member to invoke and the class members on which to perform a search.

Figure 25.6 contains a list of selected **BindingFlags** enumeration members and how they affect method **InvokeMember**. **BindingFlags** members might be combined using a bitwise OR (|) to provide more than one value.

BindingFlags Member	Use in method InvokeMember
CreateInstance	Constructs a new instance of the specified type, equivalent to class **Activator** method **CreateInstance**. Ignores member name and object instance parameters.
GetField	Returns the value of the specified field.
SetField	Sets the value of the specified field.
GetProperty	Returns the value of the specified property.
SetProperty	Sets the value of the specified property.
IgnoreCase	Ignores the case of the member name parameter while searching for a name match.
Instance	Includes instance members of the object while searching for a name match (default).
InvokeMethod	Calls a non-constructor method on the specified object instance.
NonPublic	Includes non-**public** members of the object while searching for a name match.
Public	Includes **public** members of the object while searching for a name match (default).
Static	Includes **static** members of the object while searching for a name match.

Fig. 25.6 Selected **BindingFlags** members and descriptions.

An implementation of abstract class **Binder** is used as the third argument of method **InvokeMember**. A **NULL** value causes the method to use the default system **Binder**. A **Binder** performs name resolution and type conversion to obtain the best method that matches a given name and argument list; in most cases, the default system **Binder** provides correct **Binder** mappings.

25.3 Handling COM Connection Points

COM connection point s provide a two-way communication between the COM server and client. Connection points are similar to the .NET event model: The client registers a handler with the server, and the server calls all registered handler methods when a specified event occurs. COM connection points are registered to event handlers using function pointers.

The example in this section uses the **COMTimer** example from Chapter 22, Attributed Programming in ATL/COM, to demonstrate connection point interoperability. Ensure that the **COMTimer** DLL is registered on a machine (either recompile the project or run **regsvr32.exe** on the DLL). Then, run **tlbimp.exe** on the DLL as follows:

```
tlbimp COMTimer.dll /out:InteropCOMTimer.dll
```

The generated interop assembly consists of two sets of classes: The first consists of interfaces and class implementations generated to wrap COM component classes that provide hooks into the RCW; the second set consists of generated classes designed to provide connection points through delegates.

The set of generated wrapper classes (Fig. 25.7) is similar to that generated for the previous **CStack** example. A managed interface is generated for each COM interface. An interface and an implementation class are generated for each COM class. The wrapped interfaces include **IComTimer**, **ITimerEvents** and **CComTimer**. **IComTimer** declares method **Run**. **ITimerEvents** declares the connect point method **TimerTick**, and **CComTimer** provides the implementation class interface. The implementation class **CComTimer** provides the wrapper for method **Run** and implementations for methods **add_TimerTick** and **remove_TimerTick**, which did not exist in the native COM component. These methods were injected by **tlbimp.exe** to provide delegate hooking and unhooking methods.

Fig. 25.7   COMTimer class shown in MSIL Disassembler, part I, wrapper classes.

The second set of classes and interfaces (Fig. 25.8) are each generated by **tlbimp.exe** to provide support for COM connection points through delegates. For each event interface in the native COM component, **tlbimp.exe** generates an interface using the naming convention *EventInterfaceName* **_Event**. The generated interface declares methods to hook and unhook a delegate to each event method in the COM event interface. The method naming convention for the hook and unhook methods is **add_***EventMethod* and **remove_***EventMethod* . In this example, the **ITimerEvents_Event** interface consists of method **add_TimerTick**, method **remove_TimerTick** and a delegate instance, **TimerTick**.

In addition, **tlbimp.exe** generates two classes that implement the connection point methods. The class using the naming convention *EventInterface* **_EventProvider** pro-

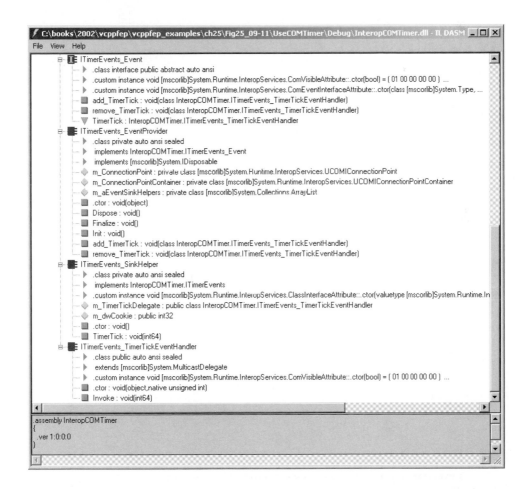

Fig. 25.8 **COMTimer** class MSIL Disassembler output, part II, generated classes.

vides the add and remove delegate implementations that register and unregister the managed delegate with the COM connection point. The class using the naming convention *EventInterface* **_SinkHelper** provides the managed implementation of **Timer-Tick** to fire the event through a managed delegate. Finally, **tlbimp.exe** generates a delegate class for each event method in the COM event interface using the naming convention, *EventInterface _EventMethod* **EventHandler**.

Figure 25.9 presents a managed class declaration that contains the managed event handler and hook/unhook methods.

Line 8 includes the **tlbimp.exe**-generated interop assembly—**InteropCOM-Timer.dll**. Line 19 declares method **HookSource**, which creates and attaches a delegate to the **TimerTick** event of the passed **CComTimerClass** object. Line 22 declares method **UnhookSource**, which detaches the **TimerTick** event handler from the source

```
1   // Fig. 25.9: CManagedTimeReceiver.h
2   // Managed COM event-sink class declaration.
3
4   #pragma once
5
6   #using <mscorlib.dll>
7   #using <System.dll>
8   #using "InteropCOMTimer.dll"
9
10  using namespace InteropCOMTimer;
11  using namespace System;
12
13  // event-sink class
14  public __gc class CTimerReceiver
15  {
16  public:
17
18     // hooks event source to sink
19     void HookSource( CComTimerClass *source );
20
21     // unhooks event source from sink
22     void UnhookSource();
23
24     // TimerTick event handler displays current time after
25     // each tick
26     void TimerTick( __int64 unformattedTime );
27
28  private:
29
30     // timer event source
31     CComTimerClass *timer;
32
33     // event handler delegate
34     ITimerEvents_TimerTickEventHandler *handler;
35  }; // end class CTimerReceiver
```

Fig. 25.9   CTimerReceiver managed COM connection point sink.

object. Line 26 declares method **TimerTick**, which receives the time of the tick event and displays the current system time.

Figure 25.10 presents the method definitions for class **CTimerReceiver**. Notice that the **tlbimp.exe**-generated wrapper classes allow the managed class to seamlessly use the COM connection point as a delegate.

Method **HookSource** (lines 7–17) attaches method **TimerTick** as an event handler delegate to the passed **CComTimerClass TimerTick** connection point. Lines 12–13 construct a new **ITimerEvents_TimerTickEventHandler** delegate class, passing

```
1   // Fig. 25.10: CManagedTimeReceiver.cpp
2   // Method implementations for class CTimerReceiver
3
4   #include "CManagedTimeReceiver.h"
5
6   // method hooks this receiver to event source
7   void CTimerReceiver::HookSource( CComTimerClass *source )
8   {
9      timer = source;
10
11     // create delegate
12     handler = new ITimerEvents_TimerTickEventHandler( this,
13        &CTimerReceiver::TimerTick );
14
15     // attach delegate
16     source->TimerTick += handler;
17  } // end method HookSource
18
19  // method unhooks this receiver from event source
20  void CTimerReceiver::UnhookSource()
21  {
22
23     // detach delegate
24     timer->TimerTick -= handler;
25  } // end method UnHookSource
26
27  // TimerTick event handler displays current time after
28  // each tick
29  void CTimerReceiver::TimerTick( __int64 unformattedTime )
30  {
31
32     // obtain current time from unmanaged time data
33     DateTime managedTime = DateTime( 1970, 1, 1, 0, 0, 0 );
34     DateTime adjustedTime = TimeZone::CurrentTimeZone->
35        ToLocalTime( managedTime.AddSeconds(
36        ( double )unformattedTime ) );
37
38     // display tick event and current time
39     Console::WriteLine( String::Concat( S"Tick! ",
40        adjustedTime.ToString() ) );
41  } // end method TimerTick
```

Fig. 25.10 CTimerReceiver class method definitions.

reference to method **TimerTick** as the handler method. Line 16 assigns the delegate to the **TimerTick** member of class **CComTimerClass**.

Method **UnhookSource** (lines 20–25) uses the **-=** operator to unregister the handler delegate from the COM connection point.

Method **TimerTick** (lines 29–41) handles the **TimerTick** COM event by converting the unmanaged time format to a managed **DateTime** object and displaying its value. Variable **unformattedTime** sent through the COM connection point is a 64-bit integer containing the number of seconds elapsed from January 1, 1970 until the time of the event. Managed class **DateTime** does not have a method to perform the direct conversions, so we initialize a **DateTime** object to January 1, 1970 at 12 A.M (line 33) and use method **AddSeconds** to add the value of **unformattedTime**. Then, we adjust the resulting value for the local timezone (lines 34–36).

The application entry point (Fig. 25.11) demonstrates class **CComTimerClass** and class **CTimerReceiver**. The application hooks and unhooks the managed delegate to the COM connection point. [*Note*: For simplicity, this example does not run the timer on a separate thread. Therefore, the program must be terminated manually by closing the console window or by pressing *Ctrl-C*.]

```
1    // Fig. 25.11: UseCOMTimer.cpp
2    // Early-binds COM timer and attaches it to managed
3    // event sink.
4
5    #using <mscorlib.dll>
6    #using "InteropCOMTimer.dll"
7
8    using namespace System;
9    using namespace InteropCOMTimer;
10
11   #include <tchar.h>
12   #include "CManagedTimeReceiver.h"
13
14   // entry point for application
15   int main()
16   {
17
18      // COM object
19      CComTimerClass *timer = new CComTimerClass();
20
21      // managed event sink
22      CTimerReceiver *receiver = new CTimerReceiver();
23
24      // hook source
25      receiver->HookSource( timer );
26
27      // run timer
28      timer->Run( 2 );
29
30      // unhook source
```

Fig. 25.11 Connection point interoperability application entry point. (Part 1 of 2.)

```
31      receiver->UnhookSource();
32
33      return 0;
34   } // end function main
```

```
Starting the timer. Will fire TimerTick every 2 seconds.
Tick! 6/4/2002 3:42:27 PM
Tick! 6/4/2002 3:42:29 PM
Tick! 6/4/2002 3:42:31 PM
Tick! 6/4/2002 3:42:33 PM
Tick! 6/4/2002 3:42:35 PM
```

Fig. 25.11 Connection point interoperability application entry point. (Part 2 of 2.)

25.4 ActiveX Controls in Windows Forms

ActiveX controls make up the body of reusable GUI components in Windows. The Windows platform comes with a number of pre-installed ActiveX controls, such as the **Web-Browser** and **MediaPlayer** controls. These controls provide impressive functionality and are not easily duplicated in managed code.

Whereas managed Windows Forms do not provide direct ActiveX control containment support, the Framework SDK includes the tool **aximp.exe**, which provides a managed wrapper for an ActiveX control. The **aximp.exe** tool generates two libraries from an ActiveX control, an interop assembly and a wrapper assembly. The interop assembly contains the data-type metadata and RCW hooks to the COM component. The interop assembly also could be generated using the **tlbimp** tool. The wrapper assembly provides a wrapper class for the ActiveX control that can be hosted on a Windows Form. The Windows Form wrapper extends class **AxHost**, which extends class **Control** to provide a hostable wrapper and default method implementations. The default method implementations only set the managed control's state, they do not make any call to the underlying ActiveX control. If the underlying control provides a method implementation, the **aximp.exe** Windows Forms wrapper class overrides the **AxHost** implementation and makes the call into the underlying control. The combination of default managed implementations and native calls often results in a managed wrapper around the underlying control that has more functionality than the original control.

In this section, we demonstrate hosting the **BookContentsScroller** control, created in Chapter 22, Attributed Programming in ATL/COM, in a Windows Form application. To ensure that the **BookContentsScroller** control is registered on your machine, either recompile the application or run **regsvr32.exe** on the provided **ContentsScroller.dll**. Use **aximp.exe** to generate an interop assembly and Windows Forms wrapper class for the control. The following command generates both assemblies:

> **aximp** *ContentsScroller_location* **\Debug\ContentsScroller.dll**

The **AxImp.exe** utility uses the original library name for the interop assembly name and names the Windows Forms wrapper assembly by prefixing **Ax** to the interop assembly name. In addition, specifying the **/source** option in the **aximp.exe** command line causes the utility to generate a C# source file containing the generated code for the Windows Forms wrapper. Use the **/source** option if the default control wrapper requires customization. You may want to view the generated assemblies using **ildasm.exe** to see the generated classes and metadata.

Create a new managed application solution, **ActiveXInterop**, and copy the **aximp.exe**-generated assemblies into the project's **Debug** directory. (Remember to set the **Resolve #using References** project property.)

Figure 25.12 declares class **ActiveXInteropForm**, a Windows Form designed to host the **ContentsScroller** control. The class hosts the control, handles connection point events and displays property pages at run time.

```
1   // Fig. 25.12: ActiveXInterop.h
2   // Class definition for ActiveX control hosting Form.
3
4   #using <mscorlib.dll>
5   #using <system.dll>
6   #using <system.drawing.dll>
7   #using <system.windows.forms.dll>
8   #using "AxContentsScroller.dll"
9   #using "ContentsScroller.dll"
10
11  #include <tchar.h>
12
13  using namespace System;
14  using namespace System::Windows::Forms;
15  using namespace ContentsScroller;
16  using namespace AxContentsScroller;
17
18  // Windows Form containing an ActiveX control
19  public __gc class ActiveXInteropForm : public Form
20  {
21  public:
22     ActiveXInteropForm();
23
24  protected:
25
26     // handles component scrollticked event
27     void ScrollTicked( Object *,
28        _IBookContentsScrollerEvents_ScrollTickEvent * );
29
30     // initializes GUI components
31     void InitializeComponent();
32
33  private:
34     AxCBookContentsScroller *scroller; // ActiveX Control
35  }; // end class ActiveXInteropForm
```

Fig. 25.12 ActiveXInteropForm class demonstrates ActiveX control on a Windows Form.

Lines 8–9 include the **aximp.exe**-generated assemblies, and lines 15–16 include the assembly namespaces. Class **ActiveXInteropForm** (lines 19–35) declares a constructor and a **ScrollTicked** event handler, and contains a pointer to the ActiveX control Windows Forms wrapper class, **AxCBookContentsScroller**. Figure 25.13 presents class **ActiveXInteropForm** method implementations.

```
1    // Fig. 25.13: ActiveXInterop.cpp
2    // Implementation of Form containing Book Contents Scroller
3    // ActiveX Control.
4
5    #using <mscorlib.dll>
6
7    // include axImp.exe generated assemblies
8    #using "AxContentsScroller.dll"
9    #using "ContentsScroller.dll"
10
11   #include "ActiveXInterop.h"
12
13   using namespace System::Drawing;
14
15   // initialize component
16   ActiveXInteropForm::ActiveXInteropForm()
17   {
18      InitializeComponent();
19
20      scroller->BackColor = Color::Blue;
21
22      // display ActiveX control property pages
23      if ( scroller->HasPropertyPages() )
24         scroller->ShowPropertyPages();
25
26      // add ScrollTick event handler
27      scroller->ScrollTick += new AxContentsScroller::
28         _IBookContentsScrollerEvents_ScrollTickEventHandler(
29         this, this->ScrollTicked );
30   } // end constructor
31
32   // ScrollTicked event, displays event properties
33   void ActiveXInteropForm::ScrollTicked( Object *sender,
34      _IBookContentsScrollerEvents_ScrollTickEvent *event )
35   {
36      Console::WriteLine(
37         String::Concat( S"ScrollTick! \ndirection: ",
38         event->direction.ToString() ) );
39   } // end method ScrollTicked
40
41   // initialize Form and Control
42   void ActiveXInteropForm::InitializeComponent()
43   {
44
```

Fig. 25.13 ActiveXInteropForm class method definitions. (Part 1 of 2.)

```
45        // create ActiveX control Object
46        this->scroller = new AxCBookContentsScroller();
47
48        // begin control initialization
49        this->scroller->BeginInit();
50        this->SuspendLayout();
51
52        // scroller
53        this->scroller->Enabled = true;
54        this->scroller->Location = Point( 24, 16 );
55        this->scroller->Name = S"scroller";
56        this->scroller->Size = Drawing::Size( 454, 227 );
57        this->scroller->TabIndex = 0;
58
59        // ActiveXInteropForm
60        this->AutoScaleBaseSize = Drawing::Size( 5, 13 );
61        this->ClientSize = Drawing::Size( 512, 269 );
62        this->Controls->Add( scroller );
63
64        this->Name = S"ActiveXInteropForm";
65        this->Text = S"Book Contents Scroller ActiveX Control";
66        this->scroller->EndInit();
67        this->ResumeLayout();
68     } // end method InitializeComponent
```

Fig. 25.13 **ActiveXInteropForm** class method definitions. (Part 2 of 2.)

Class **ActiveXInteropForm** constructor (lines 16–30) initializes the GUI, displays the control property pages and attaches a managed delegate to the control's connection point. Line 18 initializes the **Form**'s GUI, and line 20 sets the ActiveX control's **BackColor** property. Do not set a property managed by the underlying ActiveX control until after the control's initialization during **InitializeComponents**; the underlying control is not instantiated until the **Form**'s **ResumeLayout** call. Any scroller properties changed before this point will only be applied to the managed wrapper around the control, not the control itself. Lines 23–24 call the superclass **AxHost** methods *HasPropertyPages* and *ShowPropertyPages* to display the underlying control's property pages to allow property setting at runtime. [*Note*: The **ContentsScroller** control does not support property persistence, the properties must be set at run time by the client application.] Lines 27–29 declare a new **ScrollTick** delegate to event-handler method **ScrollTicked**, then attach the delegate to the control's **ScrollTick** member.

Method **ScrollTicked** (lines 33–39) displays the scrolling direction sent by the control's **ScrollTick** event. The second argument to the handler method is a variable of type **_IBookContentsScrollerEvents_ScrollTickEvent**. A class using this naming convention will appear for each event method in the ActiveX control. The argument for the event class contains public variables that contain the data members passed through the connection point by the control. In this example, the class contains a single data member **direction** that is **1** if the text scrolled up, and **-1** if the text scrolled down.

Method **InitializeComponent** (lines 42–68) constructs the Windows **Form** ActiveX control wrapper and sets the properties of the **Form** and control. Line 49 calls method **BeginInit** on the ActiveX wrapper. Method *BeginInit*, similar to **Form** method **SuspendLayout**, locks the control's display to the property state when the method is called. The application can then set the control's properties one at a time without affecting the displayed control. When the application calls method *EndInit* (line 66), all the property changes to the control made after the call to **BeginInit** are simultaneously applied. This prevents the visual side-effects of one-at-a-time property initialization. Lines 53–57 set the ActiveX control wrapper's properties. Note that the underlying control is not initialized at this point in the application's execution, only set properties that are not overridden by the wrapper method to make calls in the native component. Lines 60–65 set the managed **Form**'s properties. Line 67 applies all the changes to the managed **Form**. When the ActiveX wrapper is added to the form, it will initialize the underlying control to enable calls on its methods.

Figure 25.14 presents the application entry point and output. ActiveX controls are designed to run in a *single thread apartment (STA)* threading model. To initialize the control properly, the application must be run in a STA threading model. Although MC++ includes attribute **STAThread**, which is designed to set the threading model, the attribute currently is not fully functional in MC++. Line 16 presents a work-around that obtains the current thread and explicitly sets the apartment model using enumeration **Apartment-State**.

```
1   // Fig. 25.14: ActiveXInteropTest.cpp
2   // ActiveX Control window form test application.
3
4   #using <mscorlib.dll>
5   #using <system.dll>
6
7   #include "ActiveXInterop.h"
8
9   using namespace System::Threading;
10
11  // entry point for application
12  int main()
13  {
14
15      // set program to single threaded execution
16      Thread::CurrentThread->ApartmentState = ApartmentState::STA;
17
18      Application::Run( new ActiveXInteropForm() );
19
20      return 0;
21  } // end function main
```

Fig. 25.14 ActiveX interoperability example entry point. (Part 1 of 3.)

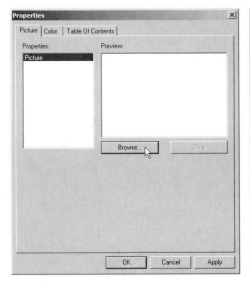
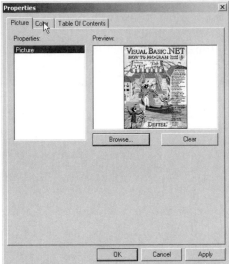

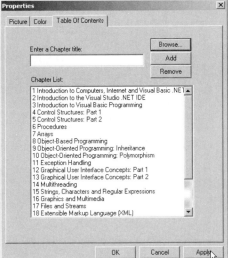

Fig. 25.14 ActiveX interoperability example entry point. (Part 2 of 3.)

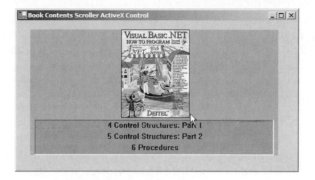

```
ScrollTick!
Direction: 0
ScrollTick!
Direction: -1
ScrollTick!
Direction: 1
ScrollTick!
Direction: 1
ScrollTick!
Direction: 1
ScrollTick!
Direction: 1
ScrollTick!
Direction: 1
ScrollTick!
Direction: 1
```

Fig. 25.14 ActiveX interoperability example entry point. (Part 3 of 3.)

25.5 .NET Components as COM

Although most Visual C++ .NET interoperability features support transition from a managed application to native code, there are situations where a native application might need to access .NET components. For instance, if an application makes heavy use of existing COM components, it may not be practical to provide an interop assembly for each component, and the performance impact may be too high. In addition, a component provider might choose to create a component in .NET, but still provide access to the component through COM. To account for these situations, Visual C++ .NET provides a set of tools and features designed to make a .NET component "visible" to a COM-aware native application.

This section provides a brief overview of the tools and technology behind .NET as COM interoperability and concludes with a large case study that demonstrates type library customization, data marshaling and event handling.

25.5.1 COM Callable Wrapper

The basis of the .NET as COM technology is the *COM Callable Wrapper (CCW)* . The CCW provides similar functionality for native code that the RCW performs for managed code. The CCW performs object lifetime management and native to managed method call marshaling, including calling convention, parameter and return data type marshaling.

A CCW is generated for each natively referenced .NET object. The runtime creates the CCW on the unmanaged heap with a reference to the managed object that it wraps. The garbage collector will not destroy the managed object while the CCW maintains its reference. The CCW uses COM-style reference counting for life-cycle management.

25.5.2 Type-Library Generation and Registration

Applications that use COM components obtain data type descriptions and behaviors by late binding using the object's ID and the ***IDispatch*** interface, or early binding by importing the COM object's type library. The .NET as COM interoperability features allow both types of access to a .NET object through the CCW. However, by default, .NET assemblies are not globally accessible to the system and are not represented in the system registry. Without a system registry entry or system-wide presence, COM-aware applications are unable to locate the component. In addition, without a type library, an application cannot early bind to the component. To overcome these difficulties, the Framework SDK includes the tools **gacutil.exe**, **tlbexp.exe** and **regasm.exe**.

The ***tlbexp.exe*** tool generates a type library that describes the data types and methods stored in a managed assembly. The tool generates a type-library description for each public class, interface, method and event in the managed assembly. However, type libraries require a large body of information that cannot be obtained from the managed assembly, such as unique identifiers, interface types and dispatch IDs. Managed C++ .NET supports a large number of attributes designed to provide control over how a class, method or assembly is exported to a type library. Figure 25.15 lists several COM export attributes and descriptions.

Attribute	Applies to	Description
ClassInterface	class	Specifies the type of interface generated for a class. Takes a member of the **ClassInterfaceType** enumeration as a parameter. Default value is **ClassInterfaceType::AutoDispatch**.
ComSourceInterfaces	class	Specifies the interface used to provide the events for the managed object, exports designated interface as **dispinterface** in type library. Takes the name of the event interface as a string parameter.
ComVisible	assembly or any type	Sets the visibility level of the entire assembly or attributed type. Takes a boolean parameter; a false value makes the attributed data invisible from COM. By default, all **public** classes, interfaces and members are visible.

Fig. 25.15 Selected COM export attributes. (Part 1 of 2.)

Attribute	Applies to	Description
DispId	interface method	Takes an integer that explicitly sets the dispatch ID of the interface method. Default value is generated.
Guid	assembly, class, interface	Takes a string value and sets the GUID of the attributed assembly, class or interface. Default value; generated GUID.
InterfaceType	interface	Sets the type of the exported interface, both, **IUnknown** or **IDispatch**. Takes a member of The **ComInterfaceType** enumeration as a parameter. Default value: **ComInterfaceType::InterfaceIsDual**.
PreserveSig	method	Prevents type-library name mangling. Methods without this attribute are converted from a managed representation to a COM representation by changing the return type to **HRESULT** and adding an out, **retval** parameter.
ProgId	class	Explicitly sets out the programmatic ID of the class. By default, **ProgId** is set to the object's namespace name plus class name.

Fig. 25.15 Selected COM export attributes. (Part 2 of 2.)

Each managed value type has a default native type. When **tlbexp.exe** converts an assembly's data member, it converts each type to its default native representation. However, many types, most notably **Strings** and **Object**s, have multiple native representations. Attribute **MarshalAs**, discussed in Chapter 24, Managed and Unmanaged Interoperability, causes **tlbexp.exe** to use the selected **UnmanagedType** in the type-library representation.

In COM, all objects must have at least one interface, because COM applications never access an object directly. They must access the object through its interface. However, in .NET, interfaces are not necessary, and many classes do not use them. To provide a .NET component to COM, the **tlbexp.exe** tool must generate an interface for .NET classes. Attribute **ClassInterface** specifies how the tool generates an interface. If the **ClassInterface** parameter is set to **ClassInterfaceType::AutoDispatch**, the tool generates an interface for the method based on its **public** methods. This is the default behavior, but is not recommended. The generated interface may break COM versioning and backwards compatibility rules, because the interface is regenerated each time, and does not increment interface numbers. However, **ClassInterfaceType::None** prevents the tool from generating an interface from the class. Instead, it defines the class interface from the first inherited interface.

For a COM component to be accessible to COM clients, various information concerning it must be entered into the system registry. The tool *regasm.exe* registers a

.NET assembly in the system registry as a COM object. The tool provides all required entries for each class and interface. In addition, **regasm.exe** can generate, and register the type-library as well, using the **/tlb** option. **regasm.exe** generates the type library in the same manner as **tlbexp.exe**, but also registers it, enabling early binding.

The *gacutil.exe* tool registers an assembly in the *Global Assembly Cache* (GAC), a system-wide assembly location. COM components can use registered assemblies only if they exist in the GAC. To register an assembly in the GAC use the command:

    gacutil /i *assembly_name* .dll

To remove an assembly from the GAC, use the command:

    gacutil -u *assembly_name*

While the GAC allows side-by-side versioning of components, it is suggested that the GAC be used sparingly, only for assemblies that must be used by several applications, or as COM components.

25.5.3 Case Study: Using ManagedContentsScroller as COM

In this case study, we present a managed implementation of the **BookContentsScroller**, designed in Chapter 22, Attributed Programming in ATL/COM. We then export and use the control from a COM-aware application. This release of Visual C++ .NET does not support hosting managed controls in a native container; thus, we will run the control from COM as its own form, not as an embedded control.

The managed application consists of two classes, the **ManagedContentsScroller** class, which extends **Form** and provides the scroller GUI and logic code, and class **COMContentsWrapper**, which provides the interfaces, attributes and properties to allow COM access to the contents scroller. It is possible, and perfectly valid, to forego the wrapper class and allow COM direct access to the implementation class. However, the wrapper class makes it easier on the developer to determine the methods provided to COM, to provide custom code between the interface and implementation and presents cleaner implementation code. The code is not "cluttered" with COM attributes.

Figure 25.16 provides the **ManagedContentsScroller** class declaration. The class is invisible to COM because of the **ComVisible** attribute; access to this class will be provided by a wrapper class. [*Note*: This case study write-around only focuses on the COM interoperability features, not the application logic.]

```
1   // Fig. 25.16: ManagedContentsScroller.h
2   // Managed UserControl that displays a book cover and
3   // allows the user to scroll its table of contents.
4
5   #pragma once
6
7   #using <mscorlib.dll>
8   #using <system.dll>
9   #using <system.windows.forms.dll>
10  #using <system.drawing.dll>
11
```

Fig. 25.16 ManagedContentsScroller class declaration. (Part 1 of 3.)

```
12   using namespace System;
13   using namespace System::Drawing;
14   using namespace System::Windows::Forms;
15   using namespace System::Runtime::InteropServices;
16
17   #include <tchar.h>
18
19   #define UP 1
20   #define DOWN -1
21
22   // delegate for ScrollTick handler
23   __delegate void DirectionDelegate( int );
24
25   // ManagedContentsScroller custom control
26   [ ComVisible( false ) ]
27   public __gc class ManagedContentsScroller : public Form
28   {
29   public:
30
31      // property Picture
32      __property Image *get_Picture()
33      {
34         return picture;
35      }
36
37      __property void set_Picture( Image *value )
38      {
39
40         // store image
41         picture = value;
42         BookImage->Image = picture;
43
44         // resize and reposition PictureBox
45         BookImage->Size = picture->Size;
46         BookImage->Location = Point(
47            ( this->Size.Width - BookImage->Size.Width ) / 2, 0 );
48
49         // reposition contents scroller panel
50         contentsScroller->Location = Point( 0,
51            BookImage->Size.Height );
52
53         // refresh control
54         this->Invalidate();
55      }
56
57      // property ContentsTable
58      __property String *get_ContentsTable()[]
59      {
60         return contents;
61      }
62
63      __property void set_ContentsTable( String *value[] )
64      {
```

Fig. 25.16 ManagedContentsScroller class declaration. (Part 2 of 3.)

```
65        contents = value; // store contents
66        currentIndex = 0; // reset scroll index
67        offset = -20;      // reset scroll offset
68     }
69
70     // declare event ScrollTick using DirectionDelegate
71     __event DirectionDelegate *ScrollTick;
72
73     // constructor initializes control
74     ManagedContentsScroller();
75
76     // initializes GUI components
77     void InitializeComponent();
78
79     // handles control drawing
80     void contentsScroller_Paint( Object *, PaintEventArgs * );
81
82     // scrolls control as user moves mouse
83     void ManagedContentsScroller_MouseMove( Object *,
84        MouseEventArgs * );
85
86     // repositions components when control is resized
87     void ManagedContentsScroller_Resize( Object *, EventArgs * );
88
89  private:
90     PictureBox *BookImage;
91     String *contents[];
92     Image *picture;
93     Panel *contentsScroller;
94     int currentIndex, direction, offset, lastY;
95     DateTime lastTime;
96  }; // end class ManagedContentsScroller
```

Fig. 25.16 **ManagedContentsScroller** class declaration. (Part 3 of 3.)

Line 23 declares **DirectionDelegate**, a delegate that is used in the class to fire a **ScrollTicked** event. The event sends the scrolling direction of the table of contents. Line 26 uses attribute **ComVisible** to prevent the export of the class into a type library. Class **ManagedContentsScroller** (lines 27–96) provides several properties designed to allow cusomization of the scroller, setting the book cover image, table of contents and background color. In addition, the control handles the **Paint**, **MouseMove** and **Resize** events. Class **ManagedContentsScroller** method definitions (Fig. 25.17) provide the GUI and logic code for the **Form**.

```
1   // Fig. 25.17: ManagedContentsScroller.cpp
2   // Method implementations for managed contents scroller
3   // control.
4
5   #include "ManagedContentsScroller.h"
6
```

Fig. 25.17 **ManagedContentsScroller** class method definitions. (Part 1 of 4.)

```
7    // constructor initializes values
8    ManagedContentsScroller::ManagedContentsScroller()
9    {
10      contents = NULL;
11      picture = NULL;
12      lastTime = DateTime::Now;
13      InitializeComponent();
14   } // end constructor
15
16   // InitializeComponent initializes control's GUI
17   void ManagedContentsScroller::InitializeComponent()
18   {
19      BookImage = new PictureBox();
20      contentsScroller = new Panel();
21      this->SuspendLayout();
22
23      // PictureBox properties
24      BookImage->Size = Drawing::Size( 0, 0 );
25      BookImage->Location = Point( 0, 0 );
26      BookImage->Name = S"BookImage";
27      BookImage->MouseMove += new MouseEventHandler( this,
28         &ManagedContentsScroller::
29         ManagedContentsScroller_MouseMove );
30
31      // Panel properties
32      contentsScroller->BackColor = Color::Gray;
33      contentsScroller->Size = Drawing::Size( 600, 60 );
34      contentsScroller->Location = Point( 0, 0 );
35      contentsScroller->Name = S"contentsScroller";
36      contentsScroller->BorderStyle = BorderStyle::Fixed3D;
37      contentsScroller->Paint += new PaintEventHandler( this,
38         &ManagedContentsScroller::contentsScroller_Paint );
39      contentsScroller->MouseMove += new MouseEventHandler( this,
40         &ManagedContentsScroller::
41         ManagedContentsScroller_MouseMove );
42
43      // UserControl properties
44      this->Name = S"ManagedContentsScroller";
45      this->Size = Drawing::Size( 600, 300 );
46      this->Location = Point( 0, 0 );
47      this->MouseMove += new MouseEventHandler( this,
48         &ManagedContentsScroller::
49         ManagedContentsScroller_MouseMove );
50      this->Resize += new EventHandler( this,
51         &ManagedContentsScroller::ManagedContentsScroller_Resize );
52      this->Controls->Add( contentsScroller );
53      this->Controls->Add( BookImage );
54
55      this->ResumeLayout();
56   } // end method InitializeComponent
57
58   // resizes contained components as control is resized
59   void ManagedContentsScroller::ManagedContentsScroller_Resize(
```

Fig. 25.17 ManagedContentsScroller class method definitions. (Part 2 of 4.)

```
60         Object *sender, EventArgs *arguments )
61    {
62
63         // resize inner panel to extend to width of control
64         contentsScroller->Size = Drawing::Size(
65            this->Size.Width, 60 );
66
67         // reposition PictureBox to center image
68         BookImage->Location = Point(
69            ( this->Size.Width - BookImage->Size.Width ) / 2, 0 );
70    } // end method ManagedContentsScroller_Resize
71
72    // scrolls contents table if one exists
73    void ManagedContentsScroller::contentsScroller_Paint(
74         Object *sender, PaintEventArgs *event )
75    {
76
77         // scrolls and displays contents table on panel
78         if ( contents != NULL ) {
79
80            // obtain Panels graphics context
81            Graphics *context = event->Graphics;
82
83            // modify text position offset
84            offset += 5 * direction;
85
86            // decrement starting title index when
87            // a title scrolls of bottom of panel
88            if ( offset > 20 ) {
89               offset = 0;
90
91               // increment index, prevent overflow
92               currentIndex = ( currentIndex + 1 ) %
93                  contents->Count;
94            }
95
96            // increment starting title index when
97            // previous starting chapter scrolls off panel
98            else if ( offset < 0 ) {
99               offset = 20;
100              currentIndex--;
101
102              if ( currentIndex < 0 )
103                 currentIndex = contents->Count - 1;
104           }
105
106           // initialize starting drawing point using offset
107           PointF drawPoint = PointF( 0.0f, ( float ) -offset );
108           Brush *text = new SolidBrush( Color::Black );
109
110           // loop through and display four chapter titles
111           for ( int i = 0; i < 4 ; i++ ) {
112
```

Fig. 25.17 ManagedContentsScroller class method definitions. (Part 3 of 4.)

```
113              // draw chapter title
114              context->DrawString(
115                 contents[ (currentIndex + i) % contents->Count ],
116                 this->Font, text, drawPoint );
117
118              // change drawing point
119              drawPoint.Y += 20;
120          } // end for
121
122          // fire ScrollTick event
123          __raise ScrollTick( direction );
124          direction = 0;
125       } // end if
126  } // end method contentsScroller_Paint
127
128  // event handler to scroll text when user clicks and drags
129  // mouse
130  void ManagedContentsScroller::ManagedContentsScroller_MouseMove(
131     Object *sender, MouseEventArgs *event )
132  {
133     DateTime eventTime = DateTime::Now;
134
135     // set scroll direction if user is holding left mouse
136     // button and 10 milliseconds have elapsed
137     if ( event->Button == MouseButtons::Left &&
138        ( eventTime.Millisecond - lastTime.Millisecond ) > 10 ) {
139
140        if ( event->Y < lastY )
141           direction = UP;
142        else
143           direction = DOWN;
144
145        // refresh text area
146        contentsScroller->Invalidate();
147     } // end if
148
149     lastTime = eventTime;
150
151     // store mouse y location
152     lastY = event->Y;
153  } // end method ManagedContentsScroller_MouseMove
```

Fig. 25.17 ManagedContentsScroller class method definitions. (Part 4 of 4.)

The class constructor (lines 8–14) initializes the starting table of contents and book cover picture to **NULL** and stores the current time. Method **InitializeComponent** (lines 17–56) constructs the **Form**'s GUI and wires the event handlers. The GUI consists of a **PictureBox** and a **Panel**. The **PictureBox** stores a book cover image and is always placed at the top center of the control, ensured by property **set_Picture**. The **Panel** provides a container to display and scroll the table of contents. The **Panel** is always placed below the cover picture and extends the width of the form. In addition, each component and **Form** is wired to **ManagedContentsScroller_MouseMove** for the mouse move event. This captures the moving mouse location on the component and enables contents scrolling.

Method **ManagedContentsScroller_Resize** (lines 59–70) fires when the size of the **Form** is adjusted. The handler repositions the book cover image to the center of the form and resizes the width of the contents **Panel** to extend across the **Form**'s width.

Method **contentsScroller_Paint** (lines 73–126) handles the contents **Panel**'s **Paint** event. Event **Paint** is fired each time the **MouseMove** event detects the user attempting to drag the table of contents. The handler draws four titles from the contents list. Each time the handler is called, the starting location for the first title is changed based on the users mouse direction. When a title becomes completely scrolled off the control, the next or previous title is displayed. Each time the **paint** method is called, it fires the **ScrollTick** event sending the direction of the scroll.

Method **ManagedContentsScroller_MouseMove** (lines 130–153) handles each component and the **Form**'s **MouseMove** event. The handler detects whether the user is holding down the left mouse button and that at least 10 milliseconds have passed since the last scrolling. Then, it refreshes the control, after setting the direction to scroll the table of contents based upon the current and previous mouse locations.

The following class and interfaces will be exposed to the COM application. The class provides a wrapper around the events, methods and properties in the **ManagedContentsScroller** form. In addition, it enables a native application to run the managed form as an application using method **ShowControl**. Figure 25.18 presents class **COMContentsWrapper** and its interface declarations.

```
1   // Fig. 25.18: ContentsScrollerWrapper.h
2   // Wrapper designed to allow COM to access the
3   // ManagedContentsScroller control.
4
5   #pragma once
6
7   #include "ManagedContentsScroller.h"
8
9   // event interface defines event methods
10  [ InterfaceType( ComInterfaceType::InterfaceIsIDispatch )   ]
11  public __gc __interface IContentsScrollerEvents
12  {
13     [ DispId( 1 ) ]
14     void ScrollTicked( int );
15  }; // end interface IContentsScrollerEvents
16
17  // wrapper interface, works as default interface for
18  // exported COM type library
19  public __gc __interface ICOMContentsWrapper
20  {
21
22     // set and retrieve book cover image through a filename
23     __property String *get_PictureFileName();
24     __property void set_PictureFileName(
25        [ MarshalAs( UnmanagedType::LPStr ) ] String * );
26
```

Fig. 25.18 COMContentsWrapper class and interfaces provide COM exporting attributes. (Part 1 of 3.)

```
27     // set and get form background color
28     __property Color get_BackColor();
29     __property void set_BackColor( Color );
30
31     // get table of contents
32     __property String *get_ContentsTable()[];
33
34     // sets table of contents
35     __property void set_ContentsTable( String *[] );
36
37     // displays form
38     void ShowControl();
39  }; // end interface ICOMContentsWrapper
40
41  [
42     // declares class event source
43     ComSourceInterfaces( S"IContentsScrollerEvents" ),
44
45     // exports first inherited interface as default
46     ClassInterface( ClassInterfaceType::None ),
47
48     // sets control ID
49     Guid( "F1471F14-40BB-40cc-B3FB-DA6EA5CF2507" ),
50  ]
51
52  // provides property and method implementations
53  // for COMContentsWrapper
54  public __gc class COMContentsWrapper :
55     public ICOMContentsWrapper
56  {
57  public:
58
59     // initialize data
60     COMContentsWrapper();
61
62     // declare event source
63     __event DirectionDelegate *ScrollTicked;
64
65     // get pictureName value
66     __property String *get_PictureFileName()
67     {
68        return pictureName;
69     } // end property pictureName
70
71     // sets pictureName value, creates image from filename,
72     // sets underlying scroller form Picture property
73     __property void set_PictureFileName( String *value )
74     {
75        pictureName = value;
76        scroller->Picture = new Bitmap( value );
77     } // end property set_PictureFileName
78
```

Fig. 25.18 COMContentsWrapper class and interfaces provide COM exporting attributes. (Part 2 of 3.)

```
79        // gets underlying form's BackColor
80        __property Color get_BackColor()
81        {
82           return scroller->BackColor;
83        } // end property get_BackColor
84
85        // sets underlying form's BackColor
86        __property void set_BackColor( Color value )
87        {
88           scroller->BackColor = value;
89        } // end property set_BackColor
90
91        // gets underlying form's table of contents
92        __property String *get_ContentsTable()[]
93        {
94           return scroller->ContentsTable;
95        } // end property get_ContentsTable
96
97        // sets underlying form's table of contents
98        __property void set_ContentsTable( String *value[] )
99        {
100          scroller->ContentsTable = value;
101       } // end property set_ContentsTable
102
103       // displays underlying form
104       void ShowControl();
105
106  private:
107
108       // handles underlying control ScrollTick, fires
109       // ScrollTicked event
110       void COMContentsWrapper_ScrollTick( int );
111
112       ManagedContentsScroller *scroller;
113       String *pictureName;
114  }; // end class COMContentsWrapper
```

Fig. 25.18 COMContentsWrapper class and interfaces provide COM exporting attributes. (Part 3 of 3.)

Interface **IContentsScrollerEvents** (lines 11–15) defines the event interface for the exported library. Attribute **InterfaceType** (line 10) takes a **ComInterface-Type** value as a parameter and defines which base COM interfaces the exported interface supports. The value **ComInterfaceType::InterfaceIsIDispatch** forces the generated type-library interface representation to support only **IDispatch**; omitting this attribute or setting its parameter to **ComInterfaceType::Both** results in an interface that supports **IUnknown** and **IDispatch**. Line 13 uses attribute **DispId** to set the dispatch identifier of the **ScrollTicked** method. We use the **ScrollTicked** method as a connection point with the COM event model; thus, we need the dispatch identifier of the method. In most cases, it is permissible to allow the exporter to generate the **DispId** value for each method.

Interface **ICOMContentsWrapper** (lines 19–39) provides the default interface for the exported type-library representation of **COMContentsWrapper**. The interface does not use any COM attributes and will be exported as a dual interface with a generated GUID. The interface provides the set of properties that allow the COM application to customize and display the **ManagedContentsScroller**. Line 25 uses attribute **MarshalAs** with the **UnmanagedType** member **LPStr** to force the **set_PictureFileName** property to take a C-style string, instead of the default for COM, a **BSTR**.

Class **COMContentsWrapper** (lines 54–114) provides the implementation of the wrapper methods for the **ManagedContentsScroller Form**. Attribute **Com-SourceInterfaces** (line 43) indicates the interface name that contains the event methods. The interface indicated by this parameter is exported to the type library as the default **dispinterface** for the class. The class uses the **ClassInterface** parameter **ClassInterfaceType::None** to prevent the generation of a class interface. Instead, the type-library exporter uses the first implemented interface as the default class interface. Line 49 uses attribute **Guid** to set the unique identifier for the class; this prevents the application from generating a new identifier each time. To generate a valid GUID, use the Visual Studio .NET **Create GUID** tool from the **Tools** menu. Line 63 declares event delegate **ScrollTicked**; this is accessible to the COM application as a connection point. Lines 66–101 define the class properties. Each property, except **set_PictureFileName**, corresponds directly with a wrapper class variable or the underlying **ManagedContentsScroller**. Property **set_PictureFileName** demonstrates the power of the wrapper class. It is a complex procedure to generate a valid managed **Bitmap** class from the COM application; thus, for the sake of simplicity, the application passes a string referencing a file name. The wrapper class then creates the managed **Bitmap** object from the specified image file. Figure 25.19 presents the method definitions for the constructor, **ShowControl** and **ScrollTick** event of class **COMContentsWrapper**.

```
1    // Fig. 25.19: ContentsScrollerWrapper.cpp
2    // Provides method implementations for COMContentsWrapper
3    // control.
4
5    #include "ContentsScrollerWrapper.h"
6
7    // constructs new underlying ManagedContentsScroller
8    COMContentsWrapper::COMContentsWrapper()
9    {
10       scroller = new ManagedContentsScroller();
11   } // end method constructor
12
13   // creates and runs scroller
14   void COMContentsWrapper::ShowControl()
15   {
16       scroller->ScrollTick += new DirectionDelegate( this,
17          &COMContentsWrapper::COMContentsWrapper_ScrollTick );
18
19       // run scroller as an application
20       Application::Run( scroller );
21   } // end method ShowControl
22
```

Fig. 25.19 COMContentsWrapper class method definitions. (Part 1 of 2.)

```
23   // receives scroller's ScrollTick event and fires
24   // ScrollTicked event with direction
25   void COMContentsWrapper::COMContentsWrapper_ScrollTick(
26      int direction )
27   {
28      if ( ScrollTicked != NULL )
29         __raise ScrollTicked( direction );
30   } // end method COMContentsWrapper_ScrollTick
```

Fig. 25.19 **COMContentsWrapper** class method definitions. (Part 2 of 2.)

The class constructor (lines 8–11) instantiates a new control of the underlying type and registers the wrapper **ScrollTick** method to the underlying control **ScrollTick** event. Method **ShowControl** (lines 14–21) uses **static** method **Run** of class **Application** to display and manage the form. This prevents the method from returning until the form has closed. Method **COMContentsWrapper_ScrollTick** (lines 25–30) handles the **ManagedContentsScroller ScrollTick** event and raises its own **ScrollTicked** event to be received by the COM application.

Before compiling the application, create a strong name for the assembly. A *strong name* uniquely identifies an assembly and version number. An assembly must have a strong name to be used in COM interop. To generate a strong name, use the **sn.exe** Framework SDK tool as follows:

```
sn -k strongName.snk
```

Copy the generated **.snk** file to your project directory. Then, set parameter **AssemblyKeyFileAttribute** to **"strongName.snk"** in the project's **AssemblyInfo.cpp** file. (If a project does not include an **AssemblyInfo.cpp** file, add the attribute to any source file.)

After creating and compiling the **ManagedContentsScroller** assembly, generate the type library, and register the assembly and type library. Use the **regasm.exe** tool with the following command:

```
regasm ManagedContentsScroller.dll /tlb
```

If the assembly and type-library generation are successful, the assembly is almost ready to be accessed from a COM application. By default, .NET assemblies are not available at the system-wide level. To make the assembly accessible from COM, add the component to the *Global Assembly Cache*—a system-wide location for .NET assemblies—using the **gacutil.exe** tool as follows:

```
gacutil /i ManagedContentsScroller.dll
```

Before creating the COM application, open the generated type library with the Visual Studio .NET tool **OLE/COM object viewer**, located in the **Tools** menu. Then, select **File > View TypeLib** to locate and view the type library. The viewer shows the generated **.idl** file for the type library (Fig. 25.20). Notice how the method signatures are converted to the COM format and the marshalled data types. The type-library exporter marshals the Color value type as a native **OLE_COLOR**, the string parameters as **BSTR**s and the arrays as **SAFEARRAY**s.

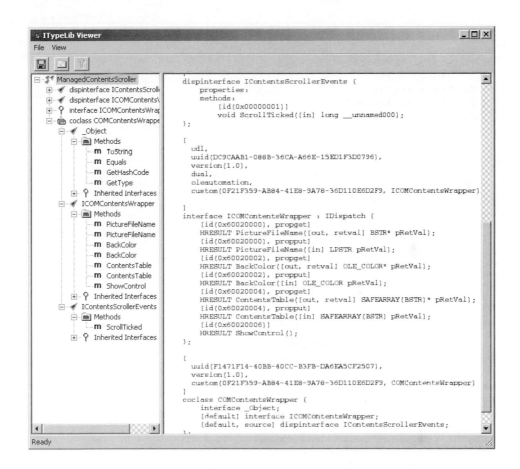

Fig. 25.20 **ManagedContentsScroller** type library.

The next example consumes the .NET component in a COM application. Create a new empty Win32 console application. The application consists of two parts: an **event_source** class designed to sink the connection point provided through the type-library (Fig. 25.21) and the application logic (Fig. 25.22), which creates and uses the **ContentsScroller**.

```
1   // Fig. 25.21: ScrollTickReceiver.h
2   // COM class to handler exported event.
3
4   #pragma once
5
6   // indicate application uses ATL attributes
7   #define _ATL_ATTRIBUTES
8
```

Fig. 25.21 **CScrollTickReceiver** COM class provides event handler for connection point. (Part 1 of 2.)

```
 9    // import exported type library, force GUID name generation
10    #import "../../Fig25_16-19/ManagedContentsScroller/Debug/
ManagedContentsScroller.tlb" named_guids, embedded_idl
11
12    #include <tchar.h>
13    #include <atlbase.h>
14    #include <atlcom.h>
15    #include <iostream>
16
17    // type library namespace
18    using namespace ManagedContentsScroller;
19    using std::cout;
20    using std::endl;
21
22    // handles ScrollTicked event
23    [ event_receiver( com ) ]
24    class CScrollTickReceiver
25    {
26    public:
27
28       // attach handler to event source
29       void Hook( ICOMContentsWrapperPtr wrapper )
30       {
31          __hook( IContentsScrollerEvents::ScrollTicked, wrapper,
32             &CScrollTickReceiver::ScrollTicked );
33       } // end method Hook
34
35       // remove handler from event source
36       void UnHook( ICOMContentsWrapperPtr wrapper )
37       {
38          __unhook( IContentsScrollerEvents::ScrollTicked, wrapper,
39             &CScrollTickReceiver::ScrollTicked );
40       } // end method UnHook
41
42       // ScrollTicked event sink
43       void __stdcall ScrollTicked( long direction )
44       {
45          char stringDirection[ 5 ];
46
47          // get string representation of direction int
48          if ( direction == -1 )
49             strcpy( stringDirection, "Down" );
50          else if ( direction == 1 )
51             strcpy( stringDirection, "Up" );
52          else if ( direction == 0 )
53             strcpy( stringDirection, "None" );
54
55          cout << "Scrolling Direction: " << stringDirection << endl;
56       } // end method ScrollTicked
57    }; // end class CScrollTickReceiver
```

Fig. 25.21 **CScrollTickReceiver** COM class provides event handler for connection point. (Part 2 of 2.)

To use COM event attributes, define **_ATL_ATTRIBUTES** (line 7). If this is not defined before including the ATL headers, the compiler will not inject the attributed code. Line 10 uses directive **#import** to provide the class definitions and identifiers to the application. Directive **#import** forces the compiler to generate a set of classes that correspond to the information in the type library. These generated classes are placed in the application's output directory (usually **\Debug**) and have the extension **.tlh** and **.tli**. The **named_guids** option after the type-library filename forces the generated class files to include a set of declarations containing the interface and class identifiers. The **embedded_idl** option forces the generated code to maintain attributes. This option is required to use attributed event handling. When the type-library is imported, it will be placed in a namespace corresponding to the library block in the **.idl** file. Line 18 declares the application using the **ManagedContentsScroller** namespace.

Class **CScrollTickReceiver** (lines 24–57) defines the event receiver class for the event source. Method **Hook** (lines 29–33) uses keyword **__hook** to provide the connection point between an event source and the sink method. Method **UnHook** (lines 36–40) removes the connection point, using keyword **__unhook**. For more information on COM event handling using the Unified Event Model, refer to Chapter 22, Attributed Programming in ATL/COM.

Method **ScrollTicked** (lines 43–56) acts as the event sink for the **Scroll- Ticked** event source. The event-sink method signature must match the type-library source signature. The method itself simply prints a string showing the direction of scrolling.

Figure 25.22 presents the logic for the COM-aware application. The program constructs a **SAFEARRAY** of **BSTR**s, initializes the event-sink object and the CCW managed object, sets the control properties, registers the event sink, and displays the form.

```
1   // Fig. 25.22: UseContentsScroller.cpp
2   // Application that uses managed object as COM.
3
4   #include "ScrollTickReceiver.h"
5   #include <iostream>
6
7   using std::cout;
8
9   // places application in module for COM component
10  [ module( name = "TickSink" ) ];
11
12  // entry point for application
13  int main( int argc, _TCHAR *argv[] )
14  {
15
16      // initialize COM
17      if ( !SUCCEEDED( CoInitialize( NULL ) ) ) {
18          cout << "Unable to initialize COM.\n";
19          return 1;
20      }
21
22      // safe array for table of contents
23      SAFEARRAY *contents = NULL;
```

Fig. 25.22 COM application that uses exported .NET type library. (Part 1 of 3.)

```
24      SAFEARRAYBOUND bounds;
25      FILE *contentsFile = NULL;
26      char title[ 100 ];
27
28      // use smart pointer to create COMContentsWrapper
29      ICOMContentsWrapperPtr wrapper(
30         __uuidof( COMContentsWrapper ) );
31
32      // create light blue OLE_COLOR object
33      OLE_COLOR color = RGB( 99, 167, 218 );
34
35      // set background color
36      wrapper->put_BackColor( color );
37
38      // set picture name property
39      wrapper->put_PictureFileName( "images/vbnethtp2e.jpg" );
40
41      // initialize array bounds
42      bounds.lLbound = 0;
43      bounds.cElements = 20;
44
45      // create safe array
46      contents = SafeArrayCreate( VT_BSTR, 1, &bounds );
47
48      // open contents file
49      contentsFile = fopen( "VB.NET.CNTS", "r" );
50
51      // check for file open error
52      if ( contentsFile == NULL ) {
53         cout << "Unable to open file VB.NET.CNTS.\n";
54         return 1;
55      }
56
57      // read first 20 titles into character buffer
58      for ( long i = 0; i < 20 &&
59         fscanf( contentsFile, "%[^\n]\n", title ) > 0; i++ ) {
60
61         // allocate a BSTR for each title, and add it to array
62         BSTR string = ::SysAllocString( CA2W( title ) );
63         SafeArrayPutElement( contents, &i, string );
64         ::SysFreeString( string );
65      }
66
67      // close file
68      fclose( contentsFile );
69
70      // set ContentsTable property
71      wrapper->put_ContentsTable( contents );
72
73      // create instance of COM event receiver object
74      CScrollTickReceiver receiver;
75
```

Fig. 25.22 COM application that uses exported .NET type library. (Part 2 of 3.)

```
76      // register event sink
77      receiver.Hook( wrapper );
78
79      // display control, function returns when user
80      // closes managed form
81      wrapper->ShowControl();
82
83      // unregister event sink
84      receiver.UnHook( wrapper );
85
86      SafeArrayDestroy( contents );
87
88      // unload COM
89      CoUninitialize();
90
91      return 0;
92  } // end function main
```

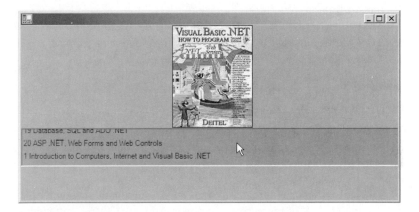

```
Scrolling Direction: None
Scrolling Direction: Down
Scrolling Direction: Down
Scrolling Direction: Down
Scrolling Direction: Down
Scrolling Direction: Up
Scrolling Direction: Up
Scrolling Direction: Down
Scrolling Direction: Down
Scrolling Direction: Down
Scrolling Direction: Down
Scrolling Direction: Down
Scrolling Direction: Down
```

Fig. 25.22 COM application that uses exported .NET type library. (Part 3 of 3.)

Line 10 uses attribute **module**, which is required to use COM events. Lines 29–30 construct the managed component, through the CCW, using the generated smart pointer.

When directive **#import** generates the **.tlh** and **.tli** files, it also generates smart pointer wrappers for each interface. The *smart wrappers* use the naming convention *interfaceName* **Ptr**, and their constructors take a COM object UUID. The smart pointers handle object construction and lifetime through reference counting.

Lines 33–36 construct a new light blue **OLE_COLOR** object using the **RGB** macro, then set the **BackColor** property on the scroller wrapper. Line 39 sets the **PictureFile-Name** property of the scroller. Note that the path specified should be relative to the managed DLL, not the current application. Lines 42–65 create a new **SAFEARRAY** of **BSTR**s and fill it with the contents of the file **VB.NET.CNTS**. Line 71 sets the **ContentsTable** property on the scroller wrapper. Lines 74–77 construct a new event-sink object and hook the event source and sink. Line 81 displays the managed control, and lines 84–89 provide cleanup after the user closes the control.

In this chapter, we discussed COM interoperability services and the interactions between the component architectures. Readers should be able to use COM components in .NET applications, and vice versa. The ability to develop in managed code, without sacrificing existing libraries and components, is a fundamental strength of Visual C++ .NET.

Well, that's it for now. We sincerely hope that you have enjoyed learning with *Visual C++ .NET for Experienced Programmers*. We would be most grateful if you would send your comments, criticisms and suggestions for improvement of this publication to **deitel@deitel.com**. Good luck!

25.6 Summary

The .NET component architecture was designed to resolve most of the problems presented by COM. It eliminates reference counting, simplifies component deployment and resolves versioning issues. The primary use of COM interoperability services is in accessing COM components from managed code.

A fundamental difference in the COM and .NET component architectures is the location techniques and layout of respective component files. A COM component consists of three distinct parts: the binary executable code, the type-library description of the component and the registered unique IDs in the system registry.

A .NET component consists of a single file—the assembly. An assembly contains all the component's type descriptions, identification and versioning information, in addition to one or more modules, which contain the component's executable code.

The **tlbimp** tool produces an assembly that contains .NET metadata to describe the types, interfaces, methods and properties defined in the specified type library. Also, the **tlbimp** tool converts each COM interface into a managed interface and each COM class into a managed **coclass** interface and implementation class.

A managed COM implementation class provides method implementations that delegate managed calls to the Runtime Callable Wrapper (RCW). To support COM objects successfully, an application must have a means of locating and instantiating the object, maintaining a reference count on the object, marshaling data types to COM types and handling COM errors. The RCW provides each of these services.

In most situations, early binding with an interop assembly is the optimal technique for COM interop. However, it is not always possible to construct interop assemblies for COM components. An application can locate a COM object through its **ProgID** or **GUID** and dynamically create and use the object. Late binding uses an RCW to manage reference counting, type marshaling and error handling, but cannot rely on the interop assembly for the object metadata and compile-time syntax checks.

To access a member on a late-bound COM object, use method **InvokeMember** of object **Type**. Enumeration **BindingFlags** specifies the type of the class data member to invoke and which class members to search for a match. A **Binder** performs name resolution and type conversion to obtain the best method that matches a given name and argument list.

COM connection points are the method of two-way communication between the COM server and client. Connection points are similar to the .NET event model. Much like managed events, COM connection points are registered to event handlers using delegates.

For each event interface in the native COM component, **tlbimp.exe** generates an interface using the naming convention *EventInterfaceName* **_Event**. The generated interface declares methods to hook and unhook a delegate to each event method in the COM event interface. Finally, **tlbimp.exe** generates a delegate class for each event method in the COM event interface.

The **aximp.exe** tool generates two libraries from an ActiveX control, an interop assembly and a wrapper assembly. The interop assembly contains the data-type metadata and RCW hooks to the COM component, the interop assembly could also be generated using the **tlbimp** tool. The wrapper assembly provides a wrapper class for the ActiveX control that can be hosted on a Windows Form.

Wrapper superclass **AxHost** methods, **HasPropertyPages** and **ShowPropertyPages**, display the underlying control's property pages to allow property setting during runtime. ActiveX controls are designed to run in a single thread apartment (STA) state. Although Managed Extensions for C++ .NET include the **STAThread** property, designed to set the threading state, currently it does not work.

If an application makes heavy use of existing COM components, it might not be practical to provide an interop assembly for each component. In addition, a component provider may choose to create a component in .NET, yet still provide access to the component through COM. To provide for these situations, Visual C++ .NET includes a set of tools and features designed to make a .NET component "visible" to a COM-aware native application.

The basis of the .NET as a COM technology is the COM Callable Wrapper (CCW), which provides similar functionality for native code that the RCW performs for managed code. The CCW performs object lifetime management and native to managed method call marshaling, including calling convention, parameter and return data type marshaling.

Applications that use COM components obtain data-type descriptions and behaviors by late binding using the object's ID and the **IDispatch** interface, or early binding by importing the COM object's type library.

This release of Visual C++ .NET does not support hosting managed controls in a native container; thus, we run the control from COM as its own form, not as an embedded control.

By default, .NET assemblies are not available at the system-wide level. To make the assembly accessible from COM, add the component to the Global Assembly Cache, using the **gacutil.exe** tool.

Operator Precedence Chart

MC++ operators are shown in decreasing order of precedence from top to bottom, with each level of precedence separated by a horizontal line.

Operator	Type	Associativity
::	binary scope resolution	left-to-right
::	unary scope resolution	
( )	parenthesized expression	left-to-right
[ ]	element access	
.	member selection via object	
->	member selection via pointer	
++	unary post-increment	
--	unary post-decrement	
typeid	run-time type information	
dynamic_cast< type >	run-time type-checked cast	
static_cast< type >	compile-time type-checked cast	
reinterpret_cast< type >	cast for non-standard conversions	
const_cast< type >	cast away **const**-ness	
++	unary pre-increment	right-to-left
--	unary pre-decrement	
+	unary plus	
-	unary minus	
!	unary logical negation	

Fig. A.1   Operator precedence chart. (Part 1 of 3.)

Operator	Type	Associativity
~	unary bitwise complement	right-to-left
(*type*)	C-style unary cast	
sizeof	determine size in bytes	
&	address	
*	dereference	
new	dynamic memory allocation	
new[]	dynamic array allocation	
delete	dynamic memory deallocation	
delete[]	dynamic array deallocation	
.*	pointer to member via object	left-to-right
->*	pointer to member via pointer	
*	multiplication	left-to-right
/	division	
%	modulus	
+	addition	left-to-right
-	subtraction	
<<	bitwise left shift	left-to-right
>>	bitwise right shift	
<	relational less than	left-to-right
<=	relational less than or equal to	
>	relational greater than	
>=	relational greater than or equal to	
==	relational is equal to	left-to-right
!=	relational is not equal to	
&	bitwise AND	left-to-right
^	bitwise exclusive OR	left-to-right
|	bitwise inclusive OR	left-to-right
&&	logical AND	left-to-right
||	logical OR	left-to-right
?:	ternary conditional	right-to-left

Fig. A.1   Operator precedence chart. (Part 2 of 3.)

Operator	Type	Associativity
=	assignment	right-to-left
+=	addition assignment	
-=	subtraction assignment	
*=	multiplication assignment	
/=	division assignment	
%=	modulus assignment	
&=	bitwise AND assignment	
^=	bitwse exclusive OR assignment	
|=	bitwise inclusive OR assignment	
<<=	bitwise left shift assignment	
>>=	bitwise right shift assignment	
,	comma	left-to-right

Fig. A.1   Operator precedence chart. (Part 3 of 3.)

Number Systems

Objectives

- To understand basic number system concepts, such as base, positional value and symbol value.
- To understand how to work with numbers represented in the binary, octal and hexadecimal number systems.
- To abbreviate binary numbers as octal numbers or hexadecimal numbers.
- To convert octal numbers and hexadecimal numbers to binary numbers.
- To convert back and forth between decimal numbers and their binary, octal and hexadecimal equivalents.
- To understand binary arithmetic and how negative binary numbers are represented in twos-complement notation.

Here are only numbers ratified.
William Shakespeare

Nature has some sort of arithmetic-geometrical coordinate system, because nature has all kinds of models. What we experience of nature is in models, and all of nature's models are so beautiful.
It struck me that nature's system must be a real beauty, because in chemistry we find that the associations are always in beautiful whole numbers—there are no fractions.
Richard Buckminster Fuller

Outline

B.1 Introduction

B.2 Abbreviating Binary Numbers as Octal Numbers and Hexadecimal Numbers

B.3 Converting Octal Numbers and Hexadecimal Numbers to Binary Numbers

B.4 Converting from Binary, Octal or Hexadecimal to Decimal

B.5 Converting from Decimal to Binary, Octal or Hexadecimal

B.6 Negative Binary Numbers: Twos-Complement Notation

B.7 Summary

B.1 Introduction

In this appendix, we introduce the key number systems that programmers use, especially when they are working on software projects that require close interaction with "machine-level" hardware. Projects like this include operating systems, computer networking software, compilers, database systems and applications requiring high performance.

When we write an integer such as 227 or –63 in a program, the number is assumed to be in the *decimal (base 10) number system*. The *digits* in the decimal number system are 0, 1, 2, 3, 4, 5, 6, 7, 8, and 9. The lowest digit is 0 and the highest digit is 9—one less than the *base* of 10. Internally, computers use the *binary (base 2) number system*. The binary number system has only two digits, namely 0 and 1. Its lowest digit is 0 and its highest digit is 1—one less than the base of 2. Fig. B.1 summarizes the digits used in the binary, octal, decimal and hexadecimal number systems.

As we will see, binary numbers tend to be much longer than their decimal equivalents. Programmers who work in assembly languages and in high-level languages that enable programmers to reach down to the "machine level" find it cumbersome to work with binary numbers. So two other number systems—the *octal number system (base 8)* and the *hexadecimal number system (base 16)*—are popular, primarily because they make it convenient to abbreviate binary numbers.

In the octal number system, the digits range from 0 to 7. Because both the binary number system and the octal number system have fewer digits than the decimal number system, their digits are the same as the corresponding digits in decimal.

The hexadecimal number system poses a problem because it requires sixteen digits—a lowest digit of 0 and a highest digit with a value equivalent to decimal 15 (one less than the base of 16). By convention, we use the letters A through F to represent the hexadecimal digits corresponding to decimal values 10 through 15. Thus, in hexadecimal, we can have numbers like 876 consisting solely of decimal-like digits, numbers like 8A55F consisting of digits and letters, and numbers like FFE consisting solely of letters. Occasionally, a hexadecimal number spells a common word, such as FACE or FEED—this can appear strange to programmers accustomed to working with numbers. Fig. B.2 summarizes each of the number systems.

Each of these number systems uses *positional notation*—each position in which a digit is written has a different positional value. For example, in the decimal number 937 (the 9, the 3, and the 7 are referred to as symbol values), we say that the 7 is written in the ones position, the 3 is written in the tens position, and the 9 is written in the hundreds position. Notice that each of these positions is a power of the base (base 10) and that these powers begin at 0 and increase by 1 as we move left in the number (Fig. B.3).

For longer decimal numbers, the next positions to the left would be the thousands position (10 to the 3rd power), the ten-thousands position (10 to the 4th power), the hundred-thousands position (10 to the 5th power), the millions position (10 to the 6th power), the ten-millions position (10 to the 7th power) and so on.

In the binary number 101, we say that the rightmost 1 is written in the ones position, the 0 is written in the twos position, and the leftmost 1 is written in the fours position. Notice that each of these positions is a power of the base (base 2), and that these powers begin at 0 and increase by 1 as we move left in the number (Fig. B.4).

For longer binary numbers, the next positions to the left would be the eights position (2 to the 3rd power), the sixteens position (2 to the 4th power), the thirty-twos position (2 to the 5th power), the sixty-fours position (2 to the 6th power) and so on.

In the octal number 425, we say that the 5 is written in the ones position, the 2 is written in the eights position, and the 4 is written in the sixty-fours position. Notice that each of these positions is a power of the base (base 8) and that these powers begin at 0 and increase by 1 as we move left in the number (Fig. B.5).

Binary digit	Octal digit	Decimal digit	Hexadecimal digit
0	0	0	0
1	1	1	1
	2	2	2
	3	3	3
	4	4	4
	5	5	5
	6	6	6
	7	7	7
		8	8
		9	9
			A (decimal value of 10)
			B (decimal value of 11)
			C (decimal value of 12)
			D (decimal value of 13)
			E (decimal value of 14)
			F (decimal value of 15)

Fig. B.1   Digits of the binary, octal, decimal and hexadecimal number systems.

Attribute	Binary	Octal	Decimal	Hexadecimal
Base	2	8	10	16
Lowest digit	0	0	0	0
Highest digit	1	7	9	F

Fig. B.2   Comparison of the binary, octal, decimal and hexadecimal number systems.

Positional values in the decimal number system			
Decimal digit	9	3	7
Position name	Hundreds	Tens	Ones
Positional value	100	10	1
Positional value as a power of the base (10)	10^2	10^1	10^0

Fig. B.3   Positional values in the decimal number system.

For longer octal numbers, the next positions to the left would be the five-hundred-and-twelves position (8 to the 3rd power), the four-thousand-and-ninety-sixes position (8 to the 4th power), the thirty-two-thousand-seven-hundred-and-sixty-eights position (8 to the 5th power) and so on.

In the hexadecimal number 3DA, we say that the A is written in the ones position, the D is written in the sixteens position, and the 3 is written in the two-hundred-and-fifty-sixes position. Notice that each of these positions is a power of the base (base 16) and that these powers begin at 0 and increase by 1 as we move left in the number (Fig. B.6).

For longer hexadecimal numbers, the next positions to the left would be the four-thousand-and-ninety-sixes position (16 to the 3rd power), the sixty-five-thousand-five-hundred-and-thirty-sixes position (16 to the 4th power) and so on.

Positional values in the binary number system			
Binary digit	1	0	1
Position name	Fours	Twos	Ones
Positional value	4	2	1
Positional value as a power of the base (2)	2^2	2^1	2^0

Fig. B.4   Positional values in the binary number system.

Positional values in the octal number system			
Decimal digit	4	2	5
Position name	Sixty-fours	Eights	Ones
Positional value	64	8	1
Positional value as a power of the base (8)	8^2	8^1	8^0

Fig. B.5   Positional values in the octal number system.

Positional values in the hexadecimal number system			
Decimal digit	3	D	A
Position name	Two-hundred-and-fifty-sixes	Sixteens	Ones
Positional value	256	16	1
Positional value as a power of the base (16)	16^2	16^1	16^0

Fig. B.6   Positional values in the hexadecimal number system.

B.2 Abbreviating Binary Numbers as Octal Numbers and Hexadecimal Numbers

The main use for octal and hexadecimal numbers in computing is for abbreviating lengthy binary representations. Figure B.7 highlights the fact that lengthy binary numbers can be expressed concisely in number systems with bases higher than that of the binary number system.

Decimal number	Binary representation	Octal representation	Hexadecimal representation
0	0	0	0
1	1	1	1
2	10	2	2
3	11	3	3
4	100	4	4
5	101	5	5
6	110	6	6

Fig. B.7   Decimal, binary, octal, and hexadecimal equivalents. (Part 1 of 2.)

Decimal number	Binary representation	Octal representation	Hexadecimal representation
7	111	7	7
8	1000	10	8
9	1001	11	9
10	1010	12	A
11	1011	13	B
12	1100	14	C
13	1101	15	D
14	1110	16	E
15	1111	17	F
16	10000	20	10

Fig. B.7   Decimal, binary, octal, and hexadecimal equivalents. (Part 2 of 2.)

A particularly important relationship that both the octal number system and the hexadecimal number system have to the binary system is that the bases of octal and hexadecimal (8 and 16 respectively) are powers of the base of the binary number system (base 2). Consider the following 12-digit binary number and its octal and hexadecimal equivalents. See if you can determine how this relationship makes it convenient to abbreviate binary numbers in octal or hexadecimal. The answer follows the numbers.

Binary Number	Octal equivalent	Hexadecimal equivalent
100011010001	4321	8D1

To see how the binary number converts easily to octal, simply break the 12-digit binary number into groups of three consecutive bits each, and write those groups over the corresponding digits of the octal number as follows

```
100     011     010     001
 4       3       2       1
```

Notice that the octal digit you have written under each group of thee bits corresponds precisely to the octal equivalent of that 3-digit binary number as shown in Fig. B.7.

The same kind of relationship may be observed in converting numbers from binary to hexadecimal. In particular, break the 12-digit binary number into groups of four consecutive bits each, and write those groups over the corresponding digits of the hexadecimal number as follows

```
1000    1101    0001
 8       D       1
```

Notice that the hexadecimal digit you wrote under each group of four bits corresponds precisely to the hexadecimal equivalent of that 4-digit binary number as shown in Fig. B.7.

B.3 Converting Octal Numbers and Hexadecimal Numbers to Binary Numbers

In the previous section, we saw how to convert binary numbers to their octal and hexadecimal equivalents by forming groups of binary digits and simply rewriting these groups as their equivalent octal digit values or hexadecimal digit values. This process may be used in reverse to produce the binary equivalent of a given octal or hexadecimal number.

For example, the octal number 653 is converted to binary simply by writing the 6 as its 3-digit binary equivalent 110, the 5 as its 3-digit binary equivalent 101, and the 3 as its 3-digit binary equivalent 011 to form the 9-digit binary number 110101011.

The hexadecimal number FAD5 is converted to binary simply by writing the F as its 4-digit binary equivalent 1111, the A as its 4-digit binary equivalent 1010, the D as its 4-digit binary equivalent 1101, and the 5 as its 4-digit binary equivalent 0101 to form the 16-digit 1111101011010101.

B.4 Converting from Binary, Octal or Hexadecimal to Decimal

Because we are accustomed to working in decimal, it is often convenient to convert a binary, octal, or hexadecimal number to decimal to get a sense of what the number is "really" worth. Our diagrams in Section B.1 express the positional values in decimal. To convert a number to decimal from another base, multiply the decimal equivalent of each digit by its positional value, and sum these products. For example, the binary number 110101 is converted to decimal 53, as shown in Fig. B.8.

To convert octal 7614 to decimal 3980, we use the same technique, this time using appropriate octal positional values, as shown in Fig. B.9.

To convert hexadecimal AD3B to decimal 44347, we use the same technique, this time using appropriate hexadecimal positional values, as shown in Fig. B.10.

Converting a binary number to decimal					
Positional values:	32	16	8	4	2	1
Symbol values:	1	1	0	1	0	1
Products:	1*32=32	1*16=16	0*8=0	1*4=4	0*2=0	1*1=1
Sum:	= 32 + 16 + 0 + 4 + 0 + 1 = 53					

Fig. B.8   Converting a binary number to decimal.

Converting an octal number to decimal			
Positional values:	512	64	8	1
Symbol values:	7	6	1	4
Products	7*512=3584	6*64=384	1*8=8	4*1=4
Sum:	= 3584 + 384 + 8 + 4 = 3980			

Fig. B.9   Converting an octal number to decimal.

Converting a hexadecimal number to decimal			
Positional values:	4096	256	16	1
Symbol values:	A	D	3	B
Products	A*4096=40960	D*256=3328	3*16=48	B*1=11
Sum:	= 40960 + 3328 + 48 + 11 = 44347			

Fig. B.10   Converting a hexadecimal number to decimal.

B.5 Converting from Decimal to Binary, Octal or Hexadecimal

The conversions of the previous section follow naturally from the positional notation conventions. Converting from decimal to binary, octal or hexadecimal also follows these conventions.

Suppose we wish to convert decimal 57 to binary. We begin by writing the positional values of the columns right to left until we reach a column whose positional value is greater than the decimal number. We do not need that column, so we discard it. Thus, we first write

Positional values: **64 32 16 8 4 2 1**

Then, we discard the column with positional value 64, leaving

Positional values: **32 16 8 4 2 1**

Next we work from the leftmost column to the right. We divide 32 into 57 and observe that there is one 32 in 57 with a remainder of 25, so we write 1 in the 32 column. We divide 16 into 25 and observe that there is one 16 in 25 with a remainder of 9 and write 1 in the 16 column. We divide 8 into 9 and observe that there is one 8 in 9 with a remainder of 1. The next two columns each produce quotients of zero when their positional values are divided into 1 so we write 0s in the 4 and 2 columns. Finally, 1 into 1 is 1, so we write 1 in the 1 column. This yields

Positional values: **32 16 8 4 2 1**
Symbol values: **1   1 1 0 0 1**

and thus decimal 57 is equivalent to binary 111001.

To convert decimal 103 to octal, we begin by writing the positional values of the columns until we reach a column whose positional value is greater than the decimal number. We do not need that column, so we discard it. Thus, we first write

Positional values: **512 64 81**

Then, we discard the column with positional value 512, yielding

Positional values: **64 81**

Next, we work from the leftmost column to the right. We divide 64 into 103 and observe that there is one 64 in 103 with a remainder of 39, so we write 1 in the 64 column. We divide 8 into 39 and observe that there are four 8s in 39 with a remainder of 7 and write 4 in the 8 column. Finally, we divide 1 into 7 and observe that there are seven 1s in 7 with no remainder, so we write 7 in the 1 column. This yields

Positional values: **64 8   1**
Symbol values: **1 4   7**

and thus decimal 103 is equivalent to octal 147.

To convert decimal 375 to hexadecimal, we begin by writing the positional values of the columns until we reach a column whose positional value is greater than the decimal number. We do not need that column, so we discard it. Thus, we first write

Positional values: **4096 256 161**

Then, we discard the column with positional value 4096, yielding

Positional values: **256 16 1**

Next, we work from the leftmost column to the right. We divide 256 into 375 and observe that there is one 256 in 375 with a remainder of 119, so we write 1 in the 256 column. We divide 16 into 119 and observe that there are seven 16s in 119 with a remainder of 7 and write 7 in the 16 column. Finally, we divide 1 into 7 and observe that there are seven 1s in 7 with no remainder, so we write 7 in the 1 column. This yields

Positional values: **256 16 1**
Symbol values: **1   7 1**

and thus decimal 375 is equivalent to hexadecimal 177.

B.6 Negative Binary Numbers: Twos-Complement Notation

The discussion in this appendix has been focussed on positive numbers. In this section, we explain how computers represent negative numbers in *twos-complement notation*. First we explain how the twos complement of a binary number is formed,then we show why it represents the negative value of the given binary number.

Consider a 32-bit integer. Suppose

```
int number = 13;
```

The 32-bit representation of **number** is

```
00000000 00000000 00000000 00001101
```

To form the negative of **number**, we first form its *ones complement* by applying MC++'s bitwise complement operator (~), which is also called the *bitwise NOT operator*:

```
onesComplement = ~number;
```

Internally, **onesComplement** is now **number** with each of its bits reversed—ones become zeros and zeros become ones, as follows:

```
number:
00000000 00000000 00000000 00001101

onesComplement:
11111111 11111111 11111111 11110010
```

To form the twos complement of **number**, we simply add one to **number**'s ones complement. Thus

```
Twos complement of number:
11111111 11111111 11111111 11110011
```

Now if this is in fact equal to –13, we should be able to add it to binary 13 and obtain the result 0. Let us try this:

```
 00000000 00000000 00000000 00001101
+11111111 11111111 11111111 11110011
------------------------------------
 00000000 00000000 00000000 00000000
```

The carry bit coming out of the leftmost column is discarded, and we indeed get zero as a result. If we add the ones complement of a number to the number, the result would be all 1s. The key to getting a result of all zeros is that the twos complement is 1 more than the ones complement. The addition of 1 causes each column to add to 0 with a carry of 1. The carry keeps moving leftward until it is discarded from the leftmost bit, and hence the resulting number is all zeros.

Computers actually perform a subtraction such as

```
x = a - number;
```

by adding the twos complement of **number** to **a** as follows:

```
x = a + ( onesComplement + 1 );
```

Suppose **a** is 27 and **number** is 13 as before. If the twos complement of **number** is actually the negative of **number**, then adding the twos complement of value to **a** should produce the result 14. Let us try this:

```
a  (i.e., 27)                 00000000 00000000 00000000 00011011
+( onesComplement + 1 ) +11111111 11111111 11111111 11110011
                              ------------------------------------
                              00000000 00000000 00000000 00001110
```

which is indeed equal to 14.

B.7 Summary

When we write an integer such as 19 or 227 or –63 in a program, the number is automatically assumed to be in the decimal (base-10) number system. The digits in the decimal number system are 0, 1, 2, 3, 4, 5, 6, 7, 8, and 9. The lowest digit is 0 and the highest digit is 9—one less than the base of 10. Internally, computers use the binary (base 2) number system. The binary number system has only two digits, namely 0 and 1. Its lowest digit is 0 and its highest digit is 1—one less than the base of 2. The octal number system (base 8) and the hexadecimal number system (base 16) are popular primarily because they make it convenient to abbreviate binary numbers. The digits of the octal number system range from 0 to 7. The hexadecimal number system poses a problem because it requires sixteen digits—a lowest digit of 0 and a highest digit with a value equivalent to decimal 15 (one less than the base of 16). By convention, we use the letters A through F to represent the hexadecimal digits corresponding to decimal values 10 through 15. Each number system uses positional notation—each position in which a digit is written has a different positional value.

A particularly important relationship that both the octal number system and the hexadecimal number system have to the binary system is that the bases of octal and hexadecimal (8 and 16 respectively) are powers of the base of the binary number system (base 2). To convert an octal number to a binary number, simply replace each octal digit with its three-digit binary equivalent. To convert a hexadecimal number to a binary number, simply replace each hexadecimal digit with its four-digit binary equivalent. Because we are accustomed to working in decimal, it is convenient to convert a binary, octal or hexadecimal number to decimal to get a sense of the number's "real" worth. To convert a number to decimal from another base, multiply the decimal equivalent of each digit by its positional value, and sum these products.

Computers represent negative numbers using twos-complement notation. To form the negative of a value in binary, first form its ones complement by applying MC++'s bitwise complement operator (~). This reverses the bits of the value. To form the twos complement of a value, simply add one to the value's ones complement.

ASCII Character Set

	0	1	2	3	4	5	6	7	8	9
0	nul	soh	stx	etx	eot	enq	ack	bel	bs	ht
1	nl	vt	ff	cr	so	si	dle	dc1	dc2	dc3
2	dc4	nak	syn	etb	can	em	sub	esc	fs	gs
3	rs	us	sp	!	"	#	$	%	&	`
4	(	)	*	+	,	-	.	/	0	1
5	2	3	4	5	6	7	8	9	:	;
6	<	=	>	?	@	A	B	C	D	E
7	F	G	H	I	J	K	L	M	N	O
8	P	Q	R	S	T	U	V	W	X	Y
9	Z	[	\	]	^	_	'	a	b	c
10	d	e	f	g	h	i	j	k	l	m
11	n	o	p	q	r	s	t	u	v	w
12	x	y	z	{	|	}	~	del		

Fig. C.1   ASCII character set.

The digits at the left of the table are the left digits of the decimal equivalent (0–127) of the character code, and the digits at the top of the table are the right digits of the character code. For example, the character code for "**F**" is 70, and the character code for "**&**" is 38.

Most users of this book are interested in the ASCII character set used to represent English characters on many computers. The ASCII character set is a subset of the Unicode® character set used to represent characters from most of the world's languages. For more information on the Unicode® character set, see Appendix D.

Unicode®

Objectives

- To become familiar with Unicode®.
- To discuss the mission of the Unicode® Consortium.
- To discuss the design basis of Unicode®.
- To understand the three Unicode® encoding forms: UTF-8, UTF-16 and UTF-32.
- To introduce characters and glyphs.
- To discuss the advantages and disadvantages of using Unicode®.
- To provide a brief tour of the Unicode® Consortium's Web site.

Outline

D.1 Introduction

The use of inconsistent character *encodings* (i.e., numeric values associated with characters) when developing global software products causes serious problems because computers process information using numbers. For example, the character "a" is converted to a numeric value so that a computer can manipulate that piece of data. Many countries and corporations have developed their own encoding systems that are incompatible with the encoding systems of other countries and corporations. For example, the Microsoft Windows operating system assigns the value 0xC0 to the character "A with a grave accent," while the Apple Macintosh operating system assigns that same value to an upside-down question mark. This results in the misrepresentation and possible corruption of data, because the data is not processed as intended.

In the absence of a widely implemented universal character encoding standard, global software developers had to *localize* their products extensively before distribution. Localization includes the language translation and cultural adaptation of content. The process of localization usually includes significant modifications to the source code (such as the conversion of numeric values and the underlying assumptions made by programmers), which results in increased costs and delays releasing the software. For example, some English-speaking programmers might design global software products assuming that a single character can be represented by one byte. However, when those products are localized for Asian markets, the programmer's assumptions are no longer valid; thus, the majority, if not the entirety, of the code needs to be rewritten. Localization is necessary with each release of a version. By the time a software product is localized for a particular market, a newer version, which needs to be localized as well, may be ready for distribution. As a result, it is cumbersome and costly to produce and distribute global software products in a market where there is no universal character-encoding standard.

In response to this situation, the *Unicode® Standard*, an encoding standard that facilitates the production and distribution of software, was created. The Unicode® Standard outlines a specification to produce consistent encoding of the world's characters and *symbols*. Software products that handle text encoded in the Unicode® Standard need to be localized, but the localization process is simpler and more efficient because the numeric values need not be converted and the assumptions made by programmers about the character encoding are universal. The Unicode® Standard is maintained by a nonprofit organization called the *Unicode® Consortium*, whose members include Apple, IBM, Microsoft, Oracle, Sun Microsystems, Sybase and many others.

When the Consortium envisioned and developed the Unicode® Standard, they wanted an encoding system that was *universal, efficient, uniform* and *unambiguous*. A universal encoding system encompasses all commonly used characters. An efficient encoding system allows text files to be parsed easily. A uniform encoding system assigns fixed values to all characters. An unambiguous encoding system represents a given character in a consistent manner. These four terms are referred to as the Unicode® Standard *design basis*.

D.2 Unicode® Transformation Formats

Although Unicode® incorporates the limited ASCII *character set* (i.e., a collection of characters), it encompasses a more comprehensive character set. In ASCII, each character is represented by a byte containing 0s and 1s. One byte is capable of storing the binary numbers from 0 to 255. Each character is assigned a number between 0 and 255; thus, ASCII-based systems can support only 256 characters, a tiny fraction of the world's characters. Unicode® extends the ASCII character set by encoding the vast majority of the world's characters. The Unicode® Standard encodes all of those characters in a uniform numerical space from 0 to 10FFFF hexadecimal. An implementation will express these numbers in one of several transformation formats, choosing the one that best fits the particular application at hand.

Three such formats are in use, called *UTF-8, UTF-16* and *UTF-32*, depending on the size of the units—in *bits*—being used. UTF-8, a variable-width encoding form, requires one to four bytes to express each Unicode® character. UTF-8 data consists of 8-bit bytes (sequences of one, two, three or four bytes, depending on the character being encoded) and is well suited for ASCII-based systems, where there is a predominance of one-byte characters (ASCII represents characters as one byte). Currently, UTF-8 is widely implemented in UNIX systems and in databases. [*Note*: Currently, Internet Explorer 5.5 and Netscape Communicator 6 support only UTF-8, so document authors should use UTF-8 for encoding XML and XHTML documents.]

The variable-width UTF-16 encoding form expresses Unicode® characters in units of 16 bits (i.e., as two adjacent bytes, or a short integer in many machines). Most characters of Unicode® are expressed in a single 16-bit unit. However, characters with values above FFFF hexadecimal are expressed with an ordered pair of 16-bit units called *surrogates*. Surrogates are 16-bit integers in the range D800 through DFFF, which are used solely for the purpose of "escaping" into higher-numbered characters. Approximately one million characters can be expressed in this manner. Although a surrogate pair requires 32 bits to represent characters, it is space-efficient to use these 16-bit units. Surrogates are rare characters in current implementations. Many string-handling implementations are written in terms of UTF-16. [*Note*: Details and sample code for UTF-16 handling are available on the Unicode® Consortium Web site at **www.unicode.org**.]

Implementations that require significant use of rare characters or entire scripts encoded above FFFF hexadecimal should use UTF-32, a 32-bit, fixed-width encoding form that usually requires twice as much memory as UTF-16 encoded characters. The major advantage of the fixed-width UTF-32 encoding form is that it expresses all characters uniformly, so it is easy to handle in arrays.

There are few guidelines that state when to use a particular encoding form. The best encoding form to use depends on computer systems and business protocols, not on the data. Typically, the UTF-8 encoding form should be used where computer systems and business protocols require data to be handled in 8-bit units, particularly in legacy systems being upgraded, because it often simplifies changes to existing programs. For this reason, UTF-8 has become the encoding form of choice on the Internet. Likewise, UTF-16 is the encoding form of choice on Microsoft Windows applications. UTF-32 is likely to become more widely used in the future as more characters are encoded with values above FFFF hexadecimal. Also, UTF-32 requires less sophisticated handling than UTF-16 in the presence of surrogate pairs. Figure D.1 shows the different ways in which the three encoding forms handle character encoding.

D.3 Characters and Glyphs

The Unicode® Standard consists of *characters*, written components (i.e., alphabetic letters, numerals, punctuation marks, accent marks, etc.) that can be represented by numeric values. Examples of characters include U+0041 LATIN CAPITAL LETTER A. In the first character representation, U+*yyyy* is a *code value*, in which U+ refers to Unicode® code values, as opposed to other hexadecimal values. The *yyyy* represents a four-digit hexadecimal number of an encoded character. Code values are bit combinations that represent encoded characters. Characters are represented using *glyphs*, various shapes, fonts and sizes for displaying characters. There are no code values for glyphs in the Unicode® Standard. Examples of glyphs are shown in Fig. D.2.

The Unicode® Standard encompasses the alphabets, ideographs, syllabaries, punctuation marks, *diacritics*, mathematical operators, etc. that comprise the written languages and scripts of the world. A diacritic is a special mark added to a character to distinguish it from another letter or to indicate an accent (e.g., in Spanish, the tilde "~" above the character "n"). Currently, Unicode® provides code values for 94,140 character representations, with more than 880,000 code values reserved for future expansion.

Character	UTF-8	UTF-16	UTF-32
LATIN CAPITAL LETTER A	0x41	0x0041	0x00000041
GREEK CAPITAL LETTER ALPHA	0xCD 0x91	0x0391	0x00000391
CJK UNIFIED IDEOGRAPH-4E95	0xE4 0xBA 0x95	0x4E95	0x00004E95
OLD ITALIC LETTER A	0xF0 0x80 0x83 0x80	0xDC00 0xDF00	0x00010300

Fig. D.1   Correlation between the three encoding forms.

Fig. D.2   Various glyphs of the character A.

D.4 Advantages and Disadvantages of Unicode®

The Unicode® Standard has several significant advantages that promote its use. One is the impact it has on the performance of the international economy. Unicode® standardizes the characters for the world's writing systems to a uniform model that promotes transferring and sharing data. Programs developed using such a schema maintain their accuracy because each character has a single definition (i.e., *a* is always U+0061, % is always U+0025). This enables corporations to manage the high demands of international markets by processing different writing systems at the same time. Also, all characters can be managed in an identical manner, thus avoiding any confusion caused by different character code architectures. Moreover, managing data in a consistent manner eliminates data corruption, because data can be sorted, searched and manipulated using a consistent process.

Another advantage of the Unicode® Standard is *portability* (i.e., the ability to execute software on disparate computers or with disparate operating systems). Most operating systems, databases, programming languages and Web browsers currently support, or are planning to support, Unicode®. Additionally, Unicode® includes more characters than any other character set in common use (although it does not yet include all of the world's characters).

A disadvantage of the Unicode® Standard is the amount of memory required by UTF-16 and UTF-32. ASCII character sets are 8 bits in length, so they require less storage than the default 16-bit Unicode® character set. However, the *double-byte character set (DBCS)* and the *multi-byte character set (MBCS)* that encode Asian characters (ideographs) require two to four bytes, respectively. In such instances, the UTF-16 or the UTF-32 encoding forms may be used with little hindrance on memory and performance.

D.5 Unicode® Consortium's Web Site

If you would like to learn more about the Unicode® Standard, visit **www.unicode.org**. This site provides a wealth of information about the Unicode® Standard. Currently, the home page is organized into various sections: *New to Unicode*, *General Information*, *The Consortium*, *The Unicode Standard*, *Work in Progress* and *For Members*.

The *New to Unicode* section consists of two subsections: **What is Unicode?** and **How to Use this Site**. The first subsection provides a technical introduction to Unicode® by describing design principles, character interpretations and assignments, text processing and Unicode® conformance. This subsection is recommended reading for anyone new to Unicode®. Also, this subsection provides a list of related links that provide the reader with additional information about Unicode®. The **How to Use this Site** subsection contains information about using and navigating the site as well hyperlinks to additional resources.

The *General Information* section contains seven subsections: **Where is my Character?**, **Display Problems?**, **Useful Resources**, **Enabled Products**, **Technical Notes**, **Mail Lists** and **Conferences**. The main areas covered in this section include a link to the Unicode® code charts (a complete listing of code values) assembled by the Unicode® Consortium, as well as a detailed outline on how to locate an encoded character in the code chart. Also, the section contains advice on how to configure different operating systems and Web browsers so that the Unicode® characters can be viewed properly. Moreover, from this section, the user can navigate to other sites that provide information on various topics such as, fonts, linguistics and other standards such as the *Armenian Standards Page* and the *Chinese GB 18030 Encoding Standard*.

The Consortium section consists of five subsections: **Who we are**, **Our Members**, **How to Join**, **Press Info** and **Contact Us**. This section provides a list of the current Unicode® Consortium members as well as information on how to become a member. Privileges for each member type—*full*, *associate*, *specialist* and *individual*—and the fees assessed to each member are listed here.

The Unicode® Standard section consists of nine subsections: **Start Here**, **Latest Version**, **Technical Reports**, **Code Charts**, **Unicode Data**, **Updates & Errata**, **Unicode Policies**, **Glossary** and **FAQ**. This section describes the updates applied to the latest version of the Unicode® Standard, as well as categorizing all defined encoding. The user can learn how the latest version has been modified to encompass more features and capabilities. For instance, one enhancement of Version 3.1 is that it contains additional encoded characters. Also, if users are unfamiliar with vocabulary terms used by the Unicode® Consortium, then they can navigate to the **Glossary** subsection.

The Work in Progress section consists of three subsections: **Calendar of Meetings**, **Proposed Characters** and **Submitting Proposals**. This section presents the user with a catalog of the recent characters included into the Unicode® Standard scheme as well as those characters being considered for inclusion. If users determine that a character has been overlooked, then they can submit a written proposal for the inclusion of that character. The **Submitting Proposals** subsection contains strict guidelines that must be adhered to when submitting written proposals.

The For Members section consists of two subsections: **Member Resources** and **Working Documents**. These subsections are password protected; only consortium members can access these links.

D.6 Using Unicode®

The MC++ application in Fig. D.3–Fig. D.5 displays the text "Welcome to Unicode!" in eight different languages: English, French, German, Japanese, Portuguese, Russian, Spanish and Simplified Chinese. The necessary characters are specified using their UTF-16 encoding values. [*Note*: The Unicode® Consortium's Web site contains a link to code charts that lists the 16-bit Unicode® code values.]

```
1    // Fig. D.3: Unicode.h
2    // Using unicode encoding.
3
4    #pragma once
5
6    #using <system.dll>
7    #using <mscorlib.dll>
8    #using <system.drawing.dll>
9    #using <system.windows.forms.dll>
10
```

Fig. D.3   **Unicode** class demonstrates Unicode values for multiple languages. (Part 1 of 2.)

```
11   using namespace System;
12   using namespace System::Drawing;
13   using namespace System::Windows::Forms;
14
15   public __gc class Unicode : public Form
16   {
17   public:
18      Unicode();
19
20   private:
21      Label *lblChinese, *lblSpanish, *lblRussian, *lblPortuguese,
22         *lblJapanese, *lblGerman, *lblFrench, *lblEnglish;
23
24      void InitializeComponent();
25      void Unicode_Load( Object *sender, EventArgs *e );
26   }; // end class Unicode
```

Fig. D.3   **Unicode** class demonstrates Unicode values for multiple languages. (Part 2 of 2.)

```
1    // Fig. D.4: Unicode.h
2    // Method definitions for class Unicode.
3
4    #include "Unicode.h"
5
6    Unicode::Unicode()
7    {
8       InitializeComponent();
9    } // end constructor
10
11   void Unicode::InitializeComponent()
12   {
13      this->lblChinese = new Label();
14      this->lblSpanish = new Label();
15      this->lblRussian = new Label();
16      this->lblPortuguese = new Label();
17      this->lblJapanese = new Label();
18      this->lblGerman = new Label();
19      this->lblFrench = new Label();
20      this->lblEnglish = new Label();
21      this->SuspendLayout();
22
23      // lblChinese
24      this->lblChinese->Font = new Drawing::Font(
25         S"Microsoft Sans Serif", 14.25, FontStyle::Regular,
26         GraphicsUnit::Point, 0 );
27      this->lblChinese->Location = Point( 336, 152 );
28      this->lblChinese->Name = S"lblChinese";
29      this->lblChinese->Size = Drawing::Size( 280, 32 );
30      this->lblChinese->TabIndex = 17;
31
```

Fig. D.4   **Unicode** class method definitions. (Part 1 of 4.)

```
32        // lblSpanish
33        this->lblSpanish->Font = new Drawing::Font(
34           S"Microsoft Sans Serif", 14.25, FontStyle::Regular,
35           GraphicsUnit::Point, 0 );
36        this->lblSpanish->Location = Point( 336, 104 );
37        this->lblSpanish->Name = S"lblSpanish";
38        this->lblSpanish->Size = Drawing::Size( 280, 32 );
39        this->lblSpanish->TabIndex = 16;
40
41        // lblRussian
42        this->lblRussian->Font = new Drawing::Font(
43           S"Microsoft Sans Serif", 14.25, FontStyle::Regular,
44           GraphicsUnit::Point, 0 );
45        this->lblRussian->Location = Point( 336, 56 );
46        this->lblRussian->Name = S"lblRussian";
47        this->lblRussian->Size = Drawing::Size( 280, 32 );
48        this->lblRussian->TabIndex = 15;
49
50        // lblPortuguese
51        this->lblPortuguese->Font = new Drawing::Font(
52           S"Microsoft Sans Serif", 14.25, FontStyle::Regular,
53           GraphicsUnit::Point, 0 );
54        this->lblPortuguese->Location = Point( 336, 8 );
55        this->lblPortuguese->Name = S"lblPortuguese";
56        this->lblPortuguese->Size = Drawing::Size( 280, 32 );
57        this->lblPortuguese->TabIndex = 14;
58
59        // lblJapanese
60        this->lblJapanese->Font = new Drawing::Font(
61           S"Microsoft Sans Serif", 14.25, FontStyle::Regular,
62           GraphicsUnit::Point, 0 );
63        this->lblJapanese->Location = Point( 8, 152 );
64        this->lblJapanese->Name = S"lblJapanese";
65        this->lblJapanese->Size = Drawing::Size( 304, 32 );
66        this->lblJapanese->TabIndex = 13;
67
68        // lblGerman
69        this->lblGerman->Font = new Drawing::Font(
70           S"Microsoft Sans Serif", 14.25, FontStyle::Regular,
71           GraphicsUnit::Point, 0 );
72        this->lblGerman->Location = Point( 8, 104 );
73        this->lblGerman->Name = S"lblGerman";
74        this->lblGerman->Size = Drawing::Size( 304, 32 );
75        this->lblGerman->TabIndex = 12;
76
77        // lblFrench
78        this->lblFrench->Font = new Drawing::Font(
79           S"Microsoft Sans Serif", 14.25, FontStyle::Regular,
80           GraphicsUnit::Point, 0 );
81        this->lblFrench->Location = Point( 8, 56 );
82        this->lblFrench->Name = S"lblFrench";
83        this->lblFrench->Size = Drawing::Size( 304, 32 );
84        this->lblFrench->TabIndex = 11;
85
```

Fig. D.4   **Unicode** class method definitions. (Part 2 of 4.)

```
 86       // lblEnglish
 87       this->lblEnglish->Font = new Drawing::Font(
 88          S"Microsoft Sans Serif", 14.25, FontStyle::Regular,
 89          GraphicsUnit::Point, 0 );
 90       this->lblEnglish->Location = Point( 8, 8 );
 91       this->lblEnglish->Name = S"lblEnglish";
 92       this->lblEnglish->Size = Drawing::Size( 304, 32 );
 93       this->lblEnglish->TabIndex = 10;
 94
 95       // Unicode
 96       this->AutoScaleBaseSize = Drawing::Size( 5, 13 );
 97       this->ClientSize = Drawing::Size( 624, 197 );
 98
 99       Control *tempControl[] = { this->lblChinese,
100          this->lblSpanish, this->lblRussian, this->lblPortuguese,
101          this->lblJapanese, this->lblGerman, this->lblFrench,
102          this->lblEnglish };
103
104       this->Controls->AddRange( tempControl );
105       this->Name = S"Unicode";
106       this->Text = S"Unicode";
107       this->Load += new EventHandler( this, Unicode_Load );
108
109       this->ResumeLayout();
110    } // end method InitializeComponent
111
112    void Unicode::Unicode_Load( Object *sender, EventArgs *e )
113    {
114       // exclamation point
115       __wchar_t exclamation = 0x0021;
116
117       // English
118       __wchar_t english __gc[] = { 0x0057, 0x0065, 0x006C,  0x0063,
119          0x006F, 0x006D, 0x0065, 0x0020, 0x0074, 0x006F, 0x0020 };
120
121       lblEnglish->Text = String::Concat( new String( english ),
122          S"Unicode", exclamation.ToString() );
123
124       // French
125       __wchar_t french __gc[] = { 0x0042, 0x0069, 0x0065, 0x006E,
126          0x0076, 0x0065, 0x006E, 0x0075, 0x0065, 0x0020, 0x0061,
127          0x0075, 0x0020 };
128
129       lblFrench->Text = String::Concat( new String( french ),
130          S"Unicode", exclamation.ToString() );
131
132       // German
133       __wchar_t german __gc[] = { 0x0057, 0x0069, 0x006C, 0x006B,
134          0x006F, 0x006D, 0x006D, 0x0065, 0x006E, 0x0020, 0x007A,
135          0x0075, 0x0020 };
136
137       lblGerman->Text =  String::Concat( new String( german ),
138          S"Unicode", exclamation.ToString() );
139
```

Fig. D.4   **Unicode** class method definitions. (Part 3 of 4.)

```
140       // Japanese
141       __wchar_t japanese __gc[] = { 0x3078,  0x3087, 0x3045, 0x3053,
142          0x305D, 0x0021 };
143
144       lblJapanese->Text = String::Concat( S"Unicode",
145          new String( japanese ) );
146
147       // Portuguese
148       __wchar_t portuguese __gc[] = { 0x0053, 0x0065, 0x006A, 0x0061,
149          0x0020, 0x0062, 0x0065, 0x006D, 0x0020, 0x0076, 0x0069,
150          0x006E, 0x0064, 0x006F, 0x0020, 0x0061, 0x0020 };
151
152       lblPortuguese->Text = String::Concat( new String( portuguese ),
153          S"Unicode", exclamation.ToString() );
154
155       // Russian
156       __wchar_t russian __gc[] = { 0x0414, 0x043E, 0x0431, 0x0440,
157          0x043E, 0x0020, 0x043F, 0x043E, 0x0436, 0x0430, 0x043B,
158          0x043E, 0x0432, 0x0430, 0x0442, 0x044A, 0x0020, 0x0432,
159          0x0020 };
160
161       lblRussian->Text = String::Concat( new String( russian ),
162          S"Unicode", exclamation.ToString() );
163
164       // Spanish
165       __wchar_t spanish __gc[] = { 0x0042, 0x0069, 0x0065, 0x006E,
166          0x0076, 0x0065, 0x006E, 0x0069, 0x0064, 0x006F, 0x0020,
167          0x0061, 0x0020 };
168
169       lblSpanish->Text = String::Concat( new String( spanish ),
170          S"Unicode", exclamation.ToString() );
171
172       // Simplified Chinese
173       __wchar_t chinese __gc[] = { 0x6B22, 0x8FCE, 0x4F7F, 0x7528,
174          0x0020 };
175
176       lblChinese->Text = String::Concat( new String( chinese ),
177          S"Unicode", exclamation.ToString() );
178 } // end method Unicode_Load
```

Fig. D.4   Unicode class method definitions. (Part 4 of 4.)

```
1  // Fig. D.5: Unicode.h
2  // Entry point for application.
3
4  #include "Unicode.h"
5
6  int __stdcall WinMain()
7  {
8     Application::Run( new Unicode() );
9
10     return 0;
11 } // end function WinMain
```

Fig. D.5   Unicode class driver. (Part 1 of 2.)

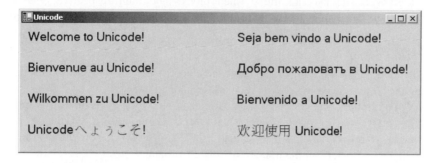

Fig. D.5   `Unicode` class driver. (Part 2 of 2.)

Lines 118–119 contain the hexadecimal codes for the English text. The **Code Charts** page on the Unicode® Consortium Web site contains a document that lists the code values for the **Basic Latin** *block* (or category), which includes the English alphabet. The first seven hexadecimal codes in lines 118–119 equate to "**Welcome** ". For specifying hexadecimal values in MC++, the format `0xyyyy` is used, where *yyyy* represents the hexadecimal number. For example, the letter "W" (with hexadecimal code `0057`) is denoted by `0x0057`. Line 36 contains the hexadecimal for the *space* character (`0x0020`). Lines 121–122 create a new string from the character array and append the word "Unicode." "Unicode" is not encoded because it is a registered trademark and has no equivalent translation in most languages. Line 122 also uses variable `exclamation` (line 115), a `__wchar_t` containing the `0x0021` notation for the exclamation mark (`!`).

The remaining welcome messages (lines 125–174) contain the Unicode® values for the other seven languages. The code values used for the French, German, Portuguese and Spanish text are located in the **Basic Latin** block, the code values used for the Simplified Chinese text are located in the **CJK Unified Ideographs** block, the code values used for the Russian text are located in the **Cyrillic** block and the code values used for the Japanese text are located in the **Hiragana** block.

[*Note*: To render the Asian characters in a Windows application, you may need to install the proper language files on your computer. To do this in Windows 2000, open the **Regional Options** dialog from the **Control Panel** (**Start > Settings > Control Panel**). At the bottom of the **General** tab is a list of languages. Check the **Japanese** and the **Traditional Chinese** checkboxes, and press **Apply**. Follow the directions of the install wizard to install the languages. For additional assistance, visit `www.unicode.org/help/display_problems.html`.]

D.7 Character Ranges

The Unicode® Standard assigns code values, which range from `0000` (**Basic Latin**) to `E007F` (*Tags*), to the written characters of the world. Currently, there are code values for 94,140 characters. To simplify the search for a character and its associated code value, the Unicode® Standard generally groups code values by *script* and function (i.e., Latin characters are grouped in a block, mathematical operators are grouped in another block, etc.). As a rule, a script is a single writing system that is used for multiple languages (e.g., the Latin script is used for English, French, Spanish, etc.) The **Code Charts** page on the Unicode®

Consortium Web site lists all the defined blocks and their respective code values. Figure D.6 lists some blocks (scripts) from the Web site and their ranges of code values.

D.8 Summary

Before Unicode®, software developers were plagued by the use of inconsistent character encoding (i.e., numeric values for characters). Most countries and organizations had their own encoding systems, which were incompatible. A good example is the different encoding systems on the Windows and Macintosh platforms. Computers process data by converting characters to numeric values. For instance, the character "a" is converted to a numeric value so that a computer can manipulate that piece of data.

Without Unicode®, localization of global software requires significant modifications to the source code, which results in increased cost and in delays releasing the product. Localization is necessary with each release of a version. By the time a software product is localized for a particular market, a newer version, which needs to be localized as well, is ready for distribution. As a result, it is cumbersome and costly to produce and distribute global software products in a market where there is no universal character encoding standard.

Script	Range of Code Values
Arabic	U+0600–U+06FF
Basic Latin	U+0000–U+007F
Bengali (India)	U+0980–U+09FF
Cherokee (Native America)	U+13A0–U+13FF
CJK Unified Ideographs (East Asia)	U+4E00–U+9FAF
Cyrillic (Russia and Eastern Europe)	U+0400–U+04FF
Ethiopic	U+1200–U+137F
Greek	U+0370–U+03FF
Hangul Jamo (Korea)	U+1100–U+11FF
Hebrew	U+0590–U+05FF
Hiragana (Japan)	U+3040–U+309F
Khmer (Cambodia)	U+1780–U+17FF
Lao (Laos)	U+0E80–U+0EFF
Mongolian	U+1800–U+18AF
Myanmar	U+1000–U+109F
Ogham (Ireland)	U+1680–U+169F
Runic (Germany and Scandinavia)	U+16A0–U+16FF
Sinhala (Sri Lanka)	U+0D80–U+0DFF
Telugu (India)	U+0C00–U+0C7F
Thai	U+0E00–U+0E7F

Fig. D.6   Some character ranges.

The Unicode® Consortium developed the Unicode® Standard in response to the serious problems created by multiple character encodings and the use of those encodings. The Unicode® Standard facilitates the production and distribution of localized software. It outlines a specification for the consistent encoding of the world's characters and symbols. Software products that handle text encoded in the Unicode® Standard need to be localized, but the localization process is simpler and more efficient because the numeric values need not be converted. The Unicode® Standard is designed to be universal, efficient, uniform and unambiguous.

A universal encoding system encompasses all commonly used characters; an efficient encoding system parses text files easily; a uniform encoding system assigns fixed values to all characters; and an unambiguous encoding system represents the same character for any given value.

Unicode® extends the limited ASCII character set to include all the major characters of the world. Unicode® makes use of three Unicode® Transformation Formats (UTF): UTF-8, UTF-16 and UTF-32, each of which may be appropriate for use in different contexts. UTF-8 data consists of 8-bit bytes (sequences of one, two, three or four bytes depending on the character being encoded) and is well suited for ASCII-based systems when there is a predominance of one-byte characters (ASCII represents characters as one-byte). UTF-8 is a variable-width encoding form that is more compact for text involving mostly Latin characters and ASCII punctuation.

UTF-16 is the default encoding form of the Unicode® Standard. It is a variable-width encoding form that uses 16-bit code units instead of bytes. Most characters are represented by a single unit, but some characters require surrogate pairs. Surrogates are 16-bit integers in the range D800 through DFFF, which are used solely for the purpose of "escaping" into higher-numbered characters. Without surrogate pairs, the UTF-16 encoding form can only encompass 65,000 characters, but with the surrogate pairs, this is expanded to include over a million characters.

UTF-32 is a 32-bit encoding form. The major advantage of the fixed-width encoding form is that it uniformly expresses all characters, so that they are easy to handle in arrays and so forth.

The Unicode® Standard consists of characters. A character is any written component that can be represented by a numeric value. Characters are represented using glyphs, various shapes, fonts and sizes for displaying characters.

Code values are bit combinations that represent encoded characters. The Unicode® notation for a code value is U+yyyy in which U+ refers to the Unicode® code values, as opposed to other hexadecimal values. The yyyy represents a four-digit hexadecimal number. When specifying hexadecimal values in MC++, the format 0xyyyy is used, where yyyy represents the hexadecimal number. Currently, the Unicode® Standard provides code values for 94,140 character representations.

An advantage of the Unicode® Standard is its impact on the overall performance of the international economy. Applications that conform to an encoding standard can be processed easily by computers anywhere. Another advantage of the Unicode® Standard is its portability. Applications written in Unicode® can easily be transferred to different operating systems, databases, Web browsers, etc. Most companies currently support, or are planning to support, Unicode®.

```
 6    <!-- Our first Web page. -->
 7
 8    <html xmlns = "http://www.w3.org/1999/xhtml">
 9       <head>
10          <title>Welcome</title>
11       </head>
12
13       <body>
14          <p>Welcome to XHTML!</p>
15       </body>
16    </html>
```

Fig. E.1   First XHTML example. (Part 2 of 2.)

XHTML markup contains text that represents the content of a document and *elements* that specify a document's structure. Some important elements of an XHTML document include the **html** element, the **head** element and the **body** element. The **html** element encloses the *head section* (represented by the **head** *element*) and the *body section* (represented by the **body** *element*). The head section contains information about the XHTML document, such as the *title* of the document. The head section also can contain special document-formatting instructions called *style sheets* and client-side programs called *scripts* for creating dynamic Web pages. The body section contains the page's content that the browser displays when the user visits the Web page.

XHTML documents delimit an element with *start* and *end* tags. A start tag consists of the element name in angle brackets (e.g., **<html>**). An end tag consists of the element name preceded by a **/** in angle brackets (e.g., **</html>**). In this example, lines 8 and 16 define the start and end of the **html** element. Note that the end tag on line 16 has the same name as the start tag, but is preceded by a **/** inside the angle brackets. Many start tags define *attributes* that provide additional information about an element. Browsers can use this additional information to determine how to process the element. Each attribute has a *name* and a *value* separated by an equal sign (**=**). Line 8 specifies a required attribute (**xmlns**) and value (**http://www.w3.org/1999/xhtml**) for the **html** element in an XHTML document. For now, simply copy and paste the **html** element start tag on line 8 into your XHTML documents. We discuss the details of the **html** element's **xmlns** attribute in Chapter 15, Extensible Markup Language (XML).

Common Programming Error E.1

Not enclosing attribute values in either single or double quotes is a syntax error.

Common Programming Error E.2

Using uppercase letters in an XHTML element or attribute name is a syntax error.

An XHTML document divides the **html** element into two sections—head and body. Lines 9–11 define the Web page's head section with a **head** element. Line 10 specifies a **title** element. This is called a *nested element*, because it is enclosed in the **head** element's start and end tags. The **head** element also is a nested element, because it is enclosed in the **html** element's start and end tags. The **title** element describes the Web page. Titles usually appear in the *title bar* at the top of the browser window and also as the text identifying a page when users add the page to their list of **Favorites** or **Bookmarks**, which enable users to return to their favorite sites. Search engines (i.e., sites that allow users to search the Web) also use the **title** for cataloging purposes.

Good Programming Practice E.3

Indenting nested elements emphasizes a document's structure and promotes readability.

Common Programming Error E.3

XHTML does not permit tags to overlap—a nested element's end tag must appear in the document before the enclosing element's end tag. For example, the nested XHTML tags **<head><title>hello</head></title>** *cause a syntax error, because the enclosing* **head** *element's ending* **</head>** *tag appears before the nested* **title** *element's ending* **</title>** *tag.*

Good Programming Practice E.4

Use a consistent **title** *naming convention for all pages on a site. For example, if a site is named "Bailey's Web Site," then the* **title** *of the main page might be "Bailey's Web Site—Links." This practice can help users better understand the Web site's structure.*

Line 13 opens the document's **body** element. The body section of an XHTML document specifies the document's content, which may include text and tags.

Some tags, such as the *paragraph tags* (**<p>** and **</p>**) in line 14, mark up text for display in a browser. All text placed between the **<p>** and **</p>** tags form one paragraph. When the browser renders a paragraph, a blank line usually precedes and follows paragraph text.

This document ends with two closing tags (lines 15–16). These tags close the **body** and **html** elements, respectively. The ending **</html>** tag in an XHTML document informs the browser that the XHTML markup is complete.

To view this example in Internet Explorer, perform the following steps:

1. Copy the Appendix E examples onto your machine by downloading the examples from **www.deitel.com**.

2. Launch Internet Explorer, and select **Open...** from the **File** Menu. This displays the **Open** dialog.

3. Click the **Open** dialog's **Browse...** button to display the **Microsoft Internet Explorer** file dialog.

4. Navigate to the directory containing the Appendix E examples and select the file **main.html**; then, click **Open**.

5. Click **OK** to have Internet Explorer render the document. Other examples are opened in a similar manner.

At this point your browser window should appear similar to the sample screen capture shown in Fig. E.1. (Note that we resized the browser window to save space in the book.)

E.4 W3C XHTML Validation Service

Programming Web-based applications can be complex, and XHTML documents must be written correctly to ensure that browsers process them properly. To promote correctly written documents, the World Wide Web Consortium (W3C) provides a *validation service* (**validator.w3.org**) for checking a document's syntax. Documents can be validated either from a URL that specifies the location of the file or by uploading a file to the site **validator.w3.org/file-upload.html**. Uploading a file copies the file from the user's computer to another computer on the Internet. Figure E.2 shows **main.html** (Fig. E.1) being uploaded for validation. Although the W3C's Web page indicates that the service name is **HTML Validation Service**,[3] the validation service is able to validate the syntax of XHTML documents. All the XHTML examples in this book have been validated successfully through **validator.w3.org**.

By clicking **Browse...**, users can select files on their own computers for upload. After selecting a file, clicking the **Validate this document** button uploads and validates the file. Figure E.3 shows the results of validating **main.html**. This document does not contain any syntax errors. If a document does contain syntax errors, the Validation Service displays error messages describing the errors.

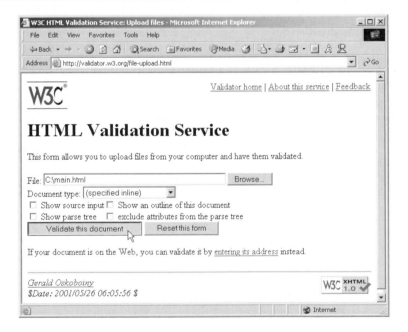

Fig. E.2   Validating an XHTML document. (Courtesy of World Wide Web Consortium (W3C).)

---

3. HTML (HyperText Markup Language) is the predecessor of XHTML designed for marking up Web content. HTML is a deprecated technology.

Testing and Debugging Tip E.1

Use a validation service, such as the W3C HTML Validation Service, to confirm that an XHTML document is syntactically correct.

E.5 Headers

Some text in an XHTML document may be more important than some other. For example, the text in this section is considered more important than a footnote. XHTML provides six *headers*, called *header elements*, for specifying the relative importance of information. Figure E.4 demonstrates these elements (**h1** through **h6**).

Portability Tip E.1

The text size used to display each header element can vary significantly between browsers.

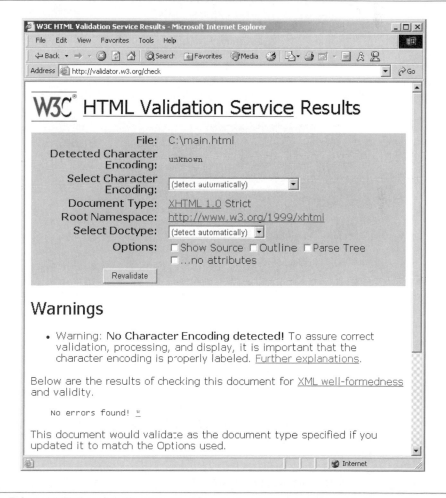

Fig. E.3   XHTML validation results. (Courtesy of World Wide Web Consortium (W3C).)

```
1   <?xml version = "1.0"?>
2   <!DOCTYPE html PUBLIC "-//W3C//DTD XHTML 1.0 Strict//EN"
3       "http://www.w3.org/TR/xhtml11/DTD/xhtml11-strict.dtd">
4
5   <!-- Fig. E.4: header.html -->
6   <!-- XHTML headers.          -->
7
8   <html xmlns = "http://www.w3.org/1999/xhtml">
9       <head>
10          <title>Headers</title>
11      </head>
12
13      <body>
14
15          <h1>Level 1 Header</h1>
16          <h2>Level 2 header</h2>
17          <h3>Level 3 header</h3>
18          <h4>Level 4 header</h4>
19          <h5>Level 5 header</h5>
20          <h6>Level 6 header</h6>
21
22      </body>
23   </html>
```

Fig. E.4   Header elements **h1** through **h6**.

Header element **h1** (line 15) is considered the most significant header and is rendered in a larger font than the other five headers (lines 16–20). Each successive header element (i.e., **h2**, **h3**, etc.) is rendered in a smaller font.

Look-and-Feel Observation E.1

Placing a header at the top of every XHTML page helps viewers understand the purpose of each page.

Look-and-Feel Observation E.2

Use larger headers to emphasize more important sections of a Web page.

E.6 Linking

One of the most important XHTML features is the *hyperlink,* which references (or *links* to) other resources, such as XHTML documents and images. In XHTML, both text and images can act as hyperlinks. Web browsers typically underline text hyperlinks and color their text blue by default, so that users can distinguish hyperlinks from plain text. In Fig. E.5, we create text hyperlinks to four different Web sites.

Line 17 introduces the **<strong>** tag. Browsers typically display text marked up with **<strong>** in a bold font.

```
1   <?xml version = "1.0"?>
2   <!DOCTYPE html PUBLIC "-//W3C//DTD XHTML 1.0 Strict//EN"
3      "http://www.w3.org/TR/xhtml1/DTD/xhtml1-strict.dtd">
4
5   <!-- Fig. E.5: links.html        -->
6   <!-- Introduction to hyperlinks. -->
7
8   <html xmlns = "http://www.w3.org/1999/xhtml">
9      <head>
10        <title>Links</title>
11     </head>
12
13     <body>
14
15        <h1>Here are my favorite sites</h1>
16
17        <p><strong>Click a name to go to that page.</strong></p>
18
19        <!-- create four text hyperlinks -->
20        <p>
21           <a href = "http://www.deitel.com">Deitel</a>
22        </p>
23
24        <p>
25           <a href = "http://www.prenhall.com">Prentice Hall</a>
26        </p>
27
28        <p>
29           <a href = "http://www.yahoo.com">Yahoo!</a>
30        </p>
31
32        <p>
33           <a href = "http://www.usatoday.com">USA Today</a>
34        </p>
35
36     </body>
37  </html>
```

Fig. E.5   Linking to other Web pages. (Part 1 of 2.)

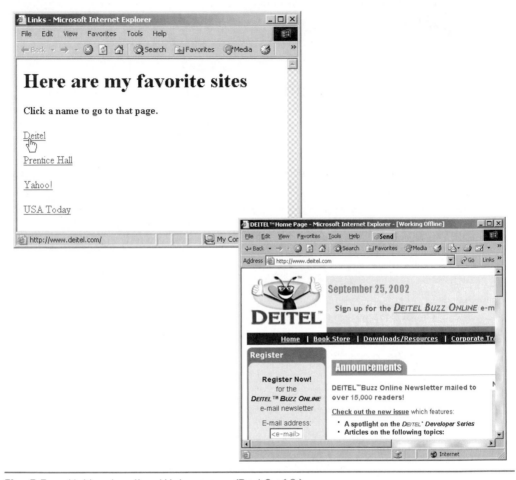

Fig. E.5   Linking to other Web pages. (Part 2 of 2.)

Links are created with the ***a*** (*anchor*) *element*. Line 21 defines a hyperlink that links the text **Deitel** to the URL assigned to attribute ***href***, which specifies the location of a linked resource, such as a Web page, a file or an e-mail address. This particular anchor element links to a Web page located at **http://www.deitel.com**. When a URL does not indicate a specific document on the Web site, the Web server returns a default Web page. This pages often is called **index.html**; however, most Web servers can be configured to to use any file as the default Web page for the site. (Open **http://www.deitel.com** in one browser window and **http://www.deitel.com/index.html** in a second browser window to confirm that they are identical.) If the Web server cannot locate a requested document, the server returns an error indication to the Web browser, and the browser displays an error message to the user.

Anchors can link to e-mail addresses through a ***mailto:*** URL. When someone clicks this type of anchored link, most browsers launch the dcfault e-mail program (e.g., Outlook Express) to enable the user to write an e-mail message to the linked address. Figure E.6 demonstrates this type of anchor.

```
 1    <?xml version = "1.0"?>
 2    <!DOCTYPE html PUBLIC "-//W3C//DTD XHTML 1.0 Strict//EN"
 3        "http://www.w3.org/TR/xhtml1/DTD/xhtml1-strict.dtd">
 4
 5    <!-- Fig. E.6: contact.html   -->
 6    <!-- Adding email hyperlinks. -->
 7
 8    <html xmlns = "http://www.w3.org/1999/xhtml">
 9        <head>
10            <title>Contact Page</title>
11            </title>
12        </head>
13
14        <body>
15
16            <p>My email address is
17                <a href = "mailto:deitel@deitel.com">
18                    deitel@deitel.com
19                </a>
20                . Click the address and your browser will
21                open an e-mail message and address it to me.
22            </p>
23        </body>
24    </html>
```

Fig. E.6   Linking to an e-mail address.

Lines 17–19 contain an e-mail link. The form of an e-mail anchor is **<a href = "mailto:**_emailaddress_**">...</a>**. In this case, we link to the e-mail address **deitel@deitel.com**.

E.7 Images

The examples discussed so far demonstrated how to mark up documents that contain only text. However, most Web pages contain both text and images. In fact, images are an equal and essential part of Web-page design. The two most popular image formats used by Web developers are Graphics Interchange Format (GIF) and Joint Photographic Experts Group (JPEG) images. Users can create images through specialized pieces of software, such as Adobe PhotoShop Elements and Jasc Paint Shop Pro (**www.jasc.com**). Images may also be acquired from various Web sites, such as **gallery.yahoo.com**. Figure E.7 demonstrates how to incorporate images into Web pages.

Lines 16–17 use an *img* element to insert an image in the document. The image file's location is specified with the **img** element's *src* attribute. In this case, the image is located in the same directory as this XHTML document, so only the image's file name is required. Optional attributes *width* and *height* specify the image's width and height, respectively. The document author can scale an image by increasing or decreasing the values of the image **width** and **height** attributes. If these attributes are omitted, the browser uses the image's actual width and height. Images are measured in *pixels* ("picture elements"), which represent dots of color on the screen. The image in Fig. E.7 is **300** pixels wide and **300** pixels high.

```
1   <?xml version = "1.0"?>
2   <!DOCTYPE html PUBLIC "-//W3C//DTD XHTML 1.0 Strict//EN"
3      "http://www.w3.org/TR/xhtml1/DTD/xhtml1-strict.dtd">
4
5   <!-- Fig. E.7: picture.html    -->
6   <!-- Adding images with XHTML. -->
7
8   <html xmlns = "http://www.w3.org/1999/xhtml">
9      <head>
10        <title>Images</title>
11     </head>
12
13     <body>
14
15        <p>
16           <img src = "pyramid.jpg" height = "300" width = "300"
17              alt = "digital art of a pyramid" />
18
19           <img src = "spaceship.jpg" height = "300" width = "300"
20              alt = "digital art of a spaceship" />
21        </p>
22
23     </body>
24  </html>
```

Fig. E.7   Placing images in XHTML files. (Part 1 of 2.)

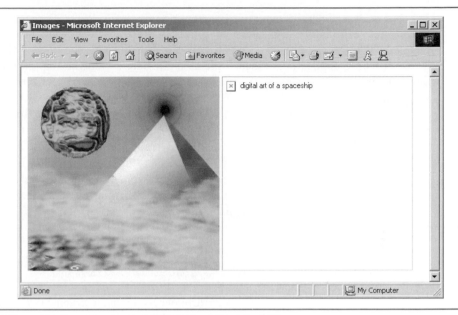

Fig. E.7   Placing images in XHTML files. (Part 2 of 2.)

Good Programming Practice E.5

*Always include the **width** and the **height** of an image inside the **<img>** tag. When the browser loads the XHTML file, it will know immediately from these attributes how much screen space to provide for the image and will lay out the page properly, even before it downloads the image.*

Performance Tip E.1

*Including the **width** and **height** attributes in an **<img>** tag will help the browser load and render pages faster.*

Common Programming Error E.4

Entering new dimensions for an image that change its inherent width-to-height ratio distorts the appearance of the image. For example, if your image is 200 pixels wide and 100 pixels high, you should ensure that any new dimensions have a 2:1 width-to-height ratio.

Every **img** element in an XHTML document has an **alt** attribute. If a browser cannot render an image, the browser displays the **alt** attribute's value. A browser might not be able to render an image for several reasons. It might not support images—as is the case with a *text-based browser* (i.e., a browser that can display only text)—or the client might have disabled image viewing to reduce download time. Figure E.7 shows Internet Explorer rendering the **alt** attribute's value when a document references a nonexistent image file (**spaceship.jpg**).

The **alt** attribute is important for creating *accessible* Web pages for users with disabilities, especially those with vision impairments and text-based browsers. Specialized software called *speech synthesizers* often are used by people with disabilities. These software applications "speak" the **alt** attribute's value so that the user knows what the browser is displaying. We discuss accessibility issues in detail in Chapter 20, Accessibility.

Some XHTML elements (called *empty elements*) contain only attributes and do not mark up text (i.e., text is not placed between the start and end tags). Empty elements (e.g., **img**) must be terminated, either by using the *forward slash character* (**/**) inside the closing right angle bracket (**>**) of the start tag or by explicitly including the end tag. When using the forward slash character, we add a space before the forward slash to improve readability (as shown at the ends of lines 17 and 20). Rather than using the forward slash character, lines 19–20 could be written with a closing **</img>** tag as follows:

```
<img src = "spaceship.jpg" height = "300" width = "300"
    alt = "digital art of a spaceship"></img>
```

By using images as hyperlinks, Web developers can create graphical Web pages that link to other resources. In Fig. E.8, we create six different image hyperlinks.

```
1   <?xml version = "1.0"?>
2   <!DOCTYPE html PUBLIC "-//W3C//DTD XHTML 1.0 Strict//EN"
3       "http://www.w3.org/TR/xhtml1/DTD/xhtml1-strict.dtd">
4
5   <!-- Fig. E.8: nav.html              -->
6   <!-- Using images as link anchors. -->
7
8   <html xmlns = "http://www.w3.org/1999/xhtml">
9       <head>
10          <title>Navigation Bar
11          </title>
12      </head>
13
14      <body>
15
16          <p>
17              <a href = "links.html">
18                  <img src = "buttons/links.jpg" width = "65"
19                      height = "50" alt = "Links Page" />
20              </a><br />
21
22              <a href = "list.html">
23                  <img src = "buttons/list.jpg" width = "65"
24                      height = "50" alt = "List Example Page" />
25              </a><br />
26
27              <a href = "contact.html">
```

Fig. E.8   Using images as link anchors. (Part 1 of 2.)

```
28                          <img src = "buttons/contact.jpg" width = "65"
29                              height = "50" alt = "Contact Page" />
30                      </a><br />
31
32                      <a href = "header.html">
33                          <img src = "buttons/header.jpg" width = "65"
34                              height = "50" alt = "Header Page" />
35                      </a><br />
36
37                      <a href = "table.html">
38                          <img src = "buttons/table.jpg" width = "65"
39                              height = "50" alt = "Table Page" />
40                      </a><br />
41
42                      <a href = "form.html">
43                          <img src = "buttons/form.jpg" width = "65"
44                              height = "50" alt = "Feedback Form" />
45                      </a><br />
46                  </p>
47
48              </body>
49          </html>
```

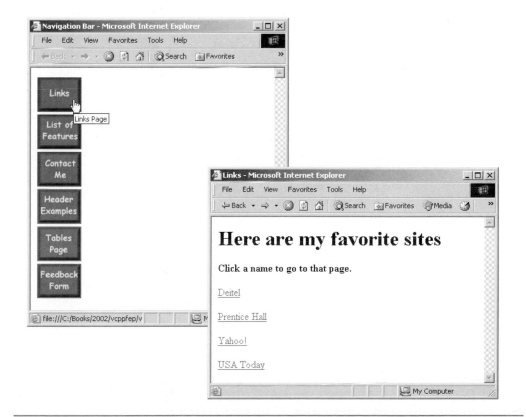

Fig. E.8   Using images as link anchors. (Part 2 of 2.)

Lines 17–20 create an *image hyperlink* by nesting an **img** element within an anchor (**a**) element. The value of the **img** element's **src** attribute value specifies that this image (**links.jpg**) resides in a directory named **buttons**. The **buttons** directory and the XHTML document are in the same directory. Images from other Web documents also can be referenced (after obtaining permission from the document's owner) by setting the **src** attribute to the name and location of the image.

On line 20, we introduce the ***br** element*, which most browsers render as a *line break*. Any markup or text following a **br** element is rendered on the next line. Like the **img** element, **br** is an example of an empty element terminated with a forward slash. We add a space before the forward slash to enhance readability.

E.8 Special Characters and More Line Breaks

When marking up text, certain characters or symbols (e.g., **<**) may be difficult to embed directly into an XHTML document. Some keyboards may not provide these symbols, or the presence of these symbols may cause syntax errors. For example, the markup

> **<p>if x < 10 then increment x by 1</p>**

results in a syntax error, because it uses the less-than character (**<**), which is reserved for start tags and end tags such as **<p>** and **</p>**. XHTML provides *special characters* or *entity references* (in the form **&***code***;**) for representing these characters. We could correct the previous line by writing

> **<p>if x < 10 then increment x by 1</p>**

which uses the special character ***<*** for the less-than symbol.

Figure E.9 demonstrates how to use special characters in an XHTML document. For a list of special characters, see Appendix G, XHTML Special Characters.

```
1   <?xml version = "1.0"?>
2   <!DOCTYPE html PUBLIC "-//W3C//DTD XHTML 1.0 Strict//EN"
3       "http://www.w3.org/TR/xhtml1/DTD/xhtml1-strict.dtd">
4
5   <!-- Fig. E.9: contact2.html       -->
6   <!-- Inserting special characters. -->
7
8   <html xmlns = "http://www.w3.org/1999/xhtml">
9      <head>
10        <title>Contact Page
11        </title>
12     </head>
13
14     <body>
15
16        <!-- special characters are   -->
17        <!-- entered using form &code; -->
18        <p>
```

Fig. E.9   Inserting special characters into XHTML. (Part 1 of 2.)

```
19              Click
20              <a href = "mailto:deitel@deitel.com">here
21              </a> to open an e-mail message addressed to
22              deitel@deitel.com.
23          </p>
24
25          <hr /> <!-- inserts a horizontal rule -->
26
27          <p>All information on this site is <strong>&copy;</strong>
28              Deitel <strong>&amp;</strong> Associates, Inc. 2003.</p>
29
30          <!-- to strike through text use <del> tags    -->
31          <!-- to subscript text use <sub> tags         -->
32          <!-- to superscript text use <sup> tags       -->
33          <!-- these tags are nested inside other tags -->
34          <p><del>You may download 3.14 x 10<sup>2</sup>
35              characters worth of information from this site.</del>
36              Only <sub>one</sub> download per hour is permitted.</p>
37
38          <p>Note: <strong>&lt; &frac14;</strong> of the information
39              presented here is updated daily.</p>
40
41      </body>
42  </html>
```

Fig. E.9   Inserting special characters into XHTML. (Part 2 of 2.)

Lines 27–28 contain other special characters, which are expressed as either word abbreviations (e.g., **amp** for ampersand and **copy** for copyright) or *hexadecimal (hex)* values (e.g., **&** is the hexadecimal representation of **&**). Hexadecimal numbers are base-16 numbers—digits in a hexadecimal number have values from 0 to 15 (a total of 16 different values). The letters A–F represent the hexadecimal digits corresponding to decimal values 10–15. Thus, in hexadecimal notation we can have numbers like 876 consisting solely of decimal-like digits, numbers like DA19F consisting of digits and letters, and numbers like DCB consisting solely of letters. We discuss hexadecimal numbers in detail in Appendix B, Number Systems.

In lines 34–36, we introduce three new elements. Most browsers render the **del** element as strike-through text. With this format, users can easily indicate document revisions. To *superscript* text (i.e., raise text on a line with a decreased font size) or *subscript* text (i.e., lower text on a line with a decreased font size), use the **sup** and **sub** elements, respectively. We also use special characters **<** for a less-than sign and **¼** for the fraction 1/4 (line 38).

In addition to special characters, this document introduces a *horizontal rule*, indicated by the **<hr />** tag in line 25. Most browsers render a horizontal rule as a horizontal line. The **<hr />** tag also inserts a line break above and below the horizontal line.

E.9 Unordered Lists

Up to this point, we have presented basic XHTML elements and attributes for linking to resources, creating headers, using special characters and incorporating images. In this section, we discuss how to organize information on a Web page using lists. In Appendix F, Introduction to XHTML: Part 2, we introduce another feature for organizing information, called a table. Figure E.10 displays text in an *unordered list* (i.e., a list that does not order its items by letter or number). The *unordered list element* **ul** creates a list in which each item begins with a bullet symbol (called a *disc*).

Each entry in an unordered list (element **ul** in line 20) is an **li** (*list item*) element (lines 23, 25, 27 and 29). Most Web browsers render these elements with a line break and a bullet symbol indented from the beginning of the new line.

```
1   <?xml version = "1.0"?>
2   <!DOCTYPE html PUBLIC "-//W3C//DTD XHTML 1.0 Strict//EN"
3      "http://www.w3.org/TR/xhtml1/DTD/xhtml1-strict.dtd">
4
5   <!-- Fig. E.10: links2.html              -->
6   <!-- Unordered list containing hyperlinks. -->
7
8   <html xmlns = "http://www.w3.org/1999/xhtml">
9      <head>
10        <title>Links</title>
11     </head>
12
13     <body>
14
15        <h1>Here are my favorite sites</h1>
16
17        <p><strong>Click on a name to go to that page.</strong></p>
18
19        <!-- create an unordered list -->
20        <ul>
21
22           <!-- add four list items -->
23           <li><a href = "http://www.deitel.com">Deitel</a></li>
24
```

Fig. E.10   Unordered lists in XHTML. (Part 1 of 2.)

```
25              <li><a href = "http://www.w3.org">W3C</a></li>
26
27              <li><a href = "http://www.yahoo.com">Yahoo!</a></li>
28
29              <li><a href = "http://www.cnn.com">CNN</a></li>
30
31          </ul>
32
33      </body>
34  </html>
```

Fig. E.10   Unordered lists in XHTML. (Part 2 of 2.)

E.10 Nested and Ordered Lists

Lists may be nested to represent hierarchical relationships, as in an outline format.
Figure E.11 demonstrates nested lists and *ordered lists* (i.e., list that order their items by
letter or number).

```
1   <?xml version = "1.0"?>
2   <!DOCTYPE html PUBLIC "-//W3C//DTD XHTML 1.0 Transitional//EN"
3      "http://www.w3.org/TR/xhtml1/DTD/xhtml1-transitional.dtd">
4
5   <!-- Fig. E.11: list.html            -->
6   <!-- Advanced Lists: nested and ordered. -->
7
8   <html xmlns = "http://www.w3.org/1999/xhtml">
9      <head>
10        <title>Lists</title>
11     </head>
12
13     <body>
14
15        <h1>The Best Features of the Internet</h1>
16
```

Fig. E.11   Nested and ordered lists in XHTML. (Part 1 of 3.)

```
17          <!-- create an unordered list -->
18          <ul>
19             <li>You can meet new people from countries around
20                the world.</li>
21
22             <li>
23                You have access to new media as it becomes public:
24
25                <!-- start nested list, use modified bullets -->
26                <!-- list ends with closing </ul> tag         -->
27                <ul>
28                   <li>New games</li>
29                   <li>
30                      New applications
31
32                      <!-- ordered nested list -->
33                      <ol type = "I">
34                         <li>For business</li>
35                         <li>For pleasure</li>
36                      </ol>
37
38                   </li>
39
40                   <li>Around the clock news</li>
41                   <li>Search engines</li>
42                   <li>Shopping</li>
43                   <li>
44                      Programming
45
46                      <!-- another nested ordered list -->
47                      <ol type = "a">
48                         <li>XML</li>
49                         <li>Visual C++</li>
50                         <li>XHTML</li>
51                         <li>Scripts</li>
52                         <li>New languages</li>
53                      </ol>
54
55                   </li>
56
57                </ul> <!-- ends nested list started in line 27 -->
58
59             </li>
60
61             <li>Links</li>
62             <li>Keeping in touch with old friends</li>
63             <li>It is the technology of the future!</li>
64
65          </ul>    <!-- ends unordered list started in line 18 -->
66
67          <h1>My 3 Favorite <em>CEOs</em></h1>
68
```

Fig. E.11   Nested and ordered lists in XHTML. (Part 2 of 3.)

```
69              <!-- ol elements without type attribute have -->
70              <!-- numeric sequence type (i.e., 1, 2, ...) -->
71              <ol>
72                 <li>Ant Chovy</li>
73                 <li>CeCe Sharp</li>
74                 <li>Albert Antstein</li>
75              </ol>
76
77         </body>
78    </html>
```

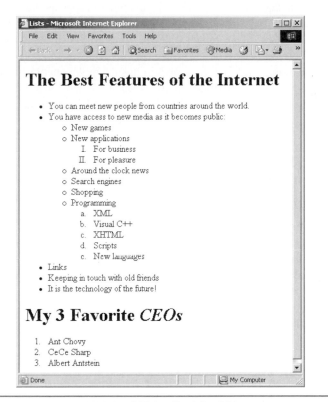

Fig. E.11   Nested and ordered lists in XHTML. (Part 3 of 3.)

The first ordered list begins in line 33. Attribute **type** specifies the *sequence type* (i.e., the set of numbers or letters used in the ordered list). In this case, setting **type** to **"I"** specifies upper-case roman numerals. Line 47 begins the second ordered list and sets attribute **type** to **"a"**, specifying lowercase letters for the list items. The last ordered list (lines 71–75) does not use attribute **type**. By default, the list's items are enumerated from one to three.

A Web browser indents each nested list to indicate a hierarchal relationship. By default, the items in the outermost unordered list (line 18) are preceded by discs. List items nested inside the unordered list of line 18 are preceded by *circles*. Although not demonstrated in this example, subsequent nested list items are preceded by *squares*. Unordered list items may be explicitly set to discs, circles or squares by setting the **ul** element's **type** attribute to **"disc"**, **"circle"** or **"square"**, respectively.

Note: XHTML is based on HTML (HyperText Markup Language)—a legacy technology of the World Wide Web Consortium (W3C). In HTML, it was common to specify the document's content, structure and formatting. Formatting might specify where the browser places an element in a Web page or the fonts and colors used to display an element. The so-called *strict* form of XHTML allows only a document's content and structure to appear in a valid XHTML document, and not that document's formatting. Our first several examples used only the strict form of XHTML. In fact, the purpose of lines 2–3 in each of the examples before Fig. E.11 was to indicate to the browser that each document conformed to the strict XHTML definition. This enables the browser to confirm that the document is valid. There are other XHTML document types as well. This particular example uses the XHTML *transitional* document type. This document type exists to enable XHTML document creators to use legacy HTML technologies in an XHTML document. In this example, the **type** attribute of the **ol** element (lines 33 and 47) is a legacy HTML technology. Changing lines 2–3, as shown in this example, enables us to demonstrate ordered lists with different numbering formats. Normally, such formatting is specified with style sheets. Most examples in this book adhere to strict HTML form.

Testing and Debugging Tip E.2

Most current browsers still attempt to render XHTML documents, even if they are invalid.

E.11 Summary

XHTML (Extensible Hypertext Markup Language) is a markup language for creating Web pages. In XHTML, text is marked up with elements, delimited by tags that are names contained in pairs of angle brackets. Some elements may contain additional markup called attributes, which provide additional information about the element. A key issue when using XHTML is the separation of the presentation of a document (i.e., the document's appearance when rendered by a browser) from the structure of the information in the document. A machine that runs specialized piece of software called a Web server stores XHTML documents.

Validation services (e.g., **validator.w3.org**) ensure that an XHTML document is syntactically correct. XHTML documents that are syntactically correct are guaranteed to render properly. XHTML documents that contain syntax errors may not display properly.

Every XHTML document contains a start **<html>** tag and an end **</html>** tag. Comments in XHTML always begin with **<!--** and end with **-->**. The browser ignores all text inside a comment.

Every XHTML document has a **head** element, which generally contains information, such as a title, and a **body** element, which contains the page content. Information in the **head** element generally is not rendered in the display window, but it could be made available to the user through other means.

The **title** element names a Web page. The title usually appears in the colored bar (called the title bar) at the top of the browser window and also appears as the text identifying a page when users add your page to their list of **Favorites** or **Bookmarks**.

The body of an XHTML document is the area in which the document's content is placed. The content may include text and tags. All text placed between the **<p>** and **</p>** tags forms one paragraph. The **<strong>** tag renders text in a bold font.

XHTML provides six headers (**h1** through **h6**) for specifying the relative importance of information. Header element **h1** is considered the most significant header and is rendered in a larger font than the other five headers. Each successive header element (i.e., **h2**, **h3**, etc.) is rendered in a smaller font.

Users can insert links with the **a** (anchor) element. The most important attribute for the **a** element is **href**, which specifies the resource (e.g., page, file or e-mail address) being linked. Web browsers typically underline text hyperlinks and color them blue by default. Anchors can link to an e-mail address, using a **mailto** URL. When someone clicks this type of anchored link, most browsers launch the default e-mail program (e.g., Outlook Express) to initiate an e-mail message to the linked address.

The **img** element's **src** attribute specifies an image's location. Optional attributes **width** and **height** specify the image width and height, respectively. Images are measured in pixels ("picture elements"), which represent dots of color on the screen. Every **img** element in a valid XHTML document must have an **alt** attribute, which contains text that is displayed if the client cannot render the image. The **alt** attribute makes Web pages more accessible to users with disabilities, especially those with vision impairments.

Some XHTML elements are empty elements, contain only attributes and do not mark up text. Empty elements (e.g., **img**) must be terminated, either by using the forward slash character (**/**) or by explicitly writing an end tag.

The **br** element causes most browsers to render a line break. Any markup or text following a **br** element is rendered on the next line.

XHTML provides special characters or entity references (in the form **&***code***;**) for representing characters that cannot be marked up. For example, the special character **<** represents the less-than symbol.

Most browsers render a horizontal rule, indicated by the **<hr />** tag, as a horizontal line. The **hr** element also inserts a line break above and below the horizontal line.

The unordered list element **ul** creates a list in which each item in the list begins with a bullet symbol (called a disc). Each entry in an unordered list is an **li** (list item) element. Most Web browsers render these elements with a line break and a bullet symbol at the beginning of the line. Lists may be nested to represent hierarchical data relationships. Attribute **type** specifies the sequence type (i.e., the set of numbers or letters used in the ordered list).

E.12 Internet and Web Resources

www.w3.org/TR/xhtml1
The *XHTML 1.0 Recommendation* contains XHTML 1.0 general information, compatibility issues, document type definition information, definitions, terminology and much more.

www.xhtml.org
XHTML.org provides XHTML development news and links to other XHTML resources, which include books and articles.

www.w3schools.com/xhtml/default.asp
The *XHTML School* provides XHTML quizzes and references. This page also contains links to XHTML syntax, validation and document type definitions.

validator.w3.org
This is the W3C XHTML validation-service site.

hotwired.lycos.com/webmonkey/00/50/index2a.html
This site provides an article about XHTML. Key sections of the article overview XHTML and discuss tags, attributes and anchors.

wdvl.com/Authoring/Languages/XML/XHTML
The Web Developers Virtual Library provides an introduction to XHTML. This site also contains articles, examples and links to other technologies.

www.w3.org/TR/1999/xhtml-modularization-19990406/DTD/doc
The XHTML 1.0 DTD documentation site provides links to DTD documentation for the strict, transitional and frameset document-type definitions.

Introduction to XHTML: Part 2

Objectives

- To create tables with rows and columns of data.
- To control table formatting.
- To create and use forms.
- To create and use image maps to aid in Web-page navigation.
- To make Web pages accessible to search engines through **`<meta>`** tags.
- To use the **`frameset`** element to display multiple Web pages in a single browser window.

Yea, from the table of my memory
I'll wipe away all trivial fond records.
William Shakespeare

Outline

F.1 Introduction

In the previous appendix, we introduced XHTML. We built several complete Web pages featuring text, hyperlinks, images, horizontal rules and line breaks. In this appendix, we discuss more substantial XHTML features, including presentation of information in *tables* and *incorporating forms* for collecting information from a Web-page visitor. We also introduce *internal linking* and *image maps* for enhancing Web-page navigation and *frames* for displaying multiple documents in the browser. By the end of this appendix, you will be familiar with the most commonly used XHTML features and will be able to create more complex Web documents. In this appendix, we do not present any MC++ programming.

F.2 Basic XHTML Tables

This section presents the XHTML *table*—a frequently used feature that organizes data into rows and columns. Our first example (Fig. F.1) uses a table with six rows and two columns to display price information for fruit.

```
1    <?xml version = "1.0"?>
2    <!DOCTYPE html PUBLIC "-//W3C//DTD XHTML 1.0 Strict//EN"
3        "http://www.w3.org/TR/xhtml1/DTD/xhtml1-strict.dtd">
4
5    <!-- Fig. F.1: table1.html   -->
6    <!-- Creating a basic table. -->
7
8    <html xmlns = "http://www.w3.org/1999/xhtml">
9       <head>
10          <title>A simple XHTML table</title>
11       </head>
```

Fig. F.1   XHTML table. (Part 1 of 3.)

```
12
13      <body>
14
15          <!-- the <table> tag begins table -->
16          <table border = "1" width = "40%"
17              summary = "This table provides information about
18                  the price of fruit">
19
20              <!-- <caption> tag summarizes table's    -->
21              <!-- contents to help visually impaired -->
22              <caption><strong>Price of Fruit</strong></caption>
23
24              <!-- <thead> is first section of table -->
25              <!-- it formats table header area        -->
26              <thead>
27                  <tr> <!-- <tr> inserts one table row -->
28                      <th>Fruit</th> <!-- insert heading cell -->
29                      <th>Price</th>
30                  </tr>
31              </thead>
32
33              <!-- all table content is enclosed within <tbody> -->
34              <tbody>
35                  <tr>
36                      <td>Apple</td> <!-- insert data cell -->
37                      <td>$0.25</td>
38                  </tr>
39
40                  <tr>
41                      <td>Orange</td>
42                      <td>$0.50</td>
43                  </tr>
44
45                  <tr>
46                      <td>Banana</td>
47                      <td>$1.00</td>
48                  </tr>
49
50                  <tr>
51                      <td>Pineapple</td>
52                      <td>$2.00</td>
53                  </tr>
54              </tbody>
55
56              <!-- <tfoot> is last section of table -->
57              <!-- it formats table footer           -->
58              <tfoot>
59                  <tr>
60                      <th>Total</th>
61                      <th>$3.75</th>
62                  </tr>
63              </tfoot>
64
```

Fig. F.1   XHTML table. (Part 2 of 3.)

```
65            </table>
66
67       </body>
68  </html>
```

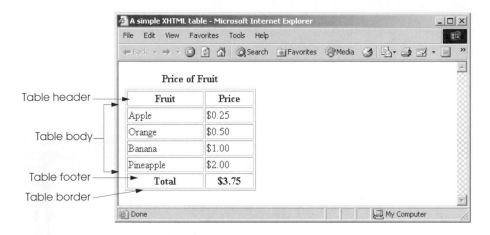

Fig. F.1   XHTML table. (Part 3 of 3.)

Tables are defined with the **table** element. Lines 16–18 specify the start tag for a table element that has several attributes. The ***border*** attribute specifies the table's border width in pixels. To create a table without a border, set **border** to **"0"**. This example assigns attribute **width "40%"**, to set the table's width to 40 percent of the browser's width. A developer can also set attribute **width** to a specified number of pixels.

Testing and Debugging Tip F.1

Try resizing the browser window to see how the width of the window affects the width of the table.

As its name implies, attribute ***summary*** (line 17) describes the table's contents. Speech devices use this attribute to make the table more accessible to users with visual impairments. The ***caption*** element (line 22) describes the table's content and helps text-based browsers interpret the table data. Text inside the **<caption>** tag is rendered above the table by most browsers. Attribute **summary** and element **caption** are two of many XHTML features that make Web pages more accessible to users with disabilities. We discuss accessibility programming in detail in Chapter 20, Accessibility.

A table has three distinct sections—*head*, *body* and *foot*. The head section (or *header cell*) is defined with a ***thead*** element (lines 26–31), which contains header information, such as column names. Each ***tr*** element (lines 27–30) defines an individual *table row*. The columns in the head section are defined with **th** elements. Most browsers center text formatted by **th** (table header column) elements and display it in bold. Table header elements are nested inside table row elements.

The body section, or *table body*, contains the table's primary data. The table body (lines 34–54) is defined in a **tbody** element. *Data cells* contain individual pieces of data and are defined with **td** (*table data*) elements.

The foot section (lines 58–63) is defined with a ***tfoot*** (table foot) element and represents a footer. Text commonly placed in the footer includes calculation results and footnotes. Like other sections, the foot section can contain table rows and each row can contain columns.

F.3 Intermediate XHTML Tables and Formatting

In the previous section, we explored the structure of a basic table. In Fig. F.2, we enhance our discussion of tables by introducing elements and attributes that allow the document author to build more complex tables.

The table begins on line 17. Element ***colgroup*** (lines 22–27) groups and formats columns. The ***col*** element (line 26) specifies two attributes in this example. The ***align*** attribute determines the alignment of text in the column. The ***span*** attribute determines how many columns the ***col*** element formats. In this case, we set **align**'s value to **"right"** and **span**'s value to **"1"** to right-align text in the first column (the column containing the picture of the camel in the sample screen capture).

Table cells are sized to fit the data they contain. Document authors can create larger data cells by using attributes ***rowspan*** and ***colspan***. The values assigned to these attributes specify the number of rows or columns occupied by a cell. The **th** element at lines 36–39 uses the attribute **rowspan = "2"** to allow the cell containing the picture of the python to use two vertically adjacent cells (thus, the cell *spans* two rows). The **th** element at lines 42–45 uses the attribute **colspan = "4"** to widen the header cell (containing **Python comparison** and **Approximate as of 12/2001**) to span four cells.

```
1   <?xml version = "1.0"?>
2   <!DOCTYPE html PUBLIC "-//W3C//DTD XHTML 1.0 Strict//EN"
3       "http://www.w3.org/TR/xhtml1/DTD/xhtml1-strict.dtd">
4
5   <!-- Fig. F.2: table2.html        -->
6   <!-- Intermediate table design. -->
7
8   <html xmlns = "http://www.w3.org/1999/xhtml">
9      <head>
10         <title>Tables</title>
11      </head>
12
13      <body>
14
15         <h1>Table Example Page</h1>
16
17         <table border = "1">
18            <caption>Here is a more complex sample table.</caption>
19
20            <!-- <colgroup> and <col> tags are used to -->
21            <!-- format entire columns                 -->
22            <colgroup>
23
```

Fig. F.2   Complex XHTML table. (Part 1 of 3.)

```
24              <!-- span attribute determines how many columns -->
25              <!-- the <col> tag affects                      -->
26              <col align = "right" span = "1" />
27          </colgroup>
28
29          <thead>
30
31              <!-- rowspans and colspans merge the specified    -->
32              <!-- number of cells vertically or horizontally   -->
33              <tr>
34
35                  <!-- merge two rows -->
36                  <th rowspan = "2">
37                      <img src = "snake.gif" width = "220"
38                          height = "100" alt = "python picture" />
39                  </th>
40
41                  <!-- merge four columns -->
42                  <th colspan = "4" valign = "top">
43                      <h1>Python comparison</h1><br />
44                      <p>Approximate as of 12/2001</p>
45                  </th>
46              </tr>
47
48              <tr valign = "bottom">
49                  <th>Average Length (Feet)</th>
50                  <th>Indigenous region</th>
51                  <th>Arboreal?</th>
52              </tr>
53
54          </thead>
55
56          <tbody>
57
58              <tr>
59                  <th>Indian Python</th>
60                  <td>20</td>
61                  <td>southeast Asia</td>
62                  <td rowspan = "2">Indian Python</td>
63              </tr>
64
65              <tr>
66                  <th>Royal Python</th>
67                  <td>4</td>
68                  <td>equatorial West Africa</td>
69              </tr>
70
71          </tbody>
72
73      </table>
74
75  </body>
76 </html>
```

Fig. F.2   Complex XHTML table. (Part 2 of 3.)

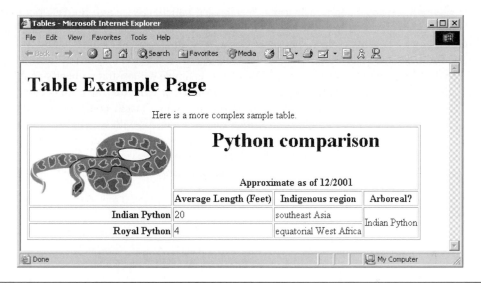

Fig. F.2   Complex XHTML table. (Part 3 of 3.)

Common Programming Error F.1

*When using **colspan** and **rowspan** to adjust the size of table data cells, keep in mind that the modified cells will occupy more than one column or row; other rows or columns of the table must compensate for the extra rows or columns spanned by individual cells. If you do not, the formatting of your table will be distorted, and you could inadvertently create more columns and rows than you originally intended.*

Line 42 introduces attribute **valign**, which aligns data vertically and may be assigned one of four values—**"top"** aligns data with the top of the cell, **"middle"** vertically centers data (the default for all data and header cells), **"bottom"** aligns data with the bottom of the cell and **"baseline"** ignores the fonts used for the row data and sets the bottom of all text in the row on a common *baseline* (i.e., the horizontal line to which each character in a word is aligned).

F.4 Basic XHTML Forms

When browsing Web sites, users often need to provide information such as e-mail addresses, search keywords and zip codes. XHTML provides a mechanism, called a *form*, for collecting such user information.

Data that users enter on a Web page normally is sent to a Web server that provides access to a site's resources (e.g., XHTML documents or images). These resources are located either on the same machine as the Web server or on a machine that the Web server can access through the network. When a browser requests a Web page or file that is located on a server, the server processes the request and returns the requested resource. A request contains the name and path of the desired resource and the method of communication (called a *protocol*). XHTML documents use the HyperText Transfer Protocol (HTTP).

Figure F.3 sends the form data to the Web server, which passes the form data to a *CGI* (*Common Gateway Interface*) script (i.e., a program) written in Perl, C or some other language. The script processes the data received from the Web server and typically returns information to the Web server. The Web server then sends the information in the form of an XHTML document to the Web browser. [*Note*: This example demonstrates client-side functionality. If the form is submitted (by clicking **Submit Your Entries**), an error occurs.]

Forms can contain visual and non-visual components. Visual components include clickable buttons and other graphical user interface components with which users interact. Non-visual components, called *hidden inputs*, store any data that the document author specifies, such as e-mail addresses and XHTML document file names that act as links. The form begins on line 23 with the *form* element. Attribute *method* specifies how the form's data is sent to the Web server.

```
 1   <?xml version = "1.0"?>
 2   <!DOCTYPE html PUBLIC "-//W3C//DTD XHTML 1.0 Strict//EN"
 3      "http://www.w3.org/TR/xhtml1/DTD/xhtml1-strict.dtd">
 4
 5   <!-- Fig. F.3: form.html    -->
 6   <!-- Form design example 1. -->
 7
 8   <html xmlns = "http://www.w3.org/1999/xhtml">
 9      <head>
10         <title>Forms</title>
11      </head>
12
13      <body>
14
15         <h1>Feedback Form</h1>
16
17         <p>Please fill out this form to help
18            us improve our site.</p>
19
20         <!-- <form> tag begins form, gives -->
21         <!-- method of sending information -->
22         <!-- and location of form scripts  -->
23         <form method = "post" action = "/cgi-bin/formmail">
24
25            <p>
26
27               <!-- hidden inputs contain non-visual -->
28               <!-- information                       -->
29               <input type = "hidden" name = "recipient"
30                  value = "deitel@deitel.com" />
31
32               <input type = "hidden" name = "subject"
33                  value = "Feedback Form" />
34
35               <input type = "hidden" name = "redirect"
36                  value = "main.html" />
37            </p>
38
```

Fig. F.3   Simple form with hidden fields and a textbox. (Part 1 of 2.)

```
39                  <!-- <input type = "text"> inserts text box -->
40                  <p>
41                      <label>Name:
42                          <input name = "name" type = "text" size = "25"
43                              maxlength = "30" />
44                      </label>
45                  </p>
46
47                  <p>
48
49                      <!-- input types "submit" and "reset" -->
50                      <!-- insert buttons for submitting    -->
51                      <!-- and clearing form's contents      -->
52                      <input type = "submit" value =
53                          "Submit Your Entries" />
54
55                      <input type = "reset" value =
56                          "Clear Your Entries" />
57                  </p>
58
59              </form>
60
61          </body>
62      </html>
```

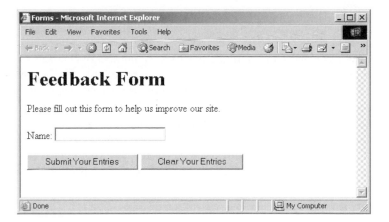

Fig. F.3   Simple form with hidden fields and a textbox. (Part 2 of 2.)

Using **method = "post"** appends form data to the browser request, which contains the protocol (i.e., HTTP) and the requested resource's URL. Scripts located on the Web server's computer (or on a computer accessible through the network) can access the form data sent as part of the request. For example, a script may take the form information and update an electronic mailing list. The other possible value, **method = "get"**, appends the form data directly to the end of the URL. For example, the URL **/cgi-bin/formmail** might have the form information **name = bob** appended to it.

The ***action*** attribute in the **<form>** tag specifies the URL of a script on the Web server; in this case, it specifies a script that e-mails form data to an address. Most Internet Service Providers (ISPs) have a script like this on their site; ask the Web-site system administrator how to set up an XHTML document to use its script correctly.

Lines 29–36 define three ***input*** elements that specify data to provide to the script that processes the form (also called the *form handler*). These three **input** element have ***type*** attribute **"hidden"**, which allows the document author to send form data that is not entered by a user to a script.

The three hidden inputs are an e-mail address to which the data will be sent, the e-mail's subject line and a URL where the browser will be redirected after submitting the form. Two other **input** attributes are ***name***, which identifies the **input** element, and ***value***, which provides the value that will be sent (or posted) to the Web server.

Good Programming Practice F.1

*Place hidden **input** elements at the beginning of a form, immediately after the opening **<form>** tag. This placement allows document authors to locate hidden **input** elements quickly.*

We introduce another **type** of **input** in lines 38–39. The **"text" input** inserts a *text box* into the form. Users can type data in text boxes. The ***label*** element (lines 37–40) provides users with information about the **input** element's purpose.

Common Programming Error F.2

*Forgetting to include a **label** element for each form element is a design error. Without these labels, users cannot determine the purpose of individual form elements.*

The **input** element's ***size*** attribute specifies the number of characters visible in the text box. Optional attribute ***maxlength*** limits the number of characters input into the text box. In this case, the user is not permitted to type more than **30** characters into the text box.

There are two types of **input** elements in lines 52–56. The **"submit" input** element is a button. When the user presses a **"submit"** button, the browser sends the data in the form to the Web server for processing. The ***value*** *attribute* sets the text displayed on the button (the default value is **Submit**). The **"reset" input** element allows a user to reset all **form** elements to their default values. The ***value*** attribute of the **"reset" input** element sets the text displayed on the button. (The default value is **Reset**.)

F.5 More Complex XHTML Forms

In the previous section, we introduced basic forms. In this section, we introduce elements and attributes for creating more complex forms. Figure F.4 contains a form that solicits user feedback about a Web site.

The ***textarea*** element (lines 42–44) inserts a multiline text box, called a *textarea*, into the form. The number of rows is specified with the ***rows*** *attribute* and the number of columns (i.e., characters) is specified with the ***cols*** *attribute*. In this example, the **textarea** is four rows high and 36 characters wide. To display default text in the text area, place the text between the **<textarea>** and **</textarea>** tags. Default text can be specified in other **input** types, such as textboxes, by using the **value** attribute.

The *"password"* input in lines 52–53 inserts a password box with the specified **size**. A password box allows users to enter sensitive information, such as credit-card numbers and passwords, by "masking" the information input with asterisks. The actual value input is sent to the Web server, not the asterisks that mask the input.

Lines 60–78 introduce the *checkbox* **form** element. Checkboxes enable users to select from a set of options. When a user selects a checkbox, a check mark appears in the check box. Otherwise, the checkbox remains empty. Each *"checkbox" input* creates a new checkbox. Checkboxes can be used individually or in groups. Checkboxes that belong to a group are assigned the same **name** (in this case, **"thingsliked"**).

```
1    <?xml version = "1.0"?>
2    <!DOCTYPE html PUBLIC "-//W3C//DTD XHTML 1.0 Strict//EN"
3        "http://www.w3.org/TR/xhtml1/DTD/xhtml1-strict.dtd">
4
5    <!-- Fig. F.4: form2.html    -->
6    <!-- Form design example 2. -->
7
8    <html xmlns = "http://www.w3.org/1999/xhtml">
9        <head>
10           <title>Forms</title>
11       </head>
12
13       <body>
14
15          <h1>Feedback Form</h1>
16
17          <p>Please fill out this form to help
18             us improve our site.</p>
19
20          <form method = "post" action = "/cgi-bin/formmail">
21
22             <p>
23                <input type = "hidden" name = "recipient"
24                   value = "deitel@deitel.com" />
25
26                <input type = "hidden" name = "subject"
27                   value = "Feedback Form" />
28
29                <input type = "hidden" name = "redirect"
30                   value = "main.html" />
31             </p>
32
33             <p>
34                <label>Name:
35                   <input name = "name" type = "text" size = "25" />
36                </label>
37             </p>
38
```

Fig. F.4   Form with textareas, password boxes and checkboxes. (Part 1 of 3.)

```
39              <!-- <textarea> creates multiline textbox -->
40              <p>
41                 <label>Comments:<br />
42                    <textarea name = "comments" rows = "4"
43                       cols = "36">Enter your comments here.
44                    </textarea>
45                 </label></p>
46
47              <!-- <input type = "password"> inserts -->
48              <!-- textboxwhose display is masked     -->
49              <!-- with asterisk characters -->
50              <p>
51                 <label>E-mail Address:
52                    <input name = "email" type = "password"
53                       size = "25" />
54                 </label>
55              </p>
56
57              <p>
58                 <strong>Things you liked:</strong><br />
59
60                 <label>Site design
61                 <input name = "thingsliked" type = "checkbox"
62                    value = "Design" /></label>
63
64                 <label>Links
65                 <input name = "thingsliked" type = "checkbox"
66                    value = "Links" /></label>
67
68                 <label>Ease of use
69                 <input name = "thingsliked" type = "checkbox"
70                    value = "Ease" /></label>
71
72                 <label>Images
73                 <input name = "thingsliked" type = "checkbox"
74                    value = "Images" /></label>
75
76                 <label>Source code
77                 <input name = "thingsliked" type = "checkbox"
78                    value = "Code" /></label>
79              </p>
80
81              <p>
82                 <input type = "submit" value =
83                    "Submit Your Entries" />
84
85                 <input type = "reset" value =
86                    "Clear Your Entries" />
87              </p>
88
89        </form>
90
```

Fig. F.4   Form with textareas, password boxes and checkboxes. (Part 2 of 3.)

```
91      </body>
92    </html>
```

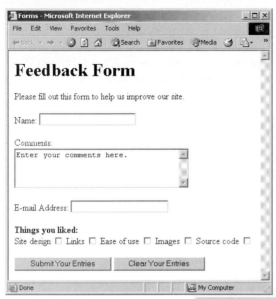

Fig. F.4   Form with textareas, password boxes and checkboxes. (Part 3 of 3.)

Common Programming Error F.3

*When your **form** has several checkboxes with the same **name**, you must make sure that they have different **value**s, or the scripts running on the Web server will not be able to distinguish between them.*

We continue our discussion of forms by presenting a third example that introduces several more form elements from which users can make selections (Fig. F.5). In this example,
we introduce two new **input** types. The first type is the *radio button* (lines 90–113), specified with type **"radio"**. Radio buttons are similar to checkboxes, except that only one radio
button in a group of radio buttons may be selected at any time. All radio buttons in a group
have the same **name** attribute; they are distinguished by their different **value** attributes. The
attribute–value pair **checked = "checked"** (line 92) indicates which radio button, if any,
is selected initially. The **checked** attribute also applies to checkboxes.

```
1   <?xml version = "1.0"?>
2   <!DOCTYPE html PUBLIC "-//W3C//DTD XHTML 1.0 Strict//EN"
3      "http://www.w3.org/TR/xhtml1/DTD/xhtml1-strict.dtd">
4
5   <!-- Fig. F.5: form3.html    -->
6   <!-- Form design example 3. -->
7
8   <html xmlns = "http://www.w3.org/1999/xhtml">
9      <head>
10        <title>Forms</title>
11     </head>
12
13     <body>
14
15        <h1>Feedback Form</h1>
16
17        <p>Please fill out this form to help
18           us improve our site.</p>
19
20        <form method = "post" action = "/cgi-bin/formmail">
21
22           <p>
23              <input type = "hidden" name = "recipient"
24                 value = "deitel@deitel.com" />
25
26              <input type = "hidden" name = "subject"
27                 value = "Feedback Form" />
28
29              <input type = "hidden" name = "redirect"
30                 value = "main.html" />
31           </p>
32
33           <p>
34              <label>Name:
35                 <input name = "name" type = "text" size = "25" />
36              </label>
37           </p>
38
39           <p>
40              <label>Comments:<br />
41                 <textarea name = "comments" rows = "4"
42                    cols = "36"></textarea>
43              </label>
44           </p>
```

Fig. F.5   Form including radio buttons and drop-down lists. (Part 1 of 4.)

```
45
46          <p>
47              <label>E-mail Address:
48                  <input name = "email" type = "password"
49                      size = "25" />
50              </label>
51          </p>
52
53          <p>
54              <strong>Things you liked:</strong><br />
55
56              <label>Site design
57                  <input name = "thingsliked" type = "checkbox"
58                      value = "Design" />
59              </label>
60
61              <label>Links
62                  <input name = "thingsliked" type = "checkbox"
63                      value = "Links" />
64              </label>
65
66              <label>Ease of use
67                  <input name = "thingsliked" type = "checkbox"
68                      value = "Ease" />
69              </label>
70
71              <label>Images
72                  <input name = "thingsliked" type = "checkbox"
73                      value = "Images" />
74              </label>
75
76              <label>Source code
77                  <input name = "thingsliked" type = "checkbox"
78                      value = "Code" />
79              </label>
80
81          </p>
82
83          <!-- <input type = "radio" /> creates one radio   -->
84          <!-- button. The difference between radio buttons -->
85          <!-- and checkboxes is that only one radio button -->
86          <!-- in a group can be selected.                  -->
87          <p>
88              <strong>How did you get to our site?:</strong><br />
89
90              <label>Search engine
91                  <input name = "howtosite" type = "radio"
92                      value = "search engine" checked = "checked" />
93              </label>
94
95              <label>Links from another site
96                  <input name = "howtosite" type = "radio"
97                      value = "link" />
98              </label>
```

Fig. F.5   Form including radio buttons and drop-down lists. (Part 2 of 4.)

```
99
100            <label>Deitel.com Web site
101                <input name = "howtosite" type = "radio"
102                   value = "deitel.com" />
103            </label>
104
105            <label>Reference in a book
106                <input name = "howtosite" type = "radio"
107                   value = "book" />
108            </label>
109
110            <label>Other
111                <input name = "howtosite" type = "radio"
112                   value = "other" />
113            </label>
114
115        </p>
116
117        <p>
118            <label>Rate our site:
119
120                <!-- <select> tag presents a drop-down -->
121                <!-- list with choices indicated by      -->
122                <!-- <option> tags                       -->
123                <select name = "rating">
124                   <option selected = "selected">Amazing</option>
125                   <option>10</option>
126                   <option>9</option>
127                   <option>8</option>
128                   <option>7</option>
129                   <option>6</option>
130                   <option>5</option>
131                   <option>4</option>
132                   <option>3</option>
133                   <option>2</option>
134                   <option>1</option>
135                   <option>Awful</option>
136                </select>
137
138            </label>
139        </p>
140
141        <p>
142            <input type = "submit" value =
143               "Submit Your Entries" />
144
145            <input type = "reset" value = "Clear Your Entries" />
146        </p>
147
148     </form>
149
150    </body>
151 </html>
```

Fig. F.5   Form including radio buttons and drop-down lists. (Part 3 of 4.)

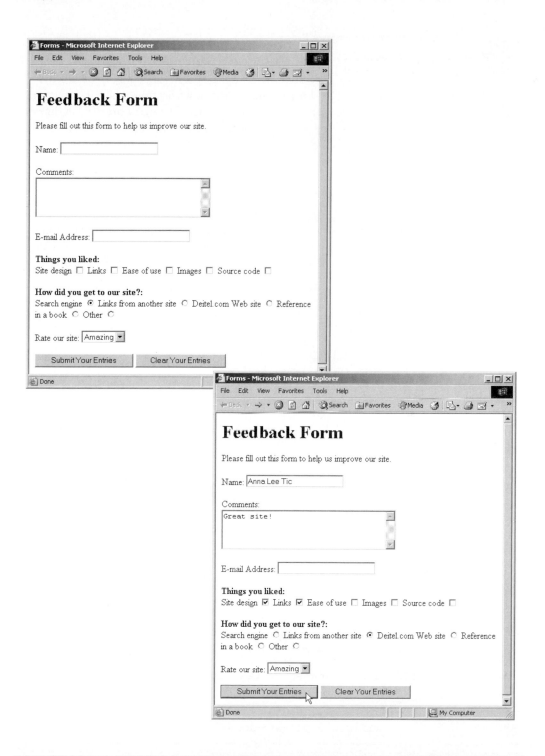

Fig. F.5   Form including radio buttons and drop-down lists. (Part 4 of 4.)

Common Programming Error F.4

*When using a group of radio buttons in a form, forgetting to set the **name** attributes to the same name lets the user select all of the radio buttons at the same time, which is a logic error.*

The **select** element (lines 123–136) provides a drop-down list from which the user can select an item. The **name** attribute identifies the drop-down list. The **option** element (lines 124–135) adds items to the drop-down list. The **option** element's **selected** attribute specifies which item initially is displayed as the selected item in the **select** element.

F.6 Internal Linking

In Appendix E, we discussed how to hyperlink one Web page to another. Figure F.6 introduces *internal linking*—a mechanism that enables the user to jump between locations in the same document. Internal linking is useful for long documents that contain many sections. Clicking an internal link enables users to find a section without scrolling through the entire document.

```
1   <?xml version = "1.0"?>
2   <!DOCTYPE html PUBLIC "-//W3C//DTD XHTML 1.0 Strict//EN"
3      "http://www.w3.org/TR/xhtml1/DTD/xhtml1-strict.dtd">
4
5   <!-- Fig. F.6: links.html -->
6   <!-- Internal linking.    -->
7
8   <html xmlns = "http://www.w3.org/1999/xhtml">
9      <head>
10        <title>List</title>
11     </head>
12
13     <body>
14
15        <!-- <a name = ".."></a> creates internal hyperlink -->
16        <p><a name = "features"></a></p>
17
18        <h1>The Best Features of the Internet</h1>
19
20        <!-- address of internal link is "#linkname" -->
21        <p>
22           <a href = "#ceos">Go to <em>Favorite CEOs</em></a>
23        </p>
24
25        <ul>
26           <li>You can meet people from countries
27              around the world.</li>
28
29           <li>You have access to new media as it becomes public:
30
31              <ul>
32                 <li>New games</li>
33                 <li>New applications
```

Fig. F.6   Internal hyperlinks used to make pages more easily navigable. (Part 1 of 3.)

```
34
35                    <ul>
36                        <li>For Business</li>
37                        <li>For Pleasure</li>
38                    </ul>
39
40                </li>
41
42                <li>Around the clock news</li>
43                <li>Search Engines</li>
44                <li>Shopping</li>
45                <li>Programming
46
47                    <ul>
48                        <li>XHTML</li>
49                        <li>Visual C++</li>
50                        <li>Java</li>
51                        <li>Scripts</li>
52                        <li>New languages</li>
53                    </ul>
54
55                </li>
56              </ul>
57
58          </li>
59
60          <li>Links</li>
61          <li>Keeping in touch with old friends</li>
62          <li>It is the technology of the future!</li>
63      </ul>
64
65      <!-- named anchor -->
66      <p><a name = "ceos"></a></p>
67
68      <h1>My 3 Favorite <em>CEOs</em></h1>
69
70      <p>
71
72          <!-- internal hyperlink to features -->
73          <a href = "#features">
74              Go to <em>Favorite Features</em>
75          </a>
76      </p>
77
78      <ol>
79          <li>Ant Chovy</li>
80          <li>CeCe Sharp</li>
81          <li>Albert Antstein</li>
82      </ol>
83
84    </body>
85 </html>
```

Fig. F.6   Internal hyperlinks used to make pages more easily navigable. (Part 2 of 3.)

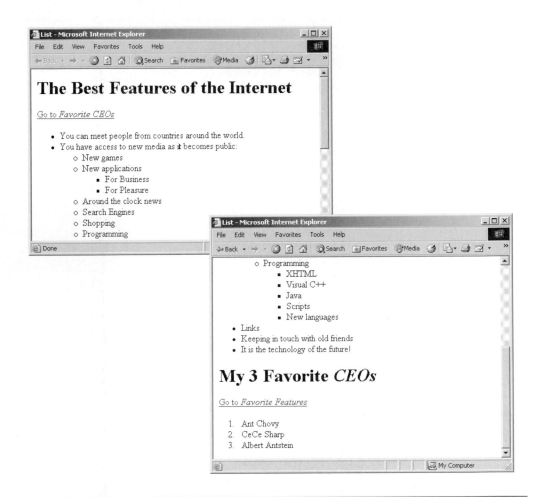

Fig. F.6   Internal hyperlinks used to make pages more easily navigable. (Part 3 of 3.)

Line 16 contains a *named anchor* (called **features**) for an internal hyperlink. To link to this type of anchor inside the same Web page, the **href** attribute of another anchor element includes the named anchor preceded with a pound sign (as in **#features**). Lines 73–74 contain a hyperlink with the anchor **features** as its target. Selecting this hyperlink in a Web browser scrolls the browser window to the **features** anchor at line 16.

Look-and-Feel Observation F.1

Internal hyperlinks are useful in XHTML documents that contain large amounts of information. Internal links to various sections on the page make it easier for users to navigate the page: They do not have to scroll to find a specific section.

Although not demonstrated in this example, a hyperlink can specify an internal link in another document by specifying the document name followed by a pound sign and the named anchor, as in

```
href = "page.html#name"
```

For example, to link to a named anchor called **booklist** in **books.html**, **href** is assigned **"books.html#booklist"**.

F.7 Creating and Using Image Maps

In Appendix E, we demonstrated how images can be used as hyperlinks to link to other resources on the Internet. In this section, we introduce another technique for image linking, called the *image map*, which designates certain areas of an image (called *hotspots*) as links. Figure F.7 introduces image maps and hotspots.

```
1   <?xml version = "1.0" ?>
2   <!DOCTYPE html PUBLIC "-//W3C//DTD XHTML 1.0 Strict//EN"
3       "http://www.w3.org/TR/xhtml1/DTD/xhtml1-strict.dtd">
4
5   <!-- Fig. F.7: picture.html         -->
6   <!-- Creating and using image maps. -->
7
8   <html xmlns = "http://www.w3.org/1999/xhtml">
9       <head>
10          <title>Image Map
11          </title>
12      </head>
13
14      <body>
15
16          <p>
17
18              <!-- <map> tag defines image map -->
19              <map id = "picture">
20
21                  <!-- shape = "rect" indicates rectangular  -->
22                  <!-- area, with coordinates for upper-left -->
23                  <!-- and lower-right corners               -->
24                  <area href = "form.html" shape = "rect"
25                      coords = "2,123,54,143"
26                      alt = "Go to the feedback form" />
27
28                  <area href = "contact.html" shape = "rect"
29                      coords = "126,122,198,143"
30                      alt = "Go to the contact page" />
31
32                  <area href = "main.html" shape = "rect"
33                      coords = "3,7,61,25" alt = "Go to the homepage" />
34
35                  <area href = "links.html" shape = "rect"
36                      coords = "168,5,197,25"
37                      alt = "Go to the links page" />
38
```

Fig. F.7   Image with links anchored to an image map. (Part 1 of 2.)

```
39                  <!-- value "poly" creates hotspot in shape -->
40                  <!-- of polygon, defined by coords          -->
41                  <area shape = "poly" alt = "E-mail the Deitels"
42                    coords = "162,25,154,39,158,54,169,51,183,39,161,26"
43                      href = "mailto:deitel@deitel.com" />
44
45                  <!-- shape = "circle" indicates a circular -->
46                  <!-- area with the given center and radius -->
47                  <area href = "mailto:deitel@deitel.com"
48                      shape = "circle" coords = "100,36,33"
49                      alt = "E-mail the Deitels" />
50              </map>
51
52              <!-- <img src =... usemap = "#id"> indicates that -->
53              <!-- specified image map is used with this image  -->
54              <img src = "deitel.gif" width = "200" height = "144"
55                  alt = "Deitel logo" usemap = "#picture" />
56          </p>
57
58      </body>
59  </html>
```

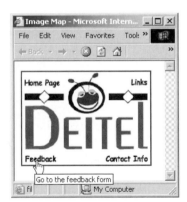

Fig. F.7   Image with links anchored to an image map. (Part 2 of 2.)

Lines 19–50 define an image map via a **map** element. Attribute **id** (line 19) identifies the image map. If **id** is omitted, the map cannot be referenced by an image. Shortly, we discuss how to reference an image map. Hotspots are defined with **area** elements (as shown on lines 24–26). Attribute **href** (line 24) specifies the link's target (i.e., the resource to which to link). Attributes **shape** (line 24) and **coords** (line 25) specify the hotspot's shape and coordinates, respectively. Attribute **alt** (line 26) provides alternative text for the link.

Common Programming Error F.5

*Not specifying an **id** attribute for a **map** element prevents an **img** element from using the **map**'s **area** elements to define hotspots.*

The markup on lines 24–26 creates a *rectangular hotspot* (**shape = "rect"**) for the *coordinates* specified in the **coords** attribute. A coordinate pair consists of two numbers representing the location of a point on the *x*-axis and the *y*-axis, respectively. The *x*-axis extends horizontally and the *y*-axis extends vertically from the upper-left corner of the image. Every point on an image has a unique *x*–*y* coordinate. For rectangular hotspots, the required coordinates are those of the upper-left and lower-right corners of the rectangle. In this case, the upper-left corner of the rectangle is located at 2 on the *x*-axis and 123 on the *y*-axis, annotated as *(2, 123)*. The lower-right corner of the rectangle is at *(54, 143)*. Coordinates are measured in pixels.

Common Programming Error F.6

Overlapping the coordinates of an image map causes the browser to render the first hotspot it encounters for the area.

The map **area** (lines 41–43) assigns the **shape** attribute *"poly"* to create a hotspot in the shape of a polygon, using the coordinates in attribute **coords**. These coordinates represent each *vertex*, or corner, of the polygon. The browser connects these points with lines to form the hotspot's area.

The map **area** (lines 47–49) assigns the **shape** attribute *"circle"* to create a *circular hotspot*. In this case, the **coords** attribute specifies the circle's center coordinates and the circle's radius, in pixels.

To use an image map with an **img** element, the **img** element's *usemap* attribute is assigned the **id** of a **map**. Lines 54–55 reference the image map named **"picture"**. The image map is located within the same document, so internal linking is used.

F.8 meta Elements

People use search engines to find useful Web sites. Search engines usually catalog sites by following links from page to page and saving identification and classification information for each page. One way that search engines catalog pages is by reading the content in each page's *meta* elements, which specify information about a document.

Two important attributes of the **meta** element are *name*, which identifies the type of **meta** element and *content*, which provides the information search engines use to catalog pages. Figure F.8 introduces the **meta** element.

Lines 14–16 demonstrate a *"keywords"* **meta** element. The *content* attribute of such a **meta** element provides search engines with a list of words that describe a page. These words are compared with words in search requests. Thus, including **meta** elements and their **content** information can draw more viewers to your site.

```
1   <?xml version = "1.0"?>
2   <!DOCTYPE html PUBLIC "-//W3C//DTD XHTML 1.0 Strict//EN"
3       "http://www.w3.org/TR/xhtml1/DTD/xhtml1-strict.dtd">
4
5   <!-- Fig. F.8: main.html -->
6   <!-- Using meta tags.      -->
7
```

Fig. F.8   **meta** used to provide keywords and a description. (Part 1 of 2.)

```
 8   <html xmlns = "http://www.w3.org/1999/xhtml">
 9      <head>
10         <title>Welcome</title>
11
12         <!-- <meta> tags provide search engines with -->
13         <!-- information used to catalog site        -->
14         <meta name = "keywords" content = "Web page, design,
15            XHTML, tutorial, personal, help, index, form,
16            contact, feedback, list, links, frame, deitel" />
17
18         <meta name = "description" content = "This Web site will
19            help you learn the basics of XHTML and Web page design
20            through the use of interactive examples and
21            instruction." />
22
23      </head>
24
25      <body>
26
27         <h1>Welcome to Our Web Site!</h1>
28
29         <p>
30            We have designed this site to teach about the wonders
31            of <strong><em>XHTML</em></strong>. <em>XHTML</em> is
32            better equipped than <em>HTML</em> to represent complex
33            data on the Internet. <em>XHTML</em> takes advantage of
34            XML's strict syntax to ensure well-formedness. Soon you
35            will know about many of the great new features of
36            <em>XHTML.</em>
37         </p>
38
39         <p>Have Fun With the Site!</p>
40
41      </body>
42   </html>
```

Fig. F.8   **meta** used to provide keywords and a description. (Part 2 of 2.)

Lines 18–21 demonstrate a ***"description"* meta** element. The **content** attribute of such a **meta** element provides a three- to four-line description of a site, written in sentence form. Search engines also use this description to catalog your site and sometimes display this information as part of the search results.

Software Engineering Observation F.1

*meta elements are not visible to users and must be placed inside the **head** section of your XHTML document. If **meta** elements are not placed in this section, they will not be read by search engines.*

F.9 **frameset** Element

All of the Web pages we have presented in this book have the ability to link to other pages, but can display only one page at a time. Figure F.9 uses *frames*, which allow the browser to display more than one XHTML document simultaneously, to display the documents in Fig. F.8 and Fig. F.10.

Most of our prior examples adhered to the strict XHTML document type. This particular example uses the *frameset* document type—a special XHTML document type specifically for framesets. This new document type is specified in lines 2–3 and is required for documents that define framesets.

A document that defines a frameset normally consists of an **html** element that contains a **head** element and a ***frameset*** element. The ***<frameset>*** tag (line 24) informs the browser that the page contains frames. Attribute ***cols*** specifies the frameset's column layout. The value of **cols** gives the width of each frame, either in pixels or as a percentage of the browser width. In this case, the attribute **cols = "110,*"** informs the browser that there are two vertical frames. The first frame extends **110** pixels from the left edge of the browser window, and the second frame fills the remainder of the browser width (as indicated by the asterisk). Similarly, **frameset** attribute ***rows*** can be used to specify the number of rows and the size of each row in a frameset.

```
1   <?xml version = "1.0"?>
2   <!DOCTYPE html PUBLIC "-//W3C//DTD XHTML 1.0 Frameset//EN"
3       "http://www.w3.org/TR/xhtml11/DTD/xhtml11-frameset.dtd">
4
5   <!-- Fig. F.9: index.html -->
6   <!-- XHTML frames I.        -->
7
8   <html xmlns = "http://www.w3.org/1999/xhtml">
9       <head>
10          <title>Main</title>
11
12          <meta name = "keywords" content = "Webpage, design,
13              XHTML, tutorial, personal, help, index, form,
14              contact, feedback, list, links, frame, deitel" />
15
16          <meta name = "description" content = "This Web site will
17              help you learn the basics of XHTML and Web page design
18              through the use of interactive examples
19              and instruction." />
20
21      </head>
22
23      <!-- <frameset> tag sets frame dimensions -->
24      <frameset cols = "110,*">
25
26          <!-- frame elements specify which pages -->
27          <!-- are loaded into given frame        -->
28          <frame name = "leftframe" src = "nav.html" />
29          <frame name = "main" src = "main.html" />
30
31          <noframes>
32              <p>This page uses frames, but your browser does not
33              support them.</p>
34
35              <p>Please, <a href = "nav.html">follow this link to
36              browse our site without frames</a>.</p>
37          </noframes>
38
```

Fig. F.9   Web document containing two frames—navigation and content. (Part 1 of 2.)

```
39        </frameset>
40    </html>
```

Fig. F.9   Web document containing two frames—navigation and content. (Part 2 of 2.)

The documents that will be loaded into the **frameset** are specified with **frame** elements (lines 28–29 in this example). Attribute **src** specifies the URL of the page to display in the frame. Each frame has **name** and **src** attributes. The first frame (which covers **110** pixels on the left side of the **frameset**) is named **leftframe** and displays the page **nav.html** (Fig. F.10). The second frame is named **main** and displays the page **main.html**.

Attribute **name** identifies a frame, enabling hyperlinks in a **frameset** to specify the *target frame* in which a linked document should display when the user clicks the link. For example,

```
<a href = "links.html" target = "main">
```

loads **links.html** in the frame whose **name** is **"main"**.

Not all browsers support frames. XHTML provides the *noframes* element (lines 31–37) to enable XHTML document designers to specify alternative content for browsers that do not support frames.

 Portability Tip F.1

*Some browsers do not support frames. Use the **noframes** element inside a **frameset** to direct users to a nonframed version of your site.*

Fig. F.10 is the Web page displayed in the left frame of Fig. F.9. This XHTML document provides the navigation buttons that, when clicked, determine which document is displayed in the right frame.

```
1   <?xml version = "1.0"?>
2   <!DOCTYPE html PUBLIC "-//W3C//DTD XHTML 1.0 Transitional//EN"
3       "http://www.w3.org/TR/xhtml1/DTD/xhtml1-transitional.dtd">
4
5   <!-- Fig. F.10: nav.html              -->
6   <!-- Using images as link anchors. -->
7
8   <html xmlns = "http://www.w3.org/1999/xhtml">
9
10      <head>
11          <title>Navigation Bar
12          </title>
13      </head>
14
15      <body>
16
17          <p>
18              <a href = "links.html" target = "main">
19                  <img src = "buttons/links.jpg" width = "65"
20                      height = "50" alt = "Links Page" />
21              </a><br />
22
23              <a href = "list.html" target = "main">
24                  <img src = "buttons/list.jpg" width = "65"
25                      height = "50" alt = "List Example Page" />
26              </a><br />
27
```

Fig. F.10   XHTML document displayed in the left frame of Fig. F.9. (Part 1 of 2.)

```
28              <a href = "contact.html" target = "main">
29                  <img src = "buttons/contact.jpg" width = "65"
30                      height = "50" alt = "Contact Page" />
31              </a><br />
32
33              <a href = "header.html" target = "main">
34                  <img src = "buttons/header.jpg" width = "65"
35                      height = "50" alt = "Header Page" />
36              </a><br />
37
38              <a href = "table1.html" target = "main">
39                  <img src = "buttons/table.jpg" width = "65"
40                      height = "50" alt = "Table Page" />
41              </a><br />
42
43              <a href = "form.html" target = "main">
44                  <img src = "buttons/form.jpg" width = "65"
45                      height = "50" alt = "Feedback Form" />
46              </a><br />
47          </p>
48
49      </body>
50  </html>
```

Fig. F.10   XHTML document displayed in the left frame of Fig. F.9. (Part 2 of 2.)

Line 29 (Fig. F.9) displays the XHTML page in Fig. F.10. Anchor attribute **target** (line 18 in Fig. F.10) specifies that the linked documents are loaded in frame **main** (line 30 in Fig. F.9). A **target** can be set to a number of preset values: **"_blank"** loads the page into a new browser window, **"_self"** loads the page into the frame in which the anchor element appears and **"_top"** loads the page into the full browser window (i.e., removes the **frameset**).

F.10 Nested frameset

You can use the **frameset** element to create more complex layouts in a Web page by nesting **frameset**s, as in Fig. F.11. The nested **frameset** in this example displays the XHTML documents in Fig. F.7, Fig. F.8 and Fig. F.10.

The outer frameset element (lines 23–41) defines two columns. The left frame extends over the first 110 pixels from the left edge of the browser, and the right frame occupies the rest of the window's width. The **frame** element on line 24 specifies that the document **nav.html** (Fig. F.10) will be displayed in the left column.

Lines 28–31 define a nested **frameset** element for the second column of the outer frameset. This **frameset** defines two rows. The first row extends 175 pixels from the top of the browser window, and the second occupies the remainder of the browser window's height, as is indicated by **rows = "175,*"**. The **frame** element at line 29 specifies that the first row of the nested **frameset** will display **picture.html** (Fig. F.7). The **frame** element at line 30 specifies that the second row of the nested **frameset** will display **main.html** (Fig. F.8).

Testing and Debugging Tip F.2

When using nested **frameset** *elements, indent every level of* **<frame>** *tag. This practice makes the page clearer and easier to debug.*

In this appendix, we presented XHTML for marking up information in tables, creating forms for gathering user input, linking to sections within the same document, using **<meta>** tags and creating frames.

```
1   <?xml version = "1.0"?>
2   <!DOCTYPE html PUBLIC "-//W3C//DTD XHTML 1.0 Frameset//EN"
3       "http://www.w3.org/TR/xhtml1/DTD/xhtml1-frameset.dtd">
4
5   <!-- Fig. F.11: index2.html -->
6   <!-- XHTML frames II.        -->
7
8   <html xmlns = "http://www.w3.org/1999/xhtml">
9       <head>
10          <title>Main</title>
11
12          <meta name = "keywords" content = "Webpage, design,
13              XHTML, tutorial, personal, help, index, form,
14              contact, feedback, list, links, frame, deitel" />
15
16          <meta name = "description" content = "This Web site will
17              help you learn the basics of XHTML and Web page design
18              through the use of interactive examples
19              and instruction." />
20
21      </head>
22
23      <frameset cols = "110,*">
24          <frame name = "leftframe" src = "nav.html" />
25
26          <!-- nested framesets are used to change -->
27          <!-- formatting and layout of frameset  -->
28          <frameset rows = "175,*">
29              <frame name = "picture" src = "picture.html" />
30              <frame name = "main" src = "main.html" />
31          </frameset>
32
33          <noframes>
34              <p>This page uses frames, but your browser does not
35              support them.</p>
36
37              <p>Please, <a href = "nav.html">follow this link to
38              browse our site without frames</a>.</p>
39          </noframes>
40
41      </frameset>
42  </html>
```

Fig. F.11   Framed Web site with a nested frameset. (Part 1 of 2.)

Left frame **leftframe**

Right frame contains these two nested frames

Fig. F.11   Framed Web site with a nested frameset. (Part 2 of 2.)

F.11 Summary

XHTML tables mark up tabular data and are one of the most frequently used features in XHTML. The **table** element defines an XHTML table. Attribute **border** specifies the table's border width, in pixels. Tables without borders set this attribute to **"0"**. Element **summary** summarizes the table's contents and is used by speech devices to make the table more accessible to users with visual impairments. Element **caption** describe's the table's content. The text inside the **<caption>** tag is rendered above the table in most browsers.

A table can be split into three distinct sections: head (**thead**), body (**tbody**) and foot (**tfoot**). The head section contains such information as table titles and column headers. The table body contains the primary table data. The table foot contains secondary information, such as footnotes.

Element **tr**, or table row, defines individual table rows. Element **th** defines a header cell. Text in **th** elements usually is centered and displayed in bold by most browsers. This element can be present in any section of the table. Data within a row are defined with **td**, or table data, elements.

Element **colgroup** groups and formats columns. Each **col** element can format any number of columns (specified with the **span** attribute). The document author has the ability to merge data cells with the **rowspan** and **colspan** attributes. The values assigned to these attributes specify the number of rows or columns occupied by the cell. These attributes can be placed inside any data-cell tag.

XHTML provides forms for collecting information from users. Forms contain visual components, such as buttons that users click. Forms may also contain nonvisual components, called hidden inputs, which are used to store any data, such as e-mail addresses and XHTML document file names used for linking. A form begins with the **form** element. Attribute **method** specifies how the form's data is sent to the Web server.

The **"text"** input inserts a textbox into the form. Textboxes allow the user to input data. The **input** element's **size** attribute specifies the number of characters visible in the **input** element. Optional attribute **maxlength** limits the number of characters input into a textbox.

The **"submit"** input submits the data entered in the form to the Web server for processing. Most Web browsers create a button that submits the form data when clicked. The **"reset"** input allows a user to reset all **form** elements to their default values.

The **textarea** element inserts a multiline textbox, called a textarea, into a form. The number of rows in the textarea is specified with the **rows** attribute, the number of columns (i.e., characters) with the **cols** attribute.

The **"password"** input inserts a password box into a form. A password box allows users to enter sensitive information, such as credit-card numbers and passwords, by "masking" the information input with another character. Asterisks are the masking character used for most password boxes. The actual value input is sent to the Web server, not the asterisks that mask the input.

The checkbox input allows the user to make a selection. When the checkbox is selected, a check mark appears in the checkbox. Otherwise, the checkbox is empty. Checkboxes can be used individually and in groups. Checkboxes that are part of the same group have the same **name**.

A radio button is similar in function and use to a checkbox, except that only one radio button in a group can be selected at any time. All radio buttons in a group have the same **name** attribute value, but different attribute **value**s.

The **select** input provides a drop-down list of items. The **name** attribute identifies the drop-down list. The **option** element adds items to the drop-down list. The **selected** attribute, like the **checked** attribute for radio buttons and checkboxes, specifies which list item is displayed initially.

Image maps designate certain sections of an image as links. These links are more properly called hotspots. Image maps are defined with **map** elements. Attribute **id** identifies the image map. Hotspots are defined with the **area** element. Attribute **href** specifies the link's target. Attributes **shape** and **coords** specify the hotspot's shape and coordinates, respectively, and **alt** provides alternative text.

One way that search engines catalog pages is by reading the **meta** elements's contents. Two important attributes of the **meta** element are **name**, which identifies the type of **meta** element, and **content**, which provides information a search engine uses to catalog a page.

Frames allow the browser to display more than one XHTML document simultaneously. The **frameset** element informs the browser that the page contains frames. Not all browsers support frames. XHTML provides the **noframes** element to specify alternative content for browsers that do not support frames.

F.12 Internet and Web Resources

courses.e-survey.net.au/xhtml/index.html
The *Web Page Design—XHTML* site provides descriptions and examples for various XHTML features, such as links, tables, frames and forms. Users can e-mail questions or comments to the Web Page Design support staff.

www.vbxml.com/xhtml/articles/xhtml_tables
The *VBXML.com* Web site contains a tutorial on creating XHTML tables.

www.webreference.com/xml/reference/xhtml.html
This Web page contains a list of the frequently used XHTML tags, such as header tags, table tags, frame tags and form tags. It also provides a description of each tag.

G

XHTML
Special Characters

The table in Fig. G.1 shows many commonly used XHTML special characters—called *character entity references* by the World Wide Web Consortium. For a complete list of character entity references, see the site

www.w3.org/TR/REC-html40/sgml/entities.html

Character	XHTML encoding	Character	XHTML encoding
non-breaking space	` `	ê	`&#234;`
§	`&#167;`	ì	`&#236;`
©	`&#169;`	í	`&#237;`
®	`&#174;`	î	`&#238;`
π	`&#188;`	ñ	`&#241;`
∫	`&#189;`	ò	`&#242;`
Ω	`&#190;`	ó	`&#243;`
à	`&#224;`	ô	`&#244;`
á	`&#225;`	õ	`&#245;`
â	`&#226;`	÷	`&#247;`
ã	`&#227;`	ù	`&#249;`
å	`&#229;`	ú	`&#250;`
ç	`&#231;`	û	`&#251;`
è	`&#232;`	•	`&#8226;`
é	`&#233;`	™	`&#8482;`

Fig. G.1 XHTML special characters.

XHTML Colors

Colors may be specified by using a standard name (such as **aqua**) or a hexadecimal RGB value (such as **#00FFFF** for **aqua**). Of the six hexadecimal digits in an RGB value, the first two represent the amount of red in the color, the middle two represent the amount of green in the color and the last two represent the amount of blue in the color. For example, **black** is the absence of color and is defined by **#000000**, whereas **white** is the maximum amount of red, green and blue and is defined by **#FFFFFF**. Pure **red** is **#FF0000**, pure green (which is called **lime**) is **#00FF00** and pure **blue** is **#0000FF**. Note that **green** in the standard is defined as **#008000**. Figure H.1 contains the XHTML standard color set. Figure H.2 contains the XHTML extended color set.

Color name	Value	Color name	Value
aqua	#00FFFF	navy	#000080
black	#000000	olive	#808000
blue	#0000FF	purple	#800080
fuchsia	#FF00FF	red	#FF0000
gray	#808080	silver	#C0C0C0
green	#008000	teal	#008080
lime	#00FF00	yellow	#FFFF00
maroon	#800000	white	#FFFFFF

Fig. H.1   XHTML standard colors and hexadecimal RGB values.

Color name	Value	Color name	Value
aliceblue	#F0F8FF	deeppink	#FF1493
antiquewhite	#FAEBD7	deepskyblue	#00BFFF
aquamarine	#7FFFD4	dimgray	#696969
azure	#F0FFFF	dodgerblue	#1E90FF
beige	#F5F5DC	firebrick	#B22222
bisque	#FFE4C4	floralwhite	#FFFAF0
blanchedalmond	#FFEBCD	forestgreen	#228B22
blueviolet	#8A2BE2	gainsboro	#DCDCDC
brown	#A52A2A	ghostwhite	#F8F8FF
burlywood	#DEB887	gold	#FFD700
cadetblue	#5F9EA0	goldenrod	#DAA520
chartreuse	#7FFF00	greenyellow	#ADFF2F
chocolate	#D2691E	honeydew	#F0FFF0
coral	#FF7F50	hotpink	#FF69B4
cornflowerblue	#6495ED	indianred	#CD5C5C
cornsilk	#FFF8DC	indigo	#4B0082
crimson	#DC1436	ivory	#FFFFF0
cyan	#00FFFF	khaki	#F0E68C
darkblue	#00008B	lavender	#E6E6FA
darkcyan	#008B8B	lavenderblush	#FFF0F5
darkgoldenrod	#B8860B	lawngreen	#7CFC00
darkgray	#A9A9A9	lemonchiffon	#FFFACD
darkgreen	#006400	lightblue	#ADD8E6
darkkhaki	#BDB76B	lightcoral	#F08080
darkmagenta	#8B008B	lightcyan	#E0FFFF
darkolivegreen	#556B2F	lightgoldenrodyellow	#FAFAD2
darkorange	#FF8C00	lightgreen	#90EE90
darkorchid	#9932CC	lightgrey	#D3D3D3
darkred	#8B0000	lightpink	#FFB6C1
darksalmon	#E9967A	lightsalmon	#FFA07A
darkseagreen	#8FBC8F	lightseagreen	#20B2AA
darkslateblue	#483D8B	lightskyblue	#87CEFA
darkslategray	#2F4F4F	lightslategray	#778899
darkturquoise	#00CED1	lightsteelblue	#B0C4DE
darkviolet	#9400D3	lightyellow	#FFFFE0

Fig. H.2   XHTML extended colors and hexadecimal RGB values. (Part 1 of 2.)

Color name	Value	Color name	Value
limegreen	#32CD32	peru	#CD853F
mediumaquamarine	#66CDAA	pink	#FFC0CB
mediumblue	#0000CD	plum	#DDA0DD
mediumorchid	#BA55D3	powderblue	#B0E0E6
mediumpurple	#9370DB	rosybrown	#BC8F8F
mediumseagreen	#3CB371	royalblue	#4169E1
mediumslateblue	#7B68EE	saddlebrown	#8B4513
mediumspringgreen	#00FA9A	salmon	#FA8072
mediumturquoise	#48D1CC	sandybrown	#F4A460
mediumvioletred	#C71585	seagreen	#2E8B57
midnightblue	#191970	seashell	#FFF5EE
mintcream	#F5FFFA	sienna	#A0522D
mistyrose	#FFE4E1	skyblue	#87CEEB
moccasin	#FFE4B5	slateblue	#6A5ACD
navajowhite	#FFDEAD	slategray	#708090
oldlace	#FDF5E6	snow	#FFFAFA
olivedrab	#6B8E23	springgreen	#00FF7F
orange	#FFA500	steelblue	#4682B4
orangered	#FF4500	tan	#D2B48C
orchid	#DA70D6	thistle	#D8BFD8
palegoldenrod	#EEE8AA	tomato	#FF6347
palegreen	#98FB98	turquoise	#40E0D0
paleturquoise	#AFEEEE	violet	#EE82EE
palevioletred	#DB7093	wheat	#F5DEB3
papayawhip	#FFEFD5	whitesmoke	#F5F5F5
peachpuff	#FFDAB9	yellowgreen	#9ACD32

Fig. H.2   XHTML extended colors and hexadecimal RGB values. (Part 2 of 2.)

7

Bit Manipulation

Objectives

- To understand the concept of bit manipulation.
- To be able to use bitwise operators.
- To be able to use class **BitArray** to perform bit manipulation.

Outline	
I.1	Introduction
I.2	Bit Manipulation and the Bitwise Operators
I.3	Class **BitArray**
I.4	Summary

I.1 Introduction

In this appendix, we present an extensive discussion of bit manipulation and the *bitwise operators* that enable it. We also discuss class **BitArray**, from which we create objects useful for manipulating sets of bits.

I.2 Bit Manipulation and the Bitwise Operators

MC++ provides extensive bit-manipulation capabilities for programmers who must work at the "bits-and-bytes" level. Operating systems, test-equipment software, networking software and many other kinds of software require that programmers communicate "directly with the hardware." In this section and the next, we discuss MC++'s bit-manipulation capabilities. After introducing MC++'s bitwise operators, we demonstrate the use of the operators in live-code examples.

Computers represent data internally as sequences of bits. Arithmetic Logic Units (ALUs), Central Processing Units (CPUs) and other pieces of hardware in a computer process data as bits or groups of bits. Each bit can assume either the value **0** or the value **1**. On all systems, a sequence of 8 bits forms a *byte*—the standard storage unit for a variable of type **char**. Other data types require larger numbers of bytes for storage. The bitwise operators manipulate the bits of integral operands (**char**, **short**, **int** and **long**; both **signed** and **unsigned**). Unsigned integers are normally used with the bitwise operators. Note that the discussion of bitwise operators in this section illustrates the binary representations of the integer operands. For a detailed explanation of the binary (also called base-2) number system, see Appendix B, Number Systems.

The operators *bitwise AND* (**&**), *bitwise inclusive OR* (**|**) and *bitwise exclusive OR* (**^**) operate similarly to their logical counterparts, except that the bitwise versions operate on the level of bits. The bitwise AND operator sets each bit in the result to 1 if the corresponding bits in both operands are 1 (Fig. I.2). The bitwise inclusive OR operator sets each bit in the result to 1 if the corresponding bits in either (or both) operand(s) are 1 (Fig. I.3). The bitwise exclusive OR operator sets each bit in the result to 1 if the corresponding bit in exactly one operand is 1 (Fig. I.4). Exclusive OR is also known as *XOR*.

The *left-shift* (**<<**) operator shifts the bits of its left operand to the left by the number of bits specified in its right operand. The *right-shift* (**>>**) operator shifts the bits in its left operand to the right by the number of bits specified in its right operand. If the left operand is negative, **1**s are shifted in from the left, whereas, if the left operand is positive **0**s are shifted in from the left. The bitwise *complement* (**~**) operator sets all **0** bits in its operand to **1** and all **1** bits to **0** in the result; this process sometimes is referred to as "taking the *ones* *complement* of the value." A detailed discussion of each bitwise operator appears in the examples that follow. The bitwise operators and their functions are summarized in Fig. I.1.

Operator	Name	Description
&	bitwise AND	Each bit in the result is set to **1** if the corresponding bits in the two operands are both **1**. Otherwise, the bit is set to **0**.
|	bitwise inclusive OR	Each bit in the result is set to **1** if at least one of the corresponding bits in the two operands is **1**. Otherwise, the bit is set to **0**.
^	bitwise exclusive OR	Each bit in the result is set to **1** if exactly one of the corresponding bits in the two operands is **1**. Otherwise, the bit is set to **0**.
<<	left shift	Shifts the bits of the first operand to the left by the number of bits specified by the second operand; fill from the right with **0** bits.
>>	right shift	Shifts the bits of the first operand to the right by the number of bits specified by the second operand. If the first operand is negative, **1**s are shifted in from the left; otherwise, **0**s are shifted in from the left.
~	complement	All **0** bits are set to **1**, and all **1** bits are set to **0**.

Fig. I.1   Bitwise operators.

Bit 1	Bit 2	Bit 1 & Bit 2
0	0	0
1	0	0
0	1	0
1	1	1

Fig. I.2   Results of combining two bits with the bitwise AND operator (**&**).

Bit 1	Bit 2	Bit 1 | Bit 2
0	0	0
1	0	1
0	1	1
1	1	1

Fig. I.3   Results of combining two bits with the bitwise inclusive OR operator (**|**).

Bit 1	Bit 2	Bit 1 ^ Bit 2
0	0	0
1	0	1
0	1	1
1	1	0

Fig. I.4   Results of combining two bits with the bitwise exclusive OR operator (^).

When using the bitwise operators, it is useful to display values in their binary representations to illustrate the effects of these operators. The application in Fig. I.5—Fig. I.7 displays integers in their binary representations as groups of eight bits each. Method **Get-Bits** (lines 88–111 of Fig. I.6) of class **PrintBits** uses the bitwise AND operator (line 100) to combine variable **number** with variable **displayMask**. Often, the bitwise AND operator is used with a *mask* operand—an integer value with specific bits set to **1**. Masks hide some bits in a value and select other bits. In line 90, **GetBits** assigns mask variable **displayMask** the value **1 << 31** (**10000000 00000000 00000000 00000000**). The left-shift operator shifts the value **1** from the low-order (rightmost) bit to the high-order (leftmost) bit in **displayMask** and fills in **0** bits from the right. Because the second operand is 31, 31 bits (each is **0**) are filled in from the right. The word "fill," in this context, means that we add a bit to the right end and delete one from the left end. Every time we add a **0** to the right end, we remove the bit at the left end.

The statement on line 100 determines whether a **1** or a **0** should be appended to **StringBuilder *output** for the leftmost bit of variable **number**. For this example, assume that **number** contains **11111** (**00000000 00000000 00101011 01100111**). When **number** and **displayMask** are combined using **&**, all the bits except the high-order bit in variable **number** are "masked off" (hidden), because any bit "ANDed" with **0** yields **0**. If the leftmost bit is **0**, **number & displayMask** evaluates to **0**, and **0** is appended; otherwise, **1** is appended. Line 104 then left shifts variable **val** one bit with the expression **number <<= 1**. (This is equivalent to **number = number << 1**.) These steps are repeated for each bit in variable **number**. At the end of method **GetBits**, line 110 returns the **String *** representation of the **StringBuilder**.

```
1   // Fig. I.5: PrintBits.h
2   // Printing the bits that constitute an integer.
3
4   #pragma once
5
6   #using <system.dll>
7   #using <mscorlib.dll>
8   #using <system.drawing.dll>
9   #using <system.windows.forms.dll>
10
11  using namespace System;
12  using namespace System::Drawing;
```

Fig. I.5   **PrintBits** class displays the bit representation of an integer. (Part 1 of 2.)

```
13    using namespace System::Windows::Forms;
14    using namespace System::Text;
15
16    // displays bit representation of user input
17    public __gc class PrintBits : public Form
18    {
19    public:
20       PrintBits();
21       String* GetBits( int );
22
23    private:
24       Label *promptLabel;
25       Label *viewLabel;
26
27       // bit representation displayed here
28       Label *displayLabel;
29
30       // for user input
31       TextBox *inputTextBox;
32
33       void InitializeComponent();
34       void inputTextBox_KeyDown( Object *, KeyEventArgs * );
35    }; // end class PrintBits
```

Fig. I.5   PrintBits class displays the bit representation of an integer. (Part 2 of 2.)

```
1     // Fig. I.6: PrintBits.cpp
2     // Method definitions for class PrintBits.
3
4     #include "PrintBits.h"
5
6     // default constructor
7     PrintBits::PrintBits()
8     {
9        InitializeComponent();
10    }
11
12    void PrintBits::InitializeComponent()
13    {
14       this->promptLabel = new Label();
15       this->inputTextBox = new TextBox();
16       this->viewLabel = new Label();
17       this->displayLabel = new Label();
18
19       this->SuspendLayout();
20
21       // promptLabel
22       this->promptLabel->AutoSize = true;
23       this->promptLabel->Location = Point( 8, 16 );
24       this->promptLabel->Name = S"promptLabel";
25       this->promptLabel->Size = Drawing::Size( 88, 13 );
26       this->promptLabel->TabIndex = 0;
```

Fig. I.6   PrintBits class method definitions. (Part 1 of 3.)

```cpp
27       this->promptLabel->Text = S"Enter an integer:";
28
29       // inputTextBox
30       this->inputTextBox->Location = Point( 104, 16 );
31       this->inputTextBox->Name = S"inputTextBox";
32       this->inputTextBox->TabIndex = 1;
33       this->inputTextBox->Text = S"";
34       this->inputTextBox->KeyDown += new KeyEventHandler( this,
35          inputTextBox_KeyDown );
36
37       // viewLabel
38       this->viewLabel->AutoSize = true;
39       this->viewLabel->Location = Point( 208, 16 );
40       this->viewLabel->Name = S"viewLabel";
41       this->viewLabel->Size = Drawing::Size( 108, 13 );
42       this->viewLabel->TabIndex = 2;
43       this->viewLabel->Text = S"The integer in bits is:";
44
45       // displayLabel
46       this->displayLabel->BorderStyle = BorderStyle::FixedSingle;
47       this->displayLabel->Location = Point( 320, 16 );
48       this->displayLabel->Name = S"displayLabel";
49       this->displayLabel->Size = Drawing::Size( 224, 23 );
50       this->displayLabel->TabIndex = 3;
51
52       // PrintBits
53       this->AutoScaleBaseSize = Drawing::Size( 5, 13 );
54       this->ClientSize = Drawing::Size( 552, 53 );
55
56       Control *tempControl[] = { this->displayLabel, this->viewLabel,
57          this->inputTextBox, this->promptLabel };
58
59       this->Controls->AddRange( tempControl );
60       this->Name = S"PrintBits";
61       this->Text = S"PrintBits";
62
63       this->ResumeLayout();
64    } // end method InitializeComponent
65
66    // process integer when user presses Enter
67    void PrintBits::inputTextBox_KeyDown( Object *sender,
68       KeyEventArgs *e )
69    {
70       // if user pressed Enter
71       if ( e->KeyCode == Keys::Enter ) {
72
73          // test whether user enetered an integer
74          try {
75             displayLabel->Text = GetBits(
76                Convert::ToInt32( inputTextBox->Text ) );
77          }
78
79          // if value is not integer, exception is thrown
```

Fig. I.6   PrintBits class method definitions. (Part 2 of 3.)

```
80          catch ( FormatException * ) {
81             MessageBox::Show( S"Please Enter an Integer", S"Error",
82                MessageBoxButtons::OK, MessageBoxIcon::Error );
83          } // end catch
84       } // end if
85    } // end method inputTextBox_KeyDown
86
87    // convert integer to its bit representation
88    String* PrintBits::GetBits( int number )
89    {
90       int displayMask = 1 << 31;
91
92       StringBuilder *output = new StringBuilder();
93
94       // get each bit, add space every 8 bits
95       // for display formatting
96       for ( int c = 1; c <= 32; c++ ) {
97
98          // append 0 or 1 depending on result of masking
99          output->Append(
100            ( number & displayMask ) == 0 ? S"0" : S"1" );
101
102         // shift left so that mask will find bit of
103         // next digit during next iteration of loop
104         number <<= 1;
105
106         if ( c % 8 == 0 )
107            output->Append( S" " );
108      } // end for
109
110      return output->ToString();
111   } // end method GetBits
```

Fig. I.6   PrintBits class method definitions. (Part 3 of 3.)

```
1    // Fig. I.7: PrintBitsTest.cpp
2    // Entry point for application.
3
4    #include "PrintBits.h"
5
6    int __stdcall WinMain()
7    {
8       Application::Run( new PrintBits() );
9
10      return 0;
11   } // end function WinMain
```

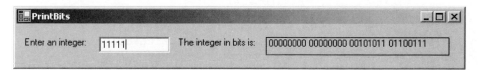

Fig. I.7   PrintBits class driver.

Common Programming Error I.1

*Using the logical AND operator (**&&**) in place of the bitwise AND operator (**&**) is a common programming error.*

Common Programming Error I.2

*Using the logical OR operator (**||**) in place of the bitwise inclusive OR operator (**|**) is a common programming error.*

The application in Fig. I.8–Fig. I.10 demonstrates the bitwise AND operator, the bitwise inclusive OR operator, the bitwise exclusive OR operator and the bitwise complement operator. The program uses method **GetBits** (lines 290–313 of Fig. I.9), which returns a **String *** that contains the bit representation of its integer argument. Users enter values into **TextBox**es and press the button corresponding to the operation they would like to test. The program displays the result in both integer and bit representations.

```
1   // Fig. I.8: BitOperations.h
2   // A class that demonstrates miscellaneous bit operations.
3
4   #pragma once
5
6   #using <system.dll>
7   #using <mscorlib.dll>
8   #using <system.drawing.dll>
9   #using <system.windows.forms.dll>
10
11  using namespace System;
12  using namespace System::Drawing;
13  using namespace System::Windows::Forms;
14  using namespace System::Text;
15
16  // allows user to test bit operators
17  public __gc class BitOperations : public Form
18  {
19  public:
20     BitOperations();
21     void InitializeComponent();
22     void andButton_Click( Object *, EventArgs * );
23     void inclusiveOrButton_Click( Object *, EventArgs * );
24     void exclusiveOrButton_Click( Object *, EventArgs * );
25     void complementButton_Click( Object *, EventArgs * );
26     String* GetBits( int );
27     void SetFields();
28
29  private:
30     Label *promptLabel, *representationLabel, *value1Label,
31        *value2Label, *resultLabel;
32
33     // display bit reprentations
34     Label *bit1Label, *bit2Label, *resultBitLabel;
35
```

Fig. I.8   Demonstrating the bitwise AND, bitwise inclusive OR, bitwise exclusive OR and bitwise complement operators. (Part 1 of 2.)

```
36      // allow user to perform bit operations
37      Button *andButton, *inclusiveOrButton, *exclusiveOrButton,
38         *complementButton;
39
40      // user inputs two integers
41      TextBox *bit1TextBox, *bit2TextBox;
42
43      TextBox *resultTextBox;
44
45      int value1, value2;
46   }; // end class BitOperations
```

Fig. I.8   Demonstrating the bitwise AND, bitwise inclusive OR, bitwise exclusive OR and bitwise complement operators. (Part 2 of 2.)

```
1    // Fig. I.9: BitOperations.cpp
2    // Method definitions for class BitOperations.
3
4    #include "BitOperations.h"
5
6    BitOperations::BitOperations()
7    {
8       InitializeComponent();
9    } // end constructor
10
11   void BitOperations::InitializeComponent()
12   {
13      this->promptLabel = new Label();
14      this->representationLabel = new Label();
15      this->value1Label = new Label();
16      this->value2Label = new Label();
17      this->resultLabel = new Label();
18      this->bit1Label = new Label();
19      this->bit2Label = new Label();
20      this->resultBitLabel = new Label();
21      this->bit1TextBox = new TextBox();
22      this->bit2TextBox = new TextBox();
23      this->resultTextBox = new TextBox();
24      this->andButton = new Button();
25      this->inclusiveOrButton = new Button();
26      this->exclusiveOrButton = new Button();
27      this->complementButton = new Button();
28
29      this->SuspendLayout();
30
31      // promptLabel
32      this->promptLabel->AutoSize = true;
33      this->promptLabel->Font = new Drawing::Font(
34         S"Microsoft Sans Serif", 9, FontStyle::Regular,
35         GraphicsUnit::Point, 0 );
36      this->promptLabel->Location = Point( 64, 8 );
37      this->promptLabel->Name = S"promptLabel";
```

Fig. I.9   **BitOperations** class method definitions. (Part 1 of 7.)

```
38       this->promptLabel->Size = Drawing::Size( 107, 14 );
39       this->promptLabel->TabIndex = 0;
40       this->promptLabel->Text = S"Enter two integers:";
41
42       // representationLabel
43       this->representationLabel->AutoSize = true;
44       this->representationLabel->Font = new Drawing::Font(
45          S"Microsoft Sans Serif", 9, FontStyle::Regular,
46          GraphicsUnit::Point, 0 );
47       this->representationLabel->Location = Point( 296, 8 );
48       this->representationLabel->Name = S"representationLabel";
49       this->representationLabel->Size = Drawing::Size( 111, 14 );
50       this->representationLabel->TabIndex = 1;
51       this->representationLabel->Text = S"Bit representations:";
52
53       // value1Label
54       this->value1Label->AutoSize = true;
55       this->value1Label->BorderStyle = BorderStyle::FixedSingle;
56       this->value1Label->Font = new Drawing::Font(
57          S"Microsoft Sans Serif", 9, FontStyle::Regular,
58          GraphicsUnit::Point, 0 );
59       this->value1Label->Location = Point( 16, 40 );
60       this->value1Label->Name = S"value1Label";
61       this->value1Label->Size = Drawing::Size( 52, 16 );
62       this->value1Label->TabIndex = 2;
63       this->value1Label->Text = S"Value 1:";
64
65       // value2Label
66       this->value2Label->AutoSize = true;
67       this->value2Label->BorderStyle = BorderStyle::FixedSingle;
68       this->value2Label->Font = new Drawing::Font(
69          S"Microsoft Sans Serif", 9, FontStyle::Regular,
70          GraphicsUnit::Point, 0 );
71       this->value2Label->Location = Point( 16, 72 );
72       this->value2Label->Name = S"value2Label";
73       this->value2Label->Size = Drawing::Size( 52, 16 );
74       this->value2Label->TabIndex = 3;
75       this->value2Label->Text = S"Value 2:";
76
77       // resultLabel
78       this->resultLabel->AutoSize = true;
79       this->resultLabel->BorderStyle = BorderStyle::FixedSingle;
80       this->resultLabel->Font = new Drawing::Font(
81          S"Microsoft Sans Serif", 9, FontStyle::Regular,
82          GraphicsUnit::Point, 0 );
83       this->resultLabel->Location = Point( 16, 104 );
84       this->resultLabel->Name = S"resultLabel";
85       this->resultLabel->Size = Drawing::Size( 45, 16 );
86       this->resultLabel->TabIndex = 4;
87       this->resultLabel->Text = S"Result:";
88
89       // bit1Label
90       this->bit1Label->BorderStyle = BorderStyle::FixedSingle;
```

Fig. I.9   **BitOperations** class method definitions. (Part 2 of 7.)

```
91      this->bit1Label->Font = new Drawing::Font(
92         S"Microsoft Sans Serif", 9, FontStyle::Regular,
93         GraphicsUnit::Point, 0 );
94      this->bit1Label->Location = Point( 200, 40 );
95      this->bit1Label->Name = S"bit1Label";
96      this->bit1Label->Size = Drawing::Size( 248, 16 );
97      this->bit1Label->TabIndex = 5;
98
99      // bit2Label
100     this->bit2Label->BorderStyle = BorderStyle::FixedSingle;
101     this->bit2Label->Font = new Drawing::Font(
102        S"Microsoft Sans Serif", 9, FontStyle::Regular,
103        GraphicsUnit::Point, 0 );
104     this->bit2Label->Location = Point( 200, 72 );
105     this->bit2Label->Name = S"bit2Label";
106     this->bit2Label->Size = Drawing::Size( 248, 16 );
107     this->bit2Label->TabIndex = 6;
108
109     // resultBitLabel
110     this->resultBitLabel->BorderStyle = BorderStyle::FixedSingle;
111     this->resultBitLabel->Font = new Drawing::Font(
112        S"Microsoft Sans Serif", 9, FontStyle::Regular,
113        GraphicsUnit::Point, 0 );
114     this->resultBitLabel->Location = Point( 200, 104 );
115     this->resultBitLabel->Name = S"resultBitLabel";
116     this->resultBitLabel->Size = Drawing::Size( 248, 16 );
117     this->resultBitLabel->TabIndex = 7;
118
119     // bit1TextBox
120     this->bit1TextBox->Font = new Drawing::Font(
121        S"Microsoft Sans Serif", 9, FontStyle::Regular,
122        GraphicsUnit::Point, 0 );
123     this->bit1TextBox->Location = Point( 88, 40 );
124     this->bit1TextBox->Name = S"bit1TextBox";
125     this->bit1TextBox->TabIndex = 8;
126     this->bit1TextBox->Text = S"";
127
128     // bit2TextBox
129     this->bit2TextBox->Font = new Drawing::Font(
130        S"Microsoft Sans Serif", 9, FontStyle::Regular,
131        GraphicsUnit::Point, 0 );
132     this->bit2TextBox->Location = Point( 88, 72 );
133     this->bit2TextBox->Name = S"bit2TextBox";
134     this->bit2TextBox->TabIndex = 9;
135     this->bit2TextBox->Text = S"";
136
137     // resultTextBox
138     this->resultTextBox->Font = new Drawing::Font(
139        S"Microsoft Sans Serif", 9, FontStyle::Regular,
140        GraphicsUnit::Point, 0 );
141     this->resultTextBox->Location = Point( 88, 104 );
142     this->resultTextBox->Name = S"resultTextBox";
143     this->resultTextBox->TabIndex = 10;
```

Fig. I.9   **BitOperations** class method definitions. (Part 3 of 7.)

```
144        this->resultTextBox->Text = S"";
145
146        // andButton
147        this->andButton->Font = new Drawing::Font(
148           S"Microsoft Sans Serif", 10, FontStyle::Regular,
149           GraphicsUnit::Point, 0 );
150        this->andButton->Location = Point( 16, 136 );
151        this->andButton->Name = S"andButton";
152        this->andButton->Size = Drawing::Size( 96, 40 );
153        this->andButton->TabIndex = 11;
154        this->andButton->Text = S"AND";
155        this->andButton->Click += new EventHandler( this,
156           andButton_Click );
157
158        // inclusiveOrButton
159        this->inclusiveOrButton->Font = new Drawing::Font(
160           S"Microsoft Sans Serif", 10, FontStyle::Regular,
161           GraphicsUnit::Point, 0 );
162        this->inclusiveOrButton->Location = Point( 128, 136 );
163        this->inclusiveOrButton->Name = S"inclusiveOrButton";
164        this->inclusiveOrButton->Size = Drawing::Size( 96, 40 );
165        this->inclusiveOrButton->TabIndex = 12;
166        this->inclusiveOrButton->Text = S"Inclusive OR";
167        this->inclusiveOrButton->Click += new EventHandler( this,
168           inclusiveOrButton_Click );
169
170        // exclusiveOrButton
171        this->exclusiveOrButton->Font = new Drawing::Font(
172           S"Microsoft Sans Serif", 10, FontStyle::Regular,
173           GraphicsUnit::Point, 0 );
174        this->exclusiveOrButton->Location = Point( 240, 136 );
175        this->exclusiveOrButton->Name = S"exclusiveOrButton";
176        this->exclusiveOrButton->Size = Drawing::Size( 96, 40 );
177        this->exclusiveOrButton->TabIndex = 13;
178        this->exclusiveOrButton->Text = S"Exclusive Or";
179        this->exclusiveOrButton->Click += new EventHandler( this,
180           exclusiveOrButton_Click );
181
182        // complementButton
183        this->complementButton->Font = new Drawing::Font(
184           S"Microsoft Sans Serif", 10, FontStyle::Regular,
185           GraphicsUnit::Point, 0 );
186        this->complementButton->Location = Point( 352, 136 );
187        this->complementButton->Name = S"complementButton";
188        this->complementButton->Size = Drawing::Size( 96, 40 );
189        this->complementButton->TabIndex = 14;
190        this->complementButton->Text = S"Complement";
191        this->complementButton->Click += new EventHandler( this,
192           complementButton_Click );
193
194        // BitOperations
195        this->AutoScaleBaseSize = Drawing::Size( 5, 13 );
196        this->ClientSize = Drawing::Size( 472, 189 );
```

Fig. I.9   **BitOperations** class method definitions. (Part 4 of 7.)

```
197
198        Control *tempControl[] = { this->complementButton,
199           this->exclusiveOrButton, this->inclusiveOrButton,
200           this->andButton, this->resultTextBox, this->bit2TextBox,
201           this->bit1TextBox, this->resultBitLabel, this->bit2Label,
202           this->bit1Label, this->resultLabel, this->value2Label,
203           this->value1Label, this->representationLabel,
204           this->promptLabel };
205
206        this->Controls->AddRange( tempControl );
207        this->Name = S"BitOperations";
208        this->Text = S"BitOperations";
209
210        this->ResumeLayout();
211 } // end method InitializeComponent
212
213 // AND
214 void BitOperations::andButton_Click( Object *sender, EventArgs *e )
215 {
216     try {
217        SetFields();
218
219        // update resultTextBox
220        resultTextBox->Text = ( value1 & value2 ).ToString();
221        resultBitLabel->Text = GetBits( value1 & value2 );
222     }
223
224     // if value is not integer, exception is thrown
225     catch ( FormatException * ) {
226        MessageBox::Show( S"Please Enter Two Integers", S"Error",
227           MessageBoxButtons::OK, MessageBoxIcon::Error );
228     } // end catch
229 } // end method andButton_Click
230
231 // inclusive OR
232 void BitOperations::inclusiveOrButton_Click( Object *sender,
233     EventArgs *e )
234 {
235     try {
236        SetFields();
237
238        // update resultTextBox
239        resultTextBox->Text = ( value1 | value2 ).ToString();
240        resultBitLabel->Text = GetBits( value1 | value2 );
241     }
242
243     // if value is not integer, exception is thrown
244     catch ( FormatException * ) {
245        MessageBox::Show( S"Please Enter Two Integers", S"Error",
246           MessageBoxButtons::OK, MessageBoxIcon::Error );
247     } // end catch
248 } // end method inclusiveOrButton_Click
249
```

Fig. I.9   **BitOperations** class method definitions. (Part 5 of 7.)

```
250   // exclusive OR
251   void BitOperations::exclusiveOrButton_Click( Object *sender,
252      EventArgs *e )
253   {
254      try {
255         SetFields();
256
257         // update resultTextBox
258         resultTextBox->Text = ( value1 ^ value2 ).ToString();
259         resultBitLabel->Text = GetBits( value1 ^ value2 );
260      }
261
262      // if value is not integer, exception is thrown
263      catch ( FormatException * ) {
264         MessageBox::Show( S"Please Enter Two Integers", S"Error",
265            MessageBoxButtons::OK, MessageBoxIcon::Error );
266      } // end catch
267   } // end method exclusiveOrButton_Click
268
269   // complement of first integer
270   void BitOperations::complementButton_Click( Object *sender,
271      EventArgs *e )
272   {
273      try {
274         value1 = Convert::ToInt32( bit1TextBox->Text );
275         bit1Label->Text = GetBits( value1 );
276
277         // update resultTextBox
278         resultTextBox->Text = ( ~value1 ).ToString();
279         resultBitLabel->Text = GetBits( ~value1 );
280      }
281
282      // if value is not integer, exception is thrown
283      catch ( FormatException * ) {
284         MessageBox::Show( S"Please Enter Two Integers", S"Error",
285            MessageBoxButtons::OK, MessageBoxIcon::Error );
286      } // end catch
287   } // end method complementButton_Click
288
289   // convert integer to its bit representation
290   String *BitOperations::GetBits( int number )
291   {
292      int displayMask = 1 << 31;
293
294      StringBuilder *output = new StringBuilder();
295
296      // get each bit, add space every 8 bits
297      // for display formatting
298      for ( int c = 1; c <= 32; c++ ) {
299
300         // append 0 or 1 depending on the result of masking
301         output->Append(
302            ( number & displayMask ) == 0 ? S"0" : S"1" );
```

Fig. I.9   **BitOperations** class method definitions. (Part 6 of 7.)

```
303
304          // shift left so that mask will find bit of
305          // next digit in the next iteration of loop
306          number <<= 1;
307
308          if ( c % 8 == 0 )
309              output->Append( S" " );
310      } // end for
311
312      return output->ToString();
313  } // end method GetBits
314
315  // set fields of Form
316  void BitOperations::SetFields()
317  {
318      // retrieve input values
319      value1 = Convert::ToInt32( bit1TextBox->Text );
320      value2 = Convert::ToInt32( bit2TextBox->Text );
321
322      // set labels to display bit representations of integers
323      bit1Label->Text = GetBits( value1 );
324      bit2Label->Text = GetBits( value2 );
325  } // end method SetFields
```

Fig. I.9   **BitOperations** class method definitions. (Part 7 of 7.)

```
1   // Fig. I.10: BitOperations.h
2   // Entry point for application.
3
4   #include "BitOperations.h"
5
6   int __stdcall WinMain()
7   {
8       Application::Run( new BitOperations() );
9
10      return 0;
11  } // end function WinMain
```

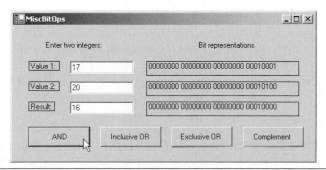

Fig. I.10   **BitOperations** class driver. (Part 1 of 2.)

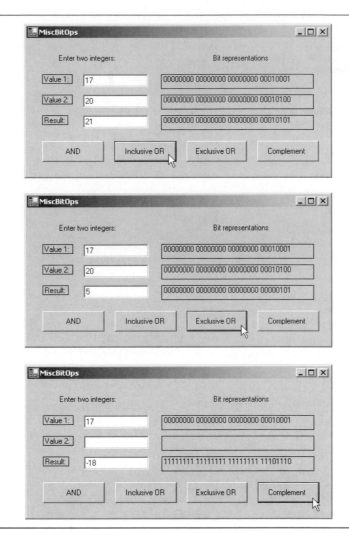

Fig. I.10   BitOperations class driver. (Part 2 of 2.)

The first output window of Fig. I.10 shows the results of combining the value **17** and the value **20** through the bitwise AND operator (**&**); the result is **16**. The second output window shows the results of combining the value **17** and the value **20** through the bitwise OR operator; the result is **21**. The third output shows the results of combining the value **17** and the value **20** through the exclusive OR operator; the result is **5**. The fourth output window shows the results of taking the ones complement of the value **17**. The result is **-18**.

The program in Fig. I.11–Fig. I.13 demonstrates the use of the left-shift operator (**<<**) and the right-shift operator (**>>**). Method **GetBits** (Fig. I.12, lines 144–167) returns a **String*** containing the bit representation of an integer value passed to it as an argument. When users enter an integer in a **TextBox** and press *Enter*, the program displays the bit representation of the specified integer in a **Label**.

```
1   // Fig. I.11: BitShift.h
2   // Demonstrates bitshift operators.
3
4   #pragma once
5
6   #using <system.dll>
7   #using <mscorlib.dll>
8   #using <system.drawing.dll>
9   #using <system.windows.forms.dll>
10
11  using namespace System;
12  using namespace System::Drawing;
13  using namespace System::Windows::Forms;
14  using namespace System::Text;
15
16  // shifts bits to the right or left
17  public __gc class BitShift : public Form
18  {
19  public:
20     BitShift();
21
22  private:
23     Label *inputLabel;
24
25     // accepts user input
26     TextBox *inputTextBox;
27
28     // displays integer in bits
29     Label *displayLabel;
30     Button *leftButton;
31     Button *rightButton;
32
33     void InitializeComponent();
34     void inputTextBox_KeyDown( Object *, KeyEventArgs * );
35     void leftButton_Click( Object *, EventArgs * );
36     void rightButton_Click( Object *, EventArgs * );
37     String *GetBits( int );
38  }; // end class BitShift
```

Fig. I.11 **BitShift** class demonstrates the bitshift operators.

```
1   // Fig. I.12: BitShift.cpp
2   // Method definitions for class BitShift.
3
4   #include "BitShift.h"
5
6   BitShift::BitShift()
7   {
8      InitializeComponent();
9   } // end constructor
10
```

Fig. I.12 **BitShift** class method definitions. (Part 1 of 4.)

```
11    void BitShift::InitializeComponent()
12    {
13        this->inputLabel = new Label();
14        this->displayLabel = new Label();
15        this->leftButton = new Button();
16        this->rightButton = new Button();
17        this->inputTextBox = new TextBox();
18
19        this->SuspendLayout();
20
21        // inputLabel
22        this->inputLabel->Location = Point( 24, 24 );
23        this->inputLabel->Name = S"inputLabel";
24        this->inputLabel->TabIndex = 0;
25        this->inputLabel->Text = S"Integer to shift:";
26
27        // displayLabel
28        this->displayLabel->BorderStyle = BorderStyle::FixedSingle;
29        this->displayLabel->Location = Point( 32, 64 );
30        this->displayLabel->Name = S"displayLabel";
31        this->displayLabel->Size = Drawing::Size( 224, 23 );
32        this->displayLabel->TabIndex = 1;
33
34        // leftButton
35        this->leftButton->Location = Point( 40, 112 );
36        this->leftButton->Name = S"leftButton";
37        this->leftButton->Size = Drawing::Size( 88, 48 );
38        this->leftButton->TabIndex = 2;
39        this->leftButton->Text = S"<<";
40        this->leftButton->Click += new EventHandler( this,
41           leftButton_Click );
42
43        // rightButton
44        this->rightButton->Location = Point( 152, 112 );
45        this->rightButton->Name = S"rightButton";
46        this->rightButton->Size = Drawing::Size( 88, 48 );
47        this->rightButton->TabIndex = 3;
48        this->rightButton->Text = S">>";
49        this->rightButton->Click += new EventHandler( this,
50           rightButton_Click );
51
52        // inputTextBox
53        this->inputTextBox->Location = Point( 152, 24 );
54        this->inputTextBox->Name = S"inputTextBox";
55        this->inputTextBox->TabIndex = 4;
56        this->inputTextBox->Text = S"";
57        this->inputTextBox->KeyDown += new KeyEventHandler( this,
58           inputTextBox_KeyDown );
59
60        // BitShift
61        this->AutoScaleBaseSize = Drawing::Size( 5, 13 );
62        this->ClientSize = Drawing::Size( 292, 181 );
63
```

Fig. I.12   **BitShift** class method definitions. (Part 2 of 4.)

```
64      Control *tempControl[] = { this->inputTextBox,
65         this->rightButton, this->leftButton,
66         this->displayLabel, this->inputLabel };
67
68      this->Controls->AddRange( tempControl );
69      this->Name = S"BitShift";
70      this->Text = S"BitShift";
71
72      this->ResumeLayout();
73   } // end method InitializeComponent
74
75   // process user input
76   void BitShift::inputTextBox_KeyDown( Object *sender,
77      KeyEventArgs *e )
78   {
79      try {
80
81         if ( e->KeyCode == Keys::Enter )
82            displayLabel->Text = GetBits( Convert::ToInt32(
83               inputTextBox->Text ) );
84      }
85
86      // if value is not integer, exception is thrown
87      catch ( FormatException * ) {
88         MessageBox::Show( S"Please Enter an Integer", S"Error",
89            MessageBoxButtons::OK, MessageBoxIcon::Error );
90      } // end catch
91   } // end method inputTextBox_KeyDown
92
93   // do left shift
94   void BitShift::leftButton_Click( Object *sender, EventArgs *e )
95   {
96      try {
97
98         // retrieve user input
99         int number = Convert::ToInt32( inputTextBox->Text );
100
101         // do left shift operation
102         number <<= 1;
103
104         // convert to integer and display in textbox
105         inputTextBox->Text = number.ToString();
106
107         // display bits in label
108         displayLabel->Text = GetBits( number );
109      }
110
111      // if value is not integer, exception is thrown
112      catch ( FormatException * ) {
113         MessageBox::Show( S"Please Enter an Integer", S"Error",
114            MessageBoxButtons::OK, MessageBoxIcon::Error );
115      } // end catch
116   } // end method leftButton_Click
```

Fig. I.12   **BitShift** class method definitions. (Part 3 of 4.)

```cpp
117
118   // do right shift
119   void BitShift::rightButton_Click( Object *sender, EventArgs *e )
120   {
121      try {
122
123         // retrieve user input
124         int number = Convert::ToInt32( inputTextBox->Text );
125
126         // do right shift operation
127         number >>= 1;
128
129         // convert to integer and display in textbox
130         inputTextBox->Text = number.ToString();
131
132         // display bits in label
133         displayLabel->Text = GetBits( number );
134      }
135
136      // if value is not integer, exception is thrown
137      catch ( FormatException * ) {
138         MessageBox::Show( S"Please Enter an Integer", S"Error",
139            MessageBoxButtons::OK, MessageBoxIcon::Error );
140      } // end catch
141   } // end method rightButton_Click
142
143   // convert integer to its bit representation
144   String* BitShift::GetBits( int number )
145   {
146      int displayMask = 1 << 31;
147
148      StringBuilder *output = new StringBuilder();
149
150      // get each bit, add space every 8 bits
151      // for display formatting
152      for ( int c = 1; c <= 32; c++ ) {
153
154         // append a 0 or 1 depending on the result of masking
155         output->Append(
156            ( number & displayMask ) == 0 ? S"0" : S"1" );
157
158         // shift left so that mask will find bit of
159         // next digit during next iteration of loop
160         number <<= 1;
161
162         if ( c % 8 == 0 )
163            output->Append( S" " );
164      } // end for
165
166      return output->ToString();
167   } // end method GetBits
```

Fig. I.12   BitShift class method definitions. (Part 4 of 4.)

```cpp
1   // Fig. I.13: BitShiftTest.cpp
2   // Entry point for application.
3
4   #include "BitShift.h"
5
6   int __stdcall WinMain()
7   {
8       Application::Run( new BitShift() );
9
10      return 0;
11  } // end function WinMain
```

Fig. I.13   **BitShift** class driver.

Each shift operator has its own button on the application's GUI. As a user clicks each button, the bits in the integer shift left or right by one bit. The **TextBox** and **Label** display the new integer value and new bit representation, respectively.

The left-shift operator (**<<**) shifts the bits of its left operand to the left by the number of bits specified in its right operand. The rightmost bits are replaced with **0**s; **1**s shifted off the left are lost. The first two output windows in Fig. I.13 demonstrate the left-shift operator. To produce the output, the user entered the value **23** and clicked the left-shift button, resulting in the value **46**.

The right-shift operator (**>>**) shifts the bits of its left operand to the right by the number of bits specified in its right operand. **0**s replace vacated bits on the left side if the number is positive, and **1**s replace the vacated bits if the number is negative. Any **1**s shifted off the right are lost. The third and fourth output windows depict the result of shifting **184** to the right once.

Each bitwise operator (except the bitwise complement operator) has a corresponding assignment operator. Figure I.14 describes these *bitwise assignment operators*, which are used in a manner similar to the arithmetic assignment operators introduced in Chapter 2, Visual Studio® .NET IDE and Visual C++ .NET Programming.

Bitwise assignment operators	
`&=`	Bitwise AND assignment operator.
`|=`	Bitwise inclusive OR assignment operator.
`^=`	Bitwise exclusive OR assignment operator.
`<<=`	Left-shift assignment operator.
`>>=`	Right-shift assignment operator.

Fig. I.14   Bitwise assignment operators.

I.3 Class `BitArray`

Class ***BitArray*** (located in namespace **System::Collections**) facilitates the creation and manipulation of *bit sets*, which programmers often use to represent a set of *boolean flags*. A boolean flag is a variable that keeps track of a certain boolean decision. **BitArray**s are resizable dynamically—more bits can be added once a **BitArray** object is created, causing the object to grow to accommodate the additional bits.

Class **BitArray** provides several constructors, one of which accepts an **int** as an argument. The **int** specifies the number of bits that the **BitArray** represents, all of which are initially set to **false**.

Method ***Set*** of **BitArray** can change the value of an individual bit; it accepts the index of the bit to change and its new **bool** value. Class **BitArray** also includes an indexer that allows us to get and set individual bit values. The indexer returns **true** if the specified bit is on (i.e., the bit has value 1) and returns **false** otherwise (i.e., the bit has value 0 or "off").

Class **BitArray** method ***And*** performs a bitwise AND between two **BitArray**s and returns the **BitArray** result of the operation. Methods ***Or*** and ***Xor*** perform bitwise inclusive OR and bitwise exclusive OR operations, respectively. Class **BitArray** also provides a ***Length*** property, which returns the number of elements in the **BitArray**.

Figure I.15–Figure I.17 demonstrates the *Sieve of Eratosthenes*, which is a technique for finding prime numbers. A prime number is an integer larger than 1 that is divisible evenly only by itself and one. The Sieve of Eratosthenes operates as follows:

> *a) Create an array with all elements initialized to 1 (true). Array elements with prime subscripts remain 1. All other array elements eventually are set to 0.*
> *b) Starting with array subscript 2 (subscript 1 must not be prime), every time an array element is found with a value of 1, loop through the remainder of the array and set to 0 every element whose subscript is a multiple of the subscript for the element with value 1. For example, for array subscript 2, all elements after 2 in the array that are multiples of 2 are set to 0 (subscripts 4, 6, 8, 10, etc.); for array subscript 3, all elements after 3 in the array that are multiples of 3 are set to 0 (subscripts 6, 9, 12, 15, etc.); and so on.*

At the end of this process, the subscripts of the array elements that are one are prime numbers. The list of prime numbers can then be displayed by locating and printing these subscripts.

```
1    // Fig. I.15: BitArrayTest.h
2    // Demonstrates BitArray class.
3
4    #pragma once
5
6    #using <system.dll>
7    #using <mscorlib.dll>
8    #using <system.drawing.dll>
9    #using <system.windows.forms.dll>
10
11   using namespace System;
12   using namespace System::Drawing;
13   using namespace System::Windows::Forms;
14   using namespace System::Collections;
15
16   // implements Sieve of Eratosthenes
17   public __gc class BitArrayTest : public Form
18   {
19   public:
20      BitArrayTest();
21
22   private:
23      Label *promptLabel;
24
25      // user inputs integer
26      TextBox *inputTextBox;
27
28      // display prime numbers
29      TextBox *outputTextBox;
30
31      // displays whether input integer is prime
32      Label *displayLabel;
33
34      BitArray *sieve;
35
36      void InitializeComponent();
37      void inputTextBox_KeyDown( Object *, KeyEventArgs * );
38   }; // end class BitArrayTest
```

Fig. I.15 **BitArrayTest** class implements the Sieve of Eratosthenes, using class **BitArray**.

```
1    // Fig. I.16: BitArrayTest.cpp
2    // Method definitions for class BitArrayTest.
3
4    #include "BitArrayTest.h"
5
6    // default constructor
7    BitArrayTest::BitArrayTest()
8    {
9       InitializeComponent();
10
```

Fig. I.16 **BitArrayTest** class method definitions. (Part 1 of 4.)

```cpp
11          // create BitArray and set all bits to true
12          sieve = new BitArray( 1024 );
13          sieve->SetAll( true );
14
15          int finalBit = static_cast< int >(
16             Math::Sqrt( sieve->Length ) );
17
18          // perform sieve operation
19          for ( int i = 2; i < finalBit; i++ )
20
21             if ( sieve->Get( i ) )
22
23                for ( int j = 2 * i; j < sieve->Length; j += i )
24                   sieve->Set( j, false );
25
26          int counter = 0;
27
28          // display prime numbers
29          for ( int i = 2; i < sieve->Length; i++ )
30
31             if ( sieve->Get( i ) )
32                outputTextBox->Text = String::Concat(
33                   outputTextBox->Text, i.ToString(),
34                   ( ++counter % 7 == 0 ? S"\r\n" : S"    " ) );
35       } // end constructor
36
37       void BitArrayTest::InitializeComponent()
38       {
39          this->promptLabel = new Label();
40          this->inputTextBox = new TextBox();
41          this->outputTextBox = new TextBox();
42          this->displayLabel = new Label();
43
44          this->SuspendLayout();
45
46          // promptLabel
47          this->promptLabel->AutoSize = true;
48          this->promptLabel->Location = Point( 8, 16 );
49          this->promptLabel->Name = S"promptLabel";
50          this->promptLabel->Size = Drawing::Size( 146, 13 );
51          this->promptLabel->TabIndex = 0;
52          this->promptLabel->Text = S"Enter a value from 1 to 1023";
53
54          // inputTextBox
55          this->inputTextBox->Location = Point( 160, 8 );
56          this->inputTextBox->Name = S"inputTextBox";
57          this->inputTextBox->TabIndex = 1;
58          this->inputTextBox->Text = S"";
59          this->inputTextBox->KeyDown += new KeyEventHandler( this,
60             inputTextBox_KeyDown );
61
62          // outputTextBox
63          this->outputTextBox->Location = Point( 16, 48 );
```

Fig. I.16 **BitArrayTest** class method definitions. (Part 2 of 4.)

```
64        this->outputTextBox->Multiline = true;
65        this->outputTextBox->Name = S"outputTextBox";
66        this->outputTextBox->ReadOnly = true;
67        this->outputTextBox->ScrollBars = ScrollBars::Both;
68        this->outputTextBox->Size = Drawing::Size( 240, 160 );
69        this->outputTextBox->TabIndex = 2;
70        this->outputTextBox->Text = S"";
71
72        // displayLabel
73        this->displayLabel->Location = Point( 16, 216 );
74        this->displayLabel->Name = S"displayLabel";
75        this->displayLabel->Size = Drawing::Size( 176, 16 );
76        this->displayLabel->TabIndex = 3;
77
78        // BitArrayTest
79        this->AutoScaleBaseSize = Drawing::Size( 5, 13 );
80        this->ClientSize = Drawing::Size( 288, 245 );
81
82        Control *tempControl[] = { this->displayLabel,
83           this->outputTextBox, this->inputTextBox,
84           this->promptLabel };
85
86        this->Controls->AddRange( tempControl );
87        this->Name = S"BitArrayTest";
88        this->Text = S"BitArrayTest";
89
90        this->ResumeLayout();
91   } // end method InitializeComponent
92
93   void BitArrayTest::inputTextBox_KeyDown( Object *sender,
94      KeyEventArgs *e )
95   {
96      // if user pressed Enter
97      if ( e->KeyCode == Keys::Enter ) {
98
99         try {
100            int number = Convert::ToInt32( inputTextBox->Text );
101
102            // if sieve is true at index of integer
103            // input by user, then number is prime
104            if ( sieve->Get( number ) )
105               displayLabel->Text = String::Concat(
106                  number.ToString(), S" is a prime number" );
107            else
108               displayLabel->Text = String::Concat(
109                  number.ToString(), S" is not a prime number" );
110         }
111
112         // if value is not integer, exception is thrown
113         catch ( FormatException * ) {
114            MessageBox::Show( S"Please Enter an Integer", S"Error",
115               MessageBoxButtons::OK, MessageBoxIcon::Error );
116         } // end catch
```

Fig. I.16   BitArrayTest class method definitions. (Part 3 of 4.)

```
117
118          // if value is not in range, exception is thrown
119          catch ( ArgumentOutOfRangeException * ) {
120             MessageBox::Show( S"Not in valid range", S"Error",
121                MessageBoxButtons::OK, MessageBoxIcon::Error );
122          } // end catch
123       } // end if
124    } // end method inputTextBox_KeyDown
```

Fig. I.16 **BitArrayTest** class method definitions. (Part 4 of 4.)

```
1    // Fig. I.17: BitArrayTestMain.cpp
2    // Entry point for application.
3
4    #include "BitArrayTest.h"
5
6    int __stdcall WinMain()
7    {
8       Application::Run( new BitArrayTest() );
9
10      return 0;
11   } // end function WinMain
```

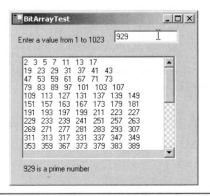

Fig. I.17 **BitArrayTest** class driver.

We use a **BitArray** to implement the algorithm. The program displays the prime numbers in the range 1–1023 in a **TextBox**. The program also provides a **TextBox** in which users can type any number from 1–1023 to determine whether that number is prime. (In which case, it displays a message indicating that the number is prime.)

The statement on line 12 (of Fig. I.15) creates a **BitArray** of **1024** bits. **BitArray** method **SetAll** sets all the bits to **true** on line 13; then, lines 15–24 determine all prime numbers occurring between 1 and 1023. The integer **finalBit** determines when the algorithm is complete.

When the user inputs a number and presses *Enter*, line 104 tests whether the input number is prime. This line uses the **Get** method of class **BitArray**, which takes a number and returns the value of that bit in the array. Lines 105–106 and 108–109 display an appropriate response.

I.4 Summary

Computers represent data internally as sequences of bits. Each bit can assume the value **0** or the value **1**. On all systems, a sequence of 8 bits forms a byte—the standard storage unit for a variable of type **char**. Other data types require larger numbers of bytes for storage.

The bitwise AND operator sets each bit in the result to 1 if the corresponding bits in both operands are 1. Often, the bitwise AND operator is used with a mask operand—an integer value with specific bits set to **1**. Masks hide some bits in a value and select other bits. The bitwise inclusive OR operator sets each bit in the result to 1 if the corresponding bit in either (or both) operand(s) are 1. The bitwise exclusive OR operator sets each bit in the result to 1 if the corresponding bit in exactly one operand is 1. Exclusive OR is also known as XOR. The left-shift (**<<**) operator shifts the bits of its left operand to the left by the number of bits specified in its right operand. The right-shift (**>>**) operator shifts the bits in its left operand to the right by the number of bits specified in its right operand. If the left operand is negative, **1**s are shifted in from the left, whereas, if the left operand is positive, **0**s are shifted in from the left. The bitwise complement (**~**) operator sets all **0** bits in its operand to **1** in the result and sets all **1** bits to **0** in the result; this process is sometimes referred to as "taking the ones complement of the value." Each bitwise operator (except the bitwise complement operator) has a corresponding assignment operator.

Class **BitArray** facilitates the creation and manipulation of bit sets, which programmers often use to represent a set of boolean flags. A boolean flag is a variable that keeps track of a certain boolean decision. **BitArray**s are resizable dynamically—more bits can be added once a **BitArray** object is created, causing the object to grow to accommodate the additional bits. Method **Set** of **BitArray** can change the value of an individual bit— it accepts the index of the bit to change and the **bool** value to which the bit should change. **BitArray** method **And** performs a bitwise AND between two **BitArray**s. It returns the **Bit-Array** that is the result of performing this operation. Methods **Or** and **Xor**, perform bitwise inclusive OR and bitwise exclusive OR, respectively. **BitArray** method **SetAll** sets all the bits in the **BitArray** to **true**.

Index

The DEITEL™
Suite of Products...

Web Services
A Technical Introduction

© 2003, 400 pp., paper (0-13-046135-0)

Web Services A Technical Introduction from the DEITEL™ Developer Series familiarizes programmers, technical managers and project managers with key Web services concepts, including what Web services are and why they are revolutionary. The book covers the business case for Web services—the underlying technologies, ways in which Web services can provide competitive advantages and opportunities for Web services-related lines of business. Readers learn the latest Web-services standards, including XML, SOAP, WSDL and UDDI; learn about Web services implementations in .NET and Java; benefit from an extensive comparison of Web services products and vendors; and read about Web services security options. Although this is not a programming book, the appendices show .NET and Java code examples to demonstrate the structure of Web services applications and documents. In addition, the book includes numerous case studies describing ways in which organizations are implementing Web services to increase efficiency, simplify business processes, create new revenue streams and interact better with partners and customers.

Java™ Web Services
for Experienced Programmers

© 2003, 700 pp., paper (0-13-046134-2)

Java™ Web Services for Experienced Programmers from the DEITEL™ Developer Series provides the experienced Java programmer with 103 LIVE-CODE™ examples and covers industry standards including XML, SOAP, WSDL and UDDI. Learn how to build and integrate Web services using the Java API for XML RPC, the Java API for XML Messaging, Apache Axis and the Java Web Services Developer Pack. Develop and deploy Web services on several major Web services platforms. Register and discover Web services through public registries and the Java API for XML Registries. Build Web Services clients for several platforms, including J2ME. Significant Web Services case studies also are included.

Visual Basic® .NET
for Experienced Programmers

©2003, paper, approximately 1150 pp., (0-13-046131-8)

Visual Basic .NET for Experienced Programmers from the DEITEL™ Developer Series presents experienced programmers with a concise introduction to programming fundamentals before delving into more sophisticated topics. Learn how to create reusable software components with assemblies, modules and dynamic link libraries. Learn Visual Basic .NET through LIVE-CODE™ examples of ASP.NET, multi-threading, object-oriented programming, XML processing, mobile application development and Web services.

Visual C++ .NET
A Managed Code Approach for
Experienced Programmers

© 2003, 1500 pp., paper (0-13-045821-X)

Visual C++ .NET A Managed Code Approach for Experienced Programmers from the DEITEL™ Developer Series teaches programmers with C++ programming experience how to develop Visual C++ applications for Microsoft's new .NET Framework. The book begins with a condensed introduction to Visual C++ programming fundamentals, then covers more sophistcated .NET application-development topics in detail. Key topics include: creating reusable software components with assemblies, modules and dynamic link libraries; using classes from the Framework Class Library (FCL); building graphical user interfaces (GUIs) with the FCL; implementing multithreaded applications; building networked applications; manipulating databases with ADO .NET and creating XML Web services. In addition, the book provides several chapters on unmanaged code in Visual C++ .NET. These chapters demonstrate how to use "attributed programming" to simplify common tasks (such as connecting to a database) and improve code readability; how to integrate managed- and unmanaged-code software components; and how to use ATL Server to create Web-based applications and Web services with unmanaged code. The book features detailed LIVE-CODE™ examples that highlight crucial .NET-programming concepts and demonstrate Web services at work. A substantial introduction to XML also is included.

www·deitel·com/newsletter/subscribe·html

C++
How to Program
Fourth Edition

©2003, 1400 pp., paper
(0-13-038474-7)

The world's best selling C++ textbook is now even better! Designed for beginning through intermediate courses, this comprehensive, practical introduction to C++ includes hundreds of hands-on exercises, and uses 267 LIVE-CODE™ programs to demonstrate C++'s powerful capabilities. This edition includes a new chapter—Web Programming with CGI—that provides everything readers need to begin developing their own Web-based applications that will run on the Internet! Readers will learn how to build so-called n-tier applications, in which the functionality provided by each tier can be distributed to separate computers across the Internet or executed on the same computer. This edition uses a new code-highlighting style with a yellow background to focus the reader on the C++ features introduced in each program. The book provides a carefully designed sequence of examples that introduces inheritance and polymorphism and helps students understand the motivation and implementation of these key object-oriented programming concepts. In addition, the OOD/UML case study has been upgraded to UML 1.4 and all flowcharts and inheritance diagrams in the text have been converted to their UML counterparts. The book presents an early introduction to strings and arrays as objects using standard C++ classes string and vector. The book also covers key concepts and techniques standard C++ developers need to master, including control structures, functions, arrays, pointers and strings, classes and data abstraction, operator overloading, inheritance, virtual functions, polymorphism, I/O, templates, exception handling, file processing, data structures and more. The book includes a detailed introduction to Standard Template Library (STL) containers, container adapters, algorithms and iterators. It also features insight into good programming practices, maximizing performance, avoiding errors, debugging and testing.

Java™ How
to Program
Fourth Edition

©2002, 1546 pp., paper
(0-13-034151-7)

The world's best-selling Java text is now even better! The Fourth Edition of *Java How to Program* includes a new focus on object-oriented design with the UML, design patterns, full-color program listings and figures and the most up-to-date Java coverage available.

Readers will discover key topics in Java programming, such as graphical user interface components, exception handling, multithreading, multimedia, files and streams, networking, data structures and more. In addition, a new chapter on design patterns explains frequently recurring architectural patterns—information that can help save designers considerable time when building large systems.

The highly detailed optional case study focuses on object-oriented design with the UML and presents fully implemented working Java code.

Updated throughout, the text includes new and revised discussions on topics such as Swing, graphics and socket- and packet-based networking. Three introductory chapters heavily emphasize problem solving and programming skills. The chapters on RMI, JDBC™, servlets and JavaBeans have been moved to *Advanced Java 2 Platform How to Program*, where they are now covered in much greater depth. (See *Advanced Java 2 Platform How to Program* below.)

Advanced Java™ 2
Platform How
to Program

©2002, 1811 pp., paper
(0-13-089560-1)

Expanding on the world's best-selling Java textbook—*Java How to Program*—*Advanced Java 2 Platform How To Program* presents advanced Java topics for developing sophisticated, user-friendly GUIs; significant, scalable enterprise applications; wireless applications and distributed systems. Primarily based on Java 2 Enterprise Edition (J2EE), this textbook integrates technologies such as XML, JavaBeans, security, Java Database Connectivity (JDBC), JavaServer Pages (JSP), servlets, Remote Method Invocation (RMI), Enterprise JavaBeans™ (EJB) and design patterns into a production-quality system that allows developers to benefit from the leverage and platform independence Java 2 Enterprise Edition provides. The book also features the development of a complete, end-to-end e-business solution using advanced Java technologies. Additional topics include Swing, Java 2D and 3D, XML, design patterns, CORBA, Jini™, JavaSpaces™, Jiro™, Java Management Extensions (JMX) and Peer-to-Peer networking with an introduction to JXTA. This textbook also introduces the Java 2 Micro Edition (J2ME™) for building applications for handheld and wireless devices using MIDP and MIDlets. Wireless technologies covered include WAP, WML and i-mode.

Visual C++ .NET How to Program

`BOOK / CD-ROM`

©2003, 1600 pp., paper (0-13-437377-4)

Visual C++® .NET How to Program provides a comprehensive introduction to building Visual C++ applications for Microsoft's new .NET Framework. The book begins with a strong foundation in introductory and intermediate programming principles, including control structures, functions, arrays, pointers, strings, classes and data abstraction, inheritance, virtual methods, polymorphism, I/O, exception handling, file processing, data structures and more. The book discusses program development with the Microsoft® Visual Studio® .NET integrated development environment (IDE) and shows how to edit, compile and debug applications with the IDE. The book then explores more sophisticated .NET application-development topics in detail. Key topics include: creating reusable software components with assemblies, modules and dynamic link libraries; using classes from the Framework Class Library (FCL); building graphical user interfaces (GUIs) with the FCL; implementing multithreaded applications; building networked applications; manipulating databases with ADO .NET and creating XML Web services. The first 75% of the book covers programming with Microsoft's new managed-code approach. The five chapters in the last quarter of the book focus on programming with unmanaged code in Visual C++ .NET. These chapters demonstrate how to use "attributed programming" to simplify common tasks (such as connecting to databases) and to improve code readability; how to integrate managed- and unmanaged-code software components; and how to use ATL Server to create Web-based applications and Web services with unmanaged code. The book features LIVE-CODE ™ examples that highlight crucial .NET-programming concepts and demonstrate Web services at work. Substantial introductions to XML and XHTML also are included.

C# How to Program

`BOOK / CD-ROM`

©2002, 1568 pp., paper (0-13-062221-4)

An exciting new addition to the How to Program series, *C# How to Program* provides a comprehensive introduction to Microsoft's new object-oriented language. C# builds on the skills already mastered by countless C++ and Java programmers, enabling them to create powerful Web applications and components—ranging from XML-based Web services on Microsoft's .NET platform to middle-tier business objects and system-level applications. *C# How to Program* begins with a strong foundation in the introductory and intermediate programming principles students will need in industry. It then explores such essential topics as object-oriented programming and exception handling. Graphical user interfaces are extensively covered, giving readers the tools to build compelling and fully interactive programs. Internet technologies such as XML, ADO .NET and Web services are also covered as well as topics including regular expressions, multithreading, networking, databases, files and data structures.

Visual Basic .NET How to Program Second Edition

`BOOK / CD-ROM`

©2002, 1400 pp., paper (0-13-029363-6)

Teach Visual Basic .NET programming from the ground up! This introduction of Microsoft's .NET Framework marks the beginning of major revisions to all of Microsoft's programming languages. This book provides a comprehensive introduction to the next version of Visual Basic—Visual Basic .NET—featuring extensive updates and increased functionality. *Visual Basic .NET How to Program, Second Edition* covers introductory programming techniques as well as more advanced topics, featuring enhanced treatment of developing Web-based applications. Other topics discussed include an extensive treatment of XML and wireless applications, databases, SQL and ADO .NET, Web forms, Web services and ASP .NET.

C How to Program Third Edition

`BOOK / CD-ROM`

©2001, 1253 pp., paper (0-13-089572-5)

Highly practical in approach, the Third Edition of the world's best-selling C text introduces the fundamentals of structured programming and software engineering and gets up to speed quickly. This comprehensive book not only covers the full C language, but also reviews library functions and introduces object-based and object-oriented programming in C++ and Java. The Third Edition includes a new 346-page introduction to Java 2 and the basics of GUIs, and the 298-page introduction to C++ has been updated to be consistent with the most current ANSI/ISO C++ standards. Plus, icons throughout the book point out valuable programming tips such as Common Programming Errors, Portability Tips and Testing and Debugging Tips.

Getting Started with Microsoft® Visual C++™ 6 with an Introduction to MFC

`BOOK / CD-ROM`

©2000, 163 pp., paper
(0-13-016147-0)

Internet & World Wide Web How to Program, Second Edition

`BOOK / CD-ROM`

©2002, 1428 pp., paper
(0-13-030897-8)

The revision of this groundbreaking book in the Deitels' *How to Program Series* offers a thorough treatment of programming concepts that yield visible or audible results in Web pages and Web-based applications. This book discusses effective Web-based design, server- and client-side scripting, multitier Web-based applications development, ActiveX® controls and electronic commerce essentials. This book offers an alternative to traditional programming courses using markup languages (such as XHTML, Dynamic HTML and XML) and scripting languages (such as JavaScript, VBScript, Perl/CGI, Python and PHP) to teach the fundamentals of programming "wrapped in the metaphor of the Web."

Updated material on `www.deitel.com` and `www.prenhall.com/deitel` provides additional resources for instructors who want to cover Microsoft® or non-Microsoft technologies. The Web site includes an extensive treatment of Netscape® 6 and alternate versions of the code from the Dynamic HTML chapters that will work with non-Microsoft environments as well.

Wireless Internet & Mobile Business How to Program

©2002, 1292 pp., paper
(0-13-062226-5)

While the rapid expansion of wireless technologies, such as cell phones, pagers and personal digital assistants (PDAs), offers many new opportunities for businesses and programmers, it also presents numerous challenges related to issues such as security and standardization. This book offers a thorough treatment of both the management and technical aspects of this growing area, including coverage of current practices and future trends. The first half explores the business issues surrounding wireless technology and mobile business, including an overview of existing and developing communi-

cation technologies and the application of business principles to wireless devices. It also discusses location-based services and location-identifying technologies, a topic that is revisited throughout the book. Wireless payment, security, legal and social issues, international communications and more are also discussed. The book then turns to programming for the wireless Internet, exploring topics such as WAP (including 2.0), WML, WMLScript, XML, XHTML™, wireless Java programming (J2ME)™, Web Clipping and more. Other topics covered include career resources, wireless marketing, accessibility, Palm™, PocketPC, Windows CE, i-mode, Bluetooth, MIDP, MIDlets, ASP, Microsoft .NET Mobile Framework, BREW™, multimedia, Flash™ and VBScript.

Python How to Program

`BOOK / CD-ROM`

©2002, 1376 pp., paper
(0-13-092361-3)

This exciting new book provides a comprehensive introduction to Python—a powerful object-oriented programming language with clear syntax and the ability to bring together various technologies quickly and easily. This book covers introductory-programming techniques and more advanced topics such as graphical user interfaces, databases, wireless Internet programming, networking, security, process management, multithreading, XHTML, CSS, PSP and multimedia. Readers will learn principles that are applicable to both systems development and Web programming. The book features the consistent and applied pedagogy that the *How to Program Series* is known for, including the Deitels' signature LIVE-CODE™ Approach, with thousands of lines of code in hundreds of working programs; hundreds of valuable programming tips identified with icons throughout the text; an extensive set of exercises, projects and case studies; two-color four-way syntax coloring and much more.

e-Business & e-Commerce for Managers

©2001, 794 pp., cloth
(0-13-032364-0)

This comprehensive overview of building and managing e-businesses explores topics such as the decision to bring a business online, choosing a business model, accepting payments, marketing strategies and security, as well as many other important issues (such as career resources). The book features Web resources and online demonstrations that supplement the text and direct readers to additional materials. The book also includes an appendix that develops a complete

Web-based shopping-cart application using HTML, JavaScript, VBScript, Active Server Pages, ADO, SQL, HTTP, XML and XSL. Plus, company-specific sections provide "real-world" examples of the concepts presented in the book.

XML How to Program

BOOK / CD-ROM

©2001, 934 pp., paper (0-13-028417-3)

This book is a comprehensive guide to programming in XML. It teaches how to use XML to create customized tags and includes chapters that address standard custom-markup languages for science and technology, multimedia, commerce and many other fields. Concise introductions to Java, JavaServer Pages, VBScript, Active Server Pages and Perl/CGI provide readers with the essentials of these programming languages and server-side development technologies to enable them to work effectively with XML. The book also covers cutting-edge topics such as XSL, DOM™ and SAX, plus a real-world e-commerce case study and a complete chapter on Web accessibility that addresses Voice XML. It includes tips such as Common Programming Errors, Software Engineering Observations, Portability Tips and Debugging Hints. Other topics covered include XHTML, CSS, DTD, schema, parsers, XPath, XLink, namespaces, XBase, XInclude, XPointer, XSLT, XSL Formatting Objects, JavaServer Pages, XForms, topic maps, X3D, MathML, OpenMath, CML, BML, CDF, RDF, SVG, Cocoon, WML, XBRL and BizTalk™ and SOAP™ Web resources.

Perl How to Program

BOOK / CD-ROM

©2001, 1057 pp., paper (0-13-028418-1)

This comprehensive guide to Perl programming emphasizes the use of the Common Gateway Interface (CGI) with Perl to create powerful, dynamic multi-tier Web-based client/server applications. The book begins with a clear and careful introduction to programming concepts at a level suitable for beginners, and proceeds through advanced topics such as references and complex data structures. Key Perl topics such as regular expressions and string manipulation are covered in detail. The authors address important and topical issues such as object-oriented programming, the Perl database interface (DBI), graphics and security. Also included is a treatment of XML, a bonus chapter introducing the Python programming language, supplemental material on career resources and a complete chapter on Web accessibility. The text includes tips such as Common Programming Errors, Software Engineering Observations, Portability Tips and Debugging Hints.

e-Business & e-Commerce How to Program

BOOK / CD-ROM

©2001, 1254 pp., paper (0-13-028419-X)

This innovative book explores programming technologies for developing Web-based e-business and e-commerce solutions, and covers e-business and e-commerce models and business issues. Readers learn a full range of options, from "build-your-own" to turnkey solutions. The book examines scores of the top e-businesses (examples include Amazon, eBay, Priceline, Travelocity, etc.), explaining the technical details of building successful e-business and e-commerce sites and their underlying business premises. Learn how to implement the dominant e-commerce models—shopping carts, auctions, name-your-own-price, comparison shopping and bots/ intelligent agents—by using markup languages (HTML, Dynamic HTML and XML), scripting languages (JavaScript, VBScript and Perl), server-side technologies (Active Server Pages and Perl/CGI) and database (SQL and ADO), security and online payment technologies. Updates are regularly posted to **www·deitel·com** and the book includes a CD-ROM with software tools, source code and live links.

www·deitel·com/newsletter/subscribe·html

Complete Training Courses

Each complete package includes the corresponding *How to Program Series* book and interactive multimedia CD-ROM Cyber Classroom. *Complete Training Courses* are perfect for anyone interested Web and e-commerce programming. They are affordable resources for college students and professionals learning programming for the first time or reinforcing their knowledge.

Each *Complete Training Course* is compatible with Windows 95, Windows 98, Windows NT and Windows 2000 and includes the following features:

Intuitive Browser-Based Interface

You'll love the *Complete Training Courses'* new browser-based interface, designed to be easy and accessible to anyone who's ever used a Web browser. Every *Complete Training Course* features the full text, illustrations and program listings of its corresponding *How to Program* book—all in full color—with full-text searching and hyperlinking.

Further Enhancements to the Deitels' Signature LIVE-CODE™ Approach

Every code sample from the main text can be found in the interactive, multimedia, CD-ROM-based *Cyber Classrooms* included in the *Complete Training Courses*. Syntax coloring of code is included for the *How to Program* books that are published in full color. Even the recent two-color and one-color books use effective multi-way syntax shading. The *Cyber Classroom* products always are in full color.

Audio Annotations

Hours of detailed, expert audio descriptions of thousands of lines of code help reinforce concepts.

Easily Executable Code

With one click of the mouse, you can execute the code or save it to your hard drive to manipulate using the programming environment of your choice. With selected *Complete Training Courses*, you can also load all of the code into a development environment such as Microsoft® Visual C++™, enabling you to modify and execute the programs with ease.

Abundant Self-Assessment Material

Practice exams test your understanding with hundreds of test questions and answers in addition to those found in the main text. Hundreds of self-review questions, all with answers, are drawn from the text; as are hundreds of programming exercises, half with answers.

www.phptr.com/phpinteractive

Sign up now for the new *DEITEL™ Buzz Online* newsletter at:

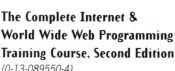
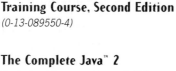

Future Publications

Here are some new titles we are considering for 2002/2003 release:

Computer Science Series: *Operating Systems 3/e, Data Structures in C++, Data Structures in Java, Theory and Principles of Database Systems.*

Database Series: *Oracle, SQL Server, MySQL.*

Internet and Web Programming Series: *Open Source Software Development: Apache, Linux, MySQL and PHP.*

Programming Series: *Flash™.*

.NET Programming Series: *ADO .NET with Visual Basic .NET, ASP .NET with Visual Basic .NET, ADO .NET with C#, ASP .NET with C#.*

Object Technology Series: *OOAD with the UML, Design Patterns, Java™ and XML.*

Advanced Java™ Series: *JDBC, Java 2 Enterprise Edition, Java Media Framework (JMF), Java Security and Java Cryptography (JCE), Java Servlets, Java2D and Java3D, JavaServer Pages™ (JSP), JINI and Java 2 Micro Edition™ (J2ME).*

DEITEL™ BUZZ ONLINE Newsletter

The Deitel and Associates, Inc. free opt-in newsletter includes:

- Updates and commentary on industry trends and developments
- Resources and links to articles from our published books and upcoming publications.
- Information on the Deitel publishing plans, including future publications and product-release schedules
- Support for instructors
- Resources for students
- Information on Deitel Corporate Training

To sign up for the Deitel™ Buzz Online newsletter, visit www.deitel.com/newsletter/subscribe.html.

E-Books

We are committed to providing our content in traditional print formats and in emerging electronic formats, such as e-books, to fulfill our customers' needs. Our R&D teams are currently exploring many leading-edge solutions.

Visit www.deitel.com and read the DEITEL™ BUZZ ONLINE for periodic updates.

Turn the page to find out more about Deitel & Associates!